LITERATURE AS EXPERIENCE

An Anthology

LITERATURE AS EXPERIENCE

An Anthology

55029

IRVING HOWE

City University of New York

JOHN HOLLANDER

Yale University

DAVID BROMWICH

Princeton University

HARCOURT BRACE JOVANOVICH, INC.

New York   San Diego   Chicago   San Francisco   Atlanta

Our main purpose in editing this book is a simple one: to teach students ways of making vital connections with the great traditions of literature. But if the purpose is simple, the methods of achieving it, as every teacher of literature knows, must sometimes be complex. Some instructors prefer to stress the formal properties of a literary work as a way of revealing its values and pleasures; others prefer to emphasize the direct and immediate experience of reading, turning afterward to formal properties in order to sustain and deepen the initial response. Both approaches have merit, and we think this book enables a teacher to take either one or to combine the two.

Literature as Experience is meant for introductory courses. The selections in each unit have been made with care to reveal something of the range and variety possible within a given literary genre, as well as to capture different kinds of human experience. The instructor should be able to organize the materials thematically, chronologically, or by genre. Our aim has been not to advance a critical theory, either in or out of fashion, but to suggest something of the amplitude, the richness, the complexity, and, above all, the deep and abiding *interest* of literature.

Literature, we believe, is both reflection and illumination, mirror and lamp, of human experience. It is not something apart from experience as such, since for many people it forms a significant portion of their lives. Yet it is a special *kind* of experience, in some ways different from daily living, working, loving. To be genuinely engaged with literature is an experience that draws upon yet lights up other aspects of the human enterprise. What we want, above all else, is to persuade students—better yet, enable students themselves to see— that literature matters, that to read well and reflectively is to gain in understanding, insight, pleasure, and the capacity to feel.

We have attended to problems of form, structure, and unity; to constructs such as plot, character, scene, imaginative world; to the relations between abstract idea and concrete detail; to such matters as what a narrative ending is, or how point of view is controlled in a story and tone in a poem, or how stanza forms can display patterns of argument. From this book, a student should learn something about the role of tradition—that, for instance, texts are not written in isolation from other texts and that the presence of earlier writers, looming predecessors, can be decisive for a poet or novelist. Literature as a realm more or less autonomous, with its own interests, procedures, myths, gossip, history— some sense of this ought also to emerge from the use of this book.

Still, our main interest can be put in two words: *connect* and *respond*. If, as experienced teachers know, this sometimes happens through initial uneasiness, even hostility, so be it. If, when we are fortunate, it happens through a burst of enthusiasm and love, that is even better. But what matters is that students living in the United States in the last third of the twentieth century should come to see that a story by Chekhov or a poem by Shelley or a play by Molière offers an imaginative structure that can reach our feelings and illuminate our experience. Our book is meant as an introduction to a new kind of pleasure, the pleasure of reading intelligently, with sensitive openness of mind and heart.

I.H., J.H., D.B.

CONTENTS

The Comic Vision

The Solitary Self

The Human Situation

POETRY

Parable, 361

Song, 366

Sonnet, 379

Repetition and Refrain, 395

Narrative, 413

Dramatic Monologue, 442

THEMES AND VARIATIONS, 457

Love's Occasions, 459

Elegy and Epitaph, 475

The Poetry of Earth, 493

Postscript: The Nature of the City, 521

Meditation, 528

Poem and Picture, 561

A NOTE ON PROSODY: Scheme, Pattern, and Form, 575

POEMS FOR FURTHER READING, 597

DRAMA

FICTION

INTRODUCTION

Consisting of a few low-keyed remarks on literature, how it comes about, why it's read, ways of treating it, and the short story as a distinctive kind of writing—remarks which the student can go through at the beginning, or read in part when working with some of the stories, or let alone.

This is a book whose main purpose is to give pleasure, a certain kind of pleasure, the kind that comes from reading literature. To some people this kind of pleasure comes easily, quickly, spontaneously. To others it comes slowly and only after effort and training. But whichever sort of reader you may be, please remember: you will be asked to read, to think about, to discuss, and perhaps write papers dealing with these stories in order to heighten your capacity for pleasure. It's something that can be learned or cultivated—just the way you can cultivate a taste for music, or learn to ice skate or dance. The process of cultivation, the effort of learning, leads to an increased capacity for response and awareness. Which brings pleasure.

We have brought together in this book a wide range of stories, different in character, tone, method, and subject matter. Some of these stories are great; others, very good; still others, flawed but interesting. Our purpose here is not to make any of you into budding literary critics, or to push for any special approach to literature. Very few "technical" terms of literary criticism appear in this book; perhaps your teacher will introduce a few of them in class, perhaps not. But we have assumed that literature is accessible to every intelligent person who has learned to read, and that it can best be discussed through ordinary language—the language of daily speech. Even when you become expert in your approach to a literary work, you can still express yourself perfectly well without using jargon, or "technical" terms. Or so it seems to us.

What is literature?

It would be foolhardy for us to try to define literature. The great eighteenth-century English critic, Dr. Samuel Johnson, once said that literature is

1

like light: everyone knows what light is but few can define or even describe it. Let's just say that by literature we mean imaginative writings—stories, novels, poems, plays—which portray or reflect or deal with human existence. Think about it for a few minutes and you can probably punch holes into that last sentence; but no matter, since at least it helps us get started.

Literature, as distinct from, say, a report in a newspaper about yesterday's shoplifting, has some lasting interest and value. We assume, also, that literature is serious—which doesn't at all mean murky or solemn, and which certainly can include the comic.

Serious means here that a story or poem tries to get at something important, perhaps lasting, about our perceptions of the world or our situations as human beings. Through a story or an imagined situation or a striking use of language, the writer wants to portray or suggest something significant—this is how things are when you're young and in love, this is how you feel when your father dies, this is the way growing up as a black man or woman makes you think about the United States, and the like. The story dealing with such topics can be sad or happy, tragic or comic; but if it leaves us with a greater insight into the human situation, we call it serious.

And then, literature as an art form has distinct characteristics of its own. A movie is made with a camera; the print consists of a certain number of "frames" which, if run at a certain speed, make a "moving picture." The movie has to be shown in a dark place, it goes on for a certain length of time, and so forth. The film itself provides a series of visual images within a given span of time, and these images are so arranged as to tell a story, yield information, or present a lyrical impression. Or consider the ballet: it has to be performed on a stage, it consists of a fixed series of steps and gestures, and like the film, it can tell a story or provide a lyrical impression. All of these comprise what we call the tradition—the inherited procedures and assumptions—of a given art form.

A story is also characterized according to its own tradition. But of course, no tradition is fixed for all time. Changes occur. These determine what a particular writer or group of writers may feel appropriate to put into a work or leave out of it; how they organize or structure their material; how they build up suspense and curiosity; what kinds of language they use (simple or elaborate, informal or formal, etc.).

Because traditions change, we may find it harder to read works that were written several centuries ago than those written last year. But we may also find that the older stories, poems, or plays—once we get past problems of changing vocabulary or changing moral attitudes—can yield us permanent (or seemingly permanent) insights. Consider, for instance, the fables composed by the Greek slave, Aesop, in ancient times. They are witty and enticing, and despite the passage of centuries, anyone can recognize himself or herself in the mirror of Aesop's fables. The vanities, pretensions, failings, and also occasional decencies that Aesop portrays in his fables about animals—who in the twentieth century would not admit that these also pertain to us?

> *Why do writers write?*
> *And readers read?*

We may speculate why it is that people want to create works of literature, or any other art—though we can never be sure. What drives people to tell stories, make songs, paint pictures? Here are a few possible answers.

In prehistoric times, apparently, an important function of storytelling was magical—to please the gods, to make sure the rains came in the spring, to bring a good harvest. In cultures such as these, storytelling, painting, or composing poems was inseparable from the rest of life. These activities were seen not as something decorative or as a luxury possible in moments of leisure; they were deeply grounded in the basic rhythms of existence.

Epics of ancient peoples tell stories about great heroes who founded nations, thereby creating a mythic account of how a people came into existence and what its claims are to a distinctive role in history.

All of us seem to have a deep psychological need for leaving some mark or record of our existence. (During the Second World War, American soldiers would scratch the words, "Kilroy Was Here," on walls, the sides of ships, wherever they happened to be—which was a way of saying, any one of us was here, Smith or Cohen or Robinson or Lopez or Palewski.) The French writer André Malraux has described the same impulse in more elegant language: human beings want to "leave a scar on the map," even though they realize the scar will fade and the map shrivel.

Telling stories or releasing emotions in poetry is a way of recognizing and organizing our deepest responses to human existence. These responses heighten, dramatize, and reveal our common situation as men and women; but they also reflect those elements of class, race, nationality, and sex which divide us.

Take the Biblical story of Jacob, who worked for seven years to get Rachel and instead, poor fellow, got Leah. Who hasn't lived through an experience like that: sweating for Rachel and ending with Leah? It is the experience of disappointment, or being "taken," and sooner or later it happens to everyone alike. It is, as we say, an *archetypal* story: that is, characteristic of a whole portion of human experience.

Or consider the black spiritual:

> When Israel was in Egypt land,
>   Let my people go!
> Oppressed so hard they could not stand,
>   Let my people go!

It was perhaps with such spirituals in mind that the great black leader of the nineteenth century, Frederick Douglass, said that songs relieve an aching heart. Certainly, this song served that purpose, and one way it did so was to link references from the Bible (Jews enslaved by Pharaoh) with the ordeal of black slaves in the United States. This sort of relief also holds true for good stories and poems about other kinds of experience, ranging from love to death.

And, of course, there's still pleasure. We're not always quite sure why it should be, yet the fact remains that telling stories and listening to stories can give pleasure. What happens next? How did the hero feel about this? How did the heroine react to that? What did they do together, and what did their parents think?

Nor is it mainly the suspense of not knowing what happens next that holds our attention. Often we do know that the hero and heroine will marry and live happily—or if it is a modern book, unhappily—ever after. What matters is the way the story is told. Bad storytelling can be a form of torture: everyone has friends who are expert at wrecking stories and jokes. Sometimes the trouble is that they don't know what to leave out ("so she said to me and I said to her"— the sheer wordiness and the bulk of unimportant detail can drive you crazy). Other times the trouble consists of an inability to focus properly on what matters, to place the necessary stress on the telling detail.

There is great artistry in telling a good story: the artistry of selection, timing, choice of words, tone of voice. As we get more experienced in the reading of literature, we respond less to the mere facts of a story and more to the manner of its narration or the nuances of meaning it accumulates. Finally, we come to see that the manner of telling and the implied meanings are inseparable.

The greatest novels, for example, use the same old story over and over again: the hero and heroine were short of money, they fell in and out of love, they were short of money, they married the wrong people and then she decided to "find herself," they were short of money, he killed a nobleman or a millionaire, they ran away and they were still short of money, and so on, and so forth. These, in comically simplified form, are the plots of Leo Tolstoy's *Anna Karenina* and Gustave Flaubert's *Madame Bovary*—two of the greatest European novels we have. There is no surprise in the events themselves, but endless surprise in the unfolding, the detail, the texture of the events.

But let us admit something which you're likely to discover anyway as you read the stories in this book: the idea of "pleasure" with regard to literature can be tricky. We go, for instance, to see a performance of Shakespeare's *King Lear,* which is about an aging king who surrenders his power too quickly to his daughters, then suffers humiliation at their hands, partly because they are selfish, partly because he is himself vain and foolish. At the end, Lear is crying out that life is unbearable, it's better not to have been born. And we suffer along with him.

And *that* you call pleasure? Yes; in a way. For it is in the nature of literature that it presents human experience through *imagined* circumstances. We reenact, we share, we act out our most fundamental feelings—our fears, hopes, desires, joys, fantasies—all through *imagined* circumstances. Every father has a streak of Lear in him; every young man overcome by moral scruples has a bit of Hamlet in him; and even the most sober couples shopping for furniture at Macy's can sometimes glimpse the ecstasy of Romeo and Juliet.

Literature casts, then, an artificial light on our existence. That artificial light is "better" than a natural one because it can be regulated with regard to strength, direction, intensity. To have our awareness as human beings increased without *directly* experiencing in our own lives the events and circumstances that move us, is an achievement possible only to literature.

But stop a minute and return to that last sentence. The key word is *directly*. That means that when you go to see a performance of *King Lear* you may make comparisons with the ingratitude of your own children, or your neighbor's children, but after all, you know that "it's just a play," something that has been "made up"—otherwise, you ought to rush up to the stage and prevent the old man from being tormented. But the truth is that even though, in one way, you may believe or almost believe that what's going on up there on the stage (or on the film screen) is "real"—and sometimes it can shake and move you much more than the actual events of your own life—still, you also know that, literally, it's not real, it's a make-believe about the real.

On getting involved
with stories and poems

Reading a good story or poem, we become involved. What does that mean?

On the simplest level, we get caught up with the story or the situation; we hope things will turn out as they should; we fear they won't; we identify with the characters of the story or the speaker in the poem. Inexperienced readers identify in a simple daydream fashion. If the hero is all heroism and strength or the heroine all sweetness, then this sort of identification is easy. But suppose the characters are drawn more subtly, with a greater sense of life's complications. Then inexperienced readers get into trouble. They read Jane Austen's *Emma*, for example, and they feel that the heroine of that novel, Emma Wodehouse, is vain and snobbish: they wouldn't want her for a friend or a roommate. But the author knows, of course, that her heroine is vain and snobbish, and you're not supposed to like Emma in any simple-minded way. You're supposed to see her as an interesting and complicated person with virtues and vices. Again, if you read W. Somerset Maugham's novel *Of Human Bondage,* which has a cripple for its main character, and you happen yourself to have a similar disadvantage, it's not at all easy to avoid an uncritical identification with the character. What we call esthetic distance—the ability to become interested in a character in a novel or story while yet retaining some critical judgments about him or her and remembering that, finally, it's just a character in a novel or story—that is something which comes only after some experience or training in responding to literature. Ideally, the experienced reader does become involved, deeply involved. Yet this reader doesn't allow accidental personal elements to enter his or her involvement, or to blind him or her to the flaws in the character, or to keep those flaws from destroying interest in the character.

This balance or tension of conflicting impulses—involvement *and* distance, strong personal feeling *and* critical objectivity—is one of the marks of a good reader of literature. You can't just decide to have it. It's something that comes from immersing yourself in novels and stories, poems and plays.

What, finally,
do you "get" out of it?

It would be foolish, and fanatical, to suppose that people read works of literature for any single reason, or that they "must" read it for a single reason. Tastes vary, experiences differ. But it may be worth while to glance at some of the possible reasons for reading stories, poems, and plays, and to see how far each of these reasons can take us toward a just or a full appreciation.

Do we read for information? Yes, sometimes. Charles Dickens's novels give us a good deal of material about the Industrial Revolution in early nineteenth-century England; Theodore Dreiser's novels, about the early American factory system. Yet information in itself is rarely the main reason that we read works of fiction. As a rule, we can get more reliable and accurate information elsewhere, in works of history or sociology. And what is more, we know that novelists and story-writers have to adapt the information they use; have to transform it for their own creative purposes, so that, for example, the picture Dickens gives us of the Industrial Revolution, while vivid and penetrating, is not always reliable in precise details. Information, yes; but more. . . .

Entertainment? Again, yes; but again, tricky. The popular humorist Art Buchwald is often entertaining, but his daily columns are hardly literature. The comic strip "Peanuts" is often entertaining, but it too isn't literature. There are various kinds of popular amusements, ranging from comic strips to television, from journalism to musical comedy, which can be pleasing, charming, and entertaining, but which we hesitate to describe as art—though sometimes the boundaries between art (or literature) and popular entertainments can be very blurred. A serious novel, a powerful story, a stirring poem can and should be entertaining, but they are also more, reaching us at deeper levels of our awareness and feeling.

How about "true to life"? That's a phrase that students who have done some reading would be inclined to use, and it's a valuable phrase because it stresses the deep relationship between literature and reality. Surely, a story that seems to us to have no connection with our sense of the way "things really are" isn't likely to seem important to us, even if it is written with clever phrases and is smoothly structured.

But there are problems here. Case histories of a psychiatric examination, newspaper reports, tapes of family conversations around the kitchen table—all these are, in one or another way, "true to life," yet few of us would think of them as literature.

A novel or story must indeed be "true to life," but it can satisfy this requirement in a great many ways: through realism, through fantasy, through humor, through fable, and so on. And besides, our sense of what is "true to life" can itself be modified and enlarged by our experience of the work of literature itself. Most of us have fairly narrow ranges of experience; and we ought to hesitate before judging the works of novelists by the limitations of our experience.

Even in the most realistic works of fiction, there is an element of *selection* because:

(a) not everything can or should be put in;
(b) a novel or story is written from a certain point of view which determines how it will shape and evaluate its material;
(c) a major interest lies in the "making" of the work of literature, how the techniques of selection establish the meanings of the work.

The great American novelist Herman Melville writes: "It is with fiction as with religion: it should present another world, and yet one to which we feel the tie." That "other world" is the one imagined by the writer, and our interest in it will depend partly on the extent to which it illuminates this world, the one we live in day by day.

The imagined world of the writer, the real world in which we live—it's not as if each is fixed forever in our minds, or as if we can ever fully know either of them, or as if both don't complicate and sometimes confuse our sense of one another. But it's probably useful to stress the extent to which the imagined world of the writer is not just a mere copy of the world of daily reality. What writers create is shaped by their vision, that is, their characteristic way of regarding experience; and it is shaped, as well, by the *conventions* of the form they use, that is, the conventions appropriate to the novel or the short story or the lyric poem or the three-act play. By conventions we mean those literary devices and procedures that have become accepted through general use in the development of a given form.

For instance: part of Shakespeare's *Henry IV,* Part I, takes place in a tavern. On the modern stage there are generally three walls visible to the audience, with the fourth wall removed, so that the audience can see what is happening. The audience makes a kind of agreement with the author to assume that it is in fact watching a tavern. It is a convention of the stage that the fourth wall of a tavern or a house or whatever be missing.

Another example: a short poem of 14 lines—usually divided into two groups, of 8 and 6 lines—with certain rhyme schemes and certain customary subjects (love, age, etc.,) is called a sonnet. You can hardly expect an elaborate plot in a sonnet, and one reason for being familiar with the conventions of literature is to avoid such false expectations.

Still another example: a novelist starts his book by telling you that just as Mr. Smith was walking across the hills of Scotland one snowy evening in the winter of 1846, so at the same time Mrs. Jones (who, as it will turn out, has a secret passion for Mr. Smith) is sitting in her armchair in London. How does the novelist know what's happening in two different places at the same time? We simply assume that he can know this—it's a convention of the novel.

Some people say that such conventions stifle their souls, they want simply to write freely, without rules. Well, too often poems without rules turn out to be no poems at all. If a soccer player demanded, as a sign of his freedom, that he be allowed to throw the ball with his hands, or a tennis player that she be allowed to kick the ball with her feet, we'd say: that's foolish. The game has certain rules and if you're going to play that game, you just have to obey the rules. Otherwise, there's no game. The same holds for literature, but with this proviso: that in the history of literature the rules do change as writers work out innovations and experiments, and as new social and moral circumstances arise.

So, let's go back to literature again. It is a symbolic expression, through an imaginative rendering or presentation, of aspects of human experience. Two words are crucial here: *symbolic*—the imaginative presentation has to have some significance beyond its particular events. The story of Jack and Jill would mean little or nothing to us if it were confined just to Jack and Jill. Only after you've learned that all of us, sooner or later, fall down hills, do we find it interesting to hear that Jack and Jill fell down the hill. And *presentation:* the action of the story concerning Jack and Jill has to be concrete, it has to be about this Jack and that Jill, not an essay about the general dilemma of human beings falling down hills. Before we can begin to sense that what has happened to Jack and Jill has some larger or "symbolic" significance, we first have to be persuaded that Jack and Jill *did* fall down that hill. We have to be persuaded of the immediate, concrete reality of the incident being presented.

*And a few words
about the short story*

Storytelling, as we've already suggested, seems to be deeply ingrained in human life, part of our need to make sense of our experience, to leave some sort of record of what has happened to us and what we have done. There are stories in the oldest writings—wonderful ones, for example, like the story of Joseph and his brothers in the Bible. But the modern short story—brief enough to appear in a magazine or newspaper—really begins in the nineteenth century with the work of writers like Washington Irving, Edgar Allan Poe, and Nathaniel Hawthorne in the United States, Sir Walter Scott in England, Honoré de Balzac and Guy de Maupassant in France. Perhaps the greatest and certainly the most influential of short story writers is Anton Chekhov, the Russian writer who lived and worked in Russia during the late nineteenth and early twentieth centuries.

There are many kinds of short stories. Some move according to a slick or pat formula, often with a "surprise" ending. More serious are those that seek to reflect a moment of experience, a "slice of life," in realistic ways (in this book, the stories by Wright, Paley, O'Hara). Then there are "symbolic" short stories, which try to communicate a vision of existence through suggestion and indirection (the stories by Calisher, Aiken).

Still, if only for the fun of it, let's try to put down some of the main characteristics of the short story as a literary form:

It ranges in length from, say, 1,000 to 15,000 words (two selections in this book, "The Dead" and "Brigitta," are longer and might even be called novelettes or novellas or short novels).

It usually focuses on a dramatic moment, a single incident or group of incidents through which character is revealed or some insight about life brought out. Obviously, the short story cannot contain the sort of extended plot, with complicated turns of action, that one finds in a novel. Nor is it reasonable to expect in a short story the kind of detailed and prolonged analysis of human character, or the complicated process by which a character is shown to change, that one finds in a novel. The short story has to achieve its effects quickly.

But this need not follow from a sharply focused action or incident. Sometimes, as in Chekhov's "The Bishop," it seems as if "almost nothing happens"—there is very little external action. What we get, instead, is a moment of experience, a sort of snapshot which captures a life at a significant point of crisis. The result is sometimes very much like that achieved by a story with a sharply focused plot which comes to a quick dramatic climax.

These few introductory remarks about literature as a distinctive kind of writing have been put down here not because they are complete in any way—far from it—but because they may help you get into the stories that follow. And perhaps you will want to read further about the nature and problems of literature. If so, your teacher will be able to suggest plenty of good books and articles. But meanwhile, we'll stop talking and turn to the stories themselves.

VIEWS OF VIOLENCE

ERNEST HEMINGWAY

Hills Like White Elephants

Introduction

It wouldn't be hard to write a full-length novel, probably a bad one, about the characters in this story, telling all that happened before they found themselves quarreling in a little Spanish town and all that's likely to happen after the girl has had her "awfully simple operation." Such a novel would fill out all the details that Ernest Hemingway deliberately chose to suppress—what the characters look like, where they have come from, how they earn a living, what their past history is, and the like. Such a full-length novel would do the work of explanation which, in the story as Hemingway wrote it, is thrust upon the reader, who must fill out in imagination what is suggested through hints and oblique turns of phrase.

The art of "Hills Like White Elephants" is essentially an art of compression, denial, and silence. The characters don't tell us what their problem is, nor does Hemingway himself stop to do so. Instead, he *shows* us—not in full-face, not in detail, but at a moment of high tension, when the characters, through their distracted chatter, reveal more about themselves than they know. They engage in seemingly random conversation under the pressure of having to make a crucial choice in their lives together, but they no longer have (it's not clear that they ever did have) the mutual confidence and courage to speak openly. So everything comes out a little twisted, as a sour sideswipe of irritation and frustration. In the seemingly irrelevant but painfully abrasive snatches of talk, we can see a human relationship being unravelled. And seeing this, we come to share their anxiety, their sense of crumbling.

The man is trying to persuade the woman—but also himself—that he is proposing a reasonable course. Yet he also feels guilty. The woman isn't sure: perhaps it *is* a reasonable course, perhaps having the baby would really spoil their relationship by limiting their freedom. (But while she doesn't put it this way, the thought that seems to be bouncing around in her mind is that all human involvements necessarily entail a limitation upon freedom.) In any case, she is afraid—and why not? The operation will be performed on her, not him. "They just let a little air in," he says, meaning to reassure her but only adding to the grisliness of the scene. And she, who has observed other people in similar situations, knows that the usual outcome is sadness and disaffection. All too often the result is to destroy the love in whose name the operation is undertaken.

The man talks too much. He talks too much because he is troubled, miserable, guilty. He gets on her nerves. He betrays his uneasiness and, after a while, his bad faith. And then we see something quite remarkable, though all too familiar: in the course of pressing the girl to do something that she doesn't want to and that he himself suspects may be wrong, he tries to gain reassurance from her. And because she, in turn, is miserable, the girl thrusts out against him with sarcastic little digs. They are sharp enough to inflame his guilt, but not fierce enough to force a showdown. It's a familiar situation: a partly controlled exchange of hostility.

So what we get to see—quickly, as if through a few snapshots—is the spectacle of two people trapped in a relationship. The man's anxiety leads him into selfishness; the girl grows more and more bitter and then resigned, as she sees there is no way out. In a few pages, Hemingway charts the death of love.

At the end, when the woman says she is "fine," what has happened is that she has resigned herself to the likelihood that no matter what she does—agree to or refuse the abortion—things will go bad. Her final politeness is a form of withdrawal, as if to say, "O.K., I won't argue any more, I see that we're lost."

The story is told obliquely; rather, it's not told at all. We come upon a critical moment in its unfolding, when nothing is made explicit but everything is made clear. All you have to do, as you read, is listen to the overtones, to the bitter music of the voices: the suppressed, needling tone, for instance, of the girl when, thinking about the people she knows who have had abortions, she says, "And afterward they were all so happy."

A word about those "white elephants." In common speech, a white elephant suggests something that is expensive but not of much use or value—perhaps the girl sees the unwanted child, or indeed, her whole relationship with the man, as a kind of white elephant. Or the "white elephant" may also suggest the swelling shape of a pregnant woman, something that could give the eye pleasure. There may be other suggestions raised in the reader's mind by the comparison between the hills and the white elephants—which we leave to you to reflect upon.

The final effect of the story is one of intense pain and loss, a glimpse of human waste through the scrim of casual talk. The kind of talk that reveals the torment of two souls.

Hills Like White Elephants

The hills across the valley of the Ebro[1] were long and white. On this side there was no shade and no trees and the station was between two lines of rails in the sun. Close against the side of the station there was the warm shadow of the building and a curtain, made of strings of bamboo beads, hung across the open door into the bar, to keep out flies. The American and the girl with him sat at a table in the shade, outside the building. It was very hot and the express from Barcelona would come in forty minutes. It stopped at this junction for two minutes and went on to Madrid.

"What should we drink?" the girl asked. She had taken off her hat and put it on the table.

"It's pretty hot," the man said.

"Let's drink beer."

"Dos cervezas," the man said into the curtain.

"Big ones?" a woman asked from the doorway.

"Yes. Two big ones."

The woman brought two glasses of beer and two felt pads. She put the felt pads and the beer glasses on the table and looked at the man and the girl. The girl was looking off at the line of hills. They were white in the sun and the country was brown and dry.

"They look like white elephants," she said.

"I've never seen one," the man drank his beer.

"No, you wouldn't have."

"I might have," the man said. "Just because you say I wouldn't have doesn't prove anything."

The girl looked at the bead curtain. "They've painted something on it," she said. "What does it say?"

"Anis del Toro. It's a drink."

"Could we try it?"

The man called "Listen" through the curtain. The woman came out from the bar.

"Four reales."

"We want two Anis del Toro."

"With water?"

"Do you want it with water?"

"I don't know," the girl said. "Is it good with water?"

"It's all right."

[1] Largest river in Spain.

"You want them with water?" asked the woman.

"Yes, with water."

"It tastes like licorice," the girl said and put the glass down.

"That's the way with everything."

"Yes," said the girl. "Everything tastes of licorice. Especially all the things you've waited so long for, like absinthe."

"Oh, cut it out."

"You started it," the girl said. "I was being amused. I was having a fine time."

"Well, let's try and have a fine time."

"All right. I was trying. I said the mountains looked like white elephants. Wasn't that bright?"

"That was bright."

"I wanted to try this new drink. That's all we do, isn't it—look at things and try new drinks?"

"I guess so."

The girl looked across at the hills.

"They're lovely hills," she said. "They don't really look like white elephants. I just meant the coloring of their skin through the trees."

"Should we have another drink?"

"All right."

The warm wind blew the bead curtain against the table.

"The beer's nice and cool," the man said.

"It's lovely," the girl said.

"It's really an awfully simple operation, Jig," the man said. "It's not really an operation at all."

The girl looked at the ground the table legs rested on.

"I know you wouldn't mind it, Jig. It's really not anything. It's just to let the air in."

The girl did not say anything.

"I'll go with you and I'll stay with you all the time. They just let the air in and then it's all perfectly natural."

"Then what will we do afterward?"

"We'll be fine afterward. Just like we were before."

"What makes you think so?"

"That's the only thing that bothers us. It's the only thing that's made us unhappy."

The girl looked at the bead curtain, put her hand out and took hold of two of the strings of beads.

"And you think then we'll be all right and be happy."

"I know we will. You don't have to be afraid. I've known lots of people that have done it."

"So have I," said the girl. "And afterward they were all so happy."

"Well," the man said, "if you don't want to you don't have to. I wouldn't have you do it if you didn't want to. But I know it's perfectly simple."

"And you really want to?"

"I think it's the best thing to do. But I don't want you to do it if you don't really want to."

"And if I do it you'll be happy and things will be like they were and you'll love me?"

"I love you now. You know I love you."

"I know. But if I do it, then it will be nice again if I say things are like white elephants, and you'll like it?"

"I'll love it. I love it now but I just can't think about it. You know how I get when I worry."

"If I do it you won't ever worry?"

"I won't worry about that because it's perfectly simple."

"Then I'll do it. Because I don't care about me."

"What do you mean?"

"I don't care about me."

"Well, I care about you."

"Oh, yes. But I don't care about me. And I'll do it and then everything will be fine."

"I don't want you to do it if you feel that way."

The girl stood up and walked to the end of the station. Across, on the other side, were fields of grain and trees along the banks of the Ebro. Far away, beyond the river, were mountains. The shadow of a cloud moved across the field of grain and she saw the river through the trees.

"And we could have all this," she said, "And we could have everything and every day we make it more impossible."

"What did you say?"

"I said we could have everything."

"We can have everything."

"No, we can't."

"We can have the whole world."

"No, we can't."

"We can go everywhere."

"No, we can't. It isn't ours any more."

"It's ours."

"No, it isn't. And once they take it away, you never get it back."

"But they haven't taken it away."

"We'll wait and see."

"Come on back in the shade," he said. "You mustn't feel that way."

"I don't feel any way," the girl said. "I just know things."

"I don't want you to do anything that you don't want to do——"

"Nor that isn't good for me," she said. "I know. Could we have another beer?"

"All right. But you've got to realize——"

"I realize," the girl said. "Can't we maybe stop talking?"

They sat down at the table and the girl looked across at the hills on the dry side of the valley and the man looked at her and at the table.

"You've got to realize," he said, "that I don't want you to do it if you don't want to. I'm perfectly willing to go through with it if it means anything to you."

"Doesn't it mean anything to you? We could get along."

"Of course it does. But I don't want anybody but you. I don't want any one else. And I know it's perfectly simple."

"Yes, you know it's perfectly simple."

"It's all right for you to say that, but I do know it."

"Would you do something for me now?"

"I'd do anything for you."

"Would you please please please please please please please stop talking?"

He did not say anything but looked at the bags against the wall of the station. There were labels on them from all the hotels where they had spent nights.

"But I don't want you to," he said, "I don't care anything about it."

"I'll scream," the girl said.

The woman came out through the curtains with two glasses of beer and put them down on the damp felt pads. "The train comes in five minutes," she said.

"What did she say?" asked the girl.

"That the train is coming in five minutes."

The girl smiled brightly at the woman, to thank her.

"I'd better take the bags over to the other side of the station," the man said. She smiled at him.

"All right. Then come back and we'll finish the beer."

He picked up the two heavy bags and carried them around the station to the other tracks. He looked up the tracks but could not see the train. Coming back, he walked through the barroom, where people waiting for the train were drinking. He drank an Anis at the bar and looked at the people. They were all waiting reasonably for the train. He went out through the bead curtain. She was sitting at the table and smiled at him.

"Do you feel better?" he asked.

"I feel fine," she said. "There's nothing wrong with me. I feel fine."

Questions for Writing and Discussion

1. On page 16, the man and the woman start arguing about the taste of licorice. Clearly, neither really cares about that, but just as clearly, something tense and important is happening here. What do you think it is?

2. The word "fine," one of Hemingway's favorites, keeps recurring throughout the story. Each use of this vague yet suggestive word carries a different meaning, a different implication. Go through the story with an eye to the different uses of this word and see how it helps bring out the larger meanings.

3. On page 17, the girl agrees to go ahead with the operation, yet she can't let the matter rest there and adds (with apparent bitterness), "Because I don't care about

me." That leads to a renewed tension between them, an opening-up of hemmed-in feeling, a discussion of whether they "can have the whole world." Focusing on this part of the story, discuss what is happening here.

4.   At the end of the story Hemingway remarks that the other people at the station "were all waiting reasonably for the train." That adverb, "reasonably," is one of the very few places where the author tips his hand, though in a somewhat strange way. What do you think he means by saying that the other people were waiting "reasonably?" What illumination may it shed upon the man and woman who have been in the foreground of the action?

5.   Is there anything about the way in which the story is written that reminds you of a scene in a movie and the way that scene is developed? Think especially of the relation between the snatches of dialogue and the passages of description.

6.   Throughout the story, the phrase "it's perfectly simple," or a variation of it, keeps recurring. How does Hemingway intend us to take this phrase? Are things really simple for either character? Why does the man keep using it?

D. H. LAWRENCE

Tickets, Please

Introduction

First a few tips, and then some brief analysis of the story.

The Midlands is the industrialized and rather ugly section of England, which cuts across the middle of the country. Industrialization came here before it did to most other countries, with the result that by the time of the First World War, when the action of "Tickets, Please" occurs, there was already considerable decay.

Occasionally, but mostly as a joke, one or two of the characters lapses into the Midland dialect. In England, as in the United States, there are a number of dialects and accents, so that in some instances it is hard for people from one area to understand what people from another area are saying.

Work is a major preoccupation in this story—the way young people experience it, the relationships among those who share it. But finally, work is not the most important concern of the story.

As you read, pay attention to the rhythm of Lawrence's narrative and the way he makes his language taut, giving it an effect of nervousness and excitement.

There is a possible mythological source or model for the action of the story—the myth of Orpheus. At the end of this introduction, you'll find a P.S. which provides more information about this. Now some analytical remarks about the story itself.

The story begins rather mildly, with Lawrence setting the place and tone. We learn that the "single-line tramway" cuts through the Midlands; that it is a rather adventurous run, since the young men and women who work on it enjoy speeding across the country; that the women who work as conductors are "fearless young hussies," decidedly different from the Victorian model of the bashful young girl; and—a bit later in the story—that because of the war there is a sexual imbalance, with the women far outnumbering the men. Nothing in this rather amiable beginning prepares us for the ferocity—indeed, the terror—of the ending.

21

Clearly we see, or sense, that even though work provides, so to say, the background of the story, or the setting in which characters act, it will be the relations between the sexes—and especially the relations between Annie and John Thomas—that will form the central concern of the story. Those relations are strained. Finding men in short supply, the women struggle for them. But they are working women. No longer blushing damsels, they have become independent and tough. They don't want to be pushed around, and naturally they find unsatisfactory the kind of "program" that John Thomas has in mind— that he remain, as Lawrence puts it, "a nocturnal presence," rather than "an all-round individual." For this feisty, attractive, and overconfident young man, the situation seems made to order: there he is, the superior of all these young women and consequently in a position to command their respect, and there he is, full of charm and sexual energy, and consequently in a position (or so he thinks) to take his pick. Above all, to keep picking. Not for him any "steady relationship" or becoming "an all-round individual" to a single person. It's hit and run, one evening with one of the women, another with another. His vanity blown up, he behaves like a cock of the walk. (By the way, it'll help you appreciate the humor of the story if you know that his name, John Thomas, and especially his nickname, Coddy, signify in British slang the male sexual organ. It's as if he is that organ on a rampage, intent on picking and choosing among the "harem" of the female conductors, without having to take either social or emotional responsibility.)

The young women decide on their act of revenge—it is a brutal revenge and most readers will feel a little sickened by it, even if they recognize a certain rough justice. What the women are doing is not, historically, so improbable, for remember that the story is set at the time when the suffragette movement was strong among English women. Some of the suffragettes (women, and sometimes men, demanding the right to vote for women) could get pretty rough with their umbrellas and put up a good fight when the police tried to arrest them. The idea of women's rights is in the air, even up in the Midlands; and behind D. H. Lawrence there are also several decades of writings by Ibsen, Strindberg, and Shaw emphasizing the clash, sometimes the deep and ineradicable hostilities, between men and women.

But the relationship of "Tickets, Please" to the issue of women's rights is decidedly ambiguous and complex, for Lawrence was not a great admirer of the women's movement, even though he clearly admires the spunk and energy of the young women in his story. The final scene is brilliantly managed, first, to show the full violence and joy of the revenge the women act out upon John Thomas, and second, to show that in acting out this revenge the women are doing something that leaves them in confusion, uneasiness, and perhaps even despair. For while they have shown their independence by teaching John Thomas his lesson, they have also broken something in him—some independence of spirit, some masculine pride, even arrogance—which first made him attractive in their eyes.

The young women are trapped. Is it they alone, or all such women? They need to humble this insufferable male, they need to teach him he just can't go around picking and choosing as if he were a sultan, and they need, above all, to "persuade" him (with their fists and buckles) that a man has to acquiesce in the rites of marriage, which means, to surrender his freedom and, at least in theory, limit himself to one woman. Well, says Lawrence in effect, they succeed in doing this, but the price they pay is to make him lose precisely the qualities they had found so attractive in him. And at the end, John Thomas does win a sort of victory. Forced to choose, he chooses Annie. This leaves her profoundly disquieted, since, as we may surmise, she has wanted him to choose her, as all the other women have wanted him to choose them. "Something," writes Lawrence, "was broken" in Annie—what it is, he does not say.

The story ends unresolved, perhaps because the battle between the sexes never is quite resolved. Lawrence does not take sides in any simple, direct way; he seems to want us to respond, not so much to the ideas that whirl around the clash between men and women, as to the intensity, energy, and pleasure that are involved in that clash. At the end, we feel a curious mixture of responses—a certain horror at the punishment suffered by John Thomas, an amusement at seeing him brought down a peg or two, a sympathy for the complicated feelings of the young women who seem to suffer bewilderment at the very moment of their victory, and finally, a bemused, contemplative witnessing of how perilous yet fragile is our life together: men and women.

P.S.—The Roman poet Ovid has a passage about the story of Orpheus which can be seen as a prototype of Lawrence's story, and surely Lawrence knew the myth on which Ovid's passage is based. You may remember that Orpheus was the fabled master poet-musician of the ancient world, whose skill was so great that he could affect humans and animals, and even trees and rocks, with his playing. Orpheus's wife, Eurydice, was carried off to the underworld; by his skill he brought her out, but disobeyed instructions not to look back at her along the way. As a result he lost her forever, went into mourning, renounced the love of women, and turned to homosexuality. This so enraged a band of women called the Maenads that when they saw him playing his lyre and singing,

> One of them, her tresses
> Streaming in the light air, cried out: "Look there!
> There is our despiser!" and she flung a spear
> Straight at the singing mouth, but the leafy wand
> Made only a mark and did no harm. Another
> Let fly a stone, which, even as it flew,
> Was conquered by the sweet harmonious music,
> Fell at his feet, as if to ask for pardon.
> But still the warfare raged, there was no limit,
> Mad fury reigned, and even so, all weapons
> Would have been softened by the singer's music,
> But there was other orchestration: flutes
> Shrilling, and trumpets braying loud, and drums,
> Beating of breasts, and howling, so the lyre
> Was overcome, and then at last the stones

Reddened with blood, the blood of the singer, heard
No more through all that outcry. All the birds
Innumerable, fled, and the charmed snakes,
The train of beast, Orpheus' glory, followed.
The Maenads stole the show. Their bloody hands
Were turned against the poet; they came thronging
Like birds who see an owl, wandering in daylight;
They bayed him down, as in the early morning,
Hounds circle the doomed stag beside the game-pits.
They rushed him, threw the wands, wreathed with green leaves,
Not meant for such a purpose; some threw clods,
Some branches torn from the tree, and some threw stones,
And they found fitter weapons for their madness.
Not far away there was a team of oxen
Plowing the field, and near them farmers, digging
Reluctant earth, and sweating over their labor,
Who fled before the onrush of this army
Leaving behind them hoe and rake and mattock
And these the women grabbed and slew the oxen
Who lowered horns at them in brief defiance
And were torn limb from limb, and then the women
Rushed back to murder Orpheus, who stretched out
His hands in supplication, and whose voice,
For the first time, moved no one. They struck him down,
And through those lips to which the rocks had listened,
To which the hearts of savage beasts responded,
His spirit found its way to winds and air.

*Translated by Rolfe Humphries**

Tickets, Please

There is in the Midlands[1] a single-line tramway[2] system which boldly
leaves the county town and plunges off into the black, industrial country-side,
up hill and down dale, through the long ugly villages of workmen's houses, over
canals and railways, past churches perched high and nobly over the smoke and
shadows, through stark, grimy cold little market-places, tilting away in a rush

*Reprinted from Ovid, *Metamorphoses,* translated by Rolfe Humphries. Copyright 1955, Indiana
University Press. Reprinted by permission.

[1]An industrial area in the middle of England.
[2]A kind of trolley car covering this area.

past cinemas and shops down to the hollow where the collieries[3] are, then up again, past a little rural church, under the ash trees, on in a rush to the terminus, the last little ugly place of industry, the cold little town that shivers on the edge of the wild, gloomy country beyond. There the green and creamy coloured tram-cars seem to pause and purr with curious satisfaction. But in a few minutes—the clock on the turret of the Co-operative Wholesale Society's shops gives the time—away it starts once more on the adventure. Again there are the reckless swoops downhill, bouncing the loops: again the chilly wait in the hill-top market-place: again the breathless slithering round the precipitous drop under the church: again the patient halts at the loops, waiting for the outcoming car: so on and on, for two long hours, till at last the city looms beyond the fat gas-works, the narrow factories draw near, we are in the sordid streets of the great town, once more we sidle to a standstill at our terminus, abashed by the great crimson and cream-coloured city cars, but still perky, jaunty, somewhat dare-devil, green as a jaunty sprig of parsley out of a black colliery garden.

To ride on these cars is always an adventure. Since we are in war-time,[4] the drivers are men unfit for active service: cripples and hunchbacks. So they have the spirit of the devil in them. The ride becomes a steeplechase. Hurray! we have leapt in a clear jump over the canal bridge—now for the four-lane corner. With a shriek and a trail of sparks we are clear again. To be sure, a tram often leaps the rails—but what matter! It sits in a ditch till other trams come to haul it out. It is quite common for a car, packed with one solid mass of living people, to come to a dead halt in the midst of unbroken blackness, the heart of nowhere on a dark night, and for the driver and the girl conductor to call: "All get off—car's on fire!" Instead, however, of rushing out in a panic, the passengers stolidly reply: "Get on—get on! We're not coming out. We're stopping where we are. Push on, George." So till flames actually appear.

The reason for this reluctance to dismount is that the nights are howlingly cold, black, and windswept, and a car is a haven of refuge. From village to village the miners travel, for a change of cinema, of girl, of pub. The trams are desperately packed. Who is going to risk himself in the black gulf outside, to wait perhaps an hour for another tram, then to see the forlorn notice 'Depot Only,' because there is something wrong! Or to greet a unit of three bright cars all so tight with people that they sail past with a howl of derision. Trams that pass in the night.

This, the most dangerous tram-service in England, as the authorities themselves declare, with pride, is entirely conducted by girls, and driven by rash young men, a little crippled, or by delicate young men, who creep forward in terror. The girls are fearless young hussies. In their ugly blue uniform, skirts up to their knees, shapeless old peaked caps on their heads, they have all the *sang-froid* of an old non-commissioned officer. With a tram packed with howling colliers, roaring hymns downstairs and a sort of antiphony of obscenities upstairs, the lasses are perfectly at their ease. They pounce on the youths who

[3]Coal mines.
[4]World War I.

try to evade their ticket-machine. They push off the men at the end of their distance. They are not going to be done in the eye—not they. They fear nobody—and everybody fears them.

"Hello, Annie!"

"Hello, Ted!"

"Oh, mind my corn. Miss Stone. It's my belief you've got a heart of stone, for you've trod on it again."

"You should keep it in your pocket," replies Miss Stone, and she goes sturdily upstairs in her high boots.

"Tickets, please."

She is peremptory, suspicious, and ready to hit first. She can hold her own against ten thousand. The step of that tram-car is her Thermopylae.[5]

Therefore, there is a certain wild romance aboard these cars—and in the sturdy bosom of Annie herself. The time for soft romance is in the morning, between ten o'clock and one, when things are rather slack: that is, except market-day and Saturday. Thus Annie has time to look about her. Then she often hops off her car and into a shop where she has spied something, while the driver chats in the main road. There is very good feeling between the girls and the drivers. Are they not companions in peril, shipmates aboard this careering vessel of a tram-car, for ever rocking on the waves of a stormy land.

Then, also, during the easy hours, the inspectors are most in evidence. For some reason, everybody employed in this tram-service is young: there are no grey heads. It would not do. Therefore the inspectors are of the right age, and one, the chief, is also good-looking. See him stand on a wet, gloomy morning, in his long oilskin, his peaked cap well down over his eyes, waiting to board a car. His face ruddy, his small brown moustache is weathered, he has a faint impudent smile. Fairly tall and agile, even in his waterproof, he springs aboard a car and greets Annie.

"Hello, Annie! Keeping the wet out?"

"Trying to."

There are only two people in the car. Inspecting is soon over. Then for a long and impudent chat on the foot-board, a good, easy, twelve-mile chat.

The inspector's name is John Thomas Raynor—always called John Thomas, except sometimes, in malice, Coddy. His face sets in fury when he is addressed, from a distance, with this abbreviation. There is considerable scandal about John Thomas in half a dozen villages. He flirts with the girl conductors in the morning, and walks out with them in the dark night, when they leave their tram-car at the depôt. Of course, the girls quit the service frequently. Then he flirts and walks out with the newcomer: always providing she is sufficiently attractive, and that she will consent to walk. It is remarkable, however, that most of the girls are quite comely, they are all young, and this roving life aboard the car gives them a sailor's dash and recklessness. What matter how they behave when the ship is in port? To-morrow they will be aboard again.

Annie, however, was something of a Tartar, and her sharp tongue had kept

---

[5] A narrow pass in Greece, where a small number of Spartans held off a large Persian army (480 B.C.).

John Thomas at arm's length for many months. Perhaps, therefore, she liked him all the more: for he always came up smiling, with impudence. She watched him vanquish one girl, then another. She could tell by the movement of his mouth and eyes, when he flirted with her in the morning, that he had been walking out with this lass, or the other, the night before. A fine cock-of-the-walk he was. She could sum him up pretty well.

In this subtle antagonism they knew each other like old friends, they were as shrewd with one another almost as man and wife. But Annie had always kept him sufficiently at arm's length. Besides, she had a boy of her own.

The Statutes fair, however, came in November, at Bestwood. It happened that Annie had the Monday night off. It was a drizzling ugly night, yet she dressed herself up and went to the fair-ground. She was alone, but she expected soon to find a pal of some sort.

The roundabouts were veering round and grinding out their music, the side-shows were making as much commotion as possible. In the coconut shies[6] there were no coconuts, but artificial war-time substitutes, which the lads declared were fastened into the irons. There was a sad decline in brilliance and luxury. None the less, the ground was muddy as ever, there was the same crush, the press of faces lighted up by the flares and the electric lights, the same smell of naphtha[7] and a few potatoes, and of electricity.

Who should be the first to greet Miss Annie on the show-ground but John Thomas. He had a black overcoat buttoned up to his chin, and a tweed cap pulled down over his brows, his face between was ruddy and smiling and handy as ever. She knew so well the way his mouth moved.

She was very glad to have a 'boy.' To be at the Statutes without a fellow was no fun. Instantly, like the gallant he was, he took her on the Dragons, grim-toothed, roundabout switchbacks. It was not nearly so exciting as a tram-car actually. But, then, to be seated in a shaking, green dragon, uplifted above the sea of bubble faces, careering in a rickety fashion in the lower heavens, whilst John Thomas leaned over her, his cigarette in his mouth, was after all the right style. She was a plump, quick, alive little creature. So she was quite excited and happy.

John Thomas made her stay on for the next round. And therefore she could hardly for shame repulse him when he put his arm round her and drew her a little nearer to him, in a very warm and cuddly manner. Besides, he was fairly discreet, he kept his movement as hidden as possible. She looked down, and saw that his red, clean hand was out of sight of the crowd. And they knew each other so well. So they warmed up to the fair.

After the dragons they went on the horses. John Thomas paid each time, so she could but be complaisant. He, of course, sat astride on the outer horse—named 'Black Bess'—and she sat sideways, towards him, on the inner horse—named 'Wildfire'. But of course John Thomas was not going to sit discreetly on 'Black Bess', holding the brass bar. Round they spun and heaved, in the light. And round he swung on his wooden steed, flinging one leg across her mount,

[6]A carnival game—coconuts thrown at a target.
[7]Cooking gas.

and perilously tipping up and down, across the space, half lying back, laughing at her. He was perfectly happy; she was afraid her hat was on one side, but she was excited.

He threw quoits on a table, and won for her two large, pale blue hat-pins. And then, hearing the noise of the cinemas, announcing another performance, they climbed the boards and went in.

Of course, during these performances pitch darkness falls from time to time, when the machine goes wrong. Then there is a wild whooping, and a loud smacking of simulated kisses. In these moments John Thomas drew Annie towards him. After all, he had a wonderfully warm, cosy way of holding a girl with his arm, he seemed to make such a nice fit. And, after all, it was pleasant to be so held: so very comforting and cosy and nice. He leaned over her and she felt his breath on her hair; she knew he wanted to kiss her on the lips. And, after all, he was so warm and she fitted in to him so softly. After all, she wanted him to touch her lips.

But the light sprang up; she also started electrically, and put her hat straight. He left his arm lying nonchalantly behind her. Well, it was fun, it was exciting to be at the Statutes with John Thomas.

When the cinema was over they went for a walk across the dark, damp fields. He had all the arts of love-making. He was especially good at holding a girl, when he sat with her on a stile in the black, drizzling darkness. He seemed to be holding her in space, against his own warmth and gratification. And his kisses were soft and slow and searching.

So Annie walked out with John Thomas, though she kept her own boy dangling in the distance. Some of the tram-girls chose to be huffy. But there, you must take things as you find them, in this life.

There was no mistake about it, Annie liked John Thomas a good deal. She felt so rich and warm in herself whenever he was near. And John Thomas really liked Annie, more than usual. The soft, melting way in which she could flow into a fellow, as if she melted into his very bones, was something rare and good. He fully appreciated this.

But with a developing acquaintance there began a developing intimacy. Annie wanted to consider him a person, a man: she wanted to take an intelligent interest in him, and to have an intelligent response. She did not want a mere nocturnal presence, which was what he was so far. And she prided herself that he could not leave her.

Here she made a mistake. John Thomas intended to remain a nocturnal presence; he had no idea of becoming an all-round individual to her. When she started to take an intelligent interest in him and his life and his character, he sheered off. He hated intelligent interest. And he knew that the only way to stop it was to avoid it. The possessive female was aroused in Annie. So he left her.

It is no use saying she was not surprised. She was at first startled, thrown out of her count. For she had been so *very* sure of holding him. For a while she was staggered, and everything became uncertain to her. Then she wept with fury, indignation, desolation, and misery. Then she had a spasm of despair. And then, when he came, still impudently, on to her car, still familiar, but letting her see by the movement of his head that he had gone away to somebody else for the time being, and was enjoying pastures new, then she determined to have her own back.

She had a very shrewd idea what girls John Thomas had taken out. She went to Nora Purdy. Nora was a tall, rather pale, but well-built girl, with beautiful yellow hair. She was rather secretive.

"Hey!" said Annie, accosting her; then softly: "Who's John Thomas on with now?"

"I don't know," said Nora.

"Why, tha does," said Annie, ironically lapsing into dialect. "Tha knows as well as I do."

"Well, I do, then," said Nora. "It isn't me, so don't bother."

"It's Cissy Meakin, isn't it?"

"It is, for all I know."

"Hasn't he got a face on him!" said Annie. "I don't half like his cheek. I could knock him off the foot-board when he comes round at me."

"He'll get dropped on one of these days," said Nora.

"Ay, he will, when somebody makes up their mind to drop it on him. I should like to see him taken down a peg or two, shouldn't you?"

"I shouldn't mind," said Nora.

"You've got quite as much cause to as I have," said Annie. "But we'll drop on him one of these days, my girl. What? Don't you want to?"

"I don't mind," said Nora.

But as a matter of fact, Nora was much more vindictive than Annie.

One by one Annie went the round of the old flames. It so happened that Cissy Meakin left the tramway service in quite a short time. Her mother made her leave. Then John Thomas was on the *qui vive.*[8] He cast his eyes over his old flock. And his eyes lighted on Annie. He thought she would be safe now. Besides, he liked her.

She arranged to walk home with him on Sunday night. It so happened that her car would be in the depot at half-past nine: the last car would come in at 10.15. So John Thomas was to wait for her there.

At the depot, the girls had a little waiting-room of their own. It was quite rough, but cosy, with a fire and an oven and a mirror, and table and wooden chairs. The half-dozen girls who knew John Thomas only too well had arranged to take service this Sunday afternoon. So, as the cars began to come in, early, the girls dropped into the waiting-room. And instead of hurrying off home, they sat around the fire and had a cup of tea. Outside was the darkness and lawlessness of war-time.

John Thomas came on the car after Annie, at about a quarter to ten. He poked his head easily into the girls' waiting-room.

"Prayer-meeting?" he asked.

"Ay," said Laura Sharp. "Ladies only."

"That's me!" said John Thomas. It was one of his favourite exclamations.

[8]French phrase: on the alert.

"Shut the door, boy," said Muriel Baggaley.

"Oh, which side of me?" said John Thomas.

"Which tha likes," said Polly Birkin.

He had come in and closed the door behind him. The girls moved in their circle, to make a place for him near the fire. He took off his great-coat and pushed back his hat.

"Who handles the teapot?" he said.

Nora Purdy silently poured him out a cup of tea.

"Want a bit o' my bread and drippin'?" said Muriel Baggaley to him.

"Ay, give us a bit."

And he began to eat his piece of bread.

"There's no place like home, girls," he said.

They all looked at him as he uttered this piece of impudence. He seemed to be sunning himself in the presence of so many damsels.

"Especially if you're not afraid to go home in the dark," said Laura Sharp.

"Me! By myself I am."

They sat till they heard the last tram come in. In a few minutes Emma Houselay entered.

"Come on, my old duck!" cried Polly Birkin.

"It *is* perishing,"[9] said Emma, holding her fingers to the fire.

"But—I'm afraid to, go home in, the dark," sang Laura Sharp, the tune having got into her mind.

"Who're you going with to-night, John Thomas?" asked Muriel Baggaley coolly.

"To-night?" said John Thomas. "Oh, I'm going home by myself to-night—all on my lonely-o."

"That's me!" said Nora Purdy, using his own ejaculation.

The girls laughed shrilly.

"Me as well, Nora," said John Thomas.

"Don't know what you mean," said Laura.

"Yes, I'm toddling," said he, rising and reaching for his overcoat.

"Nay," said Polly. "We're all here waiting for you."

"We've got to be up in good time in the morning," he said, in the benevolent official manner.

They all laughed.

"Nay," said Muriel. "Don't leave us all lonely, John Thomas. Take one!"

"I'll take the lot, if you like," he responded gallantly.

"That you won't either," said Muriel. "Two's company; seven's too much of a good thing."

"Nay—take one," said Laura. "Fair and square, all above board and say which."

"Ay," cried Annie, speaking for the first time. "Pick, John Thomas; let's hear thee."

"Nay," he said. "I'm going home quiet to-night. Feeling good, for once."

[9]British colloquialism: It's cold.

"Whereabouts?" said Annie. "Take a good 'un, then. But tha's got to take one of us!"

"Nay, how can I take one," he said, laughing uneasily. "I don't want to make enemies."

"You'd only make *one,*" said Annie.

"The chosen *one,*" added Laura.

"Oh, my! Who said girls!" exclaimed John Thomas, again turning, as if to escape. "Well—good-night."

"Nay, you've got to make your pick," said Muriel. "Turn your face to the wall, and say which one touches you. Go on—we shall only just touch your back—one of us. Go on—turn your face to the wall, and don't look, and say which one touches you."

He was uneasy, mistrusting them. Yet he had not the courage to break away. They pushed him to a wall and stood him there with his face to it. Behind his back they all grimaced, tittering. He looked so comical. He looked around uneasily.

"Go on!" he cried.

"You're looking—you're looking!" they shouted.

He turned his head away. And suddenly, with a movement like a swift cat, Annie went forward and fetched him a box on the side of the head that sent his cap flying and himself staggering. He started round.

But at Annie's signal they all flew at him, slapping him, pinching him, pulling his hair, though more in fun than in spite or anger. He, however, saw red. His blue eyes flamed with strange fear as well as fury, and he butted through the girls to the door. It was locked. He wrenched at it. Roused, alert, the girls stood round and looked at him. He faced them, at bay. At that moment they were rather horrifying to him, as they stood in their short uniforms. He was distinctly afraid.

"Come on, John Thomas! Come on! Choose!" said Annie.

"What are you after? Open the door," he said.

"We shan't—not till you've chosen!" said Muriel.

"Chosen what?" he said.

"Chosen the one you're going to marry," she replied.

He hesitated a moment.

"Open the blasted door," he said, "and get back to your senses." He spoke with official authority.

"You've got to choose!" cried the girls.

"Come on!" cried Annie, looking him in the eye. "Come on! Come on!"

He went forward, rather vaguely. She had taken off her belt, and swinging it, she fetched him a sharp blow over the head with the buckle end. He sprang and seized her. But immediately the other girls rushed upon him, pulling and tearing and beating him. Their blood was now thoroughly up. He was their sport now. They were going to have their own back, out of him. Strange, wild creatures, they hung on him and rushed at him to bear him down. His tunic was torn right up the back, Nora had hold at the back of his collar, and was actually strangling him. Luckily the button burst. He struggled in a wild frenzy of fury and terror, almost mad terror. His tunic was simply torn off his back, his shirt-sleeves were torn away, his arms were naked. The girls rushed at him, clenched their hands on him and pulled at him: or they rushed at him and pushed him, butted him with all their might: or they struck him wild blows. He ducked and cringed and struck sideways. They became more intense.

At last he was down. They rushed on him, kneeling on him. He had neither breath nor strength to move. His face was bleeding with a long scratch, his brow was bruised.

Annie knelt on him, the other girls knelt and hung on to him. Their faces were flushed, their hair wild, their eyes were all glittering strangely. He lay at last quite still, with face averted, as an animal lies when it is defeated and at the mercy of the captor. Sometimes his eye glanced back at the wild faces of the girls. His breast rose heavily, his wrists were torn.

"Now, then, my fellow!" gasped Annie at length. "Now then—now——"

At the sound of her terrifying, cold triumph, he suddenly started to struggle as an animal might, but the girls threw themselves upon him with unnatural strength and power, forcing him down.

"Yes—now, then!" gasped Annie at length.

And there was a dead silence, in which the thud of heartbeating was to be heard. It was a suspense of pure silence in every soul.

"Now you know where you are," said Annie.

The sight of his white, bare arm maddened the girls. He lay in a kind of trance of fear and antagonism. They felt themselves filled with supernatural strength.

Suddenly Polly started to laugh—to giggle wildly—helplessly—and Emma and Muriel joined in. But Annie and Nora and Laura remained the same, tense, watchful, with gleaming eyes. He winced away from these eyes.

"Yes," said Annie, in a curious low tone, secret and deadly. "Yes! You've got it now. You know what you've done, don't you? You know what you've done."

He made no sound nor sign, but lay with bright, averted eyes, and averted, bleeding face.

"You ought to be *killed,* that's what you ought," said Annie, tensely. "You ought to be *killed.*" And there was a terrifying lust in her voice.

Polly was ceasing to laugh, and giving long-drawn Oh-h-hs and sighs as she came to herself.

"He's got to choose," she said vaguely.

"Oh, yes, he has," said Laura, with vindictive decision.

"Do you hear—do you hear?" said Annie. And with a sharp movement, that made him wince, she turned his face to her.

"Do you hear?" she repeated, shaking him.

But he was quite dumb. She fetched him a sharp slap on the face. He started, and his eyes widened. Then his face darkened with defiance, after all.

"Do you hear?" she repeated.

He only looked at her with hostile eyes.

"Speak!" she said, putting her face devilishly near his.

"What?" he said, almost overcome.

"You've got to *choose!*" she cried, as if it were some terrible menace, and as if it hurt her that she could not exact more.

"What?" he said, in fear.

"Choose your girl, Coddy. You've got to choose her now. And you'll get your neck broken if you play any more of your tricks, my boy. You're settled now."

There was a pause. Again he averted his face. He was cunning in his overthrow. He did not give in to them really—no, not if they tore him to bits.

"All right, then," he said, "I choose Annie." His voice was strange and full of malice. Annie let go of him as if he had been a hot coal.

"He's chosen Annie!" said the girls in chorus.

"Me!" cried Annie. She was still kneeling, but away from him. He was still lying prostrate, with averted face. The girls grouped uneasily around.

"Me!" repeated Annie, with a terrible bitter accent.

Then she got up, drawing away from him with strange disgust and bitterness.

"I wouldn't touch him," she said.

But her face quivered with a kind of agony, she seemed as if she would fall. The other girls turned aside. He remained lying on the floor, with his torn clothes and bleeding, averted face.

"Oh, if he's chosen——" said Polly.

"I don't want him—he can choose again," said Annie, with the same rather bitter hopelessness.

"Get up," said Polly, lifting his shoulder. "Get up."

He rose slowly, a strange, ragged, dazed creature. The girls eyed him from a distance, curiously, furtively, dangerously.

"Who wants him?" cried Laura, roughly.

"Nobody," they answered, with contempt. Yet each one of them waited for him to look at her, hoped he would look at her. All except Annie, and something was broken in her.

He, however, kept his face closed and averted from them all. There was a silence of the end. He picked up the torn pieces of his tunic, without knowing what to do with them. The girls stood about uneasily, flushed, panting, tidying their hair and their dress unconsciously, and watching him. He looked at none of them. He espied his cap in a corner, and went and picked it up. He put it on his head, and one of the girls burst into a shrill, hysteric laugh at the sight he presented. He, however, took no heed, but went straight to where his overcoat hung on a peg. The girls moved away from contact with him as if he had been an electric wire. He put on his coat and buttoned it down. Then he rolled his tunic-rags into a bundle, and stood before the locked door, dumbly.

"Open the door, somebody," said Laura.

"Annie's got the key," said one.

Annie silently offered the key to the girls. Nora unlocked the door.

"Tit for tat, old man" she said. "Show yourself a man, and don't bear a grudge."

But without a word or sign he had opened the door and gone, his face closed, his head dropped.

"That'll learn him," said Laura.

"Coddy!" said Nora.

"Shut up, for God's sake!" cried Annie fiercely, as if in torture.

"Well, I'm about ready to go, Polly. Look sharp!" said Muriel.

The girls were all anxious to be off. They were tidying themselves hurriedly, with mute, stupefied faces.

Questions for Writing and Discussion

1.   Read the first four paragraphs with special care; they provide the setting, tone, pace, rhythm for the entire story. By focusing on a few key phrases or sentences in these paragraphs, show how they serve to prepare the atmosphere for all that follows in the story.

2.   On p. 26, Lawrence speaks of "a certain wild romance aboard these cars." What is there about the situation in which these young people find themselves that helps make for "a certain wild romance"? Is this description borne out by the rest of the story?

3.   Somewhat later, on p. 27, Lawrence writes about Annie and John Thomas that "in this subtle antagonism they knew each other like old friends, they were as shrewd with one another almost as man and wife." This may be a key sentence in the story, preparing us for the clash that is to follow. Relate this sentence to the central action (not just to the way the women conductors beat up John Thomas, but also to the response that Annie finally has when he is forced to "choose.").

4.   Read in the 1970s, this story could be seen as an act of feminist revenge by a group of outraged young women who have been mistreated by a charming but irresponsible young man. And that certainly seems to be a legitimate way to read the story. Yet we also know that D. H. Lawrence would almost certainly have been hostile to many aspects of contemporary feminism. What, then, do you suppose he intended to suggest through the climax of his story? Is it sometimes possible that a great writer can compose a story which turns out (perhaps even against his will) to contradict his own ideas? (Lawrence said: trust the tale, not the teller.)

THOMAS HARDY

The Fiddler of the Reels

Introduction

Thomas Hardy was one of the great English novelists and poets; he also wrote short stories, a few of which are very good. One of the best, though almost forgotten, is "Fiddler of the Reels."

It is set, like most of Hardy's fiction, in Wessex, his fictional name for the Dorset section of southwest England—rural, traditional—in which he grew up. Its pattern of narrative is a familiar one in all storytelling: a stranger arrives in a more or less stable community and the result is disruption and excitement. And its theme is also familiar, borrowed from the tradition of English fiction and especially the outlook of Romanticism: the idea of sexual attraction as an obsession, an irresistible power.

Into the placid village of Stickleford comes a handsome stranger, "from nobody knew where." Wat or "Mop" Ollamoor, "musician, dandy and company-man," plays the violin with ravishing beauty, his "chromatic subtleties" lending him a demonic power over listeners, "especially young women of fragile and responsive organization." One such young woman, Car'line Aspent, abandons her village sweetheart because she has become hopelessly enchanted by Mop's fiddle. A few years later, abandoned in turn by Mop, she arranges a marriage with the former sweetheart, now soberly employed in London, and brings with her to the city, as a dowry of sorts, the child she has had by the wizard-musician. All seems stable and quiet, until Car'line again chances upon Mop, and there follows a scene of "witchery," with Car'line abandoning herself in dance to Mop's music, "defiantly as she thought but in truth slavishly and abjectly. . . ." When she collapses, Mop seizes the little girl and races off: and Car'line, still safe with her worthy if wearied husband, seems relieved that her child remains with Mop.

It is a country tale, told with ironic severity and sophistication. The rhythms speed up, the language swells, a note of tentative abandon is struck. Not even in the placidity of Wessex can there be assurance that a life will not be

35

disordered, or quickened, by some intruding power, some obsession bearing possibilities of the unknown. Mop himself is shrewdly kept at a distance, ominous but unexplained: a demon-lover of country taverns, for whom music and sexuality flow together and the lure of abandon speeds through the scrape of a bow.

We have summarized the story here, not because anyone is likely to experience difficulty in making it out, but because we want to stress Hardy's special tone—a tone of quizzical irony toward the Romantic materials he uses, a tone that half-yields to the idea of obsession and half-mocks it. That may explain why the narrative voice keeps a considerable distance from the events it describes, why it never yields itself entirely to the idea of obsession yet acknowledges the force of that idea. Hardy's prose seems deliberately formal, as if to strike a contrast with the disorder he is representing. Still, that doesn't quite account for the first two paragraphs, which employ the familiar convention of starting out with a storyteller within the story, a convention that in fact isn't carried through sufficiently in the rest of the story.

The Fiddler of the Reels

"Talking of Exhibitions, World's Fairs, and what not," said the old gentleman, "I would not go round the corner to see a dozen of them nowadays. The only exhibition that ever made, or ever will make, any impression upon my imagination was the first of the series, the parent of them all, and now a thing of old times—the Great Exhibition of 1851, in Hyde Park, London. None of the younger generation can realize the sense of novelty it produced in us who were then in our prime. A noun substantive went so far as to become an adjective in honor of the occasion. It was "exhibition" hat, "exhibition" razor-strop, "exhibition" watch; nay, even "exhibition" weather, "exhibition" spirits, sweethearts, babies, wives—for the time.

"For South Wessex, the year formed in many ways an extraordinary chronological frontier or transit-line, at which there occurred what one might call a precipice in Time. As in a geological 'fault,' we had presented to us a sudden bringing of ancient and modern into absolute contact, such as probably in no other single year since the Conquest was ever witnessed in this part of the country."

These observations led us onward to talk of the different personages, gentle and simple, who lived and moved within our narrow and peaceful horizon at that time; and of three people in particular, whose queer little history was oddly touched at points by the Exhibition, more concerned with it than that of anybody else who dwelt in those outlying shades of the world, Stickleford, Mellstock, and Egdon. First in prominence among these three came Wat Ollamoor—if that were his real name.

He was a woman's man—supremely so—and externally very little else. To men he was not attractive; perhaps a little repulsive at times. Musician, dandy, and company-man in practice; veterinary surgeon in theory, he lodged awhile in Mellstock village, coming from nobody knew where; though some said his first appearance in this neighborhood had been as fiddleplayer in a show at Greenhill Fair.

Many a worthy villager envied him his power over unsophisticated maidenhood—a power which seemed sometimes to have a touch of the weird and wizardly in it. Personally he was not ill-favored, though rather un-English, his complexion being a rich olive, his rank hair dark and rather clammy—made still clammier by secret ointments, which, when he came fresh to a party, caused him to smell like "boys'-love" (southernwood) steeped in lamp-oil. On occasion he wore curls—a double row—running almost horizontally around his head. But as these were sometimes noticeably absent, it was concluded that they were not altogether of Nature's making. By girls whose love for him had turned to hatred he had been nicknamed "Mop," from this abundance of hair, which was long enough to rest upon his shoulders; as time passed, the name more and more prevailed.

His fiddling, possibly, had the most to do with the fascination he exercised, for, to speak fairly, it could claim for itself a most peculiar and personal quality, like that in a moving preacher. There were tones in it which bred the immediate conviction that indolence and averseness to systematic application were all that lay between "Mop" and the career of a second Paganini.[1]

While playing he invariably closed his eyes; using no notes, and, as it were, allowing the violin to wander on at will into the most plaintive passages ever heard by rustic man. There was a certain lingual character in the supplicatory expressions he produced, which would wellnigh have drawn an ache from the heart of a gate-post. He could make any child in the parish, who was at all sensitive to music, burst into tears in a few minutes by simply fiddling one of the old dance-tunes he almost entirely affected—country jigs, reels, and "Favorite Quick-Steps" of the last century—some mutilated remains of which even now reappear as nameless phantoms in new quadrilles and gallops, where they are recognized only by the curious, or by such old-fashioned and far-between people as have been thrown with men like Wat Ollamoor in their early life.

His date was a little later than that of the old Mellstock choir-band, which comprised the Dewys, Mail, and the rest—in fact, he did not rise above the horizon thereabout till those well-known muscians were disbanded as ecclesiastical functionaries. In their honest love of thoroughness they despised the new man's style. Theophilus Dewy (Reuben the tranter's younger brother) used to say there was no "plumness" in it—no bowing, no solidity—it was all fantastical. And probably this was true. Anyhow, Mop had, very obviously, never bowed a note of church-music from his birth; he never once sat in the gallery of Mellstock church, where the others had tuned their venerable psalmody so many hundreds of times; had never, in all likelihood, entered a church at all. All

[1]Niccolò Paganini (1782–1840), celebrated violin virtuoso, also composer.

were devil's tunes in his repertory. "He could no more play the 'Wold Hun-
dredth' to his true time than he could play the brazen serpent," the tranter
would say. (The brazen serpent was supposed in Mellstock to be a musical
instrument particularly hard to blow.)

Occasionally Mop could produce the aforesaid moving effect upon the
souls of grown-up persons, especially young women of fragile and responsive
organization. Such a one was Car'line Aspent. Though she was already engaged
to be married before she met him, Car'line, of them all, was the most influenced
by Mop Ollamoor's heart-stealing melodies, to her discomfort, nay, positive
pain and ultimate injury. She was a pretty, invocating, weak-mouthed girl,
whose chief defect as a companion with her sex was a tendency to peevishness
now and then. At this time she was not a resident in Mellstock parish, where
Mop lodged, but lived some miles off at Stickleford, farther down the river.

How and where she first made acquaintance with him and his fiddling is
not truly known, but the story was that it either began or was developed on one
spring evening, when, in passing through Lower Mellstock, she chanced to pause
on the bridge near his house to rest herself, and languidly leaned over the
parapet. Mop was standing on his door-step, as was his custom, spinning the
insidious thread of semi- and demi-semi-quavers from the E string of his fiddle
for the benefit of passers-by, and laughing as the tears rolled down the cheeks of
the little children hanging around him. Car'line pretended to be engrossed with
the rippling of the stream under the arches, but in reality she was listening, as he
knew. Presently the aching of the heart seized her simultaneously with a wild
desire to glide airily in the mazes of an infinite dance. To shake off the
fascination she resolved to go on, although it would be necessary to pass him as
he played. On stealthily glancing ahead at the performer, she found to her relief
that his eyes were closed in abandonment to instrumentation, and she strode on
boldly. But when closer her step grew timid, her tread convulsed itself more and
more accordantly with the time of the melody, till she very nearly danced along.
Gaining another glance at him when immediately opposite, she saw that *one* of
his eyes was open, quizzing her as he smiled at her emotional state. Her gait
could not divest itself of its compelled capers till she had gone a long way past
the house; and Car'line was unable to shake off the strange infatuation for hours.

After that day, whenever there was to be in the neighborhood a dance to
which she could get an invitation, and where Mop Ollamoor was to be the
muscian, Car'line contrived to be present, though it sometimes involved a walk
of several miles; for he did not play so often in Stickleford as elsewhere.

The next evidences of his influence over her were singular enough, and it
would require a neurologist to fully explain them. She would be sitting quietly,
any evening after dark, in the house of her father, the parish-clerk, which stood
in the middle of Stickleford village street, this being the high-road between
Lower Mellstock and Moreford, six miles eastward. Here, without a moment's
warning, and in the midst of a general conversation between her father, sister,
and the young man before alluded to, who devotedly wooed her in ignorance of
her infatuation, she would start from her seat in the chimney-corner as if she had

received a galvanic shock, and spring convulsively towards the ceiling; then she would burst into tears, and it was not till some half-hour had passed that she grew calm as usual. Her father, knowing her hysterical tendencies, was always excessively anxious about this trait in his youngest girl, and feared the attack to be a species of epileptic fit. Not so her sister Julia. Julia had found out what was the cause. At the moment before the jumping, only an exceptionally sensitive ear situated in the chimney-nook could have caught from down the flue the beat of a man's footstep along the highway without. But it was in that foot-fall, for which she had been waiting, that the origin of Car'line's involuntary springing lay. The pedestrian was Mop Ollamoor, as the girl well knew; but his business that way was not to visit her; he sought another woman, whom he spoke of as his Intended, and who lived at Moreford, two miles farther on. On one, and only one, occasion did it happen that Car'line could not control her utterance; it was when her sister alone chanced to be present. "Oh—oh—oh—!" she cried. "He's going to *her*, and not coming to *me!*"

To do the fiddler justice, he had not at first thought greatly of, or spoken much to, this girl of impressionable mould. But he had soon found out her secret, and could not resist a little by-play with her too easily hurt heart, as an interlude between his more serious performances at Moreford. The two became well acquainted, though only by stealth, hardly a soul in Stickleford except her sister, and her lover Ned Hipcroft, being aware of the attachment. Her father disapproved of her coldness to Ned; her sister, too, hoped she might get over this nervous passion for a man of whom so little was known. The ultimate result was that Car'line's manly and simple wooer Edward found his suit becoming practically hopeless. He was a respectable mechanic in a far sounder position than Mop the nominal horse-doctor; but when, before leaving her, Ned put his flat and final question, would she marry him, then and there, now or never, it was with little expectation of obtaining more than the negative she gave him. Though her father supported him and her sister supported him, he could not play the fiddle so as to draw your soul out of your body like a spider's thread, as Mop did, till you felt as limp as withy-wind and yearned for something to cling to. Indeed, Hipcroft had not the slightest ear for music; could not sing two notes in tune, much less play them.

The No he had expected and got from her, in spite of a preliminary encouragement, gave Ned a new start in life. It had been uttered in such a tone of sad entreaty that he resolved to persecute her no more; she should not even be distressed by a sight of his form in the distant perspective of the street and lane. He left the place, and his natural course was to London.

The railway to South Wessex was in process of construction, but it was not as yet opened for traffic; and Hipcroft reached the capital by a six days' trudge on foot, as many a better man had done before him. He was one of the last of the artisan class who used that now extinct method of travel to the great centres of labor, so customary then from time immemorial.

In London he lived and worked regularly at his trade. More fortunate than many, his disinterested willingness recommended him from the first. During the ensuing four years he was never out of employment. He neither advanced nor receded in the modern sense; he improved as a workman, but he did not shift one jot in social position. About his love for Car'line he maintained a rigid silence. No doubt he often thought of her; but being always occupied, and having no relations at Stickleford, he held no communication with that part of the country, and showed no desire to return. In his quiet lodging in Lambeth he moved about after working-hours with the facility of a woman, doing his own cooking, attending to his stocking-heels, and shaping himself by degrees to a life-long bachelorhood. For this conduct one is bound to advance the canonical reason that time could not efface from his heart the image of little Car'line Aspent—and it may be in part true; but there was also the inference that his was a nature not greatly dependent upon the ministrations of the other sex for its comforts.

The fourth year of his residence as a mechanic in London was the year of the Hyde-Park Exhibition already mentioned, and at the construction of this huge glass-house, then unexampled in the world's history, he worked daily. It was an era of great hope and activity among the nations and industries. Though Hipcroft was, in his small way, a central man in the movement, he plodded on with his usual outward placidity. Yet for him, too, the year was destined to have its surprises, for when the bustle of getting the building ready for the opening day was past, the ceremonies had been witnessed, and people were flocking thither from all parts of the globe, he received a letter from Car'line. Till that day the silence of four years between himself and Stickleford had never been broken.

She informed her old lover, in an uncertain penmanship which suggested a trembling hand, of the trouble she had been put to in ascertaining his address, and then broached the subject which had prompted her to write. Four years ago, she said, with the greatest delicacy of which she was capable, she had been so foolish as to refuse him. Her wilful wrong-headedness had since been a grief to her many times, and of late particularly. As for Mr. Ollamoor, he had been absent almost as long as Ned—she did not know where. She would gladly marry Ned now if he were to ask her again, and be a tender little wife to him till her life's end.

A tide of warm feeling must have surged through Ned Hipcroft's frame on receipt of this news, if we may judge by the issue. Unquestionably he loved her still, even if not to the exclusion of every other happiness. This from his Car'line, she who had been dead to him these many years, alive to him again as of old, was in itself a pleasant, gratifying thing. Ned had grown so resigned to, or satisfied with, his lonely lot, that he probably would not have shown much jubilation at anything. Still, a certain ardor of preoccupation, after his first surprise, revealed how deeply her confession of faith in him had stirred him. Measured and methodical in his ways, he did not answer the letter that day, nor the next, nor the next. He was having "a good think." When he did answer it, there was a great deal of sound reasoning mixed in with the unmistakable tenderness of his reply; but the tenderness itself was sufficient to reveal that he was pleased with her straightforward frankness; that the anchorage she had once obtained in his heart was renewable, if it had not been continuously firm.

He told her—and as he wrote his lips twitched humorously over the few gentle words of raillery he indited among the rest of his sentences—that it was all very well for her to come round at this time of day. Why wouldn't she have him when he wanted her? She had no doubt learned that he was not married, but suppose his affections had since been fixed on another? She ought to beg his pardon. Still, he was not the man to forget her. But, considering how he had been used, and what he had suffered, she could not quite expect him to go down to Stickleford and fetch her. But if she would come to him, and say she was sorry, as was only fair; why, yes, he would marry her, knowing what a good little woman she was to the core. He added that the request for her to come to him was a less one to make than it would have been when he first left Stickleford, or even a few months ago; for the new railway into South Wessex was now open, and there had just begun to be run wonderfully contrived special trains, called excursion-trains, on account of the Great Exhibition; so that she could come up easily alone.

She said in her reply how good it was of him to treat her so generously, after her hot-and-cold treatment of him; that though she felt frightened at the magnitude of the journey, and was never as yet in a railway-train, having only seen one pass at a distance, she embraced his offer with all her heart; and would, indeed, own to him how sorry she was, and beg his pardon, and try to be a good wife always, and make up for lost time.

The remaining details of when and where were soon settled, Car'line informing him, for her ready identification in the crowd, that she would be wearing "my new sprigged-laylock cotton gown," and Ned gayly responding that, having married her the morning after her arrival, he would make a day of it by taking her to the Exhibition. One early summer afternoon, accordingly, he came from his place of work, and hastened towards Waterloo Station to meet her. It was as wet and chilly as an English June day can occasionally be, but as he waited on the platform in the drizzle he glowed inwardly, and seemed to have something to live for again.

The "excursion-train"—an absolutely new departure in the history of travel—was still a novelty on the Wessex line, and probably everywhere. Crowds of people had flocked to all the stations on the way up to witness the unwonted sight of so long a train's passage, even where they did not take advantage of the opportunity it offered. The seats for the humbler class of travellers in these early experiments in steam-locomotion were open trucks, without any protection whatever from the wind and rain; and damp weather having set in with the afternoon, the unfortunate occupants of these vehicles were, on the train drawing up at the London terminus, found to be in a pitiable condition from their long journey; blue-faced, stiff-necked, sneezing, rain-beaten, chilled to the marrow, many of the men being hatless; in fact, they resembled people who had been out all night in an open boat on a rough sea, rather than inland excursionists for pleasure. The women had in some degree protected themselves by turning up the skirts of their gowns over their heads, but as by this arrangement they were additionally exposed about the hips, they were all more or less in a sorry plight.

In the bustle and crush of alighting forms of both sexes which followed the entry of the huge concatenation into the station, Ned Hipcroft soon discerned the slim little figure his eye was in search of in the sprigged lilac, as described. She came up to him with a frightened smile—still pretty, though so damp, weather-beaten, and shivering from long exposure to the wind.

"Oh, Ned!" she sputtered, "I—I—" He clasped her in his arms and kissed her, whereupon she burst into a flood of tears.

"You are wet, my poor dear! I hope you'll not get cold," he said. And surveying her and her multifarious surrounding packages, he noticed that by the hand she led a toddling child—a little girl of three or so—whose hood was as clammy and tender face as blue as those of the other travellers.

"Who is this—somebody you know?" asked Ned, curiously.

"Yes, Ned. She's mine."

"Yours?"

"Yes—my own!"

"Your own child?"

"Yes!"

"Well—as God's in—"

"Ned, I didn't name it in my letter, because, you see, it would have been so hard to explain. I thought that when we met I could tell you how she happened to be born, so much better than in writing. I hope you'll excuse it this once, dear Ned, and not scold me, now I've come so many, many miles!"

"This means Mr. Mop Ollamoor, I reckon!" said Hipcroft, gazing palely at them from the distance of the yard or two to which he had withdrawn with a start.

Car'line gasped. "But he's been gone away for years!" she supplicated. "And I never had a young man before! And I was so onlucky to be catched the first time, though some of the girls down there go on like anything!"

Ned remained in silence, pondering.

"You'll forgive me, dear Ned?" she added, beginning to sob outright. "I haven't taken 'ee in after all, because you can pack us back again, if you want to; though 'tis hundreds o' miles, and so wet, and night a-coming on, and I with no money!"

"What the devil can I do?" Hipcroft groaned.

A more pitiable picture than the pair of helpless creatures presented was never seen on a rainy day, as they stood on the great, gaunt, puddled platform, a whiff of drizzle blowing under the roof upon them now and then; the pretty attire in which they had started from Stickleford in the early morning bemuddled and sodden, weariness on their faces, and fear of him in their eyes; for the child began to look as if she thought she too had done some wrong, remaining in an appalled silence till the tears rolled down her chubby cheeks.

"What's the matter, my little maid?" said Ned, mechanically.

"I do want to go home!" she let out, in tones that told of a bursting heart.

"And my totties be cold, an' I sha'nt have no bread-an'-butter no more!"

"I don't know what to say to it all!" declared Ned, his own eye moist as he turned and walked a few steps with his head down; then regarded them again point-blank. From the child escaped troubled breaths and silently welling tears.

"Want some bread-and-butter, do 'ee?" he said, with factitious hardness.

"Ye-e-s!"

"Well, I dare say I can get 'ee a bit. Naturally, you must want some. And you, too, for that matter, Car'line."

"I do feel a little hungered. But I can keep it off," she murmured.

"Folk shouldn't do that," he said, gruffly. . . . "There, come along!" He caught up the child as he added. "You must bide here to-night, anyhow, I s'pose! What can you do otherwise? I'll get 'ee some tea and victuals; and as for this job, I'm sure I don't know what to say. This is the way out."

They pursued their way, without speaking, to Ned's lodgings, which were not far off. There he dried them and made them comfortable, and prepared tea; they thankfully sat down. The ready-made household of which he suddenly found himself the head imparted a cosey aspect to his room, and a paternal one to himself. Presently he turned to the child and kissed her now blooming cheeks; and, looking wistfully at Car'line, kissed her also.

"I don't see how I can send 'ee back all them miles," he growled, "now you've come all the way o' purpose to join me. But you must trust me, Car'line, and show you've real faith in me. Well, do you feel better now, my little woman?"

The child nodded, her mouth being otherwise occupied.

"I did trust you, Ned, in coming; and I shall always!"

Thus, without any definite agreement to forgive her, he tacitly acquiesced in the fate that Heaven had sent him; and on the day of their marriage (which was not quite so soon as he had expected it could be, on account of the time necessary for banns) he took her to the Exhibition when they came back from church, as he had promised. While standing near a large mirror in one of the courts devoted to furniture, Car'line started, for in the glass appeared the reflection of a form exactly resembling Mop Ollamoor's—so exactly that it seemed impossible to believe anybody but that artist in person to be the original. On passing round the objects which hemmed in Ned, her, and the child from a direct view, no Mop was to be seen. Whether he were really in London or not at that time was never known; and Car'line always stoutly denied that her readiness to go and meet Ned in town arose from any rumor that Mop had also gone thither; which denial there was no reasonable ground for doubting.

And then the year glided away, and the Exhibition folded itself up and became a thing of the past. The park trees that had been enclosed for six months were again exposed to the winds and storms, and the sod grew green anew. Ned found that Car'line resolved herself into a very good wife and companion, though she had made herself what is called cheap to him; but in that she was like another domestic article, a cheap teapot, which often brews better tea than a dear one. One autumn Hipcroft found himself with but little work to do, and a prospect of less for the winter. Both being country born and bred, they fancied they would like to live again in their natural atmosphere. It was accordingly decided between them that they should leave the pent-up London lodging, and that Ned should seek out employment near his native place, his wife and her daughter staying with Car'line's father during the search for occupation and an abode of their own.

Tinglings of pleasure pervaded Car'line's spasmodic little frame as she journeyed down with Ned to the place she had left two or three years before in silence and under a cloud. To return to where she had once been despised, a smiling London wife with a distinct London accent, was a triumph which the world did not witness every day.

The train did not stop at the petty road-side station that lay nearest to Stickleford, and the trio went on to Casterbridge. Ned thought it a good opportunity to make a few preliminary inquiries for employment at workshops in the borough where he had been known; and feeling cold from her journey, and it being dry underfoot and only dusk as yet, with a moon on the point of rising, Car'line and her little girl walked on towards Stickleford, leaving Ned to follow at a quicker pace, and pick her up at a certain half-way house, widely known as an inn.

The woman and child pursued the well-remembered way comfortably enough, though they were both becoming wearied. In the course of three miles they had passed Heedless William's Pond, the familiar landmark by Bloom's End, and were drawing near the Quiet Woman Inn, a lone road-side hostel on the lower verge of the Egdon Heath, since and for many years abolished. In stepping up towards it Car'line heard more voices within than had formerly been customary at such an hour, and she learned that an auction of fat stock had been held near the spot that afternoon. The child would be the better for a rest as well as herself, she thought, and she entered.

The guests and customers overflowed into the passage, and Car'line had no sooner crossed the threshold than a man whom she remembered by sight came forward with a glass and mug in his hands towards a friend leaning against the wall; but, seeing her, very gallantly offered her a drink of the liquor, which was gin-and-beer hot, pouring her out a tumblerful and saying, in a moment or two: "Surely, 'tis little Car'line Aspent that was—down at Stickleford?"

She assented, and, though she did not exactly want this beverage, she drank it since it was offered, and her entertainer begged her to come in farther and sit down. Once within the room she found that all the persons present were seated close against the walls, and there being a chair vacant she did the same. An explanation occurred the next moment. In the opposite corner stood Mop, rosining his bow and looking just the same as ever. The company had cleared the middle of the room for dancing, and they were about to dance again. As she wore a veil to keep off the wind she did not think he had recognized her, or could possibly guess the identity of the child; and to her satisfied surprise she found that she could confront him quite calmly—mistress of herself in the dignity her London life had given her. Before she had quite emptied her glass the dance was called, the dancers formed in two lines, the music sounded, and the figure began.

Then matters changed for Car'line. A tremor quickened itself to life in her, and her hand so shook that she could hardly set down her glass. It was not the dance nor the dancers, but the notes of that old violin which thrilled the London wife, these having still all the witchery that she had so well known of yore, and under which she had used to lose her power of independent will. How it all came back! There was the fiddling figure against the wall; the large, oily, mop-like head of him, and beneath the mop the face with closed eyes.

After the first moments of paralyzed reverie the familiar tune in the familiar rendering made her laugh and shed tears simultaneously. Then a man at the bottom of the dance, whose partner had dropped away, stretched out his hand and beckoned to her to take the place. She did not want to dance; she entreated by signs to be left where she was, she was entreating of the tune and its player rather than of the dancing man. The saltatory tendency which the fiddler and his cunning instrument had ever been able to start in her was seizing Car'line just as it had done in earlier years, possibly assisted by the gin-and-beer hot. Tired as she was she grasped her little girl by the hand, and, plunging in at the bottom of the figure, whirled about with the rest. She found that her companions were mostly people of the neighboring hamlets and farms—Bloom's End, Mellstock, Lewgate, and elsewhere; and by degrees she was recognized as she convulsively danced on, wishing that Mop would cease and let her heart rest from the aching he caused, and her feet also.

After long and many minutes the dance ended, when she was urged to fortify herself with more gin-and-beer; which she did, feeling very weak and overpowered with hysteric emotion. She refrained from unveiling, to keep Mop in ignorance of her presence, if possible. Several of the guests having left, Car'line hastily wiped her lips and also turned to go; but, according to the account of some who remained, at that very moment a five-handed reel was proposed, in which two or three begged her to join.

She declined on the plea of being tired and having to walk to Stickleford, when Mop began aggressively tweedling "My Fancy Lad," in D major, as the air to which the reel was to be footed. He must have recognized her, though she did not know it, for it was the strain of all seductive strains which she was least able to resist—the one he had played when she was leaning over the bridge at the date of their first acquaintance. Car'line stepped despairingly into the middle of the room with the other four.

Reels were resorted to hereabouts at this time by the more robust spirits for the reduction of superfluous energy which the ordinary figure-dances were not powerful enough to exhaust. As everybody knows, or does not know, the five reelers stood in the form of a cross, the reel being performed by each line of three alternately, the persons who successively came to the middle place dancing in both directions. Car'line soon found herself in this place, the axis of the whole performance, and could not get out of it, the tune turning into the first part without giving her opportunity. And now she began to suspect that Mop did know her, and was doing this on purpose, though whenever she stole a glance at him his closed eyes betokened obliviousness to everything outside his own brain. She continued to wend her way through the figure of eight that was formed by her course, the fiddler introducing into his notes the wild and agonizing sweetness of a living voice in one too highly wrought; its pathos running high and running low in endless variation, projecting through her nerves excruciating spasms—a sort of blissful torture. The room swam, the tune was endless; and in about a quarter of an hour the only other woman in the figure dropped out exhausted, and sank panting on a bench.

The reel instantly resolved itself into a four-handed one. Car'line would have given anything to leave off; but she had, or fancied she had, no power, while Mop played such tunes; and thus another ten minutes slipped by, a haze of dust now clouding the candles, the floor being of stone, sanded. Then another dancer fell out—one of the men—and went into the passage, in a frantic search for liquor. To turn the figure into a three-handed reel was the work of a second, Mop modulating at the same time into "The Fairy Dance," as better suited to the contracted movement, and no less one of those foods of love which, as manufactured by his bow, had always intoxicated her.

In a reel for three there was no rest whatever, and four or five minutes were enough to make her remaining two partners, now thoroughly blown, stamp their last bar, and, like their predecessors, limp off into the next room to get something to drink. Car'line, half-stifled inside her veil, was left dancing alone, the apartment now being empty of everybody save herself, Mop, and their little girl.

She flung up the veil, and cast her eyes upon him, as if imploring him to withdraw himself and his acoustic magnetism from the atmosphere. Mop opened one of his own orbs, as though for the first time, fixed it peeringly upon her, and smiling dreamily, threw into his strains the reserve of expression which he could not afford to waste on a big and noisy dance. Crowds of little chromatic subleties, capable of drawing tears from a statue, proceeded straightway from the ancient fiddle, as if it were dying of the emotion which had been pent up within it ever since its banishment from some Italian city where it first took shape and sound. There was that in the look of Mop's one dark eye which said: "You cannot leave off, dear, whether you would or no," and it bred in her a paroxysm of desperation that defied him to tire her down.

She thus continued to dance alone, defiantly as she thought, but in truth slavishly and abjectly, subject to every wave of the melody, and probed by the gimlet-like gaze of her fascinator's open eye; keeping up at the same time a feeble smile in his face, as a feint to signify it was still her own pleasure which led her on. A terrified embarrassment as to what she could say to him if she were to leave off, had its unrecognized share in keeping her going. The child, who was beginning to be distressed by the strange situation, came up and said: "Stop, mother, stop, and let's go home!" as she seized Car'line's hand.

Suddenly Car'line sank staggering to the floor; and rolling over on her face, prone she remained. Mop's fiddle thereupon emitted an elfin shriek of finality; stepping quickly down from the nine-gallon beer-cask which had formed his rostrum, he went to the little girl, who disconsolately bent over her mother.

The guests who had gone into the backroom for liquor and change of air, hearing something unusual, trooped back hitherward, where they endeavored to revive poor, weak Car'line by blowing her with the bellows and opening the window. Ned, her husband, who had been detained in Casterbridge, as aforesaid, came along the road at this juncture, and hearing excited voices through the open window, and, to his great surprise, the mention of his wife's name, he entered amid the rest upon the scene. Car'line was now in convulsions, weeping violently, and for a long time nothing could be done with her. While he was sending for a cart to take her onward to Stickleford, Hipcroft anxiously inquired how it had all happened; and then the assembly explained that a fiddler formerly known in the locality had lately revisited his old haunts, and had taken upon himself without invitation to play that evening at the inn.

Ned demanded the fiddler's name, and they said Ollamoor.

"Ah!" exclaimed Ned, looking round him. "Where is he, and where—where's my little girl?"

Ollamoor had disappeared, and so had the child. Hipcroft was in ordinary a quiet and tractable fellow, but a determination which was to be feared settled in his face now. "Blast him!" he cried. "I'll beat his skull in for'n, if I swing for it to-morrow!"

He had rushed to the poker which lay on the hearth, and hastened down the passage, the people following. Outside the house, on the other side of the highway, a mass of dark heath-land rose sullenly upward to its not easily accessible interior, a ravined plateau, whereon jutted into the sky, at the distance of a couple of miles, the fir-woods of Mistover backed by the Yalbury coppices—a place of Dantesque gloom at this hour, which would have afforded secure hiding for a battery of artillery, much less a man and a child.

Some other men plunged thitherward with him, and more went along the road. They were gone about twenty minutes altogether, returning without result to the inn. Ned sat down in the settle, and clasped his forehead with his hands.

"Well—what a fool the man is, and hev been all these years, if he thinks the child his, as a' do seem to!" they whispered. "And everybody else knowing otherwise!"

"No, I don't think 'tis mine!" cried Ned, hoarsely, as he looked up from his hands. "But she is mine, all the same! Ha'nt I nussed her? Ha'nt I fed her and teached her? Ha'nt I played wi' her? Oh, little Carry—gone with that rogue—gone!"

"You ha'n't lost your mis'ess, anyhow," they said to console him. "She's throwed up the sperrits, and she is feeling better, and she's more to 'ee than a child that isn't yours."

"She isn't! She's not so particular much to me, especially now she's lost the little maid! But Carry's everything!"

"Well, ver' like you'll find her to-morrow."

"Ah—but shall I? Yet he *can't* hurt her—surely he can't! Well—how's Car'line now? I am ready. Is the cart here?"

She was lifted into the vehicle, and they sadly lumbered on towards

Stickleford. Next day she was calmer; but the fits were still upon her; and her will seemed shattered. For the child she appeared to show singularly little anxiety, though Ned was nearly distracted. It was nevertheless quite expected that the impish Mop would restore the lost one after a freak of a day or two; but time went on, and neither he nor she could be heard of, and Hipcroft murmured that perhaps he was exercising upon her some unholy musical charm, as he had done upon Car'line herself. Weeks passed, and still they could obtain no clew either to the fiddler's whereabouts or the girl's; and how he could have induced her to go with him remained a mystery.

Then Ned, who had obtained only temporary employment in the neighborhood, took a sudden hatred towards his native district, and a rumor reaching his ears through the police that a somewhat similar man and child had been seen at a fair near London, he playing a violin, she dancing on stilts, a new interest in the capital took possession of Hipcroft with an intensity which would scarcely allow him time to pack before returning thither. He did not, however, find the lost one, though he made it the entire business of his over-hours to stand about in by-streets in the hope of discovering her, and would start up in the night, saying, "That rascal's torturing her to maintain him!" To which his wife would answer, peevishly, "Don't 'ee raft yourself so, Ned! You prevent my getting a bit o' rest! He won't hurt her!" and fall asleep again.

That Carry and her father had emigrated to America was the general opinion; Mop, no doubt, finding the girl a highly desirable companion when he had trained her to keep him by her earnings as a dancer. There, for that matter, they may be performing in some capacity now, though he must be an old scamp verging on threescore-and-ten, and she a woman of four-and-forty.

Questions for Writing and Discussion

1.   Take a look at the fifth and sixth paragraphs of the story, starting with "Many a worthy villager. . . ." Considering the details offered about "Mop" Ollamoor—his downy hair, his false curls, his indolence, the comparison with Paganini—we can get a pretty good preliminary sense of how the narrator is trying to place him. In what ways is the tone of the story being prepared here?

2.   A little later, on pp. 38–39, Hardy describes how Car'line, sitting at home, "would start from her seat in the chimney-corner as if she had received a galvanic shock," simply because she could hear Mop's footsteps as he passed by to visit another girl. Here Hardy verges on farce, taking a chance that by making Car'line so susceptible, and perhaps even silly, he will undermine the effect he wants at the climax. Do you think this passage really threatens the effectiveness of Hardy's conclusion?

3.   Poor Ned Hipcroft—he does seem to be the helpless victim throughout. Yet even with regard to him there's an element of surprise. This occurs at the end of the story (p. 47) where he compares his feelings for Car'line and "little Carry." What do you think Hardy is doing here?

4. What do you make of the story's ending? Does it strike you as a romantic fulfillment of a romantic story? If not, specify the ways in which the ending turns an ironic, or quizzical, eye upon the story of Car'line's obsession with Mop. (Can you imagine the lover of a great romance being called Mop? Does the fact that Hardy gives him this name suggest something about his intentions?)

THE PROBLEM OF BELIEF

HORTENSE CALISHER

Heartburn

Introduction

We won't try to say what this strange but gripping story is "really" about. For one thing, half the fun of reading and thinking about it is to struggle with its puzzlements and to be willing to remain in a state of relative uncertainty. Yet, while clearly a story that entices us as a remarkable performance or brilliant stunt, it is also quite as clearly trying to reach some important meanings.

A few possible clues:

1. The first page or two of "Heartburn" is cleverly arranged so as to communicate a kind of cultivated, modern atmosphere—that atmosphere of sophistication and skepticism which prevails among educated people, the sort who suppose they know all about human delusions, obsessions, and compulsions, who have a ready Freudian tag for every human trouble, and who are therefore inclined to see physical pains as mere signs of psychological disturbance. One of the apparent targets of the story is the glibness of this modern outlook, an easy rationalism which tends to reduce everything—religion, politics, human grief—to psychological categories (for instance, the doctor's first response to the psychologist's complaint). It is a glib modern outlook which habitually refuses to believe in anything that might be unfamiliar, spooky, or beyond the reach of the ordinary mind. In a general sense, then, "Heartburn" may entail a plea for the powers of the human imagination.

The patient who comes with the affliction, the frog that moves, is himself a psychiatrist—one of those who minister over and help spread this modern outlook of sophisticated skepticism. (Mention that someone has a frog in his chest, a real, breathing frog, and of course he'll have a fistful of Freudian categories ready for explanation. But so, to be honest about it, would most of us.) Through painful experience, however, he has learned better. He knows—and don't try to convince him otherwise—that he *does* have a frog in his chest, even though nothing in his experience or professional training has prepared him for any such thing.

53

2.   In a sense, then, the victim is trapped in a conflict between truth and need. If he can get the doctor to believe him, he must continue to bear his burden; if he can get the doctor to disbelieve him, he is freed of his burden. In the first case, he will be vindicated and not suspected of being merely "crazy." In the second case, he will gain the comfort of being relieved of his frog. The climax of the story comes about two pages before the end, when the doctor says, "Do you mean you *want* me to tell you you're crazy!,", and the patient—who has already seen that he can't genuinely get the doctor to believe his story—now decides in favor of personal comfort. With deceptive meekness, he says, "In my spot, which would you prefer?" Obviously, comfort is easier to live with than truth, especially a strange and unfamiliar truth. The doctor yells out, "I don't believe you!"; the patient thereby gets rid of his frog; and the doctor now suffers his punishment for a failure of sympathy and imagination.

3.   This is far from the whole of it. But suppose we stop here, suppose we can't really go any further, suppose we feel in reading the story that much remains to be explored. Should that leave us dissatisfied and restless, or should we recognize that Hortense Calisher has created a fable that may be hard to illuminate entirely but is nevertheless absorbing as only true fables can be?

Heartburn

The light, gritty wind of a spring morning blew in on the doctor's shining, cleared desk, and on the tall buttonhook of a man who leaned agitatedly toward him.

"I have some kind of small animal lodged in my chest," said the man. He coughed, a slight, hollow apologia to his ailment, and sank back in his chair.

"Animal?" said the doctor, after a pause which had the unfortunate quality of comment. His voice, however, was practiced, deft, colored only with the careful suspension of judgment.

"Probably a form of newt or toad," answered the man, speaking with clipped distaste, as if he would disassociate himself from the idea as far as possible. His face quirked with sad foreknowledge. "Of course, you don't believe me."

The doctor looked at him noncommittally. Paraphrased, an old refrain of the poker table leapt erratically in his mind. "Nits"—no—"newts and gnats and one-eyed jacks," he thought. But already the anecdote was shaping itself, trim and perfect, for display at the clinic luncheon table. "Go on," he said.

"Why won't any of you come right out and say what you think!" the man

HEARTBURN   From *In the Absence of Angels* by Hortense Calisher. Copyright 1951 by Hortense Calisher. Reprinted by permission of Candida Donadio & Associates, Inc.

said angrily. Then he flushed, not hectically, the doctor noted, but with the well-bred embarrassment of the normally reserved. "Sorry. I didn't mean to be rude."

"You've already had an examination?" The doctor was a neurologist, and most of his patients were referrals.

"My family doctor. I live up in Boston."

"Did you tell him—er . . . ?" The doctor sought gingerly for a phrase.

One corner of the man's mouth lifted, as if he had watched others in the same dilemma. "I went through the routine first. Fluoroscope, metabolism, cardiograph. Even gastroscopy." He spoke, the doctor noted, with the regrettable glibness of the patient who has shopped around.

"And—the findings?" said the doctor, already sure of the answer.

The man leaned forward, holding the doctor's glance with his own. A faint smile riffled his mouth. "Positive."

"Positive!"

"Well," said the man, "machines have to be interpreted after all, don't they?" He attempted a shrug, but the quick eye of the doctor saw that the movement masked a slight contortion within his tweed suit, as if the man writhed away from himself but concealed it quickly, as one masks a hiccup with a cough. "A curious flutter in the cardiograph, a strange variation in the metabolism, an alien shadow under the fluoroscope." He coughed again and put a genteel hand over his mouth, but this time the doctor saw it clearly—the slight, cringing motion.

"You see," added the man, his eyes helpless and apologetic above the polite covering hand. "It's alive. It *travels.*"

"Yes. Yes, of course," said the doctor, soothingly now. In his mind hung the word, ovoid and perfect as a drop of water about to fall. Obsession. A beautiful case. He thought again of the luncheon table.

"What did your doctor recommend?" he said.

"A place with more resources, like the Mayo Clinic. It was then that I told him I knew what it was, as I've told you. And how I acquired it." The visitor paused. "Then, of course, he was forced to pretend he believed me."

"Forced?" said the doctor.

"Well," said the visitor, "actually, I think he did believe me. People tend to believe anything these days. All this mass media information gives them the habit. It takes a strong individual to disbelieve evidence."

The doctor was confused and annoyed. Well, "What then?" he said peremptorily, ready to rise from his desk in dismissal.

Again came the fleeting bodily grimace and the quick cough. "He—er . . . he gave me a prescription."

The doctor raised his eyebrows, in a gesture he was swift to retract as unprofessional.

"For heartburn, I think it was," added his visitor demurely.

Tipping back in his chair, the doctor tapped a pencil on the edge of the desk. "Did he suggest you seek help—on another level?"

"Many have suggested it," said the man.

"But I'm not a psychiatrist!" said the doctor irritably.

"Oh, I know that. You see, I came to you because I had the luck to hear one of your lectures at the Academy. The one on 'Overemphasis on the Non-somatic[1] Causes of Nervous Disorder.' It takes a strong man to go against the tide like that. A disbeliever. And that's what I sorely need." The visitor shuddered, this time letting the *frisson* pass uncontrolled. "You see," he added, thrusting his clasped hands forward on the desk, and looking ruefully at the doctor, as if he would cushion him against his next remark, "you see—I am a psychiatrist."

The doctor sat still in his chair.

"Ah, I can't help knowing what you are thinking," said the man. "I would think the same. A streamlined version of the Napoleonic delusion." He reached into his breast pocket, drew out a wallet, and fanned papers from it on the desk.

"Never mind. I believe you!" said the doctor hastily.

"Already?" said the man sadly.

Reddening, the doctor hastily looked over the collection of letters, cards of membership in professional societies, licenses, and so on—very much the same sort of thing he himself would have had to amass, had he been under the same necessity of proving his identity. Sanity, of course, was another matter. The documents were all issued to Dr. Curtis Retz at a Boston address. Stolen, possibly, but something in the man's manner, in fact everything in it except his unfortunate hallucination, made the doctor think otherwise. Poor guy, he thought. Occupational fatigue, perhaps. But what a form! The Boston variant, possibly. "Suppose you start from the beginning," he said benevolently. "If you can spare the time . . ."

"I have no more appointments until lunch." And what a lunch that'll be, the doctor thought, already cherishing the pop-eyed scene—Travis the clinic's director (that plethoric Nestor), and young Gruenberg (all of whose cases were unique), his hairy nostrils dilated for once in a *mise-en-scène* which he did not dominate.

Holding his hands pressed formally against his chest, almost in the attitude of one of the minor placatory figures in a *Pietà,* the visitor went on. "I have the usual private practice," he said, "and clinic affiliations. As a favor to an old friend of mine, headmaster of a boys' school nearby, I've acted as guidance consultant there for some years. The school caters to boys of above average intelligence and is run along progressive lines. Nothing's ever cropped up except run-of-the-mill adolescent problems, colored a little, perhaps, by the type of parents who tend to send their children to a school like that—people who are—well—one might say, almost tediously aware of their commitments as parents."

The doctor grunted. He was that kind of parent himself.

"Shortly after the second term began, the head asked me to come down. He was worried over a sharp drop of morale which seemed to extend over the whole school—general inattention in classes, excited note-passing, nightly disturbances in the dorms—all pointing, he had thought at first, to the existence of

[1]Non-bodily.

some fancier than usual form of hazing, or to one of those secret societies, sometimes laughable, sometimes with overtones of the corrupt, with which all schools are familiar. Except for one thing. One after the other, a long list of boys had been sent to the infirmary by the various teachers who presided in the dining room. Each of the boys had shown a marked debility, and what the resident doctor called 'All the stigmata of pure fright. Complete unwillingness to confide.' Each of the boys pleaded stubbornly for his own release, and a few broke out of their own accord. The interesting thing was that each child did recover shortly after his own release, and it was only after this that another boy was seen to fall ill. No two were afflicted at the same time."

"Check the food?" said the doctor.

"All done before I got there. According to my friend, all the trouble seemed to have started with the advent of one boy, John Hallowell, a kid of about fifteen, who had come to the school late in the term with a history of having run away from four other schools. Records at these classed him as very bright, but made oblique references to 'personality difficulties' which were not defined. My friend's school, ordinarily pretty independent, had taken the boy at the insistence of old Simon Hallowell, the boy's uncle, who is a trustee. His brother, the boy's father, is well known for his marital exploits which have nourished the tabloids for years. The mother lives mostly in France and South America. One of these perennial dryads, apparently, with a youthfulness maintained by money and a yearly immersion in the fountains of American plastic surgery. Only time she sees the boy . . . Well, you can imagine. What the feature articles call a Broken Home."

The doctor shifted in his chair and lit a cigarette.

"I won't keep you much longer," said the visitor. "I saw the boy." A violent fit of coughing interrupted him. This time his curious writhing motion went frankly unconcealed. He got up from his chair and stood at the window, gripping the sill and breathing heavily until he had regained control, and went on, one hand pulling unconsciously at his collar. "Or, at least, I think I saw him. On my way to visit him in his room I bumped into a tall red-headed boy in a football sweater, hurrying down the hall with a windbreaker and a poncho slung over his shoulder. I asked for Hallowell's room; he jerked his thumb over his shoulder at the door just behind him, and continued past me. It never occurred to me . . . I was expecting some adenoidal gangler with acne . . . or one of these sinister little angel faces, full of neurotic sensibility.

"The room was empty. Except for its finicky neatness, and a rather large amount of livestock, there was nothing unusual about it. The school, according to the current trend, is run like a farm, with the boys doing the chores, and pets are encouraged. There was a tank with a couple of turtles near the window, beside it another, full of newts, and in one corner a large cage of well-tended, brisk white mice. Glass cases, with carefully mounted series of lepidoptera and hymenoptera, showing the metamorphic stages, hung on the walls, and on a drawing board there was a daintily executed study of Branchippus, the 'fairy shrimp.'

"While I paced the room, trying to look as if I wasn't prying, a greenish little wretch, holding himself together as if he had an imaginary shawl draped around him, slunk into the half-dark room and squeaked 'Hallowell?' When he saw me he started to duck, but I detained him and found that he had had an appointment with Hallowell too. When it was clear, from his description, that Hallowell must have been the redhead I'd seen leaving, the poor urchin burst into tears.

"'I'll never get rid of it now!' he wailed. From then on it wasn't hard to get the whole maudlin story. It seems that shortly after Hallowell's arrival at school he acquired a reputation for unusual proficiency with animals and for out-of-the way lore which would impress the ingenuous. He circulated the rumor that he could swallow small animals and regurgitate them at will. No one actually saw him swallow anything, but it seems that in some mumbo-jumbo with another boy who had shown cynicism about the whole thing, it was claimed that Hallowell had, well, divested himself of something, and passed it on to the other boy, with the statement that the latter would only be able to get rid of his cargo when he in turn found a boy who would disbelieve *him*."

The visitor paused, calmer now, and leaving the window sat down again in the chair opposite the doctor, regarding him with such fixity that the doctor shifted uneasily, with the apprehension of one who is about to be asked for a loan.

"My mind turned to the elementary sort of thing we've all done at times. You know, circle of kids in the dark, piece of cooked cauliflower passed from hand to hand with the statement that the stuff is the fresh brains of some neophyte who hadn't taken his initiation seriously. My young informer, Moulton his name was, swore however that this hysteria (for of course, that's what I thought it) was passed on singly, from boy to boy, without any such séances. He'd been home to visit his family, who are missionaries on leave, and had been infected by his roommate on his return to school, unaware that by this time the whole school had protectively turned believers, en masse. His own terror came, not only from his conviction that he was possessed, but from his inability to find anybody who would take his dare. And so he'd finally come to Hallowell. . . .

"By this time the room was getting really dark and I snapped on the light to get a better look at Moulton. Except for an occasional shudder, like a bodily tic, which I took to be the aftereffects of hard crying, he looked like a healthy enough boy who'd been scared out of his wits. I remember that a neat little monograph was already forming itself in my mind, a group study on mass psychosis, perhaps, with effective anthropological references to certain savage tribes whose dances include a rite known as 'eating evil.'

"The kid was looking at me. 'Do you believe me?' he said suddenly. 'Sir?' he added, with a naive cunning which tickled me.

"'Of course,' I said, patting his shoulder absently. 'In a way.'

"His shoulder slumped under my hand. I felt its tremor, direct misery palpitating between my fingers.

"'I thought . . . maybe for a man . . . it wouldn't be . . .' His voice trailed off.

"'Be the same? . . . I don't know,' I said slowly, for of course, I was answering, not his actual question, but the overtone of some cockcrow of meaning that evaded me.

"He raised his head and petitioned me silently with his eyes. Was it guile, or simplicity, in his look, and was it for conviction, or the lack of it, that he arraigned me? I don't know. I've gone back over what I did then, again and again, using all my own knowledge of the mechanics of decision, and I know that it wasn't just sympathy, or a pragmatic reversal of therapy, but something intimately important for me, that made me shout with all my strength—'Of course I don't believe you!'

"Moulton, his face contorted, fell forward on me so suddenly that I stumbled backwards, sending the tank of newts crashing to the floor. Supporting him with my arms, I hung on to him while he heaved, face downwards. At the same time I felt a tickling, sliding sensation in my own ear, and an inordinate desire to follow it with my finger, but both my hands were busy. It wasn't a minute 'til I'd gotten him onto the couch, where he drooped, a little white about the mouth, but with that chastened, purified look of the physically relieved, although he hadn't actually upchucked.

"Still watching him, I stooped to clear up the debris, but he bounded from the couch with amazing resilience.

"'I'll do it,' he said.

"'Feel better?'

"He nodded, clearly abashed, and we gathered up the remains of the tank in a sort of mutual embarrassment. I can't remember that either of us said a word, and neither of us made more than a halfhearted attempt to search for the scattered pests which had apparently sought crannies in the room. At the door we parted, muttering as formal a goodnight as was possible between a grown man and a small boy. It wasn't until I reached my own room and sat down that I realized, not only my own extraordinary behavior, but that Moulton, standing, as I suddenly recalled, for the first time quite straight, had sent after me a look of pity and speculation.

"Out of habit, I reached into my breast pocket for my pencil, in order to take notes as fresh as possible. And then I felt it . . . a skittering, sidling motion, almost beneath my hand. I opened my jacket and shook myself, thinking that I'd picked up something in the other room . . . but nothing. I sat quite still, gripping the pencil, and after an interval it came again—an inchoate creeping, a twitter of movement almost *lackadaisical,* as of something inching itself lazily along—but this time on my other side. In a frenzy, I peeled off my clothes, inspected myself wildly, and enumerating to myself a reassuring abracadabra of explanation—skipped heartbeat, intercostal pressure of gas—I sat there naked, waiting. And after a moment, it came again, that wandering, aquatic motion, as if something had flipped itself over just enough to make me aware, and then settled itself, this time under the sternum, with a nudge like that of some inconceivable foetus. I jumped up and shook myself again, and as I did so I caught a glimpse of myself in the mirror in the closet door. My face, my own face, was ajar with fright, and I was standing there, hooked over, as if I were wearing an imaginary shawl."

In the silence after his visitor's voice stopped, the doctor sat there in the painful embarrassment of the listener who has played confessor, and whose expected comment is a responsibility he wishes he had evaded. The breeze from the open window fluttered the papers on the desk. Glancing out at the clean, regular facade of the hospital wing opposite, at whose evenly shaded windows the white shapes of orderlies and nurses flickered in consoling routine, the doctor wished petulantly that he had fended off the man and all his papers in the beginning. What right had the man to arraign *him?* Surprised at his own inner vehemence, he pulled himself together. "How long ago?" he said at last.

"Four months."

"And since?"

"It's never stopped." The visitor now seemed brimming with a tentative excitement, like a colleague discussing a mutually puzzling case. "Everything's been tried. Sedatives do obtain some sleep, but that's all. Purgatives. Even emetics." He laughed slightly, almost with pride. "Nothing like that works," he continued, shaking his head with the doting fondness of a patient for some symptom which has confounded the best of them. "It's too cagey for that."

With his use of the word "it," the doctor was propelled back into that shapely sense of reality which had gone admittedly askew during the man's recital. To admit the category of "it," to dip even a slightly co-operative finger in another's fantasy, was to risk one's own equilibrium. Better not to become involved in argument with the possessed, lest one's own apertures of belief be found to have been left ajar.

"I am afraid," the doctor said blandly, "that your case is outside my field."

"As a doctor?" said his visitor. "Or as a man?"

"Let's not discuss me, if you please."

The visitor leaned intently across the desk. "Then you admit that to a certain extent, we *have* been—?"

"I admit nothing!" said the doctor, stiffening.

"Well," said the man disparagingly, "of course, that too is a kind of stand. The commonest, I've found." He sighed, pressing one hand against his collarbone. "I suppose you have a prescription too, or a recommendation. Most of them do."

The doctor did not enjoy being judged. "Why don't you hunt up young Hallowell?" he said, with malice.

"Disappeared. Don't you think I tried?" said his vis-à-vis ruefully. Something furtive, hope, perhaps, spread its guileful corruption over his face. "That means you do give a certain credence—"

"Nothing of the sort!"

"Well then," said his interrogator, turning his palms upward.

The doctor leaned forward, measuring his words with exasperation. "Do you mean you *want* me to tell you you're crazy!"

"In my spot," answered his visitor meekly, "which would you prefer?"

Badgered to the point of commitment, the doctor stared back at his inconvenient Diogenes.[2] Swollen with irritation, he was only half conscious of

---

[2] A Greek philosopher famous for unconventional ideas and habits.

an uneasy, vestigial twitching of his ear muscles, which contracted now as they sometimes did when he listened to atonal music.

"O.K., O.K . . .!" he shouted suddenly, slapping his hand down on the desk and thrusting his chin forward. "Have it your way then! I don't believe you!"

Rigid, the man looked back at him cataleptically, seeming, for a moment, all eye. Then, his mouth stretching in that medieval grimace, risorial and equivocal, whose mask appears sometimes on one side of the stage, sometimes on the other, he fell forward on the desk, with a long, mewing sigh.

Before the doctor could reach him, he had raised himself on his arms and their foreheads touched. They recoiled, staring downward. Between them on the desk, as if one of its mahogany shadows had become animate, something seemed to move—small, seal-colored, and ambiguous. For a moment it filmed back and forth, arching in a crude, primordial inquiry; then, homing straight for the doctor, whose jaw hung down in a rictus of shock, it disappeared from view.

Sputtering, the doctor beat the air and his own person wildly with his hands, and staggered upward from his chair. The breeze blew hypnotically, and the stranger gazed back at him with such perverse calm that already he felt an assailing doubt of the lightning, untoward event. He fumbled back over his sensations of the minute before, but already piecemeal and chimerical, they eluded him now, as they might forever.

"It's unbelievable," he said weakly.

His visitor put up a warding hand, shaking it fastidiously. *"Au contraire!"*[3] he replied daintily, as though by the use of another language he would remove himself still further from commitment. Reaching forward, he gathered up his papers into a sheaf, and stood up, stretching himself straight with an all-over bodily yawn of physical ease that was like an affront. He looked down at the doctor, one hand fingering his wallet. "No," he said reflectively, "guess not." He tucked the papers away. "Shall we leave it on the basis of—er—professional courtesy?" he inquired delicately.

Choking on the sludge of his rage, the doctor looked back at him, inarticulate.

Moving toward the door, the visitor paused. "After all," he said, "with your connections . . . try to think of it as a temporary inconvenience." Regretfully, happily, he closed the door behind him.

The doctor sat at his desk, humped forward. His hands crept to his chest and crossed. He swallowed, experimentally. He hoped it was rage. He sat there, waiting. He was thinking of the luncheon table.

Questions for Writing and Discussion

1. The doctor's first response to his patient's story is disbelief, then a quick professional glibness—"Obsession. A beautiful case." Then follows the half-hidden

[3]French: on the contrary.

contempt of seeing the patient's trouble as material for a good anecdote at lunch. By referring to specific details, describe how the doctor is here being "set up" for the conclusion of the story.

2.   It comes as an amusing surprise that the patient turns out to be a psychiatrist himself. What do you think is the significance of this? See especially the paragraph on page 56 where he says that what he very much needs is a "disbeliever." In view of what happens later, do you think Calisher is indulging in a little joke here?

3.   In the first sentence of the paragraph that starts, "In the silence after his visitor's voice stopped . . .", on pp. 59–60, the author comes as close as she wants or needs to a statement of her main theme. In the story there are two places where the word "commitment" is used, once with regard to the doctor and once, the patient. If we think of this story as being partly about "commitment" (or responsibility), what cues do these uses of the word give us here?

4.   You will find in this book a story by Nathaniel Hawthorne, "Young Goodman Brown," which seems to have certain similarities of technique to "Heartburn." Read the two stories together and see if you can work up some useful comparisons between them.

5.   What do you think the author wanted to suggest through the title? Usually the term "heartburn" refers to pain in the upper stomach, but suppose we were to take it literally—what then, given the events of the story, might it signify?

FLANNERY O'CONNOR

Parker's Back

Introduction

Let's start with the title. It opens up several possibilities:

1. On Parker's back there is tattooed the Byzantine Christ, King and Judge, as well as a figure of martyrdom.

2. After leaving Sarah Ruth, Parker finds that he misses her very much, even though she has also irritated him very much, and he therefore decides to come back to her.

3. Though Parker's first names are taken from biblical prophets, he has slipped into a thoughtless kind of indifference. Yet now he is being stirred, in his own confused way, to turn back to Christ, even if it's only by the feeble device of having a tattooed Christ on his back. If he can't get to the reality of Christ, at least he wants a picture, a likeness, of Him.

Now, if you put these items back to back, you may find your way into the idea of the story.

The story itself is vivid, playful, amusing, full of country humor, with its slyness, exaggeration, understatement, and grotesquerie. But precisely through the by-play—the incidental comedy—of the story, O'Connor reaches a level of serious suggestion about modern religious and moral problems. It's a story, we think, about the absurd way in which lost souls (Parker is certainly that!) fumble their way back to God, or fumble God onto their backs, as well as about the absurd ways that petty fanaticisms, in the name of Christianity, can succeed in keeping lost souls away from Christ.

O. E. Parker is an ordinary lout, an ignorant redneck, a country bumpkin, common clay and lazy. He is chosen deliberately by Flannery O'Connor as a specimen of debased humanity—but humanity still. His one notable characteristic at the outset seems to be that the initials of his name indicate that he has come out of, though he no longer has much real connection with, a religious culture.

Yet . . . somewhere in this sad sack of an O. E. Parker there has been a stirring of imagination, almost as if imagination were a power or faculty within our life that had a will or energy of its own. At the age of 14, O. E. Parker, "ordinary as a loaf of bread," has seen a man with tattoos, intricate in their designs and colors, and he "was filled with emotion," just as other people may be filled with emotion at seeing a beautiful view of mountains or an elegant scene at the ballet. In however primitive a form, Parker's imagination has been opened to the possible beauties of this world—he who "had never before felt the least motion of wonder in himself." His imagination has been stirred by something we might regard as gross, but it has been stirred nevertheless. Yet there has been no equivalent exaltation of spirit within him, and when his mother tries to get him to go to church, he "jerked out of her hand and ran."

In the navy, Parker goes from one tattoo to another, advancing from crossed rifles to more imaginative designs of tigers and panthers on each shoulder, a cobra on his chest, hawks on his thighs, and kings and queens on his stomach and liver. (It's not every Southern boy—or Northern one, either—who has kings on his stomach, queens on his liver.) Each tattoo is more colorful, more garish than the previous one. Yet none add up to a coherent design. "The effect was [still] . . . of something haphazard and botched." Such, then, are the limits to the pleasures and colors of this world if they don't take shape (or meaning) from a spiritual end.

Parker meets Sarah Ruth, raised in an obscure revivalist sect, an offshoot of Southern Protestantism. Her religion is literalistic, hard-spirited, fanatical, without savor or grace; yet something about her attracts him. Something touches his undisciplined yet active imagination. What can it be? Her seeming assurance? Her undeviating self-righteousness? Her angular narrowness? Where he is drift and chaos, she is fixed and clenched.

Married to her, Parker still cannot understand her, let alone subdue her. He can't even understand those confusions of feelings she stirs up in him. He is angry with himself, even "ashamed," at remaining with her, yet she draws him, stirring his imagination in ways that may not be so different from the tattoos. Away from her, he longs to be back with her: "Her sharp tongue and icepick eyes were the only comfort he could bring to mind."

He seeks to win her, to gain her approval, to show that he too can open himself to the words she speaks (though he doesn't yet see that for her they're just words, life-denying and mean-spirited). So he goes off to get still another tattoo, his last tattoo—the tattoo of revelation, of grace, of God.

It's really a stunning idea, a brilliant invention on O'Connor's part. If in the past Parker's inchoate sense of beauty was gratified by mere tattoos of animals, now his incipient sense of religious belief is to be gratified by a tattoo of "him." (Or is this a bit of an exaggeration? Is it simply that Parker wishes to please Sarah Ruth? But if so, why should he choose anything as unlikely, and as little connected with Sarah Ruth, as the Byzantine Christ?)

Parker's heart opens up, "as if it were being brought to life by a subtle power." Just as the tattoos of the animals and the kings and queens were debased versions of worldly beauty, so the tattoo of the Christ represents a debased version of religious beauty. Not that Parker is consciously aware of this, or ready to acknowledge it. When teased by the men in the pool hall, he denies that he has turned to religion, for he does not himself grasp the meaning, let alone appreciate the boldness, of what his imagination has driven him to.

Like a child bearing a gift, he brings his tattooed back to Sarah Ruth. To get into the house, he must accept the humiliation of whispering the full, Biblical name which he hates so much—as if thereby to register the religious association he has allowed to lapse. When Parker shows Sarah Ruth the image of Christ on his back, she answers—more significantly than she knows—"It ain't anybody I know." Indeed, it's not.

When Parker insists that it is a tattoo of "him," that is, of God, Sarah Ruth answers: "He's a spirit. No man shall see his face," and then she screams "idolatry." Formally, according to the letter of the faith, she is right. But she has utterly failed to grasp what has happened to Parker. She has failed to see, because she herself is devoid of the spirit of grace, that in his own coarse and bumbling way Parker has brushed against the wings of that spirit.

Defeated, he cries against a tree—"[he] who called himself Obadiah Elihue." God's word may come in unexpected ways, and none shall be less able to hear it than those who think they possess it.

Parker's Back

Parker's wife was sitting on the front porch floor, snapping beans. Parker was sitting on the step, some distance away, watching her sullenly. She was plain, plain. The skin on her face was thin and drawn as tight as the skin on an onion and her eyes were grey and sharp like the points of two icepicks. Parker understood why he had married her—he couldn't have got her any other way—but he couldn't understand why he stayed with her now. She was pregnant and pregnant women were not his favorite kind. Nevertheless, he stayed as if she had him conjured. He was puzzled and ashamed of himself.

The house they rented sat alone save for a single tall pecan tree on a high embankment overlooking a highway. At intervals a car would shoot past below and his wife's eyes would swerve suspiciously after the sound of it and then come back to rest on the newspaper full of beans in her lap. One of the things she did not approve of was automobiles. In addition to her other bad qualities, she was forever sniffing up sin. She did not smoke or dip, drink whiskey, use bad language or paint her face, and God knew some paint would have improved it, Parker thought. Her being against color, it was the more remarkable she had married him. Sometimes he supposed that she had married him because she meant to save him. At other times he had a suspicion that she actually liked

PARKER'S BACK From *Everything That Rises Must Converge* by Flannery O'Connor. Copyright © 1965 by the Estate of Mary Flannery O'Connor. Reprinted by permission of Farrar, Straus & Giroux, Inc.

everything she said she didn't. He could account for her one way or another; it was himself he could not understand.

She turned her head in his direction and said, "It's no reason you can't work for a man. It don't have to be a woman."

"Aw shut your mouth for a change," Parker muttered.

If he had been certain she was jealous of the woman he worked for he would have been pleased but more likely she was concerned with the sin that would result if he and the woman took a liking to each other. He had told her that the woman was a hefty young blonde; in fact she was nearly seventy years old and too dried up to have an interest in anything except getting as much work out of him as she could. Not that an old woman didn't sometimes get an interest in a young man, particularly if he was as attractive as Parker felt he was, but this old woman looked at him the same way she looked at her old tractor—as if she had to put up with it because it was all she had. The tractor had broken down the second day Parker was on it and she had set him at once to cutting bushes, saying out of the side of her mouth to the nigger, "Everything he touches, he breaks." She also asked him to wear his shirt when he worked; Parker had removed it even though the day was not sultry; he put it back on reluctantly.

This ugly woman Parker married was his first wife. He had had other women but he had planned never to get himself tied up legally. He had first seen her one morning when his truck broke down on the highway. He had managed to pull it off the road into a neatly swept yard on which sat a peeling two-room house. He got out and opened the hood of the truck and began to study the motor. Parker had an extra sense that told him when there was a woman nearby watching him. After he had leaned over the motor a few minutes, his neck began to prickle. He cast his eye over the empty yard and porch of the house. A woman he could not see was either nearby beyond a clump of honeysuckle or in the house, watching him out the window.

Suddenly Parker began to jump up and down and fling his hand about as if he had mashed it in the machinery. He doubled over and held his hand close to his chest. "God dammit!" he hollered, "Jesus Christ in hell! Jesus God Almighty damm! God dammit to hell!" he went on, flinging out the same few oaths over and over as loud as he could.

Without warning a terrible bristly claw slammed the side of his face and he fell backwards on the hood of the truck. "You don't talk no filth here!" a voice close to him shrilled.

Parker's vision was so blurred that for an instant he thought he had been attacked by some creature from above, a giant hawk-eyed angel wielding a hoary weapon. As his sight cleared, he saw before him a tall raw-boned girl with a broom.

"I hurt my hand," he said. "I HURT my hand." He was so incensed that he forgot that he hadn't hurt his hand. "My hand may be broke," he growled although his voice was still unsteady.

"Lemme see it," the girl demanded.

Parker stuck out his hand and she came closer and looked at it. There was no mark on the palm and she took the hand and turned it over. Her own hand was dry and hot and rough and Parker felt himself jolted back to life by her touch. He looked more closely at her. I don't want nothing to do with this one, he thought.

The girl's sharp eyes peered at the back of the stubby reddish hand she held. There emblazoned in red and blue was a tattooed eagle perched on a cannon. Parker's sleeve was rolled to the elbow. Above the eagle a serpent was coiled about a shield and in the spaces between the eagle and the serpent there were hearts, some with arrows through them. Above the serpent there was a spread hand of cards. Every space on the skin of Parker's arm, from wrist to elbow, was covered in some loud design. The girl gazed at this with an almost stupefied smile of shock, as if she had accidentally grasped a poisonous snake; she dropped the hand.

"I got most of my other ones in foreign parts," Parker said. "These here I mostly got in the United States. I got my first one when I was only fifteen year old."

"Don't tell me," the girl said, "I don't like it. I ain't got any use for it."

"You ought to see the ones you can't see," Parker said and winked.

Two circles of red appeared like apples on the girl's cheeks and softened her appearance. Parker was intrigued. He did not for a minute think that she didn't like the tattoos. He had never yet met a woman who was not attracted to them.

Parker was fourteen when he saw a man in a fair, tattooed from head to foot. Except for his loins which were girded with a panther hide, the man's skin was patterned in what seemed from Parker's distance—he was near the back of the tent, standing on a bench—a single intricate design of brilliant color. The man, who was small and sturdy, moved about on the platform, flexing his muscles so that the arabesque of men and beasts and flowers on his skin appeared to have a subtle motion of its own. Parker was filled with emotion, lifted up as some people are when the flag passes. He was a boy whose mouth habitually hung open. He was heavy and earnest, as ordinary as a loaf of bread. When the show was over, he had remained standing on the bench, staring where the tattooed man had been, until the tent was almost empty.

Parker had never before felt the least motion of wonder in himself. Until he saw the man at the fair, it did not enter his head that there was anything out of the ordinary about the fact that he existed. Even then it did not enter his head, but a peculiar unease settled in him. It was as if a blind boy had been turned so gently in a different direction that he did not know his destination had been changed.

He had his first tattoo some time after—the eagle perched on the cannon. It was done by a local artist. It hurt very little, just enough to make it appear to Parker to be worth doing. This was peculiar too for before he had thought that only what did not hurt was worth doing. The next year he quit school because he was sixteen and could. He went to the trade school for a while, then he quit the trade school and worked for six months in a garage. The only reason he worked at all was to pay for more tattoos. His mother worked in a laundry and could support him, but she would not pay for any tattoo except her name on a heart, which he had put on, grumbling. However, her name was Betty Jean and nobody had to know it was his mother. He found out that the tattoos were attractive to the kind of girls he liked but who had never liked him before. He began to drink beer and get in fights. His mother wept over what was becoming of him. One night she dragged him off to a revival with her, not telling him where they were going. When he saw the big lighted church, he jerked out of her grasp and ran. The next day he lied about his age and joined the navy.

Parker was large for the tight sailor's pants but the silly white cap, sitting low on his forehead, made his face by contrast look thoughtful and almost intense. After a month or two in the navy, his mouth ceased to hang open. His features hardened into the features of a man. He stayed in the navy five years and seemed a natural part of the grey mechanical ship, except for his eyes, which were the same pale slate-color as the ocean and reflected the immense spaces around him as if they were a microcosm of the mysterious sea. In port Parker wandered about comparing the run-down places he was in to Birmingham, Alabama. Everywhere he went he picked up more tattoos.

He had stopped having lifeless ones like anchors and crossed rifles. He had a tiger and a panther on each shoulder, a cobra coiled about a torch on his chest, hawks on his thighs, Elizabeth II and Philip over where his stomach and liver were respectively. He did not care much what the subject was so long as it was colorful; on his abdomen he had a few obscenities but only because that seemed the proper place for them. Parker would be satisfied with each tattoo about a month, then something about it that had attracted him would wear off. Whenever a decent-sized mirror was available, he would get in front of it and study his overall look. The effect was not of one intricate arabesque of colors but of something haphazard and botched. A huge dissatisfaction would come over him and he would go off and find another tattooist and have another space filled up. The front of Parker was almost completely covered but there were no tattoos on his back. He had no desire for one anywhere he could not readily see it himself. As the space on the front of him for tattoos decreased, his dissatisfaction grew and became general.

After one of his furloughs, he didn't go back to the navy but remained away without official leave, drunk, in a rooming house in a city he did not know. His dissatisfaction, from being chronic and latent, had suddenly become acute and raged in him. It was as if the panther and the lion and the serpents and the eagles and the hawks had penetrated his skin and lived inside him in a raging warfare. The navy caught up with him, put him in the brig for nine months and then gave him a dishonorable discharge.

After that Parker decided that country air was the only kind fit to breathe. He rented the shack on the embankment and bought the old truck and took various jobs which he kept as long as it suited him. At the time he met his future wife, he was buying apples by the bushel and selling them for the same price by the pound to isolated homesteaders on back country roads.

"All that there," the woman said, pointing to his arm, "is no better than what a fool Indian would do. It's a heap of vanity." She seemed to have found the word she wanted. "Vanity of vanities," she said.

Well what the hell do I care what she thinks of it? Parker asked himself, but he was plainly bewildered. "I reckon you like one of these better than another anyway," he said, dallying until he thought of something that would impress her. He thrust the arm back at her. "Which you like best?"

"None of them," she said, "but the chicken is not as bad as the rest."

"What chicken?" Parker almost yelled.

She pointed to the eagle.

"That's an eagle," Parker said. "What fool would waste their time having a chicken put on themself?"

"What fool would have any of it?" the girl said and turned away. She went slowly back to the house and left him there to get going. Parker remained for almost five minutes, looking agape at the dark door she had entered.

The next day he returned with a bushel of apples. He was not one to be outdone by anything that looked like her. He liked women with meat on them, so you didn't feel their muscles, much less their old bones. When he arrived, she was sitting on the top step and the yard was full of children, all as thin and poor as herself; Parker remembered it was Saturday. He hated to be making up to a woman when there were children around, but it was fortunate he had brought the bushel of apples off the truck. As the children approached him to see what he carried, he gave each child an apple and told it to get lost; in that way he cleared out the whole crowd.

The girl did nothing to acknowledge his presence. He might have been a stray pig or goat that had wandered into the yard and she too tired to take up the broom and send it off. He set the bushel of apples down next to her on the step. He sat down on a lower step.

"Hep yourself," he said, nodding at the basket; then he lapsed into silence.

She took an apple quickly as if the basket might disappear if she didn't make haste. Hungry people made Parker nervous. He had always had plenty to eat himself. He grew very uncomfortable. He reasoned he had nothing to say so why should he say it? He could not think now why he had come or why he didn't go before he wasted another bushel of apples on the crowd of children. He supposed they were her brothers and sisters.

She chewed the apple slowly but with a kind of relish of concentration, bent slightly but looking out ahead. The view from the porch stretched off across a long incline studded with iron weed and across the highway to a vast vista of hills and one small mountain. Long views depressed Parker. You look out into space like that and you begin to feel as if someone were after you, the navy or the government or religion.

"Who them children belong to, you?" he said at length.

"I ain't married yet," she said. "They belong to momma." She said it as if it were only a matter of time before she would be married.

Who in God's name would marry her? Parker thought.

A large barefooted woman with a wide gap-toothed face appeared in the door behind Parker. She had apparently been there for several minutes.

"Good evening," Parker said.

The woman crossed the porch and picked up what was left of the bushel of apples. "We thank you," she said and returned with it into the house.

"That your old woman?" Parker muttered.

The girl nodded. Parker knew a lot of sharp things he could have said like "You got my sympathy," but he was gloomily silent. He just sat there, looking at the view. He thought he must be coming down with something.

"If I pick up some peaches tomorrow I'll bring you some," he said.

"I'll be much obliged to you," the girl said.

Parker had no intention of taking any basket of peaches back there but the next day he found himself doing it. He and the girl had almost nothing to say to each other. One thing he did say was, "I ain't got any tattoo on my back."

"What you got on it?" the girl said.

"My shirt," Parker said. "Haw."

"Haw, haw," the girl said politely.

Parker thought he was losing his mind. He could not believe for a minute that he was attracted to a woman like this. She showed not the least interest in anything but what he brought until he appeared the third time with two cantaloups. "What's your name?" she asked.

"O. E. Parker," he said.

"What does the O.E. stand for?"

"You can just call me O.E.," Parker said. "Or Parker. Don't nobody call me by my name."

"What's it stand for?" she persisted.

"Never mind," Parker said. "What's yours?"

"I'll tell you when you tell me what them letters are the short of," she said. There was just a hint of flirtatiousness in her tone and it went rapidly to Parker's head. He had never revealed the name to any man or woman, only to the files of the navy and the government, and it was on his baptismal record which he got at the age of a month; his mother was a Methodist. When the name leaked out of the navy files, Parker narrowly missed killing the man who used it.

"You'll go blab it around," he said.

"I'll swear I'll never tell nobody," she said. "On God's holy word I swear it."

Parker sat for a few minutes in silence. Then he reached for the girl's neck, drew her ear close to his mouth and revealed the name in a low voice.

"Obadiah," she whispered. Her face slowly brightened as if the name came as a sign to her. "Obadiah," she said.

The name still stank in Parker's estimation.

"Obadiah Elihue," she said in a reverent voice.

"If you call me that aloud, I'll bust your head open," Parker said. "What's yours?"

"Sarah Ruth Cates," she said.

"Glad to meet you, Sarah Ruth," Parker said.

Sarah Ruth's father was a Straight Gospel preacher but he was away, spreading it in Florida. Her mother did not seem to mind his attention to the girl so long as he brought a basket of something with him when he came. As for Sarah Ruth herself, it was plain to Parker after he had visited three times that she was crazy about him. She liked him even though she insisted that pictures on the skin were vanity of vanities and even after hearing him curse, and even after she had asked him if he was saved and he had replied that he didn't see it was anything in particular to save him from. After that, inspired, Parker had said, "I'd be saved enough if you was to kiss me."

She scowled. "That ain't being saved," she said.

Not long after that she agreed to take a ride in his truck. Parker parked it on a deserted road and suggested to her that they lie down together in the back of it.

"Not until after we're married," she said—just like that.

"Oh that ain't necessary," Parker said and as he reached for her, she thrust him away with such force that the door of the truck came off and he found himself flat on his back on the ground. He made up his mind then and there to have nothing further to do with her.

They were married in the County Ordinary's office because Sarah Ruth thought churches were idolatrous. Parker had no opinion about that one way or the other. The Ordinary's[1] office was lined with cardboard file boxes and record books with dusty yellow slips of paper hanging on out of them. The Ordinary was an old woman with red hair who had held office for forty years and looked as dusty as her books. She married them from behind the iron-grill of a stand-up desk and when she finished, she said with a flourish, "Three dollars and fifty cents and till death do you part!" and yanked some forms out of a machine.

Marriage did not change Sarah Ruth a jot and it made Parker gloomier than ever. Every morning he decided he had had enough and would not return that night; every night he returned. Whenever Parker couldn't stand the way he felt, he would have another tattoo, but the only surface left on him now was his back. To see a tattoo on his own back he would have to get two mirrors and stand between them in just the correct position and this seemed to Parker a good way to make an idiot of himself. Sarah Ruth who, if she had had better sense, could have enjoyed a tattoo on his back, would not even look at the ones he had elsewhere. When he attempted to point out especial details of them, she would shut her eyes tight and turn her back as well. Except in total darkness, she preferred Parker dressed and with his sleeves rolled down.

"At the judgement seat of God, Jesus is going to say to you, 'What you been doing all your life besides have pictures drawn all over you?'" she said.

"You don't fool me none," Parker said, "you're just afraid that hefty girl I work for'll like me so much she'll say, 'Come on, Mr. Parker, let's you and me . . .'"

"You're tempting sin," she said, "and at the judgement seat of God you'll have to answer for that too. You ought to go back to selling the fruits of the earth."

Parker did nothing much when he was at home but listen to what the judgement seat of God would be like for him if he didn't change his ways. When he could, he broke in with tales of the hefty girl he worked for. "'Mr. Parker,'" he said she said, "'I hired you for your brains.'" (She had added, "So why don't you use them?")

"And you should have seen her face the first time she saw me without my shirt," he said. "'Mr. Parker,' she said, 'you're a walking panner-rammer!'" This

[1] A county judge.

had, in fact, been her remark but it had been delivered out of one side of her mouth.

Dissatisfaction began to grow so great in Parker that there was no containing it outside of a tattoo. It had to be his back. There was no help for it. A dim half-formed inspiration began to work in his mind. He visualized having a tattoo put there that Sarah Ruth would not be able to resist—a religious subject. He thought of an open book with HOLY BIBLE tattooed under it and an actual verse printed on the page. This seemed just the thing for a while; then he began to hear her say, "Ain't I already got a real Bible? What you think I want to read the same verse over and over for when I can read it all?" He needed something better even than the Bible! He thought about it so much that he began to lose sleep. He was already losing flesh—Sarah Ruth just threw food in the pot and let it boil. Not knowing for certain why he continued to stay with a woman who was both ugly and pregnant and no cook made him generally nervous and irritable, and he developed a little tic in the side of his face.

Once or twice he found himself turning around abruptly as if someone were trailing him. He had had a granddaddy who had ended in the state mental hospital, although not until he was seventy-five, but as urgent as it might be for him to get a tattoo, it was just as urgent that he get exactly the right one to bring Sarah Ruth to heel. As he continued to worry over it, his eyes took on a hollow preoccupied expression. The old woman he worked for told him that if he couldn't keep his mind on what he was doing, she knew where she could find a fourteen-year-old colored boy who could. Parker was too preoccupied even to be offended. At any time previous, he would have left her then and there, saying drily, "Well, you go ahead on and get him then."

Two or three mornings later he was baling hay with the old woman's sorry baler and her broken down tractor in a large field, cleared save for one enormous old tree standing in the middle of it. The old woman was the kind who would not cut down a large old tree because it was a large old tree. She had pointed it out to Parker as if he didn't have eyes and told him to be careful not to hit it as the machine picked up hay near it. Parker began at the outside of the field and made circles inward toward it. He had to get off the tractor every now and then and untangle the baling cord or kick a rock out of the way. The old woman had told him to carry the rocks to the edge of the field, which he did when she was there watching. When he thought he could make it, he ran over them. As he circled the field his mind was on a suitable design for his back. The sun, the size of a golf ball, began to switch regularly from in front to behind him, but he appeared to see it both places as if he had eyes in the back of his head. All at once he saw the tree reaching out to grasp him. A ferocious thud propelled him into the air, and he heard himself yelling in an unbelievably loud voice, "GOD ABOVE!"

He landed on his back while the tractor crashed upside-down into the tree and burst into flame. The first thing Parker saw were his shoes, quickly being eaten by the fire; one was caught under the tractor, the other was some distance away, burning by itself. He was not in them. He could feel the hot breath of the burning tree on his face. He scrambled backwards, still sitting, his eyes cavernous, and if he had known how to cross himself he would have done it.

His truck was on a dirt road at the edge of the field. He moved toward it, still sitting, still backwards, but faster and faster; halfway to it he got up and began a kind of forward-bent run from which he collapsed on his knees twice. His legs felt like two old rusted rain gutters. He reached the truck finally and took off in it, zigzagging up the road. He drove past his house on the embankment and straight for the city, fifty miles distant.

Parker did not allow himself to think on the way to the city. He only knew that there had been a great change in his life, a leap forward into a worse unknown, and that there was nothing he could do about it. It was for all intents accomplished.

The artist had two large cluttered rooms over a chiropodist's office on a back street. Parker, still barefooted, burst silently in on him at a little after three in the afternoon. The artist, who was about Parker's own age—twenty-eight—but thin and bald, was behind a small drawing table, tracing a design in green ink. He looked up with an annoyed glance and did not seem to recognize Parker in the hollow-eyed creature before him.

"Let me see the book you got with all the pictures of God in it," Parker said breathlessly. "The religious one."

The artist continued to look at him with his intellectual, superior stare. "I don't put tattoos on drunks," he said.

"You know me!" Parker cried indignantly. "I'm O. E. Parker! You done work for me before and I always paid!"

The artist looked at him another moment as if he were not altogether sure. "You've fallen off some," he said. "You must have been in jail."

"Married," Parker said.

"Oh," said the artist. With the aid of mirrors the artist had tattooed on the top of his head a miniature owl, perfect in every detail. It was about the size of a half-dollar and served him as a show piece. There were cheaper artists in town but Parker had never wanted anything but the best. The artist went over to a cabinet at the back of the room and began to look over some art books. "Who are you interested in?" he said, "saints, angels, Christs or what?"

"God," Parker said.

"Father, Son or Spirit?"

"Just God," Parker said impatiently. "Christ. I don't care. Just so it's God."

The artist returned with a book. He moved some papers off another table and put the book down on it and told Parker to sit down and see what he liked. "The up-to-date ones are in the back," he said.

Parker sat down with the book and wet his thumb. He began to go through it, beginning at the back where the up-to-date pictures were. Some of them he recognized—The Good Shepherd, Forbid Them Not, The Smiling Jesus, Jesus the Physician's Friend, but he kept turning rapidly backwards and the pictures became less and less reassuring. One showed a gaunt green dead face streaked with blood. One was yellow with sagging purple eyes. Parker's heart began to beat faster and faster until it appeared to be roaring inside him like a great generator. He flipped the pages quickly, feeling that when he reached the one ordained, a sign would come. He continued to flip through until he had almost reached the front of the book. On one of the pages a pair of eyes glanced at him swiftly. Parker sped on, then stopped. His heart too appeared to cut off; there was absolute silence. It said as plainly as if silence were a language itself, GO BACK.

Parker returned to the picture—the haloed head of a flat stern Byzantine Christ with all-demanding eyes. He sat there trembling; his heart began slowly to beat again as if it were being brought to life by a subtle power.

"You found what you want?" the artist asked.

Parker's throat was too dry to speak. He got up and thrust the book at the artist, opened at the picture.

"That'll cost you plenty," the artist said. "You don't want all those little blocks though, just the outline and some better features."

"Just like it is," Parker said, "just like it is or nothing."

"It's your funeral," the artist said, "but I don't do that kind of work for nothing."

"How much?" Parker asked.

"It'll take maybe two days work."

"How much?" Parker said.

"On time or cash?" the artist asked. Parker's other jobs had been on time, but he had paid.

"Ten down and ten for every day it takes," the artist said.

Parker drew ten dollar bills out of his wallet; he had three left in.

"You come back in the morning," the artist said, putting the money in his own pocket. "First I'll have to trace that out of the book."

"No no!" Parker said. "Trace it now or gimme my money back," and his eyes blared as if he were ready for a fight.

The artist agreed. Any one stupid enough to want a Christ on his back, he reasoned, would be just as likely as not to change his mind the next minute, but once the work was begun he could hardly do so.

While he worked on the tracing, he told Parker to go wash his back at the sink with the special soap he used there. Parker did it and returned to pace back and forth across the room, nervously flexing his shoulders. He wanted to go look at the picture again but at the same time he did not want to. The artist got up finally and had Parker lie down on the table. He swabbed his back with ethyl chloride and then began to outline the head on it with his iodine pencil. Another hour passed before he took up his electric instrument. Parker felt no particular pain. In Japan he had had a tattoo of the Buddha done on his upper arm with ivory needles; in Burma, a little brown root of a man had made a peacock on each of his knees using thin pointed sticks, two feet long; amateurs had worked on him with pins and soot. Parker was usually so relaxed and easy under the hand of the artist that he often went to sleep, but this time he remained awake, every muscle taut.

At midnight the artist said he was ready to quit. He propped one mirror, four feet square, on a table by the wall and took a smaller mirror off the lavatory wall and put it in Parker's hands. Parker stood with his back to the one on the table and moved the other until he saw a flashing burst of color reflected from his back. It was almost completely covered with little red and blue and ivory and saffron squares; from them he made out the lineaments of the face—a mouth, the beginning of heavy brows, a straight nose, but the face was empty; the eyes had not yet been put in. The impression for the moment was almost as if the artist had tricked him and done the Physician's Friend.

"It don't have eyes," Parker cried out.

"That'll come," the artist said, "in due time. We have another day to go on it yet."

Parker spent the night on a cot at the Haven of Light Christian Mission. He found these the best places to stay in the city because they were free and included a meal of sorts. He got the last available cot and because he was still bare-footed, he accepted a pair of second-hand shoes which, in his confusion, he put on to go to bed; he was still shocked from all that had happened to him. All night he lay awake in the long dormitory of cots with lumpy figures on them. The only light was from a phosphorescent cross glowing at the end of the room. The tree reached out to grasp him again, then burst into flame; the shoe burned quiety by itself; the eyes in the book said to him distinctly GO BACK and at the same time did not utter a sound. He wished that he were not in this city, not in this Haven of Light Mission, not in a bed by himself. He longed miserably for Sarah Ruth. Her sharp tongue and icepick eyes were the only comfort he could bring to mind. He decided he was losing it. Her eyes appeared soft and dilatory compared with the eyes in the book, for even though he could not summon up the exact look of those eyes, he could still feel their penetration. He felt as though, under their gaze, he was as transparent as the wing of a fly.

The tattooist had told him not to come until ten in the morning, but when he arrived at that hour, Parker was sitting in the dark hallway on the floor, waiting for him. He had decided upon getting up that, once the tattoo was on him, he would not look at it, that all his sensations of the day and night before were those of a crazy man and that he would return to doing things according to his own sound judgement.

The artist began where he left off. "One thing I want to know," he said presently as he worked over Parker's back, "why do you want this on you? Have you gone and got religion? Are you saved?" he asked in a mocking voice.

Parker's throat felt salty and dry. "Naw," he said, "I ain't got no use for none of that. A man can't save his self from whatever it is he don't deserve none of my sympathy." These words seemed to leave his mouth like wraiths and to evaporate at once as if he had never uttered them.

"Then why . . ."

"I married this woman that's saved," Parker said. "I never should have done it. I ought to leave her. She's done gone and got pregnant."

"That's too bad," the artist said. "Then it's her making you have this tattoo."

"Naw," Parker said, "she don't know nothing about it. It's a surprise for her."

"You think she'll like it and lay off you a while?"

"She can't hep herself," Parker said. "She can't say she don't like the looks of God." He decided he had told the artist enough of his business. Artists were all right in their place but he didn't like them poking their noses into the affairs of regular people. "I didn't get no sleep last night," he said. "I think I'll get some now."

That closed the mouth of the artist but it did not bring him any sleep. He lay there, imagining how Sarah Ruth would be struck speechless by the face on his back and every now and then this would be interrupted by a vision of the tree of fire and his empty shoe burning beneath it.

The artist worked steadily until nearly four o'clock, not stopping to have lunch, hardly pausing with the electric instrument except to wipe the dripping dye off Parker's back as he went along. Finally he finished. "You can get up and look at it now," he said.

Parker sat up but he remained on the edge of the table.

The artist was pleased with his work and wanted Parker to look at it at once. Instead Parker continued to sit on the edge of the table, bent forward slightly but with a vacant look. "What ails you?" the artist said. "Go look at it."

"Ain't nothing ail me," Parker said in a sudden belligerent voice. "That tattoo ain't going nowhere. It'll be there when I get there." He reached for his shirt and began gingerly to put it on.

The artist took him roughly by the arm and propelled him between the two mirrors. "Now *look*," he said, angry at having his work ignored.

Parker looked, turned white and moved away. The eyes in the reflected face continued to look at him—still, straight, all-demanding, enclosed in silence.

"It was your idea, remember," the artist said. "I would have advised something else."

Parker said nothing. He put on his shirt and went out the door while the artist shouted, "I'll expect all of my money!"

Parker headed toward a package shop on the corner. He bought a pint of whiskey and took it into a nearby alley and drank it all in five minutes. Then he moved on to a pool hall nearby which he frequented when he came to the city. It was a well-lighted barn-like place with a bar up one side and gambling machines on the other and pool tables in the back. As soon as Parker entered, a large man in a red and black checkered shirt hailed him by slapping him on the back and yelling, "Yeyyyyyy boy! O. E. Parker!"

Parker was not yet ready to be struck on the back. "Lay off," he said, "I got a fresh tattoo there."

"What you got this time?" the man asked and then yelled to a few at the machines. "O.E.'s got him another tattoo."

"Nothing special this time," Parker said and slunk over to a machine that was not being used.

"Come on," the big man said, "let's have a look at O.E.'s tattoo," and while Parker squirmed in their hands, they pulled up his shirt. Parker felt all the hands drop away instantly and his shirt fell again like a veil over the face. There was a silence in the pool room which seemed to Parker to grow from the circle around him until it extended to the foundations under the building and upward through the beams in the roof.

Finally some one said, "Christ!" Then they all broke into noise at once. Parker turned around, an uncertain grin on his face.

"Leave it to O.E.!" the man in the checkered shirt said. "That boy's a real card!"

"Maybe he's gone and got religion," some one yelled.

"Not on your life," Parker said.

"O.E.'s got religion and is witnessing for Jesus, ain't you, O.E.?" a little man with a piece of cigar in his mouth said wryly. "An o-riginal way to do it if I ever saw one."

"Leave it to Parker to think of a new one!" the fat man said.

"Yyeeeeeeyyyyyyy boy!" someone yelled and they all began to whistle and curse in compliment until Parker said, "Aaa shut up."

"What'd you do it for?" somebody asked.

"For laughs," Parker said. "What's it to you?"

"Why ain't you laughing then?" somebody yelled. Parker lunged into the midst of them and like a whirlwind on a summer's day there began a fight that raged amid overturned tables and swinging fists until two of them grabbed him and ran to the door with him and threw him out. Then a calm descended on the pool hall as nerve shattering as if the long barn-like room were the ship from which Jonah had been cast into the sea.

Parker sat for a long time on the ground in the alley behind the pool hall, examining his soul. He saw it as a spider web of facts and lies that was not at all important to him but which appeared to be necessary in spite of his opinion. The eyes that were now forever on his back were eyes to be obeyed. He was as certain of it as he had ever been of anything. Throughout his life, grumbling and sometimes cursing, often afraid, once in rapture, Parker had obeyed whatever instinct of this kind had come to him—in rapture when his spirit had lifted at the sight of the tattooed man at the fair, afraid when he had joined the navy, grumbling when he had married Sarah Ruth.

The thought of her brought him slowly to his feet. She would know what he had to do. She would clear up the rest of it, and she would at least be pleased. It seemed to him that, all along, that was what he wanted, to please her. His truck was still parked in front of the building where the artist had his place, but it was not far away. He got in it and drove out of the city and into the country night. His head was almost clear of liquor and he observed that his dissatisfaction was gone, but he felt not quite like himself. It was as if he were himself but a stranger to himself, driving into a new country though everything he saw was familiar to him, even at night.

He arrived finally at the house on the embankment, pulled the truck under the pecan tree and got out. He made as much noise as possible to assert that he was still in charge here, that his leaving her for a night without word meant nothing except it was the way he did things. He slammed the car door, stamped up the two steps and across the porch and rattled the door knob. It did not respond to his touch. "Sarah Ruth!" he yelled, "let me in."

There was no lock on the door and she had evidently placed the back of a chair against the knob. He began to beat on the door and rattle the knob at the same time.

He heard the bed springs screak and bent down and put his head to the keyhole, but it was stopped up with paper. "Let me in!" he hollered, bamming on the door again. "What you got me locked out for?"

A sharp voice close to the door said, "Who's there?"

"Me," Parker said, "O.E."

He waited a moment.

"Me," he said impatiently, "O.E."

Still no sound from inside.

He tried once more. "O.E.," he said, bamming the door two or three more times. "O. E. Parker. You know me."

There was a silence. Then the voice said slowly, "I don't know no O.E."

"Quit fooling," Parker pleaded. "You ain't got any business doing me this way. It's me, old O.E., I'm back. You ain't afraid of me."

"Who's there?" the same unfeeling voice said.

Parker turned his head as if he expected someone behind him to give him the answer. The sky had lightened slightly and there were two or three streaks of yellow floating above the horizon. Then as he stood there, a tree of light burst over the skyline.

Parker fell back against the door as if he had been pinned there by a lance.

"Who's there?" the voice from inside said and there was a quality about it now that seemed final. The knob rattled and the voice said peremptorily, "Who's there, I ast you?"

Parker bent down and put his mouth near the stuffed keyhole. "Obadiah," he whispered and all at once he felt the light pouring through him, turning his spider web soul into a perfect arabesque of colors, a garden of trees and birds and beasts.

"Obadiah Elihue!" he whispered.

The door opened and he stumbled in. Sarah Ruth loomed there, hands on her hips. She began at once, "That was no hefty blonde woman you was working for and you'll have to pay her every penny on her tractor you busted up. She don't keep insurance on it. She came here and her and me had us a long talk and I . . ."

Trembling, Parker set about lighting the kerosene lamp.

"What's the matter with you, wasting that keresene this near daylight?" she demanded. "I ain't got to look at you."

A yellow glow enveloped them. Parker put the match down and began to unbutton his shirt.

"And you ain't going to have none of me this near morning," she said.

"Shut your mouth," he said quietly. "Look at this and then I don't want to hear no more out of you." He removed the shirt and turned his back to her.

"Another picture," Sarah Ruth growled. "I might have known you was off after putting some more trash on yourself."

Parker's knees went hollow under him. He wheeled around and cried, "Look at it! Don't just say that! *Look* at it!"

"I done looked," she said.

"Don't you know who it is?" he cried in anguish.

"No, who is it?" Sarah Ruth said. "It ain't nobody I know."

"It's him," Parker said.

"Him who?"

"God!" Parker cried.

"God? God don't look like that!"

"What do you know how he looks?" Parker moaned. "You ain't seen him."

"He don't *look*," Sarah Ruth said. "He's a spirit. No man shall see his face."

"Aw listen," Parker groaned, "this is just a picture of him."

"Idolatry!" Sarah Ruth screamed. "Idolatry! Enflaming yourself with idols under every green tree! I can put up with lies and vanity but I don't want no idolator in this house!" and she grabbed up the broom and began to thrash him across the shoulders with it.

Parker was too stunned to resist. He sat there and let her beat him until she had nearly knocked him senseless and large welts had formed on the face of the tattooed Christ. Then he staggered up and made for the door.

She stamped the broom two or three times on the floor and went to the window and shook it out to get the taint of him off it. Still gripping it, she looked toward the pecan tree and her eyes hardened still more. There he was—who called himself Obadiah Elihue—leaning against the tree, crying like a baby.

Questions for Writing and Discussion

1. Read the first paragraph of this story with a special view toward O'Connor's use of language—for instance, the repetitions in the third sentence, the similes in the fourth sentence, the irony of the fifth sentence, the understatement in the sixth sentence, and the comic preposterousness of the concluding phrase, "ashamed of himself." Sticking just to these sentences, see if you can work up a preliminary description of O'Connor's methods as a writer.

2. On pp. 70–71 there is an amusing description of Parker's strategies in courtship and Sarah Ruth's counterstrategies in coping with him. From this passage, can you make a pretty good guess as to the likely outcome of their sparring?

3. What is it that keeps driving Parker to get more and more tattoos?

4. What do you make of Parker being named Obadiah Elihue? What does it suggest about Southern culture, or at least part of it? And why should he be so ashamed of his name?

5. How would you describe the marriage between Parker and Sarah Ruth?

NATHANIEL HAWTHORNE

Young Goodman Brown

Introduction

"Young Goodman Brown" seems different from all the other stories in this book, if only because it is farthest away from the kind of fiction we call "realism." By realism we mean a fiction that is set in a recognizable, ordinary, familiar world, such as we all live in; that contains events which we suppose to be possible or plausible within that world; and that has characters who strike us as recognizable, ordinary, familiar men and women. No work of fiction is merely a photographic copy of external social reality, but the kind we call realism comes closest to being that. Hortense Calisher's "Heartburn," on page 54, is also somewhat distant from "realism," though considerably less so than "Young Goodman Brown." A live frog in a doctor's chest is, after all, not something we can easily take to be part of the ordinary world; but except for this one thing, Calisher's story occurs in a quite ordinary setting and is populated with quite ordinary characters.)

There have, of course, been kinds of literature which are not realistic or which can even be called antirealistic. (Indeed, what we call realism nowadays is fairly recent in literary history, coinciding with the rise of the novel in the eighteenth and nineteenth centuries.) Fantasy, romance, fable, allegory—these are nonrealistic kinds of literature. And there are others. All depart from the standards and expectations of realism, though all seek finally to illuminate or to penetrate reality. A fable about an ant and a grasshopper can turn out, on reflection, to tell us a great deal about human conduct. A fantasy about a superman landing on the planet Jupiter may do the same. There is nothing necessarily better or worse about one or another kind of writing, so that to say a story is realistic or is not realistic is simply to offer a description of its kind, not a judgment of its value. The word "realism" should not be used as a term of praise or dispraise.

One kind of fiction, very popular in the Middle Ages but to be found in literature before and after that time, is the allegory. Nathaniel Hawthorne, the

first major writer of American fiction, was greatly influenced by such practition-
ers of the allegory as Edmund Spenser, the English poet, and John Bunyan, the
English writer of religious narratives; but Hawthorne himself, though his stories
show an obvious debt to the form, did not, strictly speaking, compose allegories.

Deriving from medieval Christian writing, the traditional allegory in
English presents a line of action which is clearly meant to serve as the equivalent
or parallel to another line of moral or philosophical ideas. There are close and
systematic connections between action and meaning throughout the work. The
characters in such fiction tend to embody abstract and distinct qualities (greed,
charity, hypocrisy, goodness). As a result, in reading allegories we focus not only
upon the depiction of a complex human situation in its own right but also upon
the working-out of a set of fixed and familiar moral premises. Allegory tends to
subordinate story to idea. Yet, to say all this, it should be stressed, is not at all to
say that allegory is inferior to or less subtle than other literary forms. It merely
serves different purposes and employs different techniques.

It is not hard to see why Nathaniel Hawthorne should have been attracted
to the allegory. He was a spiritual descendant of the New England Puritans, to
whom all existence seemed a moral drama in which absolute good was pitted
against absolute evil—a view of life that easily lent itself to allegorical representation. In general, religious thought, insofar as it assumes there is an invisible
world behind and better than the visible world, encourages one or another kind
of allegory. The relation between the visible and invisible world can be depicted,
in an allegorical story, as a relation between human action and religious or moral
ideas. And while Hawthorne himself was probably not religious, certainly not
religious in any precise or practicing sense, the hold of religious faith, religious
ceremonies, religious ideas and symbols upon his imagination remained very
strong. So we find him using allegory, but in a new way, as a mixed and impure
form.

Hawthorne's stories follow the traditional pattern of allegory, but only up
to a point. In the best of them, like "Young Goodman Brown," he enriches and
complicates this form with elements of doubt, ambiguity, and slyness, mostly
because he no longer possesses the religious certainty which is essential to a
pure allegory. Extremely clever in his quiet way, Hawthorne both employs and
undercuts allegory, so that in a story like "Young Goodman Brown" we get the
structure of the original form but not the solid assurance and undoubting truth
which often characterized traditional Christian allegory. Hawthorne is well on
the way toward a modern version of skepticism.

It is not hard to detect the allegorical element in "Young Goodman
Brown." Brown goes to the forest, meets a man who turns out to be the devil,
and this devil carries a staff or stick "which bore the likeness of a great black
snake, so curiously wrought that it might almost be seen to twist and wriggle
itself like a living serpent." Notice immediately the way Hawthorne hedges: the
snake *"might almost* be seen to twist . . . like a living serpent." And the next
sentence reads: "This, of course, must have been an ocular deception, assisted
by the uncertain light." Having presented a man who turns out to be the devil,
and thereby perhaps tried the credence of his nineteenth-century readers,

Hawthorne writes in such a way as to allow them to take the story at its face value (supernaturalistic) or to give it a naturalistic or rationalistic reading. It's as if Hawthorne were saying: "You sophisticated readers, of course, aren't inclined to believe in any supernatural phenomena, so I'm offering you an explanation which will make you more comfortable; but still, you'd better consider the possibility, at least, that it *is* supernatural. . . ."

At the devil's gathering, Brown encounters all the notables of Salem Village: the leading officials, the Puritan divines, the pious old ladies. He experiences there what is called in German *Schadenfreude,* or glee at discovering scandal. It is a thrill of recognition that one can reach upon concluding, with or without sufficient evidence, that everyone you know—parents, teachers, friends, lovers—is evil. The Puritan doctrine of "total depravity" is here given a dramatic rendering, or distortion: it becomes a sort of black mass with suggestions of blood rites and sexual orgies. Step by step, Brown's resistance is broken down by the subtle arguments of the devil, who shows him—or seems to show him—that everyone he has ever respected or loved has joined the devil's party.

Brown tries to resist. He cries out, "With heaven above and Faith below, I will yet stand firm against the devil." It is a neat touch that his wife should be named Faith, since the name serves at least two purposes: it suggests that the love of a wife can protect one from evil and that a submission to faith, even if one cannot summon a clear argument in its behalf, can also protect one from evil.

There follows the striking little incident in which Brown, screaming out for his Faith, sees something fluttering down in the woods—it turns out to be, or rather, he *perceives* it to be—Faith's pink ribbon, which she had worn when he left home. He abandons himself to despair since, as it seems to him, even Faith is tainted. "My Faith is gone! There is no good on earth; and sin is but a name. Come, devil; for to thee is this world given."

It is as if Hawthorne were slyly saying: How terrible that a man should lose his faith because of a mere ribbon such as the devil could easily counterfeit! How foolish that a man should give up faith in his wife, or Faith his wife, on no evidence other than a mere pink ribbon! And meanwhile, though Hawthorne keeps silent on this score, we should notice that Brown, as he grows increasingly skeptical about the moral claims of all the town's citizens, never stops to express skepticism about the show which the devil is staging for him. Why does he not ask himself whether these are "really" the townspeople he thinks they are, or perhaps are merely spectral shadows contrived by the devil in order to destroy his faith? Because he himself has already taken a long step toward the devil!

As the portion of the story depicting the ceremony in the woods comes to an end, Brown cries out, begging Faith to "look to heaven, and resist the wicked one." And then, with characteristic slyness, Hawthorne writes: "Whether Faith obeyed he knew not."

Yet, the next morning when he is back in Salem, Brown assumes, in fact, that she has not obeyed, that she and everyone else there are hypocrites, and that their claims to goodness and morality are merely masks for their inner submission to the devil. Undone by an excess of skepticism toward men and a lack of skepticism toward the devil, Brown becomes "a stern, a sad, a darkly meditative, a distrustful, if not a desperate man." So overwhelmed is he now by what he thinks is his discovery of the truth that he cannot even hear the singing of the holy psalms.

Whether Brown had "actually" encountered a witches' sabbath in the woods at night or had "only dreamed a wild dream" Hawthorne leaves open. It does not really matter as far as the point of the story is concerned. For Brown has been overcome by his own sudden conviction that sin is universal and unqualified. The consequences of discovering, or supposing that he has discovered, that all men are in the devil's grip is to lose any capacity for . . . resisting the devil! In his own way, then, Goodman Brown is guilty of the sin of pride: he supposes he sees the truth so much more fully than anyone else that, as the devil says in his speech, "the whole earth [is no more than] one stain of guilt, one mighty blood spot." This leads him into a complete gloom, destroying his capacity for affection, for living together with other human beings, for any sort of complex or balanced moral existence.

About this aspect of Hawthorne's work the critic Newton Arvin has written well:

> The penalty of intellectual pride and of all other forms of egotism—indeed, of guilt in general—is the deepest misery Hawthorne can conceive, the misery of estrangement, of separateness, of insulation from the normal life of mankind. . . . The simplest and truest thing to say of Hawthorne's human vision is that for him the essence of wrong is aloneness; you begin and you end with that.

The power of "Young Goodman Brown" lies in bringing together the pattern of allegory with complicating strands of intellectual doubt and uncertainty. Especially notable is the cleverness of detail with which Hawthorne manages this (e.g., Faith's pink ribbon). Traditional morality and modern psychology coexist in an uneasy but fruitful relationship, so that while the story is not "realistic" in method, it moves deeply and surely into inner areas of human reality.

Young Goodman Brown

Young Goodman[1] Brown came forth at sunset into the street at Salem village; but put his head back, after crossing the threshold, to exchange a parting kiss with his young wife. And Faith, as the wife was aptly named, thrust her own pretty head into the street, letting the wind play with the pink ribbons of her cap while she called to Goodman Brown.

[1] A term used in New England for people of middle social position.

"Dearest heart," whispered she, softly and rather sadly, when her lips were close to his ear, "prithee put off your journey until sunrise and sleep in your own bed to-night. A lone woman is troubled with such dreams and such thoughts that she's afeard of herself sometimes. Pray tarry with me this night, dear husband, of all nights in the year."

"My love and my Faith," replied young Goodman Brown, "of all nights in the year, this one night must I tarry away from thee. My journey, as thou callest it, forth and back again, must needs be done 'twixt now and sunrise. What, my sweet, pretty wife, dost thou doubt me already, and we but three months married?"

"Then God bless you!" said Faith, with the pink ribbons; "and may you find all well when you come back."

"Amen!" cried Goodman Brown. "Say thy prayers, dear Faith, and go to bed at dusk, and no harm will come to thee."

So they parted; and the young man pursued his way until, being about to turn the corner by the meeting-house, he looked back and saw the head of Faith still peeping after him with a melancholy air, in spite of her pink ribbons.

"Poor little Faith!" thought he, for his heart smote him. "What a wretch am I to leave her on such an errand! She talks of dreams, too. Methought as she spoke there was trouble in her face, as if a dream had warned her what work is to be done to-night. But no, no; 't would kill her to think it. Well, she's a blessed angel on earth; and after this one night I'll cling to her skirts and follow her to heaven."

With this excellent resolve for the future, Goodman Brown felt himself justified in making more haste on his present evil purpose. He had taken a dreary road, darkened by all the gloomiest trees of the forest, which barely stood aside to let the narrow path creep through, and closed immediately behind. It was all as lonely as could be; and there is this peculiarity in such a solitude, that the traveller knows not who may be concealed by the innumerable trunks and the thick boughs overhead; so that with lonely footsteps he may yet be passing through an unseen multitude.

"There may be a devilish Indian behind every tree," said Goodman Brown to himself; and he glanced fearfully behind him as he added, "What if the devil himself should be at my very elbow!"

His head being turned back, he passed a crook of the road, and, looking forward again, beheld the figure of a man, in grave and decent attire, seated at the foot of an old tree. He arose at Goodman Brown's approach and walked onward side by side with him.

"You are late, Goodman Brown," said he. "The clock of the Old South was striking as I came through Boston, and that is full fifteen minutes agone."

"Faith kept me back a while," replied the young man, with a tremor in his voice, caused by the sudden appearance of his companion, though not wholly unexpected.

It was now deep dusk in the forest, and deepest in that part of it where these two were journeying. As nearly as could be discerned, the second traveller was about fifty years old, apparently in the same rank of life as Goodman Brown, and bearing a considerable resemblance to him, though perhaps more in expression than features. Still they might have been taken for father and son. And yet, though the elder person was as simply clad as the younger, and as simple in manner too, he had an indescribable air of one who knew the world, and who would not have felt abashed at the governor's dinner table or in King William's[2] court, were it possible that his affairs should call him thither. But the only thing about him that could be fixed upon as remarkable was his staff, which bore the likeness of a great black snake, so curiously wrought that it might almost be seen to twist and wriggle itself like a living serpent. This, of course, must have been an ocular deception, assisted by the uncertain light.

"Come, Goodman Brown," cried his fellow-traveller, "this is a dull pace for the beginning of a journey. Take my staff, if you are so soon weary."

"Friend," said the other, exchanging his slow pace for a full stop, "having kept covenant by meeting thee here, it is my purpose now to return whence I came. I have scruples touching the matter thou wot'st of."

"Sayest thou so?" replied he of the serpent, smiling apart. "Let us walk on, nevertheless, reasoning as we go; and if I convince thee not thou shalt turn back. We are but a little way in the forest yet."

"Too far! too far!" exclaimed the goodman, unconsciously resuming his walk. "My father never went into the woods on such an errand, nor his father before him. We have been a race of honest men and good Christians since the days of the martyrs; and shall I be the first of the name of Brown that ever took this path and kept"—

"Such company, thou wouldst say," observed the elder person, interpreting his pause. "Well said, Goodman Brown! I have been as well acquainted with your family as with ever a one among the Puritans; and that's no trifle to say. I helped your grandfather, the constable, when he lashed the Quaker woman so smartly through the streets of Salem[3]; and it was I that brought your father a pitch-pine knot, kindled at my own hearth, to set fire to an Indian village, in King Philip's war.[4] They were my good friends, both; and many a pleasant walk have we had along this path, and returned merrily after midnight. I would fain be friends with you for their sake."

"If it be as thou sayest," replied Goodman Brown, "I marvel they never spoke of these matters; or, verily, I marvel not, seeing that the least rumor of the sort would have driven them from New England. We are a people of prayer, and good works to boot, and abide no such wickedness."

"Wickedness or not," said the traveller with the twisted staff, "I have a very general acquaintance here in New England. The deacons of many a church have drunk the communion wine with me; the selectmen of divers towns make me their chairman; and a majority of the Great and General Court are firm supporters of my interest. The governor and I, too—But these are state secrets."

"Can this be so?" cried Goodman Brown, with a stare of amazement at his

[2]William III, 1650–1702, King of England.
[3]Hawthorne's grandfather persecuted Quakers in New England.
[4]War between New England colonists and Indians, 1676.

undisturbed companion. "Howbeit, I have nothing to do with the governor and council; they have their own ways, and are no rule for a simple husbandman like me. But, were I to go on with thee, how should I meet the eye of that good old man, our minister, at Salem village? Oh, his voice would make me tremble both Sabbath day and lecture day."

Thus far the elder traveller had listened with due gravity; but now burst into a fit of irrepressible mirth, shaking himself so violently that his snake-like staff actually seemed to wriggle in sympathy.

"Ha! ha! ha!" shouted he again and again; then composing himself, "Well, go on, Goodman Brown, go on; but, prithee, don't kill me with laughing."

"Well, then, to end the matter at once," said Goodman Brown, considerably nettled, "there is my wife, Faith. It would break her dear little heart; and I'd rather break my own."

"Nay, if that be the case," answered the other, "e'en go thy ways, Goodman Brown. I would not for twenty old women like the one hobbling before us that Faith should come to any harm."

As he spoke he pointed his staff at a female figure on the path, in whom Goodman Brown recognized a very pious and exemplary dame, who had taught him his catechism in youth, and was still his moral and spiritual adviser, jointly with the minister and Deacon Gookin.

"A marvel, truly, that Goody Cloyse[5] should be so far in the wilderness at nightfall," said he. "But with your leave, friend, I shall take a cut through the woods until we have left this Christian woman behind. Being a stranger to you, she might ask whom I was consorting with and whither I was going."

"Be it so," said his fellow-traveller. "Betake you to the woods, and let me keep the path."

Accordingly the young man turned aside, but took care to watch his companion, who advanced softly along the road until he had come within a staff's length of the old dame. She, meanwhile, was making the best of her way, with singular speed for so aged a woman, and mumbling some indistinct words—a prayer, doubtless—as she went. The traveller put forth his staff and touched her withered neck with what seemed the serpent's tail.

"The devil!" screamed the pious old lady.

"Then Goody Cloyse knows her old friend?" observed the traveller, confronting her and leaning on his writhing stick.

"Ah, forsooth, and is it your worship indeed?" cried the good dame. "Yea, truly is it, and in the very image of my old gossip, Goodman Brown, the grandfather of the silly fellow that now is. But—would your worship believe it?—my broomstick hath strangely disappeared, stolen, as I suspect, by that unhanged witch, Goody Cory, and that, too, when I was all anointed with the juice of smallage, and cinquefoil, and wolf's bane"—

"Mingled with fine wheat and the fat of a new-born babe," said the shape of old Goodman Brown.

"Ah, your worship knows the recipe," cried the old lady, cackling aloud.

---

[5]Sentenced to death in Salem for witchcraft, 1692.

"So, as I was saying, being all ready for the meeting, and no horse to ride on, I made up my mind to foot it; for they tell me there is a nice young man to be taken into communion to-night. But now your good worship will lend me your arm, and we shall be there in a twinkling."

"That can hardly be," answered her friend. "I may not spare you my arm, Goody Cloyse; but here is my staff, if you will."

So saying, he threw it down at her feet, where, perhaps, it assumed life, being one of the rods which its owner had formerly lent to the Egyptian magi. Of this fact, however, Goodman Brown could not take cognizance. He had cast up his eyes in astonishment, and, looking down again, beheld neither Goody Cloyse nor the serpentine staff, but his fellow-traveller alone, who waited for him as calmly as if nothing had happened.

"That old woman taught me my catechism," said the young man; and there was a world of meaning in this simple comment.

They continued to walk onward, while the elder traveller exhorted his companion to make good speed and persevere in the path, discoursing so aptly that his arguments seemed rather to spring up in the bosom of his auditor than to be suggested by himself. As they went, he plucked a branch of maple to serve for a walking stick, and began to strip it of the twigs and little boughs, which were wet with evening dew. The moment his fingers touched them they became strangely withered and dried up as with a week's sunshine. Thus the pair proceeded, at a good free pace, until suddenly, in a gloomy hollow of the road, Goodman Brown sat himself down on the stump of a tree and refused to go any farther.

"Friend," said he, stubbornly, "my mind is made up. Not another step will I budge on this errand. What if a wretched old woman do choose to go to the devil when I thought she was going to heaven: is that any reason why I should quit my dear Faith and go after her?"

"You will think better of this by and by," said his acquaintance, composedly. "Sit here and rest yourself a while; and when you feel like moving again, there is my staff to help you along."

Without more words, he threw his companion the maple stick, and was as speedily out of sight as if he had vanished into the deepening gloom. The young man sat a few moments by the roadside, applauding himself greatly, and thinking with how clear a conscience he should meet the minister in his morning walk, nor shrink from the eye of good old Deason Gookin. And what calm sleep would be his that very night, which was to have been spent so wickedly, but so purely and sweetly now, in the arms of Faith! Amidst these pleasant and praiseworthy meditations, Goodman Brown heard the tramp of horses along the road, and deemed it advisable to conceal himself within the verge of the forest, conscious of the guilty purpose that had brought him thither, though now so happily turned from it.

On came the hoof tramps and the voices of the riders, two grave old voices, conversing soberly as they drew near. These mingled sounds appeared to pass along the road, within a few yards of the young man's hiding-place; but, owing doubtless to the depth of the gloom at that particular spot, neither the travellers nor their steeds were visible. Though their figures brushed the small boughs by the wayside, it could not be seen that they intercepted, even for a moment, the faint gleam from the strip of bright sky athwart which they must have passed. Goodman Brown alternately crouched and stood on tiptoe, pulling aside the branches and thrusting forth his head as far as he durst without discerning so much as a shadow. It vexed him the more, because he could have sworn, were such a thing possible, that he recognized the voices of the minister and Deacon Gookin, jogging along quietly, as they were wont to do, when bound to some ordination or ecclesiastical council. While yet within hearing, one of the riders stopped to pluck a switch.

"Of the two, reverend sir," said the voice like the deacon's, "I had rather miss an ordination dinner than to-night's meeting. They tell me that some of our community are to be here from Falmouth and beyond, and others from Connecticut and Rhode Island, besides several of the Indian powwows, who, after their fashion, know almost as much deviltry as the best of us. Moreover, there is a goodly young woman to be taken into communion."

"Mighty well, Deacon Gookin!" replied the solemn old tones of the minister. "Spur up, or we shall be late. Nothing can be done, you know, until I get on the ground."

The hoofs clattered again; and the voices, talking so strangely in the empty air, passed on through the forest, where no church had ever been gathered or solitary Christian prayed. Whither, then, could these holy men be journeying so deep into the heathen wilderness? Young Goodman Brown caught hold of a tree for support, being ready to sink down on the ground, faint and overburdened with the heavy sickness of his heart. He looked up to the sky, doubting whether there really was a heaven above him. Yet there was the blue arch, and the stars brightening in it.

"With heaven above and Faith below, I will yet stand firm against the devil!" cried Goodman Brown.

While he still gazed upward into the deep arch of the firmament and had lifted his hands to pray, a cloud, though no wind was stirring, hurried across the zenith and hid the brightening stars. The blue sky was still visible, except directly overhead, where this black mass of cloud was sweeping swiftly northward. Aloft in the air, as if from the depths of the cloud, came a confused and doubtful sound of voices. Once the listener fancied that he could distinguish the accents of towns-people of his own, men and women, both pious and ungodly, many of whom he had met at the communion table, and had seen others rioting at the tavern. The next moment, so indistinct were the sounds, he doubted whether he had heard aught but the murmur of the old forest, whispering without a wind. Then came a stronger swell of those familiar tones, heard daily in the sunshine at Salem village, but never until now from a cloud of night. There was one voice, of a young woman, uttering lamentations, yet with an uncertain sorrow, and entreating for some favor, which, perhaps, it would grieve her to obtain; and all the unseen multitude, both saints and sinners, seemed to encourage her onward.

"Faith!" shouted Goodman Brown, in a voice of agony and desparation;

and the echoes of the forest mocked him, crying "Faith! Faith!" as if bewildered wretches were seeking her all through the wilderness.

The cry of grief, rage, and terror was yet piercing the night, when the unhappy husband held his breath for a response. There was a scream, drowned immediately in a louder murmur of voices, fading into far-off laughter, as the dark cloud swept away, leaving the clear and silent sky above Goodman Brown. But something fluttered lightly down through the air and caught on the branch of a tree. The young man seized it, and beheld a pink ribbon.

"My Faith is gone!" cried he, after one stupefied moment. "There is no good on earth; and sin is but a name. Come, devil; for to thee is this world given."

And, maddened with despair, so that he laughed loud and long, did Goodman Brown grasp his staff and set forth again, at such a rate that he seemed to fly along the forest path rather than to walk or run. The road grew wilder and drearier and more faintly traced, and vanished at length, leaving him in the heart of the dark wilderness, still rushing onward with the instinct that guides mortal man to evil. The whole forest was peopled with frightful sounds—the creaking of the trees, the howling of wild beasts, and the yell of Indians; while sometimes the wind tolled like a distant church bell, and sometimes gave a broad roar around the traveller, as if all Nature were laughing him to scorn. But he was himself the chief horror of the scene, and shrank not from its other horrors.

"Ha! ha! ha!" roared Goodman Brown when the wind laughed at him. "Let us hear which will laugh loudest. Think not to frighten me with your deviltry. Come witch, come wizard, come Indian powwow, come devil himself, and here comes Goodman Brown. You may as well fear him as he fear you."

In truth, all through the haunted forest there could be nothing more frightful than the figure of Goodman Brown. On he flew among the black pines, brandishing his staff with frenzied gestures, now giving vent to an inspiration of horrid blasphemy, and now shouting forth such laughter as set all the echoes of the forest laughing like demons around him. The fiend in his own shape is less hideous than when he rages in the breast of man. Thus sped the demoniac on his course, until, quivering among the trees, he saw a red light before him, as when the felled trunks and branches of a clearing have been set on fire, and throw up their lurid blaze against the sky, at the hour of midnight. He paused, in a lull of the tempest that had driven him onward, and heard the swell of what seemed a hymn, rolling solemnly from a distance with the weight of many voices. He knew the tune; it was a familiar one in the choir of the village meeting-house. The verse died heavily away, and was lengthened by a chorus, not of human voices, but of all the sounds of the benighted wilderness pealing in awful harmony together. Goodman Brown cried out, and his cry was lost to his own ear by its unison with the cry of the desert.

In the interval of silence he stole forward until the light glared full upon his eyes. At one extremity of an open space, hemmed in by the dark wall of the forest, arose a rock, bearing some rude, natural resemblance either to an altar or a pulpit, and surrounded by four blazing pines, their tops aflame, their stems untouched, like candles at an evening meeting. The mass of foliage that had overgrown the summit of the rock was all on fire, blazing high into the night and fitfully illuminating the whole field. Each pendent twig and leafy festoon was in a blaze. As the red light arose and fell, a numerous congregation alternately shone forth, then disappeared in shadow, and again grew, as it were, out of the darkness, peopling the heart of the solitary woods at once.

"A grave and dark-clad company," quoth Goodman Brown.

In truth they were such. Among them, quivering to and fro between gloom and splendor, appeared faces that would be seen next day at the council board of the province, and others which, Sabbath after Sabbath, looked devoutly heavenward, and benignantly over the crowded pews, from the holiest pulpits in the land. Some affirm that the lady of the governor was there. At least there were high dames well known to her, and wives of honored husbands, and widows, a great multitude, and ancient maidens, all of excellent repute, and fair young girls, who trembled lest their mothers should espy them. Either the sudden gleams of light flashing over the obscure field bedazzled Goodman Brown, or he recognized a score of the church members of Salem village famous for their especial sanctity. Good old Deacon Gookin had arrived, and waited at the skirts of that venerable saint, his revered pastor. But, irreverently consorting with these grave, reputable, and pious people, these elders of the church, these chaste dames and dewy virgins, there were men of dissolute lives and women of spotted fame, wretches given over to all mean and filthy vice, and suspected even of horrid crimes. It was strange to see that the good shrank not from the wicked, nor were the sinners abashed by the saints. Scattered also among their pale-faced enemies were the Indian priests, or powwows, who had often scared their native forest with more hideous incantations than any known to English witchcraft.

"But where is Faith?" thought Goodman Brown; and, as hope came into his heart, he trembled.

Another verse of the hymn arose, a slow and mournful strain, such as the pious love, but joined to words which expressed all that our nature can conceive of sin, and darkly hinted at far more. Unfathomable to mere mortals is the lore of fiends. Verse after verse was sung; and still the chorus of the desert swelled between like the deepest tone of a mighty organ; and with the final peal of that dreadful anthem there came a sound, as if the roaring wind, the rushing streams, the howling beasts, and every other voice of the unconcerted wilderness were mingling and according with the voice of guilty man in homage to the prince of all. The four blazing pines threw up a loftier flame, and obscurely discovered shapes and visages of horror on the smoke wreaths above the impious assembly. At the same moment the fire on the rock shot redly forth and formed a glowing arch above its base, where now appeared a figure. With reverence be it spoken, the figure bore no slight similitude, both in garb and manner, to some grave divine of the New England churches.

"Bring forth the converts!" cried a voice that echoed through the field and rolled into the forest.

At the word, Goodman Brown stepped forth from the shadow of the trees and approached the congregation, with whom he felt a loathful brotherhood by the sympathy of all that was wicked in his heart. He could have well-nigh sworn that the shape of his own dead father beckoned him to advance, looking downward from a smoke wreath, while a woman, with dim features of despair, threw out her hand to warn him back. Was it his mother? But he had no power to retreat one step, nor to resist, even in thought, when the minister and good old Deacon Gookin seized his arms and led him to the blazing rock. Thither came also the slender form of a veiled female, led between Goody Cloyse, that pious teacher of the catechism, and Martha Carrier,[6] who had received the devil's promise to be queen of hell. A rampant hag was she. And there stood the proselytes beneath the canopy of fire.

"Welcome, my children," said the dark figure, "to the communion of your race. Ye have found thus young your nature and your destiny. My children, look behind you!"

They turned; and flashing forth, as it were, in a sheet of flame, the fiend worshippers were seen; the smile of welcome gleamed darkly on every visage.

"There," resumed the sable form, "are all whom ye have reverenced from youth. Ye deemed them holier than yourselves, and shrank from your own sin, contrasting it with their lives of righteousness and prayerful aspirations heavenward. Yet here are they all in my worshipping assembly. This night it shall be granted you to know their secret deeds: how hoary-bearded elders of the church have whispered wanton words to the young maids of their households; how many a woman, eager for widows' weeds, has given her husband a drink at bedtime and let him sleep his last sleep in her bosom; how beardless youths have made haste to inherit their fathers' wealth; and how fair damsels—blush not, sweet ones—have dug little graves in the garden, and bidden me, the sole guest, to an infant's funeral. By the sympathy of your human hearts for sin ye shall scent out all the places—whether in church, bed-chamber, street, field, or forest—where crime has been committed, and shall exult to behold the whole earth one stain of guilt, one mighty blood spot. Far more than this. It shall be yours to penetrate, in every bosom, the deep mystery of sin, the fountain of all wicked arts, and which inexhaustibly supplies more evil impulses than human power—than my power at its utmost—can make manifest in deeds. And now, my children, look upon each other."

They did so; and, by the blaze of the hell-kindled torches, the wretched man beheld his Faith, and the wife her husband, trembling before that unhallowed altar.

"Lo, there ye stand, my children," said the figure, in a deep and solemn tone, almost sad with its despairing awfulness, as if his once angelic nature could yet mourn for our miserable race. "Depending upon one another's hearts, ye had still hoped that virtue were not all a dream. Now are ye undeceived. Evil is the nature of mankind. Evil must be your only happiness. Welcome again, my children, to the communion of your race."

"Welcome," repeated the fiend worshippers, in one cry of despair and triumph.

[6]Hanged as witch in Salem, 1692.

And there they stood, the only pair, as it seemed, who were yet hesitating on the verge of wickedness in this dark world. A basin was hollowed, naturally, in the rock. Did it contain water, reddened by the lurid light? or was it blood? or, perchance, a liquid flame? Herein did the shape of evil dip his hand and prepare to lay the mark of baptism upon their foreheads, that they might be partakers of the mystery of sin, more conscious of the secret guilt of others, both in deed and thought, than they could now be of their own. The husband cast one look at his pale wife, and Faith at him. What polluted wretches would the next glance show them to each other, shuddering alike at what they disclosed and what they saw!

"Faith! Faith!" cried the husband, "look up to heaven, and resist the wicked one."

Whether Faith obeyed he knew not. Hardly had he spoken when he found himself amid calm night and solitude, listening to a roar of the wind which died heavily away through the forest. He staggered against the rock, and felt it chill and damp; while a hanging twig, that had been all on fire, besprinkled his cheek with the coldest dew.

The next morning young Goodman Brown came slowly into the street of Salem village, staring around him like a bewildered man. The good old minister was taking a walk along the graveyard to get an appetite for breakfast and meditate his sermon, and bestowed a blessing, as he passed, on Goodman Brown. He shrank from the venerable saint as if to avoid an anathema. Old Deacon Gookin was at domestic worship, and the holy words of his prayer were heard through the open window. "What God doth the wizard pray to?" quoth Goodman Brown. Goody Cloyse, that excellent old Christian, stood in the early sunshine at her own lattice, catechizing a little girl who had brought her a pint of morning's milk. Goodman Brown snatched away the child as from the grasp of the fiend himself. Turning the corner by the meeting-house, he spied the head of Faith, with the pink ribbons, gazing anxiously forth, and bursting into such joy at sight of him that she skipped along the street and almost kissed her husband before the whole village. But Goodman Brown looked sternly and sadly into her face, and passed on without a greeting.

Had Goodman Brown fallen asleep in the forest and only dreamed a wild dream of a witch-meeting?

Be it so if you will; but, alas! it was a dream of evil omen for young Goodman Brown. A stern, a sad, a darkly meditative, a distrustful, if not a desperate man did he become from the night of that fearful dream. On the Sabbath day, when the congregation were singing a holy psalm, he could not listen because an anthem of sin rushed loudly upon his ear and drowned all the blessed strain. When the minister spoke from the pulpit with power and fervid eloquence, and, with his hand on the open Bible, of the sacred truths of our religion, and of saint-like lives and triumphant deaths, and of future bliss or misery unutterable, then did Goodman Brown turn pale, dreading lest the roof should thunder down upon the gray blasphemer and his hearers. Often, awaking suddenly at midnight, he shrank from the bosom of Faith; and at morning or eventide, when the family knelt down at prayer, he scowled and muttered to himself, and gazed sternly at his wife, and turned away. And when he had lived long, and was borne to his grave a hoary corpse, followed by Faith, an aged woman, and children and grandchildren, a goodly procession, besides neighbors not a few, they carved no hopeful verse upon his tombstone, for his dying hour was gloom.

Questions for Writing and Discussion

1. At no point in the story does Hawthorne offer a fully worked-out or coherent explanation of why Brown goes off to the devil's gathering in the woods at night. Do you regard this as a flaw? Or is Hawthorne simply assuming that the human inclination toward evil is so deep and pervasive it need hardly be explained in any given instance? More important, is the motivation of Brown's conduct crucial for the story as it is actually written? Would a paragraph or two of explanation help us?

2. Look at the first sentence in the eighth paragraph, which appears on p. 85 and starts, "With this excellent resolve for the future...." Hawthorne put this sentence directly after Brown makes his resolve that "after this one night [of consorting with the devil] I'll cling to [Faith's] skirts and follow her to heaven"— it's like the fellow who says, "One last drink and never again!" When Hawthorne remarks about this, that it was an "excellent resolve for the future," what tone of voice do you hear him using? Looking through the remainder of the story, see if you can find other examples of similar comment by the author, and then discuss how these comments help to shape our responses to the story.

3. The story is set at some point in the history of New England; we can tell by Hawthorne's reference to "King William's court" on p. 86. In one important paragraph, a disciple of the devil—or so Brown imagines him to be—speaks about the role of Brown's family in New England history, especially its earlier history of persecution and injustice. How does this passage contribute to the point of the story?

4. On pp. 85–86, when Brown meets the devil, Hawthorne notes that they seem to bear a family resemblance. Indeed, "they might have been taken for father and son." Later in the story, Hawthorne writes that the devil bore "the shape of old Goodman Brown," that is, the father of young Goodman Brown. What do you make of this shadowy identification between father and devil? Is it something that Hawthorne wants to insist upon or something that young Goodman Brown, in his need to justify his plunge into the devil's company, is fantasizing? (That is, if he imagines his father also to be tainted with evil, and indeed playing the role of the devil, does that make it easier for him to justify his surrender in the woods?)

5. On what evidence does Brown conclude that Faith too is a communicant of the devil? What is the role of the pink ribbon? (O ye of little faith, to condemn Faith because of a pink ribbon!) What does Hawthorne gain by having Brown's wife named Faith?

VARIETIES OF LOVE

RICHARD WRIGHT

Big Boy Leaves Home

Introduction

Richard Wright was the first major black writer in America to produce fiction that fully revealed the anger of his people. When he published his early stories in the 1930s and then his famous novel, *Native Son,* in 1940, the response of American readers was a kind of cultural shock, an awakening from apathy and complacence. They now were compelled to recognize for the first time that the seemingly passive American blacks—passive, that it, in the eyes of the whites—were actually charged with rage and grief against the oppression they had to endure.

"Big Boy Leaves Home," which Wright first published in 1936 and which formed the opening story in his book *Uncle Tom's Children* (1938), is a story of uncontainable violence, suffering, martyrdom—but also of humor, tenderness, and lyricism. There can be no difficulty in grasping what happens within the story, though there may be differences of judgment as to its implications and value. These we leave to our readers, to make out for themselves. All that may be necessary to add is that, despite its subsequent violence, the story opens with a sadly mocking parallel to the classic American pastoral—some boys are singing in the summer, horsing around, wrestling playfully, making up nonsense ("a qualls a quall"), farting amiably, and getting ready to go, just as if they were Huck Finn and Tom Sawyer, to the nearby swimming hole. All is pleasant and easy; even the summer earth feels warm, "lika bed." Savoring the speech and good nature of these black boys, Wright was deliberately recalling here what one of his critics, Dan McCall, describes as "the soft mythic pastures of familiar American boyhood reverie," the going to the swimming hole for pleasure and refreshment. What follows in the story is a ghastly reminder of how the American dream can become, for blacks, a racial nightmare.

Big Boy Leaves Home

I

Yo mama don wear no drawers . . .

Clearly, the voice rose out of the woods, and died away. Like an echo another voice caught it up:

Ah seena when she pulled em off . . .

Another, shrill, cracking, adolescent:

N she washed 'em in alcohol . . .

Then a quartet of voices, blending in harmony, floated high above the tree tops:

N she hung 'em out in the hall . . .

Laughing easily, four black boys came out of the woods into cleared pasture. They walked lollingly in bare feet, beating tangled vines and bushes with long sticks.

"Ah wished Ah knowed some mo lines t tha song."

"Me too."

"Yeah, when yuh gits t where she hangs em out in the hall yuh has t stop."

"Shucks, whut goes wid *hall?*"

"*Call.*"

"*Fall.*"

"*Wall.*"

"*Quall.*"

They threw themselves on the grass, laughing.

"Big Boy?"

"Huh?"

"Yuh know one thing?"

"Whut?"

"Yuh sho is crazy!"

"Crazy?"

"Yeah, yuh crazys a bed-bug!"

"Crazy bout what?"

"Man, whoever hearda *quall?*"

"Yuh said yuh wanted something to go wid *hall,* didn't yuh?"

"Yeah, but whuts a *quall?*"

"Nigger, a *qualls* a *quall.*"

They laughed easily, catching and pulling long green blades of grass with their toes.

"Waal, ef a *qualls* a *quall,* whut IS a *quall?*"

"Oh, Ah know."

"Whut?"

"Tha ol song goes something like this:

> Yo mama don wear no drawers,
> 　Ah seena when she pulled em off,
> N she washed em in alcohol,
> 　N she hung em out in the hall,
> N then she put em back on her QUALL!"

They laughed again. Their shoulders were flat to the earth, their knees propped up, and their faces square to the sun.

"Big Boy, yuhs CRAZY!"

"Don ax me nothin else."

"Nigger, yuhs CRAZY!"

They fell silent, smiling, dropping the lids of their eyes softly against the sunlight.

"Man, don the groun feel warm?"

"Jus lika bed."

"Jeeesus, Ah could stay here ferever."

"Me too."

"Ah kin feel tha ol sun goin all thu me."

"Feels like mah bones is warm."

In the distance a train whistled mournfully.

"There goes number fo!"

"Hittin on all six!"

"Highballin it down the line!"

"Boun fer up Noth, Lawd, bound fer up Noth!"

They began to chant, pounding bare heels in the grass.

> Dis train bound fo Glory
> Dis train, Oh Hallelujah
> Dis train bound fo Glory
> Dis train, Oh Hallelujah
> Dis train bound fo Glory
> Ef yuh ride no need fer fret er worry
> Dis train, Oh Hallelujah
> Dis train . . .
> Dis train don carry no gambler
> Dis train, Oh Hallelujah

Dis train don carry no gambler
Dis train, Oh Hallelujah
Dis train don carry no gambler
No fo day creeper er midnight rambler
Dis train, Oh Hallelujah
Dis train . . .

When the song ended they burst out laughing, thinking of a train bound
for Glory.

"Gee, thas a good ol song!"

"Huuuuummmmmmmman . . ."

"Whut?"

"Geeee whiiiiiiz . . ."

"Whut?"

"Somebody done let win! Das whut!"

Buck, Bobo and Lester jumped up. Big Boy stayed on the ground,
feigning sleep.

"Jeeesus, tha sho stinks!"

"Big Boy!"

Big Boy feigned to snore.

"Big Boy!"

Big Boy stirred as though in sleep.

"Big Boy!"

"Hunh?"

"Yuh rotten inside!"

"Rotten?"

"Lawd, cant yuh smell it?"

"Smell whut?"

"Nigger, yuh mus gotta bad col!"

"Smell whut?"

"NIGGER, YUH BROKE WIN!"

Big Boy laughed and fell back on the grass, closing his eyes.

"The hen whut cackles is the hen whut laid the egg."

"We ain no hens."

"Yuh cackled, didnt yuh?"

The three moved off with noses turned up.

"C mon!"

"Where yuh-all goin?"

"T the creek fer a swim."

"Yeah, les swim."

"Naw buddy naw!" said Big Boy, slapping the air with a scornful palm.

"Aa, c mon! Don be a heel!"

"N git *lynched?* Hell naw!"

"He ain gonna see us."

"How yuh know?"

"Cause he ain."

"Yuh-all go on. Ahma stay right here," said Big Boy.

"Hell, let im stay! C mon, les go," said Buck.

The three walked off, swishing at grass and bushes with sticks. Big Boy looked lazily at their backs.

"Hey!"

Walking on, they glanced over their shoulders.

"Hey, niggers!"

"C mon!"

Big Boy grunted, picked up his stick, pulled to his feet, and stumbled off.

"Wait!"

"C mon!"

He ran, caught up with them, leaped upon their backs, bearing them to the ground.

"Quit, Big Boy!"

"Gawddam, nigger!"

"Git t hell offa me!"

Big Boy sprawled in the grass beside them, laughing and pounding his heels in the ground.

"Nigger, whut yuh think we is, hosses?"

"How come yuh awways hoppin on us?"

"Lissen, wes gonna doubt-team on yuh one of these days n beat yo ol ass good."

Big Boy smiled.

"Sho nough?"

"Yeah, don yuh like it?"

"We gonna beat yuh sos yuh cant walk!"

"N dare yuh t do nothin erbout it!"

Big Boy bared his teeth.

"C mon! Try it now!"

The three circled around him.

"Say, Buck, yuh grab his feets!"

"N yuh git his head, Lester!"

"N Bobo, yuh get berhin n grab his arms!"

Keeping more than arm's length, they circled round and round Big Boy.

"C mon!" said Big Boy, feinting at one and then the other.

Round and round they circled, but could not seem to get any closer. Big Boy stopped and braced his hands on his hips.

"Is all three of yuh-all scareda me?"

"Les git im some other time," said Bobo, grinning.

"Yeah, we kin ketch yuh when yuh ain thinkin," said Lester.

"We kin trick yuh," said Buck.

They laughed and walked together.

Big Boy belched.

"Ahm hongry," he said.

"Me too."

"Ah wished Ah hada big hot pota belly-busters!"

"Cooked wid some good ol saltry ribs . . ."

"N some good ol egg cornbread . . ."

"N some buttermilk . . ."

"N some hot peach cobbler swimmin in juice . . ."

"Nigger, hush!"

They began to chant, emphasizing the rhythm by cutting at grass with sticks.

> Bye n bye
> Ah wanna piece of pie
> Pies too sweet
> Ah wanna piece of meat
> Meats too red
> Ah wanna piece of bread
> Breads too brown
> Ah wanna go t town
> Towns too far
> Ah wanna ketch a car
> Cars too fas
> Ah fall n break mah ass
> Ahll understan it better bye n bye . . .

They climbed over a barbed-wire fence and entered a stretch of thick woods. Big Boy was whistling softly, his eyes half-closed.

"LES GIT IM!"

Buck, Lester, and Bobo whirled, grabbed Big Boy about the neck, arms, and legs, bearing him to the ground. He grunted and kicked wildly as he went back into weeds.

"Hol im tight!"

"Git his arms! Git his arms!"

"Set on his legs so he cant kick!"

Big Boy puffed heavily, trying to get loose.

"WE GOT YUH NOW, GAWDDAMMIT, WE GOT YUH NOW!"

"Thas a Gawddam lie!" said Big Boy. He kicked, twisted, and clutched for a hold on one and then the other.

"Say, yuh-all hep me hol his arms!" said Bobo.

"Aw, we got this bastard now!" said Lester.

"Thas a Gawddam lie!" said Big Boy again.

"Say, yuh-all hep me hol his arms!" called Bobo.

Big Boy managed to encircle the neck of Bobo with his left arm. He tightened his elbow scissors-like and hissed through his teeth:

"Yuh got me, ain yuh?"

"Hol im!"

"Les beat this bastard's ass!"

"Say, hep me hol his *arms!* Hes got aholda mah *neck!*" cried Bobo.

Big Boy squeezed Bobo's neck and twisted his head to the ground.

"Yuh got me, ain yuh?"

"Quit, Big Boy, yuh chokin me! Yuh hurtin mah neck!" cried Bobo.

"Turn me loose!" said Big Boy.

"Ah ain got yuh! Its the others whut got yuh!" pleaded Bobo.

"Tell them others t git t hell offa me or Ahma break yo neck," said Big Boy.

"Ssssay, yyyuh-al gggit oooooffa Bbig Boy. Hhhes got me," gurgled Bobo.

"Cant yuh hol im?"

"Nnaw, hhes ggot mmah nneck . . ."

Big Boy squeezed tighter.

"N Ahma break it too les yuh tell em t git t hell offa me!"

"Ttturn mmmeee lllloose," panted Bobo, tears gushing.

"Cant yuh hol im, Bobo?" asked Buck.

"Nnaw, yuh-all tturn im lloose; hhhes got mah nnneck . . ."

"Grab his neck, Bobo . . ."

"Ah cant; yugurgur . . ."

To save Bobo, Lester and Buck got up and ran to a safe distance. Big Boy released Bobo, who staggered to his feet, slobbering and trying to stretch a crick out of his neck.

"Shucks, nigger, yuh almos broke mah neck," whimpered Bobo.

"Ahm gonna break yo ass nex time," said Big Boy.

"Ef Bobo coulda hel yuh we woulda had yuh," yelled Lester.

"Ah waznt gonna let im do that," said Big Boy.

They walked together again, swishing sticks.

"Yuh see," began Big Boy, "when a ganga guys jump on yuh, all yuh gotta do is put the heat on one of them n make im tell the others t let up, see?"

"Gee, thas a good idee!"

"Yeah, thas a good idee!"

"But yuh almos broke mah neck, man," said Bobo.

"Ahma smart nigger," said Big Boy, thrusting out his chest.

II

They came to the swimming hole.

"Ah ain goin in," said Bobo.

"Done got scared?" asked Big Boy.

"Naw, Ah ain scared . . ."

"How come yuh ain goin in?"

"Yuh know ol man Harvey don erllow no niggers t swim in this hole."

"N jus las year he took a shot at Bob fer swimming in here," said Lester.

"Shucks, ol man Harvey ain studyin bout us niggers," said Big Boy.

"Hes at home thinking about his jelly-roll," said Buck.

They laughed.

"Buck, yo mins lowern a snakes belly," said Lester.

"Ol man Harveys too doggone ol t think erbout jelly-roll," said Big Boy.

"Hes dried up; all the saps done lef im," said Bobo.

"C mon, les go!" said Big Boy.

Bobo pointed. "See tha sign over yonder?"

"Yeah."

"Whut it say?"

"NO TRESPASSIN," read Lester.

"Know whut tha mean?"

"Mean ain no dogs n niggers erllowed," said Buck.

"Waal, wes here now," said Big Boy. "Ef he ketched us even like this thered be trouble, so we just as waal go on in . . ."

"Ahm wid the nex one!"

"Ahll go ef anybody else goes!"

Big Boy looked carefully in all directions. Seeing nobody, he began jerking off his overalls.

"LAS ONE INS A OL DEAD DOG!"

"THAS YO MA!"

"THAS YO PA!"

"THAS BOTH YO MA N YO PA!"

They jerked off their clothes and threw them in a pile under a tree. Thirty seconds later they stood, black and naked, on the edge of the hole under a sloping embankment. Gingerly Big Boy touched the water with his foot.

"Man, this waters col," he said.

"Ahm gonna put mah cloes back on," said Bobo, withdrawing his foot.

Big Boy grabbed him about the waist.

"Like hell yuh is!"

"Git outta the way, nigger!" Bobo yelled.

"Thow im in!" said Lester.

"Duck im!"

Bobo crouched, spread his legs, and braced himself against Big Boy's body. Locked in each other's arms, they tussled on the edge of the hole, neither able to throw the other.

"C mon, les me n yuh push em in."

"O.K."

Laughing, Lester and Buck gave the two locked bodies a running push. Big Boy and Bobo splashed, sending up silver spray in the sunlight. When Big Boy's head came up he yelled:

"Yuh bastard!"

"Tha wuz yo ma yuh pushed!" said Bobo, shaking his head to clear the water from his eyes.

They did a surface dive, came up and struck out across the creek. The muddy water foamed. They swam back, waded into shallow water, breathing heavily and blinking eyes.

"C mon in!"

"Man, the water's fine!"

Lester and Buck hesitated.

"Les wet em," Big Boy whispered to Bobo.

Before Lester and Buck could back away, they were dripping wet from handfuls of scooped water.

"Hey, quit!"

"Gawddam, nigger; tha waters col!"

"C mon in!" called Big Boy.

"We just as waal go on in now," said Buck.

"Look n see ef anybody's comin."

Kneeling, they squinted among the trees.

"Ain nobody."

"C mon, les go."

They waded in slowly, pausing each few steps to catch their breath. A desperate water battle began. Closing eyes and backing away, they shunted water into one another's faces with the flat palms of hands.

"Hey, cut it out!"

"Yeah, Ahm bout drownin!"

They came together in water up to their navels, blowing and blinking. Big Boy ducked, upsetting Bobo.

"Look out, nigger!"

"Don holler so loud!"

"Yeah, they kin hear yo ol big mouth a mile erway."

"This waters too col fer me."

"Thas cause it rained yistiddy."

They swam across and back again.

"Ah wish we hada bigger place t swim in."

"The white folks got plenty swimming pools n we ain got none."

"Ah useta swim in the ol Missippi when we lived in Vicksburg."

Big Boy put his head under the water and blew his breath. A sound came like that of a hippopotamus.

"C'mon, les be hippos."

Each went to a corner of the creek and put his mouth just below the surface and blew like a hippopotamus. Tiring, they came and sat under the embankment.

"Look like Ah gotta chill."

"Me too."

"Les stay here n dry off."

"Jeeesus, Ahm col!"

They kept still in the sun, suppressing shivers. After some of the water had dried off their bodies they began to talk through clattering teeth.

"Whut would yuh do ef ol man Harveyd come erlong right now?"

"Run like hell!"

"Man, Ahd run so fas hed thinka black streaka lightnin shot pass im."

"But spose he hada gun?"

"Aw, nigger, shut up!"

They were silent. They ran their hands over wet, trembling legs, brushing water away. Then their eyes watched the sun sparkling on the restless creek.

Far away a train whistled.

"There goes number seven!"

"Headin fer up Noth!"

"Blazin it down the line!"

"Lawd, Ahm goin Noth some day."

"Me too, man."

"They say colored folks up Noth is got ekual rights."

They grew pensive. A black winged butterfly hovered at the water's edge. A bee droned. From somewhere came the sweet scent of honeysuckles. Dimly they could hear sparrows twittering in the woods. They rolled from side to side, letting sunshine dry their skins and warm their blood. They plucked blades of grass and chewed them.

"Oh!"

They looked up, their lips parting.

"Oh!"

A white woman, poised on the edge of the opposite embankment, stood directly in front of them, her hat in her hand and her hair lit by the sun.

"Its a woman!" whispered Big Boy in an underbreath. "A *white* woman!"

They stared, their hands instinctively covering their groins. Then they scrambled to their feet. The white woman backed slowly out of sight. They stood for a moment, looking at one another.

"Les git outta here!" Big Boy whispered.

"Wait till she goes erway."

"Les run, theyll ketch us here naked like this!"

"Mabbe theres a man wid her."

"C mon, les git our cloes," said Big Boy.

They waited a moment longer, listening.

"What t hell! Ahma git mah cloes," said Big Boy.

Grabbing at short tufts of grass, he climbed the embankment.

"Don run out there now!"

"C mon back, fool!"

Bobo hesitated. He looked at Big Boy, and then at Buck and Lester.

"Ahm goin wid Big Boy n git mah cloes," he said.

"Don run out there naked like tha, fool!" said Buck. "Yuh don know whos out there!"

Big Boy was climbing over the edge of the embankment.

"C mon," he whispered.

Bobo climbed after. Twenty-five feet away the woman stood. She had one hand over her mouth. Hanging by fingers, Buck and Lester peeped over the edge.

"C mon back; that womans scared," said Lester.

Big Boy stopped, puzzled. He looked at the woman. He looked at the bundle of clothes. Then he looked at Buck and Lester.

"C mon, les git our cloes!"

He made a step.

"Jim!" the woman screamed.

Big Boy stopped and looked around. His hands hung loosely at his side. The woman, her eyes wide, her hand over her mouth, backed away to the tree where their clothes lay in a heap.

"Big Boy, come back here n wait till shes gone!"

Bobo ran to Big Boy's side.

"Les go home! Theyll ketch us here," he urged.

Big Boy's throat felt tight.

"Lady, we wanna git our cloes," he said.

Buck and Lester climbed the embankment and stood indecisively. Big Boy ran toward the tree.

"Jim!" the woman screamed. "Jim! Jim!"

Black and naked, Big Boy stopped three feet from her.

"We wanna git our cloes," he said again, his words coming mechanically.

He made a motion.

"You go away! You go away! I tell you, you go away!"

Big Boy stopped again, afraid. Bobo ran and snatched the clothes. Buck and Lester tried to grab theirs out of his hands.

"You go away! You go away! You go away!" the woman screamed.

"Les go!" said Bobo, running toward the woods.

CRACK!

Lester grunted, stiffened, and pitched forward. His forehead struck a toe of the woman's shoes.

Bobo stopped, clutching the clothes. Buck whirled. Big Boy stared at Lester, his lips moving.

"Hes gotta gun; hes gotta gun!" yelled Buck, running wildly.

CRACK!

Buck stopped at the edge of the embankment, his head jerked backward, his body arched stiffly to one side; he toppled headlong, sending up a shower of bright spray to the sunlight. The creek bubbled.

Big Boy and Bobo backed away, their eyes fastened fearfully on a white man who was running toward them. He had a rifle and wore an army officer's uniform. He ran to the woman's side and grabbed her hand.

"You hurt, Bertha, you hurt?"

She stared at him and did not answer.

The man turned quickly. His face was red. He raised the rifle and pointed it at Bobo. Bobo ran back, holding the clothes in front of his chest.

"Don shoot me, Mistah, don shoot me . . ."

Big Boy lunged for the rifle, grabbing the barrel.

"You black sonofabitch!"

Big Boy clung desperately.

"Let go, you black bastard!"

The barrel pointed skyward.

CRACK!

The white man, taller and heavier, flung Big Boy to the ground. Bobo dropped the clothes, ran up, and jumped onto the white man's back.

"You black sonsofbitches!"

The white man released the rifle, jerked Bobo to the ground, and began to batter the naked boy with his fists. Then Big Boy swung, striking the man in the mouth with the barrel. His teeth caved in, and he fell, dazed. Bobo was on his feet.

"C mon, Big Boy, les go!"

Breathing hard, the white man got up and faced Big Boy. His lips were trembling, his neck and chin wet with blood. He spoke quietly.

"Give me that gun, boy!"

Big Boy leveled the rifle and backed away.

The white man advanced.

"Boy, I say give me that gun!"

Bobo had the clothes in his arms.

"Run, Big Boy, run!"

The man came at Big Boy.

"Ahll kill yuh; Ahll kill yuh!" said Big Boy .

His fingers fumbled for the trigger.

The man stopped, blinked, spat blood. His eyes were bewildered. His face whitened. Suddenly, he lunged for the rifle, his hands outstretched.

CRACK!

He fell forward on his face.

"Jim!"

Big Boy and Bobo turned in surprise to look at the woman.

"Jim!" she screamed again, and fell weakly at the foot of the tree.

Big Boy dropped the rifle, his eyes wide. He looked around. Bobo was crying and clutching the clothes.

"Big Boy, Big Boy . . ."

Big Boy looked at the rifle, started to pick it up, but didn't. He seemed at a loss. He looked at Lester, then at the white man; his eyes followed a thin stream of blood that seeped to the ground.

"Yuh done killed im," mumbled Bobo.

"Les go home!"

Naked, they turned and ran toward the wood. When they reached the barbed-wire fence they stopped.

"Les git our cloes on," said Big Boy.

They slipped quickly into overalls. Bobo held Lester's and Buck's clothes.

"Whut we gonna do wid these?"

Big Boy stared. His hands twitched.

"Leave em."

They climbed the fence and ran through the woods. Vines and leaves switched their faces. Once Bobo tripped and fell.

"C mon!" said Big Boy.

Bobo started crying, blood streaming from his scratches.

"Ahm scared!"

"C mon! Don cry! We wanna git home fo they ketches us!"

"Ahm scared!" said Bobo again, his eyes full of tears.

Big Boy grabbed his hand and dragged him along.

"C mon!"

III

They stopped when they got to the end of the woods. They could see the open road leading home, to ma and pa. But they hung back, afraid. The thick shadows cast from the trees were friendly and sheltering. But the wide glare of sun stretching out over the fields was pitiless. They crouched behind an old log.

"We gotta git home," said Big Boy.

"Theys gonna lynch us," said Bobo, half-questioningly.

Big Boy did not answer.

"Theys gonna lynch us," said Bobo again.

Big Boy shuddered.

"Hush!" he said. He did not want to think of it. He could not think of it; there was but one thought, and he clung to that one blindly. He had to get home, home to ma and pa.

Their heads jerked up. Their ears had caught the rhythmic jingle of a wagon. They fell to the ground and clung flat to the side of a log. Over the crest of the hill came the top of a hat. A white face. Then shoulders in a blue shirt. A wagon drawn by two horses pulled into full view.

Big Boy and Bobo held their breath, waiting. Their eyes followed the wagon till it was lost in dust around a bend of the road.

"We gotta git home," said Big Boy.

"Ahm scared," said Bobo.

"C mon! Les keep t the fields."

They ran till they came to the cornfields. Then they went slower, for last year's corn stubbles bruised their feet.

They came in sight of a brickyard.

"Wait a minute," gasped Big Boy.

They stopped.

"Ahm goin on t mah home n yuh better go on t yos."

Bobo's eyes grew round.

"Ahm scared!"

"Yuh better go on!"

"Lemme go wid yuh; theyll ketch me . . ."

"Ef yuh kin git home mabbe yo folks kin hep yuh t git erway."

Big Boy started off. Bobo grabbed him.

"Lemme go wid yuh!"

Big Boy shook free.

"Ef yuh stay here theys gonna lynch yuh!" he yelled, running.

After he had gone about twenty-five yards he turned and looked; Bobo was flying through the woods like the wind.

Big Boy slowed when he came to the railroad. He wondered if he ought to go through the streets or down the track. He decided on the tracks. He could dodge a train better than a mob.

He trotted along the ties, looking ahead and back. His cheek itched, and he felt it. His hand came away smeared with blood. He wiped it nervously on his overalls.

When he came to his back fence he heaved himself over. He landed among a flock of startled chickens. A bantam rooster tried to spur him. He slipped and fell in front of the kitchen steps, grunting heavily. The ground was slick with greasy dishwater.

Panting, he stumbled through the doorway.

"Lawd, Big Boy, whuts wrong wid yuh?"

His mother stood gaping in the middle of the floor. Big Boy flopped wordlessly onto a stool, almost toppling over. Pots simmered on the stove. The kitchen smelled of food cooking.

"Whuts the matter, Big Boy?"

Mutely, he looked at her. Then he burst into tears. She came and felt the scratches on his face.

"Whut happened t yuh, Big Boy? Somebody been botherin yuh?"

"They after me, Ma! They after me . . ."

"Who!"

"Ah . . . Ah . . . We . . ."

"Big Boy, whuts wrong wid yuh?"

"He killed Lester n Buck," he muttered simply.

"Killed!"

"Yessum."

"Lester n Buck!"

"Yessum, Ma!"

"How killed?"

"He shot em, Ma!"

"Lawd Gawd in Heaven, have mercy on us all! This is mo trouble, mo trouble," she moaned, wringing her hands.

"N Ah killed im, Ma . . ."

She stared, trying to understand.

"Whut happened, Big Boy?"

"We tried t git our cloes from the tree . . ."

"Whut tree?"

"We wuz swimmin, Ma. N the white woman . . ."

"*White* woman? . . ."

"Yessum. She wuz at the swimmin hole . . ."

"Lawd have mercy! Ah knowed yuh boys wuz gonna keep on till yuh got into somethin like this!"

She ran into the hall.

"Lucy!"

"Mam?"

"C mere!"

"Mam?"

"C mere, Ah say!"

"Whutcha wan, Ma? Ahm sewin."

"Chile, will yuh c mere like Ah ast yuh?"

Lucy came to the door holding an unfinished apron in her hands. When she saw Big Boy's face she looked wildly at her mother.

"Whuts the matter?"

"Wheres Pa?"

"He's out front, Ah reckon."

"Git im, quick!"

"Whuts the matter, Ma?"

"Go git yo Pa, Ah say!"

Lucy ran out. The mother sank into a chair, holding a dish rag. Suddenly, she sat up.

"Big Boy, Ah thought yuh wuz at school?"

Big Boy looked at the floor.

"How come yuh didn't go t school?"

"We went t the woods."

She sighed.

"Ah done done all Ah kin fer yuh, Big Boy. Only Gawd kin help yuh now."

"Ma, don let em git me; don let em git me . . ."

His father came into the doorway. He stared at Big Boy, then at his wife.

"Whuts Big Boy inter now?" he asked sternly.

"Saul, Big Boys done n got inter trouble wid the white folks."

The old man's mouth dropped, and he looked from one to the other.

"Saul, we gotta git im erway from here."

"Open yo mouth n talk! Whut yuh been doin?" The old man gripped Big Boy's shoulders and peered at the scratches on his face.

"Me n Lester n Buck n Bobo wuz out on ol man Harveys place swimmin . . ."

"Saul, its a *white* woman!"

Big Boy winced. The old man compressed his lips and stared at his wife. Lucy gaped at her brother as though she had never seen him before.

"Whut happened? Cant yuh all talk?" the old man thundered, with a certain helplessness in his voice.

"We wuz swimmin," Big Boy began, "n then a white woman comes up t the hole. We got up right erway to git our cloes sos we could git erway, n she started screamin. Our cloes wuz right by the tree where she wuz standin, n when we started t git em she jus screamed. We told her we wanted our cloes . . . Yuh see, Pa, she was standin' right *by* our cloes; n when we went t git em she jus screamed . . . Bobo got the cloes, n then he shot Lester . . ."

"*Who* shot Lester?"

"The white man."

"Whut white man?"

"Ah dunno, Pa. He wuz a soljer, n he had a rifle."

"A soljer?"

"Yessuh."

"A *soljer?*"

"Yessuh, Pa. A soljer."

The old man frowned.

"N then what yuh-all do?"

"Waal, Buck said, 'Hes gotta gun!' N we started runnin. N then he shot Buck, n he fell in the swimmin hole. We didn't see im no mo . . . He wuz close on us then. He looked at the white woman n then he started t shoot Bobo. Ah grabbed the gun, n we started fightin. Bobo jumped on his back. He started beatin Bobo. Then Ah hit im wid the gun. Then he started at me n Ah shot im. Then we run . . ."

"Who seen?"

"Nobody."

"Wheres Bobo?"

"He went home."

"Anybody run after yuh-all?"

"Nawsuh."

"Yuh see anybody?"

"Nawsuh. Nobody but a white man. But he didnt see us."

"How long fo yuh-all lef the swimmin hole?"

"Little while ergo."

The old man nervously brushed his hand across his eyes and walked to the door. His lips moved, but no words came.

"Saul, whut we gonna do?"

"Lucy," began the old man, "go t Brother Sanders n tell im Ah said c mere; n go t Brother Jenkins n tell im Ah said c mere; n go t Elder Peters n tell im Ah said c mere. N don say nothin t nobody but whut Ah tol yuh. N when yuh git thu come straight back. Now go!"

Lucy dropped her apron across the back of a chair and ran down the steps. The mother bent over, crying and praying. The old man walked slowly over to Big Boy.

"Big Boy?"

Big Boy swallowed.

"Ahm talkin t yuh!"

"Yessuh."

"How come yuh didnt go t school this mawnin?"

"We went t the woods."

"Didnt yo ma send yuh t school?"

"Yessuh."

"How come yuh didnt go?"

"We went t the woods."

"Don yuh know thas wrong?"

"Yessuh."

"How come yuh go?"

Big Boy looked at his fingers, knotted them, and squirmed in his seat.

"AHM TALKIN T YUH!"

His wife straightened up and said reprovingly:

"Saul!"

The old man desisted, yanking nervously at the shoulder straps of his overalls.

"How long wuz the woman there?"

"Not long."

"Wuz she young?"

"Yessuh. Lika gal."

"Did yuh-all say anythin t her?"

"Nawsuh. We jes said we wanted our cloes."

"N what she say?"

"Nothin, Pa. She jus backed erway t the tree n screamed."

The old man stared, his lips trying to form a question.

"Big Boy, did yuh-all bother her?"

"Nawsuh, Pa. We didnt *touch* her."

"How long fo the white man come up?"

"Right erway."

"Whut he say?"

"Nothin. He jus cussed us."

Abruptly the old man left the kitchen.

"Ma, cant Ah go fo they ketches me?"

"Sauls doin whut he kin."

"Ma, Ma, Ah don want em t ketch me . . ."

"Sauls doin what he kin. Nobody but the good Lawd kin hep us now."

The old man came back with a shotgun and leaned it in a corner. Fascinatedly, Big Boy looked at it.

There was a knock at the front door.

"Liza, see whos there."

She went. They were silent, listening. They could hear her talking.

"Whos there?"

"Me."

"Who?"

"Me, Brother Sanders."

"C mon in. Sauls waitin fer yuh."

Sanders paused in the doorway, smiling.

"Yuh sent fer me, Brother Morrison?"

"Brother Sanders, wes in deep trouble here."

Sanders came all the way into the kitchen.

"Yeah?"

"Big Boy done gone n killed a white man."

Sanders stopped short, then came forward, his face thrust out, his mouth open. His lips moved several times before he could speak.

"A *white* man?"

"They gonna kill me; they gonna kill me!" Big Boy cried, running to the old man.

"Saul, cant we git im erway somewhere?"

"Here now, take it easy; take it easy," said Sanders, holding Big Boy's wrists.

"They gonna kill me, they gonna lynch me!"

Big Boy slipped to the floor. They lifted him to a stool. His mother held him closely, pressing his head to her bosom.

"Whut we gonna do?" asked Sanders.

"Ah done sent fer Brother Jenkins n Elder Peters."

Sanders leaned his shoulders against the wall. Then, as the full meaning of it came to him, he exclaimed:

"Theys gonna git a mob! . . ." His voice broke off and his eyes fell on the shotgun.

Feet came pounding on the steps. They turned toward the door. Lucy ran in crying. Jenkins followed. The old man met him in the middle of the room, taking his hand.

"Wes in bad trouble here, Brother Jenkins. Big Boy's done gone n killed a white man. Yuh-alls gotta hep me . . ."

Jenkins looked hard at Big Boy.

"Elder Peters says hes comin," said Lucy.

"When all this happen?" asked Jenkins.

"Near bout an hour ergo, now," said the old man.

"Whut we gonna do?" asked Jenkins.

"Ah wanna wait till Elder Peters come," said the old man helplessly.

"But we gotta work fas ef we gonna do anythin," said Sanders. "We'll git in trouble jus standin here like this."

Big Boy pulled away from his mother.

"Pa, lemma go now! Lemma go now!"

"Be still, Big Boy!"

"Where kin yuh go?"

"Ah could ketch a freight!"

"Thas *sho* death!" said Jenkins. "They'll be watchin em all!"

"Kin yuh-all hep me wid some money?" the old man asked.

They shook their heads.

"Saul, whut kin we do? Big Boy cant stay here."

There was another knock at the door.

The old man backed stealthily to the shotgun.

"Lucy, go!"

Lucy looked at him, hesitating.

"Ah better go," said Jenkins.

It was Elder Peters. He came in hurriedly.

"Good evenin, everybody!"

"How yuh, Elder?"

"Good evenin."

"How yuh today?"

Peters looked around the crowded kitchen.

"Whuts the matter?"

"Elder, wes in deep trouble," began the old man. "Big Boy n some mo boys . . ."

" . . . Lester n Buck n Bobo . . ."

" . . . wuz over on ol man Harveys place swimmin . . ."

'N he don like us niggers *none*," said Peters emphatically. He widened his legs and put his thumbs in the armholes of his vest.

" . . . n some white woman . . ."

"Yeah?" said Peters, coming closer.

" . . . comes erlong n the boys tries t git their cloes where they done lef them under a tree. Waal, she started screamin n all, see? Reckon she thought the boys wuz after her. Then a white man in a soljers suit shoots two of em . . ."

" . . . Lester n Buck . . ."

"Huummm," said Peters. "Tha wuz old man Harveys son."

"Harveys son?"

"Yuh mean the one that wuz in the Army?"

"Yuh mean Jim?"

"Yeah," said Peters. "The papers said he wuz here fer a vacation from his regiment. N tha woman the boys saw wuz jus erbout his wife . . ."

They stared at Peters. Now that they knew what white person had been killed, their fears became definite.

"N whut else happened?"

"Big Boy shot the man . . ."

"Harveys *son?*"

"He had t, Elder. He wuz gonna shoot im ef he didnt . . ."

"Lawd!" said Peters. He looked around and put his hat back on.

"How long ergo wuz this?"

"Mighty near an hour now, Ah reckon."

"Do the white folks know yit?"

"Don know, Elder."

"Yuh-all better git this boy outta here right now," said Peters. "Cause ef yuh don theres gonna be a lynchin . . ."

"Where kin Ah go, Elder?" Big Boy ran up to him.

They crowded around Peters. He stood with his legs wide apart, looking up at the ceiling.

"Mabbe we kin hide im in the church till he kin git erway," said Jenkins.

Peters' lips flexed.

"Naw, Brother, thall never do! Theyll git im in there sho. N anyhow, ef they ketch im there itll ruin us all. We gotta git the boy outta town . . ."

Sanders went up to the old man.

"Lissen," he said in a whisper. "Mah son, Will, the one whut drives fer the Magnolia Express Comny, is takin a truck o goods t Chicawgo in the mawnin. If we kin hide Big Boy somewhere till then, we kin put him on the truck . . ."

"Pa, please, lemme go wid Will when he goes in the mawnin," Big Boy begged.

The old man stared at Sanders.

"Yuh reckon thas safe?"

"Its the only thing yuh *kin* do," said Peters.

"But where we gonna hide im till then?"

"Whut time yo boy leavin out in the mawnin?"

"At six."

They were quiet, thinking. The water kettle on the stove sang.

"Pa, Ah knows where Will passes erlong wid the truck out on Bullards Road. Ah kin hide in one of them ol kilns . . ."

"Where?"

"In one of them kilns we built . . ."

"But they'll git yuh there," wailed the mother.

"But there ain no place else fer im t go."

"Theres some holes big enough fer me t git in n stay till Will comes erlong," said Big Boy. "Please, Pa, lemme go fo they ketches me. . ."

"Let im go!"

"Please, Pa . . ."

The old man breathed heavily.

"Lucy, git his things!"

"Saul, theyll git im out there!" wailed the mother, grabbing Big Boy.

Peters pulled her away.

"Sister Morrison, ef yuh don let im go n git erway from here hes gonna be caught shos theres a Gawd in Heaven!"

Lucy came running with Big Boy's shoes and pulled them on his feet. The old man thrust a battered hat on his head. The mother went to the stove and dumped the skillet of corn pone into her apron. She wrapped it, and unbuttoning Big Boy's overalls, pushed it into his bosom.

"Heres something fer yuh t eat; n pray, Big Boy, cause thas all anybody kin do now . . ."

Big Boy pulled to the door, his mother clinging to him.

"Let im go, Sister Morrison!"

"Run fas, Big Boy!"

Big Boy raced across the yard, scattering the chickens. He paused at the fence and hollered back:

"Tell Bobo where Ahm hidin n tell im t c mon!"

IV

He made for the railroad, running straight toward the sunset. He held his left hand tightly over his heart, holding the hot pone of corn bread there. At times he stumbled over the ties, for his shoes were tight and hurt his feet. His throat burned from thirst; he had had no water since noon.

He veered off the track and trotted over the crest of a hill, following Bullard's Road. His feet slipped and slid in the dust. He kept his eyes straight ahead, fearing every clump of shrubbery, every tree. He wished it were night. If he could only get to the kilns without meeting anyone. Suddenly a thought came to him like a blow. He recalled hearing the old folks tell tales of blood-hounds, and fear made him run slower. Non of them had thought of that. Spose blood-houns wuz put on his trail? Lawd! Spose a whole pack of em, foamin n howlin, tore im t pieces? He went limp and his feet dragged. Yeah, thas whut they wuz gonna send after im, blood-houns! N then thered be no way fer im t dodge! Why hadnt Pa let im take tha shotgun? He stopped. He oughta go back n git tha shotgun. And then when the mob came he would take some with him.

In the distance he heard the approach of a train. It jarred him back to a sharp sense of danger. He ran again, his big shoes sopping up and down in the dust. He was tired and his lungs were bursting from running. He wet his lips, wanting water. As he turned from the road across a plowed field he heard the train roaring at his heels. He ran faster, gripped in terror.

He was nearly there now. He could see the black clay on the sloping hillside. Once inside a kiln he would be safe. For a little while, at least. He thought of the shotgun again. If he only had something! Someone to talk to . . . Thas right! Bobo! Bobod be wid im. Hed almost fergot Bobo. Bobod bringa gun; he knowed he would. N tergether they could kill the whole mob. Then in the mawnin theyd git inter Will's truck n go fer erway, t Chicawgo . . .

He slowed to a walk, looking back and ahead. A light wind skipped over the grass. A beetle lit on his cheek and he brushed it off. Behind the dark pines hung a red sun. Two bats flapped against that sun. He shivered, for he was growing cold; the sweat on his body was drying.

He stopped at the foot of the hill, trying to choose between two patches of black kilns high above him. He went to the left, for there lay the ones he, Bobo, Lester, and Buck had dug only last week. He looked around again; the landscape was bare. He climbed the embankment and stood before a row of black pits sinking four and five feet deep into the earth. He went to the largest and peered in. He stiffened when his ears caught the sound of a whir. He ran back a few steps and poised on his toes. Six foot of snake slid out of the pit and went into coil. Big Boy looked around wildly for a stick. He ran down the slope, peering into the grass. He stumbled over a tree limb. He picked it up and tested it by striking it against the ground.

Warily, he crept back up the slope, his stick poised. When about seven feet from the snake he stopped and waved the stick. The coil grew tighter, the whir sounded louder, and a flat head reared to strike. He went to the right, and the flat head followed him, the blue-black tongue darting forth; he went to the left, and the flat head followed him there too.

He stopped, teeth clenched. He had to kill this snake. Jus had t kill im! This wuz the safest pit on the hillside. He waved the stick again, looking at the snake before, thinking of a mob behind. The flat head reared higher. With stick over shoulder, he jumped in, swinging. The stick sang through the air, catching the snake on the side of the head, sweeping him out of coil. There was a brown writhing mass. Then Big Boy was upon him, pounding blows home, one on top of the other. He fought viciously, his eyes red, his teeth bared in a snarl. He beat till the snake lay still; then he stomped it with his heel, grinding its head into the dirt.

He stopped, limp, wet. The corners of his lips were white with spittle. He spat and shuddered.

Cautiously, he went to the hole and peered. He longed for a match. He imagined whole nests of them in there waiting. He put the stick into the hole and waved it around. Stooping, he peered again. It mus be awright. He looked over the hillside, his eyes coming back to the dead snake. Then he got to his knees and backed slowly into the hole.

When inside he felt there must be snakes about him, ready to strike. It seemed he could see and feel them there, waiting tensely in coil. In the dark he imagined long, white fangs ready to sink into his neck, his side, his legs. He wanted to come out, but kept still. Shucks, he told himself, ef there wuz any snakes in here they sho woulda done bit me by now. Some of his fear left, and he relaxed.

With elbows on ground and chin on palms, he settled. The clay was cold to his knees and thighs, but his bosom was kept warm by the hot pone of corn bread. His thirst returned and he longed for a drink. He was hungry, too. But he did not want to eat the corn pone. Naw, not now. Mabbe after erwhile, after Bobo came. Then theyd both eat the corn pone.

The view from his hole was fringed by the long tufts of grass. He could see all the way to Bullard's Road, and even beyond. The wind was blowing, and in the east the first touch of dusk was rising. Every now and then a bird floated past, a spot of wheeling black printed against the sky. Big Boy sighed, shifted his weight, and chewed at a blade of grass. A wasp droned. He heard number nine, far away and mournful.

The train made him remember how they had dug these kilns on long hot summer days, how they had made boilers out of big tin cans, filled them with water, fixed stoppers for steam, cemented them in holes with wet clay, and built fires under them. He recalled how they had danced and yelled when a stopper blew out of a boiler, letting out a big spout of steam and a shrill whistle. There were times when they had the whole hillside blazing and smoking. Yeah, yuh see, Big Boy wuz Casey Jones n wuz speedin it down the gleamin rails of the Southern Pacific. Bobo had number two on the Santa Fe. Buck wuz on the Illinoy Central. Lester the Nickel Plate. Lawd, how they sheveled the wood in! The boiling water would almost jar the cans loose from the clay. More and more pine-knots and dry leaves would be piled under the cans. Flames would grow so tall they would have to shield their eyes. Sweat would pour off their faces. Then, suddenly, a peg would shoot high into the air, and

Pssseeeezzzzzzzzzzzzzzzz . . .

Big Boy sighed and stretched out his arm, quenching the flames and scattering the smoke. Why didnt Bobo c mon? He looked over the fields; there was nothing but dying sunlight. His mind drifted back to the kilns. He remembered the day when Buck, jealous of his winning, had tried to smash his kiln. Yeah, that ol sonofabitch! Naw, Lawd! He didnt go t say tha! Whut wu he thinkin erbout? Cussin the dead! Yeah, po ol Buck wuz dead now. N Lester too. Yeah, it wuz awright fer Buck t smash his kiln. Sho. N he wished he hadnt socked ol Buck so hard tha day. He wuz sorry fer Buck now. N he sho wished he hadnt cussed po ol Bucks ma, neither. Tha wuz sinful! Mabbe Gawd would git im fer that? But he didnt go t do it! Po Buck! Po Lester! Hed never treat anybody like tha ergin, never . . .

Dusk was slowly deepening. Somewhere, he could not tell exactly where, a cricket took up a fitful song. The air was growing soft and heavy. He looked over the fields, longing for Bobo . . .

He shifted his body to ease the cold damp of the ground, and thought back over the day. Yeah, hed been dam right erbout not wantin t go swimmin. N ef hed followed his right min hed neverve gone n got inter all this trouble. At first hed said naw. But shucks, somehow hed just went on wid the res. Yeah he shoulda went on t school tha mawnin, like Ma told im t do. But, hell, who wouldnt git tireda awways drivin a guy t school! Tha wuz the big trouble awways drivin a guy t school! He wouldnt be in all this trouble now if it wuznt fer that Gawddam school! Impatiently, he took the grass out of his mouth and threw it away, demolishing the little red school house . . .

Yeah, if they had all kept still n quiet when tha ol white woman showed-up, mabbe shedve went on off. But yuh never kin tell erbout these white folks. Mabbe she wouldntve went. Mabbe tha white man woulda killed all of em! All *fo* of em! Yeah, yuh never kin tell erbout white folks. Then, ergin, mabbe tha white woman woulda went off n laffed. Yeah, mabbe tha white man woulda said: *Yuh nigger bastards git t hell outta here! Yuh know Gawddam well yuh don berlong here!* N then they woulda grabbed their cloes n run like all hell . . . He blinked the white man away. Where wuz Bobo? Why didnt he hurry up n c mon?

He jerked another blade and chewed. Yeah, ef Pa had only let im have tha shotgun! He could stan off a whole mob wid a shotgun. He looked at the ground as he turned a shotgun over in his hands. Then he leveled it at an advancing white man. *Booooom!* The man curled up. Another came. He reloaded quickly, and let him have what the other had got. He too curled up. Then another came. He got the same medicine. Then the whole mob swirled around him, and he blazed away, getting as many as he could. They closed in; but, by Gawd, he had done his part, hadnt he? N the newspapersd say: NIGGER KILLS DOZEN OF MOB BEFO LYNCHED! Er mabbe theyd say: TRAPPED NIGGER SLAYS TWENTY BEFO KILLED! He smiled a little. Tha wouldnt be so bad, would it? Blinking the newspaper away, he looked over the fields. Where wuz Bobo? Why didnt he hurry up n c mon?

He shifted, trying to get a crick out of his legs. Shucks, he wuz gettin tireda this. N it wuz almos dark now. Yeah, there wuz a little bittie star way over yonder in the eas. Mabbe tha white man wuznt dead? Mabbe they wuznt even lookin fer im? Mabbe he could go back home now? Naw, better wait erwhile. Thad be bes. But, Lawd, ef he only had some water! He could hardly swallow, his throat was so dry. Gawddam them white folks! That all they wuz good fer, t run a nigger down like a rabbit! Yeah, they git yuh in a corner n then they let yuh have it. A thousan of em! He shivered, for the cold of the clay was chilling his bones. Lawd, spose they found im here in this hole? N wid nobody t help im? . . . But ain no use in thinkin erbout tha; wait till trouble come fo yuh start fightin it. But if tha mob came one by one hed wipe em all out. Clean up the whole bunch. He caught one by the neck and choked him long and hard, choked him till his tongue and eyes popped out. Then he jumped upon his chest and stomped him like he had stomped that snake. When he had finished with one, another came. He choked him too. Choked till he sank slowly to the ground, gasping . . .

"Hoalo!"

Big Boy snatched his fingers from the white man's neck and looked over the fields. He saw nobody. Had someone spied him? He was sure that somebody had hollered. His heart pounded. But, shucks, nobody couldnt see im here in this hole . . . But mabbe theyd seen im when he wuz comin n had laid low n wuz now closin in on im! Praps they wuz signalin fer the others? Yeah, they wuz creepin up on im! Mabbe he oughta git up n run . . . Oh! Mabbe tha wuz Bobo! Yeah, Bobo! He oughta clim out n see if Bobo wuz lookin fer im . . . He stiffened.

"Hoalo!"

"Hoalo!"

"Wheres yuh?"

"Over here on Bullards Road!"

"C mon over!"

"Awright!"

He heard foot steps. Then voices came again, low and far away this time.

"Seen anybody?"

"Naw. Yuh?"

"Naw."

"Yuh reckon they got erway?"

"Ah dunno. Its hard t tell."

"Gawddam them sonofabitchin niggers!"

"We oughta kill ever black bastard in this country!"

"Wall, Jim got two of em, anyhow."

"But Bertha said there wuz *fo!*"

"Where in hell they hidin?"

"She said one of em wuz named Big Boy, or somthin like tha."

"We went t his shack lookin fer im."

"Yeah?"

"But we didnt fin im."

"These niggers stick tergether; they don never tell on each other."

"We looked all thu the shack n couldnt fin hide ner hair of im. Then we drove the ol woman n man out n set the shack on fire . . ."

"Jeesus! Ah wished Ah coulda been there!"

"Yuh shoulda heard the ol nigger woman howl . . ."

"Hoalo!"

"C mon over!"

Big Boy eased to the edge and peeped. He saw a white man with a gun slung over his shoulder running down the slope. Wuz they gonna search the hill?

Lawd, there wuz no way fer im t git erway now; he wuz caught! He shoulda knowed theyd git im here. N he didnt hava thing, notta thing t fight wid. Yeah, soon as the blood-houns came theyd fin im. Lawd, have mercy! Theyd lynch im right here on the hill . . . Theyd git im n tie im t a stake n burn im erlive! Lawd! Nobody but the good Lawd could hep im now, nobody . . .

He heard more feet running. He nestled deeper. His chest ached. Nobody but the good Lawd could hep now. They wuz crowdn all round im n when they hada big crowd theyd close in on im. Then itd be over . . . The good Lawd would have t hep im, cause nobody could hep im now, nobody . . .

And then he went numb when he remembered Bobo. Spose Bobod come now? Hed be caught sho! Both of em would be caught! Theyd make Bobo tell where he wuz! Bobo oughta not try to come now. Somebody oughta tell im . . . But there wuz nobody; there wuz no way . . .

He eased slowly back to the opening. There was a large group of men. More were coming. Many had guns. Some had coils of rope slung over shoulders.

"Ah tell yuh they still here, somewhere . . ."

"But we looked all over!"

"What t hell! Wouldnt do t let em git erway!"

"Naw. Ef they git erway notta woman in this town would be safe."

"Say, whuts tha yuh got?"

"Er pillar."

"Fer whut?"

"Feathers, fool!"

"Chris! Thisll be hot if we kin ketch them niggers!"

"Ol Anderson said he wuz gonna bringa barrela tar!"

"Ah got some gasolin in mah car if yuh need it."

Big Boy had no feelings now. He was waiting. He did not wonder if they were coming after him. He just waited. He did not wonder about Bobo. He rested his cheek against the cold clay, waiting.

A dog barked. He stiffened. It barked again. He balled himself into a knot at the bottom of the hole, waiting. Then he heard the patter of dog feet.

"Look!"

"Whuts he got?"

"Its a snake!"

"Yeah, the dogs foun a snake!"

"Gee, its a big one!"

"Shucks, Ah wish he could fin one of them sonofabitchin niggers!"

The voices sank to low murmurs. Then he heard number twelve, its bell tolling and whistle crying as it slid along the rails. He flattened himself against the clay. Someone was singing:

> We'll hang ever nigger t a sour apple tree . . .

When the song ended there was hard laughter. From the other side of the hill he heard the dog barking furiously. He listened. There was more than one dog now. There were many and they were barking their throats out.

"Hush. Ah hear them dogs!"

"When theys barkin like tha theys foun somethin!"

"Here they come over the hill!"

"WE GOT IM! WE GOT IM!"

There came a roar. Tha mus be Bobo; tha mus be Bobo . . . In spite of his fear, Big Boy looked. The road, and half of the hillside across the road, were covered with men. A few were at the top of the hill, stenciled against the sky. He could see dark forms moving up the slopes. They were yelling.

"By Gawd, we got im!"

"C mon!"

"Where is he?"

"Theyre bringin im over the hill!"

"Ah got a rope fer im!"

"Say, somebody go n git the others!"

"Where is he? Cant we seem im, Mister?"

"They say Berthas comin, too."

"Jack! Jack! Don leave me! Ah wanna see im!"

"Theyre bringin im over the hill, sweetheart!"

"AH WANNA BE THE FIRST T PUT A ROPE ON THA BLACK BASTARDS NECK!"

"Les start the fire!"

"Heat the tar!"

"Ah got some chains t chain im."

"Bring im over this way!"

"Chris, Ah wished Ah hada drink . . ."

Big Boy saw men moving over the hill. Among them was a long dark spot. Tha mus be Bobo; tha mus be Bobo theys carryin . . . Theyll git im here. He oughta git up n run. He clamped his teeth and ran his hand across his forehead, bringing it away wet. He tried to swallow, but could not; his throat was dry.

They had started the song again:

> We'll hang ever nigger t a sour apple tree . . .

There were women singing now. Their voices made the song round and full. Song waves rolled over the top of pine trees. The sky sagged low, heavy with clouds. Wind was rising. Sometimes cricket cries cut surprisingly across the mob song. A dog had gone to the utmost top of the hill. At each lull of the song his howl floated full into the night.

Big Boy shrank when he saw the first flame light the hillside. Would they see im here? Then he remembered you could not see into the dark if you were standing in the light. As flames leaped higher he saw two men rolling a barrel up the slope.

"Say, gimme a han here, will yuh?"

"Awright, heave!"

"C mon! Straight up! Git t other end!"

"Ah got the feathers here in this pillar!"

"BRING SOME MO WOOD!"

Big Boy could see the barrel surrounded by flames. The mob fell back, forming a dark circle. Theyd fin im here! He had a wild impulse to climb out and fly across the hills. But his legs would not move. He stared hard, trying to find Bobo. His eyes played over a long dark spot near the fire. Fanned by wind, flames leaped higher. He jumped. That dark spot had moved. Lawd, thas Bobo; thas Bobo . . .

He smelt the scent of tar, faint at first, then stronger. The wind brought it full into his face, then blew it away. His eyes burned and he rubbed them with his knuckles. He sneezed.

"LES GIT SOURVINEERS!"

He saw the mob close in around the fire. Their faces were hard and sharp in the light of the flames. More men and women were coming over the hill. The long, dark spot was smudged out.

"Everybody git back!"

"Look! Hes gotta finger!"

"C MON! GIT THE GALS BACK FROM THE FIRE!"

"He's got one of his ears, see?"

"Whuts the matter!"

"A woman fell out! Fainted, Ah reckon . . ."

The stench of tar permeated the hillside. The sky was black and the wind was blowing hard.

"HURRY UP N BURN THE NIGGER FO IT RAINS!"

Big Boy saw the mob fall back, leaving a small knot of men about the fire. Then, for the first time, he had a full glimpse of Bobo. A black body flashed in the light. Bobo was struggling, twisting; they were binding his arms and legs.

When he saw them tilt the barrel he stiffened. A scream quivered. He knew the tar was on Bobo. The mob fell back. He saw a tar-drenched body glistening and turning.

"THE BASTARDS GOT IT!"

There was sudden quiet. Then he shrank violently as the wind carried, like a flurry of snow, a widening spiral of white feathers into the night. The flames leaped tall as the trees. The scream came again. Big Boy trembled and looked. The mob was running down the slopes, leaving the fire clear. Then he saw a writhing white mass cradled in yellow flame, and heard screams, one on top of the other, each shriller and shorter than the last. The mob was quiet now, standing still, looking up the slopes at the writhing white mass gradually growing black, growing black in a cradle of yellow flame.

"PO ON MO GAS!"

"Gimme a lif, will yuh!"

Two men were struggling, carrying between them a heavy can. They set it down, tilted it, leaving it so that the gas would trickle down to the hollowed earth around the fire.

Big Boy slid back into the hole, his face buried in clay. He had no feelings now, no fears. He was numb, empty, as though all blood had been drawn from him. Then his muscles flexed taut when he heard a faint patter. A tiny stream of cold water seeped to his knees, making him push back to a drier spot. He looked up; rain was beating in the grass.

"It's rainin!"

"C mon, les git t town!"

" . . . don worry, when the fire git thu wid im hell be gone . . ."

"Wait, Charles! Don leave me; its slippery here . . ."

"Ahll take some of yuh ladies back in mah car . . ."

Big Boy heard the dogs barking again, this time closer. Running feet pounded past. Cold water chilled his ankles. He could hear raindrops steadily hissing.

Now a dog was barking at the mouth of the hole, barking furiously, sensing a presence there. He balled himself into a knot and clung to the bottom, his knees and shins buried in water. The bark came louder. He heard paws scraping and felt the hot scent of dog breath on his face. Green eyes glowed and drew nearer as the barking, muffled by the closeness of the hole, beat upon his eardrums. Backing till his shoulders pressed against the clay, he held his breath. He pushed out his hands, his fingers stiff. The dog yawped louder, advancing, his bark rising sharp and thin. Big Boy rose to his knees, his hands before him. Then he flattened out still more against the bottom, breathing lungsful of hot dog scent, breathing it slowly, hard, but evenly. The dog came closer, bringing hotter dog scent. Big Boy could go back no more. His knees were slipping and slopping in the water. He braced himself, ready. Then, he never exactly knew how—he never knew whether he had lunged or the dog had lunged—they were together, rolling in the water. The green eyes were beneath him, between his legs. Dognails bit into his arms. His knees slipped backward and he landed full on the dog; the dog's breath left in a heavy gasp. Instinctively, he fumbled for the throat as he felt the dog twisting between his knees. The dog snarled, long and low, as though gathering strength. Big Boy's hands traveled swiftly over the dog's back, groping for the throat. He felt dognails again and saw green eyes, but his fingers had found the throat. He choked, feeling his fingers sink; he choked, throwing back his head and stiffening his arms. He felt the dog's body heave, felt dognails digging into his loins. With strength flowing from fear, he closed his fingers, pushing his full weight on the dog's throat. The dog heaved again, and lay still . . . Big Boy heard the sound of his own breathing filling the hole, and heard shouts and footsteps above him going past.

For a long time he held the dog, held it long after the last footstep had died out, long after the rain had stopped.

V

Morning found him still on his knees in a puddle of rainwater, staring at the stiff body of a dog. As the air brightened he came to himself slowly. He held still for a long time, as though waking from a dream, as though trying to remember.

The chug of a truck came over the hill. He tried to crawl to the opening.

His knees were stiff and a thousand needlelike pains shot from the bottom of his feet to the calves of his legs. Giddiness made his eyes blur. He pulled up and looked. Through brackish light he saw Will's truck standing some twenty-five yards away, the engine running. Will stood on the running board, looking over the slopes of the hill.

Big Boy scuffled out, falling weakly in the wet grass. He tried to call to Will, but his dry throat would make no sound. He tried again.

"Will!"

Will heard, answering:

"Big Boy, c mon!"

He tried to run, and fell. Will came, meeting him in the tall grass.

"C mon," Will said, catching his arm.

They struggled to the truck.

"Hurry up!" said Will, pushing him onto the running-board.

Will pushed back a square trapdoor which swung above the back of the driver's seat. Big Boy pulled through, landing with a thud on the bottom. On hands and knees he looked around in the semi-darkness.

"Wheres Bobo?"

Big Boy stared.

"Wheres Bobo?"

"They got im."

"When?"

"Las night."

"The mob?"

Big Boy pointed in the direction of a charred sapling on the slope of the opposite hill. Will looked. The trapdoor fell. The engine purred, the gears whined, and the truck lurched forward over the muddy road, sending Big Boy on his side.

For a while he lay as he had fallen, on his side, too weak to move. As he felt the truck swing around a curve he straightened up and rested his back against a stack of wooden boxes. Slowly, he began to make out objects in the darkness. Through two long cracks fell thin blades of daylight. The floor was of smooth steel, and cold to his thighs. Splinters and bits of sawdust danced with the rumble of the truck. Each time they swung around a curve he was pulled over the floor; he grabbed at corners of boxes to steady himself. Once he heard the crow of a rooster. It made him think of home, of ma and pa. He thought he remembered hearing somewhere that the house had burned, but could not remember where . . . It all seemed unreal now.

He was tired. He dozed, swaying with the lurch. Then he jumped awake. The truck was running smoothly, on gravel. Far away he heard two short blasts from the Buckeye Lumber Mill. Unconciously, the thought sang through his mind: Its six erclock . . .

The trapdoor swung in. Will spoke through a corner of his mouth.

"How yuh comin?"

"Awright."

"How they git Bobo?"

"He wuz comin over the hill."

"Whut they do?"

"They burnt im . . . Will, Ah wan some water; mah throats like fire . . ."

"Well git some when we pas a fillin station."

Big Boy leaned back and dozed. He jerked awake when the truck stopped. He heard Will get out. He wanted to peep through the trapdoor, but was afraid. For a moment, the wild fear he had known in the hole came back. Spose theyd search n fin im? He quieted when he heard Will's footsteps on the running board. The trapdoor pushed in. Will's hat came through, dripping.

"Take it, quick!"

Big Boy grabbed, spilling water into his face. The truck lurched. He drank. Hard cold lumps of brick rolled into his hot stomach. A dull pain made him bend over. His intestines seemed to be drawing into a tight knot. After a bit it eased, and he sat up, breathing softly.

The truck swerved. He blinked his eyes. The blades of daylight had turned brightly golden. The sun had risen.

The truck sped over the asphalt miles, sped northward, jolting him, shaking out of his bosom the crumbs of corn bread, making them dance with the splinters and sawdust in the golden blades of sunshine.

He turned on his side and slept.

Questions for Writing and Discussion

1. In the first part of the story, the boys sing, or improvise three songs. Read each of them carefully, and see how each relates to a particular moment or incident at the beginning of the story; also how each song seems to anticipate the later events of the story.

2. In Section II, as the boys read the sign, "No Trespassin'," one of them says it "mean ain no dogs n niggers erllowed." In what tone of voice do you take this remark to be made? What does it suggest about the speaker's sense of self? His sense of the place of blacks in American society? His sense of the moral values of the dominant whites?

3. Section III of the story contains an extremely vivid portrait of the inner life of a black community at a moment when it feels itself threatened by external violence: we see the relationships within Big Boy's family, the inner ties among the black families, their shared, unspoken assumptions about the whites. Go through this section carefully and list, in detail, some of the characteristics of Southern black life as Wright presents it.

4. At one point in Section IV, as Big Boy is hiding and thinking about his situation, he says to himself, "yuh never kin tell erbout these white folks." It wouldn't be an exaggeration to say that this is the key sentence of the whole story, the clue to the deepest feelings, the most vulnerable situation, of the black characters in the story, perhaps of all blacks in American life. Do you agree with this emphasis on the quoted sentence? Why—or why not?

JOHN O'HARA

Sportmanship

Introduction

Detail counts. It counts in life, it counts in literature. A seemingly casual gesture, a commonplace word used slightly off-key, an ironic repetition by a minor character of something that has been said by a major one—these are among the devices of "Sportmanship." Limited in scope, it is nevertheless expertly done. There is not a wasted word, not a single touch that has not been carefully planned. John O'Hara was a writer like those crafty baseball pitchers who win 12–15 games a year just because they're so professional.

So it pays to keep a sharp eye on this story, watching for the ways O'Hara builds up to his climax of brutality. Here are a few examples:

1. Jerry straightens his tie at the very beginning—a man is getting ready, nervously, to undertake something he knows is dubious and fears may be dangerous.

2. Frank, after Jerry approaches him, looks around the place "a little too carefully"—after all, it's *his* place, which Jerry (in ways we don't yet know) has threatened or violated; and meanwhile an idea is beginning to come to him for retaliation. But Frank is in no hurry: there is a Spanish proverb which goes, "Revenge is a dish best eaten cold."

3. The elaborate exchange, a sort of put-on, between Frank and Tom as they pretend not to know Jerry. Frank speaks of him, significantly, as a "stranger"—nothing is said openly, they're just toying with Jerry in their heavy-handed way, and we gain a sense of their contempt, their outrage, their unwillingness to forgive.

4. Frank wonders whether Jerry wants a job as "cashier," and later remarks that "one of us" is "gonna get a good beating"—sharp little thrusts of irony spoken by a man with strong but coarse feelings.

And so it continues. The dialogue is arranged with the precision of a well-scored piece of music; first, a motif is stated and then there follow a series of controlled variations. O'Hara wants us to hear the subtle shifts of emphasis and

127

attitude that accompany, or derive from, the repetition of words and phrases, as Frank and Tom toss them back and forth and the not-very-bright Jerry half-understands that he is being threatened. Speech here is very mannered, or stylized, and it serves to move the action forward. By the time we get to the game of billiards toward the end of the story, we have learned as much as we need to know about the values, conduct, and intelligence of the characters—"as much as we need to know" meaning as much as we need for the story to work itself out into a sharp, intelligible climax. (What might happen after the last sentence isn't our business. Nothing can happen, since characters exist only within the limits of the story in which they appear.)

None of the characters is meant to be likable. With none are we invited to identify or even sympathize. We are looking at them from a considerable moral and emotional distance, yet we must also recognize some parallels with our own lives, since what the story seems finally to be about is the way the violation of a commonly accepted code is punished within a tight little social group. It is interesting that Frank and Tom don't turn Jerry over to the police to be arraigned for his crime of theft. Instead, they punish him themselves, in their own crude way, for breaking their code of trust, or fair dealing, which they want to maintain among themselves.

There's an old saying about "honor among thieves," and of course there has to be that, since otherwise thieves couldn't go about their business. In "Sportmanship" Frank and Tom, so far as we know, aren't quite thieves; they are just pool-room characters, and they have their own code of conduct—you might even say, code of honor. When that code is violated, they act to punish, according to their lights.

It is not very pretty, it is only true.

Sportmanship

Jerry straightened his tie and brushed the sleeves of his coat, and went down the stairway where it said "The Subway Arcade." The sign was misleading only to strangers to that neighborhood; there was no subway anywhere near, and it was no arcade.

It was early in the afternoon and there were not many people in the place. Jerry walked over to where a man with glasses, and a cigar in an imitation amber holder, was sitting quietly with a thin man, who also had a cigar.

"Hyuh, Frank" said Jerry.

"Hyuh," said the man with glasses.

"Well, how's every little thing?" said Jerry.

Frank looked around the place, a little too carefully and slowly. "Why," he said finally, "it looks like every little thing is fine. How about it, Tom? Would you say every little thing was O.K.?"

"Me?" said Tom. "Yes, I guess so. I guess every little thing is—No. No. I think I smell sumpn. Do you smell sumpn, Frank? I think I do."

"Aw, you guys. I get it," said Jerry. "Still sore. I don't blame you."

"Who? Me? Me sore?" said Frank. "Why, no. Would you say I was sore, Tom? This stranger here says I'm sore. Oh, no, stranger. That's my usual way of looking. Of course you wouldn't have no way of knowing that, being a stranger. It's funny, though, speaking of looks. You look the dead spit of a guy I used to know, to my sorrow. A rat by the name of Jerry. Jerry—Jerry, uh, Daley. You remember that Jerry Daley rat I told you about one time? Remember him, Tom?"

"Oh, yes. Come to think of it," said Tom, "I recall now I did hear you speak of a heel by that name. I recall it now. I would of forgot all about the rat if you wouldn't of reminded me. What ever did happen to him? I heard he was drowned out City Island."

"Oh, no," said Frank. "They sent him to Riker's Island, the party I mean."

"All right. I get it. Still sore. Well, if that's the way you feel about it," said Jerry. He lit a cigarette and turned away. "I only come back to tell you, Frank, I wanted to tell you I'd be satisfied to work out the dough I owe you if you leave me have a job."

"Hmm," said Frank, taking the cigar out of his mouth. "Hear that, Tom? The stranger is looking for work. Wants a job."

"Well, waddia know about that? Wants a job. What doing, I wonder," said Tom.

"Yeah. What doing? Cashier?" said Frank.

"Aw, what the hell's the use trying to talk to you guys? I came here with the best intention, but if that's your attitude, *so long.*"

"Guess he's not satisfied with the salary you offered, Frank" said Tom.

Jerry was back on the stairway when Frank called him. "Wait a minute." Jerry returned. "What's your proposition?" said Frank. Tom looked surprised.

"Give me the job as house man. Twenty-five a week. Take out ten a week for what I owe you. I'll come here in the mornings and clean up, and practice up my game, and then when I get my eye back, I'll shoot for the house—"

"Using house money, of course," said Tom.

"Let him talk, Tom," said Frank.

"Using house money. What else? And the house and I split what I make." Jerry finished his proposition and his cigarette.

"How long id take you to get shooting good again?" said Frank.

"That's pretty hard to say. Two weeks at least," said Jerry.

Frank thought a minute while Tom watched him incredulously. Then he said, "Well, I might take a chance on you, Daley. Tell you what I'll do. You're on the nut. All right. Here's my proposition: the next two weeks, you can sleep here and I'll give you money to eat on, but no pay. You practice up, and in two weeks I'll play you, say, a hundred points. If you're any good, I'll give you thirty bucks cash and credit you with twenty bucks against what you're in me for. Then you can use your thirty to play with. That oughta be enough to start on, if you're any good. I seen you go into many a game when you were shooting on your nerve and come out the winner, so thirty bucks oughta be plenty. *But* if you're no good at the end of two weeks, then I'll have to leave you go. I'll charge up twenty bucks against what you owe me, and you can go out in the wide, wide world and look for adventure, the way you did once before. Is that a deal?"

"Sure. What can I lose?" said Jerry.

"Sure, what can you lose? How long since you ate last?"

In two weeks Jerry had lost the tan color of his face, and his hands were almost white again, but he looked healthier. Eating regularly was more important than the sun. The regulars who had known Jerry before he stole the hundred and forty dollars from Frank were glad to see him and made no cracks. They may have figured Frank for a real sucker, some of them, but some of the others said there were a lot of angles in a thing like that; nobody knew the whole story in a thing of that kind, and besides, Frank was no dope. It didn't look like it. Jerry was brushing off the tables, putting the cues in their right bins—the twenty-ounce cues into bins marked 20, the nineteen-ouncers in the 19 bins, and so on—and retipping cues, and cleaning garboons[1] and filling them with water, and dusting everywhere. He caught on soon about the new regulars, who wanted what table, and what they usually played. For instance, every afternoon at three o'clock two guys in Tuxedos would come in and play two fifty-point games, and the rest of the afternoon, before they had to go and play in an orchestra, they would play rotation. Well, you had to keep an eye on them. They paid by the hour, of course, but if you didn't watch them, they would use the ivory cue ball to break with in the games of rotation, instead of using the composition ball, which did not cost as much as the ivory ball and stood the hard usage better. The ivory ball cost Frank around twenty bucks, and you can't afford to have an ivory ball slammed around on the break in a game of rotation. Things like that, little things—that was where an experienced house man like Jerry could save Frank money.

Meanwhile he practiced up and his game came back to him, so that at the end of the two weeks he could even do massé shots almost to his own satisfaction. He hardly ever left except to go out to a place, a Coffee Pot on Fordham Road, for his meals. Frank gave him a "sayfitty" razor and a tube of no-brush-needed cream. He slept on the leather couch in front of the cigar counter.

He also observed that Frank was shooting just about the same kind of game he always shot—no better, and no worse. Jerry therefore was confident of beating Frank, and when the day came that ended the two weeks agreed upon, he reminded Frank of the date, and Frank said he would be in at noon the next day to play the hundred points.

Next day, Frank arrived a little after twelve. "I brought my own referee," said Frank. "Shake hands with Jerry Daley," he said, and did not add the name of the burly man, who might have been Italian, or even an octoroon. The man was dressed quietly, except for a fancy plaid cap. Frank addressed him as Doc, Jerry

[1]Slang term for spittoon.

first thought, but then he realized that Frank, who was originally from Worcester, Massachusetts, was calling the man Dark.

Dark sat down on one of the high benches, and did not seem much interested in the game. He sat there smoking cigarettes, wetting them almost halfway down their length with his thick lips. He hardly looked at the game, and with two players like Frank and Jerry there wasn't much use for a referee. Jerry had Frank forty-four to twenty before Dark even looked up at the marker. "Geez," he said. "Forty-four to twenty. This kid's good, eh?"

"Oh, yeah," said Frank. "I told you one of us was gonna get a good beating."

"Maybe the both of you, huh?" said Dark, and showed that he could laugh. Then Jerry knew there was something wrong. He missed the next two times up, on purpose. "There they are, Frank," said Dark. Frank ran six or seven. "Got a mistake in the score, there," said Dark. He got up and took a twenty-two-ounce cue out of the bin, and reached up and slid the markers over so that the score was even.

"Hey," said Jerry. "What is it?"

"That's the right score, ain't it?" said Dark. "Frank just run twenty-four balls. I seen him, and I'm the referee. Neutral referee."

"What is it, Frank? The works or something?" said Jerry.

"He's the referee," said Frank. "Gotta abide by his decision in all matters. Specially the scoring. You have to abide by the referee, specially on matters of scoring. You know that."

"So it's the works," said Jerry. "O.K. I get it. Pick up the marbles." He laid down his cue. "What a sap I been. I thought this was on the up-and-up."

"I hereby declare this game is forfeited. Frank wins the match. Congratulate the winner, why don't you, kid?"

"This means I'm out, I guess, eh, Frank?" said Jerry.

"Well, you know our agreement," said Frank. "We gotta abide by the decision of the referee, and he says you forfeited, so I guess you don't work here any more."

"Congratulate the winner," said Dark. "Where's your sportmanship, huh? Where's your sportmanship?"

"Don't look like he has any," said Frank, very sadly. "Well, that's the way it goes."

"Maybe we better teach him a little sportsmanship," said Dark.

"All right by me," said Frank. "One thing I thought about Mr. Daley, I thought he'd be a good loser, but it don't look that way. It don't look that way one bit, so maybe you better teach him a little sportsmanship. Only a little, though. Just give him a little bit of a lesson."

Jerry reached for the cue that he had laid on the table, but as he did, Dark brought his own cue down on Jerry's hands. "Shouldn't do that," said Dark. "You oughtn't to scream, either. Cops might hear you, and you don't want any cops. You don't want any part of the cops, wise guy."

"You broke me hands, you broke me hands!" Jerry screamed. The pain was awful, and he was crying.

"Keep them out of other people's pockets," said Frank. "Beat it."

Questions for Writing and Discussion

1.   What do you think is the point of this story? Do you think the author approves of the brutal incident at the end? Is there any way of telling what sort of judgment he wishes to encourage, or is he indifferent to the whole matter of judgment? Is he simply showing a group of unattractive people in an unattractive situation?

2.   What is the role of Dark (or "Doc") in the story? Is he just a goon employed to do a dirty job, or does Frank see him in a somewhat more complicated role? Is the author slyly suggesting anything in his use of this character's name?

3.   Why did O'Hara put Tom into the story? He doesn't seem to do much of anything, but just keeps repeating what Frank says. When Frank makes Jerry his offer, Tom watches "incredulously," since he doesn't see what Frank is up to. Would you say that Tom serves as a kind of echo-board or reverberator, a minor character whose main function is to help illuminate a major one? If so, how does he do this?

4.   Once Jerry goes back to work for Frank, there is a very detailed listing or catalogue, on p. 130, of exactly what Jerry does in the pool hall. Why does O'Hara put that in there?

5.   Why does Frank go to such elaborate lengths in setting up the billiard game with Jerry? Is it just a cat-and-mouse strategy, a complicated way of tasting his revenge? Or does the idea of "sportmanship" count in some strange way? After all, O'Hara uses the word for his title, and we know that in this little story everything has been carefully worked out.

ISAAC BABEL

My First Goose

Introduction

Some preliminary information:

This story is set in 1920; the recently created Soviet Union, brimming with revolutionary zeal, is waging a brief (and disastrous) war against Poland; the narrator, clearly the author himself, has just joined a unit of Cossacks in the Red Army.

The Cossacks are a people from southern Russia, famous for their skill on horseback. During the reign of the Tsars, they often served as elite troops and became notorious, among Jews and other oppressed minorities, for their brutality. In "My First Goose," however, a number of these Cossacks are fighting in a special detachment of the Red Army.

And the author? Isaac Babel was born in 1894 into a Jewish family in Odessa, a port city on the Black Sea. As a youth Babel went to St. Petersburg (later Leningrad) where he became a protégé of the Russian writer Maxim Gorky and started writing stories himself. A Bolshevik sympathizer, Babel fought with the Red Army in 1920. His most famous book, *Red Cavalry,* consists of loosely connected, brilliantly colored stories and sketches drawn from his experiences on the Polish front. Almost every story juxtaposes the contemplative and pacific values of a Jewish intellectual (Babel himself) with the rough manners and graceful bearing of the Cossacks. Babel also wrote other kinds of stories, notably about Jewish toughs in Odessa. Later, during the years of terror under the Stalin dictatorship, Babel remained silent. But it seems that he held views critical of the regime, and in 1937 he was arrested. Two or three years later he died in a concentration camp.

Now the story itself:

It is about war—the brutalities and (a little) the attractions of war. But more important, it is a story that is at war with itself, or in which the narrator is at war with himself. At the center of the action is a mind torn between two opposing ways of life, two opposing systems of value. The narrator is a man with

133

"specs" (glasses); the "specs" are part of what mark him as an intellectual, the kind of person who believes in thoughtfulness, discussion, reflection, and above all, peacefulness. The narrator lives by those values because he is an intellectual, and also because he is a Jew. Long oppressed in Russia, the Jews cultivated a view of human existence radically different from the Russians and Poles surrounding them. The Jews lived by the values of endurance, patience, prayer, study, and a little guile—the kind of resources that helpless people cultivate.

Now comes the Russian Revolution of 1917. Some young Jews, like young Russians, are captivated by its promise, its excitement, its rhetoric. They pledge themselves to a life of action and, where necessary, violence. But for the young Jews, like the narrator of "My First Goose," there is a conflict, as there must be, between what they have been made by their upbringing and what they wish now to make of themselves. "One of those grinds," says the Cossack commander about the narrator: which is to say, literary man, intellectual, a reader of books, a talker. But the narrator is also someone who wishes to prove himself in the arts of blood, the skills of war, precisely those which his whole training as a Jew and his whole commitment as an intellectual make him feel to be distasteful, perhaps dishonorable.

He joins a Cossack unit, and is received coolly. Who needs a fellow with "specs"?

The narrator is immediately attracted to the Cossacks, for they represent all that he is not. They are superbly physical, wonderfully graceful, utterly prepared to do violence. He responds not only to the immediate strength of these simple men; he also views them in terms of certain literary notions, perhaps idealizations. We sense in the background the greatest of Russian writers, Leo Tolstoy, who saw the Cossacks as men symbolic of energy and directness, men of the body—noble savages. As Lionel Trilling, one of Babel's best critics, remarks: "Babel's view of the Cossack was more consonant with that of Tolstoy than with the traditional view of his own people. For him the Cossack was indeed the noble savage, all too savage, not often noble, yet having in his savagery some quality that might raise strange questions in a Jewish mind."

From these men, the narrator must learn—not how to suffer or be ready for death, that he already knows—but how to kill without hesitation. In another of the "Red Cavalry" stories he begs fate to "grant me the simplest of proficiencies—the ability to kill my fellowmen." It is not a skill he has learned from his culture.

There follows a kind of initiation. The Cossacks haze him, and he in turn slaughters a goose—his "first goose"—in order to show that he can be just like them. They take him into their circle, asking him to share a meal with them. That is a sign of their acceptance, and in response he reads to them from Lenin's latest speech. A friendliness seems to have settled upon them.

But has the narrator really become "one of them"? Hardly. After killing his goose, he is "depressed." His heart is stained "with bloodshed," it has "grated and brimmed over." To grate is to rub raw, and to brim over is to be out of control. His old self has not been lost or buried. Yes, he has learned to kill, but with a troubled and trembling hand.

The structure of this story is very simple: a brief preparation or introduction of the characters, the central anecdote of killing the goose and eating with the Cossacks, and then a rapid closing with the narrator's reflections. But upon this simple structure Babel has thrust a very complicated sense of things and a very brilliant prose style. The story is taut with nervousness. The writing gleams. The narrative moves quickly, hard as a fist. And the language seems to dance around the action, to dance with sharp, startling images, words that shine and sparkle, phrases that bristle with ferocity and surprise. It is in the play of language that the story's full power emerges.

My First Goose

Savitsky, Commander of the VI Division,[1] rose when he saw me, and I wondered at the beauty of his giant's body. He rose, the purple of his riding breeches and the crimson of his little tilted cap and the decorations stuck on his chest cleaving the hut as a standard cleaves the sky. A smell of scent and the sickly sweet freshness of soap emanated from him. His long legs were like girls sheathed to the neck in shining riding boots.

He smiled at me, struck his riding whip on the table, and drew toward him an order that the Chief of Staff had just finished dictating. It was an order for Ivan Chesnokov to advance on Chugunov-Dobryvodka with the regiment entrusted to him, to make contact with the enemy and destroy the same.

"For which destruction," the Commander began to write, smearing the whole sheet, "I make this same Chesnokov entirely responsible, up to and including the supreme penalty, and will if necessary strike him down on the spot; which you, Chesnokov, who have been working with me at the front for some months now, cannot doubt."

The Commander signed the order with a flourish, tossed it to his orderlies and turned upon me gray eyes that danced with merriment.

I handed him a paper with my appointment to the Staff of the Division.

"Put it down in the Order of the Day," said the Commander. "Put him down for every satisfaction save the front one. Can you read and write?"

"Yes, I can read and write," I replied, envying the flower and iron of that youthfulness. "I graduated in law from St. Petersburg University."

"Oh, are you one of those grinds?" he laughed. "Specs on your nose, too! What a nasty little object! They've sent you along without making any enquiries; and this is a hot place for specs. Think you'll get on with us?"

"I'll get on all right," I answered, and went off to the village with the quartermaster to find a billet for the night.

[1] A division of the Red Army, in 1920.

The quartermaster carried my trunk on his shoulder. Before us stretched the village street. The dying sun, round and yellow as a pumpkin, was giving up its roseate ghost to the skies.

We went up to a hut painted over with garlands. The quartermaster stopped, and said suddenly, with a guilty smile:

"Nuisance with specs. Can't do anything to stop it, either. Not a life for the brainy type here. But you go and mess up a lady, and a good lady too, and you'll have the boys patting you on the back."

He hesitated, my little trunk on his shoulder; then he came quite close to me, only to dart away again despairingly and run to the nearest yard. Cossacks were sitting there, shaving one another.

"Here, you soldiers," said the quartermaster, setting my little trunk down on the ground. "Comrade Savitsky's orders are that you're to take this chap in your billets, so no nonsense about it, because the chap's been through a lot in the learning line."

The quartermaster, purple in the face, left us without looking back. I raised my hand to my cap and saluted the Cossacks. A lad with long straight flaxen hair and the handsome face of the Ryazan[2] Cossacks went over to my little trunk and tossed it out at the gate. Then he turned his back on me and with remarkable skill emitted a series of shameful noises.

"To your guns—number double-zero!" an older Cossack shouted at him, and burst out laughing. "Running fire!"

His guileless art exhausted, the lad made off. Then, crawling over the ground, I began to gather together the manuscripts and tattered garments that had fallen out of the trunk. I gathered them up and carried them to the other end of the yard. Near the hut, on a brick stove, stood a cauldron in which pork was cooking. The steam that rose from it was like the far-off smoke of home in the village, and it mingled hunger with desperate loneliness in my head. Then I covered my little broken trunk with hay, turning it into a pillow, and lay down on the ground to read in *Pravda*[3] Lenin's speech at the Second Congress of the Comintern.[4] The sun fell upon me from behind the toothed hillocks, the Cossacks trod on my feet, the lad made fun of me untiringly, the beloved lines came toward me along a thorny path and could not reach me. Then I put aside the paper and went out to the landlady, who was spinning on the porch.

"Landlady," I said, "I've got to eat."

The old woman raised to me the diffused whites of her purblind eyes and lowered them again.

"Comrade," she said, after a pause, "what with all this going on, I want to go and hang myself."

"Christ!" I muttered, and pushed the old woman in the chest with my fist. "You don't suppose I'm going to go into explanations with you, do you?"

And turning around I saw somebody's sword lying within reach. A severe-looking goose was waddling about the yard, inoffensively preening its feathers. I overtook it and pressed it to the ground. Its head cracked beneath my boot,

---

[2]A city and region in western Russia.
[3]Russian: *Truth,* title of Communist newspaper.
[4]Communist International.

cracked and emptied itself. The white neck lay stretched out in the dung, the wings twitched.

"Christ!" I said, digging into the goose with my sword. "Go and cook it for me, landlady."

Her blind eyes and glasses glistening, the old woman picked up the slaughtered bird, wrapped it in her apron, and started to bear it off toward the kitchen.

"Comrade," she said to me, after a while, "I want to go and hang myself." And she closed the door behind her.

The Cossacks in the yard were already sitting around their cauldron. They sat motionless, stiff as heathen priests at a sacrifice, and had not looked at the goose.

"The lad's all right," one of them said, winking and scooping up the cabbage soup with his spoon.

The Cossacks commenced their supper with all the elegance and restraint of peasants who respect one another. And I wiped the sword with sand, went out at the gate, and came in again, depressed. Already the moon hung above the yard like a cheap earring.

"Hey, you," suddenly said Surovkov, an older Cossack. "Sit down and feed with us till your goose is done."

He produced a spare spoon from his boot and handed it to me. We supped up the cabbage soup they had made, and ate the pork.

"What's in the newspaper?" asked the flaxen-haired lad, making room for me.

"Lenin writes in the paper," I said, pulling out *Pravda*. "Lenin writes that there's a shortage of everything."

And loudly, like a triumphant man hard of hearing, I read Lenin's speech out to the Cossacks.

Evening wrapped about me the quickening moisture of its twilight sheets; evening laid a mother's hand upon my burning forehead. I read on and rejoiced, spying out exultingly the secret curve of Lenin's straight line.

"Truth tickles everyone's nostrils," said Surovkov, when I had come to the end. "The question is, how's it to be pulled from the heap. But he goes and strikes at it straight off like a hen pecking at a grain!"

This remark about Lenin was made by Surovkov, platoon commander of the Staff Squadron; after which we lay down to sleep in the hayloft. We slept, all six of us, beneath a wooden roof that let in the stars, warming one another, our legs intermingled. I dreamed; and in my dreams saw women. But my heart, stained with bloodshed, grated and brimmed over.

Translated by Walter Morison

Questions for Writing and Discussion

1. What, finally, is the attitude that the "I" of the story takes toward violence? Do you think this attitude can be summed up neatly, or not so neatly? Can you specify

some of the mixed feelings, assuming there are mixed feelings, toward violence? Can you indicate a few specific passages where these emerge most vividly or clearly?

2.   Look at the first paragraph. There is some remarkable writing here, brilliant similes, bold descriptions. What, concretely, do you make of the character of Savitsky? What does it show about the narrator's attitude toward the Cossacks? Consider especially the phrase which occurs about a page later, when Babel refers to "the flower and iron" of Savitsky's youthfulness. Could you think of a better mixture of qualities for a young soldier than "flower and iron?"

3.   When Savitsky says about Babel, "What a nasty little object!", is he simply expressing hostility? Or is there a certain touch of amiability also? Remember that he is laughing as he makes this remark, though we don't know what *kind* of laughter it is.

4.   One of the ways of reading "My First Goose" is to see it as an initiation rite. A young person enters a group which, in some way, regards itself as special, or distinguished, or elite; he cannot be admitted to the group until he has proved himself or undergone a certain amount of discomfort, perhaps even torment, in order to earn his fellowship in the group; and then, after some ritual difficulties, he is finally accepted. To what extent does the story follow this pattern? If you read it this way, are there important elements which suffer neglect?

5.   Look now at the last sentence of the story. What does it tell us about Babel's estimate of the experience he has gone through? Is he likely now to be accepted by the Cossacks as "one of them"? Or will their attitude toward him always be somewhat uneasy and critical? Does he really want complete acceptance by them? What would be the price of gaining it? And can he, in turn, wholly accept them now?

THE COMIC VISION

GRACE PALEY

An Interest in Life

Introduction

There's a certain slant of voice in big-city American life, especially in the life of New York City, which Grace Paley captures expertly. It is the voice of people who have been bruised and beaten by the sheer effort to survive in the city; by the noise, the subways, the dirt, the lack of money, the heat; by the bad jobs, bad food, bad marriages. These people are weaving and feinting, on the defensive. They are punch-drunk. But even though they probably are losing in the battle to get along, they retain a certain fondness for the city and its ways of life. They complain, they groan, but they do not want to leave.

Through her use of the monologue, Grace Paley brings this urban voice into sharp and comic focus. Virginia is a woman drenched with urban skepticism, urban weariness, urban irony. But she persists. Talking a blue streak, and scraping together all the bits of caustic reflection that she can, Virginia still tries to take care of her family and even snatch a few moments of pleasure.

She has been abandoned by a husband who first appealed to her—and still does—for "his winking looks." She doesn't delude herself into thinking he is very good or very responsible, but she can't help responding to his deviltry: "I would do a lot for him." She even shares some of his resentments. She feels some sympathy for his sense of being crowded by life and his wish to escape responsibilities. When he leaves, she turns to neighbors, the welfare, and John Raftery, pretty much in that order.

And she keeps talking. That, in fact, is one of the things the story is about: the way people in trouble keep talking in order to validate—to make real—their own presence and thereby gain a bit of comic relief. Virginia is not in love with John Raftery; but still, he is a decent sort, he shows up regularly, he is nice to the kids, and if the way to make sure that he will continue to drop in is for her to give out, then she will give out. A loser she may be, but a fool she is not.

Her speech bristles with irony, much of it directed against herself. When John says that he wants to do something for her, she answers, with her elbows

141

dipping into the dish water, "Tell me I'm the most gorgeous thing." We know from Virginia herself that she is not exactly the most gorgeous thing; she is putting on too much weight. Still, there is a kind of resilience to her, a tough playfulness, which makes her likable. And that is the spirit which dominates the story.

What we like about Virginia is not just that she keeps fighting for her morale, nor even that she rarely lapses into self-pity, nor even that she is able to laugh at herself. What we like about her is that, despite all the weariness and skepticism the city forces upon her, she remains a romantic—wry, self-mocking, but an incorrigible romantic.

The story ends with her fantasy of the husband coming back and the two of them having a good time on the kitchen floor. The kitchen floor isn't the usual place where people have good times; but Virginia has been around long enough to know that there's usually a considerable distance between real life and fantasy. Anyway, we can almost hear her say with a grin, "you get your pleasures as you can." But since she retains her wit even in her fantasy, she also foresees that they'll forget "the precautions" and perhaps get into further trouble. Which, for a young couple that already has four children, is no small matter.

Nevertheless, in its own sweet-and-sour way, disabused and disillusioned, this is a love story.

An Interest in Life

My husband gave me a broom one Christmas. This wasn't right. No one can tell me it was meant kindly.

"I don't want you not to have anything for Christmas while I'm away in the Army," he said. "Virginia, please look at it. It comes with this fancy dustpan. It hangs off a stick. Look at it, will you? Are you blind or cross-eyed?"

"Thanks, chum," I said. I had always wanted a dustpan hooked up that way. It was a good one. My husband doesn't shop in bargain basements or January sales.

Still and all, in spite of the quality, it was a mean present to give a woman you planned on never seeing again, a person you had children with and got onto all the time, drunk or sober, even when everybody had to get up early in the morning.

I asked him if he could wait and join the Army in a half hour, as I had to get the groceries. I don't like to leave kids alone in a three-room apartment full of gas and electricity. Fire may break out from a nasty remark. Or the oldest decides to get even with the youngest.

"Just this once," he said. "But you better figure out how to get along without me."

"You're a handicapped person mentally," I said. "You should've been institutionalized years ago" I slammed the door. I didn't want to see him pack his underwear and ironed shirts.

I never got further than the front stoop, though, because there was Mrs. Raftery, wringing her hands, tears in her eyes as though she had a monopoly on all the good news.

"Mrs. Raftery!" I said, putting my arm around her. "Don't cry." She leaned on me because I am such a horsy build. "Don't cry, Mrs. Raftery, please!" I said.

"That's like you, Virginia. Always looking at the ugly side of things. 'Take in the wash. It's rainin'!' That's you. You're the first one knows it when the dumb-waiter breaks."

"Oh, come on now, that's not so. It just isn't so," I said. "I'm the exact opposite."

"Did you see Mrs. Cullen yet?" she asked, paying no attention.

"Where?"

"Virginia!" she said, shocked. "She's passed away. The whole house knows it. They've got her in white like a bride and you never saw a beautiful creature like that. She must be eighty. Her husband's proud."

"She was never more than an acquaintance; she didn't have any children," I said.

"Well, I don't care about that. Now, Virginia, you do what I say now, you go downstairs and you say like this—listen to me—say, 'I hear, Mr. Cullen, your wife's passed away. I'm sorry.' Then ask him how he is. Then you ought to go around the corner and see her. She's in Witson & Wayde. Then you ought to go over to the church when they carry her over."

"It's not my church," I said.

"That's no reason, Virginia. You go up like this," she said, parting from me to do a prancy dance. "Up the big front steps, into the church you go. It's beautiful in there. You can't help kneeling only for a minute. Then round to the right. Then up the other stairway. Then you come to a great oak door that's arched above you, then," she said, seizing a deep, deep breath, for all the good it would do her, "and then turn the knob slo-owly and open the door and see for yourself: Our Blessed Mother is in charge. Beautiful. Beautiful. Beautiful."

I sighed in and I groaned out, so as to melt a certain pain around my heart. A steel ring like arthritis, at my age.

"You are a groaner," Mrs. Raftery said, gawking into my mouth.

"I am not," I said. I got a whiff of her, a terrible cheap wine lush.

My husband threw a penny at the door from the inside to take my notice from Mrs. Raftery. He rattled the glass door to make sure I looked at him. He had a fat duffel bag on each shoulder. Where did he acquire so much worldly possession? What was in them? My grandma's goose feathers from across the ocean? Or all the diaper-service diapers? To this day the truth is shrouded in mystery.

"What the hell are you doing, Virginia?" he said, dumping them at my feet. "Standing out here on your hind legs telling everybody your business? The Army gives you a certain time, for God's sakes, they're not kidding." Then he said, "I beg your pardon," to Mrs. Raftery. He took hold of me with his two arms as though in love and pressed his body hard against mine so that I could feel him for the last time and suffer my loss. Then he kissed me in a mean way to nearly split my lip. Then he winked and said, "That's all for now," and skipped off into the future, duffel bags full of rags.

He left me in an embarrassing situation, nearly fainting, in front of that old widow, who can't even remember the half of it. "He's a crock," said Mrs. Raftery. "Is he leaving for good or just temporarily, Virginia?"

"Oh, he's probably deserting me," I said, and sat down on the stoop, pulling my big knees up to my chin.

"If that's the case, tell the Welfare right away," she said. "He's a bum, leaving you just before Christmas. Tell the cops," she said. "They'll provide the toys for the little kids gladly. And don't forget to let the grocer in on it. He won't be so hard on you expecting payment."

She saw that sadness was stretched world-wide across my face. Mrs. Raftery isn't the worst person. She said, "Look around for comfort, dear." With a nervous finger she pointed to the truckers eating lunch on their haunches across the street, leaning on the loading platforms. She waved her hand to include in all the men marching up and down in search of a decent luncheonette. She didn't leave out the six longshoremen loafing under the fish-market marquee. "If their lungs and stomachs ain't crushed by overwork, they disappear somewhere in the world. Don't be disappointed, Virginia. I don't know a man living'd last you a lifetime."

Ten days later Girard asked, "Where's Daddy?"

"Ask me no questions, I'll tell you no lies." I didn't want the children to know the facts. Present or past, a child should have a father.

"Where *is* Daddy?" Girard asked the week after that.

"He joined the Army," I said.

"He made my bunk bed," said Phillip.

"The truth shall make ye free," I said.

Then I sat down with pencil and pad to get in control of my resources. The facts, when I added and subtracted them, were that my husband had left me with fourteen dollars, and the rent unpaid, in an emergency state. He'd claimed he was sorry to do this, but my opinion is, out of sight, out of mind. "The city won't let you starve," he'd said. "After all, you're half the population. You're keeping up the good work. Without you the race would die out. Who'd pay the taxes? Who'd keep the streets clean? There wouldn't be no Army. A man like me wouldn't have no place to go."

I sent Girard right down to Mrs. Raftery with a request about the whereabouts of Welfare. She responded RSVP with an extra comment in left-handed script: "Poor Girard . . . he's never the boy my John was!"

Who asked her?

I called on Welfare right after the new year. In no time I discovered that they're rigged up to deal with liars, and if you're truthful it's disappointing to them. They may even refuse to handle your case if you're too truthful.

They asked sensible questions at first. They asked where my husband had enlisted. I didn't know. They put some letter writers and agents after him. "He's not in the United States Army," they said. "Try the Brazilian Army," I suggested.

They have no sense of kidding around. They're not the least bit light-hearted and they tried. "Oh no," they said. "That was incorrect. He is not in the Brazilian Army."

"No?" I said. "How strange! He must be in the Mexican Navy."

By law, they had to hound his brothers. They wrote to his brother who has a first-class card in the Teamsters and owns an apartment house in California. They asked his two brothers in Jersey to help me. They have large families. Rightfully they laughed. Then they wrote to Thomas, the oldest, the smart one (the one they all worked so hard for years to keep him in college until his brains could pay off). He was the one who sent ten dollars immediately, saying, "What a bastard! I'll send something time to time, Ginny, but whatever you do, don't tell the authorities." Of course I never did. Soon they began to guess they were better people than me, that I was in trouble because I deserved it, and then they liked me better.

But they never fixed my refrigerator. Every time I called I said patiently, "The milk is sour . . ." I said, "Corn beef went bad." Sitting in that beer-stinking phone booth in Felan's for the sixth time (sixty cents) with the baby on my lap and Barbie tapping at the glass door with an American flag, I cried into the secretary's hardhearted ear, "I bought real butter for the holiday, and it's rancid . . ." They said, "You'll have to get a better bid on the repair job."

While I waited indoors for a man to bid, Girard took to swinging back and forth on top of the bathroom door, just to soothe himself, giving me the laugh, dreamy, nibbling calcimine off the ceiling. On first sight Mrs. Raftery said, "Whack the monkey, he'd be better off on arsenic."

But Girard is my son and I'm the judge. It means a terrible thing for the future, though I don't know what to call it.

It was from constantly thinking of my foreknowledge on this and other subjects, it was from observing when I put my lipstick on daily, how my face was just curling up to die, that John Raftery came from Jersey to rescue me.

On Thursdays, anyway, John Raftery took the tubes in to visit his mother. The whole house knew it. She was cheerful even before breakfast. She sang out loud in a girlish brogue that only came to tongue for grand occasions. Hanging out the wash, she blushed to recall what a remarkable boy her John had been. "Ask the sisters around the corner," she said to the open kitchen windows. "They'll never forget John."

That particular night after supper Mrs. Raftery said to her son, "John, how come you don't say hello to your old friend Virginia? She's had hard luck and she's gloomy."

"Is that so, Mother?" he said, and immediately climbed two flights to knock at my door.

"Oh, John," I said at the sight of him, hat in hand in a white shirt and blue-striped tie, spick-and-span, a Sunday-school man. "Hello!"

"Welcome, John!" I said. "Sit down. Come right in. How are you? You look awfully good. You do. Tell me, how've you been all this time, John?"

"How've I been?" he asked thoughtfully. To answer within reason, he described his life with Margaret, marriage, work, and children up to the present day.

I had nothing good to report. Now that he had put the subject around before my very eyes, every burnt-up day of my life smoked in shame, and I couldn't even get a clear view of the good half hours.

"Of course," he said, "you do have lovely children. Noticeable-looking, Virginia. Good looks is always something to be thankful for."

"Thankful?" I said. "I don't have to thank anything but my own foolishness for four children when I'm twenty-six years old, deserted, and poverty-struck, regardless of looks. A man can't help it, but I could have behaved better."

"Don't be so cruel on yourself, Ginny," he said. "Children come from God."

"You're still great on holy subjects, aren't you? You know damn well where children come from."

He did know. His red face reddened further. John Raftery has had that color coming out on him boy and man from keeping his rages so inward.

Still he made more sense in his conversation after that, and I poured fresh tea to tell him how my husband used to like me because I was a passionate person. That was until he took a look around and saw how in the long run this life only meant more of the same thing. He tried to turn away from me once he came to this understanding, and make me hate him. His face changed. He gave up his brand of cigarettes, which we had in common. He threw out the two pairs of socks I knitted by hand. "If there's anything I hate in this world, it's navy blue," he said. Oh, I could have dyed them. I would have done anything for him, if he were only not too sorry to ask me.

"You were a nice kid in those days," said John, referring to certain Saturday nights. "A wild, nice kid."

"Aaah," I said, disgusted. Whatever I was then, was on the way to where I am now. "I was fresh. If I had a kid like me, I'd slap her cross-eyed."

The very next Thursday John gave me a beautiful radio with a record player. "Enjoy yourself," he said. That really made Welfare speechless. We didn't own any records, but the investigator saw my burden was lightened and he scribbled a dozen pages about it in his notebook.

On the third Thursday he brought a walking doll (twenty-four inches) for Linda and Barbie with a card inscribed, "A baby doll for a couple of dolls." He had also had a couple of drinks at his mother's, and this made him want to dance. "La-la-la," he sang, a ramrod swaying in my kitchen chair. "La-la-la, let yourself go . . ."

"You gotta give a little," he sang, "live a little . . ." He said, "Virginia, may I have this dance?"

"Sssh, we finally got them asleep. Please, turn the radio down. Quiet. Deathly silence, John Raftery."

"Let me do your dishes, Virginia."

"Don't be silly, you're a guest in my house," I said. "I still regard you as a guest."

"I want to do something for you, Virginia."

"Tell me I'm the most gorgeous thing," I said, dipping my arm to the funny bone in dish soup.

He didn't answer. "I'm having a lot of trouble at work," was all he said. Then I heard him push the chair back. He came up behind me, put his arms around my waistline, and kissed my cheek. He whirled me around and took my hands. He said, "An old friend is better than rubies." He looked me in the eye. He held my attention by trying to be honest. And he kissed me a short sweet kiss on my mouth.

"Please sit down, Virginia," he said. He kneeled before me and put his head in my lap. I was stirred by so much activity. Then he looked up at me and, as though proposing marriage for life, he offered—because he was drunk—to place his immortal soul in peril to comfort me.

First I said, "Thank you." Then I said, "No."

I was sorry for him, but he's devout, a leader of the Fathers' Club at his church, active in all the lay groups for charities, orphans, etc. I knew that if he stayed late to love with me, he would not do it lightly but would in the end pay terrible penance and ruin his long life. The responsibility would be on me.

So I said no.

And Barbie is such a light sleeper. All she has to do, I thought, is wake up and wander in and see her mother and her new friend John with his pants around his knees, wrestling on the kitchen table. A vision like that could affect a kid for life.

I said no.

Everyone in this building is so goddamn nosy. That evening I had to say no.

But John came to visit, anyway, on the fourth Thursday. This time he brought the discarded dresses of Margaret's daughters, organdy party dresses and glazed cotton for every day. He gently admired Barbara and Linda, his blue eyes rolling to back up a couple of dozen oohs and ahs.

Even Phillip, who thinks God gave him just a certain number of hellos and he better save them for the final judgment, Phillip leaned on John and said, "Why don't you bring your boy to play with me? I don't have nobody to play with." Phillip's a liar. There must be at least seventy-one children in this house, pale pink to medium brown, English-talking and gibbering in Spanish, rough-and-tough boys, the Lone Ranger's bloody pals, or the exact picture of Super-mouse. If a boy wanted a friend, he could pick the very one out of his neighbors.

Also, Girard is a cold fish. He was in a lonesome despair. Sometimes he looked in the mirror and said, "How come I have such an ugly face? My nose is funny. Mostly people don't like me." He was a liar too. Girard has a face like his father's. His eyes are the color of those little blue plums in August. He looks like an advertisement in a magazine. He could be a child model and make a lot of money. He is my first child, and if he thinks he is ugly, I think I am ugly.

John said, "I can't stand to see a boy mope like that. . . . What do the sisters say in school?"

"He doesn't pay attention is all they say. You can't get much out of them."

"My middle boy was like that," said John. "Couldn't take an interest. Aaah, I wish I didn't have all that headache on the job. I'd grab Girard by the collar and make him take notice of the world. I wish I could ask him out to Jersey to play in all that space."

"Why not?" I said.

"Why, Virginia, I'm surprised you don't know why not. You know I can't take your children out to meet my children."

I felt a lot of strong arthritis in my ribs.

"My mother's the funny one, Virginia." He felt he had to continue with the subject matter. "I don't know. I guess she likes the idea of bugging Margaret. She says, 'You goin' up, John?' 'Yes, Mother,' I say. 'Behave yourself, John,' she says. 'That husband might come home and hack-saw you into hell. You're a Catholic man, John,' she says. But I figured it out. She likes to know I'm in the building. I swear, Virginia, she wishes me the best of luck."

"I do too, John," I said. We drank a last glass of beer to make sure of a peaceful sleep. "Good night, Virginia," he said, looping his muffler neatly under his chin. "Don't worry. I'll be thinking of what to do about Girard."

John was sincere. That's true. He paid a lot of attention to Girard, smoking out all his sneaky sorrows. He registered him into a wild pack of cub scouts that went up to the Bronx once a week to let off steam. He gave him a Junior Erector Set. And sometimes when his family wasn't listening he prayed at great length for him.

One Sunday, Sister Veronica said in her sweet voice from another life, "He's not worse. He might even be a little better. How are *you*, Virginia?" putting her hand on mine. Everybody around here acts like they know everything.

"Just fine," I said.

"We ought to start on Phillip," John said, "if it's true Girard's improving."

"You should've been a social worker, John."

"A lot of people have noticed that about me," said John.

"Your mother was always acting so crazy about you, how come she didn't knock herself out a little to see you in college? Like we did for Thomas?"

"Now, Virginia, be fair. She's a poor old woman. My father was a weak earner. She had to have my wages, and I'll tell you, Virginia, I'm not sorry. Look at Thomas. He's still in school. Drop him in this jungle and he'd be devoured. He hasn't had a touch of real life. And here I am with a good chunk of a family, a home of my own, a name in the building trades. One thing I have to tell you, the poor old woman is sorry. I said one day (oh, in passing—years ago) that I might marry you. She stuck a knife in herself. It's a fact. Not more than an eighth of an inch. You never saw such a gory Sunday. One thing—you would have been a better daughter-in-law to her than Margaret."

"Marry me?" I said.

"Well, yes. . . . Aaah—I always liked you, then . . . Why do you think I'd sit in the shade of this kitchen every Thursday night? For God's sakes, the only warm thing around here is this teacup. Yes, sir, I did want to marry you, Virginia."

"No kidding, John? Really?" It was nice to know. Better late than never, to learn you were desired in youth.

I didn't tell John, but the truth is, I would never have married him. Once I met my husband with his winking looks, he was my only interest. Wild as I had been with John and others, I turned all my wildness over to him and then there was no question in my mind.

Still, face facts, if my husband didn't budge on in life, it was my fault. On me, as they say, be it. I greeted the morn with a song. I had a hello for everyone but the landlord. Ask the people on the block, come or go—even the Spanish ones, with their sad dark faces—they have to smile when they see me.

But for his own comfort, he should have done better lifewise and money-wise. I was happy, but I am now in possession of knowledge that this is wrong. Happiness isn't so bad for a woman. She gets fatter, she gets older, she could lie down, nuzzling a regiment of men and little kids, she could just die of the pleasure. But men are different, they have to own money, or they have to be famous, or everybody on the block has to look up to them from the cellar stairs.

A woman counts her children and acts snotty, like she invented life, but men *must* do well in the world. I know that men are not fooled by being happy.

"A funny guy," said John, guessing where my thoughts had gone. "What stopped him up? He was nobody's fool. He had a funny thing about him, Virginia, if you don't mind my saying so. He wasn't much distance up, but he was all set and ready to be looking down on us all."

"He was very smart, John. You don't realize that. His hobby was cross-word puzzles, and I said to him real often, as did others around here, that he ought to go out on the '$64 Question.' Why not? But he laughed. You know what he said? He said, 'That proves how dumb you are if you think I'm smart.'"

"A funny guy," said John. "Get if all off your chest," he said. "Talk it out, Virginia; it's the only way to kill the pain."

By and large, I was happy to oblige. Still I could not carry through about certain cruel remarks. It was like trying to move back into the dry mouth of a nightmare to remember that the last day I was happy was the middle of a week in March, when I told my husband I was going to have Linda. Barbara was five months old to the hour. The boys were three and four. I had to tell him. It was the last day with anything happy about it.

Later on, he said, "Oh, you make me so sick, you're so goddamn big and fat, you look like a goddamn brownstone, the way you're squared off in front."

"Well, where are you going tonight?" I asked.

"How should I know? he said. "Your big ass takes up the whole goddamn bed," he said. "There's no room for me." He bought a sleeping bag and slept on the floor.

I couldn't believe it. I would start every morning fresh. I couldn't believe that he would turn against me so, while I was still young and even his friends still liked me.

But he did, he turned absolutely against me and became no friend of mine. "All you ever think about is making babies. This place stinks like the men's room in the BMT. It's a fucking *pissoir*." He was strong on truth all through the year. "That kid eats more than the five of us put together," he said. "Stop stuffing your face, you fat dumbbell," he said to Phillip.

Then he worked on the neighbors. "Get that nosy old bag out of here," he said. "If she comes on once more with 'my son in the building trades' I'll squash her for the cat."

Then he turned on Spielvogel, the checker, his oldest friend, who only visited on holidays and never spoke to me (shy, the way some bachelors are). "That sonofabitch, don't hand me that friendship crap, all he's after is your ass. That's what I need—a little shitmaker of his using up the air in this flat."

And then there was no one else to dispose of. We were left alone fair and square, facing each other.

"Now, Virginia," he said, "I come to the end of my rope. I see a black wall ahead of me. What the hell am I supposed to do? I only got one life. Should I lie down and die? I don't know what to do any more. I'll give it to you straight, Virginia, if I stick around, you can't help it, you'll hate me . . ."

"I hate you right now," I said. "So do whatever you like."

"This place drives me nuts," he munbled. "I don't know what to do around here. I want to get you a present. Something."

"I told you, do whatever you like. Buy me a rattrap for rats."

That's when he went down to the House Appliance Store, and he brought back a new broom and a classy dustpan.

"A new broom sweeps clean," he said. "I got to get out of here," he said. "I'm going nuts." Then he began to stuff the duffel bags, and I went to the grocery store but was stopped by Mrs. Raftery, who had to tell me what she considered so beautiful—death—then he kissed and went to join some army somewhere.

I didn't tell John any of this, because I think it makes a woman look too bad to tell on how another man has treated her. He begins to see her through the other man's eyes, a sitting duck, a skinful of flaws. After all, I had come to depend on John. All my husband's friends were strangers now, though I had always said to them, "Feel welcome."

And the family men in the building looked too cunning, as though they had all personally deserted me. If they met me on the stairs, they carried the heaviest groceries up and helped bring Linda's stroller down, but they never asked me a question worth answering at all.

Besides that, Girard and Phillip taught the girls the days of the week: Monday, Tuesday, Wednesday, Johnday, Friday. They waited for him once a week, under the hallway lamp, half asleep like bugs in the sun, sitting in their little chairs with their names on in gold, a birth present from my mother-in-law. At fifteen after eight he punctually came, to read a story, pass out some kisses, and tuck them into bed.

But one night, after a long Johnday of them squealing my eardrum split, after a rainy afternoon with brother constantly raising up his hand against brother, with the girls near ready to go to court over the proper ownership of Melinda Lee, the twenty-four-inch walking doll, the doorbell rang three times. Not any of those times did John's face greet me.

I was too ashamed to call down to Mrs. Raftery, and she was too mean to knock on my door and explain.

He didn't come the following Thursday either. Girard said sadly, "He must've run away, John."

I had to give him up after two weeks' absence and no word. I didn't know how to tell the children: something about right and wrong, goodness and meanness, men and women. I had it all at my finger tips, ready to hand over. But I didn't think I ought to take mistakes and truth away from them. Who knows? They might make a truer friend in this world somewhere than I have ever made. So I just put them to bed and sat in the kitchen and cried.

In the middle of my third beer, searching in my mind for the next step, I found the decision to go on "Strike It Rich." I scrounged some paper and pencil from the toy box and I listed all my troubles, which must be done in order to qualify. The list when complete could have brought tears to the eye of God if He had a minute. At the sight of it my bitterness began to improve. All that is really necessary for survival of the fittest, it seems, is an interest in life, good, bad, or peculiar.

As always happens in these cases where you have begun to help yourself with plans, news comes from an opposite direction. The doorbell rang, two short and two long—meaning John.

My first thought was to wake the children and make them happy. "No! No!" he said. "Please don't put yourself to that trouble. Virginia, I'm dog-tired," he said. "Dog-tired. My job is a damn headache. It's too much. It's all day and it scuttles my mind at night, and in the end who does the credit go to?

"Virginia," he said, "I don't know if I can come any more. I've been wanting to tell you. I just don't know. What's it all about? Could you answer me if I asked you? I can't figure this whole thing out at all."

I started the tea steeping because his fingers when I touched them were cold. I didn't speak. I tried looking at it from his man point of view, and I thought he had to take a bus, the tubes, and a subway to see me; and then the subway, the tubes, and a bus to go back home at 1 A.M. It wouldn't be any trouble at all for him to part with us forever. I thought about my life, and I gave strongest consideration to my children. If given the choice, I decided to choose not to live without him.

"What's that?" he asked, pointing to my careful list of troubles. "Writing a letter?"

"Oh no," I said, "it's for 'Strike It Rich.' I hope to go on the program."

"Virginia, for goodness' sakes," he said, giving it a glance, "you don't have a ghost. They'd laught you out of the studio. Those people really suffer."

"Are you sure, John?" I asked.

"No question in my mind at all," said John. "Have you ever seen that program? I mean, in addition to all of this—the little disturbances of man"—he waved a scornful hand at my list—"they *suffer*. They live in the forefront of tornadoes, their lives are washed off by floods—catastrophes of God. Oh, Virginia."

"Are you sure, John?"

"For goodness' sake . . ."

Sadly, I put my list away. Still, if things got worse, I could always make use of it.

Once that was settled, I acted on an earlier decision. I pushed his cup of scalding tea aside. I wedged myself onto his lap between his hard belt buckle and the table. I put my arms around his neck and said, "How come you're so cold, John?" He has a kind face and he knew how to look astonished. He said, "Why, Virginia, I'm getting warmer." We laughed.

John became a lover to me that night.

Mrs. Raftery is sometimes silly and sick from her private source of cheap wine. She expects John often. "Honor your mother, what's the matter with you, John?" she complains. "Honor. Honor."

"Virginia dear," she says. "You never would've taken John away to Jersey like Margaret. I wish he'd've married you."

"You didn't like me much in those days."

"That's a lie," she says. I know she's a hypocrite, but no more than the rest of the world.

What is remarkable to me is that it doesn't seem to conscience John as I thought it might. It is still hard to believe that a man who sends out the Ten Commandments every year for a Christmas card can be so easy buttoning and unbuttoning.

Of course we must be very careful not to wake the children or disturb the neighbors who will enjoy another person's excitment just so far, and then the pleasure enrages them. We must be very careful for ourselves too, for when my husband comes back, realizing the babies are in school and everything easier, he won't forgive me if I've started it all up again—noisy signs of life that are so much trouble to a man.

We haven't seen him in two and a half years. Although people have suggested it, I do not want the police or Intelligence or a private eye or anyone to go after him to bring him back. I know that if he expected to stay away forever he would have written and said so. As it is, I just don't know what evening, any time, he may appear. Sometimes, stumbling over a blockbuster of a dream at midnight, I wake up to vision his soft arrival.

He comes in the door with his old key. He gives me a strict look and says,

"Well, you look older, Virginia." "So do you," I say, although he hasn't changed a bit.

He settles in the kitchen because the children are asleep all over the rest of the house. I unknot his tie and offer him a cold sandwich. He raps my backside, paying attention to the bounce. I walk around him as though he were a Maypole, kissing as I go.

"I didn't like the Army much," he says. "Next time I think I might go join the Merchant Marine."

"What army?" I say.

"It's pretty much the same everywhere," he says.

"I wouldn't be a bit surprised," I say.

"I lost my cuff link, goddamnit," he says, and drops to the floor to look for it. I go down too on my knees, but I know he never had a cuff link in his life. Still I would do a lot for him.

"Got you off your feet that time," he says, laughing. "Oh yes, I did." And before I can even make myself half comfortable on that polka-dotted linoleum, he got onto me right where we were, and the truth is, we were so happy, we forgot the precautions.

Questions for Writing and Discussion

1. Why did Grace Paley choose to write this story in the first person singular? What might have been lost (or gained) if it had been told in the third person? How does Virginia's tone of voice substantiate what she tells us about her half-comic, half-tragic experiences with men?

2. The beginning is very sharp and amusing. About to leave Virginia, the husband gives her a broom for Christmas, whereupon, with her usual irony, she remarks, "No one can tell me it was meant kindly." What, in the context of the story, does the broom suggest? How does it indicate the husband's attitude toward the marriage?

3. Now, Mrs. Raftery. What role does she play in the story? Could it have been told just as well without her? Apart from getting son John to visit Virginia (which might have been managed some other way), what purpose does she serve? A gossipy old lush, of course, but what about her remark to Virginia: "I don't know a man living'd last you a lifetime"?

4. John Raftery becomes Virginia's lover, but what is her attitude toward him? Is she just "using" him? Is she fond of him?

JAMES THURBER

The Secret Life of Walter Mitty

Introduction: Walter Mitty Talks Back

I resent every word of it, James Thurber, and don't think that just because you've convinced the whole world I'm a timid, hen-pecked soul, I won't talk back. I will. I really will.

I admit right off that "The Secret Life of Walter Mitty" is very clever. By now, everyone has recognized the cleverness of the story, the way you show me succumbing to a series of fantasies of "heroism" interspersed with grim and humiliating realities. One minute I'm daydreaming that I'm Commander Mitty of the hydroplane on a daredevil assignment, and the next minute my wife pesters me to buy overshoes. Then I'm Dr. Mitty the great surgeon, cool as ice and handy with the scalpel, and next I'm a poor devil who can't even park the car right. I even think of wearing my right arm in a sling so that the car attendants won't make fun of me.

And then I'm Captain Mitty getting ready to "fly alone," and philosophizing that "we only live once, Sergeant . . . or do we?" and before you know it I've tumbled back into reality and am buying puppy biscuits. *Puppy biscuits!*

Your cleverest touch comes at the end when I fancy myself before the firing squad, "erect and motionless, proud and disdainful, Walter Mitty the Undefeated." Everyone gets the point—that it's in real life that I'm facing the firing squad, with my wife at the trigger and the circumstances of my existence pressing closer and closer. I'm being executed every day, every minute, over and over again. . . . So, after having laughed at me through the accumulation of incidents that you so skilfully put together, people will even feel a little sorry for me. They'll say, oh yes, that Thurber, he's *so* compassionate, *so* understanding, *so* ready to drop a tear for poor ridiculous Walter Mitty.

But I reject the whole thing. I reject your ridicule and I reject your compassion. I know everyone is with you; by now it's probably as impossible for me to straighten out the record as it would be for George Washington to come back to life and insist that he did tell a lie. And your story makes everyone feel

155

superior, feel that he or she is, at least, stronger and happier than Walter Mitty. But I defy you all—I Walter Mitty the Undefeated, "inscrutable to the last," defy you all!

You probably suppose I'm going to deny your story and claim I never fantasized about being a great surgeon or fearless warrior. But I won't. Every detail of your story, I happily admit, is true. When I go to town with my wife I do imagine myself all those heroic, fearless, gallant chaps whom you portray. And if someone were to say, "They all seem to come straight out of the movies, Ronald Coleman or John Wayne or Paul Newman," then I'd reply, "Of course, where do you think we Americans get our fantasies from, anyway?" Even those little "nonchalant" remarks you put into my mouth, those modest touches by which the hero makes light of his heroism—even those are true. Smile if you want to!

Why then do I reject everything you have written about me? Because if true to the letter, it is false to the spirit. I daydream for the same reason that everyone else daydreams—life is intolerable! I daydream for the reason you, Thurber, and you, unknown reader victimized by Thurber, daydream—life is intolerable!

It's not the big problems that wear me down. I earn a living, there's no serious illness in the family, my wife and I get along, more or less. It's the little things, the endless round of irritations and trivialities, the lists one has to keep in mind while shopping, the mild whining of one's wife, the boasting of the people in my office, the boring chatter of my neighbors, the bills unpaid, the faucets that leak, the toilet bowl that won't flush, the zippers that get stuck—that's what wears me down. And what can be done about it? Religion, politics, utopia, dictatorship, contemplation? Will any of these take care of the bills, the whining voices, the zippers, the toilet bowls? Will any of these remove the stream of irritation, soon to become a flood of defeat, which gathers about our lives?

The only solution, the only human way, the only path to a kind of heroism is to . . . daydream. What distinguishes men from the beasts? Some say our capacity to think. Nonsense! Most people can't think at all. *But everyone can daydream.* And in our daydreams we fulfill ourselves, we realize our finest aspirations.

Do you suppose this is true only for me? Not at all. I, Walter Mitty of suburban Connecticut, stand proudly with the greatest poets, the most brilliant generals, the profoundest statesmen. What do you suppose Napoleon did before his greatest victories? Daydream! What do you think Milton did before writing "Paradise Lost"? Daydream! And George Washington just before accepting the American Presidency? Daydream!

Or listen to the voice of that master daydreamer, William Butler Yeats, the supreme poet in English during the twentieth century:

> Sometimes I told myself very adventurous love-stories with myself for hero, and at other times I planned out a life of lonely austerity, and at other times mixed the ideals and planned a life of lonely austerity mitigated by periodic lapses.

You thought, James Thurber, that by afflicting this most common of human activities upon a sad sack named Walter Mitty, you'd isolate the danger and allow yourself and others to laugh at it. Not at all! The last laugh is on you, my creator and tormentor, and on you, thousands of readers who smile pityingly at me, as if you were in any way superior. For what you expected to mock as the secret life of Walter Mitty is actually the secret life of yourselves.

And you, James Thurber, how about your life? What is it you do before sitting down to write? You daydream. For once, tell the truth. Let the world know your secret: *Walter Mitty, c'est vous!**

The Secret Life of Walter Mitty

"We're going through!" The Commander's voice was like thin ice breaking. He wore his full-dress uniform, with the heavily braided white cap pulled down rakishly over one cold gray eye. "We can't make it, sir. It's spoiling for a hurricane, if you ask me." "I'm not asking you, Lieutenant Berg," said the Commander. "Throw on the power lights! Rev her up to 8,500! We're going through!" The pounding of the cylinders increased: ta-pocketa-pocketa-pocketa-*pocketa-pocketa.* The Commander stared at the ice forming on the pilot window. He walked over and twisted a row of complicated dials. "Switch on No. 8 auxiliary!" he shouted. "Switch on No. 8 auxiliary!" repeated Lieutenant Berg. "Full strength in No. 3 turret!" shouted the Commander, "Full strength in No. 3 turret!" The crew, bending to their various tasks in the huge, hurtling eight-engined Navy hydroplane, looked at each other and grinned. "The Old Man'll get us through," they said to one another. "The Old Man ain't afraid of Hell!" . . .

"Not so fast! You're driving too fast!" said Mrs. Mitty. "What are you driving so fast for?"

"Hmm?" said Walter Mitty. He looked at his wife, in the seat beside him, with shocked astonishment. She seemed grossly unfamiliar, like a strange woman who had yelled at him in a crowd. "You were up to fifty-five," she said. "You know I don't like to go more than forty. You were up to fifty-five." Walter Mitty drove on toward Waterbury in silence, the roaring of the SN202 through

*After feats of research, we have discovered what Mitty is doing here. The great French novelist Gustave Flaubert once said about his daydreaming, mediocre heroine Emma Bovary—"Emma Bovary, c'est moi," Emma Bovary, she is I. And Mitty is challenging Thurber to admit that he, Mitty, far from being some alien or distant creature, is actually a version or double of himself, James Thurber.

the worst storm in twenty years of Navy flying fading in the remote, intimate airways of his mind. "You're tensed up again," said Mrs. Mitty. "It's one of your days. I wish you'd let Dr. Renshaw look you over."

Walter Mitty stopped the car in front of the building where his wife went to have her hair done. "Remember to get those overshoes while I'm having my hair done," she said. "I don't need overshoes," said Mitty. She put her mirror back into her bag. "We've been all through that," she said, getting out of the car. "You're not a young man any longer." He raced the engine a little. "Why don't you wear your gloves? Have you lost your gloves?" Walter Mitty reached in a pocket and brought out the gloves. He put them on, but after she had turned and gone into the building and he had driven on to a red light, he took them off again. "Pick it up, brother!" snapped a cop as the light changed, and Mitty hastily pulled on his gloves and lurched ahead. He drove around the streets aimlessly for a time, and then he drove past the hospital on his way to the parking lot.

. . . "It's the millionaire banker, Wellington McMillan," said the pretty nurse. "Yes?" said Walter Mitty, removing his gloves slowly. "Who has the case?" "Dr. Renshaw and Dr. Benbow, but there are two specialists here, Dr. Remington from New York and Mr. Pritchard-Mitford from London. He flew over." A door opened down a long, cool corridor and Dr. Renshaw came out. He looked distraught and haggard. "Hello, Mitty," he said. "We're having the devil's own time with McMillan, the millionaire banker and close personal friend of Roosevelt. Obstreosis of the ductal tract. Tertiary. Wish you'd take a look at him." "Glad to," said Mitty.

In the operating room there were whispered introductions: "Dr. Remington, Dr. Mitty. Mr. Pritchard-Mitford, Dr. Mitty." "I've read your book on streptothricosis," said Pritchard-Mitford, shaking hands. "A brilliant performance, sir." "Thank you," said Walter Mitty. "Didn't know you were in the States, Mitty," grumbled Remington. "Coals to Newcastle, bringing Mitford and me up here for a tertiary." "You are very kind," said Mitty. A huge, complicated machine, connected to the operating table, with many tubes and wires, began at this moment to go pocketa-pocketa-pocketa. "The new anesthetizer is giving way!" shouted an interne. "There is no one in the East who knows how to fix it!" "Quiet, man!" said Mitty, in a low, cool voice. He sprang to the machine, which was now going pocketa-pocketa-queep-pocketa-queep. He began fingering delicately a row of glistening dials. "Give me a fountain pen!" he snapped. Someone handed him a fountain pen. He pulled a faulty piston out of the machine and inserted the pen in its place. "That will hold for ten minutes," he said. "Get on with the operation." A nurse hurried over and whispered to Renshaw, and Mitty saw the man turn pale. "Coreopsis has set in," said Renshaw nervously. "If you would take over, Mitty?" Mitty looked at him and at the craven figure of Benbow, who drank, and at the grave, uncertain faces of the two great specialists. "If you wish," he said. They slipped a white gown on him; he adjusted a mask and drew on thin gloves; nurses handed him shining . . .

"Back it up, Mac! Look out for that Buick!" Walter Mitty jammed on the brakes. "Wrong lane, Mac," said the parking-lot attendant, looking at Mitty closely. "Gee. Yeh," muttered Mitty. He began cautiously to back out of the lane marked "Exit Only." "Leave her sit there," said the attendant. "I'll put her away." Mitty got out of the car. "Hey, better leave the key." "Oh," said Mitty, handing the man the ignition key. The attendant vaulted into the car, backed it up with insolent skill, and put it where it belonged.

They're so damn cocky, thought Walter Mitty, walking along Main Street; they think they know everything. Once he had tried to take his chains off, outside New Milford, and he had got them wound around the axles. A man had had to come out in a wrecking car and unwind them, a young, grinning garageman. Since then Mrs. Mitty always made him drive to a garage to have the chains taken off. The next time, he thought, I'll wear my right arm in a sling; they won't grin at me then. I'll have my right arm in a sling and they'll see I couldn't possibly take the chains off myself. He kicked at the slush on the sidewalk. "Overshoes," he said to himself, and he began looking for a shoe store.

When he came out into the street again, with the overshoes in a box under his arm, Walter Mitty began to wonder what the other thing was his wife had told him to get. She had told him twice, before they set out from their house in Waterbury. In a way he hated these weekly trips to town—he was always getting something wrong. Kleenex, he thought, Squibb's, razor blades? No. Toothpaste, toothbrush, bicarbonate, carborundum, initiative and referendum? He gave it up. But she would remember it. "Where's the what's-its-name?" she would ask. "Don't tell me you forgot the what's-its-name." A newsboy went by shouting something about the Waterbury trial.

. . . "Perhaps this will refresh your memory." The District Attorney suddenly thrust a heavy automatic at the quiet figure on the witness stand. "Have you ever seen this before?" Walter Mitty took the gun and examined it expertly. "This is my Webley-Vickers 50.80," he said calmly. An excited buzz ran around the courtroom. The judge rapped for order. "You are a crack shot with any sort of firearms, I believe?" said the District Attorney, insinuatingly. "Objection!" shouted Mitty's attorney. "We have shown that the defendant could not have fired the shot. We have shown that he wore his right arm in a sling on the night of the fourteenth of July." Walter Mitty raised his hand briefly and the bickering attorneys were stilled. "With any known make of gun," he said evenly, "I could have killed Gregory Fitzhurst at three hundred feet *with my left hand.*" Pandemonium broke loose in the courtroom. A woman's scream rose above the bedlam and suddenly a lovely, dark-haired girl was in Walter Mitty's arms. The District Attorney struck at her savagely. Without rising from his chair, Mitty let the man have it on the point of the chin. "You miserable cur!" . . .

"Puppy biscuit," said Walter Mitty. He stopped walking and the buildings of Waterbury rose up out of the misty courtroom and surrounded him again. A woman who was passing laughed. "He said 'Puppy biscuit,'" she said to her companion. "That man said 'Puppy biscuit' to himself." Walter Mitty hurried on. He went into an A. & P., not the first one he came to but a smaller one farther up the street. "I want some biscuit for small, young dogs," he said to the clerk. "Any special brand, sir?" The greatest pistol shot in the world thought a moment. "It says 'Puppies Bark for It' on the box," said Walter Mitty.

His wife would be through at the hairdresser's in fifteen minutes, Mitty saw in looking at his watch, unless they had trouble drying it; sometimes they had trouble drying it. She didn't like to get to the hotel first; she would want him to be there waiting for her as usual. He found a big leather chair in the lobby, facing a window, and he put the overshoes and the puppy biscuit on the floor beside it. He picked up an old copy of *Liberty* and sank down into the chair. "Can Germany Conquer the World Through the Air?" Walter Mitty looked at the pictures of bombing planes and of ruined streets.

. . . "The cannonading has got the wind up in young Raleigh, sir," said the sergeant. Captain Mitty looked up at him through tousled hair. "Get him to bed," he said wearily. "With the others. I'll fly alone." "But you can't, sir," said the sergeant anxiously. "It takes two men to handle that bomber and the Archies are pounding hell out of the air. Von Richtman's circus is between here and Saulier." "Somebody's got to get that ammunition dump," said Mitty. "I'm going over. Spot of brandy?" He poured a drink for the sergeant and one for himself. War thundered and whined around the dugout and battered at the door. There was a rending of wood and splinters flew through the room. "A bit of a near thing," said Captain Mitty carelessly. "The box barrage is closing in," said the sergeant. "We only live once, Sergeant," said Mitty, with his faint, fleeting smile. "Or do we?" He poured another brandy and tossed it off. "I never see a man could hold his brandy like you, sir," said the sergeant. "Begging your pardon, sir." Captain Mitty stood up and strapped on his huge Webley-Vickers automatic. "It's forty kilometers through hell, sir," said the sergeant. Mitty finished one last brandy. "After all," he said softly, "What isn't?" The pounding of the cannon increased; there was the rat-tat-tatting of machine guns, and from somewhere came the menacing pocketa-pocketa-pocketa of the new flamthrowers. Walter Mitty walked to the door of the dugout humming "Auprès de Ma Blonde." He turned and waved to the sergeant. "Cheerio!" he said. . . .

Something struck his shoulder. "I've been looking all over this hotel for you," said Mrs. Mitty. "Why do you have to hide in this old chair? How did you expect me to find you?" "Things close in," said Walter Mitty vaguely. "What?" Mrs. Mitty said. "Did you get the what's-its-name? The puppy biscuit? What's in that box?" "Overshoes," said Mitty. "Couldn't you have put them on in the store?" "I was thinking," said Walter Mitty. "Does it ever occur to you that I am sometimes thinking?" She looked at him. "I'm going to take your temperature when I get you home," she said.

They went out through the revolving doors that made a faintly derisive whistling sound when you pushed them. It was two blocks to the parking lot. At the drugstore on the corner she said, "Wait here for me. I forgot something. I won't be a minute." She was more than a minute. Walter Mitty lighted a cigarette. It began to rain, rain with sleet in it. He stood up against the wall of the drugstore, smoking. . . . He put his shoulders back and his heels together. "To hell with the handkerchief," said Walter Mitty scornfully. He took one last drag on his cigarette and snapped it away. Then, with that faint, fleeting smile playing about his lips, he faced the firing squad; erect and motionless, proud and disdainful, Walter Mitty the Undefeated, inscrutable to the last.

Questions for Writing and Discussion

1.   One of the decisions a writer has to make is how to start a story. Thurber starts his in the very middle of a Walter Mitty fantasy—with a vivid phrase, "We're going through," that will seem familiar to anyone who has seen certain kinds of movies or read certain kinds of adventure fiction. But suppose Thurber had started with Walter Mitty as he is in reality, what would he have gained or lost? Why do some stories start "at the beginning" and others "in the middle"? Is this just an arbitrary decision?

2.   One of the things Mitty admires most in his fantasy heroes is the aplomb with which they face a crisis—while in real life he gets upset when the smallest thing goes wrong. Consider, for example, the second fantasy, Dr. Mitty with the anesthetizer "giving way," and relate it to the incident of Mitty and the car that immediately follows. How has Thurber aligned each incident of fantasy with each incident of reality?

3.   Once you get the idea of the story—the alternation of grandiose fantasy and miserable reality—there isn't much chance that it will yield many surprises for you. How, then, does Thurber succeed in holding your interest? Consider, especially, details of language—the throw-away lines that the fantasy Mitty speaks, or, by contrast, the hilarious business about the brand of puppy food he buys.

4.   In the imaginary reply that Walter Mitty writes to James Thurber (pp. 155–157), Mitty indicates a certain view about the ending of the story. Do you agree with this? Do you see other possible ways of regarding the last few sentences?

SHOLOM ALEICHEM

On Account of a Hat

Introduction

In reading this story, the first thing you're likely to notice is a voice. It is the voice of the narrator, a rather shrewd fellow who likes to think of himself as worldly, though he comes from the same obscure little town as the "scatter-brain" about whom he tells his story. This voice is sly, clever, self-assured. It reaches out for the attention of its listener partly through a series of buttonhol-ing parenthetical phrases ("now listen to this," "get a load of this"). It speaks with the air of the skilled storyteller who keeps prodding the listener as if to say, "wait, wait, this will really be a good one." And we keep listening, as the voice sticks to the main line of the story and as it goes off occasionally on a side path to follow some general observation. For, gradually, we're persuaded that it's a voice with a wry, expert knowledge of the way the world really is.

Sholom Aleichem (which in Hebrew means "Peace Unto You") was the pen-name of the greatest Yiddish writer, Sholom Rabinowitz, who lived most of his life in Tsarist Russia, and the last few years in the United States. He was a master of Yiddish speech: pithy, idiomatic, drenched with ironies. Like no one else, he caught the outlook of modern Jews, their complex mixture of the idealistic and the hard-headed, the sentimental and the sardonic. All translations of his stories lose a good deal of the original verbal play and cleverness, but this one by Isaac Rosenfeld manages to work out a lively English equivalent.

The main character about whom the narrator tells his anecdote is Sholem Shachnah, a harassed fellow trying to earn a few pennies with which to feed wife and children, yet by nature hopeful and optimistic. In Yiddish he would be called a *luftmensh,* literally, a man of the air, which means a fellow who gets by on his wits, doing an odd job here, making a trivial deal there, talking big and earning little. He's a ne'er-do-well, not because he's lazy, but because he lives in Tsarist Russia a few years before the turn of the twentieth century, where most Jews did not have much opportunity to earn a living. So he scrapes through, bites his nails, and dreams.

163

Now comes the anecdote at the heart of Sholom Aleichem's story. Our bumbling Sholem Shachnah gets ready for his trip home for the Passover holiday; he's made a few cents; and then there occurs the complication with Buttons' hat, which then leads everyone to think that he, Sholem Shachnah, is an official meriting the title "Your Excellency," which then leads him, Sholem Shachnah, to look in the mirror and think, poor rattle-brain that he is, that it's not he who is staring back at him out of the mirror (for how could a poor Jew be wearing an official's hat?), but Buttons himself and that he, Sholem Shachnah, is still asleep at the station, having missed his train. So finally this leads him to go back and actually miss the train, whereupon he spends a miserable Passover with strangers and ends up with an earful from his wife and a razzing from his townspeople.

It's a funny story, but a funny story with a sad twist. For, after all, Sholem Shachnah is a nice fellow and his wife, despite her abrasive tongue, isn't so terrible either, and their misfortunes make us sympathize with them. But more: it's a story which, like most good stories, has hidden or half-hidden depths of implication. As long as he's dressed in the clothes of a poor Jew, Sholem Shachnah can expect to be treated like dirt. Yet when he puts on the official's hat "with the red band," everyone treats him as if he were a man of power and dignity. What then is the difference between those who give orders and those who must obey them? A red band, a cardboard visor, a mere badge!

Another detail. When Sholem Shachnah finally gets back home, his wife laces into him, in the great tradition of angry wives. As the narrator remarks, in one of his amusing asides, "Well, that's what wives are for." But she has a more serious complaint: "the telegram! And not so much the telegram—you hear what I say?—as the one short phrase, *without fail*. What possessed him to put that into the wire: *Arriving home Passover without fail*. Was he trying to make the telegraph company rich? And besides, how dare a human being say 'without fail' in the first place?"

In that last sentence is compressed a whole tradition of wisdom: life is precarious, life is often beyond our control, life is beset by constant peril—you hear what I say?

On Account of a Hat

"Did I hear you say absent-minded? Now, in our town, that is, in Kasri-levke,[1] we've really got someone for you—do you hear what I say? His name is Sholem Shachnah, but we call him Sholem Shachnah Rattlebrain, and is he

---

[1] A fictional small town in the Ukraine.

ON ACCOUNT OF A HAT by Sholom Aleichem, translated by Isaac Rosenfeld. From *A Treasury of Yiddish Stories,* edited by Irving Howe and Eliezer Greenberg. Copyright 1954 by The Viking Press, Inc. Reprinted by permission of the publishers.

absent-minded, is this a distracted creature, Lord have mercy on us! The stories they tell about him, about this Sholem Shachnah—bushels and baskets of stories—I tell you, whole crates full of stories and anecdotes! It's too bad you're in such a hurry on account of the Passover, because what I could tell you, Mr. Sholom Aleichem—do you hear what I say?—you could go on writing it down forever. But if you can spare a moment I'll tell you a story about what happened to Sholem Shachnah on a Passover eve—a story about a hat, a true story, I should live so, even if it does sound like someone made it up."

These were the words of a Kasrilevke merchant, a dealer in stationery, that is to say, snips of paper. He smoothed out his beard, folded it down over his neck, and went on smoking his thin little cigarettes, one after the other.

I must confess that this true story, which he related to me, does indeed sound like a concocted one, and for a long time I couldn't make up my mind whether or not I should pass it on to you. But I thought it over and decided that if a respectable merchant and dignitary of Kasrilevke, who deals in stationery and is surely no *litterateur*[2]—if he vouches for a story, it must be true. What would he be doing with fiction? Here it is in his own words. I had nothing to do with it.

This Sholem Shachnah I'm telling you about, whom we call Sholem Shachnah Rattlebrain, is a real-estate broker—you hear what I say? He's always with landowners, negotiating transactions. Transactions? Well, at least he hangs around the landowners. So what's the point? I'll tell you. Since he hangs around the landed gentry, naturally some of their manner has rubbed off on him, and he always has a mouth full of farms, homesteads, plots, acreage, soil, threshing machines, renovations, woods, timber, and other such terms having to do with estates.

One day God took pity on Sholem Shachnah, and for the first time in his career as a real-estate broker—are you listening?—he actually worked out a deal. That is to say, the work itself, as you can imagine, was done by others, and when the time came to collect the fee, the big rattler turned out to be not Sholem Shachnah Rattlebrain, but Drobkin, a Jew from Minsk province, a great big fearsome rattler, a real-estate broker from way back—he and his two brothers, also brokers and also big rattlers. So you can take my word for it, there was quite a to-do. A Jew has contrived and connived and has finally, with God's help, managed to cut himself in—so what do they do but come along and cut him out! Where's Justice? Sholem Shachnah wouldn't stand for it—are you listening to me? He set up such a holler and an outcry—"Look what they've done to me!"—that at last they gave in to shut him up, and good riddance it was too.

When he got his few cents Sholem Shachnah sent the greater part of it home to his wife, so she could pay off some debts, shoo the wolf from the door, fix up new outfits for the children, and make ready for the Passover holidays. And as for himself, he also needed a few things, and besides he had to buy presents for his family, as was the custom.

---

[2]French: literary person.

Meanwhile the time flew by, and before he knew it, it was almost Passover. So Sholem Shachnah—now listen to this—ran to the telegraph office and sent home a wire: *Arriving home Passover without fail.* It's easy to say "arriving" and "without fail" at that. But you just try it! Just try riding out our way on the new train and see how fast you'll arrive. Ah, what a pleasure! Did they do us a favor! I tell you, Mr. Sholom Aleichem, for a taste of Paradise such as this you'd gladly forsake your own grandchildren! You see how it is: until you get to Zlodievka there isn't much you can do about it, so you just lean back and ride. But at Zlodievka the fun begins, because that's where you have to change, to get onto the new train, which they did us such a favor by running out to Kasrilevke. But not so fast. First, there's the little matter of several hours' wait, exactly as announced in the schedule—provided, of course, that you don't pull in after the Kasrilevke train has left. And at what time of night may you look forward to this treat? The very middle, thank you, when you're dead tired and disgusted, without a friend in the world except sleep—and there's not one single place in the whole station where you can lay your head, not one. When the wise men of Kasrilevke quote the passage from the Holy Book, *"Tov shem meshemon tov,"* they know what they're doing. I'll translate it for you: We were better off without the train.

To make a long story short, when our Sholem Shachnah arrived in Zlodievka with his carpetbag he was half dead; he had already spent two nights without sleep. But that was nothing at all to what was facing him—he still had to spend the whole night waiting in the station. What shall he do? Naturally he looked around for a place to sit down. Whoever heard of such a thing? Nowhere. Nothing. No place to sit. The walls of the station were covered with soot, the floor was covered with spit. It was dark, it was terrible. He finally discovered one miserable spot on a bench where he had just room enough to squeeze in, and no more than that, because the bench was occupied by an official of some sort in a uniform full of buttons, who was lying there all stretched out and snoring away to beat the band. Who this Buttons was, whether he was coming or going, he hadn't the vaguest idea, Sholem Shachnah, that is. But he could tell that Buttons was no dime-a-dozen official. This was plain by his cap, a military cap with a red band and a visor. He could have been an officer or a police official. Who knows? But surely he had drawn up to the station with a ringing of bells, had staggered in, full to the ears with meat and drink, laid himself out on the bench, as in his father's vineyard, and worked up a glorious snoring.

It's not such a bad life to be a gentile, and an official one at that, with buttons, thinks he, Sholem Shachnah, that is, and he wonders, dare he sit next to this Buttons, or hadn't he better keep his distance? Nowadays you never can tell whom you're sitting next to. If he's no more than a plain inspector, that's still all right. But what if he turns out to be a district inspector? Or a provincial commander? Or even higher than that? And supposing this is even Purishke-vitch[3] himself, the famous anti-Semite, may his name perish? Let someone else

---

[3]A notorious Russian anti-semite.

deal with him and Sholem Shachnah turns cold at the mere thought of falling into such a fellow's hands. But then he says to himself—now listen to this—Buttons, he says, who the hell is Buttons? And who gives a hang for Purishkevitch? Don't I pay my fare the same as Purishkevitch? So why should he have all the comforts of life and I none? If Buttons is entitled to a delicious night's sleep, then doesn't he, Sholem Shachnah that is, at least have a nap coming? After all, he's human too, and besides, he's already gone two nights without a wink. And so he sits down, on a corner of the bench, and leans his head back, not, God forbid, to sleep, but just like that, to snooze. But all of a sudden he remembers—he's supposed to be home for Passover, and tomorrow is Passover eve! What if, God have mercy, he should fall asleep and miss his train? But that's why he's got a Jewish head on his shoulders—are you listening to me or not?—so he figures out the answer to that one too, Sholem Shachnah, that is, and goes looking for the porter, a certain Yeremei, he knows him well, to make a deal with him. Whereas he, Sholem Shachnah, is already on his third sleepless night and is afraid, God forbid, that he may miss his train, therefore let him, Yeremei, that is, in God's name, be sure to wake him, Sholem Shachnah, because tomorrow night is a holiday, Passover. "Easter," he says to him in Russian and lays a coin in Yeremei's mitt. "Easter, Yeremei, do you understand, *goyisher kop?*[4] Our Easter." The peasant pockets the coin, no doubt about that, and promises to wake him at the first sign of the train—he can sleep soundly and put his mind at rest. So Sholem Shachnah sits down in his corner of the bench, gingerly, pressed up against the wall, with his carpetbag curled around him so that no one should steal it. Little by little he sinks back, makes himself comfortable, and half shuts his eyes—no more than forty winks, you understand. But before long he's got one foot propped up on the bench and then the other; he stretches out and drifts off to sleep. Sleep? I'll say sleep, like God commanded us: with his head thrown back and his hat rolling away on the floor, Sholem Shachnah is snoring like an eight-day wonder. After all, a human being, up two nights in a row—what would you have him do?

He had a strange dream. He tells this himself, that is, Sholem Shachnah does. He dreamed that he was riding home for Passover—are you listening to me?—but not on the train, in a wagon, driven by a thievish peasant, Ivan Zlodi we call him. The horses were terribly slow, they barely dragged along. Sholem Shachnah was impatient, and he poked the peasant between the shoulders and cried, "May you only drop dead, Ivan darling! Hurry up, you lout! Passover is coming, our Jewish Easter!" Once he called out to him, twice, three times. The thief paid him no mind. But all of a sudden he whipped his horses to a gallop and they went whirling away, up hill and down, like demons. Sholem Shachnah lost his hat. Another minute of this and he would have lost God knows what. "Whoa, there, Ivan old boy! Where's the fire? Not so fast!" cried Sholem Shachnah. He covered his head with his hands—he was worried, you see, over his lost hat. How can he drive into town bareheaded? But for all the good it did him, he could have been hollering at a post. Ivan the Thief was racing the horses as if

---

[4]Yiddish: literally, gentile head, but used as a term indicating slow wits.

forty devils were after him. All of a sudden—tppprrru!—they came to a dead stop, right in the middle of the field—you hear me?—a dead stop. What's the matter? Nothing. "Get up," said Ivan, "time to get up."

Time? What time? Sholem Shachnah is all confused. He wakes up, rubs his eyes, and is all set to step out of the wagon when he realizes he has lost his hat. Is he dreaming or not? And what's he doing here? Sholem Shachnah finally comes to his senses and recognizes the peasant—this isn't Ivan Zlodi at all but Yeremei the porter. So he concludes that he isn't on the high road after all, but in the station at Zlodievka, on the way home for Passover, and that if he means to get there he'd better run to the window for a ticket, but fast. Now what? No hat. The carpetbag is right where he left it, but his hat? He pokes around under the bench, reaching all over, until he comes up with a hat—not his own, to be sure, but the official's, with the red band and the visor. But Sholem Shachnah has no time for details and he rushes off to buy a ticket. The ticket window is jammed, everybody and his cousins are crowding in. Sholem Shachnah thinks he won't get to the window in time, perish the thought, and he starts pushing forward, carpetbag and all. The people see the red band and the visor and they make way for him. "Where to, Your Excellency?" asks the ticket agent. What's this Excellency, all of a sudden? wonders Sholem Shachnah, and he rather resents it. Some joke, a gentile poking fun at a Jew. All the same he says, Sholem Shachnah, that is, "Kasrilevke." "Which class, Your Excellency?" The ticket agent is looking straight at the red band and the visor. Sholem Shachnah is angrier than ever. I'll give him an Excellency, so he'll know how to make fun of a poor Jew! But then he thinks, Oh, well, we Jews are in Diaspora—do you hear what I say?—let it pass. And he asks for a ticket third class. "Which class?" The agent blinks at him, very much surprised. This time Sholem Shachnah gets good and sore and he really tells him off. "Third!" says he. All right, thinks the agent, third is third.

In short, Sholem Shachnah buys his ticket, takes up his carpetbag, runs out onto the platform, plunges into the crowd of Jews and gentiles, no comparison intended, and goes looking for the third-class carriage. Again the red band and the visor work like a charm, everyone makes way for the official. Sholem Shachnah is wondering, What goes on here? But he runs along the platform till he meets a conductor carrying a lantern. "Is this third class?" asks Sholem Shachnah, putting one foot on the stairs and shoving his bag into the door of the compartment. "Yes, Your Excellency," says the conductor, but he holds him back. "If you please, sir, it's packed full, as tight as your fist. You couldn't squeeze a needle into that crowd." And he takes Sholem Shachnah's carpetbag—you hear what I'm saying?—and sings out, "Right this way, Your Excellency, I'll find you a seat." "What the Devil!" cries Sholem Shachnah. "Your Excellency and Your Excellency!" But he hasn't much time for the fine points; he's worried about his carpetbag. He's afraid, you see, that with all these Excellencies he'll be swindled out of his belongings. So he runs after the conductor with the lantern, who leads him into a second-class carriage. This is also packed to the rafters, no room even to yawn in there. "This way please, Your Excellency!" And again the conductor grabs the bag and Sholem Shachnah lights out after him. "Where in blazes is he taking me?" Sholem Shachnah is racking his brains over this Excellency business, but meanwhile he keeps his eye on the main thing—the carpetbag. They enter the first-class carriage, the conductor sets down the bag, salutes, and backs away, bowing. Sholem Shachnah bows right back. And there he is, alone at last.

Left alone in the carriage, Sholem Shachnah looks around to get his bearings—you hear what I say? He has no idea why all these honors have suddenly been heaped on him—first class, salutes, Your Excellency. Can it be on account of the real-estate deal he just closed? That's it! But wait a minute. If his own people, Jews, that is, honored him for this, it would be understandable. But gentiles! The conductor! The ticket agent! What's it to them? Maybe he's dreaming. Sholem Shachnah rubs his forehead, and while passing down the corridor glances into the mirror on the wall. It nearly knocks him over! He sees not himself but the official with the red band. That's who it is! "All my bad dreams on Yeremei's head and on his hands and feet, that lug! Twenty times I tell him to wake me and I even give him a tip, and what does he do, that dumb ox, may he catch cholera in his face, but wake the official instead! And me he leaves asleep on the bench! Tough luck, Sholem Shachnah old boy, but this year you'll spend Passover in Zlodievka, not at home."

Now get a load of this. Sholem Shachnah scoops up his carpetbag and rushes off once more, right back to the station where he is sleeping on the bench. He's going to wake himself up before the locomotive, God forbid, lets out a blast and blasts his Passover to pieces. And so it was. No sooner had Sholem Shachnah leaped out of the carriage with his carpetbag than the locomotive did let go with a blast—do you hear me?—one followed by another, and then, good night!

The paper dealer smiled as he lit a fresh cigarette, thin as a straw. "And would you like to hear the rest of the story? The rest isn't so nice. On account of being such a rattlebrain, our dizzy Sholem Shachnah had a miserable Passover, spending both Seders among strangers in the house of a Jew in Zlodievka. But this was nothing—listen to what happened afterward. First of all, he has a wife, Sholem Shachnah, that is, and his wife—how shall I describe her to you? *I* have a wife, *you* have a wife, we all have wives, we've had a taste of Paradise, we know what it means to be married. All I can say about Sholem Shachnah's wife is that she's A Number One. And did she give him a royal welcome! Did she lay into him! Mind you, she didn't complain about his spending the holiday away from home, and she said nothing about the red band and the visor. She let that stand for the time being; she'd take it up with him later. The only thing she complained about was—the telegram! And not so much the telegram—you hear what I say?—as the one short phrase, *without fail.* What possessed him to put that into the wire: *Arriving home Passover without fail.* Was he trying to make the telegraph company rich? And besides, how dare a human being say 'without fail' in the first place? It did him no good to answer and explain. She buried him alive. Oh, well, that's what wives are for. And not that she was altogether wrong—after all, she had been waiting so anxiously. But this was nothing compared with what he caught from the town, Kasrilevke, that is. Even before he returned the whole town—you hear what I say?—knew all about Yeremei and the official and the red band and the visor and the conductor's Your Excellency—the whole show. He himself, Sholem Shachnah, that is, denied everything and swore up and down that the Kasrilevke smart-alecks had invented the entire story for lack of anything better to do. It was all very simple—the reason he came home late, after the holidays, was that he had made a special trip to inspect a wooded estate. Woods? Estate? Not a chance—no one bought *that!* They pointed him out in the streets and held their sides, laughing. And everybody asked him, 'How does it feel, Reb Sholem Shachnah, to wear a cap with a red band and a visor?' 'And tell us,' said others, 'what's it like to travel first class?' As for the children, this was made to order for them—you hear what I say? Wherever he went they trooped after him, shouting, 'Your Excellency! Your excellent Excellency! Your most excellent Excellency!'

"You think it's so easy to put one over on Kasrilevke?"

Translated by Isaac Rosenfeld

Questions for Writing and Discussion

1. Sholom Aleichem wrote mainly about the culture of the east European Jews in the last third of the nineteenth century and first decade of the twentieth century. It was a culture marked by poverty so extreme that in a story like "On Account of a Hat" this poverty is simply taken for granted. Still, one of the most interesting things in reading a work of fiction is to try to discover precisely those of its assumptions which are most deeply present, or buried, in the writing. In a story like this one, you can hardly understand what's happening unless you become aware of the importance of the theme of poverty. With that in mind, go through the story again and see if you can find evidence for the above statements.

2. Just as poverty is a recurrent theme or motif in the story, so too is a certain view of Jewish mind, or Jewish intelligence, or Jewish wit. We won't try to say here what that view is, except to remark that it's by no means a simple one. Again, go through the story and see if you think we're right on this one.

3. "On Account of a Hat" is written as a story within a story. We hear the voice of the narrator as he tells us about Sholem Shachnah, though at one or two points his voice breaks off and the author, Sholom Aleichem, himself speaks out in his own right before turning things over again to the narrator. What, then, is the use of the narrator? How does he help establish the tone, and thereby the meaning, of the story?

4. Reread the last sentence. Does it seem a sudden shift of focus? What do you think the author is doing with this sentence?

THE SOLITARY SELF

ANTON CHEKHOV

The Bishop

Introduction

Anton Chekhov, the Russian playwright and short story writer, is one of the very few writers about whom it can be said that he changed the course of world literature. Great short stories had of course been written before him, by Nathaniel Hawthorne in the United States, Leo Tolstoy in Russia, Guy de Maupassant in France. But the modern short story as we have come to know it derives largely from Chekhov. There is hardly a master of the short story in the twentieth century, from Ernest Hemingway to Isaac Babel, who does not bear the imprint of Chekhov. Sometimes that imprint comes through as a direct influence in style and tone; sometimes as a force that, for a later writer wishing to preserve his individuality, must be strongly resisted.

Can we describe *the* Chekhov story, not this or the other, but the typical one? It may be foolhardy to try, but let us go ahead, anyway.

The old tricks, the old devices are largely abandoned: no intricate or elaborate plotting, no melodrama, no wish-fulfilling conclusions, no flashy or precious diction, no exotic settings, no extended analysis of character, no fancy or obscure symbolism, no moralizing from on high or sensationalism from below. Chekhov is a poet of the commonplace. He is a writer who celebrates and mourns—often the two together—ordinary life. Life as it is, life in its gray, shapeless flow, is enough for him. His imagination is stirred by the seemingly trivial, and through it he breaks into a sense of the tragic.

Reading his stories, we join the life of a man or a woman at some point in mid-passage, and then, for a greater or shorter time, we share a journey. Chekhov's characters are seldom fresh to the world, seldom innocent; usually they are people who have been battered and bruised into reflectiveness, sometimes a melancholy reflectiveness. Chekhov himself comes along with us as a guide, speaking with quiet detachment, never using anything but a pure and simple language.

He notices that even in the most uneventful lives there gather forces of trouble, moments of crisis, undertows of disintegration. He watches these forces, as they emerge into the open and sometimes overwhelm the people upon whom they act. He watches from a certain distance, but not the distance of coldness. He is intensely sympathetic yet detached, like a good doctor.

The climax of a Chekhov story comes, usually, as a small event. Perhaps it is a visit to a place associated with youthful desires; perhaps it is a conversation with a man or woman, as in "The Bishop," whom the central character has loved but been separated from; perhaps it is a personal intuition that something has gone wrong, life has dribbled away, nothing can now be done but to accept one's fate with dignity and courage. Realizations of failure, recognitions that the dreams of youth will not be fulfilled, discoveries of one's inescapable limitations—such are, often, the outcomes of Chekhov's stories.

Conventional heroism plays little part in these stories. People seldom make grand gestures (except in self-mockery). They seldom engage in violent actions. They seldom display their bravery. No; Chekhov deals with ordinary people who work, yearn, dream, and see their years waste away. Still, these people do have a kind of heroism—a heroism of quiet endurance. They do their duty, they live with forebearance, they survive. Stoicism becomes their line of defense. (In "The Bishop," the leading character reveals this kind of heroism, continuing to meet his obligations even when he is in pain and accepting his own dissolution without a whimper or complaint.)

Chekhov creates the illusion of a natural flow of life. His work seems artless, though that is an illusion possible only to the greatest artists. If you look carefully at "The Bishop," you will see that the apparent jumble of detail works itself out as a seamless continuity of experience. Each little incident, each little touch serves to reveal the Bishop's feelings, and at the same time, to work out the meanings, the implications that Chekhov has in mind.

Portraying his characters, Chekhov does not "take sides." He neither blames the strong nor praises the weak; neither praises the strong nor blames the weak. He does not moralize, he is never righteous, he rejects postures of superiority. He was himself a doctor, and perhaps that training—though it surely doesn't have that effect on most doctors!—enabled him to see all people as fellow-creatures not to be dismissed, not to be condemned.

Chekhov came to Russian literature after the towering giants, Tolstoy and Dostoevsky. Both of these great writers were intent upon advancing philosophical world-views, religious ideologies. Chekhov is more modest, more the pure artist. Strong residues of Christian feeling, especially that loving-kindness called "charity" in the Bible, remained with Chekhov throughout his career, but he did not try to convert his readers to anything: not to Christianity, not to socialism, not to any system or belief. He does not twist our arms, he speaks to our hearts.

The aim of serious literature, he wrote, is "truth, unconditional and honest." The writer "should be, not the judge of his characters and their conversations, but only an unbiased witness." In a letter to a friend he said:

> I fear those who seek tendencies between the lines [of a story] and who without fail wish to see me as a liberal or a conservative. I am not a liberal, not a

conservative, not a gradualist, not a monk, and not an indifferentist. I would like to be a free artist—and that's all. . . . I regard trademarks and labels as prejudices. My holy of holies is the human body, health, mind, talent, inspiration, love and absolute freedom—freedom from violence and lies. . . . Here you have the program to which I would adhere if I were a great artist.

If ever any writer came close to realizing all this in his work, it was Anton Chekhov. One of his Russian critics, Leonid Grossman, has a passage which nicely sums up all that we have been getting at:

Chekhov's chief strength lives in a love for man which overcame all revulsion. At root, he did not bring to his creations any new philosophy. . . . Chekhov was not a thinker of genius. He did not leave humanity revelations which strike one by their newness, boldness, or depth. . . . Even in the sphere of abstract wisdom, as in his purely artistic pages, he spoke the most simple words devoid of any philosophical profundity. Everything that is said in his works about the fate of the world and of people is in essence so simple that it might enter the head of any ordinary person. . . . But Chekhov expressed this simple wisdom in words so magically beautiful, and, in their beauty, so comforting, that everyone was left with the impression that somehow he had been reassured about something, that he had been reconciled with something, that something had been set right.

Yes, that is the effect created by Chekhov's stories. Meanwhile, however, there's still "The Bishop," about which we've said very little. But what need is there for analyzing this great story? All that we have to do is read it for pleasure and illumination—better still, the pleasure of illumination.

The Bishop

It was on the eve of Palm Sunday; vespers[1] were being sung in the Staro-Petrovski Convent. The hour was nearly ten when the palm leaves were distributed, and the little shrine lamps were growing dim; their wicks had burnt low, and a soft haze hung in the chapel. As the worshippers surged forward in the twilight like the waves of the sea, it seemed to his Reverence Peter, who had been feeling ill for three days, that the people who came to him for palm leaves all looked alike, and, men or women, old or young, all had the same expression in their eyes. He could not see the doors through the haze; the endless procession rolled toward him, and seemed as if it must go on rolling for ever. A choir of women's voices was singing and a nun was reading the canon.

[1]A religious service, usually musical, in the evening.

THE BISHOP by Anton Chekhov. From *The Oxford Chekhov: Volume 9, Stories 1898–1904,* translated and edited by Ronald Hingley and published by Oxford University Press. Copyright 1975 by Ronald Hingley. Reprinted by permission of the publishers.

How hot and close the air was, and how long the prayers! His Reverence was tired. His dry, parching breath was coming quickly and painfully, his shoulders were aching, and his legs were trembling. The occasional cries of an idiot in the gallery annoyed him. And now, as a climax, his Reverence saw, as in a delirium, his own mother whom he had not seen for nine years coming toward him in the crowd. She, or an old woman exactly like her, took a palm leaf from his hands, and moved away looking at him all the while with a glad, sweet smile, until she was lost in the crowd. And for some reason the tears began to course down his cheeks. His heart was happy and peaceful, but his eyes were fixed on a distant part of the chapel where the prayers were being read, and where no human being could be distinguished among the shadows. The tears glistened on his cheeks and beard. Then some one who was standing near him began to weep, too, and then another, and then another, until little by little the chapel was filled with a low sound of weeping. Then the convent choir began to sing, the weeping stopped, and everything went on as before.

Soon afterward the service ended. The fine, jubilant notes of the heavy chapel-bells were throbbing through the moonlit garden as the bishop stepped into his coach and drove away. The white walls, the crosses on the graves, the silvery birches, and the far-away moon hanging directly over the monastery, all seemed to be living a life of their own, incomprehensible, but very near to mankind. It was early in April, and a chilly night had succeeded a warm spring day. A light frost was falling, but the breath of spring could be felt in the soft, cool air. The road from the monastery was sandy, the horses were obliged to proceed at a walk, and, bathed in the bright, tranquil moonlight, a stream of pilgrims was crawling along on either side of the coach. All were thoughtful, no one spoke. Everything around them, the trees, the sky, and even the moon, looked so young and intimate and friendly that they were reluctant to break the spell which they hoped might last for ever.

Finally the coach entered the city, and rolled down the main street. All the stores were closed but that of Erakin, the millionaire merchant. He was trying his electric lights for the first time, and they were flashing so violently that a crowd had collected in front of the store. Then came wide, dark streets in endless succession, and then the highway, and fields, and the smell of pines. Suddenly a white crenelated wall loomed before him, and beyond it rose a tall belfry flanked by five flashing golden cupolas, all bathed in moonlight. This was the Pankratievski Monastery where his Reverence Peter lived. Here, too, the calm, brooding moon was floating directly above the monastery. The coach drove through the gate, its wheels crunching on the sand. Here and there the dark forms of monks started out into the moonlight and footsteps rang along the flagstone paths.

"Your mother has been here while you were away, your Reverence," a lay brother told the bishop as he entered his room.

"My mother? When did she come?"

"Before vespers. She first found out where you were, and then drove to the convent."

"Then it was she whom I saw just now in the chapel! Oh, Father in heaven!"

And his Reverence laughed for joy.

"She told me to tell you, your Reverence," the lay brother continued, "that she would come back tomorrow. She had a little girl with her, a grandchild, I think. She is stopping at Ovsianikoff's inn."

"What time is it now?"

"It is after eleven."

"What a nuisance!"

His Reverence sat down irresolutely in his sitting-room, unwilling to believe that it was already so late. His arms and legs were racked with pain, the back of his neck was aching, and he felt uncomfortable and hot. When he had rested a few moments he went into his bedroom and there, too, he sat down, and dreamed of his mother. He heard the lay brother walking away and Father Sisoi the priest coughing in the next room. The monastery clock struck the quarter.

His Reverence undressed and began his prayers. He spoke the old, familiar words with scrupulous attention, and at the same time he thought of his mother. She had nine children, and about forty grandchildren. She had lived from the age of seventeen to the age of sixty with her husband the deacon in a little village. His Reverence remembered her from the days of his earliest childhood, and, ah, how he had loved her! Oh, that dear, precious, unforgettable childhood of his! Why did those years that had vanished for ever seem so much brighter and richer and gayer than they really had been? How tender and kind his mother had been when he was ill in his childhood and youth! His prayers mingled with the memories that burned ever brighter and brighter in his heart like a flame, but they did not hinder his thoughts of his mother.

When he had prayed he lay down, and as soon as he found himself in the dark there rose before his eyes the vision of his dead father, his mother, and Lyesopolye, his native village. The creaking of wagon wheels, the bleating of sheep, the sound of church-bells on a clear summer morning, ah, how pleasant it was to think of these things! He remembered Father Simeon, the old priest at Lyesopolye, a kind, gentle, good-natured old man. He himself had been small, and the priest's son had been a huge strapping novice with a terrible bass voice. He remembered how this young priest had scolded the cook once, and had shouted: "Ah, you she-ass of Jehovah!" And Father Simeon had said nothing, and had only been mortified because he could not for the life of him remember reading of an ass of that name in the Bible!

Father Simeon had been succeeded by Father Demian, a hard drinker who sometimes even went so far as to see green snakes. He had actually borne the nickname of "Demian the Snake-Seer" in the village. Matvei Nikolaitch had been the schoolmaster, a kind, intelligent man, but a hard drinker too. He never thrashed his scholars, but for some reason he kept a little bundle of birch twigs hanging on his wall, under which was a tablet bearing the absolutely unintelligible inscription: "Betula Kinderbalsamica Secuta." He had had a woolly black dog whom he called "Syntax."

The bishop laughed. Eight miles from Lyesopolye lay the village of Obnino possessing a miraculous icon. A procession started from Obnino every summer bearing the wonder-working icon and making the round of all the neighbouring villages. The church-bells would ring all day long first in one village, then in another, and to Little Paul (his Reverence was called Little Paul then) the air itself seemed tremulous with rapture. Barefoot, hatless, and infinitely happy, he followed the icon with a naïve smile on his lips and naïve faith in his heart.

Until the age of fifteen Little Paul had been so slow at his lessons that his parents had even thought of taking him out of the ecclesiastical school and putting him to work in the village store.

The bishop turned over so as to break the train of his thoughts, and tried to go to sleep.

"My mother has come!" he remembered, and laughed.

The moon was shining in through the window, and the floor was lit by its rays while he lay in shadow. A cricket was chirping. Father Sisoi was snoring in the next room, and there was a forlorn, friendless, even a vagrant note in the old man's cadences.

Sisoi had once been the steward of a diocesan bishop and was known as "Father Former Steward." He was seventy years old, and lived sometimes in a monastery sixteen miles away, sometimes in the city, sometimes wherever he happened to be. Three days ago he had turned up at the Pankratievski Monastery, and the bishop had kept him here in order to discuss with him at his leisure the affairs of the monastery.

The bell for matins rang at half past one. Father Sisoi coughed, growled something, and got up.

"Father Sisoi!" called the bishop.

Sisoi came in dressed in a white cassock, carrying a candle in his hand.

"I can't go to sleep," his Reverence said. "I must be ill. I don't know what the matter is; I have fever."

"You have caught cold, your Lordship. I must rub you with tallow."

Father Sisoi stood looking at him for a while and yawned: "Ah-h—the Lord have mercy on us!"

"Erakin has electricity in his store now—I hate it!" he continued.

Father Sisoi was aged, and round-shouldered, and gaunt. He was always displeased with something or other, and his eyes, which protruded like those of a crab, always wore an angry expression.

"I don't like it at all," he repeated—"I hate it."

II

Next day, on Palm Sunday, his Reverence officiated at the cathedral in the city. Then he went to the diocesan bishop's, then to see a general's wife who was very ill, and at last he drove home. At two o'clock two beloved guests were having dinner with him, his aged mother, and his little niece Kitty, a child of eight. The spring sun was peeping cheerily in through the windows as they sat at their meal, and was shining merrily on the white tablecloth, and on Kitty's red hair. Through the double panes they heard the rooks cawing, and the magpies chattering in the garden.

"It is nine years since I saw you last," said the old mother, "and yet when I caught sight of you in the convent chapel yesterday I thought to myself: God bless me, he has not changed a bit! Only perhaps you are a little thinner than you were, and your beard has grown longer. Oh, holy Mother, Queen of Heaven! Everybody was crying yesterday. As soon as I saw you, I began to cry myself, I don't know why. His holy will be done!"

In spite of the tenderness with which she said this, it was clear that she was not at her ease. It was as if she did not know whether to address the bishop by the familiar "thee" or the formal "you," and whether she ought to laugh or not. She seemed to feel herself more of a poor deacon's wife than a mother in his presence. Meanwhile Kitty was sitting with her eyes glued to the face of her uncle the bishop as if she were trying to make out what manner of man this was. Her hair had escaped from her comb and her bow of velvet ribbon, and was standing straight up around her head like a halo. Her eyes were foxy and bright. She had broken a glass before sitting down, and now, as she talked, her grandmother kept moving first a glass, and then a wine glass out of her reach. As the bishop sat listening to his mother, he remembered how, many, many years ago, she had sometimes taken him and his brothers and sisters to visit relatives whom they considered rich. She had been busy with her own children in those days, and now she was busy with her grandchildren, and had come to visit him with Kitty here.

"Your sister Varenka has four children"—she was telling him—"Kitty is the oldest. God knows why, her father fell ill and died three days before Assumption. So my Varenka has been thrown out into the cold world."

"And how is my brother Nikanor?" the bishop asked.

"He is well, thank the Lord. He is pretty well, praise be to God. But his son Nikolasha wouldn't go into the church, and is at college instead learning to be a doctor. He thinks it is best, but who knows? However, God's will be done!"

"Nikolasha cuts up dead people!" said Kitty, spilling some water into her lap.

"Sit still child!" her grandmother said, quietly taking the glass out of her hands.

"How long it is since we have seen one another!" exclaimed his Reverence, tenderly stroking his mother's shoulder and hand. "I missed you when I was abroad, I missed you dreadfully."

"Thank you very much!"

"I used to sit by my window in the evening listening to the band playing, and feeling lonely and forlorn. Sometimes I would suddenly grow so homesick that I used to think I would gladly give everything I had in the world for a glimpse of you and home."

His mother smiled and beamed, and then immediately drew a long face and said stiffly:

"Thank you very much!"

The Bishop's mood changed. He looked at his mother, and could not understand where she had acquired that deferential, humble expression of face and voice, and what the meaning of it might be. He hardly recognised her, and felt sorrowful and vexed. Besides, his head was still aching, and his legs were racked with pain. The fish he was eating tasted insipid and he was very thirsty.

After dinner two wealthy lady landowners visited him, and sat for an hour and a half with faces a mile long, never uttering a word. Then an archimandrite,[2] a gloomy, taciturn man, came on business. Then the bells rang for vespers, the sun set behind the woods, and the day was done. As soon as he got back from church the bishop said his prayers, and went to bed, drawing the covers up closely about his ears. The moonlight troubled him, and soon the sound of voices came to his ears. Father Sisoi was talking politics with his mother in the next room.

"There is a war in Japan now," he was saying. "The Japanese belong to the same race as the Montenegrins. They fell under the Turkish yoke at the same time."

And then the bishop heard his mother's voice say:

"And so, you see, when we had said our prayers, and had our tea, we went to Father Yegor——"

She kept saying over and over again that they "had tea," as if all she knew of life was tea-drinking.

The memory of his seminary and college life slowly and mistily took shape in the bishop's mind. He had been a teacher of Greek for three years, until he could no longer read without glasses, and then he had taken the vows, and had been made an inspector. When he was thirty-two he had been made the rector of a seminary,[3] and then an archimandrite. At that time his life had been so easy and pleasant, and had seemed to stretch so far, far into the future that he could see absolutely no end to it. But his health had failed, and he had nearly lost his eyesight. His doctors had advised him to give up his work and go abroad.

"And what did you do next?" asked Father Sisoi in the adjoining room.

"And then we had tea," answered his mother.

"Why, Father, your beard is green!" exclaimed Kitty suddenly. And she burst out laughing.

The bishop remembered that the colour of Father Sisoi's beard really did verge on green, and he, too, laughed.

"My goodness! What a plague that child is!" cried Father Sisoi in a loud voice, for he was growing angry. "You're a spoiled baby you are! Sit still!"

The bishop recalled the new white church in which he had officiated when he was abroad, and the sound of a warm sea. Eight years had slipped by while he was there; then he had been recalled to Russia, and now he was already a bishop, and the past had faded away into mist as if it had been but a dream.

Father Sisoi came into his room with a candle in his hand.

"Well, well!" he exclaimed, surprised. "Asleep already, your Reverence?"

"Why not?"

"It's early yet, only ten o'clock! I bought a candle this evening and wanted to rub you with tallow."

[2]Head of a monastery; abbot.
[3]Head of a religious school.

"I have a fever," the bishop said, sitting up. "I suppose something ought to be done. My head feels so queer."

Sisoi began to rub the bishop's chest and back with tallow.

"There—there—" he said. "Oh, Lord God Almighty! There! I went to town to-day, and saw that—what do you call him?—that archpresbyter Sidonski. I had tea with him. I hate him! Oh, Lord God Almighty! There! I hate him!"

III

The diocesan bishop was very old and very fat, and had been ill in bed with gout for a month. So his Reverence Peter had been visiting him almost every day, and had received his suppliants for him. And now that he was ill he was appalled to think of the futilities and trifles they asked for and wept over. He felt annoyed at their ignorance and cowardice. The very number of all those useless trivialities oppressed him, and he felt as if he could understand the diocesan bishop who had written "Lessons in Free Will" when he was young, and now seemed so absorbed in details that the memory of everything else, even of God, had forsaken him. Peter must have grown out of touch with Russian life while he was abroad, for it was hard for him to grow used to it now. The people seemed rough, the women stupid and tiresome, the novices and their teachers uneducated and often disorderly. And then the documents that passed through his hands by the hundreds of thousands! The provosts gave all the priests in the diocese, young and old, and their wives and children marks for good behaviour, and he was obliged to talk about all this, and read about it, and write serious articles on it. His Reverence never had a moment which he could call his own; all day his nerves were on edge, and he only grew calm when he found himself in church.

He could not grow accustomed to the terror which he involuntarily inspired in every breast in spite of his quiet and modest ways. Every one in the district seemed to shrivel and quake and apologise as soon as he looked at them. Every one trembled in his presence; even the old archpresbyters fell down at his feet, and not long ago one suppliant, the old wife of a village priest, had been prevented by terror from uttering a word, and had gone away without asking for anything. And he, who had never been able to say a harsh word in his sermons, and who never blamed people because he pitied them so, would grow exasperated with these suppliants, and hurl their petitions to the ground. Not a soul had spoken sincerely and naturally to him since he had been here; even his old mother had changed, yes, she had changed very much! Why did she talk so freely to Sisoi when all the while she was so serious and ill at ease with him, her own son? It was not like her at all! The only person who behaved naturally in his presence, and who said whatever came into his head was old man Sisoi, who had lived with bishops all his life, and had outlasted eleven of them. And therefore his Reverence felt at ease with Sisoi, even though he was, without doubt, a rough and quarrelsome person.

After morning prayers on Tuesday the bishop received his suppliants, and lost his temper with them. He felt ill, as usual, and longed to go to bed, but he had hardly entered his room before he was told that the young merchant Erakin, a benefactor of the monastery, had called on very important business. The bishop was obliged to receive him. Erakin stayed about an hour talking in a very loud voice, and it was hard to understand what he was trying to say.

After he had gone there came an abbess from a distant convent, and by the time she had gone the bells were tolling for vespers; it was time for the bishop to go to church.

The monks sang melodiously and rapturously that evening; a young, black-bearded priest officiated. His Reverence listened as they sang of the Bride-groom and of the chamber swept and garnished, and felt neither repentance nor sorrow, but only a deep peace of mind. He sat by the altar where the shadows were deepest, and was swept in imagination back into the days of his childhood and youth, when he had first heard these words sung. The tears trickled down his cheeks, and he meditated on how he had attained everything in life that it was possible for a man in his position to attain; his faith was unsullied, and yet all was not clear to him; something was lacking, and he did not want to die. It still seemed to him that he was leaving unfound the most important thing of all. Something of which he had dimly dreamed in the past, hopes that had thrilled his heart as a child, a schoolboy, and a traveller in foreign lands, troubled him still.

"How beautifully they are singing to-day!" he thought. "Oh, how beautifully!"

IV

On Thursday he held a service in the cathedral. It was the festival of the Washing of Feet. When the service was over, and the people had gone to their several homes, the sun was shining brightly and cheerily, and the air was warm. The gutters were streaming with bubbling water, and the tender songs of larks came floating in from the fields beyond the city, bringing peace to his heart. The trees were already awake, and over them brooded the blue, unfathomable sky.

His Reverence went to bed as soon as he reached home, and told the lay brother to close his shutters. The room grew dark. Oh, how tired he was!

As on the day before, the sound of voices and the tinkling of glasses came to him from the next room. His mother was gaily recounting some tale to Father Sisoi, with many a quaint word and saying, and the old man was listening gloomily, and answering in a gruff voice:

"Well, I never! Did they, indeed? What do you think of that!"

And once more the bishop felt annoyed, and then hurt that the old lady should be so natural and simple with strangers, and so silent and awkward with her own son. It even seemed to him that she always tried to find some pretext for standing in his presence, as if she felt uneasy sitting down. And his father? If he had been alive, he would probably not have been able to utter a word when the bishop was there.

Something in the next room fell to the floor with a crash. Kitty had evidently broken a cup or a saucer, for Father Sisoi suddenly snorted, and cried angrily:

"What a terrible plague this child is! Merciful heavens! No one could keep her supplied with china!"

Then silence fell. When he opened his eyes again, the bishop saw Kitty standing by his bedside staring at him, her red hair standing up around her head like a halo, as usual.

"Is that you, Kitty?" he asked. "Who is that opening and shutting doors down there?"

"I don't hear anything."

He stroked her head.

"So your cousin Nikolasha cuts up dead people, does he?" he asked, after a pause.

"Yes, he is learning to."

"Is he nice?"

"Yes, very, only he drinks a lot."

"What did your father die of?"

"Papa grew weaker and weaker, and thinner and thinner, and then came his sore throat. And I was ill, too, and so was my brother Fedia. We all had sore throats. Papa died, Uncle, but we got well."

Her chin quivered, her eyes filled with tears.

"Oh, your Reverence!" she cried in a shrill voice, beginning to weep bitterly. "Dear Uncle, mother and all of us are so unhappy! Do give us a little money! Help us, Uncle darling!"

He also shed tears, and for a moment could not speak for emotion. He stroked her hair, and touched her shoulder, and said:

"All right, all right, little child. Wait until Easter comes, then we will talk about it. I'll help you."

His mother came quietly and timidly into the room, and said a prayer before the icon. When she saw that he was awake, she asked:

"Would you like a little soup?"

"No, thanks," he answered. "I'm not hungry."

"I don't believe you are well—I can see that you are not well. You really mustn't fall ill! You have to be on your feet all day long. My goodness, it makes one tired to see you! Never mind, Easter is no longer over the hills and far away. When Easter comes you will rest. God will give us time for a little talk then, but now I'm not going to worry you any more with my silly chatter. Come, Kitty, let his Lordship have another forty winks——"

And the bishop remembered that, when he was a boy, she had used exactly the same half playful, half respectful tone to all high dignitaries of the church. Only by her strangely tender eyes, and by the anxious look which she gave him as she left the room could any one have guessed that she was his mother. He shut his eyes, and seemed to be asleep, but he heard the clock strike twice, and Father Sisoi coughing next door. His mother came in again, and looked shyly at him. Suddenly there came a bang, and a door slammed; a vehicle of some kind drove up to the front steps. The lay brother came into the bishop's room, and called:

"Your Reverence!"

"What is it?"

"Here is the coach! It is time to go to our Lord's Passion———"

"What time is it?"

"Quarter to eight."

The bishop dressed, and drove to the cathedral. He had to stand motionless in the centre of the church while the twelve gospels were being read, and the first and longest and most beautiful of them all he read himself. A strong, valiant mood took hold of him. He knew this gospel, beginning "The Son of Man is risen to-day—," by heart, and as he repeated it, he raised his eyes, and saw a sea of little lights about him. He heard the sputtering of candles, but the people had disappeared. He felt surrounded by those whom he had known in his youth; he felt that they would always be here until—God knew when!

His father had been a deacon, his grandfather had been a priest, and his great grandfather a deacon. He sprang from a race that had belonged to the church since Christianity first came to Russia, and his love for the ritual of the church, the clergy, and the sound of church-bells was inborn in him, deeply, irradicably implanted in his heart. When he was in church, especially when he was taking part in the service himself, he felt active and valorous and happy. And so it was with him now. Only, after the eighth gospel had been read, he felt that his voice was becoming so feeble that even his cough was inaudible; his head was aching, and he began to fear that he might collapse. His legs were growing numb; in a little while he ceased to have any sensation in them at all, and could not imagine what he was standing on, and why he did not fall down.

It was quarter to twelve when the service ended. The bishop went to bed as soon as he reached home, without even saying his prayers. As he pulled his blanket up over him, he suddenly wished that he were abroad; he passionately wished it. He would give his life, he thought, to cease from seeing these cheap, wooden walls and that low ceiling, to cease from smelling the stale scent of the monastery.

If there were only some one with whom he could talk, some one to whom he could unburden his heart!

He heard steps in the adjoining room, and tried to recall who it might be. At last the door opened, and Father Sisoi came in with a candle in one hand, and a teacup in the other.

"In bed already, your Reverence?" he asked. "I have come to rub your chest with vinegar and vodka. It is a fine thing, if rubbed in good and hard. Oh, Lord God Almighty! There—there—I have just come from our monastery. I hate it. I am going away from here to-morrow, my Lord. Oh, Lord, God Almighty—there—"

Sisoi never could stay long in one place, and he now felt as if he had been in this monastery for a year. It was hard to tell from what he said where his home was, whether there was any one or anything in the world that he loved, and whether he believed in God or not. He himself never could make out why he had become a monk, but then, he never gave it any thought, and the time when he had taken the vows had long since faded from his memory. He thought he must have been born a monk.

"Yes, I am going away to-morrow. Bother this place!"

"I want to have a talk with you—I never seem to have the time—" whispered the bishop, making a great effort to speak. "You see, I don't know any one—or anything—here——"

"Very well then, I shall stay until Sunday, but no longer! Bother this place!"

"What sort of a bishop am I?" his Reverence went on, in a faint voice. "I ought to have been a village priest, or a deacon, or a plain monk. All this is choking me—it is choking me——"

"What's that? Oh, Lord God Almighty! There—go to sleep now, your Reverence. What do you mean? What's all this you are saying? Good night!"

All night long the bishop lay awake, and in the morning he grew very ill. The lay brother took fright and ran first to the archimandrite, and then for the monastery doctor who lived in the city. The doctor, a stout, elderly man, with a long, grey beard, looked intently at his Reverence, shook his head, knit his brows, and finally said:

"I'll tell you what, your Reverence; you have typhoid."

The bishop grew very thin and pale in the next hour, his eyes grew larger, his face became covered with wrinkles, and he looked quite small and old. He felt as if he were the thinnest, weakest, puniest man in the whole world, and as if everything that had occurred before this had been left far, far behind, and would never happen again.

"How glad I am of that!" he thought. "Oh, how glad!"

His aged mother came into the room. When she saw his wrinkled face and his great eyes, she was seized with fear, and, falling down on her knees by his bedside, she began kissing his face, his shoulders, and his hands. He seemed to her to be the thinnest, weakest, puniest man in the world, and she forgot that he was a bishop, and kissed him as if he had been a little child whom she dearly, dearly loved.

"Little Paul, my dearie!" she cried. "My little son, why do you look like this? Little Paul, oh, answer me!"

Kitty, pale and severe, stood near them, and could not understand what was the matter with her uncle, and why granny wore such a look of suffering on her face, and spoke such heartrending words. And he, he was speechless, and knew nothing of what was going on around him. He was dreaming that he was an ordinary man once more, striding swiftly and merrily through the open country, a staff in his hand, bathed in sunshine, with the wide sky above him, as free as a bird to go wherever his fancy led him.

"My little son! My little Paul! Answer me!" begged his mother.

"Don't bother his Lordship," said Sisoi. "Let him sleep. What's the matter?"

Three doctors came, consulted together, and drove away. The day seemed long, incredibly long, and then came the long, long night. Just before dawn on

Saturday morning the lay brother went to the old mother who was lying on a sofa in the sitting-room, and asked her to come into the bedroom; his Reverence had gone to eternal peace.

Next day was Easter. There were forty-two churches in the city, and two monasteries, and the deep, joyous notes of their bells pealed out over the town from morning until night. The birds were carolling, the bright sun was shining. The big market place was full of noise; barrel organs were droning, concertinas were squealing, and drunken voices were ringing through the air. Trotting races were held in the main street that afternoon; in a word, all was merry and gay, as had been the year before and as, doubtless, it would be the year to come.

A month later a new bishop was appointed, and every one forgot his Reverence Peter. Only the dead man's mother, who is living now in a little country town with her son the deacon, when she goes out at sunset to meet her cow, and joins the other women on the way, tells them about her children and grandchildren, and her boy who became a bishop.

And when she mentions him she looks at them shyly, for she is afraid they will not believe her.

And, as a matter of fact, not all of them do.

Translated by Ronald Hingley

Questions for Writing and Discussion

1. Everything is foreshadowed, prepared for, hinted at in the first two paragraphs. We learn a few crucial though seemingly disconnected facts: that to the unwell Bishop it seems as if all the worshippers have the same expression in their eyes, that his body is troubling him, that a woman who seems to resemble his mother takes a palm frond, and that tears come to his eyes. How would you connect these bits of detail into a meaningful sequence which sets the story into motion?

2. The first encounter between the Bishop and his mother (in Part II of the story) is an example of Chekhov's great skill at suggesting through quiet details the interplay of emotions and moods. How does the old lady's treatment of little Kitty, the Bishop's niece, reveal this? and the facial changes with which she responds to the Bishop's statement that he has missed her? After that, why does he feel "sorrowful and vexed," and why does the fish seem to him stale and tasteless?

3. Part III of the story is crucial to understanding the Bishop's character: his reaction to the peasants; his impatience with detail and then his regret over his impatience; his sense of being oppressed by the commonplace aspects of life and then the way he overcomes this sense; and above all, his inward struggle regarding the faith he still holds yet feels, somehow, is "lacking still." (Though Chekhov doesn't quite say the last, he says "*something* was lacking still.") From this part, describe the character of the Bishop. Has Chekhov succeeded in doing something both difficult and rare in literature—to present a genuinely good man?

4. The climax of the story comes in two conversations in Part IV, that between the Bishop and Kitty and that between the Bishop and his mother. In these

conversations, not only do we reach some final insights into these particular characters, but we feel that we have come to deep truths—deep, simple, lasting—about the nature of human existence. Do you share this view? What do you make of these conversations?

5.   Reread the last two paragraphs of the story. What is the tone in which they are written? What do they suggest about fame, achievement, power in this world? Why is the Bishop's mother afraid to say that her son was a Bishop? And what does the last sentence suggest?

CONRAD AIKEN

Silent Snow, Secret Snow

Introduction

A secret journey into "another" world, a child's version of mystical transport, an ecstatic yielding to fantasy, a reach toward higher consciousness, a drop into the illness of schizophrenia—which of these phrases describes the action of "Silent Snow, Secret Snow"? All have some relevance to what happens in this story, though none fully encompasses it. Trying to reach some agreement in describing it is more important than finding a tag with which to label the story. For if we can describe it carefully enough, we may not have to label it.

A sensitive twelve-year-old boy experiences a visitation, a remarkable new presence that has come into his consciousness and which clearly is not of the day-to-day familiar world. Immediately and instinctively, he knows that this remarkable new presence must be concealed from his mother and father, first, because they will not understand, second, because they may interfere, and third, because it is something so precious he does not wish to share it with anyone. This presence is associated in the boy's mind with the silence and the whiteness—above all, the silence—of snow, and also, in some way, with the steps of the postman as he crunches the snow while making his rounds. To reach this state of ecstasy, the boy does not need to make any effort; he needs only to relax, to wait, to be receptive—and it will come to him, it will come. . . .

Let us turn from the character to the story, and more particularly, the way the story is written. Aiken's style is deeply enticing, a kind of verbal equivalent to an experience which finally is incommunicable. The sentences slide and glide and wind along, luring his readers into a state of receptivity, leading them to suspend their critical or rational powers, tempting them into a dreamlike pleasure of surrender. It's the rhythm or the music of the sentences which achieves this effect, through a velvety smoothness, a quiet eloquence that becomes the vehicle for suggesting the quality, the tone, the *feel* of the boy's slide into the silent and secret world of snow. The language is deliberately seductive, as if to beckon the reader along the path the boy has taken.

189

But Aiken is too tough-minded a writer simply to yield himself, or ask the reader to join him in yielding, to the boy's experience. The story is divided into four sections; it has a simple but disciplined plot line; it isn't a mere shapeless "trip." In Part I, Aiken abruptly introduces us to the boy's discovery, "a new world" that is "irresistible" and "miraculous," and with a "beauty . . . simply beyond anything." There is a first, rather comic bit about the way this discovery makes the boy seem absent-minded at school, but the clash between the two worlds—that of ordinary life and that of his private vision—is not yet severe. The boy still thinks in terms of bridging the two worlds. Part II plunges him somewhat into the secret world of white and silent snow as it shimmers wordlessly in his mind, and now there appears a touch of desperation: "The secret world must, *at all costs,* be preserved" [emphasis added]. Part III starts very much in the ordinary world, at home: "After supper, the inquisition began." It's not to be supposed that affectionate parents will allow their child simply to slip away from reality—reality as they see it, the reality of things you can touch and smell and measure. They bring in the family doctor, a decent enough man, and the story now is lightened with some comedy, as a relief from the intensities and immensities of the boy's visionary state. Between the doctor and the boy there can hardly be much real communication, though the doctor does begin to fumble his way toward some sense of the extraordinary, and the boy comes to feel that even the obligation to answer the doctor's questions constitutes a nuisance he has to put up with, until he can again reenter the pleasure of his privacy. The ordinary world and its affectionate people come to seem "humdrum" to the boy—"these gross intelligences . . . so bound to the usual, the ordinary." Part IV, the briefest in the story, brings everything to a climax. The boy's surrender to his vision is interrupted by "a gash of horrible light" when the door opens and "something alien" enters the room—which leads him to cry out, "Mother! Mother! Go away! I hate you!" He has made his choice. He yields to his vision (or is it his sickness?), and he encounters "peace" and "remoteness," "cold" and "sleep."

This going-back-and-forth between the boy's two worlds is a major strategy in Aiken's story. To make the boy's experience seem real—seem both beautiful and terrifying—the author must lure us a good part of the way into the boy's inner life. Otherwise, the story could have no effect upon us. But it isn't Aiken's intention to write a defense of "higher consciousness" or schizophrenia or inspired madness or whatever you want to call the boy's experience. Aiken treats the subject with the dispassionate austerity of a physician, one who genuinely wishes to understand and to *see* his patient's strange journey, but who doesn't, thereby, want to pass judgment, favorable or hostile, upon it. What this story does is to make more familiar an unfamiliar kind of event; what it does is to bring us closer to kinds of people whom we might not be able to reach in actual life; but it does not suggest that their life is better or richer or deeper than that of ordinary people—only that there are moments when they may feel so.

There is hardly another piece of fiction written in the twentieth century which uses the ideas of modern psychology so carefully and authoritatively. The tone is neither moralistic nor sentimental, neither quick to denounce nor insipid with "empathy." Reading this story, one thinks of Spinoza's famous remark that his objective as a philosopher was neither to laugh nor to cry, but to understand.

Silent Snow, Secret Snow

Just why it should have happened, or why it should have happened just when it did, he could not, of course, possibly have said; nor perhaps would it even have occurred to him to ask. The thing was above all a secret, something to be preciously concealed from Mother and Father; and to that very fact it owed an enormous part of its deliciousness. It was like a peculiarly beautiful trinket to be carried unmentioned in one's trouser pocket—a rare stamp, an old coin, a few tiny gold links found trodden out of shape on the path in the park, a pebble of carnelian, a seashell distinguishable from all others by an unusual spot or stripe—and, as if it were any one of these, he carried around with him everywhere a warm and persistent and increasingly beautiful sense of possession. Nor was it only a sense of possession—it was also a sense of protection. It was as if, in some delightful way, his secret gave him a fortress, a wall behind which he could retreat into heavenly seclusion. This was almost the first thing he had noticed about it—apart from the oddness of the thing itself—and it was this that now again, for the fiftieth time, occurred to him, as he sat in the little schoolroom. It was the half-hour for geography. Miss Buell was revolving with one finger, slowly, a huge terrestrial globe which had been placed on her desk. The green and yellow continents passed and repassed, questions were asked and answered, and now the little girl in front of him, Deirdre, who had a funny little constellation of freckles on the back of her neck, exactly like the Big Dipper, was standing up and telling Miss Buell that the equator was the line that ran round the middle.

Miss Buell's face, which was old and grayish and kindly, with gray stiff curls beside the cheeks, and eyes that swam very brightly, like little minnows, behind thick glasses, wrinkled itself into a complication of amusements.

"Ah! I see. The earth is wearing a belt, or a sash. Or someone drew a line round it!"

"Oh no—not that—I mean——"

In the general laughter, he did not share, or only a very little. He was thinking about the Arctic and Antarctic regions, which of course, on the globe, were white. Miss Buell was now telling them about the tropics, the jungles, the steamy heat of equatorial swamps, where the birds and butterflies, and even the snakes, were like living jewels. As he listened to these things, he was already, with a pleasant sense of half-effort, putting his secret between himself and the words. Was it really an effort at all? For effort implied something voluntary, and perhaps even something one did not especially want; whereas this was distinctly pleasant, and came almost of its own accord. All he needed to do was to think of that morning, the first one, and then of all the others——

But it was all so absurdly simple! It had amounted to so little. It was nothing, just an idea—and just why it should have become so wonderful, so permanent, was a mystery—a very pleasant one, to be sure, but also, in an amusing way, foolish. However, without ceasing to listen to Miss Buell, who had now moved up to the north temperate zones, he deliberately invited his memory of the first morning. It was only a moment or two after he had waked up—or perhaps the moment itself. But was there, to be exact, an exact moment? Was one awake all at once? or was it gradual? Anyway, it was after he had stretched a lazy hand up toward the headrail, and yawned, and then relaxed again among his warm covers, all the more grateful on a December morning, that the thing had happened. Suddenly, for no reason, he had thought of the postman, he remembered the postman. Perhaps there was nothing so odd in that. After all, he heard the postman almost every morning in his life—his heavy boots could be heard clumping round the corner at the top of the little cobbled hill-street, and then, progressively nearer, progressively louder, the double knock at each door, the crossings and re-crossings of the street, till finally the clumsy steps came stumbling across to the very door, and the tremendous knock came which shook the house itself.

(Miss Buell was saying, "Vast wheat-growing areas in North America and Siberia."

Deirdre had for the moment placed her left hand across the back of her neck.)

But on this particular morning, the first morning, as he lay there with his eyes closed, he had for some reason *waited* for the postman. He wanted to hear him come round the corner. And that was precisely the joke—he never did. He never came. He never had come—*round the corner*—again. For when at last the steps *were* heard, they had already, he was quite sure, come a little down the hill, to the first house; and even so, the steps were curiously different—they were softer, they had a new secrecy about them, they were muffled and indistinct; and while the rhythm of them was the same, it now said a new thing—it said peace, it said remoteness, it said cold, it said sleep. And he had understood tne situation at once—nothing could have seemed simpler—there had been snow in the night, such as all winter he had been longing for; and it was this which had rendered the postman's first footsteps inaudible, and the later ones faint. Of course! How lovely! And even now it must be snowing—it was going to be a snowy day—the long white ragged lines were drifting and sifting across the street, across the faces of the old houses, whispering and hushing, making little triangles of white in the corners between cobblestones, seething a little when the wind blew them over the ground to a drifted corner; and so it would be all day, getting deeper and deeper and silenter and silenter.

(Miss Buell was saying, "Land of perpetual snow.")

All this time, of course (while he lay in bed), he had kept his eyes closed, listening to the nearer progress of the postman, the muffled footsteps thumping and slipping on the snow-sheathed cobbles; and all the other sounds—the double knocks, a frosty far-off voice or two, a bell ringing thinly and softly as if under a sheet of ice—had the same slightly abstracted quality, as if removed by one degree from actuality—as if everything in the world had been insulated by snow. But when at last, pleased, he opened his eyes, and turned them toward the window, to see for himself this long-desired and now so clearly imagined miracle—what he saw instead was brilliant sunlight on a roof; and when, astonished, he jumped out of bed and stared down into the street, expecting to see the cobbles obliterated by the snow, he saw nothing but the bare bright cobbles themselves.

Queer, the effect this extraordinary surprise had had upon him—all the following morning he had kept with him a sense as of snow falling about him, a secret screen of new snow between himself and the world. If he had not dreamed such a thing—and how could he have dreamed it while awake?—how else could one explain it? In any case, the delusion had been so vivid as to affect his entire behavior. He could not now remember whether it was on the first or the second morning—or was it even the third?—that his mother had drawn attention to some oddness in his manner.

"But my darling"—she had said at the breakfast table—"what has come over you? You don't seem to be listening. . . ."

And how often that very thing had happened since!

(Miss Buell was now asking if anyone knew the difference between the North Pole and the Magnetic Pole. Deirdre was holding up her flickering brown hand, and he could see the four white dimples that marked the knuckles.)

Perhaps it hadn't been either the second or third morning—or even the fourth or fifth. How could he be sure? How could he be sure just when the delicious *progress* had become clear? Just when it had really *begun?* The intervals weren't very precise. . . . All he now knew was, that at some point or other— perhaps the second day, perhaps the sixth—he had noticed that the presence of the snow was a little more insistent, the sound of it clearer; and, conversely, the sound of the postman's footsteps more indistinct. Not only could he not hear the steps come round the corner, he could not even hear them at the first house. It was below the first house that he heard them; and then, a few days later, it was below the second house that he heard them; and a few days later again, below the third. Gradually, gradually, the snow was becoming heavier, the sound of its seething louder, the cobblestones more and more muffled. When he found, each morning, on going to the window, after the ritual of listening, that the roofs and cobbles were bare as ever, it made no difference. This was, after all, only what he had expected. It was even what pleased him, what rewarded him: the thing was his own, belonged to no one else. No one else knew about it, not even his mother and father. There, outside, were the bare cobbles; and here, inside, was the snow. Snow growing heavier each day, muffling the world, hiding the ugly, and deadening increasingly—above all—the steps of the postman.

"But, my darling"—she had said at the luncheon table—"what has come over you? You don't seem to listen when people speak to you. That's the third time I've asked you to pass your plate. . . ."

How was one to explain this to Mother? or to Father? There was, of course, nothing to be done about it: nothing. All one could do was to laugh embarrassedly, pretend to be a little ashamed, apologize, and take a sudden and somewhat disingenuous interest in what was being done or said. The cat had stayed out all night. He had a curious swelling on his left cheek—perhaps somebody had kicked him, or a stone had struck him. Mrs. Kempton was or was not coming to tea. The house was going to be housecleaned, or "turned out," on Wednesday instead of Friday. A new lamp was provided for his evening work— perhaps it was eyestrain which accounted for this new and so peculiar vagueness of his—Mother was looking at him with amusement as she said this, but with something else as well. A new lamp? A new lamp. Yes, Mother, No, Mother, Yes, Mother. School is going very well. The geometry is very easy. The history is very dull. The geography is very interesting—particularly when it takes one to the North Pole. Why the North Pole? Oh, well, it would be fun to be an explorer. Another Peary or Scott or Shackleton.[1] And then abruptly he found his interest in the talk at an end, stared at the pudding on his plate, listened, waited, and began once more—ah, how heavenly, too, the first beginnings—to hear or feel—for could he actually hear it?—the silent snow, the secret snow.

(Miss Buell was telling them about the search for the Northwest Passage, about Hendrik Hudson, the *Half Moon*.)[2]

This had been, indeed, the only distressing feature of the new experience; the fact that it so increasingly had brought him into a kind of mute misunderstanding, or even conflict, with his father and mother. It was as if he were trying to lead a double life. On the one hand, he had to be Paul Hasleman, and keep up the appearance of being that person—dress, wash, and answer intelligently when spoken to—; on the other, he had to explore this new world which had been opened to him. Nor could there be the slightest doubt—not the slightest—that the new world was the profounder and more wonderful of the two. It was irresistible. It was miraculous. Its beauty was simply beyond anything— beyond speech as beyond thought—utterly incommunicable. But how then, between the two worlds, of which he was thus constantly aware, was he to keep a balance? One must get up, one must go to breakfast, one must talk with Mother, go to school, do one's lessons—and, in all this, try not to appear too much of a fool. But if all the while one was also trying to extract the full deliciousness of another and quite separate existence, one which could not easily (if at all) be spoken of—how was one to manage? How was one to explain? Would it be safe to explain? Would it be absurd? Would it merely mean that he would get into some obscure kind of trouble?

[1]Explorers of North and South Poles.
[2]Northwest Passage: hoped-for route from Atlantic to Pacific oceans through the Arctic. Hendrik Hudson: English explorer who tried to find Northwest Passage; Hudson River named after him. *Half Moon:* one of Hudson's ships.

These thoughts came and went, came and went, as softly and secretly as the snow; they were not precisely a disturbance, perhaps they were even a pleasure; he liked to have them; their presence was something almost palpable, something he could stroke with his hand, without closing his eyes, and without ceasing to see Miss Buell and the schoolroom and the globe and the freckles on Deirdre's neck; nevertheless he did in a sense cease to see, or to see the obvious external world, and substituted for this vision the vision of snow, the sound of snow, and the slow, almost soundless, approach of the postman. Yesterday, it had been only at the sixth house that the postman had become audible; the snow was much deeper now, it was falling more swiftly and heavily, the sound of its seething was more distinct, more soothing, more persistent. And this morning, it had been—as nearly as he could figure—just above the seventh house— perhaps only a step or two above; at most, he had heard two or three footsteps before the knock had sounded. . . . And with each such narrowing of the sphere, each nearer approach of the limit at which the postman was first audible, it was odd how sharply was increased the amount of illusion which had to be carried into the ordinary business of daily life. Each day, it was harder to get out of bed, to go to the window, to look out at the—as always—perfectly empty and snowless street. Each day it was more difficult to go through the perfunctory motions of greeting Mother and Father at breakfast, to reply to their questions, to put his books together and go to school. And at school, how extraordinarily hard to conduct with success simultaneously the public life and the life that was secret! There were times when he longed—positively ached—to tell everyone about it—to burst out with it—only to be checked almost at once by a far-off feeling as of some faint absurdity which was inherent in it—but *was* it absurd?— and more importantly by a sense of mysterious power in his very secrecy. Yes; it must be kept secret. That, more and more, became clear. At whatever cost to himself, whatever pain to others——

(Miss Buell looked straight at him, smiling, and said, "Perhaps we'll ask Paul. I'm sure Paul will come out of his daydream long enough to be able to tell us. Won't you, Paul?" He rose slowly from his chair, resting one hand on the brightly varnished desk, and deliberately stared through the snow toward the blackboard. It was an effort, but it was amusing to make it. "Yes," he said slowly, "it was what we now call the Hudson River. This he thought to be the Northwest Passage. He was disappointed." He sat down again, and as he did so Deirdre half turned in her chair and gave him a shy smile, of approval and admiration.)

At whatever pain to others.

This part of it was very puzzling, very puzzling. Mother was very nice, and so was Father. Yes, that was all true enough. He wanted to be nice to them, to tell them everything—and yet, was it really wrong of him to want to have a secret place of his own?

At bed-time, the night before, Mother had said, "If this goes on, my lad, we'll have to see a doctor, we will! We can't have our boy—" But what was it she had said? "Live in another world"? "Live so far away"? The word "far" had been in it, he was sure, and then Mother had taken up a magazine again and laughed a little, but with an expression which wasn't mirthful. He had felt sorry for her. . . .

The bell rang for dismissal. The sound came to him through long curved parallels of falling snow. He saw Deirdre rise, and had himself risen almost as soon—but not quite as soon—as she.

II

On the walk homeward, which was timeless, it pleased him to see through the accompaniment, or counterpoint, of snow, the items of mere externality on his way. There were many kinds of brick in the sidewalks, and laid in many kinds of pattern. The garden walls, too, were various, some of wooden palings, some of plaster, some of stone. Twigs of bushes leaned over the walls: the little hard green winter-buds of lilac, on gray stems, sheathed and fat; other branches very thin and fine and black and desiccated. Dirty sparrows huddled in the bushes, as dull in color as dead fruit left in leafless trees. A single starling creaked on a weather vane. In the gutter, beside a drain, was a scrap of torn and dirty newspaper, caught in a little delta of filth; the word ECZEMA appeared in large capitals, and below it was a letter from Mrs. Amelia D. Gravath, 2100 Pine Street, Fort Worth, Texas, to the effect that after being a sufferer for years she had been cured by Caley's Ointment. In the little delta, beside the fan-shaped and deeply runneled continent of brown mud, were lost twigs, descended from their parent trees, dead matches, a rusty horse-chestnut burr, a small concentration of eggshell, a streak of yellow sawdust which had been wet and now was dry and congealed, a brown pebble, and a broken feather. Farther on was a cement sidewalk, ruled into geometrical parallelograms, with a brass inlay at one end commemorating the contractors who had laid it, and, halfway across, an irregular and random series of dog-tracks, immortalized in synthetic stone. He knew these well, and always stepped on them; to cover the little hollows with his own foot had always been a queer pleasure; today he did it once more, but perfunctorily and detachedly, all the while thinking of something else. That was a dog, a long time ago, who had made a mistake and walked on the cement while it was still wet. He had probably wagged his tail, but that hadn't been recorded. Now, Paul Hasleman, aged twelve, on his way home from school, crossed the same river, which in the meantime had frozen into rock. Homeward through the snow, the snow falling in bright sunshine. Homeward?

Then came the gateway with the two posts surmounted by egg-shaped stones which had been cunningly balanced on their ends, as if by Columbus, and mortared in the very act of balance; a source of perpetual wonder. On the brick wall just beyond, the letter H had been stenciled, presumably for some purpose. H? H.

The green hydrant, with a little green-painted chain attached to the brass screw-cap.

The elm tree, with the great gray wound in the bark, kidney-shaped, into which he always put his hand—to feel the cold but living wood. The injury, he had been sure, was due to the gnawings of a tethered horse. But now it deserved only a passing palm, a merely tolerant eye. There were more important things. Miracles. Beyond the thoughts of trees, mere elms. Beyond the thoughts of sidewalks, mere stone, mere brick, mere cement. Beyond the thoughts even of his own shoes, which trod these sidewalks obediently, bearing a burden—far above—of elaborate mystery. He watched them. They were not very well polished; he had neglected them, for a very good reason: they were one of the many parts of the increasing difficulty of the daily return to daily life, the morning struggle. To get up, having at last opened one's eyes, to go to the window, and discover no snow, to wash, to dress, to descend the curving stairs to breakfast——

At whatever pain to others, nevertheless, one must persevere in severance, since the incommunicability of the experience demanded it. It was desirable, of course, to be kind to Mother and Father, especially as they seemed to be worried, but it was also desirable to be resolute. If they should decide—as appeared likely—to consult the doctor, Doctor Howells, and have Paul inspected, his heart listened to through a kind of dictaphone, his lungs, his stomach—well, that was all right. He would go through with it. He would give them answer for question, too—perhaps such answers as they hadn't expected? No. That would never do. For the secret world must, at all costs, be preserved.

The bird-house in the apple tree was empty—it was the wrong time of year for wrens. The little round black door had lost its pleasure. The wrens were enjoying other houses, other nests, remoter trees. But this too was a notion which he only vaguely and grazingly entertained—as if, for the moment, he merely touched an edge of it; there was something further on, which was already assuming a sharper importance; something which already teased at the corners of his eyes, teasing also at the corner of his mind. It was funny to think that he so wanted this, so awaited it—and yet found himself enjoying this momentary dalliance with the bird-house, as if for a quite deliberate postponement and enhancement of the approaching pleasure. He was aware of his delay, of his smiling and detached and now almost uncomprehending gaze at the little bird-house; he knew what he was going to look at next: it was his own little cobbled hill-street, his own house, the little river at the bottom of the hill, the grocer's shop with the cardboard man in the window—and now, thinking of all this, he turned his head, still smiling, and looking quickly right and left through the snow-laden sunlight.

And the mist of snow, as he had foreseen, was still on it—a ghost of snow falling in the bright sunlight, softly and steadily floating and turning and pausing, soundlessly meeting the snow that covered, as with a transparent mirage, the bare bright cobbles. He loved it—he stood still and loved it. Its beauty was paralyzing—beyond all words, all experience, all dream. No fairy story he had ever read could be compared with it—none had ever given him this extraordinary combination of ethereal loveliness with a something else, unnameable, which was just faintly and deliciously terrifying. What was this thing? As he thought of it, he looked upward toward his own bedroom window, which was open—and it was as if he looked straight into the room and saw himself lying half awake in his bed. There he was—at this very instant he was still perhaps actually there—more truly there than standing here at the edge of the cobbled hill-street, with one hand lifted to shade his eyes against the snow-sun. Had he indeed ever left his room, in all this time? since that very first morning? Was the whole progress still being enacted there, was it still the same morning, and himself not yet wholly awake? And even now, had the postman not yet come round the corner? . . .

This idea amused him, and automatically, as he thought of it, he turned his head and looked toward the top of the hill. There was, of course, nothing there—nothing and no one. The street was empty and quiet. And all the more because of its emptiness it occurred to him to count the houses—a thing which, oddly enough, he hadn't before thought of doing. Of course, he had known there weren't many—many, that is, on his own side of the street, which were the ones that figured in the postman's progress—but nevertheless it came as something of a shock to find that there were precisely *six,* above his own house—his own house was the seventh.

Six!

Astonished, he looked at his own house—looked at the door, on which was the number thirteen—and then realized that the whole thing was exactly and logically and absurdly what he ought to have known. Just the same, the realization gave him abruptly, and even a little frighteningly, a sense of hurry. He was being hurried—he was being rushed. For—he knit his brow—he couldn't be mistaken—it was just above the *seventh* house, his *own* house, that the postman had first been audible this very morning. But in that case—in that case—did it mean that tomorrow he would hear nothing? The knock he had heard must have been the knock of their own door. Did it mean—and this was an idea which gave him a really extraordinary feeling of surprise—that he would never hear the postman again?—that tomorrow morning the postman would already have passed the house, in a snow so deep as to render his footsteps completely inaudible? That he would have made his approach down the snow-filled street so soundlessly, so secretly, that he, Paul Hasleman, there lying in bed, would not have waked in time, or waking, would have heard nothing?

But how could that be? Unless even the knocker should be muffled in the snow—frozen tight, perhaps? . . . But in that case——

A vague feeling of disappointment came over him; a vague sadness as if he felt himself deprived of something which he had long looked forward to, something much prized. After all this, all this beautiful progress, the slow delicious advance of the postman through the silent and secret snow, the knock creeping closer each day, and the footsteps nearer, the audible compass of the world thus daily narrowed, narrowed, narrowed, as the snow soothingly and beautifully encroached and deepened, after all this, was he to be defrauded of the one thing he had so wanted—to be able to count, as it were, the last two or three solemn footsteps, as they finally approached his own door? Was it all going to happen, at the end, so suddenly? or indeed, had it already happened? with no slow and subtle graduations of menace, in which he could luxuriate?

He gazed upward again, toward his own window which flashed in the sun; and this time almost with a feeling that it would be better if he *were* still in bed, in that room; for in that case this must still be the first morning, and there would be six more mornings to come—or, for that matter, seven or eight or nine— how could he be sure?—or even more.

III

After supper, the inquisition began. He stood before the doctor, under the lamp, and submitted silently to the usual thumpings and tappings.

"Now will you please say 'Ah!'?"

"Ah!"

"Now again, please, if you don't mind."

"Ah."

"Say it slowly, and hold it if you can——"

"Ah-h-h-h-h-h——"

"Good."

How silly all this was. As if it had anything to do with his throat! Or his heart, or lungs!

Relaxing his mouth, of which the corners, after all this absurd stretching, felt uncomfortable, he avoided the doctor's eyes, and stared toward the fireplace, past his mother's feet (in gray slippers) which projected from the green chair, and his father's feet (in brown slippers) which stood neatly side by side on the hearth rug.

"Hm. There is certainly nothing wrong there . . . ?"

He felt the doctor's eyes fixed upon him, and, as if merely to be polite, returned the look, but with a feeling of justifiable evasiveness.

"Now, young man, tell me—do you feel all right?"

"Yes, sir, quite all right."

"No headaches? no dizziness?"

"No, I don't think so."

"Let me see. Let's get a book, if you don't mind—yes, thank you, that will do splendidly—and now, Paul, if you'll just read it, holding it as you would normally hold it——"

He took the book and read:

"And another praise have I to tell for this the city our mother, the gift of a great god, a glory of the land most high; the might of horses, the might of young horses, the might of the sea. . . . For thou, son of Cronus, our lord Poseidon, hath throned herein this pride, since in these roads first thou didst show forth the curb that cures the rage of steeds. And the shapely oar, apt to men's hands, hath a wondrous speed on the brine, following the hundred-footed Nereids. . . . O land that art praised above all lands, now is it for thee to make those bright praises seen in deeds."

He stopped, tentatively, and lowered the heavy book.

"No—as I thought—there is certainly no superficial sign of eyestrain."

Silence thronged the room, and he was aware of the focused scrutiny of the three people who confronted him. . . .

"We could have his eyes examined—but I believe it is something else."

"What could it be?" That was his father's voice.

"It's only this curious absent-mindedness—" This was his mother's voice. In the presence of the doctor, they both seemed irritatingly apologetic.

"I believe it is something else. Now Paul—I would like very much to ask you a question or two. You will answer them, won't you—you know I'm an old, old friend of yours, eh? That's right! . . ."

His back was thumped twice by the doctor's fat fist—then the doctor was grinning at him with false amiability, while with one fingernail he was scratching the top button of his waistcoat. Beyond the doctor's shoulder was the fire, the fingers of flame making light prestidigitation against the sooty fireback, the soft sound of their random flutter the only sound.

"I would like to know—is there anything that worries you?"

The doctor was again smiling, his eyelids low against the little black pupils, in each of which was a tiny white bead of light. Why answer him? why answer him at all? "At whatever pain to others"—but it was all a nuisance, this necessity for resistance, this necessity for attention; it was as if one had been stood up on a brilliantly lighted stage, under a great round blaze of spotlight; as if one were merely a trained seal, or a performing dog, or a fish, dipped out of an aquarium and held up by the tail. It would serve them right if he were merely to bark or growl. And meanwhile, to miss these last few precious hours, these hours of which each minute was more beautiful than the last, more menacing—! He still looked, as if from a great distance, at the beads of light in the doctor's eyes, at the fixed false smile, and then, beyond, once more at his mother's slippers, his father's slippers, the soft flutter of the fire. Even here, even amongst these hostile presences, and in this arranged light, he could see the snow, he could hear it—it was in the corners of the room, where the shadow was deepest, under the sofa, behind the half-opened door which led to the dining room. It was gentler here, softer, its seethe the quietest of whispers, as if, in deference to a drawing room, it had quite deliberately put on its "manners"; it kept itself out of sight, obliterated itself, but distinctly with an air of saying, "Ah, but just wait! Wait till we are alone together! Then I will begin to tell you something new! Something white! something cold! something sleepy! something of cease, and peace, and the long bright curve of space! Tell them to go away. Banish them. Refuse to speak. Leave them, go upstairs to your room, turn out the light and get into bed—I will go with you, I will be waiting for you, I will tell you a better story than Little Kay of the Skates, or The Snow Ghost—I will surround your bed, I will close the windows, pile a deep drift against the door, so that none will ever again be able to enter. Speak to them! . . ." It seemed as if the little hissing voice came from a slow white spiral of falling flakes in the corner of the front window—but he could not be sure. He felt himself smiling, then, and said to the doctor, but without looking at him, looking beyond him still——

"Oh no, I think not——"

"But are you sure, my boy?"

His father's voice came softly and coldly then—the familiar voice of silken warning.

"You needn't answer at once, Paul—remember we're trying to help you— think it over and be quite sure, won't you?"

He felt himself smiling again, at the notion of being quite sure. What a joke! As if he weren't so sure that reassurance was no longer necessary, and all this cross-examination a ridiculous farce, a grotesque parody! What could they know about it? these gross intelligences, these humdrum minds so bound to the usual, the ordinary? Impossible to tell them about it! Why, even now, even now, with the proof so abundant, so formidable, so imminent, so appallingly present here in this very room, could they believe it?—could even his mother believe it? No—it was only too plain that if anything were said about it, the merest hint given, they would be incredulous—they would laugh—they would say "Absurd!"—think things about him which weren't true. . . .

"Why no, I'm not worried—why should I be?"

He looked then straight at the doctor's low-lidded eyes, looked from one of them to the other, from one bead of light to the other, and gave a little laugh.

The doctor seemed to be disconcerted by this. He drew back in his chair, resting a fat white hand on either knee. The smile faded slowly from his face.

"Well, Paul!" he said, and paused gravely, "I'm afraid you don't take this quite seriously enough. I think you perhaps don't quite realize—don't quite realize—" He took a deep quick breath and turned, as if helplessly, at a loss for words, to the others. But Mother and Father were both silent—no help was forthcoming.

"You must surely know, be aware, that you have not been quite yourself, of late? Don't you know that? . . ."

It was amusing to watch the doctor's renewed attempt at a smile, a queer disorganized look, as of confidential embarrassment.

"I feel all right, sir," he said, and again gave the little laugh.

"And we're trying to help you." The doctor's tone sharpened.

"Yes, sir, I know. But why? I'm all right. I'm just *thinking*, that's all."

His mother made a quick movement forward, resting a hand on the back of the doctor's chair.

"Thinking?" she said. "But my dear, about what?"

This was a direct challenge—and would have to be directly met. But before he met it, he looked again into the corner by the door, as if for reassurance. He smiled again at what he saw, at what he heard. The little spiral was still there, still softly whirling, like the ghost of a white kitten chasing the ghost of a white tail, and making as it did so the faintest of whispers. It was all right! If only he could remain firm, everything was going to be all right.

"Oh, about anything, about nothing—*you* know the way you do!"

"You mean—daydreaming?"

"Oh, no—thinking!"

"But thinking about *what?*"

"Anything."

He laughed a third time—but this time, happening to glance upward

toward his mother's face, he was appalled at the effect his laughter seemed to
have upon her. Her mouth had opened in an expression of horror. . . . This was
too bad! Unfortunate! He had known it would cause pain, of course—but he
hadn't expected it to be quite so bad as this. Perhaps—perhaps if he just gave
them a tiny gleaming hint——?

"About the snow," he said.

"What on earth?" This was his father's voice. The brown slippers came a
step nearer on the hearth-rug.

"But my dear, what do you mean?" This was his mother's voice.

The doctor merely stared.

"Just *snow,* that's all. I like to think about it."

"Tell us about it, my boy."

"But that's all it is. There's nothing to tell. *You* know what snow is?"

This he said almost angrily, for he felt that they were trying to corner him.
He turned sideways so as no longer to face the doctor, and the better to see the
inch of blackness between the window-sill and the lower curtain—the cold inch
of beckoning and delicious night. At once he felt better, more assured.

"Mother—can I go to bed, now, please? I've got a headache."

"But I thought you said——"

"It's just come. It's all these questions—! Can I, mother?"

"You can go as soon as the doctor has finished."

"Don't you think this thing ought to be gone into thoroughly, and *now?*"
This was Father's voice. The brown slippers again came a step nearer, the voice
was the well-known "punishment" voice, resonant and cruel.

"Oh, what's the use, Norman——"

Quite suddenly, everyone was silent. And without precisely facing them,
nevertheless he was aware that all three of them were watching him with an
extraordinary intensity—staring hard at him—as if he had done something
monstrous, or was himself some kind of monster. He could hear the soft
irregular flutter of the flames; the cluck-click-cluck-click of the clock; far and
faint, two sudden spurts of laughter from the kitchen, as quickly cut off as
begun; a murmur of water in the pipes; and then, the silence seemed to deepen,
to spread out, to become world-long and world-wide, to become timeless and
shapeless, and to center inevitably and rightly, with a slow and sleepy but
enormous concentration of all power, on the beginning of a new sound. What
this new sound was going to be, he knew perfectly well. It might begin with a
hiss, but it would end with a roar—there was no time to lose—he must escape.
It mustn't happen here——

Without another word, he turned and ran up the stairs.

IV

Not a moment too soon. The darkness was coming in long white waves. A
prolonged sibilance filled the night—a great seamless seethe of wild influence
went abruptly across it—a cold low humming shook the windows. He shut the

door and flung off his clothes in the dark. The bare black floor was like a little raft tossed in waves of snow, almost overwhelmed, washed under whitely, up again, smothered in curled billows of feather. The snow was laughing; it spoke from all sides at once; it pressed closer to him as he ran and jumped exulting into his bed.

"Listen to us!" it said. "Listen! We have come to tell you the story we told you about. You remember? Lie down. Shut your eyes, now—you will no longer see much—in this white darkness who could see, or want to see? We will take the place of everything. . . . Listen——"

A beautiful varying dance of snow began at the front of the room, came forward and then retreated, flattened out toward the floor, then rose fountain-like to the ceiling, swayed, recruited itself from a new stream of flakes which poured laughing in through the humming window, advanced again, lifted long white arms. It said peace, it said remoteness, it said cold—it said——

But then a gash of horrible light fell brutally across the room from the opening door—the snow drew back hissing—something alien had come into the room—something hostile. This thing rushed at him, clutched at him, shook him—and he was not merely horrified, he was filled with such a loathing as he had never known. What was this? this cruel disturbance? this act of anger and hate? It was as if he had to reach up a hand toward another world for any understanding of it—an effort of which he was only barely capable. But of that other world he still remembered just enough to know the exorcising words. They tore themselves from his other life suddenly——

"Mother! Mother! Go away! I hate you!"

And with that effort, everything was solved, everything became all right: the seamless hiss advanced once more, the long white wavering lines rose and fell like enormous whispering sea-waves, the whisper becoming louder, the laughter more numerous.

"Listen!" it said. "We'll tell you the last, the most beautiful and secret story—shut your eyes—it is a very small story—a story that gets smaller and smaller—it comes inward instead of opening like a flower—it is a flower becoming a seed—a little cold seed—do you hear? we are leaning closer to you——"

The hiss was now becoming a roar—the whole world was a vast moving screen of snow—but even now it said peace, it said remoteness, it said cold, it said sleep.

Questions for Writing and Discussion

1. This story is, in significant part, a story of sounds—the sounds that run through the boy's head, the sounds that beckon to him from "the secret world," and the "sounds" of silence. As you read through the story, make a little list of some of the main sounds, and kinds of silence, that significantly affect the boy's effort to live in "the second world" while remaining bodily in our familiar, everyday world.

2.   One of the things that makes this story so effective, indeed, so enticing, is Conrad Aiken's style. The prose seems to purr along, in an elegant hum—simple yet sophisticated, an allurement of language to represent the boy's experience. Reading the story with this aspect of it in mind, try to work up a description of the way Aiken uses language—and do it in your own words. Consider such matters as the length of sentences, his choice of words, his occasional images, the way he moves from commonplace description to semi-poetic passages, and so on.

3.   The figure of the mother is lightly sketched, yet we gain a clear sense of her— an affectionate and intelligent woman who tries to remain calm yet is deeply worried about her child. At the end of the story, the boy cries out, "Mother! Mother! Go away! I hate you!" This is perhaps the one difficult or perplexing moment in the story. Why does he cry out in this way? What does his mother represent that he wishes to leave behind?

4.   In the first question we suggested that sounds were very important in "Silent Snow, Secret Snow." But visual images are also important, especially that of the silent and white snow, which becomes for the boy a secret snow. Clearly the whiteness of the snow figures significantly in the boy's visions—whiteness which is commonly associated with the pure, blank, untouched, and also with the frightening, the terror of the unfamiliar. (If you've read Herman Melville's *Moby Dick,* you'll remember a remarkable chapter on "The Whiteness of the Whale.") Discuss the ways in which the image of the snow gradually builds up in the boy's imagination as a symbol of everything that is luring him away from the familiar— and familial—world.

ADALBERT STIFTER

Brigitta

Introduction

Glowing, serene, radiant—these are the words that come to mind when we read "Brigitta." For all its formality of manner and quietness of voice, this long story (or novella) glows with a healthy romanticism, a serene persuasion that the life of a man or woman can become radiant if he or she achieves harmony with the world of nature. Indeed, harmony is probably the main note of "Brigitta," harmony between ourselves and the external world, but also harmony within ourselves, through the disciplines of work, responsibility, and affection. "Brigitta" is a positive story, though not in some sort of foolish or soft-headed way. It recognizes fully enough the pain and losses that must occur in life; but it sets up barriers against despair, it completely refuses cynicism and nihilism. Here the traditional virtues still reign: duty, patience, faithfulness, devotion to others.

"Brigitta" is a story that may seem "old-fashioned" today, "old-fashioned" in the sense that it does not venture into the recesses or complexities of psychology as we have come to understand it in the decades since Sigmund Freud. It is "old-fashioned" in that it believes in the reality of fixed principles by which men and women, happy or not, are obliged to live. And it is "old-fashioned" in that it sees the purpose of storytelling as, in some large and generous sense, educative. (The narrator learns from the Major and Brigitta something about the possibilities of life, and the tone of modest self-assurance with which he speaks does a good deal to persuade us that, yes, he has learned something.)

"Brigitta" is "old-fashioned" in still another way: it works on the assumption that stories ought to have interesting plots, with clear beginnings, middles, and ends; that a touch here and there of the exotic (the scenery of the Hungarian *pusta,* or barren wasteland, the fight with the wolves, the encounter with the shepherds, the dress of the characters) will help hold the attention of readers; and that we will appreciate the niceties of the natural world as these emerge from the author's description, we won't be impatient, we won't be looking for some quick sensation or cheap shock. In short, that we'll appreciate the wholesome moral beauty of the ending of the story.

It is an ending which, superficially, comes close to seeming like "and they lived happily ever after." As, indeed, the Major and Brigitta do. But if we take that as some sort of wish-fulfilling fantasy, we are misreading the story. For both the Major and Brigitta have suffered a very great deal; they have lost some of the best years of their lives because of his slip and her stubbornness; and if, at the end, happiness does come to them, it is a happiness they have earned through their work, their readiness to wait and endure, their patience, their discipline. Each of the two major characters achieves an inner harmony through suffering, and it is this which they must have in order to renew their love. The story is completely romantic, but not childishly or irresponsibly so. It is a mature romanticism that emerges at the end, the romanticism of people who have lived long enough to be worthy of the other's love. And their worthiness is tested by their ability to survive—survive and remain responsible people—through all the years when they are deprived of each other's love.

Their worthiness is tested in still another way: the question of whether Brigitta's dismissal of her husband was an appropriate step, whether she was perhaps excessive in her pride, is never settled (it is not even raised) between them. They allow each other the history of their lives, which means, the history of their flaws and their faults. They do not gnaw upon the bones of the past, but simply accept that some things happened which led to painful, even tragic results, and that now they are riper, truer than in their youth. In youth love may come to people, but in their later years they learn—if they learn anything at all—that they must go to it. That is the story of "Brigitta."

Brigitta

1   Across the Steppes

There are often incidents and relationships in life whose meaning is not immediately clear to us and whose background is not readily understandable. And then, just because they are rather mysterious, they exercise a certain gentle and quite pleasant attraction on us. The features of a quite plain person often impress us as having a real inner beauty, though we are not always immediately able to say why. On the other hand, we often find a face cold and empty though all others assure us that its features are of great beauty. In the same way we will occasionally find ourselves quite strongly attracted to someone we really hardly

BRIGITTA by Adalbert Stifter, translated by Ilsa Barea. Reprinted by permission of Story Classics, A. S. Barnes & Co., Inc.

know at all. We like his bearing perhaps, or we find his personality engaging. We are sorry when the acquaintance ends, and in later years when we call him to mind we experience a feeling almost of sadness, a kind of longing, even something approaching affection. On the other hand, we sometimes find that a person whose worth is attested by many things nevertheless means little to us even after we have been acquainted with him for years.

There is no doubt that in such cases there are intangible factors at work, things that affect the heart, and we are not able to analyze the matter deliberately and arrive at logical conclusions. Psychology has now explained a great many things to us, but others remain unfathomable and still beyond our reach. It is hardly too much to say that even in our world there is a certain immeasurable and serene zone in which God and the intangible are at work still. In moments of rapture the soul will sometimes cross its borders impetuously, and in childlike artlessness poetry too will occasionally raise the veil. But stark science with its cautious calculations can never venture farther than the edge, and usually it is quite content to have neither hand nor part in such mysteries.

Such thoughts were aroused in my mind by an experience that once fell to my lot as a very young man on the estate of an old Major, a very good friend of mine. It happened at a time when the restlessness of youth was still sending me here, there and everywhere in the hope of experiencing or discovering God alone knows exactly what.

I had got to know this Major whilst I was in Italy and on several occasions he invited me to visit him in his own country. However, at the time I regarded the invitation as more or less a polite formality, the sort of amiability travelers do often exchange at their casual meetings, and I should probably have thought no more about the matter, but some long time afterward I received a friendly letter from him inquiring after my welfare and concluding by repeating once again his old invitation and suggesting that I should stay with him on his estate in Hungary for a summer, or for longer if I had a mind—for a year or for five years, since he had at last made up his mind to stay in one place, in one very small spot on this earth, and to let no other dust settle on his feet henceforth but that of his own country, where he had, so he declared, at last found an aim in life that he had sought in vain elsewhere throughout the world.

It was spring when I received this letter and I was curious to know just what was the aim to which he referred, and as, also, I was at a loss at that moment to know where to go next, I decided to do as he suggested and so I accepted his invitation.

His estate was in Eastern Hungary and for a couple of days I occupied myself with various plans for making my journey as comfortable and convenient as possible. The third day saw me in a mail coach rolling eastward, my mind greatly occupied with thoughts of heaths and woodlands, for I had never visited his country before. On the eighth day I was already crossing the famous pusta, a barren, level heath probably as magnificent and as lonely as any Hungary had to offer.

At first I was completely under the spell of its immense endlessness. A fresh breeze ceaselessly caressed my face, the smell of the steppes was constantly in my nostrils, and a uniform loneliness stretched away in all directions. And so it remained the next day and the day after that, and the day after that again, always the same faraway horizon where heaven and earth met. I therefore soon became accustomed to it and my eye grew less curious. Surfeited by the immense, unchanging emptiness my mind withdrew into itself and as the sun shone on persistently and the grass glistened endlessly in its rays, other thoughts arose. Older memories crowded in as I rolled across the heath, and, in particular, my recollections of the man to whom I was now making my way. I welcomed the memories and in that lonely expanse of heath around me I had time enough and inclination to recall all I had ever known about him and to reconstruct the former picture in my mind.

I had first met him in Southern Italy, in a barren waste almost as austere as the one through which I was now passing. In those days he had been an honored and welcome guest everywhere, and although even then he was almost fifty years of age, more than one pair of beautiful eyes had been drawn to him, for never was there a man whose build and whose features more deserved the description of handsome, or a man who bore himself with greater nobility. In addition there was a certain gentle modesty in his bearing which was so natural and so engaging that men too were won by it. And as for women, it was rumored—and I can well believe it—that in younger years his effect on them had been devastating. There were many stories current concerning his conquests and many of them were remarkable. But, they said, there was one thing lacking in him: the ability to respond truly, and it was this that made him really dangerous. No one, not even the greatest beauty, had ever succeeded in holding him for long. To the very end he would behave himself with all the charm that won him every heart and filled the lady of the moment with enraptured triumph, but then, when he was so minded, he would make his farewell, set out on his travels once more—and never return. But, far from discouraging women, this behavior seemed to attract them still more, and more than one hot-blooded woman of southern climes could hardly control her impatience or wait to offer him both heart and devotion. And the fact that no one knew from whence he came or what was his position in the world was nothing but an added ground for attraction.

But although the Graces[1] had clearly chosen him for their own, there was yet an indication of some sorrow on his brow, a sign that in the past at least his emotions had perhaps not lacked profundity. And it was just that past that puzzled and interested people so greatly, and that above all because no one had the slightest inkling of what had been his past. There were rumors, of course: he had been embroiled in matters of State; he had been unhappily married; he had shot his own brother . . . and other suggestions of a like dramatic nature. However, the only certain thing people did know was not about his past: it was that now he was keenly interested in the progress of science.

I had already heard a great deal about him before I first met him, tossing stones into the crater of Vesuvius[2] and watching the blue smoke that wreathed

[1]Mythological figures: three daughters of Zeus personifying grace, gentleness, and beauty.
[2]Volcano near the Bay of Naples.

up from time to time from the main crater and from various fissures. I recognized him at once from the descriptions I had heard and I went toward him between the yellow boulders which were strewn around. He answered amiably when I spoke to him and soon we were talking animatedly. The scene around us at the time was truly desolate, a gloomy waste, and the effect was heightened by the indescribably lovely blue of the Southern Italian sky above us into which slow billows of smoke rose sadly and erratically from the crater. We chatted for some time in a very friendly fashion but when we finally parted each went his separate way down the mountainside.

Later on opportunity arose for us to meet again and after that we exchanged a number of visits and by the time I had decided to return home we were very close friends, almost inseparable. I found that he was more or less unconscious of the effect his personality and appearance produced on those around him. Although he was then approaching fifty years of age, there was a certain youthful impetuousness in him which broke out from time to time as though even in the middle years his life and his character were far from settled. And as I became more closely acquainted with him I discovered that his nature was more generous, more that of a poet, than that of any man I had as yet encountered. Because of this there was often something childlike, something even ingenuous, about him. He was clearly quite unaware of these things and in all naturalness his language was more beautiful than any I have ever heard on human lips. Throughout my life—even later on when I associated a great deal with artists and poets—I never encountered such a sensitive feeling for beauty, though it could certainly be provoked to impatience by grossness. It was probably these gifts, of which he seemed unconscious, that won him the hearts of all women, for such brilliance is unusual in men of middle years. Now although I was a very young man at the time and really not in a position to appreciate such qualities at their true worth, he seemed to be very willingly in my company. It was, in fact, not until I grew older—and in particular when I began to set down the story of his life—that I came to understand and appreciate such things.

What truth there was in the fabulous stories of his successes with women I never discovered, because he never spoke about such things himself and I never had any personal opportunity for judging. I was also never able to discover anything about the reason for that sadness that seemed on him. All I could find out about his earlier life was that as a young man he had been always on the move. In recent years, however, he seemed more or less to have settled down in Naples, where he devoted himself to the study of volcanic lava and antiquities. It was from his own lips that I learned that he had lands in Hungary, and, as I have already said, he repeatedly invited me to come and visit him there.

We were close friends for quite a long time and when I finally went away it was not without emotion that we separated. Subsequently my mind was so occupied with many different countries and many different people that it never even occurred to me as a possibility that I should one day be traveling across the Hungarian pusta to visit him, as I was now in fact doing. With so much time to spare on my journey my mind turned more and more to my recollections of him and I reconstructed the old picture so successfully in my memory that now and again I had some difficulty in realizing that I was not once again in Italy, particularly as the steppe landscape through which I was passing was as hot and silent as Italy had been, and at the same time the bluish haze in the distance mirrored itself in my eye as an optical illusion of the Pontine Marshes.[3]

I did not make straight for the Major's estate, whose whereabouts he had described to me in detail in his letters. Instead I traveled here and there through the countryside, wishing to take advantage of the opportunity to get thoroughly acquainted with it. Because of what my friend had told me so often about it, the picture in my mind had merged more and more with what I knew about Italy, but now it began to develop its own individuality and to become an independent entity for me. Since setting out I had crossed scores of rivulets, streams and rivers and I had often shared the humble shelter of the herdsmen of the plains and their shaggy dogs. I had drunk from those steppe wells with their typical high poles jutting up into the sky at a sharp angle and I had slept under more than one of those low-eved thatched roofs that characterized the countryside. Here the bagpipe player would take his ease, there the busy carter would drive his horses rapidly over the heath, whilst in the distance glistened the white coat of the horse-minder.

I often wondered whether I should find my friend at all changed in such surroundings. I had previously seen him only in society, in company where one man looks very much like another. There he had been the polished gentleman moving amongst his kind. But here everything was so different, and often, when for whole days I saw nothing but the reddish-blue shimmer of the rolling steppes relieved only by innumerable white specks where the cattle grazed, I wondered how he would fit into it all. The soil beneath my feet was dark and rich, giving rise to a wild and luxuriant growth, and despite the country's ancient history there was something new and elemental about it all. As I traveled around in this countryside and learned to know its character and its individuality it sometimes seemed to me that I could hear the ringing blows of the hammer that was falling on the anvil as the future of this people was forged. Those things that have had their day and are passing away are tired and weary, but those things that are still becoming are fiery and vigorous. This, it seemed to me, was a country of the future and I found myself taking a keen pleasure in its innumerable villages, its fine vineyards stretching up the hillsides, its broad marshes with their luxuriant reeds, and, far in the distance, the soft blue mountains that framed it all.

After months of wandering around in this fashion I realized one day that I must be somewhere quite close to my friend's estate, and, a little tired now of my travels, I decided to make straight for where I was long expected. That afternoon I had trudged through an arid waste of stones. Far away to the left the blue summits of mountains rose into the sky. They were the Carpathians,[4] I judged. To the right was broken countryside with the peculiar reddish coloration of the steppes. Between the two was the seemingly endless sweep of the

[3]Malarial region southeast of Rome.
[4]Mountains in eastern Europe.

plains. After crossing the bed of a dried-out stream I climbed slowly out of a small valley and to the right I saw a wood of chestnut trees and a white house.

Three miles. Three miles. That was what I had been told all the afternoon when I asked the way to Unwar, which was the name of the Major's house and estate. Three miles. But by this time I had learned what a Hungarian mile was. I had certainly gone at least five ordinary miles already and I therefore hoped devoutly that the white house I could now see—previously I had been unsighted by a sand drift—would prove to be Unwar. In the middle distance tilled fields rose up to a sort of causeway on which I could see figures. I decided to ask if the white house were, in fact, Unwar, and to reach the men I could see there I cut through the verge of the chestnut wood.

Before long I observed what I had already guessed from my previous experience of the deceptive lie of this countryside: that the house was not really by the wood at all but at the other side of a level stretch of land that ran away from it. It became clear too that it must be a very large house. At that moment I saw a rider galloping across the level stretch of land toward the fields where the men were working. When this rider came up with them the men gathered round him as though he were their master. At that I looked keenly at the horseman but the figure looked nothing like that of my friend the Major. Without hurrying I made my way toward the causeway, which was farther away than I had at first thought, and as I came up with the group the rays of the sinking sun were turning red as they fell across the rich maize fields and on the group of bearded men as they stood around the rider. To my surprise this rider turned out to be a woman. She was perhaps forty years of age and she was wearing the wide trousers of the countryside and sitting astride her horse like a man. By the time I reached her the laborers were already going back to their work and she was almost alone. I therefore directed my inquiries to her. Resting my pack on my stick and raising one hand to protect my eyes from the still strong rays of the sun I looked up at her and spoke in German.

"Good evening, ma'am."

"Good evening," she replied in the same language.

"Would you be so good as to tell me whether that white house over yonder is Unwar?"

"No. That isn't Unwar. It is Unwar you want?"

"Yes. An old friend of mine lives there, a Major. He has invited me to visit him."

"Oh, yes. Very well, follow me. I will set you on your way to Unwar."

She moved off slowly on her horse so that I could keep up with her, making her way still farther up the slope between the high ears of maize. As I followed behind her I had ample opportunity to look around at the countryside and what I saw astonished me more and more. The higher we went up the hill the more the valley opened up behind us and I saw that the wood beyond the white house was very large and stretched away to the mountains. Great avenues of trees came right down to the fields and one cultivated area after the other was revealed with crops which all seemed in excellent heart. I had never seen such long, plump and healthy-looking maize before and it was obviously most carefully tended, for there was no grass or weed growing between its strong stems. The vineyard whose edge we were now approaching reminded me of the Rhineland, but I had never seen quite such rich foliage or such luscious berries; they seemed almost bursting with juice. The level ground between the chestnut trees and the house was meadowland and it looked as soft and green as though it were a stretch of fine satin. The ways across this meadowland were all fenced in neatly and between them white cattle, as smooth and shapely as deer, grazed peacefully. This rich landscape was in striking contrast to the stony waste I had previously trudged through. It lay behind me now, looking dry and parched in the red rays of the sun by comparison with the cool, green freshness of this richly cultivated soil.

In a little while we arrived at one of the small white huts I had noticed dotted around here and there against the darker green of the vineyards and the woman spoke to a young fellow who was working there. Despite the warmth of the July evening he was wearing a shaggy fur coat.

"Milosch, this gentleman wishes to get to Unwar today. Take a couple of the horses and go with him as far the gallows."

"Yes, ma'am," said the young fellow obediently, abandoning what he was doing.

"Go with him now," said the woman to me. "He will put you safely on your way."

And with that she turned her horse's head and was about to ride away. I took her to be some sort of estate overseer and I wanted to give her something in return for the service she had done me, but she smiled and shook her head and I noticed that she had very beautiful white teeth. She rode her horse slowly down the vineyard slope but soon afterward I heard the rapid beat of hoofs as she galloped away across the flat ground below.

I put my money away and turned to the young fellow she had addressed as Milosch. He now put on a broad-brimmed hat in addition to his fur coat and then he led me through the vineyard. After a while the ground sloped down again and we came to some farm buildings. Going to the stables he led out two of the small wiry horses of which there are so many in this part of the world. One he saddled for me but the other he mounted bare back and together we set off in the deepening twilight toward the darkening eastern horizon. We must have presented an odd picture as we rode along together: the German wanderer with his pack, his knotted stick and his cap, and the slim young Hungarian with his long, drooping mustaches, his round, broad-brimmed hat, his fur coat and his wide, flapping trousers.

On the other side of the vineyards was wasteland and the prosperous settlement lay behind us now like a vanished fairy land. This wasteland was actually part of the stony waste I had tramped through earlier that day and it was so much the same to the eye that I could have thought we were going back the way I had come but for the fact that the dying red across the horizon behind me told me that we really were going eastward.

"How far is Unwar?" I asked.

"About another mile and a half," the young fellow answered. I kept up with him as well as I could and we passed the same innumerable gray boulders I had already seen by the thousand that day. They now glimmered with a false light against the dark ground and we rode between them on firm moorland, the hoofs of our horses making no sound except when occasionally their shoes rang out against a stone. Our beasts were obviously used to such going, however, and they usually managed to pick their way safely between the stones. The way was level on the whole but now and again there were small depressions. We rode down one side and up the other and at the bottom of each of these small valleys there was a petrified stream of scree.

"Who owns the estate we have just left?" I asked.

"Maroshely," he answered.

He spoke without reining in and I was not certain whether that was the name of the owner or the estate, or whether I had even caught it correctly. The movement of our horses made it difficult to speak or to hear what was spoken.

An orange moon had now begun to rise and in its first faint light I distinguished a tall scaffolding looming up on the heath ahead of us. I took it to be the gallows to which my companion had been instructed to lead me, and so it was.

"This is the gallows," he said almost immediately, and he reined in his horse. "Down below there is a stream. Look, you can see it glistening. That black mass near it is an oak tree. That's where they used to hang wrongdoers at one time. It isn't used now that we've got a real gallows up here. On the other side of that oak tree you'll find a path. There are young trees on either side. Go along that for about an hour and you'll come to a gate in a fence. You'll see a bell pull there. Ring the bell, but don't go in even if the gate's unlocked—because of the dogs. Dismount now. And do up your jacket or you might catch fever."

I dismounted and although I had not had much luck with the supposed overseer I offered Milosch some money. He accepted it without question and tucked it away somewhere inside his fur jacket, murmuring a word of thanks. Then he took the reins of my horse, turned the two horses about and galloped off at once even before I had time to ask him to thank the owner of the horses for his kindness in allowing me, a complete stranger, to ride off on one of them at such a late hour. Milosch seemed anxious to get away from the neighborhood of the gallows as quickly as possible. In the yellow moonlight I could see that it consisted of nothing but two upright poles and a cross beam. I rather fancied that there was something hanging from it, but that could have been imagination and I made no attempt to find out. Nothing loath I quickly left it behind me too and went on at a good pace through the long grass, which had seemed almost to be whispering as it caressed the foot of the gallows.

There was now neither sight nor sound of Milosch and there might never have been such a person. I quickly came to the stream, which glistened and rippled through the rushes like a snake. Above it loomed the black mass of the old oak that had once been a gallows tree and on the other side I found that path Milosch had described. It was of beaten earth with a ditch on either side and it looked almost white in the moon between long lines of young poplars. My steps as they sounded on this harder ground were vaguely comforting; it was almost as though I were walking along one of the familiar paths at home.

I went forward steadily and the moon rose higher and brighter until finally it rode at full strength in the warm summer sky shining down on the heath that stretched away on either side, gray and robbed of all its normal color. I had walked for about an hour when black clumps of trees rose up ahead as though I were coming to the beginning of a wood. Soon after that I came to a gate set in a high fence that ran out of the trees. Behind it the massive crowns of many great trees stood out still and silent in the silver light of the moon. There was a bell pull at the gate, as Milosch had said, and I gave it a good tug. A bell rang somewhere at a distance and then, instead of barking, I heard a deep, snorting, snuffling sound such as big dogs make, followed immediately by a thud as the beast sprang at the gate. It was one of the most magnificent dogs I have ever seen and it stood on its hind legs with its fore paws against the bars of the gate, staring at me without making a sound as such great solemn beasts will.

After a moment or two it was joined by two younger and smaller dogs of the same breed which ran up prancing and growling. They were fine mastiff dogs and all three now stood there together and stared at me unwinkingly. After a while I heard footsteps and a man came up to the gate wearing the inevitable shaggy fur coat. In answer to his question as to my business I asked if this were Unwar and I mentioned my name. He obviously already had his instructions and at the mention of my name he immediatley called off the dogs with a few sharp words in Hungarian and opened the gate.

"The master has received your letters, sir," he said as he closed the gate behind me and led me along the path. "He has been expecting you for some time."

"I told him in my last letter that I wanted to see something of the countryside first," I replied.

"I hope you have enjoyed it, sir," he said.

"Yes, I did. Is the Major still up?"

"He isn't at home at all today, sir. He's at the session. Tomorrow morning he'll ride back. But rooms are prepared for you and we have instructions to make you as comfortable as possible should you arrive in his absence."

"Very well—if you'd be good enough to do that."

"Most certainly, sir."

This was the only conversation that took place between us during the rather long walk through the park. It put me in mind of a well-kept jungle. Enormous fir trees reared into the sky and limbs of oak as thick as a man's middle stretched out all around. The biggest dog trotted quietly along at our side, but the other two, not yet so well behaved, sniffed at my clothing from time to time and danced around us. When we had gone through the park we came to a treeless rise on which the Major's house stood. As far as I could see in the light of the moon that fell lambently upon it, it was a large four-cornered building. A flight of broad stone steps led up to a terrace and the house was surrounded by railings. The man led me to a gate in these railings and then he said a word or two to the dogs, which immediately turned about and trotted back into the park. Opening the gate the man then led me into the house.

Lights were burning on the staircase and they shone on a row of strange statues representing men in wide-topped high boots and flowing garments. They might have been former Hungarian kings. On the first floor we entered a long corridor laid out with rush matting. At the end of this corridor we went up another flight of steps and came into another such corridor. Opening a wing of one of the doors along this corridor my guide invited me to enter and informed me that these were to be my quarters. He followed me inside and after he had lit a great many more candles in each of the three rooms of which my quarters consisted he wished me good night and went away. Shortly after that another man-servant brought me wine, bread and cold roast meat. He too then bowed, bade me good night and departed. As I was obviously to be left to my own devices now I went to the doors and closed them.

After that I sat down and made a good supper and then I looked at my leisure around my new quarters. The first room, in which my meal had been laid out at one end of a long table, was very large, almost a small hall, but so many candles were burning that it was very well lit. It was furnished rather differently from the fashion I was accustomed to at home. Down the center was the long table at which I had eaten and along its sides were oaken benches. There were only one or two ordinary chairs and the general impression was formal rather than comfortable—as though the place were really intended for meetings. On the walls hung ancient weapons from various historical periods. They were probably mostly Hungarian and there were many bows and arrows. Apart from these weapons there were also costumes displayed on the walls as though in a museum. They seemed chiefly to be Hungarian costumes of other days but here and there were also silken garments that had probably been worn at one time by Turks, or perhaps Tartars.

Giving off this main chamber there were two other rooms that had been placed at my disposal and when I went into them I noticed with approval that they were rather more comfortably furnished. There were chairs, tables, wardrobes, writing accommodation and materials and washing arrangements—in fact there was everything to make a traveler feel at his ease after a long and tiring journey. There were even books on a bedside table and I noticed that they were all in German. In each of these two smaller rooms there was a bed. One of them was draped with the wide Hungarian garment known as a "Bunda" instead of the ordinary covering. This Bunda is usually a mantle of furs worn with the rough side inward, and the smooth outer skins are often decorated with gaily colored straps and with drawings on leather plaques stitched on to them.

Before I went to bed I walked over to the window to look at the lie of the land outside, a habit of mine in strange quarters. There was not a great deal to be seen, but the moonlight was strong enough to show me very clearly that the landscape was very different to that of my own homeland. Rather like another but enormous Bunda, the park lay spread out below, a dark splash over the rolling steppes, now shimmering softly in the light of the moon.

After looking out at this unfamiliar scene for a while I closed the window and turned back into the room. Undressing, I climbed into the bed which was covered by the Bunda. As I drew its soft fur gratefully up over my tired limbs and before my eyes closed in sleep I still had time to wonder what experiences might be awaiting me in this house: pleasant or disagreeable?

Then I fell asleep and everything that had already been in my life and everything for which I still so keenly longed faded together into unconsciousness.

2   *The House in the Steppes*

How long I slept I really do not know, but I do know that I slept neither soundly nor well. Perhaps over-tiredness was the cause. In any case, all night I wandered around on Vesuvius and I saw the Major, first dressed as a wanderer and sitting in Pompeii, and then in evening dress standing amidst the boulders on the mountainside and looking for stones. Toward morning the whinnying of horses and the barking of dogs mingled with my dream. After that I slept quite soundly for a while and when I woke up it was broad daylight. From my bedroom I looked out into the main chamber where the weapons and the clothing were hanging. The rays of the early morning sun came through the windows, and outside the park was filled with the singing of birds. I got up and went to the windows. The heath was colorful again in the sunlight. I began to dress, but before I had quite finished there was a knock at the door. I opened it and my old friend came in.

For days I had been consumed with curiosity to know just what he would look like in these new surroundings, and now I saw that he looked very much as one would have expected of him, namely in complete harmony with them, so much so in fact that it was almost as though I had always known him just like this. On his upper lip there was the traditional long mustache, and his eyes were, if possible, brighter than ever. He was wearing the round, broad-brimmed hat and the long wide, white trousers of the countryside. It seemed so natural that he should be dressed like this that suddenly I could no longer remember what he looked like in evening dress. His Hungarian garb so took my fancy that my own well-worn German broadcloth that lay, still dusty from my journey, over a bench beneath the faded silk garments of some old Tartar seemed quite wretched by comparison. His jacket was shorter than we were accustomed to in Germany, but it certainly suited the whole style of his dress. He looked rather older, of course, and there were strands of white in his hair, and on his face were those fine, short lines that appear at last and indicate the passing of the years in men of culture. However, his general appearance was every bit as agreeable and engaging as before.

He welcomed me warmly, even affectionately, and after we had chatted for a half an hour or so we were as intimate again as ever we had been. You might almost have thought, in fact, that we had not separated since our first meeting in Italy. Whilst completing my dressing I remaked that a trunk would arrive with the rest of my things, whereupon he proposed that until it did—or, indeed, throughout the whole period of my stay if I cared—I should wear Hungarian dress, and this I readily agreed to do. The necessary garments were soon brought and as I put them on he observed approvingly that he would see to it that I did not lack for variety whilst I was here. We then went down into the courtyard where his men, all with long mustaches and all similarly dressed, were waiting for us. As they led forward the horses for our morning ride they looked at us with such pleasure from under their bushy eyebrows and there was such a general atmosphere of pleasant and cultivated well-being that my spritis rose at once and I was greatly heartened in these new and stange surroundings.

Accompanied by the great mastiff I had seen the previous evening we now made a tour of inspection of the Major's estate. As he showed me round it was soon clear that he took a keen and personal interest in everything that was going on, giving orders, commenting on this or that, and uttering words of praise where he felt they were due. We first rode through the park. It was a friendly, orderly wilderness with well-kept paths, and beyond it we rode out into fields that were a mass of tossing green. The only country in which I had ever seen such luxuriant green was England, but there the growth had seemed less strong and vigorous than it did here in these sun-drenched fields. We rode up a long incline to where the vineyards began. From this height I could see that the cultivated area spread far and wide over the landscape, the dark green relieved by many peach trees, whilst here and there, as at Maroshely, the white huts of laborers were picked out by the sun against the dark-green background of the vines. On the heath itself we saw his cattle grazing, a vast herd scattered around almost as far as eye could see. Then an hour's riding brought us to the stables and the sheepfolds. As we rode across the heath the Major pointed to a narrow, dark stretch of green cutting across the gray steppes to the west.

"They are the vineyards of Maroshely, where they lent you the horses yesterday," he said.

We rode back a different way and on the other side of the estate he showed me the orchards, the gardens and the greenhouses. Before we came to them we rode through a rather barren and uninteresting stretch of land on which a great number of men were at work. In answer to my question he declared that they were beggars, tramps and vagabonds who had been persuaded to work for him in return for regular wages. They were engaged in draining marshland and in laying down a new road.

We returned to the house at midday and there we ate together with all the men and girls who were attached to the house. The meal was served under a large projecting roof forming a sort of veranda. Near by there was a large nut tree and one of the typical wells of the countryside. As we ate, a party of wandering gypsies grouped before the well played to us. I was not the only visitor. At our table was a youth who attracted my attention at once by his quite extraordinary beauty. He had brought letters to the house and after the meal rode away again. I noticed that the Major treated him with great consideration and something very like affection.

The sun was very hot now and we spent the heat of the day in the cool rooms of the house. When evening came my host declared that the sunset on the heath was a sight worth seeing and he ordered the horses to be brought round for us. At the same time he advised me to wear a fur coat as a precaution against the fever of the plains, despite the fact that the still warm air seemed to make such a precaution unnecessary. We rode out to a suitable spot and there we waited for a while until the sun went down. The sunset was a wonderful spectacle indeed. The tremendous dome of the heavens covered the dark heath as though with a vast curtain of red and yellow flames and the glow was so great that everything on the ground seemed black and strange. A taller blade of grass would stand out against the light as though it were a beam and a passing animal was outlined against the fiery golden background like some dark mastodon, whilst modest juniper and blackthorn bushes looked like distant turrets and battlements. After a while the fresh, cold blue of the approaching night began to spread over the eastern horizon throwing dark shadows across the brilliance of the glowing sky.

In June, when the sun stands high in the heavens, the spectacle lasts for quite a while, and when we were already back at the house, and even after we had taken our evening meal and had chatted for some time, there was still a colorful glow in the west. In fact, when I stood at my window much later, just before retiring for the night—it was already past midnight—there was still a last vestige of yellow in the western sky although in the dark blue east the orange disk of the moon was already up.

As I stood there and looked out I decided that the next day, or the day after that, or whenever a convenient opportunity arose, I would ask the Major what it was exactly that he had referred to in his letter as having found here at last to keep him forever in his own country.

He came to my room very early the next morning to ask me whether I would prefer to spend the day on my own or to share it with him. I could do whichever I pleased, today or on any other day of my stay. On any day that I wished to take part in the normal affairs of the household all I had to do was to rise at the sound of the house bell in the courtyard, which was rung every morning, and come down to the common table for breakfast. Should I, on the other hand, wish at any time to follow my own devices, then, if he were not there, his servants had been instructed to have horses ready for me, to provide me with anything I required, and to accompany me wherever I wished to go. However, should I ever have plans that would take me a long way from the house it would be as well if I would let him know beforehand so that he could advise me of any difficulties and perhaps warn me of any dangers that might be involved.

I was very grateful to him for his kindness and consideration and his readiness to assist me in everything, but I assured him that today, tomorrow and indefinitely I would prefer to spend my days with him. At the same time I should certainly let him know in good time of any change in my intentions.

When he had gone I got up, dressed and presented myself at the common table beneath the great roof for breakfast. The others had almost all finished their meal and were already going off on the various tasks of the day, but the Major had waited for me and he sat there with me until I had finished my breakfast. Saddled horses were then brought for us and we set off. I did not ask where we were going or what he intended to do; I just followed him wherever he rode.

It was no tour of inspection for my benefit this time as it had been on the first day when he had showed me round his estate and explained its running, and he declared that today we would just attend to whatever matters that arose in the ordinary course and he hoped that I would not be bored. First we rode over to a wide expanse of meadowland where haymaking was going on. The beautiful brown Hungarian horses we were riding carried us spiritedly over the level turflike ground where the long grass had been cut. The Major dismounted to examine the quality of the hay in various ricks and the man who held his horse in the meantime remarked that the hay was to be carried in that afternoon. Before we rode on the Major gave instructions that whilst the grass was short a number of trenches should be dug here and there, some to drain off surplus water, others to collect it.

Next we went to the greenhouses, which were not, as is usually the case, near the house but in a very favorable spot where a gentle slope offered protection in the mornings and at midday. Near the greenhouses was a small well-kept stable where the Major and anyone who happened to be with him could leave their horses if an extended stay in the greenhouses was intended— sometimes, when visitors were anxious to look over the houses thoroughly, the inspection might take several hours. We left our horses in this stable without having them unsaddled and went off to look at a variety of plants which were being prepared for despatch to fulfill orders. After that we entered a little office where the administrative side of the business was attended to and there the Major spent some time at a desk where various papers and correspondence were awaiting his attention. In the meantime I looked around on my own with as much, or as little, understanding for what I saw as an inveterate traveler, who has seen many greenhouses in his time, manages, willy-nilly, to acquire. Later on, back at the house, I spent some time looking through that part of the Major's library which was devoted to horticultural matters and in consequence I was soon made to realize just how little I knew about the fundamentals of the science. The Major was certainly not exaggerating when he observed on another occasion:

"It is all quite fascinating, but if you want to do anything really worth while in such a complicated branch of horticulture, where one thing leads to another endlessly, you have to go into the matter very thoroughly indeed and constantly strive to outdo all your rivals at it."

When the Major had finished his work in the office we continued our tour of inspection. We stopped to watch a number of women who were engaged in cleaning the leaves of camellia plants. In those days the camellia was quite a rare and therefore an expensive flower. The Major examined the plants that had already been wiped and made a comment or two. Then we walked along between many beds of fine white sand where seedlings were being grown, and from there on to ordinary beds where various kinds of plants and bushes were systematically cultivated. By this time we were on the far side of the gardens and there we found a lad waiting for us with the horses, which had been brought round from the stable to be ready for us. There was a large open space here where various soils were prepared and made up for particular uses. Donkeys were used to bring in earth in baskets from other localities, often from quite distant forests of fir trees, and this transport went on throughout the year except when the ground was frozen hard. Near by there was a row of great ovens for sterilizing the soil, and at a little distance there were great stacks of oak logs for use as fuel during the winter months.

Beyond the greenhouses, as I had already noticed, was the open heath and we now rode out into it. Our fine horses bore us along swiftly until soon the park was no more than a dark stretch on the horizon behind us and the great house a mere dot whilst all around the level plains rolled away and the scent of warm heather in the sun was in our nostrils. After a long gallop we fell in with the Major's herdsmen and came to a primitive hut of branches, hardly more than a recognizable spot that could be seen from afar and that served as a meeting-point. A fire of tough branches and the roots of juniper, blackthorn and other bushes was burning, or rather glowing, there and round it the herdsmen, who ate their meal early, at about eleven o'clock, were already engaged in preparing it. Sun-tanned men in short sleeves and the usual long, and in this case, rather dirty white trousers, crowded round the Major as we rode up. Their shaggy fur coats were scattered around on the ground. Others farther away had spotted the Major's arrival and now they came galloping up riding bare back on small, wiry ponies. They had neither saddles nor saddle cloths and their only bridle was often just a rope. They dismounted and, still holding their horses' heads, they joined the crowd around the Major, who had also dismounted and handed his horse to one of the men.

He asked questions and they answered him, but it was not only of their work that they talked and he seemed to know almost all of them by name. His manner toward them was very friendly, almost familiar, and their attitude to him was enthusiastic. As at home on our mountain pastures, the cattle here were kept out in the open throughout the summer months. They were long-horned beasts with white hides and they lived by cropping the grass and plants of the heath, which were, incidentally, of a pungency and flavor that our alpine herdsmen would hardly have credited. These herdsmen of the plains stayed out in the open with their cattle throughout the summer, and apart from the flimsy sort of construction I mentioned previously, and perhaps a mud hut or two, their only roof was the blue sky during the day and the bright stars of the pusta at night. Now they crowded round their master, the Lord of the Manor as he is called in these parts, and listened keenly to his instructions. When he remounted, one of the men, whose dark eyes sparkled under bushy eyebrows, held his horse's head whilst others, with long hair and thick drooping mustaches, bent down to hold his stirrup.

"Good-by, men," he called out cheerfully as we rode off. "I shall be here again soon, and when our neighbors come over we'll spend an afternoon on the heath and eat with you."

He had spoken in Hungarian of course and at my request he translated his words for me, adding:

"If you should ever feel inclined to come out here on your own to spend a day with the men and get to know their lives a bit better—take care of their dogs. They aren't usually as docile and friendly as they were today, and certainly not to strangers. In fact if you paid an unexpected visit it could go hard with you, so if you feel like riding out here at any time let me know beforehand so that I can go with you or arrange for one of the men to accompany you if I should be unable to."

I had, in fact, taken particular note of the lean and shaggy dogs that had sat around us by the fire and behaved themselves so intelligently and so obediently. They seemed to know what was going on and to have their share in it. In all my travels I had never seen such impressive beasts.

We turned our horses' heads toward the house, for it was approaching midday and the time for the midday meal was drawing near. As we passed the place where the men were at work draining the marshland and laying out the new road the Major pointed to a field of wheat close by. The ears of grain seemed to be particularly full and heavy.

"Good fields like that have to produce the money to enable us to make improvements elsewhere," he said. "The hired men over there work on the marshland all the year through. They are paid daily and they prepare their food on the job in the open air. At nights they sleep in those wooden huts you can see over there. In winter when it begins to freeze we move them to the lower lying ground where nothing can be done in summer because of the stagnant water. They then cart stones and debris from the heath and the vineyards to make a firmer surface."

I looked around and I could see the wooden huts to which he referred, and in various spots on the brow of the heath thin wisps of smoke were rising from where the day laborers were preparing their midday meal.

As we turned into the park the dogs ran up to welcome us, leaping up and dancing around our horses, and at that moment the bell in the courtyard began to ring to call us and the others to our midday meal. That afternoon was spent as usual in the house, though at five o'clock the Major set off along the avenue of poplars I had used to approach the house on the night of my arrival. I had no idea where he was going, or on what errand, and I spent the time he was away in looking through the books he was sending in to me in increasing numbers from his library. Although I had firmly determined to do so the evening before when I went to bed, I had found no opportunity of asking the Major what it was he had found here which had caused him to settle down so definitely, altogether abandoning his former mode of life.

The next day the Major had a good deal of writing to do and I spent the whole day with the horses in his stables and in getting to know his many servants.

The morning after that I went with him to the sheep-folds, which were situated a good two hours' ride away from the house, and there we spent the whole day. There were obviously a number of very capable men to look after this branch of his activities. They were devoted to their work and able to discuss it with him from all angles. It was here that I discovered that each of the various activities of his estate had its own separate accounting and that a surplus from one would be used to further the progress of the other. The sheep rearing, for example, was assisted in this way. A very careful accounting was kept and the Major's books would always provide an exact picture of the state of affairs prevailing in any branch of the estate's operations.

On another occasion we inspected the stud farm and then went out to the meadows where the horses of lesser value were looked after by his men in the same way as his cattle were looked after by his herdsmen.

In this way I gradually obtained a very good picture of all the activities on his estate, and the sum-total was not inconsiderable. I was astonished again and again at the great care and attention to details he showed in practical matters, for previously I had known him as interested only in literary and scientific affairs.

"As I see it," he said to me on one occasion, "we owe a duty to our land. Our country and our history are already old, but there is still a great deal left for us to do. The country is like a jewel—perhaps a more valuable jewel than you might think—but it still has to be given a proper setting. The whole world is striving to make the most of itself and we, too, have to play our part in the struggle. There are great latent capacities in our country but they must first be developed and brought out. I have no doubt that on your long way here you did not fail to observe those possibilities. These heaths make splendid agricultural land, and those hills with their bright stones that roll away to the blue mountains you can see in the north are full of hidden metals, whilst the soil itself offers rich nourishment to our vines. Two great streams flow through the land, but the sky above it is empty, so to speak, as though awaiting the fluttering of many triumphant flags. Different types of people inhabit the country and some of them are like children—they have first to be shown what to do before they will do it. Since I have lived amongst my people—over whom I have more rights than you might think—since I have worn their clothing, shared their customs and learned to know their ways, I have won their respect and affection, and in doing so I have found that good fortune I once searched for in vain in so many other lands."

These few earnest words made it unnecessary for me to ask any direct questions concerning the wholly satisfying aim he had found in life and to which he had referred in his letters to me.

He had devoted himself in particular to improving the yield of the grain and he had experimented with various sorts. They now grew on all sides vigorously as a living tribute to the success of his activities. The ears were full and heavy and I was curious to know when the fields would be ripe for the reapers and the harvest brought in.

The single-minded devotion he showed to his lonely task often made me think of those sturdy early Romans, who also loved agricultural pursuits and who, in the early years of their history at least, were quite prepared to suffer the natural loneliness of the busy husbandman at work on his own lands.

How admirable and truly elemental is the destiny of the countryman! I thought. And how wonderful when he brings a ripe understanding to his tasks which can lift them from the rut and ennoble and refine them! In its simplicity and yet diversity and in its close contact with dispassionate nature it approaches the paradisal state.

Gradually I got to know the life on the Major's estate as though it had always been my own; I understood what was going on; I could watch the growth of the crops with an understanding eye and do my part to assist their progress. And soon the uneventful passage of the days in simple tasks so captured me that I felt happy and at peace with the world, forgetful of the towns I had left behind, as though I had turned my back on nothing of importance.

One day we were again on the heath amongst the horses and their guardians, and as it happened the latter were joined by the herdsmen who tended the cattle so that an unusually large number of the Major's men were gathered around us. As we drove home—this time we were not on horseback but in a broad-based carriage whose wheels rolled safely over the heath as it was drawn along by a pair of fine horses in full harness—the Major referred to his men.

"I could lead those men into battle if I cared to place myself at their head," he declared. "They are absolutely devoted to me, and so are all the servants and laborers around the house. They would let themselves be cut into pieces rather than have anything happen to me. And if I add those who are subject to me by feudal right and are equally devoted to me—as they have shown on many occasions—I could muster quite a large army of men who love me. And remember: I did not come to them until my hair was going gray, and after long years of forgetfulness. What must it be like to lead hundreds of thousands of such men and guide their steps toward a noble aim? Once they trust a leader they are generally like children and they will follow loyally wherever they are led—to good or evil."

After a while he spoke again:

"At one time I imagined that I would be an artist or a scholar, but then I realized that such men must have a deep and earnest message for humanity, a message to arouse enthusiasm, to make men greater and nobler. The scholar at least must discover and reveal things that will further the material well-being of humanity and improve the means to attain it. But in the one case and the other the man himself must first possess a big and simple heart. As I was convinced that I possessed no such thing, I let my opportunities pass by—and now it is too late."

As he spoke these words it seemed to me as though a shadow passed over his face, and at that moment it was as though he looked out into the world with that same ecstatic reverie I had known in him in former years when, sitting idly on the Epomeo,[5] we had talked together of the innumerable wishes and dreams of youth whilst all around us the heavens were almost solemnly blue and the sea glittered in the sun below us. And suddenly I wondered whether the happiness he had thought to find here was altogether so complete after all.

[5]Volcanic mountain on island of Ischia, off Naples, Italy.

This was the only occasion throughout our whole acquaintanceship that he had made any reference to his past life. Before that he had never given even the slightest indication. For my part I had never asked any questions, nor did I do so now. A man who has traveled widely learns to treat others with consideration and never to refer to the initimate personal affairs of a man's life, for they are never revealed except voluntarily.

I had already been with the Major for quite a time now, and very gladly too, for I had come to take a great interest in the management of his estate and I had often taken an active hand in the work connected with it. Whilst not so engaged I had devoted myself to keeping a diary of my travels and my experiences. As a result of my stay at Unwar there was now one thing of which I felt fairly confident: as simple and active as the life was that the Major led here, there was some faintly disturbing element present which had not yet been altogether resolved, and at the same time a certain sadness which, in such a man, expressed itself in serene and earnest resignation.

In all other matters that arose during our life together at Unwar he was frank and open with me and there was no question of reserve or dissimulation. I often visited him in his study, where we would spend the heat of the day or the cool of the evening by candlelight before retiring for the night, chatting about a great variety of matters. On his desk there was a small portrait of a young woman in the early 'twenties. To me the most interesting feature of this portrait was that although the artist had no doubt done his best to gloss over the fact, it was not the portrait of a beautiful young woman but rather that of a plain one. But there was vitality in the face and strength of character, too. The dark complexion and the shape of the forehead were unusual and the eyes were proud and untamed. It was certainly the portrait of a determined woman.

It was not difficult to imagine that this young woman must have played some role in his former life, and the sight of that portrait made me wonder—as I had wondered during our stay in Italy together—why such a man had never married. But on principle I had not asked him then and for the same reason I made no comment now. The fact that the picture was there openly on his writing desk meant nothing, for none of his people ever came into the room. If any of his men had anything to say to him and he was in his study they had to wait in an anteroom where their entrance rang a little bell which announced their presence. He also never received visitors in his study in the ordinary way and it was therefore an indication of some intimacy that I was allowed to enter the room. In fact it was perhaps this signal mark of his confidence and trust in me that saved me from pondering and speculating.

Harvesting had now begun and I shall never forget the cheerful, happy days that accompained it. Now and again the Major had to visit places in the neighborhood and he always invited me to accompany him. There are few contries in Europe where the distances between the inhabited centers are so great, but we would cover them in a comparatively short time either on horseback or driving fast over the heath in a light carriage. For one such journey the Major dressed himself in the close-fitting national costume of Hungary and at his side he wore a saber. The handsome garb suited him very well. It was to a meeting of the local administrative body that we went and there he delivered a speech in Hungarian. It was always my endeavor in whatever land I came to learn as much of the language as I could and as quickly as possible. I had therefore picked up quite a little Hungarian from the Major's men and from everyone else with whom I came into contact, with the result that I was able to understand quite a lot of what he said. The reception accorded to his words varied from warm approval and admiration to no less warm disapproval. On the way back he translated the whole speech into German for me. That evening he once again wore evening dress and he was as I had known him in Italy. Most of the others present had put off their Hungarian costumes and were also in ordinary European evening dress.

I accompanied him on other journeys and I learned that there were four estates in the neighborhood, of which the Major's was one. A few years back the owners of these estates had agreed that they would work together to raise agricultural standards and improve the quality of the local crops. This they proposed to do by setting a practical example on their own estates and encouraging others to follow it, which they would most likely do when they observed that it led to prosperity and a better life for all. This association of estates had developed its own rules and from time to time its members came together to discuss whatever matters happened to arise. As yet only these four large estates were actually members of the association, but a number of smaller landowners had already begun to follow the example of their bigger neighbors without formally joining the association. Those landowners and farmers of the neighborhood who were not members of the association were at liberty to attend its meetings, listen to the proceedings and ask for advice and information, the only condition being that they should give notice in good time of their intention to be present, and, as I saw when I went to such a meeting, very many of them took advantage of this privilege. This particular meeting took place on another estate about four hours' ride from Unwar. It belonged to a local worthy named Gömör, who was a member of the association. The only members present at this meeting were the Major and this Gömör, but it was well attended by an audience of interested parties who had come to listen to the proceedings.

I had already got to know this Gömör quite well and I had visited his estate on two previous occasions. On the second I had even stayed there for a few days.

When the harvesting was almost over and there was less to attend to, the Major broached a new project.

"We shall be having more time to ourselves now," he said, "and next week we will ride over to my neighbor Brigitta Maroshely's estate on a visit. When you meet her I think you will agree with me that she is the most wonderful woman in the world."

Two days after this earnest remark he made me acquainted with Brigitta Maroshely's son, who happened to have come over to Unwar for some reason. It was the handsome youngster who had eaten at our table on the first day after my arrival and whom I had noticed in particular at the time because of his exceptional good looks. This time he remained at Unwar throughout the day and went with us on our visits to various parts of the estate. He was, as I had already noted, still very young indeed, little more than a boy and hardly even a stripling as yet. I took to him at once. His eye was dark and amiable and when he sat on horseback there was something at the same time so vigorous and yet so modest about his demeanor that my heart went out to him. I had once had a very good friend, whose fate had been to go to an early grave, and Gustave—for such was the name of Brigitta Maroshely's son—reminded me of him very strongly.

Since the Major had praised Brigitta Maroshely so highly, and now that I had made the acquaintance of her son, I was very anxious to meet the mother in person.

Whilst I was the guest of Gömör I had learnt something of the Major's past. Gömör, like so many of the people I met here, was of a frank and open disposition, and he spoke to me freely and without prompting of what he knew. The Major, it appeared, was not of a local family at all. His parents had been very rich and from his youth he had traveled around constantly. No one really knew where his travels had taken him or in whose service he had attained the rank of Major. In his youth he had never been to Unwar at all, having first come there only a few years previously. However, once there, he had settled down and joined the association of those landowners who styled themselves the friends of agriculture. At that time the association had consisted of two members only: he, Gömör, and Brigitta Maroshely. In fact, in those days it had not really been an association at all, and the rules and the holding of formal meetings was to come only later. It had all started because two good neighbors, he, Gömör, and Brigitta Maroshely, had talked the matter over and decided to work together to improve their property in this rather barren part of the country. Incidentally, the initiative in the matter had come from Brigitta Maroshely.

Although a very agreeable and intelligent woman, he went on, she was not beautiful, and her husband, a frivolous scamp to whom she had been married when she was very young, had soon left her and never returned. After this desertion she had come to Maroshely, which was the name of the estate, with her son, who had then been only a very small child. She had taken over the management of the estate as efficiently as any man and soon introduced new methods and improvements. In fact, she had begun to dress like a man and she rode astride like a man. She worked hard herself from morning to night and she kept a firm rein on her servants and her laborers. She had shown what persistent hard work can do and she had achieved wonders on what had been little more than a stony waste. He, Gömör, had got to know her well and he had followed her example and introduced her methods on his own estate, and up to the present he had seen no cause to regret it.

When the Major had first come to settle in Unwar he had never ridden over to Maroshely to visit his neighbor, but when he had already been at Unwar for a number of years Brigitta Maroshely had fallen seriously ill. She had been at death's door and then the Major had ridden over to Maroshely and attended to her until she was well again. From that time on he had visited her frequently. Her recovery under his care had been so remarkable that at the time there had been a good deal of talk of animal magnetism, at which the Major was said to be an adept. However, no one had known anything for certain about his methods. In any case, an unusually close and intimate friendship had developed between the two. Brigitta Maroshely was certainly worthy of the profoundest feelings of friendship, but whether of the passionate attachment the Major had conceived for the already ageing and far from beautiful woman was another matter. But passion was undoubtedly the right word to describe the Major's feelings for her and everyone who knew them both could plainly see it. The Major would undoubtedly marry Brigitta if he could, and he was obviously deeply grieved at not being able to do so. Nothing was known about the husband's whereabouts or his fate and there was therefore no possibility of a divorce, nor could his death be assumed. It said a good deal for Brigitta Maroshely's qualities that she, whose husband had once so irresponsibly left her, should now be sought after by such a serious wooer.

Such was the story Gömör told me about the affairs of Brigitta Maroshely and the Major, and it made me more than ever anxious to meet her. Whilst out visiting I saw her son again on one or two occasions, and then the day came which had been fixed for our ride over to Maroshely to visit his mother.

The night before as I lay in bed and the chirping of myriads of crickets filled my drowsy ear before I fell asleep my thoughts dwelt on her and all I had heard. And when I fell asleep she appeared in my dreams. I stood once again on the heath before the strange rider who had lent me the horse and the escort to take me to Unwar and her beautiful eyes held me so in thrall that I was rooted to the spot and aware that I was condemned to spend the rest of my days there on the heath, unable to stir. But then my dream ceased and I fell into an untroubled sleep to wake up feeling fresh and vigorous the next morning. After breakfast our horses were brought round and in my heart I was delighted to know that at last I was to see face to face the woman who had so occupied my thoughts, even to appearing in my dreams in the night.

3   *A Past in the Steppes*

Before I describe how we came to Maroshely, how I made the acquaintance of Brigitta and how I came to be so often on her estate after that, I must first tell something at least of her earlier life, for without that it would be impossible to understand what follows. How I obtained such a detailed knowledge of the circumstances which are about to be described will result naturally from my relationship to the Major and to Brigitta Maroshely and develop as my story goes along. It is not necessary that I should reveal beforehand what I myself did not learn prematurely but from the unfolding of the events themselves.

The human race possesses an extraordinary and wonderful quality which we know as beauty. We are all attracted by a felicity in appearance though we are not always able to say just in what the attraction consists. Beauty is everywhere around us. It lies in the eye of the beholder. Yet sometimes it is not present in features which seem formed according to all the canons that normally produce it. Sometimes beauty goes unperceived because it blossoms in the desert, or because the seeing eye has not yet lighted upon it. And often it is praised and near idolized where in reality it is lacking. But where a heart beats high in ecstasy and passion, and where two hearts beat as one, it is ever present, or the heart would fail and the love of twin souls perish.

It is a strange flower and often it blooms in unlikely places, but, whatever the soil, once it burgeons it can hardly be destroyed. Remove it from one spot and it will blossom again in another, and often in the least considered place. It is proper to mankind alone and it magnifies the man who kneels before it, pouring into his trembling and ecstatic heart all the things that make the life of man worth while. To have it not, or know it not, is a tragedy, and he in whom no other eye can perceive it is an object of pity. Even the heart of a mother can turn away from a child in whom she cannot—or can no longer—divine even the faintest shimmer of its glory.

And so it was with the child Brigitta. When she was born her mother had no feelings for her child. To her it was not the helpless, appealing little creature that calls out all the love and tenderness in a normal mother's heart. And later when the child lay amidst the snow-white linen in its beautiful gilded cot its face was clouded over because of this deprivation and it was as though a wicked fairy had breathed over it. Almost unwittingly the mother would turn her glance away to where her two other little children played together on the deep, rich carpet. They were the vessels of beauty to her.

When strangers came they neither praised nor criticized the newborn child but turned their attention to its sisters. And so the child grew up. The father often went through the room indifferently on his affairs, and when the mother sometimes embraced and fondled the other children in despairing ardor she did not observe the dark eyes of Brigitta as they stared at her unwinkingly as though the small child already understood and resented the slight it put upon her. When the child cried her wants were attended to; when she remained quiet she was left alone. The others had their own affairs that interested them and the child lay there, staring at the gilt decorations on her cot or at the intricate patterns on the wallpaper.

When her limbs grew stronger and her cot was no longer the one place in which she stayed, she would sit in a corner and play with her bricks and utter strange sounds she had heard from no one. As her games became more complicated her rebellious eyes would often bear that look that boys have when they intend some forbidden thing. If her sisters ever tried to join her games she would reject them roughly, even striking them. And when, in a belated surge of love and pity, her mother would take her into her arms and weep over her the child would go stiff and cry and struggle to escape from the clinging arms around her. Because of this rejection and frustration the mother now grew more loving, but also more embittered. She did not realize that when the first small soft roots had sought the warm soil of mother love and found themselves rebuffed they had turned in on themselves and found an obstinate hold in the stoniness of a lonely heart.

And now the stony waste spread still farther.

As the children grew up and the period of fine clothes began, those for Brigitta were always thought to be good enought for her. But the clothes of her sisters were altered and adjusted again and again before they were finally considered perfect. Great care was taken to teach the other children how to behave and they were praised when their conduct was pleasing. Brigitta was not even blamed, although she often creased her clothes and made them dirty.

When the time came for learning lessons and the mornings were devoted to them, Brigitta would sit there staring at book or map with the only beautiful feature she possessed: her dark, glowing eyes. And if the teacher suddenly asked her a question she would start, as though out of a reverie, and not know what to answer. During the long evenings, and at other times when the family was in the drawing room and she was not missed, she would lie at full length on the floor, sprawling on books or pictures, or on torn cards her sisters no longer wanted. And all the while a fantastic but crippled world festered in her heart. The library door was never locked and, although no one suspected it, she had read half her father's books, though most of them she could not as yet understand. Now and again pieces of paper were found lying around with strange and wild drawings on them, and these she must have made.

As the young girls began to become young ladies Brigitta was like some strange plant in a conventional bed. Her sisters were now soft-fleshed beautiful creatures, made to grace a drawing room, but Brigitta was strong and slim. Her strength was almost that of a youth, and if her sisters teased her, or wanted to embrace her affectionately, she would put them away firmly with her strong slim arms. Manual labor attracted her and often she would work until beads of sweat stood on her forhead. She took no music lessons as her sisters did, but she rode a horse with spirit and as well as any youth. Often she would lie in the grass, wearing her best clothes, talking to herself and declaiming to the silent bushes.

It was about this time that her father began to make her reproaches for her wayward and obstinate behavior. Even when she did talk she would sometimes fall silent suddenly and her mood would become sullen and resentful. It was no use her mother's making encouraging signs to her or expressing helplessness and bitter despair by wringing her hands; her daughter still remained silent. On one occasion her angry father so far forgot himself as to chastise her, the grown girl, because she refused to go into the drawing room when her presence was desired there. She just looked at him with hot, dry eyes, and still refused to go. Whatever he did would have made no difference; she would have remained unmoved.

If there had been just one person around her with an understanding eye for her hidden self, just one who could see the beauty that was there, just one person for whom she could have felt something beyond contempt and resentment . . . But there was no one. The others could not help her and there was nothing she could do for them.

The family lived in town and had always done, and there they led a life of brilliance and fashion. As the daughters grew up and became young women of marriageable age, reports of their beauty spread and soon many people were coming to the house on their account, and the social gatherings and entertainments became more numerous and more brilliant than before. The heart of more than one young man beat higher and longed for possession of one of the treasures the house contained. But the girls were unmoved; as yet they were too young to understand such things. However, they gave themselves up gladly to the pleasure such parties brought with them, and the ordering of a new gown and all the preliminaries of a party would occupy their rapt attention for days in advance. Not so Brigitta. In any case, as the youngest she was never consulted, as though she were still too young to know and understand anything about such matters. Sometimes she was present on such social occasions and then she would always wear a full-skirted black silk dress she had made herself, but usually she avoided company and remained in her own room, and no one knew how she occupied her time there.

A number of years passed in this way and then one day a certain young man who had already caused quite a fluttering in various circles appeared in the town. His name was Stephen Murai and he had been brought up on his father's country estate. When his formal education was completed he was sent out on the Grand Tour in preparation for taking his place in the select society of his own country. It was on his return that he came to the capital, where Brigitta and her family lived. Before long he became the main subject of conversation in society. Some praised his intelligence and others praised his good manners, his charm and his modesty. And many people declared that they had never seen anyone quite so handsome as this young newcomer. But, of course, there were those who preferred malice and slander, and they said that there was something wild and arrogant about him. You could see quite plainly, they said, that he had been brought up in the country. He was also proud, they said, and, if it came to the point, probably deceitful. But one way or the other, more than one young woman who had not yet had the opportunity was very anxious to make his acquaintance when she heard of his reputation.

Brigitta's father knew this young man's family quite well, and as a young man, when he too had traveled a good deal, he had often stayed on their estate, though later, when he settled down in town for good, he had rather lost touch with them. He knew that at that time this family had been wealthy and now he made discreet inquiries about their present state, finding, to his satisfaction, that they were now wealthier than ever, for the simple life they led on their country estates had caused their fortunes to increase still further. Should this young man prove personally acceptable, therefore, he would obviously make a very suitable candidate for the hand of one of the girls. It was quite obvious, of course, that in view of the young man's expectations other mothers and fathers would be moved by similar ideas and so Brigitta's father lost no time but promptly invited the young man to visit the house.

This Stephen Murai did on a number of occasions, but at first Brigitta did not meet him because for some time she had practically given up her in any case rare appearances in the drawing room. However, at about this time she accepted an invitation to a social gathering at the house of an uncle. This was unusual, but as a younger girl she had sometimes stayed with this uncle and found his company agreeable. She was therefore present that evening and she sat there in her usual black silk dress watching what was going on around her. She was also wearing a headdress she had made for herself. It was not the fashion to wear such a headdress and her sisters found it unbecoming, even ugly, but, in fact, it suited her dark complexion very well.

Many guests were present and when she casually looked toward a little group not far away from where she was sitting she noticed that a young man with dark, romantic eyes was looking at her. Modestly she looked away at once, but a little later she observed that the young man was again looking at her. It was Stephen Murai.

About a week later her father gave a ball and Stephen Murai was invited. He arrived when most of the other guests were already present and the dancing had already begun. The gentlemen were just taking their partners for the second dance and looking around he saw Brigitta. He went up to her immediately and asked her respectfully for the honor of the dance, but she refused, saying that she had never learned to dance. He then bowed silently and went away. Brigitta sat down on a couch behind a table and watched the glittering scene around her. Murai chatted happily with various people and danced with some of the young ladies. That evening he seemed more than usually agreeable and courteous to everyone. At last the ball came to an end and the guests departed.

Brigitta went up to her room—it had cost her a great deal of pleading and persistence to persuade her parents to let her have a room to herself in which she could be alone as she desired. As she undressed now—she could not bear to have a maid around her—she looked into the mirror and studied her dark-complexioned face in its frame of jet black curls. When she went to bed—it was not a soft couch, but firm, as she liked it—she drew up the white linen sheets and lay down with her arms behind her head and stared with sleepless eyes at the ceiling.

Other parties followed, and now Brigitta was always there and so was Stephen Murai. He continued to pay attention to her, greeting her respectfully, and when she rose to go he would always be at hand to help her with her shawl or give her her fan. Once she had left the room it was not long before the wheels of Stephen Murai's carriage sounded in the courtyard below as he was driven home.

This went on for some time until one evening she was again at a party given by her uncle. It was a warm evening and it was hot in the ballroom so Brigitta went out on to the balcony through the open French windows. Hearing a step behind her she turned and found Stephen Murai had followed her. Standing there on the balcony away from the lights they talked of unimportant matters, but there was an unusual timidity in his voice. He referred to the night then and said that it was unjust to speak harshly of the darkness. On the contrary, it was a kind and lovely thing and it soothed and comforted the anxious heart. Then he fell silent and she fell silent with him. After a while they went back into the ballroom and he stood for a long time by himself at a window.

When Brigitta went home that night she undressed in her room, slowly discarding one piece of finery after the other, and putting on her nightdress. Then once again she looked at herself in the mirror, for a long time. Tears welled to her eyes and soon she was weeping uncontrollably. They were the first tears she had ever wept in her life and now they ran down her cheeks freely as though she were making up for all the bitter but unshed tears of her life. She had sunk to the floor and she sat there crouched down with her feet under her and cried her heart out as though relief would come when she could cry no more. It was a place where she often sat crouched in reverie and by chance there was a picture on the floor there, a child's picture and it showed one brother sacrificing himself for the other. Impulsively, and hardly knowing why, she picked it up and pressed it to her lips until it was creased from her kisses and wet from her tears.

At last she ceased to weep, but although the candles had burnt low she still crouched there on the floor before her mirror like a heart-broken child that has cried itself out and feels relief. Her hands lay crossed and motionless in her lap and the ribbons and pleats of her nightdress were damp from her tears and hung disconsolately over her ripening bosom. There she remained sunk in reverie, but after a long while she sighed deeply once or twice as though drawing new breath into her body. Then she passed her hand over her eyes, rose and went to bed. Lying there by the faint glow of a night light she had placed behind a small screen after having put out the candles she murmured to herself incredulously:

"It can't be true. It can't be true."

And then she fell asleep.

When she met Stephen Murai again after that nothing seemed to have changed outwardly between them, but he sought her company more than ever and there was now something shy and almost hesitant in his manner. He said very little to her and she gave him no encouragement, not even the slightest.

There were many opportunities for him to speak to her alone, but he let them all pass unutilized until one day another arose and then he summoned up courage and spoke. He said that he felt that she was not very amiably disposed toward him, and if that were really so all he asked was that she should allow herself to get to know him better. Perhaps then he might not prove entirely unworthy of her attention. Perhaps, after all, he had qualities, or could develop them, which would win her respect . . . her respect at least, if not something he would desire a thousand times more earnestly.

"No, Stephen," she answered. "It is not that I am not well disposed toward you. Oh, no! Far from it. But there is one thing I must beg of you. Do not seek my hand. Do not, I beg of you, for if you do you will most surely have cause to regret it."

"But why, Brigitta? Why do you say that?" the young man asked in amazement.

It was a moment or two before she replied and then she spoke slowly:

"Because no love but the very deepest would be at all acceptable to me. You see, I know that I am not beautiful, and just because of that I would demand a love greater than that you could feel for the most beautiful girl in the world. How deep such a love would have to be I cannot tell, but I feel that it would have no limit and no end. And now you know how impossible it is that you should pay court to me. You are the only one who has ever taken it for granted that I even had a heart at all, and because of that I would never deceive you."

Perhaps she would have said more, but at that moment others approached and he saw that her lips were trembling as though in pain.

It is clear that far from discouraging Stephen Murai such words were calculated to increase his ardor. He began to worship her almost as though she were an angel of light and always he ignored the greater beauties so willingly around him, looking instead beyond them in the hope of meeting her eyes. And so it went on until in her breast the dark irresistible power began to stir and cause her arid heart to blossom and tremble. It was soon impossible for either of them to conceal such feelings altogether. Those around them began incredulously to suspect the unbelievable and when at last they were convinced their astonishment knew no bounds.

For his part Stephen Murai took no pains to conceal his feelings for Brigitta. On the contrary, he seemed anxious that all the world should know. One day as they stood alone in a room from which they could hear in the distance the sound of the music the company had come together to enjoy, he took her hand and drew her to him wordlessly. She made no attempt to resist the gentle pressure and their faces came closer and closer together until she felt his lips on hers and softly answered his kiss.

It was the first time in her life that she had ever kissed a living soul, not even her mother or her sisters. And many years later Murai declared that never in his life either before or since had he experienced such pure and deep emotion as he did the first time those lonely, untouched lips met his.

With this first kiss the barrier that had been between the two was gone. There was no further hindrance to their union. Within a few days the two were openly affianced and Brigitta was the intended bride of the man who had been so widely and so earnestly sought after. Both families readily gave their approval to the match and a serener relationship developed between the two young people. A warm and heartening glow gradually arose in the lonely heart of the neglected girl, and then steadily developed into something rich and gay.

The instinct that had drawn Stephen Murai to her had not deceived him. Her character was stronger and purer than that of most women, and because her heart had never been burdened by premature thoughts and imaginings of love, real love, now that it had come, could flourish in it all the more strongly. The intimate association that now developed between the two was more than usually delightful to him. Because she had always been alone she had built up a world of her own into which no one else had entered, but now he was privileged to do so and it was something new and strange and sweet that had previously belonged to her alone. Her personality began to flower richly before his eyes and he gratefully recognized the warmth and profundity of her love, which rose like a stream of pure gold as though between banks that had long been deserted. The hearts of others were divided amongst a great many things and a great many people, but hers had remained whole, and as he had been the only one to recognize its very presence so now he was the only one to possess it.

Time passed on light and delicate wings and he lived in joy and elation throughout the days of their betrothal. At last came their wedding day and at the church portals after the solemn ceremony Stephen Murai took his silent bride into his arms and lifted her into the carriage that was to take them to their new home.

The two young people had decided to live in town, and thanks to his father's generosity Stephen Murai had been able to take a fine house and furnish it magnificently. His father had long been a widower living alone on his country estate and never coming to the capital; but for his son's wedding he made the journey. Brigitta's father and mother were there too, together with her sisters, her favorite uncle and a number of other close relations. Both Murai's father and Brigitta's had desired that the marriage should be solemnized in great state and so it had been and afterward there was a splendid reception for all the wedding guests.

When the last guests had departed, Stephen Murai led his bride through the brilliantly lit reception rooms to their own private apartments and there he sat alone with the girl who until then had had only one room that she could really call her own and who was now his wife.

"How beautiful everything was, Brigitta! And how wonderfully everything has come to pass! I knew the first moment I saw you. Something told me at once that you were a woman to whom I could not remain indifferent. But I did not realize at once that I must either love you or hate you forever. How happy I am that it is love and not hate!"

Brigitta made no reply, but she held his hand in hers and her fine dark eyes looked serenely around her.

After a while Murai called the servants and ordered them to clear away all signs of the wedding reception, to extinguish the unnecessary lights and to turn the festive house into the living place they were now to occupy together. When this was done the servants were sent to their quarters and the first night descended on the new home and on the new family of two who had shared it for but a few hours.

From then on Stephen Murai and his bride lived almost wholly in their own home, visiting the houses of others only rarely. When they had first made each other's acquaintance they had always been in the company of others, and even during their engagement they had been together only in public. Now they retired gladly into the privacy of their own home and neither felt that anything outside themselves or outside their walls was necessary to their happiness.

Although the house had been well furnished and lavishly equipped, there was still a great deal to be done to make it exactly as they wanted it, an addition here, an improvement there, a rearrangement elsewhere. They thought over what was still to be done, consulted each other on all points and discussed what was still to be obtained, until in this way their surroundings were gradually ordered to their liking and their guests were received in an atmosphere of domestic comfort and simplicity which was at the same time refined and beautiful.

Within a year of their marriage Brigitta bore her husband a son, and this new marvel kept them more than ever in their own home. Brigitta was taken up with the care for her child, and Murai now had his affairs to attend to, for his father had handed over part of the estate and this Murai now administered from the town.

When the boy was old enough not to need quite the same constant attention, and when Murai had put his own affairs so far into order that they no longer needed his every spare moment, he began to take his wife out again; into society, to public places, to the theater and so on. On such occasions Brigitta noticed that he treated her if possible with even greater consideration and more marked affection than he did at home and her heart moved to him in gratitude for his understanding.

In the following spring he took her and the boy away into the country and when they returned in the autumn he proposed that they should now live in the country rather than the town, making their home on one of his estates. After all, he declared, it was much more beautiful in the country than in the town and life was, on the whole, more agreeable there. Brigitta agreed and so they went into the country to live.

Once they were there Murai settled down to the life of a country gentleman on his estate, in which he now took a deep interest, developing it and introducing many changes for the better. His chief recreation was shooting and he often went out alone with his gun, sometimes on foot and sometimes on horseback. It was thus that fate led him to make the acquaintance of another woman, a being totally different to anything he had known before. It was on one such shooting expedition that he first saw her.

His horse was picking its way carefully down a wooded slope when suddenly he turned his head involuntarily and his eyes met those of a beautiful woman who was regarding him through the foliage of the surrounding bushes. They were like the eyes of some shy and untamed gazelle, and before he could take a second and closer look they were gone. The woman was also on horseback and in a moment she had turned her horse and galloped away across the heath.

Her name was Gabrielle, he discovered, and she was the only daughter of an old Count who had his estate in the neighborhood. She had, like him, been brought up in the country and she was a wild creature, for her father had allowed her to do as she pleased, believing that in this way she would best develop her natural qualities and not grow up to be an animated doll like the women of the town, for whom the Count had nothing but contempt. Gabrielle's beauty was renowned throughout the neighborhood, but no word of it had as yet come to Murai's ears, for he had never lived on this estate before and quite recently he had been traveling to his other estates.

A few days later the two met again, at the very same spot. After that they met often and became acquainted. They asked no questions of each other and they were not curious to know who they were or where they came from. They just accepted each other, and the girl, unsophisticated and ingenuous, laughed, joked and teased Murai, urging him on to ride wild and daring races with her and galloping along madly at his side, an untamed and heavenly enigma. He fell in gaily with her high spirits and usually let her win. One day when they were racing wildly over the heath and she was too exhausted and out of breath to speak she could bring him to a halt only by grasping repeatedly at his bridle. He reined in his horse and dismounted. As he lifted her out of the saddle she leaned against him and whispered softly that she was defeated. Her stirrup leather needed adjustment and as he put it right she stood against a tree, breathless, but glowing with life and vitality. When he straightened himself he seized her impulsively and pressed her to him fiercely. Then, without waiting to see whether she was pleased or angry, he leapt into the saddle and galloped off.

It was sheer high spirits and the impulse of a moment that had made him act so, but as he held her there was an indescribable ecstasy in his heart, and as he rode back his mind was filled with thoughts of her soft cheeks, her sweet breath and her sparkling eyes.

After that they no longer sought each other's company, and when by chance they met again in the house of a neighbor they both flushed a deep red. Murai then went away to visit one of his other estates a long way off, and there he stayed for some time in a fever of reorganization and rearrangement.

Brigitta was aware of what had happened and her heart went numb. A bitter feeling of shame arose in her bosom and when she went about the house on her affairs it was as though a dark shadow were moving through the rooms. But at last she ruthlessly crushed the gnawing pain in her heart and made her decision.

When Murai returned from the storm of activity on his distant estate she went to him in his room and gently proposed that they should part. It took him by surprise and shocked him deeply, but he argued with her, pleaded with her, begged her to change her mind. In vain. All she would say was, "I warned you that you would have cause to regret it if you married me. I warned you that you would regret it."

At last he sprang to his feet, seized her hands and declared with deep emotion, "Woman, I hate you more than words can say. I hate you."

She made no reply to his impassioned outburst but just looked at him with dry, reddened eyes.

He packed his trunk and sent it on ahead and three days afterwards, toward evening, he left the house in his traveling clothes. When he had gone she threw herself to the floor and lay there as she had once lain in the grass declaiming to the silent bushes the feelings that filled her heart. But now they were feelings of pain and humiliation and the scalding tears ran from her eyes unchecked. They were the last tears she shed for the man she loved so much and after that her eyes were dry.

In the meantime he galloped wildly over the heath, and a hundred times he was sorely tempted to draw the saddle pistol from its holster and blow his fevered brains out. On his way, and whilst it was still daylight, he had passed

Gabrielle standing on the balcony of her father's house and looking out. He did not even raise his eyes but rode on past her without a sign of recognition.

Six months later he sent back formal agreement to the divorce and his consent to his wife's retaining the boy. Perhaps he felt that the child would be better taken care of in her hands, or perhaps his old love for her made him unwilling to deprive her of the last dear thing she possessed. After all, for him the whole world now lay open again. At the same time he made generous provision for both her and the boy, sending her all the necessary documents containing the arrangements. This was the first sign she had received from him since his departure, and it was the last. Nor did she see him again. She learned later from his lawyer that the funds he needed for himself had been transferred to a banking house at Amsterdam. More she never learned.

Not long after this parting Brigitta's father, mother and two sisters all died within a very short space of time. And a little while after that Murai's father, who was already an old man, died too. Brigitta was now completely alone in the world with her child.

Far away from the capital she owned an estate in a barren part of the country where she was unknown. The house and the estate were known as Maroshely and it was the place from which her own family took its name. She decided to go there where she could live unknown to the rest of the world and this she did, resuming her maiden name.

As a child when they had given her, perhaps out of pity, a beautiful doll, she had played with it happily for a while, but then discarded it in favor of things that were dearer to her, simple things, strangely shaped sticks and stones. Now she took with her to Maroshely the greatest treasure she possessed, her son, abandoning all else. And there she watched over him, caring for him devotedly, with eyes only for him and his needs. But as he grew older and his own world extended so did hers. She began to pay more attention to the running of her estate and to the development of the barren heathlands around her. She put on man's clothing, rode astride as she had done in her youth, and began to appear more freely amongst her people.

As soon as the boy could ride a horse he went everywhere with her, and the vigorous, creative, longing soul of the mother now gradually flowered in the son. Her interests and her activities grew wider and a paradise of creative activity surrounded her and rewarded her efforts. The bare hills around grew green with the vines and gushing streams watered the plains until what had been a stony waste became a rich and heroic poem of human effort. And like all real poetry it brought its own blessings.

Others followed her shining example and an association of like-minded landowners grew up to carry her efforts still further. Even those who lived farther away were now moved to enthusiasm and emulation and on the blind and barren heathlands there were increasing signs of vigorous human activity as though a friendly eye were opening in the wasteland.

Brigitta had lived and worked at Maroshely for fifteen years when my friend the Major came to his neglected estate at Unwar and elected to settle down for the rest of his life there where he had never lived before, and where, he assured me, he learned application and persistence from this strange woman to whom he was soon deeply attracted by the belated affection I have previously recorded.

4   *A Present in the Steppes*

The Major and I rode over to Maroshely. Brigitta was really the woman I had seen on horseback on the day of my arrival. Her friendly smile showed that she recalled our short acquaintance and I blushed, remembering my unfortunate attempt to give her money. There were no other guests present and the Major introduced me as an old acquaintance of his travels in whose company he had spent a good deal of time—an acquaintance, he added, who was about, he flattered himself to think, to develop into a friend.

I was very gratified—and it was really no small thing for me—to learn that she already knew almost everything relating to my earlier acquaintance with him. He must therefore have talked to her about me quite a lot and it indicated that he recalled our days together with real pleasure and that on her part she regarded it as worth while to remember such things.

She declared amiably that she did not propose to take me on a tour of inspection of the house and the estate because I could see everything that interested me when we rode out in the ordinary way and on the many occasions that she hoped I would now ride over from Unwar as her guest, which she now invited me to be whenever I pleased.

She then reproached the Major for not having visited her for some time and he excused himself, pleading the pressure of work at the harvest and saying in particular that he had not wished to come over without me but that at the same time he had wished to judge first how well or how indifferently I might suit her company.

We then went into a large hall in which we rested for a while after our ride. The Major took advantage of the occasion to produce a writing tablet and ask Brigitta a number of questions, noting down her replies, which were clear, very simply couched and to the point. It was then her turn to ask various questions relating to this or that neighbor, to the business of the moment and to the forthcoming Diet. The discussion gave me an opportunity of observing how earnestly she dealt with such matters and what weight the Major attached to her opinions. When she was uncertain on this or that point she did not hesitate to say so openly and to ask the Major his views.

The Major finally put away his writing tablet and as we were now rested we got up to take a walk on the estate. On the way the talk between them turned to certain alterations she had made on her property since his last visit, and when she spoke of her estate and the things connected with it there was a certain pride and warmth, almost a tenderness, in her tone. She showed us a wooden veranda she had had built on the garden side of the house and she asked the Major whether he thought it would be a good idea to train vines up the pillars, adding that he might well have something of the sort built at his own house as it had proved a very agreeable place to sit in the late autumn sun.

She then led us into the park, which, it appeared, had been just a forest of oak trees ten years previously. Now there were carefully-kept paths laid out through it and banked streams. Deer were grazing there in safety, for in the course of time she had caused a high wall to be built right round it to keep out the wolves. The considerable expense the building of the wall had entailed had been met from the profits of her maize crops and her cattle breeding, both of which she had greatly developed and improved. When the buidling of the wall had been concluded, huntsmen had thoroughly quartered the whole park to make sure that no wolves—perhaps a mother wolf with her whelps—had been enclosed by the wall, but nothing had been found. Only after that had the deer been established and bred there. It seemed almost as though the deer knew that she was their benefactor, for those we saw on our walk were not in the least timid. As we came near they raised their heads and looked at us with their large velvety eyes but they made no attempt to flee.

Brigitta was obviously very proud of this park and she took great pleasure in showing it to her guests. From there we went on to the pheasantry and as we walked along the wooded paths with little white clouds showing through the oak trees above our heads I took the opportunity of observing her more closely than I had as yet been able to do. Her eyes struck me as even more darkly liquid and more glowing than those of the deer, and perhaps at that moment they were more sparkling than ever because at her side walked a man who understood and appreciated her and knew what she was striving for. Her teeth were very white and her body was still lithe and supple although she was no longer young and she impressed me as having an inexhaustible fund of strength and vitality. As she had expected our visit she was wearing woman's clothes and she had put aside her affairs in order to devote the day to us.

As we walked through the park the talk turned to a great variety of subjects: the future of the country, the raising of the common man and the improvement of his conditions, the tilling and betterment of the soil, the conservancy work for the regulation of the Danube, and the personalities of the prominent men of the country. In this pleasant fashion we went through the greater part of the park, though, as she had said, she made no attempt to show us round on a formal tour of inspection and was interested only in keeping us company.

When we returned to the house it was time to eat. Gustave, her son, appeared at the table. He was bronzed from the sun and the slim, engaging youth looked the picture of health. He had taken his mother's place to supervise the work in the fields that day and now he briefly reported this and that item of interest to her. Otherwise he sat modestly at table with us and listened rather than spoke. In him one could sense a tremendous enthusiasm for the present and an unbounded confidence in the future. Here too, as in the Major's house, it was the custom for the servants attached to the house to eat at the common table and I noticed my old acquaintance Milosch, who acknowledged our previous meeting by greeting me respectfully.

The greater part of the afternoon was then spent inspecting various innovations which the Major had not seen before, and in visits to the gardens and the vineyards.

Toward evening we made ready to ride back to Unwar, and as we were gathering our things together Brigitta reproached the Major with having ridden home one evening from Gömör's estate too lightly clothed for the cool of the evening. He knew very well how treacherous the dewy air of the steppes was at that time of the day so why did he expose himself unnecessarily to its vagaries? The Major made no attempt to excuse himself but merely replied that in the future he would take better care of himself. I remembered the occasion to which Brigitta referred and I happened to know that when it turned out that her son Gustave had come to Gömör's estate without his Bunda, the Major had insisted that Gustave should take his, declaring, untruthfully, that he had another one to hand in the stables. This time, however, we were both well provided with warm clothing for our return journey in the cool of the evening. Brigitta assured herself that this was really so and stood outside the house with us until we were safely in the saddle wearing our warm jackets. Just before we set off she gave the Major one or two commissions and then she took leave of us amiably and without fuss and went back into the house.

Their conversation throughout the day had been serene and cheerful, but it had seemed to me that when they addressed each other there was a certain inner warmth which neither of them cared to show openly, perhaps regarding themselves as too old for demonstrations of affection. The Major and I rode back together in the moonlight and when I said a few sincere words of admiration for Brigitta which I had been unable to withhold he declared simply:

"My friend, in my life I have often been deeply desired, though whether I was as deeply loved I cannot say, but the society and the regard of that woman have meant more to me than anything else I have ever encountered in this world."

He spoke calmly and without emotion but with such certainty and deep conviction that it was quite clear that what he said was the simple truth. At that moment, though it is not my nature, I think I envied the Major for this deep friendship and for his good fortune in having been able to settle down so happily, for at that time I had no firm footing anywhere in the world, or anything to which I could cling, except perhaps the stick that accompanied me on my travels through so many countries.

That day, after we had arrived back at Unwar, the Major suggested that I should stay on as his guest throughout the winter as well. He had begun to treat me with still greater intimacy and to open his heart to me, whilst my feelings of regard and affection for him were growing even stronger. I therefore gladly accepted his offer. He then told me that he would like me to take a definite part in the management of his estate, to take over one branch of his activities and to run it entirely. I should have no cause to regret this and in the future it might come in useful. I agreed at once to this suggestion too, and in fact it did prove useful to me. It is largely the Major I have to thank that I now have a household of my own and a loving wife to help me.

Once I had agreed to take a definite and more settled share in the happy and harmonious life he had built up at Unwar I was anxious to do my share to the very best of my ability. I worked hard and enthusiastically and as I became more experienced so I became more capable and was able to be more and more useful. In this way I learnt the profound satisfaction and pleasure of creative activity and my self-respect increased. I realized more and more how much better it is to take up the work at hand and do it thoroughly rather than to idle around from place to place as I had previously been doing on the pretext of gaining experience of life. For the first time I became capable of really sustained and persistent effort.

My life at Unwar was very happy and the time passed almost unnoticeably. I was also a frequent guest at Maroshely, where I came to be looked on almost as a member of the family. At the same time the relationship between Brigitta and the Major became more and more clear to me. There was no question of any secret passion or any feverish desires, and certainly not a trace of the animal magnetism of which I had heard rumors. However, the relationship between the two was certainly unusual and I had never previously encountered anything of the sort. The nature of that relationship was beyond all question what, in the ordinary way and between two people of opposite sexes, we should call love, and yet it did not express itself in the usual way. The Major treated the ageing woman with a tenderness and respect that was reminiscent more of the devotion a man pays to a higher being, and it was clear that it filled her with a profound inner joy. Her happiness showed itself in her face like the blossoming of some late flower and it gave her features an expression of confidence and serenity, and at the same time a radiance that was quite astonishing. She clearly returned his affection and respect in full measure, but in her attitude toward him there was occasionally a trace of anxiety which expressed itself in solicitude for his health and in attention to those minor needs of life, both so typical of a woman when she loves. So much was obvious in the feelings of each for the other, but beyond that there was nothing further in the behavior or attitude of either.

The Major once confided in me that, at a moment when they had come to talk together of each other in a more intimate fashion than people usually do, they had agreed that they should be united by friendship of the deepest kind, by co-operation toward the same end and by a like striving, but by nothing further. They were both anxious that this calm relationship should remain firmly founded—if possible to the end of their days. They were determined to ask no more of fate, and then there need be no barb, no disappointment. It had been like that between them for a good many years now, he said, and that was how they desired that it should remain.

But man proposes . . . It was not long after he had told me this that that fate of which they had both decided to ask no more acted in despite of them and brought about a happening which swiftly and unexpectedly gave matters a very different complexion.

It was already late autumn, in fact winter had really begun, and one day I was riding with the Major along the new road with its double line of poplars. We had proposed to do a little shooting but a thick mist lay over the already frozen steppes. Suddenly as we rode the sound of two shots boomed dully through the mist.

"They were my pistols," declared the Major. "I would know the reports anywhere," and he immediately urged his horse into a furious gallop along the avenue, riding as hard as I have ever seen a man ride. I had a foreboding of evil and I quickly galloped after him toward the spot from where the sound of the shots had come. When I came up with him after a moment or two my eyes saw a spectacle so terrible and yet so thrilling that even now I shudder at it in recollection and my heart beats higher.

By the old gallows tree, where the rush-grown stream flowed past, the Major had come upon the youngster Gustave defending himself against a pack of fierce wolves, but the lad was already clearly tiring. He had killed two wolves with his pistols and slashed open a third with his blade as the beast sprang at his horse's head. Now they were standing round him irresolutely for a moment, held off only by the look of fierce desperation in his eyes. Licking their slavering chops they looked at him and waited their opportunity. A slight movement, anything or nothing, and they would have sprung at him all together and the boy would have been lost. But in this critical situation the Major thundered up. He had already dismounted when I arrived and I was just in time to see him fling himself at the wolves almost as though he were a wild animal himself. I had heard two more reports and the Major had fired from the saddle, killing two more wolves. Now I saw his hunting blade flash left and right amongst the ravening beasts. From his arrival the whole affair lasted three or four seconds, no more. I had just time to empty my hunting piece into the pack and they were gone, swallowed up by the thick mist all around, and all that was left of them was the dead bodies of those that had been killed.

"Reload," shouted the Major. "They'll attack again."

He recovered his own pistol, a double-barreled model, and rammed home the cartridges. Gustave and I also reloaded. No sooner had we done so and were waiting there for a moment or so listening than we heard the soft footfall of wolves from beyond the gallows tree. The famished but intimidated brutes had now surrounded us. At any moment they would attack again. When they are not driven on by hunger, as they were now, wolves are cowardly creatures and more likely to flee than to attack. However, we were not equipped for wolf hunting and the wretched all-pervading mist made it impossible to see very far so we decided to get back to the house. We mounted and set our horses into a gallop. The frightened beasts needed no urging and they galloped along madly and more than once as we rode I caught a glimpse of a gray shadow loping along silently beside us in the mist. The wolves were tracking us relentlessly and we had to be on our guard the whole time. Once the Major discharged his pistol to the left, but it was impossible to see whether he hit his mark and there was no time for talk. Finally we reached the park gates and the dogs which had been waiting there rushed out and chased after the wolves. A moment later we heard angry howling behind us and then it died away in the distance as the wolves fled from the dogs over the steppes.

"To horse all of you," shouted the Major to his men as they ran up. "Let the wolfhounds loose. I don't want my dogs to come to any harm. Rouse the neighborhood and set the hunt going. Hunt them as long as you please. A double reward for every dead wolf except those lying near the gallows tree, for we killed them ourselves. One of the pistols I gave Gustave last year must be lying around there somewhere. I see he had only one and the other holster is empty. See if you can find the other pistol."

Then the Major turned to me.

"It's five years since wolves ventured so close to the house," he said. "We were beginning to feel fairly secure. It looks as though there's going to be a hard winter. It must already have set in to the north to bring them so far south so early in the season."

The men had rushed off to carry out their master's orders, and in less time than I would have believed possible a party of eager men was on horseback accompanied by a pack of those great shaggy dogs which are so typical of the Hungarian pusta and so necessary to the men who live and work on it. They made arrangements for rousing the neighborhood and then they set off on a hunt which could last a week, a fortnight, and even longer.

Without dismounting we sat there and watched the rapid preparations, but as we finally turned away from the out-buildings and made our way toward the house we observed that Gustave was faint from a wound he had received. As we turned in under the archway which led to the living quarters he suffered a fit of giddiness and almost fell from his horse. One of the servants caught him and helped him from the saddle and then we saw that the saddle and the flanks of the horse were stained with blood.

We carried the lad into one of the rooms on the garden floor and the Major ordered a bed to be prepared and a fire lit. The Major gently removed the boy's clothing and examined the wound. It proved to be a bite in the thigh; nothing very dangerous, but the loss of blood and the excitement had weakened the lad, who was now fighting against the faintness it induced. He was then made as comfortable as possible in bed and the local doctor was sent for whilst another servant rode over to Maroshely to let Brigitta know what had happened. In the meantime the Major remained by the boy's bedside and did his best for him until the doctor arrived. After examining the patient the doctor declared that there was no danger. All the boy needed was a stimulant. Far from being serious, the loss of blood was a good thing: it would help to counteract the inflammation that so often set in after such bites. The chief trouble was the shock and excitement, but a day or two in bed would put the boy right and dispose of any feverishness. It wouldn't be long before he was on his feet again.

We were all very much relieved to hear this good report and the doctor then left with our warm thanks, for there was not one of us in the house who was not deeply attached to the lad.

Toward evening Brigitta appeared, and in her usual thorough and conscientious fashion she was not satisfied until she had examined her son very carefully to make quite certain that there was nothing else wrong with him beyond the bite. When she had finished her examination she stayed by her son's bedside and gave him the medicine the doctor had prescribed. A second bed was quickly made up for her in the same room and there she spent the night. The next morning she was once again sitting by the boy's bedside and listening to his breathing. It was perfectly regular and he was sleeping soundly and peacefully.

And then something happened that made an ineradicable impression on me. I can still see the scene clearly before my eyes. I had come down early in order to inquire how the patient was doing and I had gone into the room adjoining the sick-room. The latter, as I have already said, gave on to the garden. The mist had gone and a red winter's sun was shining into the room through the leafless branches of the trees in the garden. The Major was also in the room with me and he stood at the window and seemed to be looking out into the garden. I could see through the open door into the sick-room where the early-morning light had been subdued a little by light curtains drawn over the windows. Brigitta was sitting by the bed and looking closely at her son. Suddenly she gave a sigh of relief and as I looked at her I glimpsed the light of happy love and devotion in her eyes as she saw that the boy had woken up out of his long sleep and was looking around serenely.

Then I heard a slight sound, almost like a stifled groan, from where the Major had been standing and I looked round. He had half turned back into the room and I saw that there were tears in his eyes. I went toward him, anxiously asking if anything were wrong.

"I have no child," he said softly.

Brigitta's hearing was very keen and she must have heard the half-whispered words, for at that moment she appeared in the doorway. She looked a little uncertainly at my friend and then with an expression I cannot describe, as though she wanted to say something and hardly dared, she said simply:

"Stephen."

The Major turned toward her and they looked at each other wordlessly for a moment, but no more than a moment. Then he strode resolutely toward her and they were in each other's arms. She held him tightly to her and I heard him utter a low sound, and this time there was no room for doubt: it was a sob. At that she embraced him even more closely.

"We shall never part again, Brigitta," I heard him say. "Neither now nor ever."

"Never, Stephen," she replied fervently. "Never."

I was very ill at ease at being present at such an intimate moment and I moved silently toward the door, but she raised her hand.

"Don't go, my friend," she said. "Stay here."

The serious, high-minded woman had been weeping with her head on my friend's shoulder. Her eyes were still wet with tears as she looked at me and her face was radiant with indescribable beauty, for on it there was forgiveness, the most beautiful quality we poor miserable creatures here below can aspire to. At the sight my own feelings were deeply moved.

"My poor wife," exclaimed the Major. "For fifteen long years I have had to do without you, and for fifteen years you were sacrificed."

She smiled gently up at him.

"I was at fault," she said softly. "Forgive me, Stephen. It was the sin of pride. But I had no conception of how good you are. And, after all, the thing was quite natural. We are all drawn irresistibly by what is beautiful."

He put his hand over her lips.

"How can you say such a thing, Brigitta! Yes, it is true, we are all attracted by the beautiful, but I had to wander all over the world before I learnt that it was in our own hearts and that I had abandoned it in one heart that loved me loyally and steadfastly, a heart I thought I had lost forever but which still went with me through all those years and all those many countries. Brigitta, my wife and the mother of my child, you were always with me, by day and by night."

"Yes, I was not lost to you," she replied. "But I have spent sad and regretful years. How good you are, Stephen! Now that I know you, how good you are!"

And they embraced again as though they could never embrace enough, as though they could still hardly believe in the good fortune that had come to them again. They were like two people from whom a great burden has been suddenly lifted. Once again the world stood open to them. They were happy as children are happy, and at that moment they were as innocent children, for the highest bloom of love, and only the highest form of love, is forgiveness, and therefore man will always find it in God and in a mother. Great hearts will forgive again and again; poor creatures never.

Husband and wife had forgotten my presence again and they now turned to the sick-room where Gustave lay in bed, half-guessing what had happened and eagerly awaiting their coming.

"Gustave! Gustave!" exclaimed Brigitta as they entered the room. "It was your father all the time and you did not know it."

Deeply moved at what I had seen and heard I now took the opportunity of going unobtrusively out into the garden. For the first time in my life I truly realized what a noble thing the love of husband and wife is and I counted myself wretched that up to then all I had known of love was the dark, smoldering flame of passion.

I stayed away from the house for some time and when I finally returned everything was calm and serene and all emotional tension had been resolved. Happy and bustling activity now filled the rooms like cheerful sunshine after a storm. I was received with open arms as a dear witness of the joyful thing that had taken place. Once they had discovered that in their preoccupation with each other I had gone they had searched for me everywhere. Gradually I learned everything that had happened then and before. Some of it I learned at once there and then in their elation; the rest I learned in the days that followed until I was able to piece together all the details and set down my story.

My old friend the Major was thus Stephen Murai. After leaving his wife he had called himself Stephen Bathori, which was his family name on the distaff side, and that was the name under which I had always known him. He had won the rank of Major in Spain, and everyone had always referred to him by it. He had traveled all over Europe under the name of Bathori and when he finally went to his neglected estate at Unwar, where no one knew him and to which he seemed drawn by some inner necessity, it was as Stephen Bathori. Although no one on his own estate there knew him, or had ever seen him there, he knew that he would be the neighbor of his wife Brigitta. But even after he had settled in Unwar he did not visit her on the estate at Maroshely she was managing so efficiently, and it was not until he heard the news of her serious illness that he did so. But then he mounted his horse and rode over at once. Her temperature was so high when he arrived that she was already wandering and she did not recognize him. After that he remained day and night at Maroshely and tended her devotedly until she recovered.

It was then that, deeply moved by their first meeting after so many years, and still deeply attached to each other by a love that had never really ceased, but also a little frightened at the thought of their future, for they were still uncertain of each other and both feared that something might again happen to separate them, they made the strange pact by which they should remain no more than firm friends. For years they had both strictly respected it and neither of them had dared to call it into question—until fate suddenly struck at both of them through their son Gustave. Their common anxiety for what they both loved so deeply then threw them into each other's arms and brought them together once again in the more natural and more beautiful relationship of the married couple and dissipated all doubts and all fears.

After a fortnight the news was made known in the neighborhood and well-wishers began to come in from near and far to present their congratulations.

I remained with them throughout the winter, but at Maroshely, to which they now all moved. It was the Major's firm intention never to take his wife away from the little world she had built up for herself in his absence. Perhaps the most obviously delighted and happy of them all was Gustave. He had always been deeply attached to the Major and with the earnest and burning enthusiasm of youth he had always declared him to be the finest man on God's earth. And now the man he had almost worshiped proved to be his father.

That winter I watched two hearts grow more closely together than ever before in a splendid if belated blossoming of married happiness.

I will never forget any of them as long as I live.

But when spring came again I resumed my old German traveling garb, took my stout German stick and turned my steps in the direction of my own Fatherland once again. On my way I visited the grave of the lovely Gabrielle, who had died twelve years previously in the full bloom of all her youthful beauty. Two white lilies lay on the marble slab of her grave.

With melancholy but gentle thoughts I continued my journey and soon I was across the Leitha and in the distance I could see the blue haze that I knew to be the mountains of my own dear Fatherland.

Translated by Ilsa Barea

Questions for Writing and Discussion

1. This story differs strikingly from a good many of the others in this book, especially, in that it has little dramatic action, not much dialogue, and is largely told through the voice of a narrator. Discuss what the role of the narrator is in

"Brigitta," how he serves to "frame" the action, how he brings to bear upon the rather exotic atmosphere of eastern Hungary a perspective of distance and curiosity, and how he serves as the intelligence upon whom the events register, the character who learns from the experiences of the other characters.

2.   The relationship between the Major and the people who work for him is one that might be a little difficult for us to grasp—it is a premodern relationship, somewhat like that of a feudal lord and his retainers, but it also has some aspects that might surprise us because of their democratic simplicity. Analyze these relationships with special emphasis on how they contribute to the total effect of the story.

3.   The idea of work—work as an activity good in itself, work as a form of self-discipline, work as a healing for troubled souls—seems very important in "Brigitta." Show how and where this idea appears in the story and relate it to other aspects of the story, especially the love between Brigitta and the Major.

4.   Why should a woman like Brigitta demand stricter faithfulness and greater moral probity than ordinary women? What is the reason she gives for this? What do you thing of her reason? Do you think such a reason could easily be given or accepted in our own time?

THE HUMAN SITUATION

THOMAS MANN

Disorder and Early Sorrow

Introduction

This story, first published in German in 1925, is set in the years immediately after the First World War. Defeated by the Allies and subjected by them to punitive terms of settlement, Germany changed from a monarchy to a republic, but a republic under extremely adverse conditions. A large portion of its population remained hostile to democracy, still clinging to one or another authoritarian outlook. A terrible inflation overtook the economy, so that people would count their salaries in hundreds of thousands, even millions of marks, and the savings of a lifetime could be swallowed up overnight. In general, there was an atmosphere in Weimar Germany (as it came to be called) of social instability, feverishness, and violence.

All of these matters are reflected, obliquely, in Mann's story. We gain from it a sense of malaise and precariousness, as if people are living at the edge of collapse. Mann himself rarely makes explicit statements, but we can sense from the way the characters speak and act that they find themselves caught in abnormal times. (To some readers it seems that in "Disorder and Early Sorrow" Mann anticipated those conditions of social breakdown which would lead to the triumph of Nazism a few years later.) And then there are passing references which tell us a great deal, such as the mention in the very first sentence of croquettes made from turnip greens, neither a very appetizing nor nutritious food.

In such circumstances it was only natural that people should cherish more than ever the stabilities of family life, falling back upon the simple affections between parents and children. This attitude, though not without a certain critical irony, dominates Mann's story. In the story's foreground there is a tender presentation of a close-knit family and of those little touches of good feeling and respect which lighten up even their casual conversations (the way the young people call their middle-aged parents "old folks," the way the young people improvise comic routines in order to divert their parents, etc.). It would be almost impossible to make too much of this aspect of "Disorder and Early Sorrow," since everything else in the story, everything that might seem difficult and problematic, depends first of all on a portrayal of the family's inner strength and coherence.

Yet, in showing the relations between children and parents, Mann's tone is not exactly light-hearted or carefree. All sorts of problems hover in the background: Bert is uncertain as to his career, little Snapper suffers from temper tantrums, Mrs. Cornelius becomes exhausted from coping with economic troubles, and Professor Cornelius feels a pervasive anxiety at having to support the members of his family. And then there are the "natural," unavoidable problems all the children face in growing up, problems that would be irksome under the best of circumstances. With his reflective mind and long-established habit of relating his immediate experience to the history of Europe, Professor Cornelius comes to feel that somehow there is a close connection, even if one that is hard to specify, between the difficulties experienced by his children and the social feverishness and instability which characterize the moment in which they live.

What we have, then, in this gravely lyrical story is an intimate portrait of middle-class life: its kindliness, cultivation, anxieties, confusions. Except perhaps in Mann's early novel, *Buddenbrooks,* there can hardly be a more authoritative and compassionate portrait of that way of life. And perhaps it is also a kind of elegy for it.

Mann understands that no family can ever exist in isolation from the social conditions of the moment. Precisely insofar as its members turn to the family for support and shelter do they reveal the extent to which they are vulnerable to the pressures of society and the blows of history. The family protects; the family is helpless. All through the story Mann shrewdly plants little details, seemingly casual remarks which indicate the dual role of the family—as, for instance, in his remark about little Snapper: "Born and brought up in these desolate, distracted times, he has been endowed by them with an unstable and hypersensitive nervous system and suffers greatly under life's disharmonies."

One reason the story is so moving, then, is that Mann keeps in balance the two possible roles of the family. He shows the charms and pleasures of the young people at their party, but also the emotional and financial strain that accompanies that party. He shows the closeness of relationship between children and parents, but also the damage which bad times can inflict on those relationships.

So that if "Disorder and Early Sorrow" is to be read as a celebration of family life, it is by no means an unqualified, and certainly not a sentimental, celebration. And all this comes through not merely in the brief scenes and encounters among the members of the family, but still more in the brooding consciousness of Professor Cornelius. That consciousness hovers over the story like a gray cloud, measuring the costs and erosions to which his loved ones are exposed and making it all seem a good deal more than just a story about a few individuals. For through Professor Cornelius's reflections we come to understand that what is being shown in this story are the inevitable tensions and troubles which the sheer fact of social existence, the necessity human beings have for living together, must exact.

At its climax the story moves to an incident of a kind that everyone has probably experienced in one form or another. Who does not remember from childhood a sudden outcropping of emotion, barely understood and clearly out of control, which one had felt toward some adult, an attractive older cousin, a beautiful aunt, a handsome uncle? Who does not remember tears shed for reasons not really grasped, and the responses of sympathetic but also smiling grown-ups, who felt that they understood this outburst in a way no child could? And then would come the reassurance, as it comes at the end of Mann's story, that in a little while, darling, everything will be all right, you'll feel better and will return to your "normal" ways.

It is such an experience that little Ellie undergoes toward the end of the story. She yearns to make the young man, Max Hergesell, her "brother." Gallant or pleased to play at being gallant, Hergesell is very nice to the child. But he also calls her "little Lorelei," invoking the name of a legendary siren of the Rhine river—as if to show that he is aware of the ambiguities of the child's response. Professor Cornelius, stirred out of his usual composure, feels for the young man "a most singular mixture of thankfulness, embarrassment, and hatred." The last word is very telling: for if the life of the family is being shown in idyllic terms, it is by no means an undisturbed idyll. In any case, Professor Cornelius takes comfort from the thought that tomorrow his little Ellie will again be "normal" and that "young Hergesell will be a pale shadow," even though he also knows that his little girl cannot remain innocent forever.

Interwoven with this "family romance" are a series of musings and reflections by Professor Cornelius (perhaps actually those of Thomas Mann?). These have to do with the nature of human existence, the complexities of family life, the course of human history, the temptations and limitations of Cornelius's conservative thought, and so forth. These reflections come through in brief parenthetical clauses, occasional sentences tucked away in the folds of the narrative; but they are important, for they lift the story out of the small-gauged routines of middle-class existence and give it a larger, more problematic significance. They are like hidden ties of intelligence binding the Cornelius family to the turmoil of European history.

In these reflections Professor Cornelius does not assert himself with unqualified conviction and strong energy. Like Mann himself, he can be slyly ironic toward his own thought and sufficiently self-doubting to call into question his own values. In a remarkable paragraph which appears on page 259 (beginning, "But he understood more"), Professor Cornelius ties in his personal feelings with his views about history. "His devotion to [Ellie] this priceless little morsel of life and new growth has something to do with death, it clings to death as against life; and that is neither right nor beautiful—in a sense."

In what sense? He reasons that his devotion to the past and its history as something timeless and eternal has become absorbed into, or confused with, his love for the child. Because "father love, and a little child on its mother's breast—

are not these timeless, and thus very, very holy and beautiful?" But this love of the timeless and the beautiful also seems to Professor Cornelius a source of his hostility to "the history of today, which is still in the making. . . ." The fixity of the past and the wish to see his little girl's beauty as something exempt from the ravages of time—these come to seem frail allies against the harshness of the contemporary world, with its noise, its violence, its foolishness.

Such, in brief summary, are some of Professor Cornelius's reflections, as they contribute to the meditative temper of the story. But there is another and perhaps more fundamental order of meditativeness in "Disorder and Early Sorrow." As we read from paragraph to paragraph, we come to see that Mann is concerned not merely with telling a story about a middle-class family in a difficult historical moment, but also with making this very act of telling into a kind of sustained meditation. He is concerned not just with the question, "What happens next?" but also with the question, "What does it all mean and how can we even suppose that we know what it means?" The two questions gradually fuse into one, and what we are finally listening to is the music of a reflective mind, the meditation of a writer who holds a fragment of life in his hands and contemplates its mystery.

Disorder and Early Sorrow

The principal dish at dinner had been croquettes made of turnip greens. So there follows a trifle,[1] concocted out of one of those dessert powders we use nowadays, that taste like almond soap.[2] Xaver, the youthful manservant, in his outgrown striped jacket, white woolen gloves, and yellow sandals, hands it round, and the "big folk" take this opportunity to remind their father, tactfully, that company is coming today.

The "big folk" are two, Ingrid and Bert. Ingrid is brown-eyed, eighteen, and perfectly delightful. She is on the eve of her exams, and will probably pass them, if only because she knows how to wind masters, and even headmasters, round her finger. She does not, however, mean to use her certificate once she gets it; having leanings toward the stage, on the ground of her ingratiating smile, her equally ingratiating voice, and a marked and irresistible talent for burlesque. Bert is blond and seventeen. He intends to get done with school somehow, anyhow, and fling himself into the arms of life. He will be a dancer, or a cabaret actor, possibly even a waiter—but not a waiter anywhere else save at the Cairo,

[1]A dessert.
[2]The years after the First World War were marked by a terrible inflation in Germany.

DISORDER AND EARLY SORROW From *Death in Venice and Seven Other Stories* by Thomas Mann, translated by H. T. Lowe-Porter. Copyright 1936, renewed 1964 by Alfred A. Knopf, Inc. Reprinted by permission of the publisher.

the nightclub, whither he has once already taken flight, at five in the morning, and been brought back crestfallen. Bert bears a strong resemblance to the youthful manservant Xaver Kleinsgutl, of about the same age as himself; not because he looks common—in features he is strikingly like his father, Professor Cornelius—but by reason of an approximation of types, due in its turn to far-reaching compromises in matters of dress and bearing generally. Both lads wear their heavy hair very long on top, with a cursory parting in the middle, and give their heads the same characteristic toss to throw it off the forehead. When one of them leaves the house, by the garden gate, bare-headed in all weathers, in a blouse rakishly girt with a leather strap, and sheers off bent well over with his head on one side; or else mounts his push-bike—Xaver makes free with his employers', of both sexes, or even, in acutely irresponsible mood, with the Professor's own—Dr. Cornelius from his bedroom window cannot, for the life of him, tell whether he is looking at his son or his servant. Both, he thinks, look like young moujiks.[3] And both are impassioned cigarette-smokers, though Bert has not the means to compete with Xaver, who smokes as many as thirty a day, of a brand named after a popular cinema star. The big folk call their father and mother the "old folk"—not behind their backs, but as a form of address and in all affection: "Hullo, old folks," they will say; though Cornelius is only forty-seven years old and his wife eight years younger. And the Professor's parents, who lead in his household the humble and hesitant life of the really old, are on the big folk's lips the "ancients." As for the "little folk," Ellie and Snapper, who take their meals upstairs with blue-faced Ann—so-called because of her prevailing facial hue—Ellie and Snapper follow their mother's example and address their father by his first name, Abel. Unutterably comic it sounds, in its pert, confiding familiarity; particularly on the lips, in the sweet accents, of five-year-old Eleanor, who is the image of Frau Cornelius's baby pictures and whom the Professor loves above everything else in the world.

"Darling old thing," says Ingrid affably, laying her large but shapely hand on his, as he presides in proper middle-class style over the family table, with her on his left and the mother opposite: "Parent mine, may I ever so gently jog your memory, for you have probably forgotten: this is the afternoon we were to have our little jollification, our turkey-trot with eats to match. You haven't a thing to do but just bear up and not funk it; everything will be over by nine o'clock."

"Oh—ah!" says Cornelius, his face falling. "Good!" he goes on, and nods his head to show himself in harmony with the inevitable. "I only meant—is this really the day? Thursday, yes. How time flies! Well, what time are they coming?"

"Half past four they'll be dropping in, I should say," answers Ingrid, to whom her brother leaves the major role in all dealings with the father. Upstairs, while he is resting, he will hear scarcely anything, and from seven to eight he takes his walk. He can slip out by the terrace if he likes.

"Tut!" says Cornelius deprecatingly, as who should say: "You exaggerate."

[3]Russian word for *peasants*.

But Bert puts in: "It's the one evening in the week Wanja doesn't have to play. Any other night he'd have to leave by half past six, which would be painful for all concerned."

Wanja is Ivan Herzl, the celebrated young leading man at the Stadt-theater. Bert and Ingrid are on intimate terms with him, they often visit him in his dressing-room and have tea. He is an artist of the modern school, who stands on the stage in strange and, to the Professor's mind, utterly affected dancing attitudes, and shrieks lamentably. To a professor of history, all highly repugnant; but Bert has entirely succumbed to Herzl's influence, blackens the lower rim of his eyelids—despite painful but fruitless scenes with the father—and with youthful carelessness of the ancestral anguish declares that not only will he take Herzl for his model if he becomes a dancer, but in case he turns out to be a waiter at the Cairo he means to walk precisely thus.

Cornelius slightly raises his brows and makes his son a little bow—indicative of the unassumingness and self-abnegation that befits his age. You could not call it a mocking bow or suggestive in any special sense. Bert may refer it to himself or equally to his so talented friend.

"Who else is coming?" next inquires the master of the house. They mention various people, names all more or less familiar, from the city, from the suburban colony, from Ingrid's school. They still have some telephoning to do, they say. They have to phone Max. This is Max Hergesell, an engineering student; Ingrid utters his name in the nasal drawl which according to her is the traditional intonation of all the Hergesells. She goes on to parody it in the most abandonedly funny and lifelike way, and the parents laugh until they nearly choke over the wretched trifle. For even in these times when something funny happens people have to laugh.

From time to time the telephone bell rings in the Professor's study, and the big folk run across, knowing it is their affair. Many people had to give up their telephones the last time the price rose, but so far the Corneliuses have been able to keep theirs, just as they have kept their villa, which was built before the war, by dint of the salary Cornelius draws as professor of history—a million marks, and more or less adequate to the chances and changes of post-war life. The house is comfortable, even elegant, though sadly in need of repairs that cannot be made for lack of materials, and at present disfigured by iron stoves with long pipes. Even so, it is still the proper setting of the upper middle class, though they themselves look odd enough in it, with their worn and turned clothing and altered way of life. The children, of course, know nothing else; to them it is normal and regular, they belong by birth to the "villa proletariat." The problem of clothing troubles them not at all. They and their like have evolved a costume to fit the time, by poverty out of taste for innovation: in summer it consists of scarcely more than a belted linen smock and sandals. The middle-class parents find things rather more difficult.

The big folk's table-napkins hang over their chair-backs, they talk with their friends over the telephone. These friends are the invited guests who have rung up to accept or decline or arrange; and the conversation is carried on in the jargon of the clan, full of slang and high spirits, of which the old folk understand hardly a word. These consult together meantime about the hospitality to be offered to the impending guests. The Professor displays a middle-class ambitiousness: he wants to serve a sweet—or something that looks like a sweet—after the Italian salad and brown-bread sandwiches. But Frau Cornelius says that would be going too far. The guests would not expect it, she is sure—and the big folk, returning once more to their trifle, agree with her.

The mother of the family is of the same general type as Ingrid, though not so tall. She is languid; the fantastic difficulties of the housekeeping have broken and worn her. She really ought to go and take a cure, but feels incapable; the floor is always swaying under her feet, and everything seems upside down. She speaks of what is uppermost in her mind: the eggs, they simply must be bought today. Six thousand marks apiece they are, and just so many are to be had on this one day of the week at one single shop fifteen minutes' journey away. Whatever else they do, the big folk must go and fetch them immediately after luncheon, with Danny, their neighbor's son, who will soon be calling for them; and Xaver Kleinsgutl will don civilian garb and attend his young master and mistress. For no single household is allowed more than five eggs a week; therefore the young people will enter the shop singly, one after another, under assumed names, and thus wring twenty eggs from the shopkeeper for the Cornelius family. This enterprise is the sporting event of the week for all participants, not excepting the moujik Kleinsgutl, and most of all for Ingrid and Bert, who delight in misleading and mystifying their fellowmen and would revel in the performance even if it did not achieve one single egg. They adore impersonating fictitious characters; they love to sit in a bus and carry on long lifelike conversations in a dialect which they otherwise never speak, the most commonplace dialogue about politics and people and the price of food, while the whole bus listens open-mouthed to this incredibly ordinary prattle, though with a dark suspicion all the while that something is wrong somewhere. The conversation waxes ever more shameless, it enters into revolting detail about these people who do not exist. Ingrid can make her voice sound ever so common and twittering and shrill as she impersonates a shop-girl with an illegitimate child, said child being a son with sadistic tendencies, who lately out in the country treated a cow with such unnatural cruelty that no Christian could have borne to see it. Bert nearly explodes at her twittering, but restrains himself and displays a grisly sympathy; he and the unhappy shop-girl entering into a long, stupid, depraved, and shuddery conversation over the particular morbid cruelty involved; until an old gentleman opposite, sitting with his ticket folded between his index finger and his seal ring, can bear it no more and makes public protest against the nature of the themes these young folk are discussing with such particularity. He uses the Greek plural: "themata." Whereat Ingrid pretends to be dissolving in tears, and Bert behaves as though his wrath against the old gentleman was with difficulty being held in check and would probably burst out before long. He clenches his fists, he gnashes his teeth, he shakes from head to foot; and the unhappy old gentleman, whose intentions had been of the best, hastily leaves the bus at the next stop.

Such are the diversions of the big folk. The telephone plays a prominent part in them: they ring up any and everybody—members of government, opera singers, dignitaries of the Church—in the character of shop assistants, or perhaps as Lord or Lady Doolittle. They are only with difficulty persuaded that they have the wrong number. Once they emptied their parents' card-tray[4] and distributed its contents among the neighbors' letter-boxes, wantonly, yet not without impish sense of the fitness of things to make it highly upsetting. God only knowing why certain people should have called where they did.

Xaver comes to clear away, tossing the hair out of his eyes. Now that he has taken off his gloves you can see the yellow chain-ring on his left hand. And as the Professor finishes his watery eight-thousand-mark beer and lights a cigarette, the little folk can be heard scrambling down the stair, coming, by established custom, for their after-dinner call on Father and Mother. They storm the dining-room, after a struggle with the latch, clutched by both pairs of little hands at once; their clumsy small feet twinkle over the carpet, in red felt slippers with the socks falling down on them. With prattle and shoutings each makes for his own place: Snapper to Mother, to climb on her lap, boast of all he has eaten, and thump his fat little tum; Ellie to her Abel, so much hers because she is so very much his; because she consciously luxuriates in the deep tenderness—like all deep feeling, concealing a melancholy strain—with which he holds her small form embraced; in the love in his eyes as he kisses her little fairy hand or the sweet brow with its delicate tracery of tiny blue veins.

The little folk look like each other, with the strong undefined likeness of brother and sister. In clothing and hair-cut they are twins. Yet they are sharply distinguished after all, and quite on sex lines. It is a little Adam and a little Eve. Not only is Snapper the sturdier and more compact, he appears consciously to emphasize his four-year-old masculinity in speech, manner, and carriage, lifting his shoulders and letting the little arms hang down quite like a young American athlete, drawing down his mouth when he talks and seeking to give his voice a gruff and forthright ring. But all this masculinity is the result of effort rather than natively his. Born and brought up in these desolate, distracted times, he has been endowed by them with an unstable and hypersensitive nervous system and suffers greatly under life's disharmonies. He is prone to sudden anger and outbursts of bitter tears, stamping his feet at every trifle; for this reason he is his mother's special nursling and care. His round, round eyes are chestnut brown and already inclined to squint, so that he will need glasses in the near future. His little nose is long, the mouth small—the father's nose and mouth they are, more plainly than ever since the Professor shaved his pointed beard and goes smooth-faced. The pointed beard had become impossible—even professors must make some concession to the changing times.

But the little daughter sits on her father's knee, his Eleonorchen,[5] his little Eve, so much more gracious a little being, so much sweeter-faced than her brother—and he holds his cigarette away from her while she fingers his glasses with her dainty wee hands. The lenses are divided for reading and distance, and each day they tease her curiosity afresh.

[4]Which holds calling cards of visitors.
[5]"Little Eleanor," a diminutive used affectionately.

At bottom he suspects that his wife's partiality may have a firmer basis than his own: that Snapper's refractory masculinity perhaps is solider stuff than his own little girl's more explicit charm and grace. But the heart will not be commanded, that he knows; and once and for all his heart belongs to the little one, as it has since the day she came, since the first time he saw her. Almost always when he holds her in his arms he remembers that first time: remembers the sunny room in the Women's Hospital, where Ellie first saw the light, twelve years after Bert was born. He remembers how he drew near, the mother smiling the while, and cautiously put aside the canopy of the diminutive bed that stood beside the large one. There lay the little miracle among the pillows: so well formed, so encompassed, as it were, with the harmony of sweet proportions, with little hands that even then, though so much tinier, were beautiful as now; with wide-open eyes blue as the sky and brighter than the sunshine—and almost in that very second he felt himself captured and held fast. This was love at first sight, love everlasting: a feeling unknown, unhoped for, unexpected—in so far as it could be a matter of conscious awareness; it took entire possession of him, and he understood, with joyous amazement, that this was for life.

But he understood more. He knows, does Dr. Cornelius, that there is something not quite right about this feeling, so unaware, so undreamed of, so involuntary. He has a shrewd suspicion that it is not by accident it has so utterly mastered him and bound itself up with his existence; that he had—even subconsciously—been preparing for it, or, more precisely, been prepared for it. There is, in short, something in him which at a given moment was ready to issue in such a feeling; and this something, highly extraordinary to relate, is his essence and quality as a professor of history. Dr. Cornelius, however, does not actually say this, even to himself; he merely realizes it, at odd times, and smiles a private smile. He knows that history professors do not love history because it is something that comes to pass, but only because it is something that *has* come to pass; that they hate a revolution like the present one because they feel it is lawless, incoherent, irrelevant—in a word, unhistoric; that their hearts belong to the coherent, disciplined, historic past. For the temper of timelessness, the temper of eternity—thus the scholar communes with himself when he takes his walk by the river before supper—that temper broods over the past; and it is a temper much better suited to the nervous system of a history professor than are the excesses of the present. The past is immortalized; that is to say, it is dead; and death is the root of all godliness and all abiding significance. Dr. Cornelius, walking alone in the dark, has a profound insight into this truth. It is this conservative instinct of his, his sense of the eternal, that has found in his love for his little daughter a way to save itself from the wounding inflicted by the times. For father love, and a little child on its mother's breast—are not these timeless, and thus very, very holy and beautiful? Yet Cornelius, pondering there in the dark, descries something not perfectly right and good in his love. Theoretically, in the interests of science, he admits it to himself. There is something ulterior about it, in the nature of it; that something is hostility, hostility against the history of today, which is still in the making, and thus not history at all, in behalf of the genuine history that has already happened—that is to say, death. Yes, passing strange though all this is, yet it is true; true in a sense, that is. His devotion to this priceless little morsel of life and new growth has something to do with death, it clings to death as against life; and that is neither right nor beautiful—in a sense. Though only the most fanatical asceticism could be capable, on no other ground than such casual scientific perception, of tearing this purest and most precious of feelings out of his heart.

He holds his darling on his lap and her slim rosy legs hang down. He raises his brows as he talks to her, tenderly, with a half-teasing note of respect, and listens enchanted to her high, sweet little voice calling him Abel. He exchanges a look with the mother, who is caressing her Snapper and reading him a gentle lecture. He must be more reasonable, he must learn self-control; today again, under the manifold exasperations of life, he has given way to rage and behaved like a howling dervish. Cornelius casts a mistrustful glance at the big folk now and then, too; he thinks it not unlikely they are not unaware of those scientific preoccupations of his evening walks. If such be the case they do not show it. They stand there leaning their arms on their chair-backs and with a benevolence not untinctured with irony look on at the parental happiness.

The children's frocks are of a heavy, brick-red stuff, embroidered in modern "arty" style. They once belonged to Ingrid and Bert and are precisely alike, save that little knickers come out beneath Snapper's smock. And both have their hair bobbed. Snapper's is a streaky blond, inclined to turn dark. It is bristly and sticky and looks for all the world like a droll, badly fitting wig. But Ellie's is chestnut brown, glossy and fine as silk, as pleasing as her whole little personality. It covers her ears—and these ears are not a pair, one of them being the right size, the other distinctly too large. Her father will sometimes uncover this little abnormality and exclaim over it as though he had never noticed it before, which both makes Ellie giggle and covers her with shame. Her eyes are now golden brown, set far apart and with sweet gleams in them—such a clear and lovely look! The brows above are blond; the nose still unformed, with thick nostrils and almost circular holes; the mouth large and expressive, with a beautifully arching and mobile upper lip. When she laughs, dimples come in her cheeks and she shows her teeth like loosely strung pearls. So far she has lost but one tooth, which her father gently twisted out with his handkerchief after it had grown very wobbling. During this small operation she had paled and trembled very much. Her cheeks have the softness proper to her years, but they are not chubby; indeed, they are rather concave, due to her facial structure, with its somewhat prominent jaw. On one, close to the soft fall of her hair, is a downy freckle.

Ellie is not too well pleased with her looks—a sign that already she troubles about such things. Sadly she thinks it is best to admit it once for all, her face is "homely"; though the rest of her, "on the other hand," is not bad at all. She loves expressions like "on the other hand"; they sound choice and grown-up to her, and she likes to string them together, one after the other: "very likely," "probably," "after all." Snapper is self-critical too, though more in the moral sphere: he suffers from remorse for his attacks of rage and considers himself a tremendous sinner. He is quite certain that heaven is not for such as he; he is sure to go to "the bad place" when he dies, and no persuasions will convince him to the contrary—as that God sees the heart and gladly makes allowances. Obstinately he shakes his head, with the comic, crooked little peruke,[6] and vows there is no place for him in heaven. When he has a cold he is immediately quite choked with mucus; rattles and rumbles from top to toe if you even look at him; his temperature flies up at once and he simply puffs. Nursy is pessimistic on the score of his constitution: such fat-blooded children as he might get a stroke any minute. Once she even thought she saw the moment at hand: Snapper had been in one of his berserker rages, and in the ensuing fit of penitence stood himself in the corner with his back to the room. Suddenly Nursy noticed that his face had gone all blue, far bluer, even, than her own. She raised the alarm, crying out that the child's all too rich blood had at length brought him to his final hour; and Snapper, to his vast astonishment, found himself, so far from being rebuked for evil-doing, encompassed in tenderness and anxiety—until it turned out that his color was not caused by apoplexy but by the distempering on the nursery wall, which had come off on his tear-wet face.

Nursy had come downstairs too, and stands by the door, sleek-haired, owl-eyed, with her hands folded over her white apron, and a severely dignified manner born of her limited intelligence. She is very proud of the care and training she gives her nurslings and declares that they are "enveloping wonderfully." She has had seven suppurated teeth lately removed from her jaws and been measured for a set of symmetrical yellow ones in dark rubber gums; these now embellish her peasant face. She is obsessed with the strange conviction that these teeth of hers are the subject of general conversation, that, as it were, the sparrows on the housetops chatter of them. "Everybody knows I've had a false set put in," she will say; "there has been a great deal of foolish talk about them." She is much given to dark hints and veiled innuendo: speaks, for instance, of a certain Dr. Bleifuss, whom every child knows, and "there are even some in the house who pretend to be him." All one can do with talk like this is charitably to pass it over in silence. But she teaches the children nursery rhymes: gems like:

> Puff, puff, here comes the train!
> Puff, puff, toot, toot,
> Away it goes again.

Or that gastronomical jingle, so suited, in its sparseness, to the times, and yet seemingly with a blitheness of its own:

> Monday we begin the week,
> Tuesday there's a bone to pick.
> Wednesday we're half way through,
> Thursday what a great do-do!
> Friday we eat what fish we're able,
> Saturday we dance round the table.

[6] A wig.

> Sunday brings us pork and greens—
> Here's a feast for kings and queens!

Also a certain four-line stanza with a romantic appeal, unutterable and unuttered:

> Open the gate, open the gate
> And let the carriage drive in,
> Who is it in the carriage sits?
> A lordly sir with golden hair.

Or, finally that ballad about golden-haired Marianne who sat on a, sat on a, sat on a stone, and combed out her, combed out her, combed out her hair; and about blood-thirsty Rudolph, who pulled out a, pulled out a, pulled out a knife—and his ensuing direful end. Ellie enunciates all these ballads charmingly, with her mobile little lips, and sings them in her sweet little voice—much better than Snapper. She does everything better than he does, and he pays her honest admiration and homage and obeys her in all things except when visited by one of his attacks. Sometimes she teaches him, instructs him upon the birds in the picture-book and tells him their proper names: "This is a chaffinch, Buddy, this is a bullfinch, this is a cowfinch." He has to repeat them after her. She gives him medical instruction too, teaches him the names of diseases, such as inflammation of the lungs, inflammation of the blood, inflammation of the air. If he does not pay attention and cannot say the words after her, she stands him in the corner. Once she even boxed his ears, but was so ashamed that she stood herself in the corner for a long time. Yes, they are fast friends, two souls with but a single thought, and have all their adventures in common. They come home from a walk and relate as with one voice that they have seen two moollies and a teenty-weenty baby calf. They are on familiar terms with the kitchen, which consists of Xaver and the ladies Hinterhofer, two sisters once of the lower middle class who, in these evil days, are reduced to living *"au pair"*[7] as the phrase goes and officiating as cook and housemaid for their board and keep. The little ones have a feeling that Xaver and the Hinterhofers are on much the same footing with their father and mother as they are themselves. At least sometimes, when they have been scolded, they go downstairs and announce that the master and mistress are cross. But playing with the servants lacks charm compared with the joys of playing upstairs. The kitchen could never rise to the height of the games their father can invent. For instance, there is "four gentlemen taking a walk." When they play it Abel will crook his knees until he is the same height with themselves and go walking with them, hand in hand. They never get enough of this sport; they could walk round and round the dining-room a whole day on end, five gentlemen in all, counting the diminished Abel.

Then there is the thrilling cushion game. One of the children, usually Ellie, seats herself, unbeknownst to Abel, in his seat at table. Still as a mouse she

---

[7]Working without pay.

awaits his coming. He draws near with his head in the air, descanting in loud, clear tones upon the surpassing comfort of his chair; and sits down on top of Ellie. "What's this, what's this?" says he. And bounces about, deaf to the smothered giggles exploding behind him. "Why have they put a cushion in my chair? And what a queer, hard, awkward-shaped cushion it is!" he goes on. "Frightfully uncomfortable to sit on!" And keeps pushing and bouncing about more and more on the astonishing cushion and clutching behind him into the rapturous giggling and squeaking, until at last he turns round, and the game ends with a magnificent climax of discovery and recognition. They might go through all this a hundred times without diminishing by an iota its power to thrill.

Today is no time for such joys. The imminent festivity disturbs the atmosphere, and besides there is work to be done, and, above all, the eggs to be got. Ellie has just time to recite "Puff, puff," and Cornelius to discover that her ears are not mates, when they are interrupted by the arrival of Danny, come to fetch Bert and Ingrid. Xaver, meantime, has exchanged his striped livery for an ordinary coat, in which he looks rather rough-and-ready, though as brisk and attractive as ever. So then Nursy and the children ascend to the upper regions, the Professor withdraws to his study to read, as always after dinner, and his wife bends her energies upon the sandwiches and salad that must be prepared. And she has another errand as well. Before the young people arrive she has to take her shopping-basket and dash into town on her bicycle, to turn into provisions a sum of money she has in hand, which she dares not keep lest it lose all value.

Cornelius reads, leaning back in his chair, with his cigar between his midlle and index fingers. First he reads Macaulay[8] on the origin of the English public debt at the end of the seventeenth century; then an article in a French periodical on the rapid increase in the Spanish debt toward the end of the sixteenth. Both these for his lecture on the morrow. He intends to compare the astonishing prosperity which accompanied the phenomenon in England with its fatal effects a hundred years earlier in Spain, and to analyze the ethical and psychological grounds of the difference in results. For that will give him a chance to refer back from the England of William III, which is the actual subject in hand, to the time of Philip II and the Counter-Reformation,[9] which is his own special field. He has already written a valuable work on this period; it is much cited and got him his professorship. While his cigar burns down and gets strong, he excogitates a few pensive sentences in a key of gentle melancholy, to be delivered before his class next day: about the practically hopeless struggle carried on by the belated Philip against the whole trend of history: against the new, the kingdom-disrupting power of the Germanic ideal of freedom and individual liberty. And about the persistent, futile struggle of the aristocracy, condemned by God and rejected of man, against the forces of progress and change. He savors his sentences; keeps on polishing them while he puts back the books he has been using; then goes upstairs for the usual pause in his day's work, the hour with drawn blinds and closed eyes, which he so imperatively needs. But today, he recalls, he will rest

[8]Thomas Macaulay (1800–1859), English historian.
[9]Catholic response or reaction to the Protestant Reformation, sixteenth century.

under disturbed conditions, amid the bustle of preparations for the feast. He smiles to find his heart giving a mild flutter at the thought. Disjointed phrases on the theme of black-clad Philip and his times mingle with a confused consciousness that they will soon be dancing down below. For five minutes or so he falls asleep.

As he lies and rests he can hear the sound of the garden gate and the repeated ringing at the bell. Each time a little pang goes through him, of excitement and suspense, at the thought that the young people have begun to fill the floor below. And each time he smiles at himself again—though even his smile is slightly nervous, is tinged with the pleasurable anticipations people always feel before a party. At half past four—it is already dark—he gets up and washes at the wash-stand. The basin has been out of repair for two years. It is supposed to tip, but has broken away from its socket on one side and cannot be mended because there is nobody to mend it; neither replaced because no shop can supply another. So it has to be hung up above the vent and emptied by lifting in both hands and pouring out the water. Cornelius shakes his head over this basin, as he does several times a day—whenever, in fact, he has occasion to use it. He finishes his toilet with care, standing under the ceiling light to polish his glasses till they shine. Then he goes downstairs.

On his way to the dining-room he hears the gramophone already going, and the sound of voices. He puts on a polite, society air; at his tongue's end is the phrase he means to utter: "Pray don't let me disturb you," as he passes directly into the dining-room for his tea. "Pray don't let me disturb you"—it seems to him precisely the *mot juste;* toward the guests cordial and considerate, for himself a very bulwark.

The lower floor is lighted up, all the bulbs in the chandelier are burning save one that has burned out. Cornelius pauses on a lower step and surveys the entrance hall. It looks pleasant and cozy in the bright light, with its copy of Marées[10] over the brick chimney-piece, its wainscoted walls—wainscoted in soft wood—and red-carpeted floor, where the guests stand in groups, chatting, each with his tea-cup and slice of bread-and-butter spread with anchovy paste. There is a festal haze, faint scents of hair and clothing and human breath come to him across the room, it is all characteristic and familiar and highly evocative. The door into the dressing-room is open, guests are still arriving.

A large group of people is rather bewildering at first sight. The Professor takes in only the general scene. He does not see Ingrid, who is standing just at the foot of the steps, in a dark silk frock with a pleated collar falling softly over the shoulders, and bare arms. She smiles up at him, nodding and showing her lovely teeth.

"Rested?" she asks, for his private ear. With a quite unwarranted start he recognizes her, and she presents some of her friends.

"May I introduce Herr Zuber?" she says. "And this is Fräulein Plaichinger."

---

[10]Hans von Marées (1837–1887), German painter.

Herr Zuber is insignificant. But Fräulein Plaichinger is a perfect Germania, blond and voluptuous, arrayed in floating draperies. She has a snub nose, and answers the Professor's salutation in the high, shrill pipe so many stout women have.

"Delighted to meet you," he says. "How nice of you to come! A classmate of Ingrid's I suppose?"

And Herr Zuber is a golfing partner of Ingrid's. He is in business; he works in his uncle's brewery. Cornelius makes a few jokes about the thinness of the beer and professes to believe that Herr Zuber could easily do something about the quality if he would. "But pray don't let me disturb you," he goes on, and turns toward the dining-room.

"There comes Max," says Ingrid. "Max, you sweep, what do you mean by rolling up at this time of day?" For such is the way they talk to each other, offensively to an older ear; of social forms, of hospitable warmth, there is no faintest trace. They all call each other by their first names.

A young man comes up to them out of the dressing-room and makes his bow; he has an expanse of white shirt-front and a little black string tie. He is as pretty as a picture, dark, with rosy cheeks, clean-shaven of course, but with just a sketch of side-whisker. Not a ridiculous or flashy beauty, not like a gypsy fiddler, but just charming to look at, in a winning, well-bred way, with kind dark eyes. He even wears his dinner-jacket a little awkwardly.

"Please don't scold me, Cornelia," he says; "it's the idiotic lectures." And Ingrid presents him to her father as Herr Hergesell.

Well, and so this is Herr Hergesell. He knows his manners, does Herr Hergesell, and thanks the master of the house quite ingratiatingly for his invitation as they shake hands. "I certainly seem to have missed the bus," says he jocosely. "Of course I have lectures today up to four o'clock; I would have; and after that I had to go home to change." Then he talks about his pumps, with which he has just been struggling in the dressing-room.

"I brought them with me in a bag," he goes on. "Mustn't tramp all over the carpet in our brogues—it's not done. Well, I was ass enough not to fetch along a shoe-horn, and I find I simply can't get in! What a sell! They are the tightest I've ever had, the numbers don't tell you a thing, and all the leather today is just cast iron. It's not leather at all. My poor finger"—he confidingly displays a reddened digit and once more characterizes the whole thing as a "sell," and a putrid sell into the bargain. He really does talk just as Ingrid said he did, with a peculiar nasal drawl, not affectedly in the least, but merely because that is the way of all the Hergesells.

Dr. Cornelius says it is very careless of them not to keep a shoe-horn in the cloak-room and displays proper sympathy with the mangled finger. "But now you *really* must not let me disturb you any longer," he goes on. "*Auf wiedersehen!*" And he crosses the hall into the dining-room.

There are guests there too, drinking tea; the family table is pulled out. But the Professor goes at once to his own little upholstered corner with the electric light bulb above it—the nook where he usually drinks his tea. His wife is sitting there talking with Bert and two other young men, one of them Herzl, whom Cornelius knows and greets; the other a typical "Wandervogel"[11] named Möller, a youth who obviously neither owns nor cares to own the correct evening dress of the middle classes (in fact, there is no such thing any more), nor to ape the manners of a gentleman (and, in fact, there is no such thing any more either). He has a wilderness of hair, horn spectacles, and a long neck, and wears golf stockings and a belted blouse. His regular occupation, the Professor learns, is banking, but he is by way of being an amateur folk-lorist and collects folk-songs from all localities and in all languages. He sings them, too, and at Ingrid's command has brought his guitar; it is hanging in the dressing-room in an oilcloth case. Herzl, the actor, is small and slight, but he has a strong growth of black beard, as you can tell by the thick coat of powder on his cheeks. His eyes are larger than life, with a deep and melancholy glow. He has put on rouge besides the powder—those dull carmine high-lights on the cheeks can be nothing but a cosmetic. "Queer," thinks the Professor. "You would think a man would be one thing or the other—not melancholic and use face paint at the same time. It's a psychological contradiction. How can a melancholy man rouge? But here we have a perfect illustration of the abnormality of the artist soul-form. It can make possible a contradiction like this—perhaps it even consists in the contradiction. All very interesting—and no reason whatever for not being polite to him. Politeness is a primitive convention—and legitimate. . . . Do take some lemon, Herr Hofschauspieler!"[12]

Court actors and court theaters—there are no such things any more, really. But Herzl relishes the sound of the title, notwithstanding he is a revolutionary artist. This must be another contradiction inherent in his soul-form; so, at least, the Professor assumes, and he is probably right. The flattery he is guilty of is a sort of atonement for his previous hard thoughts about the rouge.

"Thank you so much—it's really too good of you, sir," says Herzl, quite embarrassed. He is so overcome that he almost stammers; only his perfect enunciation saves him. His whole bearing toward his hostess and the master of the house is exaggeratedly polite. It is almost as though he had a bad conscience in respect of his rouge; as though an inward compulsion had driven him to put it on, but now, seeing it through the Professor's eyes, he disapproves of it himself, and thinks, by an air of humility toward the whole of unrouged society, to mitigate its effect.

They drink their tea and chat: about Möller's folk-songs, about Basque folk-songs and Spanish folk-songs; from which they pass to the new production of *Don Carlos*[13] at the Stadttheater, in which Herzl plays the title-rôle. He talks about his own rendering of the part and says he hopes his conception of the character has unity. They go on to criticize the rest of the cast, the setting, and the production as a whole; and Cornelius is struck, rather painfully, to find the conversation trending toward his own special province, back to Spain and the Counter-Reformation. He has done nothing at all to give it this turn, he is

[11]German word meaning a person who flits about, with no fixed social position.
[12]German word for court actor.
[13]A play by Friedrich Schiller (1759–1805).

perfectly innocent, and he hopes it does not look as though he had sought an occasion to play the professor. He wonders, and falls silent, feeling relieved when the little folk come up to the table. Ellie and Snapper have on their blue velvet Sunday frocks; they are permitted to partake in the festivities up to bedtime. They look shy and large-eyed as they say how-do-you-do to the strangers and, under pressure, repeat their names and ages. Herr Möller does nothing but gaze at them solemnly, but Herzl is simply ravished. He rolls his eyes up to heaven and puts his hands over his mouth; he positively blesses them. It all, no doubt, comes from his heart, but he is so addicted to theatrical methods of making an impression and getting an effect that both words and behavior ring frightfully false. And even his enthusiasm for the little folk looks too much like part of his general craving to make up for the rouge on his cheeks.

The tea-table has meanwhile emptied of guests, and dancing is going on in the hall. The children run off, the Professor prepares to retire. "Go and enjoy yourselves," he says to Möller and Herzl, who have sprung from their chairs as he rises from his. They shake hands and he withdraws into his study, his peaceful kingdom, where he lets down the blinds, turns on the desk lamp, and sits down to work.

It is work which can be done, if necessary, under disturbed conditions: nothing but a few letters and a few notes. Of course, Cornelius's mind wanders. Vague impressions float through it: Herr Hergesell's refractory pumps, the high pipe in that plump body of the Plaichinger female. As he writes, or leans back in his chair and stares into space, his thoughts go back to Herr Möller's collection of Basque folk-songs, to Herzl's posings and humility, to "his" Carlos and the court of Philip II. There is something strange, he thinks, about conversations. They are so ductile, they will flow of their own accord in the direction of one's dominating interest. Often and often he has seen this happen. And while he is thinking, he is listening to the sounds next door—rather subdued, he finds them. He hears only voices, no sound of footsteps. The dancers do not glide or circle round the room; they merely walk about over the carpet, which does not hamper their movements in the least. Their way of holding each other is quite different and strange, and they move to the strains of the gramophone, to the weird music of the new world. He concentrates on the music and makes out that it is a jazz-band record, with various percussion instruments and the clack and clatter of castanets, which, however, are not even faintly suggestive of Spain, but merely jazz like the rest. No, not Spain. . . . His thoughts are back at the old round.

Half an hour goes by. It occurs to him it would be no more than friendly to go and contribute a box of cigarettes to the festivities next door. Too bad to ask the young people to smoke their own—though they have probably never thought of it. He goes into the empty dining-room and takes a box from his supply in the cupboard: not the best ones, nor yet the brand he himself prefers, but a certain long, thin kind he is not averse to getting rid of—after all, they are nothing but youngsters. He takes the box into the hall, holds it up with a smile, and deposits it on the mantel-shelf. After which he gives a look round and returns to his own room.

There comes a lull in dance and music. The guests stand about the room in groups or round the table at the window or are seated in a circle by the fireplace. Even the built-in stairs, with their worn velvet carpet, are crowded with young folk as in an amphitheater: Max Hergesell is there, leaning back with one elbow on the step above and gesticulating with his free hand as he talks to the shrill, voluptuous Plaichinger. The floor of the hall is nearly empty, save just in the center: there, directly beneath the chandelier, the two little ones in their blue velvet frocks clutch each other in an awkward embrace and twirl silently round and round, oblivious of all else. Cornelius, as he passes, strokes their hair, with a friendly word; it does not distract them from their small solemn preoccupation. But at his own door he turns to glance round and sees young Hergesell push himself off the stair by his elbow—probably because he noticed the Professor. He comes down into the arena, takes Ellie out of her brother's arms, and dances with her himself. It looks very comic, without the music, and he crouches down just as Cornelius does when he goes walking with the four gentlemen, holding the fluttered Ellie as though she were grown up and taking little "shimmying" steps. Everybody watches with huge enjoyment, the gramophone is put on again, dancing becomes general. The Professor stands and looks, with his hand on the door-knob. He nods and laughs; when he finally shuts himself into his study the mechanical smile still lingers on his lips.

Again he turns over pages by his desk lamp, takes notes, attends to a few simple matters. After a while he notices that the guests have forsaken the entrance hall for his wife's drawing-room, into which there is a door from his own study as well. He hears their voices and the sounds of a guitar being tuned. Herr Möller, it seems, is to sing—and does so. He twangs the strings of his instrument and sings in a powerful bass a ballad in a strange tongue, possibly Swedish. The Professor does not succeed in identifying it, though he listens attentively to the end, after which there is great applause. The sound is deadened by the portière that hangs over the dividing door. The young bank-clerk begins another song. Cornelius goes softly in.

It is half-dark in the drawing-room; the only light is from the shaded standard lamp, beneath which Möller sits, on the divan, with his legs crossed, picking his strings. His audience is grouped easily about; as there are not enough seats, some stand, and more, among them many young ladies, are simply sitting on the floor with their hands clasped round their knees or even with their legs stretched out before them. Hergesell sits thus, in his dinner jacket, next the piano, with Fräulein Plaichinger beside him. Frau Cornelius is holding both children on her lap as she sits in her easy-chair opposite the singer. Snapper, the Boeotian,[14] begins to talk loud and clear in the middle of the song and has to be intimidated with hushings and finger-shakings. Never, never would Ellie allow herself to be guilty of such conduct. She sits there daintily erect and still on her mother's knee. The Professor tries to catch her eye and exchange a private signal with his little girl; but she does not see him. Neither does she seem to be looking at the singer. Her gaze is directed lower down.

---

[14]Dullard or clown; residents of the ancient Greek city of Boeotia were supposed to be like that.

Möller sings the "joli tambour":[15]

"Sire, mon roi, donnez-moi votre fille—"

They are all enchanted. "How good!" Hergesell is heard to say, in the odd, nasally condescending Hergesell tone. The next one is a beggar ballad, to a tune composed by young Möller himself; it elicits a storm of applause:

Gypsy lassie a-goin' to the fair, Huzza!
Gypsy laddie a-goin' to be there—
Huzza, diddlety umpty dido!

Laughter and high spirits, sheer reckless hilarity, reigns after this jovial ballad. "Frightfully good!" Hergesell comments again, as before. Follows another popular song, this time a Hungarian one; Möller sings it in its own outlandish tongue, and most effectively. The Professor applauds with ostentation. It warms his heart and does him good, this outcropping of artistic, historic, and cultural elements all amongst the shimmying. He goes up to young Möller and congratulates him, talks about the songs and their sources, and Möller promises to lend him a certain annotated book of folk-songs. Cornelius is the more cordial because all the time, as fathers do, he has been comparing the parts and achievements of this young stranger with those of his own son, and being gnawed by envy and chagrin. This young Möller, he is thinking, is a capable bank-clerk (though about Möller's capacity he knows nothing whatever) and has this special gift besides, which must have taken talent and energy to cultivate. "And here is my poor Bert, who knows nothing and can do nothing and thinks of nothing except playing the clown, without even talent for that!" He tries to be just; he tells himself that after all, Bert has innate refinement; that probably there is a good deal more to him than there is to the successful Möller; that perhaps he has even something of the poet in him, and his dancing and table-waiting are due to mere boyish folly and the distraught times. But paternal envy and pessimism win the upper hand; when Möller begins another song, Dr. Cornelius goes back to his room.

He works as before, with divided attention, at this and that, while it gets on for seven o'clock. Then he remembers a letter he may just as well write, a short letter and not very important, but letter-writing is wonderful for the way it takes up the time, and it is almost half past when he has finished. At half past eight the Italian salad will be served; so now is the prescribed moment for the Professor to go out into the wintry darkness to post his letters and take his daily quantum of fresh air and exercise. They are dancing again, and he will have to pass through the hall to get his hat and coat; but they are used to him now, he need not stop and beg them not to be disturbed. He lays away his papers, takes up the letters he has written, and goes out. But he sees his wife sitting near the door of his room and pauses a little by her easy-chair.

[15]An old French folk song.

She is watching the dancing. Now and then the big folk or some of their guests stop to speak to her; the party is at its height, and there are more onlookers than these two: blue-faced Ann is standing at the bottom of the stairs, in all the dignity of her limitations. She is waiting for the children, who simply cannot get their fill of these unwonted festivities, and watching over Snapper, lest his all too rich blood be churned to the danger-point by too much twirling round. And not only the nursery but the kitchen takes an interest: Xaver and the two ladies Hinterhofer are standing by the pantry door looking on with relish. Fräulein Walburga, the elder of the two sunken sisters (the culinary section— she objects to being called a cook), is a whimsical, good-natured sort, brown-eyed, wearing glasses with thick circular lenses; the nose-piece is wound with a bit of rag to keep it from pressing on her nose. Fräulein Cecilia is younger, though not so precisely young either. Her bearing is as self-assertive as usual, this being her way of sustaining her dignity as a former member of the middle class. For Fräulein Cecilia feels acutely her descent into the ranks of domestic service. She positively declines to wear a cap or other badge of servitude, and her hardest trial is on the Wednesday evening when she has to serve the dinner while Xaver has his afternoon out. She hands the dishes with averted face and elevated nose—a fallen queen; and so distressing is it to behold her degradation that one evening when the little folk happened to be at table and saw her they both with one accord burst into tears. Such anguish is unknown to young Xaver. He enjoys serving and does it with an ease born of practice as well as talent, for he was once a "piccolo."[16] But otherwise he is a thorough-paced good-for-nothing and windbag—with quite distinct traits of character of his own, as his long-suffering employers are always ready to concede, but perfectly impossible and a bag of wind for all that. One must just take him as he is, they think, and not expect figs from thistles. He is the child and product of the disrupted times, a perfect specimen of his generation, follower of the revolution, Bolshevist sympathizer. The Professor's name for him is the "minute-man," because he is always to be counted on in any sudden crisis, if only it address his sense of humor or love of novelty, and will display therein amazing readiness and resource. But he utterly lacks a sense of duty and can as little be trained to the performance of the daily round and common task as some kinds of dog can be taught to jump over a stick. It goes so plainly against the grain that criticism is disarmed. One becomes resigned. On grounds that appealed to him as unusual and amusing he would be ready to turn out of his bed at any hour of the night. But he simply cannot get up before eight in the morning, he cannot do it, he will not jump over the stick. Yet all day long the evidence of this free and untrammeled existence, the sound of his mouth-organ, his joyous whistle, or his raucous but expressive voice lifted in song, rises to the hearing of the world above-stairs; and the smoke of his cigarette fills the pantry. While the Hinterhofer ladies work he stands and looks on. Of a morning while the Professor is breakfasting, he tears the leaf off the study calendar—but does not lift a finger to

---

[16]An apprentice waiter.

dust the room. Dr. Cornelius has often told him to leave the calendar alone, for he tends to tear off two leaves at a time and thus to add to the general confusion. But young Xaver appears to find joy in this activity, and will not be deprived of it.

Again, he is fond of children, a winning trait. He will throw himself into games with the little folk in the garden, make and mend their toys with great ingenuity, even read aloud from their books—and very droll it sounds in his thick-lipped pronunciation. With his whole soul he loves the cinema; after an evening spent there he inclines to melancholy and yearning and talking to himself. Vague hopes stir in him that some day he may make his fortune in that gay world and belong to it by rights—hopes based on his shock of hair and his physical agility and daring. He likes to climb the ash tree in the front garden, mounting branch by branch to the very top and frightening everybody to death who sees him. Once there he lights a cigarette and smokes it as he sways to and fro, keeping a look-out for a cinema director who might chance to come along and engage him.

If he changed his striped jacket for mufti, he might easily dance with the others and no one would notice the difference. For the big folk's friends are rather anomalous in their clothing: evening dress is worn by a few, but it is by no means the rule. There is quite a sprinkling of guests, both male and female, in the same general style as Möller the ballad-singer. The Professor is familiar with the circumstances of most of this young generation he is watching as he stands beside his wife's chair; he has heard them spoken of by name. They are students at the high school or at the School of Applied Art; they lead, at least the masculine portion, that precarious and scrambling existence which is purely the product of the time. There is a tall, pale, spindling youth, the son of a dentist, who lives by speculation. From all the Professor hears, he is a perfect Aladdin. He keeps a car, treats his friends to champagne suppers, and showers presents upon them on every occasion, costly little trifles in mother-of-pearl and gold. So today he has brought gifts to the young givers of the feast: for Bert a gold lead-pencil, and for Ingrid a pair of ear-rings of barbaric size, great gold circlets that fortunately do not have to go through the little ear-lobe, but are fastened over it by means of a clip. The big folk come laughing to their parents to display these trophies; and the parents shake their heads even while they admire—Aladdin bowing over and over from afar.

The young people appear to be absorbed in their dancing—if the performance they are carrying out with so much still concentration can be called dancing. They stride across the carpet, slowly, according to some unfathomable prescript, strangely embraced; in the newest attitude, tummy advanced and shoulders high, waggling the hips. They do not get tired, because nobody could. There is no such thing as heightened color or heaving bosoms. Two girls may dance together or two young men—it is all the same. They move to the exotic strains of the gramophone, played with the loudest needles to procure the maximum of sound: shimmies, foxtrots, one-steps, double foxes, African shimmies, Java dances, and Creole polkas, the wild musky melodies follow one another, now furious, now languishing, a monotonous Negro program in unfamiliar rhythm, to a clacking, clashing, and strumming orchestral accompaniment.

"What is that record?" Cornelius inquires of Ingrid, as she passes him by in the arms of the pale young speculator, with reference to the piece then playing, whose alternate languors and furies he finds comparatively pleasing and showing a certain resourcefulness in detail.

"*Prince of Pappenheim:* 'Console thee, dearest child,'" she answers, and smiles pleasantly back at him with her white teeth.

The cigarette smoke wreathes beneath the chandelier. The air is blue with a festal haze compact of sweet and thrilling ingredients that stir the blood with memories of green-sick pains and are particularly poignant to those whose youth—like the Professor's own—has been over-sensitive. . . . The little folk are still on the floor. They are allowed to stop up until eight, so great is their delight in the party. The guests have got used to their presence; in their own way, they have their place in the doings of the evening. They have separated, anyhow: Snapper revolves all alone in the middle of the carpet, in his little blue velvet smock, while Ellie is running after one of the dancing couples, trying to hold the man fast by his coat. It is Max Hergesell and Fräulein Plaichinger. They dance well, it is a pleasure to watch them. One has to admit that these mad modern dances, when the right people dance them, are not so bad after all— they have something quite taking. Young Hergesell is a capital leader, dances according to rule, yet with individuality. So it looks. With what aplomb can he walk backward—when space permits! And he knows how to be graceful standing still in a crowd. And his partner supports him well, being unsuspectedly lithe and buoyant, as fat people often are. They look at each other, they are talking, paying no heed to Ellie, though others are smiling to see the child's persistence. Dr. Cornelius tries to catch up his little sweetheart as she passes and draw her to him. But Ellie eludes him, almost peevishly; her dear Abel is nothing to her now. She braces her little arms against his chest and turns her face away with a persecuted look. Then escapes to follow her fancy once more.

The Professor feels an involuntary twinge. Uppermost in his heart is hatred for this party, with its power to intoxicate and estrange his darling child. His love for her—that not quite disinterested, not quite unexceptionable love of his—is easily wounded. He wears a mechanical smile, but his eyes have clouded, and he stares fixedly at a point in the carpet, between the dancers' feet.

"The children ought to go to bed," he tells his wife. But she pleads for another quarter of an hour; she has promised already, and they do love it so! He smiles again and shakes his head, stands so a moment and then goes across to the cloak-room, which is full of coats and hats and scarves and overshoes. He has trouble in rummaging out his own coat, and Max Hergesell comes out of the hall, wiping his brow.

"Going out, sir?" he asks, in Hergesellian accents, dutifully helping the older man on with his coat. "Silly business this, with my pumps," he says. "They pinch like hell. The brutes are simply too tight for me, quite apart from the bad leather. They press just here on the ball of my great toe"—he stands on one foot and holds the other in his hand—"it's simply unbearable. There's nothing for it but to take them off; my brogues will have to do the business. . . . Oh, let me help you, sir."

"Thanks," says Cornelius. "Don't trouble. Get rid of your own tormentors. . . . Oh, thanks very much!" For Hergesell has gone on one knee to snap the fasteners of his snowboots.

Once more the Professor expresses his gratitude; he is pleased and touched by so much sincere respect and youthful readiness to serve. "Go and enjoy yourself," he counsels. "Change your shoes and make up for what you have been suffering. Nobody can dance in shoes that pinch. Good-by, I must be off to get a breath of fresh air."

"I'm going to dance with Ellie now," calls Hergesell after him. "She'll be a first-rate dancer when she grows up, and that I'll swear to."

"Think so?" Cornelius answers, already half out. "Well, you are a connoisseur, I'm sure. Don't get curvature of the spine with stooping."

He nods again and goes. "Fine lad," he thinks as he shuts the door. "Student of engineering. Knows what he's bound for, got a good clear head, and so well set up and pleasant too." And again paternal envy rises as he compares his poor Bert's status with this young man's, which he puts in the rosiest light that his son's may look the darker. Thus he sets out on his evening walk.

He goes up the avenue, crosses the bridge, and walks along the bank on the other side as far as the next bridge but one. The air is wet and cold, with a little snow now and then. He turns up his coat-collar and slips the crook of his cane over the arm behind his back. Now and then he ventilates his lungs with a long deep breath of the night air. As usual when he walks, his mind reverts to his professional preoccupations, he thinks about his lectures and the things he means to say tomorrow about Philip's struggle against the Germanic revolution, things steeped in melancholy and penetratingly just. Above all just, he thinks. For in one's dealings with the young it behooves one to display the scientific spirit, to exhibit the principles of enlightenment—not only for purposes of mental discipline, but on the human and individual side, in order not to wound them or indirectly offend their political sensibilities; particularly in these days, when there is so much tinder in the air, opinions are so frightfully split up and chaotic, and you may so easily incur attacks from one party or the other, or even give rise to scandal, by taking sides on a point of history. "And taking sides is unhistoric anyhow," so he muses. "Only justice, only impartiality is historic." And could not, properly considered, be otherwise. . . . For justice can have nothing of youthful fire and blithe, fresh, loyal conviction. It is by nature melancholy. And, being so, has secret affinity with the lost cause and the forlorn hope rather than with the fresh and blithe and loyal—perhaps this affinity is its very essence and without it it would not exist at all! . . . "And is there then no such thing as justice?" the Professor asks himself, and ponders the question so deeply that he absently posts his letters in the next box and turns round to go home. This thought of his is unsettling and disturbing to the scientific mind—but is it not after all itself scientific, psychological, conscientious, and therefore to be accepted without prejudice, no matter how upsetting? In the midst of which musings Dr. Cornelius finds himself back at his own door.

On the outer threshold stands Xaver, and seems to be looking for him.

"Herr Professor," says Xaver, tossing back his hair, "go upstairs to Ellie straight off. She's in a bad way."

"What's the matter?" asks Cornelius in alarm. "Is she ill?"

"No-o, not to say ill," answers Xaver. "She's just in a bad way and crying fit to bust her little heart. It's along o' that chap with the shirt-front that danced with her—Herr Hergesell. She couldn't be got to go upstairs peaceably, not at no price at all, and she's b'en crying bucketfuls."

"Nonsense," says the Professor, who has entered and is tossing off his things in the cloak-room. He says no more; opens the glass door and without a glance at the guests turns swiftly to the stairs. Takes them two at a time, crosses the upper hall and the small room leading into the nursery. Xaver follows at his heels, but stops at the nursery door.

A bright light still burns within, showing the gay frieze that runs all round the room, the large row of shelves heaped with a confusion of toys, the rocking-horse on his swaying platform, with red-varnished nostrils and raised hoofs. On the linoleum lie other toys—building blocks, railway trains, a little trumpet. The two white cribs stand not far apart, Ellie's in the window corner, Snapper's out in the room.

Snapper is asleep. He has said his prayers in loud, ringing tones, prompted by Nurse, and gone off at once into vehement, profound, and rosy slumber—from which a cannonball fired at close range could not rouse him. He lies with both fists flung back on the pillows on either side of the tousled head with its funny crooked little slumber-tossed wig.

A circle of females surrounds Ellie's bed: not only blue-faced Ann is there, but the Hinterhofer ladies too, talking to each other and to her. They make way as the Professor comes up and reveal the child sitting all pale among her pillows, sobbing and weeping more bitterly than he has ever seen her sob and weep in her life. Her lovely little hands lie on the coverlet in front of her, the nightgown with its narrow lace border has slipped down from her shoulder—such a thin, birdlike little shoulder—and the sweet head Cornelius loves so well, set on the neck like a flower on its stalk, her head is on one side, with the eyes rolled up to the corner between wall and ceiling above her head. For there she seems to envisage the anguish of her heart and even to nod to it—either on purpose or because her head wobbles as her body is shaken with the violence of her sobs. Her eyes rain down tears. The bow-shaped lips are parted, like a little *mater dolorosa's,*[17] and from them issue long, low wails that in nothing resemble the unnecessary and exasperating shrieks of a naughty child, but rise from the deep extremity of her heart and wake in the Professor's own a sympathy that is well-nigh intolerable. He has never seen his darling so before. His feelings find immediate vent in an attack on the ladies Hinterhofer.

"What about the supper?" he asks sharply. "There must be a great deal to do. Is my wife being left to do it alone?"

For the acute sensibilities of the former middle class this is quite enough.

---

[17]Latin phrase: Our Lady of Sorrow, the Virgin Mary mourning for Christ.

The ladies withdraw in righteous indignation, and Xaver Kleinsgutl jeers at them as they pass out. Having been born to low life instead of achieving it, he never loses a chance to mock at their fallen state.

"Childie, childie," murmurs Cornelius, and sitting down by the crib enfolds the anguished Ellie in his arms. "What is the trouble with my darling?"

She bedews his face with her tears.

"Abel . . . Abel . . ." she stammers between sobs. "Why—isn't Max—my brother? Max ought to be—my brother!"

Alas, alas! What mischance is this? Is this what the party has wrought, with its fatal atmosphere? Cornelius glances helplessly up at blue-faced Ann standing there in all the dignity of her limitations with her hands before her on her apron. She purses up her mouth and makes a long face. "It's pretty young," she says, "for the female instincts to be showing up."

"Hold your tongue," snaps Cornelius, in his agony. He has this much to be thankful for, that Ellie does not turn from him now; she does not push him away as she did downstairs, but clings to him in her need, while she reiterates her absurd, bewildered prayer that Max might be her brother, or with a fresh burst of desire demands to be taken downstairs so that he can dance with her again. But Max, of course, is dancing with Fräulein Plaichinger, that behemoth who is his rightful partner and has every claim upon him; whereas Ellie—never, thinks the Professor, his heart torn with the violence of his pity, never has she looked so tiny and birdlike as now, when she nestles to him shaken with sobs and all unaware of what is happening in her little soul. No, she does not know. She does not comprehend that her suffering is on account of Fräulein Plaichinger, fat, overgrown, and utterly within her rights in dancing with Max Hergesell, whereas Ellie may only do it once, by way of a joke, although she is incomparably the more charming of the two. Yet it would be quite mad to reproach young Hergesell with the state of affairs or to make fantastic demands upon him. No, Ellie's suffering is without help or healing and must be covered up. Yet just as it is without understanding, so it is also without restraint—and that is what makes it so horribly painful. Xaver and blue-faced Ann do not feel this pain, it does not affect them—either because of native callousness or because they accept it as the way of nature. But the Professor's fatherly heart is quite torn by it, and by a distressful horror of this passion, so hopeless and so absurd.

Of no avail to hold forth to poor Ellie on the subject of the perfectly good little brother she already has. She only casts a distraught and scornful glance over at the other crib, where Snapper lies vehemently slumbering, and with fresh tears calls again for Max. Of no avail either the promise of a long, long walk tomorrow, all five gentlemen, round and round the dining-room table; or a dramatic description of the thrilling cushion games they will play. No, she will listen to none of all this, nor to lying down and going to sleep. She will not sleep, she will sit bolt upright and suffer. . . . But on a sudden they stop and listen, Abel and Ellie; listen to something miraculous that is coming to pass, that is approaching by strides, two strides, to the nursery door, that now overwhelmingly appears. . . .

It is Xaver's work, not a doubt of that. He has not remained by the door where he stood to gloat over the ejection of the Hinterhofers. No, he has bestirred himself, taken a notion; likewise steps to carry it out. Downstairs he has gone, twitched Herr Hergesell's sleeve, and made a thick-lipped request. So here they both are. Xaver, having done his part, remains by the door; but Max Hergesell comes up to Ellie's crib; in his dinner-jacket, with his sketchy side-whisker and charming black eyes; obviously quite pleased with his rôle of swan knight and fairy prince,[18] as one who should say: "See, here am I, now all losses are restored and sorrows end."

Cornelius is almost as much overcome as Ellie herself.

"Just look," he says feebly, "look who's here. This is uncommonly good of you, Herr Hergesell."

"Not a bit of it," says Hergesell. "Why shouldn't I come to say good night to my fair partner?"

And he approaches the bars of the crib, behind which Ellie sits struck mute. She smiles blissfully through her tears. A funny, high little note that is half a sigh of relief comes from her lips, then she looks dumbly up at her swan knight with her golden-brown eyes—tear-swollen though they are, so much more beautiful than the fat Plaichinger's. She does not put up her arms. Her joy, like her grief, is without understanding; but she does not do that. The lovely little hands lie quiet on the coverlet, and Max Hergesell stands with his arms leaning over the rail as on a balcony.

"And now," he says smartly, "she need not 'sit the livelong night and weep upon her bed'!"[19] He looks at the Professor to make sure he is receiving due credit for the quotation. "Ha ha!" he laughs, "she's beginning young. 'Console thee, dearest child!' Never mind, you're all right! Just as you are you'll be wonderful! You've only got to grow up. . . . And you'll lie down and go to sleep like a good girl, now I've come to say good night? And not cry any more, little Lorelei?"[20]

Ellie looks up at him, transfigured. One birdlike shoulder is bare; the Professor draws the lace-trimmed nighty over it. There comes into his mind a sentimental story he once read about a dying child who longs to see a clown he had once, with unforgettable ecstasy, beheld in a circus. And they bring the clown to the bedside marvelously arrayed embroidered before and behind with silver butterflies; and the child dies happy. Max Hergesell is not embroidered, and Ellie, thank God, is not going to die, she has only "been in a bad way." But, after all, the effect is the same. Young Hergesell leans over the bars of the crib and rattles on, more for the father's ear than the child's, but Ellie does not know that—and the father's feelings toward him are a most singular mixture of thankfulness, embarrassment, and hatred.

"Good night, little Lorelei," says Hergesell, and gives her his hand through the bars. Her pretty, soft, white little hand is swallowed up in the grasp of his big, strong, red one. "Sleep well," he says, "and sweet dreams! But don't dream

[18]A reference to Richard Wagner's opera *Lohengrin,* in which the hero arrives in a boat drawn by swans in order to rescue a lady.
[19]Quoted from a poem that appears in Goethe's novel, *Wilhelm Meister's Apprenticeship.*
[20]Legendary siren of the Rhine river, whose beauty distracted sailors from the dangers of navigation.

about me—God forbid! Not at your age—ha ha!" And then the fairy clown's visit is at an end. Cornelius accompanies him to the door. "No, no, positively, no thanks called for, don't mention it," he large-heartedly protests; and Xaver goes downstairs with him, to help serve the Italian salad.

But Dr. Cornelius returns to Ellie, who is now lying down, with her cheek pressed into her flat little pillow.

"Well, wasn't that lovely?" he says as he smooths the covers. She nods, with one last little sob. For a quarter of an hour he sits beside her and watches while she falls asleep in her turn, beside the little brother who found the right way so much earlier than she. Her silky brown hair takes the enchanting fall it always does when she sleeps; deep, deep lie the lashes over the eyes that late so abundantly poured forth their sorrow; the angelic mouth with its bowed upper lip is peacefully relaxed and a little open. Only now and then comes a belated catch in her slow breathing.

And her small hands, like pink and white flowers, lie so quietly, one on the coverlet, the other on the pillow by her face—Dr. Cornelius, gazing, feels his heart melt with tenderness as with strong wine.

"How good," he thinks, "that she breathes in oblivion with every breath she draws! That in childhood each night is a deep, wide gulf between one day and the next. Tomorrow, beyond all doubt, young Hergesell will be a pale shadow, powerless to darken her little heart. Tomorrow, forgetful of all but present joy, she will walk with Abel and Snapper, all five gentlemen, round and round the table, will play the ever-thrilling cushion game."

Heaven be praised for that!

Translated by H. T. Lowe-Porter

Questions for Writing and Discussion

1. Most stories are written in the past tense, as if to suggest that the author, or the narrator within the story, is looking back upon a completed action. But this story is written in the present tense. Can you see any strong reasons for Mann's use of the present tense? Do you think it would have been a less effective story if he had written in the more conventional way?

2. The party which is described in the middle of the story is there, partly, to prepare the way for Ellie's unhappy wish that Hergesell be "her brother." But it also serves another purpose: it is a kind of sounding-board, a test, for Professor Cornelius. Responding to the young people, their manners and their outlooks, he finds himself forced to think about the social and moral distance between generations. Trace these reflections in the story itself and indicate what they contribute to its overall significance.

3. Examine the last five or six paragraphs of the story, with special attention to the small shifts in tone which Mann achieves through a word here, a phrase there. How do these concluding paragraphs contribute to the resolution of the conflicts that the

story has established? Consider, for example, the conflicts in Cornelius's mind between the traditional values he clings to and his feeling that one should be sympathetic to the ways of life that young people work out.

4.　Among all twentieth-century writers, Thomas Mann was one of the most closely acquainted with the ideas of Sigmund Freud, the founder of psychoanalysis. Do you find much evidence of Freudian thought in this story? Could the relationships among the characters have been described just as well, or perhaps better, by a writer who had never read or heard of Freud? Do you find that the evidence of Freudianism in this story juts out uncomfortably, like some pellets of thought that have not been absorbed into the stream of the narrative, or do you think that whatever Freudian insights Mann may have borrowed were smoothly absorbed in the story? Offer some instances in the text to support your conclusion.

JAMES JOYCE

The Dead

Introduction

Let us start toward the end of the story, at the point where the Christmas party is breaking up. It is the point where Joyce visibly pulls together the threads of his narrative, until then deliberately allowed to hang loose. The conflicts and tensions among the characters have been slowly accumulating beneath a surface of small talk and holiday pleasantries; but now the time has come to drive the narrative directly toward its climax.

Bartell d'Arcy is singing an old Irish air and Gabriel Conroy, the central figure of "The Dead," is looking up the stairs to see his wife listening intently to the song, which braids love and death into words of wistfulness:

> Oh, the rains fall on my heavy locks,
> And the dew wets my skin,
> My babe lies cold . . .

Looking up the stairs, Gabriel is surprised to see that "there was color on [Gretta's] cheeks and that her eyes were shining." He is stirred by her apparent excitement—it is the first strong and spontaneous feeling he has had all evening long. "A sudden tide of joy went leaping out of his heart." It's as if he were seeing his faded, middle-aged wife in her original freshness; as if he, the somewhat fussy, middle-aged man, were now open to unexpected emotions.

The point of which we speak comes on page 306, about four-fifths of the way through the story. Until now, everything has seemed diffuse, weary, and trivial, the sort of scatter of words and responses one expects at social occasions. In fact, as we shall see, the early portions of the story are by no means diffuse, weary, and trivial: Joyce is using every word for clearly thought-out purposes. But right now let us focus on what happens in the last few pages.

Something has occurred which breaks the mild routine of the party: Gabriel has been stirred by the sight of his wife, by his perception that there is

279

"grace and mystery in her attitude as if she were a symbol of something." A surge of renewed life sweeps over him, though he does not quite know why.

Husband and wife walk together toward the hotel where they are to spend the night, and he feels himself to be young, even amorous, wanting to whisper foolishly into her ear. Memories overcome him, happy moments from the past, flickering incidents of no importance to anyone but Gretta and himself. He wants "to make her forget the years of their dull existence together." And he remembers the lyricism of an early love letter he had sent her: "Why is it that words like these seem to me so dull and cold? Is it because there is no word tender enough to be your name?"

Entering the hotel, Gabriel feels "a keen pang of lust." The excitement, the holiday atmosphere, the upsurge of his thoughts and feelings, all stir him sexually. Perhaps a little fatuously—but who would care to judge?—he hopes that in the hotel, place of honeymoons and liaisons, there may occur "a new adventure."

The spell is broken for Gabriel by the porter's clumsiness and his wife's evident distance, which she calls "tiredness." He blunders into irrelevant chatter about Freddie Malins owing him some money. He cannot name his true feelings, for he is uncertain, diffident, fearful of rejection. Gretta responds with a kiss, affectionate but not passionate, saying that he is generous for having lent money to Malins. Which is all very well, but serves only to put off Gabriel still further.

And then come Gretta's memories. She had been thinking about the song, but not in connection with Gabriel, not in any way that he might have hoped, for it is not her husband who has stirred her emotions or made her cry. At first Gabriel speaks in a gentle way, but when he asks whether "the person" she remembers was "someone you were in love with," he protects himself behind a shield of irony. It is becoming clear to him, as it already is to the reader, that what Gabriel had hoped would be a series of steps leading to renewed intimacy is actually a retreat into separateness.

For it is Michael Furey whom Gretta remembers, the "delicate" boy who loved her when they were young. As Gretta recalls the boy's love, Gabriel can only respond with the dulled needle of his irony: so the unknown rival was merely an employee of the "gasworks"!

It is a blow to his self-esteem. "While he had been full of memories of their secret life together . . . she had been comparing him in her mind with another." He sees himself now as a ludicrous figure, a sentimentalist, a fearful middle-aged weakling who worries about his galoshes when it gets wet—while Michael Furey, in the abandonment of youthful passion, had risked his skin in the rain for the girl he loved.

"I think he died for me," says Gretta, and a sense of terror descends upon Gabriel when he hears these words. For he knows that he never could have been what Michael Furey was; yet he is sensitive enough to appreciate the attractiveness of Furey's romanticism and to understand, even if it threatens him, why Gretta should remember the boy with strong feelings.

And now comes Gabriel's vision, the ending of the story, which James

Joyce called an epiphany. Originally, an epiphany signified a religious revelation, and in Christianity it refers to the twelfth night after Christmas, when Jesus was revealed as the Christ to the Magi at Bethlehem; but as Joyce uses the term, and as it has come to be used in modern literary discussion, it refers to a moment of intense illumination, religious or nonreligious. It is a moment in the story that merits close inspection.

Gabriel now looks at his wife with a curious detachment. He feels very little pain to learn that she had had a youthful lover, and the face he sees on the bed, he acknowledges to himself, is no longer young or beautiful. Not out of indifference but out of a growing comprehension, Gabriel begins to distance himself from the experience he has been having, and as he does this, he feels for his sleeping wife "a strange, friendly pity." He feels that pity because he recognizes in the passage of her life, in the pathos and hopelessness of her memories, the damage wrought by the common human condition. "One by one, they were all becoming shades." The faces he remembers at the party are faces on which oncoming death has already left its mark. And the thought strikes him, perhaps the central thought of the story: "Better pass boldly into that other world, in the full glory of some passion, than fade and wither dismally with age." When we say that this is the central thought of the story, we do not mean to suggest that Joyce wants it to seem as if he endorses it uncritically. Not at all. It is merely that Joyce understands how powerful such a thought can be to a man who has himself begun to fade and wither into age.

"The full glory of some passion" is not for Gabriel Conroy. He recognizes, with "generous tears," the strength and genuineness of the youthful encounter that his wife has suddenly remembered, though he is also honest enough to admit to himself that he has never felt anything like what Michael Furey did. As he now summons in imagination a picture of Michael Furey "standing under a dripping tree" and waiting for the young Gretta, Gabriel is no longer thinking merely of himself or his wife or even the dead boy; he is no longer in the grip merely of personal complaints or griefs; no, his imagination has been fired and purified by the pain occasioned through Gretta's recollections, and he sees the whole of humanity, both those gone and those still here, as companions in yearning and suffering. "His own identity was fading out into a grey impalpable world"—if you wish, you can call this a religious or a mystical experience. In any case, it is an experience embodying the democracy of fate. Time dissolves and eternity creeps in.

Two phrases that had been spoken casually by Mary Jane earlier in the story—"snow was general all over Ireland" and "to remind them of their last end"—are now used in their literal sense, like a painful and ironic echo.

Looking toward the window, Gabriel sees the drops of snow. In its soothing, hypnotic, encompassing fall, the snow keeps coming down equally upon the living and the dead. There had been notations of snow earlier in the story, signifying different things at various points: the vigorousness of life, as people entering the house brush snow off their clothes; the hope for mystery and change, as Gabriel looks out the window during the party and thinks how much more pleasant it would be to be outside, walking through the night. But here, at the story's end, the snow becomes an inclusive symbol, a kind of mothering and silencing motion of nature which reconciles us to all that we are and must become, in our life and in our death. It is a wonderful stroke of symbolism on Joyce's part—this concluding soft beat of snow, comforting as a caress, inexorable as time.

We have gone into so detailed an account of the concluding section of "The Dead" because we believe that to grasp firmly what happens there is to enable the reader to understand what Joyce has been doing in the early portions of the story. Now, when we know the outcome of the story, we can see why Joyce put in the early chaos and buzz of chatter, the trivial encounters at the party, the idle and boastful talk of the guests. It is all a prelude to the great crisis at the end, all a preparation for Gabriel's transforming and purifying illumination. And now too we can better understand the title of the story.

Who are the dead? All the living. All those who feel, like Gabriel at one point, that his life is a kind of empty shadow-play, a life-in-death. All those who live, like the guests at the party, without adequate consciousness and who waste the time given them by reducing their lives to mere routine, flatness, deadness. All those who, like the Misses Morkan, are withering into age, moving closer to dissolution.

At best there is only a temporary escape from this common fate, through the illuminations of a heightened awareness and the communions of shared love which are the privilege, or possibility, of humanity. But even then, it would be foolish and fanatical to expect that we can live out most of our days at such peaks of intensity. If Joyce is romantic in forever looking toward those peaks, he is realistic in knowing that most of the time we have to settle for the drabness of the plains. That is why, finally, despite the ironic ways in which he displays the characters of his story, he does not propose to judge or condemn them. All are shown to have their failings, their secret (and sometimes not-so-secret) anxieties, their moments of affection and good feeling. They are common clay, humans and not gods; and the snow falls upon all.

Nor does Joyce invite us to pass judgment on Gabriel Conroy. For the final triumph of the story resides in the complexity and humaneness with which Joyce evokes the figure of this man. Let there be no mistake about it: Gabriel is a mediocre man. His posturings, his rhetoric, his little fears, his incapacity to reach out to other people, his excessive need to be liked and admired, his desire to be thought intellectually distinguished (when, in fact, he is merely educated), his sentimentalism and timidity (those galoshes!)—all these are the traits of a mediocre man. Nothing about him is large or impressive, certainly nothing is heroic. No furies have ever seized him, none ever will. And there is every reason to expect, even after the illumination that comes to him at the story's end, that Gabriel will fall back into his usual rut. What else could he do? Had Michael Furey lived longer, he too might well have become a mediocre man; the glamour he has in Gretta's memory may well be a result of having died young.

Yet we also know that Gabriel is, in many ways, a decent and sensitive man. If he cannot live up to the standards that he perceives and appreciates, he is at least capable of perceiving and appreciating them. Indeed, we may feel that

Gabriel is a figure typical of many educated or semi-educated people of the twentieth century: all those who have been taught to honor the "creative" life and to value personal sensitivity, yet cannot themselves quite realize them. As a result, such people live in a state of constant dissatisfaction, somehow aware that they are failures and sometimes tormenting themselves excessively.

Still, let us stress again that Gabriel Conroy is an affectionate and decent man, one who is generous, considerate, and cultivated. Modern civilization has produced far, far worse than Gabriel Conroy, and it would be a very self-righteous reader who simply dismissed him with contempt. Still more to the point, there is hardly a complaint or criticism to be launched against Gabriel that has not occurred to him already. His distinctive trait is precisely that his self-knowledge serves to make him unhappy.

The judgment that Joyce demands of us with regard to Conroy may be severe, but the response of feeling that intertwines itself with that judgment ought to be compassionate. Gabriel Conroy is a part, larger or smaller, of all of us—a part, also, of James Joyce. He is that part of us which becomes a little more slothful with each passing year. He is that part of us which goes about the business of daily life, neither exalted nor debased, neither saintly nor devilish, just commonplace. We cannot live without the Gabriel Conroy within us, though at some points in our lives we hope to become more than him.

It is notable, in "The Dead," that even after having shown Gabriel in all his limitations and failures, Joyce moves very close to him at the end of the story. (Perhaps he moves close to him *because* he has shown his failures.) In the concluding paragraphs there is barely a touch of irony on Joyce's part, barely any effort to distance himself from Gabriel. The language seems equally Joyce's and Gabriel's. The sorrow, the sense of suffering, the relief that comes from recognizing that the sorrow and suffering are shared by all human beings: these are equally the author's and the character's. At the end of "The Dead" Joyce seems to be saying that Gabriel Conroy is part of him and that as we approach the end we are all one.

The Dead

Lily, the caretaker's daughter, was literally run off her feet. Hardly had she brought one gentleman into the little pantry behind the office on the ground floor and helped him off with his overcoat than the wheezy hall-door bell clanged again and she had to scamper along the bare hallway to let in another guest. It was well for her she had not to attend to the ladies also. But Miss Kate and Miss Julia had thought of that and had converted the bathroom upstairs into a ladies' dressing-room. Miss Kate and Miss Julia were there, gossiping and laughing and fussing, walking after each other to the head of the stairs, peering down over the banisters and calling down to Lily to ask her who had come.

It was always a great affair, the Misses Morkan's annual dance. Everybody who knew them came to it, members of the family, old friends of the family, the members of Julia's choir, any of Kate's pupils that were grown up enough, and even some of Mary Jane's pupils too. Never once had it fallen flat. For years and years it had gone off in splendid style, as long as anyone could remember; ever since Kate and Julia, after the death of their brother Pat, had left the house in Stoney Batter and taken Mary Jane, their only niece, to live with them in the dark, gaunt house on Usher's Island,[1] the upper part of which they had rented from Mr. Fulham, the corn-factor[2] on the ground floor. That was a good thirty years ago if it was a day. Mary Jane, who was then a little girl in short clothes, was now the main prop of the household, for she had the organ in Haddington Road. She had been through the Academy and gave a pupils' concert every year in the upper room of the Antient Concert Rooms. Many of her pupils belonged to the better-class families on the Kingstown and Dalkey line. Old as they were, her aunts also did their share. Julia, though she was quite grey, was still the leading soprano in Adam and Eve's,[3] and Kate, being too feeble to go about much, gave music lessons to beginners on the old square piano in the back room. Lily, the caretaker's daughter, did housemaid's work for them. Though their life was modest, they believed in eating well; the best of everything: diamond-bone sirloins, three-shilling tea and the best bottled stout. But Lily seldom made a mistake in the orders, so that she got on well with her three mistresses. They were fussy, that was all. But the only thing they would not stand was back answers.

Of course, they had good reason to be fussy on such a night. And then it was long after ten o'clock and yet there was no sign of Gabriel and his wife. Besides they were dreadfully afraid that Freddy Malins might turn up screwed.[4] They would not wish for worlds that any of Mary Jane's pupils should see him under the influence; and when he was like that it was sometimes very hard to manage him. Freddy Malins always came late, but they wondered what could be keeping Gabriel: and that was what brought them every two minutes to the banisters to ask Lily had Gabriel or Freddy come.

"O, Mr. Conroy," said Lily to Gabriel when she opened the door for him, "Miss Kate and Miss Julia thought you were never coming. Good-night, Mrs. Conroy."

"I'll engage they did," said Gabriel, "but they forget that my wife here takes three mortal hours to dress herself."

He stood on the mat, scraping the snow from his goloshes, while Lily led his wife to the foot of the stairs and called out:

"Miss Kate, here's Mrs. Conroy."

[1] One of the banks of the Liffey River, within Dublin.
[2] Merchant of grain.
[3] A church in Dublin.
[4] Drunk.

Kate and Julia came toddling down the dark stairs at once. Both of them kissed Gabriel's wife, said she must be perished alive, and asked was Gabriel with her.

"Here I am as right as the mail, Aunt Kate! Go on up. I'll follow," called out Gabriel from the dark.

He continued scraping his feet vigorously while the three women went upstairs, laughing, to the ladies' dressing-room. A light fringe of snow lay like a cape on the shoulders of his overcoat and like toecaps on the toes of his goloshes; and, as the buttons of his overcoat slipped with a squeaking noise through the snow-stiffened frieze, a cold, fragrant air from out-of-doors escaped from crevices and folds.

"Is it snowing again, Mr. Conroy?" asked Lily.

She had preceded him into the pantry to help him off with his overcoat. Gabriel smiled at the three syllables she had given his surname and glanced at her. She was a slim, growing girl, pale in complexion and with hay-coloured hair. The gas in the pantry made her look still paler. Gabriel had known her when she was a child and used to sit on the lowest step nursing a rag doll.

"Yes, Lily," he answered, "and I think we're in for a night of it."

He looked up at the pantry ceiling, which was shaking with the stamping and shuffling of feet on the floor above, listened for a moment to the piano and then glanced at the girl, who was folding his overcoat carefully at the end of a shelf.

"Tell me, Lily," he said in a friendly tone, "do you still go to school?"

"O no, sir," she answered. "I'm done schooling this year and more."

"O, then," said Gabriel gaily, "I suppose we'll be going to your wedding one of these fine days with your young man, eh?"

The girl glanced back at him over her shoulder and said with great bitterness:

"The men that is now is only all palaver and what they can get out of you."

Gabriel coloured, as if he felt he had made a mistake and, without looking at her, kicked off his goloshes and flicked actively with his muffler at his patent-leather shoes.

He was a stout, tallish young man. The high colour of his cheeks pushed upwards even to his forehead, where it scattered itself in a few formless patches of pale red; and on his hairless face there scintillated restlessly the polished lenses and the bright gilt rims of the glasses which screened his delicate and restless eyes. His glossy black hair was parted in the middle and brushed in a long curve behind his ears where it curled slightly beneath the groove left by his hat.

When he had flicked lustre into his shoes he stood up and pulled his waistcoat down more tightly on his plump body. Then he took a coin rapidly from his pocket.

"O Lily," he said, thrusting it into her hands, "it's Christmas-time, isn't it? Just . . . here's a little. . . ."

He walked rapidly towards the door.

"O no, sir!" cried the girl, following him. "Really, sir, I wouldn't take it."

"Christmas-time! Christmas-time!" said Gabriel, almost trotting to the stairs and waving his hand to her in deprecation.

The girl, seeing that he had gained the stairs, called out after him: "Well, thank you, sir."

He waited outside the drawing-room door until the waltz should finish, listening to the skirts that swept against it and to the shuffling of feet. He was still discomposed by the girl's bitter and sudden retort. It had cast a gloom over him which he tried to dispel by arranging his cuffs and the bows of his tie. He then took from his waistcoat pocket a little paper and glanced at the headings he had made for his speech. He was undecided about the lines from Robert Browning, for he feared they would be above the heads of his hearers. Some quotation that they would recognise from Shakespeare or from the Melodies[5] would be better. The indelicate clacking of the men's heels and the shuffling of their soles reminded him that their grade of culture differed from his. He would only make himself ridiculous by quoting poetry to them which they could not understand. They would think that he was airing his superior education. He would fail with them just as he had failed with the girl in the pantry. He had taken up a wrong tone. His whole speech was a mistake from first to last, an utter failure.

Just then his aunts and his wife came out of the ladies' dressing-room. His aunts were two small, plainly dressed old women. Aunt Julia was an inch or so the taller. Her hair, drawn low over the tops of her ears, was grey; and grey also, with darker shadows, was her large flaccid face. Though she was stout in build and stood erect, her slow eyes and parted lips gave her the appearance of a woman who did not know where she was or where she was going. Aunt Kate was more vivacious. Her face, healthier than her sister's, was all puckers and creases, like a shrivelled red apple, and her hair, braided in the same old-fashioned way, had not lost its ripe nut colour.

They both kissed Gabriel frankly. He was their favourite nephew, the son of their dead elder sister, Ellen, who had married T. J. Conroy of the Port and Docks.

"Gretta tells me you're not going to take a cab back to Monkstown to-night, Gabriel," said Aunt Kate.

"No," said Gabriel, turning to his wife, "we had quite enough of that last year, hadn't we? Don't you remember, Aunt Kate, what a cold Gretta got out of it? Cab windows rattling all the way, and the east wind blowing in after we passed Merrion. Very jolly it was. Gretta caught a dreadful cold."

Aunt Kate frowned severely and nodded her head at every word.

"Quite right, Gabriel, quite right," she said. "You can't be too careful."

"But as for Gretta there," said Gabriel, "she'd walk home in the snow if she were let."

Mrs. Conroy laughed.

"Don't mind him, Aunt Kate," she said. "He's really an awful bother, what with green shades for Tom's eyes at night and making him do the dumb-bells,

---

[5] *The Irish Melodies* of Thomas Moore (1779–1852), romantic-sentimental verses popular in Ireland.

and forcing Eva to eat the stirabout.[6] The poor child! And she simply hates the sight of it! . . . O, but you'll never guess what he makes me wear now!"

She broke out into a peal of laughter and glanced at her husband, whose admiring and happy eyes had been wandering from her dress to her face and hair. The two aunts laughed heartily, too, for Gabriel's solicitude was a standing joke with them.

"Goloshes!" said Mrs. Conroy. "That's the latest. Whenever it's wet underfoot I must put on my goloshes. To-night even, he wanted me to put them on, but I wouldn't. The next thing he'll buy me will be a diving suit."

Gabriel laughed nervously and patted his tie reassuringly, while Aunt Kate nearly doubled herself, so heartily did she enjoy the joke. The smile soon faded from Aunt Julia's face and her mirthless eyes were directed towards her nephew's face. After a pause she asked:

"And what are goloshes, Gabriel?"

"Goloshes, Julia!" exclaimed her sister. "Goodness me, don't you know what goloshes are? You wear them over your . . . over your boots, Gretta, isn't it?"

"Yes," said Mrs. Conroy. "Guttapercha things. We both have a pair now. Gabriel says everyone wears them on the continent."

"O, on the continent," murmured Aunt Julia, nodding her head slowly.

Gabriel knitted his brows and said, as if he were slightly angered:

"It's nothing very wonderful, but Gretta thinks it very funny because she says the word reminds her of Christy Minstrels."[7]

"But tell me, Gabriel," said Aunt Kate, with brisk tact. "Of course, you've seen about the room. Gretta was saying . . ."

"O, the room is all right," replied Gabriel. "I've taken one in the Gresham."[8]

"To be sure," said Aunt Kate, "by far the best thing to do. And the children, Gretta, you're not anxious about them?"

"O, for one night," said Mrs. Conroy. "Besides, Bessie will look after them."

"To be sure," said Aunt Kate again. "What a comfort it is to have a girl like that, one you can depend on! There's that Lily, I'm sure I don't know what has come over her lately. She's not the girl she was at all."

Gabriel was about to ask his aunt some questions on this point, but she broke off suddenly to gaze after her sister, who had wandered down the stairs and was craning her neck over the banisters.

"Now, I ask you," she said almost testily, "where is Julia going? Julia! Julia! Where are you going?"

Julia, who had gone half way down one flight, came back and announced blandly:

"Here's Freddy."

At the same moment a clapping of hands and a final flourish of the pianist

[6]Porridge.
[7]A blackface minstrel troupe, popular at the time.
[8]Dublin hotel, middle-range in price.

told that the waltz had ended. The drawing-room door was opened from within and some couples came out. Aunt Kate drew Gabriel aside hurriedly and whispered into his ear:

"Slip down, Gabriel, like a good fellow and see if he's all right, and don't let him up if he's screwed. I'm sure he's screwed. I'm sure he is."

Gabriel went to the stairs and listened over the banisters. He could hear two persons talking in the pantry. Then he recognised Freddy Malins' laugh. He went down the stairs noisily.

"It's such a relief," said Aunt Kate to Mrs. Conroy, "that Gabriel is here. I always feel easier in my mind when he's here. . . . Julia, there's Miss Daly and Miss Power will take some refreshment. Thanks for your beautiful waltz, Miss Daly. It made lovely time."

A tall wizen-faced man, with a stiff grizzled moustache and swarthy skin, who was passing out with his partner, said:

"And may we have some refreshment, too, Miss Morkan?"

"Julia," said Aunt Kate summarily, "and here's Mr. Browne and Miss Furlong. Take them in, Julia, with Miss Daly and Miss Power."

"I'm the man for the ladies," said Mr. Browne, pursing his lips until his moustache bristled and smiling in all his wrinkles. "You know, Miss Morkan, the reason they are so fond of me is——"

He did not finish his sentence, but, seeing that Aunt Kate was out of earshot, at once led the three young ladies into the back room. The middle of the room was occupied by two square tables placed end to end, and on these Aunt Julia and the caretaker were straightening and smoothing a large cloth. On the sideboard were arrayed dishes and plates, and glasses and bundles of knives and forks and spoons. The top of the closed square piano served also as a sideboard for viands and sweets. At a smaller sideboard in one corner two young men were standing, drinking hop-bitters.[9]

Mr. Browne led his charges thither and invited them all, in jest, to some ladies' punch, hot, strong and sweet. As they said they never took anything strong, he opened three bottles of lemonade for them. Then he asked one of the young men to move aside, and, taking hold of the decanter, filled out for himself a goodly measure of whisky. The young men eyed him respectfully while he took a trial sip.

"God help me," he said, smiling, "it's the doctor's orders."

His wizened face broke into a broader smile, and the three young ladies laughed in musical echo to his pleasantry, swaying their bodies to and fro, with nervous jerks of their shoulders. The boldest said:

"O, now, Mr. Browne, I'm sure the doctor never ordered anything of the kind."

Mr. Browne took another sip of his whisky and said, with sidling mimicry:

"Well, you see, I'm like the famous Mrs. Cassidy, who is reported to have said: 'Now, Mary Grimes, if I don't take it, make me take it, for I feel I want it.'"

His hot face had leaned forward a little too confidentially and he had

[9]An Irish soft drink.

assumed a very low Dublin accent so that the young ladies, with one instinct, received his speech in silence. Miss Furlong, who was one of Mary Jane's pupils, asked Miss Daly what was the name of the pretty waltz she had played; and Mr. Browne, seeing that he was ignored, turned promptly to the two young men who were more appreciative.

A red-faced young woman, dressed in pansy, came into the room, excitedly clapping her hands and crying:

"Quadrilles! Quadrilles!"[10]

Close on her heels came Aunt Kate, crying:

"Two gentlemen and three ladies, Mary Jane!"

"O, here's Mr. Bergin and Mr. Kerrigan," said Mary Jane. "Mr. Kerrigan, will you take Miss Power? Miss Furlong, may I get you a partner, Mr. Bergin. O, that'll just do now."

"Three ladies, Mary Jane," said Aunt Kate.

The two young gentlemen asked the ladies if they might have the pleasure, and Mary Jane turned to Miss Daly.

"O, Miss Daly, you're really awfully good, after playing for the last two dances, but really we're so short of ladies to-night."

"I don't mind in the least, Miss Morkan."

"But I've a nice partner for you, Mr. Bartell D'Arcy, the tenor. I'll get him to sing later on. All Dublin is raving about him."

"Lovely voice, lovely voice!" said Aunt Kate.

As the piano had twice begun the prelude to the first figure Mary Jane led her recruits quickly from the room. They had hardly gone when Aunt Julia wandered slowly into the room, looking behind her at something.

"What is the matter, Julia?" asked Aunt Kate anxiously. "Who is it?"

Julia, who was carrying in a column of table-napkins, turned to her sister and said, simply, as if the question had surprised her:

"It's only Freddy, Kate, and Gabriel with him."

In fact right behind her Gabriel could be seen piloting Freddy Malins across the landing. The latter, a young man of about forty, was of Gabriel's size and build, with very round shoulders. His face was fleshy and pallid, touched with colour only at the thick hanging lobes of his ears and at the wide wings of his nose. He had coarse features, a blunt nose, a convex and receding brow, tumid and protruded lips. His heavy-lidded eyes and the disorder of his scanty hair made him look sleepy. He was laughing heartily in a high key at a story which he had been telling Gabriel on the stairs and at the same time rubbing the knuckles of his left fist backwards and forwards into his left eye.

"Good-evening, Freddy," said Aunt Julia.

Freddy Malins bade the Misses Morkan good-evening in what seemed an offhand fashion by reason of the habitual catch in his voice and then, seeing that Mr. Browne was grinning at him from the sideboard, crossed the room on rather shaky legs and began to repeat in an undertone the story he had just told to Gabriel.

---

[10]A dance, like a reel.

"He's not so bad, is he?" said Aunt Kate to Gabriel.

Gabriel's brows were dark but he raised them quickly and answered: "O, no, hardly noticeable."

"Now, isn't he a terrible fellow!" she said. "And his poor mother made him take the pledge[11] on New Year's Eve. But come on, Gabriel, into the drawing-room."

Before leaving the room with Gabriel she signalled to Mr. Browne by frowning and shaking her forefinger in warning to and fro. Mr. Browne nodded in answer and, when she had gone, said to Freddy Malins:

"Now, then, Teddy, I'm going to fill you out a good glass of lemonade just to buck you up."

Freddy Malins, who was nearing the climax of his story, waved the offer aside impatiently but Mr. Browne, having first called Freddy Malins' attention to a disarray in his dress, filled out and handed him a full glass of lemonade. Freddy Malins' left hand accepted the glass mechanically, his right hand being engaged in the mechanical readjustment of his dress. Mr. Browne, whose face was once more wrinkling with mirth, poured out for himself a glass of whisky while Freddy Malins exploded, before he had well reached the climax of his story, in a kink of high-pitched bronchitic laughter and, setting down his untasted and overflowing glass, began to rub the knuckles of his left fist backwards and forwards into his left eye, repeating words of his last phrase as well as his fit of laughter would allow him.

*   *   *

Gabriel could not listen while Mary Jane was playing her Academy piece, full of runs and difficult passages, to the hushed drawing-room. He liked music but the piece she was playing had no melody for him and he doubted whether it had any melody for the other listeners, though they had begged Mary Jane to play something. Four young men, who had come from the refreshment-room to stand in the doorway at the sound of the piano, had gone away quietly in couples after a few minutes. The only persons who seemed to follow the music were Mary Jane herself, her hands racing along the key-board or lifted from it at the pauses like those of a priestess in momentary imprecation, and Aunt Kate standing at her elbow to turn the page.

Gabriel's eyes, irritated by the floor, which glittered with beeswax under the heavy chandelier, wandered to the wall above the piano. A picture of the balcony scene in *Romeo and Juliet* hung there and beside it was a picture of the two murdered princes in the Tower which Aunt Julia had worked in red, blue and brown wools when she was a girl. Probably in the school they had gone to as girls that kind of work had been taught for one year. His mother had worked for him as a birthday present a waistcoat of purple tabinet,[12] with little foxes' heads upon it, lined with brown satin and having round mulberry buttons. It was strange that his mother had had no musical talent though Aunt Kate used to call her the brains carrier of the Morkan family. Both she and Julia had always

---

[11]Vow to stop drinking.
[12]An Irish cloth made of cotton.

seemed a little proud of their serious and matronly sister. Her photograph stood before the pierglass.[13] She held an open book on her knees and was pointing out something in it to Constantine who, dressed in a man-o'-war suit, lay at her feet. It was she who had chosen the names of her sons for she was very sensible of the dignity of family life. Thanks to her, Constantine was now senior curate in Balbriggan and, thanks to her, Gabriel himself had taken his degree in the Royal University. A shadow passed over his face as he remembered her sullen opposition to his marriage. Some slighting phrases she had used still rankled in his memory; she had once spoken of Gretta as being country cute and that was not true of Gretta at all. It was Gretta who had nursed her during all her last long illness in their house at Monkstown.

He knew that Mary Jane must be near the end of her piece for she was playing again the opening melody with runs of scales after every bar and while he waited for the end the resentment died down in his heart. The piece ended with a trill of octaves in the treble and a final deep octave in the bass. Great applause greeted Mary Jane as, blushing and rolling up her music nervously, she escaped from the room. The most vigorous clapping came from the four young men in the doorway who had gone away to the refreshment-room at the beginning of the piece but had come back when the piano had stopped.

Lancers[14] were arranged. Gabriel found himself partnered with Miss Ivors. She was a frank-mannered talkative young lady, with a freckled face and prominent brown eyes. She did not wear a low-cut bodice and the large brooch which was fixed in the front of her collar bore on it an Irish device and motto.

When they had taken their places she said abruptly:

"I have a crow to pluck[15] with you."

"With me?" said Gabriel.

She nodded her head gravely.

"What is it?" asked Gabriel, smiling at her solemn manner.

"Who is G. C.?" answered Miss Ivors, turning her eyes upon him.

Gabriel coloured and was about to knit his brows, as if he did not understand, when she said bluntly:

"O, innocent Amy! I have found out that you write for *The Daily Express.* Now, aren't you ashamed of yourself?"

"Why should I be ashamed of myself?" asked Gabriel, blinking his eyes and trying to smile.

"Well, I'm ashamed of you," said Miss Ivors frankly. "To say you'd write for a paper like that. I didn't think you were a West Briton."[16]

A look of perplexity appeared on Gabriel's face. It was true that he wrote a literary column every Wednesday in *The Daily Express,* for which he was paid fifteen shillings. But that did not make him a West Briton surely. The books he received for review were almost more welcome than the paltry cheque. He

[13]Vertical mirror.
[14]A dance.
[15]"I want to quarrel"; a bone to pick.
[16]Someone who thought of himself as a "West Briton" would be an Irishman loyal to England, i.e., hostile to Irish nationalism. Miss Ivors is an Irish nationalist.

loved to feel the covers and turn over the pages of newly printed books. Nearly every day when his teaching in the college was ended he used to wander down the quays to the second-hand booksellers, to Hickey's on Bachelor's Walk, to Webb's or Massey's on Aston's Quay, or to O'Clohissey's in the by-street. He did not know how to meet her charge. He wanted to say that literature was above politics. But they were friends of many years' standing and their careers had been parallel, first at the University and then as teachers: he could not risk a grandiose phrase with her. He continued blinking his eyes and trying to smile and murmured lamely that he saw nothing political in writing reviews of books.

When their turn to cross had come he was still perplexed and inattentive. Miss Ivors promptly took his hand in a warm grasp and said in a soft friendly tone:

"Of course, I was only joking. Come, we cross now."

When they were together again she spoke of the University question and Gabriel felt more at ease. A friend of hers had shown her his review of Browning's poems. That was how she had found out the secret: but she liked the review immensely. Then she said suddenly:

"O, Mr. Conroy, will you come for an excursion to the Aran Isles[17] this summer? We're going to stay there a whole month. It will be splendid out in the Atlantic. You ought to come. Mr. Clancy is coming, and Mr. Kilkelly and Kathleen Kearney. It would be splendid for Gretta too if she'd come. She's from Connacht, isn't she?"

"Her people are," said Gabriel shortly.

"But you will come, won't you?" said Miss Ivors, laying her warm hand eagerly on his arm.

"The fact is," said Gabriel, "I have just arranged to go——"

"Go where?" asked Miss Ivors.

"Well, you know, every year I go for a cycling tour with some fellows and so——"

"But where?" asked Miss Ivors.

"Well, we usually go to France or Belgium or perhaps Germany," said Gabriel awkwardly.

"And why do you go to France and Belgium," said Miss Ivors, "instead of visiting your own land?"

"Well," said Gabriel, "it's partly to keep in touch with the languages and partly for a change."

"And haven't you your own language to keep in touch with—Irish?" asked Miss Ivors.

"Well," said Gabriel, "if it comes to that, you know, Irish is not my language."

Their neighbours had turned to listen to the cross-examination. Gabriel glanced right and left nervously and tried to keep his good humour under the ordeal which was making a blush invade his forehead.

"And haven't you your own land to visit," continued Miss Ivors, "that you know nothing of, your own people, and your own country?"

[17]Islands off Ireland, where Gaelic (the original Irish language) was still spoken; hence a place Miss Ivors would want to visit.

"O, to tell you the truth," retorted Gabriel suddenly, "I'm sick of my own country, sick of it!"

"Why?" asked Miss Ivors.

Gabriel did not answer for his retort had heated him.

"Why?" repeated Miss Ivors.

They had to go visiting together and, as he had not answered her, Miss Ivors said warmly:

"Of course, you've no answer."

Gabriel tried to cover his agitation by taking part in the dance with great energy. He avoided her eyes for he had seen a sour expression on her face. But when they met in the long chain he was surprised to feel his hand firmly pressed. She looked at him from under her brows for a moment quizzically until he smiled. Then, just as the chain was about to start again, she stood on tiptoe and whispered into his ear:

"West Briton!"

When the lancers were over Gabriel went away to a remote corner of the room where Freddy Malins' mother was sitting. She was a stout feeble old woman with white hair. Her voice had a catch in it like her son's and she stuttered slightly. She had been told that Freddy had come and that he was nearly all right. Gabriel asked her whether she had had a good crossing. She lived with her married daughter in Glasgow and came to Dublin on a visit once a year. She answered placidly that she had had a beautiful crossing and that the captain had been most attentive to her. She spoke also of the beautiful house her daughter kept in Glasgow, and of all the friends they had there. While her tongue rambled on Gabriel tried to banish from his mind all memory of the unpleasant incident with Miss Ivors. Of course the girl or woman, or whatever she was, was an enthusiast but there was a time for all things. Perhaps he ought not to have answered her like that. But she had no right to call him a West Briton before people, even in joke. She had tried to make him ridiculous before people, heckling him and staring at him with her rabbit's eyes.

He saw his wife making her way towards him through the waltzing couples. When she reached him she said into his ear:

"Gabriel, Aunt Kate wants to know won't you carve the goose as usual. Miss Daly will carve the ham and I'll do the pudding."

"All right," said Gabriel.

"She's sending in the younger ones first as soon as this waltz is over so that we'll have the table to ourselves."

"Were you dancing?" asked Gabriel.

"Of course I was. Didn't you see me? What row had you with Molly Ivors?"

"No row. Why? Did she say so?"

"Something like that. I'm trying to get that Mr. D'Arcy to sing. He's full of conceit, I think."

"There was no row," said Gabriel moodily, "only she wanted me to go for a trip to the west of Ireland and I said I wouldn't."

His wife clasped her hands excitedly and gave a little jump.

"O, do go, Gabriel," she cried. "I'd love to see Galway again."

"You can go if you like," said Gabriel coldly.

She looked at him for a moment, then turned to Mrs. Malins and said:

"There's a nice husband for you, Mrs. Malins."

While she was threading her way back across the room Mrs. Malins, without adverting to the interruption, went on to tell Gabriel what beautiful places there were in Scotland and beautiful scenery. Her son-in-law brought them every year to the lakes and they used to go fishing. Her son-in-law was a splendid fisher. One day he caught a beautiful big fish and the man in the hotel cooked it for their dinner.

Gabriel hardly heard what she said. Now that supper was coming near he began to think again about his speech and about the quotation. When he saw Freddy Malins coming across the room to visit his mother Gabriel left the chair free for him and retired into the embrasure of the window. The room had already cleared and from the back room came the clatter of plates and knives. Those who still remained in the drawing-room seemed tired of dancing and were conversing quietly in little groups. Gabriel's warm trembling fingers tapped the cold pane of the window. How cool it must be outside! How pleasant it would be to walk out alone, first along by the river and then through the park! The snow would be lying on the branches of the trees and forming a bright cap on the top of the Wellington Monument.[18] How much more pleasant it would be there than at the supper-table!

He ran over the headings of his speech: Irish hospitality, sad memories, the Three Graces, Paris, the quotation from Browning. He repeated to himself a phrase he had written in his review: "One feels that one is listening to a thought-tormented music." Miss Ivors had praised the review. Was she sincere? Had she really any life of her own behind all her propagandism? There had never been any ill-feeling between them until that night. It unnerved him to think that she would be at the supper-table, looking up at him while he spoke with her critical quizzing eyes. Perhaps she would not be sorry to see him fail in his speech. An idea came into his mind and gave him courage. He would say, alluding to Aunt Kate and Aunt Julia: "Ladies and Gentlemen, the generation which is now on the wane among us may have had its faults but for my part I think it had certain qualities of hospitality, of humour, of humanity, which the new and very serious and hypereducated generation that is growing up around us seems to me to lack." Very good: that was one for Miss Ivors. What did he care that his aunts were only two ignorant old women?

A murmur in the room attracted his attention. Mr. Browne was advancing from the door, gallantly escorting Aunt Julia, who leaned upon his arm, smiling and hanging her head. An irregular musketry of applause escorted her also as far as the piano and then, as Mary Jane seated herself on the stool, and Aunt Julia, no longer smiling, half turned so as to pitch her voice fairly into the room, gradually ceased. Gabriel recognised the prelude. It was that of an old song of Aunt Julia's—*Arrayed for the Bridal.* Her voice, strong and clear in tone, attacked with great spirit the runs which embellish the air and though she sang very rapidly she did not miss even the smallest of the grace notes. To follow the

---

[18]Obelisk in Phoenix Park, Dublin.

voice, without looking at the singer's face, was to feel and share the excitement of swift and secure flight. Gabriel applauded loudly with all the others at the close of the song and loud applause was borne in from the invisible supper-table. It sounded so genuine that a little colour struggled into Aunt Julia's face as she bent to replace in the music-stand the old leather-bound song-book that had her initials on the cover. Freddy Malins, who had listened with his head perched sideways to hear her better, was still applauding when everyone else had ceased and talking animatedly to his mother who nodded her head gravely and slowly in acquiescence. At last, when he could clap no more, he stood up suddenly and hurried across the room to Aunt Julia whose hand he seized and held in both his hands, shaking it when words failed him or the catch in his voice proved too much for him.

"I was just telling my mother," he said, "I never heard you sing so well, never. No, I never heard your voice so good as it is to-night. Now! Would you believe that now? That's the truth. Upon my word and honour that's the truth. I never heard your voice sound so fresh and so . . . so clear and fresh, never."

Aunt Julia smiled broadly and murmured something about compliments as she released her hand from his grasp. Mr. Browne extended his open hand towards her and said to those who were near him in the manner of a showman introducing a prodigy to an audience:

"Miss Julia Morkan, my latest discovery!"

He was laughing very heartily at this himself when Freddy Malins turned to him and said:

"Well, Browne, if you're serious you might make a worse discovery. All I can say is I never heard her sing half so well as long as I am coming here. And that's the honest truth."

"Neither did I," said Mr. Browne. "I think her voice has greatly improved."

Aunt Julia shrugged her shoulders and said with meek pride:

"Thirty years ago I hadn't a bad voice as voices go."

"I often told Julia," said Aunt Kate emphatically, "that she was simply thrown away in that choir. But she never would be said by me."

She turned as if to appeal to the good sense of the others against a refractory child while Aunt Julia gazed in front of her, a vague smile of reminiscence playing on her face.

"No," continued Aunt Kate, "she wouldn't be said or led by anyone, slaving there in that choir night and day, night and day. Six o'clock on Christmas morning! And all for what?"

"Well, isn't it for the honour of God, Aunt Kate?" asked Mary Jane, twisting round on the piano-stool and smiling.

Aunt Kate turned fiercely on her niece and said:

"I know all about the honour of God, Mary Jane, but I think it's not at all honourable for the pope to turn out the women out of the choirs that have slaved there all their lives and put little whipper-snappers of boys over their heads. I suppose it is for the good of the Church if the pope does it. But it's not just, Mary Jane, and it's not right."

She had worked herself into a passion and would have continued in defence of her sister for it was a sore subject with her but Mary Jane, seeing that all the dancers had come back, intervened pacifically:

"Now, Aunt Kate, you're giving scandal to Mr. Browne who is of the other persuasion."[19]

Aunt Kate turned to Mr. Browne, who was grinning at this allusion to his religion, and said hastily:

"O, I don't question the pope's being right. I'm only a stupid old woman and I wouldn't presume to do such a thing. But there's such a thing as common everyday politeness and gratitude. And if I were in Julia's place I'd tell that Father Healey straight up to his face . . ."

"And besides, Aunt Kate," said Mary Jane, "we really are all hungry and when we are hungry we are all very quarrelsome."

"And when we are thirsty we are also quarrelsome," added Mr. Browne.

"So that we had better go to supper," said Mary Jane, "and finish the discussion afterwards."

On the landing outside the drawing-room Gabriel found his wife and Mary Jane trying to persuade Miss Ivors to stay for supper. But Miss Ivors, who had put on her hat and was buttoning her cloak, would not stay. She did not feel in the least hungry and she had already overstayed her time.

"But only for ten minutes, Molly," said Mrs. Conroy. "That won't delay you."

"To take a pick itself," said Mary Jane, "after all your dancing."

"I really couldn't," said Miss Ivors.

"I am afraid you didn't enjoy yourself at all," said Mary Jane hopelessly.

"Ever so much, I assure you," said Miss Ivors, "but you really must let me run off now."

"But how can you get home?" asked Mrs. Conroy.

"O, it's only two steps up the quay."

Gabriel hesitated a moment and said:

"If you will allow me, Miss Ivors, I'll see you home if you are really obliged to go."

But Miss Ivors broke away from them.

"I won't hear of it," she cried. "For goodness' sake go in to your suppers and don't mind me. I'm quite well able to take care of myself."

"Well, you're the comical girl, Molly," said Mrs. Conroy frankly.

"*Beannacht libh,*"[20] cried Miss Ivors, with a laugh, as she ran down the staircase.

Mary Jane gazed after her, a moody puzzled expression on her face, while Mrs. Conroy leaned over the banisters to listen for the hall-door. Gabriel asked himself was he the cause of her abrupt departure. But she did not seem to be in ill humour: she had gone away laughing. He stared blankly down the staircase.

At the moment Aunt Kate came toddling out of the supper-room, almost wringing her hands in despair.

[19]That is, a Protestant.
[20]"Blessing on you," in Gaelic.

"Where is Gabriel?" she cried. "Where on earth is Gabriel? There's everyone waiting in there, stage to let, and nobody to carve the goose!"

"Here I am, Aunt Kate!" cried Gabriel, with sudden animation, "ready to carve a flock of geese, if necessary."

A fat brown goose lay at one end of the table and at the other end, on a bed of creased paper strewn with sprigs of parsley, lay a great ham, stripped of its outer skin and peppered over with crust crumbs, a neat paper frill round its shin and beside this was a round of spiced beef. Between these rival ends ran parallel lines of side-dishes: two little minsters of jelly, red and yellow; a shallow dish full of blocks of blancmange and red jam, a large green leaf-shaped dish with a stalk-shaped handle, on which lay bunches of purple raisins and peeled almonds, a companion dish on which lay a solid rectangle of Smyrna figs, a dish of custard topped with grated nutmeg, a small bowl full of chocolates and sweets wrapped in gold and silver papers and a glass vase in which stood some tall celery stalks. In the centre of the table there stood, as sentries to a fruit-stand which upheld a pyramid of oranges and American apples, two squat old-fashioned decanters of cut glass, one containing port and the other dark sherry. On the closed square piano a pudding in a huge yellow dish lay in waiting and behind it were three squads of bottles of stout and ale and minerals, drawn up according to the colours of their uniforms, the first two black, with brown and red labels, the third and smallest squad white, with transverse green sashes.

Gabriel took his seat boldly at the head of the table and, having looked to the edge of the carver, plunged his fork firmly into the goose. He felt quite at ease now for he was an expert carver and liked nothing better than to find himself at the head of a well-laden table.

"Miss Furlong, what shall I send you?" he asked. "A wing or a slice of the breast?"

"Just a small slice of the breast."

"Miss Higgins, what for you?"

"O, anything at all, Mr. Conroy."

While Gabriel and Miss Daly exchanged plates of goose and plates of ham and spiced beef Lily went from guest to guest with a dish of hot floury potatoes wrapped in a white napkin. This was Mary Jane's idea and she had also suggested apple sauce for the goose but Aunt Kate had said that plain roast goose without any apple sauce had always been good enough for her and she hoped she might never eat worse. Mary Jane waited on her pupils and saw that they got the best slices and Aunt Kate and Aunt Julia opened and carried across from the piano bottles of stout and ale for the gentlemen and bottles of minerals for the ladies. There was a great deal of confusion and laughter and noise, the noise of orders and counter-orders, of knives and forks, of corks and glass-stoppers. Gabriel began to carve second helpings as soon as he had finished the first round without serving himself. Everyone protested loudly so that he compromised by taking a long draught of stout for he had found the carving hot work. Mary Jane settled down quietly to her supper but Aunt Kate and Aunt Julia were still toddling round the table, walking on each other's heels, getting in each other's way and giving each other unheeded orders. Mr. Browne begged of them to sit down and eat their suppers and so did Gabriel but they said there was time enough, so that, at last, Freddy Malins stood up and, capturing Aunt Kate, plumped her down on her chair amid general laughter.

When everyone had been well served Gabriel said, smiling:

"Now, if anyone wants a little more of what vulgar people call stuffing let him or her speak."

A chorus of voices invited him to begin his own supper and Lily came forward with three potatoes which she had reserved for him.

"Very well," said Gabriel amiably, as he took another preparatory draught, "kindly forget my existence, ladies and gentlemen, for a few minutes."

He set to his supper and took no part in the conversation with which the table covered Lily's removal of the plates. The subject of talk was the opera company which was then at the Theatre Royal. Mr. Bartell D'Arcy, the tenor, a dark-complexioned young man with a smart moustache, praised very highly the leading contralto of the company but Miss Furlong thought she had a rather vulgar style of production. Freddy Malins said there was a negro chieftain singing in the second part of the Gaiety pantomime who had one of the finest tenor voices he had ever heard.

"Have you heard him?" he asked Mr. Bartell D'Arcy across the table.

"No," answered Mr. Bartell D'Arcy carelessly.

"Because," Freddy Malins explained, "now I'd be curious to hear your opinion of him. I think he has a grand voice."

"It takes Teddy to find out the really good things," said Mr. Browne familiarly to the table.

"And why couldn't he have a voice too?" asked Freddy Malins sharply. "Is it because he's only a black?"

Nobody answered this question and Mary Jane led the table back to the legitimate opera. One of her pupils had given her a pass for *Mignon.* Of course it was very fine, she said, but it made her think of poor Georgina Burns. Mr. Browne could go back farther still, to the old Italian companies that used to come to Dublin—Tietjens, Ilma de Murzka, Campanini, the great Trebelli Giuglini, Ravelli, Aramburo. Those were the days, he said, when there was something like singing to be heard in Dublin. He told too of how the top gallery of the old Royal used to be packed night after night, of how one night an Italian tenor had sung five encores to *Let me like a Soldier fall,* introducing a high C every time, and of how the gallery boys would sometimes in their enthusiasm unyoke the horses from the carriage of some great *prima donna* and pull her themselves through the streets to her hotel. Why did they never play the grand old operas now, he asked, *Dinorah, Lucrezia Borgia?* Because they could not get the voices to sing them: that was why.

"O, well," said Mr. Bartell D'Arcy, "I presume there are as good singers to-day as there were then."

"Where are they?" asked Mr. Browne defiantly.

"In London, Paris, Milan," said Mr. Bartell D'Arcy warmly. "I suppose Caruso, for example, is quite as good, if not better than any of the men you have mentioned."

"Maybe so," said Mr. Browne. "But I may tell you I doubt it strongly."

"O, I'd give anything to hear Caruso sing," said Mary Jane.

"For me," said Aunt Kate, who had been picking a bone, "there was only one tenor. To please me, I mean. But I suppose none of you ever heard of him."

"Who was he, Miss Morkan?" asked Mr. Bartell D'Arcy politely.

"His name," said Aunt Kate, "was Parkinson. I heard him when he was in his prime and I think he had then the purest tenor voice that was ever put into a man's throat."

"Strange," said Mr. Bartell D'Arcy. "I never even heard of him."

"Yes, yes, Miss Morkan is right," said Mr. Browne. "I remember hearing of old Parkinson but he's too far back for me."

"A beautiful, pure, sweet, mellow English tenor," said Aunt Kate with enthusiasm.

Gabriel having finished, the huge pudding was transferred to the table. The clatter of forks and spoons began again. Gabriel's wife served out spoonfuls of the pudding and passed the plates down the table. Midway down they were held up by Mary Jane, who replenished them with raspberry or orange jelly or with blancmange and jam. The pudding was of Aunt Julia's making and she received praises for it from all quarters. She herself said that it was not quite brown enough.

"Well, I hope, Miss Morkan," said Mr. Browne, "that I'm brown enough for you because, you know, I'm all brown."

All the gentlemen, except Gabriel, ate some of the pudding out of compliment to Aunt Julia. As Gabriel never ate sweets the celery had been left for him. Freddy Malins also took a stalk of celery and ate it with his pudding. He had been told that celery was a capital thing for the blood and he was just then under doctor's care. Mrs. Malins, who had been silent all through the supper, said that her son was going down to Mount Melleray in a week or so. The table then spoke of Mount Melleray, how bracing the air was down there, how hospitable the monks were and how they never asked for a penny-piece from their guests.

"And do you mean to say," asked Mr. Browne incredulously, "that a chap can go down there and put up there as if it were a hotel and live on the fat of the land and then come away without paying anything?"

"O, most people give some donation to the monastery when they leave," said Mary Jane.

"I wish we had an institution like that in our Church," said Mr. Brown candidly.

He was astonished to hear that the monks never spoke, got up at two in the morning and slept in their coffins. He asked what they did it for.

"That's the rule of the order," said Aunt Kate firmly.

"Yes, but why?" asked Mr. Browne.

Aunt Kate repeated that it was the rule, that was all. Mr. Browne still seemed not to understand. Freddy Malins explained to him, as best he could, that the monks were trying to make up for the sins committed by all the sinners in the outside world. The explanation was not very clear for Mr. Browne grinned and said:

"I like that idea very much but wouldn't a comfortable spring bed do them as well as a coffin?"

"The coffin," said Mary Jane, "is to remind them of their last end."

As the subject had grown lugubrious it was buried in a silence of the table during which Mrs. Malins could be heard saying to her neighbour in an indistinct undertone:

"They are very good men, the monks, very pious men."

The raisins and almonds and figs and apples and oranges and chocolates and sweets were now passed about the table and Aunt Julia invited all the guests to have either port or sherry. At first Mr. Bartell D'Arcy refused to take either but one of his neighbours nudged him and whispered something to him upon which he allowed his glass to be filled. Gradually as the last glasses were being filled the conversation ceased. A pause followed, broken only by the noise of the wine and by unsettlings of chairs. The Misses Morkan, all three, looked down at the tablecloth. Someone coughed once or twice and then a few gentlemen patted the table gently as a signal for silence. The silence came and Gabriel pushed back his chair and stood up.

The patting at once grew louder in encouragement and then ceased altogether. Gabriel leaned his ten trembling fingers on the tablecloth and smiled nervously at the company. Meeting a row of upturned faces he raised his eyes to the chandelier. The piano was playing a waltz tune and he could hear the skirts sweeping against the drawing-room door. People, perhaps, were standing in the snow on the quay outside, gazing up at the lighted windows and listening to the waltz music. The air was pure there. In the distance lay the park where the trees were weighted with snow. The Wellington Monument wore a gleaming cap of snow that flashed westward over the white field of Fifteen Acres.

He began:

"Ladies and Gentlemen,

"It has fallen to my lot this evening, as in years past, to perform a very pleasing task but a task for which I am afraid my poor powers as a speaker are all too inadequate."

"No, no!" said Mr. Browne.

"But, however that may be, I can only ask you to-night to take the will for the deed and to lend me your attention for a few moments while I endeavour to express to you in words what my feelings are on this occasion.

"Ladies and Gentlemen, it is not the first time that we have gathered together under this hospitable roof, around this hospitable board. It is not the first time that we have been the recipients—or perhaps, I had better say, the victims—of the hospitality of certain good ladies."

He made a circle in the air with his arm and paused. Everyone laughed or smiled at Aunt Kate and Aunt Julia and Mary Jane who all turned crimson with pleasure. Gabriel went on more boldly:

"I feel more strongly with every recurring year that our country has no tradition which does it so much honour and which it should guard so jealously as that of its hospitality. It is a tradition that is unique as far as my experience goes (and I have visited not a few places abroad) among the modern nations. Some would say, perhaps, that with us it is rather a failing than anything to be boasted of. But granted even that, it is, to my mind, a princely failing, and one that I trust will long be cultivated among us. Of one thing, at least, I am sure. As long as this one roof shelters the good ladies aforesaid—and I wish from my heart it may do so for many and many a long year to come—the tradition of genuine warm-hearted courteous Irish hospitality, which our forefathers have handed down to us and which we in turn must hand down to our descendants, is still alive among us."

A hearty murmur of assent ran round the table. It shot through Gabriel's mind that Miss Ivors was not there and that she had gone away discourteously: and he said with confidence in himself:

"Ladies and Gentlemen,

"A new generation is growing up in our midst, a generation actuated by new ideas and new principles. It is serious and enthusiastic for these new ideas and its enthusiasm, even when it is misdirected, is, I believe, in the main sincere. But we are living in a sceptical and, if I may use the phrase, a thought-tormented age: and sometimes I fear that this new generation, educated or hypereducated as it is, will lack those qualities of humanity, of hospitality, of kindly humour which belonged to an older day. Listening to-night to the names of all those great singers of the past it seemed to me, I must confess, that we were living in a less spacious age. Those days might, without exaggeration, be called spacious days: and if they are gone beyond recall let us hope, at least, that in gatherings such as this we shall still speak of them with pride and affection, still cherish in our hearts the memory of those dead and gone great ones whose fame the world will not willingly let die."

"Hear, hear!" said Mr. Browne loudly.

"But yet," continued Gabriel, his voice falling into a softer inflection, "there are always in gatherings such as this sadder thoughts that will recur to our minds: thoughts of the past, of youth, of changes, of absent faces that we miss here to-night. Our path through life is strewn with many such sad memories: and were we to brood upon them always we could not find the heart to go on bravely with our work among the living. We have all of us living duties and living affections which claim, and rightly claim, our strenuous endeavours.

"Therefore, I will not linger on the past. I will not let any gloomy moralising intrude upon us here to-night. Here we are gathered together for a brief moment from the bustle and rush of our everyday routine. We are met here as friends, in the spirit of good-fellowship, as colleagues, also to a certain extent, in the true spirit of *camaraderie*, and as the guests of—what shall I call them?—the Three Graces of the Dublin musical world."

The table burst into applause and laughter at this allusion. Aunt Julia vainly asked each of her neighbours in turn to tell her what Gabriel had said.

"He says we are the Three Graces, Aunt Julia," said Mary Jane.

Aunt Julia did not understand but she looked up, smiling, at Gabriel, who continued in the same vein:

"Ladies and Gentlemen,

"I will not attempt to play to-night the part that Paris played on another occasion. I will not attempt to choose between them. The task would be an invidious one and one beyond my poor powers. For when I view them in turn, whether it be our chief hostess herself, whose good heart, whose too good heart, has become a byword with all who know her, or her sister, who seems to be gifted with perennial youth and whose singing must have been a surprise and a revelation to us all to-night, or, last but not least, when I consider our youngest hostess, talented, cheerful, hard-working and the best of nieces, I confess, Ladies and Gentlemen, that I do not know to which of them I should award the prize."

Gabriel glanced down at his aunts and, seeing the large smile on Aunt Julia's face and the tears which had risen to Aunt Kate's eyes, hastened to his close. He raised his glass of port gallantly, while every member of the company fingered a glass expectantly, and said loudly:

"Let us toast them all three together. Let us drink to their health, wealth, long life, happiness and prosperity and may they long continue to hold the proud and self-won position which they hold in their profession and the position of honour and affection which they hold in our hearts."

All the guests stood up, glass in hand, and turning towards the three seated ladies, sang in unison, with Mr. Browne as leader:

> "For they are jolly gay fellows,
> For they are jolly gay fellows,
> For they are jolly gay fellows,
>   Which nobody can deny."

Aunt Kate was making frank use of her handkerchief and even Aunt Julia seemed moved. Freddy Malins beat time with his pudding-fork and the singers turned towards one another, as if in melodious conference, while they sang with emphasis:

> "Unless he tells a lie,
> Unless he tells a lie,"

Then, turning once more towards their hostesses, they sang:

> "For they are jolly gay fellows,
> For they are jolly gay fellows,
> For they are jolly gay fellows,
>   Which nobody can deny."

The acclamation which followed was taken up beyond the door of the supper-room by many of the other guests and renewed time after time, Freddy Malins acting as officer with his fork on high.

* * *

The piercing morning air came into the hall where they were standing so that Aunt Kate said:

"Close the door, somebody. Mrs. Malins will get her death of cold."

"Browne is out there, Aunt Kate," said Mary Jane.

"Browne is everywhere," said Aunt Kate, lowering her voice.

Mary Jane laughed at her tone.

"Really," she said archly, "he is very attentive."

"He has been laid on here like the gas," said Aunt Kate in the same tone, "all during the Christmas."

She laughed herself this time good-humouredly and then added quickly:

"But tell him to come in, Mary Jane, and close the door. I hope to goodness he didn't hear me."

At that moment the hall-door was opened and Mr. Browne came in from the doorstep, laughing as if his heart would break. He was dressed in a long green overcoat with mock astrakhan cuffs and collar and wore on his head an oval fur cap. He pointed down the snow-covered quay from where the sound of shrill prolonged whistling was borne in.

"Teddy will have all the cabs in Dublin out," he said.

Gabriel advanced from the little pantry behind the office, struggling into his overcoat and, looking round the hall, said:

"Gretta not down yet?"

"She's getting on her things, Gabriel," said Aunt Kate.

"Who's playing up there?" asked Gabriel.

"Nobody. They're all gone."

"O no, Aunt Kate," said Mary Jane. "Bartell D'Arcy and Miss O'Callaghan aren't gone yet."

"Someone is fooling at the piano anyhow," said Gabriel.

Mary Jane glanced at Gabriel and Mr. Browne and said with a shiver:

"It makes me feel cold to look at you two gentlemen muffled up like that. I wouldn't like to face your journey home at this hour."

"I'd like nothing better this minute," said Mr. Browne stoutly, "than a rattling fine walk in the country or a fast drive with a good spanking goer between the shafts."

"We used to have a very good horse and trap at home," said Aunt Julia sadly.

"The never-to-be-forgotten Johnny," said Mary Jane, laughing.

Aunt Kate and Gabriel laughed too.

"Why, what was wonderful about Johnny?" asked Mr. Browne.

"The late lamented Patrick Morkan, our grandfather, that is," explained Gabriel, "commonly known in his later years as the old gentleman, was a glue-boiler."

"O, now, Gabriel," said Aunt Kate, laughing, "he had a starch mill."

"Well, glue or starch," said Gabriel, "the old gentleman had a horse by the name of Johnny. And Johnny used to work in the old gentleman's mill, walking round and round in order to drive the mill. That was all very well; but now comes the tragic part about Johnny. One fine day the old gentleman thought he'd like to drive out with the quality to a military review in the park."

"The Lord have mercy on his soul," said Aunt Kate compassionately.

"Amen," said Gabriel. "So the old gentleman, as I said, harnessed Johnny and put on his very best tall hat and his very best stock collar and drove out in grand style from his ancestral mansion somewhere near Back Lane, I think."

Everyone laughed, even Mrs. Malins, at Gabriel's manner and Aunt Kate said:

"O, now, Gabriel, he didn't live in Back Lane, really. Only the mill was there."

"Out from the mansion of his forefathers," continued Gabriel, "he drove with Johnny. And everything went on beautifully until Johnny came in sight of King Billy's statue:[21] and whether he fell in love with the horse King Billy sits on or whether he thought he was back again in the mill, anyhow he began to walk round the statue."

Gabriel paced in a circle round the hall in his goloshes amid the laughter of the others.

"Round and round he went," said Gabriel, "and the old gentleman, who was a very pompous old gentleman, was highly indignant. 'Go on, sir! What do you mean, sir? Johnny! Johnny! Most extraordinary conduct! Can't understand the horse!'"

The peals of laughter which followed Gabriel's imitation of the incident was interrupted by a resounding knock at the hall door. Mary Jane ran to open it and let in Freddy Malins. Freddy Malins, with his hat well back on his head and his shoulders humped with cold, was puffing and steaming after his exertions.

"I could only get one cab," he said.

"O, we'll find another along the quay," said Gabriel.

"Yes," said Aunt Kate. "Better not keep Mrs. Malins standing in the draught."

Mrs. Malins was helped down the front steps by her son and Mr. Browne and, after many manoeuvres, hoisted into the cab. Freddy Malins clambered in after her and spent a long time settling her on the seat, Mr. Browne helping him with advice. At last she was settled comfortably and Freddy Malins invited Mr. Browne into the cab. There was a good deal of confused talk, and then Mr. Browne got into the cab. The cabman settled his rug over his knees, and bent down for the address. The confusion grew greater and the cabman was directed differently by Freddy Malins and Mr. Browne, each of whom had his head out through a window of the cab. The difficulty was to know where to drop Mr. Browne along the route, and Aunt Kate, Aunt Julia and Mary Jane helped the discussion from the doorstep with cross-directions and contradictions and abundance of laughter. As for Freddy Malins he was speechless with laughter. He popped his head in and out of the window every moment to the great danger of his hat, and told his mother how the discussion was progressing, till at last Mr. Browne shouted to the bewildered cabman above the din of everybody's laughter:

"Do you know Trinity College?"

"Yes, sir," said the cabman.

"Well, drive bang up against Trinity College gates," said Mr. Browne, "and then we'll tell you where to go. You understand now?"

[21]King William III (1650–1700), conqueror of Ireland. The statue of him mounted on a horse, erected in 1701, was an object of Irish nationalist derision, defacement, and damage.

"Yes, sir," said the cabman.

"Make like a bird for Trinity College."

"Right, sir," said the cabman.

The horse was whipped up and the cab rattled off along the quay amid a chorus of laughter and adieus.

Gabriel had not gone to the door with the others. He was in a dark part of the hall gazing up the staircase. A woman was standing near the top of the first flight, in the shadow also. He could not see her face but he could see the terracotta and salmon-pink panels of her skirt which the shadow made appear black and white. It was his wife. She was leaning on the banisters, listening to something. Gabriel was surprised at her stillness and strained his ear to listen also. But he could hear little save the noise of laughter and dispute on the front steps, a few chords struck on the piano and a few notes of a man's voice singing.

He stood still in the gloom of the hall, trying to catch the air that the voice was singing and gazing up at his wife. There was grace and mystery in her attitude as if she were a symbol of something. He asked himself what is a woman standing on the stairs in the shadow, listening to distant music, a symbol of. If he were a painter he would paint her in that attitude. Her blue felt hat would show off the bronze of her hair against the darkness and the dark panels of her skirt would show off the light ones. *Distant Music* he would call the picture if he were a painter.

The hall-door was closed; and Aunt Kate, Aunt Julia and Mary Jane came down the hall, still laughing.

"Well, isn't Freddy terrible?" said Mary Jane. "He's really terrible."

Gabriel said nothing but pointed up the stairs towards where his wife was standing. Now that the hall-door was closed the voice and the piano could be heard more clearly. Gabriel held up his hand for them to be silent. The song seemed to be in the old Irish tonality and the singer seemed uncertain both of his words and of his voice. The voice, made plaintive by distance and by the singer's hoarseness, faintly illuminated the cadence of the air with words expressing grief:

> "O, the rain falls on my heavy locks
> And the dew wets my skin,
> My babe lies cold . . ."

"O," exclaimed Mary Jane. "It's Bartell D'Arcy singing and he wouldn't sing all the night. O, I'll get him to sing a song before he goes."

"O, do, Mary Jane," said Aunt Kate.

Mary Jane brushed past the others and ran to the staircase, but before she reached it the singing stopped and the piano was closed abruptly.

"O, what a pity!" she cried. "Is he coming down, Gretta?"

Gabriel heard his wife answer yes and saw her come down towards them. A few steps behind her were Mr. Bartell D'Arcy and Miss O'Callaghan.

"O, Mr. D'Arcy," cried Mary Jane, "it's downright mean of you to break off like that when we were all in raptures listening to you."

"I have been at him all the evening," said Miss O'Callaghan, "and Mrs. Conroy, too, and he told us he had a dreadful cold and couldn't sing."

"O, Mr. D'Arcy," said Aunt Kate, "now that was a great fib to tell."

"Can't you see that I'm as hoarse as a crow?" said Mr. D'Arcy roughly.

He went into the pantry hastily and put on his overcoat. The others, taken aback by his rude speech, could find nothing to say. Aunt Kate wrinkled her brows and made signs to the others to drop the subject. Mr. D'Arcy stood swathing his neck carefully and frowning.

"It's the weather," said Aunt Julia, after a pause.

"Yes, everybody has colds," said Aunt Kate readily, "everybody."

"They say," said Mary Jane, "we haven't had snow like it for thirty years; and I read this morning in the newspapers that the snow is general all over Ireland."

"I love the look of snow," said Aunt Julia sadly.

"So do I," said Miss O'Callaghan. "I think Christmas is never really Christmas unless we have the snow on the ground."

"But poor Mr. D'Arcy doesn't like the snow," said Aunt Kate smiling.

Mr. D'Arcy came from the pantry, fully swathed and buttoned, and in a repentant tone told them the history of his cold. Everyone gave him advice and said it was a great pity and urged him to be very careful of his throat in the night air. Gabriel watched his wife, who did not join in the conversation. She was standing right under the dusty fanlight and the flame of the gas lit up the rich bronze of her hair, which he had seen her drying at the fire a few days before. She was in the same attitude and seemed unaware of the talk about her. At last she turned towards them and Gabriel saw that there was colour on her cheeks and that her eyes were shining. A sudden tide of joy went leaping out of his heart.

"Mr. D'Arcy," she said, "what is the name of that song you were singing?"

"It's called *The Lass of Aughrim*,"[22] said Mr. D'Arcy, "but I couldn't remember it properly. Why? Do you know it?"

"*The Lass of Aughrim*," she repeated. "I couldn't think of the name."

"It's a very nice air," said Mary Jane. "I'm sorry you were not in voice to-night."

"Now, Mary Jane," said Aunt Kate, "don't annoy Mr. D'Arcy. I won't have him annoyed."

Seeing that all were ready to start she shepherded them to the door, where good-night was said:

"Well, good-night, Aunt Kate, and thanks for the pleasant evening."

"Good-night, Gabriel. Good-night, Gretta!"

"Good-night, Aunt Kate, and thanks ever so much. Good-night, Aunt Julia."

"O, good-night, Gretta, I didn't see you."

"Good-night, Mr. D'Arcy. Good-night, Miss O'Callaghan."

---

[22]A ballad about a girl who drowns herself after being betrayed by a lord. The song becomes very significant in the crisis that is to follow between Gabriel and Gretta.

"Good-night, Miss Morkan."

"Good-night, again."

"Good-night, all. Safe home."

"Good-night. Good night."

The morning was still dark. A dull, yellow light brooded over the houses and the river; and the sky seemed to be descending. It was slushy underfoot; and only streaks and patches of snow lay on the roofs, on the parapets of the quay and on the area railings. The lamps were still burning redly in the murky air and, across the river, the palace of the Four Courts stood out menacingly against the heavy sky.

She was walking on before him with Mr. Bartell D'Arcy, her shoes in a brown parcel tucked under one arm and her hands holding her skirt up from the slush. She had no longer any grace of attitude, but Gabriel's eyes were still bright with happiness. The blood went bounding along his veins; and the thoughts went rioting through his brain, proud, joyful, tender, valorous.

She was walking on before him so lightly and so erect that he longed to run after her noiselessly, catch her by the shoulders and say something foolish and affectionate into her ear. She seemed to him so frail that he longed to defend her against something and then to be alone with her. Moments of their secret life together burst like stars upon his memory. A heliotrope envelope was lying beside his breakfast-cup and he was caressing it with his hand. Birds were twittering in the ivy and the sunny web of the curtain was shimmering along the floor: he could not eat for happiness. They were standing on the crowded platform and he was placing a ticket inside the warm palm of her glove. He was standing with her in the cold, looking in through a grated window at a man making bottles in a roaring furnace. It was very cold. Her face, fragrant in the cold air, was quite close to his; and suddenly he called out to the man at the furnace:

"Is the fire hot, sir?"

But the man could not hear with the noise of the furnace. It was just as well. He might have answered rudely.

A wave of yet more tender joy escaped from his heart and went coursing in warm flood along his arteries. Like the tender fire of stars moments of their life together, that no one knew of or would ever know of, broke upon and illumined his memory. He longed to recall to her those moments, to make her forget the years of their dull existence together and remember only their moments of ecstasy. For the years, he felt, had not quenched his soul or hers. Their children, his writing, her household cares had not quenched all their souls' tender fire. In one letter that he had written to her then he had said: "Why is it that words like these seem to me so dull and cold? Is it because there is no word tender enough to be your name?"

Like distant music these words that he had written years before were borne towards him from the past. He longed to be alone with her. When the others had gone away, when he and she were in the room in the hotel, then they would be alone together. He would call her softly:

"Gretta!"

Perhaps she would not hear at once: she would be undressing. Then something in his voice would strike her. She would turn and look at him. . . .

At the corner of Winetavern Street they met a cab. He was glad of its rattling noise as it saved him from conversation. She was looking out of the window and seemed tired. The others spoke only a few words, pointing out some building or street. The horse galloped along wearily under the murky morning sky, dragging his old rattling box after his heels, and Gabriel was again in a cab with her, galloping to catch the boat, galloping to their honeymoon.

As the cab drove across O'Connell Bridge Miss O'Callaghan said:

"They say you never cross O'Connell Bridge without seeing a white horse."

"I see a white man this time," said Gabriel.

"Where?" asked Mr. Bartell D'Arcy.

Gabriel pointed to the statue, on which lay patches of snow. Then he nodded familiarly to it and waved his hand.

"Good-night, Dan," he said gaily.

When the cab drew up before the hotel, Gabriel jumped out and, in spite of Mr. Bartell D'Arcy's protest, paid the driver. He gave the man a shilling over his fare. The man saluted and said:

"A prosperous New Year to you, sir."

"The same to you," said Gabriel cordially.

She leaned for a moment on his arm in getting out of the cab and while standing at the curbstone, bidding the others good-night. She leaned lightly on his arm, as lightly as when she had danced with him a few hours before. He had felt proud and happy then, happy that she was his, proud of her grace and wifely carriage. But now, after the kindling again of so many memories, the first touch of her body, musical and strange and perfumed, sent through him a keen pang of lust. Under cover of her silence he pressed her arm closely to his side; and, as they stood at the hotel door, he felt that they had escaped from their lives and duties, escaped from home and friends and run away together with wild and radiant hearts to a new adventure.

An old man was dozing in a great hooded chair in the hall. He lit a candle in the office and went before them to the stairs. They followed him in silence, their feet falling in soft thuds on the thickly carpeted stairs. She mounted the stairs behind the porter, her head bowed in the ascent, her frail shoulders curved as with a burden, her skirt girt tightly about her. He could have flung his arms about her hips and held her still, for his arms were trembling with desire to seize her and only the stress of his nails against the palms of his hands held the wild impulse of his body in check. The porter halted on the stairs to settle his guttering candle. They halted, too, on the steps below him. In the silence Gabriel could hear the falling of the molten wax into the tray and the thumping of his own heart against his ribs.

The porter led them along a corridor and opened a door. Then he set his unstable candle down on a toilet-table and asked at what hour they were to be called in the morning.

"Eight," said Gabriel.

The porter pointed to the tap of the electric-light and began a muttered apology, but Gabriel cut him short.

"We don't want any light. We have light enough from the street. And I say," he added, pointing to the candle, "you might remove that handsome article, like a good man."

The porter took up his candle again, but slowly, for he was surprised by such a novel idea. Then he mumbled good-night and went out. Gabriel shot the lock to.

A ghastly light from the street lamp lay in a long shaft from one window to the door. Gabriel threw his overcoat and hat on a couch and crossed the room towards the window. He looked down into the street in order that his emotion might calm a little. Then he turned and leaned against a chest of drawers with his back to the light. She had taken off her hat and cloak and was standing before a large swinging mirror, unhooking her waist. Gabriel paused for a few moments, watching her, and then said:

"Gretta!"

She turned away from the mirror slowly and walked along the shaft of light towards him. Her face looked so serious and weary that the words would not pass Gabriel's lips. No, it was not the moment yet.

"You looked tired," he said.

"I am a little," she answered.

"You don't feel ill or weak?"

"No, tired: that's all."

She went on to the window and stood there, looking out. Gabriel waited again and then, fearing that diffidence was about to conquer him, he said abruptly:

"By the way, Gretta!"

"What is it?"

"You know that poor fellow Malins?" he said quickly.

"Yes. What about him?"

"Well, poor fellow, he's a decent sort of chap, after all," continued Gabriel in a false voice. "He gave me back that sovereign I lent him, and I didn't expect it, really. It's a pity he wouldn't keep away from that Browne, because he's not a bad fellow, really."

He was trembling now with annoyance. Why did she seem so abstracted? He did not know how he could begin. Was she annoyed, too, about something? If she would only turn to him or come to him of her own accord! To take her as she was would be brutal. No, he must see some ardour in her eyes first. He longed to be master of her strange mood.

"When did you lend him the pound?" she asked, after a pause.

Gabriel strove to restrain himself from breaking out into brutal language about the sottish Malins and his pound. He longed to cry to her from his soul, to crush her body against his, to overmaster her. But he said:

"O, at Christmas, when he opened that little Christmas-card shop in Henry Street."

He was in such a fever of rage and desire that he did not hear her come from the window. She stood before him for an instant, looking at him strangely. Then, suddenly raising herself on tip-toe and resting her hands lightly on his shoulders, she kissed him.

"You are a very generous person, Gabriel," she said.

Gabriel, trembling with delight at her sudden kiss and at the quaintness of her phrase, put his hands on her hair and began smoothing it back, scarcely touching it with his fingers. The washing had made it fine and brilliant. His heart was brimming over with happiness. Just when he was wishing for it she had come to him of her own accord. Perhaps her thoughts had been running with his. Perhaps she had felt the impetuous desire that was in him, and then the yielding mood had come upon her. Now that she had fallen to him so easily, he wondered why he had been so diffident.

He stood, holding her head between his hands. Then, slipping one arm swiftly about her body and drawing her towards him, he said softly:

"Gretta, dear, what are you thinking about?"

She did not answer nor yield wholly to his arm. He said again, softly:

"Tell me what it is, Gretta. I think I know what is the matter. Do I know?"

She did not answer at once. Then she said in an outburst of tears:

"O, I am thinking about that song, *The Lass of Aughrim*."

She broke loose from him and ran to the bed and, throwing her arms across the bed-rail, hid her face. Gabriel stood stock-still for a moment in astonishment and then followed her. As he passed in the way of the cheval-glass[23] he caught sight of himself in full length, his broad, well-filled shirt-front, the face whose expression always puzzled him when he saw it in a mirror, and his glimmering gilt-rimmed eyeglasses. He halted a few paces from her and said:

"What about the song? Why does that make you cry?"

She raised her head from her arms and dried her eyes with the back of her hand like a child. A kinder note than he had intended went into his voice.

"Why, Gretta?" he asked.

"I am thinking about a person long ago who used to sing that song."

"And who was the person long ago?" asked Gabriel, smiling.

"It was a person I used to know in Galway when I was living with my grandmother," she said.

The smile passed away from Gabriel's face. A dull anger began to gather again at the back of his mind and the dull fires of his lust began to glow angrily in his veins.

"Someone you were in love with?" he asked ironically.

"It was a young boy I used to know," she answered, "named Michael Furey. He used to sing that song, *The Lass of Aughrim*. He was very delicate."

Gabriel was silent. He did not wish her to think that he was interested in this delicate boy.

"I can see him so plainly," she said, after a moment. "Such eyes as he had: big, dark eyes! And such an expression in them—an expression!"

"O, then, you are in love with him?" said Gabriel.

---

[23]Long, tilted mirror.

"I used to go out walking with him," she said, "when I was in Galway."

A thought flew across Gabriel's mind.

"Perhaps that was why you wanted to go to Galway with that Ivors girl?" he said coldly.

She looked at him and asked in surprise:

"What for?"

Her eyes made Gabriel feel awkward. He shrugged his shoulders and said:

"How do I know? To see him, perhaps."

She looked away from him along the shaft of light towards the window in silence.

"He is dead," she said at length. "He died when he was only seventeen. Isn't it a terrible thing to die so young as that?"

"What was he?" asked Gabriel, still ironically.

"He was in the gasworks," she said.

Gabriel felt humiliated by the failure of his irony and by the evocation of this figure from the dead, a boy in the gasworks. While he had been full of memories of their secret life together, full of tenderness and joy and desire, she had been comparing him in her mind with another. A shameful consciousness of his own person assailed him. He saw himself as a ludicrous figure, acting as a pennyboy for his aunts, a nervous, well-meaning sentimentalist, orating to vulgarians and idealising his own clownish lusts, the pitiable fatuous fellow he had caught a glimpse of in the mirror. Instinctively he turned his back more to the light lest she might see the shame that burned upon his forehead.

He tried to keep up his tone of cold interrogation, but his voice when he spoke was humble and indifferent.

"I suppose you were in love with this Michael Furey, Gretta," he said.

"I was great with him at that time," she said.

Her voice was veiled and sad. Gabriel, feeling now how vain it would be to try to lead her whither he had purposed, caressed one of her hands and said, also sadly:

"And what did he die of so young, Gretta? Consumption, was it?"

"I think he died for me," she answered.

A vague terror seized Gabriel at this answer, as if, at that hour when he had hoped to triumph, some impalpable and vindictive being was coming against him, gathering forces against him in its vague world. But he shook himself free of it with an effort of reason and continued to caress her hand. He did not question her again, for he felt that she would tell him of herself. Her hand was warm and moist: it did not respond to his touch, but he continued to caress it just as he had caressed her first letter to him that spring morning.

"It was in the winter," she said, "about the beginning of the winter when I was going to leave my grandmother's and come up here to the convent. And he was ill at the time in his lodgings in Galway and wouldn't be let out, and his people in Oughterard were written to. He was in decline, they said, or something like that. I never knew rightly."

She paused for a moment and sighed.

"Poor fellow," she said. "He was very fond of me and he was such a gentle boy. We used to go out together, walking, you know, Gabriel, like the way they do in the country. He was going to study singing only for his health. He had a very good voice, poor Michael Furey."

"Well; and then?" asked Gabriel.

"And then when it came to the time for me to leave Galway and come up to the convent he was much worse and I wouldn't be let see him so I wrote him a letter saying I was going up to Dublin and would be back in the summer, and hoping he would be better then."

She paused for a moment to get her voice under control, and then went on:

"Then the night before I left, I was in my grandmother's house in Nuns' Island, packing up, and I heard gravel thrown up against the window. The window was so wet I couldn't see, so I ran downstairs as I was and slipped out the back into the garden and there was the poor fellow at the end of the garden, shivering."

"And did you not tell him to go back?" asked Gabriel.

"I implored of him to go home at once and told him he would get his death in the rain. But he said he did not want to live. I can see his eyes as well as well! He was standing at the end of the wall where there was a tree."

"And did he go home?" asked Gabriel.

"Yes, he went home. And when I was only a week in the convent he died and he was buried in Oughterard, where his people came from. O, the day I heard that, that he was dead!"

She stopped, choking with sobs, and, overcome by emotion, flung herself face downward on the bed, sobbing in the quilt. Gabriel held her hand for a moment longer, irresolutely, and then, shy of intruding on her grief, let it fall gently and walked quietly to the window.

She was fast asleep.

Gabriel, leaning on his elbow, looked for a few moments unresentfully on her tangled hair and half-open mouth, listening to her deep-drawn breath. So she had had that romance in her life: a man had died for her sake. It hardly pained him now to think how poor a part he, her husband, had played in her life. He watched her while she slept, as though he and she had never lived together as man and wife. His curious eyes rested long upon her face and on her hair: and, as he thought of what she must have been then, in that time of her first girlish beauty, a strange, friendly pity for her entered his soul. He did not like to say even to himself that her face was no longer beautiful, but he knew that it was no longer the face for which Michael Furey had braved death.

Perhaps she had not told him all the story. His eyes moved to the chair over which she had thrown some of her clothes. A petticoat string dangled to the floor. One boot stood upright, its limp upper fallen down: the fellow of it lay upon its side. He wondered at his riot of emotions of an hour before. From what had it proceeded? From his aunt's supper, from his own foolish speech, from the wine and dancing, the merry-making when saying good-night in the hall, the pleasure of the walk along the river in the snow. Poor Aunt Julia! She, too, would soon be a shade with the shade of Patrick Morkan and his horse. He had caught that haggard look upon her face for a moment when she was singing *Arrayed for the Bridal.* Soon, perhaps, he would be sitting in that same drawing-room, dressed in black, his silk hat on his knees. The blinds would be drawn down and Aunt Kate would be sitting beside him, crying and blowing her nose and telling him how Julia had died. He would cast about in his mind for some words that might console her, and would find only lame and useless ones. Yes, yes: that would happen very soon.

The air of the room chilled his shoulders. He stretched himself cautiously along under the sheets and lay down beside his wife. One by one, they were all becoming shades. Better pass boldly into that other world, in the full glory of some passion, than fade and wither dismally with age. He thought of how she who lay beside him had locked in her heart for so many years that image of her lover's eyes when he had told her that he did not wish to live.

Generous tears filled Gabriel's eyes. He had never felt like that himself towards any woman, but he knew that such a feeling must be love. The tears gathered more thickly in his eyes and in the partial darkness he imagined he saw the form of a young man standing under a dripping tree. Other forms were near. His soul had approached that region where dwell the vast hosts of the dead. He was conscious of, but could not apprehend, their wayward and flickering existence. His own identity was fading out into a grey impalpable world: the solid world itself, which these dead had one time reared and lived in, was dissolving and dwindling.

A few light taps upon the pane made him turn to the window. It had begun to snow again. He watched sleepily the flakes, silver and dark, falling obliquely against the lamplight. The time had come for him to set out on his journey westward. Yes, the newspapers were right: snow was general all over Ireland. It was falling on every part of the dark central plain, on the treeless hills, falling softly upon the Bog of Allen and, farther westward, softly falling into the dark mutinous Shannon waves. It was falling, too, upon every part of the lonely churchyard on the hill where Michael Furey lay buried. It lay thickly drifted on the crooked crosses and headstones, on the spears of the little gate, on the barren thorns. His soul swooned slowly as he heard the snow falling faintly through the universe and faintly falling, like the descent of their last end, upon all the living and the dead.

Questions for Writing and Discussion

1. The story is punctuated by several disconcerting encounters which Gabriel Conroy has with women. First, there is the servant girl Lily, to whom he tries to be polite but who embarrasses him with her bitterness; there is Miss Ivors, the Irish nationalist with whom he has a sort of flirtatious quarrel; and finally, there is his wife Gretta. Each of these encounters reveals something important about Conroy's character: his strengths and weaknesses, his decencies and failures. Discuss them in

sequence, showing how they lead into one another and how they build up to Joyce's final view of Conroy.

2. At no point in the story does Joyce openly express his opinions of the characters, yet if we read "The Dead" with reasonable attention we can discover what judgments we are meant to make, or what judgments to suspend, about even the least significant of the characters. How does Joyce do this? Consider especially the bits of crucial dialogue he allots them.

3. Turn to the section of the story in which Gabriel makes his speech—apparently a speech that, with one or another variation, he has made several times before. What do you think Joyce wants us to feel about this speech? Do you accept this proposed judgment? Do you think Conroy is deeply proud of his performance? What is the nature of the response which the other guests make to it?

4. There are a number of things in this story that can be regarded both as ordinary objects in the scene or the action and also as symbols suggesting something of Joyce's deeper intentions. Let's say, the galoshes, and still more important, the snow. If a writer is going to show human beings in their ordinary world, there will of course have to be furniture, clothing, weather, all the external materials and circumstances that condition our existence. And in Dublin it seems reasonable that there should be galoshes and snow during December. Yet when we read "The Dead" we may well feel that the galoshes and the snow take on an importance, a suggestiveness beyond their immediate use or presence. By checking several instances where the galoshes and the snow figure, can you indicate what symbolic purpose they may serve in the story?

5. Turn to the last two pages of "The Dead," at the point where Gretta has fallen asleep crying and Gabriel reflects upon their lives. By what or whom has Gabriel been moved? Is he simply feeling sorry for himself? Does he reach some larger vision of the human situation which makes him understand, perhaps, his own problems? How does the concluding vision of Gabriel give point and meaning to the entire story?

POETRY

POETRY

INTRODUCTION

The poems in this section of *Literature as Experience* are grouped somewhat differently from the stories in the previous one. You will notice that the titles of the various sections do not refer so directly to some aspect of our lives as human individuals living among the interconnections of family, love, friendship, and the institutions of society. Rather, these poems are arranged in sections of a different sort. The sections define various subregions of one domain of experience, that of utterance itself. The many different kinds of utterance—telling tales; being warmly or derisively funny; sighing with desire or regret; crying out in pain or outrage; urging or cajoling another person; addressing a god, a scene or an object, or an inner self, whether any of these can respond in kind or not; meditating half-audibly or explaining—are all modes of expressing our state of being alive.

Poetry inhabits the regions of utterance, the various modes and forms of putting things. Originally, in the world of Biblical and early Greek literature, narrative, drama, lyric, both public and private, even history and science, were all poetic forms or genres. It is only since the seventeenth century that prose has carved a world of its own. But while a poem can concern an event, an occasion, a kind of experience as much as a story can, poetry has a very different kind of relation to its mode of utterance than narrative prose does. Just as laughing, crying, murmuring, pleading, shouting, and denouncing are areas of human experience as much as the cause of the crying or pleading or arguing is, so it is with various poetic kinds. Getting to understand this is part of getting to understand how poetry much more than prose involves a complex interpenetration of what is said with the way of saying it. In poetry, the *way* something is said or asked or pondered or exclaimed comes to be a most important part of *what* is being said. These ways can be *generic:* is the poem a kind of taletelling or a purported address to someone loved or something said at a funeral, a birth, a ceremony of some private sort? There are also ways of saying that are *formal:*

317

how do the patterns and structures of language, phonetic and graphic, which make all poetry more like song and which are so different from the patterns and structures of prose, enter into the matter of what is being said?

The divisions of the table of poetic contents reflect, as you can see, these complex relations of mode of discourse to way of life. We start out with the apparently primitive category of the small or short form, the elementary or atomic aspects of poetry, and move on to groupings that are generic, formal, or even, like those of the stories, thematic. Just as narrative depends upon certain conventions—such as the rule that effects follow their causes in time—so does poetic utterance. These conventions are like the ground rules of a tennis match or a baseball game: while in one sense they may be thought of as constraints, in another they may be seen as giving birth to the power and force of the game itself. (There can be no human power—as opposed to brute strength—in hitting a home run if there is no foul line to be avoided.) The conventions of genre and form, and the ways in which these are modified to give rise to new conventions by individual poems throughout the history of poetry, come themselves to represent the condition of being human.

But something further needs to be said about the way poetry comprehends our lives, and how this way differs from that of prose fiction. Our experience of life is intimately connected with our sense of time, and our sense of time is far from simple. We have a steady consciousness of what we may call "clock-time," the time that measures the hours and days of our lives and the passage from season to season and from youth to age; but we are conscious also of a very different kind of time, one in which we have our moments of intense emotion or sudden recognition. The first kind of time is inexorable and regular; the second is unpredictable, so that its appearances always catch us by surprise. We could not live without either: the long plateau which is alternately tedious and reassuring, the peaks and valleys which may be at once dreadful and exhilarating. The first kind of time is responsible for our sense of continuity, the second for our sense of change, and we require both equally. Without the contrasting mood and tone of our necessary daily action, we would gain nothing from the flashing moment of "ecstasy": a portentous-sounding word that means something really quite simple—a departure from our ordinary state, a stepping out of ourselves.

Let us suggest the reductive but perhaps helpful formula that prose fiction was invented to deal with the first kind of time, and poetry with the second, each with a sure knowledge of the other's existence in the background. This would explain why we often find ourselves speaking of a poet's "inspiration," in contrast with a novelist's "vision of life." Or why we can think of poetry as the world of the mirror and prose fiction as that of the window. It is in poetry that we expect above all things *concentration.* For the mirror's image to be coherent, so that all the parts seem to contribute to a logical whole, the objects before it have to be consciously arranged; whereas the window's image is so large that we cannot possibly take in all the parts at once, and our need to understand its principle of arrangement is less immediately urgent. Having a narrow space in which to reflect, every poem tries to communicate to its readers the attention to detail that was necessary for its composition and to produce the effect that we associate with moments which exist outside ordinary time. That is why the greatest critics of poetry employ as their terms of praise "elevation" or "sublimity" (both of which refer to the cause of our astonishment at these moments), while critics of fiction, and the great novelists themselves, are more inclined to speak of "imitation" (by which they mean truth to life). Poetry, of course, has its own truth to life, but we are apt to feel helpless when we start to talk about it. One mark of a good poem is that it makes us feel "This is true" *without* making it easy for us to answer the questions: true of what? why? for whom?

"It is not metres," wrote Ralph Waldo Emerson, "but a metre-making argument, that makes a poem." Every reader, as he or she grows more confident with poetry, builds up a definition of poetic argument. In some respects, it resembles verbal argument, for it has a design upon us (though like the finest rhetoricians, the best poets do not have a "palpable design"). While seeming to amuse, instruct, or delight, it persuades; and it proceeds by leaving out everything irrelevant to its purpose while inclining us to believe that on its own terms, to which we have been converted, it is wholly inclusive. *What* are we convinced of at the end of a poem? Not to change our minds about anything in particular; perhaps, then, to admit that we have seen something we could not possibly have seen for ourselves. The means by which a poem argues us into its perception are as various as the men and women who make poems. From the intransigent meter and storming verbs of Blake's "London" (p. 526), to the alternation of formal address with lyric vignette in Hart Crane's "To Brooklyn Bridge" (p. 539), no pattern that the poet may choose is forbidden, so long as it can move readers up what Emerson called "the stairway of surprise"—until, at the top, they are able to see both the new landscape beneath them and the way they took in achieving their view of it. But all genuine poems share at least this feature: they hurry us along, and impress us with their power, long before we can be sure where they will lead. Every poem, the first time we read it, is like a darkened room filled with objects. It is we who bring the light to it by reading, and by retracing our path, again and again.

FORMS AND STRUCTURES

Short Forms: The Atoms of Poetry

Poetry is essentially more intense, compact, and compressed a form of writing than prose. The very notion of having, as a unit of utterance, a fixed line or group of lines instead of an open-ended sentence or paragraph implies a formal limit, if only on length. Ideally, a poem can be as short as one line; but that single line, framed or given context by its title, would make a pair with that title.

A minimal unit or atom of poetry, rather than of a kind of verse form, probably has to consist of two parts—something said of something else. Even if the saying is a question or an exclamation, this will probably hold true: a mere "What?" or "Ouch!" however intensely felt, does not make poetry. But some way of representing that questioning impulse, or feeling, in other terms allows it to survive beyond the time and place of the impulse or emotion. And that representation may be quite minimal and still do its work.

Extremely compact poetry is often wise and witty, rather than elaborately expressive of broad feeling. Conciseness itself, being a kind of elegance, makes for this wisdom and wit. An *epigram* is a compact piece of wisdom, in prose or verse, that, as one poet put it, has to be witty, but not necessarily true (as opposed to an *aphorism,* which *has to* be true and *may* be funny). In English, verse epigrams are frequently put in the form of *heroic couplets* (see pp. 581–82), like Alexander Pope's own epigram *about* epigrammatic poetry:

> True wit is nature to advantage dressed,
> What oft was thought, but ne'er so well expressed.

We can notice that even in these two lines much is implied: We *might* think wit to be artificial and plain speaking natural, but it is much more complicated than that. The artificiality is all in the mode of expression, so that thought is to the (natural) body as language is to (artful) clothes, which do not

323

hide the body but rather show it off to its best advantage. This relationship is embodied in the tight, neat rhyming form and the parallelism of the second line ("What oft . . . but ne'er. . . ."). The force of this epigram depends upon contrastive statement, denying what one would ordinarily think about wit and nature. Frequently, epigrams will take some obvious truism, folk saying, or well-known proverb and show, very sharply, how the opposite or antithesis is *really* the case. The great eighteenth-century French aphorist, La Rochefoucauld remarked that "We always hate those to whom we have done an injury," and the power and profundity of the observation comes not only from its truth but from its reversal of a normal sequence (we injure those we hate).

Such *antithetical* or paradoxical power is, of course, not confined to wit in verse. Consider for a moment the following paragraph from a novel by Elizabeth Bowen in which is presented a view of innocent people who, we feel, are always manipulated by circumstances and by other people less innocent than themselves:

> Innocence so constantly finds itself in a false position that inwardly innocent people learn to be disingenuous. Finding no language in which to speak in their own terms, they resign themselves to being translated imperfectly. They exist alone; when they try to enter into relations they compromise falsifyingly—through anxiety, through desire to impart and to feel warmth. The system of our affections is too corrupt for them. They are bound to blunder, then to be told they cheat. In love, the sweetness and violence they have to offer involves a thousand betrayals for the less innocent. Incurable strangers to the world, they never cease to exact a heroic happiness. Their singleness, their ruthlessness, their one continuous wish makes them bound to be cruel, and to suffer cruelty. The innocent are so few that two of them seldom meet—when they do meet, their victims lie strewn all round.

The last line of this paragraph is like an epigram, paradoxical at first, a strange inversion of what we would naturally expect. But in this case, the whole passage gives it context. Frequently, epigrammatic poetry or prose will leave out—as understood—the context, like a riddle. Indeed, as we will see, riddles are a kind of basic poetic device themselves.

Witty revisions of received or traditional wisdom can be a first stage of one sort of poetic thought. Many aphorisms or epigrams have the form of definitions, but they assign new meanings to words whose definition is already known; the *force* of the wit depends upon the missing word "really" or "not what we usually think, but. . . ." Thus, "Genius is the infinite capacity for taking pains" is a redefinition of the notion that genius is an inspired condition that flies above or transcends mere work or devotion. William Blake's proverb, "Joys impregnate, sorrows bring forth" depends on a reversal of the Judeo-Christian tradition that what we do in joy and with no thought for the moment will bear a fruit of sorrow or pain. Blake reverses this to mean something more complex and profound.

Or consider Cardinal Newman's observation that a gentleman is someone who never causes pain in others. This is a revision of an older meaning of "gentleman"—a man, born into the upper classes in a society which values social class, whose speech, manners, and dress distinguish him from members of the lower classes. Newman revises this into a sort of *gentle man,* thus implying that there is a Christian aristocracy of love of fellow men that is far more important than social nobility. Now consider a famous witticism ascribed to Oscar Wilde, which simply adds to Newman's aphorism, "a gentleman is someone who never causes pain—*unintentionally.*" This implicitly redefines "gentleman" back again into a person so in control of his manners, of his way of dealing with others, that he never slips up; he possesses a kind of coldness, is capable of cruelty but never of messiness. In short, this is the old notion of aristocracy. Wilde takes the process around once again, as if to show that things really cannot change, or that a merely *ethical* revision of such ideas as nobility will not be able to change the reality they refer to.

This revisionary process lies at the heart of epigrammatic pungency. Sometimes proverbs come in pairs, the first one providing the context, the second, the revision. Thus, from the Biblical Book of Proverbs,

> Answer not a fool according to his folly, lest thou be like unto him.
> Answer a fool according to his folly, lest he be wise in his own conceit.

Or, in modern colloquial English, *Don't talk to a fool in his own language or you'll be foolish AND Talk to a fool in his own language or he'll think he's smarter than he is.* William Blake's "The Question Answered" has this same form: The first epigram sets us up for thinking that the answer to the second must be very different.

> What is it men in women do require?
> The lineaments of gratified desire.
> What is it women do in men require?
> The lineaments of gratified desire.

In other words, conventional cynicism about the war between the sexes would lead us to think that while men want women to be sexually satisfied, women want something very different for themselves. But Blake rebukes the reader for thinking that the epigram would merely be clever and witty in a wiseacre way.

Even when we can predict the direction of epigrammatic wit, the actual working out of the observation happens so quickly that we are surprised by its neatness and rapidity. Here are some epigrams, rather like those of the Roman satirist Martial, by the contemporary American poet J. V. Cunningham:

> Naked I came, naked I leave the scene,
> And naked was my pastime in between.

Even without knowing the source (Job 1:21), most of us know the traditional utterance about entering the world naked and leaving it in the same way. But the poet reminds us of an other, erotic, dimension of nakedness, which serves as a kind of inevitable light of hope. Here are two more of Cunningham's elegantly turned verse epigrams:

You ask me how Contempt who claims to sleep
With every woman that has ever been
Can still maintain that women are skin deep?
They never let him any deeper in.

Good Fortune, when I hailed her recently,
Passed by me with the intimacy of shame
As one that in the dark had handled me
And could no longer recollect my name.

Both of these epigrams, incidentally, depend upon what is called *personifi-cation,* the turning of an abstract entity—usually a moral term—into a briefly described fictional being. Biblical proverbs and verses from the Psalms are full of these personifications; thus, from the Twenty-third Psalm, "Surely Goodness and Mercy will follow me all the days of my life; and I shall dwell in the house of the Lord forever." We could, if we wanted, print "goodness" and "mercy" in lower case and make them seem less like kindly attendants who follow one; the meaning is at any rate clear—"Whatever I may do, good and merciful effects will result." But the personification makes this thought more forceful. (Even the proverbial little boy in the joke—he came home from school having learned by rote "Surely good Mrs. Murphy will follow me all the days of my life"—was somehow right in his obvious mistake: he had retained the poetic presence of a benevolent Being named, in this case, Good Mrs. Murphy.) Personifications can be very powerful and, in proverbs or epigrams, can generate a kind of miniature *parable* or *allegory* of their own.

Here is the first of two examples of personification:

Mercy and Truth are met together; Righteousness and Peace have kissed each other.

In this case, the meeting and embracing of the members of the two pairs is a powerful notion when we remember a fact about our lives: Truth is ordinarily merciless, and social wrongs, as well as private ones, are made right only by a disruption of peace. The verse from the Psalm thus envisions an ideal situation when virtues, positive concepts, do not exist at each other's expense. This is what the image of meeting and love implies. In the image, a little story or parable is condensed. To fill it out, we must think for ourselves, and remember some truths.

Here is the other powerful personification momentarily created in a proverb. Again, William Blake revises a previous notion:

Prudence is a rich, ugly old maid, courted by Incapacity.

In reading this, we must not only ask ourselves what we had previously thought Prudence to be (a neat, modestly dressed, industrious housewife? a busy ant working all summer instead of singing away the time?). In addition, we must read the little story very carefully, realizing that every word means exactly what it says. Only then can we understand what Blake is saying about prudence in opposition to earlier ideas.

This aspect of epigram and proverb—their way of being like a brief parable or allegory—extends beyond personification. An abstract term can be poetically conceived as a place, say, or a thing. Samuel Johnson's famous remark, "Patriotism is the last refuge of a scoundrel," means exactly what it says: not that all patriots are scoundrels, but that dishonest and immoral men, having failed to justify their action in any other way, will inevitably turn to the argument that they did what they did for the good of their country. But we must read the words carefully—the epigram does *not* say that patriotism is a place inhabited exclusively by scoundrels (although some people today might believe this to be true).

Very often a short, witty utterance will be like an atom of poetry in another way: an implied comparison or *simile* will be presented in condensed form, and the reader must do the work of elaborating the comparison. When we say, "X is like Y," *it is always with respect to some mutual quality, a or b.* When this mutual quality seems obvious, then the comparison has little strength, as for example in "The Amazon is like the Nile" (they're both great tropical rivers). When it is clear, but not obvious, the simile can be very effective: "My love is like a red, red rose/That's newly sprung in June." Robert Burns's simile does not merely liken the girl to a flower but to a newly blossomed fresh one, with the added overtone that his love for her is also newly sprung. Sometimes a comparison can be enigmatic and riddling, when the *a* or *b* term seems impossible to discern. "Why is a raven like a writing desk?" Alice is asked at the Mad Tea Party, and the answer is never given (nor can be—save for some trivial and exasperating solution such as "they both begin with an 'r' sound even if the second isn't spelled that way"). But some of the best poetic comparisons do make us dwell over them, rather than yielding up their point immediately, like a quick joke.

Here are some aphorisms, epigrams, and proverbs. In thinking about them, try to discern those elements of personification, comparison, and so forth which make the text both pointed and true.

> As the door turneth upon his hinges, so doth the slothful upon his bed.
>
> When a father gives to his son, both laugh; when a son gives to his father, both cry.
>
> When a poor man eats a chicken, one of them is sick.
>
> As a thorn goeth up into the hand of a drunkard, so is a proverb in the mouth of a fool.

William Blake

> Her whole life is an epigram, smack, smooth and neatly penned,
> Plaited quite neat to catch applause with a sliding noose at the end.

Oscar Wilde, from *Lady Windermere's Fan*

In this world there are only two tragedies.
One is not getting what one wants. The other is getting it.

ON A BOY NAMED ASTER

(Greek for "star")

Plato, translated by Percy Bysshe Shelley

Sweet star, thou child of love and beauty bright,
   Alone thou lookest on the midnight skies;
O! that I might be yonder heaven of light
   To look upon thee with a thousand eyes!

FOR THE TOMB OF THOSE SPARTANS WHO DIED DEFENDING GREECE AT THERMOPYLAE

Simonides

Tell them in Sparta, thou that passest by,
That here, obedient to their word, we lie.

ON JOHN 2:1-11   WATERS TURNED INTO WINE

from the Latin of Richard Crashaw

Whence comes this redness here? What rose so strange
   And new has made these wondering waters change?
O Guests, acknowledge God, for it is he
   The water-nymph looked at, and blushed to see.

In many epigrams and proverbs there is an element of *paradox.* A paradox in literature is a statement that would seem not to be true but actually is. In philosophy—in logic in particular—paradox has a limited meaning: a logical paradox is a statement that leads to an absolute self-contradiction. It indicates that the logical machinery of our language is not functioning right at this point, and that there have to be some repairs—new definitions of what we mean, etc.

Famous historical paradoxes have been those of the Greek philosopher Zeno's arrow (which, since its tip as it moves from bow to target is at any particular instant always at one particular point along that path, cannot possibly be "in motion") or that of Epimenedes the Cretan, who said "All Cretans are liars" (if that's true, then he is lying when he says that it's true). This last paradox has been represented by modern logicians in a neater way:

> THE SENTENCE IN THIS BOX IS FALSE.

This can be true, like Epimenedes' remark, *if and only if it isn't.* (Work it out.) Logical paradoxes like this (1) tend to reduce to a self-contradiction, and an ultimately fruitless one at that, and (2) seem to involve an element of self-reference; that is, they will always be statements about themselves.

In poetry, "paradox" is used in a looser and more fruitful way. There can be self-reference, of course, as "Physician, heal thyself" (Luke 4:23) or John Donne's "Death, thou shalt die." But more often, the self-contradiction can be resolved, as strictly logical ones cannot, by recognizing that the contradiction occurs only if both terms are taken literally. When the Greek poet Sappho invented the word "bittersweet" to talk about her feeling of love, she knew that a literal physical taste couldn't be both bitter and sweet at once. But both "bitter" and "sweet" are words we also use figuratively, to talk about feelings in certain ways; when those words are conjoined, a statement is made about those feelings. Her great Roman follower Catullus wrote, also of love:

> I'm in hate and I'm in love. How so? you ask.
> —Well, I don't know. But I feel it, and I'm in agony.

What the poem does is remind us that love and hate are *not* mutually exclusive. (If we personified them, it might be as siblings, sometimes rivals, sometimes sharing their attachment to people; their common enemy would be Indifference.) Sometimes paradoxes in poetry can have a witty, riddling quality. The seventeenth-century poets John Donne and Richard Crashaw delighted in such paradoxes. Crashaw once wrote, in one of his many religious epigrams, about the bashfulness, the lowered gaze, of the Virgin Mary in pictures; observe the way in which the poem provides a context for the final paradox about looking up and down:

> That on her lap she casts her humble eye,
> 'Tis the sweet pride of her humility.
> The fair star is well fixed, for where, O where
> Could she have fixed it on a fairer sphere?
> 'Tis heaven, 'tis Heaven she sees, heaven's God there lies,

She can see heaven, and ne'er lift up her eyes:
This new guest to her eyes new laws hath given,
'Twas once *look up*, 'Tis now *look down* to heaven.

The context for the poem, of course, is the Christian story—itself para-doxical—of the incarnation of a transcendent God in a little baby on earth; this baby would go to an early death that would, in Christian terms, put an end to all death (hence, for John Donne, death shall die). Another kind of paradox is present in the phrase "sweet pride of her humility." The close conjunction of a term and its apparent opposite is called an *oxymoron*, an extremely condensed paradox. "Bittersweet" is an oxymoron, so is the phrase "victor-victim" in James Shirley's poem (p. 374). The seventeenth century was very fond of the rhyme of "womb" and "tomb" because it implied a paradoxical simile.

Minimal units of poetry have a puzzling, enigmatic, or riddling element in them, and riddles have an essentially poetic quality to them. A seemingly irreconcilable paradox can be resolved as is a riddle. This riddle is as old as Homer: "All we caught we took away, and left behind all we didn't catch." The answer, so Greek tradition goes, is "fleas." Usually, an enigma teases us into demanding a solution; we want to dissolve the paradox or the impossibility and turn the riddle into something more familiar and understandable. Poetic rid-dling, by contrast, takes a certain delight in the puzzle before it is resolved. The nursery rhyme about Humpty Dumpty is, after all, a riddle: its solution is "an egg"; but we find that a proverbial notion of Humpty Dumpty as a personifica-tion of pride or ambition (that exists before a fall) keeps coming to mind even more than the mere instability and fragility of an egg on a flat surface. Many nursery rhymes are riddles, and yet their solutions are less satisfying than the interesting, grotesque, or paradoxical images they present. You may remember this one:

Little Nancy Etticoat
In a white petticoat,
And a red nose;
She has no feet or hands,
And the longer she stands
The shorter she grows.

The solution is "a candle," but the unexplained riddle and its answer seem to coexist equally for us—there is a sense almost of disappointment as the verbal "trick" is "explained." The enjoyment of riddles is part of the most basic tradition of *oral poetry*, of the body of song and story that existed even before writing, and whose forms written literature has inherited.

The earliest English poetry included riddles among its other forms. Here is one, translated from the Anglo-Saxon language in something like the *accentual verse* (see pp. 576, 585) of the original:

My house is silent   nor am I loud
But the Lord's injunction   joined our fates:

> I'm swifter than he   and sometimes stronger;
> He labors slowly   and lasts longer;
> Sometimes I rest: my house runs on.
> I live in him   as long as I live,
> If we're divided   I'm doomed to die.

Without the solution, the poem sounds like a little lyric of friendship or love. The solution points out just what is to be taken figuratively, and what literally, in the language of the riddle. (The answer here is "fish and river.") Sometimes the text of a riddle creates a visionary or dreamlike scene. Here is another one from the Mother Goose collections:

> I saw a peacock with a fiery tail
> I saw a blazing comet drop down hail
> I saw a cloud with ivy circled round
> I saw a sturdy oak creep on the ground
> I saw a pismire swallow up a whale
> I saw a raging sea brim full of ale
> I saw a Venice glass sixteen foot deep
> I saw a well full of men's tears that weep
> I saw their eyes all in a flame of fire
> I saw a house as big as the moon and higher
> I saw the sun even in the midst of night
> I saw the man that saw this wondrous sight

Before we even consider the solution, we might observe that the *form* of the poem—a rhymed list of reports—sounds like a series of dreams or prophecies, incongruities that *mean something* but that need decoding. The Greek oracles, like the famous one at Delphi, that foretold the future or gave advice, always spoke in veiled terms, in something like riddles that required interpretation. The great poetry of the Old Testament prophets like Isaiah and Ezekiel frequently reported visions which needed expounding; the most famous instance of this in the Old Testament is Joseph's interpretation of Pharaoh's dream of seven scrawny cows eating up seven fat ones as a vision of seven years of plenty followed by seven of famine.

This series of frightful visions, starting off with such prophetic-sounding wonders as a comet raining hail and an ivy-crowned cloud, all resolve into perfectly ordinary occurrences when the poem is punctuated with a semicolon or period after the object of "I saw" in each line. (For example, "I saw a peacock; with a fiery tail /I saw a blazing comet".) The traditional inversion of seventeenth-century English style (this riddle dates at least from then) allows the rewriting, although the original text, with its normal word order, misleads us. The role of rhyme here is also misleading; it stops the ends of the lines and makes us think that each vision ends at the rhyming word.

The idea that the puzzling, unsolved riddle is *imaginatively more important than the solution itself* is basic to poetry's whole way of saying something and meaning more, or other, than what is said. In Greek mythology, the Sphinx, lying in wait for travelers along a road, allowed them to pass only if they could answer her horrible riddle: *What walks on four legs in the morning, two legs at noon, and three in the evening?* Only Oedipus could answer this (see p. 654); he knew that the uncanny monster presented in the riddle is a representation of something familiar and homely—man himself (crawling, walking, and using a cane or stick). Moreover, he understood that the times of day were metaphors for the phases of a human life. But the force of the riddle is never dissolved: man is still an outlandish creature, and the realization that the riddle has an easy, familiar answer itself leads to a new sense of strangeness.

We might have presented the Sphinx's riddle as a story—"There was once a creature who changed its appearance strangely: in the morning. . . ."—and the solution as after the story—"Dear reader: the creature is man, who, in infancy. . . ." In that case, the riddle would have been the kind of narration we call a *parable* or a *fable*. Parables are most familiar to us from the Bible; Jesus did most of his moral teaching in parables, and he was using a form that rabbis had employed for hundreds of years before. Here is an interesting parable from the Old Testament (Ecclesiastes 12:1-7):

> Remember now thy Creator in the days of thy youth, while the evil days come not, nor the years draw nigh, when thou shalt say, I have no pleasure in them;
>
> 2 While the sun, or the light, or the moon, or the stars, be not darkened, nor the clouds return after the rain:
>
> 3 In the day when the keepers of the house shall tremble, and the strong men shall bow themselves, and the grinders cease because they are few, and those that look out of the windows be darkened.
>
> 4 And the doors shall be shut in the streets, when the sound of the grinding is low, and he shall rise up at the voice of the bird, and all the daughters of musick shall be brought low;
>
> 5 Also when they shall be afraid of that which is high, and fears shall be in the way, and the almond tree shall flourish, and the grasshopper shall be a burden, and desire shall fail: because man goeth to his long home, and the mourners go about the streets:
>
> 6 Or ever the silver cord be loosed, or the golden bowl be broken, or the pitcher be broken at the fountain, or the wheel broken at the cistern.
>
> 7 Then shall the dust return to the earth as it was: and the spirit shall return unto God who gave it.

The solution or interpretation of this beautiful riddling passage is an account of the decay of the human body with age. "Those that look out of the windows" are eyes; "the daughters of musick" are the lips; "the grasshopper" is the sex organs; "silver cord" and "golden bowl" are spinal cord and skull, and so forth. Yet the images, the details of the parable, have always had a poetic and evocative power in their own right, and many people have quoted and used the parable without knowing what it "meant." We must, then, in considering poetic meaning, be able to deal with both the surface and the depth of fables, parables, and riddling verses.

In the twenty-fifth chapter of the Gospel according to Matthew, Jesus tells two parables about the nature of the Kingdom of Heaven. They are reprinted below, in the King James version.

Then shall the kingdom of heaven be likened unto ten virgins, which took their lamps, and went forth to meet the bridegroom.

2 And five of them were wise, and five were foolish.

3 They that were foolish took their lamps, and took no oil with them:

4 But the wise took oil in their vessels with their lamps.

5 While the bridegroom tarried, they all slumbered and slept.

6 And at midnight there was a cry made, Behold, the bridegroom cometh; go ye out to meet him.

7 Then all those virgins arose, and trimmed their lamps.

8 And the foolish said unto the wise, Give us of your oil; for our lamps are gone out.

9 But the wise answered, saying, Not so; lest there be not enough for us and you: but go ye rather to them that sell, and buy for yourselves.

10 And while they went to buy, the bridegroom came; and they that were ready went in with him to the marriage: and the door was shut.

11 Afterward came also the other virgins, saying, Lord, Lord, open to us.

12 But he answered and said, Verily I say unto you, I know you not.

13 Watch therefore, for ye know neither the day nor the hour wherein the Son of man cometh.

14 ¶ For the kingdom of heaven is as a man travelling into a far country, who called his own servants, and delivered unto them his goods.

15 And unto one he gave five talents,° to another two, and to another one: to every man according to his several ability; and straightway took his journey.

16 Then he that had received the five talents went and traded with the same, and made them other five talents.

talents: one talent was a large sum of gold

17 And likewise he that had received two, he also gained other two.

18 But he that had received one went and digged in the earth, and hid his lord's money.

19 After a long time the lord of those servants cometh, and reckoneth with them.

20 And so he that had received five talents came and brought other five talents, saying, Lord, thou deliveredst unto me five talents: behold, I have gained beside them five talents more.

21 His lord said unto him, Well done, thou good and faithful servant: thou hast been faithful over a few things, I will make thee ruler over many things: enter thou into the joy of thy lord.

22 He also that had received two talents came and said, Lord, thou deliveredst unto me two talents: behold, I have gained two other talents beside them.

23 His lord said unto him, Well done, good and faithful servant; thou hast been faithful over a few things, I will make thee ruler over many things: enter thou into the joy of thy lord.

24 Then he which had received the one talent came and said, Lord, I knew thee that thou art an hard man, reaping where thou hast not sown, and gathering where thou hast not strawed:

25 And I was afraid, and went and hid thy talent in the earth: lo, there thou hast that is thine.

26 His lord answered and said unto him, Thou wicked and slothful servant, thou knewest that I reap where I sowed not, and gather where I have not strawed:

27 Thou oughtest therefore to have put my money to the exchangers, and then at my coming I should have received mine own with usury.

28 Take therefore the talent from him, and give it unto him which hath ten talents.

29 For unto every one that hath shall be given, and he shall have abundance: but from him that hath not shall be taken away even that which he hath.

30 And cast ye the unprofitable servant into outer darkness: there shall be weeping and gnashing of teeth.

Like parables, the fables that the Greeks called *allegory* have both a surface and a deeper interpretation. Greek myths were themselves treated allegorically. For example, the story of the mourning of Demeter, the goddess of grain and harvests, for the loss of her daughter Persephone to Hades, god of the underworld, who carried her away to be his queen, is a myth of winter coming over the land; Persephone is finally restored to Demeter for half of every year, and the explanation is fully worked out in terms of actual seasons. More frequently, allegorical stories involve not gods and goddesses as personifications of natural or human forces, but the kinds of personification we noticed earlier: ethical abstractions. There are also other elements in parables and allegories: places, objects, actions, situations. When they are understood in terms of their parabolic or allegorical meaning, we tend to speak of them as *symbols.* Thus, in the parable of the wise and foolish virgins (p. 333), getting oil and trimming the wick of the lamp are symbolic of spiritual preparation for the coming of the messiah. Extremely brief parables or presentations of moral symbols can occur in epigrams and proverbs, as we have seen. In all our modern literature—from the Renaissance on, in fact—symbols can function independently of allegorical or parabolic stories, just as personifications can. (*Emblems* were Renaissance pictorial symbols: see p. 561; their method of expounding the meaning of a picture was very close to that of a riddle, asking "What does this mean?")

The term "symbol" can be used in a number of ways to mean anything from an extremely ordinary and conventional sign, like

→ or ✝ or ☀ or a halo, or "Uncle Sam"

to a more opaque representation—as the ⊂⟩ symbol

of early Christianity; the letters of the Greek word for "fish" were the initials of a phrase used to describe Christ. This last symbol is much more like a poetic one than a simple sign can be. Like the riddles we explored earlier, *the unexplained meaning has as much force and presence as the explained one;* in contrast, when we read signs, we read *through* them to the meaning, almost throwing away the outer form in the process.

Symbolization—one thing standing for another—is a way of describing an element of poetic substance. Another way of talking about the language of poetry involves consideration of the process called *figuration.* We know that we can use words literally or figuratively, even in ordinary speech. Consider:

(1) *Said of an office on a hot summer day when the air conditioning has failed—* "It's a furnace in there!"

(2) *Said of the third rainy day in a row—* "Yeah, it's a *beautiful* day!"

(3) *Asked in the hope of getting a ride home—* "Have you got wheels?"

None of these is meant literally, and to say "No, it isn't a furnace" or "No, it's an unpleasant day" or "No, I have a car, though" would be not to understand the way in which the words were being used. All of these figurative uses of language, in which a word is being used in another sense, are called *tropes.* The three exemplified above are *metaphor* ("furnace" to mean "a place hotter than usual"); *irony*—here in its crudest form, *sarcasm* ("beautiful" to mean just the opposite); and *synecdoche* ("wheels," part of a car, to mean the whole one). Frequently, writers on language will use *metaphor* to stand for all tropes. (*Trope* means "turn" in Greek, by the way.) Another informal term that will be used throughout this book is *image,* which can be embodied in a trope, simile, or symbol. The simile mentioned on page 327, "My love is like a red, red rose," can be loosely characterized as a piece of imagery without specifying the way in which the language is used nonliterally. But from this linguistic point of view, the essence of poetry is its nonliteralness.

We might observe that in ordinary, nonpoetic speech, nonliteralness is seldom puzzling. We read, or hear, *through* it the way we read through simple signs, to the meaning behind it. Often we can find ordinary, literally used words that were clearly once metaphorical: thus we speak of the *arm* of a chair, the *leg* of a table, the *blade* of a sword, without thinking of the dead or mummified metaphor. Not only is there no other word for what the chair stands on, but, when we use the word, we forget that it refers to part of a human being or animal. In the case of the sword blade, the shift or turn of meaning is historical: the ancestor of "blade" in Old English meant "leaf." If we try to awaken the dead metaphor, it will be in a bit of verbal wit: "Did you scratch the chair's leg?" "No, only its toe." This kind of wit we recognize as epigrammatic and sometimes paradoxical; at any rate, it awakens an image in the literal term "leg."

A single image in isolation—like one half of a simile or an enigmatic metaphor—can be rather like a riddle; riddles, like paradoxes, are built out of mixtures of the literal and the figurative. In all images, we have two balanced desires as readers: to consider the image in itself; and to allow it to direct us to what it stands for. An image in isolation can be a sort of miniature puzzle or poem in itself; the "solution" will complete the reading without causing us to throw away the fragmentary image. Here is an image from an ancient Greek handbook on poetic style:

The cicadas are singing on the ground.

This doesn't seem to us like an image at all, until it is made clear that its meaning is *allusive*—in this case, to a natural fact. Cicadas sing in trees; if they are singing on the ground, it means that the trees have been felled and are lying on the ground themselves. This is a little like a kind of riddle, which presents a fragment and asks what is it a fragment of.

Here is one last example of a very short poetic unit. It is somewhat like a Japanese *haiku* (p. 586) in form, but it poses a beautiful riddle about fragmentariness itself.

PAPYRUS

Ezra Pound

Spring . . .
Too long . . .
Gongula . . .

"Gongula" is a girl's name in Greek. The title identifies the poem as a fragment of Greek poetry—like one of the many fragments of poems by Sappho and other ancient Greek poets—found on small pieces of papyrus that have been studiously transcribed by scholars who have had to conjecture what an original line or poem was. Ezra Pound's little poem suggests, from the name in it and the title, that this is some Sapphic fragment. But everyone is to make his or her own story of it. Is it a letter? a plea? a report? from—or to—or about Gongula? What is its tone? (Consider also its elegant structure: even though a fragment, the papyrus was, Pound is suggesting, torn so as to give us lines of one, two, and three syllables successively. What about the relations of the sounds in the tiny lines?) You can compare this little poem with the great anonymous love song called "Western Wind" (p. 367).

Epigram and Riddle

THE TUFT OF KELP

Herman Melville

All dripping in tangles green,
  Cast up by a lonely sea
If purer for that, O Weed,
  Bitterer, too, are ye?

Questions for Writing and Discussion

1. Here is a paraphrase of the poem: "Those who suffer the tumult of life, and are made wretched by it, may at last triumph over circumstances, but they will triumph in the lonely purity of an integrity that they might rather not have gained, since the cost of survival is permanent bitterness and the sense that purity can never be had without bitterness." In what way, apart from its length, is that paraphrase inferior to "The Tuft of Kelp"?

2. What does Melville gain by using the phrase "O Weed" instead of "O Tuft" or "O Kelp"?

STARS, I HAVE SEEN THEM FALL

A. E. Housman

Stars, I have seen them fall,
  But when they drop and die

No star is lost at all
    From all the star-sown sky.
The toil of all that be   5
    Helps not the primal fault;°
It rains into the sea,
    And still the sea is salt.

Questions for Writing and Discussion

1. Would the poem gain in directness if we altered the first line to "I have seen the stars fall"? What, if anything, would it lose?

2. In lines 1–4, Housman speaks of stars that apparently (but not actually) are lost from the sky; in the last two lines, of clear water that apparently (but not actually) weakens the saltwater of the sea. In both instances he points to a continuing stability beneath every appearance of change. How is the "primal fault" related to this continuity? What would be the effect of alluding to the primal fault at the *very* end of the poem?

THE LATEST DECALOGUE

Arthur Hugh Clough

Thou shalt have one God only; who
Would be at the expense of two?
No graven images may be
Worshipped, except the currency:
Swear not at all; for for thy curse   5
Thine enemy is none the worse:

At church on Sunday to attend
Will serve to keep the world thy friend:
Honour thy parents; that is, all
From whom advancement may befall: 10

Thou shalt not kill; but needst not strive
Officiously to keep alive:
Do not adultery commit;
Advantage rarely comes of it:
Thou shalt not steal; an empty feat,   15
When it's so lucrative to cheat:
Bear not false witness; let the lie
Have time on its own wings to fly:

primal fault: original sin

Thou shalt not covet; but tradition
Approves all forms of competition.   20

The sum of all is, thou shalt love,
If any body, God above:
At any rate shall never labour
More than thyself to love thy neighbour.

Questions for Writing and Discussion

1.   What does the poet mean by his title? Aren't these the same commandments that were given to Moses on Mount Sinai? Wouldn't obeying them make one a moral person?

2.   How does the qualification on the first commandment set the tone for the rest? (In place of the semicolon in line 1, read "After all, I mean. . . . ") What kind of "advantage" is mentioned in line 14?

3.   Even without knowing anything of middle-class Victorian England, what, from this poem alone, can you say about the society being satirized in it?

NUANCES OF A THEME BY WILLIAMS

Wallace Stevens

It's a strange courage
you give me, ancient star:

Shine alone in the sunrise
toward which you lend no part!

I

Shine alone, shine nakedly, shine like bronze,   5
that reflects neither my face nor any inner part
of my being, shine like fire, that mirrors nothing

II

Lend no part to any humanity that suffuses
you in its own light.
Be not chimera of morning,   10
Half-man, half-star.
Be not an intelligence,°

intelligence: a bit of information or of perception

Like a widow's bird
Or an old horse.

Discussion

Poets are always conscious of other poems, even those of the recent past. This consciousness is not like rivalry, nor does it show up obviously or superficially in poems themselves. Often, a serious poem is engaged in a sort of revision of the elements in other poems. These elements may be forms, images, or, more deeply, the way in which images are used to represent a vision of life. For major poetry, this interaction between poems can be a matter of great importance as far as the power of the imagination is concerned.

Wallace Stevens' epigrammatic little poem is quite clearly just such a revision of an earlier text, in this case by his friend and fellow poet William Carlos Williams. Williams' "theme" is the epigram which has the title of "El Hombre," which means in Spanish, "the man." It is a poem addressed to the morning star, which is not truly a "star" at all but a planet, often Venus, that can be seen shining brightly in the sky after all the stars have set.

Since classical antiquity, the morning star has had certain mythological associations. For the ancient Greeks, it was associated with Prometheus, who brought fire to man in defiance of the will of Zeus; for the followers of early Latin Christianity, with Lucifer or Satan, the fallen angel who led the rebellion against God. This overtone of defiance is certainly present in Williams' four lines about the star. But Williams believed that the imagination of modern poetry must avoid old mythologies and seek, instead, to find its metaphors in things as they appear to the senses. His view of Lucifer, the Latin name of the morning star, starts out by admitting its effect on him—it gives him "a strange courage." We are reminded by these words that the "ancient star" Williams addresses refers not to the trivial fact that stars are billions of years old but to an ancient tradition of regarding the star as an image of defiant rebellion.

The second two lines spell out this interpretation quite precisely, but in Williams' characteristic manner. "Shine alone in the sunrise/toward which you lend no part!" The star is urged to refuse, even in its shining, to have anything to do with the sunrise; it already lends no part to the light of the day (for, as we know, it is doomed to be bleached out by the general brightness of the fully risen sun). The morning star has hung on all through the end of darkness. Williams implies that to think of it as contributing to the sun's light would be both insulting and injurious. If the morning star still shines while the sun is beginning to light the sky, it is its own shining—a last, bright bit of the shining of night.

Suppose, for example, that one were to write of the morning star: *"You teach me a great moral lesson, bright star. You add your last half-hour of shining to the great sun's daylight, even though you will cease to be seen; you sacrifice your glory for the grand general triumph of Light over Darkness."* This would be one way of "reading," or interpreting, the same visual phenomenon. It is just the opposite, or antithesis, of Williams'. Perhaps we can see how Williams would interpret the star if we think about the "strange" quality of the courage the star inspires. This is not the courage of heroism but of understanding. The star "gives" it to the observer not by its light nor by some astrological "influence," but by means of its myth, its "ancientness," which is meditated upon poetically. The courage is not simply that of defiance of authority—that too often can be the easiest and least brave thing to do. Williams' courage concerns, more profoundly, behaving brightly in the face of the inevitable, and thereby, as it were, depriving the triumphant sunlight of all the fruits of victory.

Ultimately, Williams is saying that the star should not be thought of as a god, titan, angel, or demon, but as "El Hombre," or "Man." Wallace Stevens grants this, and everything we have observed above, even as he starts out to revise Williams. He calls his poem "nuances" of his predecessor's theme (not, as one might expect, "variations" on that "theme" in a musical sense). Stevens takes up, in Part I of his own poem, the phrase "Shine alone," and, following Williams' imperative form, urges the morning star one step further. "Don't even be Man," says Stevens, implying that Williams' way of seeing defiance and integrity in the star is after all only seeing some human quality mirrored in it. "Shine like fire, that mirrors nothing," continues Stevens; and indeed, fire mirrors nothing, but shines with its own light. If the evening star is to be a metaphor for a kind of imaginative independence, it must be free even of old interpretations of it. *And that is the way it can more truly represent what Lucifer and El Hombre were supposed to mean.*

And so with the phrase "Lend no part": the earlier poem's identification of the star with humanity is one imaginative approach to stars, trees, rocks, or clouds. It is a way of seeing human impulses in them. But Stevens is urging the star to stand for another kind of imagination, one which would not be satisfied with giving human qualities to natural things. In this case the star would not represent human feelings, such as courage, in the first type of imagination (which can be thought of as sentimental, although Williams does not make it seem so). In Stevens' poem, this type of sentimental imagination is likened to the sun when he says to the star: "Lend no part to any humanity that suffuses/you in its own light." Only when considered unsentimentally can the star be what it makes poets like Shelley, Williams, and Stevens feel it is.

A "chimera" is a nonexistent, imaginary, perhaps even frightening, presence. The word comes from the name of a mythological creature, part lion, part serpent, and part bird, who spat fire. Stevens is using the word in both its modern and its classical senses: the star as "El Hombre" is not a metaphor, but a mere chimera in the modern sense, an unrealizable fantasy; it is also a chimera like the ancient Greek fiction because it is a composite, "Half-man, half-star." Stevens urges it not to be that and goes on with his final injunction: "Be not an intelligence, /Like a widow's bird/Or an old horse." "Intelligence" is used here, as the gloss notes, in the sense of a unit of something known, rather than that which does the knowing. But we must still ask ourselves what sort of knowledge the examples would produce. A widow's parrot or canary and a poor, tired, old horse—these are familiar objects of sentimental attention, suffused in the light of our own feelings. Stevens knows the star to be something other than these. He wants it not to be thought of as involving itself in any way in the sentimentalizing process.

Williams' imperative to the star has the tone of encouragement; it says in essence, "Go on, shining and refusing at once." Stevens' command is of a different sort. It is almost as if it were addressed to a person considering the star rather than merely to the star itself. And finally, the imperative completes Williams' formulation by revising it. Only by being considered in its *naked* shining can the star give us the "strange courage" which comes from the true relation of poetry to natural fact. Only then can the morning star remain a potent myth instead of a piece of lofty but shallow eloquence. Stevens' nuances of Williams' theme have, by varying its tones, allowed its basic hue to prevail, even under a changing kind of light.

EPISTLE

TO A LADY

Of the Characters of Women

Alexander Pope

Nothing so true as what you once let fall,°
"Most Women have no Characters at all."
Matter too soft a lasting mark to bear,
And best distinguished by black, brown, or fair.
　How many pictures of one Nymph we view,   5
All how unlike each other, all how true!
Arcadia's Countess, here, in ermined pride,
Is, there, Pastora by a fountain side.
Here Fannia, leering on her own good man,
And there, a naked Leda with a Swan.   10
Let then the Fair one beautifully cry,
In Magdalen's loose hair and lifted eye,
Or dressed in smiles of sweet Cecilia shine,°
With simpering Angels, Palms, and Harps divine;
Whether the Charmer sinner it, or saint it,   15
If Folly grow romantic, I must paint it.
　Come then, the colours and the ground prepare!
Dip in the Rainbow, trick her off in Air;
Choose a firm Cloud, before it fall, and in it

---

let fall: casually observed   How many . . . shine: "Attitudes in which several ladies affected to be drawn, and sometimes one lady in them all" (Pope's note)

Catch, ere she change, the Cynthia of this minute.   20
  Rufa, whose eye quick-glancing o'er the Park,
Attracts each light gay meteor of a Spark,
Agrees as ill with Rufa studying Locke,
As Sappho's diamonds with her dirty smock;
Or Sappho at her toilet's greasy task,°   25
With Sappho fragrant at an evening Masque:
So morning Insects that in muck begun,
Shine, buzz, and flyblow° in the setting sun.
  How soft is Silia! fearful to offend;
The Frail one's advocate, the Weak one's friend: 30
To her, Calista proved her conduct nice;
And good Simplicius asks of her advice.
Sudden, she storms! she raves! You tip the wink,
But spare your censure; Silia does not drink.
All eyes may see from what the change arose,   35
All eyes may see—a Pimple on her nose.
  Papillia° wedded to her amorous spark,
Sighs for the shades—"How charming is a Park!"
A Park is purchased, but the Fair he sees
All bathed in tears—"Oh, odious, odious Trees!"   40
  Ladies, like variegated Tulips, show;
'Tis to their Changes half their charms we owe;
Fine by defect, and delicately weak,
Their happy Spots the nice admirer take,
'Twas thus Calypso° once each heart alarmed,   45
Awed without Virtue, without Beauty charmed;
Her tongue bewitched as oddly as her Eyes,
Less Wit than Mimic, more a Wit than wise;
Strange graces still, and stranger flights she had,
Was just not ugly, and was just not mad;   50
Yet ne'er so sure our passion to create,
As when she touched the brink of all we hate.
  Narcissa's nature, tolerably mild,
To make a wash, would hardly stew a child;
Has even been proved to grant a Lover's prayer,   55
And paid a Tradesman once to make him stare;
Gave alms at Easter, in a Christian trim,°
And made a Widow happy, for a whim.
Why then declare Good nature is her scorn,
When 'tis by that alone she can be borne?   60
Why pique all mortals, yet affect a name?

---

greasy task: making up a face   **flyblow:** grow filthy   **Papillia:** from the Latin for "butterfly"
Calypso: she kept Odysseus on her island, away from home, for seven years after the Trojan War
was over   **trim:** compromise

A fool to Pleasure, yet a slave to Fame:
Now deep in Taylor° and the Book of Martyrs,
Now drinking citron with his Grace and Chartres:°
Now Conscience chills her, and now Passion burns;   65
And Atheism and Religion take their turns;
A very Heathen in the carnal part,
Yet still a sad, good Christian at her heart.
   See Sin in State, majestically drunk;
Proud as a Peeress, prouder as a Punk;°   70
Chaste to her Husband, frank° to all beside,
A teeming Mistress, but a barren Bride.
What then? let Blood and Body bear the fault,
Her Head's untouched, that noble Seat of Thought:
Such this day's doctrine—in another fit   75
She sins with Poets through pure Love of Wit.
What has not fired her bosom or her brain?
Caesar and Tallboy,° Charles° and Charlemagne.
As Helluo,° late Dictator of the Feast,
The Nose of Hautgout, and the Tip of Taste,   80
Critiqued your wine, and analysed your meat,
Yet on plain Pudding deigned at home to eat;
So Philomedé, lecturing all mankind
On the soft Passion, and the Taste refined,
Th' Address, the Delicacy—stoops at once,   85
And makes her hearty meal upon a Dunce.
   Flavia's a Wit, has too much sense to Pray;
To Toast our wants and wishes, is her way;
Nor asks of God, but of her Stars, to give
The mighty blessing, "while we live, to live."   90
Then all for Death, that Opiate of the soul!
Lucretia's dagger,° Rosamonda's bowl.°
Say, what can cause such impotence of mind?
A spark too fickle, or a Spouse too kind.
Wise Wretch! with Pleasures too refined to please;   95
With too much Spirit to be e'er at ease;
With too much Quickness ever to be taught;
With too much Thinking to have common Thought:
You purchase Pain with all that Joy can give,
And die of nothing but a Rage to live.   100

Taylor: Jeremy Taylor, seventeenth-century Anglican divine, whose sermons became part of the accepted reading for cultivated eighteenth-century taste   **Chartres:** Francis Chartres, whose name Pope used to denote "libertine," as we say "Kleenex" for "tissue"   **Punk:** whore   **frank:** open, generous; hence, loose   **Tallboy:** a coarse young man in Richard Brome's comedy of 1641, *The Jovial Crew*   **Charles:** generic name for "footman"   **Helluo:** Latin for "glutton"   **Lucretia:** raped by Tarquin, she committed suicide   **Rosamonda:** the mistress of Henry II, she is said to have drunk poison at the (forcible) bidding of Queen Eleanor; Lucretia and Rosamonda thus exemplify suicide caused by an involuntary loss of chastity and a deliberate infidelity, respectively.

Turn then from Wits; and look on Simo's Mate,
No Ass so meek, no Ass so obstinate.
Or her, that owns her Faults, but never mends,
Because she's honest, and the best of Friends.
Or her, whose life the Church and Scandal share,   105
For ever in a Passion, or a Prayer.
Or her, who laughs at Hell, but (like her Grace)
Cries, "Ah! how charming, if there's no such place!"
Or who in sweet vicissitude° appears
Of Mirth and Opium, Ratafie° and Tears,   110
The daily Anodyne, and nightly Draught,
To kill those foes to Fair ones, Time and Thought.
Woman and Fool are two hard things to hit;
For true No-meaning puzzles more than Wit.
But what are these to great Atossa's mind?   115
Scarce once herself, by turns all Womankind!
Who, with herself, or others, from her birth
Finds all her life one warfare upon earth:
Shines, in exposing Knaves, and painting Fools,
Yet is, whate'er she hates and ridicules.   120
No Thought advances, but her Eddy Brain
Whisks it about, and down it goes again.
Full sixty years the World has been her Trade,
The wisest Fool much Time has ever made.
From loveless youth to unrespected age,   125
No passion gratified except her Rage.
So much the Fury still outran the Wit,
The Pleasure missed her, and the Scandal hit.
Who breaks with her, provokes Revenge from Hell,
But he's a bolder man who dares be well.°   130
Her every turn with Violence pursued,
Nor more a storm her Hate than Gratitude:
To that each Passion turns, or soon or late;
Love, if it makes her yield, must make her hate:
Superiors? death! and Equals? what a curse!   135
But an Inferior not dependant? worse.
Offend her, and she knows not to forgive;
Oblige her, and she'll hate you while you live:
But die, and she'll adore you—Then the Bust
And Temple rise—then fall again to dust.   140
Last night, her Lord was all that's good and great;
A Knave this morning, and his Will a Cheat.
Strange! by the Means defeated of the Ends,
By Spirit robbed of Power, by Warmth of Friends,

vicissitude: alternation   **Ratafie:** an apricot liqueur   **well:** kind

By Wealth of Followers! without one distress   145
Sick of herself through very selfishness!
Atossa, cursed with every granted prayer,
Childless with all her Children, wants an Heir.
To Heirs unknown descends th' unguarded store,
Or wanders, Heaven-directed, to the Poor.   150
   Pictures like these, dear Madam, to design,
Asks no firm hand, and no unerring line;
Some wandering touches, some reflected light,
Some flying stroke alone can hit 'em right:
For how should equal Colours do the knack?°   155
Chameleons who can paint in white and black?
   "Yet Chloe sure was formed without a spot"—
Nature in her then erred not, but forgot.
"With every pleasing, every prudent part,
Say, what can Chloe want?"—She wants a Heart.   160
She speaks, behaves, and acts just as she ought;
But never, never, reached one generous Thought.
Virtue she finds too painful an endeavour,
Content to dwell in Decencies for ever.
So very reasonable, so unmoved,   165
As never yet to love, or to be loved.
She, while her Lover pants upon her breast,
Can mark the figures on an Indian chest;
And when she sees her Friend in deep despair,
Observes how much a Chintz exceeds Mohair.   170
Forbid it Heaven, a Favour or a Debt
She e'er should cancel—but she may forget.
Safe is your Secret still in Chloe's ear;
But none of Chloe's shall you ever hear.
Of all her Dears she never slandered one,   175
But cares not if a thousand are undone.
Would Chloe know if you're alive or dead?
She bids her Footman put it in her head.
Chloe is prudent—Would you too be wise?
Then never break your heart when Chloe dies.   180
   One certain Portrait may (I grant) be seen,
Which Heaven has varnished out, and made a *Queen:*°
THE SAME FOR EVER! and described by all
With Truth and Goodness, as with Crown and Ball.
Poets heap Virtues, Painters Gems at will,   185
And show their zeal, and hide their want of skill.

---

knack: trick   **Queen:** Queen Caroline, whose warmth to Pope's political enemies kept on unabated until her death; her portrait looks good only when every trace of the model has been "varnished out"

'Tis well—but, Artists! who can paint or write,
To draw the Naked is your true delight.
That robe of Quality so struts and swells,
None see what Parts of Nature it conceals: 190
Th' exactest traits of Body or of Mind,
We owe to models of an humble kind.
If QUEENSBURY° to strip there's no compelling,
'Tis from a Handmaid we must take a Helen.
From Peer or Bishop 'tis no easy thing   195
To draw the man who loves his God, or King:
Alas! I copy (or my draught would fail)
From honest Máhomet,° or plain Parson Hale.°
    But grant, in Public Men sometimes are shown,
A Woman's seen in Private life alone: 200
Our bolder Talents in full light displayed;
Your Virtues open fairest in the shade.
Bred to disguise, in Public 'tis you hide;
There, none distinguish twixt your Shame or Pride,
Weakness or Delicacy; all so nice,   205
That each may seem a Virtue, or a Vice.
    In Men, we various Ruling Passions° find;
In Women, two almost divide the kind;
Those, only fixed, they first or last obey,
The Love of Pleasure, and the Love of Sway.°   210
    That, Nature gives; and where the lesson taught
Is but to please, can Pleasure seem a fault?
Experience, this; by Man's oppression curst,
They seek the second not to lose the first.
    Men, some to Business, some to Pleasure take;   215
But every Woman is at heart a Rake:
Men, some to Quiet, some to public Strife;
But every Lady would be Queen for life.
    Yet mark the fate of a whole Sex of Queens!
Power all their end, but Beauty all the means: 220
In youth they conquer, with so wild a rage,
As leaves them scarce a subject in their Age:
For foreign glory, foreign joy, they roam;
No thought of peace or happiness at home.
But Wisdom's triumph is well-timed Retreat,   225
As hard a science to the Fair as Great!

Queensbury: the Duchess of Queensbury, a celebrated beauty whom Pope honored for her
kindness to his friend John Gay   **Máhomet:** Turkish servant to George I   **Parson Hale:** an
Anglican clergyman and friend of Pope   **Ruling Passions:** in many of his Moral Epistles, Pope
alludes to his theory that every man has a single obsessive passion—that is, an interest or aim—which
dictates all of his actions, so that he may be said to be "ruled" by it   **Sway:** power over others

Beauties, like Tyrants, old and friendless grown,
Yet hate repose, and dread to be alone,
Worn out in public, weary every eye,
Nor leave one sigh behind them when they die.   230
    Pleasures the sex, as children Birds, pursue,
Still out of reach, yet never out of view;
Sure, if they catch, to spoil the Toy at most,
To covet flying, and regret when lost:
At last, to follies Youth could scarce defend,   235
It grows their Age's prudence to pretend;
Ashamed to own they gave delight before,
Reduced to feign it, when they give no more:
As Hags hold Sabbaths, less for joy than spite,
So these their merry, miserable Night;   240
Still round and round the Ghosts of Beauty glide,
And haunt the places where their Honour died.
    See how the World its Veterans rewards!
A Youth of Frolics, an old Age of Cards;
Fair to no purpose, artful to no end,   245
Young without Lovers, old without a Friend;
A Fop their Passion, but their Prize a Sot;
Alive, ridiculous, and dead, forgot!
    Ah! Friend! to dazzle let the Vain design;
To raise the Thought, and touch the Heart be thine!   250
That Charm shall grow, while what fatigues the Ring,°
Flaunts and goes down, an unregarded thing:
So when the Sun's broad beam has tired the sight,
All mild ascends the Moon's more sober light,
Serene in Virgin Modesty she shines,   255
And unobserved the glaring Orb declines.
    Oh! blest with Temper, whose unclouded ray
Can make tomorrow cheerful as today;
She, who can love a Sister's charms, or hear
Sighs for a Daughter with unwounded ear;   260
She, who ne'er answers till a Husband cools,
Or, if she rules him, never shows she rules;
Charms by accepting, by submitting sways,
Yet has her humour most, when she obeys;
Lets Fops or Fortune fly which way they will;   265
Disdains all loss of Tickets, or Codille;°
Spleen, Vapours, or Smallpox, above them all,
And Mistress of herself, though China° fall.

---

the Ring: a fashionable circular drive in Hyde Park   **Disdains. . . Codille:** refuses to be disturbed
by losing in the lottery or a hand at the card games of ombre or quadrille   **China:** both the country
and the breakable ware sought after by fashionable women

And yet, believe me, good as well as ill,
Woman's at best a Contradiction still.   270
Heaven, when it strives to polish all it can
Its last best work, but forms a softer Man;
Picks from each sex, to make the Favorite blest,
Your love of Pleasure, our desire of Rest:
Blends, in exception to all general rules,   275
Your Taste of Follies, with our Scorn of Fools:
Reserve with Frankness, Art with Truth allied,
Courage with Softness, Modesty with Pride;
Fixed Principles, with Fancy ever new;
Shakes all together, and produces—You.   280
    Be this a Woman's Fame: with this unblest,
Toasts live a scorn, and Queens may die a jest.
This Phoebus promised (I forget the year)
When those blue eyes first opened on the sphere;
Ascendant Phoebus watched that hour with care,   285
Averted half your Parents' simple Prayer;
And gave you Beauty, but denied the Pelf
That buys your sex a Tyrant o'er itself.
The generous God, who Wit and Gold refines,
And ripens Spirits as he ripens Mines,°   290
Kept Dross for Duchesses, the world shall know it,
To you gave Sense, Good Humour, and a Poet.

Discussion

When William Blake wrote of a woman he detested, "Her whole life is an epigram" (p. 327), he implied several judgments at once: that the pattern of her life revealed an extraordinary consistency; that her moral nature was not so complex as to elude a brisk and witty summing-up; that finally she had come to seem identical with a certain nasty quip about her, so that now that she is dead the epigram brings back all there ever was of her. In constructing the dazzling sequence of portraits that occupy the first two-thirds of his "Epistle," Alexander Pope takes for granted that a life can be reduced to an epigram if it has seemed already to reduce itself to one.

Many of Pope's epigrams might indeed be imagined as fierce or ironic epitaphs which correct and, by their sheer rhetorical power, replace the sweet and sentimental words that are found on most of the gravestones in a cemetery. An epitaph, like an epigram, sums up a life by reducing it to a phrase.

The generous God ... Mines: Apollo, god of the sun and of poetry, who, by simply shining, refines gold and ripens both fruit (which turns to spirits) and, metaphorically, the ore of metal underground; Apollo's warmth is felt all the while by the wit of poets

NARCISSA

A very Heathen in the carnal part,
Yet still a sad, good Christian at her heart.

SIN IN STATE

Chaste to her Husband, frank to all beside,
A teeming Mistress, but a barren Bride.

ATOSSA

Atossa, cursed with every granted prayer,
Childless with all her Children, wants an Heir.

CHLOE

Chloe is prudent—Would you too be wise?
Then never break your heart when Chloe dies.

In the last of these epigrams, we may find the concluding line about Chloe especially difficult, since "never break your heart when Chloe dies" seems to say: "Never once break your heart over Chloe, no matter how often she dies." But of course Pope does not mean simply this particular Chloe, but rather "women like Chloe," whom as an aggregate he has chosen to call by that name. Indeed, all of his portraits have been built up from a close observation of individuals; but they are intended to represent types, and his hope is that they will be universal enough for us to recognize them by their epigrams.

If we lose something when we classify the types by their traits—thus making the poem more abstract than Pope has made it—we at the same time gain an appreciation of the wide range of "characters" that the "Epistle" sets before us. We have, then, affectation in the "many pictures of one Nymph"; a *secret* vulgarity in Rufa; vanity in Silia; flightiness in Papillia; promiscuity—personal, emotional, and intellectual instability—in Narcissa; coarseness mingled with fastidiousness in Sin in State; suicidal passion in Flavia; and finally the two climactic portraits of shattering self-will in Atossa and devastating indifference in Chloe. What seems most to absorb Pope in sketching these portraits is the *perverseness* of his subjects: the word would not, in Pope's day, have meant sexual peculiarity so much as a willfulness in the self that is turned against the self—a tendency to negate or set at defiance that which comes most naturally to one's own nature, and become *un*natural. But however perverse or self-destructive these women may be, they are in no sense hypocritical. For it is not hypocrisy but merely weakness to fail in the effort to practice what one preaches or be what one wishes to be. Hypocrisy is rather the preaching of what one does not believe, or even of what one scorns; it is pretense for the sake of tangible gain, a deception of others that involves no deception of oneself. And hypocrisy is perhaps the one vice that Pope does *not* find in his survey of women.

Bewildered by the variety and self-contradictoriness of the characters he has to describe, Pope, in a slightly self-mocking attempt at scientific analysis, tries to master his subject by subdividing it. He calls upon the theory of "Ruling Passions," which he has set forth in other verse epistles, and decides that where women are concerned, two Passions "almost divide the kind": these are "The Love of Pleasure and the Love of Sway"—and women "seek the second not to lose the first." It is because these two passions are apt to be confused with each other, because beauty is the only instrument women have for attaining both and yet beauty is fleeting, that women may so often—as Pope insists—be seen to sacrifice the only attainment for which men admire them at all times of life: their dignity.

> At last, to follies Youth could scarce defend,
> It grows their Age's prudence to pretend;
> Ashamed to own they gave delight before,
> Reduced to feign it, when they give no more:
> As Hags hold Sabbaths, less for joy than spite,
> So these their merry, miserable Night;
> Still round and round the Ghosts of Beauty glide,
> And haunt the places where their Honour died.
> See how the World its Veterans rewards!
> A Youth of Frolics, an old Age of Cards;
> Fair to no purpose, artful to no end,
> Young without Lovers, old without a Friend;
> A Fop their Passion, but their Prize a Sot;
> Alive, ridiculous, and dead, forgot!

Beauty is worth having only so long as it keeps its "Honour"; but women in their youth too willingly make honor the stalking horse of pleasure and personal ascendency; and young beauties may be said to become "Hags" from the moment their honor is lost. At that moment, their lives begin to turn into epigrams: the process by which this happens, together with the kind of epigram that results, are what we see in the great line—"Alive, ridiculous, and dead, forgot!" An equation is set up between the two groups of adjectives: to be ridiculous when alive is to be forgotten when dead—the bleakest of all possible fates, since if we are ridiculous we wish at least to be memorable. But Pope has so constructed the line that we may read it in a slightly different way, with the first three words describing the course of a life wholly given over to being ridiculous and the last word reading out the verdict on that life: "Alive, ridiculous, and dead—forgot!"

This is the central passage of the "Epistle," the passage on which Pope clearly wished the whole moral weight of his poem to rest. In thinking about it we need to ask ourselves how thoroughly and how fairly it summarizes the portraits we have found earlier in the poem. Perhaps it is enough to recall what Pope has already confessed, that nothing he knows can account for the appeal to men (including himself) of all that is most perverse or "contrary" about women: "Yet ne'er so sure our passion to create,/As when she touched the brink of all we hate." The bafflement that prompted these lines is in no way dispelled by the formula that traces women's actions back to "the Love of Pleasure and the Love of Sway." The bafflement is only, somewhat arbitrarily, pushed to one side. And yet we also need to ask ourselves if in fact it spoils our experience of the poem to discover that Pope cannot avoid oversimplifying his task. The answer to this will depend on whether we read the poem as a moral investigation of a serious subject, which promises its readers a definite conclusion by which they may profit, or as an urbane and more or less relaxed session between one man—a notably witty, observant, sympathetic man, and doubtless a good talker—and his readers. We may want to make allowances for the self-contradictoriness which the poem shares with its subject when we remind ourselves that Pope imagines he has only one reader—the lady to whom his poem is addressed—and that with her as an audience he may assume the freedom of friendship, which includes the freedom to organize one's thoughts in no very strict or self-consistent order so long as one continues to be amusing.

It is to this lady (Martha Blount) that he turns at the end of his poem, with the exasperated cry, "Woman's at best a contradiction still," and the assurance that he will find in her, at any rate, something of the steadiness that he associates with the masculine temperament, along with another quality that men seldom possess. He calls it, simply, "Good Humour." Sympathy, resilience, wit, endurance, shrewdness, self-possession, and a long temper: all of these are contained in Pope's notion of good humor. Of course, good humor also means the ability to "humor," by seeming to follow the whim of, a person not lucky enough to be blessed by good humor—and this is likely to be a man. Heaven, he tells his lady, has to concoct a creature like her by following the instructions of a kind of recipe for the perfect woman; and when it does its work right, it "Shakes all together, and produces—You." This is just flippant enough to remove the patina of mawkishness from what sounds like an overwhelming and possibly embarrassing compliment. As he brings his "Epistle" to a close, Pope lifts the emphasis from "women" and restores it to "character" with the presentation of his poem and himself to someone whose worth, like his own, cannot be measured in vulgar pleasure or sway, in wealth or titles.

> The generous God, who Wit and Gold refines,
> And ripens Spirits as he ripens Mines,
> Kept Dross for Duchesses, the world shall know it,
> To you gave Sense, Good Humour, and a Poet.

The last word conceals a private compliment beneath the resounding public one, for it is a feminine rhyme. (See the Note on Prosody.)

We ought to mention the "epistolary" form in which Pope cast his poem. An epistle is a letter, and in letters we can speak our minds and ramble a little. If we are at all tempted to call this poem a heap of brilliant fragments, or condemn Pope as a bigot, we ought to remember that the form of the verse epistle gives him a certain license: he is not expected to be either as logical or as civic-minded as the writer of a didactic poem. In any case, the impression will persist with most readers that the poem *is* a coherent whole; if it were not, they will ask, how could they be so moved by its conclusion?

We offer two reasons for the strength of this impression. First, the follies that Pope describes often lead to disaster, and one may satirize follies but not disaster: the generally satiric mood of the poem is always subject to the tug of a powerful tragic undercurrent; and the alternation of these moods, the sense we have of each poised on the other's brink, remains throughout the poem and gives it a satisfying consistency of tone. And second, the "Epistle" has at its center two impressive passages of very different kinds: the portrait of Atossa and the description of the Hags' Sabbath. The descriptive passage which we have quoted is all the more astonishing when we hold it alongside the vivid and terrible account of Atossa's fate. These are among the greatest moments in eighteenth-century poetry, and they support each other's claims within this poem.

There is, finally, a source of pleasure in the "Epistle" which we have neglected entirely: it is the appealing contrast between the tightness, the pressure, the concision of the epigrammatic form and the easy expansiveness proper to a verse epistle. Most readers of the poem have felt this pleasure without being able to analyze it. And perhaps, after all, analysis has to stop here. There are times when criticism, to keep itself honest, can only point to the things it admires and leave them to speak for themselves.

FURTHER IN SUMMER

Emily Dickinson

Further in Summer than the Birds
Pathetic from the Grass
A minor Nation celebrates
Its unobtrusive Mass.

No Ordinance° be seen   5
So gradual the Grace
A pensive Custom it becomes
Enlarging Loneliness.

Antiquest° felt at Noon

Ordinance: a sign of ordainment, a ritual of religious communion **Antiquest:** most antique

When August burning low 10
Arise this spectral Canticle°
Repose to typify.

Remit as yet no Grace
No Furrow on the Glow
Yet a Druidic° Difference 15
Enhances Nature now.

Discussion

Some poems are riddles; and we know that Emily Dickinson wrote many of her poems for an audience that liked to be entertained by riddles of a homely kind. This audience, coming upon a poem that began—"A Route of Evanescence/With a revolving Wheel—/A Resonance of Emerald—/And Rush of Cochineal"— would know at once that the poet was describing a hummingbird. And having discovered this, they would feel that they had "solved" the poem and concluded their business with it. Perhaps, at the start of one of her greatest poems, Dickinson wrote with this audience in mind; at any rate she seems to have begun it simply as another riddle.

Further in Summer than the Birds
Pathetic from the Grass/
A minor Nation celebrates
Its unobtrusive Mass.

It is an exquisite description of a natural music with which we are all familiar: the noise of crickets.

Yet these lines contain disturbing elements which do not vanish with the solution of the riddle. The obvious reading of "A minor Nation"—the reading favored by the audience we have mentioned—would call it a quaint paraphrase of "a species of little creatures." But if we adopt this reading, we ignore the religious metaphor that is implied elsewhere in the stanza: the nation is singing hymns at its own "unobtrusive Mass," and hymns filled with "pathetic" feeling would probably be sung in a minor key. There are other ambiguities, of a more disturbing kind. How can a mass be at once pathetic—a word derived from "pathos" or scene of suffering—and yet "unobtrusive"? Why does the metaphor of celebration, and specifically of *religious* celebration, occur in a poem about the summer sounds of crickets? Above all, what are we to make of the phrase "Further in Summer"? Does it mean "further away, during the summer"—that is, "more distant-sounding than the birds"? Or can it imply also "further into the summer; more deeply imbued with the moods of summer"—because we grow

Canticle: a hymn whose words come directly from the Bible   **Druidic:** of the nature of Druids, an ancient Celtic priesthood of sorcerers and bards influential before Christianity; hence, primitive and powerful in a way allied to poetry and forbidden by Christianity

attentive to the sounds of crickets in the dog days of August, when the singing of birds has become too familiar to be noticed? We may return once more to the curious word, "pathetic": it indicates an emotional disturbance in the poem's speaker, even if she will not confess to any emotion deeper than ingenuity; and it exerts a pressure on the poem to continue after this stanza and offer some account of the speaker's mood. This can be done only through metaphor.

In the second and third stanzas, the religious metaphor that we have noticed is pursued with an astonishing persistence. We are hardly aware, the speaker tells us, of the effect of this music—so gradual is it, so without "Ordinance" or announced significance—before it confers on us a peculiar "Grace," a sense of blessedness that seems to make loneliness itself more generous and more spacious. Grace becomes a "pensive Custom," a familiar attribute, almost without our knowing it. The crickets are scarcely audible at noon—they are most remarkable at night—but even at noon, their voices come to us from the depths of the last month of the season and are full of meaning: "When August burning low/Arise this spectral Canticle." And these voices seem to "typify" or represent the ideal form of a repose that we long to have. One thought that may disturb us here is that an ideal repose can be found only in death, or else by God when the work of creation has ceased. But we dismiss this doubt and expect it like the others to be resolved by an inclusive movement at the end of the poem, where the religious metaphor will at last be completed, and the blessings of nature and of God will be shown to coincide.

The poem leads us to expect some such resolution. What it gives us instead, however, is yet another jarring and difficult moment, more sustained than any of the earlier ones, which makes us return to the opening of the poem with a renewed uneasiness. "Remit as yet no Grace" is the crucial line, and it is a difficult one. In reading it we ought to bear in mind several overlapping meanings of "remit": (1) to surrender or give up; (2) to lay aside; (3) to abate; and (4) to send back. However we understand the word, we are made aware of a strange uncertainty about the "Grace" we have found in the second stanza. Grace is not to be remitted—*as yet.* But at some point it will be. And even now, if we look closely we will see that "Nature" is enhanced not by the religious celebration this poem has seemed to offer us but by what Dickinson calls "a Druidic Difference." The phrase suggests a nature filled with primitive force, enchantment, and poetry—but not with Grace, in any Christian understanding of the term. Religion and bad poetry alike comfort man by exhibiting his harmony with the world he lives in: if (they say) man feels lonely, so does nature, and this gives him company; if crickets seem to him "Pathetic," that is because they are celebrating a kind of mass. These are pleasing thoughts; but, at the end of her poem Dickinson tells us that we must reject them as illusions. If we acknowledge what is disturbing in the noise of the crickets—from the point of view of "now," without reference to anything outside the present moment—we will say that our awareness of nature teaches us only its difference: difference *from us.* We must "remit" Grace just as a church "remits" a sin by agreeing not to use it against the sinner. And perhaps, by seeking a Christian Grace in nature, we were ourselves commiting a sin against it.

What do we find when we look at the entire poem in the light of its closing lines? Dickinson has shown us, subtly and yet unmistakably, that "Grace" is more real to our imaginings than it can ever be to nature itself. We may have taken "Enlarging Loneliness" to mean "making loneliness less miserable by giving it company," but the words only said "making loneliness more intense." We may have wanted to find a "Canticle" reassuring, but all we really heard was a "spectral Canticle," a shadow cast by our own need to be reassured. Yet Dickinson is so careful of our need to *mis*understand nature by viewing it in a human or religious scale, that she tells us, in effect: "Persist in your easy comforts for as long as you wish; I refuse to tell you they are all lies; and after all, why should you know this, as yet?"

We can appreciate Dickinson's enormous rigor of workmanship by remarking on two features of the poem which, though they are apt to escape notice, contribute decisively to its power. First, unlike this essay, the poem itself avoids a single use of the personal pronoun: we are never referred to an "I" or a "we" that feels the things described—an omission that quietly emphasizes our difference from nature. And second, the poem is set at a particular time, the end of summer, just before the fall. The fall, we remember, shares a name with the Biblical Fall, after which a number of things that had not happened as yet began to happen for the first time. Seasons changed; the sights and sounds of earth became variable rather than constant; man and woman were separated from nature and compelled to recognize their difference. The sounds of the "minor Nation" are *further in summer* in a sense we could not have imagined when we read this poem's opening lines.

SOME LAST QUESTIONS

W. S. Merwin

What is the head
      a. Ash
What are the eyes
      a. The wells have fallen in and have
           Inhabitants   5
What are the feet
      a. Thumbs left after the auction
No what are the feet
      a. Under them the impossible road is moving
           Down which the broken necked mice push   10
           Balls of blood with their noses
What is the tongue
      a. The black coat that fell off the wall
           With sleeves trying to say something
What are the hands   15
      a. Paid

No what are the hands
    a. Climbing back down the museum wall
        To their ancestors the extinct shrews that will
        Have left a message   20
What is the silence
    a. As though it had a right to more
Who are the compatriots
    a. They make the stars of bone

Questions for Writing and Discussion

This poem is a kind of catechism or interrogation in which the Questioner and the Answerer are undefined, unnamed, and undescribed. All we know from the title is the word "Last," and its full meaning will emerge only as we read through the poem. We can observe that the Answerer's way of answering subtly changes after the first question—we might say that his interpretation of the meaning of the word "what" in the questions keeps changing. Certainly the answers get stranger toward the end.

1.   What is the effect in the poem of the Questioner's words in lines 8 and 17? Do the answers to these have any image in common?

2.   How does the Answerer's way of answering change? What does he substitute for fact or material description after the first question?

3.   What kind of finality does the "Last" of the title call up? the death of a person? a thermonuclear holocaust? one of these seen in terms of the other?

O WHERE ARE YOU GOING?

W. H. Auden

"O where are you going?" said reader to rider,
"That valley is fatal when furnaces burn,
Yonder's the midden° whose odours will madden,
That gap is the grave where the tall return."

"O do you imagine," said fearer to farer,   5
"That dusk will delay on your path to the pass,
Your diligent looking discover the lacking
Your footsteps feel from granite to grass?"

"O what was that bird," said horror to hearer,

---

midden: burial mound

"Did you see that shape in the twisted trees?   10
Behind you swiftly the figure comes softly,
The spot on your skin is a shocking disease."

"Out of this house"—said rider to reader,
"Yours never will"—said farer to fearer,
"They're looking for you"—said hearer to horror,   15
As he left them there, as he left them there.

Questions for Writing and Discussion

1.   Assuming that "rider," "farer," and "hearer" are all the same person setting out on a quest of some sort, what sort of relation do the questioners have to him? What effect is gained by the assonance and alliteration (see pp. 580–81) which connect the names of questioner and questioned?

2.   In the last stanza, how are the questioners treated? The first question in stanza 1 is clearly answered. What about the others?

3.   What is the effect of the nursery-rhymelike quality of this poem?

CARDINAL IDEOGRAMS

May Swenson

0   A mouth.   Can blow or breathe,
     be funnel, or Hello.

1   A grass blade or a cut.

2   A question seated.   And a proud
     bird's neck.

3   Shallow mitten for two-fingered hand.

4   Three-cornered hut
     on one stilt.   Sometimes built
     so the roof gapes.

5   A policeman.   Polite.
     Wearing visored cap.

6   O unrolling,
     tape of ambiguous length
     on which is written the mystery
     of everything curly.

7 A step,
   detached from its stair.

8 The universe in diagram:
   A cosmic hourglass.
   (Note enigmatic shape,
   absence of any valve of origin,
   how end overlaps beginning.)
   Unknotted like a shoelace
   and whipped back and forth,
   can serve as a model of time.

9 Lorgnette for the right eye.
   In England or if you are Alice
   the stem is on the left.

10 A grass blade or a cut
    companioned by a mouth.
    Open? Open. Shut? Shut.

Questions for Writing and Discussion

1. In her title, the poet pretends that our arabic numerals (representing cardinal numbers) were originally pictograms like Chinese characters and Egyptian hieroglyphics. Each stanza of the poem is a "reading" of the number. How, in particular, do 6, 8, and 9 differ in tone from the others?

2. What is the meaning of "In England or if you are Alice" in 9?

3. Is there an additional visual emblem in 7?

4. Aside from the individual readings, is there any point at which the poem builds to a climax before its end? How is it unified?

THE CLOD AND THE PEBBLE

William Blake

Love seeketh not Itself to please,
Nor for itself hath any care;
But for another gives its ease,
And builds a Heaven in Hell's despair.

So sang a little Clod of Clay,   5
Trodden with the cattle's feet;
But a Pebble of the brook,
Warbled out these metres meet.

Love seeketh only Self to please,
To bind another to its delight;   10
Joys in another's loss of ease,
And builds a Hell in Heaven's despite.

Questions for Writing and Discussion

Proverbs and other flat moral assertions, cast in absolute terms, can be given poetic life (and perhaps greater moral force) in many ways. One way is to make a more complex statement about life out of a simple one, but without turning the simpler statement upside down. Instead of asserting that "X should be done" or "Y will always happen to Z," the poet—like the playwright or novelist—will do something like this: "'X should be done,' says A." In this case, the whole statement is about a human or personal perception that will produce a sense of what is right. Here is a little poem which does this very elegantly and powerfully.

1.   How does passive and self-sacrificing love "build a Heaven in Hell's despair"?

2.   What do lines 5–6 tell you about the poet's attitude toward the Wisdom about love in lines 1–4? Why didn't he start out with lines 5–6?

3.   What is the character of the pebble as opposed to that of the clod?

4.   Do you think that the poet wanted the pebble to have the last word? Compare this poem with Blake's two Nurses' Songs, (p. 369).

SONG OF MYSELF   11

Walt Whitman

Twenty-eight young men bathe by the shore,
Twenty-eight young men and all so friendly;
Twenty-eight years of womanly life and all so lonesome.

She owns the fine house by the rise of the bank,
She hides handsome and richly drest aft the blinds of the window.   5

Which of the young men does she like the best?
Ah the homeliest of them is beautiful to her.

Where are you off to, lady? for I see you,
You splash in the water there, yet stay stock still in your room.

Dancing and laughing along the beach came the twenty-ninth
      bather,   10
The rest did not see her, but she saw them and loved them.

The beards of the young men glisten'd with wet, it ran from their
      long hair,
Little streams pass'd all over their bodies.

An unseen hand also pass'd over their bodies,
It descended tremblingly from their temples and ribs.   15

The young men float on their backs, their white bellies bulge to the
      sun, they do not ask who seizes fast to them,
They do not know who puffs and declines with pendant and
      bending arch,
They do not think whom they souse with spray

Questions for Writing and Discussion

1.   The paradoxes of lines 9, 14, and 15 are resolved if we follow a clue given us at the beginning: Why are there twenty-eight young men? How does that number occur in nature? If the young men are days, then who is the woman who loves them?

2.   Comment on the image of moonlight as a twenty-ninth bather. How does it extend through line 18?

3.   Compare this poem with Hart Crane's "Voyages 1" (p. 507), which seems to echo this poem's scene but not its theme or tone. Also, compare Whitman's poem with Conrad Aiken's "Sea Holly" (p. 506). In what way are they somewhat alike?

UP-HILL

Christina Rossetti

Does the road wind up-hill all the way?
   Yes, to the very end.
Will the day's journey take the whole long day?
   From morn to night, my friend.

But is there for the night a resting-place?   5
   A roof for when the slow dark hours begin.
May not the darkness hide it from my face?
   You cannot miss that inn.

Shall I meet other wayfarers at night?
   Those who have gone before.   10
Then must I knock, or call when just in sight?
   They will not keep you standing at that door.

Shall I find comfort, travel-sore and weak?
   Of labour you shall find the sum.
Will there be beds for me and all who seek?   15
   Yea, beds for all who come.

Questions for Writing and Discussion

1.   Is the up-hill road the route of a particular journey? Could you name "that inn"? And name the road itself?

2.   With this in mind, consider the final line in each stanza: How does the meaning shift as one becomes aware of the significance of the journey?

3.   Is there anything about some uses of the words "road" or "path" that help you read this poem? (Consider this: The word "way" used to have only the sense of "road," for example, as in "highway.")

THE TWO SPIRITS: AN ALLEGORY

Percy Bysshe Shelley

FIRST SPIRIT

O thou, who plumed° with strong desire
  Wouldst float above the earth, beware!
A Shadow° tracks thy flight of fire—
    Night is coming!
  Bright are the regions of the air,   5
And among the winds and beams
  It were delight to wander there—
    Night is coming!

SECOND SPIRIT

The deathless stars are bright above;
  If I would cross the shade of night,°   10
Within my heart is the lamp of love,°
    And that is day!
  And the moon will smile with gentle light
On my golden plumes where'er they move;
  The meteors will linger round my flight,   15
    And make night day.

FIRST SPIRIT

But if the whirlwinds of darkness waken
  Hail, and lightning, and stormy rain;
See, the bounds of the air are shaken—
    Night is coming!   20
  The red swift clouds of the hurricane
Yon declining sun have overtaken,
  The clash of the hail sweeps over the plain—
    Night is coming!

---

plumed: literally, adorned with feathers; by extension, rendered proud   **Shadow:** the negation of desire   **shade of night:** the cone of darkness formed by the earth as it blocks the sun's light   **lamp of love:** the planet Venus, associated with love, where the cast shadow of night cannot reach

SECOND SPIRIT

I see the light, and I hear the sound;　　　　　　　　　　25
　　I'll sail on the flood of the tempest dark,
With the calm within and the light around
　　　　Which makes night day:
　　And thou, when the gloom is deep and stark,
Look from thy dull earth, slumber-bound,　　　　　　30
　　My moon-like flight thou then mayst mark
　　　　On high, far away.

Some say there is a precipice
　　Where one vast pine is frozen to ruin
O'er piles of snow and chasms of ice　　　　　　　　35
　　　　Mid Alpine mountains;
　　And that the languid storm pursuing
That wingèd shape, forever flies
　　Round those hoar branches, aye renewing
　　　　Its aery fountains.　　　　　　　　　　　40

Some say when nights are dry and clear,
　　And the death-dews sleep on the morass,
Sweet whispers are heard by the traveller,
　　　　Which make night day:
　　And a silver shape like his early love doth pass　　45
Upborne by her wild and glittering hair,
　　And when he awakes on the fragrant grass,
　　　　He finds night day.

Questions for Writing and Discussion

1. What is the attitude of the First Spirit toward the Second's adventure?

2. The Second Spirit assures the First that he knows what day will be like (lines 11–16). When he says, "If I would cross the shade of night . . .", does he seem to be sure that he will see day for himself?

3. Are the elements of hail, lightning, and rain, the perils invoked in the third stanza, intended to be entirely literal? Can you find any hint that Shelley may have wanted to suggest a battle fought by armies?

4. How would you characterize the Second Spirit's attitude toward the First in his final speech (lines 24–32)?

5. The last two stanzas of the poem are a commentary delivered by someone other than the First or Second Spirit. If you read these stanzas as more "objective" than the rest of the poem, and judge the claims of the First and Second Spirit by the evidence of these stanzas, which Spirit seems to have the deeper understanding of his own limitations, of the truth of what his antagonist says, and of his destiny?

Song

Originally, all poetry was song of some kind: solo or choral, religious chant or love song, work songs (like sea chanties or harvest songs), comic or tragic drama. Musical patterns and the metrical or rhythmic arrangements of verse were one and the same, and the rhythm of the music was that of the words. But poetry began to be independent of music some twenty-five hundred years ago, and songlike poems, written to the "music" of their own rhythmic patterns, are as traditional in literature as actual songs themselves. A "lyric" poem meant a solo song in classical times (sung by one person to his or her own accompaniment on a lyre). From the Renaissance on, a lyric poem has been a text which might or might not be set to music, but which need not be. Songs sung in actual dramas, for example, frequently outlive their musical settings, and even their dramatic contexts, and survive independently as poems. What remains important is the notion of a single speaker, revealing or expressing, like someone overheard, feelings we often associate with music. A poet may indeed write a song for himself or herself to sing; more frequently, writers will mean by the "I" of a lyric some imaginary speaker, almost like a character from a play. In the songs which follow we can see how very complex a matter the expression of an emotion or belief can be.

THE LONG NIGHT

Anonymous

It's lovely while summer can last
With the birds' song;
But now comes the windy blast
And the weather strong.

Ay, ay! How this night is long!   5
And I having been done wrong,
Sorrow and mourn and fast.

Questions for Writing and Discussion

1.   Line 5 refers to a literal fact that accompanies what is mentioned in lines 3 and
4. How is it figurative as well? How does the poem depend on this exchange
between the literal and figurative to give it coherence?

2.   Compare this little song with "Western Wind" (below). What is the difference
between the relationships, in the two poems, of natural fact and human feeling?

WESTERN WIND

Anonymous

Western wind, when will thou blow,
    The small° rain down can rain?
Christ, if my love were in my arms
    And I in my bed again!

Questions for Writing and Discussion

This great, anonymous love song has been celebrated as a simple, powerful
expression of longing. It is as brief as an epigram, but not pointed or witty. Yet,
like an epigram, it has two elements. The first is a question asked of nature; the
second is an exclamation of desire, *given as if in answer* to the first question that
was probably rhetorical to begin with. The song is certainly as powerful, and
nowhere nearly as simple, as has been suggested. It is very compressed and very
elliptical—that is, it leaves out all sorts of verbal elements that must be
understood, or supplied, by the hearer or reader. For example, words like "and
then" or "so that" are missing between lines 1 and 2. The "and" in line 4 is also
misleadingly simple.

1.   What could that "and" mean? Is there anything about the relation of the wind
and the rain in lines 1–2 that might be paralleled in lines 3–4? that might confirm
our knowledge that the bed here is one of love and not of slumber?

2.   What season of the year is being invoked? Consider the relation between the
weather and the singer's feelings.

small: thin, light

MISTRESS, SINCE YOU SO MUCH DESIRE

Thomas Campion

Mistress, since you so much desire
To know the place of Cupid's fire,
In your fair shrine that flame doth rest,
Yet never harboured in your breast.
It bides not in your lips so sweet,   5
Nor where the rose and lilies meet,
　　But a little higher,
There, O there, lies Cupid's fire.

E'en in those starry piercing eyes,
There Cupid's sacred fire lies.   10
Those eyes I strive not to enjoy,
For they have power to destroy.
Nor woo I for a smile or kiss,
So meanly triumphs not my bliss.
　　But a little higher   15
I climb to crown my chaste desire.

BEAUTY, SINCE YOU SO MUCH DESIRE

Thomas Campion

Beauty, since you so much desire
To know the place of Cupid's fire,
About you somewhere doth it rest,
Yet never harboured in your breast,
Nor gout-like in your heel or toe.   5
What fool would seek Love's flame so low?
　　But a little higher,
There, O there lies Cupid's fire.

Think not, when Cupid most you scorn,
Men judge that you of ice were born.   10
For though you cast Love at your heel,
His fury yet sometime you feel.
And whereabouts, if you would know,
I tell you still, not in your toe,
　　But a little higher,   15
There, O there lies Cupid's fire.

Questions for Writing and Discussion

These two songs were written by the same poet-composer, about eighteen years or so apart. The second is a kind of parody of the first. The notion that an idealized love was reflected in a lady's eyes (see Carew, "Ask Me No More" on page 397) was common in Renaissance poetry. What was "higher" was more noble and abstract.

1. Where do "the rose and lilies meet" in line 6 of the first poem?

2. How does the second poem mock the first one's concept of "higher"?

NURSE'S SONG I

William Blake

When the voices of children are heard on the green
And laughing is heard on the hill,
My heart is at rest within my breast
    And everything else is still.

"Then come home, my children, the sun is gone down   5
And the dews of night arise;
Come, come, leave off play, and let us away
Till the morning appears in the skies."

"No, no, let us play, for it is yet day
And we cannot go to sleep;   10
Besides, in the sky the little birds fly
And the hills are all cover'd with sheep."

"Well, well, go & play till the light fades away
And then go home to bed."
The little ones leaped & shouted & laugh'd   15
    And all the hills echoed.

NURSE'S SONG II

William Blake

When the voices of children are heard on the green
And whisp'rings are in the dale,

The days of my youth rise fresh in my mind,
My face turns green and pale.

Then come home, my children, the sun is gone down,   5
And the dews of night arise;
Your spring & your day are wasted in play,
And your winter and night in disguise.

Questions for Writing and Discussion

These two "songs" are very different from Campion's on the preceding
pages, and the relation between them is more complex. They are imaginary
songs supposedly sung by a nursemaid. Like a majority of English poems after
the early eighteenth century that were called "songs," they were not intended to
be sung. They represent different views of the world, and perhaps different
degrees of awareness.

1.   How does the Nurse in the first poem react to nightfall? Does it seem to have
any other meaning for her? What about the Nurse in II?

2.   How does Nurse II react to the children's voices? What are the "whisperings"
she hears? What does she think, do you suppose, they are about?

3.   Why could Nurse II feel that childhood is "wasted in play"? (Is there any clue
to this in the fact that she couples "childhood and day"?) What sorts of "disguises"
do children adopt? Are those the ones she is concerned about?

4.   Do you see any significance in the difference between two kinds of "song"
here? Nurse I sings to the children; in the poem, they answer. To whom is Nurse II
singing?

5.   What does Nurse II seem to feel about Nurse I's knowledge of life?

6.   Not only did William Blake wish to show how a childlike nurse can herself
grow up, he also wanted to imply that being grown up involves its own ways of not
seeing things. Can you imagine a Nurse III who would "know" much more about
life and death, cycles of nature and stages of learning things, piety and cynicism,
than Nurse II? in fact, as much more as Nurse II does than Nurse I? What attitude
would *she,* Nurse III, then have to Nurse I?

SPRING

William Shakespeare

When daisies pied and violets blue
And lady-smocks all silver-white

And cuckoo-buds of yellow hue
  Do paint the meadows with delight,
The cuckoo then, on every tree,   5
Mocks married men; for thus sings he,
      Cuckoo,
Cuckoo, cuckoo! O word of fear
Unpleasing to a married ear!

When shepherds pipe on oaten straws,   10
  And merry larks are ploughmen's clocks,
When turtles tread, and rooks, and daws,°
  And maidens bleach their summer smocks,
The cuckoo then, on every tree,
Mocks married men; for thus sings he,   15
      Cuckoo,
Cuckoo, cuckoo! O word of fear,
Unpleasing to a married ear!

WINTER

William Shakespeare

When icicles hang by the wall,
  And Dick the shepherd blows his nail,
And Tom bears logs into the hall,
  And milk comes frozen home in pail,
When blood is nipped, and ways° be foul,   5
Then nightly sings the staring owl,
      Tu-whit, to-who,
      A merry note,
While greasy Joan doth keel° the pot

When all aloud the wind doth blow,   10
  And coughing drowns the parson's saw,°
And birds sit brooding in the snow,
  And Marian's nose looks red and raw,
When roasted crabs° hiss in the bowl,
Then nightly sings the staring owl,   15
      Tu-whit, to-who,
      A merry note,
While greasy Joan doth keel the pot.

turtles ... daws: doves and other birds mate

ways: roads   keel: cool, by skimming   saw: proverb   crabs: crabapples

Questions for Writing and Discussion

1.   What is the exact image in line 4 of "Spring"? Does it mean "delightedly"?

2.   The cuckoo proverbially mocks married men because his call sounds like the word "cuckold." What is unusual about the relation of these two songs as celebrations of summer and winter? Which is usually the pleasanter season? Which seems the pleasanter one in the poems?

3.   The details in both songs are all natural ones, or possible facts. How do these details function as images or metaphors?

Barnaby Googe and Billie Holiday: A Comparison

Here are two short lyrics. Their authors lived almost four centuries apart, and Billie Holiday (the great American blues singer) probably did not know the work of Barnaby Googe (an Elizabethan poet and translator). Nevertheless, these two lyrics are strikingly close to each other in tone and sentiment. As you read them, ask yourself how, through her use of the refrain, Billie Holiday is able to show us certain contrasts which Googe, since he is writing a poem and not a song, has to show us through syntax and rhyme.

OF MONEY

Barnaby Googe

Give money me, take friendship whoso list,
For friends are gone come once adversity,
When money yet remaineth safe in chest,
That quickly can thee bring from misery.
Fair face show friends, when riches do abound;   5
Come time of proof,° farewell they must away.
Believe me well, they are not to be found
If God but send thee once a lowring day.
Gold never starts aside, but in distress,
Finds ways enough to ease thine heaviness.   10

GOD BLESS THE CHILD

Billie Holiday

Them that's got shall have,
Them that's not shall lose;

proof: testing

So the Bible says
And it still is news.
Mama may have,   5
Papa may have,
But God bless the child that's got his own,
That's got his own.

Yes the strong gets more
While the weak ones fade;   10
Empty pockets don't
Ever make the grade.
Mama may have,
Papa may have,
But God bless the child that's got his own,   15
That's got his own.

Money, you've got lots of friends,
They're crowded round your door.
But when you're gone and spending ends
They don't come round no more.   20

Rich relations give
Crusts of bread and such;
You can help yourself
But don't take too much.
Mama may have,   25
Papa may have,
But God bless the child that's got his own,
That's got his own.

He just don't worry 'bout nothing
'Cause he's got his own.   30
Yes, he's got his own.

Questions for Writing and Discussion

1. Compare lines 5–8 in "Of Money" with the third stanza of "God Bless the Child." Do you think "Money" in Billie Holiday's lyric might be a condensed expression for "when riches do abound"? Or is this whole stanza of "God Bless the Child" addressing "money" as "you," as if it were a person? What would be the purpose of doing that?

2. Both Googe and Holiday write in the *plain* style of their day. But, within that style, there are modulations of tone. For example, Googe tells us in a rather offhand way to "Believe me well," and again that gold will find "ways enough" to ease our distress. Where might you locate a similar modulation in the first stanza of "God Bless the Child"? In the fourth stanza?

3. "You can help yourself/But don't take too much" brings together, in a sudden quiet joke, the worlds of the dinner table and of St. Matthew's parable of the talents (see p. 333: from him that has shall be taken even that which he has). Is there anything comparable to this in "Of Money"? Wit has been defined as the faculty of yoking together two objects or qualities unexpectedly and yet fittingly. According to this definition, which poem would you describe as the more witty of the two, Googe's or Holiday's?

SONG

James Shirley

The glories of our blood and state
   Are shadows,° not substantial things,
There is no armour against Fate,
   Death lays his icy hand on Kings;
      Scepter and crown,   5
      Must tumble down,
And in the dust be equal made
With the poor crooked scythe and spade.

Some men with swords may reap the field,
   And plant fresh laurels where they kill,   10
But their strong nerves° at last must yield,
   They tame but one another still;
      Early or late;
      They stoop to fate,
And must give up their murmuring breath   15
When they, pale captives, creep to death.

The garlands wither on your brow,
   Then boast no more your mighty deeds;
Upon death's purple° altar now,
   See where the victor-victim bleeds;   20
      Your heads must come
      To the cold tomb;
Only the actions of the just
Smell sweet, and blossom in their dust.°

shadows: images, appearances, as opposed to "substances" or tangible, actual things or persons nerves: muscles, sinews purple: red dust: the clay from which Man was shaped and to which every person returns

Discussion

This is a famous seventeenth-century poem by a dramatist who today is known mostly to scholars and historians. It has remained attractive to several centuries of readers for a number of reasons: in earlier times, its sentiments were highly prized; in the last fifty years it has come to be regarded as a model of elegance and conciseness. We shall examine the compression and intensity of statement brought about by its images and by some of the relations between these images.

The poem was originally written as a song at the end of a brief play, but the context need not concern us at the beginning. You will observe from the notes that four words in the poem had slightly different meanings from those that they bear today. Each of the lines in which these words occur can, of course, be read clearly—and slightly mistakenly—with the modern senses slightly blurring the points in question. In the opening line, for example, the glories of nobility and condition are not the shadows that lie on the ground when the sun, say, hits whatever it is that casts them. Rather, they are hallucinations of our pride, illusions generated in the world by our absorption with it and by our constant avoidance, in life, of thoughts of death.

What is immediately apparent about the poetic language in these stanzas is the balance between abstract conceptions like *Fate, Death,* and *Glories,* and extremely concrete, durable objects like *armor, swords, crown, scythe, spade,* and *garlands of laurel.* Yet from the very outset, the relation between the shadowy abstractions and the substantial things is complex. *Fate,* which is abstract and general (rather than concrete, like a strong soldier or a piece of artillery), cannot be warded off with armor. In contrast, *Death* (line 4), which is usually abstract, is personified and made concrete (by reference to "his icy hand"). "Scepter and crown" are specific objects belonging to a king, but the assertion that they "tumble down" is by no means a literal one. If we take lines 5–6 literally, they would yield only the ridiculously obvious conclusion that heavy golden objects can and will fall to the ground. No, it is a particular figure of speech that is at work here, the trope called *synecdoche* (see pp. 335–36). What these lines say is that kings themselves, and indeed kingdoms and kingship, succumb to time and history.

But the last two lines of the first stanza present a further complexity. The "poor crooked scythe and spade" make another metonymic image: they stand for the humblest farmer, who in death is equal to a king. We should also note that scythes and spades are more directly powerful objects than crowns and sceptres, which are only emblems of power; the former can actually cut and tear (as indeed they did in peasants' revolts throughout European history when they were used as makeshift weapons). We get an interesting kind of crisscross of figurative and literal power here: the passive crown commands more force in life than the active scythe, yet the men who wield them are alike in death. It is the particular genius of these lines, however, to make us feel a final irony. Consider "And in the dust be equal made/With the poor crooked scythe and spade": We assume that it means "be made equal *to*," but the word "with" could also mean "by means of." There is in these lines a sense of "emblems of kingship are made equal to the implements of lowly farm wokers, and *by means of* the scythe and the spade." But how do scythes and spades do this, particularly when a popular revolt has not overthrown a king? Because of another figurative use of "scythe," in this case, the scythe of the old personification of Time (with a scythe and an hourglass). Time with his scythe (which mows down flesh as it does grass) and a purely literal spade (now that of a gravedigger) are the objects with which the bodies of men of both high and low estate are consigned to the same "dust," earth, or mud. This additional set of meanings works like a soft echo of the primary one, and it makes the whole, initially clear statement of the first stanza much richer.

The next stanza presents the same theme as the first, which is amplified in its images. In line 9, "Some men with swords may reap the fields," the language momentarily turns the (literal) swords into smaller, human instances of Time's (metaphoric) scythe; killing men on the (battle)field is here equated with mowing the field of life. But just as reaping in agriculture is part of a larger cycle (plowing, planting, etc.), so is human participation in the actions of time. The sword seems to "become" a scythe in that it mows and reaps, and also a spade in line 10, which turns over the earth to plant future laurels. The laurel garland was the badge of victory for the Romans; thus, killing men, which is metaphorically the same as reaping a harvest, is also, by extension, the same as planting the seeds of laurels of military victory.

But actual garlands, made of green leaves, eventually wither, just as human bodies finally rot and die, even in peacetime, if not in battle. Death's altar (line 19) is "purple" because of the blood of its victims and because it is royal, "death" being a kind of king to whom all creep as "pale captives" (line 16). The phrase "victor-victim" in line 20 is a perfect case of the old rhetorical device known as *oxymoron,* in which a word is joined with its apparent opposite (see "paradox" on pages 328–30). In this case, all military victors are in their turn victims of death, whether dying in battle at the hand of a stronger victor or later, at the icy hand of personified Death.

Only at the end of the poem is there some relief. Although garlands of laurel have neither fragrance nor flowers, fragrant blossoming will occur when the deeds of just men come to fruition after them by figuratively growing out of the earth in which their bodies decay. Again there is the delicate interplay, which we have observed before, between the figurative and literal uses of "blossom" and "dust"; and again this interplay gives strength and depth to what might otherwise be an empty cliché, no matter how noble the sentiment. And we may also observe that without the context of the earlier portions of the poem, the image of "blossoming" in "dust"—indeed, even the very way in which we come to understand that image—would lose a great deal.

We might say a few words about "context" here. There are several "contexts" for a poem, or for that matter any work of literature or art. First, the poem as a whole serves as a kind of ground for the meanings of particular words, images, lines, stanzas, or whatever occurs in the poem. We have just seen how the context of Shirley's poem affected the words "blossom" and "dust." Another instance can be found in the shift of the grammatical person in the poem. The ways in which the first and third persons are used in stanzas I and II help establish general statements, which are then brought home in stanza III by use of the second person. The "you" of line 17 is clearly the reader, the consciousness being addressed by the poem. The whole structure is like that of a *syllogism,* or logical chain: (stanza I) *Since* all persons come to death, *and* (stanza II) even those persons who seek to outdo Death by being like him also die, *then* (stanza III) you (or "we" or "one") must not boast of valor, for that implicitly declares your mortality. The stanzas are related to one another as are propositions in a logical chain of reasoning. But, having explored the poem and the reasons for its force, let us turn to its "context" in a larger sense.

This poem, usually entitled simply "Song" in anthologies, is in fact taken from a short play called *The Contention of Ajax and Ulysses,* which dramatized an episode from the myth of the Trojan War as told by the Roman poet Ovid. The Greek hero Ajax and the wily and clever Ulysses debate before the Greek chieftains their rights to the armor of the slain hero Achilles. In Ovid's story, Ajax loses the debate: "the power of eloquence was evident, and the eloquent man carried off the brave man's arms. Then he (Ajax) who had so often stood all alone against the great Hector, against sword and fire and Jove himself, couldn't hold out against his own anger: sorrow conquered the unconquered hero. He then drew out his sword, crying "At least this is mine—or does Ulysses claim it too? I must use it on me; the sword so often wet with Trojan blood will be wet with its master's—no man but Ajax will ever conquer Ajax!" With that, Ajax stabs himself, and his blood, spreading over the green turf, gives rise to the red hyacinth flowers. In Shirley's play, the song is sung by a priest over the body of Ajax, and the "you" of stanza III clearly refers to the assembled Greek princes (including Ulysses). "Your heads must come/To the cold tomb" applies to them.

Shirley's seventeenth-century audience would certainly have known the story from Ovid and its conclusion in the hyacinth blossoming from Ajax's blood as well as his military heroism falling victim first to clever speech and then to violent passion. Ovid's story would have been almost as familiar at that time as, say, George Washington's mythical cherry tree and its accompanying story is today. The last couplet of the poem and the lines about the "purple altar" and the "victor-victim" would have spoken directly to the original audience's memory of the story and their memory of Ovid's images and paradoxes. The meaning of the images as discussed earlier is not changed in any essential way by our knowledge of the poem's theatrical and classical contexts. Our added knowledge provides us only with another set of reasons for the shift of address in the last stanza, and another layer of reference—in this case, outside of the poem itself rather than within it—in the blossoms at the close.

The poem's survival out of its context is attributable to its moral statement: not only do human wars continue, but social strife still provides basic images for describing human activity. The leveling of social status by death is an old story, but it has continually to be relearned. The tight organization and interlocking images that we have traced also have a kind of basic appeal. Moreover, the poem's verbal music is as memorable as that of a catchy tune: the short lines in each stanza ("Scepter and crown/Will tumble down," for example) make a compact jingle, complete in itself, although qualified and amplified by the following longer couplet. And just as the lines from Ovid must have echoed in the chamber, as it were, of the last stanza for Shirley's original audience, readers since then would most likely have heard one more set of resonances. Two Biblical texts that most literate people until about a generation ago would have found familiar concern themselves with the matter of the poem's images: one "all flesh is grass . . . the grass withereth" is from Isaiah 40:6–7, and the other, a profound image of returning from wartime to peace, is from Isaiah 2:4: "And they shall beat their swords into ploughshares, and their spears into pruning hooks." We will not work out in detail the way in which these texts help reinforce the poem's images and make them seem even richer; this is one of the many things that the student can now do for him or herself.

Sonnet

One particular form of lyric has fascinated the greatest poets in the English language for over four hundred years. The sonnet, in fourteen lines of iambic pentameter (see pp. 578–79), and with a number of fixed rhyme schemes, is a short, intense kind of poem that shares some of the properties of song and epigram. Its "scanty plot of ground"—as Wordsworth called it—provides ample meeting place for cries of feeling and whispers of wit. Whether emotions and thoughts meet there to do battle, or to perform a dance with each other, the sonnet has remained a kind of poetic world of its own.

Sonnets were originally about love. The fourteenth-century Italian poet Petrarch had written a great cycle of sonnets to an idealized lady named Laura, who was a muse for his poetry as well as the object of his love. Each poem of the sequence explored a different aspect of the relationship between poet-lover and lady. When these poems were translated and imitated in English in the sixteenth century, English writers invented ideal ladies of their own in sonnet cycles. Sometimes resembling a love song, sometimes a philosophical argument, sonnets continued to deal with matters of love—both erotic and, in Christian terms, divine.

Later, in the eighteenth and nineteenth centuries—largely because of the influence of John Milton's very original sonnets—the form became associated with a wide variety of subjects. Aspects of nature, historical and mythological events, great or representative people fell under the scrutiny of a kind of intense meditation that had been originally directed at human love, the speaker's own and those of others. The sonnet is an interesting case of a poetic form which—unlike, say, blank verse or a rhymed quatrain—has by its very history taken on, for poets, the quality of a particular kind of experience.

379

THAT TIME OF YEAR
THOU MAYST IN ME BEHOLD

William Shakespeare

That time of year thou mayst in me behold
When yellow leaves, or none, or few, do hang
Upon those boughs which shake against the cold,
Bare ruined choirs, where late the sweet birds sang.
In me thou seest the twilight of such day   5
As after sunset fadeth in the west;
Which by and by black night doth take away,
Death's second self, that seals up all in rest.
In me thou seest the glowing of such fire,
That° on the ashes of his youth doth lie,   10
As the death-bed whereon it must expire,
Consumed with that which it was nourished by.
   This thou perceiv'st, which makes thy love more strong,
   To love that well which thou must leave ere long.

Discussion

This is one of a group of sonnets by Shakespeare in which the speaker addresses a younger friend. The poems are concerned with time and mortality, with their consequences for beauty and love. In particular, the poems compare, contrast, and interweave the youth of the friend and the understanding by the older speaker of both the strength and fragility of that youthful state. This poem differs slightly—and interestingly—from the other sonnets in the group.

To grasp this difference, let us first consider the phrase "in me." Here the speaker clearly does not mean to say "in my body," "in my bloodstream," or so forth. Nor does he mean to use a familiar metaphor like "in my heart" or "in the back of my mind." These, by becoming part of ordinary speech, have lost all of their poetic quality and are now mere idioms. The first element of the poem's unfolding pattern is unnamed directly, but unmistakable. "That time of year . . . when . . ." is autumn, and the speaker says that his friend may "behold" that season "in" him. The speaker may mean that he is literally very old, at the autumn of his life. Or that he himself is like a picture "in" which autumn is represented by the depiction of a fall scene. What, by the way, does an autumn scene really look like? It can be a time when yellow leaves (October, say) or else no leaves at all (December) or perhaps a few last remaining ones (mid-November) appear on the trees. Perhaps the hesitations in line 2 have to do with what we think of as being the essence of autumn.

That: as

But the rest of the quatrain concentrates on the tree branches and likens them to the ruins of gothic stone abbeys and their churches. The "choirs" would have been the section at one end where the choristers, choirboys in ceremonial vestments, would have sat. From them could have been heard the sounds of singing. The appearance in gothic tracery and arched stonework of tree and vinelike patterns helps enhance the comparison. But the unusual beauty, resonance, and effectiveness of line 4 depend on some very complex elements of organization, working beneath the surface even of our careful reading.

Now, let us turn to the second quatrain and look at "In me thou seest the twilight of such day/As after sunset fadeth in the west." The grammar is ambiguous; both "day" and "sunset" seem to be the subject of "fadeth." The image of late, failing daylight, however, is very clear and perhaps made even clearer by the flickering of the grammatical reference. Night is "death's second self" (line 8), because Sleep, in Greek mythology, was personified as the brother of Death. This is a powerful reminder that all we the living can know about being dead is by an inadequate resemblance to slumber. Here it is night who, half-personified, "seals up" everything in repose. (In Shakespeare's day, the term "seal" meant "to stitch up the eyelids of a hawk," as part of its training; in the poem, this sense of the word reinforces the sense of "seal" in rest or sleep.)

The young man has been told in the first two quatrains, then, that he "may" or "can" see, "in" his older friend, both autumn and twilight. The autumn is full of visible memories of a vanished music, the twilight barely holding onto a world about to be darkened. The final term in the sequence of comparisons is "fire": fire comprehended not so much as light but as the source of heat and, thereby, sexual and youthful passion. But this fire is not a fierce, high crackling flame of youth—literally, a young fire—but rather the glowing coals or embers, lying on the ashes of its own "youth." But there is another comparison here, which follows the direction suggested by night in lines 7–8: the ashes on which the late, old fire lies (we usually speak of "a bed" of ashes or embers) is not a bed of repose or lovemaking, but a deathbed. Furthermore, the fire, dying and choking off into the ashes, will be "consumed with" its fuel. How? In two senses: it will be consumed *by* the ashes of its wood, and it will be consumed *at the same time as* its wood is burned (*with* its wood). And just as a familiar phrase, "bed of ashes," is unstated but lurking in these lines, so is the notion of being "consumed with passion." What we must finally remember, too, is that although embers are the late, "twilight," "autumnal" phase of an open fire, they are also the hottest.

The major images in the sonnet's three quatrains are thus *autumn, evening twilight,* and *glowing coals.* Each of these images represents a state or condition "in" which a human being may find him or herself. Moreover each seems to refer to and to contain elements of the previous image. The embers sum up the other two and add the final note of passion which had been missing from the earlier quatrains. In introducing it, the poem replaces evocations of memory, fading light and heat, and life yielding to death with a more forceful sense of a powerful life, hardly vibrant and not to last too long, but nonetheless "glowing." As the images have unrolled, the overall image of the speaker's "interior" has grown more complex as well. The young friend is invited, by the sonnet itself, to consider what it is about the speaker that is autumnal, fading, late, secondary (and perhaps experienced and even wise).

What, then, does the final couplet proclaim to be the effect of the young man's "reading" of the picture book of his older companion? It will strengthen his love, whether for his friend (the speaker), a woman or anyone else he loves, his own youth or beauty—perhaps even for his own life itself. All of these are "objects" of love—not in the sense of "object" as an impersonal "thing," but rather as a human being or abstract entity toward which love of various sorts is directed. They will either depart from him or be abandoned by him. Given the added dimensions of the heat in the third quatrain, the final line not only maintains "You'd better love well what you won't have soon" but "What you won't have soon may be worth loving more because it can love better in return." In other words, the opening of the poem, which appears to ask for tender consideration, if not for pity, is replaced by what, at the end, has become a potent display of worth.

A final comment on the fourth line. We mentioned earlier that the lingering melody of the line resulted from internal complexities. These are of two sorts. The first pertains to the image of the birds. Lines 3 and 4 can be read in two ways, in one of which the "birds" are literally birds, in the other, a metaphor for choirboys. It is a matter of where, in reading, we draw the boundaries of the figure of speech. We might diagram it in the following way, putting what is metaphorical in italics:

> *boughs* which shake against the cold . . . where late the sweet birds sang: [as it were,] *bare, ruined choirs*

Here, the boughs on which the birds literally sang in summer are figuratively invoked as ruined churches. On the other hand, the syntax of the lines allows us to extend the metaphor:

> boughs which shake against the cold: [as it were,] *bare, ruined choirs where choirboys used to sing:* [as it were,] *sweet birds*

Here, on the other hand, we have two different metaphors. The trees are *choirs,* the boys that once sang in them are *birds.* In other words, whether the literal birdsong of summer or the figurative *birdsong* of choirboys in the old days, there is only a memory of singing in those trees. The lingering effect of either reading, once we have chosen it over the other one, reinforces the general sense of lost music: the readings echo each other.

The other complexity in line 4 is in the delicate patterning of the sounds of its words. The line is composed of monosyllables, and in assigning a metrical role to the accentuation of each word, we have no contrast of stresses—as we have in a disyllabic word—to guide us. "Bare, ruined choirs, where late the sweet birds sang" not only tempts us to accentuate the first three and last three words in the same slow cadence, but also arranges a pattern of "r" sounds throughout the line. *"R" sounds mean nothing in themselves.* But when they are the "r" 's of the word "bare," they keep harking back to it and echo meaningfully. Similarly, the half-rhyme of "late" and "sweet" tends to make those two syllables more prominent than merely their positions as stressed syllables in the line could do. Finally, the last word in the line is the only one that refers to sound, which thereby makes us take the word "sweet" in its Elizabethan musical sense of "being in tune"; and the word "sang" lingers on with its more open nasal sound (instead of a "stop" consonant like "p" "t" or "k"). It is this kind of effective placement of word-sounds which makes some readers say that the line imitates in its verbal "music" the meanings of its words.

This sonnet, like all of Shakespeare's, is of the type which has 3 quatrains and a final couplet, and this formal pattern generally influences the poem's logical and seemingly "narrative" structure. Often, the three quatrains frame a logical argument with two premises and a conclusion, such as "Since A is the case, and B is the case, therefore C is true." The closing couplet then works like a kind of epigram to tie it all up, or perhaps to add a qualification. In the case of this sonnet, the pattern varies a bit and looks something like this: "In me you see A (autumn); in me you see B (twilight); in me you see C (embers). You see me in terms of all these, which has effect D upon you." In the course of the sonnet's unrolling, we see how A, B, and C are all related: they are late phases of the year, day, and fire. It is the fire which more generally embraces the others, since the sun's varying heat and light shape the course of day and year. The couplet argues that there is value in what will vanish soon, perhaps added value because of its transitoriness.

But another kind of point, an implicit one, is made by the course of the poem's metaphors. There is in each of these autumnal images a powerful beauty, like that of the verbal "music" which accompanies the description of the lost, absent bird-and-choir song in line 4. This beauty gives the autumnal state a value which transcends even that claimed for it by the end of the poem itself.

YE TRADEFUL MERCHANTS

Edmund Spenser

Ye tradeful merchants, that with weary toil
Do seek most precious things to make your gain,
And both the Indias° of their treasures spoil,
What needeth you to seek so far in vain?
For lo! my love doth in herself contain   5
All this world's riches that may far be found:

Indias: East and West Indies

If saphires, lo! her eyes be saphires plain;
If rubies, lo! her lips be rubies sound;
If pearls, her teeth be pearls both pure and round;
If ivory, her forehead ivory ween,°   10
If gold, her locks are finest gold on ground;
If silver, her fair hands are silver sheen:
But that which fairest is but few behold,
Her mind, adorned with virtues manifold.

Questions for Writing and Discussion

1.   The catalog of the lady's beauties in this poem extends through the second quatrain. Does it break off at the couplet (lines 13–14)? What happens there to the extended comparison begun in lines 5–6?

2.   What relation of mind to body is suggested by this change of metaphor? (Consider the implications of "but few behold.")

3.   If in reading the poem you had stopped at line 13, what might you have expected the last line to mention? How does the mild surprise of "Her mind" coming at the beginning of line 14 emphasize the meaning of the couplet?

MY MISTRESS' EYES
ARE NOTHING LIKE THE SUN

William Shakespeare

My mistress' eyes are nothing like the sun;
Coral is far more red than her lips' red;
If snow be white, why then her breasts are dun;°
If hairs be wires, black wires grow on her head;
I have seen roses damasked,° red and white,   5
But no such roses see I in her cheeks;
And in some perfumes is there more delight
Than in the breath that from my mistress reeks;
I love to hear her speak, yet well I know
That music hath a far more pleasing sound;   10
I grant I never saw a goddess go
(My mistress when she walks treads on the ground).
   And yet by heaven I think my love as rare
   As any she belied with false compare.

ween: know (i.e., "know that it is")

dun: dully colored   **damasked:** of varied color

Questions for Writing and Discussion

1.   Compare this sonnet with the preceding one. Which of the two seems more down-to-earth? Which one seems more "literary"?

2.   What tone does Shakespeare adopt in this sonnet? Compare the tone of this sonnet to that of the same poet's "That Time of Year" on page 380. How do these two poems differ in tone?

ONE DAY I WROTE HER NAME

Edmund Spenser

One day I wrote her name upon the strand,°
But came the waves and washèd it away;
Again I wrote it with a second hand,°
But came the tide, and made my pains his prey.
"Vain man," said she "that dost in vain essay   5
A mortal thing so to immortalize,
For I my self shall like to° this decay,
And eek° my name be wipèd out likewise."
"Not so," quoth I, "let baser things devise°
To die in dust, but you shall live by fame: 10
My verse your virtues rare shall éternize,
And in the heavens write your glorious name.
Where, whenas death shall all the world subdue,
Our love shall live, and later life renew."

Questions for Writing and Discussion

1.   The central fiction of this sonnet is that of writing a poem to somebody. How does the poem connect the actuality of writing poetry with the metaphors of writing a name in the sand and of "writing" it in the heavens?

2.   What is unusual about the rhyme scheme of this sonnet?

WHO WILL IN FAIREST BOOK

Sir Philip Sidney

Who will in fairest book of Nature know
How virtue may best lodged in beauty be,

strand: beach   second hand: a second time   like to: liken to   eek: also   devise: plan

Let him but learn of love to read in thee,
Stella, those fair lines which true goodness show.
There shall he find all vices' overthrow,   5
Not by rude force, but sweetest sovereignty
Of reason, from whose light those night-birds fly,
That inward sun in thine eyes shineth so.
And, not content to be perfection's heir
Thyself, dost strive all minds that way to move,   10
Who mark in thee what is in thee most fair.
So while thy beauty draws the heart to love,
   As fast thy virtue bends that love to good.
   But, ah, Desire still cries, 'Give me some food.'

Questions for Writing and Discussion

This sonnet is from a long sequence entitled *Astrophel and Stella.* In all of the poems, the speaker, Astrophel (Greek for "star lover"), invokes his muse, or ideal love, Stella (Latin for "star").

1.   Point out the conceit in lines 1–4. What is the moral problem about beautiful women and goodness ("virtue lodged in beauty")?

2.   What are the "night-birds" of line 7? What is the "inward sun" of line 8?

3.   Does the last line seem abrupt? In what ways? What relation does it have to the argument that Stella's virtue diverts sexual desire into spiritual channels?

BATTER MY HEART

John Donne

Batter my heart, three personed God; for, you
As yet but knock, breathe, shine, and seek to mend;
That I may rise, and stand, overthrow me, and bend
Your force, to break, blow, burn and make me new.
I, like an usurped town, to another due,   5
Labour to admit you, but Oh, to no end,
Reason your viceroy in me, me should defend,
But is captived, and proves weak or untrue,
Yet dearly I love you, and would be loved faine,°

faine: with joy

But am betrothed unto your enemy,   10
Divorce me, untie, or break that knot again,
Take me to you, imprison me, for I
Except you enthrall° me, never shall be free,
Nor ever chaste, except you ravish me.

Questions for Writing and Discussion

1.   The major pattern of metaphors (called a *conceit*) in this sonnet is of a besieged, walled city. Discuss the relation of attacker and defender. Who is the speaker? Whose side is she on?

2.   How is the conceit modified in the sestet of the sonnet (lines 9–14)?

3.   Explain the paradoxes of lines 3 and 14. How do they make sense?

4.   How does the rhythm of lines 2 and 4 make itself heard and meaningful?

PRAYER

George Herbert

Prayer, the Church's banquet, Angel's age,
   God's breath in man returning to his birth,
The soul in paraphrase, heart in pilgrimage,
   The Christian plummet,° sounding heaven and earth;
Engine against the Almighty, sinner's tower,   5
   Reversèd thunder, Christ-side-piercing spear,
The six-days' world transposing in an hour,
   A kind of tune, which all things hear and fear;
Softness, and peace, and joy, and love, and bliss,
   Exalted manna, gladness of the best,   10
   Heaven in ordinary, man well dressed°
The milky way, the bird of Paradise,
   Church-bells beyond the stars heard, the soul's blood,
   The land of spices; something understood.

---

enthrall: subjugate

plummet: lead weight on a line for sounding the depth of water   **Heaven . . . dressed:** God at dinner, man served for his meal

Questions for Writing and Discussion

1.   Where is the main verb in this poem of one long sentence? Does the peculiar construction weaken or strengthen the various metaphors in it?

2.   How does prayer "transpose" the first six days of the working week (line 7)?

3.   Are the various paraphrases of "prayer' in a random order, or do they build up in sequence in any way? Comment, in this connection, on the last line.

ON HIS BLINDNESS

John Milton

When I consider how my light is spent,
   Ere half my days, in this dark world and wide,
   And that one talent which is death to hide
   Lodged with me useless, though my soul more bent
To serve therewith my Maker, and present   5
   My true account, lest he returning chide,
   'Doth God exact day-labour, light denied?'
   I fondly ask. But Patience, to prevent
That murmur, soon replies: 'God doth not need
   Either man's work or his own gifts; who best   10
   Bear his mild yoke, they serve him best. His state
Is kingly: thousands at his bidding speed,
   And post o'er land and ocean without rest;
   They also serve who only stand and wait.'

Questions for Writing and Discussion

1.   Read the New Testament parable of the talents (p. 333). How is it used in this poem? What is the poet's "talent" that has, against his will, been buried? How does line 10 allude to the parable?

2.   Notice the construction "dark world and wide" in line 2. Aside from the change of rhyme, can you see any difference of meaning arising from a more usual, conversational word order (say, "dark, wide world")?

3.   What is the effect of the use of "that murmur" (instead of, say, "this murmur") in line 9?

4.   This is a sonnet of the so-called Italian type: the lines rhyme *abba abba cde cde.* What unifies the sestet, which starts, here, in the middle of line 9?

TO THE EVENING STAR

William Blake

Thou fair-hair'd angel of the evening,
Now, whilst the sun rests on the mountains, light
Thy bright torch of love; thy radiant crown
Put on, and smile upon our evening bed!
Smile on our loves, and, while thou drawest the   5
Blue curtains of the sky, scatter thy silver dew
On every flower that shuts its sweet eyes
In timely sleep. Let thy west wind sleep on
The lake; speak silence with thy glimmering eyes,
And wash the dusk with silver. Soon, full soon,   10
Dost thou withdraw; then the wolf rages wide,
And the lion glares thro' the dun forest:
The fleeces of our flocks are cover'd with
Thy sacred dew: protect them with thine influence.

Questions for Writing and Discussion

This poem in 14 lines of unrhymed verse is almost a kind of blank-verse sonnet. In its fluid movement from line to line it is reminiscent of John Milton's sonnets. But it goes a step beyond Milton's fluidity. There is no real break between octave and sestet, and the enjambments, or straddling of the syntax at the line endings, are very striking. At line 5, for example, and line 13, the terminal words "the" and "with" are unstressed and even auxiliary (and line 6 has six stresses, because "Blue" takes a stress from the preceding line). All of these lines are metrically irregular in some delicate way or other.

But the most remarkable enjambments occur in lines 2 and 8. There the lines might read one way if we think of them as end stopped and another way if we see them as going over to the next line. (End stopping occurs if the line break comes at the end of a phrase, between subject and predicate, etc.) In line 2, we expect the word "light" to be a noun—as if perhaps the next line would follow something like this:

> Now, whilst the sun rests on the mountains, light
> Prepares for its departure . . .

But the next line shows us that "light" is an imperative verb. Even more surprisingly, "let thy west wind sleep on" in line 8 seems complete enough: to "sleep on" is intransitive. But the new line "reveals" that "on" is not part of the verb but of a prepositional phrase adverbially modifying the verb. The whole poem is full of experimental modifications of Milton's kind of verse.

1.   How is the evening star personified? Comment on the use of "thy" to qualify so many different things in the poem.

2.   Comment on the image in Line 9.

3.   Compare this poem with Wallace Stevens' "Nuances of a Theme of Williams" (pp. 340–41).

BRIGHT STAR

John Keats

Bright star, would I were stedfast as thou art—
   Not in lone splendour hung aloft the night
And watching, with eternal lids apart,
   Like nature's patient, sleepless Eremite,°
The moving waters at their priestlike task   5
   Of pure ablution° round earth's human shores,
Or gazing on the new soft-fallen mask
   Of snow upon the mountains and the moors—
No—yet still stedfast, still unchangeable,
   Pillowed upon my fair love's ripening breast,   10
To feel forever its soft fall and swell,
   Awake forever in a sweet unrest,
Still, still to hear her tender-taken breath,
And so live ever—or else swoon to death.

Questions for Writing and Discussion

1.   After a sustained aspiration to the "stedfast" bearing of the bright star, Keats turns back on himself and says that he aspires to something rather different, though equally stedfast. The reversal takes place at "No—" (line 9). What do you think prompts it?

2.   Suppose instead of "or else swoon to death," Keats had written: "or else love till death." Is love implied in swooning? In what sense does his repose upon his lover's breast imply a patience like that of the Eremite?

Eremite: a hermit or recluse, often with a religious connotation   **ablution:** the act of washing a thing clean, again with a religious connotation

IF BY DULL RHYMES
OUR ENGLISH MUST BE CHAINED

John Keats

If by dull rhymes our English must be chained,
And, like Andromeda,° the Sonnet sweet
Fettered, in spite of painèd loveliness,
Let us find out, if we must be constrained,
Sandals more interwoven and complete   5
To fit the naked foot of Poesy:
Let us inspect the lyre, and weigh the stress
Of every chord,° and see what may be gained
By ear industrious, and attention meet;
Misers of sound and syllable, no less   10
Than Midas° of his coinage, let us be
Jealous of° dead leaves in the bay wreath° crown;
So, if we may not let the Muse be free,
She will be bound with garlands of her own.

Questions for Writing and Discussion

1. How does this poem actually try to free the form of the sonnet from some of its fetters? Consider the unusual and original rhyme scheme in lines 1–10. What is the effect on the reader's ear of these rhymes?

2. Trace the image of a chain through the poem. How does the image change its quality and meaning? What is the sense of "bound" in line 14? Does it mean "constrained?"

3. This poem may be making a statement about poetry generally, in its relation to the constraints of formal pattern. What do you think this general statement might be?

4. Keats omits mention of two elements of the Andromeda story: (1) Pegasus, the winged horse ridden by Perseus that has come to symbolize the poetic imagination, and (2) the sea monster that threatens Andromeda. Even though present only by allusion, could they be fitted into the sonnet's fable in any way?

Andromeda: in Greek myth her mother praised her beauty, and in punishment Andromeda was chained to a rock guarded by a monster; she was rescued by Perseus **chord:** string **Midas:** he wished all he touched to turn to gold **Jealous of:** jealousy lest there be **bay wreath:** the laurel crown of poetry

DESIGN

Robert Frost

I found a dimpled spider, fat and white,
On a white heal-all,° holding up a moth
Like a white piece of rigid satin cloth—
Assorted characters of death and blight
Mixed ready to begin the morning right,   5
Like the ingredients of a witches' broth—
A snow-drop spider, a flower like a froth,
And dead wings carried like a paper kite.

What had that flower to do with being white,
The wayside blue and innocent heal-all?   10
What brought the kindred spider to that height,
Then steered the white moth thither in the night?
What but design of darkness to appall?—
If design govern in a thing so small.

Questions for Writing and Discussion

1.   In an earlier version of this poem, called "White," Frost ended the sonnet with the line "Design, design! Do I use the word aright?" How is the word used in this version of the poem? Does it mean pattern? plan or intention?

2.   What does "characters" (line 4) mean?

3.   What is the effect of the last line of the poem? Does it seem to break away from the rest of the argument? Compare it with the last line of Frost's "Never Again Would Birds' Song Be the Same" (below).

NEVER AGAIN WOULD BIRDS' SONG BE THE SAME

Robert Frost

He would declare and could himself believe
That the birds there in all the garden round
From having heard the daylong voice of Eve
Had added to their own an oversound,

heal-all: a violet-blue wildflower, also called Prunella, or "self-heal"

Her tone of meaning but without the words.   5
Admittedly an eloquence so soft
Could only have had an influence on birds
When call or laughter carried it aloft
Be that as may be, she was in their song.
Moreover her voice upon their voices crossed   10
Had now persisted in the woods so long
That probably it never would be lost.
Never again would birds' song be the same.
And to do that to birds was why she came.

Discussion

Songs, words, and the quality somewhere between them that Frost calls "tone of meaning" are the subjects of this sonnet. One result of the Fall from Paradise has been the loss to nature of its own song, which was innocent of meaning, and the addition to it of human meaning without human words. The last two lines suggest, first, that the "influence" of human emotions has made nature participate in—by echoing—human complexities; and second, that while this is a loss for nature (something Eve does *to* birds, not *for* them), it is also a gain when we regard nature with human eyes and ears—which is of course the only way we can regard it.

This is a very serious myth-making poem. It describes the supposed occasion upon which nature first started to appear human: when birds' noises became "song" (or when running brooks started to "babble" or "chatter," the wind to "whisper" or "sigh" in trees, and so forth). But it is also a poem that is always struggling with its own playfulness. It hints that Eve's influence on birds was part of a providential scheme, which the speaker has come to reveal. The "he" of the opening line is Adam, who is uneasy with the daring of imagination—"He would declare and could himself believe"—and the speaker of the poem begins to think and speak for Adam. He goes through an elaborate hedging with which he nevertheless makes his version of the myth of Adam and Eve in paradise as persuasive as possible. (John Milton, in *Paradise Lost,* had shown them to be in total harmony with an environment which had not yet become humanized as Nature.) Those strangely casual and conversational-sounding words, "Admittedly," "moreover," and the phrase "be that as may be," are symptoms of this struggle between the wondrous and the skeptical; they are interjections of an easy tone of rational argument.

"Admittedly" . . . and we expect the voice to continue "admittedly, this is all Adam's little story that he's preparing for Eve, out of love for her." But the proposition that the speaker grants is directed toward the story itself, not toward the frame of how it got to be told; it continues, "admittedly, qualities of human voice could only have been imprinted on nature when some deep emotional force made the utterance sublime or lofty." (The word "aloft" is not merely picturesque or archaic here.) In other words, no language like "pass the lettuce, Adam" could ever have had "an influence on birds."

One interpretation of these gambits might be that the division between the naturalness of song and the artificiality of words has gone as far as it can go in the speaker. He belongs thoroughly to the world of words—of "admittedly" and "moreover." But it could also be argued that the division between song and words, which seemed unnatural before the Fall, has now come to seem part of our nature. This would account for the ease with which those words fall into the poem's strict metrical pattern.

The final lines present a fascinating instance of the kind of closing couplet which seems to divide itself in half logically (like the one at the end of Sir Philip Sidney's "Who Will in Fairest Book," p. 385). The penultimate line, which also gives Frost's poem its title, would seem to sum it all up. But we have forgotten Adam, whom we left at the end of the first line. His playful remark—"I do declare, Eve, those birds must have learned to sing from you"—the easy kind of joking compliment that is still part of the rhetoric of affection, here becomes a myth, a story with a meaning about our lives and our world, which Adam "could himself believe." He is almost a kind of poet as maker-of-explanations (in contrast to, say, the poet as giver-of-names portrayed in John Hollander's "Adam's Task," p. 645). But in working through this original notion, in following the process by which the poem takes seriously the playful fable—almost as if to say "Now suppose that little story were true, what then?"—we have moved through the admittedlys and moreovers and forgotten what Eve meant for Adam in the first place. The very last line, capping the climax of the previous one, brings us back, wittily and outrageously, to that: it was to be, as the bible says, "a help meet for Adam" that Eve was created, not "to do that to birds." But in a very deep sense, perhaps "to do that to birds" was a necessary and crucial part of human existence in paradise, particularly if we view Adam and Eve not as the First Man and the First Woman, but as two component parts of, and partners in, human existence.

Repetition and Refrain

No matter what its form or apparent "subject," poetry constantly directs our attention to what we would consider simple, primary, basic, or elementary in human experience, but almost always with a view to reminding us that the truth is never simple. Very complex poetic visions or interpretations of basic processes like death and love make use of devices which can be themselves intricate or simple. Repetition is such a device; it is as primitive as the pounding of drum beats, which can hammer on our feelings or our understanding; and yet repetitions, spaced at the right intervals and in varying contexts, can have soothing or otherwise pleasant effects. Some of the most complicated poems will employ patterns of repetition, either in the regular recurrences of refrains—marking out stanzas or other units like the chimes of a clock—or in arrangements of other kinds.

Repeating something often enough can make its meaning seem less important because more predictable; repeating it a few times can make it more meaningful. Apparent repetitions, because of changes in the meaning of what is repeated, can have a very different effect from the original statement. For example, when Othello, in Shakespeare's tragedy, is about to kill his wife because of her supposed infidelity, he enters her room with a candle and says "Put out the light, and then put out the light." The first statement is literal—he is referring to the night light which he will extinguish; the second is figurative—it refers to the light of life.

The following group of poems uses formal refrain and informal patterns of repetition in various ways. (The Note on Prosody contains a detailed discussion of some of these forms.) What is important throughout is the range of meanings that the actual fact of repetition displays—from a kind of merely "musical" *fa-la-la* to shifts of sense like Othello's.

CHERRY-RIPE

Thomas Campion

There is a garden in her face,
    Where roses and white lilies grow;
A heavenly paradise is that place,
    Wherein all pleasant fruits do flow.
There cherries grow which none may buy,   5
Till 'Cherry-ripe' themselves do cry.°

Those cherries fairly do enclose
    Of orient° pearl a double row,
Which when her lovely laughter shows,
    They look like rosebuds filled with snow.   10
Yet them nor peer nor prince can buy,
Till 'Cherry-ripe' themselves do cry.

Her eyes like angels watch them still;
    Her brows like bended bows do stand,
Threatening with piercing frowns to kill   15
    All that attempt with eye or hand
Those sacred cherries to come nigh,
Till 'Cherry-ripe' themselves do cry.

Questions for Writing and Discussion

1. This kind of extended comparison is called a *conceit.* (The word is related to "concept.") In the comparison of the face to the garden, what are the cherries and the pearls? What, figuratively speaking, constitutes buying the cherries in this case? Why is it that "none may buy" until the cherries sing their own sales commercial, as it were?

2. Comment on "heavenly" in line 3. What does it mean here?

3. Angels were set at the gates of Paradise to prevent Adam and Eve from reentering. Comment on line 13 and its place in the conceit.

4. Trace the slight changes of tone in the refrain. How does the content of the stanzas influence this changing tone?

cry: to call out one's wares as a peddler does   **orient:** shining

SONG

Thomas Carew

Ask me no more where Jove bestows,
When June is past, the fading rose;
For in your beauty's orient deep
These flowers, as in their causes, sleep.

Ask me no more whither do stray   5
The golden atoms of the day;
For in pure love heaven did prepare
Those powders to enrich your hair.

Ask me no more whither doth haste
The nightingale when May is past;   10
For in your sweet dividing throat
She winters and keeps warm her note.

Ask me no more where those stars 'light
That downwards fall in dead of night;
For in your eyes they sit, and there   15
Fixèd become as in their sphere.

Ask me no more if east or west
The Phoenix builds her spicy nest;
For unto you at last she flies,
And in your fragrant bosom dies.   20

ASK ME NO MORE

Alfred, Lord Tennyson

Ask me no more: the moon may draw the sea;
The cloud may stoop from heaven and take the shape,
With fold to fold, of mountain or of cape;
But O too fond, when have I answered thee?
  Ask me no more.   5

Ask me no more: what answer should I give?
I love not hollow cheek or faded eye:
Yet, O my friend, I will not have thee die!
Ask me no more, lest I should bid thee live;
  Ask me no more.   10

Ask me no more: thy fate and mine are sealed;

I strove against the stream and all in vain;
Let the great river take me to the main.
No more, dear love, for at a touch I yield;
                    Ask me no more.   15

Questions for Writing and Discussion

Both of these poems start out with the same phrase, although in the second it is a kind of refrain, repeated not only initially but at the ends of stanzas. In Carew's poem, the phrase introduces a repeated form of question—"Don't ask me what happens to beautiful event A, B, or C when it is over." The second half of each stanza takes this up with an unstated "Why not? Well, —" and an explanation: "They have all been translated into some feature of the beauty of the woman being praised."

The beautiful things in question are related in several ways:

1. They are all transient
2. They are cyclical in their disappearance and return
3. They are preserved during their term of absence (the period of the roses' "sleep" in the fourth line) *by being associated with the lady's beauty.*

This association is figurative, and the poem is wittily suggesting that the falling stars don't go out because they survive in the metaphor of *starry eyes.* And so with all the stanzas.

Notice, too, that the associations are almost clichés (and were so even in Carew's time): the poem is all the more effective in avoiding the simple statement of those trite gestures of praise (e.g., "your voice is like a nightingale's"). Instead, it says something more outrageous—"When May is over and the nightingale no longer sings, she is transformed, as it were, into the concept of herself as Vocal Beauty, and *thereby* "in your throat." And so with all the stanzas.

Comparisons to the phoenix were popular in the seventeenth century. The mythical bird generally stood for resurrection. As the last of Carew's comparisons, it underlines one more subtle, but sharp, point: these famous, gorgeous happenings all "vanish" or "die" and become poetic metaphors for the unnamed woman's beauty. But they will all reappear in nature (metaphorically awaken from death or sleep). They thus become physical actualities again—and are thereby "resurrected"—instead of remaining merely beautiful language about feminine beauty.

Coming at the end of the poem, this point may cause us to reflect on the purpose of poems—what happens after they are over—as well. Complex statements about human life and experience "fall," "die," break, or trail off. Perhaps we *must* ask, at least once more, where they go: into the memory? the mind? the intellect?

Tennyson's poem "echoes" Carew's. But the echoing refrain is used in a very different way, for a very different kind of poem. For one thing, this is both a bit of a song and a bit of a dramatic monologue (see p. 442). The speaker is a woman, and the man she addresses has been doing the asking. But *we* must ask: is he asking her something? or asking something *of* her?

1.   The "hollow cheek" and "faded eye" in line 7 are traditionally associated with pining away for unrequited love. Do the images in lines 1–2 have anything to do with this? What do they suggest about the relations between men and women?

2.   In lines 12–13, what does the force of water currents have to do with erotic feelings? With conflicting emotions?

3.   Does Tennyson's refrain gather any meaning as it is repeated throughout the poem? What about the very last repetition?

VERSES IN THE STYLE OF THE DRUIDS°

Sir Walter Scott

I ask'd of my harp, "Who hath injured thy chords?"°
And she replied, "The crooked finger, which I mocked in my tune."
A blade of silver may be bended—a blade of steel abideth:
Kindness fadeth away, but vengeance endureth.

The sweet taste of mead° passeth from the lips,   5
But they are long corroded by the juice of wormwood;°
The lamb is brought to the shambles,° but the wolf rangeth the
        mountain;
Kindness fadeth away, but vengeance endureth.

I asked the red-hot iron, when it glimmer'd on the anvil,
"Wherefore glowest thou longer than the firebrand?"   10
"I was born in the dark mine, and the brand in the pleasant
        greenwood."
Kindness fadeth away, but vengeance endureth.

I ask'd the green oak of the assembly wherefore its boughs were dry
        and sear'd like the horns of the stag:
And it show'd me that a small worm had gnaw'd its roots.
The boy who remembered the scourge undid the wicket of the castle
        at midnight.   15
Kindness fadeth away, but vengeance endureth.

Verses . . . Druids: Supposedly in the manner of the poetry of the pre-Christian cult of England, venerating oak groves and mistletoe **chords:** archaic form for "strings" (of a musical instrument) **mead:** fermented drink made from honey **wormwood:** a bitter bark **shambles:** slaughterhouse

Lightning destroyeth temples, though their spires pierce the clouds;
Storms destroy armadas, though their sails intercept the gale.
He that is in his glory falleth, and that by a contemptible enemy.
Kindness fadeth away, but vengeance endureth.   20

Questions for Writing and Discussion

1.   The language of these lines is quite Biblical. Is their wisdom that of The Book of Proverbs? In what sort of society would they constitute good counsel?

2.   Specifically, how does "vengeance" endure or prevail in the two "proverbs" of the fourth stanza? in the third?

3.   The verse form of these lines has no regular measure or beat. Is there anything else about their organization which seems to give the lines all a similar form?

LONG-LEGGED FLY

William Butler Yeats

That civilisation may not sink,
Its great battle lost,
Quiet the dog, tether the pony
To a distant post;
Our master Caesar is in the tent   5
Where the maps are spread,
His eyes fixed upon nothing,
A hand under his head.
Like a long-legged fly upon the stream
His mind moves upon silence.   10

That the topless towers° be burnt
And men recall that face,
Move most gently if move you must
In this lonely place.
She thinks, part woman, three parts a child,   15
That nobody looks; her feet
Practise a tinker shuffle
Picked up on a street.
Like a long-legged fly upon the stream
Her mind moves upon silence.   20

topless towers: of Troy—Yeats is quoting the famous lines with which Marlowe's *Dr. Faustus* greets Helen of Troy: "Is this the face that launched a thousand ships/ And burned the topless towers of Ilium?"

That girls at puberty may find
The first Adam in their thought,
Shut the door of the Pope's chapel,
Keep those children out.
There on that scaffolding reclines   25
Michael Angelo.
With no more sound than the mice make
His hand moves to and fro.
Like a long-legged fly upon the stream
His mind moves upon silence.   30

Questions for Writing and Discussion

1. The form of each of these stanzas might be diagrammed as:
    a. Hush! Genius at work!
    b. The genius is shown at a characteristic moment
    c. The refrain
What is the remarkable person actively *doing* in the second four lines of each
stanza? How would each of them ordinarily be represented, in a heroic poem or in
a public statue, for example?

2. What aspects of human genius do Caesar, Helen, and Michelangelo represent?
Is the order of the stanzas significant?

3. Does the refrain gain or lose significance as it is repeated? Does it become
more like a repeated "tra-la-la," or does the comparison stated in it take on new
dimensions? What makes that comparison particularly effective in this poem?

DO NOT GO GENTLE INTO THAT GOOD NIGHT

Dylan Thomas

Do not go gentle into that good night,
Old age should burn and rave at close of day;
Rage, rage against the dying of the light.

Though wise men at their end know dark is right,
Because their words had forked no lightning they   5
Do not go gentle into that good night.

Good men, the last wave by, crying how bright
Their frail deeds might have danced in a green bay,
Rage, rage against the dying of the light.

Wild men who caught and sang the sun in flight,   10

And learn, too late, they grieved it on its way,
Do not go gentle into that good night.

Grave man, near death, who see with blinding sight
Blind eyes could blaze like meteors and be gay,
Rage, rage against the dying of the light.   15

And you, my father, there on the sad height,
Curse, bless, me now with your fierce tears, I pray.
Do not go gentle into that good night.
Rage, rage against the dying of the light.

Questions for Writing and Discussion

1. This poem is a *villanelle* in form (see p. 593): it has two refrains recurring alternately. As stated in lines 1–3 and 18–19, do they produce declarative or imperative sentences? What happens in lines 5–6 to change this?

2. The middle four tercets, or groups of three lines, envision the different ways of life—and of approaching death—of four different kinds of men. Each is summed up in a powerful but dense image; each of those images is a miniature fable or parable. Discuss each one.

3. In lines 5–6, "wise men" and "words" are related; is there any such parallel connection with the other men? Is there a pun on "grave" in line 13? Is it meant to be witty?

ON THE HILL BELOW THE LIGHTHOUSE

James Dickey

Now I can be sure of my sleep;
I have lost the blue sea in my eyelids.
From a place in the mind too deep
For thought, a light like a wind is beginning.
        Now I can be sure of my sleep.   5

When the moon is held strongly within it,
The eye of the mind opens gladly.
Day changes to dark, and is bright,
And miracles trust to the body,
        When the moon is held strongly within it.   10

A woman comes true when I think her.
Her eyes on the window are closing.
She has dressed the stark wood of a chair.

Her form and my body are facing.
   A woman comes true when I think her.   15

Shade swings, and she lies against me.
The lighthouse has opened its brain.
A browed light travels the sea.
Her clothes on the chair spread their wings.
   Shade swings, and she lies against me.   20

Let us lie in returning light,
As a bright arm sweeps through the moon.
The sun is dead, thinking of night
Swung round like a thing on a chain.
   Let us lie in returning light.   25

Let us lie where your angel is walking
In shadow, from wall onto wall,
Cast forth from your off-cast clothing
To pace the dim room where we fell.
   Let us lie where your angel is walking.   30

Coming back, coming back, going over.
An arm turns the light world around
The dark. Again we are waiting to hover
In a blaze in the mind like a wind
   Coming back, coming back, going over.   35

   Now I can be sure of my sleep;
   The moon is held strongly within it.
   A woman comes true when I think her.
   Shade swings, and she lies against me.
   Let us lie in returning light;   40
   Let us lie where your angel is walking,
   Coming back, coming back, going over.

Questions for Writing and Discussion

1.   The speaker in this poem imagines—somewhere between thinking and dreaming—a woman coming to him to make love at night. At the same time he watches the periodic sweep of a lighthouse beam across sea, sky, and land. Where in the poem are these sweeps indicated? How, in the imagined realm of the poet's night thoughts, are they transformed by imagery?

2.   The pattern of repeated lines in this poem is quite intricate. The first line of each stanza is repeated as a refrain. But also notice how lines 10 and 35 in particular modify their meanings slightly on repetition because of their relation to the preceding lines. What is the effect of the refrains being gathered into a final stanza at the end?

3. Does the poem rhyme? How would you characterize the rhythm of its lines? the larger rhythm of its stanzas and themes? Do you detect the periodic sweep of the light beam in any other elements of the poem?

MNEMOSYNE

Trumbull Stickney

It's autumn in the country I remember.

How warm a wind blew here about the ways!°
And shadows on the hillside lay to slumber
During the long sun-sweetened summer-days.

It's cold abroad the country I remember.   5

The swallows veering skimmed the golden grain
At midday with a wing aslant and limber;
And yellow cattle browsed upon the plain.

It's empty down the country I remember.

I had a sister lovely in my sight: 10
Her hair was dark, her eyes were very sombre;
We sang together in the woods at night.

It's lonely in the country I remember.

The babble of our children fills my ears,
And on our hearth I stare the perished ember   15
To flames that show all starry thro' my tears.

It's dark about the country I remember.

There are the mountains where I lived. The path
Is slushed with cattle-tracks and fallen timber,
The stumps are twisted by the tempests' wrath.   20

But° that I knew these places are my own,
I'd ask how came such wretchedness to cumber
The earth, and I to people it alone.
It rains across the country I remember.

Questions for Writing and Discussion

1. *Mnemosyne,* "memory," was in Greek mythology the mother of the Muses, which is to say that, in the language of mythology, memory is a necessary cause of

ways: roads   But: except

art. The refrain line maintains that the country is a remembered region of the world or of life. Does considering the meaning of lines 21–23 raise any questions about this?

2.   What is the exact grammatical sense of "I stare the perished ember / To flames that . . ." (lines 15–16)? What shift of time and place occurs at lines 14–15?

3.   Is "sister" in line 10 literal? Where in the Bible does the phrase "my sister, my spouse" occur?

4.   The refrain, with its variations, works as both a kind of title for the three lines of verse which follow it and a burden or summation of what has gone before. Trace the connection of each repetition of the refrain with the preceding and following lines.

5.   In each tercet, the middle line rhymes with the refrain. Which of these, unlike the others, rhymes exactly?

SESTINA

Elizabeth Bishop

September rain falls on the house.
In the failing light, the old grandmother
sits in the kitchen with the child
beside the Little Marvel Stove,
reading the jokes from the almanac,   5
laughing and talking to hide her tears.

She thinks that her equinoctial tears
and the rain that beats on the roof of the house
were both foretold by the almanac,
but only known to a grandmother.   10
The iron kettle sings on the stove.
She cuts some bread and says to the child,

It's time for tea now; but the child
is watching the teakettle's small hard tears
dance like mad on the hot black stove,   15
the way the rain must dance on the house.
Tidying up, the old grandmother
hangs up the clever almanac

on its string. Birdlike, the almanac
hovers half open above the child,   20
hovers above the old grandmother
and her teacup full of dark brown tears.
She shivers and says she thinks the house
feels chilly, and puts more wood in the stove.

It was to be, says the Marvel Stove.   25
I know what I know, says the almanac.
With crayons the child draws a rigid house
and a winding pathway. Then the child
puts in a man with buttons like tears
and shows it proudly to the grandmother.   30

But secretly, while the grandmother
busies herself about the stove,
the little moons fall down like tears
from between the pages of the almanac
into the flower bed the child   35
has carefully placed in the front of the house.

Time to plant tears, says the almanac.
The grandmother sings to the marvellous stove
and the child draws another inscrutable house.

Questions for Writing and Discussion

1.   What does the poet mean by "equinoctial tears" in line 7? The causes of the
grandmother's weeping are not shown in the poem. What might some of these be?

2.   A *sestina* is an intricate verse form from the Middle Ages. It uses six stanzas of
six lines, the final words of the first six lines repeated in a series of changes
throughout the following stanzas; the pattern involves the last word of each stanza
being the final word of the first line of the next stanza. A final short stanza of three
lines contains all six words, three of them in the middle, three at the end of the
lines. Is the repetition merely formal in this poem? Do the repeated words act like
those of a repeated refrain? Do changes in meaning or use affect the "musical"
quality of the repetition?

3.   Aside from the terminal words, what other repetitions and variations occur in
the poem? What seems to be occurring in the sixth stanza? What other transforma-
tions momentarily occur in the poem's imagery?

SESTINA (AFTER DANTE)
Of the Lady Pietra degli Scrovigni°

Dante Gabriel Rossetti

To the dim light and the large circle of shade
I have clomb,° and to the whitening of the hills,

Pietra degli Scrovigni: her Christian name means "stone" in Italian   clomb: climbed

There where we see no colour in the grass.
Natheless my longing loses not its green,
It has so taken root in the hard stone   5
Which talks and hears as though it were a lady.

Utterly frozen is this youthful lady,
Even as the snow that lies within the shade;
For she is no more moved than is the stone
By the sweet season which makes warm the hills   10
And alters them afresh from white to green,
Covering their sides again with flowers and grass.

When on her hair she sets a crown of grass
The thought has no more room for other lady,
Because she weaves the yellow with the green   15
So well that Love sits down there in the shade,—
Love who has shut me in among low hills
Faster than between walls of granite-stone.

She is more bright than is a precious stone;
The wound she gives may not be healed with grass.   20
I therefore have fled far o'er plains and hills
For refuge from so dangerous a lady;
But from her sunshine nothing can give shade,—
Not any hill, nor wall, nor summer-green.

A while ago, I saw her dressed in green,—   25
So fair, she might have wakened in a stone
This love which I do feel even for her shade;
And therefore, as one woos a graceful lady,
I wooed her in a field that was all grass
Girdled about with very lofty hills.   30

Yet shall the streams turn back and climb the hills
Before Love's flame in this damp wood and green
Burn, as it burns within a youthful lady,
For my sake, who would sleep away in stone
My life, or feed like beasts upon the grass,   35
Only to see her garments cast a shade.

How dark soe'er the hills throw out their shade,
Under her summer-green the beautiful lady
Covers it, like a stone covered in grass.

Questions for Writing and Discussion

1. This is another example of the form which Elizabeth Bishop employed in the preceding poem. Rossetti's poem is a translation from a great lyric by Dante

Alighieri, accurate and yet a magnificent English poem in its own right. How do the final words of the lines differ in character from those in the contemporary poet's sestina? Do any of the words in Rossetti's poem almost rhyme?

2.   In line 39, the phrase "like a stone covered in grass" may apply to the shade or the lady. Discuss the way the image applies in each case. Does anything else in the poem lead you to think that it might apply to both?

3.   What changes in connotation or quality do the words at the ends of lines undergo as they reappear throughout the poem? (Start out with "shade," which can mean "shadow" or even "image" or "ghost.")

4.   How does the tone of the poem change in the sixth stanza? Where else in the poem does the narrator also display shifts of feeling for the lady?

THE POET'S CAT

Christopher Smart

For I will consider my Cat Jeoffry.
For he is the servant of the Living God duly and daily serving him.
For at the first glance of the glory of God in the East he worships in
    his way.
For is this done by wreathing his body seven times round with
    elegant quickness.
For then he leaps up to catch the musk, which is the blessing of God
    upon his prayer.   5
For he rolls upon prank to work it in.
For having done duty and received blessing he begins to consider
    himself.
For this he performs in ten degrees.
For first he looks upon his fore-paws to see if they are clean.
For secondly he kicks up behind to clear away there.   10
For thirdly he works it upon stretch with the fore-paws extended.
For fourthly he sharpens his paws by wood.
For fifthly he washes himself.
For sixthly he rolls upon wash.
For seventhly he fleas himself, that he may not be interrupted upon
    the beat.°   15
For eighthly he rubs himself against a post.
For ninthly he looks up for his instructions.
For tenthly he goes in quest of food.
For having considered God and himself he will consider his
    neighbour.
For if he meets another cat he will kiss her in kindness.   20

upon the beat: in his activity

For when he takes his prey he plays with it to give it a chance.
For one mouse in seven escapes by his dallying.
For when his day's work is done his business more properly begins.
For he keeps the Lord's watch in the night against the adversary.
For he counteracts the powers of darkness by his electrical skin and
      glaring eyes. 25
For he counteracts the Devil, who is death, by brisking about the life.
For in his morning orisons he loves the sun and the sun loves him.
For he is of the tribe of Tiger.
For the Cherub Cat is a term of the Angel Tiger.
For he has the subtlety and hissing of a serpent, which in goodness
      he suppresses. 30
For he will not do destruction if he is well-fed, neither will he spit
      without provocation.
For he purrs in thankfulness, when God tells him he's a good Cat.
For he is an instrument for the children to learn benevolence upon.
For every house is incomplete without him and a blessing is lacking
      in the spirit.
For the Lord commanded Moses concerning the cats at the departure
      of the Children of Israel from Egypt. 35
For every family had one cat at least in the bag.
For the English Cats are the best in Europe.
For he is the cleanest in the use of his fore-paws of any quadruped.
For the dexterity of his defence is an instance of the love of God to
      him exceedingly.
For he is the quickest to his mark of any creature. 40
For he is tenacious of his point.
For he is a mixture of gravity and waggery.
For he knows that God is his Saviour.
For there is nothing sweeter than his peace when at rest.
For there is nothing brisker than his life when in motion. 45
For he is of the Lord's poor and so indeed is he called by benevo-
      lence perpetually—Poor Jeoffry! poor Jeoffry! the rat has bit
      thy throat.
For I bless the name of the Lord Jesus that Jeoffry is better.
For the divine spirit comes about his body to sustain it in complete
      cat.
For his tongue is exceeding pure so that it has in purity what it wants
      in music.
For he is docile and can learn certain things. 50
For he can set up with gravity which is patience upon approbation.
For he can fetch and carry, which is patience in employment.
For he can jump over a stick which is patience upon proof positive.
For he can spraggle upon waggle at the word of command.
For he can jump from an eminence into his master's bosom. 55
For he can catch the cork and toss it again.

For he is hated by the hypocrite and miser.
For the former is afraid of detection.
For the latter refuses the charge.
For he camels his back to bear the first notion of business.   60
For he is good to think on, if a man would express himself neatly.
For he made a great figure in Egypt for his signal services.
For he killed the Ichneumon-rat° very pernicious by land.
For his ears are so acute that they sting again.
For from this proceeds the passing quickness of his attention.   65
For by stroking of him I have found out electricity.
For I perceived God's light about him both wax and fire.
For the electrical fire is the spiritual substance, which God sends
    from heaven to sustain the bodies both of man and beast.
For God has blessed him in the variety of his movements.
For, though he cannot fly, he is an excellent clamberer.   70
For his motions upon the face of the earth are more than any other
    quadruped.
For he can tread to all the measures upon the music.
For he can swim for life.
For he can creep.

Questions for Writing and Discussion

1. This is part of an experimental poem by an eighteenth-century poet, writing while confined in a madhouse. (Some of the strange words and expressions are usual for his day, some very idiosyncratic and personal.) The verse form is influenced by the unmeasured but still patterned poetry of the Old Testament. Indeed, the whole poem is like a secular Psalm. What kind of patterns can you discern among various groups of lines here? (The common opening, "For," which links them all, is called an *anaphora*.) See p. 587.

2. Does this seem to be about an actual cat? or about an abstract idea of catness? Has the poet observed cats very closely?

3. Which of these lines are literal? Which figurative? How does the whole section develop the theme of the first two lines?

DOMINATION OF BLACK

Wallace Stevens

At night, by the fire,
The colors of the bushes

Ichneumon-rat: a kind of weasel

And of the fallen leaves,
Repeating themselves,
Turned in the room,   5
Like the leaves themselves
Turning in the wind.
Yes: but the color of the heavy hemlocks
Came striding.
And I remembered the cry of the peacocks.   10

The colors of their tails
Were like the leaves themselves
Turning in the wind,
In the twilight wind.
They swept over the room,   15
Just as they flew from the boughs of the hemlocks
Down to the ground.
I heard them cry—the peacocks.
Was it a cry against the twilight
Or against the leaves themselves   20
Turning in the wind,
Turning as the flames
Turned in the fire,
Turning as the tails of the peacocks
Turned in the loud fire,   25
Loud as the hemlocks
Full of the cry of the peacocks?
Or was it a cry against the hemlocks?

Out of the window,
I saw how the planets gathered   30
Like the leaves themselves
Turning in the wind.
I saw how the night came,
Came striding like the color of the heavy hemlocks
I felt afraid.   35
And I remembered the cry of the peacocks.

Questions for Writing and Discussion

1. The only color named in the poem is in the title. What are the other colors to which the poem keeps referring? How do the relations among these colors, and of them to black, develop during the course of the poem?

2. Sound first enters the poem explicitly when the speaker is reminded of "the

cry of the peacocks" (line 10)—not of their color or shape. What seems to remind him of them? How does sound interweave with color in the rest of the poem?

3. Of what is the speaker afraid in line 35?

4. What does the speaker agree to in line 8 when he says "Yes"? And how does he go on to qualify his assent? What does the "but" clause mean?

5. Consider the various kinds of "turning" in the poem. The word itself seems a kind of refrain, starting out with the *colors* of the leaves turning in the wind but emerging definitely as "the leaves themselves" do so. How would you connect this refrain with the blackness of the title, with lines 33–34, and with your answer to question 3 above? Are there other refrains?

Narrative

The earliest oral poetry was sung, and often danced as well. Prayers, work songs, spells and enchantments, riddles, all of which were originally oral, continue to exist in written, literary poetry. One of the most important modes of oral poetry was narrative; epic tales in both our classical and Biblical traditions were composed and sung in lines, with an instrumental accompaniment.

The survival of narrative poetry in English literature was largely occasioned by the English and Scottish ballad, a narrative form with its roots in the Middle Ages, but which achieved the form in which we know it rather later than that. By the eighteenth century, most ballads conformed to the so-called *ballad stanza* of four lines rhymed *abcb,* and some had refrains while some did not; most told tragic or violent stories, reflecting heroic or demonic visions of former days, and preserving old themes and motifs.

But the eighteenth century was also the period of the rise of the novel. By 1800, narrative poems began to be associated with supernatural, highly imaginative story telling as well as with some of the heroic aspects of simple life, leaving the more direct representation of men and women in society to prose fiction. The title of the great experimental book of poems by William Wordsworth and Samuel Taylor Coleridge, *Lyrical Ballads* (1798), suggests that narrative verse could become evocative, rather than primarily informative or creative of suspense. The more fully developed and complex the novel became in the following centuries, the less straightforward and more allusive narrative poems grew. Romantic and later poetic stories range far beyond the ballad in form and structure, recalling variously heroic romance, epic, and even, in some of the poems which follow (Browning, Rossetti, Hardy, Robinson), the narrative methods and concerns of the modern short story.

Yet the English ballad remains a central form in our literature, and we may well start out with an example of it. A favorite structural device of the ballad is the catechism, a rhythm of question and answer overheard by the reader or

413

listener. Here, with its two refrains throughout, is one of the most famous ballads in the language.

LORD RANDAL

Anonymous

O where ha' you been, Lord Randal my son?
And where ha' you been, my handsome young man?
I ha' been at the greenwood; mother, make my bed soon,
For I'm wearied wi' hunting and fain wad lie down.

An' wha met ye there, Lord Randal my son?   5
An' wha met you there, my handsome young man?
O I met wi my true-love; mother, mak my bed soon,
For I'm wearied wi' huntin' an' fain wad lie down.

And what did she give you, Lord Randal my son?
And what did she give you, my handsome young man?   10
Eels fried in a pan; mother, mak my bed soon,
For I'm wearied wi' huntin' and fain wad lie down.

And wha gat your leavins, Lord Randal my son?
And wha gat your leavins, my handsome young man?
My hawks and my hounds; mother, mak my bed soon,   15
For I'm wearied wi' hunting and fain wad lie down.

And what becam of them, Lord Randal my son?
And what becam of them, my handsome young man?
They stretched their legs out an' died; mother, mak my bed soon,
For I'm wearied wi' huntin' and fain wad lie down.   20

O I fear you are poisoned, Lord Randal my son,
I fear you are poisoned, my handsome young man.
O yes, I am poisoned; mother, mak my bed soon,
For I'm sick at the heart and I fain wad lie down.

What d'ye leave to your mother, Lord Randal my son?   25
What d'ye leave to your mother, my handsome young man?
Four and twenty milk kye; mother, mak my bed soon,
For I'm sick at the heart and I fain wad lie down.

What d'ye leave to your sister, Lord Randal my son?
What d'ye leave to your sister, my handsome young man?   30
My gold and my silver; mother, make my bed soon,
For I'm sick at the heart an' I fain wad lie down.

What d'ye leave to your brother, Lord Randal my son?
What d'ye leave to your brother, my handsome young man?
My houses and my lands; mother, mak my bed soon,   35
For I'm sick at the heart and I fain wad lie down.

What d'ye leave to your true-love, Lord Randal my son?
What d'ye leave to your true-love, my handsome young man?
I leave her hell and fire; mother, mak my bed soon,
For I'm sick at the heart and I fain wad lie down.   40

Questions for Writing and Discussion

1. What is the effect of the shift in the refrain at line 24?

2. How do the repetitions in the seventh, eight, and ninth stanzas work to build up toward the tenth and final one?

3. There are many versions of all these ballads, and "Lord Randal" has shown up in many guises over the centuries, in Britain and America (the hero variously known as Durandal, even Durango—you can see how these stories were all transmitted by ear). One recent version was an English music hall rendering in cockney dialect about "Henry, my son." One stanza went like this:

> Them eels was snakes, 'Enery my son,
> Them eels was snakes, my pretty one.
> Oooooooooow, dear muvver, Ooooow dear muvver,
> Ow muvver come quick, I'm gonna be sick, I'm gonna
>   lay down—and die,

Aside from the dialect, what dramatic gains or losses do you find in a version which includes this stanza?

'CHILDE ROLAND TO THE DARK TOWER CAME'
(See Edgar's Song in *Lear*)

Robert Browning

I
My first thought was, he lied in every word,
    That hoary cripple, with malicious eye
    Askance to watch the working of his lie
On mine, and mouth scarce able to afford
Suppression of the glee, that pursed and scored   5
    Its edge, at one more victim gained thereby.

II

What else should he be set for, with his staff?
   What, save to waylay with his lies, ensnare
   All travellers who might find him posted there,
And ask the road? I guessed what skull-like laugh   10
Would break, what crutch 'gin° write my epitaph
   For pastime in the dusty thoroughfare.

III

If at his counsel I should turn aside
   Into that ominous tract which, all agree,
   Hides the Dark Tower. Yet acquiescingly   15
I did turn as he pointed: neither pride
Nor hope rekindling at the end descried,
   So much as gladness that some end might be.

IV

For, what with my whole world-wide wandering,
   What with my search drawn out through years, my hope   20
   Dwindled into a ghost not fit to cope
With that obstreperous joy success would bring,—
I hardly tried now to rebuke the spring
   My heart made, finding failure in its scope.

V

As when a sick man very near to death   25
   Seems dead indeed, and feels begin and end
   The tears and takes the farewell of each friend,
And hears one bid the other go, draw breath
Freelier outside, ('since all is o'er,' he saith,
   'And the blow fallen no grieving can amend');   30

VI

While some discuss if near the other graves
   Be room enough for this, and when a day
   Suits best for carrying the corpse away,
With care about the banners, scarves and staves:
And still the man hears all, and only craves   35
   He may not shame such tender love and stay.

gin: begin to

VII

Thus, I had so long suffered in this quest,
　Heard failure prophesied so oft, been writ
　So many times among 'The Band'—to wit,
The knights who to the Dark Tower's search addressed　　40
Their steps—that just to fail as they, seemed best,
　And all the doubt was now—should I be fit?

VIII

So, quiet as despair, I turned from him,
　That hateful cripple, out of his highway
　Into the path he pointed. All the day　　45
Had been a dreary one at best, and dim
Was settling to its close, yet shot one grim
　Red leer to see the plain catch its estray.°

IX

For mark! no sooner was I fairly found
　Pledged to the plain, after a pace or two,　　50
　Than, pausing to throw backward a last view
O'er the safe road, 'twas gone; grey plain all round:
Nothing but plain to the horizon's bound.
　I might go on; nought else remained to do.

X

So, on I went. I think I never saw　　55
　Such starved ignoble nature; nothing throve:
　For flowers—as well expect a cedar grove!
But cockle, spurge,° according to their law
Might propagate their kind, with none to awe,
　You'd think; a burr had been a treasure-trove.　　60

XI

No! penury, inertness and grimace,
　In some strange sort, were the land's portion. 'See
　Or shut your eyes,' said Nature peevishly,
'It nothing skills: I cannot help my case:
'Tis the Last Judgment's fire must cure this place,　　65
　Calcine° its clods and set my prisoners free.'

---

estray: a strayed animal, vulnerable for having left the flock **cockle, spurge:** rough
weeds **Calcine:** pulverize

XII

If there pushed any ragged thistle-stalk
   Above its mates, the head was chopped; the bents°
   Were jealous else. What made those holes and rents
In the dock's harsh swarth leaves, bruised as to baulk   70
All hope of greenness? 'tis a brute must walk
   Pashing° their life out, with a brute's intents.

XIII

As for the grass, it grew as scant as hair
   In leprosy; thin dry blades pricked the mud
   Which underneath looked kneaded up with blood.   75
One stiff blind horse, his every bone a-stare,
Stood stupefied, however he came there:
   Thrust out past service from the devil's stud!

XIV

Alive? he might be dead for aught I know,
   With that red gaunt and colloped° neck a-strain,   80
   And shut eyes underneath the rusty mane;
Seldom went such grotesqueness with such woe;
I never saw a brute I hated so;
   He must be wicked to deserve such pain.

XV

I shut my eyes and turned them on my heart.   85
   As a man calls for wine before he fights,
   I asked one draught of earlier, happier sights,
Ere fitly I could hope to play my part.
Think first, fight afterwards—the soldier's art:
   One taste of the old time sets all to rights.   90

XVI

Not it! I fancied Cuthbert's reddening face
   Beneath its garniture of curly gold,
   Dear fellow, till I almost felt him fold
An arm in mine to fix me to the place,
That way he used. Alas, one night's disgrace!   95
   Out went my heart's new fire and left it cold.

---

bents: coarse grass **Pashing:** trampling **colloped:** ridged

XVII

Giles then, the soul of honour—there he stands
 Frank as ten years ago when knighted first.
 What honest men should dare (he said) he durst.
Good—but the scene shifts—faugh! what hangman-hands   100
Pin to his breast a parchment? his own bands
 Read it. Poor traitor, spit upon and curst!

XVIII

Better this present than a past like that;
 Back therefore to my darkening path again!
 No sound, no sight as far as eye could strain.   105
Will the night send a howlet or a bat?
I asked: when something on the dismal flat
 Came to arrest my thoughts and change their train.

XIX

A sudden little river crossed my path
 As unexpected as a serpent comes.   110
 No sluggish tide congenial to the glooms;
This, as it frothed by, might have been a bath
For the fiend's glowing hoof—to see the wrath
 Of its black eddy bespate° with flakes and spumes.

XX

So petty yet so spiteful! All along,   115
 Low scrubby alders kneeled down over it:
 Drenched willows flung them headlong in a fit
Of mute despair, a suicidal throng:
The river which had done them all the wrong,
 Whate'er that was, rolled by, deterred no whit.   120

XXI

Which, while I forded,—good saints, how I feared
 To set my foot upon a dead man's cheek,
 Each step, or feel the spear I thrust to seek
For hollows, tangled in his hair or beard!
—It may have been a water-rat I speared,   125
 But, ugh! it sounded like a baby's shriek.

bespate: bespattered

XXII

Glad was I when I reached the other bank.
  Now for a better country. Vain presage!
  Who were the strugglers, what war did they wage,
Whose savage trample thus could pad the dank   130
Soil to a plash? Toads in a poisoned tank,
  Or wild cats in a red-hot iron cage—

XXIII

The fight must so have seemed in that fell cirque.°
  What penned them there, with all the plain to choose?
  No foot-print leading to the horrid mews,°   135
None out of it. Mad brewage set to work
Their brains, no doubt, like galley-slaves the Turk
  Pits for his pastime, Christians against Jews.

XXIV

And more than that—a furlong on—why, there!
  What bad use was that engine for, that wheel,   140
  Or brake, not wheel—that harrow fit to reel
Men's bodies out like silk? with all the air
Of Tophet's° tool, on earth left unaware,
  Or brought to sharpen its rusty teeth of steel.

XXV

Then came a bit of stubbed ground, once a wood,   145
  Next a marsh, it would seem, and now mere earth
  Desperate and done with; (so a fool finds mirth,
Makes a thing and then mars it, till his mood
Changes and off he goes!) within a rood°—
  Bog, clay and rubble, sand and stark black dearth.   150

XXVI

Now blotches rankling, coloured gay and grim,
  Now patches where some leanness of the soil's
  Broke into moss or substances like boils;
Then came some palsied oak, a cleft in him
Like a distorted mouth that splits its rim   155
  Gaping at death, and dies while it recoils.

---

cirque: circus   **mews:** a sort of narrow stable-area   **Tophet:** hell   **rood:** quarter-acre

XXVII

And just as far as ever from the end!
  Nought in the distance but the evening, nought
  To point my footstep further! At the thought,
A great black bird, Apollyon's° bosom-friend,   160
Sailed past, nor beat his wide wing dragon-penned°
  That brushed my cap—perchance the guide I sought.

XXVIII

For, looking up, aware I somehow grew,
  'Spite of the dusk, the plain had given place
  All round to mountains—with such name to grace   165
Mere ugly heights and heaps now stolen in view.
How thus they had surprised me,—solve it, you!
  How to get from them was no clearer case.

XXIX

Yet half I seemed to recognize some trick
  Of mischief happened to me, God knows when—   170
  In a bad dream perhaps. Here ended, then,
Progress this way. When, in the very nick
Of giving up, one time more, came a click
  As when a trap shuts—you're inside the den!

XXX

Burningly it came on me all at once,   175
  This was the place! those two hills on the right,
Crouched like two bulls locked horn in horn in fight;
While to the left, a tall scalped mountain . . . Dunce,
Dotard, a-dozing at the very nonce,
  After a life spent training for the sight!   180

XXXI

What in the midst lay but the Tower itself?
  The round squat turret, blind as the fool's heart,
  Built of brown stone, without a counterpart
In the whole world. The tempest's mocking elf
Points to the shipman thus the unseen shelf   185
  He strikes on, only when the timbers start.

Apollyon: a name for the Devil   **dragon-penned:** dragon-winged

XXXII

Not see? because of night perhaps?—why, day
  Came back again for that! before it left,
  The dying sunset kindled through a cleft:
The hills, like giants at a hunting, lay,   190
Chin upon hand, to see the game at bay,—
  'Now stab and end the creature—to the heft!'

XXXIII

Not hear? when noise was everywhere! it tolled
  Increasing like a bell. Names in my ears
  Of all the lost adventurers my peers,—   195
How such a one was strong, and such was bold,
And such was fortunate, yet each of old
  Lost, lost! one moment knelled the woe of years.

XXXIV

There they stood, ranged along the hill-sides, met
  To view the last of me, a living frame   200
  For one more picture! in a sheet of flame
I saw them and I knew them all. And yet
Dauntless the slug-horn° to my lips I set,
  And blew. *'Childe Roland to the Dark Tower came.'*

Questions for Writing and Discussion

1. The "Tower itself" is partially described in lines 181–84; what else do we know of the hero's quest? of his goal and its relation to the tower? Would the poem be stronger if that quest were for a treasure, a hidden land, a great religious relic, or to free another human being in a condition of terror?

2. The last line of the poem may be ambiguously punctuated. If the period after "blew" is made a colon, what effect would this have on the italicized words? What can they mean as the punctuation stands?

3. What is Roland's relation to the "the Band" first mentioned in stanza VII?

4. Childe Roland's journey takes him through unpleasant and menacing terrain. What kind of hostile regions are these? What are their specific dangers, and to what or whom are they dangerous?

5. What relation does this quest or mission story have to others you may have known since childhood—fairytale, fable, science-fiction adventure, etc.?

lug-horn: an imaginary instrument

6.   Discuss Roland's account of his adventure from the point of view of his tone in telling it and his reliability as a narrator. (You might consider this poem as a dramatic monologue, like "My Last Duchess" (p. 445), as well as a narrative.)

LA BELLE DAME SANS MERCI°
A Ballad

John Keats

O, what can ail thee, knight-at-arms,
    Alone and palely loitering?
The sedge° has withered from the lake,
    And no birds sing.

O, what can ail thee, knight-at-arms,   5
    So haggard and so woe-begone?
The squirrel's granary is full,
    And the harvest's done.

I see a lily on thy brow,
    With anguish moist and fever dew;   10
And on thy cheeks a fading rose
    Fast withereth too.

I met a lady in the meads,°
    Full beautiful—a faery's child,
Her hair was long, her foot was light,   15
    And her eyes were wild.

I made a garland for her head,
    And bracelets too, and fragrant zone;°
She looked at me as she did love,
    And made sweet moan.   20

I set her on my pacing steed,
    And nothing else saw all day long;
For sidelong would she bend, and sing
    A faery's song.

She found me roots of relish sweet,   25
    And honey wild, and manna dew,
And sure in language strange she said—
    'I love thee true.'

La Belle Dame Sans Merci: the beautiful lady without mercy   **sedge:** marsh grass   **meads:** meadows   **zone:** girdle

She took me to her elfin grot,°
  And there she wept and sighed full sore   30
And there I shut her wild wild eyes
  With kisses four.

And there she lullèd me asleep
  And there I dreamed—Ah! woe betide!
The latest dream I ever dreamed   35
  On the cold hill side.

I saw pale kings and princes too,
  Pale warriors, death-pale were they all;
They cried—'La Belle Dame sans Merci
  Hath thee in thrall!'   40

I saw their starved lips in the gloam,°
  With horrid warning gapèd wide,
And I awoke and found me here,
  On the cold hill's side.

And this is why I sojourn here   45
  Alone and palely loitering,
Though the sedge has withered from the lake,
  And no birds sing.

Questions for Writing and Discussion

1. How is the landscape at the opening of the poem made to correspond to the emotional state of the knight-at-arms? Has the knight sought out this landscape? Or has it sought him out?

2. Why do you think Keats used the curious expression, "fever dew" (line 10)? Does it correspond to any details of the landscape later in the poem (stanzas IV–XI)?

3. "Latest" (line 35) is an archaic word for "last"; but it also carries our more modern connotation of "too late." What advantage might Keats have seen in a word that covered both meanings?

4. In Milton's great poem, *Paradise Lost,* Adam dreams of Eden before actually setting eyes on it. In one of his letters, Keats made a celebrated comment on the nature of the imagination when he wrote: "The Imagination may be compared to Adam's dream—he awoke and found it truth." How might this comment be applied to the dream of the knight-at-arms?

5. Is the knight-at-arms, like the singer of Kubla Khan (p. 427), an object of dread to all who behold him? At what point in the poem does he seem most fiercely "possessed"—and why does he cease to be so?

grot: grotto or bower   gloam: twilight dusk

KUBLA KHAN:
Or, a Vision in a Dream. A Fragment.

Samuel Taylor Coleridge

The following fragment is here published at the request of a poet° of great and deserved celebrity, and, as far as the Author's own opinions are concerned, rather as a psychological curiosity, than on the ground of any supposed *poetic* merits.

In the summer of the year 1797, the Author, then in ill health, had retired to a lonely farm-house between Porlock and Linton, on the Exmoor confines of Somerset and Devonshire. In consequence of a slight indisposition, an anodyne had been prescribed, from the effects of which he fell asleep in his chair at the moment that he was reading the following sentence, or words of the same substance, in 'Purchas's Pilgrimage': 'Here the Khan Kubla commanded a palace to be built, and a stately garden thereunto. And thus ten miles of fertile ground were inclosed with a wall.'° The Author continued for about three hours in a profound sleep,° at least of the external senses, during which time he has the most vivid confidence, that he could not have composed less than from two to three hundred lines; if that indeed can be called composition in which all the images rose up before him as *things,* with a parallel production of the correspondent expressions, without any sensation or consciousness of effort. On awaking he appeared to himself to have a distinct recollection of the whole, and taking his pen, ink, and paper, instantly and eagerly wrote down the lines that are here preserved. At this moment he was unfortunately called out by a person on business from Porlock, and detained by him above an hour, and on his return to his room, found, to his no small surprise and mortification, that though he still retained some vague and dim recollection of the general purport of the vision, yet, with the exception of some eight or ten scattered lines and images, all the rest had passed away like the images on the surface of a stream into which a stone has been cast, but, alas! without the after restoration of the latter!

> Then all the charm
> Is broken—all that phantom-world so fair
> Vanishes, and a thousand circlets spread,
> And each mis-shape[s] the other. Stay awhile,
> Poor youth! who scarcely dar'st lift up thine eyes—

a poet: Lord Byron   **"Here . . . wall":** quoted by memory from Samuel Purchas, *Purchas His Pilgrimage* (1613); Coleridge also relied on Purchas' account of Alvadine, the Old Man of the Mountain, whose walled garden was a training ground for assassins whom he sent to murder his enemies   **profound sleep:** induced by opium, as Coleridge admitted in a manuscript note

The stream will soon renew its smoothness, soon
The visions will return! And lo, he stays,
And soon the fragments dim of lovely forms
Come trembling back, unite, and now once more
The pool becomes a mirror.

[From *The Picture; or, the Lover's Resolution,* 11. 91–100.]

Yet from the still surviving recollections in his mind, the Author has frequently purposed to finish for himself what had been originally, as it were, given to him. Σαμερον αδιον ασω [Αὔριον ἄδιον ἄσω° *1834*]: but the tomorrow is yet to come.

In Xanadu did Kubla Khan
A stately pleasure-dome decree:
Where Alph,° the sacred river, ran
Through caverns measureless to man
   Down to a sunless sea.   5
So twice five miles of fertile ground
With walls and towers were girdled round:
And there were gardens bright with sinuous rills,
Where blossomed many an incense-bearing tree;
And here were forests ancient as the hills,   10
Enfolding sunny spots of greenery.

But oh! that deep romantic chasm which slanted
Down the green hill athwart a cedarn cover!
A savage place! as holy and enchanted
As e'er beneath a waning moon was haunted   15
By woman wailing for her demon-lover!
And from this chasm, with ceaseless turmoil seething,
As if this earth in fast thick pants were breathing,
A mighty fountain momently° was forced:
Amid whose swift half-intermitted burst   20
Huge fragments vaulted like rebounding hail,
Or chaffy grain beneath the thresher's flail:
And 'mid these dancing rocks at once and ever
It flung up momently the sacred river.
Five miles meandering with a mazy motion   25
Through wood and dale the sacred river ran,
Then reached the caverns measureless to man,
And sank in tumult to a lifeless ocean:
And 'mid this tumult Kubla heard from far

Σαμερου . . . ἄσω: from the Greek, "I'll sing to you a sweeter song another day [I'll sing to you a sweeter song tomorrow.]"   **Alph:** a compounding of "Alpha," the first letter of the Greek alphabet, with "Alpheus," the underground river of classical lore   **momently:** at moments

Ancestral voices prophesying war!   30
The shadow of the dome of pleasure
Floated midway on the waves;
Where was heard the mingled measure°
From the fountain and the caves.
It was a miracle of rare device,   35
A sunny pleasure-dome with caves of ice!

A damsel with a dulcimer°
In a vision once I saw:
It was an Abyssinian° maid,
And on her dulcimer she played,   40
Singing of Mount Abora.°
Could I revive within me
Her symphony and song,
To such a deep delight 'twould win me,
That with music loud and long,   45
I would build that dome in air,
That sunny dome! those caves of ice!
And all who heard should see them there,
And all should cry, Beware! Beware!
His flashing eyes, his floating hair!   50
Weave a circle round him thrice,
And close your eyes with holy dread,
For he on honey-dew hath fed,
And drunk the milk of Paradise.°

Questions for Writing and Discussion

1. How does Coleridge's prose introduction affect the way you read the poem? Do you think he intended it as an apology, or is he calling attention to the risk inherent in certain kinds of vision? How, in particular, does the last line quoted from *The Picture* ("The pool becomes a mirror") bear upon "Kubla Khan"?

2. A plot seems to be alluded to, without being revealed, in parts of "Kubla Khan." How much of it can you reconstruct? Does it help or hinder the effect of the poem as a unified vision?

mingled measure: the mingled sound of the prophetic voices and the bubbling fountain, or of the fountain and the echoing caves   **dulcimer:** a musical instrument on which strings are stretched across a sounding board and struck with two hammers; as Coleridge probably did not intend us to visualize his damsel armed with two hammers, we may assume that he meant "lute" or "lyre" rather than "dulcimer," but chose the latter word for its sound   **Abyssinian:** Ethiopian; the Garden of Eden, where language itself began, was supposed to have been in Abyssinia, according to some mythological speculations   **Mount Abora:** the mountain that commands a view of a Paradise different from, and rivaling, Eden   **And . . . Paradise:** in Plato's *Ion,* the inspired poet is compared to those ecstatic women who worshiped Bacchus, the god of wine, and who, "when possessed, draw milk and honey from the rivers, but not when in their sense."

3.   An ancient critic, whom we know by the name of Longinus, praised the sublime—the quality in poetry that can *astonish* and *move* us by the display of verbal and imaginative power—as the defining characteristic of the greatest poetry. He believed that sublimity could not be sustained but could only occur in moments of sudden and passionate elevation. It was partly as a result of Longinus' influence that the lyric poem, in the late eighteenth and early nineteenth centuries, came to replace epic and drama as the dominant form of poetic speech: only in a shorter form was there an occasion for sublimity to be sustained throughout. Assuming that Coleridge shared Longinus' belief about the nature of the sublime, where in "Kubla Khan" itself does he exhibit the energy of a profound imagination as a necessarily sudden and unsteady phenomenon?

4.   Who is the Abyssinian maid, and what does her appearance at the end of this poem signify? In what way might you associate her with Keats's "La Belle Dame Sans Merci" (p. 423)?

THE HARLOT'S HOUSE

Oscar Wilde

We caught the tread of dancing feet,
We loitered down the moonlit street,
And stopped beneath the harlot's house.

Inside, above the din and fray,
We heard the loud musicians play   5
The "Treues Liebes Herz" of Strauss.°

Like strange mechanical grotesques,
Making fantastic arabesques,
The shadows raced across the blind.

We watched the ghostly dancers spin   10
To sound of horn and violin,
Like black leaves wheeling in the wind.

Like wire-pulled automatons,
Slim silhouetted skeletons
Went sidling through the slow quadrille.

                                                                          15
They took each other by the hand,
And danced a stately saraband;°
Their laughter echoed thin and shrill.

Strauss: a waltz of Johann Strauss called "The True, Dear Heart"   **saraband:** like "quadrille," an archaic dance

Sometimes a clockwork puppet pressed
A phantom lover to her breast,   20
Sometimes they seemed to try to sing.

Sometimes a horrible marionette
Came out, and smoked its cigarette
Upon the steps like a live thing.

Then, turning to my love, I said,   25
"The dead are dancing with the dead,
The dust is whirling with the dust."

But she—she heard the violin,
And left my side and entered in:
Love passed into the house of lust.   30

Then suddenly the tune went false,
The dancers wearied of the waltz,
The shadows ceased to wheel and whirl.

And down the long and silent street,
The dawn, with silver-sandalled feet,   35
Crept like a frightened girl.

Questions for Writing and Discussion

1. Trace the course of the *simile* in line 7 as it runs throughout the poem. Who, by implication, is pulling the wires in line 13 and playing the violin?

2. In lines 34–36, the narrative takes a strange turn: we are not told what happens to the speaker's lover once she gets inside the house, but instead there is a simile of the arrival of morning. Discuss this ending. How does it relate to the rest of the poem?

3. Consider line 30. Is this a general abstract statement? If so, what is the statement line 30 makes about love and lust? Does this statement describe the action of the narrative?

IMPERIAL ADAM

A. D. Hope

Imperial Adam, naked in the dew,
Felt his brown flanks and found the rib was gone.

Puzzled he turned and saw where, two and two,
The mighty spoor of Jahweh° marked the lawn.

Then he remembered through mysterious sleep   5
The surgeon fingers probing at the bone,
The voice so far away, so rich and deep:
"It is not good for him to live alone."

Turning once more he found Man's counterpart
In tender parody breathing at his side.   10
He knew her at first sight, he knew by heart
Her allegory of sense unsatisfied.

The pawpaw drooped its golden breasts above
Less generous than the honey of her flesh;
The innocent sunlight showed the place of love;   15
The dew on its dark hairs winked crisp and fresh.

This plump gourd severed from his virile root,
She promised on the turf of Paradise
Delicious pulp of the forbidden fruit;
Sly as the snake she loosed her sinuous thighs,   20

And waking, smiled up at him from the grass;
Her breasts rose softly and he heard her sigh—
From all the beasts whose pleasant task it was
In Eden to increase and multiply

Adam had learned the jolly deed of kind: 25
He took her in his arms and there and then,
Like the clean beasts, embracing from behind,
Began in joy to found the breed of men.

Then from the spurt of seed within her broke
Her terrible and triumphant female cry,   30
Split upward by the sexual lightning stroke.
It was the beasts now who stood watching by:

The gravid elephant, the calving hind,
The breeding bitch, the she-ape big with young
Were the first gentle midwives of mankind;   35
The teeming lioness rasped her with her tongue;

The proud vicuña nuzzled her as she slept
Lax on the grass; and Adam watching too
Saw how her dumb breasts at their ripening wept,
The great pod of her belly swelled and grew,   40

Jahweh: the God of Genesis, usually rendered in English as "Jehovah"

And saw its water break, and saw, in fear,
Its quaking muscles in the act of birth.
Between her legs a pigmy face appear,
And the first murderer lay upon the earth.

Questions for Writing and Discussion

1.   Explain the metaphors of parody and allegory in lines 10 and 12. (The *sense* that is "unsatisfied" in the latter line represents all of the senses except for sight, which alone is satisfied by the act of seeing Eve.)

2.   The shock of the last line reminds us that Cain was born before Abel. What light does the end of the poem cast back on the rest of it? Is the reader *rebuked* in any way—aside from being surprised—for his or her feelings about the earlier part of the poem?

3.   What are some of the relations of the vegetable and animal kingdoms, as we still call them, to "imperial" man in this poem's version of Eden?

DURING WIND AND RAIN

Thomas Hardy

They sing their dearest songs—
He, she, all of them—yea,
Treble and tenor and bass,
And one to play;
With the candles mooning each face. . . .   5
Ah, no; the years O!
How the sick leaves reel down in throngs!

They clear the creeping moss—
Elders and juniors—aye,
Making the pathways neat   10
And the garden gay;
And they build a shady seat. . . .
Ah, no; the years, the years;
See, the white stormbirds wing across!

They are blithely breakfasting all—   15
Men and maidens—yea,
Under the summer tree,
With a glimpse of the bay,

While pet fowl come to the knee. . . .
    Ah, no; the years O!   20
And the rotten rose is ripped from the wall.

They change to a high new house,
He, she, all of them—aye,
Clocks and carpets and chairs
    On the lawn all day,   25
And brightest things that are theirs. . . .
    Ah, no; the years, the years;
Down their carved names the raindrop plows.

Discussion

This great lyric poem by Thomas Hardy tells a story and sings a song at the same time. The two run along together. But the voice that does the singing, in the last two lines of each stanza, knows much more than the voice of the storyteller. The singer even sees more of the story than the narrator does. Whether or not the narrator and singer in the poem are two different *personae* (characters invented by the poet), or whether the poet is breaking off his narration and interrupting himself in each stanza with an old refrain that a wiser part of him knows, the reader will eventually have to decide. The two voices differ from each other in many ways. Although both speak in verse, one tells with approval a story that seems to be happy, while the other interrupts to groan wearily and report a sorrowful vision. One is a chronicler of hope; the other is a singer of sad memories which he knows will repeat themselves in the future.

The "They" of line 1 are unidentified. As with "He" and "She" in Edwin Arlington Robinson's "Eros Turannos" on page 434 (another short story in verse, with which this poem should be compared), we are introduced to a couple, a family even, without the background of names, places, or times. Many modern short stories, of course, do just this. In Hardy's poem, we are given a series of discrete pictures, scenes of family life separated by years and decades. The "wind and rain" of the title do not occur in any of these scenes. The condition of the weather and of the human spirit defined in the title apply, as we discover on reading the poem, to the refrain.

It is night in the first stanza. "He" and "she," presumably with another couple, represented by the three singing voices and the piano player, are singing songs indoors. From the romantic setting, we can guess that the "dearest songs" of the first line are about love. The "candles mooning each face" supply a touch of conventional romantic moonlight, but made actual rather than mythical: at the time at which this poem was written, candlelight had already begun to acquire something of the purely sentimental and ceremonial character it now has for us. Here, though, the narrator's voice breaks off and is interrupted by the refrain of the poem itself. If it were only that the singer of the refrain were aware that time would pass, that the young people would grow old ("Ah, no; the years O!"), the interjection would be a simple matter. It would be like a *memento mori,* a reminder of death, in orthodox Christian scenes of the vanity of material things, frequently represented by a skull sitting among valuable objects in a still-life picture.

But line 7 yields a more subtle image: falling autumn leaves that are likened to people ("sick," "throngs") through the common aspects of their death. In both cases sickness and death come to multitudes. The time of this, the autumn of wind and rain, is evoked in the title. For Hardy himself, the image of the leaves had an additional dimension that he knew some, but not all, of his readers might also see. The autumn leaves belong appropriately to this poem, but by the associations of "sick" and "throngs," he is alluding to the autumn leaves, "Yellow, and black, and pale,—and hectic red," of Shelley's "Ode to the West Wind," which in that poem are connected with dying multitudes (see p. 509). Hardy also knew, incidentally, that Shelley himself had been thinking of John Milton's description of Satan's "fallen" army of defeated rebel angels in *Paradise Lost,* who were as "thick as autumnal leaves" that Milton had seen in Italy. The leaves in Hardy's refrain may also suggest, by extension, the years themselves.

The following stanzas are all in daylight, in a sunlight of happiness and continually expanding hope. The growth of peace, prosperity, and pleasure is developed through minute details in a kind of cameo narrative. The family rebuilds and improves an old house (by clearing the creeping moss, making the pathways neat and the garden gay), enjoys the fruits of its labor (by blithely breakfasting under the summer tree, with a glimpse of the bay, while pet fowl come to the knee), and moves to a grander estate (by changing to a high new house with clocks, carpets, and chairs on the lawn). The movement from the hopeful "dearest song" (line 1) to the fulfilled "brightest things that are theirs" (line 25) seems a progress which anyone might desire. But the true cycle of things is revealed in the interjections. Prophetic, fearfully white stormbirds fly across the scene of pleasant, dim shade in the second stanza; in the third, the roses of summer, traditional representations of maidens, are "ripped from the wall" by the fall wind; in the fourth, the carpets and furniture on the lawn are horribly mocked by the hard furniture of the tombstone on which "the raindrop plows."

The final word of the poem is a brilliant last term in the powerful series of verbs used in the refrains: "reel," "wing," "is ripped." But it is also more: plowing initiates cycles of birth, growth, and death by burying the old growth, turning up new earth, and making way for planting new seed. The word "plowing," as used by Hardy, also suggests additional meanings to the life cycle: there is no life after death. Instead of the rain dripping slowly down the tombstone, like the sympathetic tears of a nature saddened by the death of people and their hopes, it plows down the furrowed lines that spell their names. It is a horrible irony that while cutting deeper into the stone, marking out the inscriptions to the memory of the dead, the rain and wind also erode the stone. After less than a hundred years, their names will be illegible.

The structure of Hardy's poem, then, is that of a series of scenes (almost like glimpses into separate rooms, both indoors and outdoors, reminding us that the word "stanza" means "room" in Italian). Most novelists, Hardy himself included, would write at great length and with great power of what was going on in the white spaces between the stanzas, so to speak. They would describe all of the details of life, love, careers, ambitions, work, the surrounding world of other people's lives and aspirations, the shaping forces of society. Hardy moves in this poem beyond society to nature. His rhythmic organization of the four stanzas is subtle but powerful: notice how in the first and third stanzas "yea" in the second line goes with one version of the refrain, while in the second and fourth, "aye" goes with the varied form. It is almost as if the odd and even stanzas were like material read or sung responsively in a church service, as if they were what is called antiphonal. And in each refrain, as we have seen, a powerful, purely independent image does the work of commentary. This poem is both extremely modernist, in its use of an image instead of exposition, and strangely old-fashioned, in telling a story in a complicated stanza form.

EROS TURANNOS°

Edwin Arlington Robinson

She fears him, and will always ask
   What fated her to choose him;
She meets in his engaging mask
   All reasons to refuse him;
But what she meets and what she fears   5
Are less than are the downward years,
Drawn slowly to the foamless weirs°
   Of age, were she to lose him.

Between a blurred sagacity
   That once had power to sound him,   10
And Love, that will not let him be
   The Judas that she found him,
Her pride assuages her almost,
   As if it were alone the cost.—
He sees that he will not be lost,   15
   And waits and looks around him.

A sense of ocean and old trees
   Envelops and allures him;
Tradition, touching all he sees,
   Beguiles and reassures him;   20

Eros Turannos: (Greek) "Love the Tyrant"   weirs: low dams, over which river water gently falls

And all her doubts of what he says
Are dimmed with what she knows of days—
Till even prejudice delays
   And fades, and she secures him.

The falling leaf inaugurates   25
   The reign of her confusion;
The pounding wave reverberates
   The dirge of her illusion;
And home, where passion lived and died,
Becomes a place where she can hide,   30
While all the town and harbor side
   Vibrate with her seclusion.

We tell you, tapping on our brows,
   The story as it should be,—
As if the story of a house   35
   Were told, or ever could be;
We'll have no kindly veil between
Her visions and those we have seen,—
As if we guessed what hers have been,
   Or what they are or would be.   40

Meanwhile we do no harm; for they
   That with a god have striven,
Not hearing much of what we say,
   Take what the god has given;
Though like waves breaking it may be,   45
Or like a changed familiar tree,
Or like a stairway to the sea
   Where down the blind are driven.

Questions for Writing and Discussion

1. This is the story of a bad marriage in a New England seaside town. The woman presumably has wealth and position. What are her deepest fears, as expressed in the first stanza?

2. The man is not to be trusted; perhaps he merely wants her money and status. She knows this and yet marries him anyway. What does line 20 mean in this connection?

3. What is the relation between the images in lines 17–18, and lines 25–28? How are these images reintroduced at the end of the poem?

4. What is the meaning of "vibrate" in line 32?

5. In this poem we find a profound analysis of character; questions are raised about understanding people's motives, and even about the ways in which people

maintain relationships (see lines 37–40, for example). But these are all handled in a kind of neat, singsong light verse, perhaps suggesting a Gilbert and Sullivan song. Does this singsong quality undermine the seriousness of the narration? What effect does it have?

THE FALL OF ROME
(for Cyril Connolly)

W. H. Auden

The piers are pummelled by the waves;
In a lonely field the rain
Lashes an abandoned train;
Outlaws fill the mountain caves.

Fantastic grow the evening gowns;   5
Agents of the Fisc° pursue
Absconding tax-defaulters through
The sewers of provincial towns.

Private rites of magic send
The temple prostitutes to sleep;   10
All the literati keep
An imaginary friend.

Cerebrotonic Cato° may
Extol the Ancient Disciplines
But the muscle-bound Marines   15
Mutiny for food and pay.

Caesar's double-bed is warm
As an unimportant clerk
Writes *I DO NOT LIKE MY WORK*
On a pink official form.   20

Unendowed with wealth or pity,
Little birds with scarlet legs,
Sitting on their speckled eggs,
Eye each flu-infected city.

Altogether elsewhere, vast   25
Herds of reindeer move across
Miles and miles of golden moss,
Silently and very fast.

Fisc: the Roman state treasury **Cerebrotonic Cato:** Cato was a venerated Roman senator and rhetorician, the sort of man who might well have used the word "Cerebrotonic," which is here applied to him and means "headstrong" or muscle-bound-in-the-brain

Questions for Writing and Discussion

1. Why is "pummelled" an unexpected word in line 1? With what sort of action do we ordinarily connect the word? Is there a similar surprise in "*Unendowed* with wealth and pity" (line 21)? How would you describe the effect that both words achieve?

2. How do lines 15–16 comment on the two lines directly before them? Is a similar comment suggested by lines 18–20 as they refer to "Caesar's double-bed is warm"?

3. What does Auden's final stanza have to do with the rest of the poem? Remembering that this is a poem about the fall of Rome, can you speculate *why* the reindeer are in flight? Are they afraid of something?

NOT WAVING BUT DROWNING

Stevie Smith

Nobody heard him, the dead man,
But still he lay moaning:
I was much farther out than you thought
And not waving but drowning.

Poor chap, he always loved larking   5
And now he's dead
It must have been too cold for him his heart gave way,
They said.

Oh, no no no, it was too cold always
(Still the dead one lay moaning)   10
I was much too far out all my life
And not waving but drowning.

Questions for Writing and Discussion

1. The drowning man is "farther out" from shore than anyone thought; but "far out" also has a colloquial sense. He is drowning in the ocean; but again, we can speak colloquially of a man "drowning" or "going down." How do these colloquial meanings help characterize the dead man's plight?

2. How deeply concerned about the drowning man are the voices that we hear in the second stanza? What is the effect of the unusually long line in the form of a quasi-medical diagnosis followed by the short line "They said"?

3. In the final stanza, perhaps unexpectedly, the dead man refuses to be still. Why

do you think he renews his complaint? Remember that "always" originally meant *all ways*. What has the man found "too cold always"?

CAPTAIN CARPENTER

John Crowe Ransom

Captain Carpenter rose up in his prime
Put on his pistols and went riding out
But had got wellnigh nowhere at that time
Till he fell in with ladies in a rout.

It was a pretty lady and all her train   5
That played with him so sweetly but before
An hour she'd taken a sword with all her main
And twined him of his nose for evermore.

Captain Carpenter mounted up one day
And rode straightway into a stranger rogue   10
That looked unchristian but be that as may
The Captain did not wait upon prologue.

But drew upon him out of his great heart
The other swung against him with a club
And cracked his two legs at the shinny part   15
And let him roll and stick like any tub.

Captain Carpenter rode many a time
From male and female took he sundry harms
He met the wife of Satan crying "I'm
The she-wolf bids you shall bear no more arms."   20

Their strokes and counters whistled in the wind
I wish he had delivered half his blows
But where she should have made off like a hind
The bitch bit off his arms at the elbows.

And Captain Carpenter parted with his ears   25
To a black devil that used him in this wise
O Jesus ere his threescore and ten years
Another had plucked out his sweet blue eyes.

Captain Carpenter got up on his roan°
And sallied from the gate in hell's despite°   30
I heard him asking in the grimmest tone
If any enemy yet there was to fight?

roan: roan stallion   **in hell's despite:** despite the resistance of hell

"To any adversary it is fame
If he risk to be wounded by my tongue
Or burnt in two beneath my red heart's flame   35
Such are the perils he is cast among.

"But if he can he has a pretty choice
From an anatomy with little to lose
Whether he cut my tongue and take my voice
Or whether it be my round red heart he choose."   40

It was the neatest knave that ever was seen
Stepping in perfume from his lady's bower
Who at this word put in his merry mien
And fell on Captain Carpenter like a tower.

I would not knock old fellows in the dust   45
But there lay Captain Carpenter on his back
His weapons were the old heart in his bust
And a blade shook between rotten teeth alack.

The rogue in scarlet and grey soon knew his mind
He wished to get his trophy and depart   50
With gentle apology and touch refined
He pierced him and produced the Captain's heart.

God's mercy rest on Captain Carpenter now
I thought him Sirs an honest gentleman
Citizen husband soldier and scholar enow°   55
Let jangling kites eat of him if they can.

But God's deep curses follow after those
That shore him of his godly nose and ears
His legs and strong arms at the two elbows
And eyes that had not watered seventy years.   60

The curse of hell upon the sleek upstart
That got the Captain finally on his back
And took the red red vitals of his heart
And made the kites to whet their beaks clack clack.

Questions for Writing and Discussion

"Captain Carpenter" adopts, in order to throw into relief, certain conventions of a familiar kind of ballad: the ballad of love, contest, and pilgrimage that once would have been sung by a traveling minstrel, and altered a little with each new telling. It has the deliberately anonymous surface of such a ballad, while

enow: enough

allowing us to see, in strokes like the rhyme of "rogue" with "prologue," the deftness of a consciously witty modern poet. The poem incorporates elements of parody (the mimicking of a style by exposing the faults of the style and at the same time exploiting it faithfully). In this poem, the sudden springing into humanity of a nonsense world makes us aware of a grotesqueness that we take for granted in our human world, even if as a rule we turn our eyes away from it. This is a grotesqueness not only in the stiff, mechanical quality that some of our actions can seem to acquire, if we allow ourselves to look at them from the outside, but also in the sense we occasionally have that the whole pattern of our lives is at once arbitrary and repetitive.

1.   What is the significance—the fun—of the name Captain Carpenter? Does the name itself help account for any of the poem's episodes?

2.   Judging by the final three stanzas of "Captain Carpenter," would you say that the narrator of the poem has a fixed or a coherent view of his hero?

THE WOODSPURGE

Dante Gabriel Rossetti

The wind flapped loose, the wind was still,
Shaken out dead from tree and hill:
I had walked on at the wind's will,—
I sat now, for the wind was still.

Between my knees my forehead was,—   5
My lips, drawn in, said not Alas!
My hair was over in the grass,
My naked ears heard the day pass.

My eyes, wide open, had the run
Of some ten weeds to fix upon;   10
Among these few, out of the sun,
The woodspurge flowered, three cups in one.

From perfect grief there need not be
Wisdom or even memory:
One thing then learnt remains to me,—   15
The woodspurge has a cup of three.

Questions for Writing and Discussion

1.   Lines 5–8 describe the speaker outwardly, as lines 3–4 say something about the aimlessness of his or her walking. What are the inner feelings?

2.   Comment on the phrase "my naked ears" in line 8: does this mean that they have been uncovered by long hair falling forward?

3.   What, indeed, has the speaker "learnt"? A botanical lesson? Does the flower symbolize anything?

Dramatic Monologue

A dramatic monologue is a poetic speech that seems to create its own context—a fragment from which we may infer the rest of a drama. We are present at a performance which the speaker of the poem does not know to be a performance: by his words, by his tone, he leaves us with a vivid sense of his character, and so draws an unconscious self-portrait. One way of defining the special dramatic perspective of such a poem is by contrasting it with a *soliloquy*.

In a soliloquy, a single character from a play stands on stage alone and says what he could never say in front of the other characters: this may be self-revelation, self-chastisement, a confidential opinion, the unveiling of a plot. At any rate, there is a tacit agreement between the character and his audience: what the character says is heard by the audience and not by the other characters. Suppose, however, that not even this tacit agreement existed—suppose that instead of hearing a character speak to us in terms made familiar by the rest of the drama, we *overheard* a speech which the character himself might not consider characteristic, but which a third party, outside of the character and ourselves—namely, the author—had allowed us to hear, for the way it brought out the essence of the character and his situation. We would then have a dramatic monologue.

To extend the comparison: when we hear Hamlet, in a soliloquy, declaim against himself "O what a rogue and peasant slave am I," we know it is Hamlet in *one* of his moods. But when the speaker of a monologue by Robert Browning opens a poem with a literal growl—"*Grr-r-r*"—we recognize *the* mood that will be sustained through the poem and that will form our whole sense of this character. He is telling us more than he imagines (since he does not know we are listening at all), and he thus opens up the possibility of irony: a distinct separation between his view of himself and our view of him, both of which are based on the same evidence. The poet is telling us something about the character "over the head" of the character himself, and we read the poet's signals in the character's speech. It is this clear-cut division between the poet and the

442

speaker of a poem which marks off the province of the dramatic monologue. Obviously, songs like Clare's "Secret Love" (p. 471) or Yeats' "Crazy Jane Talks with the Bishop" (p. 469) or a dramatic piece like Shelley's "The Two Spirits: An Allegory" (p. 364)—poems spoken by voices, which imply a larger drama from which they have been deliberately cut off—have to be read with something of the same tact, the feeling for every nuance of characterization, which dramatic monologues teach us.

ULYSSES°

Alfred, Lord Tennyson

It little profits that an idle king,
By this still hearth, among these barren crags,
Matched with an aged wife, I mete and dole
Unequal laws° unto a savage race,
That hoard, and sleep, and feed, and know not me.   5

I cannot rest from travel; I will drink
Life to the lees. All times I have enjoyed
Greatly, have suffered greatly, both with those
That loved me, and alone: on shore, and when
Through scudding drifts the rainy Hyades°   10
Vexed the dim sea. I am become a name;
For always roaming with a hungry heart
Much have I seen and known—cities of men
And manners, climates, councils, governments,
Myself not least, but honored of them all—   15
And drunk delight of battle with my peers,
Far on the ringing plains of windy Troy.
I am a part of all that I have met;
Yet all experience is an arch wherethrough
Gleams that untraveled world whose margin fades   20
Forever and forever when I move.
How dull it is to pause, to make an end,
To rust unburnished, not to shine in use!
As though to breathe were life! Life piled on life
Were all too little, and of one to me   25

Ulysses: or Odysseus, ruler of Ithaca, a cunning warrior and master of rhetoric, was an important secondary character in the *Iliad* and central figure in the *Odyssey*. In *The Divine Comedy,* Dante added another episode to the Ulysses legend, according to which Ulysses grew restless after his return to Ithaca and in old age embarked with a band of loyal followers upon a new voyage.   **Unequal laws:** rewards and punishments   **Hyades:** constellation formed by the Nymphs (daughters of Atlas) whom Zeus installed in the heavens; their rising with the sun was taken to be a sign that rainy weather was coming

Little remains; but every hour is saved
From that eternal silence, something more,
A bringer of new things; and vile it were
For some three suns to store and hoard myself,
And this gray spirit yearning in desire   30
To follow knowledge like a sinking star,
Beyond the utmost bound of human thought.

This is my son, mine own Telemachus,
To whom I leave the scepter and the isle—
Well-loved of me, discerning to fulfill   35
This labor, by slow prudence to make mild
A rugged people, and through soft degrees
Subdue them to the useful and the good.
Most blameless is he, centered in the sphere
Of common duties, decent not to fail   40
In offices of tenderness, and pay
Meet adoration to my household gods,
When I am gone. He works his work, I mine.

There lies the port; the vessel puffs her sail;
There gloom the dark, broad seas. My Mariners,   45
Souls that have toiled, and wrought, and thought with me—
That ever with a frolic welcome took
The thunder and the sunshine, and opposed
Free hearts, free foreheads—you and I are old;
Old age hath yet his honor and his toil.   50
Death closes all; but something ere the end,
Some work of noble note, may yet be done,
Not unbecoming men that strove with Gods.
The lights begin to twinkle from the rocks;
The long day wanes; the slow moon climbs; the deep   55
Moans round with many voices. Come, my friends,
'Tis not too late to seek a newer world.
Push off, and sitting well in order smite
The sounding furrows; for my purpose holds
To sail beyond the sunset, and the baths   60
Of all the western stars,° until I die.
It may be that the gulfs will wash us down;
It may be we shall touch the Happy Isles,°
And see the great Achilles, whom we knew.
Though much is taken, much abides; and though   65

---

the baths . . . stars: in Greek cosmology, the belt of waters surrounding the flat circle of the earth
into which the stars descended   **Happy Isles:** Elysium, or the Islands of the Blessed, where Achilles
resided after his death

We are not now that strength which in old days
Moved earth and heaven, that which we are, we are—
One equal temper of heroic hearts,
Made weak by time and fate, but strong in will
To strive, to seek, to find, and not to yield.   70

Questions for Writing and Discussion

1. Does Ulysses reveal a high opinion of his accomplishments only when he means to, or are some of his revelations unwitting? What do you think is implied in the phrase "I am become a name" (line 11)—what does Ulysses think is implied in it?

2. What tone does Ulysses adopt toward Telemachus?

3. Does Ulysses' meditation on the boundlessness of man's thirst for knowledge and adventure (lines 19–32) adequately prepare you for the speech on embarkation (beginning "There lies the port . . .")? Why does the third-person address to Telemachus intervene between these two longer passages?

4. What does Ulysses think ought not to be yielded (line 70)? What—consciously or not—is he afraid of yielding *to?*

5. Taking the poem as a whole, to what extent do you find Ulysses an admirable hero? In what ways is he less than admirable? How would you describe the differences between your understanding of Ulysses and his understanding of himself?

MY LAST DUCHESS
Ferrara°

Robert Browning

That's my last Duchess painted on the wall,
Looking as if she were alive. I call
That piece a wonder, now: Frà Pandolf's° hands
Worked busily a day, and there she stands.
Will't please you sit and look at her? I said   5
"Frà Pandolf " by design, for never read
Strangers like you that pictured countenance,
The depth and passion of its earnest glance,

Ferrara: Alfonso d'Este, Duke of Ferrara, a historical figure of the sixteenth century   Frà Pandolf: "Brother Pandolf," a fictional monkish painter

But to myself they turned (since none puts by
The curtain I have drawn for you, but I)   10
And seemed as they would ask me, if they durst,
How such a glance came there; so, not the first
Are you to turn and ask thus. Sir, 'twas not
Her husband's presence only, called that spot
Of joy into the Duchess' cheek: perhaps   15
Fràn Pandolf chanced to say "Her mantle laps
Over my lady's wrist too much," or "Paint
Must never hope to reproduce the faint
Half-flush that dies along her throat:" such stuff
Was courtesy, she thought, and cause enough   20
For calling up that spot of joy. She had
A heart—how shall I say?—too soon made glad,
Too easily impressed; she liked whate'er
She looked on, and her looks went everywhere.
Sir, 'twas all one! My favour at her breast,   25
The dropping of the daylight in the West,
The bough of cherries some officious fool
Broke in the orchard for her, the white mule
She rode with round the terrace—all and each
Would draw from her alike the approving speech,   30
Or blush, at least. She thanked men,—good! but thanked
Somehow—I know not how—as if she ranked
My gift of a nine-hundred-years-old name
With anybody's gift. Who'd stoop to blame
This sort of trifling? Even had you skill   35
In speech—(which I have not)—to make your will
Quite clear to such an one, and say, "Just this
Or that in your disgusts me; here you miss,
Or there exceed the mark"—and if she let
Herself be lessoned so, nor plainly set   40
Her wits to yours, forsooth, and made excuse,
—E'en then would be some stooping; and I choose
Never to stoop. Oh sir, she smiled, no doubt,
Whene'er I passed her; but who passed without
Much the same smile? This grew; I gave commands;   45
Then all smiles stopped together. There she stands
As if alive. Will't please you rise? We'll meet
The company below, then. I repeat,
The Count your master's known munificence
Is ample warrant that no just pretence   50
Of mine for dowry will be disallowed;
Though his fair daughter's self, as I avowed
At starting, is my object. Nay, we'll go

Together down, sir. Notice Neptune, though,
Taming a sea-horse, thought a rarity,   55
Which Claus of Innsbruck° cast in bronze for me!

Questions for Writing and Discussion

1.   In a dramatic monologue like this, the reader must infer a whole dramatic
situation from what is said. Here, it is obvious at the beginning that the Duke is
conducting a visitor through his palace; it is only at the end of the poem that we
learn who the visitor is and why he is there. What is the effect of this delayed
discovery?

2.   The visitor's reactions to the Duke's monologue can only be surmised; what do
you suppose is happening in lines 54–55, though, when the Duke says "Nay, we'll
go/Together down, sir"?

3.   The Duke's revelations are framed at the beginning and end of the poem by his
attention to works of art. Is there any significance to the particular subject of the
bronze in the final lines? If so, what is that significance? If not, why not?

4.   Do you think that the Duke is fully aware of what he is revealing about
himself? Explain your answer.

HAWK ROOSTING

Ted Hughes

I sit in the top of the wood, my eyes closed.
Inaction, no falsifying dream
Between my hooked head and hooked feet:
Or in sleep rehearse perfect kills and eat.

The convenience of the high trees!   5
The air's buoyancy and the sun's ray
Are of advantage to me;
And the earth's face upward for my inspection.

My feet are locked upon the rough bark.
It took the whole of Creation   10
To produce my foot, my each feather:
Now I hold Creation in my foot

Claus of Innsbruck: a fictional sculptor

Or fly up, and revolve it all slowly—
I kill where I please because it is all mine.
There is no sophistry in my body: 15
My manners are tearing off heads—

The allotment of death.
For the one path of my flight is direct
Through the bones of the living.
No arguments assert my right: 20

The sun is behind me.
Nothing has changed since I began.
My eye has permitted no change.
I am going to keep things like this.

Questions for Writing and Discussion

1. What is the point of the word "convenience" (line 5)? How does it help
establish the speaker's tone?

2. What is the logical relation between lines 20 and 21?

3. Consider this as a dramatic monologue. Is the speaker self-deluded in any way?
Does he betray himself by what he says?

4. Compare this poem with "The Yachts" by William Carlos Williams (p. 637), as
representations of true and false nobility.

MIRROR

James Merrill

I grow old under an intensity
Of questioning looks. *Nonsense,*
I try to say, *I cannot teach you children*
How to live.—If not you, who will?
Cries one of them aloud, grasping my gilded   5
Frame till the world sways. *If not you, who will?*
Between their visits the table, its arrangement
Of Bible, fern and Paisley, all past change,
Does very nicely. If ever I feel curious
As to what others endure,   10
Across the parlor *you* provide examples,
Wide open, sunny, of everything I am
Not. You embrace a whole world without once caring
To set it in order. That takes thought. Out there

Something is being picked. The red-and-white bandannas   15
Go to my heart. A fine young man
Rides by on horseback. Now the door shuts. Hester
Confides in me her first unhappiness.
This much, you see, would never have been fitted
Together, but for me. Why then is it   20
They more and more neglect me? Late one sleepless
Midsummer night I strained to keep
Five tapers from your breathing. *No,* the widowed
Cousin said, *Let them go out.* I did.
The room brimmed with gray sound, all the instreaming   25
Muslin of your dream . . .
Years later now, two of the grown grandchildren
Sit with novels face-down on the sill,
Content to muse upon your tall transparence,
Your clouds, brown fields, persimmon far   30
And cypress near. One speaks. *How superficial
Appearances are!* Since then, as if a fish
Had broken the perfect silver of my reflectiveness,
I have lapses. I suspect
Looks from behind, where nothing is, cool gazes   35
Through the blind flaws of my mind. As days,
As decades lengthen, this vision
Spreads and blackens. I do not know whose it is,
But I think it watches for my last silver
To blister, flake, float leaf by life, each milling-   40
Downward dumb conceit, to a standstill
From which not even you strike any brilliant
Chord in me, and to a faceless will,
Echo of mine, I am amenable.

Discussion

One of the most ancient symbols of art has been the mirror. In the past, art—whether literature or the visual arts—was thought to imitate nature. It served as a kind of mirror of reality. But imitation is never simple. The artist always "added" some quality to the imitation. For many, this added quality was the artist's thought or understanding. Through the exercise of his or her thought, the artist brought "order" to the "chaos" of nature.

The audience for literature and art, schooled in imitation theory, came to expect, indeed to demand, that the arts *teach people how to live.* At this point, not only must art and literature reflect reality but they must also serve as a guide to life. The modern arts, however, have rejected the role of teacher or guide. They insist that their only function is to reflect reality in a coherent fashion by "fitting together" the separate pieces of experience that would otherwise not make sense. Art and literature, so the modern view holds, cannot answer the questions of life.

It is this situation that James Merrill deals with in his poem. As is the custom in poetry, however, Merrill treats the problem of art and its relation to its audience indirectly. First, he sets up two extended metaphors: one of a mirror representing art and the other of a window representing life or reality. Then he establishes the central contrast between them in a few deft lines: "Across the parlor *you* provide examples,/Wide open, sunny, of everything I am/Not. You embrace a whole world without once caring/To set it in order. That takes thought . . ." Finally, Merrill places the problem of art within the frame of a dramatic monologue. Now, let us look more closely at his poem.

A mirror is the speaker of this monologue. But it is not just any mirror. We need to read through the first twenty lines of the poem before we can discover just what kind of mirror it is. A tall looking glass, standing on the floor in a gilded frame, in a large family house, surviving several generations, it grows old, it says, "under" the fierce, questioning gaze of the inhabitants of the house. "Under" (line 1), brilliantly used here in several senses, can mean (a) "during" or "in the course of," (b) "worn out by," or even (c) "beneath the surface of." What mirrors always show us is the surface of things. Yet from the start, this mirror is full of profundities—ideas and insights that lie under the surface of things. The children of the house, who have asked the mirror over the years "how to live," seem overinsistent on its importance as some kind of teacher for them. But we cannot tell from the mirror's response whether its refusal to accept the role of teacher is an instance of prudence, false modesty, or simple recognition of its own limitations.

Between the visits of the children, the mirror seems content (lines 7–9) with the scene before it, which it can compose into a sort of still-life painting. In lines 9–14, we discover something absolutely crucial about the room that the mirror is in, and its position in that room. Across the parlor from the mirror there is a window, and through it the mirror sees the world of daily life in an *unreflecting,* open manner. We are reminded that although the mirror, unlike the window glass, is opaque, it can act more like a mind or a complex consciousness. When we look into a mirror, we see within its framed glass the reflection of a world with clear boundaries. These boundaries provide us with an immediate sense of form, which is lost in the world outside the window. We can also remember that no one ever consults a window for knowledge of himself or herself, but only about what is going on outside.

This view of the mirror as an organizing consciousness in contrast to the window is developed in lines 9–20:

> If ever I feel curious
> As to what others endure,
> Across the parlor *you* provide examples,
> Wide open, sunny, of everything I am

Not. You embrace a whole world without once caring
To set it in order. That takes thought. Out there
Something is being picked. The red-and-white bandannas
Go to my heart. A fine young man
Rides by on horseback. Now the door shuts. Hester
Confides in me her first unhappiness.
This much, you see, would never have been fitted
Together, but for me. . . .

Because the window does not care to "set the world in order," it is merely an opening to reality across which images flit in random profusion. Only our minds can "fit" these random images "together" into some kind of order. Works of art are products of our minds; they bring order out of the chaos of our sensations, much as the mirror does with the chaotic images seen through the window. The details in lines 15–18 are like disconnected scenes from a romantic novel, which the mirror, like a good novelist, brings together in a reflective, meditative way by putting them within a frame. By placing reality within the frame of a novel, for example, we gain a perspective on the world.

"Why then is it/They more and more neglect me?" becomes an especially poignant question here. Through a complex system of metaphoric associations, the poem suggests a possible answer. Immediately following the question, the mirror describes a death scene, but in interestingly oblique terms. It uses a number of words and refers to a number of objects that are usually connected with death: "five tapers," the lighted candles often used at a wake or around a coffin; "keep from your breathing"—the wind, of course, would put out the candles, which is a kind of death—but the words "keep from breathing" themselves suggest death; "widowed cousin" is connected with death in a still more obvious way; "gray sound" suggests the muted talk of persons in the presence of death. Clearly, the death which is suggested is that of a member of the family, although this is never made explicit. The only things we actually see "dying" in the poem are the five tapers. Their light has been allowed to go out.

Light, whether candlelight, lamplight, or sunlight, is an ancient symbol of knowledge. Since it appears immediately after the mirror's poignant question, we can safely assume that the dying light is a metaphoric answer to that question. This interpretation of the dying light as a metaphor of knowledge is reinforced when we recognize that it is only in the death of the light that the mirror actually claims to have taken an active part. Up to that point, the mirror had passively reflected whatever came before it, except for the neutral act of "fitting things together." Now, it "strained" to keep the tapers from being blown out by the breeze coming through the window, but when commanded to let the light go out, *the mirror did so.* The mirror, representing art and literature, therefore had control over the light, standing for knowledge. By letting the light go out, the mirror reverts to the opening refusal to teach. Here the poem seems to be saying that by refusing to serve as either a guide to life or a source of knowledge, art and literature cannot satisfy the demands of their audience.

We can now move to the next scene. The grown grandchildren sit on the windowsill "with novels face down" and muse upon the reality outside the window. Novels, of course, are forms of art, which according to the poem can no longer provide answers to troubling questions. Like the mirror, they can only reflect appearances. The contemptuous remark of one of the grandchildren, "How superficial/Appearances are," has a devastating effect on the mirror, whose sole purpose has been to reflect appearances. From this point on the mirror describes its decline.

In a sense we can say that this poem is about the consequences of rejecting the traditional roles of art and literature. Since traditional values are central to the poem, it is only proper that the poem use, in some fashion, traditional forms. We saw one level of this in the use of the mirror and window as main characters in the poem. We can also see this on a more subtle level if we consider the lines in which the mirror speaks. As we noted earlier, this poem is in the form of a dramatic monologue, and the greatest exponent of this form was Robert Browning. His dramatic monologue, "My Last Duchess" (p. 445), is in heroic couplets, although until the final lines, those couplets are never end stopped (which itself is a modification of the tradition established by John Dryden, page 483, and Alexander Pope, page 343). Merrill's poem is also very much a dramatic monologue—perhaps in some ways, more like Tennyson's "Ulysses" (p. 443) than like Browning's "My Last Duchess." By its verse form, Merrill's poem makes some allusion to these earlier works. The lines of the poem *are* couplets, but they are delicately muted, both by their special way of rhyming and by their varied length. The odd-numbered lines are all loose iambic pentameter (except for line 37), and the even-numbered ones have anywhere from three to five stresses. Moreover, the rhymes are so delicate that we scarcely hear them on a first reading. The second line of each "couplet" ends in a syllable which rhymes not with the final one of the previous line but with the next to last syllable, or even (lines 33–34) with the third from the end on the preceding line. For example:

> I grow old under an in*tens*ity
> Of questioning looks. Non*sense.*

OR

> Between their visits the table, its ar*range*ment
> Of Bible, fern and Paisley, all past *change*

This system provides a smoothly flowing, flexible verse for the mirror's musings, uninterrupted by sharper and more obvious end rhymes. The half-heard rhymes work in an evocative way, like memories or reflections. The memories suggested by the rhymes are also echoed in the overall structure of the poem. The effect of "framing" (as it is sometimes called) this poem in a version of an older formal scheme is to remind us of the tradition to which the poem belongs and from which it has departed.

As we go through the mirror's monologue, fitting it all together for ourselves, we as readers are doing something of the mirror's own work. From fragments and allusions we put its story together. It is as if the poem had enlisted us as interpreters who continue the poetic process. One can, in a way, say that this process holds true for all poetry. Poems are never completed on the page. They continue in our minds.

SKUNK HOUR
(For Elizabeth Bishop)

Robert Lowell

Nautilus Island's hermit
heiress still lives through winter in her Spartan cottage;
her sheep still graze above the sea.
Her son's a bishop. Her farmer
is first selectman in our village;   5
she's in her dotage.

Thirsting for
the hierarchic privacy
of Queen Victoria's century,
she buys up all   10
the eyesores facing her shore,
and lets them fall.

The season's ill—
we've lost our summer millionaire,
who seemed to leap from an L. L. Bean   15
catalogue. His nine-knot yawl
was auctioned off to lobstermen.
A red fox stain covers Blue Hill.

And now our fairy°
decorator brightens his shop for fall;   20
his fishnet's filled with orange cork,
orange, his cobbler's bench and awl;
there is no money in his work,
he'd rather marry.

One dark night,   25
my Tudor° Ford climbed the hill's skull;
I watched for love-cars. Lights turned down,
they lay together, hull to hull,
where the graveyard shelves on the town. . . .
My mind's not right.   30

fairy: slang for homosexual **Tudor:** two-door

A car radio bleats,
"Love, O careless Love. . . ." I hear
my ill-spirit sob in each blood cell,
as if my hand were at its throat. . . .
I myself am hell;°   35
nobody's here—

only skunks, that search
in the moonlight for a bite to eat.
They march on their soles up Main Street:
white stripes, moonstruck eyes' red fire   40
under the chalk-dry and spar spire
of the Trinitarian Church.

I stand on top
of our back steps and breathe the rich air—
a mother skunk with her column of kittens swills the   45
        garbage pail.
She jabs her wedge-head in a cup
of sour cream, drops her ostrich tail,
and will not scare.

Discussion

"Skunk Hour" may be taken to exemplify the continuing energy, in poetry as in the other arts, of *expressionism:* a mode defined by the special authority, and depth of self-revelation, with which an author declares: "What I say is both myself in truth and creates a new world" (to borrow the phrase of a modern critic, R. P. Blackmur). The title of the poem suggests the title of a painting: we see a New England fishing town at evening, at the hour when the skunks go foraging. We are told all the conversational facts about the speaker's dwelling place, the small talk of his life. And at first, the voice that tells us this is an objective-seeming "we." In the fifth stanza, however, rather quietly and without warning, the "we" becomes an "I," a revealer of unexpected intimacies. It is this "I" that has led many readers to think of Lowell as a "confessional poet"—a man you hardly know, ready to tell you all his secrets. But, at least in this poem, the speaker is a highly dramatic presence, who cannot be associated *in any simple way* with the poet himself. Lowell is writing of a madness that is peculiarly modern, and peculiarly his own. The speaker of "Skunk Hour" emphatically dramatizes Lowell's own condition, although we cannot point to any one-to-one correspondence between Lowell's life and the life of the speaker.

The details which this speaker observes need several readings to sink in and be recalled or talked about. They seem plain enough; a line like "A red fox

myself am hell: said by Satan, in the great Soliloquy of Book IV of *Paradise Lost*

stain covers Blue Hill," for instance, can seem easy to the point of prose. Yet if we look at the line a second time, this directness or simplicity has the made-up coherence of madness. Notice, too, how the local characters appear, to the speaker's eyes, to suffer from the very aimlessness that he will later reveal afflicts him: the fairy decorator who'd as soon marry as do anything; the hermit heiress who buys up all the eyesores only to let them fall down.

Madness, indeed, is the explicit subject of the poem. It is a madness which may seem to us not only disturbing, and shocking, but also enigmatic. Yet there is a clue in the quotation from Milton's *Paradise Lost.* Not long after Satan says "myself am hell," he will look in upon Eden, spy Adam and Eve "imparadised" in each other's arms, and utter the terrible lament: "Oh Hell! What do mine eyes with grief behold?" This is the cry of a self-conscious and morally complex voyeur; and Lowell's speaker, watching for "love-cars," is in the same position. His own lament is "nobody's here," that is: "They, who love, are there; I, who would love, am here, merely a watcher. I hardly exist on my own, I am nothing, yet I must say 'I'." And this is hell. The close observation of the skunks in the final stanzas may be seen as an attempt by the speaker to extricate himself from this hell by an act of objective scrutiny—investigation, at last, rather than peeping. But even this attempt fails; it too becomes merely obsessive.

the way to hump a cow

e. e. cummings

<pre>
the way to hump a cow is not
to get yourself a stool
but draw a line around the spot
and call it beautifool

to multiply because and why   5
dividing thens by nows
and adding and (i understand)
is hows to hump a cows

the way to hump a cow is not
to elevate your tool   10
but drop a penny in the slot
and bellow like a bool

to lay a wreath from ancient greath
on insulated brows
(while tossing boms at uncle toms)   15
is hows to hump a cows
</pre>

the way to hump a cow is not
to push and then to pull
but practicing the art of swot
to preach the golden rull   20

so vote for me all decent mem
and wonens will allows
which if they dont to hell with them
is hows to hump a cows

Questions for Writing and Discussion

1.   How do you envision the speaker of these lines? How does the last stanza put him in clearer focus?

2.   What is the comic effect of the misspellings, grammatical confusions, and so forth throughout this poem?

3.   What kind of statement does the poet make, through the speaker, about the relation of sex to politics?

THEMES AND VARIATIONS

Poetry continually makes some of the most ordinary experiences of life into ceremonies; in that way, it is like a kind of religion of its own, worshiping human life and its awareness of itself. Love poems are usually ceremonies of desire, celebrated in the absence of someone wanted, or in the denial of a person's love. But physical, sublimated, and domestic love present many other occasions to the participants or their observers: meeting, parting, remembering, anticipating, even regretting can all be experienced as ceremonies of the birth, death, education, initiation, or transformation of feeling. Love has its universal aspects as well as those which we all feel are peculiarly our own, and its occasions are both public and private; erotic emotions can seem ritualized to an outside observer and totally original to lovers. Among the poems that follow are those which celebrate, imagine, or even create occasions for love, and those in which poets, imagining themselves as lovers, tell us more truths about love than if they really were lovers.

SINCE THERE'S NO HELP

Michael Drayton

Since there's no help, come let us kiss and part.
    Nay, I have done; you get no more of me,
And I am glad, yea, glad with all my heart,
    That thus so cleanly I myself can free;
Shake hands for ever, cancel all our vows,   5
    And when we meet at any time again,
Be it not seen in either of our brows

That we one jot of former love retain.
Now at the last gasp of Love's latest breath,
    When, his pulse failing, Passion speechless lies,   10
When Faith is kneeling by his bed of death,
    And Innocence is closing up his eyes,
        Now if thou wouldst, when all have given him over,
        From death to life thou mightst him yet recover.

Questions for Writing and Discussion

1. Like a sonnet by Shakespeare, this poem is arranged in three quatrains and a closing couplet. It seems, however, to divide naturally into an *octave* of eight lines, and a *sestet* of six. How does the poem change at line 9?

2. If the end of the poem seems to revoke the opening, what connections might you draw between the kind of language used in the first eight lines and that used in lines 9–12?

3. Compare the closing of this poem with that of the sonnet by Sir Philip Sidney (p. 385).

4. Can you imagine a painting or sculpture of the personifications—the turning of Love, Passion, Faith, and Innocence into allegorical figures—in lines 9–12? Does what you imagine resemble any well-known subject of painting or sculpture?

TO LUCASTA, GOING TO THE WARS

Richard Lovelace

Tell me not, sweet, I am unkind,°
    That from the nunnery
Of thy chaste breast and quiet mind,
    To war and arms I fly.

True, a new mistress now I chase,   5
    The first foe in the field;
And with a stronger faith embrace
    A sword, a horse, a shield.

Yet this inconstancy is such
    As you too shall adore;   10
I could not love thee, dear, so much,
    Loved I not honour more.

unkind: unnatural as well as harsh

Questions for Writing and Discussion

1.   This is the essential soldierly farewell. How does the graceful paradox of its conclusion deal with the speaker's conflicting feelings?

2.   What is the relation of love, religion, and warfare in the poem's images?

3.   Compare this poem with Drayton's preceding sonnet on leave-taking. How do they differ in tone?

'SO WE'LL GO NO MORE A-ROVING'

George Gordon, Lord Byron

So we'll go no more a-roving
   So late into the night,
Though the heart be still as loving,
   And the moon be still as bright.

For the sword outwears its sheath,   5
   And the soul wears out the breast,
And the heart must pause to breathe,
   And Love itself have rest.

Though the night was made for loving,
   And the day returns too soon,   10
Yet we'll go no more a-roving
   By the light of the moon.

Questions for Writing and Discussion

1.   Look up the various senses of "rove" and "roving" in the *Oxford English Dictionary* or any other unabridged dictionary. Which ones are implied in the poem?

2.   Under what circumstances does "day," as in line 10, return "too soon"?

3.   Byron sent this poem in a letter to his friend Tom Moore at the end of carnival season in Venice in 1817. Considering that the poem is about sexual exhaustion, interpret the image in line 5 and its relation to the following line.

THE FLEA

John Donne

Mark but this flea, and mark in this.
How little that which thou deny'st me is:
Me it sucked first, and now sucks thee,
And in this flea, our two bloods mingled be;
Confess it, this cannot be said°   5
A sin, or shame, or loss of maidenhead,
   Yet this enjoys before it woo,
   And pampered swells with one blood made of two,
   And this, alas, is more than we would do.

Oh stay, three lives in one flea spare,   10
Where we almost, nay more than married are.
This flea is you and I, and this
Our marriage bed, and marriage temple is;
Though parents grudge, and you, we are met,
And cloistered in these living walls of jet.   15
   Though use° make you apt to kill me,
   Let not to this, self murder added be,
   And sacrilege, three sins in killing three.

Cruel and sudden, hast thou since
Purpled° thy nail, in blood of innocence?   20
In what could this flea guilty be,
Except in that drop which it sucked from thee?
Yet thou trimph'st, and say'st that thou
Find'st not thyself, nor me the weaker now;
   'Tis true, then learn how false, fears be;   25
   Just so much honour, when thou yield'st to me,
   Will waste, as this flea's death took life from thee.

Questions for Writing and Discussion

1. Donne is famous for his use of "conceits," a word derived from the Italian *concetto* (concept) and used in English to denote an extended and often intricately developed metaphor. In this poem, the flea is a conceit. Trace, in the first stanza, the development of this conceit. What is meant by "that which thou deny'st me," "swells with one blood made of two," and "this, alas, is more than we would do"? What is the line of argument in this stanza?

said: said to be **use:** habit **purpled:** reddened

2.   In the second stanza, this poem becomes more like a dramatic monologue. How does the relation between the speaker and the woman become clearer?

3.   What happens in the "action" between stanzas I and II: between II and III?

TO HIS COY MISTRESS

Andrew Marvell

Had we but world enough, and time,
This coyness, Lady, were no crime.
We would sit down, and think which way
To walk, and pass our long love's day.
Thou by the Indian Ganges' side   5
Shouldst rubies find; I by the tide
Of Humber° would complain. I would
Love you ten years before the Flood,
And you should, if you please, refuse
Till the Conversion of the Jews.   10
My vegetable love should grow
Vaster than empires and more slow;
An hundred years should go to praise
Thine eyes, and on thy forehead gaze;
Two hundred to adore each breast,   15
But thirty thousand to the rest;
An age at least to every part,
And the last age should show your heart.
For, Lady, you deserve this state,
Nor would I love at lower rate.   20
   But at my back I always hear
Time's wingèd chariot hurrying near;
And yonder all before us lie
Deserts of vast eternity.
Thy beauty shall no more be found,   25
Nor, in thy marble vault, shall sound
My echoing song; then worms shall try
That long-preserved virginity,
And your quaint honour turn to dust,
And into ashes all my lust: 30
The grave's a fine and private place,
But none, I think, do there embrace.
   Now therefore, while the youthful hue

Humber: river in the north of England

Sits on thy skin like morning dew,
And while thy willing soul transpires   35
At every pore with instant fires,
Now let us sport us while we may,
And now, like amorous birds of prey,
Rather at once our time devour
Than languish in his slow-chapt° power.   40
Let us roll all our strength and all
Our sweetness up into one ball,
And tear our pleasures with rough strife
Thorough° the iron gates of life;
Thus, though we cannot make our sun   45
Stand still, yet we will make him run.

Discussion

This is one of the most celebrated short poems in the English language, and certainly one of the most remarkable poems about love ever written. We shall consider it from a number of different points of view, each of which can be applied to the study of other poems. We shall also look at the ways in which the poem is put together and the ways in which the patterns of structure yield up knowledge and excitement for a reader. Finally, we shall try to say something about the poem's uniqueness.

The overall point of the poem is as clear as its major structure: the speaker wants the lady addressed in the poem to sleep with him; she has been "coy" (shy or reticent, rather than in the more modern sense of *pretending* to be shy, reserved, or evasive); and, instead of reporting his feelings, describing them, or "expressing" them in something like a song, he resorts to argument. The logical pattern of that argument is very tight:

A: *If* there were time enough, I'd write endless poems praising you and making verbal love to you unil the very end of history (lines 1–20).

B: *But* time moves on, we're both going to die, and there is no lovemaking—nor indeed, even poetry about lovemaking—in the grave (lines 21–32).

C: *Therefore,* we'd better make love and have our pleasure now; since we can't make time stand still, we can at least make it pass quickly in erotic activity (lines 33–46).

The longest part of the poem is the first one, concerning how talk about, before, and perhaps in place of love might go on if we were immortal. The short middle section is about death; the slightly longer final one envisions in metaphorical terms the act of love itself.

slow-chapt: slowly munching jaws   thorough: through

But a prose analysis like this is similar to a skeletal X-ray of a person; it is reductive, showing the lines of argument but not *how* the argument is made. In the case of a poem, the *how* (the way in which) an argument is made is a part of and as important as the *what* (the content) of the argument itself; the figurative language used in presenting an argument enters its logic in ways that are powerful even though subtle and complex. The kind of argument about love made in "To His Coy Mistress" is so conventional in poetry from the third century B.C. on that there is even a standard name for it, *carpe diem* (Latin for "seize the day," after a poem by Horace on just this subject). This theme counsels the loved one to make hay while the sun shines or "Gather ye rosebuds while ye may," to borrow the words of Robert Herrick, another seventeenth-century poet. Reducing Marvell's poem to its logical skeleton makes it look just like other *carpe diem* poems. We could even consider it an elaboration of an epigram by the Greek poet Aesclepiades, the first such verse we have:

> Love's joys are for the living: in the grave
> You won't have a virginity to save.

While recognizing common themes can be a help in understanding a poem, it can also sometimes be a kind of trap. Instead of considering the conventional pattern of argument, let's turn to the *how* of the argument, to the actual unrolling of the language of the poem and try to see what is going on.

The first section starts mildly enough, with the speaker saying that there is neither space ("world") nor time enough for the lady to be shy. To give his statement bite, he also suggests that the delays caused by her shyness are criminal. He then catalogs the various ways he would woo her if he had time, and it immediately appears that the catalog is to be developed by means of parallels that may even contain contrasts. Space and time are paired throughout the first two sections of the poem: "which way/To walk" suggests space, and "our long love's day" implies time; the lady can roam across the world to find actual rubies in India, while the poet remains in his home city of Hull, by the unexotic river, to write poems that complain of his unreturned love. If their "long love's day" is eternity, then it is appropriate to delay and substitute for the act of love the elaborate praise of each part of the woman's body (called a *blazon* in earlier poetry—see Spenser's "Ye Tradeful Merchants" and Shakespeare's parody of it, "My Mistress' Eyes Are Nothing Like the Sun," on pages 383–84).

The poet is usually paired with time, the lady with space: he would love her from before the Biblical deluge, which spread out over the whole earth, and she could travel all over the world saying "no" until, as tradition held it, all of the Jews would be converted in the last age before the end of time. The poet continues to link time and space throughout his catalog: he would love the lady ten years before the deluge, which, because it covered the earth, suggests space as well as time; his love would cover a larger area and grow more slowly than do empires (here we should note Marvell's wonderfully fanciful use of the word "vegetable" to suggest slowness in a context in which our erotic natures are thought of as animal); he would devote a hundred, two hundred, and then thirty thousand years to the praise and adoration of her body (bodies, of course, occupy space and have spatial dimensions themselves). This last is a fine piece of exaggeration or hyperbole, which the poet half-acknowledges when he says in lines 19–20 that the lady deserves "this state," which here means "elaborate ceremonial treatment," and that he would not love her at a "lower rate," which refers to both speed and his expenditure of language. We get a sense that the extravagance and slowness are being slightly ridiculed here. The ridicule is slight only because the note of mockery occurs about 20 lines away from the opening "Had we but . . . time," as if the speaker had forgotten his mortality. So it is, the poem implies, with all our delays and elaborations: they can occur only because we forget that we are to die.

The middle section of the poem introduces another traditional theme, but one that is not common to erotic poetry. We might call this the "reminder of death" theme, or we can borrow a term from the fine arts and call it *memento mori* (Latin for "remember you must die"). In painting, for example, *memento mori* were still-lifes that often showed a table, littered with the fallen petals of dying flowers, on which rested rotting fruit and a skull. This image was usually understood as a reminder of human mortality and often associated with Christian meditation. Love poetry, especially *carpe diem* poems, also used emblems that served as reminders of human mortality. The most common, perhaps, was the short-lived rose. Marvell has, in this poem, invented another reminder of human mortality—"Time's chariot," which ushers in his vision of the grave and his meditation on the urgency of love. At the beginning of this meditation, in lines 25–27, the grammar is slightly tricky because of the inversion of a phrase. We can make this perfectly clear with a minor adjustment: "In thy marble vault" (a) your beauty will not be visible, and (b) my love poetry will not be audible.

And then something rather complex and remarkable happens in the poem's use of language. The terms "virginity," "honour," and "lust" (lines 28–30) are all abstract words, applying to conditions or states of human life. ("Honour" means, in the context of Marvell's poem, chastity.) And yet, in the images of lines 27–30, these abstract terms are coupled with powerful concrete objects—worms, dust, and ashes—all of which are traditionally associated with the decay of the body after death. Worms will "try" (in the various senses of "test," "attempt," "strain," "experience") the lady's virginity by invading the body that had refused all sexual penetration in life. In this image, the abstract word "virginity" is a euphemism for the physical impediment to sex, the hymen. So too with "quaint honour" and "lust": they are also euphemisms. Abstract entities, such as virtue, reputation, anger, wisdom, do not decay into earth as do the bodies that, when living, manifest or engender them. To say that fame crumbles is to say, metaphorically, that a statue or monument does. In Marvell's lines, the multiple meanings of "quaint" ("fastidious," but with a pun on "cunt") tend to make concrete the lady's chastity, and, by implication, the poet's desire, as the two sets of sexual organs, both of which will, without question, decay or turn to "dust" and "ashes." The final couplet of the poem's middle section continues this suggestion with the overtones of the words "fine" (in the sense of "narrow") and "private" (as in "private parts," the old euphemism for genitalia).

The remarkable way in which these terms work both abstractly and concretely is part of the poem's argument: if we, in our evasive language about bodies, use abstract terms as euphemisms, death will have the last word by reducing chastity and desire to the vagina and the penis, and these to dust after all.

While reading the middle section, we can observe a continuation of the parallel treatment of time and space introduced in the first line. One kind of anatomy chart for the structure of the poem is the skeleton of its argument that we outlined earlier. Here is another diagram—if not of the poem's skeleton, then perhaps of its nervous system:

SPACE	TIME
World	*time*
(she)	*(he)*
walk	*pass*
Ganges' side	*Humber* ("tide" also means "time")
Flood	*Conversion of the Jews*
vaster	*more slow*
state	*rate*
deserts	*Time's wingèd chariot*
beauty found	*echoing song* heard

Virginity
Honour
lust
worms
dust
ashes
fine
private

It is as if time narrows down to death, and space narrows down to the grave. In death, at any rate, the distinctions between time and space vanish. In the center column we have all the images that cannot be assigned to the temporal or spatial sides of the diagram. Just as the lovers will come together in the grave, by separately decaying into the same substance, so do the image patterns that divide the poem's language join at the end. Even before we come to the "Now therefore . . ." conclusion, then, we have been shown an implicit argument through the images: lovers might as well come together joyfully and alive in bed, instead of joylessly and dead in the grave.

Images in the final section are much more allusive than those in the first two. Lines 35–36 imply that the lady's reticence cannot prevent her own erotic feeling from revealing itself in her blushes. By comparing the lovers to the fierce image of birds of prey, the speaker urges the lady to join him in devouring the great beast of time ("Devouring Time," Shakespeare calls him in a sonnet) before they themselves get eaten. The strength referred to in line 41 is not simply his and the sweetness hers: both qualities belong to each character. Also, Marvell's readers would have known that in the Book of Judges (Chapter 14),

Samson sets a riddle about bringing sweetness out of strength by presenting the image of a honeycomb in the carcass of a lion. The point is that all the oppositions and polarities—of sex, time, and space—are to be affirmatively joined, rather than allowed to fall together in death. The final images underline this joining: *strength, sweetness,* the *ball* (both a kind of cannonball and a pomander, or fragrant orange stuck with cloves and other spices), the *gates,* etc. Strength, rather than sweetness, seems to set the tone for the poem's last lines. The phrase "iron gates of life" is wonderfully evocative, whether or not we consider it allusive. The realities and difficulties of daily life always seem to keep gates locked against pleasure. In classical literature the twin gates of ivory and horn were the portals of sleep though which false (ivory) and true (horn) dreams came into the world; Marvell's iron gates seem even stronger. The final couplet alludes to the Biblical tale of Joshua (10:12–14), who commanded the sun to stand still in order to win a battle. This allusion underscores the conclusion to the argument: "We can't halt time, but we can make it whiz by in pleasure." What is unstated is the undertone that lingers from the middle section of the poem: "And the fact that this whizzing by of time also hastens us toward the grave is, for the moment, forgotten and irrelevant."

It is not only the images and their patterns that mark out the different sections of the poem. Each section has a distinct tone. We might think of the first as being a kind of verbal strolling, the second a sort of involuntary shuddering at death, and the final one a sweet-strong, almost violent, verbal equivalent of physical contact. The rhythm of the verse throughout the poem underscores this. The *tetrameter,* four-beat and eight-syllabled couplets, is varied rhythmically in certain significant ways. An early instance is

> My vegetable love should grow
> Vaster than empires and more slow

where instead of the normal cadence in the first line—de *dum* de *dum* de *dum* de *dum*—we get *dum* de de *dum* de, de *dum dum,* and if we shift the stress to "*and*" in an effort to hear the line as being more regular, it makes for an emphasis of "*and* more slow"; in either event, we seem to feel a rhythmic slowness.

More obvious is the celebrated shift of movement in lines 21–22:

> But at my back I always hear
> Time's wingèd Chariot hurrying near

The extra syllables set up a beat of *dum* de de that repeats itself and makes us "always hear" the speeding up of things. In this case, it is only the verse which speeds up, but we implicitly take it as a kind of acceleration of a clock's ticking.

This poem is interesting not only because of its great compression and terseness but also because the relation of its *poetic* thought, the energies of the words and images themselves, to the *logical* thought, revealed in our opening analysis, is so vital. Moreover, it is a poem which used to be admired because it seemed to represent the opposite of sentimentality and because any feelings the poet may have had were completely externalized in the poem's language. There are also many other grounds for admiring it; some of these may emerge if you think about what the poem—rather than its outward argument—seems to suggest about the relation of love poetry, of language, to feeling and to death itself.

CRAZY JANE TALKS WITH THE BISHOP

William Butler Yeats

I met the Bishop on the road
And much said he and I.
'Those breasts are flat and fallen now,
Those veins must soon be dry;
Live in a heavenly mansion,   5
Not in some foul sty.'

'Fair and foul are near of kin,
And fair needs foul,' I cried.
'My friends are gone, but that's a truth
Nor° grave nor bed denied,   10
Learned in bodily lowliness
And in the heart's pride.

'A woman can be proud and stiff
When on love intent;
But Love has pitched his mansion in   15
The place of excrement;
For nothing can be sole or whole
That has not been rent.'

Questions for Writing and Discussion

1. In this encounter, the Bishop counsels the spiritual, rather than the bodily life; what is the old hag's answer? What does she mean by the last two lines?

2. What is Crazy Jane saying in lines 15–16? Is she making an abstract, general statement about love personified? Do the "mansion" of love and "the place of excrement" refer to human anatomy in a specific way?

3. Consider the words "pitched" and "mansion" in line 15: what effect is gained by their use? (Try the line out with synonyms, such as "Love has built his palace" for example.)

Nor: neither

I CANNOT LIVE WITH YOU

Emily Dickinson

I cannot live with You—
It would be Life—
And Life is over there—
Behind the Shelf

The Sexton keeps the Key to—   5
Putting up
Our Life—His Porcelain—
Like a Cup—

Discarded of the Housewife—
Quaint—or Broke—   10
A newer Sèvres° pleases—
Old Ones crack—

I could not die—with You—
For One must wait
To shut the Other's Gaze down—   15
You—could not—

And I—Could I stand by
And see You—freeze—
Without my Right of Frost—
Death's privilege?   20

Nor could I rise—with You—
Because Your Face
Would put out Jesus'—
That New Grace

Glow plain—and foreign   25
On my homesick Eye—
Except that You than He
Shone closer by—

They'd judge Us—How—
For You—served Heaven—You know,   30
Or sought to—
I could not—

Because You saturated Sight—
And I had no more Eyes
For sordid excellence   35
As Paradise

Sèvres: a costly porcelain, light blue in color, manufactured in France

And were You lost, I would be—
Though My Name
Rang loudest
On the Heavenly fame—   40

And were You—saved—
And I—condemned to be
Where You were not—
That self—were Hell to Me—

So We must meet apart—   45
You there—I—here—
With just the Door ajar
That Oceans are—and Prayer—
And that White Sustenance—
Despair—   50

Questions for Writing and Discussion

1. Emily Dickinson's own idiosyncratic use of dashes is preserved here. Repunctuate the poem to make the syntax apparent.

2. The dense argumentative structure of this poem suggests a deliberate inversion of the conventions of a courtly lyric, in which a man tries to persuade a woman to give up her chastity because *it stands to reason* that she should. Is Emily Dickinson in love with the person she addresses as "you"? Or is she merely playful and intent on putting that person off?

3. Why are oceans like a door ajar (lines 47–48)? Why is despair called a "White Sustenance" (line 49)?

SECRET LOVE

John Clare

I hid my love when young while I
Couldn't bear the buzzing of a fly;
I hid my love to my despite
Till I could not bear to look at light:
I dare not gaze upon her face   5
But left her memory in each place;
Where'er I saw a wild flower lie
I kissed and bade my love good-bye.

I met her in the greenest dells,

Where dewdrops pearl the wood bluebells;   10
The lost breeze kissed her bright blue eye,
The bee kissed and went singing by,
A sunbeam found a passage there,
A gold chain round her neck so fair;
As secret as the wild bee's song   15
She lay there all the summer long.

I hid my love in field and town
Till e'en the breeze would knock me down;
The bees seemed singing ballads o'er,
The fly's buss° turned a lion's roar;   20
And even silence found a tongue,
To haunt me all the summer long;
The riddle nature could not prove
Was nothing else but secret love.

THE SICK ROSE

William Blake

O Rose thou art sick.
The invisible worm,
That flies in the night
In the howling storm:

Has found out thy bed   5
Of crimson joy:
And his dark secret love
Does thy life destroy.

Discussion

Clare's exquisite little song is one of the easiest poems to read in this
anthology, and one of the hardest to understand. It is, of course, about an
obsessive love, the nature of which the speaker has never revealed to himself. In
this as in other respects, the poem is very close to Blake's "The Sick Rose." The
love of "Secret Love" is the "dark secret love" of Blake's poem: it is not a
comfortable secret, which is kept up by being discreet; rather, the speaker
makes his love secret by alienating himself from his own deepest impulse. The

buss: buzz

difficulty of the poem is that this alienation is made to seem attractive—pretty, that is, and delicate in its effect.

Instead of finding his love where, and as, she truly is, the speaker finds her in the forms of nature: the wind, the flowers, the sun. And all of these are scaled down to a reassuring size. An act of erotic displacement is performed in the second stanza: the body of the lover is rendered vivid, and at the same time inaccessibly mysterious, when the speaker thinks of it as the body of nature. In this way he succeeds in evading his desire without seeming to avert his gaze.

Nature takes its revenge in the final stanza by growing immense and terrible. Where the speaker once found comfort in gazing on what could never seem to him overtly erotic, he is now rewarded for this self-deception by the presence of a nature that is neither erotic nor comforting. The "secret" of his love has turned into a riddle; he is left alone in the world, with no true image of desire, and no false one.

You may wish to chart the poem's progress—so deceptive, because its diction seems all of a piece—by the central words in each stanza. It is a poem that moves from "gaze" and "love" and "memory," to "lost" and "bright" and "chain," to "haunt" and "riddle" and "nothing."

A courtly tradition in poetry makes available to us the comparison of a chaste and beautiful lady to a rose. In Blake's poem, the first half of the comparison is only implied, but the self-corrupting nature of a purity that isolates itself from all knowledge is something we know by our experience of the human world. The poem is a statement, contained in one line, followed by an explanation, contained in seven. And yet, the explanation is more devious than we at first suspect; perhaps, after all, it brings us back to the simple statement, "O Rose thou art sick." In reading the poem we have to ask ourselves how "crimson joy" may differ from joy, and "dark secret love" from love. Does the worm alone destroy the rose? Or is there something in the rose itself that carries the seeds of its destruction?

LIVING IN SIN

Adrienne Rich

She had thought the studio would keep itself;
no dust upon the furniture of love.
Half heresy, to wish the taps less vocal,
the panes relieved of grime. A plate of pears,
a piano with a Persian shawl, a cat   5
stalking the picturesque amusing mouse
had risen at his urging.
Not that at five each separate stair would writhe
under the milkman's tramp; that morning light

so coldly would delineate the scraps   10
of last night's cheese and three sepulchral bottles;
that on the kitchen shelf among the saucers
a pair of beetle-eyes would fix her own—
envoy from some black village in the mouldings . . .
Meanwhile, he, with a yawn,   15
sounded a dozen notes upon the keyboard,
declared it out of tune, shrugged at the mirror,
rubbed at his beard, went out for cigarettes;
while she, jeered by the minor demons,
pulled back the sheets and made the bed and found   20
a towel to dust the table-top,
and let the coffee-pot boil over on the stove.
By evening she was back in love again,
though not so wholly but throughout the night
she woke sometimes to feel the daylight coming   25
like a relentless milkman up the stairs.

Questions for Writing and Discussion

1. Having read the poem, what tone do you suppose the speaker would give to the phrase that she adopts as her title?

2. In the narrative movement of this poem, do you find any of the conventions of a novel (e.g., "once upon a time"; description of the hero or heroine's financial state; etc.)?

3. How closely bound does the poem imply "she" and "he" are? (By how many lines are they separated in the poem itself? What is the effect of "meanwhile"?)

4. What about the speaker's attitude toward herself and her lover is implied by the way she chooses to connect her last two sentences: "and let the coffee-pot boil over on the stove./By evening she was back in love again"?

5. Does the milkman on the stairs—every day at dawn—carry a suggestion of constancy or fidelity? If so, does the same hold true of the "relentless milkman" at the end of the poem?

Elegy and Epitaph

Death is inevitable and, for humans, universal. We lose other people to death, we cause their deaths or struggle to prevent them, we watch others die. But all we know of dying is a kind of hearsay. It is inevitable that poetry, whether religious, secular, private, or public, should be continually absorbed with death: to die oneself is a literal experience, but everything the living say of dying or death is some kind of figurative utterance. When someone dies, there is in one profound sense absolutely nothing to say. And yet the need somehow to celebrate life at every instance of its termination, whether a welcomed or a ghastly death, leads to post-mortem utterance. Once silence is broken, the modes of utterance can vary widely: language can be used to console others, to console oneself, to question and to answer, to understand and to reconcile; it can be an extension of—or replacement for—some more elaborate ceremony. For example, an elaborate poem can take the place of a tomb of great proportions or elegance, and in the past, poems (poesy) have frequently been attached like, and with, flowers (posies) to a coffin, hearse, or grave.

Many religious ceremonies are symbolic enactments of a larger, explanatory scheme of reconciliation to death. Ceremonies can symbolize some kind of resurrection or a continuing process of another sort. The poetic language attending on such enactments can be very powerful and exemplary even out of its ceremonial context. Here, for example, is part of the burial service from the Book of Common Prayer of the Church of England. As you can see, it starts out by confronting the transitoriness of life.

At the grave.

When they come to the Grave, while the Body is made ready to be laid into the earth, shall be sung or said,

475

Man, that is born of a woman, hath but a short time to live, and is full of misery. He cometh up, and is cut down, like a flower; he fleeth as it were a shadow, and never continueth in one stay.

In the midst of life we are in death; of whom may we seek for succour, but of thee, O Lord, who for our sins art justly displeased?

Yet, O Lord God most holy, O Lord most mighty, O holy and most merciful Saviour, deliver us not into the bitter pains of eternal death.

Thou knowest, Lord, the secrets of our hearts; shut not thy merciful ears to our prayer; but spare us, Lord most holy, O God most mighty, O holy and merciful Saviour, thou most worthy Judge eternal, suffer us not, at our last hour, for any pains of death, to fall from thee.

Then, while the earth shall be cast upon the Body by some standing by, the Minister shall say,

Unto Almighty God we commend the soul of our *brother* departed, and we commit *his* body to the ground; earth to earth, ashes to ashes, dust to dust; in sure and certain hope of the Resurrection unto eternal life, through our Lord Jesus Christ; at whose coming in glorious majesty to judge the world, the earth and the sea shall give up their dead; and the corruptible bodies of those who sleep in him shall be changed, and made like unto his own glorious body; according to the mighty working whereby he is able to subdue all things unto himself.

Then shall be said or sung,

I heard a voice from heaven, saying unto me, Write, From henceforth blessed are the dead who die in the Lord: even so saith the Spirit; for they rest from their labours.

Then the Minister shall say,

The Lord be with you.
Answer. And with thy spirit.

The imagery of these passages survives by allusion in much of the poetry in our language. The redemptive pattern it leads to is part of the Christian view of death and resurrection. But there are also other elements of our tradition of *elegy,* or poetry for the dead, that come from pre- or non-Christian sources. Consider this little epigram by Plato (translated by Shelley) to the same boy, Aster, celebrated in the loving epigram on page 328:

> Thou wert the morning star among the living
> Ere thy fair light had fled;
> Now, having died, thou art as Hesperus, giving,
> New splendour to the dead.

(Hesperus is the evening star.) This epigram is elegant, witty, gently resigned, and, despite its elaborate metaphor—itself based on a pun on Aster's name— reserved in what it makes of death's finality. This kind of funerary epigram may or not be an actual *epitaph,* or gravestone inscription, but it will frequently function like one. In the poems which follow, a variety of attitudes are taken toward particular deaths and death in general. We will see running through the poems a never-ending struggle between the literalness of death and the figurative powers of language.

ON SOLOMON PAVY

A Child of Queen Elizabeth's Chapel

Ben Jonson

Weep with me, all you that read
    This little story;
And know, for whom a tear you shed
    Death's self is sorry.
'Twas a child that so did thrive   5
    In grace and feature,
As Heaven and Nature seemed to strive
    Which owned the creature.
Years he numbered scarce thirteen
    When Fates turned cruel,   10
Yet three filled Zodiacs° had he been
    The Stage's jewel;
And did act (what now we moan)
    Old men so duly,
As sooth the Parcae° thought him one,   15
    He played so truly.
So, by error, to his fate
    They all consented;
But, viewing him since, alas, too late!
    They have repented;   20
And have sought, to give new birth,
    In baths° to steep him;
But, being so much too good for earth,
    Heaven vows to keep him.

Questions for Writing and Discussion

1. This poem mourns the death of a child actor. We all tend to feel that the death of a child is a particular outrage, a particular error in nature's cycles. How does "this little story" cope with such a sense of outrage?

---

filled Zodiacs: whole (and busy) year **Parcae:** the three Fates—in Greek mythology, they spun, measured, and cut the thread of life **baths:** magical restorative baths

2.   This is like an extended epigram. At what line does it seem to divide into individual epigrams within itself?

3.   What is the tone here? Does the ingenuity of the argument, the elegance of the "story," make the whole poem seem frivolous? Why?

A REFUSAL TO MOURN THE DEATH, BY FIRE, OF A CHILD IN LONDON

Dylan Thomas

Never until the mankind making
Bird beast and flower
Fathering and all humbling darkness
Tells with silence the last light breaking
And the still hour   5
Is come of the sea tumbling in harness

And I must enter again the round
Zion of the water bead
And the synagogue of the ear of corn
Shall I let pray the shadow of a sound   10
Or sow my salt seed
In the least valley of sackcloth to mourn

The majesty and burning of the child's death.
I shall not murder
The mankind of her going with a grave truth   15
Nor blaspheme down the stations of the breath
With any further
Elegy of innocence and youth.

Deep with the first dead lies London's daughter,
Robed in the long friends,   20
The grains beyond age, the dark veins of her mother,
Secret by the unmourning water
Of the riding Thames.
After the first death, there is no other.

Questions for Writing and Discussion

1.   Pick out some of the specifically religious images here. How are they used in a personal, secular way?

2. How can "mankind making," "bird beast and flower fathering," and "all humbling" be considered attributes of darkness? What is this darkness?

3. Thomas says he will not "murder/The mankind" of this child's death "with a grave truth/Nor blaspheme down the stations of breath/With any further/Elegy of innocence and youth." What does he mean by the "the mankind of her going"? The phrase, "any further elegy" implies an awareness of earlier elegies, which are seen as different in kind from this one. Why does Thomas reject these?

DEATH OF A SON
(who died in a mental hospital aged one)

Jon Silkin

Something has ceased to come along with me.
Something like a person: something very like one.
     And there was no nobility in it
        Or anything like that.

     Something was there like a one year   5
Old house, dumb as stone. While the near buildings
     Sang like birds and laughed
        Understanding the pact

     They were to have with silence. But he
Neither sang nor laughed. He did not bless silence   10
     Like bread, with words.
        He did not forsake silence.

     But rather, like a house in mourning
Kept the eye turned in to watch the silence while
     The other houses like birds   15
        Sang around him.

And the breathing silence neither
Moved nor was still.

     I have seen stones: I have seen brick
But this house was made up of neither bricks nor stone   20
     But a house of flesh and blood
        With flesh of stone

     And bricks for blood. A house
Of stones and blood in breathing silence with the other
     Birds singing crazy on its chimneys.   25
        But this was silence,

This was something else, this was
Hearing and speaking though he was a house drawn
Into silence, this was
                Something religious in his silence,   30

Something shining in his quiet,
This was different this was altogether something else:
Though he never spoke, this
                Was something to do with death.

And then slowly the eye stopped looking   35
Inward. The silence rose and became still.
The look turned to the outer place and stopped,
                With the birds still shrilling around him.
                And as if he could speak

He turned over on his side with his one year   40
Red as a wound
He turned over as if he could be sorry for this
And out of his eyes two great tears rolled, like stones,
                and he died.

Questions for Writing and Discussion

1.   The child of this poem is mentally retarded and dies at an age before any of us reach full consciousness of ourselves. The special feeling connected with the death of a being fully human, but not quite *recognizably* human, is hinted at in the second line, where the child is called "Something like a person: something very like one." Can you find phrases in the poem that describe this child's almost-human awareness, from the child's own point of view?

2.   What is the cumulative effect of the word "something" in stanzas VIII and IX? Of the phrase "as if"?

3.   Does the poem ever ask us to pity the child? To sympathize with him?

4.   It is traditional for an elegy to portray nature as mourning the death of a human being. Does nature mourn for the death of this child? Why, or why not?

THE VOW

Anthony Hecht

In the third month, a sudden flow of blood.
The mirth of tabrets ceaseth, and the joy
Also of the harp. The frail image of God

Lay spilled and formless. Neither girl nor boy,
But yet blood of my blood, nearly my child.   5
        All that long day
Her pale face turned to the window's mild
        Featureless grey.

And for some nights she whimpered as she dreamed
The dead thing spoke, saying: "Do not recall   10
Pleasure at my conception. I am redeemed
From pain and sorrow. Mourn rather for all
Who breathlessly issue from the bone gates,
        The gates of horn,
For truly it is best of all the fates   15
        Not to be born.

"Mother, a child lay gasping for bare breath
On Christmas Eve when Santa Claus had set
Death in the stocking, and the lights of death
Flamed in the tree. O, if you can, forget   20
You were the child, turn to my father's lips
        Against the time
When his cold hand puts forth its fingertips
        Of jointed lime."

Doctors of Science, what is man that he   25
Should hope to come to a good end? *The best
Is not to have been born.* And could it be
That Jewish diligence and Irish jest
The consent of flesh and a midwinter storm
        Had reconciled,   30
Was yet too bold a mixture to inform
        A simple child?

Even as gold is tried, Gentile and Jew.
If that ghost was a girl's, I swear to it:
Your mother shall be far more blessed than you.   35
And if a boy's, I swear: The flames are lit
That shall refine us; they shall not destroy
        A living hair.
Your younger brothers shall confirm in joy
        This that I swear.   40

Questions for Writing and Discussion

1. The "gates of horn" were those through which, in classical mythology, true
dreams issued forth into the world. (False dreams came through ivory gates.) What

are the "bone gates" in the poem? What is their relation to the mythological ones? to "the iron gates" in Andrew Marvell's "To His Coy Mistress" on p. 463?

2.   Do you detect any allusions in the poem? Of what sort? Where?

3.   How does this poem differ from those you have read about the deaths of children? Is it a poem of mourning?

4.   What point is being raised about the relation of birth and death in the lines about Christmas?

ELEGY FOR JANE
My Student, Thrown by a Horse

Theodore Roethke

I remember the neckcurls, limp and damp as tendrils;
And her quick look, a sidelong pickerel smile;
And how, once startled into talk, the light syllables leaped for her,
And she balanced in the delight of her thought,
A wren, happy, tail into the wind   5
Her song trembling the twigs and small branches.
The shade sang with her;
The leaves, their whispers turned to kissing;
And the mold sang in the bleached valleys under the rose.

Oh, when she was sad, she cast herself down into such a pure depth,   10
Even a father could not find her:
Scraping her cheek against straw;
Stirring the clearest water.

My sparrow, you are not here,
Waiting like a fern, making a spiny shadow.   15
The sides of wet stones cannot console me,
Nor the moss, wound with the last light.

If only I could nudge you from this sleep,
My maimed darling, my skittery pigeon.
Over this damp grave I speak the words of my love: 20
I, with no rights in this matter,
Neither father nor lover.

Questions for Writing and Discussion

1.   The speaker of this poem compares Jane to a fish, then to a wren, a sparrow, and a pigeon. These associations ask us to imagine her as a swift, darting creature, a

spirit of air and water, whose proper home is in nature. Do the comparisons lead in a particular direction—toward or away from creatures of whom we have a common knowledge? If you think there is such a movement, what is its effect?

2.   Let us suppose that the "Elegy" is meant to be recited formally, at the graveside, with mourners listening. Does the poet's sense that he has "no rights in this matter" determine what he chooses to remember? Would the poem have been better suited to its occasion if he gave a more personal reminiscence of Jane?

3.   The speaker goes out of his way to tell us that "The sides of wet stones cannot console me,/Nor the moss, wound with the last light." Given his picture of Jane, why *might* they console him? Are the moss and wet stones part of Jane's actual life, or do they belong more properly to the sparrow to whom Jane is compared? And what does the poet's refusal to be consoled tell us about his belief, or disbelief, in the fiction of this poem, which presents Jane as inseparable from nature?

TO THE MEMORY OF MR. OLDHAM

John Dryden

Farewell, too little, and too lately known,
Whom I began to think and call my own:
For sure our souls were near allied, and thine
Cast in the same poetic mould with mine.
One common note on either lyre did strike,   5
And knaves and fools we both abhorred alike.
To the same goal did both our studies drive;
The last set out the soonest did arrive.
Thus Nisus° fell upon the slippery place,
While his young friend performed and won the race.   10
O early ripe! to thy abundant store
What could advancing age have added more?
It might (what nature never gives the young)
Have taught the numbers° of thy native tongue.
But satire needs not those, and wit will shine   15
Through the harsh cadence of a rugged line:
A noble error, and but seldom made,
When poets are by too much force betrayed.
Thy generous fruits, though gathered ere their prime,
Still showed a quickness;° and maturing time   20
But mellows what we write to the dull sweets of rhyme.
Once more, hail and farewell; farewell, thou young,
But ah too short, Marcellus° of our tongue;

Nisus: in Virgil's *Aeneid,* he slipped and fell in a footrace   **numbers:** smoothness of poetic meter   **quickness:** vitality   **Marcellus:** the young nephew and heir of the Emperor Augustus, dead at twenty

Thy brows with ivy, and with laurels bound;
But fate and gloomy night encompass thee around.   25

Questions for Writing and Discussion

1. This is Dryden's poem on the death of a poet and satirist twenty years younger than himself. How does the poem deal with the problem of mourning a young person of promise rather than of perfect accomplishments (like Mozart, for example)?

2. Is there a change of tone and subject in line 11? How is the image of ripeness used here and in lines 19–21? (Comment on the phrase "dull sweets of rhyme".) What in satirical poetry is more important than smoothness ("numbers" in line 14)?

3. Poets are traditionally thought of as crowned, like victorious Roman soldiers or athletes, with laurels. What is the effect of the last line? (Wouldn't you have expected the last two lines to be reversed, to say "You're surrounded by death's night, *but* immortal in your poetry?")

MONODY°

Herman Melville

To have known him, to have loved him
     After loneness long;
And then to be estranged in life,
     And neither in the wrong;
And now for death to set his seal—   5
     Ease me, a little ease, my song!

By wintry hills his hermit-mound
     The sheeted snow-drifts drape,
And houseless there the snow-bird flits
     Beneath the fir-trees' crape:°   10
Glazed now with ice the cloistral vine
     That hid the shyest grape.

Questions for Writing and Discussion

1. Melville associates Hawthorne's solitary spirit with the "hermit-mound" under which he now lies buried. With what part of the landscape, if any, do you think

Monody: a song carried by a single voice; Melville wrote this poem on hearing of Hawthorne's death in 1864; the two great writers had been close friends before growing estranged in middle life   crape: thin, worsted material used for the gowns of clergymen

Melville associates himself? If you agree that these associations are present *at all,* you will have noticed that they are delicately concealed. Does this imply anything about the qualities Melville found in Hawthorne's art? Does the poem make you think Melville admired these qualities unreservedly?

2.   What sort of critical observation about Hawthorne's work might be implied in the lines, "Glazed now with ice the cloistral vine/That hid the shyest grape"? What is the tone of "shyest grape"? Is it flatly descriptive? tender? reproving?

PRAISE FOR AN URN
In Memoriam: Ernest Nelson

Hart Crane

It was a kind and northern face
That mingled in such exile guise
The everlasting eyes of Pierrot°
And, of Gargantua,° the laughter.

His thoughts, delivered to me   5
From the white coverlet and pillow,
I see now, were inheritances—
Delicate riders of the storm.

The slant moon on the slanting hill
Once moved us toward presentiments   10
Of what the dead keep, living still,
And such assessments of the soul

As, perched in the crematory lobby,
The insistent clock commented on,
Touching as well upon our praise   15
Of glories proper to the time.

Still, having in mind gold hair,
I cannot see that broken brow
And miss the dry sound of bees
Stretching across a lucid space.   20

Scatter these well-meant idioms
Into the smoky spring that fills
The suburbs, where they will be lost.
They are no trophies of the sun.

Pierrot: a fool and comic butt in traditional French pantomine; his whole face was painted white; hence, the eyes would stand out   **Gargantua:** a gigantic king, hero of a vast comic tale by Rabelais, whose appetite and humor were on a scale with his size

Questions for Writing and Discussion

1.   The title of this poem informs us that Crane is addressing not the dead man but the urn that contains his ashes. Where in the poem do you find evidence of a detachment that might be suited to this mode of address? Are the ashes ever mentioned explicitly? obliquely?

2.   What does Crane mean by "exile guise"? In what sense does the man whose death Crane mourns wear that guise? How does it connect him with Pierrot and Gargantua?

3.   At the end of his "Ode to the West Wind" (p. 509), Shelley asks the wind's fierce spirit to "Drive my dead thoughts over the universe/Like withered leaves to quicken a new birth!/ . . . Scatter, as from an unextinguished hearth/Ashes and sparks, my words among mankind." How close to this is the wish that Crane expresses at the end of "Praise for an Urn"?

BECAUSE I COULD NOT STOP FOR DEATH

Emily Dickinson

Because I could not stop for Death—
He kindly stopped for me—
The Carriage held but just Ourselves—
And Immortality.

We slowly drove—He knew no haste   5
And I had put away
My labor and my leisure too,
For His Civility—

We passed the School, where Children strove
At Recess—in the Ring—   10
We passed the Fields of Gazing Grain—
We passed the Setting Sun—

Or rather—He passed Us—
The Dews drew quivering and chill—
For only Gossamer, my Gown—   15
My Tippet°—only Tulle—°

We paused before a House that seemed
A Swelling of the Ground—
The Roof was scarcely visible—
The Cornice—in the Ground—   20

Tippet: covering attached to the upper part of a gown; here, a shawl or mantle   **Tulle:** fine silk net

Since then—'tis Centuries—and yet
Feels shorter than the Day
I first surmised the Horses Heads
Were toward Eternity—

Questions for Writing and Discussion

1.   One of the "Proverbs of Hell" in William Blake's *The Marriage of Heaven and Hell* informs us: "Prudence is a rich, ugly old maid, courted by Incapacity." Construct an epigram about Death's courtship of the poet in "Because I Could Not Stop For Death."

2.   What sort of imagination would think, "We passed the Fields of Gazing Grain," and then, "We passed the Setting Sun," as if they were parallel and equally plausible statements? What do you learn about this poet's imagination by the correction that follows—"Or rather—He passed Us"? Is she anxious? or just correct? or unworried, and honestly observant, and used to restraining her own flights of fancy?

3.   Why do Death and the poet pause before the unfamiliar house, when they have passed everything else on their way? What is strange about the look of the house? Who might live there?

4.   Suppose the last lines of this poem read: "I guessed the Horses galloped toward/The land Eternity"? Would the poem be improved? ruined? Why?

IN MEMORY OF JANE FRAZER

Geoffrey Hill

When snow like sheep lay in the fold
And winds went begging at each door,
And the far hills were blue with cold,
And a cold shroud lay on the moor,

She kept the siege. And every day   5
We watched her brooding over death
Like a strong bird above its prey.
The room filled with the kettle's breath.

Damp curtains glued against the pane
Sealed time away. Her body froze   10
As if to freeze us all, and chain
Creation to a stunned repose.

She died before the world could stir.
In March the ice unloosed the brook
And water ruffled the sun's hair.   15
Dead cones upon the alder shook.

Questions for Writing and Discussion

1.   The poet tells us that Jane Frazer awaited her death "Like a strong bird above its prey." In the images of death that you recall from songs, stories, and poems, is it the dying person or death itself that is usually imagined as "prey"? What does the image in this poem tell us about Jane Frazer's attitude toward her death? Is this attitude shared by the poet?

2.   In an earlier version of this elegy, a comma appeared at the end of line 15, and the last line read: "And a few sprinkled leaves unshook." What is the emotional difference between the two versions?

ELEGY
WRITTEN IN A COUNTRY CHURCHYARD

Thomas Gray

The curfew tolls the knell of parting day,
   The lowing herd wind slowly o'er the lea,
The ploughman homeward plods his weary way,
   And leaves the world to darkness and to me.

Now fades the glimmering landscape on the sight,   5
   And all the air a solemn stillness holds,
Save where the beetle wheels his droning flight,
   And drowsy tinklings lull the distant folds;

Save that from yonder ivy-mantled tower
   The moping owl does to the moon complain   10
Of such, as wandering near her secret bower,
   Molest her ancient solitary reign.

Beneath those rugged elms, that yew-tree's shade,
   Where heaves the turf in many a mouldering heap,
Each in his narrow cell forever laid,   15
   The rude° forefathers of the hamlet sleep.

The breezy call of incense-breathing morn,
   The swallow twittering from the straw-built shed,

rude: unschooled

The cock's shrill clarion or the echoing horn,°
    No more shall rouse them from their lowly bed.   20

For them no more the blazing hearth shall burn,
    Or busy housewife ply her evening care;
No children run to lisp their sire's return,
    Or climb his knees the envied kiss to share.

Oft did the harvest to their sickle yield;   25
    Their furrow oft the stubborn glebe° has broke;
How jocund did they drive their team afield!
    How bowed the woods beneath their sturdy stroke!

Let not Ambition mock their useful toil,
    Their homely joys and destiny obscure;   30
Nor Grandeur hear with a disdainful smile
    The short and simple annals of the poor.

The boast of heraldry, the pomp of power,
    And all that beauty, all that wealth e'er gave,
Awaits alike the inevitable hour: 35
    The paths of glory lead but to the grave.

Nor you, ye proud, impute to these the fault.
    If Memory o'er their tomb no trophies° raise,
Where through the long-drawn aisle and fretted° vault
    The pealing anthem swells the note of praise.   40

Can storied urn or animated bust°
    Back to its mansion call the fleeting breath?
Can Honour's voice provoke° the silent dust,
    Or Flattery soothe the dull cold ear of Death?

Perhaps in this neglected spot is laid   45
    Some heart once pregnant with celestial fire;
Hands that the rod of empire might have swayed,
    Or waked to ecstasy the living lyre.

But Knowledge to their eyes her ample page,
    Rich with the spoils of time, did ne'er unroll;   50
Chill Penury repressed their noble rage,°
    And froze the genial current° of the soul.

Full many a gem of purest ray serene,
    The dark unfathomed caves of ocean bear;

---

echoing horn: hunter's horn, which echoes the cock's clarion **glebe:** soil **trophies:** monuments or memorials of the dead **fretted:** ornamented in relief with crossing lines **storied . . . bust:** a storied urn narrated a life in a sequence of tableaux, as one turned it; an animated bust is a piece of sculpture into which the artist has breathed a living sense of his subject **provoke:** call forth **rage:** ardor or intensity **genial current:** human potentiality

Full many a flower is born to blush unseen,   55
    And waste its sweetness on the desert air.

Some village Hampden,° that with dauntless breast
    The little tyrant of his fields withstood;
Some mute inglorious Milton° here may rest,
    Some Cromwell,° guiltless of his country's blood.   60

The applause of listening senates to command,
    The threats of pain and ruin to despise,
To scatter plenty o'er a smiling land,
    And read their history in a nation's eyes,

Their lot forbade; nor circumscribed alone   65
    Their growing virtues, but their crimes confined;
Forbade to wade through slaughter to a throne,
    And shut the gates of mercy on mankind;

The struggling pangs of conscious truth to hide,
    To quench the blushes of ingenuous shame,°   70
Or heap the shrine of Luxury and Pride
    With incense kindled at the Muse's flame.

Far from the madding crowd's ignoble strife,
    Their sober wishes never learned to stray;
Along the cool sequestered vale of life   75
    They kept the noiseless tenor of their way.

Yet even these bones from insult to protect,
    Some frail memorial still erected nigh,
With uncouth° rhymes and shapeless sculpture decked,
    Implores the passing tribute of a sigh.   80

Their name, their years, spelt by the unlettered Muse,
    The place of fame and elegy supply;
And many a holy text around she strews,
    That teach the rustic moralist to die.

For who, to dumb forgetfulness a prey,   85
    This pleasing anxious being e'er resigned,
Left the warm precincts of the cheerful day,
    Nor cast one longing lingering look behind?

Hampden: John Hampden refused to pay a tax levied by Charles I; an act of individual protest
which Gray associates with individual glory, denied to the poor **mute inglorious Milton:**
someone who might have achieved the stature of Milton had he not lived out his days illiterate and so
inarticulate **Cromwell:** the Puritan rebel against the English crown who, as ruler of England, gave
himself the title of "Lord Protector"; the "bloodshed" alluded to by Gray may refer to Cromwell's
military campaigns against the royalists in Ireland, Scotland, and England **ingenuous shame:**
shame that shows itself in blushes because it expresses an innocent soul **uncouth:** unrefined

On some fond breast the parting soul relies,
    Some pious drops° the closing eye requires;   90
Even from the tomb the voice of Nature cries,
    Even in our ashes live their wonted° fires.

For thee,° who mindful of the unhonoured dead
    Dost in these lines their artless tale relate;
If chance,° by lonely contemplation led,   95
    Some kindred spirit shall inquire thy fate,

Haply some hoary-headed swain may say,
    'Oft have we seen him at the peep of dawn
Brushing with hasty steps the dews away
    To meet the sun upon the upland lawn.   100

'There at the foot of yonder nodding beech
    That wreathes its old fantastic roots so high,
His listless length at noontide would he stretch,
    And pore upon the brook that babbles by.

'Hard by yon wood, now smiling as in scorn,   105
    Muttering his wayward fancies he would rove;
Now drooping, woeful-wan, like one forlorn,
    Or crazed with care, or crossed in hopeless love.

'One morn I missed him on the customed hill,
    Along the heath and near his favourite tree;   110
Another came; nor yet beside the rill,
    Nor up the lawn, nor at the wood was he;

'The next, with dirges due, in sad array,
    Slow through the church-way path we saw him borne.
Approach and read (for thou canst read) the lay,   115
    Graved on the stone beneath yon agèd thorn.'

THE EPITAPH

Here rests his head upon the lap of earth,
    A youth to fortune and to fame unknown;
Fair Science° frowned not on his humble birth,   120
    And Melancholy° marked him for her own.

Large was his bounty and his soul sincere;
    Heaven did a recompense as largely send:
He gave to Misery all he had, a tear;
    He gained from Heaven ('twas all he wished) a friend.   125

---

pious drops: tears of filial love and fidelity   **wonted**: accustomed   **thee**: the poet who writes these
lines **If chance**: ellipsis for "if it should chance that"   **Science**: knowledge, learning **Melancholy**: a susceptibility to feelings which implies sympathy

No farther seek his merits to disclose,
    Or draw his frailties from their dread abode,
(There they alike in trembling hope repose)
    The bosom of his Father and His God.

Questions for Writing and Discussion

1. What does the final line of Gray's first stanza—"And leaves the world to darkness and to me"—suggest about the speaker's mood by placing "darkness" and "me" in parallel grammatical positions? Is this the darkness of death? of obscurity?

2. In the march of allegorical traits that occupies much of the poem from line 28 to line 44, we hear real or imagined responses to those who are buried in the churchyard from Ambition, Grandeur, Memory, Honour, and Flattery. Later in the poem the allegorical agents of Knowledge, Penury, Luxury, and Pride are evoked. Are all of these traits equally despicable? Which of them, if any, does the context tell us may be vicious only by the *way* they are exhibited? What is the relation of these traits to the Melancholy and Science said in "The Epitaph" to be possessed by the speaker himself?

3. Is it better to be Oliver Cromwell or a "Cromwell, guiltless of his country's blood" (line 60)? John Milton or a "mute inglorious Milton"? Is the poem trying to persuade you that the two cases—the relation of John Milton to inglorious Milton and of Oliver Cromwell to guiltless Cromwell—are more similar than they really are? If so, why?

4. Some critics have found the speaker's turning back upon himself—at "For thee . . ." (line 93)—an abrupt transition in the poem. Can you justify it by considering what has come before and what comes after it? Why do you think Gray wrote "thee" instead of "me"?

5. How large a claim does the speaker make for himself in his epitaph? By casting it as a formal epitaph, and placing it at the end of his reflections, does he set himself above the village poor whom he has been describing?

The Poetry of Earth

Spring, summer, autumn, and winter: each of the seasons is naturally associated in our minds with a particular aspect of our experience of earth and of time. Spring is the time of rebirth; summer, of seemingly never-ending growth and ease; autumn, of ripening and decay; winter, of death, which can seem as permanent as summer's life, until we think of spring. Because they leave us with so complete a chronicle of birth, death, and rebirth, the seasons have been a single vast and inexhaustible store of poetic metaphors.

For Shelley in the "Ode to the West Wind," autumn *means* death, just as for William Carlos Williams in "Spring and All," spring *means* birth. Winter and summer are the steady seasons, which allow us to imagine for a moment that nature is all loss or all gain. But it is autumn and spring, the seasons of change, which have brought forth the most complex and dramatic poetry, since they include both loss and gain, and the mind likes to hold two ideas at once.

Shelley asks rhetorically at the end of his poem—"If Winter comes, can Spring be far behind?" Thus, while looking *forward* to a time of death and loss that has not yet come, he insists at the same time on looking *back* upon that time from the spring that will follow, in a heroic denial that winter's verdict can be final. Williams observes the fitful growths of early spring a little grimly, because the memory of winter is still with him: "rooted, they/grip down and begin to awaken." These examples are enough to show how unexpectedly the moods of earth correspond to our human moods. They both confirm and help us rebel against the tragic or even the comic, romantic, or ironic sense of life which we feel is uniquely ours.

493

DAYS

Ralph Waldo Emerson

Daughters of Time, the hypocritic Days,
Muffled and dumb like barefoot dervishes,
And marching single in an endless file,
Bring diadems and fagots° in their hands.
To each they offer gifts after his will,   5
Bread, kingdom, stars, and sky that holds them all.

I, in my pleached garden,° watched the pomp,
Forgot my morning wishes, hastily
Took a few herbs and apples, and the Day
Turned and departed silent. I, too late,   10
Under her solemn fillet° saw the scorn.

Questions for Writing and Discussion

1. To what sorts of persons might the Days bring sticks of wood or diadems? Does the speaker of the poem belong distinctly to either of these groups?

2. What element, in the passing spectacle of the imagined "pomp" of Days, distracts the speaker from his morning wishes? Can you guess what he might have wished for?

3. Do the phrases "I, in my pleached garden" and "I, too late" tend to isolate the speaker? To strengthen him? Why does he pick the herbs and apples "hastily"?

4. In lines 5–6 does Emerson suggest that we "will" the conditions of our life? Do we will the existence of the stars and sky too?

SPRING POOLS

Robert Frost

These pools that, though in forests, still reflect
The total sky almost without defect,
And like the flowers beside them, chill and shiver,
Will like the flowers beside them soon be gone,
And yet not out by any brook or river,   5
But up by roots to bring dark foliage on.

fagots: sticks of wood **pleached garden:** a garden covered or enclosed by intertwining branches **fillet:** a thin band encircling the hair

The trees that have it in their pent-up buds
To darken nature and be summer woods—
Let them think twice before they use their powers
To blot out and drink up and sweep away   10
These flowery waters and these watery flowers
From snow that melted only yesterday.

Questions for Writing and Discussion

1.   Line 11 arranges the words for flower and water (nouns and adjectives) in a
pattern of *abba,* a crisscrossing called *chiasmus* in old rhetoric books. How does the
purely decorative pattern of word placement embody the image in the line? In
what way are clarity and confusion both present in the line?

2.   Line 1 ends in a verb, "reflect," which can be transitive or intransitive depending on whether we stop at the end of the line or move on to the next one. What
does to *reflect* mean, other than to *reflect something?* Which is done by a mirror,
which by a mind? Similarly, what about the words "chill" and "shiver" (line 3): are
they verbs or adjectives?

3.   Is there anything playful about "Let them think twice"? Why?

THE POPLAR FIELD

William Cowper

The poplars are felled, farewell to the shade,
And the whispering sound of the cool colonnade;
The winds play no longer and sing in the leaves,
Nor Ouse° on his bosom their image receives.

Twelve years have elapsed since I last took a view   5
Of my favourite field, and the bank where they grew;
And now in the grass behold they are laid,
And the tree is my seat that once lent me a shade.

The blackbird has fled to another retreat,
Where the hazels afford him a screen from the heat,   10
And the scene where his melody charmed me before
Resounds with his sweet flowing ditty no more.

My fugitive years are all hasting away,
And I must ere long lie as lowly as they,

Ouse: an English river

With a turf on my breast, and a stone at my head,   15
Ere another such grove shall arise in its stead.

'Tis a sight to engage me if anything can,
To muse on the perishing pleasures of man;
Though his life be a dream, his enjoyments, I see,
Have a being less durable even than he.   20

BINSEY POPLARS
Felled 1879

Gerard Manley Hopkins

My aspens dear, whose airy cages quelled,
Quelled or quenched in leaves the leaping sun,
All felled, felled, are all felled:
   Of a fresh and following folded rank
      Not spared, not one   5
      That dandled a sandalled
    Shadow that swam or sank
On meadow and river and wind-wandering weed-winding bank.

  O if we but knew what we do
      When we delve or hew—   10
    Hack and rack the growing green!
     Since country is so tender
    To touch, her being só slender,
    That, like this sleek and seeing ball
    But a prick will make no eye at all,   15
    Where we, even where we mean
      To mend her we end her,
     When we hew or delve:
After-comers cannot guess the beauty been.
  Ten or twelve, only ten or twelve   20
    Strokes of havoc únselve
     The sweet especial scene,
    Rural scene, a rural scene,
    Sweet especial rural scene.

Questions for Writing and Discussion

1.   Here are two poems about the felling of a familiar grove of poplar trees. They contrast strongly in meter and rhythm, figurative language, tone, and overall view of the relation of man and nature. In "The Poplar Field," you might start out with

line 8: how does it embody the speaker's attitude throughout the poem? Is he anguished? bereaved? amused?

2.   During the nineteenth century, the meter of the poem was thought of as having the quality of a light, comic singsong. Here, it is certainly not comic. What quality of tone, then, does the meter give the poem? In what way does the meter seem to fill the vacancy left by the departed music of the wind and the blackbird?

3.   Notice how the description of vanished sights and sounds, in stanzas I and III, alternates with the meditation about time in stanzas II and IV. How are these alternating concerns maintained in stanza V? In what way does this stanza serve as a summary of the preceding stanzas?

4.   What does the poet mean in line 17 by "a sight to *engage* me if anything can"? "Engage" means neither to delight nor to repel; what exactly does it mean here? We might say that the tone of the poem is embodied in that word as well.

5.   What is the antecedent of "they" in line 14? What are the speaker's feelings as expressed in the observation in lines 14–16?

6.   Why should an eighteenth-century clergyman (as Cowper was) think human life "a dream" (line 19)? Is there any unstated comparison between human life, human "enjoyments," and the felled trees?

7.   The poem by Gerard Manley Hopkins is cast in that poet's own extremely personal version of accentual meter, which he called "sprung rhythm." Only the major stresses on words or even phrases count for beats in this meter. But the center of the poem's power is its association of the fragile woods with the vulnerable eyeball through which their beauty is perceived. What images of fragility are immediately presented in the first eight lines? Are poplars or aspens like oaks? And what of the relation of the eye to what it sees? Is this merely a more violent and precise version of Cowper's view that man's enjoyments have "a being less durable even than he"? For more on sprung rhythm see p. 585.

8.   Hopkins' own sense of language was like a kind of nature-lore for him, as it is for all true poets. In addition, he was particularly learned in the history of English and in the classics. He knew the Latin origins of the word "special" (from *species,* which itself originally meant "a way of appearing," from the verb *specere,* "to look"), and he knew that the Latin word *sylva,* while unrelated etymologically to the English word "self," meant "woods" or "forest." How do these echoed meanings affect the force of lines 21–22? Is "unselve" like "unman"?

9.   How would you compare the attitudes of the speakers toward the two chopped-down groves of trees?

NUTTING

William Wordsworth

_____ It seems a day
(I speak of one from many singled out)
One of those heavenly days that cannot die;

When, in the eagerness of boyish hope,
I left our cottage-threshold, sallying forth   5
With a huge wallet° o'er my shoulders slung,
A nutting-crook° in hand; and turned my steps
Toward some far-distant wood, a Figure quaint,
Tricked out in proud disguise of cast-off weeds
Which for that service had been husbanded,   10
By exhortation of my frugal Dame°—
Motley accoutrement, of power to smile
At thorns, and brakes, and brambles,—and, in truth,
More ragged than need was! O'er pathless rocks,
Through beds of matted fern, and tangled thickets,   15
Forcing my way, I came to one dear nook
Unvisited, where not a broken bough
Drooped with its withered leaves, ungracious sign
Of devastation; but the hazels rose
Tall and erect, with tempting clusters hung,   20
A virgin scene!—A little while I stood,
Breathing with such suppression of the heart
As joy delights in; and, with wise restraint
Voluptuous, fearless of a rival, eyed
The banquet;—or beneath the trees I sate   25
Among the flowers, and with the flowers I played;
A temper known to those who, after long
And weary expectation, have been blest
With sudden happiness beyond all hope.
Perhaps it was a bower beneath whose leaves   30
The violets of five seasons re-appear
And fade, unseen by any human eye;
Where fairy water-breaks do murmur on
Forever; and I saw the sparkling foam,
And—with my cheek on one of those green stones 35
That, fleeced with moss, under the shady trees,
Lay round me, scattered like a flock of sheep—
I heard the murmur and the murmuring sound,
In that sweet mood when pleasure loves to pay
Tribute to ease; and, of its joy secure,   40
The heart luxuriates with indifferent things,°
Wasting its kindliness on stocks and stones,
And on the vacant air. Then up I rose,
And dragged to earth both branch and bough, with crash
And merciless ravage: and the shady nook   45

---

wallet: sack **nutting-crook:** a staff with a hook at one end, used in gathering nuts **Dame:** guardian, or foster mother **indifferent things:** things not deliberately selected

Of hazels, and the green and mossy bower,
Deformed and sullied, patiently gave up
Their quiet being: and, unless I now
Confound my present feelings with the past,
Ere from the mutilated bower I turned   50
Exulting, rich beyond the wealth of kings,
I felt a sense of pain when I beheld
The silent trees, and saw the intruding sky.—
Then, dearest Maiden,° move along these shades
In gentleness of heart; with gentle hand   55
Touch—for there is a spirit in the woods.

Discussion

Several episodes in William Wordsworth's long autobiographical poem, *The Prelude,* focus on the growth of the moral sense in childhood. For Wordsworth, this sense drew much of its strength from an almost superstitious reverence for the spirit of Nature, together with a faith in the "renovating virtue" which human beings may derive from that spirit. In one of his greatest lyrics, the "Immortality Ode," Wordsworth described Nature as a "Nurse" to the growing child, and at the same time a foster mother; and in a celebrated passage of "Tintern Abbey," he found in Nature "The anchor of my purest thoughts, the nurse, /The guide, the guardian of my heart, and soul/Of all my moral being," and rested his hope for the survival of his own imagination on this article of faith: "Nature never did betray/The heart that loved her." The fragment called "Nutting" was to have formed one of the many childhood episodes in *The Prelude* where the moral sense is fostered and affirmed by an unforced communion with Nature. It was never incorporated into the larger poem, however, and has come to be read as a separate lyric.

Wordsworth tells us of a single experience that has isolated itself in his memory. The day of this experience is so vividly present to him that he cannot bring himself to say "Once upon a time," or "It so happened"—rather, "It seems a day." Quite early in the account of this day we recognize that for the child, his "sallying forth" toward "some far-distant wood" is in no way quaint; it is glorious and to his mind allegorically significant: indeed it is no ordinary sallying forth, but a Quest. (For an example of the Quest see "Childe Roland to the Dark Tower Came," p. 415.) The child's motherly guardian has become "my frugal Dame"; he himself, far from being simply a child, is "a Figure"; later, the imaginary traveler whom he salutes will be elevated into another allegorical shape familiar to the questing knight, a "dearest Maiden." For the child, then,

---

Maiden: any woman ("maiden" may imply virgin) who passes by; perhaps Wordsworth's sister Dorothy

this journey is full of dignity and meaning: his own seriousness toward it forbids our condescension. He is an intrepid explorer who, if fitted out with "motley accoutrement," is nevertheless convinced that even his clothes have "power to smile/At thorns, and brakes, and brambles."

In the secluded spot that he finds after "Forcing my way" past every obstacle, he has a place of contemplation worthy of his own power. It is

> one dear nook
> Unvisited, where not a broken bough
> Drooped with its withered leaves, ungracious sign
> Of devastation. . . .

This is a place *naturally* sacred, and sacred to Nature. Whether it has survived as "A virgin scene" because no one has visited it before or because no one visiting it would dare to mutilate it makes little difference. It is a scene to which the very thought of devastation is ungracious: to damage this place would reveal an absence of grace in the passer-by who laid rough hands upon it. And when we hear that the child looks on it "with such suppression of the heart/As joy delights in," and sets himself apart from it "with wise restraint"—and, further on, that he allows himself to repose "In that sweet mood when pleasure loves to pay/ Tribute to ease," and lets his heart waste "its kindliness on stocks and stones"— we may feel that the scene has found the perfect soul to honor it and preserve its sanctity.

But the description of the child's mood is subtly deceptive. If we read carefully, we can see that he delights in the joy that comes of being "fearless of a rival"—which is not necessarily the joy of restraint. Again, if we follow past the ending of line 23, as the punctuation encourages us to do, we are made aware that what the child feels is not in fact "wise restraint" but a very different thing: "wise restraint/Voluptuous." The child's self-sufficient happiness may owe less to his awe of the place than to his selfish knowledge that however he may use it, this virgin scene belongs to him alone. He thinks of it as a bower—traditionally, a place of sexual fulfillment—and there is a sexual undercurrent in the playfulness or mere dallying that follows the "weary expectation" of his journey and the "sudden happiness" of his discovery. His mood completes itself in an act of symbolic violation:

> Then up I rose,
> And dragged to earth both branch and bough, with crash
> And merciless ravage. . . .

The repetition of short *a*-sounds, with the violent crowding and repetition of consonants ("dragged to earth both branch and bough, with crash"), heighten our sense of a harsh and peculiarly *obsessive* moment of destruction. Now the entire scene appears to the child "Deformed and sullied" and, as if the scene were conscious of this, its constituents "patiently gave up their quiet being."

One cannot account for the change simply by saying that a few overhanging branches were lost to a nook that had never once been touched. It is a loss of something greater and less easily described.

The child, in one part of himself, resists the knowledge of any world more complex than that of the heroic Quest, in which he began his journey. He turns from the bower "Exulting, rich beyond the wealth of kings," having satisfied his wish to devour something of the "banquet" that lay before him. But in another part of himself—a part so closely allied to the adult's moral sense that Wordsworth asks himself if he may not be confounding "present feelings with the past"—the child feels that he has betrayed a Nature that offered him pleasures which he loved. Nature has set its pleasures before him while seeming to demand in return only that he leave the source of those pleasures intact. This he has not done: and, seeing the sky as an intrusion and knowing that he has made it so, he feels—"a sense of pain." Nothing more than that. And yet, nothing more is needed; for a sense of pain that is not merely physical and that follows from one's own actions and not someone else's, is the beginning of moral self-knowledge.

The poem ends with a memorial of Nature's teaching on this particular day. The child who has learned a new kind of reverence for things outside himself—or else the poet, recollecting the child's emotions—imparts a message to whoever may pass there that may almost seem an inscription left at the scene of his learning and spoken by him on behalf of Nature itself. "Move along these shades/In gentleness of heart; with gentle hand/Touch." The spirit of these woods is a spirit of place, no less exalted than the soul of a person and holding perhaps the profoundest source of vitality for the human imagination. If Wordsworth chooses to address this moral to a "Maiden," that may be his way of including the world of the Quest—which would involve just such a maiden—in the world of Nature that he has found beyond it.

SPRING AND ALL

William Carlos Williams

By the road to the contagious hospital
under the surge of the blue
mottled clouds driven from the
northeast—a cold wind. Beyond, the
waste of broad, muddy fields   5
brown with dried weeds, standing and fallen

patches of standing water
the scattering of tall trees

All along the road the reddish
purplish, forked, upstanding, twiggy   10

stuff of bushes and small trees
with dead, brown leaves under them
leafless vines—

Lifeless in appearance, sluggish
dazed spring approaches—   15

They enter the new world naked,
cold, uncertain of all
save that they enter. All about them
the cold, familiar wind—

Now the grass, tomorrow   20
the stiff curl of wildcarrot leaf

One by one objects are defined—
It quickens: clarity, outline of leaf

But now the stark dignity of
entrance—Still, the profound change   25
has come upon them: rooted they
grip down and begin to awaken

Discussion

Modern poems that seem unconventional often are concerned with
renewing a previously established convention. This opening poem of William
Carlos Williams' sequence, "Spring and All," takes the advent of spring as its
subject; in doing so, it reminds the reader of other such poems. Traditionally,
these poems celebrate spring as the time of renewal or rebirth. As we shall see,
Williams' poem is concerned with taking a very close look at the instant of
spring's onset, a period that retains winter's deathlike look while faintly showing
forth spring's renewal of life. The coming of spring is treated here as a gradual
realization that what the speaker sees about him adds up to life, emergence, and
hope, rather than to the death it seems to embody.

It seems inevitable that an awareness of returning spring should kindle in
the imagination the idea of a renewal of life for the individual. Like other spring
poems, this one centers on an awareness of concrete things and events, but here
the kind of awareness is itself made appropriate to the start of the season. The
consciousness shown in the poem is not swift, responsive, and impassioned, but
rather slow, an uncoiling realization, as if the winter's own tired understanding
had come to recognize its own transformation. As a spring song, this poem's
theme is that in the midst of death we are in life.

Traditionally, spring poems emphasize the poet's own response to the
arrival of the new season. Williams' poem differs from these poems as a

consequence of his great principle of poetic honesty, "no ideas but in things." He deliberately writes a poetry of natural appearances. Natural objects or events are seldom addressed, invoked, or conceptualized, but rather *named* by being described. Unlike traditional poems, Williams' poem contains no "I." The bushes, trees, grass, and deceptive buds take the place of that "I" and are elevated by the process.

The intersection of Whitman's legacy and an older tradition of spring song is apparent in the formal aspects of this poem. Williams' poem is written in free verse (see pp. 587–90), which came into English poetry in the early decades of this century, following the influence of Whitman and some French and Japanese poetry. The poets who used free verse associated it with the kind of concrete delineation of images that we see in Williams' poem.

But a little more needs to be said about Williams' structure. Although there is no point in counting stressed syllables in this or other free verse poems, it is important to notice several things. First, the paired lines (7–8, 14–15, 20–21, and 22–23) seem at first glance rather like a short, varied refrain to the "stanzas." Second, these "refrain" lines grow increasingly more general and abstract as the poem goes on: the first pair presents an image; the second narrates, using more general terms; the third predicts, alluding to the relatively abstract concept of time; and the fourth, using the most abstract words in any of the pairs ("objects," "defined"), describes the kind of mental process that is actually happening in the poem. Third, the relationship of line endings to ordinary syntax provides rhythmic force (this is true in varying degrees of all free verse, and of measured kinds of line patterning as well). Here we have patterns of various line endings (see the sections on free verse in A Note on Prosody, also p. 579): the clearly enjambed line, as in " . . . Beyond, the/waste of broad, muddy fields"; the line ending that corresponds to a grammatical juncture of some prominence, as in lines 14–15; or the line division which is the only clue we might have to the grammar at that point, as in lines 12–13, where "leafless vines" is to be considered partly in series with and partly in apposition to the preceding material. The rhythm of line breaks becomes highly expressive at the poem's most dramatic points, as for example in "But now the stark dignity of/ entrance," where the reader's discovery of the object of the preposition "of" makes the word "entrance" more resonant.

Even more significant is the transition from line 2 to line 3. After reading the first line, we expect that each of the following ones will stop at the end of a phrase. Therefore, when we come to "under the surge of the blue" in line 2, with its dactylic rhythm (*dum* de de *dum* de de *dum*), we read "blue" as a noun; it seems to refer to the sky (as in "the wild blue yonder") and, particularly in association with "surge," suggests a powerfully cheerful and invigorating sight. But the line is not end stopped. As we read on, we discover that the object of the preposition "of" is not "blue" but "clouds," and that "blue" has joined the adjective "mottled" in describing a chill, unpleasant, wintry sky, contributing to the overriding gray, brown and reddish-purplish colors of the bleak landscape.

The tone of the poem depends upon an aspect of language that is so subtle we tend not to notice it. The opening line, for example, contains the phrase, "the contagious hospital," which refers, of course, to some institution probably named "The James B. So-and-So Memorial Hospital for Contagious Diseases." Only doctors (like Williams himself, who was a general practitioner in New Jersey) or their poorer and less literate patients would call it "the contagious hospital." But in that version of the name there lurks an image that governs the whole poem: it is *as if* the hospital itself is "contagious" and would infect the surrounding countryside with the look of death and sickness. The hospital also suggests human birth in lines 16–19; there the images of new spring buds and growth merge with the actualities of human birth. The pronoun "they" is kept purposely ambiguous and can be thought of as referring to a human newborn as well as to nature's new growth.

Although the image of the hospital opens the poem, the grammatical subject of the poem's first sentence is actually "a cold wind." The place from which the wind blows and the time of year are quickly made specific in naturalistic terms. It is an early spring wind from the northeast, with the cold of late winter still in it. But "a cold wind" also serves symbolically as the wind of births and entrances and transitions. It comes forcefully upon the barren scene so powerfully described in lines 5–13 and carries with it the beginnings of a spring as sluggishly dazed as the scene it approaches.

With line 16, the tone changes. "They" are the fresh growths of spring, after all. The "reddish/purplish, forked, upstanding, twiggy/stuff" turns out to be budding material, not dried and dead as we might have thought; not diseases of the branch, even as the whole scene in lines 1–14 has looked like a disease of the land. Buds do indeed have a way of looking like dead growth at first, and it is often impossible to visualize anything green coming from their stubby reddish or brown lumps. We feel the courage and uncertainty of these growths as they emerge, for the poet is humanizing them and comparing them implicitly to newborn babies.

At line 20, the poem's final movement begins. The transition from "now the grass" to "tomorrow/the stiff curl of wildcarrot leaf " is a movement from the general word "grass"—not separate blades, but a blended, more abstract greenness—to a sharply outlined specific bit of that green. It is almost as if the poet were focusing binoculars or rubbing his eyes to dispel a blur. The remarkable line "One by one objects are defined" seems to confirm the image of looking through binoculars. The mysterious "It" of the next line perhaps refers back to the grass and forward to "clarity, outline of leaf." But we certainly feel that "It" is not limited to these; rather "It" seems to encompass the world in spring and, ultimately, the power of consciousness itself.

After its swift but highly suggestive glance ahead, the poem returns to its present moment in the final four lines. The phrase "the stark dignity of/ entrance" is an epitome of the whole poem and is justified by the poet's skillful placement of "awaken," the poem's final word. This word adds a broader element to the climax and underlines "the profound change" that is taking place. The change has occurred not only in the season but in the level of consciousness expressed in the poem about the nature of what is observed.

GRAVELLY RUN

A. R. Ammons

I don't know somehow it seems sufficient
to see and hear whatever coming and going is,
losing the self to the victory
    of stones and trees,
of bending sandpit lakes, crescent   5
round groves of dwarf pine:

for it is not so much to know the self
as to know it as it is known
    by galaxy and cedar cone,
as if birth had never found it   10
and death could never end it:

the swamp's slow water comes
down Gravelly Run fanning the long
    stone-held algal°
hair and narrowing roils between   15
the shoulders of the highway bridge:

holly grows on the banks in the woods there,
and the cedars' gothic-clustered
    spires could make
green religion in winter bones: 20

so I look and reflect, but the air's glass
jail seals each thing in its entity:

no use to make any philosophies here:
    I see no
god in the holly, hear no song from   25
the snowbroken weeds: Hegel° is not the winter
yellow in the pines: the sunlight has never
heard of trees: surrendered self among
    unwelcoming forms: stranger,
hoist your burdens, get on down the road.   30

Questions for Writing and Discussion

1. Is there a possible double meaning of "reflect" in line 21? (See also Robert
Frost's "Spring Pools," page 494.) Is there anything in the landscape that, conversely, mirrors a human watcher?

algal: algaelike   **Hegel:** G. W. F. Hegel (1770–1831), a German philosopher; the poet feels him to
have contributed heavily to modern theories of consciousness

2.   Comment on the phrase, "the air's glass/jail."

3.   Is the poet advocating a common-sense, unreflective approach to natural scenes, to "whatever coming and going is"?

4.   Lines 23–28 recommend unburdening oneself of philosophizing. What does the last line suggest about the consequences of this advice? Is "the road" simply a road of walking and doing rather than thinking?

SEA HOLLY

Conrad Aiken

Begotten by the meeting of rock with rock,
The mating of rock and rock, rocks gnashing together;
Created so, and yet forgetful, walks
The seaward path, puts up her left hand, shades
Blue eyes, the eyes of rock, to see better   5
In slanting light the ancient sheep (which kneels
Biting the grass) the while her other hand,
Hooking the wicker handle, turns the basket
Of eggs. The sea is high to-day. The eggs
Are cheaper. The sea is blown from the southwest,   10
Confused, taking up sand and mud in waves,
The waves break, sluggish, in brown foam, the wind
Disperses (on the sheep and hawthorn) spray,—
And on her cheeks, the cheeks engendered of rock,
And eyes, the colour of rock. The left hand   15
Falls from the eyes, and undecided slides
Over the left breast on which muslin lightly
Rests, touching the nipple, and then down
The hollow side, virgin as rock, and bitterly
Caresses the blue hip.   20

                        It was for this,
This obtuse taking of the seaward path,
This stupid hearing of larks, this hooking
Of wicker, this absent observation of sheep
Kneeling in harsh sea-grass, the cool hand shading   25
The spray-stung eyes—it was for this the rock
Smote itself. The sea is higher to-day,
And eggs are cheaper. The eyes of rock take in
The seaward path that winds toward the sea,
The thistle-prodder, old woman under a bonnet,   30
Forking the thistles, her back against the sea,

Pausing, with hard hands on the handle, peering
With rock eyes from her bonnet.

                              It was for this,
This rock-lipped facing of brown waves, half sand   35
And half water, this tentative hand that slides
Over the breast of rock, and into the hollow
Soft side of muslin rock, and then fiercely
Almost as rock against the hip of rock—
It was for this in midnight the rocks met,   40
And dithered together, cracking and smoking.

                              It was for this
Barren beauty, barrenness of rock that aches
On the seaward path, seeing the fruitful sea,
Hearing the lark of rock that sings, smelling   45
The rock-flower of hawthorn, sweetness of rock—
It was for this, stone pain in the stony heart,
The rock loved and laboured; and all is lost.

Questions for Writing and Discussion

1.   Whether or not the title is the grammatical subject of the verb "walks" in the first sentence, that verb is still ambiguous: it could mean that a woman walks along the path or that the path itself "walks" up the rocks by the sea. How does this ambiguity lead into something central to the whole poem?

2.   Describe the scene evoked in the poem as if it were a photograph. Is there an actual woman in the picture?

3.   Trace the sequence of interpretations of the scene beginning "It was for this . . ." (lines 20, 32, 39). How do the last seven lines of the poem help resolve the puzzle about the woman, the path, the vegetation creeping up the clefts in the rocks? Is the beauty indeed totally barren?

4.   What has been "lost" at the very end of the poem?

VOYAGES   I

Hart Crane

Above the fresh ruffles of the surf
Bright striped urchins flay each other with sand.
They have contrived a conquest for shell shucks,

And their fingers crumble fragments of baked weed
Gaily digging and scattering.   5

And in answer to their treble interjections
The sun beats lightning on the waves,
The waves fold thunder on the sand;
And could they hear me I would tell them:

O brilliant kids, frisk with your dog,   10
Fondle your shells and sticks, bleached
By time and the elements; but there is a line
You must not cross nor ever trust beyond it
Spry cordage of your bodies to caresses
Too lichen-faithful from too wide a breast.   15
The bottom of the sea is cruel.

Questions for Writing and Discussion

1. What kinds of danger does this poem of a beach scene imply are on the other side of the "line/You must not cross"?

2. Explain the image "lichen-faithful." In what way is the sea's breast "too wide"?

3. How do the surf's "fresh ruffles" and the "bright striped" boys on the beach combine in a larger image? How does that image become more significant by the end of the poem?

4. It is likely that Crane had in mind the episode from Walt Whitman's "Song of Myself" (p. 622). If so, how does his version of Whitman's erotic parable contrast with the original?

TO AUTUMN

William Blake

O Autumn, laden with fruit, and stained
With the blood of the grape, pass not, but sit
Beneath my shady roof; there thou may'st rest,
And tune thy jolly voice to my fresh pipe;
And all the daughters of the year shall dance!   5
Sing now the lusty song of fruits and flowers.

"The narrow bud opens her beauties to
The sun, and love runs in her thrilling veins;
Blossoms hang round the brows of morning, and

Flourish down the bright cheek of modest eve,   10
Till clust'ring Summer breaks forth into singing,
And feather'd clouds strew flowers round her head.

"The spirits of the air live on the smells
Of fruit; and joy, with pinions light, roves round
The gardens, or sits singing in the trees."   15
Thus sang the jolly Autumn as he sat;
Then rose, girded himself, and o'er the bleak
Hills fled from our sight; but left his golden load.

Questions for Writing and Discussion

1. In what way is Autumn's song "lusty"? Why is it a song of spring and summer?

2. Comment on the "bleak hills" in lines 17–18.

3. Compare this poem with Keats's on p. 515: how do the personifications differ?

ODE TO THE WEST WIND

Percy Bysshe Shelley

I

O wild West Wind, thou breath of Autumn's being,
Thou, from whose unseen presence the leaves dead
Are driven, like ghosts from an enchanter fleeing,

Yellow, and black, and pale, and hectic red,
Pestilence-stricken multitudes: O thou,   5
Who chariotest to their dark wintry bed

The wingèd seeds, where they lie cold and low,
Each like a corpse within its grave, until
Thine azure sister of the Spring shall blow

Shelley's note: This poem was conceived and chiefly written in a wood that skirts the Arno, near Florence, and on a day when that tempestuous wind, whose temperature is at once mild and animating, was collecting the vapours which pour down the autumnal rains. They began, as I foresaw, at sunset with a violent tempest of hail and rain, attended by that magnificent thunder and lightning peculiar to the Cisalpine regions.

The phenomenon alluded to at the conclusion of the third stanza is well known to naturalists. The vegetation at the bottom of the sea, of rivers, and of lakes, sympathizes with that of the land in the change of seasons, and is consequently influenced by the winds which announce it.

Her clarion o'er the dreaming earth, and fill   10
(Driving sweet buds like flocks to feed in air)
With living hues and odours plain and hill:

Wild Spirit, which art moving everywhere;
Destroyer and preserver; hear, oh, hear!

II

Thou on whose stream, mid the steep sky's commotion,   15
Loose clouds like earth's decaying leaves are shed,
Shook from the tangled boughs of Heaven and
Ocean,

Angels° of rain and lightning: there are spread
On the blue surface of thine aery surge,
Like the bright hair uplifted from the head   20

Of some fierce Maenad,° even from the dim verge
Of the horizon to the zenith's height,
The locks of the approaching storm. Thou dirge

Of the dying year, to which this closing night
Will be the dome of a vast sepulchre,   25
Vaulted with all thy congregated might

Of vapours, from whose solid atmosphere
Black rain, and fire, and hail will burst: oh, hear!

III

Thou who didst waken from his summer dreams
The blue Mediterranean, where he lay,   30
Lulled by the coil of his crystàlline streams,

Beside a pumice° isle in Baiae's° bay,
And saw in sleep old palaces and towers
Quivering within the wave's intenser day.

All overgrown with azure moss and flowers   35
So sweet, the sense faints picturing them! Thou
For whose path the Atlantic's level powers

Cleave themselves into chasms, while far below
The sea-blooms and the oozy woods which wear
The sapless foliage of the ocean, know   40

Thy voice, and suddenly grow grey with fear,
And tremble and despoil themselves: oh, hear!

Angels: literally, "messengers" **Maenad:** frenzied followers of the Greek god Dionysus **pumice:** volcanic stone **Baiae:** a seaside resort near Naples even in Imperial Roman times

IV

If I were a dead leaf thou mightest bear;
If I were a swift cloud to fly with thee;
A wave to pant beneath thy power, and share   45

The impulse of thy strength, only less free
Than thou, O uncontrollable! If even
I were as in my boyhood, and could be

The comrade of thy wanderings over Heaven,
As then, when to outstrip thy skiey speed   50
Scarce seemed a vision; I would ne'er have striven

As thus with thee in prayer in my sore need.
Oh, lift me as a wave, a leaf, a cloud!
I fall upon the thorns of life! I bleed!

A heavy weight of hours has chained and bowed   55
One too like thee: tameless, and swift, and proud.

V

Make me thy lyre,° even as the forest is:
What if my leaves are falling like its own!
The tumult of thy mighty harmonies

Will take from both a deep, autumnal tone,   60
Sweet though in sadness. Be thou, Spirit fierce,
My spirit! Be thou me, impetuous one!

Drive my dead thoughts over the universe
Like withered leaves to quicken a new birth!
And, by the incantation of this verse,   65

Scatter, as from an unextinguished hearth
Ashes and sparks, my words among mankind!
Be through my lips to unawakened earth

The trumpet of a prophecy! O, Wind,
If Winter comes, can Spring be far behind?   70

Discussion

An ode in English and American literature is often a kind of public
proclamation in verse addressed to a person. It stems from an ancient tradition.

lyre: the Aeolian harp, an instrument on which music was produced by the wind blowing through its
strings; it became an important Romantic symbol of poetic inspiration

In ancient Greece, odes or choral poems (see p. 591) were sung and danced at festivals that celebrated, for example, the winner of an athletic event. In poetry from the Renaissance on, the form of an ode, a longish poem in sections (but without music and dance), became adapted to other purposes. It could still be "public" in praising or commemorating an important person, but it might also address itself to a personification, such as Joy, Duty, Dejection, Beauty. This personification, which embodies an idea or abstract concept, would also be made into a mythological figure by the poem itself. In a sense, all our major poetry has this function of myth making, of substituting for ancient mythologies and modern religions new interpretations of our experience to outlast our own culture and perhaps become fables for later ones.

William Blake and John Keats mythologize the season of autumn in their respective odes (pp. 508 and 515). Shelley's poem invokes not the season itself, but its west wind, the "destroyer and preserver" which brings down the leaves from the trees and brings on the deadly cold of winter. At the same time, however, it scatters into new fertile ground the matured seeds of all growing things, so that they may regenerate in spring. Shelley reminds us that there is also a west wind of spring (the "azure sister" of line 9). This suggests classical myths which make related states or conditions into brothers or sisters (Death and Sleep are brothers, for example). The blue associated with the spring wind in this poem, and the black, yellow, red, and brown which color the other one, are parallel but opposed.

In making a mythological presence out of the wind, Shelley keeps in mind a major physical fact about it. Human voices are phonetically shaped breath, or wind. Moreover, the word "spirit" originally meant "breath" (thus words like "re*spir*ation"). If the poem connects modern and older senses of the word "spirit" in invoking the wind, it never leaves the physical fact far behind: the vocal wind with which a speaker addresses the natural one can certainly vanish into the larger roar. For example, a wind can blow one's words, with one's breath, back into one's face if one shouts *into* it. On the other hand, it can seem to broadcast one's spoken words by carrying them along with it, or it can broadcast one's written words by blowing leaves of books (like leaves of trees) far and wide. Thus, poetic or prophetic language (seeds of thought, as it were), as well as dead leaves and living seeds of plants, can be scattered by the autumnal wind.

A word might be said about this ode's formal structure. Usually, English odes have strophes of varied line length and rhyme scheme. Shelley has constructed his from two other formal patterns. Each strophe is really a kind of smoothly flowing sonnet. Each is also composed, as the line groupings indicate, of four *tercets* and a final couplet. Moreover, the tercets are rhymed in the interlocking pattern of *aba bcb cdc ded,* as in the following six lines:

> O wild West Wind, thou breath of Autumn's *being,*
> Thou, from whose unseen presence the leaves *dead*
> Are driven, like ghosts from an enchanter *fleeing,*

Yellow, and black, and pale, and hectic *red,*
Pestilence-stricken multitudes: O *thou,*
Who chariotest to their dark wintry *bed*

This rhyme scheme is called *terza rima* in Italian (see Note on Prosody), and is the verse form of Dante's great visionary and prophetic poem, *The Divine Comedy.* No poet can use the form without thinking of Dante in some way. Shelley's very scheme of lines and rhymes suggests that he is associating his ode not with classical Greek public odes, but with a modern tradition of imaginative prophecy.

The opening strophe, or stanzaic section, of this ode introduces us to the wind's ambivalent force of destruction and renewal. It is a force associated with natural cycles of night and day, of season, or of death and regeneration. A simple, benign view of all this is that such a force preserves *by* destroying: seeds must fall from rotting fruit, die, and be entombed in the ground before they can rise again. It is one thing to say this, another really to feel it. Shelley knows how hard it is for human beings to bear this detached view of death and suffering. The dead leaves in the first five lines are described ("hectic red" and "Pestilence-stricken multitudes") in a way that suggests hordes of sick people being blown by a wind of change. Indeed, this wind is a revolutionary one, since Shelley is committed to the overthrow of social and political tyranny. But the poem contains more than a symbolic depiction of revolution. Rather, Shelley is showing us that this annual, fierce autumn wind is among other things *like* revolution in the paradoxical nature of blowing away the old and infirm— perhaps even cruelly—in order that the new may be blown in.

The first three strophes all address the wind in a long *apostrophe,* as it is called—a long "O you, who. . . ." ending up "O hear!" The clouds of lines 15–23 are likened at first to the leaves of the opening part; then they are personified momentarily as "angels" (in the original Greek sense of "messengers"), heralding rain and lightning, whose purpose we do not yet comprehend. The clouds, like the leaves, show the visible effects of the invisible force and become "locks of the approaching storm," spread out across "the blue surface" of the wind's energy. Even the sky becomes conscripted into an army of visible aspects of the wind's might. The cloud-hair is likened to the wild locks of frenzied, violent Maenads, the followers of Dionysus whose cult celebrated the relation of death and rebirth. The wind then becomes a sound ("dirge/Of the dying year"), just as in the first strophe, his azure sister, the spring wind, has been known by her trumpet call, her "clarion o'er the dreaming earth," an awakening blast of music like that of the last trumpet of the end of the world in the Book of Revelation. The funeral song echoes in a dome of night (lines 24–26), which is both a tomb and a kind of cathedral for the "congregated might" of air pressure, winds, and the like. These "vapours" will respond to the dirge and produce the "black rain, and fire, and hail" of a by now clearly destructive and revolutionary storm.

The third strophe presents yet one more central image by which we trace the wind's effects. Here, the west wind is seen as the awakener of waves in the blue Mediterranean and in the gray Atlantic. Under the Mediterranean lie buried the remains of ancient instruments of tyranny, "old palaces and towers." They have, in time, been ruined and transformed imaginatively into a beauty they never had—a beauty of picture and memory. Again, in line 41, we have the presence of a sound, a voice, awakening the inert and dormant life under the sea. As in the previous strophes, the mention of a sound leads to the concluding invocation, "O hear!"

But the wind does not answer, and clearly something must happen in the poem to complete our sense of the strange relation of poet and wind. It is as if, until now, the speaker were standing aloof and watching the wind blow across his observed and imagined world. There has been a kind of natural rhythm to the storm in these sections as well: the pure windy force in the first strophe, the thunder and rain in the second, and the calm aftermath in the third. But with the fourth strophe, the poet rises and puts himself in the path of the wind. He is not a leaf, cloud, or wave; he is not even a child anymore, a boy whose will seemed identical with the wind's will but whose direct and unconsidered relation to nature could not survive the consequences of "a heavy weight of hours." He is a poet with a spirit, a breath of his own that enables him to, as he says he must, strive "with [the wind] in prayer." The ode is itself like a personal, secular hymn to a presence powerful in the world, yet worshiped in no churches, only in the spaces of the imagination. Ordinarily we do not think of prayer *to* something as strife *with* it. But the wind has been invoked as singer, prophet, and awakener, whose force and volume can drown out the voice of any human singer. Even to call out to it "O hear!" is somehow to contend with it.

In the final strophe, Shelley changes his poetic stance. It is as if he were now turned so that the wind is blowing from behind him. There is no need now to ask it to listen to him; he wants it to join his eloquence to its force. The wind has power, loudness, and the ability to continue throughout cycles of human life; the poet's voice is quiet and dies with him, but its words have meaning and can embody visions of things beyond themselves. The poet asks the wind to make him its lyre similar to the leaves and boughs of trees which make a kind of music when the wind blows through them. (This music was absent from the opening strophe.) "Be thou me" the poet calls out: even if his own "dead thoughts" are like fallen leaves, they will be scattered over time and space to make a seedbed for the new. And if the residue of life is ashes as well as dust, poetic language is not a matter of ashes only, but of living sparks among them. Only now that the wind is, figuratively, blowing from behind the poet—not across him nor against him—can it "be through my lips . . . the trumpet of a prophecy."

The ode ends, significantly enough, in a great rhetorical question. It is the question we always tend to ask of our most negative moments—midnight, midwinter, darkness, despair: Can any good be brought out of this evil? The imagination of mythological poetry can answer this affirmatively, but not easily. In Shelley's ode, the force of that imagination is as strong as that of the spirit of the wind it invokes. "The incantation of this verse" (line 65) succeeds because it seems to have the force of the destroying and preserving wind in it. As a presence in our thoughts, the wind has become animated by the "tumult" of the ode's own "mighty harmonies" of image, form, and verse. Certainly, the "deep autumnal tone" of a seasonal ode that celebrates the passing of the late year has been produced by the instrument of its own poetic music.

TO AUTUMN

John Keats

I

Season of mists and mellow fruitfulness,
    Close bosom-friend of the maturing° sun;
Conspiring° with him how to load and bless
    With fruit the vines that round the thatch-eves run;
To bend with apples the mossed cottage-trees,   5
    And fill all fruit with ripeness to the core;
        To swell the gourd, and plump the hazel shells
With a sweet kernel; to set budding more,
    And still more, later flowers for the bees,
    Until they think warm days will never cease,   10
        For Summer has o'er-brimmed their clammy cells.

II

Who hath not seen thee oft amid thy store?
    Sometimes whoever seeks abroad may find
Thee sitting careless on a granary floor,
    Thy hair soft-lifted by the winnowing° wind;   15
Or on a half-reaped furrow sound asleep,
    Drowsed with the fume of poppies, while thy hook
        Spares the next swath and all its twinèd flowers:
And sometimes like a gleaner thou dost keep
    Steady thy laden head across a brook;   20
Or by a cider-press, with patient look,
        Thou watchest the last oozings hours by hours.

III

Where are the songs of Spring? Aye, where are they?
    Think not of them, thou hast thy music too,—
While barred clouds bloom the soft-dying day,   25
    And touch the stubble-plains with rosy hue;
Then in a wailful choir the small gnats mourn

---

maturing: causing what it shines upon to mature   **conspiring:** breathing together   **winnowing:** separating grain from chaff

> Among the river sallows,° borne aloft
>   Or sinking as the light wind lives or dies;
> And full-grown lambs loud bleat from hilly bourn;°   30
>   Hedge-crickets sing; and now with treble soft
>   The red-breast whistles from a garden-croft;°
>   And gathering swallows twitter in the skies.

Discussion

A narrative poem like "Eros Turannos" or a dramatic monologue like "Ulysses," tells a story in an especially concentrated way. But many poems are forms of *address,* spoken to a person, an object, or an idea; and their chief aim is to show the work of the poet's imagination as he is moved to passionate speech. During the Romantic era in England (roughly 1800–1830), one kind of poem emerged to serve the need for a poetry of pure address. In the Romantic ode, of which both Shelley's "Ode to the West Wind" and Keats's "To Autumn" are examples, the drama of the poet's self-scrutiny is projected onto some force or thing beyond the poet himself, whether it is a season or a wind associated in our minds with a season. As we observed in discussing Shelley's poem, the classical ode was originally a song of celebration written for the victors of athletic contests; and though, for the Romantics, the ode became a far more comprehensive form than this original function might suggest, a part of the old sense of contest was preserved. Now, however, it was the poet's own contest with his destiny—with mortality, with duty, with the continuation of his poetic labor— which the ode was expected to observe and celebrate, with a full awareness of the dangers that the poet faced.

Keats wrote his ode "To Autumn" only a few months before his death. Both his mother and his brother Tom had died of tuberculosis—Keats, at immense personal sacrifice, had been Tom's nurse from the onset of his final illness until his death—and when he wrote the poem he had grown used to the fear that he too would die young. Yet, if we call "To Autumn" a poem about death, we feel at once that we are misrepresenting the poem by simplifying it. We shall be closer to the mark if we call it a poem about mortality, closer still, if we say that in this poem death itself is naturalized as part of a cycle of earthly loss and gain that has no end. We shall be almost equal to the subtlety of the poem if we recognize that it makes our sense of change a *condition* of our sense of the fullness of life: for only in autumn do we come to know what spring and summer have been for us.

"To Autumn" has at its very center the almost allegorical figure, or "emblem," of Autumn "sound asleep,/Drowsed with the fume of poppies, while thy hook/Spares the next swath and all its twined flowers." This may remind us of another emblematic figure: Death with his scythe, preparing to cut off the

sallows: willows   bourn: region   croft: plot of ground

human lives which to him are as grass to a mower. And yet, our experience of Keats's exquisite restraint depends on our not being able to say whether Autumn is like Death, or Death like Autumn. The single movement of the poem is, indeed, the emergence from the landscape of this by no means terrifying figure, and its gradual absorption back into the landscape. But while the scene before us remains the same, the *kind* of autumn detail that we contemplate in the third stanza is markedly different from that of the first.

In the first stanza, we see the sensuous particulars of a process—the process of ripening caught on the verge of decay—and we feel these particulars as if from the inside: the gourd swelling, the hazel shells being made plump, the "o'erbrimming" of the clammy cells of the beehive. The single sentence that winds its way through the length of the entire first stanza is without a main verb: it gives us no specific action but only an endless making that will yield at last to unmaking. The third stanza, on the contrary, is filled with verbs, with the transitive actions of things that have an end: the lambs bleat; the redbreast whistles, and swallows twitter; in an extraordinary moment, the "barred clouds bloom the soft-dying day." Throughout the poem, we are moving from the minute details of a landscape (seen and felt as if from the inside) to landscape in our usual sense of the word (seen by a painter and heard by a poet); and we are moving, at the same time, from a scene of suspended action to one of completed action.

Let us suppose that for Keats, this movement from an inward to an outward perspective corresponded to a similar movement in the life of an individual—from the inward consciousness of the living being to the outward memories that remain after death. It would then be right for him to convey this movement by evoking the reclining figure of Autumn—or, as it looks to us from a distance, the figure of Death itself—as *a central but not a conclusive image* in the poem. For Keats saw how comparatively predictable would be the appearance of this figure at the end of the poem, as a way of "clinching" it. As it is, the figure is allowed to fade as quietly as it appeared, and it joins the different worlds of the first and third stanzas—steady and apparently unchangeable process with change and farewell. So, too, the verbs of the central stanza are poised between the slow, inaudible ripenings of the first stanza and the distinct music of the third. These verbs are almost distinct, almost definite—as we learn especially from the effect of Keats's enjambment: "Sometimes whoever seeks abroad may find/Thee sitting careless"; or again, "And sometimes like a gleaner thou dost keep/Steady thy laden head across a brook." At both line endings we feel that we might well stop but cannot.

Our greatest delight in this poem comes, perhaps, from our image of Keats's own assurance as he stands poised between two states of being. Autumn has grown drowsy temporarily, or fallen asleep, careless of its task of harvesting; death itself is arrested in mid-process, its hook sparing for a moment the next swath "and all its twinèd flowers"; and for this moment, the poet can feel that he is himself a "close bosom-friend" of the season. He conspires with autumn to "load and bless" his poem with all the sensations of an overwhelming natural particularity. "Conspiring," however, is a word drawn from the same source as "inspiration" and "expire." As he adds to his own poetic career the "still more, later flowers" of his great ode, Keats knows this. He knows, too, that conspiracy is not unrelated to deception, that all wind is inconstant and all breath lasts only for the term of a human season.

BAT

D. H. Lawrence

At evening, sitting on this terrace,°
When the sun from the west, beyond Pisa, beyond the mountains of
    Carrara
Departs, and the world is taken by surprise . . .

When the tired flower of Florence is in gloom beneath the glowing
Brown hills surrounding . . .   5

When under the arches of the Ponte Vecchio
A green light enters against stream, flush from the west,
Against the current of obscure Arno. . . .

Look up, and you see things flying
Between the day and the night;   10
Swallows with spools of dark thread sewing the shadows together.

A circle swoop, and a quick parabola under the bridge arches
Where light pushes through;
A sudden turning upon itself of a thing in the air.
A dip to the water.   15

And you think:
"The swallows are flying so late!"

Swallows?

Dark air-life looping
Yet missing the pure loop . . .   20
A twitch, a twitter, an elastic shudder in flight
And serrated wings against the sky,
Like a glove, a black glove thrown up at the light,
And falling back.

Never swallows!   25
Bats!
The swallows are gone.

---

terrace: the scene is in Florence, Italy, overlooking the famous old bridge (Ponte Vecchio) across the river Arno

At a wavering instant the swallows give way to bats
By the Ponte Vecchio . . .
Changing guard.   30

Bats, and an uneasy creeping in one's scalp
As the bats swoop overhead!
Flying madly.

Pipistrello!°
Black piper on an infinitesimal pipe.   35
Little lumps that fly in air and have voices indefinite, wildly
    vindictive;
Wings like bits of umbrella.

Bats!

Creatures that hang themselves up like an old rag, to sleep;
And disgustingly upside down.   40
Hanging upside down like rows of disgusting old rags
And grinning in their sleep.
Bats!

In China the bat is symbol of happiness.

Not for me!   45

Questions for Writing and Discussion

1.   This poem is full of precise—almost wittily precise—imagery. Characterize
the images in lines 3, 4–5, and 9–15. Is there anything different about the imagery
in lines 19–24? Does it answer in any way the rhetorical question—the question
that the poem almost asks of itself—"Swallows?" in line 18?

2.   The poem not only calls attention to the "wavering instant" in line 28; it is also
itself a "wavering instant" when a sense of what twilight means gives way to a
different sense, almost to another phase or kind of twilight. What are the differences between the twilight of swallows and the twilight of bats?

3.   Read Keats's "To Autumn" (p. 515). You can then compare the swallows in
this poem with those in Lawrence's. Is there anything benevolent or reassuring
about the swallows in both poems?

4.   Assuming that there has been no misprint in line 44, provide the missing word
and explain the consequent awkwardness of expression. In general, does the
poem's style change after line 30?

Pipistrello: (Italian) bat

THE SNOW MAN

Wallace Stevens

One must have a mind of winter
To regard the frost and the boughs
Of the pine-trees crusted with snow;

And have been cold a long time
To behold the junipers shagged with ice,   5
The spruces rough in the distant glitter

Of the January sun; and not to think
Of any misery in the sound of the wind,
In the sound of a few leaves,

Which is the sound of the land   10
Full of the same wind
That is blowing in the same bare place

For the listener, who listens in the snow,
And, nothing himself, beholds
Nothing that is not there and the nothing that is. 15

Questions for Writing and Discussion

1. The title could mean both (a) a snowman made of snow, and (b) a snowy person, a man momentarily like, or in process of becoming, the snow around him. Given the same ambiguity, what could "a mind of winter" mean?

2. The whole poem is one long complex sentence. (Compare it with Robert Frost's "The Silken Tent," page 636.) In prose it might look something like this:

> One must be really *snowy* to see snow and icy trees and yet at the same time not hear misery in the sounds of wind and leaves—those sounds which are really that of the land full of the wind (that wind which is meaninglessly blowing through emptiness for some listening person, like oneself, listening and seeing).

How does the arrangement of the verbs (of seeing, thinking, hearing) in the poem fit this pattern? How do lines 7–9 function as the *center* of the poem, as well as its halfway point?

3. What would make one ordinarily think of "misery" in the sounds mentioned in lines 8–9?

4. Explain the difference, in line 15, between "nothing that is not there" and "the nothing that is."

Postscript: The Nature of the City

In the eighteenth century—and especially in the poetry of Dryden, Swift, and Pope—the city became as much a part of nature as nature itself. Perhaps more so, because there have always been two different meanings of the word "nature": (1) green things that grow, and (2) everything that is not man. If we adopt the second meaning rather than the first, we see that poets in the last two hundred years have written about cities as the part of nature that they know best.

In proportion as poets recognize the city as their home, they write of the country as a place of conscious leisure and retirement: the city ("urban") becomes the natural place for man, while the country ("pastoral") becomes the artificial place, where only the exceptionally cultivated poet lives. All poets are aware of the shifting terms of the contrast between city and country: which is natural, which is artificial? Which one provides the metaphors for the other? Blake's "London" gives us strong verbs associated with natural disasters ("blast"; "blight") when it seeks to astonish us with a catastrophic vision of the city; in Eliot's "Preludes," the several minds of the poem have neither the warmth of a human community nor the regularity of a natural one, and the nymphs culling flowers, whom we might expect to find in a classical or neoclassical "pastoral," have become old women hunting for dead wood to kindle their fires with: "The worlds revolve like ancient women/Gathering fuel in vacant lots."

A DESCRIPTION OF THE MORNING

Jonathan Swift

Now hardly here and there an hackney coach
Appearing showed the ruddy morn's approach.

521

Now Betty from her master's bed had flown,
And softly stole to discompose her own.
The slipshod 'prentice from his master's door   5
Had pared the dirt, and sprinkled round the floor.
Now Moll had whirled her mop with dexterous airs,
Prepared to scrub the entry and the stairs.
The youth with broomy stumps began to trace
The kennel-edge,° where wheels had worn the place.   10
The small-coal man was heard with cadence deep,
Till drowned in shriller notes of chimney-sweep.
Duns° at his lordship's gate began to meet;
And brick-dust Moll had screamed through half the street.
The turnkey° now his flock returning sees.   15
Duly let out a-nights to steal for fees.
The watchful bailiffs take their silent stands:
And schoolboys lag with satchels in their hands.

Questions for Writing and Discussion

1.   Did you expect this "description" to start out with the sunrise instead of an eighteenth-century taxi, bringing an all-night reveler home? Why, by the way, does Betty, in line 4, "discompose" her own bed? How do the two opening couplets prepare us for the rest of the details?

2.   What comparisons between country and city are implied by the poem? How does one become aware of morning on waking up in the country? What are the parallels here?

3.   Is it city or country life that is being mocked?

NEW YORK

Marianne Moore

the savage's romance,
accreted° where we need the space for commerce—
the center of the wholesale fur trade,°
starred with tepees of ermine and peopled with foxes,
the long guard-hairs waving two inches beyond the body of the pelt;   5
the ground dotted with deer-skins—white with white spots,

---

kennel-edge: curb   **Duns:** bill collectors   **turnkey:** jailer (he lets his prisoners out to steal for him)   **accreted:** gathered or collected   **the center . . . fur trade:** "In 1921 New York succeeded St. Louis as the center of the wholesale fur trade" [Marianne Moore's note]

"as satin needlework in a single color may carry a varied pattern,"°
and wilting eagle's-down compacted by the wind;
and picardels of beaver-skin; white ones alert with snow.
It is a far cry from the "queen full of jewels"   10
and the beau with the muff,
from the gilt coach shaped like a perfume-bottle,
to the conjunction of the Monongahela and the Allegheny,°
and the scholastic philosophy of the wilderness
to combat which one must stand outside and laugh   15
since to go in is to be lost.
It is not the dime-novel exterior,
Niagara Falls, the calico horses and the war-canoe;
it is not that "if the fur is not finer than such as one sees others wear,
one would rather be without it"°—   20
that estimated in raw meat and berries, we could feed the universe;
it is not the atmosphere of ingenuity,
the otter, the beaver, the puma skins
without shooting-irons or dogs;
it is not the plunder,   25
but "accessibility to experience."°

Questions for Writing and Discussion

1. What is "the scholastic philosophy of the wilderness" (line 14)? Why can one laugh at it only from the outside? How does it differ from "the savage's romance" (line 1)?

2. The quotations in this poem are intended to convey a sense of the apparent chaos and underlying resourcefulness of New York. Considering them one by one, would you say they are instances of the "plunder" of sources or of "accessibility to experience"? Why did you choose one over the other?

PRELUDES

T. S. Eliot

I

The winter evening settles down
With smell of steaks in passageways.

"as . . . pattern": this quotation comes from a prose description of the skin of a captured fawn
Allegheny: at Pittsburgh   "if the fur . . . without it": paraphrase of a statement by Isabella,
Duchess of Gonzaga, quoted in Frank Alvah Parsons, *The Psychology of Dress* "accessibility to
experience": a quotation from Henry James

Six o'clock.
The burnt-out ends of smoky days.
And now a gusty shower wraps   5
The grimy scraps
Of withered leaves about your feet
And newspapers from vacant lots;
The showers beat
On broken blinds and chimney-pots,   10
And at the corner of the street
A lonely cab-horse steams and stamps.
And then the lighting of the lamps.

          II

The morning comes to consciousness
Of faint stale smells of beer   15
From the sawdust-trampled street
With all its muddy feet that press
To early coffee-stands.
With the other masquerades
That time resumes,   20
One thinks of all the hands
That are raising dingy shades
In a thousand furnished rooms.

          III

You tossed a blanket from the bed,
You lay upon your back, and waited;   25
You dozed, and watched the night revealing
The thousand sordid images
Of which your soul was constituted;
They flickered against the ceiling.
And when all the world came back   30
And the light crept up between the shutters
And you heard the sparrows in the gutters,
You had such a vision of the street
As the street hardly understands;
Sitting along the bed's edge, where   35
You curled the papers from your hair,
Or clasped the yellow soles of feet
In the palms of both soiled hands.

          IV

His soul stretched tight across the skies
That fade behind a city block,   40

Or trampled by insistent feet
At four and five and six o'clock;
And short square fingers stuffing pipes,
And evening newspapers, and eyes
Assured of certain certainties,   45
The conscience of a blackened street
Impatient to assume the world.

I am moved by fancies that are curled
Around these images, and cling:
The notion of some infinitely gentle   50
Infinitely suffering thing.

Wipe your hand across your mouth, and laugh;
The worlds revolve like ancient women
Gathering fuel in vacant lots.

Questions for Writing and Discussion

1. "The morning comes to consciousness" (line 14), taken by itself, may mean either "The morning comes to be conscious" or "Someone comes to be conscious of the morning." Does the context favor one of these meanings over the other? Can you find similar ambiguities elsewhere in the poem? If so, what do they indicate about the sorts of impressions, or "fancies," that interest Eliot?

2. Is the "you" of Eliot's third stanza intended to represent a specific person in the city? the reader? anyone? or perhaps the poet himself, regarded from a distance? Are there similar possibilities for the "he" of the fourth stanza, whose soul is "stretched tight across the skies"? How might lines 48–51 help explain the presence of these second- and third-person actors?

3. Would you call the tone of the last three lines lighthearted? bitterly ironic? or something different from either of these? In what way does the image of worlds revolving "like ancient women/Gathering fuel in vacant lots" comment on the hypothetical person who is assured of more than "*certain* certainties"?

COMPOSED UPON WESTMINSTER BRIDGE, SEPTEMBER 3, 1802

William Wordsworth

Earth has not anything to show more fair:
Dull would he be of soul who could pass by
A sight so touching in its majesty:
This City now doth, like a garment, wear

The beauty of the morning; silent, bare,   5
Ships, towers, domes, theatres, and temples lie
Open unto the fields, and to the sky;
All bright and glittering in the smokeless air.
Never did sun more beautifully steep
In his first splendour, valley, rock, or hill;   10
Ne'er saw I, never felt, a calm so deep!
The river glideth at his own sweet will:
Dear God! the very houses seem asleep;
And all that mighty heart is lying still!

Discussion

Wordsworth describes the gentle beauty of the city asleep as a way of telling his readers *without exhortation* what he thinks of the grinding ugliness of the city when it is awake. The sense of power that he has in contemplating the city's industry is carried over into his description of the city at dawn, before the wheels have begun to turn, when it is still and smokeless; he responds to this power—both in his idea of the city awake and in his picture of it asleep—with an awe that is mingled with terror. The "calm so deep" by which Wordsworth feels himself exalted is the calm of death. But it is a death which *he* has dealt in imagining the city as he has; and he is afraid that this death will be replaced by an equally terrifying life.

About the quality of the light: In the early morning, as Wordsworth regards the city from a height above it, the places of work and commerce do not seem to him quite themselves before they have assumed their daily functions. Thus, while all are distinct ("bare"), their qualities or values are in some sense interchangeable (the adjectives "silent, bare" apply to all the nouns that complete the mixed catalog). This contributes to the sense of a mysterious calm and also to the suspicion that this calm has been achieved by the use of a deliberate fiction.

Here as elsewhere in the book, we do not trouble to distinguish between Wordsworth and "the speaker" because we cannot see that anything is gained by supposing that there is any distance, ironic or otherwise, between the two.

LONDON

William Blake

I wander through each chartered° street,
Near where the chartered Thames does flow,

chartered: commercially contracted for

And mark in every face I meet
Marks of weakness, marks of woe.

In every cry of every Man,   5
In every Infant's cry of fear,
In every voice, in every ban,°
The mind-forged manacles I hear.

How the Chimney-sweeper's cry
Every blackening Church appalls;   10
And the hapless Soldier's sigh
Runs in blood down Palace walls.

But most through midnight streets I hear
How the youthful Harlot's curse
Blasts the new born Infant's tear,   15
And blights with plagues the Marriage hearse.

Questions for Writing and Discussion

1. What is implied by the phrase "Marriage hearse" in line 16? Where else in the poem is marriage considered?

2. In the third stanza, the chimney sweep and the soldier are perceived as having a visionary relation to two major social institutions. Does this also hold true for the young prostitute of stanza IV?

3. The word "curse" in line 14 could have two meanings. Show how they may both be at work in the last stanza.

4. The prophetic wanderer or visionary who utters the words of the poem "marks" or *sees* things in stanza I and *hears* in stanza II. What is happening to the relation of sound and sight in the third stanza? Is there any echo or continuation of this in the last stanza?

ban: both marriage banns, or announcements, posted in churches, and all prohibitions generally

Meditation

If songs are words to be sung and dramatic monologues are speeches to be overheard by the reader, the meditation is a somber and drawn-out reflection that the poet mutters to himself. Its themes are the perennial themes of man and nature, freedom and necessity, permanence and change; its setting and ostensible subject are often a landscape; and it bears at least one interesting relation to an emblem (see Poem and Picture, pp. 561–74), since it may read a given landscape, for dramatic purposes, *as if the landscape were a picture.*

Arnold's "Dover Beach" appropriately begins this section, and its little allegory of the Sea of Faith is as clear an instance as we need of the meditative habit of "reading" a landscape, without quite crossing over into the realm of open allegory.

> But now I only hear
> Its melancholy, long, withdrawing roar,
> Retreating, to the breath
> Of the night-wind, down the vast edges drear
> And naked shingles of the world.

The Sea of Faith is *almost* a living thing mourning the spectacle of its own diminishment, *almost* an animated shape that seems to have (with the breath of the wind) a life of its own, apart from the mind that creates it. But the little allegory comes to an end, and we are left finally with the image of Arnold standing alone, speaking to his love and brooding on his fate.

528

DOVER BEACH°

Matthew Arnold

The sea is calm tonight.
The tide is full, the moon lies fair
Upon the straits;—on the French coast the light
Gleams and is gone; the cliffs of England stand,
Glimmering and vast, out in the tranquil bay.   5
Come to the window, sweet is the night-air!

Only, from the long line of spray
Where the sea meets the moon-blanched land,
Listen! you hear the grating roar
Of pebbles which the waves draw back, and fling,   10
At their return, up the high strand,
Begin, and cease, and then again begin,
With tremulous cadence slow, and bring
The eternal note of sadness in.

Sophocles long ago   15
Heard it on the Aegaean,° and it brought
Into his mind the turbid ebb and flow
Of human misery; we
Find also in the sound a thought,
Hearing it by this distant northern sea.   20

The Sea of Faith
Was once, too, at the full, and round earth's shore
Lay like the folds of a bright girdle furled.°
But now I only hear
Its melancholy, long, withdrawing roar,   25
Retreating, to the breath
Of the night-wind, down the vast edges drear
And naked shingles of the world.

Ah, love, let us be true
To one another! for the world, which seems   30
To lie before us like a land of dreams,
So various, so beautiful, so new,
Hath really neither joy, nor love, nor light,
Nor certitude, nor peace, nor help for pain;
And we are here as on a darkling plain   35

Dover Beach: the shore on the English side of the Channel facing toward France and thus all
Europe   **Sophocles . . . Aegaean:** probably an allusion to the third choral ode of *Oedipus at
Colonus,* where the constant lashings of human agony are compared to the beating of waves upon the
earth's shore   **furled:** wrapped around

Swept with confused alarms of struggle and flight,
Where ignorant armies clash by night.°

Questions for Writing and Discussion

1. Arnold withholds the identity of his listener until the final stanza. Does the poem, up to that point, lead you to believe it is his love who stands beside him? Is the urging of true love at the end of "Dover Beach" a probable—that is, a "natural" or credible—response to the moral crisis which Arnold has sought through the rest of the poem to make vivid?

2. The eternal "note of sadness" which Sophocles too has heard is never sounded altogether clearly in the poem: Arnold refers to it, in line 19, simply as "a thought," though the next stanza presumably divulges the content of this thought—that the Sea of Faith is at its lowest ebb in history, and is still withdrawing. Does this reticence over the *cause* of Arnold's melancholy seem to you a strength of the poem? Or is its effect to make the poem as confused as those armies?

THE RHODORA
On Being Asked, Whence Is the Flower?

Ralph Waldo Emerson

In May, when sea-winds pierced our solitudes,
I found the fresh Rhodora in the woods,
Spreading its leafless blooms in a damp nook,
To please the desert and the sluggish brook.
The purple petals, fallen in the pool,   5
Made the black water with their beauty gay;
Here might the red-bird come his plumes to cool,
And court the flower that cheapens his array.
Rhodora! if the sages ask thee why
This charm is wasted on the earth and sky,   10
Tell them, dear, that if eyes were made for seeing,
Then Beauty is its own excuse for being;
Why thou wert there, O rival of the rose!
I never thought to ask, I never knew;
But, in my simple ignorance, suppose   15
The self-same Power that brought me there brought you.

Where . . . night: Arnold's poem was written not long after the European revolutionary upheavals and violent suppressions of 1848; the armies, however, may be taken in a wider sense

Questions for Writing and Discussion

1. Why is the rhodora's charm "wasted" (line 10)? Does the speaker's feeling that it may be seen as wasted make the flower more attractive to him or less? Why?

2. To what sort of object might the "sages" of line 9 address a poem?

3. When the poet confesses his own ignorance of the causes of beauty, does he seem to do so regretfully? proudly? Is his "simple" ignorance available to everyone who knows little or has forgotten what he knows?

4. Does "the self-same Power" of the last line refer to God? to some all-encompassing spirit of Nature? If so, why doesn't Emerson name it? What sort of power, if any, has the poem exemplified?

5. What is the connection between the first line and the rest of the poem? Does it hint at a motive for so careful a description of something so small and so apparently slight?

THE CONVERGENCE OF THE TWAIN
(Lines on the Loss of the "Titanic")°

Thomas Hardy

I

    In a solitude of the sea
    Deep from human vanity,
And the Pride of Life that planned her, stilly couches she.

II

    Steel chambers, late the pyres
    Of her salamandrine fires,°
Cold currents thrid,° and turn to rhythmic tidal lyres.

III

    Over the mirrors meant
    To glass the opulent
The sea worm crawls—grotesque, slimed, dumb, indifferent.

Titanic: the largest and most opulent passenger liner of her era, the *Titanic* was considered unsinkable; having struck an iceberg on a night of low visibility in the North Atlantic, she went down on April 15, 1912, drowning most of those aboard **salamandrine fires:** the salamander was supposed by legend to survive (unharmed) the flames of any fire; here, it is the *fires* of the *Titanic* that are supposed by her builders to survive any catastrophe **thrid:** archaic past tense of "thread"

IV

Jewels in joy designed
To ravish the sensuous mind
Lie lightless, all their sparkles bleared and black and blind.

V

Dim moon-eyed fishes near
Gaze at the gilded gear
And query: "What does this vaingloriousness down here?"

VI

Well: while was fashioning
This creature of cleaving wing,
The Immanent Will° that stirs and urges everything

VII

Prepared a sinister mate
For her—so gaily great—
A Shape of Ice, for the time far and dissociate.

VIII

And as the smart ship grew
In stature, grace, and hue,
In shadowy silent distance grew the Iceberg too.

IX

Alien they seemed to be:
No mortal eye could see
The intimate welding of their later history,

X

Or sign that they were bent
By paths coincident
On being anon twin halves of one august event,

XI

Till the Spinner of the Years°
Said "Now!" And each one hears,
And consummation comes, and jars two hemispheres.

Immanent Will: the will of nature made present in each thing Spinner of the Years: first of the
three Fates who spin, measure, and cut the thread of individual destiny

Questions for Writing and Discussion

1.   In the second line of the poem we may read "from" to mean "away from" or "because of." Which of these meanings do you think Hardy primarily intended? Can you see a way in which both might work together?

2.   Explain the irony of the phrase "salamandrine fires." Is the irony too heavy-handed? When you have read the whole poem, does the salamander strike you as consistent with other images of animals or mythical creatures—or does it seem to you imported into the poem arbitrarily? How does the phrase "cold currents thrid" help move the poem from "fires" to "rhythmic tidal lyres"?

3.   How many images or suppressed images of spinning—of a winding or unraveling thread—do you find in the poem?

4.   The *Titanic* sank in 1912; in Hardy's *Collected Poems,* "The Convergence of the Twain" is dated "1912, 1914." What sort of resonance do you think he meant the last line of the poem to have for his contemporaries?

DULCE ET DECORUM EST

Wilfred Owen

Bent double, like old beggars under sacks,
Knock-kneed, coughing like hags, we cursed through sludge,
Till on the haunting flares we turned our backs
And towards our distant rest began to trudge.
Men marched asleep. Many had lost their boots   5
But limped on, blood-shod.° All went lame; all blind;
Drunk with fatigue; deaf even to the hoots
Of tired, outstripped Five-Nines that dropped behind.

Gas! GAS! Quick, boys!—An ecstasy of fumbling,
Fitting the clumsy helmets just in time;   10
But someone still was yelling out and stumbling
And flound'ring like a man in fire or lime . . .
Dim, through the misty panes and thick green light,
As under a green sea, I saw him drowning.

In all my dreams, before my helpless sight,   15
He plunges at me, guttering, choking, drowning.

If in some smothering dreams you too could pace
Behind the wagon that we flung him in,
And watch the white eyes writhing in his face,
His hanging face, like a devil's sick of sin;   20
If you could hear, at every jolt, the blood

blood-shod: with blood for shoes

Come gargling from the froth-corrupted lungs,
Obscene as cancer, bitter as the cud
Of vile, incurable sores on innocent tongues,—
My friend, you would not tell with such high zest   25
To children ardent for some desperate glory,
The old Lie: Dulce et decorum est
Pro patria mori.°

Discussion

Here is a place as good as any to point out that in some poems we hear the poet speaking in his own voice; and the rule determining when we are allowed to say so should be common sense. When Wordsworth addresses Coleridge "O Friend," he speaks as Wordsworth; so here with Owen. That Wilfred Owen fought in World War I; that he believed less and less in "the old Lie" as time went on; that finally he came to hate war in general, and the European trench war in particular: these facts of "background" enter into the poem very thoroughly and are part of our experience of it.

In reading the poem, we ought to pay close attention to such rhymes as sludge/trudge, or fumbling/stumbling, as a verbal equivalent of the organized ugliness of war. Note too the expressiveness or "enactment" of the three lines describing the ecstasy of fumbling; the sudden slowing down of the pace for the grotesque image of the soldier drowning in gas; the hardly noticeable shift, so essential to the poem's tone, from "hags" to "boys." The final rhyme of "glory" with "mori" is perhaps the keenest stroke of all: something like rhyming "well" with "hell."

Images of grotesque suffering may, if we abstract ourselves from them, resemble images of excited pleasure. For a terrible moment in line 14 we are meant to see the drowning man as almost beautiful. But in the next two lines, the poem turns against this beauty, offers a careful therapy in the reading of such images, and protests every separation of aesthetic measure from the human scale of things. Of the kind of art which enforces this separation, and which Owen despised and rejected, Yeats's "Leda and the Swan" is a perfect example.

CRISPUS ATTUCKS°

Jay Wright

When we speak
of those musket-draped

Dulce et decorum est pro patria mori: It is sweet and fitting to die for one's country

Attucks: a black American patriot (1723?–1770) thought to have been a runaway slave and one of five men killed in the Boston Massacre

and manqué° Englishmen;
that cloistered country;
all those common people,   5
dotting the potted stoves,
hating the king,
shifting uneasily under
the sharp sails
of the unwelcome boats,   10
sometimes we forget you.
Who asked you
for that impulsive miracle?
I form it now,
with my own motives.   15
The flag dipping in your hands,
your crafted boots
hammering up the unclaimed streets,
all that was in that unformed moment.
But it wasn't the feel of those things,   20
nor the burden of the American character;
it was somehow the sense
of an unencumbered escape,
the breaking of a Protestant host,
the ambiguous, detached   25
judgment of yourself.
Now, we think of you,
when, through the sibilant streets,
another season drums
your intense, communal daring.   30

Questions for Writing and Discussion

1. What are the two senses of "Protestant host" in line 24 (one sense of "breaking" applies traditionally to bread).

2. In line 14, what is the "it" that the poet says he will form? Why does this line and the following one occur in the very middle of the poem? How do the two halves differ in language? in detail?

3. Lines 27–30 refer to the fact that when this poem was written America was beginning to remember the heroic history of its black citizens, a history which had lain hidden, at least from popular culture. What do you suppose some of the poet's "own motives" for reimagining "that impulsive miracle" are? How is this poem more than merely an editorial complaint about the neglect of black American history?

manqué: unfulfilled, unsuccessful

CHURCH GOING

Philip Larkin

Once I am sure there's nothing going on
I step inside, letting the door thud shut.
Another church: matting, seats, and stone,
And little books; sprawlings of flowers, cut
For Sunday, brownish now; some brass and stuff   5
Up at the holy end; the small neat organ;
And a tense, musty, unignorable silence,
Brewed God knows how long. Hatless, I take off
My cycle-clips in awkward reverence,

Move forward, run my hand around the font.   10
From where I stand, the roof looks almost new—
Cleaned or restored? Someone would know: I don't.
Mounting the lectern, I peruse a few
Hectoring large-scale verses, and pronounce
'Here endeth' much more loudly than I'd meant.   15
The echoes snigger briefly. Back at the door
I sign the book, donate an Irish sixpence,°
Reflect the place was not worth stopping for.

Yet stop I did: in fact I often do,
And always end much at a loss like this,   20
Wondering what to look for; wondering, too,
When churches fall completely out of use
What we shall turn them into, if we shall keep
A few cathedrals chronically on show,
Their parchment, plate and pyx° in locked cases,   25
And let the rest rent-free to rain and sheep.
Shall we avoid them as unlucky places?

Or, after dark, will dubious women come
To make their children touch a particular stone;
Pick simples for a cancer,° or in some   30
Advised night see walking a dead one?
Power of some sort or other will go on
In games, in riddles, seemingly at random;
But superstition, like belief, must die,
And what remains when disbelief has gone?   35
Grass, weedy pavement, brambles, buttress, sky,

Irish sixpence: rather like a Canadian dime for the United States   **pyx:** box or case in which the Host is kept   **Pick . . . cancer:** simples are herbs, so called because used uncompounded; they were thought by an old tradition to cure cancer

A shape less recognisable each week,
A purpose more obscure. I wonder who
Will be the last, the very last, to seek
This place for what it was; one of the crew   40
That tap and jot and know what rood-lofts° were?
Some ruin-bibber,° randy for antique,
Or Christmas-addict, counting on a whiff
Of gown-and-bands and organ-pipes and myrrh?
Or will he be my representative,   45

Bored, uninformed, knowing the ghostly silt
Dispersed, yet tending to this cross of ground
Through suburb scrub because it held unspilt
So long and equably what since is found
Only in separation—marriage, and birth,   50
And deaths, and thoughts of these—for whom was built
This special shell? For, though I've no idea
What this accoutred frowsty barn is worth,
It pleases me to stand in silence here;

A serious house on serious earth it is,   55
In whose blent air all our compulsions meet,
Are recognized, and robed as destinies.
And that much never can be obsolete,
Since someone will forever be surprising
A hunger in himself to be more serious,   60
And gravitating with it to this ground,
Which, he once heard, was proper to grow wise in,
If only that so many dead lie round.

Discussion

Philip Larkin's delicate poem is about respect for tradition—but respect that is emptied of any specific content or association, whether social, religious, or superstitious. The need to visit and revisit old places, the speaker tells us, is one thing we can be sure will never die. Only by acts of personal homage or "awkward reverence" can we remind ourselves of death while reminding ourselves as well of the permanence of what is human.

The speaker is convincing by seeming to be "one of us," casual toward sacred and ceremonial matters. But he is, we see at the end, driven to return to places such as this church by a "seriousness" that is all the more serious since—

rood-lofts: galleries forming the head of the screens which separate the nave from the choir of a church   ruin-bibber: enthusiast of ruins; castle-and-cathedral-comber

being intensely private, a characteristic the church allows for—he keeps it hidden from himself. Note the special weight of "gravitating," which resumes the sense of "*tending* to this cross of ground," and yet suggests gravity—a more than personal seriousness. This is a seriousness which the poem believes, and encourages us to admit, we all share, at whatever level: in the superstition of those "dubious women," or the educated casualness of the speaker himself.

We include this poem because we find it moving. But we don't have an answer to arguments about the "rightness" of the poem's sudden turn in the third stanza, which leads to the more powerful turn at the end. Some readers are likely to find the last two stanzas unconvincing or unearned. If the speaker is bored, why does he come at all? Aren't the several tones of the poem (bored, observant, witty, dismissive, vastly affirmative) contradictory? It is possible to locate a flaw here. But an appeal to experience can be useful, too. Do we always know why we're serious about something, or even *that* we're serious about it, before we *see* that we are?

The tone of the last stanza owes something to Tennyson; and a comparison of this poem with "Ulysses" (p. 443) will make several points at once: about tone, the decline of faith, the various strategies available to the dramatic monologue.

A FAR CRY FROM AFRICA

Derek Walcott

A wind is ruffling the tawny pelt
Of Africa. Kikuyu,° quick as flies,
Batten upon the bloodstreams of the veldt.°
Corpses are scattered through a paradise.
Only the worm, colonel of carrion, cries: 5
"Waste no compassion on these separate dead!"
Statistics justify and scholars seize
The salients of colonial policy.
What is that to the white child hacked in bed?
To savages, expendable as Jews?   10

Threshed out by beaters, the long rushes break
In a white dust of ibises whose cries
Have wheeled since civilization's dawn
From the parched river or beast-teeming plain.
The violence of beast on beast is read   15
As natural law, but upright man
Seeks his divinity by inflicting pain.

Kikuyu: members of an east African tribe   veldt: African plain

Delirious as these worried beasts, his wars
Dance to the tightened carcass of a drum,
While he calls courage still that native dread   20
Of the white peace contracted by the dead.

Again brutish necessity wipes its hands
Upon the napkin of a dirty cause, again
A waste of our compassion, as with Spain,
The gorilla wrestles with the superman.   25

I who am poisoned with the blood of both,
Where shall I turn, divided to the vein?
I who have cursed
The drunken officer of British rule, how choose
Between this Africa and the English tongue I love?   30
Betray them both, or give back what they give?
How can I face such slaughter and be cool?
How can I turn from Africa and live?

Questions for Writing and Discussion

1. What is the point of the punning of the title? What are the two meanings of the phrase? How do they embody the point of the whole poem?

2. The holocaust in World War II in which six million Jews were killed in Europe (line 10) and the Spanish Civil War (line 24) both enter this poem as allusions. What is their function?

3. The events alluded to in the opening lines are those connected with the uprising among the Kikuyu tribe in Kenya against both whites and Africans. The poet is a West Indian with roots in both Africa and England. What does he mean by the alternative stated in line 30?

TO BROOKLYN BRIDGE

Hart Crane

How many dawns, chill from his rippling rest
The seagull's wings shall dip and pivot him,
Shedding white rings of tumult, building high
Over the chained bay waters Liberty—

Then, with inviolate curve, forsake our eyes   5
As apparitional as sails that cross

Some page of figures to be filed away;
—Till elevators drop us from our day . . .

I think of cinemas, panoramic sleights°
With multitudes bent toward some flashing scene   10
Never disclosed, but hastened to again,
Foretold to other eyes on the same screen;

And Thee, across the harbor, silver-paced
As though the sun took step of thee, yet left
Some motion ever unspent in thy stride,—   15
Implicitly thy freedom staying thee!

Out of some subway scuttle, cell or loft
A bedlamite° speeds to thy parapets,
Tilting there momently, shrill shirt ballooning,
A jest falls from the speechless caravan.   20

Down Wall,° from girder into street noon leaks,
A rip-tooth of the sky's acetylene;°
All afternoon the cloud-flown derricks turn . . .
Thy cables breathe the North Atlantic still.

And obscure as that heaven of the Jews,   25
Thy guerdon° . . . Accolade thou dost bestow
Of anonymity time cannot raise:
Vibrant reprieve and pardon thou dost show,

O harp and altar, of the fury fused,
(How could mere toil align thy choiring strings!)   30
Terrific threshold of the prophet's pledge,
Prayer of pariah, and the lover's cry,—

Again the traffic lights° that skim thy swift
Unfractioned idiom, immaculate sigh of stars,
Beading thy path—condense eternity: 35
And we have seen night lifted in thine arms.

Under thy shadow by the piers I waited;
Only in darkness is thy shadow clear.
The City's fiery parcels all undone,
Already snow submerges an iron year . . .   40

O Sleepless as the river under thee,
Vaulting the sea, the prairies' dreaming sod,
Unto us lowliest sometime sweep, descend
And of the curveship lend a myth to God.

---

panoramic sleights: movies, which involve trickery on an enormous scale   **bedlamite**: resident of an asylum for the insane   **Wall**: Wall Street   **acetylene**: fuel used to supply the flame in welding   **guerdon**: reward   **traffic lights**: not traffic signals but the headlights of cars

Discussion

This lyric forms the "proem," or poetic prologue, to a unified sequence of poems titled *The Bridge.* Myth, legend, fantasy, and casual anecdote are mingled in *The Bridge* to make what Hart Crane thought would be the appropriate homage to an ideal at once peculiarly American and peculiarly modern. The bridge itself, uniting one shore with another and, in the space between them, rising and curving like a harp, as if to unite earth with heaven, suggested to Crane a linking of ideas and things, of qualities and feelings, and of facts and ideals usually kept separate in our minds. The bridge links those who saw it once with those who see it now; ordinary life with the imagination; art (which made it) with commerce (which uses it), and therefore artist with citizen. For these reasons it may seem, like a rainbow, to express a kind of covenant. As we read "To Brooklyn Bridge," we find that Crane is especially attentive to the covenant between two ways of seeing.

A train of vivid and precise images—the wheeling of the seagull, Wall Street at noon, the poet waiting by the piers—is interrupted now and then by stanzas of abstract meditation. The fourth, seventh, and eleventh stanzas owe their power to such words as "motion," "freedom," "time," "anonymity," "reprieve," and "myth." Reading the stanzas aloud is a good test of both their power and their abstractness. Our idea of the bridge as energy controlled by form, and freedom maintained by purpose, acquires a special force in the eighth stanza in the image of an aeolian harp played by the wind. We hear the strings of an aeolian harp vibrate without the help of a musician. In the same way, we feel the most impressive qualities of the bridge, through these four stanzas, without knowing their source in experience. If we were to construct a religion for the worship of landscape—a religion something like pantheism, except that it would recognize the city as part of nature—these stanzas might be its hymns. Why then are they not enough to complete the poem?

There is a poetry that deals in ideas and a poetry that deals in impressions. Good writing is possible in either kind. But evidently there is still another kind of poetry, which shows us how impressions relate to ideas by giving words to both. Crane believed that the highest poetry is of this kind. He gives us, in the hymns of praise and the metaphor of the bridge as harp and altar, an idea of the sublimity of what he sees. But through the rest of the poem, he shows us how this idea is built up from minute impressions of the landscape. We receive the first of these impressions from the image of a seagull's dip and pivot as it rises and, with a circling motion, passes slowly from our view. The "inviolate curve" of its flight seems to linger with us, and we wish it to linger, so that we feel forsaken by its passing, at the approach of other objects and other memories. The seagull's "white rings of tumult" yield to associated images: the whiteness of sails on the water, the whiteness of a "page of figures to be filed away," perhaps by a clerk in the city who can only dream of glimpsing the seagull's freedom. With the break at "—Till elevators drop us from our day," we leave behind the seagull and all it has evoked and are plunged into the very different tumult of the city. In "elevators drop us from our day" we may discern a grotesque transformation of the stock phrases informing us that every human being is born at his appointed hour.

We have surveyed Crane's movement in the first two stanzas. That he does move any reader can see in the course of passing from one line to the next ("sails that cross/Some page of figures"). But it is the swiftness and ease that he shows in changing his focus which may strike us as extraordinary, or unaccountable, or both. Let us pursue the metaphor implied in our use of the word "focus." In "To Brooklyn Bridge" Crane avails himself of two devices essential to cinematic narration: the *fade-out* or *dissolve,* in which a vivid image grows less and less vivid, disappears, and is replaced by some other image to which the first bears no immediate or strictly visual relation; and *montage* or *cutting,* in which a vivid image is replaced, without the middle stage of fading and blending, by another equally vivid image to which the first is related. In the poem's opening stanza we follow the seagull's flight intently, as if we were tracking it with the eye of a camera; the break at "Liberty—" coincides with the seagull's wheeling in a new direction, and our shifting to a different point of view to watch it from; finally, as we lose sight of it, the moment during which it was seen becomes a self-contained vision, capable of being absorbed as an "apparition" into the reverie of another mind; and from just such a reverie we cut abruptly to the reality of the city, for a single line, and then yield gradually to the stirring of the poet's own voice ("I think of cinemas"). The narrative devices of these stanzas are at work throughout the poem, with the abrupt shift being registered by a dash and the gradual shift by suspension dots.

We move then in the opening stanzas from the witnessing eye to the dreaming mind, and in doing so we encounter the first of this poem's "flashing scene[s]/Never disclosed, but hastened to again," in the sustained glimpse of the seagull's flight. In such "panoramic sleights" as in cinemas, multitudes recognize the true shape of their imaginings. Yet Crane performs an exemplary feat of conjuring, and perhaps something more than a "sleight," in connecting those who only dream of a flashing scene with one who actually beholds it. In this respect his poem does the work of a bridge. And the poet who reveals to others what they cannot see for themselves is also a prophet. We may begin to understand why later in the poem the bridge will become "the prophet's pledge."

The phrase "Foretold to other eyes" would seem to refer not only to the several points of view within this poem but also to the vision of those who came before Crane. Whitman, a poet whom Crane loved and from whose work he learned much, identified the poet's vocation with the prophet's; and in one of his greatest poems, "Crossing Brooklyn Ferry" (pp. 624–28), Whitman spoke of "others who look back on me because I look'd forward to them." We find seagulls present as a vivid central image in "Crossing Brooklyn Ferry," and that poem, like Crane's, tells us that the imagination draws sustenance from what it calls the "necessary film" of "appearances." While deliberately evoking details of Whitman's poem, however, Crane writes "To Brooklyn Bridge" with great confidence in his own originality, and if his energy alone failed to convince us of this, we could still guess it from a single circumstance of the poem's setting.

"Crossing Brooklyn Ferry" takes place at sunset, with the sun "half an hour high." "To Brooklyn Bridge" begins, "How many dawns. . . ."

In the fourth stanza we notice that the first explicit address to the bridge is made to occur almost incidentally, as an afterthought: the bridge is an object of the sentence beginning "I think . . ." and Crane has thought of a great deal before he comes to the subject of his poem. The stance of easy indifference is a convention of courtly love poetry. The lover affects to think of everything but his beloved, and yet, in everything he describes, her image is reflected. Such poetry is always a more or less elaborate variation on the rhetorical formula: "And so I think of beauty, and of you." The bridge is the greatest of all conjuring tricks, the most panoramic of "sleights," and hence their symbol: like the sun, it seems to vault from one horizon to the other; unlike the sun, it is ever-present because stayed by its own freedom. We have encountered the paradox of freedom-through-restraint earlier, in the "chained bay waters Liberty," and it embodies what the bridge can teach us: that energy makes itself visible to us only through our awareness of form. If we regard "To Brooklyn Bridge" as a love poem, addressed not to a beloved person but to a beloved vocation and the object associated with it, most of our difficulties with the poem's tone will vanish.

We are conscious of the city, in the third stanza, only as a chaos of impressions. Gradually we come to experience its life as something painful and shattering. The vision of the bedlamite plunging to his death from the bridge's parapets, "Tilting there momently," is, we feel, an episode like any other in the city's life, and it concentrates all attention on the "jest" of the man's poor equipment for flight. The "rip-tooth" of sky above Wall Street, through which the sun leaks, introduces a touch of lively and gratuitous pain. How close is this city to hell? It is close enough, at least, for us to feel relieved when we escape from the turning of the derricks, by another fade-out, to the cables of the bridge which breathe the different air of the North Atlantic. And it is at this point that Crane praises the consolation afforded by the bridge for being as obscure as "that heaven of the Jews."

The ninth stanza sketches an alternative landscape to the city's. That it is also a literal description of the bridge at night may be concealed from us by the daring of Crane's language. Yet it is wholly in keeping with the rest of this poem to describe the lights on the bridge as an earthly condensation of the breath from heaven's "immaculate sigh of stars." "Traffic lights" is perhaps a misleading name for the headlights of cars, but here Crane most likely wanted "traffic" for its special implication of commerce. Anyone who has ever noticed the long converging lines formed by the lights of cars, which seem to meet at an infinitely distant point, will know why Crane saw in them a "condensed" image of eternity. In misusing ordinary speech we may fracture an idiom. The bridge's idiom is "unfractioned" because it is shared, as a unified and unifying vision, by all who look on it, by those who built it and those for whom it was built.

We have reached a point of balance between the bridge and the city. To the poet of the tenth stanza falls the task of subsuming the city's reality in the promise of heaven implicit in the bridge. The poet waits for something; he does not tell us what. But the entire poem has testified to a conviction that his poetic and therefore his personal destiny lies in the task to which the bridge enjoins him. It is this that he waits to perform. Exhausted by its own grinding motion, and with all its fire spent, the city is ready to retire into the long sleep of winter, while the bridge and the river under it remain sleepless. The city can be released from the grip of an "iron year" only at those privileged moments when it is absorbed into something greater than itself. This something is the work of imagination that Crane associates with the bridge. Literary critics sometimes exhibit their fondness for an especially striking or far-reaching metaphor by calling it a "symbol." As a rule this is loose talk. But we do need some such word when the resonance between the two parts of a comparison becomes so perfect that we cannot tell which represents which, or whether it is fair to speak of representation at all. In Crane's poem, the correspondences between what the poet will seek to accomplish by prophecy and what the bridge, as his inspiration, actually does accomplish, all tend to reduce the distinctions between them. We may justly speak of the bridge as a symbol. Whether the poet's dedication to his task makes him able, like the bridge, to show "vibrant reprieve and pardon" to what he looks on, only our sense of *The Bridge* as a whole, and perhaps of the larger shape of Crane's career, can begin to tell us. "To Brooklyn Bridge" is a poem of seeing and waiting.

PARADISE

George Herbert

I bless thee, Lord, because I GROW
Among thy trees, which in a ROW
To thee both fruit and order OW.

What open force, or hidden CHARM
Can blast° my fruit, or bring me HARM   5
While the enclosure is thine ARM?

Enclose me still for fear I START;
Be to me rather sharp and TART,
Than let me want° thy hand and ART.

When thou dost greater judgments SPARE,   10
And with thy knife but prune and PARE,
Even fruitful trees more fruitful ARE.

Such sharpness shows the sweetest FREND:
Such cuttings rather heal than REND;
And such beginnings touch° their END.   15

---

blast: cause to wither   **want:** be lacking in   **touch:** both "touch" and "concern"

Questions for Writing and Discussion

1. In Paradise, Adam did not have to do any work. But the tradition followed by Herbert, a seventeenth-century English clergyman, in this remarkable prayer, had it that Eden was so rich and full of all things that it needed pruning and cutting, which led to even more luxuriant foliage. The poet compares himself to a tree. What sort of pruning and paring (line 11) does he ask of God? What can he mean by asking to be cut back?

2. Explain line 15 as it relates to the above.

3. How does the form of the poem ingeniously embody the action described in it? What has the poet done to "prune and pare" the language of the poem in each tercet (three lines)? How does it apply to the poem itself?

DENIAL

George Herbert

When my devotions could not pierce
            Thy silent ears;
Then was my heart broken, as was my verse:
       My breast was full of fears
                         And disorder: 5

My bent thoughts, like a brittle bow,
            Did fly asunder:
Each took his way; some would to pleasures go,
       Some to the wars and thunder
                       Of alarms.   10

'As good go any where,' they say,
            'As to benumb
Both knees and heart, in crying night and day,
       Come, come, my God, O come,
                     But no hearing.'   15

O that thou shouldst give dust a tongue
            To cry to thee,
And then not hear it crying! all day long
       My heart was in my knee,
                     But no hearing.   20

Therefore my soul lay out of sight,
            Untuned, unstrung;
My feeble spirit, unable to look right,
       Like a nipped blossom, hung
                     Discontented.   25

O cheer and tune my heartless breast,
        Defer no time;
That so thy favours granting my request,
        They and my mind may chime,
                And mend my rhyme.   30

Questions for Writing and Discussion

1.   How does the comparison in line 3 work throughout the poem? How does the mending take place?

2.   Consider lines 5, 10, 15, 20, 25, 30: How is the meaning of each reinforced by the verse pattern? Does line 3 represent its own meaning by its rhythm in any way? How are the images of tuning, writing, and praying connected in the last 3 stanzas?

3.   What does line 19 mean?

4.   Are lines 29–30 "musical" or "tuned" in any other way than by the rhyming of "chime" and "rhyme"?

SUNDAY MORNING

Wallace Stevens

I

Complacencies of the peignoir,° and late
Coffee and oranges in a sunny chair,
And the green freedom of a cockatoo
Upon a rug mingle to dissipate
The holy hush of ancient sacrifice.   5
She dreams a little, and she feels the dark
Encroachment of that old catastrophe,°
As a calm darkens among water-lights.
The pungent oranges and bright, green wings
Seem things in some procession of the dead,   10
Winding across wide water, without sound.
The day is like wide water, without sound,
Stilled for the passing of her dreaming feet
Over the seas, to silent Palestine,
Dominion of the blood and sepulchre.   15

peignoir: dressing gown   **old catastrophe:** the Crucifixion

II

Why should she give her bounty to the dead?
What is divinity if it can come
Only in silent shadows and in dreams?
Shall she not find in comforts of the sun,
In pungent fruit and bright, green wings, or else   20
In any balm or beauty of the earth,
Things to be cherished like the thought of heaven?
Divinity must live within herself:
Passions of rain, or moods in falling snow;
Grievings in loneliness, or unsubdued   25
Elations when the forest blooms; gusty
Emotions on wet roads on autumn nights;
All pleasures and all pains, remembering
The bough of summer and the winter branch.
These are the measures destined for her soul.   30

III

Jove° in the clouds had his inhuman birth.
No mother suckled him, no sweet land gave
Large-mannered motions to his mythy mind
He moved among us, as a muttering king,
Magnificent, would move among his hinds,°   35
Until our blood, commingling, virginal,
With heaven, brought such requital° to desire
The very hinds discerned it, in a star.
Shall our blood fail? Or shall it come to be
The blood of paradise? And shall the earth   40
Seem all of paradise that we shall know?
The sky will be much friendlier then than now,
A part of labor and a part of pain,
And next in glory to enduring love,
Not this dividing and indifferent blue.   45

IV

She says, "I am content when wakened birds,
Before they fly, test the reality
Of misty fields, by their sweet questionings;
But when the birds are gone, and their warm fields
Return no more, where, then, is paradise?"   50
There is not any haunt of prophecy,

Jove: Jupiter   hinds: shepherds   requital: fulfillment

Nor any old chimera of the grave,
Neither the golden underground, nor isle
Melodious, where spirits gat° them home,
Nor visionary south, nor cloudy palm   55
Remote on heaven's hill, that has endured
As April's green endures; or will endure
Like her remembrance of awakened birds,
Or her desire for June and evening, tipped
By the consummation of the swallow's wings.   60

V

She says, "But in contentment I still feel
The need of some imperishable bliss."
Death is the mother of beauty; hence from her,
Alone, shall come fulfilment to our dreams
And our desires. Although she strews the leaves   65
Of sure obliteration on our paths,
The path sick sorrow took, the many paths
Where triumph rang its brassy phrase, or love
Whispered a little out of tenderness,
She makes the willow shiver in the sun   70
For maidens who were wont to sit and gaze
Upon the grass, relinquished to their feet.
She causes boys to pile new plums and pears
On disregarded plate. The maidens taste
And stray impassioned in the littering leaves.   75

VI

Is there no change of death in paradise?
Does ripe fruit never fall? Or do the boughs
Hang always heavy in that perfect sky,
Unchanging, yet so like our perishing earth,
With rivers like our own that seek for seas   80
They never find, the same receding shores
That never touch with inarticulate pang?
Why set the pear upon those river-banks
Or spice the shores with odors of the plum?
Alas, that they should wear our colors there,   85
The silken weavings of our afternoons,
And pick the strings of our insipid lutes!
Death is the mother of beauty, mystical,
Within whose burning bosom we devise
Our earthly mothers waiting, sleeplessly.   90

gat: deliberately archaic for "got"

VII

Supple and turbulent, a ring of men
Shall chant in orgy on a summer morn
Their boisterous devotion to the sun,
Not as a god, but as a god might be,
Naked among them, like a savage source.   95
Their chant shall be a chant of paradise,
Out of their blood, returning to the sky;
And in their chant shall enter, voice by voice,
The windy lake wherein their lord delights,
The trees, like serafin,° and echoing hills,   100
That choir among themselves long afterward.
They shall know well the heavenly fellowship
Of men that perish and of summer morn.
And whence they came and whither they shall go
The dew upon their feet shall manifest.   105

VIII

She hears, upon that water without sound,
A voice that cries, "The tomb in Palestine
Is not the porch of spirits lingering.
It is the grave of Jesus, where he lay."
We live in an old chaos of the sun,   110
Or old dependency of day and night,
Or island solitude, unsponsored, free,
Of that wide water, inescapable.
Deer walk upon our mountains, and the quail
Whistle about us their spontaneous cries;   115
Sweet berries ripen in the wilderness;
And, in the isolation of the sky,
At evening, casual flocks of pigeons make
Ambiguous undulations as they sink,
Downward to darkness, on extended wings.   120

Questions for Writing and Discussion

1. The opening lines of this poem seem to describe a nineteenth-century painting showing a lady in an interior setting; "Sunday Morning" might be its title, as might also "Not Going to Church". How does the first stanza move from a domestic scene to its transcendent subject?

serafin: seraphim, angels

2.   The questions in stanza II are still asked almost as if of the subject of a figurative painting. The speaker answers them as he does those of the lady, later on in stanzas IV–VII. How complete an answer is given in lines 23–30?

3.   In line 45, what does the blue of the sky divide? To what is it indifferent?

4.   As if unsatisfied by the previous questions and answers, the lady asks her own in stanza IV. What does she want to know or feel? In answering her, the poem's speaker rejects mythical paradises for their impermanence. But his answer is complex: *Does* "April's green" endure? If at all, how? How do the memory and desire of lines 58–60 endure? How does this weaken the case against old fables of heaven?

5.   "Death is the mother of beauty" (line 63): this is like a moral preceding the poem's anecdote about the relation of death to art and sex. But the truth of the statements in lines 70 and 73 is not obvious. How indeed is death responsible for what the poem says it or "she" does in lines 70–74?

6.   The story of the sun dancers in stanza VII closes with an image of dew. Physically, dew appears on the ground, but has condensed out of the air. How do these facts—the phenomenon and the scientific explanation—help answer the implied questions (whence? whither?) in lines 104 and 105?

7.   In stanza VIII, a third voice enters the poem. What does it assert? What does "unsponsored" mean in line 112? Why is the "wide water" from stanza I now declared to be "inescapable"? What is "ambiguous" about the flight of the pigeons at the end of the poem?

LYING IN A HAMMOCK AT WILLIAM DUFFY'S FARM IN PINE ISLAND, MINNESOTA

James Wright

Over my head, I see the bronze butterfly,
Asleep on the black trunk,
Blowing like a leaf in green shadow.
Down the ravine behind the empty house,
The cowbells follow one another   5
Into the distances of the afternoon.
To my right,
In a field of sunlight between two pines,
The droppings of last year's horses
Blaze up into golden stones.   10
I lean back, as the evening darkens and comes on.
A chicken hawk floats over, looking for home.
I have wasted my life.

Questions for Writing and Discussion

1.   What is the relation between the seen and the heard in lines 4–5?

2.   This poem in free verse (see pp. 587–90) appears to be arranged in lines of random length. Is this really true? Look at the relation between lines 5–6 and 9–10. Which is the shortest line? Can you see any rhythm in the changing line length? Any stanzalike groupings?

3.   The last line, which "moralizes" or gives a reading of the landscape that the poet sees about him, has seemed to many critics shocking, abrupt, and unjustified. Do you feel that it represents in any way a conclusion to be drawn from the scene? How?

THE FISH

Marianne Moore

wade
through black jade.
   Of the crow-blue mussel shells, one keeps
   adjusting the ash heaps;
      opening and shutting itself like   5

an
injured fan.
   The barnacles which encrust the side
   of the wave, cannot hide
      there for the submerged shafts of the   10

sun,
split like spun
   glass, move themselves with spotlight swiftness
   into the crevices—
      in and out, illuminating   15

the
turquoise sea
   of bodies. The water drives a wedge
   of iron through the iron edge
      of the cliff; whereupon the stars,   20

pink
rice-grains, ink-
   bespattered jellyfish, crabs like green
   lilies, and submarine
      toad-stools, slide each on the other.   25

All
external
   marks of abuse are present on this
   defiant edifice—
      all the physical features of   30

ac-
cident—lack
   of cornice, dynamite grooves, burns, and
   hatchet strokes, these things stand
      out on it; the chasm side is   35

dead.
Repeated
   evidence has proved that it can live
   on what can not revive
      its youth. The sea grows old in it.   40

Questions for Writing and Discussion

1.   The title of this poem is the grammatical subject of its opening sentence. What relation does it have to the "subject" or theme of the poem itself? Suggest another title.

2.   This poem is written in syllabic verse (see pp. 585–87). Its stanzas are composed of five lines of 1, 3, 9, 6, and 8 syllables in that order (in the first stanza, "opening" is made to have two syllables); the rhyme scheme is *aabbc*. Considering the rhymes, what effect does the lack of regular stress patterns have on the sound? Comment on the hyphenation across lines 22–23 and 31–32. Why did Marianne Moore break up these words?

3.   Humans and animals "wade" through water, fish "swim." Why might Marianne Moore have used so odd a word as "wade"? What is described as moving in ways that you would think fish might?

4.   Consider lines 8–9. Trace the ways in which the cliff emerges during the poem. What is the cliff's relation to the water? to that which is in the water?

THE INSTRUCTION MANUAL

John Ashbery

As I sit looking out of a window of the building
I wish I did not have to write the instruction manual on the uses of a
   new metal.

I look down into the street and see people, each walking with an
　　inner peace,
And envy them—they are so far away from me!
Not one of them has to worry about getting out this manual on
　　schedule.　　　　　　　　　　　　　　　　　　　　　　　　5
And, as my way is, I begin to dream, resting my elbows on the desk
　　and leaning out of the window a little,
Of dim Guadalajara! City of rose-colored flowers!
City I wanted most to see, and most did not see, in Mexico!
But I fancy I see, under the press of having to write the instruction
　　manual,
Your public square, city, with its elaborate little bandstand!　　10
The band is playing *Scheherazade* by Rimsky-Korsakov.
Around stand the flower girls, handing out rose- and lemon-colored
　　flowers,
Each attractive in her rose-and-blue striped dress (Oh! such shades of
　　rose and blue),
And nearby is the little white booth where women in green serve
　　you green and yellow fruit.
The couples are parading; everyone is in a holiday mood.　　15
First, leading the parade, is a dapper fellow
Clothed in deep blue. On his head sits a white hat
And he wears a mustache, which has been trimmed for the occasion.
His dear one, his wife, is young and pretty; her shawl is rose, pink,
　　and white.
Her slippers are patent leather, in the American fashion,　　20
And she carries a fan, for she is modest, and does not want the crowd
　　to see her face too often.
But everybody is so busy with his wife or loved one
I doubt they would notice the mustachioed man's wife.
Here come the boys! They are skipping and throwing little things on
　　the sidewalk
Which is made of gray tile. One of them, a little older, has a
　　toothpick in his teeth.　　　　　　　　　　　　　　　　　25
He is silenter than the rest, and affects not to notice the pretty young
　　girls in white.
But his friends notice them, and shout their jeers at the laughing
　　girls.
Yet soon all this will cease, with the deepening of their years,
And love bring each to the parade grounds for another reason.
But I have lost sight of the young fellow with the toothpick.　　30
Wait—there he is—on the other side of the bandstand,
Secluded from his friends, in earnest talk with a young girl
Of fourteen or fifteen. I try to hear what they are saying
But it seems they are just mumbling something—shy words of love,
　　probably.

She is slightly taller than he, and looks quietly down into his sincere
    eyes.   35
She is wearing white. The breeze ruffles her long fine black hair
    against her olive cheek.
Obviously she is in love. The boy, the young boy with the toothpick,
    he is in love too;
His eyes show it. Turning from this couple,
I see there is an intermission in the concert.
The paraders are resting and sipping drinks through straws   40
(The drinks are dispensed from a large glass crock by a lady in dark
    blue),
And the musicians mingle among them, in their creamy white
    uniforms, and talk
About the weather, perhaps, or how their kids are doing at school.

Let us take this opportunity to tiptoe into one of the side streets.
Here you may see one of those white houses with green trim   45
That are so popular here. Look—I told you!
It is cool and dim inside, but the patio is sunny.
An old woman in gray sits there, fanning herself with a palm leaf fan.
She welcomes us to her patio, and offers us a cooling drink.
"My son is in Mexico City," she says. "He would welcome you too   50
If he were here. But his job is with a bank there.
Look, here is a photograph of him."
And a dark-skinned lad with pearly teeth grins out at us from the
    worn leather frame.
We thank her for her hospitality, for it is getting late
And we must catch a view of the city, before we leave, from a good
    high place.   55
That church tower will do—the faded pink one, there against the
    fierce blue of the sky. Slowly we enter.
The caretaker, an old man dressed in brown and gray, asks us how
    long we have been in the city, and how we like it here.
His daughter is scrubbing the steps—she nods to us as we pass into
    the tower.
Soon we have reached the top, and the whole network of the city
    extends before us.
There is the rich quarter, with its houses of pink and white, and its
    crumbling, leafy terraces.   60
There is the poorer quarter, its homes a deep blue.
There is the market, where men are selling hats and swatting flies
And there is the public library, painted several shades of pale green
    and beige.
Look! There is the square we just came from, with the promenaders.
There are fewer of them, now that the heat of the day has increased,   65
But the young boy and girl still lurk in the shadows of the bandstand.

And there is the home of the little old lady—
She is still sitting in the patio, fanning herself.
How limited, but how complete withal, has been our experience of
    Guadalajara!
We have seen young love, married love, and the love of an aged
    mother for her son.   70
We have heard the music, tasted the drinks, and looked at colored
    houses.
What more is there to do, except stay? And that we cannot do.
And as a last breeze freshens the top of the weathered old tower, I
    turn my gaze
Back to the instruction manual which has made me dream of
    Guadalajara.

Questions for Writing and Discussion

1. Does the poem seem to change its tone from time to time? What kind of tone do lines 44–46, 54–55, and 69 have, for example? or lines 24, 30, and 31?

2. Why do you think the poet selected the instruction manual for the title of this poem? After all, the narrator does not want to write it. Is the poem itself in any way an "instruction manual"?

3. What is the effect of the poem's simple, even naive, language? of the objects and events singled out for notice?

THE RETREAT

Henry Vaughan

Happy those early days, when I
Shined in my angel-infancy!
Before I understood this place
Appointed for my second race,
Or taught my soul to fancy aught   5
But a white celestial thought;
When yet I had not walked above
A mile or two from my first love,
And looking back, at that short space,
Could see a glimpse of his bright face;   10
When on some gilded cloud, or flower,
My gazing soul would dwell an hour,
And in those weaker glories spy

Some shadows of eternity;
Before I taught my tongue to wound   15
My conscience with a sinful sound,
Or had the black art to dispense
A several sin to every sense,
But felt through all this fleshly dress
Bright shoots of everlastingness.   20

    O how I long to travel back,
And tread again that ancient track!
That I might once more reach that plain
Where first I left my glorious train;
From whence the enlightened spirit sees   25
That shady City of Palm-trees.
But ah! my soul with too much stay
Is drunk, and staggers in the way.
Some men a forward motion love,
But I by backward steps would move,   30
And when this dust falls to the urn
In that state I came, return.

Questions for Writing and Discussion

1. A retreat is a movement backward in which one's steps are retraced. It is also a place to which one may retire for solitary religious contemplation. Do you think Vaughan intends one, or both, of these meanings to apply to the lost time of childhood? to the life that remains to him?

2. Vaughan regrets having had "the black art to dispense/A several sin to every sense." Judging by the pattern of images in the poem, which of the senses predominated for him in childhood? Does it continue to predominate through his maturity? in eternity?

I WENT TO THE SUMMIT

A. R. Ammons

I went to the summit and stood in the high nakedness:
the wind tore about this
way and that in confusion and its speech could not
get through to me nor could I address it:
still I said as if to the alien in myself   5

I do not speak to the wind now:
for having been brought this far by nature I have been
brought out of nature
and nothing here shows me the image of myself:
for the word *tree* I have been shown a tree   10
and for the word *rock* I have been shown a rock,
for stream, for cloud, for star
this place has provided firm implication and answering
     but where here is the image for *longing:*
so I touched the rocks, their interesting crusts: 15
I flaked the bark of stunt-fir:
I looked into space and into the sun
and nothing answered my word *longing:*
     goodbye, I said, goodbye, nature so grand and
reticent, your tongues are healed up into their own   20
element
and as you have shut up you have shut me out: I am
as foreign here as if I had landed, a visitor:
so I went back down and gathered mud
and with my hands made an image for *longing:*   25
     I took the image to the summit: first
I set it here, on the top rock, but it completed
nothing: then I set it there among the tiny firs
but it would not fit:
so I returned to the city and built a house to set   30
the image in
and men came into my house and said
     that is an image for *longing*
and nothing will ever be the same again

Questions for Writing and Discussion

1. In line 13, what "firm implication and answering" has nature provided? In what way is nature "reticent," as in line 20?

2. How does the word "longing" differ from the name of an object, like the words "rock," "cloud," or "star"? What kind of object does the poet suggest will provide "an image for longing"? And does he mean "an image *of* it"?

3. The "summit" in line 1 is not described. What are the implications of its not being that of any particular mountain?

4. In lines 24–25, the speaker says he made a piece of sculpture. What sort of house do you imagine he built in lines 30–34? What do you think the man-made image for *"longing"* looked like?

BROTHERHOOD IN PAIN

Robert Penn Warren

Fix your eyes on any chance object. For instance,
The leaf, prematurely crimson, of the swamp maple

That dawdles down gold air to the velvet-black water
Of the moribund beaver-pond. Or the hunk

Of dead chewing gum in the gutter with the mark of a molar   5
Yet distinct on it, like the most delicate Hellenistic° chisel-work.

Or a black sock you took off last night and by mistake
Left lying, to be found in the morning, on the bathroom tiles.

Or pick up a single stone from the brookside, inspect it
Most carefully, then throw it back in. You will never   10

See it again. By the next spring flood, it may have been hurled
A mile downstream. Fix your gaze on any of these objects,

Or if you think me disingenuous in my suggestions,
Whirl around three times like a child, or a dervish,° with eyes shut,

Then fix on the first thing seen when they open.   15
In any case, you will suddenly observe an object in the obscene
     moment of birth.

It does not know what it is. It has no name. The matrix° from which
     it is torn
Bleeds profusely. It has not yet begun to breathe. Its experience

Is too terrible to recount. Only when it has completely forgotten
Everything, will it smile shyly, and try to love you,   20

For somehow it knows that you are lonely, too.
It pityingly knows that you are more lonely than it is, for

You exist only in the delirious illusion of language.

Questions for Writing and Discussion

1.   Are the leaf, the chewing gum, the sock, and the stone really "chance objects"? How are they related in the poem?

Hellenistic: a late, refined period of Greek art   **dervish:** oriental mystic who whirls   **matrix:** womb

2.   The imagery following line 13 suggests that noticing something very intensely or in a new way can be a violent event. What is the "matrix"—the background of ways of seeing—from which such an object is torn?

3.   Once the object is "born" into the observer's consciousness, what does the poem imply about its new relation to the observer? How does this help explain the suddenness of the last line?

GOD'S LITTLE MOUNTAIN

Geoffrey Hill

Below, the river scrambled like a goat,
Dislodging stones. The mountain stamped its foot,
Shaking, as from a trance. And I was shut
With wads of sound into a sudden quiet.

I thought the thunder had unsettled heaven,   5
All was so still. And yet the sky was cloven°
By flame that left the air cold and engraven.°
I waited for the word that was not given,

Pent up into a region of pure force,
Made subject to the pressure of the stars;   10
I saw the angels lifted like pale straws;
I could not stand before those winnowing eyes

And fell, until I found the world again.
Now I lack grace to tell what I have seen;
For though the head frames words the tongue has none.   15
And who will prove the surgeon to this stone?

Questions for Writing and Discussion

1.   This poem is about a thunderstorm that leads to a vision. What sort of vision is it describing? Would you call it religious? Or does it have something to do with the writing of poetry?

2.   The speaker of the poem tells us that he "waited for the word that was not given," but he hints later on that if he did not lack grace, he might tell us (presumably in words) what he has seen. What does this suggest about the nature of "the word"? of "grace"?

cloven: split   engraven: engraved; impressed or inscribed with meaning

3.   You may once have read the following passage in the New Testament (Revelation 2:17): "He that hath an ear, let him hear what the Spirit saith unto the churches; To him that overcometh I will give to eat of the hidden manna, and will give him a white stone, and in the stone a new name written, which no man knoweth save he that receiveth it." Considering this passage, how might you interpret the final line of the poem?

Poem and Picture

"Poetry is like painting," said the Roman poet Horace. Renaissance writers liked to say that a poem was a speaking picture, and painting a silent poetry. The very words we use to describe the elements of poetic language—"figurative," "image"—were originally used about visual matters rather than linguistic ones. And there are many ways in which pictures and poems relate to one another. Some of these relationships are quite complex. Some pictures, for example, are illustrations of poems or other texts, such as Rembrandt's illustrations of the Bible or Rubens' of classical mythology. On the other hand some poems are written about pictures, such as W. H. Auden's poem about Pieter Bruegel's painting called *Landscape with the Fall of Icarus.* Still other poems were written to accompany pictures, with which they formed a unit. Such poem and picture combinations are called *emblems*.

The emblem was very common in the sixteenth and seventeenth centuries. It affected the traditions by which concrete things or scenes or actions come, in poetry, to *represent* or *stand for* abstract qualities, emotions, moral concepts, states of mind, and so forth. Emblems were pictures with verses printed below them; the title or label of the picture was often in Latin, but the verses could be in any language. The poems formed the link between the picture and its "meaning" or title. In linking the two, they would often draw extended metaphorical connections between the object and its meaning. For example, a familiar emblem was a serpent biting its own tail and thus making a ring: it represented the universe, or eternity, which has no beginning or end. The seventeenth-century preacher and writer John Bunyan, in an emblem book for

561

schoolchildren, included a picture of a ring for the snake and interpreted it in this simple quatrain:

> Eternity is like unto a Ring.
> Time, like to Measure, doth itself extend;
> Measure commences, is a finite thing.
> The ring has no beginning, middle, end.

As we can see, an emblem picture without its poem can be rather like a riddle. Samson, in the Book of Judges, posed just such an emblematic riddle when he asked what the meaning was of honey found and taken from the carcass of a lion. The answer was sweetness coming from strength. Sometimes the picture in emblem books would seem strange, until the interpretation, however clear or farfetched, would draw a connection. Below is an emblem by a sixteenth-century English writer, Geoffrey Whitney. Its title, in Latin, was *"Ex Bello, Pax,"* or "After War, Peace." The woodcut picture is reproduced below, followed by the text (often called the *motto*—hence our word for a printed slogan) in modernized spelling.

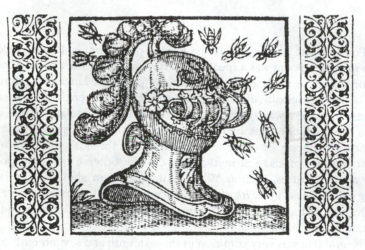

"Ex Bello, Pax." Woodcut from Geoffrey Whitney, *A Choice of Emblems* (Leyden, 1586).

> The helmet strong, that did the head defend,
> Behold, for hive the bees in quiet served;
> And when that wars, with bloody blows, had end,
> They honey wrought, where soldier was preserved;
>   Which doth declare the blessed fruits of peace,
>   How sweet she is, when mortal wars do cease.

There is a play here on two senses of "sweetness," both the literal sweetness of honey and the figurative sweetness of peace and prosperity. In emblem poems, sometimes the object talks and explains itself, sometimes the verse asks a rhetorical question of the picture—*"What are you? What do you mean?"*—and then answers its own question. In the poetry of the seventeenth century, an emblem will often be implied without the actual picture being there. The famous ending of John Donne's "A Valediction Forbidding Mourning" uses an extended metaphor of a compass to represent the mutual faithfulness of a husband and wife who are forced to be apart. After arguing that the souls of the two, husband and wife, were really one and therefore could not be thought of as parted by travel, the poem shifts its argument:

> If they be two, they are two so
>   As stiff twin compasses are two,
> Thy soul, the fixed foot, makes no show
>   To move, both doth if th'other do.
>
> And though it in the center sit,   5
>   Yet when the other far doth roam,
> It leans, and hearkens after it,
>   And grows erect as that comes home.
>
> Such wilt thou be to me, who must
>   Like the other foot obliquely run;   10
> Thy firmness makes my circle just
>   And makes me end where I begun.

If the comparison had started with the compass instead of with the souls, we could easily imagine it printed under a picture of the compass drawing a "just" or perfect circle.

Emblem as shaped poem

Occasionally, an emblem poem makes its own picture, so to speak. By arranging its words on a page in a particular shape, a poem can present a visual image of its subject. The poem itself then develops the implications of the image-subject. For example, altar-shaped poems, with images of sacrifice, offering, commemoration, etc., were frequent in the sixteenth and seventeenth centuries. Other poets, borrowing from the ancient Greeks, used the shape of cupid's wings to write about the power of love. George Herbert's poem, based on such verses, was originally printed with the lines running up and down the page, like this:

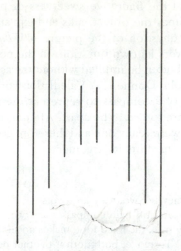

Easter celebrates Christ's passion and resurrection, which according to orthodox Christian tradition constituted a victory over all human death. The Easter story involves Christ's suffering, death, and entombment, which are only then followed by His rising. Religious meditation would reveal that the first had to be in order that the last could occur. Herbert was an Anglican priest, and his Easter poem reveals this: the wings are those of larks, angels, the holy spirit as the dove, and, metaphorically the spirit of the speaker.

EASTER-WINGS

George Herbert

Lord, who createdst man in wealth and store,°
Though foolishly he lost the same,
Decaying more and more,
Till he became
Most poor: 5
With thee
O let me rise
As larks, harmoniously,
And sing this day thy victories:
Then shall the fall further the flight in me.   10

store: plenty

My tender age in sorrow did begin:
And still with sicknesses and shame
Thou didst so punish sin,
That I became
Most thin.   15
With thee
Let me combine,
And feel this day thy victory:
For, if I imp° my wing on thine,
Affliction shall advance the flight in me.   20

We can also observe that when the lines are printed horizontally, as they always are in modern editions of this poem, the two stanzas make up an abstract shape, each one looking like this:

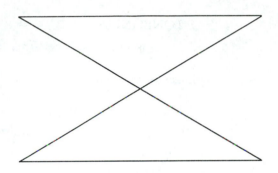

.The actual shape of the stanza on the page narrows and then widens.

1.   What are the several meanings of "fall" in line 10? How does one of them refer to the first lines of the stanza?

2.   How are lines 5–6 and 15–16 related?

3.   Aside from the interpretation of the wing pattern in the poem, how can you interpret the abstract shape? How is this abstract shape given *meaning* in the context of the poem? (Start out by considering your answer to question 2.)

The poem as visual image

A more extreme example of the way print is arranged on a page to reinforce a poetic image can be seen in the experiments of e. e. cummings (as he spelled his name). His little epigram is both delicate and intense in its effect:

imp: to graft a feather onto another one

```
                    l(a

                    le

                    af

                    fa

                    ll                                        5

                    s)

                    one

                    l

                    iness
```

The poem might be said to comprise two elements—perhaps a title and a single line, or a slightly longer line of two parts. For example, in the first instance, we could read the poem as

LONELINESS

a leaf falls

or, in the second, as a single image or emblem

What cummings has done is to so shape the poem on the page—breaking it up into minimal "lines" of, in one case, only a single letter—that it composes a kind of visual emblem of a falling leaf. This process works through several stages. In the first stage, the image of the solitary, falling leaf is put into close association with its meaning by an insertion: "l *(a leaf falls)* oneliness." Let us consider the point of insertion. If the parenthetical phrase had gone in as "lone *(a leaf falls)* liness," it might have been centered more precisely in "loneliness," true. But cummings' way of inserting the phrase reminds us that the noun stem "lone" can be broken up visually into l + one. Since the letter "l" and the numeral "1" are identical on most typewriters and in many typefaces, the word "lone" can be divided into two separate, lonely representations of singleness. The next stage is the visual representation of the dropping leaf.

1.   How does cummings' arrangement of type "depict" a leaf falling from a tree, turning as it falls? (Consider lines 2–5.)

2.   How does the sequence of lines 5–8 dramatize the "1 + one" structure described above?

3.   Why is a falling leaf an image of loneliness, after all? Does it suggest other experiences associated with being *lonely* (rather than merely *solitary*)?

The poem as commentary on a picture

Poems can also address themselves to pictures as a whole rather than, as an emblematic verse, to the object or event depicted in them. In this case, it is the artist's conception which is addressed, rather than the picture's "subject." Thus a poem or text might explain or interpret a Biblical scene shown in an engraving, but any engraving of that scene will serve. But a poem written about a particular artist's picture deals with that artist's interpretation of the scene as he has transformed it by his design and execution.

For example, Dante Gabriel Rossetti wrote a sonnet about a painting by Leonardo da Vinci which he had seen for the first time in Paris. The so-called *Madonna of the Rocks,* in the Louvre, was thought to have been painted around 1485. It is famous for the landscape background and its use of light and shadow; the figures represent the Virgin Mary, the infant Jesus, the angel Gabriel, and, on the viewer's left, the infant St. John the Baptist, whom Jesus is blessing and at whom the angel is pointing.

For
OUR LADY OF THE ROCKS
By Leonardo da Vinci

Dante Gabriel Rossetti

Mother, is this the darkness of the end,
   The Shadow of Death? and is that outer sea
   Infinite imminent Eternity?
And does the death-pang by man's seed sustained
In Time's each instant cause thy face to bend   5
   Its silent prayer upon the Son, while He
   Blesses the dead with His hand silently
To His long day which hours no more offend?

Mother of grace, the pass is difficult,
   Keen as these rocks, and the bewildered souls   10

Throng it like echoes, blindly shuddering through.
Thy name, O Lord, each spirit's voice extols,
Whose peace abides in the dark avenue
Amid the bitterness of things occult.°

occult: dark

LEONARDO DA VINCI, *The Virgin of the Rocks, c.* 1485. Oil on
wood panel, approx. 75″ × 43″. Louvre, Paris.

Rossetti's sonnet starts out by asking the Virgin Mary what the landscape means. Then, in the sestet, as if having heard the answer (or, at any rate, in place of the answer), it comments both on the landscape and on the meaning it has read in it.

One of the first things we notice about the poem is that it leaves out the infant St. John (Jesus is seen as blessing "the dead"), and the angel Gabriel as well. Instead, the poem focuses on the mood of the painting and the Christian meanings in the story of Christ.

1. What elements in the life of Christ involve death and its relation to life? How do they come up in Rossetti's question about what the landscape represents of death and life?

2. What does "the pass" (line 9) mean? How is it related to birth? to life? to death?

3. The questions asked in the octave make certain assumptions. What does line 4 assume?

Albrecht Durer's engraving called *Knight, Death, and the Devil,* done in 1513, is a religious allegory. The knight represents the devout Christian dressed in the armor of faith and righteousness (thus illustrating images from several texts in the New Testament). He moves undaunted, and even undistracted, through a hostile world on his way to the fortress of Virtue set on a hilltop. Death menaces him with an hourglass, the Devil, behind him, with a pickaxe. Here is Randall Jarrell's poem, based on the engraving.

THE KNIGHT, DEATH, AND THE DEVIL

Randall Jarrell

Cowhorn-crowned, shockheaded, cornshuck-bearded,
Death is a scarecrow—his death's-head a teetotum°
That tilts up toward man confidentially
But trimmed with adders; ringlet-maned, rope-bridled,
The mare he rides crops herbs beside a skull.   5
He holds up, warning, the crossed cones of time:
Here, narrowing into now, the Past and Future
Are quicksand.
            A hoofed pikeman trots behind.
His pike's claw-hammer mocks—in duplicate, inverted—
The pocked, ribbed, soaring crescent of his horn.   10
A scapegoat aged into a steer; boar-snouted;
His great limp ears stuck sidelong out in air;
A dewlap bunched at his breast; a ram's-horn wound

teetotum: spinning top

Beneath each ear; a spur licked up and out
From the hide of his forehead; bat-winged, but in bone;   15
His eye a ring inside a ring inside a ring
That leers up, joyless, vile, in meek obscenity—
This is the devil. Flesh to flesh, he bleats
The herd back to the pit of being.

In fluted mail; upon his lance the bush   20
Of that old fox; a sheep-dog bounding at his stirrup,
In its eyes the cast of faithfulness (our help,
Our foolish help); his dun war-horse pacing
Beneath in strength, in ceremonious magnificence;
His castle—some man's castle—set on every crag: 25
So, companioned so, the knight moves through this world.
The fiend moos in amity, Death mouths, reminding:

ALBRECHT DÜRER, *The Knight, Death and the Devil*. Copper
engraving, 1513.

He listens in assurance, has no glance
To spare for them, but looks past steadily
At—at—
        a man's look completes itself.   30

The death of his own flesh, set up outside him;
The flesh of his own soul, set up outside him—
Death and the devil, what are these to him?
His being accuses him—and yet his face is firm
In resolution, in absolute persistence;   35
The folds of smiling do for steadiness;
The face is its own fate—*a man does what he must*—
And the body underneath it says: *I am.*

1. The poem is written as a description of the picture. What details does the poet select? In what way does the very description of the details interpret them? (Consider lines 16–17, for example, or lines 6–8.)

2. The poem changes its way of looking at the engraving at line 30. What happens there? Is the poem looking at details in the picture at this point? In what way does the end of the poem give the picture a modern meaning?

BEFORE THE MIRROR
(Verses written under a Picture)
Inscribed to J. A. Whistler°
Algernon C. Swinburne

I

White rose in red rose-garden
  Is not so white;
Snowdrops that plead for pardon
  And pine for fright
Because the hard East blows   5
Over their maiden rows
  Grow not as this face grows from pale to bright.

Behind the veil, forbidden,
  Shut up from sight,
Love, is there sorrow hidden,   10
  Is there delight?
Is Joy thy dower or grief,

James A. M. Whistler: (1834–1903) American painter who lived in England

White rose of weary leaf,
   Late rose whose life is brief, whose loves are light?

Soft snows that hard winds harden 15
   Till each flake bite
Fill all the flowerless garden
   Whose flowers took flight
Long since when summer ceased,
And men rose up from feast, 20
   And warm west wind grew east, and warm day night.

JAMES MCNEILL WHISTLER, *Symphony in White No. 2: The Little White Girl,* 1864. Oil on canvas, 30″ × 20″. Tate Gallery, London.

II

"Come snow, come wind or thunder
   High up in air,
I watch my face, and wonder
   At my bright hair;   25
Nought else exalts or grieves
The rose at heart, that heaves
   With love of her own leaves and lips that pair.

"She knows not loves that kissed her
   She knows not where.   30
Art thou the ghost, my sister,
   White sister there,
Am I the ghost, who knows?
My hand, a fallen rose,
   Lies snow-white on white snows, and takes no care.   35

"I cannot see what pleasures
   Or what pains were;
What pale new loves and treasures
   New years will bear;
What beam will fall, what shower,   40
What grief or joy for dower;
   But one thing knows the flower; the flower is fair."

III

Glad, but not flushed with gladness,
   Since joys go by;
Sad, but not bent with sadness,   45
   Since sorrows die;
Deep in the gleaming glass
She sees all past things pass,
   And all sweet life that was lie down and lie.

There glowing ghosts of flowers   50
   Draw down, draw nigh;
And wings of swift spent hours
   Take flight and fly;
She sees by formless gleams,
She hears across cold streams,   55
   Dead mouths of many dreams that sing and sigh.

Face fallen and white throat lifted,
   With sleepless eye
She sees old loves that drifted,
   She knew not why,   60
Old loves and faded fears

Float down a stream that hears
The flowing of all men's tears beneath the sky.

1.   What elements in the picture are addressed by Parts I, II, and III, respectively? (Part II, to which the editors have added quotation marks, is supposedly spoken by the girl.)

2.   In what way does Part II answer the questions posed in Part I?

3.   What new dimension is given, in Part III, to what is seen in the mirror? (Compare this poem with James Merrill's "Mirror," p. 448.)

A Note on Prosody: Scheme, Pattern, and Form

We started out looking at the building blocks of poetry, but figurative language lying about in heaps, or even neatly stacked like boards in a lumberyard, does not make a structure. Structures need plans, whether detailed blueprints or, as used to be the case for centuries with the construction of houses, *internal* blueprints, which are a builder's grasp of a particular kind of scheme, a set of variations on it, and a way of putting bricks or wood together to realize it. A carpenter framing a house in nineteenth-century America might be said to have his drawings "by hand," as a blues singer has her chord patterns and verse form "by ear."

Poetry is built from trope, in and by means of schemes or patterns. We can loosely call these schemes poetic form. They include the structures of *lines* of verse, groups of lines called *strophes* or *stanzas,* patterns of *rhyme, alliteration, assonance,* overall patterns of variation and repetition (*refrains,* etc.), and even larger patterns of these (*ballad stanza. heroic couplet, sonnet form,* etc.). Over the years and even centuries, these forms have come at times to be associated with one kind of poetic use or another. Sonnets, as can be seen from those included in this volume, start out by being about a particular philosophical version of love, and end up in the twentieth century as descriptions of pictures, explanations of myths, or analytic meditations. And yet the later poems—when written by the finest poets—are always in some way aware of what the history of their form entailed.

This Note on Prosody contains examples of formal schemes of every sort and every level. Since we are concerned only with verse in English, no historical or comparative sketch of metrics and forms is given. But it should be remembered that all poetry was originally *oral.* It was sung or chanted, and poetic scheme and musical pattern were identical. Poetic form as we know it is an abstraction from, or residue of, musical form, from which it came to be divorced when writing replaced memory as a way of preserving poetic utterance in narrative, prayer, spell, and the like. The ghost of oral poetry never vanishes, even though the conventions and patterns of writing reach out across time and silence all actual voices. This is why, to go back to the earlier analogy of building, a poet is always like both the builder of houses with plans "at hand," and the designer or executor of a complicated edifice, drawing and working from complex blueprints.

Verse can be organized according to very many metrical *systems,* depending upon the structure of the language in which the verse is written. The systems we shall discuss are:

   1. *Pure accentual*—the meter of the earliest Germanic poetry; it is preserved in nursery rhymes and in much lyric verse
   2. *Accentual-syllabic*—the verse system which involves such patterns as "iambic," "dactylic," etc., all somewhat confusingly named for Greek meters in a totally different system
   3. *Pure syllabic*—the basic system of modern French and Japanese, to cite two kinds of poetry that have used it for centuries, but which has been used in English only in the last fifty years or so
   4. So-called "free verse," of which there are many varieties, developed mostly in the twentieth century

Since accentual-syllabism has been so dominant, and so important, during the course of the poetic history of the English language, we will start with it.

Accentual-syllabic verse is built up of pairs or triads of syllables, alternating or otherwise grouping stressed and unstressed ones. Syllables usually keep their word accent, or the accent they would have in phrases in normal speech. *Iambic pentameter,* a line pattern made up of five syllable pairs with the first syllable unstressed, can be illustrated by a line which most perfectly conforms to the pattern itself:

$$\overset{.}{A}\overset{/}{bout}\ \overset{.}{a}\overset{/}{bout}\ \overset{.}{a}\overset{/}{bout}\ \overset{.}{a}\overset{/}{bout}\ \overset{.}{a}\overset{/}{bout}$$

OR

$$\overset{.}{A}\ \overset{/}{boat},\ \overset{.}{a}\ \overset{/}{boat},\ \overset{.}{a}\ \overset{/}{boat},\ \overset{.}{a}\ \overset{/}{boat},\ \overset{.}{a}\ \overset{/}{boat}$$

(for a monosyllable, with its preceding article, is accented like a word of two syllables). But actual lines of iambic pentameter, because they can't simply repeat identical pairs of syllables, have individual and particular rhythms which depart from the metrical pattern slightly. It is in this variation that the sound of poetry lives. For example, a simple variation of our first example—one that has become a standard pattern in itself—is actually a reversal of stressed and unstressed syllables in the first pair:

Almost "*about about about about*"

or in the second as well:

Nearly almost "*about about about*"

But there are ways of departing that seem to obscure the pattern so that they can no longer be considered variations from it:

*Al*most the *sound* of the *line* of "*about*"s

What we hear is a rhythm of four beats, not five, and the unstressed syllables are grouped into triads of *dum* de de, *dum* de de, (called dactyls), even though there are, in fact, ten syllables in the lines.

Most interesting from the viewpoint of poetry are the variations—and almost every line of poetry exhibits them—that lie between these extremes. Any poem will be cast in one metrical form or another, and after we read three or more lines, it will be obvious which of two patterns even the most ambiguous line is a variation of. Frequently, richness and significance of sound depend upon our ear hesitating for a while between patterns; but there is real ambiguity only at the start of a poem. An extreme case is the opening of one of Keats's sonnets:

How many bards gild the lapses of time

We might think that a matching line would be:

Read this as dactyls and then it will rhyme

like the one we made up before. But in fact, the sonnet continues in iambic pentameter, and we realize that we had a wildly variant first line instead of a more patterned one. But a better example, also by Keats, can be seen in the second line of his "Ode on a Grecian Urn":

Thou foster-child of silence and slow time

Here, although only the fourth pair has its order reversed, the line nevertheless resounds with other possibilities. Thus,

Thou, foster-child of silence and slow time
Accentually pounding to so mime
An antiquated rhythm which had no rhyme

But the phrase "slow time" resolves itself in the poem because "time" rhymes there only with the monosyllable "rhyme" two lines below (there's no "slow"/"so" chiming, as in our example). When we *scan* a line of poetry, or mark the prominent syllables, we are really showing what its actual rhythm is, and then, by putting this rhythm in alignment with adjacent ones in the poem or stanza of the poem, deciding what their common pattern is. Thus, every line is at once unique and has family resemblances, usually very strong, to its companions in any one poem.

Accentual-syllabic verse is traditionally discussed as sequences of *feet;* and although the terminology is misleading, you can remember that:

A foot | is just | a group | of syl- | lables:
Trochees | (like these), | iambs, | spondees, | paired, while
Dactyls and | anapests | always are | triads of | syllables.

An iamb is a pair with a stress on the second syllable (as in "about"):

Iambic meter runs along like this:
Pentameters will have five syllables
More strongly stressed than other ones nearby—
Ten syllables all told, perhaps eleven.

BUT

Trochees simply tumble on and
Start with downbeats just like this one
(Sorry, "iamb" is trochaic).

"Dactyl" means | "finger" in | Greek, and a | foot that was | made up of | one long
Syllable followed by two, like the joints in a finger was used for
Lines made of six, just like these, in the epics of Homer and Virgil,
Except that in English we substitute downbeats and upbeats for long-short.

In an *an* | *apest* up | beats start out | in reverse
Of the dactyl's persuasion but end up no worse.
(Yes, the anapest's name is dactylic—a curse?)

Slow *spondees* are two heavy stressed downbeats
That stand shoulder to strong shoulder this way.

When the older terminology of "foot" for "syllable pair" or "triad" is used, line length is described in terms of number of feet, as for example *di*meter, *tri*meter:

If she should write
Some verse tonight
This dimeter
Would limit her.

BUT

Iambic trimeter
Is rather easier.

AND

Tetrameter allows more space
For thoughts to seat themselves with grace.

NOW

/ . . / . / . / . /
Here is *pentameter,* the line of five
That English poetry still keeps alive;
In other centuries it was official.
Now, different kinds of verse make it seem special.

. / . . / . / . . / . /
Six downbeats in a line that has twelve syllables
Make up the *alexandrine,* which, as you can hear,
Tends to fall into halves—one question, one reply.

The break that you heard in the last line is called *caesura.* Here it is at work in rhymed pairs of lines called *couplets:*

In couplets, one line often makes a point
Which hinges on its bending, like a joint;
The sentence makes that line break into two.
Here's a *caesura:* see what it can do.
(And here's a gentler one, whose pause, more slight,
Waves its two hands, and makes what's left sound right.)

Two even longer measured lines:

Fourteeners, cut from *ballad stanzas,* don't seem right for song:
Their measure rumbles on like this for just a bit too long.

and, used by early Elizabethans,

A poulter's measure (like a baker's dozen) cut
One foot off a fourteener couplet, ended in a rut.

Let us now consider groupings of lines, by rhyme or other means, remembering first that:

A line can be *end stopped,* just like this one.
Or it can show *enjambment,* just like this
One, where the sense straddles two lines: you feel
As if from shore you'd stepped into a boat.

First, then, *blank verse:*

Iambic five-beat lines are labeled *blank*
Verse (with sometimes a foot or two reversed,
Or one more syllable—"feminine ending")
Blank verse can be extremely flexible:
It tocks and tocks the time with even feet
(Or sometimes, cleverly, can end limping).

Shakespeare and others of his day explored
Blank verse in stage plays, both in regular
And rather uneven and more rough-hewn forms.
Occasionally, rhyming couplets sound
Out at scenes' endings, gongs to end the round.
Milton did other things: he made it more
Heroic than dramatic: although blind
He turned its structure into something half
Heard, half seen, as when a *chiasm*
(Words, phrases, sounds or parts of speech arranged
In mirroring) occurs in *Paradise*
Lost (he often *enjambs* this way) we see
Half a line that, reflecting its line-half
Cannot sit still to be regarded like
A well-made picture or inscription, but
Rushes ahead as sentences do, not like
Visual melody in a well-shaped line.
But back again to what blank verse can do:
In time of old, inversions it contained
Of syntax, and Wordsworth and Tennyson
More delicately such arrangements made.
But Browning, and more lately Robert Frost
Made their blank verse seem natural again,
The kind of sound our sentences would make
If only we could leave them to themselves—
The road our way of talking always takes,
Not, like a foul line or state boundary,
An artificially-drawn line at all.

Before we move into groupings made by rhyme, let us consider the ways in which syllables themselves can reach through, or across, lines. They can *alliterate:*

Alliteration lightly links
Stressed syllables with common consonants

and they can, without actually rhyming, exhibit *assonance:*

Assonance is the spirit of a rhyme
A common vowel, hovering like a sigh
After its consonantal body dies.

And we should remember the following, about rhyme itself:

The weakest way in which two words can chime
Is with the most expected kind of rhyme—
(If it's the only rhyme that you can write,
A homonym will never sound quite right.)

A rhyme is stronger when the final words
Seem less alike than pairs of mated birds.
When meaning makes a gap, which sound can span, it's
As if the rhyme words came from different planets.
But when a final verb, perhaps, will reach
Out to rhyme with some different part of speech,
Or when a word spelled in one way, like "off"
Rhymes strictly, with a sort of visual cough
Of surprise—or when a common word like "love"
Which rhymed in Shakespeare's time with "move" and "prove"
Ends up today a sight-rhyme, as above;
Some rhymes can trip you as you move along
Their lines can seem as smooth as they are strong.
Like a typewriter's final, right-hand bell,
A rhyme can stop a line, or it can tell
The sentence to go on and do its best
Till, at the next line's end it comes to rest.
And if the tone shows signs of letting up, let
There be a cute rhyme for a final couplet.
(A serious effect is often killable
By rhyming with *too* much more than one syllable).

Internal rhymes can claim a word or name
And make two words mean something of the same:
Thus *spring* can *jingle* with its *singing* birds,
Or *summer hum* with two resounding words;
The red *robes* of October's garish ball
Make *fall recall* that dropping leaves are all
We hear; the hard, dry stint of winter lasts
Through blizzards and through *slow* and *snowy* blasts,
Until lengthening sunlight hours will bring
Round in a *ring*like way again, the *spring.*

One of the most important groupings of lines we have had in English, particularly in the seventeenth through the nineteenth centuries, has been the English couplet, paired rhymed iambic pentameter:

Heroic couplets, classical and cold
Can make new matters smack of something old
And something borrowed (like a wedding, true,
But this comparison stops short of "blue"
Yet points out how the marriage of two lines
Brings forth long children as their length combines
—And sometimes triplets help to vary the designs)
This verse was called "heroic" for the way
It seemed equivalent, in Jonson's day—
The seventeenth century—to Homer's long
Unrhymed hexameters, and Virgil's song.
With Alexander Pope, we have so pure a

Way of arranging these, that a *caesura*
Makes this line pause, makes that one slowly wend
Its way to join its partner in the end.
An *end-stopped* line is one—as you'll have guessed—
Whose syntax comes, just at its end, to rest.
But when the walking sentence needs to keep
On going, the *enjambment* makes a leap
Across a line-end (here, a rhyming close).
—Milton, in his blank verse, makes use of those:
His long, dependent clauses are enjambed.
A somewhat sharp effect, as well, is damned
Easy—when, reading on, the reader learns
The maze of verse can have its sudden turns
And twists—but couplets take your hand, and then
Lead you back into end-stopped rhyme again.

Of course,

Couplets can be of any length
And shorter size gives greater strength
Sometimes—but sometimes, willy-nilly,
Four-beat couplets sound quite silly.
(Some lines really should stay single
Feminine rhymes can make them jingle.)

These *anapestic tetrameter* couplets, by the way, were used widely in the late eighteenth and the early nineteenth centuries; they can seem either active or passively elegiac:

There are rhythms like this that you'll frequently meet:
They resound with the pounding of regular feet,
And their anapests carry a narrative load
(The hoofbeats of horses, of course, on the road).
But they lie by the side of a whispering stream
Flowing slowly as time, gliding by in a dream.

Now, then

Tercets are groups of three; they are a band
—Playful, like couplets that get out of hand—
Of lines that fly far, then come back to land.

*

The *ballad stanza*'s four short lines
Are very often heard;
The second and the fourth lines rhyme
But not the first and third.

Lord Byron, seeking out a verse to dally in
    While roaming through *Don Juan,* came to see
The point of imitating the Italian
    Poets back in the sixteenth century:
Don Juan's stanza, jumping like a stallion
    Over its disyllabic rhymes, and free
Of too much room to roam in, came to seem a
Verse pattern all its own *(ottava rima).*

One more famous stanza should be described here;
It can come rhymed, unrhymed or what you will, at
Least in English; it's named for the great Greek poet
    Passionate Sappho . . .

Sapphics: four-line stanzas whose first three lines are
Heard—in our hard English at least—as heartbeats,
Then, in one more touch of a final short line,
    Tenderly ending.

A true *Spenserian stanza* wakes up well
With what will seem a quatrain first; in time
The third line rings its "a" rhyme like a bell,
The fourth, its "b" resounding like a dime
In a pay telephone—this paradigm
Demonstrating the kind of interlocking
Of quatrains doubling back on the same rhyme
Ends in an alexandrine, gently rocking
The stanza back to sleep, lest the close be too shocking.

(And so the questions that the last lines ask
The alexandrine answers, as a pleasant task.)

There is a famous way of interlocking tercets:

    The unrhymed middle line, in the tight schema
    Of tercets spinning out a lengthy text
    (Dante gave us this form, called *terza rima*)

    Rhymes, after all, with the start of the next
    Tercet, then helps set up a new unrhyme
    That, sure of foot, and not at all perplexed

    Walks across blank space, as it did last time
    (A couplet ends this little paradigm).

Here follow some other groupings, or forms of *stanza,* in which poems are constructed:

A *quatrain* has four lines
  As one can plainly see:
One of its strict designs
  Comes rhymed *abab.*

Another way of rhyme can come
  From *abba* (middle two
  Lines holding hands as lovers do)
In Tennyson's *In Memoriam.*

After the heyday of such rhyme's renown,
After the weariness of World War I,
Modern poets built in a sad letdown
By rhyming quatrains thus: *abax.*

And here is a longer one:

A *stanza* in Italian means "a room";
  In verse, they needn't keep to square
Corners, as of some dismal tomb,
  But wander anywhere:
Some stanzas can be built of many lines
  Of different length;
Their variation then combines
  With rhymes to give it strength.
   Along the way
   Short lines can play,
And, at the end, a longer and more solemn
  Line extends below, a broad base for a column.

Sonnets can be of two general sorts—the so-called Elizabethan form, with three quatrains and a couplet, or the Italian kind, with an *octave* rhymed *abba abba* and a *sestet* of various groupings of *cde.* Here are the two types:

The kind of *sonnet* form that Shakespeare wrote
—A poem of Love, or Time, in fourteen lines
Rhymed the way these are, clear, easy to quote—
Channels strong feelings into deep designs.
Three *quatrains* neatly fitting limb to joint,
Their lines cut with the sharpness of a prism,
Flash out in colors as they make their point
In what logicians call a syllogism—
(*If A, and B, then C*)—and so it goes
Unless the final quatrain starts out "But"
Or "Nevertheless," these groups of lines dispose
Themselves in reasoned sections, tightly shut.
   The final couplet's tight and terse and tends
   To sum up neatly how the sonnet ends.

*

Milton and Wordsworth made the sonnet sound
Again in a new way; not with the sighs
Of witty passion, where fierce reason lies
Entombed in end-stopped lines, or tightly bound
In chains of quatrain: more like something found
Than built—a smooth stone on a sandy rise,
A drop of dew secreted from the sky's
Altitude, unpartitioned, whole and round.
The *octave*'s over; now, gently defying
Its opening tone, the *sestet* then recalls
Old rhythms and old thoughts, enjambed, half-heard
As verses in themselves. The final word,
Five lines away from what it rhymes with, falls
Off into silence, like an echo dying.

Before we examine larger traditional forms, we might consider the way in which some of the other *systems* of verse in English can work. *Accentual* meter, which we all know from the first oral poetry we hear—nursery rhymes and so forth—measures stressed syllables only:

In accentual meter it doesn't matter
Whether each line is thin or fatter;
What you hear (this matters more)
Is *one, two, three, four.*

In medieval times,

The oldest English	accented meter
Of four, unfailing	fairly audible
Strongly stressed	syllables seldom
Attended to anything	other than
Definite downbeats:	how many dim
Unstressed upbeats	in any line
Mattered not much;	the motion was measured
With what is labeled	alliteration
Observably lurking in	every line.

Sprung rhythm is modern accentual, counting the downbeats.
Instead of pentameter, Gerard Manley Hopkins' verse
Rains down in no shower, but as the sound of a town beats
Down on the ear in a queer-clear way; his terse
Compound words, noun-to-noun-tethered, togethered with strange
Wordings (not absurdings) roamed his rhythms' range.

Strict syllabic verse—sometimes called "isosyllabic"—is an importation into English from other languages. Its lines can be of any length.

Whereas iambic verse will let you hear
Five downbeats, countable inside your ear,

Lines made up of ten syllables purely
Without any arrangement of downbeats
Will not seem to be in any meter,
And rhyme becomes something this form defeats.

Thus decasyllabic verse in French or
Japanese, unaccented, will sound like
Something strange to English ears, which still lust
For downbeats, drumbeats *(something)* in a line
A last syllable at least, stressed, which hits
The nail of a rhyme-word: thus rhyme limits,
If we are to *hear* it (not as above)
Pure syllabic wandering. W.
H. Auden and Marianne Moore both wrote
In syllabic meter like this, which can
Always regain a pure *iambic* voice
By sorting out the accents in its words
In any line, or rush into hiding
Again, in caves of accentless shadow.

*

And stanzas made
up of lines
of varying length
like this one—
with four, three, five, three, six
syllables, and then one of eight—

are quite clearly
of the same
form as each other;
but only
the counting eye can tell:
You use your fingers, not your ear.

One conventional pure syllabic form, borrowed from Japanese poetry, has been popular in English verse for over twenty years:

Haiku, with seven
Syllables in between two
Shorter lines of five,

Gently—like cherry
Blossoms in a breeze—allude
To just one season

Sometimes: they are a
Peculiarly Japanese
Form of epigram.

> In them, brevity
> Lights up with meaning briefly
> Like a firefly.

Accentual-syllabic, accentual, and pure syllabic verse all count or measure units—either syllables or just accented ones or both—to determine a line. But various kinds of unmeasured verse exist, and have for ages. The most influential of these is the verse form of the Hebrew Bible, as it was translated into English and thereby resonated throughout the language in quotation, allusion, and echo.

> The verse of the Hebrew Bible is strange; the meter of *Psalms* and *Proverbs*
>   perplexes.
> It is not a matter of number, no counting of beats or syllables.
> Its song is a music of matching, its rhythm a kind of parallelling.
> One half-line makes an assertion; the other part paraphrases it; sometimes a
>   third part will vary it.
> An abstract statement meets with its example, yes, the way a wind runs the
>   tree's moving leaves.
> One river's water is heard on the other shore; so did this Hebrew verse form
>   carry across into English.

Modern free verse, influenced by the inventiveness of Walt Whitman in English (and Arthur Rimbaud among others in French), can be of many sorts; since a line may be determined in almost any way, and since lines may be grouped on the page in any fashion, it is the mode of variation itself which is significant. Here are examples of a number of different types:

> *Free verse* is never totally "free":
> It can occur in many forms,
> All of them having in common one principle—
> Nothing is necessarily counted or measured
> (Remember Biblical verse—see above).
> One form—this one—makes each line a grammatical unit.
> This can be a clause
> Which has a subject and a predicate,
> Or a phrase
> Of prepositional type.
> The in-and-out variation of line length
> Can provide a visual "music" of its own, a rhythm
> That, sometimes, indented lines
>   like diagrammed sentences
> Can reinforce.
> Our eye—and perhaps in a funny, metaphorical way, our breath itself,
> Can be dragged far out, by some rather longer line, across the page,
> Then made to trip
> On short lines:
> The effect is often wry.

Yet such verse often tends
To fall very flat.

                              *

Another kind of free verse can play a
sort of rhythmic tune at the end
of lines, moving back and forth from those that stop
to those that are enjambed as
sharply as the first one.
Aside from the rhythmic tension
 of varying the ebb and flow of
sense along the lines, of making them seem
more (like this one), or less, like measured lines
(like this
one), this sort of free verse can direct our attention
as well as any iambic line, for
instance, to what our language is made up of:
it can break up compound words at line-ends, sometimes wittily,
(like someone talking in winter of a whole hiber-
nation of bears)
like tripping hurriedly over what, when you look
down, turns out to have been a grave
stone.

                              *

Some free verse is arranged in various
graphic patterns like this that suggest
the barely-seen but silent ghost of a
        classical verse form

like a fragment of Sapphic . . .

                              *

Free verse can, like a shrewd smuggler, contain more
measured kinds of line, hidden
inside its own more random-seeming
ones; and when a bit of song
comes, blown in on a kind of wind, it will move
across my country
'tis of thee, sweet land
of liberty,
of thee
I sing—the accented verses get cut up
by line breaks that reveal something about them we'd
never seen before: it's a little
like putting a contour map over a street plan.
(Customs inspector: are you
trained to hear heroic couplets beating
on the ear if they are hidden in the linings
of free verse, as in the case of these above?)

*

Free verse can build up various
stanzalike units without
rhyme or measured line length to hold
them together, but the power of blank

space between them marks out their rhythms
as surely as the timing of some iambic clock
but, of course, silently: the
ear alone can't tell where they end.

*

Free verse can be a way of making lines that surge
With a power of rhythmic motion, pulsing and oceanic, then
Break, as if a jetty of tumbled boulders had thrust a long finger out into the
Surf, making the rumble of water irregular, keeping
The lines from becoming too
Metrical, marked with the yardstick
Of dactyls.

*

A milder kind
of *vers libre*
as it was called
earlier in this century

Hardly ever enjambed its lines,
but used the linear unit
and even stanzalike
gatherings of lines
as a delicate way of controlling,
of slowing
the pace of the reading eye
or speeding it up across the page again.

It could single out
words
and hang them in lines all their own
like sole blossoms on branches,
made more precious
by their loneliness.

*

And to be able to wander, free
            (in a wide field, as it were)
      verse can amble about
            on a kind of nature walk
                  the lines following no
            usual path, for
            then the poem might seem
            to have wandered into

another kind of meter's backyard
                              but
                                        sometimes
                seeming
                  to map out the syntax,
                                          sometimes
                  seeming to do almost the
                                  opposite,
        this kind of meandering verse can
                                          even
  oddly

                come upon a flower
                of familiar rhythm
                                        a sight for sore
        ears, or encounter
                          a bit later
  on,
                once again a patch of
                trochees growing somewhere
                                        (like an old song)
                                                          and
                take one by the
                                  stem
              and
                        break
          it
                off

                                        *

And, finally, a unique kind of rhymed free verse, but of a sort that really
can only be considered as antiverse:

Because light verse makes meter sound easy,
And because saying something just for the rhyme is inept and, well, cheesy,
A famous comic writer whose name follows developed a deliberate and
    highly skilled method of writing lines that didn't even try to scan
    so that the general effect was that of a metrical hash:
Ogden Nash.

Repetition is a powerful and diversified element of formal structures. It is
also a very ancient one: primitive work songs, or prayers, or danced rituals, all
involved a solo singer or leader, who would chant new and developing material,
and a chorus, who would repeat some shorter element over and over as a kind of
punctuation of the new material. Before considering refrains and other modern
kinds of repetition, we should distinguish between this primitive but continuing
kind of solo-chorus structure and the vastly complex pattern of the Greek choral
ode, whether used in tragedy or in public ceremonies. Although Greek verse

used a system of syllable lengths rather than stressed accents, you can see what a typical pattern was like:

> The *choral ode*
> in ancient Greece was more
> than just a verse form: for each section
> (like this one), called a *strophe*
> was sung—not recited—and danced,
> and the dancers were singers.
> These words to their music moved
> with the dancers in one direction,
> then finished their pattern
> at the end of part of what they had to say.
>
> The second part
> of every section then
> would have the same tune, the same rhythm,
> the strophe had, and therefore
> the whole *antistrophe* would move
> with a parallel motion.
> (This matching of verse to verse
> is referred to as *contrafactum*.)
> The dancers moved back then
> as they sang with those same steps the other way.
>
> And then a last, unmatching section
> called an *epode,* or standing,
> followed the strophe (or "turn")
> and the antistrophe (or "counterturn")
> and, rather more simply, perhaps,
> completed the *triad* or section
> of which there could be one or several.

One kind of medieval dance-song was called a *carol,* or ring dance. In a carol, the leader would sing the stanzas, the dancers sing the *burden* or refrain:

> The dancers flutter about
> Like a circle of fluttering birds,
> The leader stands in place
> And remembers many more words.
> *Birdily, birdily bright*
> *Their burden is very light.*
>
> The dancers circle about
> Like a ring around the moon,
> Their singing a kind of dance,
> Their language a kind of tune.
> *Birdily, birdily bright*
> *Their burden is very light.*

Like grain when it is threshed
Like hay when it is mown
Making, instead of more sense,
A music of its own:
  Birdily, birdily bright
  Their burden is very light.

A literary lyric poem is a song only metaphorically; it is designed to be spoken or read, and a formal refrain can often serve as a kind of reminder or substitute for an earlier relation to music. Some refrains are literal imitations of music—"fa la la la la," etc. Others may be a thematic phrase or sentence; the structural richness of refrains in modern verse depends upon one simple phenomenon: repeating something often may make it *more trivial*—because more expected and therefore carrying less information, as an engineer might put it—or, because of shifting or developing context in each stanza preceding, *more important*.

What once was called a burden
Was seldom heavy to bear
It was sung by the dancers, and heard in
Between the stanzas, like air
Rushing by between cars of a train,
Again and again and again.

Like the point of a sharpened tool
Blunted by too much use,
Or a lesson learned in school
Drummed into the obtuse,
Here comes the old refrain
Again and again and again

Like a sound from the distant past
Of remembered waves on a shore,
Each echo means more than the last,
Once more, once more and once more.
But *less* is more: too much is pain
Again and again and again.
(Like the pounding of hard rain
Again and again and again.)

(Bored with this dulling song
Clever stanzas may set
Out on a walk less long
Shift their burdens, and get
Each time, with the old refrain,
A gain and a gain and a gain.)

A BRIEF DIGRESSION: The three-beat accentual rhythm of the last example reminds one of a problem mentioned at the beginning of this discussion, metrical ambiguity. Keats's line, "How many bards gild the lapses of time" was given as an example; this latest example, of refrain, provides another, reminding us how

> Some lines like houses will—for ill or good—
> Take on the look of a whole neighborhood,
> Clearing muddles in which, alone, they stood.
>
> As before, when we said a refrain
> "Rushes by between cars of a train"—
> All the anapests in it rang out
> At the other ones gathered about.
>
> But context governs, and will always reign:
> "Rushing by between cars of a train"
> Becomes a five-beat line without much pain.

But back to repetition. Two well known forms, one from medieval Provençe, one from France, delighted nineteenth-century makers of intricate verse and became important forms for meditative speculation in modern poetry. First, the *villanelle:*

> This form with two refrains in parallel?
> (Just watch the opening and the third line)
> The repetitions build the villanelle.
>
> The subject thus established, it can swell
> Across the poet-architect's design:
> This form with two refrains in parallel
>
> Must never make them jingle like a bell,
> Tuneful but empty, nor the sense resign;
> The repetitions build the villanelle
>
> By moving out beyond the tercet's cell
> (Though having two lone rhyme-sounds can confine
> This form.) With two refrains in parallel
>
> A poem can find its way into a hell
> Of ingenuity to redesign
> The repetitions. Build the villanelle
>
> Till it has told the tale it has to tell;
> Then two refrains will finally intertwine.
> This form with two refrains in parallel
> The repetitions build: The Villanelle.

The other such form is the *sestina:* six stanzas, each of six lines, and a three-line *envoi* (or "send-off"), the repetition being not of lines, as in the villanelle, but of the final words of the first stanza:

> Now we come to the complex *sestina:*
> In the first stanza, each line's final word

Will show up subsequently at the ends
Of other lines, arranged in different ways;
The words move through the maze of a dark forest,
Than crash out, at the stanza's edge, to light.

The burden of repeating words is light
To carry through the course of a sestina;
And walking through the language of a forest
One comes on the clearing of an echoed word
Refreshingly employed in various ways,
Until one's amble through the stanza ends.

The next one starts out where the last one ends
As in the other cases, with the light
Sounds of two lines, like two roads or pathways
Meeting before they drift apart. Sestina
Patterns reveal the weaving ways a word
Can take through the thick clauses of a forest.

The poet dances slowly through a forest
Of permutations, a maze that never ends
(With seven hundred twenty ways those words
Can be disposed in six-line groups). But light
Falls through the leaves into the dark sestina
Picking out only six clear trails, six ways,

Like change-ringing in bells. The words find ways
And means for coping with an endless forest
By chopping out the course of a sestina.
Walking a known trail sometimes, one emends
The route a bit to skirt a green stone, light
With covering moss; or rings changes on words—

And so it is that the first stanza's word
Order—"Sestina," "Word," "End," and then "Ways"
(Three abstract, three concrete like "Forest," and "Light"
Which interweaves with leaves high in the forest),
With the words' meanings serving different ends
Repeats its pattern through the whole sestina.

Now the *envoi*'s last word: as the sestina's
End words make way for curtain calls, in the light
That floods the forest as the whole poem ends.

One last form based on refrain: that wonderful modern mode of accentual oral poetry and song called "The Blues." Musically, a 4/4 rhythm, usually slow, moves through twelve measures in a fairly fixed chordal sequence. [Musicians would identify it as I (IV) I IV V I.] The repetition of the first line is not merely decorative, nor expressive, as you will see. Blues are improvised by the singer, like this:

Ballads from Scotland told stories and sang the news—
Ballads from Scotland told stories and sang the news,
   But black America felt and thought the blues.

Now a blues has stanzas, stanzas of a funny kind—
Yes a blues has stanzas of a very funny kind;
   (Do that line again singer, while you make up your mind) . . .

Make up your mind, while the next line gives you time,
Make up your mind, yes, while this line's giving you time,
   Then your train of thought comes running after your rhyme.

You can quote a proverb: they say a new broom sweeps clean—
Yes, that's what they say: it's the new broom that sweeps clean,
   So sing a new line—make that proverb really *mean*.[1]

You sing the blues upside-down: you begin with the refrain—
O you sing upside-down, you start out with the refrain,
   And the end of a blues is like the falling rain.

And, as a general afterthought,

        Let us talk of variation:
        In a very boring meter
        Like this blank (unrhymed) trochaic
        —Four beats, so *tetrameter*—the
        Chance for any subtle rhythm
        To develop, making any
        Line sound much more like itself than
        Like the others all around it
        Isn't very high at all (a
        Cycle written in this verse form
        By the poet Henry Wadsworth
        Longfellow—it's most well known—is
        Called *The Song of Hiawatha,*
        Imitated from the Finnish
        Meter of an epic cycle
        Called—in Finnish—*Kalevala.*

        But let us move into a form—
        Iambic, with four beats the norm—
        And listen to the way that lines
        Tap out their rhythms, while designs
        Of rhyme and reason, overlaid
        On the straight tune that's being played

---

[1]You see

   Blues are like weddings, sad as a beat-up shoe
   Blues are like weddings, sad as a beat-up shoe
     With something borrowed, and something old or new.

Blues are also witty, epigrammatic, and passionate at once.

Can make these lines (although they rhyme)
Less like a clock that ticks the time
Or wakes us up with an alarming chime.
Lines may be varied with a rare
Misplaced syllable here and there,
Even two beats together, strong
Enough to shove their words along
The line a bit, until they drop
Into the next, and finally stop.
Rhythms can shimmer, just like this;
Two lines can delicately kiss;
Some words' slow burdens make them bleed
And, fudged, bunched, clustered, hurt to read;
Each line can echo what it says;
Yet family resemblances
Still hold between the various faces
Of lines in their respective places.

SIR PATRICK SPENCE

Anonymous

The king sits in Dumferling toune,°
  Drinking the blude-reid wine:
'O whar will I get guid sailor,
  To sail this schip of mine?'

Up and spak an eldern° knicht,   5
  Sat at the kings richt° kne:
'Sir Patrick Spence is the best sailor
  That sails upon the se.'

The king has written a braid° letter,
  And signed wi' his hand,   10
And sent it to Sir Patrick Spence,
  Was walking on the sand.

The first line that Sir Patrick red,
  A loud lauch° lauched he;
The next line that Sir Patrick red,   15
  The teir blinded his ee.°

toune: town **eldern:** old **richt:** right **braid:** broad; public **lauch:** laugh **ee:** eye

'O wha is this has done this deid,
  This ill deid don to me,
To send me out this time o' the yeir,
  To sail upon the se?'   20

'Mak hast, mak hast, my mirry men all,
  Our guid schip sails the morne:'
'O say na sae, my master deir,
  For I feir a deadlie storme.'

'Late late yestreen° I saw the new moone,   25
  Wi' the auld moone in hir arme,
And I feir, I feir, my deir master,
  That we will cum to harme.'

O our Scots nobles were rich laith°
  To weet° their cork-heild schoone;   30
Bot lang owre a' the play wer playd,
  Thair hats they swam aboone.°

O lang, lang, may their ladies sit,
  Wi' thair fans into their hand,
Or eir they se Sir Patrick Spence   35
  Cum sailing to the land.

O lang, lang, may the ladies stand,
  Wi' thair gold kems° in their hair,
Waiting for their ain° deir lords,
  For they'll se thame na mair.   40

Have owre,° have owre to Aberdour,
  It's fifty fadom deip,
And thair lies guid Sir Patrick Spence,
  Wi' the Scots lords at his feit.

EDWARD

Anonymous

'Why dois° your brand° sae drap wi bluid,°
    Edward, Edward,
Why dois your brand sae drap wi bluid,
  And why sae sad gang° yee O?'

---

yestreen: last night   laith: loath   weet: wet   hats . . . aboone: their hats were floating above
their drowned heads   kems: combs   ain: own   have owre: halfway

dois: does   brand: sword   bluid: blood   gang: go

'O I hae killed my hauke° sae guid,   5
              Mither, mither,
O I hae killed my hauke sae guid,
  And I had nae mair bot hee° O.'

'Your haukis bluid was nevir sae reid,°
              Edward, Edward,   10
'Your haukis bluid was nevir sae reid,
  My deir son I tell thee O.'
'O I hae killed my reid-roan steid,°
              Mither, mither,
O I hae killed my reid-roan steid,   15
  That erst was sae fair and frie O.'

'Your steid was auld, and ye hae gat mair,
              Edward, Edward,
Your steid was auld, and ye hae gat mair,
  Sum other dule° ye drie° O.'   20
'O I hae killed my fadir deir,
              Mither, mither,
O I hae killed my fadir deir,
  Alas, and wae° is mee O!'

'And whatten penance wul ye drie° for that,   25
              Edward, Edward?
And whatten penance will ye drie for that?
  My deir son, now tell me O.'
'Ile set my feit° in yonder boat,
              Mither, mither,   30
Ile set my feit in yonder boat,
  And Ile fare ovir the sea O.'

'And what wul ye doe wi your towirs and your ha,°
              Edward, Edward?
And what wul ye doe wi your towirs and your ha,   35
  That were sae fair to see O?'
'Ile let thame stand tul they doun fa,°
              Mither, mither,
Ile let thame stand tul they doun fa,
  For here nevir mair maun I bee O.'   40

'And what wul ye leive to your bairns° and your wife,
              Edward, Edward?
And what wul ye leive to your bairns and your wife,
  Whan ye gang ovir the sea O?'

---

hauke: hawk   **nae mair bot hee:** none other than he   **reid:** red   **steid:** steed   **dule:** dole; sorrow   **drie:** suffer   **wae:** woe   **drie:** undergo   **feit:** feet   **ha:** hall; castle   **fa:** fall   **bairns:** children

'The warldis room, late them beg thrae life,°   45
    Mither, mither,
The warldis room, late them beg thrae life,
    For thame nevir mair wul I see O.'

'And what wul ye leive to your ain mither deir,
    Edward, Edward?   50
And what wul ye leive to your ain mither deir?
    My deir son, now tell me O.'
'The curse of hell frae me sall° ye beir,
    Mither, mither,
The curse of hell frae me sall ye beir,   55
    Sic counseils ye gave to me O.'

JAMES HARRIS
(The Demon Lover)

Anonymous

'O where have you been, my long, long love,
    This long seven years and mair?'°
'O I'm come to seek my former vows
    Ye granted me before.'

'O hold your tongue of your former vows,   5
    For they will breed sad strife;
O hold your tongue of your former vows,
    For I am become a wife.'

He turned him right and round about,
    And the tear blinded his ee:°   10
'I wad never hae trodden on Irish ground,
    If it had not been for thee.

'I might hae had a king's daughter,
    Far, far beyond the sea;
I might have had a king's daughter,   15
    Had it not been for love o thee.'

'If ye might have had a king's daughter,
    Yer sel ye had to blame;
Ye might have taken the king's daughter,
    For ye kend° that I was nane.°   20

warldis . . . life: "all the space in the world: let them beg through life"   **sall:** shall
mair: more   **ee:** eye   **kend:** knew   **nane:** none

'If I was to leave my husband dear,
　And my two babes also,
O what have you to take me to,
　If with you I should go?'

'I hae seven ships upon the sea—   25
　The eighth brought me to land—
With four-and-twenty bold mariners,
　And music on every hand.'

She has taken up her two little babes,
　Kiss'd them baith° cheek and chin: 30
'O fair ye weel, my ain° two babes,
　For I'll never see you again.'

She set her foot upon the ship,
　No mariners could she behold;
But the sails were o the taffetie,   35
　And the masts o the beaten gold.

They had not sailed a league, a league,
　A league but barely three,
When dismal grew his countenance,
　And drumlie° grew his ee.   40

They had not sailed a league, a league,
　A league but barely three,
Until she espied his cloven foot,
　And she wept right bitterlie.

'O hold your tongue of your weeping,' says he,   45
　'Of your weeping now let me be;
I will shew you how lilies grow
　On the banks of Italy.'

'O what hills are yon, yon pleasant hills,
　That the sun shines sweetly on?'   50
'O yon are the hills of heaven,' he said,
　'Where you will never win.'

'O whaten mountain is yon,' she said,
　'All so dreary wi frost and snow?'
'O yon is the mountain of hell,' he cried   55
　'Where you and I will go.'

He strack° the tap-mast wi his hand,
　The fore-mast wi his knee,

---

baith: both **ain:** own **drumlie:** cloudy; gloomy **strack:** struck

And he brake that gallant ship in twain,
And sank her in the sea.   60

THE CUTTY WREN

Anonymous

Oh, where are you going, says Milder to Malder,
O, I cannot tell, says Festel to Fose,
We're going to the woods, says John the Red Nose,
We're going to the woods, says John the Red Nose.

O, what will you do there, says Milder to Malder,   5
O, I cannot tell, says Festel to Fose.
We'll shoot the Cutty° Wren, says John the Red Nose,
We'll shoot the Cutty Wren, says John the Red Nose.

O, how will you shoot her, says Milder to Malder,
O, I cannot tell, says Festel to Fose.
With arrows and bows, says John the Red Nose,   10
With arrows and bows, says John the Red Nose.

O, that will not do, says Milder to Malder,
O, what will do then, says Festel to Fose,
Big guns and cannons, says John the Red Nose,   15
Big guns and cannons, says John the Red Nose.

O, how will you bring her home, says Milder to Malder,
O, I cannot tell, says Festel to Fose,
On four strong men's shoulders, says John the Red Nose,
On four strong men's shoulders, says John the Red Nose.   20

O, that will not do, says Milder to Malder,
O, what will do then, says Festel to Fose,
Big carts and wagons, says John the Red Nose,
Big carts and wagons, says John the Red Nose.

O, what will you cut her up with, says Milder to Malder,   25
O, I cannot tell, says Festel to Fose,
With knives and with forks, says John the Red Nose,
With knives and with forks, says John the Red Nose.

O, that will not do, says Milder to Malder,
O, what will do then, says Festel to Fose,   30

Cutty: little

Hatchets and cleavers, says John the Red Nose,
Hatchets and cleavers, says John the Red Nose.

O, how will you boil her, says Milder to Malder,
O, I cannot tell, says Festel to Fose,
In pots and in kettles, says John the Red Nose,   35
In pots and in kettles, says John the Red Nose.

O, that will not do, says Milder to Malder,
O, what will do then, says Festel to Fose,
Brass pans and cauldrons, says John the Red Nose,
Brass pans and cauldrons, says John the Red Nose.   40

O, who'll have the spare ribs, says Milder to Malder,
O, I cannot tell, says Festel to Fose,
We'll give them to the poor, says John the Red Nose,
We'll give them to the poor, says John the Red Nose.

ELEGY
(Written for Himself)

Chidiock Tichborne (?)

My prime of youth is but a frost of cares,
My feast of joy is but a dish of pain,
My crop of corn is but a field of tares,
And all my good is but vain hope of gain;
The day is past, and yet I saw no sun,   5
And now I live, and now my life is done.

My tale was heard and yet it was not told,
My fruit is fallen and yet my leaves are green,
My youth is spent and yet I am not old,
I saw the world and yet I was not seen;   10
My thread is cut and yet it is not spun,
And now I live, and now my life is done.

I sought my death and found it in my womb,
I looked for life and saw it was a shade,°
I trod the earth and knew it was my tomb,   15
And now I die, and now I was but made;
My glass° is full, and now my glass is run,
And now I live, and now my life is done.

shade: phantasy, hallucination   **glass:** drinking glass and hourglass

THE PEDDLER'S SONG
FROM *THE WINTER'S TALE*

William Shakespeare

When daffodils begin to peer,°
  With heigh! the doxy,° over the dale,
Why, then comes in the sweet o' the year;
  For the red blood reigns in the winter's pale.

The white sheet bleaching on the hedge,   5
  With heigh! the sweet birds, O, how they sing!
Doth set my pugging° tooth on edge,
  For a quart of ale is a dish for a king.

The lark, that tirra-lirra chants,
  With heigh! with heigh! the thrush and the jay,   10
Are summer songs for me and my aunts,°
  While we lie tumbling in the hay.

THE CLOWN'S SONG
AT THE END OF *TWELFTH NIGHT*

William Shakespeare

When that I was and a little tiny boy,
  With hey ho, the wind and the rain,
A foolish thing was but a toy°
  For the rain it raineth every day.

But when I came to man's estate,   5
  With a hey ho, the wind and the rain,
'Gainst knaves and thieves men shut their gate,
  For the rain it raineth every day.

But when I came, alas, to wive,
  With hey ho, the wind and the rain,   10
By swaggering could I never thrive,
  For the rain it raineth every day.

peer: appear **doxy:** whore **pugging:** drinking **aunts:** girlfriends
toy: fanciful thing

But when I came unto my beds,
   With hey ho, the wind and the rain,
With toss-pots° still had drunken heads,   15
   For the rain it raineth every day.

A great while ago the world began,
   With hey ho, the wind and the rain,
But that's all one, our play is done,
   And we'll strive to please you every day.   20

A SONG IN TIME OF PLAGUE

Thomas Nashe

Adieu, farewell, earth's bliss;
This world uncertain is;
Fond are life's lustful joys;
Death proves them all but toys;
None from his darts can fly;   5
I am sick, I must die.
   Lord, have mercy on us!

Rich men, trust not in wealth,
Gold cannot buy you health;
Physic° himself must fade.   10
All things to end are made,
The plague full swift goes by;
I am sick, I must die.
   Lord, have mercy on us!

Beauty is but a flower   15
Which wrinkles will devour;
Brightness falls from the air;
Queens have died young and fair;
Dust hath closed Helen's° eye.
I am sick, I must die.   20
   Lord, have mercy on us!

Strength stoops unto the grave,
Worms feed on Hector brave;
Swords may not fight with fate,
Earth still holds ope her gate.   25

toss-pots: drunkards

physic: the medical profession   **Helen:** Helen of Troy; Hector was a Trojan hero

"Come, come!" the bells do cry.
I am sick, I must die.
   Lord, have mercy on us.

Wit with his wantonness
Tasteth death's bitterness;   30
Hell's executioner
Hath no ears for to hear
What vain art can reply.
I am sick, I must die.
   Lord, have mercy on us.   35

Haste, therefore, each degree,
To welcome destiny;
Heaven is our heritage,
Earth but a player's stage;
Mount we unto the sky.   40
I am sick, I must die.
   Lord, have mercy on us.

A VALEDICTION: FORBIDDING MOURNING

John Donne

As virtuous men pass mildly away,
   And whisper to their souls, to go,
Whilst some of their sad friends do say;
   "The breath goes now," and some say, "No,"

So let us melt, and make no noise,   5
   No tear-floods, nor sigh-tempests move;
'Twere profanation of our joys
   To tell the laity° our love.

Moving of the earth° brings harms and fears,
   Men reckon what it did and meant,   10
But trepidation of the spheres,°
   Though greater far, is innocent.

Dull sublunary° lovers' love
   (Whose soul is sense) cannot admit
Absence, because it doth remove   15
   Those things which elemented it.

laity: (as if *they* were love's clergy)   **Moving . . . earth:** earthquakes   **trepidation . . . spheres:** irregularities in planetary movements   **sublunary:** below the moon; earthbound

But we by a love, so much refin'd,
   That ourselves know not what it is,
Inter-assurèd of the mind,
   Care less, eyes, lips, and hands to miss.   20

Our two souls therefore, which are one,
   Though I must go, endure not yet
A breach, but an expansion,
   Like gold to airy thinness beat.

If they be two, they are two so   25
   As stiff twin compasses are two:
Thy soul the fix'd foot, makes no show
   To move, but doth, if the other do.

And though it in the center sit,
   Yet when the other far doth roam,   30
It leans, and hearkens after it,
   And grows erect, as that comes home.

Such wilt thou be to me, who must
   Like the other foot, obliquely run;
Thy firmness makes my circle just,°   35
   And makes me end, where I begun.

PSALM 23

Old Testament

The Lord is my shepherd; I shall not want.

2 He maketh me to lie down in green pastures: he leadeth me beside the still waters.

3 He restoreth my soul: he leadeth me into the paths of righteousness for his name's sake.

4 Yea, though I walk through the valley of the shadow of death, I will fear no evil: for thou art with me; thy rod° and thy staff they comfort me.

5 Thou preparest a table for me in the presence of mine enemies: thou annointest my head with oil; my cup runneth over.

just: geometrically true

rod: a club; a defensive weapon

6 Surely goodness and mercy shall follow me all the days of my life: and I will dwell in the house of the Lord for ever.

PSALM 19
In the King James Version

Old Testament

The heavens declare the glory of God; and the firmament sheweth his handywork.

2 Day unto day uttereth speech, and night unto night sheweth knowledge.

3 There is no speech nor language, where their voice is not heard.

4 Their line° is gone out through all the earth, and their words to the end of the world. In them hath he set a tabernacle for the sun,

5 Which is as a bridegroom coming out of his chamber, and rejoiceth as a strong man to run a race.

6 His going forth is from the end of the heaven, and his circuit unto the ends of it: and there is nothing hid from the heat thereof.

7 The law of the LORD is perfect, converting the soul: the testimony of the LORD is sure, making wise the simple.

8 The statutes of the LORD are right, rejoicing the heart: the commandment of the LORD is pure, enlightening the eyes.

9 The fear of the LORD is clean, enduring for ever: the judgments of the LORD are true and righteous altogether.

10 More to be desired are they than gold, yea, than much fine gold: sweeter also than honey and the honeycomb.

11 Moreover by them is thy servant warned: and in keeping of them there is great reward.

12 Who can understand his errors? cleanse thou me from secret faults.

13 Keep back thy servant also from presumptuous sins; let them not have dominion over me: then shall I

line: a measuring line

be upright, and I shall be innocent from the great transgression.

14 Let the words of my mouth, and the meditation of my heart, be acceptable in thy sight, O LORD, my strength, and my redeemer.

PSALM 19

In the Version of The New English Bible

Old Testament

The heavens tell out the glory of God,
the vault of heaven reveals his handiwork.
One day speaks to another,
night with night shares its knowledge,
        and this without speech or language
        or sound of any voice.
Their music goes out through all the earth,
        their words reach to the end of the world.

In them a tent is fixed for the sun,
who comes out like a bridegroom from his wedding chamber,
rejoicing like a strong man to run his race.
        His rising is at one end of the heavens,
        his circuit touches their farthest ends;
        and nothing is hidden from his heat.

The law of the LORD is perfect and revives the soul.
    The LORD's instruction never fails,
        and makes the simple wise.
The precepts of the LORD are right and rejoice the heart
    The commandment of the LORD shines clear
        and gives light to the eyes.
    The fear of the LORD is pure and abides for ever.
The LORD's decrees are true and righteous every one,
more to be desired then gold, pure gold in plenty,
    sweeter than syrup or honey from the comb.
    It is these that give thy servant warning,
    and he who keeps them wins a great reward.

        Who is aware of his unwitting sins?
        Cleanse me of any secret fault.
    Hold back thy servant also from sins of self-will,
        lest they get the better of me.

Then I shall be blameless
and innocent of any great transgression.

May all that I say and think be acceptable to thee,
O LORD, my rock and my redeemer!

A SONG FROM *MARRIAGE À LA MODE*

John Dryden

I

Why should a foolish marriage vow,
   Which long ago was made,
Oblige us to each other now,
   When passion is decay'd?
We lov'd, and we lov'd, as long as we could,   5
   Till our love was lov'd out in us both;
But our marriage is dead, when the pleasure is fled:
   'T was pleasure first made it an oath.

II

If I have pleasures for a friend,
   And farther love in store,   10
What wrong has he whose joys did end,
   And who could give no more?
'T is a madness that he should be jealous of me.
   Or that I should bar him of another:
For all we can gain is to give ourselves pain,   15
   When neither can hinder the other.

LIGHT SHINING OUT OF DARKNESS

William Cowper

God moves in a mysterious way
   His wonders to perform;
He plants his footsteps in the sea,
   And rides upon the storm.

Deep in unfathomable mines   5
   Of never-failing skill,

He treasures up his bright designs,
   And works his sovereign will.

Ye fearful saints, fresh courage take,
   The clouds ye so much dread   10
Are big with mercy, and shall break
   In blessings on your head.

Judge not the Lord by feeble sense,
   But trust him for his grace:
Behind a frowning providence   15
   He hides a smiling face.

His purposes will ripen fast,
   Unfolding every hour;
The bud may have a bitter taste,
   But sweet will be the flower.   20

Blind unbelief is sure to err,
   And scan his work in vain:
God is his own interpreter,
   And he will make it plain.

ON HIS SEVENTY-FIFTH BIRTHDAY

Walter Savage Landor

I strove with none, for none was worth my strife:
   Nature I loved, and next to Nature, Art:
I warmed both hands before the fire of Life;
   It sinks; and I am ready to depart.

MEMORY

Walter Savage Landor

The Mother of the Muses, we are taught,
Is Memory: she has left me; they remain,
And shake my shoulder, urging me to sing
About the summer days, my loves of old.
Alas! alas! is all I can reply.   5
Memory has left me with that name alone,
Harmonious name, which other bards may sing,
But her bright image in my darkest hour
Comes back, in vain comes back, called or uncalled.

Forgotten are the names of visitors   10
Ready to press my hand but yesterday;
Forgotten are the names of earlier friends
Whose genial converse and glad countenance
Are fresh as ever to mine ear and eye;
To these, when I have written and besought   15
Remembrance of me, the word *Dear* alone
Hangs on the upper verge, and waits in vain.
A blessing wert thou, O oblivion,
If thy stream carried only weeds away,
But vernal and autumnal flowers alike   20
It hurries down to wither on the strand.

LINES WRITTEN IN THE BAY OF LERICI

Percy Bysshe Shelley

She left me at the silent time
When the moon had ceased to climb
The azure path of Heaven's steep,
And like an albatross asleep,
Balanced on her wings of light,   5
Hovered in the purple night,
Ere she sought her ocean nest
In the chambers of the West.
She left me, and I stayed alone
Thinking over every tone   10
Which, though silent to the ear,
The enchanted heart could hear,
Like notes which die when born, but still
Haunt the echoes of the hill;
And feeling ever—oh, too much!—   15
The soft vibration of her touch,
As if her gentle hand, even now,
Lightly trembled on my brow;
And thus, although she absent were,
Memory gave me all of her   20
That even fancy dares to claim:—
Her presence had made weak and tame
All passions, and I lived alone
In the time which is our own;
The past and future were forgot,   25
As they had been, and would be, not.
But soon, the guardian angel gone,

The daemon reassumed his throne
In my faint heart. I dare not speak
My thoughts, but thus disturbed and weak   30
I sat and saw the vessels glide
Over the ocean bright and wide,
Like spirit-wingèd chariots sent
O'er some serenest element°
For ministrations strange and far;   35
As if to some Elysian° star
Sailed for drink to medicine
Such sweet and bitter pain as mine.
And the wind that winged their flight
From the land came fresh and light,   40
And the scent of wingèd flowers,
And the coolness of the hours
Of dew, and sweet warmth left by day,
Were scattered o'er the twinkling bay,
And the fisher with his lamp   45
And spear about the low rocks damp
Crept, and struck the fish which came
To worship the delusive flame.
Too happy they, whose pleasure sought°
Extinguishes all sense and thought   50
Of the regret that pleasure leaves,
Destroying life alone, not peace!

TO A WATERFOWL

William Cullen Bryant

Whither, midst falling dew,
While glow the heavens with the last steps of day,
Far, through their rosy depths, dost thou pursue
    Thy solitary way?

Vainly the fowler's eye   5
Might mark thy distant flight to do thee wrong,
As, darkly seen against the crimson sky,
    Thy figure floats along.

Seek'st thou the plashy brink
Of weedy lake, or marge of river wide,   10

---

serenest element: a sky utterly unclouded Elysian: from "Elysium," the paradise or "fortunate fields" of Greek legend Too . . . sought: they are too happy, for whom the pleasure that is desired

Or where the rocking billows rise and sink
   On the chafed ocean-side?

   There is a Power whose care
Teaches thy way along that pathless coast—
The desert and illimitable air—   15
   Lone wandering, but not lost.

   All day thy wings have fanned,
At that far height, the cold, thin atmosphere,
Yet stoop not, weary, to the welcome land,
   Though the dark night is near.   20

   And soon that toil shall end;
Soon shalt thou find a summer home, and rest,
And scream among thy fellows; reeds shall bend,
   Soon, o'er thy sheltered nest.

   Thou'rt gone, the abyss of heaven   25
Hath swallowed up thy form; yet, on my heart
Deeply has sunk the lesson thou hast given,
   And shall not soon depart.

   He who, from zone° to zone,
Guides through the boundless sky thy certain flight,   30
In the long way that I must tread alone,
   Will lead my steps aright.

MARIANA

Mariana in the Moated Grange
(*Measure for Measure*)

Alfred, Lord Tennyson

With blackest moss the flower-plots
   Were thickly crusted, one and all:
The rusted nails fell from the knots
   That held the pear° to the gable-wall.
The broken sheds looked sad and strange: 5
   Unlifted was the clinking latch;
   Weeded and worn the ancient thatch
Upon the lonely moated grange.
     She only said, 'My life is dreary,
      He cometh not,' she said;   10

zone: region

pear: a pear tree espaliered, or caused to grow flat against a wall

She said, 'I am aweary, aweary,
  I would that I were dead!'

Her tears fell with the dews at even;
  Her tears fell ere the dews were dried;
She could not look on the sweet heaven,   15
  Either at morn or eventide.
After the flitting of the bats,
  When thickest dark did trance° the sky,
  She drew her casement-curtain by,
And glanced athwart the glooming flats.   20
    She only said, 'The night is dreary,
      He cometh not,' she said;
    She said, 'I am aweary, aweary,
      I would that I were dead!'

Upon the middle of the night,   25
  Waking she heard the night-fowl crow:
The cock sung out an hour ere light:
  From the dark fen the oxen's low
Came to her: without hope of change,
  In sleep she seemed to walk forlorn,   30
  Till cold winds woke the gray-eyed morn
About the lonely moated grange.
    She only said, 'The day is dreary,
      He cometh not,' she said;
    She said, 'I am aweary, aweary,   35
      I would that I were dead!'

About a stone-cast from the wall
  A sluice with blackened waters slept,
And o'er it many, round and small,
  The clustered marish-mosses° crept.   40
Hard by a poplar shook alway,°
  All silver-green with gnarlèd bark:
  For leagues no other tree did mark
The level waste, the rounding gray.
    She only said, 'My life is dreary,   45
      He cometh not,' she said;
    She said, 'I am aweary, aweary,
      I would that I were dead!'

And ever when the moon was low,
  And the shrill winds were up and away,   50
In the white curtain, to and fro,
  She saw the gusty shadow sway.

---

trance: entrance   **marish-mosses:** marsh mosses; algae   **alway:** always

But when the moon was very low,
    And wild winds bound within their cell,
    The shadow of the poplar fell   55
Upon her bed, across her brow.
        She only said, 'The night is dreary,
            He cometh not,' she said;
        She said, 'I am aweary, aweary,
            I would that I were dead!'   60

All day within the dreamy house,
    The doors upon their hinges creaked;
The blue fly sung in the pane; the mouse
    Behind the mouldering wainscot shrieked,
Or from the crevice peered about.   65
    Old faces glimmered through the doors,
    Old footsteps trod the upper floors,
Old voices called her from without.
        She only said, 'My life is dreary,
            He cometh not,' she said;   70
        She said, 'I am aweary, aweary,
            I would that I were dead!'

The sparrow's chirrup on the roof,
    The slow clock ticking, and the sound
Which to the wooing wind aloof   75
    The poplar made, did all confound
Her sense; but most she loathed the hour
    When the thick-moted sunbeam lay
    Athwart the chambers, and the day
Was sloping toward his western bower.   80
        Then, said she, 'I am very dreary,
            He will not come,' she said;
        She wept, 'I am aweary, aweary,
            Oh God, that I were dead!'

THE VOYAGE OF MAELDUNE
(Founded on an Irish Legend A.D. 700)

Alfred, Lord Tennyson

   I
I was the chief of the race—he had stricken my father dead—
But I gather'd my fellows together, I swore I would strike off his
    head.
Each of them look'd like a king, and was noble in birth as in worth,

And each of them boasted he sprang from the oldest race upon
    earth.
Each was as brave in the fight as the bravest hero of song,   5
And each of them liefer° had died than have done one another a
    wrong.
He lived on an isle in the ocean—we sail'd on a Friday morn—
He that had slain my father the day before I was born.

II

And we came to the isle in the ocean, and there on the shore was he.
But a sudden blast blew us out and away thro' a boundless sea.   10

III

And we came to the Silent Isle that we never had touch'd at before,
Where a silent ocean always broke on a silent shore,
And the brooks glitter'd on in the light without sound, and the long
    waterfalls
Pour'd in a thunderless plunge to the base of the mountain walls,
And the poplar and cypress unshaken by storm flourish'd up beyond
    sight,   15
And the pine shot aloft from the crag to an unbelievable height,
And high in the heaven above it there flicker'd a songless lark,
And the cock couldn't crow, and the bull couldn't low, and the dog
    couldn't bark.
And round it we went, and thro' it, but never a murmur, a breath—
It was all of it fair as life, it was all of it quiet as death,   20
And we hated the beautiful isle, for whenever we strove to speak
Our voices were thinner and fainter than any flittermouse-shriek;
And the men that were mighty of tongue and could raise such a
    battle-cry
That a hundred who heard it would rush on a thousand lances and
    die—
O, they to be dumb'd by the charm!—so fluster'd with anger were
    they   25
They almost fell on each other; but after we sail'd away.

IV

And we came to the Isle of Shouting; we landed, a score of wild birds
Cried from the topmost summit with human voices and words.
Once in an hour they cried, and whenever their voices peal'd
The steer fell down at the plow and the harvest died from the field,   30
And the men dropt dead in the valleys and half of the cattle went
    lame,

liefer: rather

And the roof sank in on the hearth, and the dwelling broke into
    flame;
And the shouting of these wild birds ran into the hearts of my crew,
Till they shouted along with the shouting and seized one another and
    slew.
But I drew them the one from the other; I saw that we could not
    stay,   35
And we left the dead to the birds, and we sail'd with our wounded
    away.

V

And we came to the Isle of Flowers; their breath met us out on the
    seas,
For the Spring and the middle Summer sat each on the lap of the
    breeze;
And the red passion-flower to the cliffs, and the dark-blue clematis,
    clung,
And starr'd with a myriad blossom the long convolvulus hung;   40
And the topmost spire of the mountain was lilies in lieu of snow,
And the lilies like glaciers winded down, running out below
Thro' the fire of the tulip and poppy, the blaze of gorse, and the
    blush
Of millions of roses that sprang without leaf or a thorn from the
    bush;
And the whole isle-side flashing down from the peak without ever a
    tree   45
Swept like a torrent of gems from the sky to the blue of the sea.
And we roll'd upon capes of crocus and vaunted our kith and our
    kin,
And we wallow'd in beds of lilies, and chanted the triumph of Finn,°
Till each like a golden image was pollen'd from head to feet
And each was as dry as a cricket, with thirst in the middle-day heat.   50
Blossom and blossom, and promise of blossom, but never a fruit!
And we hated the Flowering Isle, as we hated the isle that was mute,
And we tore up the flowers by the million and flung them in bight
    and bay,
And we left but a naked rock, and in anger we sail'd away.

VI

And we came to the Isle of Fruits; all round from the cliffs and the
    capes,   55
Purple or amber, dangled a hundred fathom of grapes,
And the warm melon lay like a little sun on the tawny sand,

Finn: legendary Irish hero

And the fig ran up from the beach and rioted over the land,
And the mountain arose like a jewell'd throne thro' the fragrant air,
Glowing with all-color'd plums and with golden masses of pear,   60
And the crimson and scarlet of berries that flamed upon bine and
    vine,
But in every berry and fruit was the poisonous pleasure of wine;
And the peak of the mountain was apples, the hugest that ever were
    seen,
And they prest, as they grew, on each other, with hardly a leaflet
    between,
And all of them redder than rosiest health or than utterest shame,   65
And setting, when Even descended, the very sunset aflame.
And we stay'd three days, and we gorged and we madden'd, till every
    one drew
His sword on his fellow to slay him, and ever they struck and they
    slew;
And myself, I had eaten but sparely, and fought till I sunder'd the
    fray,
Then I bade them remember my father's death, and we sail'd away.   70

VII

And we came to the Isle of Fire; we were lured by the light from afar,
For the peak sent up one league of fire to the Northern Star;
Lured by the glare and the blare, but scarcely could stand upright,
For the whole isle shudder'd and shook like a man in a mortal
    affright.
We were giddy besides with the fruits we had gorged, and so crazed
    that at last   75
There were some leap'd into the fire; and away we sail'd, and we past
Over that undersea isle, where the water is clearer than air.
Down we look'd—what a garden! O bliss, what a Paradise there!
Towers of a happier time, low down in a rainbow deep
Silent palaces, quiet fields of eternal sleep!   80
And three of the gentlest and best of my people, whate'er I could
    say,
Plunged head-down in the sea, and the Paradise trembled away.

VIII

And we came to the Bounteous Isle, where the heavens lean low on
    the land,
And ever at dawn from the cloud glitter'd o'er us a sun-bright hand,
Then it open'd and dropt at the side of each man, as he rose from his
    rest,   85
Bread enough for his need till the laborless day dipt under the west;
And we wander'd about it and thro' it. O, never was time so good!

And we sang of the triumphs of Finn, and the boast of our ancient
    blood,
And we gazed at the wandering wave as we sat by the gurgle of
    springs,
And we chanted the songs of the Bards° and the glories of fairy
    kings.   90
But at length we began to be weary, to sigh, and to stretch and yawn,
Till we hated the Bounteous Isle and the sun-bright hand of the
    dawn,
For there was not an enemy near, but the whole green isle was our
    own,
And we took to playing at ball, and we took to throwing the stone,
And we took to playing at battle, but that was a perilous play,   95
For the passion of battle was in us, we slew and we sail'd away.

      IX

And we came to the Isle of Witches and heard their musical cry—
"Come to us, O, come, come!" in the stormy red of a sky
Dashing the fires and the shadows of dawn on the beautiful shapes,
For a wild witch naked as heaven stood on each of the loftiest capes,   100
And a hundred ranged on the rock like white sea-birds in a row,
And a hundred gamboll'd and pranced on the wrecks in the sand
    below,
And a hundred splash'd from the ledges, and bosom'd the burst of
    the spray;
But I knew we should fall on each other, and hastily sail'd away.

      X

And we came in an evil time to the Isle of the Double Towers,   105
One was of smooth-cut stone, one carved all over with flowers,
But an earthquake always moved in the hollows under the dells,
And they shock'd on each other and butted each other with clashing
    of bells,
And the daws flew out of the towers and jangled and wrangled in
    vain,
And the clash and boom of the bells rang into the heart and the
    brain,   110
Till the passion of battle was on us, and all took sides with the
    towers,
There were some for the clean-cut stone, there were more for the
    carven flowers,
And the wrathful thunder of God peal'd over us all the day,
For the one half slew the other, and after we sail'd away.

Bards: ancient Irish poet-heroes

XI

And we came to the Isle of a Saint who had sail'd with Saint Brendan
   of yore,   115
He had lived ever since on the isle and his winters were fifteen score,
And his voice was low as from other worlds, and his eyes were sweet,
And his white hair sank to his heels, and his white beard fell to his
   feet,
And he spake to me: "O Maeldune, let be this purpose of thine!
Remember the words of the Lord when he told us, 'Vengeance is
   mine!'°   120
His fathers have slain thy fathers in war or in single strife,
Thy fathers have slain his fathers, each taken a life for a life,
Thy father had slain his father, how long shall the murder last?
Go back to the Isle of Finn and suffer the Past to be Past."
And we kiss'd the fringe of his beard, and we pray'd as we heard him
   pray,   125
And the holy man he assoil'd° us, and sadly we sail'd away.

XII

And we came to the isle we were blown from, and there on the shore
   was he,
The man that had slain my father. I saw him and let him be.
O, weary was I of the travel, the trouble, the strife, and the sin,
When I landed again with a tithe of my men, on the Isle of Finn!   130

MEETING AT NIGHT

Robert Browning

The grey sea and the long black land;
And the yellow half-moon large and low;
And the startled little waves that leap
In fiery ringlets from their sleep,
As I gain the cove with pushing prow,   5
And quench its speed i' the slushy sand.

Then a mile of warm sea-scented beach;
Three fields to cross till a farm appears;
A tap at the pane, the quick sharp scratch
And blue spurt of a lighted match,   10
And a voice less loud, thro' its joys and fears,
Than the two hearts beating each to each!

Vengeance is mine: see Romans 12:19   **assoil'd:** assailed

PARTING AT MORNING

Robert Browning

Round the cape of a sudden came the sea,
And the sun looked over the mountain's rim:
And straight was a path of gold for him,
And the need of a world of men for me.

THE PORTENT

Herman Melville

Hanging from the beam,
   Slowly swaying (such the law),
Gaunt the shadow on your green,
   Shenandoah!
The cut is on the crown   5
   (Lo, John Brown),°
And the stabs shall heal no more.

Hidden in the cap
   Is the anguish none can draw;
So your future veils its face,   10
   Shenandoah!
But the streaming beard is shown
   (Weird° John Brown),
The meteor of the war.

SONG OF MYSELF   6

Walt Whitman

A child said *What is the grass?* fetching it to me with full hands;
How could I answer the child? I do not know what it is any more
   than he.

I guess it must be the flag of my disposition, out of hopeful green
   stuff woven.

John Brown: abolitionist fanatic, whose armed raid on Harper's Ferry (to establish a stronghold for escaped slaves) helped set in motion the train of events that led to the Civil War; he was hanged for treason in 1859 **Weird:** from the noun "weird," meaning "a disastrous destiny," hence, darkly portentous

Or I guess it is the handkerchief of the Lord,
A scented gift and remembrancer designedly dropt,   5
Bearing the owner's name someway in the corners, that we may see
      and remark, and say *Whose?*

Or I guess the grass is itself a child, the produced babe of the
      vegetation.

Or I guess it is a uniform hieroglyphic,
And it means, Sprouting alike in broad zones and narrow zones,
Growing among black folks as among white,   10
Kanuck,° Tuckahoe,° Congressman, Cuff,° I give them the same, I
      receive them the same.

And now it seems to me the beautiful uncut hair of graves.

Tenderly will I use you curling grass,
It may be you transpire from the breasts of young men,
It may be if I had known them I would have loved them,   15
It may be you are from old people, or from offspring taken soon out
      of their mothers' laps,
And here you are the mothers' laps.

This grass is very dark to be from the white heads of old mothers,
Darker than the colorless beards of old men,
Dark to come from under the faint red roofs of mouths.   20

O I perceive after all so many uttering tongues,
And I perceive they do not come from the roofs of mouths for
      nothing.

I wish I could translate the hints about the dead young men and
      women,
And the hints about old men and mothers, and the offspring taken
      soon out of their laps.

What do you think has become of the young and old men?   25
And what do you think has become of the women and children?

They are alive and well somewhere,
The smallest sprout shows there is really no death,
And if ever there was it led forward life, and does not wait at the end
      to arrest it,
And ceas'd the moment life appear'd.   30

All goes onward and outward, nothing collapses,
And to die is different from what any one supposed, and luckier.

Kanuck, Tuckahoe, Cuff: colloquial terms for French Canadian, tidewater Virginian, and Negro
(none used here disrespectfully)

CROSSING BROOKLYN FERRY

Walt Whitman

I
Flood-tide below me! I see you face to face!
Clouds of the west—sun there half an hour high—I see you also face
    to face.

Crowds of men and women attired in the usual costumes, how
    curious you are to me!
On the ferry-boats the hundreds and hundreds that cross, returning
    home, are more curious to me than you suppose,
And you that shall cross from shore to shore years hence are more to
    me, and more in my meditations, than you might suppose.   5

II
The impalpable sustenance of me from all things at all hours of the
    day,
The simple, compact, well-join'd scheme, myself disintegrated,
    every one disintegrated yet part of the scheme,
The similitudes of the past and those of the future,
The glories strung like beads on my smallest sights and hearings, on
    the walk in the street and the passage over the river,
The current rushing so swiftly and swimming with me far away,   10
The others that are to follow me, the ties between me and them,
The certainty of others, the life, love, sight, hearing of others.

Others will enter the gates of the ferry and cross from shore to shore,
Others will watch the run of the flood-tide,
Others will see the shipping of Manhattan north and west, and the
    heights of Brooklyn to the south and east,   15
Others will see the islands large and small;

Fifty years hence, others will see them as they cross, the sun half an
    hour high,
A hundred years hence, or ever so many hundred years hence,
    others will see them,
Will enjoy the sunset, the pouring-in of the flood-tide, the falling-
    back to the sea of the ebb-tide.

III
It avails not, time nor place—distance avails not,   20
I am with you, you men and women of a generation, or ever so many
    generations hence,
Just as you feel when you look on the river and sky, so I felt,

Just as any of you is one of a living crowd, I was one of a crowd,
Just as you are refresh'd by the gladness of the river and the bright
    flow, I was refresh'd,
Just as you stand and lean on the rail, yet hurry with the swift
    current, I stood yet was hurried,   25
Just as you look on the numberless masts of ships and the thick-
    stemm'd pipes of steamboats, I look'd.

I too many and many a time cross'd the river of old,
Watched the Twelfth-month° sea-gulls, saw them high in the air
    floating with motionless wings, oscillating their bodies,
Saw how the glistening yellow lit up parts of their bodies and left the
    rest in strong shadow,
Saw the slow-wheeling circles and the gradual edging toward the
    south,   30
Saw the reflection of the summer sky in the water,
Had my eyes dazzled by the shimmering track of beams,
Look'd at the fine centrifugal° spokes of light round the shape of my
    head in the sunlit water,
Look'd on the haze on the hills southward and south-westward,
Look'd on the vapor as it flew in fleeces tinged with violet,   35
Look'd toward the lower bay to notice the vessels arriving,
Saw their approach, saw aboard those that were near me,
Saw the white sails of schooners and sloops, saw the ships at anchor,
The sailors at work in the rigging or out astride the spars,
The round masts, the swinging motion of the hulls, the slender
    serpentine pennants,   40
The large and small steamers in motion, the pilots in their pilot-
    houses,
The white wake left by the passage, the quick tremulous whirl of the
    wheels,
The flags of all nations, the falling of them at sunset,
The scallop-edged waves in the twilight, the ladled cups, the frolic-
    some crests and glistening,
The stretch afar growing dimmer and dimmer, the gray walls of the
    granite storehouses by the docks,   45
On the river the shadowy group, the big steam-tug closely flank'd on
    each side by the barges, the hay-boat, the belated lighter,
On the neighboring shore the fires from the foundry chimneys
    burning high and glaringly into the night,
Casting their flicker of black contrasted with wild red and yellow
    light over the tops of houses, and down into the clefts of
    streets.

Twelfth-month: end-of-year (a Quaker usage)   **centrifugal:** spinning outward from the center

IV

These and all else were to me the same as they are to you,
I loved well those cities, loved well the stately and rapid river,   50
The men and women I saw were all near to me,
Others the same—others who look back on me because I look'd
    forward to them,
(The time will come, though I stop here to-day, and to-night.)

V

What is it then between us?
What is the count of the scores or hundreds of years between us?   55

Whatever it is, it avails not—distance avails not, and place avails not,
I too lived, Brooklyn of ample hills was mine,
I too walk'd the streets of Manhattan island, and bathed in the waters
    around it,
I too felt the curious abrupt questionings stir within me,
In the day among crowds of people sometimes they came upon me,   60
In my walks home late at night or as I lay in my bed they came upon
    me,
I too had been struck from the float forever held in solution,°
I too had receiv'd identity by my body,
That I was I knew was of my body, and what I should be I knew I
    should be of my body.

VI

It is not upon you alone the dark patches fall,   65
The dark threw its patches down upon me also,
The best I had done seem'd to me blank and suspicious,
My great thoughts as I supposed them, were they not in reality
    meagre?
Nor is it you alone who know what it is to be evil,
I am he who knew what it was to be evil,   70
I too knitted the old knot of contrariety,
Blabb'd, blush'd, resented, lied, stole, grudg'd,
Had guile, anger, lust, hot wishes I dared not speak,
Was wayward, vain, greedy, shallow, sly, cowardly, malignant,
The wolf, the snake, the hog, not wanting in me,   75
The cheating look, the frivolous word, the adulterous wish, not
    wanting,

I . . . solution: I too had become isolated from the crowd involuntarily (as a person falls from a raft or "float," or as a chemical particle ceases to be suspended in a solution)

Refusals, hates, postponements, meanness, laziness, none of these
    wanting,
Was one with the rest, the days and haps of the rest,
Was call'd by my nighest name° by clear loud voices of young men as
    they saw me approaching or passing,
Felt their arms on my neck as I stood, or the negligent leaning of
    their flesh against me as I sat,   80
Saw many I loved in the street or ferry-boat or public assembly, yet
    never told them a word,
Lived the same life with the rest, the same old laughing, gnawing,
    sleeping,
Play'd the part that still looks back on the actor or actress,
The same old role, the role that is what we make it, as great as we
    like,
Or as small as we like, or both great and small.   85

VII

Closer yet I approach you,
What thought you have of me now, I had as much of you—I laid in
    my stores in advance,
I consider'd long and seriously of you before you were born.

Who was to know what should come home to me?
Who knows but I am enjoying this?   90
Who knows, for all the distance, but I am as good as looking at you
    now, for all you cannot see me?

VIII

Ah, what can ever be more stately and admirable to me than mast-
    hemm'd Manhattan?
River and sunset and scallop-edg'd waves of flood-tide?
The sea-gulls oscillating their bodies, the hay boat in the twilight, and
    the belated lighter?

What gods can exceed these that clasp me by the hand, and with
    voices I love call me promptly and loudly by my nighest name
    as I approach?   95

What is more subtle than this which ties me to the woman or man
    that looks in my face?
Which fuses me into you now, and pours my meaning into you?

We understand then do we not?
What I promis'd without mentioning it, have you not accepted?

my nighest name: Walt

What the study could not teach—what the preaching could not
  accomplish is accomplish'd, is it not?   100

IX

Flow on, river! flow with the flood-tide, and ebb with the ebb-tide!
Frolic on, crested and scallop-edg'd waves!
Gorgeous clouds of the sunset! drench with your splendor me, or
  the men and women generations after me!

You have waited, you always wait, you dumb, beautiful ministers,°
We receive you with free sense at last, and are insatiate
  henceforward,   105
Not you any more shall be able to foil us, or withhold yourselves
  from us,
We use you, and do not cast you aside—we plant you permanently
  within us,
We fathom° you not—we love you—there is perfection in you also,
You furnish your parts toward eternity,
Great or small, you furnish your parts toward the soul.   110

I HEARD A FLY BUZZ

Emily Dickinson

I heard a Fly buzz—when I died—
The Stillness in the Room
Was like the Stillness in the Air—
Between the Heaves of Storm—

The Eyes around—had wrung them dry—   5
And Breaths were gathering firm
For that last Onset—when the King
Be witnessed—in the Room—

I willed my Keepsakes—Signed away
What portion of me be   10
Assignable—and then it was
There interposed a Fly—

With Blue—uncertain stumbling Buzz—
Between the light—and me—
And then the Windows failed—and then   15
I could not see to see—

ministers: the flood-tide of phenomena that serve and watch over us fathom: measure and
understand

JABBERWOCKY

Lewis Carroll
(Charles Lutwidge Dodgson)

'Twas brillig, and the slithy toves
  Did gyre and gimble in the wabe;
All mimsy were the borogoves,
  And the mome raths outgrabe.

'Beware the Jabberwock, my son!   5
  The jaws that bite, the claws that catch!
Beware the Jubjub bird, and shun
  The frumious Bandersnatch!'

He took his vorpal sword in hand;
  Long time the manxome foe he sought—   10
So rested he by the Tumtum tree,
  And stood awhile in thought.

And, as in uffish thought he stood,
  The Jabberwock, with eyes of flame,
Came whiffling through the tulgey wood,   15
  And burbled as it came!

One, two! One, two! And through and through
  The vorpal blade went snicker-snack!
He left it dead, and with its head
  He went galumphing back.   20

'And hast thou slain the Jabberwock?
  Come to my arms, my beamish boy
O frabjous day! Callooh! Callay!'
  He chortled in his joy.

'Twas brillig, and the slithy toves   25
  Did gyre and gimble in the wabe;
All mimsy were the borogoves,
  And the mome raths outgrabe.

GEORGE MEREDITH

Thomas Hardy

Forty years back, when much had place
That since has perished out of mind,
I heard that voice and saw that face.

He spoke as one afoot will wind°
A morning horn ere men awake;   5
His note was trenchant, turning kind.

He was of those whose wit can shake
And riddle to the very core
The counterfeits that Time will break.

Of late, when we two met once more,   10
The luminous countenance and rare
Shone just as forty years before.

So that, when now all tongues declare
His shape unseen by his green hill,
I scarce believe he sits not there.   15

No matter. Further and further still
Through the world's vaporous vitiate° air
His words wing on—as live words will.

THIRTY BOB° A WEEK

John Davidson

I couldn't touch a stop and turn a screw,
    And set the blooming world a-work for me,
Like such as cut their teeth—I hope like you—
    On the handle of a skeleton gold key;
I cut mine on a leek, which I eat it every week: 5
    I'm a clerk at thirty bob as you can see.

But I don't allow it's luck and all a toss;
    There's no such thing as being starred and crossed;
It's just the power of some to be a boss,
    And the bally power of others to be bossed: 10
I face the music, sir; you bet I ain't a cur;
    Strike me lucky if I don't believe I'm lost!

For like a mole I journey in the dark,
    a-travelling along the underground
From my Pillar'd Halls and broad Suburbean Park,   15
    To come the daily dull official round;

___

wind: blow   vitiate: impure; corrupt

bob: shillings; in today's terms the speaker is almost at poverty level

And home again at night with my pipe all alight,
    A-scheming how to count° ten bob a pound.

And it's often very cold and very wet,
    And my missis stitches towels for a hunks,°   20
And the Pillar'd Halls is half of it to let—
    Three rooms about the size of travelling trunks.
And we cough, my wife and I, to dislocate a sigh,
    When the noisy little kids are in their bunks.

But you never hear her do a growl or whine,   25
    For she's made of flint and roses, very odd;
And I've got to cut my meaning rather fine,
    Or I'd blubber, for I'm made of greens and sod:
So p'r'aps we are in Hell for all that I can tell,
    And lost and damn'd and served up hot to God.   30

I ain't blaspheming, Mr. Silver-tongue;
    I'm saying things a bit beyond your art:
Of all the rummy starts you ever sprung,
    Thirty bob a week's the rummiest start!
With your science and your books and your the'ries about spooks,   35
    Did you ever hear of looking in your heart?

I didn't mean your pocket, Mr., no:
    I mean that having children and a wife,
With thirty bob on which to come and go,
    Isn't dancing to the tabor and the fife: 40
When it doesn't make you drink, by Heaven! it makes you think,
    And notice curious items about life.

I step into my heart and there I meet
    A god-almighty devil singing small,
Who would like to shout and whistle in the street,   45
    And squelch the passers flat against the wall;
If the whole world was a cake he had the power to take,
    He would take it, ask for more, and eat them all.

And I meet a sort of simpleton beside,
    The kind that life is always giving beans: 50
With thirty bob a week to keep a bride
    He fell in love and married in his teens:
At thirty bob he stuck; but he knows it isn't luck:
    He knows the seas are deeper than tureens.

And the god-almighty devil and the fool   55
    That meet me in the High Street on the strike,

count: make it worth   **hunks:** stingy person

When I walk about my heart a-gathering wool,
    Are my good and evil angels if you like.
And both of them together in every kind of weather
    Ride me like a double-seated bike.   60

That's rough a bit and needs its meaning curled.
    But I have a high old hot un in my mind—
A most engrugious° notion of the world,
    That leaves your lightning 'rithmetic behind:
I give it at a glance when I say, "There ain't no chance,   65
    Nor nothing of the lucky-lottery kind."

And it's this way that I make it out to be:
    No fathers, mothers, countries, climates—none;
Not Adam was responsible for me,
    Nor society, nor systems, nary one: 70
A little sleeping seed, I woke—I did, indeed—
    A million years before the blooming sun.

I woke because I thought the time had come;
    Beyond my will there was no other cause;
And everywhere I found myself at home,   75
    Because I chose to be the thing I was;
And in whatever shape of mollusc or of ape
    I always went according to the laws.

I was the love that chose my mother out;
    I joined two lives and from the union burst;   80
My weakness and my strength without a doubt
    Are mine alone for ever from the first:
It's just the very same with a difference in the name
    As "Thy will be done." You say it if you durst!

They say it daily up and down the land   85
    As easy as you take a drink, it's true;
But the difficultest go to understand,
    And the difficultest job a man can do,
Is to come it brave and meek with thirty bob a week,
    And feel that that's the proper thing for you.   90

It's a naked child against a hungry wolf;
    It's playing bowls upon a splitting wreck;
It's walking on a string across a gulf
    With millstones fore-and-aft about your neck;
But the thing is daily done by many and many a one;   95
    And we fall, face forward, fighting, on the deck.

engrugious: egregious; astonishing

THE BALLAD OF THE KING'S JEST

Rudyard Kipling

When spring-time flushes the desert grass,
Our kafilas° wind through the Khyber Pass.
Lean are the camels but fat the frails,
Light are the purses but heavy the bales,
As the snowbound trade of the North comes down   5
To the market-square of Peshawur° town.

In a turquoise twilight, crisp and chill,
A kafila camped at the foot of the hill.
Then blue smoke-haze of the cooking rose,
And tent-peg answered to hammer-nose;   10
And the picketed ponies, shag and wild,
Strained at their ropes as the feed was piled;
And the bubbling camels beside the load
Sprawled for a furlong adown the road;
And the Persian pussy-cats, brought for sale,   15
Spat at the dogs from the camel-bale;
And the tribesmen bellowed to hasten the food;
And the camp-fires twinkled by Fort Jumrood;
And there fled on the wings of the gathering dusk
A savour of camels and carpets and musk,   20
A murmur of voices, a reek of smoke,
To tell us the trade of the Khyber woke.

The lid of the flesh-pot chattered high,
The knives were whetted and—then came I
To Mahbub Ali, the muleteer,   25
Patching his bridles and counting his gear,
Crammed with the gossip of half a year.
But Mahbub Ali the kindly said,
"Better is speech when the belly is fed."
So we plunged the hand to the mid-wrist deep   30
In a cinnamon stew of the fat-tailed sheep,
And he who never hath tasted the food,
By Allah! he knoweth not bad from good.
We cleansed our beards of the mutton-grease,
We lay on the mats and were filled with peace,   35
And the talk slid north, and the talk slid south,
With the sliding puffs from the hookah-mouth.

Four things greater than all things are,—
Women and Horses and Power and War.

kafilas: caravans **Peshawur:** city in India below the Khyber Pass into Afghanistan

We spake of them all, but the last the most.   40
For I sought a word of a Russian post,
Of a shifty promise, an unsheathed sword,
And a grey-coat guard on the Helmund ford.
Then Mahbub Ali lowered his eyes
In the fashion of one who is weaving lies.   45
Quoth he: "Of the Russians who can say?
"When the night is gathering all is grey.
"But we look that the gloom of the night shall die
"In the morning flush of a blood-red sky.
"Friend of my heart, is it meet or wise   50
"To warn a King of his enemies?
"We know what Heaven or Hell may bring,
"But no man knoweth the mind of the King.
"That unsought counsel is cursed of God
"Attesteth the story of Wali Dad.   55

"His sire was leaky of tongue and pen,
"His dam was a clucking Khattack hen;
"And the colt bred close to the vice of each,
"For he carried the curse of an unstaunched speech.
"Therewith madness—so that he sought   60
"The favour of kings at the Kabul Court;
"And travelled, in hope of honour, far
"To the line where the grey-coat squadrons are.
"There have I journeyed too—but I
"Saw naught, said naught, and—did not die!   65
"*He* hearked to rumour, and snatched at a breath
"Of 'this one knoweth,' and 'that one saith,'—
"Legends that ran from mouth to mouth
"Of a grey-coat coming, and sack of the South.
"These have I also heard—they pass   70
"With each new spring and the winter grass.

"Hot-foot southward, forgotten of God,
"Back to the city ran Wali Dad,
"Even to Kabul—in full durbar
"The King held talk with his Chief in War.   75
"Into the press of the crowd he broke,
"And what he had heard of the coming spoke.
"Then Gholam Hyder, the Red Chief, smiled,
"As a mother might on a babbling child;
"But those who would laugh restrained their breath,   80
"When the face of the King showed dark as death.
"Evil it is in full durbar
"To cry to a ruler of gathering war!
"Slowly he led to a peach-tree small,

"That grew by a cleft of the city wall.   85
"And he said to the boy: 'They shall praise thy zeal
"'So long as the red spurt follows the steel.
"'And the Russ is upon us even now?
"'Great is thy prudence—wait them, thou.
"'Watch from the tree. Thou art young and strong.   90
"'Surely the vigil is not for long.
"'The Russ is upon us, thy clamour ran?
"'Surely an hour shall bring their van.
"'Wait and watch. When the host is near,
"'Shout aloud that my men may hear.'   95

"Friend of my heart, is it meet or wise
"To warn a King of his enemies?
"A guard was set that he might not flee—
"A score of bayonets ringed the tree.
"The peach-bloom fell in showers of snow,   100
"When he shook at his death as he looked below.
"By the power of God, Who alone is great,
"Till the seventh day he fought with his fate.
"Then madness took him, and men declare
"He mowed in the branches as ape and bear,   105
"And last as a sloth, ere his body failed,
"And he hung like a bat in the forks, and wailed,
"And sleep the cord of his hands untied,
"And he fell, and was caught on the points and died.

"Heart of my heart, is it meet or wise   110
"To warn a King of his enemies?
"We know what Heaven or Hell may bring,
"But no man knoweth the mind of the King.
"Of the grey-coat coming who can say?
"When the night is gathering all is grey.   115
"Two things greater than all things are,
"The first is Love, and the second War.
"And since we know not how War may prove,
"Heart of my heart, let us talk of Love!"

THE OVEN BIRD

Robert Frost

There is a singer everyone has heard,
Loud, a mid-summer and a mid-wood bird,
Who makes the solid tree trunks sound again.

He says that leaves are old and that for flowers
Mid-summer is to spring as one to ten.   5
He says the early petal-fall is past
When pear and cherry bloom went down in showers
On sunny days a moment overcast;
And comes that other fall we name the fall.
He says the highway dust is over all.   10
The bird would cease and be as other birds
But that he knows in singing not to sing.
The question that he frames in all but words
Is what to make of a diminished thing.

THE SILKEN TENT

Robert Frost

She is as in a field a silken tent
At midday when a sunny summer breeze
Has dried the dew and all its ropes relent,
So that in guys it gently sways at ease,
And its supporting central cedar pole,   5
That is its pinnacle to heavenward
And signifies the sureness of the soul,
Seems to owe naught to any single cord,
But strictly held by none, is loosely bound
By countless silken ties of love and thought   10
To everything on earth the compass round,
And only by one's going slightly taut
In the capriciousness of summer air
Is of the slightest bondage made aware.

OF MODERN INVENTIONS

Martin Buber

"You can learn from everything," the rabbi of Sadagora once said to
his Hasidim.° "Everything can teach us something, and not only
everything God has created. What man has made has also something
to teach us."

"What can we learn from a train?" one Hasid asked dubiously.

"That because of one second one can miss everything."

Hasidim: disciples in an Eastern-European mystical Jewish sect

"And from the telegraph?"
"That every word is counted and charged."
"And the telephone?"
"That what we say here is heard there."

ON PARABLES

Franz Kafka

Many complain that the words of the wise are always merely parables and of no use in daily life, which is the only life we have. When the sage says: "Go over," he does not mean that we should cross to some actual place, which we could do anyhow if the labor were worth it; he means some fabulous yonder, something unknown to us, something too that he cannot designate more precisely, and therefore cannot help us here in the very least. All these parables really set out to say merely that the incomprehensible is incomprehensible, and we know that already. But the cares we have to struggle with every day: that is a different matter.

Concerning this a man once said: Why such reluctance? If you only follow the parables you yourself would become parables and with that rid of all your daily cares.

Another said: I bet that is also a parable.[1]

The first said: You have won.

The second said: But unfortunately only in parable.

The first said: No, in reality: in parable you have lost.

Translated by Willa and Edwin Muir

THE YACHTS

William Carlos Williams

contend in a sea which the land partly encloses
shielding them from the too-heavy blows
of an ungoverned ocean which when it chooses

tortures the biggest hulls, the best man knows
to pit against its beatings, and sinks them pitilessly.   5
Mothlike in mists, scintillant in the minute

---

[1]The German word here means both a parable and more generally "figurative" as opposed to literal. It could be so translated; the last remark would then read, "No, literally: figuratively you have lost."

brilliance of cloudless days, with broad bellying sails
they glide to the wind tossing green water
from their sharp prows while over them the crew crawls

ant-like, solicitously grooming them, releasing,   10
making fast as they turn, lean far over and having
caught the wind again, side by side, head for the mark.

In a well guarded arena of open water surrounded by
lesser and greater craft which, sycophant, lumbering
and flittering follow them, they appear youthful, rare   15

as the light of a happy eye, live with the grace
of all that in the mind is feckless, free and
naturally to be desired. Now the sea which holds them

is moody, lapping their glossy sides, as if feeling
for some slightest flaw but fails completely.   20
Today no race. Then the wind comes again. The yachts

move, jockeying for a start, the signal is set and they
are off. Now the waves strike at them but they are too
well made, they slip through, though they take in canvas.

Arms with hands grasping seek to clutch at the prows.   25
Bodies thrown recklessly in the way are cut aside.
It is a sea of faces about them in agony, in despair

until the horror of the race dawns staggering the mind,
the whole sea become an entanglement of watery bodies
lost to the world bearing what they cannot hold. Broken,   30

beaten, desolate, reaching from the dead to be taken up
they cry out, failing, failing! their cries rising
in waves still as the skillful yachts pass over.

GERONTION°

T. S. Eliot

Thou hast nor youth nor age
But as it were an after dinner sleep
Dreaming of both.°

Gerontion: little old man   **Thou . . . both:** Shakespeare, *Measure for Measure*, III, i, 32–34; from a
speech in which Claudio, who has been condemned to death for committing fornication, is counseled
by the Duke (disguised as a friar) to accept his punishment without complaint

Here I am, an old man in a dry month,
Being read to by a boy, waiting for rain.
I was neither at the hot gates°
Nor fought in the warm rain
Nor knee deep in the salt marsh, heaving a cutlass,   5
Bitten by flies, fought.
My house is a decayed house,
And the jew° squats on the window sill, the owner,
Spawned in some estaminet° of Antwerp,
Blistered in Brussels, patched and peeled in London.   10
The goat coughs at night in the field overhead;
Rocks, moss, stonecrop, iron, merds.
The woman keeps the kitchen, makes tea,
Sneezes at evening, poking the peevish gutter.
                    I an old man,   15
A dull head among windy spaces.

   Signs are taken for wonders. "We would see a sign!"°
The word within a word, unable to speak a word,
Swaddled with darkness.° In the juvescence° of the year
Came Christ the tiger°   20

   In depraved May, dogwood and chestnut, flowering judas,
To be eaten, to be divided, to be drunk
Among whispers; by Mr. Silvero
With caressing hands, at Limoges
Who walked all night in the next room;   25

   By Hakagawa, bowing among the Titians;°
By Madame de Tornquist, in the dark room
Shifting the candles; Fräulein von Kulp
Who turned in the hall, one hand on the door.
            Vacant shuttles   30
Weave the wind. I have no ghosts,
An old man in a draughty house
Under a windy knob.

---

hot gates: Thermopylae, where in 480 B.C. the Spartans were finally defeated, after heroically defending the narrow mountain pass against an overwhelming army of Persians   jew: in lower case to represent the Jewish usurer as an archetype of all corruption; Eliot responded to charges of anti-Semitism by altering it to "Jew" in later printings   estaminet: cheap café   Signs ... sign!": miracle requested of Christ by the Scribes and Pharisees, prompting the rebuke: "An evil and adulterous generation seeketh after a sign" (Matthew 12:38–39)   The word ... Swaddled with darkness: the Christian *logos* (in a formula misremembered by Eliot from the seventeenth-century divine, Lancelot Andrewes)   juvescence: juvenescence; youth   Christ the tiger: Andrewes' Nativity Sermon of 1622 reported the speech of those who would not rush to see the newborn Christ—"Christ is no wild-cat ... what needs such haste?"   Titians: paintings by Titian, to which the fake-cosmopolitan Hakagawa pays ritual deference

After such knowledge, what forgiveness? Think now
History has many cunning passages, contrived corridors   35
And issues, deceives with whispering ambitions,
Guides us by vanities. Think now
She gives when our attention is distracted
And what she gives, gives with such supple confusions
That the giving famishes the craving. Gives too late   40
What's not believed in, or if still believed,
In memory only, reconsidered passion. Gives too soon
Into weak hands, what's thought can be dispensed with
Till the refusal propagates a fear. Think
Neither fear nor courage saves us. Unnatural vices   45
Are fathered by our heroism. Virtues
Are forced upon us by our impudent crimes.
These tears are shaken from the wrath-bearing tree.

    The tiger springs in the new year. Us he devours. Think at last
We have not reached conclusion, when I   50
Stiffen in a rented house. Think at last
I have not made this show purposelessly
And it is not by any concitation°
Of the backward devils
I would meet you upon this honestly.   55
I that was near your heart was removed therefrom
To lose beauty in terror, terror in inquisition.
I have lost my passion: why should I need to keep it
Since what is kept must be adulterated?
I have lost my sight, smell, hearing, taste and touch: 60
How should I use them for your closer contact?

    These with a thousand small deliberations
Protract the profit of their chilled delirium,
Excite the membrane, when the sense has cooled,
With pungent sauces, multiply variety   65
In a wilderness of mirrors. What will the spider do,
Suspend its operations, will the weevil
Delay? De Bailhache, Fresca, Mrs. Cammel, whirled
Beyond the circuit of the shuddering Bear°
In fractured atoms. Gull against the wind, in the windy straits   70
Of Belle Isle,° or running on the Horn,
White feathers in the snow, the Gulf claims,
And an old man driven by the Trades°

---

concitation: stirring up; conjuring   **shuddering Bear:** the constellation of the Great Bear,
shuddering because it is cold in the sky, and especially in the North   **Belle Isle:** island in the North
Atlantic   **Trades:** trade winds

To a sleepy corner.

                        Tenants of the house,   75
Thoughts of a dry brain in a dry season.

ODE TO THE CONFEDERATE DEAD

Allen Tate

Row after row with strict impunity
The headstones yield their names to the element,
The wind whirrs without recollection;
In the riven troughs the splayed leaves
Pile up, of nature the casual sacrament   5
To the seasonal eternity of death;
Then driven by the fierce scrutiny
Of heaven to their election in the vast breath,
They sough the rumor of mortality.

Autumn is desolation in the plot   10
Of a thousand acres where these memories grow
From the inexhaustible bodies that are not
Dead, but feed the grass row after rich row.
Think of the autumns that have come and gone!
Ambitious November with the humors of the year,   15
With a particular zeal for every slab,
Staining the uncomfortable angels that rot
On the slabs, a wing chipped here, an arm there:
The brute curiosity of an angel's stare
Turns you, like them, to stone,   20
Transforms the heaving air
Till plunged to a heavier world below
You shift your sea-space blindly
Heaving, turning like the blind crab.

               Dazed by the wind, only the wind   25
               The leaves flying, plunge

You know who have waited by the wall
The twilight certainty of an animal,
Those midnight restitutions of the blood
You know—the immitigable° pines, the smoky frieze   30
Of the sky, the sudden call: you know the rage,

immitigable: which cannot be made less severe

The cold pool left by the mounting flood,
Of muted Zeno and Parmenides.°
You who have waited for the angry resolution
Of those desires that should be yours tomorrow,   35
You know the unimportant shrift of death
And praise the vision
And praise the arrogant circumstance
Of those who fall
Rank upon rank, hurried beyond decision—   40
Here by the sagging gate, stopped by the wall.

    Seeing, seeing only the leaves
    Flying, plunge and expire

Turn your eyes to the immoderate past,
Turn to the inscrutable infantry rising   45
Demons out of the earth—they will not last.
Stonewall,° Stonewall, and the sunken fields of hemp,
Shiloh, Antietam, Malvern Hill, Bull Run.°
Lost in that orient of the thick and fast
You will curse the setting sun.   50

    Cursing only the leaves crying
    Like an old man in a storm

You hear the shout, the crazy hemlocks point
With troubled fingers to the silence which
Smothers you, a mummy, in time.   55
      The hound bitch
Toothless and dying, in a musty cellar
Hears the wind only.

      Now that the salt of their blood
Stiffens the saltier oblivion of the sea,   60
Seals the malignant purity of the flood,
What shall we who count our days and bow
Our heads with a commemorial woe
In the ribboned coats of grim felicity,
What shall we say of the bones, unclean,   65
Whose verdurous anonymity will grow?

The ragged arms, the ragged heads and eyes
Lost in these acres of the insane green?
The gray lean spiders come, they come and go;

Zeno and Parmenides: 5th century B.C. Greek philosophers who believed that ultimate reality was eternal and immutable, despite the illusory confusion of phenomena that change   **Stonewall:** Thomas Jonathan ("Stonewall") Jackson, got his nickname at the Battle of Bull Run in 1861   **Shiloh ... Bull Run:** only the last of these Civil War battles was won by the South

In a tangle of willows without light   70
The singular screech-owl's tight
Invisible lyric seeds the mind
With the furious murmur of their chivalry.

> We shall say only the leaves
> Flying, plunge and expire   75

We shall say only the leaves whispering
In the improbable mist of nightfall
That flies on multiple wing:
Night is the beginning and the end
And in between the ends of distraction   80
Waits mute speculation, the patient curse
That stones the eyes, or like the jaguar leaps
For his own image in a jungle pool, his victim.

What shall we say who have knowledge
Carried to the heart? Shall we take the act   85
To the grave? Shall we, more hopeful, set up the grave
In the house? The ravenous grave?

> Leave now
The shut gate and the decomposing wall:
The gentle serpent, green in the mulberry bush,   90
Riots with his tongue through the hush—
Sentinel of the grave who counts us all!

AT THE FISHHOUSES

Elizabeth Bishop

Although it is a cold evening,
down by one of the fishhouses
an old man sits netting,
his net, in the gloaming° almost invisible
a dark purple-brown   5
and his shuttle worn and polished.
The air smells so strong of codfish
it makes one's nose run and one's eyes water.
The five fishhouses have steeply peaked roofs
and narrow, cleated gangplanks slant up   10
to storerooms in the gables
for the wheelbarrows to be pushed up and down on.

gloaming: the glow of dusk

All is silver: the heavy surface of the sea,
swelling slowly as if considering spilling over,
is opaque, but the silver of the benches,   15
the lobster pots, and masts, scattered
among the wild jagged rocks,
is of an apparent translucence
like the small old buildings with an emerald moss
growing on their shoreward walls.   20
The big fish tubs are completely lined
with layers of beautiful herring scales
and the wheelbarrows are similarly plastered
with creamy iridescent coats of mail,
with small iridescent flies crawling on them.   25
Up on the little slope behind the houses,
set in the sparse bright sprinkle of grass,
is an ancient wooden capstan,°
cracked, with two long bleached handles
and some melancholy stains, like dried blood,   30
where the ironwork has rusted.
The old man accepts a Lucky Strike.
He was a friend of my grandfather.
We talk of the decline in the population
and of codfish and herring   35
while he waits for a herring boat to come in.
There are sequins on his vest and on his thumb.
He has scraped the scales, the principal beauty,
from unnumbered fish with that black old knife,
the blade of which is almost worn away.   40

Down at the water's edge, at the place
where they haul up the boats, up the long ramp
descending into the water, thin silver
tree trunks are laid horizontally
across the gray stones, down and down   45
at intervals of four or five feet.

Cold dark deep and absolutely clear,
element bearable to no mortal,
to fish and to seals . . . One seal particularly
I have seen here evening after evening.   50
He was curious about me. He was interested in music;
like me a believer in total immersion,
so I used to sing him Baptist hymns.
I also sang "A Mighty Fortress is Our God."
He stood up in the water and regarded me   55

capstan: a large, cylinder-shaped apparatus for hauling in cables and hawsers

steadily, moving his head a little.
Then he would disappear, then suddenly emerge
almost in the same spot, with a sort of shrug
as if it were against his better judgment.
Cold dark deep and absolutely clear, 60
the clear gray icy water . . . Back, behind us,
the dignified tall firs begin.
Bluish, associating with their shadows,
a million Christmas trees stand
waiting for Christmas. The water seems suspended 65
above the rounded gray and blue-gray stones.
I have seen it over and over, the same sea, the same,
slightly, indifferently swinging above the stones,
icily free above the stones,
above the stones and then the world. 70
If you should dip your hand in,
your wrist would ache immediately,
your bones would begin to ache and your hand would burn
as if the water were a transmutation of fire
that feeds on stones and burns with a dark gray flame. 75
If you tasted it, it would first taste bitter,
then briny, then surely burn your tongue.
It is like what we imagine knowledge to be:
dark, salt, clear, moving, utterly free,
drawn from the cold hard mouth 80
of the world, derived from the rocky breasts
forever, flowing and drawn, and since
our knowledge is historical, flowing, and flown.

ADAM'S TASK

John Hollander

*"And Adam gave names to all cattle, and
to the fowl of the air, and to every
beast of the field . . ."*—Gen. 2:20

Thou, paw-paw-paw; thou, glurd; thou, spotted
 Glurd; thou, whitestap, lurching through
The high-grown brush; thou, pliant-footed,
 Implex; thou, awagabu.

Every burrower, each flier 5
 Came for the name he had to give:

Gay, first work, ever to be prior,
  Not yet sunk to primitive.

Thou, verdle; thou, McFleery's pomma;
  Thou; thou; thou—three types of grawl;   10
Thou, flisket; thou, kabasch; thou, comma-
  Eared mashawk; thou, all; thou, all.

Were, in a fire of becoming,
  Laboring to be burned away,
Then work, half-measuring, half-humming,   15
  Would be as serious as play.

Thou, pambler; thou, rivarn; thou, greater
  Wherret, and thou, lesser one;
Thou, sproal; thou, zant; thou, lily-eater.
  Naming's over. Day is done.   20

DRAMA

INTRODUCTION

In this section of *Literature as Experience* you will find a sampling of plays, some of them among the greatest ever written. Our selection ranges from the ancient Greek drama to the contemporary American. It includes an Elizabethan tragedy written in English and a classical comedy written in French, though here given in a brilliant English translation. It also includes a major example of nineteenth-century European realism in the drama. This is not of course a complete representation of all the kinds of drama that we have had over the centuries, but it should serve as a handy introduction.

The drama shares with the other kinds of literature offered in this book— poetry and short prose fiction—the same general end: imaginatively to depict and illuminate human experience. But the means through which the drama proposes to achieve this end are very different. A play can be read by an individual comfortable in a chair at home, quite in the same way that he or she would read a novel or poem; but basically the play is intended for performance on a stage. It resembles, in that respect, a musical score, by existing on the page as a potentiality—as a not-completed structure of possibilities—which can be fully realized only through performance.

The major shape of the play is already present in the text. The words to be spoken (occasionally sung) by the actors are on the page, and the customary divisions into acts and scenes are indicated. A few hints for the performance may be provided by the author through stage directions. Yet, the play is fully *there,* fully alive only in actual performance. Again like a piece of music, a play can take on new and sharply different shapes and meanings with each new staging, for each director and group of actors are likely to offer a new interpretation which will be at variance, in large or small ways, with previous stagings. Even each performance under one director is likely to be somewhat different: an actor tries out a new emphasis in a crucial speech, an actress happens not to be feeling well on a given evening, the director wants to speed up the pace of a lagging second act, and so forth.

As much as possible, therefore, in reading these plays you ought to try for a two-sided approach: first, to regard them as literary works with their own intrinsic value, which can be read as you read the poems and stories; second, to imagine them being performed on a stage. And this imagining of a stage performance can itself be divided into two parts: how the play was performed in its own time and how it might now be performed. *Oedipus Rex,* like the other ancient Greek dramas, was imbedded in Greek religious ritual; it was performed in the daytime at an outdoor theatre by actors who wore masks and recited in a traditional rhythm. We could not completely reproduce such a performance even if we wanted to, and there would probably be no point in trying. So there is always the question of how closely to try to imitate what we think were the style and manner of original productions and how freely to adapt a great play to current ideas and notions of taste. You may want, as you read, to think from time to time about such matters—perhaps by imagining that you are a director who has been commissioned to produce one of the great plays and who must now decide how to go about it.

There are certain inherent characteristics—possibilities and limitations— which the play as a form imposes on the author. Over the centuries there have also accumulated a good many conventions (habitual ways of doing things) regarding the drama. These conventions change, of course—with the appearance of the modern drama in the last century, they have changed radically. So here, very briefly and incompletely, we will note just a few of the characteristics and conventions of drama as a genre or kind of literature:

A play is meant for performance on a stage, but what constitutes a stage can itself change from one period to another. Greek tragedies, as we've just remarked, were performed in the open air; there was no curtain and there was only one stage structure (called the *skene*) at the back of the performance area. Shakespeare's plays were also performed in the day-time, but with a more elaborate structure on the performance area, so that the audience could be induced to suppose parts of it were a home or a square or a balcony. Molière's plays were done on a stage that was almost entirely surrounded by the audience—spectators were grouped on three sides of the stage.

By the time we reach Ibsen's nineteenth-century theatre, the audience is seated (or cooped up) directly in front of the stage. When the curtain goes up, the spectators are supposed to imagine that they are looking through an invisible fourth wall upon the represented scene. There is also a tendency by the nineteenth century to work up elaborate stage settings: painted scenery, furniture, lights, and similar objects, all in an effort to be realistic. Directors in our own time have frequently abandoned the clutter of the realistic stage and gone back to the bare space of an older theatre. So a lot depends on how the stage is conceived of at a given time, as well as what its technical possibilities are (how many changes of scene can be managed).

A play must be of usable length, which generally means that it can be performed in one sitting (an afternoon or evening)—though within recent memory there have been plays by the American dramatist Eugene O'Neill that were so long the audience had to come in the early evening, go out to dinner, and then return to the theatre. There are also one-act plays, which don't even pretend to develop any sort of complex action or show characters in the process of change, but instead content themselves with focusing on a dramatic situation at a moment of intensity (for instance, the little play by Strindberg in this book). Still, the need for performance imposes severe limitations on playwrights. There are thousand-page novels and two-line poems, but neither extreme is available to the writer of plays.

A play, let us say, takes two-and-a-half hours to perform. That is what we call its *playing time.* But the time that is represented in the action, or story, of the play can be very different—usually, much longer. Only rarely do playing time and represented time coincide.

A play must usually have a well-defined and perceptible action, that is, a *developing conflict* between human beings. This developing conflict creates tension and excitement (with appropriate suspense at the conclusion of scenes and acts). There then occurs a *climax,* that is, the moment when the conflict reaches its sharpest point. And finally, toward the end of the play there is often a settlement or *resolution* of the conflict or of the problems that have been dramatized. Clearly, then, unity of action counts for a good deal more in a play than in a novel. (But in some contemporary plays, perhaps because their authors feel that in modern times there are no real ways to resolve human difficulties, the traditional resolution of the action is barely visible. Such plays tend simply to stop rather than to reach a significant ending.)

A play must have a reasonably limited number of roles. There cannot be as many characters in a play as are found, for instance, in some of the gigantic nineteenth-century novels, such as Dickens' *Bleak House* or Tolstoy's *War and Peace.* For one thing, it costs a lot of money to hire actors, and so every producer of a play tries to find ways of reducing their number. For another and more important reason, a great many people milling around on a stage can confuse an audience. The spectator does not have the privilege that a reader does—you cannot ask the actors to go back and redo the last ten minutes of a performance because you did not fully understand them, as you can turn back the pages of a book and read them over again.

Some things can be shown on the stage, others cannot. It depends on the moral standards and notions of taste that prevail at a given time. The

Greeks, for example, avoided violence on the stage—death, though it occurs frequently in their plays, must always take place offstage. The audience learns about it through either outcries from the wings or the report of a messenger. By contrast, in *Hamlet* there is no shortage of violence. Conventions of performance have changed still more radically in our own time. Partial or even complete nudity is now frequently accepted in the theatre, and sometimes even the simulation of sexual activity. Obscene language is now frequently accepted in the theatre, though people over fifty years of age can easily remember when it would have aroused violent opposition, even censorship. Whether these changes are good or bad is another matter; the point is that they now govern the possibilities of what the playwright can write and the director can mount on the stage.

In writing a play the author must speak through the voices of his characters; he cannot, as in other literary forms, speak directly through his own. Sometimes there will be a character (often called the *raisonneur*) who appears to be "speaking for" the author. But as we come closer to the modern theatre, in which uncertainty and ambiguity play an increasing role, we can often assume that the author's opinions and feelings have been "distributed" among various characters, sometimes even all of them. Or the author may expect the audience to reach some conclusion about the play not from any explicit statement made by one or another character but from an overall impression, a unifying sense of things.

A playwright cannot explain what is happening to the characters in the way a novelist can. A playwright cannot speak directly about his or her feelings in the way a poet can. Whatever motivating thought there may be behind the play has to be grasped by the audience through its perception of the work as a whole. But just because of such restrictions, there are also tremendous possibilities for vividness of presentation and depths of emotion in a play. It is a literary form of great directness and concentration. Instead of reading on a cold page about, say, a conflict between a king and his daughters, you can sit in a theatre and see and hear a great actor like Laurence Olivier playing the part of King Lear and speaking Shakespeare's incomparable lines. You are subject in the theatre to the emotional effect of the human voice, its capacity to move and persuade, to entice and dazzle. The playwright provides the script; the director, the guiding style of production; the actors, the immediate effect of feeling.

There is more to be said, of course, about the art of the drama, and some of it you will find in the introductions to the individual plays (discussion of tragedy in the introduction to *Oedipus Rex* and of comedy in the introduction to *A School for Wives*). Still more will occur to you as you read, think, and respond.

Oedipus Rex

Introduction

We usually use the word "tragedy" in a very loose way to mean catastrophes, misfortunes, calamities, or pathetic events of many sorts. Disaster in life is common, but true tragedy is rare. The heroic or universal—as opposed to the ordinary or common—nature of a tragic plot in dramatic literature has very different meanings for us than the daily occurrences of violence and brutality, which seem to be getting more and more familiar. A great tragic play is not like a mirror in which we see the world of our daily lives. It is rather like a high platform on which is mounted not only a mirror, but a combined telescope, X-ray, and long videotape of human history as well. When we look toward it, we will not learn whether our hair has been arranged properly, but we will know much more than a mirror can tell us about the truth of our lives.

The very word itself is connected with ancient Greek drama. In Greek, tragedy meant, literally, "goat-ode": the religious festivals at which drama was performed were sacred to the god Dionysus, or Bacchus, with whose worship goats were associated. As the philosopher Aristotle defined it, however, the essence of tragedy lay in its being the representation of an action, by dramatic rather than narrative means, that had the aim of arousing in the beholder pity and terror, *in order, at the end of the play, to purge the spectator of just those emotions.* (When we respond to "tragic" events in life—the lurid murder of children, or of helpless old people, for example—with sympathy, we may be manifesting one part of our humanity by having strong feelings, but we will probably not be learning much. The purpose of tragic art is to teach us something, if only how to learn as much about life from life itself as we can from art.)

Sophocles' *Oedipus Rex* is the representation, as we shall see, of an act of knowing or learning, although the story involves violence enough—parricide, incest, attempted infanticide. Its hero's predicament is hardly one in which mentally and socially competent people will be found. And yet Oedipus' relation to knowledge and fate, to what human beings can control in their lives and what they cannot, is universal. Oedipus stands for man, mythologically speaking.

653

"Myth" in Greek means story, and the ancient legends that come to us from classical Greece are fables with meanings for all of our lives. Poetry was the way in which the significance of these stories was shown in the ancient world, and dramatic poetry, or tragedy, was one of the most important devices for the unfolding of universal meaning. The myth of Oedipus has become more important for modern humanity than perhaps any other, and to some degree it seems impossible to separate this importance from that of Sophocles' play. There were a good many Greek tragedies composed about the Oedipus story, although only this one survives. And yet that is not the only reason for the power that *Oedipus Rex* has in shaping the story for us.

The universality of the condition of Oedipus was developed at considerable length by Sigmund Freud in the early years of this century. Oedipus (his name means "swollen-foot" in Greek, and refers to the results of his childhood injury) was the son of King Laïos and Queen Iokastê of Thebes; an oracle told Laïos that a son born to them would kill his father and marry his mother, and when a boy was indeed born, he was taken by a slave to Mount Kithairon, near Thebes, with his ankles riveted together so that he would die of exposure. But, instead of leaving the baby to die, the slave gave him to a shepherd who took him to Corinth to the court of King Polybos and Queen Meropê. There, he was raised as the prince. But on learning from an oracle that he was fated to kill his father and marry his mother, he fled, only to come to Thebes and, without knowing it, act out his doom in seeking to avoid it.

Most important in the myth is Oedipus' encounter with the Sphinx (the name means "strangler") on the way to Thebes. This monster, with the head of a woman and the body of a lion, asked a riddle of every traveller, who, if he could not answer, was destroyed by her. The riddle went: *What walks on four legs in the morning, two at noon, and three in the evening?* Oedipus answers the riddle correctly: this uncanny monster with its varying number of feet is only man—crawling in infancy, walking erect at maturity, and then with a cane in the evening of old age. Oedipus' wisdom is such that he can solve the riddle whose answer is "Man" (or "us," or "me"); his tragic fate is to unriddle another puzzle whose uncanniness lies right at his door.

Freud found Oedipus of central importance to his notion of the "family romance"—a pattern, which he felt to be universal in Western man, in which sons (a) are in psychic combat with their fathers, (b) are erotically attached to their mothers, and (c)—and this is very important—do not know that they are. The so-called Oedipus complex is a pattern of relationships, which families do not act out, as is done in the story, but for which the story stands as a strong and active representation. A second element of universality in the Oedipus myth, Freudian interpretation aside, is the way in which it constituted a parable of human knowledge. It is precisely those qualities in Oedipus enabling him to subdue the Sphinx that led him to follow the fated course of his life, even in trying so hard to resist it. Oedipus' story is one in which a crippling problem turns out to have a familiar—a horribly familiar—solution: it points to the solutions of some of the wildest monstrosities of human nature, which lie in ourselves.

The play

In order to understand the means which Sophocles employed in his version of the Oedipus story, we must first acquaint ourselves with the nature of drama in classical Greece. It was as much ritual—religious and patriotic—as entertainment. Presented at annual festivals, the dramatic performances drew audiences from far away; the atmosphere was both celebratory and intense, and to approximate it, you would have to imagine a kind of combined Easter, July Fourth, Superbowl, and World Series. The knowledge and understanding of dramatic poetry, music, and dance that the audience brought to a performance of a tragedy was not unlike the expertise of today's spectators at a Superbowl game, in fact. Just as doctors, truck drivers, teachers, students, business executives, criminals, police officers, and scholars can all discuss with knowledge and concern the elegance of the last forward pass, so could the audience in Sophocles' Athens respond to the elements of the drama. Poetry, music, dance were all directed toward the representation of the plot, which itself interpreted a well-known mythological story.

The singing and dancing were done by a chorus. In *Oedipus Rex* they are the elders of Thebes; fifteen in number, the Chorus appeared at a point shortly after the beginning of each play, called the *párados,* or formal entrance. Their leader, the *Choragos,* would speak for them all in the dialogue. Unlike Elizabethan or modern plays, divided into acts and scenes by a change of scenery, a falling curtain, or a darkened stage, Greek tragedies were composed of episodes of spoken poetic dialogue, followed by choral odes. These odes were songs of great musical and choreographic complexity in which were represented the community's attitudes, thoughts, and emotions prompted by the heroic action unfolding before them (Note on Prosody, p. 591). Sophocles' *Oedipus Rex* consists of a Prologue (lines 1–153), the *párados,* in which the chorus enters (lines 154–203), four episodes, or scenes, each followed by a chorus, and finally, the *éxodos,* or conclusion, containing the departure of the chorus (lines 1176–end). As in all Greek tragedies no violent action occurs onstage and the entire play occurs in one place and in one uninterrupted period of time.

Doing and knowing

Indeed, if we take a simple view of what dramatic action is, a good deal of the Oedipus story has taken place long before the play starts. As Oedipus himself narrates (lines 726–71), he had grown up in Corinth, the son of the King. A drunken companion at a party accused him of not being his father's son; he thereupon consulted the oracle of Apollo at Delphi, where he was told that he was fated to kill his father and marry his mother. In terror and revulsion, he fled his native Corinth to avoid contact with his parents (as he thought them to be). At a place where three roads met, he encountered Laïos and his entourage, and was insulted by being forced off the road by Laïos' chariot. In a rage, he killed all but one of the company, including Laïos, whom he did not know to be (a) the King of Thebes or (b) his own father. To continue the story beyond Oedipus' retelling, he then proceeded to Thebes, where he found the city plagued by the Sphinx, who killed all those unable to solve her riddle; answering it correctly, he delivered the city from her power (the Sphinx destroyed herself in chagrin) and was awarded the throne and the hand in marriage of the widowed queen. He had four children by her, and the city prospered until famine and a plague overtook Thebes. The elders of the city, consulting the Delphic oracle, learn that things will not improve until the murderer of Laïos is discovered.

It is at this point that the play begins, with the elders coming to their king, the famous solver of riddles, to ask him to help redeem the city again. Had Sophocles chosen to dramatize any other parts of the story outlined above, such as the actual murder of Laïos, the flight from Corinth, the triumphant arrival in Thebes, and the marriage to Iokastê, the action represented might seem more overt—a hero makes a reasoned or hasty decision with immediate consequences—than it does in *Oedipus Rex*. As it is, the action is like a kind of stationary quest: Oedipus decides to find out who killed Laïos, and thereby finds out much too much more. He discovers that, indeed, the puzzle he wants to solve entails solving another one that he hadn't even known existed. Oedipus is like a detective searching for a murderer, impatiently pushing aside warnings that he had better give up the investigation, and discovering that he had himself unwittingly committed the crime.

This most universal instance of tragic movement is an action of knowing, not of performing or committing, a deed. The violent conclusions—in the final acts of Iokastê and Oedipus—are responses to tragic knowledge, rather than tragic acts in themselves. Sophocles' audience watched the play not in order to discover what would happen to Oedipus: they all knew the myth very well. What they waited to discover was what Sophocles thought the myth meant, and how he would interpret its significance for human life. The plague and the oracle's advice are the only elements of the plot that originate with Sophocles; the continual and powerful unrolling of what is called dramatic irony in the play, and the fundamental contradiction of Oedipus' predicament—only someone who could solve riddles so well could be so horribly entrapped in the riddle of himself—are of a far greater and deeper originality.

Dramatic irony

By dramatic irony we usually mean a quality of a situation in which a speaker is not aware of the true significance of his or her remarks but an audience or reader is. Frequently this involves an inevitability of which the speaker is ignorant. In the Biblical story of the sacrifice of Isaac, Abraham obeys God's order to take his only son to the top of a mountain and sacrifice him, like a sheep or a goat, on an altar. On the way to the place of sacrifice, the young boy,

Isaac—not knowing what his father has been told to do—innocently asks, "Behold the fire and the wood: but where is the lamb for a burnt offering?" Abraham answers, "My son, God will provide himself a lamb," meaning the boy himself. We might say that there is an irony of tone here: Abraham knows that he is being metaphorical, and he knows to his own sorrow what the "lamb" here means. But also, by hiding part of the truth, he spares the boy some of the horror for a few moments at least. The dramatic irony here results from the reader's own knowledge of the outcome of the story: at the last minute, God shows Abraham a ram entangled in a thicket to use for the sacrifice, and reveals that he was only testing him. So that Abraham's "God will provide himself a lamb" is *unwittingly literal,* and if we know the story, the statement is a powerful case of dramatic irony.

Given our knowledge of the truth about Oedipus, much of what he says during the course of the play is tinged with this kind of unwitting, violent truth or falsehood. What he thinks to be true is true in ways he cannot imagine. His arguments with the blind "seer," Teiresias, are shot through with this irony, for example: only when Oedipus "sees" what the blind Teiresias sees will he know enough to blind himself. It is the dramatic irony that continually spotlights and shadows the events of discovery and confrontation in this tragedy of human knowledge.

Modern readers cannot participate in the spectacle, the music, or even some of the effects created by the poetic language of the original—there are many untranslatable puns, for example, such as those on Oedipus' own name, which keep pointing up ironic overtones. But the inexorable unrolling of the hero's fate moves on with a dramatic rhythm of its own, and as readers we can follow this rhythm in many ways. The choruses, for example, which follow the episodes, have very different characteristics: when is the chorus right about what has been going on? When wrong? Are they ever right, but for the wrong reasons? When are they simply giving voice to conventional wisdom, itself untested by any of the ultimate human horror gradually developing before them? Are they ever, on the other hand (as perhaps at lines 851–64), aware of a general *truth* about human life, without yet knowing, as Oedipus does not yet know, the specific facts? Another pattern we can follow as readers is that of doubleness: at line 405, Teiresias speaks of the figurative "double lash" of the curse of Oedipus' parents; at line 768, Oedipus himself mentions the "double goad" with which he was struck by Laïos; at line 1199 the Second Messenger bewails the "double fruit" of Iokastê's marriage; and a hideous relation extends among the prongs with which Oedipus' ankles had been "pinned together" in infancy, the prongs of the two brooches that put out his eyes, and even the double bolts on the "twin doors" of Iokastê's chamber.

It is in the opening-up of patterns like these, in the taunting interrogations that Oedipus conducts with Teiresias, the Shepherd, the Messenger where lines of verse are traded like blows, and in the reader's knowledge of Oedipus' past and future that the full dramatic force of this play lies. Its action is played out, for every reader, on the stage of what he or she knows about Oedipus, and of what we all fear about our ability to know ourselves.

Oedipus Rex

CHARACTERS OF THE PLAY

OEDIPUS, *King of Thebes, supposed son of Polybos and
    Meropê, King and Queen of Corinth*
IOKASTÊ, *wife of Oedipus and widow of the late King Laïos*
KREON, *brother of Iokastê, a prince of Thebes*
TEIRESIAS, *a blind seer who serves Apollo*
PRIEST
MESSENGER, *from Corinth*
SHEPHERD, *former servant of Laïos*
SECOND MESSENGER, *from the palace*
CHORUS OF THEBAN ELDERS
CHORAGOS, *leader of the Chorus*
ANTIGONE *and* ISMENE, *young daughters of Oedipus and
    Iokastê. They appear in the Éxodos but do not speak.*
SUPPLIANTS, GUARDS, SERVANTS

THE SCENE. *Before the palace of* OEDIPUS, *King of Thebes. A central door
and two lateral doors open onto a platform which runs the length of the façade. On
the platform, right and left, are altars; and three steps lead down into the
orchêstra, or chorus-ground. At the beginning of the action these steps are crowded
by suppliants who have brought branches and chaplets of olive leaves and who sit
in various attitudes of despair.* OEDIPUS *enters.*

Prologue

OEDIPUS   My children, generations of the living
In the line of Kadmos,° nursed at his ancient hearth:
Why have you strewn yourselves before these altars
In supplication, with your boughs and garlands?
The breath of incense rises from the city   5
With a sound of prayer and lamentation.
                                    Children,
I would not have you speak through messengers,

2 **Kadmos**: legendary founder of Thebes

THE OEDIPUS REX OF SOPHOCLES   An English Version by Dudley Fitts and Robert Fitzgerald, copyright, 1949, by Harcourt Brace Jovanovich, Inc., and reprinted with their permission.

And therefore I have come myself to hear you—
I, Oedipus, who bear the famous name.
(*To a* PRIEST) You, there, since you are eldest in the company,   10
Speak for them all, tell me what preys upon you,
Whether you come in dread, or crave some blessing:
Tell me, and never doubt that I will help you
In every way I can; I should be heartless
Were I not moved to find you suppliant here.   15

PRIEST   Great Oedipus, O powerful king of Thebes!
You see how all the ages of our people
Cling to your altar steps: here are boys
Who can barely stand alone, and here are priests
By weight of age, as I am a priest of God,   20
And young men chosen from those yet unmarried;
As for the others, all that multitude,
They wait with olive chaplets in the squares,
At the two shrines of Pallas,° and where Apollo°
Speaks in the glowing embers.   25
                                        Your own eyes
Must tell you: Thebes is tossed on a murdering sea
And can not lift her head from the death surge.
A rust consumes the buds and fruits of the earth;
The herds are sick; children die unborn,
And labor is vain. The god of plague and pyre   30
Raids like detestable lightning through the city,
And all the house of Kadmos is laid waste,
All emptied, and all darkened: Death alone
Battens upon the misery of Thebes.

You are not one of the immortal gods, we know;   35
Yet we have come to you to make our prayer
As to the man surest in mortal ways
And wisest in the ways of God. You saved us
From the Sphinx, that flinty singer, and the tribute
We paid to her so long; yet you were never   40
Better informed than we, nor could we teach you:
A god's touch, it seems, enabled you to help us.

Therefore, O mighty power, we turn to you:
Find us our safety, find us a remedy,
Whether by counsel of the gods or of men.   45
A king of wisdom tested in the past
Can act in a time of troubles, and act well.
Noblest of men, restore

---

24 **Pallas:** Athena, goddess of wisdom; she was the patroness of Athens, where her two shrines were
the Parthenon and the Erechtheum on the Acropolis   **Apollo:** god of the sun, music, poetry, and
medicine

Life to your city! Think how all men call you
Liberator for your boldness long ago;   50
Ah, when your years of kingship are remembered,
Let them not say *We rose, but later fell*—
Keep the State from going down in the storm!
Once, years ago, with happy augury,
You brought us fortune; be the same again!   55
No man questions your power to rule the land:
But rule over men, not over a dead city!
Ships are only hulls, high walls are nothing,
When no life moves in the empty passageways.

OEDIPUS   Poor children! You may be sure I know   60
All that you longed for in your coming here.
I know that you are deathly sick; and yet,
Sick as you are, not one is as sick as I.
Each of you suffers in himself alone
His anguish, not another's; but my spirit   65
Groans for the city, for myself, for you.

I was not sleeping, you are not waking me.
No, I have been in tears for a long while
And in my restless thought walked many ways.
In all my search I found one remedy,   70
And I have adopted it: I have sent Kreon,
Son of Menoikeus, brother of the queen,
To Delphi, Apollo's place of revelation,
To learn there, if he can,
What act or pledge of mine may save the city.   75
I have counted the days, and now, this very day,
I am troubled, for he has overstayed his time.
What is he doing? He has been gone too long.
Yet whenever he comes back, I should do ill
Not to take any action the god orders.   80

PRIEST   It is a timely promise. At this instant
They tell me Kreon is here.

OEDIPUS   O Lord Apollo!
May his news be fair as his face is radiant!

PRIEST   Good news, I gather! he is crowned with bay,
The chaplet is thick with berries.

OEDIPUS   We shall soon know;   85
He is near enough to hear us now.

(Enter KREON.*)*

                              O prince:
Brother: son of Menoikeus:
What answer do you bring us from the god?

KREON   A strong one. I can tell you, great afflictions
    Will turn out well, if they are taken well.   90
OEDIPUS   What was the oracle? These vague words
    Leave me still hanging between hope and fear.
KREON   Is it your pleasure to hear me with all these
    Gathered around us? I am prepared to speak,
    But should we not go in?
OEDIPUS   Speak to them all,   95
    It is for them I suffer, more than for myself.
KREON   Then I will tell you what I heard at Delphi.
    In plain words
    The god commands us to expel from the land of Thebes
    An old defilement we are sheltering.   100
    It is a deathly thing, beyond cure;
    We must not let it feed upon us longer.
OEDIPUS   What defilement? How shall we rid ourselves of it?
KREON   By exile or death, blood for blood. It was
    Murder that brought the plague-wind on the city.   105
OEDIPUS   Murder of whom? Surely the god has named him?
KREON   My lord: Laïos once ruled this land,
    Before you came to govern us.
OEDIPUS   I know;
    I learned of him from others; I never saw him.
KREON   He was murdered; and Apollo commands us now   110
    To take revenge upon whoever killed him.
OEDIPUS   Upon whom? Where are they? Where shall we find a clue
    To solve that crime, after so many years?
KREON   Here in this land, he said. Search reveals
    Things that escape an inattentive man.   115
OEDIPUS   Tell me: Was Laïos murdered in his house,
    Or in the fields, or in some foreign country?
KREON   He said he planned to make a pilgrimage
    He did not come home again.
OEDIPUS   And was there no one,
    No witness, no companion, to tell what happened?   120
KREON   They were all killed but one, and he got away
    So frightened that he could remember one thing only.
OEDIPUS   What was the one thing? One may be the key
    To everything, if we resolve to use it.
KREON   He said that a band of highwaymen attacked them,   125
    Outnumbered them, and overwhelmed the king.
OEDIPUS   Strange, that a highwayman should be so daring—
    Unless some faction here bribed him to do it.
KREON   We thought of that. But after Laïos' death
    New troubles arose and we had no avenger.
OEDIPUS   What troubles could prevent your hunting down the killers?

KREON   The riddling Sphinx's song
    Made us deaf to all mysteries but her own.
OEDIPUS   Then once more I must bring what is dark to light.
    It is most fitting that Apollo shows,   135
    As you do, this compunction for the dead.
    You shall see how I stand by you, as I should,
    Avenging this country and the god as well,
    And not as though it were for some distant friend,
    But for my own sake, to be rid of evil.   140
    Whoever killed King Laïos might—who knows?—
    Lay violent hands even on me—and soon.
    I act for the murdered king in my own interest.

    Come, then, my children: leave the altar steps,
    Lift up your olive boughs!
                         One of you go   145
    And summon the people of Kadmos to gather here.
    I will do all that I can; you may tell them that.   (*Exit a* PAGE.)
    So, with the help of God,
    We shall be saved—or else indeed we are lost.
PRIEST   Let us rise, children. It was for this we came,   150
    And now the king has promised it.
    Phoibos° has sent us an oracle; may he descend
    Himself to save us and drive out the plague.
        (*Exeunt* OEDIPUS *and* KREON *into the palace by the central door.*
        The PRIEST *and the* SUPPLIANTS *disperse R and L. After a short*
        pause the CHORUS *enters the orchêstra.*)

Párodos

STROPHE 1
CHORUS   What is God singing in his profound
    Delphi of gold and shadow?   155
    What oracle for Thebes, the sunwhipped city?
    Fear unjoints me, the roots of my heart tremble.
    Now I remember, O Healer, your power, and wonder:
    Will you send doom like a sudden cloud, or weave it
    Like nightfall of the past?   160
    Speak to me, tell me, O
    Child of golden Hope, immortal Voice.

ANTISTROPHE 1
    Let me pray to Athenê, the immortal daughter of Zeus,
    And to Artemis her sister

152 **Phoibos:** Apollo; his shrine, with its famous oracle, was at Delphi

Who keeps her famous throne in the market ring,   165
And to Apollo, archer from distant heaven—
O gods, descend! Like three streams leap against
The fires of our grief, the fires of darkness;
Be swift to bring us rest!
As in the old time from the brilliant house   170
Of air you stepped to save us, come again!

STROPHE 2
Now our afflictions have no end,
Now all our stricken host lies down
And no man fights off death with his mind;
The noble plowland bears no grain,   175
And groaning mothers can not bear—
See, how our lives like birds take wing,
Like sparks that fly when a fire soars,
To the shore of the god of evening.

ANTISTROPHE 2
The plague burns on, it is pitiless,   180
Though pallid children laden with death
Lie unwept in the stony ways,
And old gray women by every path
Flock to the strand about the altars
There to strike their breasts and cry   185
Worship of Phoibos in wailing prayers:
Be kind, God's golden child!

STROPHE 3
There are no swords in this attack by fire,
No shields, but we are ringed with cries.
Send the besieger plunging from our homes   190
Into the vast sea-room of the Atlantic
Or into the waves that foam eastward of Thrace—
For the day ravages what the night spares—
Destroy our enemy, lord of the thunder!
Let him be riven by lightning from heaven!   195

ANTISTROPHE 3
Phoibos Apollo, stretch the sun's bowstring,
That golden cord, until it sing for us,
Flashing arrows in heaven!
                           Artemis, Huntress,
Race with flaring lights upon our mountains!
O scarlet god, O golden-banded brow,   200
O Theban Bacchos° in a storm of Maenads,

201 **Bacchos:** Dionysus, god of wine and patron of the dramatic festivals; the Maenads, or Bacchae, were his female worshippers

(Enter OEDIPUS, *C.)*

Whirl upon Death, that all the Undying hate!
Come with blinding torches, come in joy!

Scene I

OEDIPUS   Is this your prayer? It may be answered. Come,
    Listen to me, act as the crisis demands,   205
    And you shall have relief from all these evils.

    Until now I was a stranger to this tale,
    As I had been a stranger to the crime.
    Could I track down the murderer without a clue?
    But now, friends,   210
    As one who became a citizen after the murder,
    I make this proclamation to all Thebans:
    If any man knows by whose hand Laïos, son of Labdakos,
    Met his death, I direct that man to tell me everything,
    No matter what he fears for having so long withheld it.   215
    Let it stand as promised that no further trouble
    Will come to him, but he may leave the land in safety.

    Moreover: If anyone knows the murderer to be foreign,
    Let him not keep silent: he shall have his reward from me.
    However, if he does conceal it; if any man   220
    Fearing for his friend or for himself disobeys this edict,
    Hear what I propose to do:

    I solemnly forbid the people of this country,
    Where power and throne are mine, ever to receive that man
    Or speak to him, no matter who he is, or let him   225
    Join in sacrifice, lustration,° or in prayer.
    I decree that he be driven from every house,
    Being, as he is, corruption itself to us: the Delphic
    Voice of Apollo has pronounced this revelation.
    Thus I associate myself with the oracle   230
    And take the side of the murdered king.

    As for the criminal, I pray to God—
    Whether it be a lurking thief, or one of a number—
    I pray that that man's life be consumed in evil and wretchedness.
    And as for me, this curse applies no less   235
    If it should turn out that the culprit is my guest here,

---

226 lustration: ritual purification

Sharing my hearth.
                    You have heard the penalty.
I lay it on you now to attend to this
For my sake, for Apollo's, for the sick
Sterile city that heaven has abandoned.   240
Suppose the oracle had given you no command:
Should this defilement go uncleansed for ever?
You should have found the murderer: your king,
A noble king, had been destroyed!
                              Now I,
Having the power that he held before me,   245
Having his bed, begetting children there
Upon his wife, as he would have, had he lived—
Their son would have been my children's brother,
If Laïos had had luck in fatherhood!
(And now his bad fortune has struck him down)—   250
I say I take the son's part, just as though
I were his son, to press the fight for him
And see it won! I'll find the hand that brought
Death to Labdakos' and Polydoros' child,
Heir of Kadmos' and Agenor's line.°   255
And as for those who fail me,
May the gods deny them the fruit of the earth,
Fruit of the womb, and may they rot utterly!
Let them be wretched as we are wretched, and worse!

For you, for loyal Thebans, and for all   260
Who find my actions right, I pray the favor
Of justice, and of all the immortal gods.
CHORAGOS   Since I am under oath, my lord, I swear
    I did not do the murder, I can not name
    The murderer. Phoibos ordained the search;   265
    Why did he not say who the culprit was?
OEDIPUS   An honest question. But no man in the world
    Can make the gods do more than the gods will.
CHORAGOS   There is an alternative, I think—
OEDIPUS   Tell me.
    Any or all, you must not fail to tell me.   270
CHORAGOS   A lord clairvoyant to the lord Apollo,
    As we all know, is the skilled Teiresias.
    One might learn much about this from him, Oedipus.
OEDIPUS.   I am not wasting time:

---

255 Kadmos . . . line: Agenor was the father of Kadmos, Thebes's founder. The line of succession
went: Kadmos—Polydoros—Labdakos—Laïos. The royal line is invoked to honor Laïos' memory;
the irony is that Oedipus himself, although he does not know this yet, is next in line.

Kreon spoke of this, and I have sent for him—   275
Twice, in fact; it is strange that he is not here.
CHORAGOS The other matter—that old report—seems useless.
OEDIPUS What was that? I am interested in all reports.
CHORAGOS The king was said to have been killed by highwaymen.
OEDIPUS I know. But we have no witnesses to that.   280
CHORAGOS If the killer can feel a particle of dread,
Your curse will bring him out of hiding!
OEDIPUS   No.
The man who dared that act will fear no curse.

(Enter the blind seer TEIRESIAS, *led by a* PAGE.)

CHORAGOS But there is one man who may detect the criminal.
This is Teiresias, this is the holy prophet   285
In whom, alone of all men, truth was born.
OEDIPUS Teiresias: seer: student of mysteries,
Of all that's taught and all that no man tells,
Secrets of Heaven and secrets of the earth:
Blind though you are, you know the city lies   290
Sick with plague; and from this plague, my lord,
We find that you alone can guard or save us.

Possibly you did not hear the messengers?
Apollo, when we sent to him,
Sent us back word that this great pestilence   295
Would lift, but only if we established clearly
The identity of those who murdered Laïos.
They must be killed or exiled.
                                  Can you use
Birdflight° or any art of divination
To purify yourself, and Thebes, and me   300
From this contagion? We are in your hands.
There is no fairer duty
Than that of helping others in distress.
TEIRESIAS How dreadful knowledge of the truth can be
When there's no help in truth! I knew this well,   305
But did not act on it: else I should not have come.
OEDIPUS What is troubling you? Why are your eyes so cold?
TEIRESIAS Let me go home. Bear your own fate, and I'll
Bear mine. It is better so: trust what I say.
OEDIPUS What you say is ungracious and unhelpful   310
To your native country. Do not refuse to speak.
TEIRESIAS When it comes to speech, your own is neither temperate
Nor opportune. I wish to be more prudent.

299 Birdflight: patterns made by flying birds were used to foretell the future

OEDIPUS   In God's name, we all beg you—
TEIRESIAS   You are all ignorant.
    No; I will never tell you what I know.   315
    Now it is my misery; then, it would be yours.
OEDIPUS   What! You do know something, and will not tell us?
    You would betray us all and wreck the State?
TEIRESIAS   I do not intend to torture myself, or you.
    Why persist in asking? You will not persuade me.   320
OEDIPUS   What a wicked old man you are! You'd try a stone's
    Patience! Out with it! Have you no feeling at all?
TEIRESIAS   You call me unfeeling. If you could only see
    The nature of your own feelings° . . .
OEDIPUS   Why,
    Who would not feel as I do? Who could endure   325
    Your arrogance toward the city?
TEIRESIAS   What does it matter?
    Whether I speak or not, it is bound to come.
OEDIPUS   Then, if "it" is bound to come, you are bound to tell me.
TEIRESIAS   No, I will not go on. Rage as you please.
OEDIPUS   Rage? Why not!
                 And I'll tell you what I think: 330
    You planned it, you had it done, you all but
    Killed him with your own hands: if you had eyes,
    I'd say the crime was yours, and yours alone.
TEIRESIAS   So? I charge you, then,
    Abide by the proclamation you have made: 335
    From this day forth
    Never speak again to these men or to me;
    You yourself are the pollution of this country.
OEDIPUS   You dare say that! Can you possibly think you have
    Some way of going free, after such insolence?   340
TEIRESIAS   I have gone free. It is the truth sustains me.
OEDIPUS   Who taught you shamelessness? It was not your craft.
TEIRESIAS   You did. You made me speak. I did not want to.
OEDIPUS   Speak what? Let me hear it again more clearly.
TEIRESIAS   Was it not clear before? Are you tempting me?   345
OEDIPUS   I did not understand it. Say it again.
TEIRESIAS   I say that you are the murderer whom you seek.
OEDIPUS   Now twice you have spat out infamy. You'll pay for it!
TEIRESIAS   Would you care for more? Do you wish to be really angry?
OEDIPUS   Say what you will. Whatever you say is worthless.   350
TEIRESIAS   I say you live in hideous shame with those
    Most dear to you. You can not see the evil.

---

324 nature . . . feelings: the Greek word for "feelings" is, literally, "anger," and the line goes
something like "You blame my anger, but you don't see what (i.e., anger) you're living with." The
Greek audience would hear an implied reference to Iokaste here as well (wife? mother? what?)

OEDIPUS   Can you go on babbling like this for ever?

TEIRESIAS   I can, if there is power in truth.

OEDIPUS   There is:

    But not for you, not for you,   355
    You sightless, witless, senseless, mad old man!

TEIRESIAS   You are the madman. There is no one here
    Who will not curse you soon, as you curse me.

OEDIPUS   You child of total night! I would not touch you;
    Neither would any man who sees the sun.   360

TEIRESIAS   True: it is not from you my fate will come.
    That lies within Apollo's competence,
    As it is his concern.

OEDIPUS   Tell me, who made
    These fine discoveries? Kreon? or someone else?

TEIRESIAS   Kreon is no threat. You weave your own doom.   365

OEDIPUS   Wealth, power, craft of statesmanship!
    Kingly position, everywhere admired!
    What savage envy is stored up against these,
    If Kreon, whom I trusted, Kreon my friend,
    For this great office which the city once   370
    Put in my hands unsought—if for this power
    Kreon desires in secret to destroy me!

    He has bought this decrepit fortune-teller, this
    Collector of dirty pennies, this prophet fraud—
    Why, he is no more clairvoyant than I am!

                                        Tell us: 375
    Has your mystic mummery ever approached the truth?
    When that hellcat the Sphinx was performing here,
    What help were you to these people?
    Her magic was not for the first man who came along:
    It demanded a real exorcist. Your birds—   380
    What good were they? or the gods, for the matter of that?
    But I came by,
    Oedipus, the simple man, who knows nothing—
    I thought it out for myself, no birds helped me!
    And this is the man you think you can destroy,   385
    That you may be close to Kreon when he's king!
    Well, you and your friend Kreon, it seems to me,
    Will suffer most. If you were not an old man,
    You would have paid already for your plot.

CHORAGOS   We can not see that his words or yours   390
    Have been spoken except in anger, Oedipus,
    And of anger we have no need. How to accomplish
    The god's will best: that is what most concerns us.

TEIRESIAS   You are a king. But where argument's concerned

I am your man, as much a king as you.   395
I am not your servant, but Apollo's.
I have no need of Kreon or Kreon's name.

Listen to me. You mock my blindness, do you?
But I say that you, with both your eyes, are blind:
You can not see the wretchedness of your life,   400
Nor in whose house you live, no, nor with whom.
Who are your father and mother? Can you tell me?
You do not even know the blind wrongs
That you have done them, on earth and in the world below.
But the double lash of your parents' curse will whip you   405
Out of this land some day, with only night
Upon your precious eyes.
Your cries then—where will they not be heard?
What fastness of Kithairon° will not echo them?
And that bridal-descant of yours—you'll know it then,   410
The song they sang when you came here to Thebes
And found your misguided berthing.
All this, and more, that you can not guess at now,
Will bring you to yourself among your children.

Be angry, then. Curse Kreon. Curse my words.   415
I tell you, no man that walks upon the earth
Shall be rooted out more horribly than you.
OEDIPUS   Am I to bear this from him?—Damnation
    Take you! Out of this place! Out of my sight!
TEIRESIAS   I would not have come at all if you had not asked me.   420
OEDIPUS   Could I have told that you'd talk nonsense, that
    You'd come here to make a fool of yourself, and of me?
TEIRESIAS   A fool? Your parents thought me sane enough.
OEDIPUS   My parents again!—Wait: who were my parents?
TEIRESIAS   This day will give you a father, and break your heart.   425
OEDIPUS   Your infantile riddles! Your damned abracadabra!
TEIRESIAS   You were a great man once at solving riddles.
OEDIPUS   Mock me with that if you like; you will find it true.
TEIRESIAS   It was true enough. It brought about your ruin.
OEDIPUS   But if it saved this town?
TEIRESIAS *(to the* PAGE)   Boy, give me your hand.   430
OEDIPUS   Yes, boy; lead him away.
                                    —While you are here
    We can do nothing. Go; leave us in peace.

---

409 Kithairon: the mountain near Thebes. Teiresias chooses this as if taking up a random example
of something that will echo voices, but he—and the audience—know that this is the place where
Oedipus was exposed as an infant. It is also where Oedipus announces the wish to be taken at the end
of the play.

TEIRESIAS   I will go when I have said what I have to say.
    How can you hurt me? And I tell you again:
    The man you have been looking for all this time,   435
    The damned man, the murderer of Laïos,
    That man is in Thebes. To your mind he is foreign-born,
    But it will soon be shown that he is a Theban,
    A revelation that will fail to please.
                          A blind man,
    Who has his eyes now; a penniless man, who is rich now;   440
    And he will go tapping the strange earth with his staff.
    To the children with whom he lives now he will be
    Brother and father—the very same; to her
    Who bore him, son and husband—the very same
    Who came to his father's bed, wet with his father's blood.   445

    Enough. Go think that over.
    If later you find error in what I have said,
    You may say that I have no skill in prophecy.
          (Exit TEIRESIAS, *led by his* PAGE. OEDIPUS *goes into the palace.)*

Ode I

STROPHE 1

CHORUS   The Delphic stone of prophecies
    Remembers ancient regicide   450
    And a still bloody hand.
    That killer's hour of flight has come.
    He must be stronger than riderless
    Coursers of untiring wind,
    For the son of Zeus° armed with his father's thunder   455
    Leaps in lightning after him;
    And the Furies° hold his track, the sad Furies.

ANTISTROPHE 1

    Holy Parnassos' peak of snow
    Flashes and blinds that secret man,
    That all shall hunt him down: 460
    Though he may roam the forest shade
    Like a bull gone wild from pasture
    To rage through glooms of stone.
    Doom comes down on him; flight will not avail him;
    For the world's heart calls him desolate,   465
    And the immortal voices follow, for ever follow.

455 son of Zeus: Apollo   **457 Furies:** avenging goddesses

STROPHE 2
But now a wilder thing is heard
From the old man skilled at hearing Fate in the wing-beat of a bird.
Bewildered as a blown bird, my soul hovers and can not find
Foothold in this debate, or any reason or rest of mind.   470
But no man ever brought—none can bring
Proof of strife between Thebes' royal house,
Labdakos' line, and the son of Polybos;°
And never until now has any man brought word
Of Laïos' dark death staining Oedipus the King.   475

ANTISTROPHE 2
Divine Zeus and Apollo hold
Perfect intelligence alone of all tales ever told;
And well though this diviner works, he works in his own night;
No man can judge that rough unknown or trust in second sight,
For wisdom changes hands among the wise.   480
Shall I believe my great lord criminal
At a raging word that a blind old man let fall?
I saw him, when the carrion woman faced him of old,
Prove his heroic mind. These evil words are lies.

Scene II

KREON   Men of Thebes: 485
   I am told that heavy accusations
   Have been brought against me by King Oedipus.

   I am not the kind of man to bear this tamely.

   If in these present difficulties
   He holds me accountable for any harm to him   490
   Through anything I have said or done—why, then,
   I do not value life in this dishonor.
   It is not as though this rumor touched upon
   Some private indiscretion. The matter is grave.
   The fact is that I am being called disloyal   495
   To the State, to my fellow citizens, to my friends.
CHORAGOS   He may have spoken in anger, not from his mind.
KREON   But did you not hear him say I was the one
   Who seduced the old prophet into lying?
CHORAGOS   The thing was said; I do not know how seriously.   500

---

473 son of Polybos: (at this point both the Chorus and Oedipus himself believe that he is the son of
Polybos of Corinth, not Laïos)

KREON   But you were watching him! Were his eyes steady?
  Did he look like a man in his right mind?
CHORAGOS   I do not know.
  I can not judge the behavior of great men.
  But here is the king himself.

(Enter OEDIPUS.)

OEDIPUS   So you dared come back.
  Why? How brazen of you to come to my house,   505
  You murderer!
                    Do you think I do not know
  That you plotted to kill me, plotted to steal my throne?
  Tell me, in God's name: am I coward, a fool,
  That you should dream you could accomplish this?
  A fool who could not see your slippery game?   510
  A coward, not to fight back when I saw it?
  You are the fool, Kreon, are you not? hoping
  Without support or friends to get a throne?
  Thrones may be won or bought: you could do neither.
KREON   Now listen to me. You have talked; let me talk, too.   515
  You can not judge unless you know the facts.
OEDIPUS   You speak well: there is one fact; but I find it hard
  To learn from the deadliest enemy I have.
KREON   That above all I must dispute with you.
OEDIPUS   That above all I will not hear you deny.   520
KREON   If you think there is anything good in being stubborn
  Against all reason, then I say you are wrong.
OEDIPUS   If you think a man can sin against his own kind
  And not be punished for it, I say you are mad.
KREON   I agree. But tell me: What have I done to you?   525
OEDIPUS   You advised me to send for that wizard, did you not?
KREON   I did. I should do it again.
OEDIPUS   Very well. Now tell me:
  How long has it been since Laïos—
KREON   What of Laïos?
OEDIPUS   Since he vanished in that onset by the road?
KREON   It was long ago, a long time.
OEDIPUS   And this prophet,   530
  Was he practicing here then?
KREON   He was; and with honor, as now.
OEDIPUS   Did he speak of me at that time?
KREON   He never did,
  At least, not when I was present.
OEDIPUS   But . . . the enquiry?
  I suppose you held one?

KREON   We did, but we learned nothing.

OEDIPUS   Why did the prophet not speak against me then?   535

KREON   I do not know; and I am the kind of man
Who holds his tongue when he has no facts to go on.

OEDIPUS   There's one fact that you know, and you could tell it.

KREON   What fact is that? If I know it, you shall have it.

OEDIPUS   If he were not involved with you, he could not say   540
That it was I who murdered Laïos.

KREON   If he says that, you are the one that knows it!—
But now it is my turn to question you.

OEDIPUS   Put your questions. I am no murderer.

KREON   First, then: You married my sister?

OEDIPUS   I married your sister.   545

KREON   And you rule the kingdom equally with her?

OEDIPUS   Everything that she wants she has from me.

KREON   And I am the third, equal to both of you?

OEDIPUS   That is why I call you a bad friend.

KREON   No. Reason it out, as I have done.   550
Think of this first: Would any sane man prefer
Power, with all a king's anxieties.
To that same power and the grace of sleep?
Certainly not I.
I have never longed for the king's power—only his rights.   555
Would any wise man differ from me in this?
As matters stand, I have my way in everything
With your consent, and no responsibilities.
If I were king, I should be a slave to policy.

How could I desire a scepter more   560
Than what is now mine—untroubled influence?
No, I have not gone mad; I need no honors,
Except those with the perquisites I have now.
I am welcome everywhere; every man salutes me,
And those who want your favor seek my ear,   565
Since I know how to manage what they ask.
Should I exchange this ease for that anxiety?
Besides, no sober mind is treasonable.
I hate anarchy
And never would deal with any man who likes it.   570
Test what I have said. Go to the priestess
At Delphi, ask if I quoted her correctly.
And as for this other thing: if I am found
Guilty of treason with Teiresias,
Then sentence me to death. You have my word   575
It is a sentence I should cast my vote for—
But not without evidence!

                                    You do wrong
When you take good men for bad, bad men for good.
A true friend thrown aside—why, life itself
Is not more precious!
                                    In time you will know this well: 580
For time, and time alone, will show the just man,
Though scoundrels are discovered in a day.
CHORAGOS   This is well said, and a prudent man would ponder it.
    Judgments too quickly formed are dangerous.
OEDIPUS   But is he not quick in his duplicity?   585
    And shall I not be quick to parry him?
    Would you have me stand still, hold my peace, and let
    This man win everything, through my inaction?
KREON   And you want—what is it, then? To banish me?
OEDIPUS   No, not exile. It is your death I want,   590
    So that all the world may see what treason means.
KREON   You will persist, then? You will not believe me?
OEDIPUS   How can I believe you?
KREON   Then you are a fool.
OEDIPUS   To save myself?
KREON   In justice, think of me.
OEDIPUS   You are evil incarnate.
KREON   But suppose that you are wrong?   595
OEDIPUS   Still I must rule.
KREON   But not if you rule badly.
OEDIPUS   O city, city!
KREON   It is my city, too!
CHORAGOS   Now, my lords, be still. I see the queen,
    Iokastê, coming from her palace chambers;
    And it is time she came, for the sake of you both.   600
    This dreadful quarrel can be resolved through her.

    (*Enter* IOKASTÊ.)

IOKASTÊ   Poor foolish men, what wicked din is this?
    With Thebes sick to death, is it not shameful
    That you should rake some private quarrel up?
    (*To* OEDIPUS) Come into the house.
                                    —And you, Kreon, go now: 605
    Let us have no more of this tumult over nothing.
KREON   Nothing? No, sister: what your husband plans for me
    Is one of two great evils: exile or death.
OEDIPUS   He is right.
                    Why, woman I have caught him squarely
                    Plotting against my life.

KREON   No! Let me die   610
    Accurst if ever I have wished you harm!
IOKASTÊ   Ah, believe it, Oedipus!
    In the name of the gods, respect this oath of his
    For my sake, for the sake of these people here!

STROPHE 1
CHORAGOS   Open your mind to her, my lord. Be ruled by her, I beg you!   615
OEDIPUS   What would you have me do?
CHORAGOS   Respect Kreon's word. He has never spoken like a fool,
    And now he has sworn an oath.
OEDIPUS   You know what you ask?
CHORAGOS   I do.
OEDIPUS   Speak on, then.
CHORAGOS   A friend so sworn should not be baited so,
    In blind malice, and without final proof.   620
OEDIPUS   You are aware, I hope, that what you say
    Means death for me, or exile at the least.

STROPHE 2
CHORAGOS   No, I swear by Helios,° first in Heaven!
    May I die friendless and accurst,
    The worst of deaths, if ever I meant that!   625
        It is the withering fields
          That hurt my sick heart:
        Must we bear all these ills,
          And now your bad blood as well?
OEDIPUS   Then let him go. And let me die, if I must,   630
    Or be driven by him in shame from the land of Thebes.
    It is your unhappiness, and not his talk,
    That touches me.
            As for him—
    Wherever he goes, hatred will follow him.
KREON   Ugly in yielding, as you were ugly in rage!   635
    Natures like yours chiefly torment themselves.
OEDIPUS   Can you not go? Can you not leave me?
KREON   I can
    You do not know me; but the city knows me,
    And in its eyes I am just, if not in yours.   *(Exit* KREON.*)*

ANTISTROPHE 1
CHORAGOS   Lady Iokastê, did you not ask the King to go to his
    chambers?   640
IOKASTÊ   First tell me what has happened.

---

623 Helios: the sun is here invoked as a kind of primary, general deity, not identified, as elsewhere
in mythology, with Apollo

CHORAGOS   There was suspicion without evidence; yet it rankled
 As even false charges will.
IOKASTÊ   On both sides?
CHORAGOS   On both.
IOKASTÊ   But what was said?
CHORAGOS   Oh let it rest, let it be done with!
 Have we not suffered enough?   645
OEDIPUS   You see to what your decency has brought you:
 You have made difficulties where my heart saw none.

ANTISTROPHE 2
CHORAGOS   Oedipus, it is not once only I have told you—
 You must know I should count myself unwise
 To the point of madness, should I now forsake you—   650
   You, under whose hand,
    In the storm of another time,
   Our dear land sailed out free.
    But now stand fast at the helm!
IOKASTÊ   In God's name, Oedipus, inform your wife as well: 655
 Why are you so set in this hard anger?
OEDIPUS   I will tell you, for none of these men deserves
 My confidence as you do. It is Kreon's work,
 His treachery, his plotting against me.
IOKASTÊ   Go on, if you can make this clear to me.   660
OEDIPUS   He charges me with the murder of Laïos.
IOKASTÊ   Has he some knowledge? Or does he speak from hearsay?
OEDIPUS   He would not commit himself to such a charge,
 But he has brought in that damnable soothsayer
 To tell his story.
IOKASTÊ   Set your mind at rest.   665
 If it is a question of soothsayers, I tell you
 That you will find no man whose craft gives knowledge
 Of the unknowable.
      Here is my proof:

An oracle was reported to Laïos once
(I will not say from Phoibos himself, but from   670
His appointed ministers, at any rate)
That his doom would be death at the hands of his own son—
His son, born of his flesh and of mine!

Now, you remember the story: Laïos was killed
By marauding strangers where three highways meet;   675
But his child had not been three days in this world
Before the king had pierced the baby's ankles
And left him to die on a lonely mountainside.

Thus, Apollo never caused that child

To kill his father, and it was not Laïos' fate   680
To die at the hands of his son, as he had feared.
This is what prophets and prophecies are worth!
Have no dread of them.
                              It is God himself
Who can show us what he wills, in his own way.

OEDIPUS   How strange a shadowy memory crossed my mind,   685
    Just now while you were speaking; it chilled my heart.

IOKASTÊ   What do you mean? What memory do you speak of?

OEDIPUS   If I understand you, Laïos was killed
    At a place where three roads meet.

IOKASTÊ   So it was said;
    We have no later story.

OEDIPUS   Where did it happen?   690

IOKASTÊ   Phokis, it is called: at a place where the Theban Way
    Divides into the roads toward Delphi and Daulia.

OEDIPUS   When?

IOKASTÊ   We had the news not long before you came
    And proved the right to your succession here.

OEDIPUS   Ah, what net has God been weaving for me?   695

IOKASTÊ   Oedipus! Why does this trouble you?

OEDIPUS   Do not ask me yet.
    First, tell me how Laïos looked, and tell me
    How old he was.

IOKASTÊ   He was tall, his hair just touched
    With white; his form was not unlike your own.

OEDIPUS   I think that I myself may be accurst   700
    By my own ignorant edict.

IOKASTÊ   You speak strangely.
    It makes me tremble to look at you, my king.

OEDIPUS   I am not sure that the blind man can not see.
    But I should know better if you were to tell me—

IOKASTÊ   Anything—though I dread to hear you ask it.   705

OEDIPUS   Was the king lightly escorted, or did he ride
    With a large company, as a ruler should?

IOKASTÊ   There were five men with him in all: one was a herald.
    And a single chariot, which he was driving.

OEDIPUS   Alas, that makes it plain enough!
                                    But who—   710
    Who told you how it happened?

IOKASTÊ   A household servant,
    The only one to escape.

OEDIPUS   And is he still
    A servant of ours?

IOKASTÊ   No; for when he came back at last
    And found you enthroned in the place of the dead king,

He came to me, touched my hand with his, and begged   715
That I would send him away to the frontier district
Where only the shepherds go—
As far away from the city as I could send him.
I granted his prayer; for although the man was a slave,
He had earned more than this favor at my hands.   720

OEDIPUS   Can he be called back quickly?

IOKASTÊ   Easily.
   But why?

OEDIPUS   I have taken too much upon myself
   Without enquiry; therefore I wish to consult him.

IOKASTÊ   Then he shall come.

                    But am I not one also
To whom you might confide these fears of yours?   725

OEDIPUS   That is your right; it will not be denied you,
   Now least of all; for I have reached a pitch
   Of wild foreboding. Is there anyone
   To whom I should sooner speak?

Polybos of Corinth is my father.   730
My mother is a Dorian: Meropê.
I grew up chief among the men of Corinth
Until a strange thing happened—
Not worth my passion, it may be, but strange.
At a feast, a drunken man maundering in his cups   735
Cries out that I am not my father's son!

I contained myself that night, though I felt anger
And a sinking heart. The next day I visited
My father and mother, and questioned them. They stormed,
Calling it all the slanderous rant of a fool;   740
And this relieved me. Yet the suspicion
Remained always aching in my mind;
I knew there was talk; I could not rest;
And finally, saying nothing to my parents,
I went to the shrine at Delphi.   745

The god dismissed my question without reply;
He spoke of other things.
                    Some were clear,

Full of wretchedness, dreadful, unbearable:
As, that I should lie with my own mother, breed
Children from whom all men would turn their eyes;   750
And that I should be my father's murderer.

I heard all this, and fled. And from that day
Corinth to me was only in the stars

Descending in that quarter of the sky,
As I wandered farther and farther on my way   755
To a land where I should never see the evil
Sung by the oracle. And I came to this country
Where, so you say, King Laïos was killed.

I will tell you all that happened there, my lady.

There were three highways   760
Coming together at a place I passed;
And there a herald came towards me, and a chariot
Drawn by horses, with a man such as you describe
Seated in it. The groom leading the horses
Forced me off the road at his lord's command;   765
But as this charioteer lurched over towards me
I struck him in my rage. The old man saw me
And brought his double goad down upon my head
As I came abreast.
                    He was paid back, and more!
Swinging my club in this right hand I knocked him   770
Out of his car, and he rolled on the ground.
                                    I killed him.

I killed them all.
Now if that stranger and Laïos were—kin,
Where is a man more miserable than I?
More hated by the gods? Citizen and alien alike   775
Must never shelter me or speak to me—
I must be shunned by all.
                         And I myself
Pronounced this malediction upon myself!

Think of it: I have touched you with these hands,
These hands that killed your husband. What defilement!   780

Am I all evil, then? It must be so,
Since I must flee from Thebes, yet never again
See my own countrymen, my own country,
For fear of joining my mother in marriage
And killing Polybos, my father.
                                Ah,   785
If I was created so, born to this fate,
Who could deny the savagery of God?

O holy majesty of heavenly powers!
May I never see that day! Never!
Rather let me vanish from the race of men   790
Than know the abomination destined me!

CHORAGOS   We too, my lord, have felt dismay at this.
    But there is hope: you have yet to hear the shepherd.
OEDIPUS   Indeed, I fear no other hope is left me.
IOKASTÊ   What do you hope from him when he comes?
OEDIPUS   This much: 795
    If his account of the murder tallies with yours,
    Then I am cleared.
IOKASTÊ   What was it that I said
    Of such importance?
OEDIPUS   Why, "marauders," you said,
    Killed the king, according to this man's story.
    If he maintains that still, if there were several,   800
    Clearly the guilt is not mine: I was alone.
    But if he says one man, singlehanded, did it,
    Then the evidence all points to me.
IOKASTÊ   You may be sure that he said there were several;
    And can he call back that story now? He can not.   805
    The whole city heard it as plainly as I.
    But suppose he alters some detail of it:
    He can not ever show that Laïos' death
    Fulfilled the oracle: for Apollo said
    My child was doomed to kill him; and my child—   810
    Poor baby!—it was my child that died first.

    No. From now on, where oracles are concerned,
    I would not waste a second thought on any.
OEDIPUS   You may be right.
                     But come: let someone go
For the shepherd at once. This matter must be settled.   815
IOKASTÊ   I will send for him.
    I would not wish to cross you in anything,
    And surely not in this.—Let us go in.   *(Exeunt into the palace.)*

Ode II

STROPHE 1
CHORUS   Let me be reverent in the ways of right,
    Lowly the paths I journey on;   820
    Let all my words and actions keep
    The laws of the pure universe
    From highest Heaven handed down.
    For Heaven is their bright nurse,
    Those generations of the realms of light;   825
    Ah, never of mortal kind were they begot,

Nor are they slaves of memory, lost in sleep:
Their Father is greater than Time, and ages not.

ANTISTROPHE 1

The tyrant is a child of Pride
Who drinks from his great sickening cup   830
Recklessness and vanity,
Until from his high crest headlong
He plummets to the dust of hope.
That strong man is not strong.
But let no fair ambition be denied;   835
May God protect the wrestler for the State
In government, in comely policy,
Who will fear God, and on His ordinance wait.

STROPHE 2

Haughtiness and the high hand of disdain
Tempt and outrage God's holy law;   840
And any mortal who dares hold
No immortal Power in awe
Will be caught up in a net of pain:
The price for which his levity is sold.
Let each man take due earnings, then,   845
And keep his hands from holy things,
And from blasphemy stand apart—
Else the crackling blast of heaven
Blows on his head, and on his desperate heart.
Though fools will honor impious men,   850
In their cities no tragic poet sings.

ANTISTROPHE 2

Shall we lose faith in Delphi's obscurities,
We who have heard the world's core
Discredited, and the sacred wood
Of Zeus at Elis° praised no more?   855
The deeds and the strange prophecies
Must make a pattern yet to be understood.
Zeus, if indeed you are lord of all,
Throned in light over night and day,
Mirror this in your endless mind: 860
Our masters call the oracle
Words on the wind, and the Delphic vision blind!
Their hearts no longer know Apollo,
And reverence for the gods has died away.

855 Elis: where Olympia (along with Delphi, the other great religious center of Greece) was situated

Scene III

(Enter IOKASTÊ.*)*

IOKASTÊ   Princes of Thebes, it has occurred to me   865
           To visit the altars of the gods, bearing
           These branches as a suppliant, and this incense.
           Our king is not himself: his noble soul
           Is overwrought with fantasies of dread,
           Else he would consider   870
           The new prophecies in the light of the old.
           He will listen to any voice that speaks disaster,
           And my advice goes for nothing.

(She approaches the altar, R.)

                                                    To you, then, Apollo,
           Lycéan lord, since you are nearest, I turn in prayer.
           Receive these offerings, and grant us deliverance   875
           From defilement. Our hearts are heavy with fear
           When we see our leader distracted, as helpless sailors
           Are terrified by the confusion of their helmsman.

(Enter MESSENGER.*)*

MESSENGER   Friends, no doubt you can direct me:
             Where shall I find the house of Oedipus,   880
             Or, better still, where is the king himself?
CHORAGOS   It is this very place, stranger; he is inside.
             This is his wife and mother of his children.
MESSENGER   I wish her happiness in a happy house,
             Blest in all the fulfillment of her marriage.   885
IOKASTÊ   I wish as much for you: your courtesy
           Deserves a like good fortune. But now, tell me:
           Why have you come? What have you to say to us?
MESSENGER   Good news, my lady, for your house and your husband.
IOKASTÊ What news? Who sent you here?
MESSENGER   I am from Corinth.   890
             The news I bring ought to mean joy for you,
             Though it may be you will find some grief in it.
IOKASTÊ   What is it? How can it touch us in both ways?
MESSENGER   The word is that the people of the Isthmus
             Intend to call Oedipus to be their king.   895
IOKASTÊ   But old King Polybos—is he not reigning still?
MESSENGER   No. Death holds him in his sepulchre.

IOKASTÊ   What are you saying? Polybos is dead?

MESSENGER   If I am not telling the truth, may I die myself.

IOKASTÊ *(to a* MAIDSERVANT*)*   Go in, go quickly; tell this to your
　　master.   900

　　O riddlers of God's will, where are you now!
　　This was the man whom Oedipus, long ago,
　　Feared so, fled so, in dread of destroying him—
　　But it was another fate by which he died.

　　(Enter OEDIPUS, *C.)*

OEDIPUS   Dearest Iokastê, why have you sent for me?   905

IOKASTÊ   Listen to what this man says, and then tell me
　　What has become of the solemn prophecies.

OEDIPUS   Who is this man? What is his news for me?

IOKASTÊ   He has come from Corinth to announce your father's death!

OEDIPUS   Is it true, stranger? Tell me in your own words.   910

MESSENGER   I can not say it more clearly: the king is dead.

OEDIPUS   Was it by treason? Or by an attack of illness?

MESSENGER   A little thing brings old men to their rest.

OEDIPUS   It was sickness, then?

MESSENGER   Yes, and his many years.

OEDIPUS   Ah!   915
　　Why should a man respect the Pythian hearth,° or
　　Give heed to the birds that jangle above his head?
　　They prophesied that I should kill Polybos,
　　Kill my own father; but he is dead and buried,
　　And I am here—I never touched him, never,   920
　　Unless he died of grief for my departure,
　　And thus, in a sense, through me. No. Polybos
　　Has packed the oracles off with him underground.
　　They are empty words.

IOKASTÊ   Had I not told you so?

OEDIPUS   You had; it was my faint heart that betrayed me.   925

IOKASTÊ   From now on never think of those things again.

OEDIPUS   And yet—must I not fear my mother's bed?

IOKASTÊ   Why should anyone in this world be afraid,
　　Since Fate rules us and nothing can be foreseen?
　　A man should live only for the present day.   930

　　Have no more fear of sleeping with your mother:
　　How many men, in dreams, have lain with their mothers!
　　No reasonable man is troubled by such things.

916 **Pythian hearth:** the oracle of Apollo at Delphi

OEDIPUS   That is true; only—
    If only my mother were not still alive!   935
    But she is alive. I can not help my dread.
IOKASTÊ   Yet this news of your father's death is wonderful.
OEDIPUS   Wonderful. But I fear the living woman.
MESSENGER   Tell me, who is this woman that you fear?
OEDIPUS   It is Meropê, man; the wife of King Polybos.   940
MESSENGER   Meropê? Why should you be afraid of her?
OEDIPUS   An oracle of the gods, a dreadful saying.
MESSENGER   Can you tell me about it or are you sworn to silence?
OEDIPUS   I can tell you, and I will.
    Apollo said through his prophet that I was the man   945
    Who should marry his own mother, shed his father's blood
    With his own hands. And so, for all these years
    I have kept clear of Corinth, and no harm has come—
    Though it would have been sweet to see my parents again.
MESSENGER   And is this the fear that drove you out of Corinth?   950
OEDIPUS   Would you have me kill my father?
MESSENGER   As for that
    You must be reassured by the news I gave you.
OEDIPUS   If you could reassure me, I would reward you.
MESSENGER   I had that in mind, I will confess: I thought
    I could count on you when you returned to Corinth.   955
OEDIPUS   No: I will never go near my parents again.
MESSENGER   Ah, son, you still do not know what you are doing—
OEDIPUS   What do you mean? In the name of God tell me!
MESSENGER   —If these are your reasons for not going home.
OEDIPUS   I tell you, I fear the oracle may come true.   960
MESSENGER   And guilt may come upon you through your parents?
OEDIPUS   That is the dread that is always in my heart.
MESSENGER   Can you not see that all your fears are groundless?
OEDIPUS   Groundless? Am I not my parents' son?
MESSENGER   Polybos was not your father.
OEDIPUS   Not my father?   965
MESSENGER   No more your father than the man speaking to you.
OEDIPUS   But you are nothing to me!
MESSENGER   Neither was he.
OEDIPUS   Then why did he call me son?
MESSENGER   I will tell you:
    Long ago he had you from my hands, as a gift.
OEDIPUS   Then how could he love me so, if I was not his?   970
MESSENGER   He had no children, and his heart turned to you.
OEDIPUS   What of you? Did you buy me? Did you find me by chance?
MESSENGER   I came upon you in the woody vales of Kithairon.
OEDIPUS   And what were you doing there?
MESSENGER   Tending my flocks.

OEDIPUS   A wandering shepherd?

MESSENGER   But your savior, son, that day.   975

OEDIPUS   From what did you save me?

MESSENGER   Your ankles should tell you that.

OEDIPUS   Ah, stranger, why do you speak of that childhood pain?

MESSENGER   I pulled the skewer that pinned your feet together.

OEDIPUS   I have had the mark as long as I can remember.

MESSENGER   That was why you were given the name you bear.°   980

OEDIPUS   God! Was it my father or my mother who did it?
     Tell me!

MESSENGER   I do not know. The man who gave you to me
     Can tell you better than I.

OEDIPUS   It was not you that found me, but another?

MESSENGER   It was another shepherd gave you to me.   985

OEDIPUS   Who was he? Can you tell me who he was?

MESSENGER   I think he was said to be one of Laïos' people.

OEDIPUS   You mean the Laïos who was king here years ago?

MESSENGER   Yes; King Laïos; and the man was one of his herdsmen.

OEDIPUS   Is he still alive? Can I see him?

MESSENGER   These men here   990
     Know best about such things.

OEDIPUS   Does anyone here
     Know this shepherd that he is talking about?
     Have you seen him in the fields, or in the town?
     If you have, tell me. It is time things were made plain.

CHORAGOS   I think the man he means is that same shepherd   995
     You have already asked to see. Iokastê perhaps
     Could tell you something.

OEDIPUS   Do you know anything
     About him, Lady? Is he the man we have summoned?
     Is that the man this shepherd means?

IOKASTÊ   Why think of him?
     Forget this herdsman. Forget it all.   1000
     This talk is a waste of time.

OEDIPUS   How can you say that,
     When the clues to my true birth are in my hands?

IOKASTÊ   For God's love, let us have no more questioning!
     Is your life nothing to you?
     My own is pain enough for me to bear.   1005

OEDIPUS   You need not worry. Suppose my mother a slave,
     And born of slaves: no baseness can touch you.

IOKASTÊ   Listen to me, I beg you: do not do this thing!

OEDIPUS   I will not listen; the truth must be made known.

IOKASTÊ   Everything that I say is for your own good!

---

980 name you bear: "Oedipus" means "swollen-foot" in Greek

OEDIPUS   My own good   1010
    Snaps my patience, then; I want none of it.
IOKASTÊ   You are fatally wrong! May you never learn who you are!
OEDIPUS   Go, one of you, and bring the shepherd here.
    Let us leave this woman to brag of her royal name.
IOKASTÊ   Ah, miserable!   1015
    That is the only word I have for you now.
    That is the only word I can ever have.   *(Exit into the palace.)*
CHORAGOS   Why has she left us, Oedipus? Why has she gone
    In such a passion of sorrow? I fear this silence:
    Something dreadful may come of it.
OEDIPUS   Let it come!   1020
    However base my birth, I must know about it.
    The Queen, like a woman, is perhaps ashamed
    To think of my low origin.° But I
    Am a child of Luck; I can not be dishonored.
    Luck is my mother; the passing months, my brothers,   1025
    Have seen me rich and poor.
                   If this is so,
    How could I wish that I were someone else?
    How could I not be glad to know my birth?

Ode III

STROPHE

CHORUS   If ever the coming time were known
    To my heart's pondering,   1030
    Kithairon, now by Heaven I see the torches
    At the festival of the next full moon,
    And see the dance, and hear the choir sing
    A grace to your gentle shade:
    Mountain where Oedipus was found,   1035
    O mountain guard of a noble race!
    May the god who heals us lend his aid,
    And let that glory come to pass
    For our king's cradling-ground.

ANTISTROPHE

Of the nymphs that flower beyond the years,   1040
    Who bore you, royal child,
    To Pan of the hills or the timberline Apollo,

1023 **low origin:** Oedipus' origin, we remember, is even higher than he thinks—he is the legitimate hereditary ruler, alas, of Thebes, not merely the proclaimed king

Cold in delight where the upland clears,
Or Hermês for whom Kyllenê's heights° are piled?
Or flushed as evening cloud,   1045
Great Dionysos, roamer of mountains,
He—was it he who found you there,
And caught you up in his own proud
Arms from the sweet god-ravisher
Who laughed by the Muses' fountains?   1050

Scene IV

OEDIPUS   Sirs: though I do not know the man,
    I think I see him coming, this shepherd we want:
    He is old, like our friend here, and the men
    Bringing him seem to be servants of my house.
    But you can tell, if you have ever seen him.   1055

(Enter SHEPHERD escorted by SERVANTS.)

CHORAGOS   I know him, he was Laïos' man. You can trust him.
OEDIPUS   Tell me first, you from Corinth: is this the shepherd
    We were discussing?
MESSENGER   This is the very man.
OEDIPUS (to SHEPHERD)   Come here. No, look at me. You must answer
    Everything I ask.—You belonged to Laïos?   1060
SHEPHERD   Yes: born his slave, brought up in his house.
OEDIPUS   Tell me: what kind of work did you do for him?
SHEPHERD   I was a shepherd of his, most of my life.
OEDIPUS   Where mainly did you go for pasturage?
SHEPHERD   Sometimes Kithairon, sometimes the hills near-by.   1065
OEDIPUS   Do you remember ever seeing this man out there?
SHEPHERD   What would he be doing there? This man?
OEDIPUS   This man standing here. Have you ever seen him before?
SHEPHERD   No. At least, not to my recollection.
MESSENGER   And that is not strange, my lord. But I'll refresh   1070
    His memory: he must remember when we two
    Spent three whole seasons together, March to September,
    On Kithairon or thereabouts. He had two flocks;
    I had one. Each autumn I'd drive mine home
    And he would go back with his to Laïos' sheepfold.—   1075
    Is this not ture, just as I have described it?

1044 Kyllenê's heights: Mount Kyllenê, sacred to Hermês, messenger of the gods

SHEPHERD   True, yes; but it was all so long ago.
MESSENGER   Well, then: do you remember, back in those days,
    That you gave me a baby boy to bring up as my own?
SHEPHERD   What if I did? What are you trying to say?   1080
MESSENGER   King Oedipus was once that little child.
SHEPHERD   Damn you, hold your tongue!
OEDIPUS   No more of that!
    It is your tongue needs watching, not this man's.
SHEPHERD   My king, my master, what is it I have done wrong?
OEDIPUS   You have not answered his question about the boy.   1085
SHEPHERD   He does not know . . . He is only making trouble . . .
OEDIPUS   Come, speak plainly, or it will go hard with you.
SHEPHERD   In God's name, do not torture an old man!
OEDIPUS   Come here, one of you; bind his arms behind him.
SHEPHERD   Unhappy king! What more do you wish to learn?   1090
OEDIPUS   Did you give this man the child he speaks of?
SHEPHERD   I did.
    And I would to God I had died that very day.
OEDIPUS   You will die now unless you speak the truth.
SHEPHERD   Yet if I speak the truth, I am worse than dead.
OEDIPUS (*to* ATTENDANT)   He intends to draw it out, apparently—   1095
SHEPHERD   No! I have told you already that I gave him the boy.
OEDIPUS   Where did you get him? From your house? From somewhere
    else?
SHEPHERD   Not from mine, no. A man gave him to me.
OEDIPUS   Is that man here? Whose house did he belong to?
SHEPHERD   For God's love, my king, do not ask me any more!   1100
OEDIPUS   You are a dead man if I have to ask you again.
SHEPHERD   Then . . . Then the child was from the palace of Laïos.
OEDIPUS   A slave child? or a child of his own line?
SHEPHERD   Ah, I am on the brink of dreadful speech!
OEDIPUS   And I of dreadful hearing. Yet I must hear.   1105
SHEPHERD   If you must be told, then . . .
                                    They said it was Laïos' child;
    But it is your wife who can tell you about that.
OEDIPUS   My wife!—Did she give it to you?
SHEPHERD   My lord, she did.
OEDIPUS   Do you know why?
SHEPHERD   I was told to get rid of it.
OEDIPUS   Oh heartless mother!
SHEPHERD   But in dread of prophecies . . .   1110
OEDIPUS   Tell me.
SHEPHERD   It was said that the boy would kill his own father.
OEDIPUS   Then why did you give him over to this old man?
SHEPHERD   I pitied the baby, my king,
    And I thought that this man would take him far away

To his own country.
He saved him—but for what a fate!   1115
For if you are what this man says you are,
No man living is more wretched than Oedipus.

OEDIPUS   Ah God!
It was true!
All the prophecies!
—Now,
O Light, may I look on you for the last time!   1120
I, Oedipus,
Oedipus, damned in his birth, in his marriage damned,
Damned in the blood he shed with his own hand!

(He rushes into the palace.)

Ode IV

STROPHE 1

CHORUS   Alas for the seed of men.
What measure shall I give these generations   1125
That breathe on the void and are void
And exist and do not exist?
Who bears more weight of joy
Than mass of sunlight shifting in images,
Or who shall make his thought stay on   1130
That down time drifts away?
Your splendor is all fallen.
O naked brow of wrath and tears,
O change of Oedipus!
I who saw your days call no man blest—   1135
Your great days like ghósts góne.

ANTISTROPHE 1

That mind was a strong bow.
Deep, how deep you drew it then, hard archer,
At a dim fearful range,
And brought dear glory down!   1140
You overcame the stranger—
The virgin with her hooking lion claws—
And though death sang, stood like a tower
To make pale Thebes take heart.
Fortress against our sorrow!   1145
True king, giver of laws,
Majestic Oedipus!
No prince in Thebes had ever such renown,
No prince won such grace of power.

STROPHE 2

And now of all men ever known   1150
Most pitiful is this man's story:
His fortunes are most changed, his state
Fallen to a low slave's
Ground under bitter fate.
O Oedipus, most royal one!   1155
The great door that expelled you to the light
Gave at night—ah, gave night to your glory:
As to the father, to the fathering son.
All understood too late.
How could that queen whom Laïos won,   1160
The garden that he harrowed at his height,
Be silent when that act was done?

ANTISTROPHE 2

But all eyes fail before time's eye,
All actions come to justice there.
Though never willed, though far down the deep past,   1165
Your bed, your dred sirings,
Are brought to book at last.
Child by Laïos doomed to die,
Then doomed to lose that fortunate little death,
Would God you never took breath in this air   1170
That with my wailing lips I take to cry:
For I weep the world's outcast.
I was blind, and now I can tell why:
Asleep, for you had given ease of breath
To Thebes, while the false years went by.   1175

Éxodos

(Enter, from the palace, SECOND MESSENGER.*)*

SECOND MESSENGER   Elders of Thebes, most honored in this land,
What horrors are yours to see and hear, what weight
Of sorrow to be endured, if, true to your birth,
You venerate the line of Labdakos!
I think neither Istros nor Phasis,° those great rivers,   1180
Could purify this place of all the evil
It shelters now, or soon must bring to light—
Evil not done unconsciously, but willed.

The greatest griefs are those we cause ourselves.

1180 *Istros . . . Phasis:* the Danube, and the Phasis, a river in the Caucasus

CHORAGOS   Surely, friend, we have grief enough already;   1185
    What new sorrow do you mean?
SECOND MESSENGER   The queen is dead.
CHORAGOS   O miserable queen! But at whose hand!
SECOND MESSENGER   Her own.
    The full horror of what happened you can not know,
    For you did not see it; but I, who did, will tell you
    As clearly as I can how she met her death.   1190

    When she had left us,
    In passionate silence, passing through the court,
    She ran to her apartment in the house,
    Her hair clutched by the fingers of both hands.
    She closed the doors behind her; then, by that bed   1195
    Where long ago the fatal son was conceived—
    That son who should bring about his father's death—
    We heard her call upon Laïos, dead so many years,
    And heard her wail for the double fruit of her marriage,
    A husband by her husband, children by her child.   1200

    Exactly how she died I do not know:
    For Oedipus burst out moaning and would not let us
    Keep vigil to the end: it was by him
    As he stormed about the room that our eyes were caught.
    From one to another of us he went, begging a sword,   1205
    Hunting the wife who was not his wife, the mother
    Whose womb had carried his own children and himself.
    I do not know: it was none of us aided him,
    But surely one of the gods was in control!
    For with a dreadful cry   1210
    He hurled his weight, as though wrenched out of himself,
    At the twin doors: the bolts gave, and he rushed in.
    And there we saw her hanging, her body swaying
    From the cruel cord she had noosed about her neck.
    A great sob broke from him, heartbreaking to hear,   1215
    As he loosed the rope and lowered her to the ground.

    I would blot out from my mind what happened next!
    For the king ripped from her gown the golden brooches
    That were her ornament, and raised them, and plunged them down
    Straight into his own eyeballs,° crying, "No more,   1220
    No more shall you look on the misery about me,
    The horrors of my own doing! Too long you have known
    The faces of those whom I should never have seen,
    Too long been blind to those for whom I was searching!

1220 eyeballs: the Greek word here, *"arthra,"* is the same one used for the ankles at lines 677 and
976

From this hour, go in darkness!" And as he spoke,   1225
He struck at his eyes—not once, but many times;
And the blood spattered his beard,
Bursting from his ruined sockets like red hail.

So from the unhappiness of two this evil has sprung,
A curse on the man and woman alike. The old   1230
Happiness of the house of Labdakos
Was happiness enough: where is it today?
It is all wailing and ruin, disgrace, death—all
The misery of mankind that has a name—
And it is wholly and for ever theirs.   1235

CHORAGOS   Is he in agony still? Is there no rest for him?

SECOND MESSENGER   He is calling for someone to open the doors wide
So that all the children of Kadmos may look upon
His father's murderer, his mother's—no,
I can not say it!

                  And then he will leave Thebes,   1240
Self-exiled, in order that the curse
Which he himself pronounced may depart from the house.
He is weak, and there is none to lead him,
So terrible is his suffering.

                  But you will see:
Look, the doors are opening; in a moment   1245
You will see a thing that would crush a heart of stone.

(The central door is opened; OEDIPUS, blinded, is led in.)

CHORAGOS   Dreadful indeed for men to see.
    Never have my own eyes
    Looked on a sight so full of fear.

    Oedipus!   1250
    What madness came upon you, what daemon°
    Leaped on your life with heavier
    Punishment than a mortal man can bear?
    No: I can not even
    Look at you, poor ruined one.   1255
    And I would speak, question, ponder,
    If I were able. No.
    You make me shudder.

OEDIPUS   God. God.
    Is there a sorrow greater?   1260
    Where shall I find harbor in this world?

1251 **daemon:** god

My voice is hurled far on a dark wind.
What has God done to me?
CHORAGOS   Too terrible to think of, or to see.

STROPHE 1
OEDIPUS   O cloud of night,   1265
 Never to be turned away: night coming on,
 I can not tell how: night like a shroud!
 My fair winds brought me here.
         O God. Again
 The pain of the spikes where I had sight,
 The flooding pain   1270
 Of memory, never to be gouged out.
CHORAGOS   This is not strange.
 You suffer it all twice over, remorse in pain,
 Pain in remorse.

ANTISTROPHE 1
OEDIPUS   Ah dear friend   1275
 Are you faithful even yet, you alone?
 Are you still standing near me, will you stay here,
 Patient, to care for the blind?
        The blind man!
 Yet even blind I know who it is attends me,
 By the voice's tone—   1280
 Though my new darkness hide the comforter.
CHORAGOS   Oh fearful act!
 What god was it drove you to rake black
 Night across your eyes?

STROPHE 2
OEDIPUS   Apollo. Apollo. Dear   1285
 Children, the god was Apollo.
 He brought my sick, sick fate upon me.
 But the blinding hand was my own!
 How could I bear to see
 When all my sight was horror everywhere?   1290
CHORAGOS   Everywhere; that is true.
OEDIPUS   And now what is left?
 Images? Love? A greeting even,
 Sweet to the senses? Is there anything?
 Ah, no friends: lead me away.   1295
 Lead me away from Thebes.
       Lead the great wreck
 And hell of Oedipus, whom the gods hate.
CHORAGOS   Your misery, you are not blind to that.
 Would God you had never found it out!

ANTISTROPHE 2

OEDIPUS   Death take the man who unbound   1300
    My feet on that hillside
    And delivered me from death to life! What life?
    If only I had died,
    This weight of monstrous doom
    Could not have dragged me and my darlings down.   1305

CHORAGOS   I would have wished the same.

OEDIPUS   Oh never to have come here
    With my father's blood upon me! Never
    To have been the man they call his mother's husband!
    Oh accurst! Oh child of evil,   1310
    To have entered that wretched bed—
                 the selfsame one!
    More primal than sin itself, this fell to me.

CHORAGOS   I do not know what words to offer you.
    You were better dead than alive and blind.

OEDIPUS   Do not counsel me any more. This punishment   1315
    That I have laid upon myself is just.
    If I had eyes,
    I do not know how I could bear the sight
    Of my father, when I came to the house of Death,
    Or my mother: for I have sinned against them both   1320
    So vilely that I could not make my peace
    By strangling my own life.
                Or do you think my children,
    Born as they were born, would be sweet to my eyes?
    Ah never, never! Nor this town with its high walls,
    Nor the holy images of the gods.
                 For I,   1325
    Thrice miserable!—Oedipus, noblest of all the line
    Of Kadmos, have condemned myself to enjoy
    These things no more, by my own malediction
    Expelling that man whom the gods declared
    To be a defilement in the house of Laïos.   1330
    After exposing the rankness of my own guilt,
    How could I look men frankly in the eyes?
    No, I swear it,
    If I could have stifled my hearing at it source,
    I would have done it and made all this body   1335
    A tight cell of misery, blank to light and sound:
    So I should have been safe in my dark mind
    Beyond external evil.
             Ah Kithairon!
    Why did you shelter me? When I was cast upon you,

Why did I not die? Then I should never   1340
Have shown the world my execrable birth.

Ah Polybos! Corinth, city that I believed
The ancient seat of my ancestors: how fair
I seemed, your child! And all the while this evil
Was cancerous within me!

       For I am sick   1345
In my own being, sick in my origin.

O three roads, dark ravine, woodland and way
Where three roads met: you, drinking my father's blood,
My own blood, spilled by my own hand: can you remember
The unspeakable things I did there, and the things   1350
I went on from there to do?

       O marriage, marriage!
The act that engendered me, and again the act
Performed by the son in the same bed—

          Ah, the net
Of incest, mingling fathers, brothers, sons,
With brides, wives, mothers: the last evil   1355
That can be known by men: no tongue can say
How evil!

    No. For the love of God, conceal me
Somewhere far from Thebes; or kill me; or hurl me
Into the sea, away from men's eyes for ever.

Come, lead me. You need not fear to touch me.   1360
Of all men, I alone can bear this guilt.

(Enter KREON.*)*

CHORAGOS Kreon is here now. As to what you ask,
  He may decide the course to take. He only
  Is left to protect the city in your place.
OEDIPUS Alas, how can I speak to him? What right have I   1365
  To beg his courtesy whom I have deeply wronged?
KREON I have not come to mock you, Oedipus,
  Or to reproach you, either. *(To* ATTENDANTS*)*
       —You, standing there:
  If you have lost all respect for man's dignity,
  At least respect the flame of Lord Helios:
  Do not allow this pollution to show itself   1370
  Openly here, an affront to the earth
  And Heaven's rain and the light of day. No, take him
  Into the house as quickly as you can.

For it is proper   1375
That only the close kindred see his grief.
OEDIPUS   I pray you in God's name, since your courtesy
Ignores my dark expectation, visiting
With mercy this man of all men most execrable:
Give me what I ask—for your good, not for mine.   1380
KREON   And what is it that you turn to me begging for?
OEDIPUS   Drive me out of this country as quickly as may be
To a place where no human voice can ever greet me.
KREON   I should have done that before now—only,
God's will had not been wholly revealed to me.   1385
OEDIPUS   But his command is plain: the parricide
Must be destroyed. I am that evil man.
KREON   That is the sense of it, yes; but as things are,
We had best discover clearly what is to be done.
OEDIPUS   You would learn more about a man like me?   1390
KREON   You are ready now to listen to the god.
OEDIPUS   I will listen. But it is to you
That I must turn for help. I beg you, hear me.

The woman in there—
Give her whatever funeral you think proper: 1395
She is your sister.
                    —But let me go, Kreon!
Let me purge my father's Thebes of the pollution
Of my living here, and go out to the wild hills,
To Kithairon, that has won such fame with me,
The tomb my mother and father appointed for me,   1400
And let me die there, as they willed I should.
And yet I know
Death will not ever come to me through sickness
Or in any natural way: I have been preserved
For some unthinkable fate. But let that be.   1405

As for my sons, you need not care for them.
They are men, they will find some way to live.
But my poor daughters, who have shared my table,
Who never before have been parted from their father—
Take care of them, Kreon; do this for me.   1410

And will you let me touch them with my hands
A last time, and let us weep together?
Be kind, my lord,
Great prince, be kind!
                    Could I but touch them,
They would be mine again, as when I had my eyes.   1415

(Enter ANTIGONE *and* ISMENE, *attended.)*

Ah, God!
Is it my dearest children I hear weeping?
Has Kreon pitied me and sent my daughters?
KREON   Yes, Oedipus: I knew that they were dear to you
In the old days, and know you must love them still.   1420
OEDIPUS   May God bless you for this—and be a friendlier
Guardian to you than he has been to me!

Children, where are you?
Come quickly to my hands: they are your brother's—
Hands that have brought your father's once clear eyes   1425
To this way of seeing—
                          Ah dearest ones,
I had neither sight nor knowledge then, your father
By the woman who was the source of his own life!
And I weep for you—having no strength to see you—,
I weep for you when I think of the bitterness   1430
That men will visit upon you all your lives.
What homes, what festivals can you attend
Without being forced to depart again in tears?
And when you come to marriageable age,
Where is the man, my daughters, who would dare   1435
Risk the bane that lies on all my children?
Is there any evil wanting? Your father killed
His father; sowed the womb of her who bore him;
Engendered you at the fount of his own existence!
That is what they will say of you.

                          Then, whom   1440
Can you ever marry? There are no bridegrooms for you,
And your lives must wither away in sterile dreaming.

O Kreon, son of Menoikeus!
You are the only father my daughters have,
Since we, their parents, are both of us gone for ever.   1445
They are your own blood: you will not let them
Fall into beggary and loneliness;
You will keep them from the miseries that are mine!
Take pity on them; see, they are only children,
Friendless except for you. Promise me this,   1450
Great prince, and give me your hand in token of it.

(KREON *clasps his right hand.*)

Children:
I could say much, if you could understand me,
But as it is, I have only this prayer for you:

Live where you can, be happy as you can—   1455
Happier, please God, than God has made your father.

KREON   Enough. You have wept enough. Now go within.

OEDIPUS   I must; but it is hard.

KREON   Time eases all things.

OEDIPUS   You know my mind, then?

KREON   Say what you desire.

OEDIPUS   Send me from Thebes!

KREON   God grant that I may!   1460

OEDIPUS   But since God hates me . . .

KREON   No, he will grant your wish.

OEDIPUS   You promise?

KREON   I can not speak beyond my knowledge.

OEDIPUS   Then lead me in.

KREON   Come now, and leave your children.

OEDIPUS   No! Do not take them from me!

KREON   Think no longer
That you are in command here, but rather think   1465
How, when you were, you served your own destruction.

(*Exeunt into the house all but the* CHORUS; *the* CHORAGOS *chants
directly to the audience.*)

CHORAGOS   Men of Thebes: look upon Oedipus.

This is the king who solved the famous riddle
And towered up, most powerful of men.
No mortal eyes but looked on him with envy,   1470
Yet in the end ruin swept over him.

Let every man in mankind's frailty
Consider his last day; and let none
Presume on his good fortune until he find
Life, at his death, a memory without pain.   1475

Translated by Dudley Fitts and Robert Fitzgerald

Questions for Writing and Discussion

1.   Once he had made his terrible final discovery, why does Oedipus put out his
eyes, rather than, say, (a) killing himself and/or Iokastê; (b) chopping off the arm
that killed Laïos; (c) castrating himself—all of which might seem to be grimly
appropriate? How does the whole play make the blinding seem most appropriate
of all?

2.   Consider the way in which we use "I see" to mean "I know" or "I understand."
Is there any pattern connecting seeing and knowing in the play? What is the
relation of Teiresias' blindness to that of Oedipus?

3. What are the connections between the Sphinx's riddle and the puzzle of Laïos' murder? (Consider this both generally and with regard to specific details, like line 441, for instance.)

4. A pattern of doubling was pointed out in the introduction. Apply this to the two messengers: how do their roles differ? How are they parallel?

5. A tragic hero for the Greeks was a man of high position—someone extraordinary—who is brought low as a result of some tragic flaw in his nature. How does this apply to Oedipus? Does Oedipus have a tragic flaw?

6. There are several myths about the origin of Teiresias' blindness. In one, he sees Athena, the virgin goddess of wisdom, bathing and is struck blind; in another, he sees two snakes copulating and is blinded; in another, he is turned into a woman by Zeus and Hera, his queen, who are arguing about whether men or women take more pleasure in sexual intercourse. Teiresias, after some experience, reports that women do; Hera strikes him blind in a fit of rage, but Zeus compensates him by giving him prophetic foresight. How are these background myths relevant to the play?

7. What do you make of the character of Iokastê? Is she an appropriate queen for such a king as Oedipus?

8. In Oedipus' speech beginning with line 1020, some critics see the hero at his most deceived, some do not; comment on the view of one of the latter who finds that the pride manifested in this speech "proclaims man's dignity on the edge of ruin."

WILLIAM SHAKESPEARE

Hamlet

Introduction

Certain questions are asked again and again of the student of *Hamlet*. Is Hamlet's melancholy caused simply by the situation in which he finds himself? Or does it exist prior to, or in excess of, the situation? Is his madness more real than he knows? Why is he unable—why does he seem to himself unable—to perform his promised revenge swiftly and without compunction? Every critic of the play has been compelled to take these questions seriously, if only to clear the ground for a consideration of other matters, such as the place of *Hamlet* in the tradition of "revenge" tragedy or in the arc of Shakespeare's career. The critic, then, ordinarily moves from the problems raised by the play to a more or less specialized interest with which the play is associated. Let us begin one step earlier, and move from the most general human concerns that the play engages and exemplifies to the means by which these are made dramatic in the play itself. Perhaps, as we go along, our initial questions will take care of themselves.

Hamlet is a portrait of the first tragic hero in literature to exhibit the full imaginative range and depth of self-doubt—the habit of restless inquiry into all motives, including his own. We have come to take this self-questioning for granted in our idea of what is human, and have at last simplified our notion of it with the help of a new word, a word that neither Hamlet nor Shakespeare would have used: *self-consciousness.* Hamlet is famous for his soliloquies, the long rhetorical speeches during which he occupies the stage alone and talks to himself about himself. Many dramatic justifications could be given for the prominence of these speeches, but *what* they dramatize is plain enough: he is constantly aware of a division in his own character between an inward and an outward self. Others in the play, Claudius and Polonius most notably, believe in a division between what the soul reveals and what it conceals; but for them the secret is a matter of information, something that may come to be known if it is not carefully guarded. For Hamlet, on the other hand, the inward self is defined by the fact that it cannot possibly be known except by itself.

701

The more often we read this play, the better we appreciate how every detail increases our knowledge of Hamlet's divided nature, and the distance at which it makes him hold the world. Thus, the very first words of the play are an exchange of suspicious warnings between two night watchmen:

BERNARDO   Who's there?
FRANCISCO   Nay, answer me. Stand, and unfold yourself.

These sentries treat identity as an unmixed essence: the name will always equal the thing named, and they can speak figuratively of a self's "unfolding" as a simple operation. But the inmost reaches of Hamlet's identity remain hidden— "folded." He might well be answering the second watchman, across a distance of two hundred lines, when, in response to his mother's advice to cast off the "nighted color" of his melancholy, he says that he can do no such thing: "I have that within which passeth show." Again, when Hamlet feigns madness, he is of course putting on an "antic disposition" as a disguise, under the protection of which he may scrutinize Claudius at liberty. But he is also dramatizing the gulf between himself and the world that his awareness of an inward self has opened up: to the world, a man who feels with this intensity of inwardness is only a man who talks to himself, in short a lunatic.

All of the dramatic action follows from Hamlet's double movement of concealment and exposure: concealment of his own nature and motives, exposure of the nature and motives of others. He suspects that Claudius has murdered his father, and while Claudius and his agents seek to discover the ground of Hamlet's suspicion and to "sound him," he is laying plans for the detection of Claudius' guilt. Of these two different acts of unmasking, Hamlet's is far and away the less problematic. For while Claudius wants to know "What *is* Hamlet, that he should bear me such malice," all that Hamlet asks is "What has Claudius *done,* that he should appear to me so guilty?" Curiously, though Hamlet is the man of reflection and Claudius the practical man of affairs, it is Hamlet who searches out the easily confirmed fact and Claudius who is forced to proceed as if he assigned a metaphysical cause to Hamlet's behavior. Hamlet acts in full knowledge of this curious reversal of roles. From his earliest appearance on stage, he is able to make Claudius the butt of his wit, taunting him almost casually:

KING   But now, my cousin Hamlet, and my son—
HAMLET [*Aside*]   A little more than kin and less than kind.

In this first exchange, Hamlet offers his own self-portrait against Claudius' official statement of their relations: to Claudius he is more than kin, since a stepfather is not quite a father; he is less than kind, since he cannot love a man who he believes has murdered his father, any more than he can be "of a kind" with such a man; beyond this, it is typical of Hamlet to note in passing that "kind" is "kin"-plus-one (the letter *d*) and to refuse Claudius even the tiny diplomatic kindness of making the addition.

Wit is indeed Hamlet's most pronounced trait—a wit always at the ready, magnificent in defense, glinting with self-mockery, propelled by the nervous exhilaration of meanings caught by surprise. Actors, especially young actors, often play Hamlet as a rather sulky character, grudging and overfastidious, like a spoiled child. This interpretation of the part cannot possibly do justice to the variable moods of Hamlet's wit (with Claudius; with Polonius; with Horatio; with Ophelia; with Rosencrantz and Guildenstern—toward each of whom he adopts a different tone). But it is misleading for an even more important reason, as it tends to reduce Hamlet to a series of attention-getting theatrical gestures, precisely the sort of gestures that he warns the players against when he tells them how to "catch the conscience of a king." By enacting on stage Claudius' murder of Hamlet's father, and shocking Claudius with the vivid memory of what he has done, the players will bring out the truth and aid Hamlet's plan. This can only happen if they act plainly, without flourishes.

> HAMLET   Speak the speech, I pray you, as I pronounced it to you, trippingly on the tongue. But if you mouth it, as many of your players do, I had as lief the town crier spoke my lines. Nor do not saw the air too much with your hand, thus, but use all gently. For in the very torrent, tempest, and, as I may say, whirlwind of passion, you must acquire and beget a temperance that may give it smoothness. . . . Suit the action to the word, the word to the action, with this special observance, that you o'erstep not the modesty of nature. For anything so o'erdone is from the purpose of playing, whose end, both at the first and now, was and is to hold as 'twere the mirror up to Nature.

This, then, is Hamlet's credo, and he is as much an actor as the players are, not only when he feigns madness, but when, in looking at the play itself, he affects the unruly high spirits of a boy at a puppet show, all the while keeping close watch on Claudius' every move.

Act III of *Hamlet* documents his astonishing success in holding the mirror up to nature. After the players have performed their pantomime-murder, Claudius retires from the scene to pray: "Oh, my offense is rank, it smells to Heaven." And when Hamlet is alone with Gertrude, he extracts from her a confession not of guilt but of overwhelming shame at having married again so soon after her husband's death: "O Hamlet, speak no more./ Thou turn'st mine eyes into my very soul,/ And there I see such black and grainèd spots/ As will not leave their tint." Initially, however, Hamlet succeeds only as an artist (he gives a horrifying and convincing portrait of both Claudius and Gertrude) and not as a hero (success in this role would entail killing the man who killed his father, and rescuing Gertrude from his arms). Indeed, Hamlet devotes so much energy to what we may call the artistic "touches" of his plan that he seems at times to lose track of its original purpose: he reasons himself out of killing Claudius at the first clear opportunity; and he has to be warned by the ghost against making too black an indictment of Gertrude, since his aim after all is not to make her despair but to lead her to salvation. Now, an Elizabethan ghost might be an evil spirit or a good one, and we can justify part of Hamlet's delay in avenging his father by his conscientious resolve to test the good faith of this particular ghost. But, once the play-within-a-play and the response to it have proved the ghost correct, we may well ask why Hamlet delays his vengeance still further.

A famous answer was given by the Romantic poet and critic Samuel Taylor Coleridge, who described *Hamlet* as a kind of morality play about the perils of irresolution, and saw Hamlet as thwarting himself from the very outset: "the great object of his life [that is, his revenge] is defeated by continually resolving to do, yet doing nothing but resolve." If we take this view of the play, we will judge Hamlet to be the unhappy owner of a brooding and speculative intelligence, which prefers analysis to action and temperamentally unfits him for true heroism. Such a judgment does not square with our sense that Hamlet is *in control* throughout the play, whatever his self-lacerations and his real or imagined lapses from resolve. Nevertheless, Coleridge's view is very much in line with modern psychoanalytic discussions which draw a parallel between Hamlet and Oedipus—discussions which have done so much to influence modern performances of Hamlet that, if only for that reason, they deserve some consideration here.

Roughly, the psychoanalytic interpretation is as follows: *Oedipus* dramatizes the two coinciding wishes that mark every man's striving for self-definition—the wish to murder his father and sleep with his mother. It is the knowledge of this unconscious wish that Oedipus at first represses, and with it the knowledge of his double crime; his discovery of all that he has repressed is like the self-discovery to which a therapist can sometimes lead a patient. The case of Hamlet is similar—his unconscious wish was to murder his father and sleep with his mother—except that to him self-discovery can never come because the crimes were never committed and have become impossible to commit. Instead, Hamlet finds his father already dead and his mother united with the man who killed him. Thus, Hamlet is disappointed of what he did not quite know he wanted, and left to baffle himself in anguish and aimless petulance.

How plausible is this account of Hamlet? Certain resemblances between Hamlet and Oedipus are hard to miss: both see before them a society that has suffered a blight—for Oedipus a literal plague, for Hamlet a metaphorical "something" that is "rotten in the state of Denmark"; both undertake the detection of the cause of this misery, and vow to extinguish it; both meet with an unexpected trial—for Oedipus the discovery that he is himself the guilty cause, for Hamlet the uneasy perception that the longer he contemplates his revenge, the more difficult it grows to perform. Also, it is true that the stress of Hamlet's anger falls most of all on Gertrude's supposed infidelity, to the point of almost forgetting Claudius' treachery:

> Oh, God! God!
> How weary, stale, flat, and unprofitable
> Seem to me all the uses of this world!
> Fie on 't, ah, fie! 'Tis an unweeded garden,
> That grows to seed, things rank and gross in nature

> Possess it merely. That it should come to this!
> But two months dead! Nay, not so much, not two.
> So excellent a King, that was, to this,
> Hyperion to a satyr. So loving to my mother
> That he might not beteem the winds of heaven
> Visit her face too roughly. Heaven and earth!
> Must I remember? Why, she would hang on him
> As if increase of appetite had grown
> By what it fed on. And yet within a month—
> Let me not think on 't.—Frailty, thy name is woman!—

To many readers, these sentiments seem altogether consistent with unrequited longings for Gertrude. Such readers construe the soliloquies as *involuntary* self-revelations and, having done so, are free to look on Hamlet's madness as more real than feigned. In the mad scenes, it is argued, he gives way utterly to the despair that is kept fitfully under control in the soliloquies; for the secret that Hamlet conceals, the inwardness "which passeth show," is something about which Hamlet himself remains in the dark. The revenge is finally accomplished, but by accident: the play ends in confusion.

It is possible for us to profit greatly from this way of reading the play—because it nicely juxtaposes two masterpieces of European literature, and asks us to view Hamlet with just the unswerving gaze he directs upon himself—but at the same time we may find its explanation of Hamlet far from convincing. When Hamlet denounces Gertrude even more vehemently than he denounces Claudius, we may suspect him of acting from an unanalyzed motive. But we may also point to an old law of human nature: we are naturally harder on the weakness of those from whom we expected much, than on the positive wickedness of those from whom nothing was to be expected. As for Hamlet's madness, let us recall that he assures us, not once but three times, that he is its stage manager: first, when he warns Horatio and Marcellus against seeming to be *in the know* if he should "think meet/ To put an antic disposition on"; second, when he tells Rosencrantz and Guildenstern that he is "but mad north-northwest. When the wind is southerly, I know a hawk from a handsaw"; and third, when he charges Gertrude by no means to let Claudius "Make you to ravel all this matter out,/ That I essentially am not in madness." As for the soliloquies, we need to ponder Hamlet's self-chastisement carefully before taking it as a disinterested judgment of his character. Is this judgment repeated by anyone else in the play? For that matter, would *we* think Hamlet slow to act if he were not there to tell us so, and the soliloquies to slow down the action? But the deepest objection to the view we have been considering is that it accuses Hamlet of a kind of inadequacy that really amounts to villainy. For Hamlet's duty is not merely the satisfaction of a personal revenge but also the discharging of a political obligation—he must rid Denmark of a murderer who has usurped the throne—and on this view of the play, he does his best to fail. But we can judge him a failure only if we regard the end of the play as a complete chaos, whereas what we feel most strongly at the end is the emergence of a new order. Moreover, it is an order that owes much to the emergence of Hamlet as precisely the bold and decisive hero that he feared he could never be.

Perhaps we can offer a summary of our earlier characterization of Hamlet as an artist, a wit, and a divided nature by saying that he is a character who must try out various postures before any of them becomes real to him: the outward show is not the same as, but helps him to form, the inward motive. This can make it look as if he cared only for postures, but in fact he cares for more than that. To play a part—the injured lover, the loyal son, the avenger—is for him a powerfully seductive means to an end: but it is a means only. For Hamlet, *acting comes before action.* But eventually action does come. In the middle of Act IV he disappears from the play, sent to his death by Claudius. But he manages to turn the tables on Claudius' agents, and he survives. At the end of Act IV we hear him speak again, in a letter that Horatio reads aloud, and then in another that Claudius reads: "High and Mighty, you shall know I am set naked on your kingdom." In his strange journey, and in the battle with the pirates where he had to "put on a compelled valor," Hamlet has played at death in spite of himself, and upon his return he is ready to die in earnest. Earlier in the play, when Polonius asked Hamlet "Will you walk out of the air, my lord," Hamlet replied: "Into my grave." And when we see him at the beginning of Act V, it is as a man reborn (an image suggested also in his letter to Claudius), but reborn for the sake of preparing to die: a grave is already being dug—it is Ophelia's, yet we think of Hamlet—by a gravedigger who began working at Elsinore on the "very day that young Hamlet was born." Starting with his letter to Claudius, and throughout Act V, we feel that Hamlet speaks for the first time as a man with his hand on his sword. Like his father's ghost, he has reentered the stage from the other side of death; and like the ghost, he has a strange power over those who have remained on stage as mortal actors.

Standing by the graveside, exchanging pleasantries with Horatio and the gravediggers, Hamlet is witty but not laceratingly so; reflective, but quietly reflective; at peace with himself, and alert for the chance to do what he must do. There are no more soliloquies. We get a very clear view of the change that has come over Hamlet if we contrast him with Laertes. For Laertes' destiny has begun to take a course parallel to Hamlet's, and, with Hamlet's inadvertent slaying of Polonius, Laertes too has found himself cast in the role of avenger. But, though by Act V their roles have merged, their styles of playing could not be more different. Laertes is impetuous, eager to strike a heroic pose, and full of melodramatic rant. Claudius asks him how he intends to dispose of Hamlet and he replies, typically, "cut his throat i' the church." In the same manner, when the priest denies Ophelia a full Christian burial, since her death may have been suicide, Laertes cries out, "I tell thee, churlish priest,/ A ministering angel shall my sister be/ When thou liest howling." We may call this sheer bluster, and yet it has its eloquence: it reminds us of nothing so much as Hamlet's defense of his father's memory in the first two acts. The truth is, Laertes has taken over the role in which we found Hamlet at the beginning of the play—though he performs it with less cunning and agility—while Hamlet has advanced beyond it. Laertes is now a "foil" to Hamlet. He is a character who by his apparent similarities to Hamlet shows us the underlying contrast between them, and sharpens our awareness of Hamlet's heroic stature: a fact Hamlet is quick to seize upon, when, with a pun on a second meaning of the word derived from fencing, he tells Laertes ironically, "I'll be your foil."

Laertes and Hamlet engage in a brief scuffle at the graveside; when Hamlet wins, it is through the power of words, with an expression of restraint that promises strength. "Words, words, words," he has said long before to Polonius, dismissively. But of all the characters in the play, Hamlet is the master of rhetoric—he is the only character whom we can imagine writing the play—and he is never more confident than in this terse encounter with Laertes. The assailant's hands are at his throat when Hamlet says,

> Thou pray'st not well.
> I prithee, take thy fingers from my throat,
> For though I am not splenitive and rash,
> Yet have I in me something dangerous,
> Which let thy wisdom fear.

This is the Hamlet of "I have that within which passeth show," but with a difference. His consciousness of an inward self is, we feel, no longer an impediment to action, and on an instant's provocation he will deal death to whoever crosses him. It is this Hamlet who can call an end to the laying of schemes, with a Stoic indifference to fortune and acceptance of fate: "we defy augury . . . The readiness is all." That he should say so to Horatio is a delicate touch, for it is Horatio all along who has resisted all forms of superstition and display, including Hamlet's; it is Horatio whom we love for his response to Marcellus' impressive account of the nocturnal habits of the spirit world, in a single line that characterizes him perfectly: "So have I heard and do in part believe it." By his calm at the end, Hamlet has earned the undying allegiance of Horatio. And as he draws his last breath in the final scene of the play, as he sees that his place at center stage will be quickly taken by Fortinbras—another "foil," more successful though less complex than Hamlet, whose march into Denmark completes his own revenge—he asks that Horatio remain alive to preserve his reputation from the injuries of rumor and legend:

> If thou didst ever hold me in thy heart,
> Absent thee from felicity a while,
> And in this harsh world draw thy breath in pain
> To tell my story.

Felicity would be to die with Hamlet; to live will be only painful, when Hamlet is not among the living. The task is hard, yet we do not for a moment doubt that Horatio will perform it. The man who is not "passion's slave," for whom the self *is* what it *seems* and acting and action are two names for the same thing, would be as little capable of telling the story wrongly as of living the life that made it.

Hamlet

CHARACTERS OF THE PLAY

CLAUDIUS, *King of Denmark*
HAMLET, *son to the late, and nephew to the present, King*
POLONIUS, *Lord Chamberlain*
HORATIO, *friend to Hamlet*
LAERTES, *son to Polonius*
VOLTIMAND
CORNELIUS
ROSENCRANTZ
GUILDENSTERN } *courtiers*
OSRIC
A GENTLEMAN
A PRIEST
MARCELLUS } *officers*
BERNARDO
FRANCISCO, *a soldier*
REYNALDO, *servant to Polonius*
PLAYERS
TWO CLOWNS, *gravediggers*
FORTINBRAS, *Prince of Norway*
A CAPTAIN
ENGLISH AMBASSADORS
GERTRUDE, *Queen of Denmark, and mother to Hamlet*
OPHELIA, *daughter to Polonius*
LORDS, LADIES, OFFICERS, SOLDIERS, SAILORS,
    MESSENGERS, *and other* ATTENDANTS
GHOST *of Hamlet's father*

SCENE—*Denmark.*

ACT I

Scene I. Elsinore. A platform before the castle.

[FRANCISCO *at his post. Enter to him* BERNARDO.]

HAMLET by William Shakespeare. From *Shakespeare: The Complete Works* edited by G. B. Harrison, copyright, 1948, 1952, by Harcourt Brace Jovanovich, Inc.; renewed, 1976 by G. B. Harrison. Reprinted by permission of the publishers.

BERNARDO   Who's there?

FRANCISCO   Nay, answer me. Stand, and unfold yourself.°

BERNARDO   Long live the King!

FRANCISCO   Bernardo?

BERNARDO   He.   5

FRANCISCO   You come most carefully upon your hour.

BERNARDO   'Tis now struck twelve. Get thee to bed, Francisco.

FRANCISCO   For this relief much thanks. 'Tis bitter cold,
    And I am sick at heart.

BERNARDO   Have you had quiet guard?

FRANCISCO   Not a mouse stirring.   10

BERNARDO   Well, good night.
    If you do meet Horatio and Marcellus,
    The rivals° of my watch, bid them make haste.

FRANCISCO   I think I hear them. Stand, ho! Who is there?

[*Enter* HORATIO *and* MARCELLUS.]

HORATIO   Friends to this ground.

MARCELLUS   And liegemen° to the Dane.   15

FRANCISCO   Give you good night.

MARCELLUS   Oh, farewell, honest soldier.
    Who hath relieved you?

FRANCISCO   Bernardo hath my place.
    Give you good night.   [*Exit.*]

MARCELLUS   Holloa! Bernardo!

BERNARDO   Say,
    What, is Horatio there?

HORATIO   A piece of him.

BERNARDO   Welcome, Horatio. Welcome, good Marcellus.   20

MARCELLUS   What, has this thing appeared again tonight?

BERNARDO   I have seen nothing.

MARCELLUS   Horatio says 'tis but our fantasy,
    And will not let belief take hold of him
    Touching this dreaded sight twice seen of us.   25
    Therefore I have entreated him along
    With us to watch the minutes of this night,
    That if again this apparition come,
    He may approve our eyes° and speak to it.

HORATIO   Tush, tush, 'twill not appear.

BERNARDO   Sit down awhile,   30
    And let us once again assail your ears,

I.i.2 unfold yourself: reveal who you are   **13 rivals:** partners   **15 liegemen:** loyal subjects   **29
approve our eyes:** verify what we have seen

That are so fortified against our story,
What we have two nights seen.
HORATIO   Well, sit we down,
And let us hear Bernardo speak of this.
BERNARDO   Last night of all,   35
When yond same star that's westward from the pole°
Had made his course to illume that part of heaven
Where now it burns, Marcellus and myself,
The bell then beating one—

[*Enter* GHOST.]

MARCELLUS   Peace, break thee off. Look where it comes again!   40
BERNARDO   In the same figure, like the King that's dead.
MARCELLUS   Thou art a scholar. Speak to it, Horatio.
BERNARDO   Looks it not like the King? Mark it, Horatio.
HORATIO   Most like. It harrows me with fear and wonder.
BERNARDO   It would be spoke to.
MARCELLUS   Question it, Horatio.   45
HORATIO   What art thou that usurp'st this time of night,
Together with that fair and warlike form
In which the majesty of buried Denmark°
Did sometimes march? By Heaven I charge thee, speak!
MARCELLUS   It is offended.
BERNARDO   See, it stalks away!   50
HORATIO   Stay! Speak, speak! I charge thee, speak!   [*Exit* GHOST.]
MARCELLUS   'Tis gone, and will not answer.
BERNARDO   How now, Horatio! You tremble and look pale.
Is not this something more than fantasy?
What think you on 't?   55
HORATIO   Before my God, I might not this believe
Without the sensible and true avouch
Of mine own eyes.°
MARCELLUS   Is it not like the King?
HORATIO   As thou art to thyself.
Such was the very armor he had on   60
When he the ambitious Norway combated.
So frowned he once when, in an angry parle,°
He smote the sledded° Polacks on the ice.
'Tis strange.
MARCELLUS   Thus twice before, and jump at this dead hour,°   65
With martial stalk hath he gone by our watch.

36 pole: Polestar   48 Denmark: the dead King   57–58 Without . . . eyes: unless my own eyes
had vouched for it; sensible: perceived by my senses   62 parle: parley   63 sledded: on sleds   65
jump . . . hour: just at deep midnight

HORATIO   In what particular thought to work I know not,
　　But in the gross and scope° of my opinion
　　This bodes some strange eruption to our state.

MARCELLUS   Good now, sit down and tell me, he that knows,　　　70
　　Why this same strict and most observant watch
　　So nightly toils the subject of the land;
　　And why such daily cast of brazen cannon
　　And foreign mart° for implements of war;
　　Why such impress° of shipwrights, whose sore task　　　75
　　Does not divide the Sunday from the week;
　　What might be toward,° that this sweaty haste
　　Doth make the night joint laborer with the day.
　　Who is 't that can inform me?

HORATIO　　　　　　　　　　　　That can I,
　　At least the whisper goes so. Our last King,　　　80
　　Whose image even but now appeared to us,
　　Was, as you know, by Fortinbras of Norway,
　　Thereto pricked on by a most emulate° pride,
　　Dared to the combat, in which our valiant Hamlet—
　　For so this side of our known world esteemed him—　　　85
　　Did slay this Fortinbras. Who by a sealed compact,°
　　Well ratified by law and heraldry,
　　Did forfeit, with his life, all those his lands
　　Which he stood seized of° to the conqueror.
　　Against the which, a moiety competent°　　　90
　　Was gagèd° by our King, which had returned
　　To the inheritance of Fortinbras
　　Had he been vanquisher, as by the same covenant
　　And carriage of the article designed°
　　His fell to Hamlet. Now, sir, young Fortinbras,　　　95
　　Of unimprovèd mettle° hot and full,
　　Hath in the skirts of Norway here and there
　　Sharked° up a list of lawless resolutes,°
　　For food and diet, to some enterprise
　　That hath a stomach in 't. Which is no other—　　　100
　　As it doth well appear unto our state—
　　But to recover of us, by strong hand
　　And terms compulsatory,° those foresaid lands
　　So by his father lost. And this, I take it,
　　Is the main motive of our preparations,　　　105

68 **gross . . . scope:** general conclusion   74 **foreign mart:** purchase abroad   75 **impress:** conscription   77 **toward:** in preparation   83 **emulate:** jealous   86 **sealed compact:** formal agreement   89 **seized of:** possessed of, a legal term   90 **moiety competent:** adequate portion   91 **gagèd:** pledged   94 **carriage . . . designed:** fulfillment of the clause in the agreement   96 **unimprovèd mettle:** untutored, wild material, nature   98 **Sharked:** collected indiscriminately, as a shark bolts its prey; **lawless resolutes:** gangsters   103 **terms compulsatory:** force

The source of this our watch and the chief head°
Of this posthaste and romage° in the land.
BERNARDO   I think it be no other but e'en so.
Well may it sort that this portentous figure
Comes armèd through our watch, so like the King   110
That was and is the question of these wars.
HORATIO   A mote it is to trouble the mind's eye.
In the most high and palmy state of Rome,
A little ere the mightiest Julius fell,
The graves stood tenantless, and the sheeted° dead   115
Did squeak and gibber° in the Roman streets.
As stars° with trains of fire and dews of blood,
Disasters° in the sun, and the moist star°
Upon whose influence Neptune's empire stands
Was sick almost to doomsday with eclipse.   120
And even the like precurse° of fierce events,
As harbingers° preceding still the fates
And prologue to the omen° coming on,
Have Heaven and earth together demonstrated
Unto our climatures° and countrymen.   125
[*Reenter* GHOST.] But soft, behold! Lo where it comes again!
I'll cross it,° though it blast me. Stay, illusion!
If thou hast any sound, or use of voice,
Speak to me.
If° there be any good thing to be done   130
That may to thee do ease and grace to me,°
Speak to me.
If thou art privy to° thy country's fate,
Which, happily,° foreknowing may avoid,
Oh, speak!   135
Or if thou hast uphoarded in thy life
Extorted° treasure in the womb of earth,
For which, they say, you spirits oft walk in death,
Speak of it. Stay, and speak! [*The cock crows.*°] Stop it, Marcellus.
MARCELLUS   Shall I strike at it with my partisan?°   140
HORATIO   Do, if it will not stand.
BERNARDO   'Tis here!

---

106 chief head: main purpose   **107 posthaste . . . romage:** urgency and bustle   **115 sheeted:** in
their shrouds   **116 gibber:** utter strange sounds   **117 As stars:** the sense of the passage is here
broken; possibly a line has been omitted after line 116   **118 Disasters:** unlucky signs; **moist star:**
the moon, which influences the tides   **121 precurse:** forewarning   **122 harbingers:** forerun-
ners   **123 omen:** disaster   **125 climatures:** regions   **127 cross it:** stand in its way   **130–39 If
. . . speak:** in popular belief there were four reasons why the spirit of a dead man should *walk:* (a) to
reveal a secret, (b) to utter a warning, (c) to reveal concealed treasure, (d) to reveal the manner of its
death; Horatio thus adjures the ghost by three potent reasons, but before he can utter the fourth the
cock crows   **131 grace to me:** bring me into a state of spiritual grace   **133 privy to:** have secret
knowledge of   **134 happily:** by good luck   **137 Extorted:** evilly acquired   **139 s.d. cock crows:**
i.e., a sign that dawn is at hand; see lines 147–64   **140 partisan:** pike

HORATIO   'Tis here!
MARCELLUS   'Tis gone!   [*Exit* GHOST.]
    We do it wrong, being so majestical,
    To offer it the show of violence,
    For it is as the air invulnerable,   145
    And our vain blows malicious mockery.
BERNARDO   It was about to speak when the cock crew.
HORATIO   And then it started like a guilty thing
    Upon a fearful summons. I have heard
    The cock, that is the trumpet to the morn,   150
    Doth with his lofty and shrill-sounding throat
    Awake the god of day, and at his warning,
    Whether in sea or fire, in earth or air,
    The extravagant and erring° spirit hies
    To his confine.° And of the truth herein   155
    This present object made probation.°
MARCELLUS   It faded on the crowing of the cock.
    Some say that ever 'gainst° that season comes
    Wherein Our Saviour's birth is celebrated,
    The bird of dawning singeth all night long.   160
    And then, they say, no spirit dare stir abroad,
    The nights are wholesome, then no planets° strike,
    No fairy takes° nor witch hath power to charm,
    So hallowed and so gracious is the time.
HORATIO   So have I heard and do in part believe it.   165
    But look, the morn, in russet mantle clad,
    Walks o'er the dew of yon high eastward hill.
    Break we our watch up, and by my advice
    Let us impart what we have seen tonight
    Unto young Hamlet, for upon my life,   170
    This spirit, dumb to us, will speak to him.
    Do you consent we shall acquaint him with it,
    As needful in our loves, fitting our duty?
MARCELLUS   Let's do 't, I pray. And I this morning know
    Where we shall find him most conveniently.   [*Exeunt.*]   175

Scene II. A room of state in the castle.

[*Flourish.*° *Enter the* KING, QUEEN, HAMLET, POLONIUS, LAERTES,
VOLTIMAND, CORNELIUS, LORDS, *and* ATTENDANTS.]

---

154 **extravagant . . . erring:** both words mean "wandering"   155 **confine:** place of confinement
156 **probation:** proof   158 **'gainst:** in anticipation of   162 **planets:** planets were supposed to
bring disaster   163 **takes:** bewitches   **I.ii.s.d. Flourish:** fanfare of trumpets

KING   Though yet of Hamlet our dear brother's death
      The memory be green, and that it us befitted
      To bear our hearts in grief and our whole kingdom
      To be contracted in° one brow of woe,
      Yet so far hath discretion fought with nature   5
      That we with wisest sorrow think on him,
      Together with remembrance of ourselves.
      Therefore our sometime sister,° now our Queen,
      The imperial jointress° to this warlike state,
      Have we, as 'twere with a defeated joy—   10
      With an auspicious° and a dropping eye,
      With mirth in funeral and with dirge in marriage,
      In equal scale weighing delight and dole°—
      Taken to wife. Nor have we herein barred
      Your better wisdoms,° which have freely gone   15
      With this affair along. For all, our thanks.
      Now follows that you know. Young Fortinbras,
      Holding a weak supposal° of our worth,
      Or thinking by our late dear brother's death
      Our state to be disjoint and out of frame,   20
      Colleagued with the dream of his advantage,°
      He hath not failed to pester us with message
      Importing the surrender of those lands
      Lost by his father, with all bonds of law,°
      To our most valiant brother. So much for him.   25
      Now for ourself, and for this time of meeting.
      Thus much the business is: We have here writ
      To Norway, uncle of young Fortinbras—
      Who, impotent and bedrid, scarcely hears
      Of this his nephew's purpose—to suppress   30
      His further gait° herein, in that the levies,
      The lists° and full proportions,° are all made
      Out of his subject.° And we here dispatch
      You, good Cornelius, and you, Voltimand,
      For bearers of this greeting to old Norway,   35
      Giving to you no further personal power
      To business with the King more than the scope°
      Of these delated articles° allow.
      Farewell, and let your haste commend° your duty.

---

4 contracted in: puckered in; also, reduced to   **8 sister:** sister-in-law   **9 jointress:** partner by marriage   **11 auspicious:** full of joy   **13 dole:** grief   **14–15 barred . . . wisdoms:** i.e., in taking this step we have not shut out your advice   **18 weak supposal:** poor opinion   **21 Colleagued . . . advantage:** uniting himself with this dream that here was a good opportunity   **24 with . . . law:** legally binding, as already explained in lines 80–95 above   **31 gait:** progress   **32 lists:** rosters; **proportions:** military establishments   **33 subject:** subjects   **37 scope:** limit   **38 delated articles:** detailed instructions   **39 commend:** display; lit., recommend

CORNELIUS, VOLTIMAND   In that and all things will we show our duty.   40
KING   We doubt it nothing. Heartily farewell.
                              [*Exeunt* VOLTIMAND *and* CORNELIUS.]
    And now, Laertes, what's the news with you?
    You told us of some suit°—what is 't, Laertes?
    You cannot speak of reason to the Dane
    And lose your voice. What wouldst thou beg, Laertes,   45
    That shall not be my offer, not thy asking?
    The head is not more native° to the heart,
    The hand more instrumental° to the mouth,
    Than is the throne of Denmark to thy father.
    What wouldst thou have, Laertes?
LAERTES   My dread° lord,   50
    Your leave and favor to return to France,
    From whence though willingly I came to Denmark
    To show my duty in your coronation,
    Yet now, I must confess, that duty done,
    My thoughts and wishes bend again toward France   55
    And bow them to your gracious leave and pardon.
KING   Have you your father's leave? What says Polonius?
POLONIUS   He hath, my lord, wrung from me my slow leave
    By laborsome petition, and at last
    Upon his will° I sealed my hard consent.°   60
    I do beseech you give him leave to go.
KING   Take thy fair hour, Laertes, time be thine,
    And thy best graces spend° it at thy will!
    But now, my cousin° Hamlet, and my son—
HAMLET [*Aside*]   A little more than kin and less than kind.°   65
KING   How is it that the clouds still hang on you?
HAMLET   Not so, my lord. I am too much i' the sun.°
QUEEN   Good Hamlet, cast thy nighted color° off,
    And let thine eye look like a friend on Denmark.
    Do not forever with thy vailèd lids°   70
    Seek for thy noble father in the dust.
    Thou know'st 'tis common—all that lives must die,
    Passing through nature to eternity.
HAMLET   Aye, madam, it is common.
QUEEN   If it be,
    Why seems it so particular with thee?   75
HAMLET   Seems, madam! Nay, it is. I know not "seems."

43 **suit:** petition   47 **native:** closely related   48 **instrumental:** serviceable   50 **dread:** dreaded, much respected   60 **will:** desire; **sealed . . . consent:** agreed to, but with great reluctance   63 **best . . . spend:** i.e., use your time well   64 **cousin:** kinsman; the word was used for any near relation   65 **A . . . kind:** too near a relation (uncle-father) and too little natural affection; see Introduction, p. 702; **kind:** pun on "natural" and "affectionate"   67 **sun:** pun on "son"   68 **nighted color:** black   70 **vailèd lids:** lowered eyelids

'Tis not alone my inky cloak, good Mother,
Nor customary suits of solemn black,
Nor windy suspiration of forced breath—
No, nor the fruitful river° in the eye,   80
Nor the dejected havior of the visage,°
Together with all forms, moods, shapes of grief—
That can denote me truly. These indeed seem,
For they are actions that a man might play.°
But I have that within which passeth show,   85
These but the trappings° and the suits of woe.
KING 'Tis sweet and commendable in your nature, Hamlet,
To give these mourning duties to your father.
But you must know your father lost a father,
That father lost, lost his, and the survivor bound   90
In filial obligation for some term
To do obsequious sorrow.° But to perséver
In obstinate condolement° is a course
Of impious stubbornness, 'tis unmanly grief.
It shows a will most incorrect to Heaven,   95
A heart unfortified,° a mind impatient,
An understanding simple and unschooled.
For what we know must be and is as common
As any the most vulgar° thing to sense,
Why should we in our peevish opposition   100
Take it to heart? Fie! 'Tis a fault to Heaven,
A fault against the dead, a fault to nature,
To reason most absurd, whose common theme
Is death of fathers, and who still hath cried,
From the first corse° till he that died today,   105
"This must be so." We pray you throw to earth
This unprevailing° woe, and think of us
As of a father. For let the world take note,
You are the most immediate to our throne,
And with no less nobility of love   110
Than that which dearest father bears his son
Do I impart toward you. For your intent
In going back to school° in Wittenberg,
It is most retrograde° to our desire.
And we beseech you bend you° to remain   115

80 **fruitful river:** stream of tears   81 **dejected . . . visage:** downcast countenance   84 **play:** act, as in a play   86 **trappings:** ornaments   92 **obsequious sorrow:** the sorrow usual at funerals   93 **obstinate condolement:** lamentation disregarding the will of God   96 **unfortified:** not strengthened with the consolation of religion   99 **vulgar:** common   105 **corse:** corpse; there is unconscious irony in this remark, for the first corpse was that of Abel, also slain by his brother   107 **unprevailing:** futile   113 **school:** university   114 **retrograde:** contrary   115 **bend you:** incline

Here in the cheer and comfort of our eye,
Our chiefest courtier, cousin, and our son.
QUEEN   Let not thy mother lose her prayers, Hamlet.
I pray thee, stay with us, go not to Wittenberg.
HAMLET   I shall in all my best obey you, madam.   120
KING   Why, 'tis a loving and a fair reply.
Be as ourself in Denmark. Madam, come,
This gentle and unforced accord of Hamlet
Sits smiling to my heart. In grace whereof,
No jocund health that Denmark drinks today   125
But the great cannon to the clouds shall tell,
And the King's rouse° the Heaven shall bruit° again,
Respeaking earthly thunder. Come away.
                              [*Flourish. Exeunt all but* HAMLET.]
HAMLET   Oh, that this too too solid flesh would melt,
Thaw, and resolve itself into a dew!   130
Or that the Everlasting had not fixed
His canon° 'gainst self-slaughter! Oh, God! God!
How weary, stale, flat, and unprofitable
Seem to me all the uses° of this world!
Fie on 't, ah, fie! 'Tis an unweeded garden,   135
That grows to seed, things rank° and gross in nature
Possess it merely.° That it should come to this!
But two months dead! Nay, not so much, not two.
So excellent a King, that was, to this,
Hyperion° to a satyr.° So loving to my mother   140
That he might not beteem° the winds of heaven
Visit her face too roughly. Heaven and earth!
Must I remember? Why, she would hang on him
As if increase of appetite had grown
By what it fed on. And yet within a month—   145
Let me not think on 't.—Frailty, thy name is woman!—
A little month, or ere those shoes were old
With which she followed my poor father's body,
Like Niobe° all tears.—Why she, even she—
Oh, God! A beast that wants discourse of reason°   150
Would have mourned longer—married with my uncle,
My father's brother, but no more like my father
Than I to Hercules. Within a month,

---

127 **rouse:** deep drink; **bruit:** sound loudly, echo   132 **canon:** rule, law   134 **uses:** ways   136
rank: coarse   137 **merely:** entirely   140 **Hyperion:** the sun god; **satyr:** a creature half man, half
goat—ugly and lecherous   141 **beteem:** allow   149 **Niobe:** she boasted of her children, to the
annoyance of the goddess Artemis, who slew them all; thereafter Niobe became so sorrowful that
she changed into a rock everlastingly dripping water   150 **wants . . . reason:** is without ability to
reason

Ere yet the salt of most unrighteous tears
Had left the flushing in her gallèd° eyes,   155
She married. Oh, most wicked speed, to post°
With such dexterity° to incestuous sheets!
It is not, nor it cannot, come to good.
But break, my heart, for I must hold my tongue!

[*Enter* HORATIO, MARCELLUS, *and* BERNARDO.]

HORATIO   Hail to your lordship!
HAMLET   I am glad to see you well.   160
    Horatio—or I do forget myself.
HORATIO   The same, my lord, and your poor servant ever.
HAMLET   Sir, my good friend—I'll change that name° with you.
    And what make you from Wittenberg, Horatio?
    Marcellus?   165
MARCELLUS   My good lord?
HAMLET   I am very glad to see you. [*To* BERNARDO] Good even, sir.
    But what, in faith, make you from Wittenberg?
HORATIO   A truant disposition, good my lord.
HAMLET   I would not hear your enemy say so,   170
    Nor shall you do my ear that violence
    To make it truster of your own report
    Against yourself. I know you are no truant.
    But what is your affair in Elsinore?
    We'll teach you to drink deep ere you depart.   175
HORATIO   My lord, I came to see your father's funeral.
HAMLET   I pray thee do not mock me, fellow student.
    I think it was to see my mother's wedding.
HORATIO   Indeed, my lord, it followed hard upon.
HAMLET   Thrift, thrift, Horatio! The funeral baked meats
    Did coldly furnish forth the marriage tables.
    Would I had met my dearest° foe in Heaven
    Or ever I had seen that day, Horatio!
    My father!—Methinks I see my father.
HORATIO   Oh, where, my lord?
HAMLET   In my mind's eye, Horatio.   185
HORATIO   I saw him once. He was a goodly King.
HAMLET   He was a man, take him for all in all.
    I shall not look upon his like again.
HORATIO   My lord, I think I saw him yesternight.
HAMLET   Saw? Who?   190

155 **gallèd:** sore   156 **post:** hasten   157 **dexterity:** nimbleness   163 **that name:** i.e., friend
182 **dearest:** best-hated

HORATIO   My lord, the King your father.
HAMLET   The King my father!
HORATIO   Season your admiration° for a while
    With an attent° ear till I may deliver,
    Upon the witness of these gentlemen,
    This marvel to you.
HAMLET   For God's love, let me hear.   195
HORATIO   Two nights together had these gentlemen,
    Marcellus and Bernardo, on their watch
    In the dead vast and middle of the night,°
    Been thus encountered. A figure like your father,
    Armed at point exactly, cap-a-pie,°   200
    Appears before them and with solemn march
    Goes slow and stately by them. Thrice he walked
    By their oppressed and fear-surprisèd eyes
    Within his truncheon's° length, whilst they, distilled°
    Almost to jelly with the act of fear,   205
    Stand dumb, and speak not to him. This to me
    In dreadful secrecy impart they did,
    And I with them the third night kept the watch.
    Where, as they had delivered, both in time,
    Form of the thing, each word made true and good,   210
    The apparition comes. I knew your father.
    These hands are not more like.
HAMLET   But where was this?
MARCELLUS   My lord, upon the platform where we watched.
HAMLET   Did you not speak to it?
HORATIO   My lord, I did,
    But answer made it none. Yet once methought   215
    It lifted up it° head and did address
    Itself to motion, like as it would speak.
    But even then the morning cock crew loud,
    And at the sound it shrunk in haste away
    And vanished from our sight.
HAMLET   'Tis very strange.   220
HORATIO   As I do live, my honored lord, 'tis true,
    And we did think it writ down in our duty
    To let you know of it.
HAMLET   Indeed, indeed, sirs, but this troubles me.
    Hold you the watch tonight?
MARCELLUS, BERNARDO   We do, my lord.   225

---

192 Season . . . admiration: moderate your wonder   **193 attent:** attentive   **198 dead . . . night:**
deep, silent midnight   **200 at . . . cap-a-pie:** complete in every detail, head to foot   **204
truncheon:** a general's staff; **distilled:** melted   **216 it:** its

HAMLET   Armed, say you?

MARCELLUS, BERNARDO   Armed, my lord.

HAMLET   From top to toe?

MARCELLUS, BERNARDO   My lord, from head to foot.

HAMLET   Then saw you not his face?

HORATIO   Oh yes, my lord, he wore his beaver° up.

HAMLET   What, looked he frowningly?   230

HORATIO   A countenance more in sorrow than in anger.

HAMLET   Pale, or red?

HORATIO   Nay, very pale.

HAMLET   And fixed his eyes upon you?

HORATIO   Most constantly.

HAMLET   I would I had been there.

HORATIO   It would have much amazed you.   235

HAMLET   Very like, very like. Stayed it long?

HORATIO   While one with moderate haste might tell° a hundred.

MARCELLUS, BERNARDO   Longer, longer.

HORATIO   Not when I saw 't.

HAMLET   His beard was grizzled?° No?

HORATIO   It was as I have seen it in his life,   240
A sable silvered.°

HAMLET   I will watch tonight.
Perchance 'twill walk again.

HORATIO   I warrant it will.

HAMLET   If it assume my noble father's person,
I'll speak to it though Hell itself should gape
And bid me hold my peace. I pray you all,   245
If you have hitherto concealed this sight,
Let it be tenable° in your silence still,
And whatsoever else shall hap tonight,
Give it an understanding, but no tongue.
I will requite° your loves. So fare you well.   250
Upon the platform, 'twixt eleven and twelve,
I'll visit you.

ALL   Our duty to your Honor.

HAMLET   Your loves, as mine to you. Farewell.

                              [*Exeunt all but* HAMLET.]
I doubt° some foul play. Would the night were come!
Till then sit still, my soul. Foul deeds will rise,   255
Though all the earth o'erwhelm them, to men's eyes.   [*Exit.*]

---

229 **beaver:** front part of the helmet, which could be raised   237 **tell:** count   239 **grizzled:**
gray   241 **sable silvered:** black mingled with white   247 **tenable:** held fast   250 **requite:**
repay   254 **doubt:** suspect

Scene III. A room in Polonius' house.

[*Enter* LAERTES *and* OPHELIA.]

LAERTES   My necessaries° are embarked. Farewell.
    And, sister, as the winds give benefit
    And convoy is assistant,° do not sleep,
    But let me hear from you.
OPHELIA   Do you doubt that?
LAERTES   For Hamlet, and the trifling of his favor,°   5
    Hold it a fashion and a toy in blood,°
    A violet in the youth of primy° nature,
    Forward, not permanent, sweet, not lasting,
    The perfume and suppliance° of a minute—
    No more.
OPHELIA   No more but so?
LAERTES   Think it no more.   10
    For Nature crescent does not grow alone
    In thews and bulk,° but as this temple° waxes
    The inward service of the mind and soul
    Grows wide withal. Perhaps he loves you now,
    And now no soil nor cautel° doth besmirch   15
    The virtue of his will.° But you must fear,
    His greatness weighed,° his will is not his own,
    For he himself is subject to his birth.
    He may not, as unvalued persons do,
    Carve° for himself, for on his choice depends   20
    The safety and health of this whole state,
    And therefore must his choice be circumscribed°
    Unto the voice and yielding of that body
    Whereof he is the head. Then if he says he loves you,
    It fits your wisdom so far to believe it   25
    As he in his particular act and place
    May give his saying deed, which is no further
    Than the main voice of Denmark goes withal.
    Then weigh what loss your honor may sustain
    If with too credent° ear you list his songs,   30
    Or lose your heart, or your chaste treasure open
    To his unmastered importunity.

I.iii.1 **necessaries:** baggage   3 **convoy ... assistant:** means of conveyance is available   5 **favor:** i.e., toward you   6 **toy in blood:** trifling impulse   6 **primy:** springtime; i.e., youthful   9 **suppliance:** pastime   11–12 **For ... bulk:** for natural growth is not only in bodily bulk   12 **temple:** i.e., the body   15 **cautel:** deceit   16 **will:** desire   17 **His ... weighed:** when you consider his high position   20 **Carve:** choose   22 **circumscribed:** restricted   30 **credent:** credulous

Fear it, Ophelia, fear it, my dear sister,
And keep you in the rear of your affection,
Out of the shot and danger of desire.   35
The chariest maid is prodigal enough
If she unmask her beauty to the moon.
Virtue itself 'scapes not calumnious strokes.
The canker galls the infants° of the spring
Too oft before their buttons° be disclosed,   40
And in the morn and liquid dew of youth
Contagious blastments° are most imminent.
Be wary, then, best safety lies in fear.
Youth to itself rebels, though none else near.°

OPHELIA   I shall the effect of this good lesson keep   45
As watchman to my heart. But, good my brother,
Do not, as some ungracious pastors do,
Show me the steep and thorny way to Heaven
Whilst, like a puffed° and reckless libertine,
Himself the primrose path of dalliance° treads   50
And recks not his own rede.°

LAERTES   Oh, fear me not.
I stay too long. But here my father comes.
[*Enter* POLONIUS.] A double blessing is a double grace,
Occasion° smiles upon a second leave.

POLONIUS   Yet here, Laertes! Aboard, aboard, for shame!   55
The wind sits in the shoulder of your sail
And you are stayed° for. There, my blessing with thee!
And these few precepts in thy memory
Look thou chárácter.° Give thy thoughts no tongue,
Nor any unproportioned° thought his act.   60
Be thou familiar, but by no means vulgar.
Those friends thou hast, and their adoption tried,°
Grapple them to thy soul with hoops of steel,
But do not dull thy palm with entertainment°
Of each new-hatched unfledged° comrade. Beware   65
Of entrance to a quarrel, but being in,
Bear 't that the opposèd may beware of thee.
Give every man thy ear, but few thy voice.°
Take each man's censure,° but reserve thy judgment.

---

39 **canker . . . infants:** maggot harms the unopened buds   40 **buttons:** buds   42 **Contagious blastments:** infectious blights   44 **though . . . near:** without anyone else to encourage it   49 **puffed:** panting   50 **dalliance:** love-making   51 **recks . . . rede:** takes no heed of his own advice   54 **Occasion:** opportunity   57 **stayed:** waited   59 **chárácter:** inscribe   60 **unproportioned:** unsuitable   62 **adoption tried:** friendship tested by experience   64 **dull . . . entertainment:** let your hand grow callous with welcome   65 **unfledged:** lit., newly out of the egg, immature   68 **Give . . . voice:** listen to everyone but commit yourself to few   69 **censure:** opinion

Costly thy habit° as thy purse can buy,   70
But not expressed in fancy°—rich, not gaudy.
For the apparel oft proclaims the man,
And they in France of the best rank and station
Are of a most select and generous chief in that.°
Neither a borrower nor a lender be,   75
For loan oft loses both itself and friend
And borrowing dulls the edge of husbandry.°
This above all: To thine own self be true,
And it must follow, as the night the day,
Thou canst not then be false to any man.   80
Farewell. My blessing season° this in thee!

LAERTES   Most humbly do I take my leave, my lord.

POLONIUS   The time invites you. Go, your servants tend.°

LAERTES   Farewell, Ophelia, and remember well
What I have said to you.

OPHELIA   'Tis in my memory locked,   85
And you yourself shall keep the key of it.

LAERTES   Farewell.   [*Exit.*]

POLONIUS   What is 't, Ophelia, he hath said to you?

OPHELIA   So please you, something touching the Lord Hamlet.

POLONIUS   Marry,° well bethought.°   90
'Tis told me he hath very oft of late
Given private time to you, and you yourself
Have of your audience been most free and bounteous.
If it be so—as so 'tis put on me,
And that in way of caution—I must tell you   95
You do not understand yourself so clearly
As it behooves° my daughter and your honor.
What is between you? Give me up the truth.

OPHELIA   He hath, my lord, of late made many tenders°
Of his affection to me.   100

POLONIUS   Affection! Pooh! You speak like a green girl,
Unsifted° in such perilous circumstance.
Do you believe his tenders, as you call them?

OPHELIA   I do not know, my lord, what I should think.

POLONIUS   Marry, I'll teach you. Think yourself a baby   105
That you have ta'en these tenders° for true pay,
Which are not sterling.° Tender yourself more dearly,

---

70 **habit:** dress   71 **expressed in fancy:** fantastic   74 **Are . . . that:** a disputed line; this is the F1 reading; Q2 reads "Or of the most select and generous, chief in that"; i.e., the best noble and gentle families are very particular in their dress; **generous:** of gentle birth; **chief:** eminence   77 **husbandry:** economy   81 **season:** bring to fruit   83 **tend:** attend   90 **Marry:** Mary, by the Virgin Mary; **well bethought:** well remembered   97 **behooves:** is the duty of   99 **tenders:** offers   102 **Unsifted:** untried   106–09 **tenders . . . tender:** Polonius puns on "tenders," counters (used for money in games); "tender," value; "tender," show   107 **sterling:** true currency

Or—not to crack the wind of the poor phrase,
Running it thus—you'll tender me a fool.°
OPHELIA   My lord, he hath importuned me with love   110
In honorable fashion.
POLONIUS   Aye, fashion° you may call it. Go to, go to.
OPHELIA   And hath given countenance to his speech,° my lord,
With almost all the holy vows of Heaven.
POLONIUS   Aye, springes° to catch woodcocks.° I do know,   115
When the blood burns, how prodigal° the soul
Lends the tongue vows. These blazes,° daughter,
Giving more light than heat, extinct in both,
Even in their promise as it is a-making,
You must not take for fire. From this time   120
Be something scanter of your maiden presence,
Set your entreatments at a higher rate
Than a command to parley.° For Lord Hamlet,
Believe so much in him, that he is young,
And with a larger tether may he walk   125
Than may be given you. In few,° Ophelia,
Do not believe his vows, for they are brokers,°
Not of that dye which their investments° show,
But mere implorators° of unholy suits,
Breathing like sanctified and pious bawds°   130
The better to beguile. This is for all.
I would not, in plain terms, from this time forth
Have you so slander any moment leisure°
As to give words or talk with the Lord Hamlet.
Look to 't, I charge you. Come your ways.
OPHELIA   I shall obey, my lord.   [*Exeunt.*]

Scene IV. The platform.

[*Enter* HAMLET, HORATIO, *and* MARCELLUS.]

HAMLET   The air bites shrewdly.° It is very cold.
HORATIO   It is a nipping and an eager° air.

---

109 tender ... fool: (a) look like a fool, (b) present me a fool, (c) present me a bastard baby   **112 fashion:** mere show   **113 given ... speech:** confirmed his words   **115 springes:** snares; **woodcocks:** foolish birds   **116 prodigal:** extravagantly   **117 blazes:** flashes, quickly extinguished (*extinct*)   **122–23 Set ... parley:** when you are asked to see him do not regard it as a command to negotiate   **126 In few:** in short   **127 brokers:** pimps   **128 investments:** garments   **129 implorators:** men who solicit   **130 bawds:** keepers of brothels   **133 slander ... leisure:** misuse any moment of leisure

I.iv.1 shrewdly: bitterly   **2 eager:** sharp

HAMLET   What hour now?
HORATIO   I thinks it lacks of twelve.
MARCELLUS   No, it is struck.
HORATIO   Indeed? I heard it not. It then draws near the season   5
   Wherein the spirit held his wont to walk.

[*A flourish of trumpets, and ordnance shot off within.*°]

   What doth this mean, my lord?
HAMLET   The King doth wake° tonight and takes his rouse,°
   Keeps wassail,° and the swaggering upspring reels.°
   And as he drains his draughts of Rhenish° down,   10
   The kettledrum and trumpet thus bray out
   The triumph of his pledge.
HORATIO   Is it a custom?
HAMLET   Aye, marry, is 't.
   But to my mind, though I am native here
   And to the manner born, it is a custom   15
   More honored in the breach than the observance.
   This heavy-headed revel° east and west
   Makes us traduced and taxed of° other nations.
   They clepe° us drunkards, and with swinish phrase
   Soil our addition,° and indeed it takes   20
   From our achievements, though performed at height,°
   The pith and marrow of our attribute.°
   So oft it chances in particular men,
   That for some vicious mole° of nature in them,
   As in their birth—wherein they are not guilty,   25
   Since nature cannot choose his origin—
   By the o'ergrowth of some complexion,°
   Oft breaking down the pales° and forts of reason,
   Or by some habit that too much o'erleavens°
   The form of plausive° manners, that these men—   30
   Carrying, I say, the stamp of one defect,
   Being Nature's livery,° or Fortune's star°—
   Their virtues else—be they as pure as grace,
   As infinite as man may undergo—
   Shall in the general censure take corruption   35

6 s.d. within: offstage   8 wake: "makes a night of it"; rouse: See I.ii.127, n.   9 wassail: revelry;
swaggering ... reels: reel in a riotous dance   10 Rhenish: Rhine wine   17 heavy-headed
revel: drinking which produces a thick head   18 traduced ... of: disgraced and censured by   19
clepe: call   20 soil ... addition: smirch our honor; addition: lit., title of honor added to a man's
name   21 though ... height: though of the highest merit   22 pith ... attribute: essential part
of our honor; i.e., we lose the honor due to our achievements because of our reputation for
drunkenness   24 mole: blemish   27 o'ergrowth ... complexion: some quality allowed to
overbalance the rest   28 pales: defenses   29 o'erleavens: mixes with   30 plausive: agreeable
32 Nature's livery: i.e., inborn; Fortune's star: the result of ill luck

From that particular fault. The dram of eale
Doth all the noble substance of a doubt
To his own scandal.°

[*Enter* GHOST.]

HORATIO   Look, my lord, it comes!
HAMLET   Angels and ministers of grace defend us!
Be thou a spirit of health or goblin damned,°   40
Bring with thee airs from Heaven or blasts from Hell,
Be thy intents wicked or charitable,
Thou comest in such a questionable° shape
That I will speak to thee. I'll call thee Hamlet,
King, Father, royal Dane. Oh, answer me!   45
Let me not burst in ignorance, but tell
Why thy canónized° bones, hearsèd° in death,
Have burst their cerements,° why the sepulcher
Wherein we saw thee quietly inurned°
Hath oped his ponderous and marble jaws   50
To cast thee up again. What may this mean,
That thou, dead corse, again, in complete steel,°
Revisit'st thus the glimpses of the moon,
Making night hideous, and we fools of nature
So horridly to shake our disposition°   55
With thoughts beyond the reaches of our souls?
Say, why is this? Wherefore? What should we do?

[GHOST *beckons* HAMLET.]

HORATIO   It beckons you to go away with it,
As if it some impartment° did desire
To you alone.
MARCELLUS   Look with what courteous action   60
It waves you to a more removèd ground.
But do not go with it.
HORATIO   No, by no means.
HAMLET   It will not speak. Then I will follow it.
HORATIO   Do not, my lord.
HAMLET   Why, what should be the fear?
I do not set my life at a pin's fee,°   65

36–38 **The . . . scandal:** this is the most famous of all disputed passages in Shakespeare's plays; the general meaning is clear: "a small portion of evil brings scandal on the whole substance, however noble"; "eale" is an Elizabethan spelling and pronunciation of "evil"   40 **spirit . . . damned:** a holy spirit or damned fiend   43 **questionable:** inviting discourse   47 **canónized:** buried with full rites according to the canon of the Church; **hearsèd:** buried   48 **cerements:** waxen shroud, used to wrap the bodies of the illustrious dead   49 **inurned:** buried   52 **complete steel:** full armor   55 **disposition:** nature   59 **impartment:** communication   65 **fee:** value

And for my soul, what can it do to that,
Being a thing immortal as itself?
It waves me forth again. I'll follow it.
HORATIO   What if it tempt you toward the flood, my lord,
Or to the dreadful summit of the cliff   70
That beetles o'er° his base into the sea,
And there assume some other horrible form
Which might deprive your sovereignty of reason°
And draw you into madness? Think of it.
The very place puts toys° of desperation,   75
Without more motive, into every brain
That looks so many fathoms to the sea
And hears it roar beneath.
HAMLET   It waves me still.
Go on. I'll follow thee.
MARCELLUS   You shall not go, my lord.
HAMLET   Hold off your hands.   80
HORATIO   Be ruled. You shall not go.
HAMLET   My fate cries out,
And makes each petty artery in this body
As hardy as the Nemean lion's nerve.°
Still am I called. Unhand me, gentlemen.
By Heaven, I'll make a ghost of him that lets° me!   85
I say, away! Go on. I'll follow thee.
                                    [*Exeunt* GHOST *and* HAMLET.]
HORATIO   He waxes desperate with imagination.
MARCELLUS   Let's follow. 'Tis not fit thus to obey him.
HORATIO   Have after. To what issue will this come?
MARCELLUS   Something is rotten in the state of Denmark.   90
HORATIO   Heaven will direct it.
MARCELLUS   Nay, let's follow him.   [*Exeunt.*]

Scene V. Another part of the platform.

[*Enter* GHOST *and* HAMLET.]

HAMLET   Whither wilt thou lead me? Speak. I'll go no further.
GHOST   Mark me.
HAMLET   I will.
GHOST   My hour is almost come

---

71 **beetles o'er:** juts out over   73 **sovereignty of reason:** control of your reason over your actions
75 **toys:** fancies   83 **Nemean . . . nerve:** sinew of a fierce beast slain by Hercules   85 **lets:**
hinders

When I to sulphurous and tormenting flames
Must render up myself.

HAMLET   Alas, poor ghost!

GHOST   Pity me not, but lend thy serious hearing   5
To what I shall unfold.

HAMLET   Speak. I am bound to hear.

GHOST   So art thou to revenge, when thou shalt hear.

HAMLET   What?

GHOST   I am thy father's spirit,
Doomed for a certain term to walk the night   10
And for the day confined to fast in fires
Till the foul crimes done in my days of nature
Are burnt and purged away. But that I am forbid
To tell the secrets of my prison house,
I could a tale unfold whose lightest word   15
Would harrow up thy soul, freeze thy young blood,
Make thy two eyes, like stars, start from their spheres,°
Thy knotted and combinèd° locks to part
And each particular° hair to stand an° end
Like quills upon the fretful porpentine.°   20
But this eternal blazon° must not be
To ears of flesh and blood. List, list, oh, list!
If thou didst ever thy dear father love—

HAMLET   Oh, God!

GHOST   Revenge his foul and most unnatural murder.   25

HAMLET   Murder!

GHOST   Murder most foul, as in the best it is,
But this most foul, strange, and unnatural.

HAMLET   Haste me to know 't, that I, with wings as swift
As meditation or the thoughts of love,   30
May sweep to my revenge.

GHOST   I find thee apt,
And duller shouldst thou be than the fat weed
That roots itself in ease on Lethe wharf°
Wouldst thou not stir in this. Now, Hamlet, hear.
'Tis given out that, sleeping in my orchard,   35
A serpent stung me—so the whole ear of Denmark
Is by a forgèd process° of my death
Rankly abused. But know, thou noble youth,
The serpent that did sting thy father's life
Now wears his crown.

I.v.17 **spheres:** in Ptolemaic astronomy, heavenly bodies were thought to be held in transparent
spheres, not orbits   18 **knotted . . . combinèd:** the hair that lies together in a mass   19
particular: individual; **an:** on   20 **porpentine:** porcupine   21 **eternal blazon:** description of
eternity   33 **Lethe wharf:** the bank of Lethe, the river of forgetfulness in the underworld   37
forgèd process: false account

HAMLET   Oh, my prophetic soul!   40
     My uncle!
GHOST   Aye, that incestuous, that adulterate beast,
     With witchcraft of his wit, with traitorous gifts—
     O wicked wit and gifts, that have the power
     So to seduce!—won to his shameful lust   45
     The will of my most seeming-virtuous Queen.
     O Hamlet, what a falling-off was there!
     From me, whose love was of that dignity
     That it went hand in hand even with the vow
     I made to her in marriage, and to decline   50
     Upon a wretch whose natural gifts were poor
     To those of mine!
     But virtue, as it never will be moved
     Though lewdness court it in a shape of Heaven,°
     So Lust, though to a radiant angel linked,   55
     Will sate itself° in a celestial bed
     And prey on garbage.
     But soft! Methinks I scent the morning air.
     Brief let me be. Sleeping within my orchard,
     My custom always of the afternoon,   60
     Upon my secure hour° thy uncle stole
     With juice of cursèd hebenon° in a vial,
     And in the porches of my ears did pour
     The leperous distillment,° whose effect
     Holds such an enmity with blood of man   65
     That swift as quicksilver it courses through
     The natural gates and alleys of the body,
     And with a sudden vigor it doth posset°
     And curd, like eager° droppings into milk,
     The thin and wholesome blood. So did it mine,   70
     And a most instant tetter° barked about,
     Most lazarlike,° with vile and loathsome crust,
     All my smooth body.
     Thus was I, sleeping, by a brother's hand
     Of life, of crown, of Queen, at once dispatched—   75
     Cut off even in the blossoms of my sin,
     Unhouseled, disappointed, unaneled,°
     No reckoning made, but sent to my account
     With all my imperfections on my head.
     Oh, horrible! Oh, horrible, most horrible!   80

---

54 **lewdness . . . Heaven:** though wooed by Lust disguised as an angel   56 **sate itself:** gorge   61
secure hour: time of relaxation   62 **hebenon:** probably henbane, a poisonous plant   64 **leperous
distillment:** distillation causing leprosy   68 **posset:** curdle   69 **eager:** acid   71 **tetter:** scab   72
lazarlike: like leprosy   77 **Unhouseled . . . unaneled:** without receiving the sacrament, not
properly prepared, unanointed—without extreme unction

If thou hast nature° in thee, bear it not.
Let not the royal bed of Denmark be
A couch for luxury° and damned incest.
But, howsoever thou pursuest this act,
Taint not thy mind, nor let thy soul contrive   85
Against thy mother aught. Leave her to Heaven
And to those thorns that in her bosom lodge
To prick and sting her. Fare thee well at once!
The glowworm shows the matin° to be near,
And 'gins to pale his uneffectual° fire.   90
Adieu, adieu, adieu! Remember me.   [*Exit.*]
HAMLET   O all you host of Heaven! O earth! What else?
And shall I couple Hell? Oh, fie! Hold, hold, my heart,
And you, my sinews, grow not instant old
But bear me stiffly up. Remember thee!   95
Aye, thou poor ghost, while memory holds a seat
In this distracted globe.° Remember thee!
Yea, from the table° of my memory
I'll wipe away all trivial fond° records,
All saws° of books, all forms,° all pressures° past,   100
That youth and observation copied there,
And thy commandment all alone shall live
Within the book and volume of my brain,
Unmixed with baser matter. Yes, by Heaven!
O most pernicious woman!   105
O villain, villain, smiling, damnèd villain!
My tables—meet it is I set it down
[*Writing*] That one may smile, and smile, and be a villain.
At least I'm sure it may be so in Denmark.
So, Uncle, there you are. Now to my word.°   110
It is "Adieu, adieu! Remember me."
I have sworn 't.
HORATIO, MARCELLUS [*Within*]   My lord, my lord!

[*Enter* HORATIO *and* MARCELLUS.]

MARCELLUS   Lord Hamlet!
HORATIO   Heaven secure him!
HAMLET   So be it!
MARCELLUS   Illo, ho, ho,° my lord!   115
HAMLET   Hillo, ho, ho, boy! Come, bird, come.
MARCELLUS   How is 't, my noble lord?

81 **nature**: natural feelings   83 **luxury**: lust   89 **matin**: morning   90 **uneffectual**: made ineffectual by daylight   97 **globe**: i.e., head   98 **table**: notebook   99 **fond**: trifling   100 **saws**: wise sayings; **forms**: images in the mind; **pressures**: impressions   110 **word**: cue   115 **Illo . . . ho**: the falconer's cry to recall the hawk

HORATIO   What news, my lord?

HAMLET   Oh, wonderful!

HORATIO   Good my lord, tell it.

HAMLET   No, you will reveal it.

HORATIO   Not I, my lord, by Heaven.

MARCELLUS   Nor I, my lord.   120

HAMLET   How say you, then, would heart of man once think it?
    But you'll be secret?

HORATIO, MARCELLUS   Aye, by Heaven, my lord.

HAMLET   There's ne'er a villain dwelling in all Denmark
    But he's an arrant° knave.

HORATIO   There needs no ghost, my lord, come from the grave   125
    To tell us this.

HAMLET   Why, right, you are i' the right.
    And so, without more circumstance° at all,
    I hold it fit that we shake hands and part—
    You as your business and desire shall point you,
    For every man hath business and desire,   130
    Such as it is. And for my own poor part,
    Look you, I'll go pray.

HORATIO   These are but wild and whirling words, my lord.

HAMLET   I'm sorry they offend you, heartily,
    Yes, faith, heartily.

HORATIO   There's no offense, my lord.   135

HAMLET   Yes, by Saint Patrick, but there is, Horatio,
    And much offense too. Touching this vision here,
    It is an honest° ghost, that let me tell you.
    For your desire to know what is between us,
    O'ermaster 't as you may. And now, good friends   140
    As you are friends, scholars, and soldiers,
    Give me one poor request.

HORATIO   What is 't, my lord? We will.

HAMLET   Never make known what you have seen tonight.

HORATIO, MARCELLUS   My lord, we will not.

HAMLET   Nay, but swear 't.

HORATIO   In faith,   145
    My lord, not I.

MARCELLUS   Nor I, my lord, in faith.

HAMLET   Upon my sword.

MARCELLUS   We have sworn, my lord, already.

HAMLET   Indeed, upon my sword,° indeed.

GHOST [*Beneath*]   Swear.

HAMLET   Ah, ha, boy! Say'st thou so? Art thou there, truepenny?°   150

---

124 **arrant:** out-and-out   127 **circumstance:** ceremony   138 **honest:** true   148 **upon . . .**
sword: on the cross made by the hilt of the sword   150 **truepenny:** old boy

Come on. You hear this fellow in the cellarage.
Consent to swear.
HORATIO   Propose the oath, my lord.
HAMLET   Never to speak of this that you have seen,
Swear by my sword.
GHOST [*Beneath*]   Swear.   155
HAMLET   *Hic et ubique?*° Then we'll shift our ground.
Come hither, gentlemen,
And lay your hands again upon my sword.
Never to speak of this that you have heard,
Swear by my sword.   160
GHOST [*Beneath*]   Swear.
HAMLET   Well said, old mole! Canst work i' the earth so fast?
A worthy pioner!° Once more remove,° good friends.
HORATIO   Oh, day and night, but this is wondrous strange!
HAMLET   And therefore as a stranger give it welcome.   165
There are more things in Heaven and earth, Horatio,
Than are dreamt of in your philosophy.
But come,
Here, as before, never, so help you mercy,
How strange or odd soe'er I bear myself,   170
As I perchance hereafter shall think meet
To put an antic disposition° on,
That you, at such times seeing me, never shall,
With arms encumbered° thus, or this headshake,
Or by pronouncing of some doubtful phrase,   175
As "Well, well, we know," or "We could an if we would,"
Or "If we list to speak," or "There be, an if they might,"
Or such ambiguous giving out, to note
That you know aught of me. This not to do,
So grace and mercy at your most need help you,   180
Swear.
GHOST [*Beneath*]   Swear.
HAMLET   Rest, rest, perturbèd spirit! [*They swear.*] So, gentlemen,
With all my love I do commend me to you.
And what so poor a man as Hamlet is   185
May do to express his love and friending° to you,
God willing, shall not lack. Let us go in together.
And still your fingers on your lips, I pray.
The time is out of joint. Oh, cursèd spite
That ever I was born to set it right!   190
Nay, come, let's go together.   [*Exeunt.*]

---

156 *Hic et ubique:* here and everywhere   163 **pioner:** miner; **remove:** move   172 **antic disposition:** mad behavior   174 **encumbered:** folded   186 **friending:** friendship

ACT II

Scene I. A room in Polonius' house.

[*Enter* POLONIUS *and* REYNALDO.]

POLONIUS   Give him this money and these notes, Reynaldo.
REYNALDO   I will, my lord.
POLONIUS   You shall do marvelous wisely, good Reynaldo,
    Before you visit him, to make inquire
    Of his behavior.
REYNALDO   My lord, I did intend it.   5
POLONIUS   Marry, well said, very well said. Look you, sir,
    Inquire me first what Danskers° are in Paris,
    And how, and who, what means,° and where they keep,°
    What company, at what expense, and finding
    By this encompassment and drift of question°   10
    That they do know my son, come you more nearer
    Than your particular demands will touch it.
    Take you, as 'twere, some distant knowledge of him,
    As thus, "I know his father and his friends,
    And in part him." Do you mark this, Reynaldo?   15
REYNALDO   Aye, very well, my lord.
POLONIUS   "And in part him, but" you may say, "not well.
    But if 't be he I mean, he's very wild,
    Addicted so and so"—and there put on him
    What forgeries° you please. Marry, none so rank°   20
    As may dishonor him, take heed of that,
    But, sir, such wanton, wild, and usual slips
    As are companions noted and most known
    To youth and liberty.
REYNALDO   As gaming, my lord.
POLONIUS   Aye, or drinking, fencing, swearing, quarreling,   25
    Drabbing.° You may go so far.
REYNALDO   My lord, that would dishonor him.
POLONIUS   Faith, no, as you may season° it in the charge.
    You must not put another scandal on him,
    That he is open to incontinency.°   30
    That's not my meaning. But breathe his faults so quaintly°
    That they may seem the taints of liberty,
    The flash and outbreak of a fiery mind.

II.i.7 **Danskers:** Danes   **8 what means:** what their income is; **keep:** live   **10 encompassment
. . . question:** roundabout method of questioning   **20 forgeries:** inventions; **rank:** gross   **26
Drabbing:** whoring   **28 season:** qualify   **30 open . . . incontinency:** so long as Laertes does his
drabbing inconspicuously Polonius would not be disturbed   **31 quaintly:** skillfully

A savageness in unreclaimèd° blood,
Of general assault.°
REYNALDO   But, my good lord—   35
POLONIUS   Wherefore should you do this?
REYNALDO   Aye, my lord,
I would know that.
POLONIUS   Marry, sir, here's my drift,°
And I believe it is a fetch of warrant.°
You laying these slight sullies° on my son,
As 'twere a thing a little soiled i' the working,   40
Mark you,
Your party in converse, him you would sound,
Having ever seen° in the prenominate° crimes
The youth you breathe of guilty, be assured
He closes with you in this consequence°—   45
"Good sir," or so, or "friend," or "gentleman,"
According to the phrase or the addition°
Of man and country.
REYNALDO   Very good, my lord.
POLONIUS   And then, sir, does he this—he does—
What was I about to say? By the mass, I was about to say something.   50
Where did I leave?
REYNALDO   At "closes in the consequence," at "friend or so," and
"gentleman."
POLONIUS   At "closes in the consequence," aye, marry,
He closes with you thus: "I know the gentleman.   55
I saw him yesterday, or t'other day,
Or then, or then, with such, or such, and, as you say,
There was a' gaming, there o'ertook in 's rouse,
There falling out at tennis." Or perchance,
"I saw him enter such a house of sale,"   60
Videlicet,° a brothel, or so forth.
See you now,
Your bait of falsehood takes this carp of truth.
And thus do we of wisdom and of reach,°
With windlasses° and with assays of bias,°   65
By indirections find directions out.°
So, by my former lecture and advice,
Shall you my son. You have me, have you not?
REYNALDO   My lord, I have.

---

34 **unreclaimed**: naturally wild   35 **Of . . . assault**: common to all men   37 **drift**: intention   38
fetch . . . warrant: trick warranted to work   39 **sullies**: blemishes   43 **Having . . . seen**: if ever
he has seen; **prenominate**: aforementioned   45 **closes . . . consequence**: follows up with this
reply   47 **addition**: title   61 **Videlicet**: namely, "viz."   64 **wisdom . . . reach**: of far-reaching
wisdom   65 **windlasses**: roundabout methods; **assays of bias**: making our bowling ball take a
curved course   66 **indirections . . . out**: by indirect means come at the direct truth

POLONIUS   God be wi' ye, fare ye well.
REYNALDO   Good my lord!   70
POLONIUS   Observe his inclination in° yourself.
REYNALDO   I shall, my lord.
POLONIUS   And let him ply his music.
REYNALDO   Well, my lord.
POLONIUS   Farewell!   [*Exit* REYNALDO.]

[*Enter* OPHELIA.]

                  How now, Ophelia! What's the matter?
OPHELIA   Oh, my lord, my lord, I have been so affrighted!   75
POLONIUS   With what, i' the name of God?
OPHELIA   My lord, as I was sewing in my closet,°
   Lord Hamlet, with his doublet° all unbraced,
   No hat upon his head, his stockings fouled,
   Ungartered and down-gyvèd° to his ankle,   80
   Pale as his shirt, his knees knocking each other,
   And with a look so piteous in purport
   As if he had been loosèd out of Hell
   To speak of horrors, he comes before me.
POLONIUS   Mad for thy love?
OPHELIA   My lord, I do not know,   85
   But truly I do fear it.
POLONIUS   What said he?
OPHELIA   He took me by the wrist and held me hard.
   Then goes he to the length of all his arm,
   And with his other hand thus o'er his brow,
   He falls to such perusal of my face   90
   As he would draw it. Long stayed he so.
   At last, a little shaking of mine arm,
   And thrice his head thus waving up and down,
   He raised a sigh so piteous and profound
   As it did seem to shatter all his bulk   95
   And end his being. That done, he lets me go.
   And with his head over his shoulder turned,
   He seemed to find his way without his eyes;
   For out o' doors he went without their helps,
   And to the last bended their light on me.   100
POLONIUS   Come, go with me. I will go seek the King.
   This is the very ecstasy° of love,
   Whose violent property fordoes° itself
   And leads the will to desperate undertakings

---

71 in: for   77 **closet**: private room   78 **doublet**: the short close-fitting coat which was braced to
the hose by laces   80 **down-gyved**: hanging around his ankles like fetters   102 **ecstasy**: frenzy
103 **property fordoes**: natural quality destroys

As oft as any passion under heaven   105
That does afflict our natures. I am sorry.
What, have you given him any hard words of late?
OPHELIA   No, my good lord, but, as you did command,
I did repel his letters and denied
His access to me.
POLONIUS   That hath made him mad.   110
I am sorry that with better heed and judgment
I had not quoted° him. I feared he did but trifle
And meant to wreck thee, but beshrew° my jealousy!
By Heaven, it is as proper° to our age
To cast beyond ourselves° in our opinions   115
As it is common for the younger sort
To lack discretion. Come, go we to the King.
This must be known, which, being kept close, might move
More grief to hide than hate to utter love.°
Come.   [*Exeunt.*]   120

Scene II. A room in the castle.

[*Flourish. Enter* KING, QUEEN, ROSENCRANTZ, GUILDENSTERN,
and ATTENDANTS.]

KING   Welcome, dear Rosencrantz and Guildenstern!
Moreover° that we much did long to see you,
The need we have to use you did provoke
Our hasty sending. Something have you heard
Of Hamlet's transformation—so call it,   5
Sith° nor the exterior nor the inward man
Resembles that it was. What it should be,
More than his father's death, that thus hath put him
So much from the understanding of himself
I cannot dream of. I entreat you both   10
That, being of so young days brought up with him
And sith so neighbored to his youth and havior°
That you vouchsafe your rest° here in our Court
Some little time, so by your companies
To draw him on to pleasures, and to gather   15

112 **quoted:** observed carefully   113 **beshrew:** a plague on   114 **proper:** natural   115 **cast . . .
ourselves:** be too clever   118–19 **which . . . love:** by being kept secret it may cause more sorrow
than it will cause anger by being revealed; i.e., the King and Queen may be angry at the thought of
the Prince's marrying beneath his proper rank

II.ii.2 Moreover: in addition to the fact that   6 **Sith:** since   12 **neighbored . . . havior:** so near
to his youthful manner of living   13 **vouchsafe . . . rest:** consent to stay

So much as from occasion you may glean,
Whether aught to us unknown afflicts him thus
That opened lies within our remedy.°
QUEEN   Good gentlemen, he hath much talked of you,
And sure I am two men there are not living   20
To whom he more adheres.° If it will please you
To show us so much gentry° and goodwill
As to expend your time with us a while
For the supply and profit of our hope,°
Your visitation shall receive such thanks   25
As fits a king's remembrance.
ROSENCRANTZ   Both your Majesties
Might, by the sovereign power you have of us,
Put your dread pleasures more into command
Than to entreaty.
GUILDENSTERN   But we both obey,
And here give up ourselves, in the full bent°   30
To lay our service freely at your feet,
To be commanded.
KING   Thanks, Rosencrantz and gentle Guildenstern.
QUEEN   Thanks, Guildenstern and gentle Rosencrantz.
And I beseech you instantly to visit   35
My too-much-changèd son. Go, some of you,
And bring these gentlemen where Hamlet is.
GUILDENSTERN   Heavens make our presence and our practices
Pleasant and helpful to him!
QUEEN   Aye, amen!
[*Exeunt* ROSENCRANTZ, GUILDENSTERN, *and some* ATTENDANTS.]

[*Enter* POLONIUS.]

POLONIUS   The ambassadors from Norway, my good lord,   40
Are joyfully returned.
KING   Thou still° hast been the father of good news.
POLONIUS   Have I, my lord? I assure my good liege
I hold my duty as I hold my soul,
Both to my God and to my gracious King.   45
And I do think, or else this brain of mine
Hunts not the trail of policy so sure
As it hath used to do,° that I have found
The very cause of Hamlet's lunacy.
KING   Oh, speak of that. That do I long to hear.   50

18 opened ... remedy: if revealed, might be put right by us   21 To ... adheres: whom he
regards more highly   22 gentry: courtesy   24 supply ... hope: to bring a profitable conclusion
to our hope   30 in ... bent: stretched to our uttermost   42 still: always   47–48 Hunts ... do:
is not so good at following the scent of political events as it used to be

POLONIUS   Give first admittance to the ambassadors.
　　My news shall be the fruit° to that great feast.
KING   Thyself do grace° to them and bring them in.   [*Exit* POLONIUS.]
　　He tells me, my dear Gertrude, he hath found
　　The head and source of all your son's distemper.°   55
QUEEN   I doubt it is no other but the main,°
　　His father's death and our o'erhasty marriage.
KING   Well, we shall sift him.

　　　[*Reenter* POLONIUS, *with* VOLTIMAND *and* CORNELIUS.]

　　　　　　　　　　　　Welcome, my good friends!
　　Say, Voltimand, what from our brother Norway?
VOLTIMAND   Most fair return of greetings and desires.   60
　　Upon our first,° he sent out to suppress
　　His nephew's levies, which to him appeared
　　To be a preparation 'gainst the Polack,
　　But better looked into, he truly found
　　It was against your Highness, whereat, grieved   65
　　That so his sickness, age, and impotence
　　Was falsely borne in hand,° sends out arrests
　　On Fortinbras; which he, in brief, obeys,
　　Receives rebuke from Norway, and in fine°
　　Makes vow before his uncle never more   70
　　To give the assay of arms° against your Majesty.
　　Whereon old Norway, overcome with joy,
　　Gives him three thousand crowns in annual fee
　　And his commission to employ those soldiers,
　　So levied as before, against the Polack.   75
　　With an entreaty, herein further shown,

　　　[*Giving a paper*]

　　That it might please you to give quiet pass°
　　Through your dominions for this enterprise,
　　On such regards of safety and allowance°
　　As therein are set down.
KING　　　　　　　　　　It likes° us well,   80
　　And at our more considered time we'll read,
　　Answer, and think upon this business.
　　Meantime we thank you for your well-took labor.

---

52 **fruit:** dessert   53 **do grace:** honor; i.e., by escorting them into the royal presence   55
distemper: mental disturbance   56 **main:** principal cause   61 **first:** i.e., audience   67 **borne in
hand:** imposed upon   69 **in fine:** in the end   71 **give . . . arms:** make an attack   77 **pass:**
passage   79 **regards . . . allowance:** safeguard and conditions   80 **likes:** pleases

Go to your rest. At night we'll feast together.
Most welcome home!

[Exeunt VOLTIMAND and CORNELIUS.]

POLONIUS   This business is well ended.   85
My liege, and madam, to expostulate°
What majesty should be, what duty is,
Why day is day, night night, and time is time,
Were nothing but to waste night, day, and time.
Therefore, since brevity is the soul of wit   90
And tediousness the limbs and outward flourishes,°
I will be brief. Your noble son is mad.
Mad call I it, for to define true madness,
What is 't but to be nothing else but mad?
But let that go.
QUEEN   More matter, with less art.°   95
POLONIUS   Madam, I swear I use no art at all.
That he is mad, 'tis true. 'Tis true 'tis pity,
And pity 'tis 'tis true—a foolish figure,°
But farewell it, for I will use no art.
Mad let us grant him, then. And now remains   100
That we find out the cause of this effect,
Or rather say the cause of this defect,
For this effect defective comes by cause.
Thus it remains and the remainder thus.
Perpend.°   105
I have a daughter—have while she is mine—
Who in her duty and obedience, mark,
Hath given me this. Now gather and surmise.°

[*Reads.*]

"To the celestial, and my soul's idol, the most beautified Ophelia—"
That's an ill phrase, a vile phrase, "beautified" is a vile phrase. But you   110
shall hear. Thus:

[*Reads.*]

"In her excellent white bosom, these," and so forth.
QUEEN   Came this from Hamlet to her?
POLONIUS   Good madam, stay awhile, I will be faithful.

---

86 **expostulate**: discuss   91 **flourishes**: ornaments   95 **art**: ornament   98 **figure**: figure of
speech   105 **Perpend**: note carefully   108 **surmise**: guess the meaning

[*Reads.*]

> "Doubt thou the stars are fire,   115
>   Doubt that the sun doth move,
> Doubt truth to be a liar,
>   But never doubt I love.

"O dear Ophelia, I am ill at these numbers,° I have not art to reckon
my groans, but that I love thee best, O most best, believe it. Adieu.   120
            "Thine evermore, most dear lady, whilst this
                    machine° is to him, HAMLET."
This in obedience hath my daughter shown me,
And more above, hath his solicitings,
As they fell out by time, by means and place,   125
All given to mine ear.
KING   But how hath she
    Received his love?
POLONIUS   What do you think of me?
KING   As of a man faithful and honorable.
POLONIUS   I would fain prove so. But what might you think,
    When I had seen this hot love on the wing—   130
    As I perceived it, I must tell you that,
    Before my daughter told me—what might you
    Or my dear Majesty your Queen here think
    If I had played the desk or table book,°
    Or given my heart awinking, mute and dumb,   135
    Or looked upon this love with idle sight—
    What might you think? No, I went round to work,
    And my young mistress thus I did bespeak:°
    "Lord Hamlet is a Prince, out of thy star.°
    This must not be." And then I prescripts° gave her   140
    That she should lock herself from his resort,
    Admit no messengers, receive no tokens.
    Which done, she took the fruits of my advice.
    And he, repulsèd, a short tale to make,
    Fell into a sadness, then into a fast,   145
    Thence to a watch, thence into a weakness,
    Thence to a lightness,° and by this declension°
    Into the madness wherein now he raves
    And all we mourn for.

---

119 **numbers:** verses   122 **machine:** i.e., body, an affected phrase   134 **desk ... book:** i.e.,
acted as silent go-between (desks and books being natural post offices for a love letter), or been a
recipient of secrets but took no action   138 **bespeak:** address   139 **out ... star:** above your
destiny   140 **prescripts:** instructions   145–47 **Fell ... lightness:** Hamlet's case history, according to Polonius, develops by stages   147 **declension:** decline

KING   Do you think this?

QUEEN   It may be, very like.   150

POLONIUS   Hath there been such a time, I'd fain know that,
That I have positively said " 'Tis so"
When it proved otherwise?

KING   Not that I know.

POLONIUS [*Pointing to his head and shoulder.*]
Take this from this, if this be otherwise.
If circumstances lead me, I will find   155
Where truth is hid, though it were hid indeed
Within the center.°

KING   How may we try it further?

POLONIUS   You know sometimes he walks four hours together
Here in the lobby.

QUEEN   So he does indeed.

POLONIUS   At such a time I'll loose° my daughter to him.   160
Be you and I behind an arras° then.
Mark the encounter. If he love her not,
And be not from his reason fall'n thereon,
Let me be no assistant for a state,
But keep a farm and carters.°

KING   We will try it.   165

QUEEN   But look where sadly the poor wretch comes reading.

POLONIUS   Away, I do beseech you, both away.
I'll board° him presently.

                    [*Exeunt* KING, QUEEN, *and* ATTENDANTS.]

[*Enter* HAMLET, *reading.*]

Oh, give me leave. How does my good Lord Hamlet?

HAMLET   Well, God-a-mercy.   170

POLONIUS   Do you know me, my lord?

HAMLET   Excellent well. You are a fishmonger.°

POLONIUS   Not I, my lord.

HAMLET   Then I would you were so honest a man.

POLONIUS   Honest, my lord!   175

HAMLET   Aye, sir, to be honest, as this world goes, is to be one man
picked out of ten thousand.

POLONIUS   That's very true, my lord.

HAMLET   For if the sun breed maggots° in a dead dog, being a god kissing
carrion°—Have you a daughter?   180

---

157 **center:** center of the earth   160 **loose:** turn loose   161 **arras:** tapestry hanging   165 **keep
. . . carters:** i.e., turn country squire   168 **board:** accost   172 **fishmonger:** (a) fish-seller, (b)
pimp   179 **sun . . . maggots:** a general belief   180 **carrion:** flesh

POLONIUS   I have, my lord.

HAMLET   Let her not walk i' the sun. Conception° is a blessing, but not as your daughter may conceive—friend, look to 't.

POLONIUS [*Aside*]   How say you by that? Still harping on my daughter. Yet he knew me not at first, he said I was a fishmonger. He is far gone, far gone. And truly in my youth I suffered much extremity for love, very near this. I'll speak to him again.—What do you read, my lord?   185

HAMLET   Words, words, words.

POLONIUS   What is the matter, my lord?   190

HAMLET   Between who?

POLONIUS   I mean the matter that you read, my lord.

HAMLET   Slanders, sir. For the satirical rogue says here that old men have gray beards, that their faces are wrinkled, their eyes purging thick amber and plum-tree gum, and that they have a plentiful lack of wit,   195 together with most weak hams. All which, sir, though I most powerfully and potently believe, yet I hold it not honesty to have it thus set down; for yourself, sir, should be old as I am if like a crab you could go backward.

POLONIUS [*Aside*]   Though this be madness, yet there is method° in 't.—   200 Will you walk out of the air, my lord?

HAMLET   Into my grave.

POLONIUS   Indeed, that's out of the air. [*Aside*] How pregnant° sometimes his replies are! A happiness° that often madness hits on, which reason and sanity could not so prosperously be delivered of. I will   205 leave him, and suddenly contrive the means of meeting between him and my daughter.—My honorable lord, I will most humbly take my leave of you.

HAMLET   You cannot, sir, take from me anything that I will more willingly part withal—except my life, except my life, except my life.   210

POLONIUS   Fare you well, my lord.

HAMLET   These tedious old fools!

[*Enter* ROSENCRANTZ *and* GUILDENSTERN.]

POLONIUS   You go to seek the Lord Hamlet. There he is.

ROSENCRANTZ [*To* POLONIUS]   God save you, sir!   [*Exit* POLONIUS.]

GUILDENSTERN   My honored lord!   215

ROSENCRANTZ   My most dear lord!

HAMLET   My excellent good friends!° How dost thou, Guildenstern? Ah, Rosencrantz! Good lads, how do you both?

ROSENCRANTZ   As the indifferent° children of the earth.

182 **Conception:** (a) thought, (b) becoming pregnant   200 **method:** order, sense   203 **pregnant:** apt, meaningful   204 **happiness:** good turn of phrase   217 **My . . . friends:** as soon as Polonius has gone, Hamlet drops his assumed madness and greets Rosencrantz and Guildenstern naturally   219 **indifferent:** neither too great nor too little

GUILDENSTERN   Happy in that we are not overhappy. On Fortune's cap   220
　　we are not the very button.°

HAMLET   Nor the soles of her shoe?

ROSENCRANTZ   Neither, my lord.

HAMLET   Then you live about her waist, or in the middle of her favors?

GUILDENSTERN   Faith, her privates° we.   225

HAMLET   In the secret parts of Fortune? Oh, most true, she is a strum-
　　pet.° What's the news?

ROSENCRANTZ   None, my lord, but that the world's grown honest.

HAMLET   Then is Doomsday near. But your news is not true. Let me
　　question more in particular. What have you, my good friends,   230
　　deserved at the hands of Fortune, that she sends you to prison hither?

GUILDENSTERN   Prison, my lord!

HAMLET   Denmark's a prison.

ROSENCRANTZ   Then is the world one.

HAMLET   A goodly one, in which there are many confines,° wards,° and   235
　　dungeons. Denmark being one o' the worst.

ROSENCRANTZ   We think not so, my lord.

HAMLET   Why, then 'tis none to you, for there is nothing either good or
　　bad but thinking makes it so. To me it is a prison.

ROSENCRANTZ   Why, then your ambition makes it one. 'Tis too narrow   240
　　for your mind.

HAMLET   Oh, God, I could be bounded in a nutshell and count myself a
　　king of infinite space were it not that I have bad dreams.

GUILDENSTERN   Which dreams indeed are ambition, for the very sub-
　　stance of the ambitious is merely the shadow of a dream.   245

HAMLET   A dream itself is but a shadow.

ROSENCRANTZ   Truly, and I hold ambition of so airy and light a quality
　　that it is but a shadow's shadow.

HAMLET   Then are our beggars bodies, and our monarchs and out-
　　stretched° heroes the beggars' shadows.° Shall we to the Court? For,   250
　　by my fay,° I cannot reason.

ROSENCRANTZ, GUILDENSTERN   We'll wait upon you.

HAMLET   No such matter. I will not sort you with the rest of my servants,
　　for, to speak to you like an honest man, I am most dreadfully
　　attended.° But in the beaten way of friendship, what make you at   255
　　Elsinore?

ROSENCRANTZ   To visit you, my lord, no other occasion.

HAMLET   Beggar that I am, I am even poor in thanks, but I thank you.
　　And sure, dear friends, my thanks are too dear a halfpenny.° Were

---

221 **button:** i.e., at the top   225 **privates:** with a pun on "private parts" and "intimate friends"
226–27 **strumpet:** whore   235 **confines:** places of confinement; **wards:** cells   249–50 **Then . . .
shadows:** i.e., by your reasoning beggars are the only men of substance, for kings and heroes are by
nature ambitious and therefore "the shadows of a dream"   250 **outstretched:** of exaggerated
reputation   251 **fay:** faith   254–55 **dreadfully attended:** my attendants are a poor crowd   259
too . . . halfpenny: not worth a halfpenny

you not sent for? Is it your own inclining? Is it a free visitation?   260
Come, deal justly with me. Come, come. Nay, speak.

GUILDENSTERN   What should we say, my lord?

HAMLET   Why, anything, but to the purpose. You were sent for, and
there is a kind of confession in your looks which your modesties have
not craft enough to color.° I know the good King and Queen have   265
sent for you.

ROSENCRANTZ   To what end, my lord?

HAMLET   That you must teach me. But let me conjure° you, by the rights
of our fellowship, by the consonancy of our youth, by the obligation
of our ever preserved love, and by what more dear a better proposer   270
could charge you withal, be even° and direct with me, whether you
were sent for, or no.

ROSENCRANTZ [*Aside to* GUILDENSTERN]   What say you?

HAMLET [*Aside*]   Nay, then, I have an eye of you.—If you love me, hold
not off.   275

GUILDENSTERN   My lord, we were sent for.

HAMLET   I will tell you why. So shall my anticipation prevent° your
discovery, and your secrecy to the King and Queen molt no feather.°
I have of late—but wherefore I know not—lost all my mirth, for-
gone all custom of exercises, and indeed it goes so heavily with my   280
disposition that this goodly frame the earth seems to me a sterile
promontory. This most excellent canopy, the air, look you, this brave
o'erhanging firmament, this majestical roof fretted° with golden fire—
why, it appears no other thing to me than a foul and pestilent
congregation of vapors. What a piece of work is a man! How noble in   285
reason! How infinite in faculty! In form and moving how express° and
admirable! In action how like an angel! In apprehension how like a
god! The beauty of the world! The paragon of animals! And yet, to
me, what is this quintessence° of dust? Man delights not me—no, nor
woman neither, though by your smiling you seem to say so.   290

ROSENCRANTZ   My lord, there was no such stuff in my thoughts.

HAMLET   Why did you laugh, then, when I said "Man delights not me"?

ROSENCRANTZ   To think, my lord, if you delight not in man, what lenten
entertainment° the players shall receive from you. We coted° them on
the way, and hither are they coming to offer you service.   295

HAMLET   He that plays the King shall be welcome, His Majesty shall
have tribute of me. The adventurous knight shall use his foil and
target,° the lover shall not sigh gratis, the humorous man° shall end his
part in peace, the clown shall make those laugh whose lungs are tickle

---

265 **color:** conceal   268 **conjure:** make solemn appeal to   271 **even:** straight   277 **prevent:**
forestall   278 **molt no feather:** be undisturbed   283 **fretted:** ornamented   286 **express:** exact
289 **quintessence:** perfection   294 **lenten entertainment:** meager welcome; **coted:** overtook
297–98 **foil . . . target:** rapier and small shield   298 **humorous man:** the man who specializes in
character parts

o' the sere,° and the lady shall say her mind freely or the blank verse   300
shall halt° for 't. What players are they?

ROSENCRANTZ   Even those you were wont to take such delight in, the
tragedians of the city.

HAMLET   How chances it they travel? Their residence, both in reputation
and profit, was better both ways.   305

ROSENCRANTZ   I think their inhibition° comes by the means of the late
innovation.°

HAMLET   Do they hold the same estimation they did when I was in the
city? Are they so followed?

ROSENCRANTZ   No, indeed are they not.   310

HAMLET   How comes it? Do they grow rusty?

ROSENCRANTZ   Nay, their endeavor keeps in the wonted pace.° But
there is, sir, an eyrie° of children, little eyases,° that cry out on the top
of question° and are most tyrannically° clapped for 't. These are now
the fashion, and so berattle° the common stages°—so they call   315
them—that many wearing rapiers are afraid of goose quills° and dare
scarce come thither.

HAMLET   What, are they children? Who maintains 'em? How are they
escoted?° Will they pursue the quality° no longer than they can sing?
Will they not say afterward, if they should grow themselves to   320
common players—as it is most like if their means are no better—their
writers do them wrong to make them exclaim against their own
succession?°

ROSENCRANTZ   Faith, there has been much to-do on both sides, and the
nation holds it no sin to tarre° them to controversy. There was for a   325
while no money bid for argument° unless the poet and the player
went to cuffs° in the question.

HAMLET   Is 't possible?

GUILDENSTERN   Oh, there has been much throwing about of brains.

HAMLET   Do the boys carry it away?   330

ROSENCRANTZ   Aye, that they do, my lord, Hercules and his load° too.

HAMLET   It is not very strange, for my uncle is King of Denmark, and
those that would make mows° at him while my father lived give
twenty, forty, fifty, a hundred ducats apiece for his picture in little.

299–300 are . . . sere: explode at a touch; the *sere* is part of the trigger mechanism of a gun which if
"ticklish" will go off at a touch   301 halt: limp   306 inhibition: formal prohibition   307
innovation: riot   312 endeavor . . . pace: they try as hard as ever   313 eyrie: nest; eyases:
young hawks; this refers to the performing groups of boy actors, rivals of Shakespeare's own
theatrical company   314 cry . . . question: either "cry in a shrill voice" or perhaps "cry out the
latest detail of the dispute"; tyrannically: outrageously   315 berattle: abuse; common stages:
the professional players; the boys acted in "private" playhouses   316 goose quills: pens; i.e., of
satirists   319 escoted: paid; quality: acting profession   322–23 exclaim . . . succession: abuse
the profession to which they will afterward belong   325 tarre: urge on to fight; generally used of
encouraging a dog   326 argument: plot of a play; see III.ii.213   327 went to cuffs: boxed each
other's ears   331 Hercules . . . load: Hercules carrying the globe on his shoulders was the sign of
the Globe Playhouse   333 mows: grimaces

'Sblood,° there is something in this more than natural, if philosophy   335
could find it out.

[*Flourish of trumpets within.*]

GUILDENSTERN   There are the players.
HAMLET   Gentlemen, you are welcome to Elsinore. Your hands. Come
then. The appurtenance of welcome is fashion and ceremony.° Let me
comply° with you in this garb,° lest my extent° to the players—which,   340
I tell you, must show fairly outward—should more appear like enter-
tainment° than yours. You are welcome. But my uncle-father and
aunt-mother are deceived.
GUILDENSTERN   In what, my dear lord?
HAMLET   I am but mad north-northwest.° When the wind is southerly,° I   345
know a hawk from a handsaw.°

[*Reenter* POLONIUS.]

POLONIUS   Well be with you, gentlemen!
HAMLET   Hark you, Guildenstern, and you too—at each ear a hearer.
That great baby you see there is not yet out of his swaddling clouts.°
ROSENCRANTZ   Happily he's the second time comes to them, for they   350
say an old man is twice a child.
HAMLET   I will prophesy he comes to tell me of the players, mark it. You
say right, sir. O' Monday morning, 'twas so indeed.
POLONIUS   My lord, I have news to tell you.
HAMLET   My lord, I have news to tell you. When Roscius° was an actor in   355
Rome—
POLONIUS   The actors are come hither, my lord.
HAMLET   Buzz, buzz!°
POLONIUS   Upon my honor—
HAMLET   Then came each actor on his ass—   360
POLONIUS   The° best actors in the world, either for tragedy, comedy,
history, pastoral, pastoral-comical, historical-pastoral, tragical-histori-
cal, tragical-comical-historical-pastoral, scene individable° or poem

335 'Sblood: by God's blood   339 appurtenance . . . ceremony: that which pertains to welcome
is formal ceremony   340 comply: use the formality of welcome; i.e., shake hands with you; garb:
fashion; extent: outward behavior   341–42 entertainment: welcome   345 north-northwest:
i.e., 327° (out of 360°) of the compass; wind is southerly: the south wind was considered
unhealthy   341 hawk . . . handsaw: either "handsaw" is a corruption of "heronshaw," heron, or a
hawk is a tool like a pickax; the phrase means "I'm not so mad as you think"   349 clouts: clothes
355 Roscius: the most famous of Roman actors   358 Buzz, buzz: slang for "stale news"   361–65
The . . . men: Polonius reads out the accomplishments of the actors from the license which they
have presented him   363 scene individable: i.e., a play preserving the unities

unlimited.° Seneca cannot be too heavy, nor Plautus° too light. For
the law of writ° and the liberty,° these are the only men.   365
HAMLET   O Jephthah,° judge of Israel, what a treasure hadst thou!
POLONIUS   What a treasure had he, my lord?
HAMLET   Why,

> "One° fair daughter, and no more,
>   The which he lovèd passing well."   370

POLONIUS [*Aside*]   Still on my daughter.
HAMLET   Am I not i' the right, old Jephthah?
POLONIUS   If you call me Jephthah, my lord, I have a daughter that I love
passing well.
HAMLET   Nay, that follows not.   375
POLONIUS   What follows, then, my lord?
HAMLET   Why,

> "As by lot, God wot,"°

and then you know,

> "It came to pass, as most like it was—"   380

the first row° of the pious chanson° will show you more, for look
where my abridgement° comes.

[*Enter four or five* PLAYERS.]

You are welcome, masters, welcome all. I am glad to see thee well.
Welcome, good friends. Oh, my old friend!° Why, thy face is val-
anced° since I saw thee last. Comest thou to beard° me in Denmark?   385
What, my young lady° and mistress! By 'r Lady, your ladyship is
nearer to Heaven than when I saw you last, by the altitude of a
chopine.° Pray God your voice, like a piece of uncurrent gold, be not
cracked within the ring.° Masters, you are all welcome. We'll e'en to 't
like French falconers,° fly at anything we see. We'll have a speech   390
straight. Come, give us a taste of your quality°—come, a passionate
speech.

363–64 **poem unlimited:** i.e., a play which disregards the rules   364 **Seneca . . . Plautus:** the
Roman writers of tragedy and comedy with whose plays every educated man was familiar   365 **law
of writ:** the critical rules; i.e., classical plays; **liberty:** plays freely written; i.e., "modern" drama
366 **Jephthah:** the story of Jephthah is told in Judges, Chapter 11; he vowed that if successful
against the Ammonites he would sacrifice the first creature to meet him on his return, which was his
daughter   369–80 **One . . . was:** quotations from a ballad of Jephthah   378 **wot:** knows   381
row: line; **pious chanson:** godly poem   382 **abridgement:** entertainment   384 **old friend:** i.e.,
the leading player   384–85 **valanced:** bearded; a valance is a fringe hung round the sides and
bottom of a bed   **beard:** dare, with a pun on "valanced"   386 **young lady:** i.e., the boy who takes
the woman's parts   388 **chopine:** lady's shoe with thick cork sole   389 **cracked . . . ring:** before
coins were milled on the rim they were liable to crack; when the crack reached the ring surrounding
the device, the coin was no longer valid   390 **French falconers:** they were famous for their skill in
hawking   391 **quality:** skill as an actor

FIRST PLAYER   What speech, my good lord?

HAMLET   I heard thee speak me a speech once, but it was never acted, or
if it was, not above once; for the play, I remember, pleased not the   395
million, 'twas caviar to the general.° But it was—as I received it, and
others, whose judgments in such matters cried in the top of mine°—
an excellent play, well digested° in the scenes, set down with as much
modesty° as cunning. I remember one said there were no sallets° in
the lines to make the matter savory, nor no matter in the phrase that   400
might indict the author of affection,° but called it an honest method,
as wholesome as sweet, and by very much more handsome than fine.°
One speech in it I chiefly loved. 'Twas Aeneas' tale to Dido,° and
thereabout of it especially where he speaks of Priam's° slaughter. If it
live in your memory, begin at this line—let me see, let me see—   405
    "The rugged Pyrrhus,° like th' Hyrcanian beast,°—"
It is not so. It begins with "Pyrrhus."
    "The rugged Pyrrhus, he whose sable° arms,
    Black as his purpose, did the night resemble
    When he lay couchèd in the ominous° horse,°   410
    Hath now this dread and black complexion smeared
    With heraldry° more dismal. Head to foot
    Now is he total gules, horridly tricked
    With blood of fathers, mothers, daughters, sons,
    Baked and impasted° with the parching streets   415
    That lend a tyrannous and a damnèd light
    To their lord's murder. Roasted in wrath and fire,
    And thus o'ersized with coagulate gore,°
    With eyes like carbuncles, the hellish Pyrrhus
    Old grandsire Priam seeks."   420
So, proceed you.

POLONIUS   'Fore God, my lord, well spoken, with good accent and good
discretion.

FIRST PLAYER   "Anon he finds him
    Striking too short at Greeks. His antique sword,   425
    Rebellious to his arm, lies where it falls,
    Repugnant to command.° Unequal matched,
    Pyrrhus at Priam drives, in rage strikes wide,

---

396 **general:** common herd   397 **cried . . . mine:** surpassed mine   398 **digested:** composed
399 **modesty:** moderation; **sallets:** salads—here, spicy jokes   400–01 **phrase . . . affection:**
nothing in the language which could charge the author with affectation   402 **fine:** subtle   403
Aeneas' . . . Dido: the story of the sack of Troy as told by Aeneas to Dido, Queen of Carthage, in
Virgil's *Aeneid*   404 **Priam:** the old King of Troy   406 **Pyrrhus:** the son of Achilles, one of the
Greeks concealed in the Wooden Horse; **Hyrcanian beast:** the tiger   408 **sable:** black   410
ominous: fateful; **horse:** the Wooden Horse by which a small Greek force was enabled to make a
secret entry into Troy   412 **heraldry:** painting; the image of heraldic painting is kept up in *gules*
(the heraldic term for red) and *tricked* (painted)   415 **impasted:** turned into a crust by the heat of
the burning city   418 **o'ersized . . . gore:** covered over with congealed blood   427 **Repugnant to
command:** refusing to be used

But with the whiff and wind of his fell sword
The unnerved father falls. Then senseless Ilium,°   430
Seeming to feel this blow, with flaming top
Stoops to his base,° and with a hideous crash
Takes prisoner Pyrrhus' ear. For, lo! his sword,
Which was declining° on the milky° head
Of reverend Priam, seemed i' the air to stick.   435
So as a painted tyrant° Pyrrhus stood,
And like a neutral to his will and matter,°
Did nothing.
But as we often see, against° some storm
A silence in the heavens, the rack° stand still,   440
The bold winds speechless and the orb° below
As hush as death, anon the dreadful thunder
Doth rend the region°—so after Pyrrhus' pause
Aroused vengeance sets him new awork.
And never did the Cyclops'° hammers fall   445
On Mars's armor, forged for proof eterne,°
With less remorse° than Pyrrhus' bleeding sword
Now falls on Priam.
Out, out, thou strumpet, Fortune! All you gods,
In general synod° take away her power,   450
Break all the spokes and fellies° from her wheel,
And bowl the round nave° down the hill of Heaven
As low as to the fiends!"
POLONIUS   This is too long.
HAMLET   It shall to the barber's, with your beard. Prithee, say on. He's   455
for a jig° or a tale of bawdry, or he sleeps. Say on. Come to Hecuba.
FIRST PLAYER   "But who, oh, who had seen the mobled° Queen—"
HAMLET   "The mobled Queen"?
POLONIUS   That's good, "mobled Queen" is good.   460
FIRST PLAYER   "Run barefoot up and down, threatening the flames
With bisson rheum,° a clout° upon that head
Where late the diadem stood, and for a robe,
About her lank and all o'erteemèd° loins
A blanket, in the alarm of fear caught up.   465
Who this had seen, with tongue in venom steeped

430 Ilium: the citadel of Troy   432 Stoops . . . base: collapses   434 declining: bending toward; milky: milk-white   436 painted tyrant: as in the painting of a tyrant   437 neutral . . . matter: one midway (*neutral*) between his desire (*will*) and action (*matter*)   439 against: just before   440 rack: the clouds in the upper air   441 orb: world   443 region: the country round   445 Cyclops': of Titans, giants who aided Vulcan, the blacksmith god, to make armor for Mars, the war god   446 proof eterne: everlasting protection   447 remorse: pity   450 synod: council   451 fellies: the pieces forming the circumference of a wooden wheel   452 nave: center of the wheel   456 jig: bawdy dance   458 mobled: muffled   462 bisson rheum: blinding moisture; clout: rag   464 o'erteemèd: exhausted by bearing children; she had borne fifty-two

'Gainst Fortune's state would treason have pronounced.°
But if the gods themselves did see her then,
When she saw Pyrrhus make malicious sport
In mincing with his sword her husband's limbs,   470
The instant burst of clamor that she made,
Unless things mortal move them not at all,
Would have made milch° the burning eyes of Heaven
And passion in the gods."

POLONIUS   Look whether he has not turned his color and has tears in 's   475
eyes. Prithee, no more.

HAMLET   'Tis well; I'll have thee speak out the rest of this soon. Good my
lord, will you see the players well bestowed?° Do you hear, let them
be well used, for they are the abstract and brief chronicles of the
time.° After your death you were better have a bad epitaph than their   480
ill report while you live.

POLONIUS   My lord, I will use them according to their desert.°

HAMLET   God's bodykins,° man, much better. Use every man after his
desert and who shall 'scape whipping? Use them after your own
honor and dignity. The less they deserve, the more merit is in your   485
bounty. Take them in.

POLONIUS   Come, sirs.

HAMLET   Follow him, friends. We'll hear a play tomorrow.
        [*Exit* POLONIUS *with all the* PLAYERS *but the* FIRST.]
Dost thou hear me, old friend? Can you play *The Murder of Gonzago?*

FIRST PLAYER   Aye, my lord.   490

HAMLET   We'll ha 't tomorrow night. You could, for a need, study a
speech of some dozen or sixteen lines which I would set down and
insert in 't, could you not?

FIRST PLAYER   Aye, my lord.

HAMLET   Very well. Follow that lord, and look you mock him not.   495
                                [*Exit* FIRST PLAYER.]
My good friends, I'll leave you till night. You are welcome to
Elsinore.

ROSENCRANTZ   Good my lord!

HAMLET   Aye, so, God be wi' ye!
                [*Exeunt* ROSENCRANTZ *and* GUILDENSTERN.]
                Now I am alone.
Oh, what a rogue and peasant slave am I!   500
Is it not monstrous that this player here,
But in a fiction, in a dream of passion,
Could force his soul so to his own conceit°

466–67 Who . . . pronounced: anyone who had seen this sight would with bitter words have
uttered treason against the tyranny of Fortune   473 milch: moist   478 bestowed: housed   479–
80 abstract. . . time: they summarize and record the events of our time; Elizabethan players were
often in trouble for too saucily commenting on their betters in plays dealing with history or
contemporary events and persons   482 desert: rank   483 God's bodykins: by God's little body
503 conceit: imagination

That from her working° all his visage wanned,°
Tears in his eyes, distraction in 's aspect,   505
A broken voice, and his whole function° suiting
With forms to his conceit? And all for nothing!
For Hecuba!
What's Hecuba to him or he to Hecuba,
That he should weep for her? What would he do   510
Had he the motive and the cue for passion
That I have? He would drown the stage with tears
And cleave the general ear° with horrid speech,
Make mad the guilty and appal the free,°
Confound the ignorant, and amaze indeed   515
The very faculties of eyes and ears.
Yet I,
A dull and muddy-mettled° rascal, peak,°
Like John-a-dreams,° unpregnant of my cause,°
And can say nothing—no, not for a King   520
Upon whose property° and most dear life
A damned defeat was made. Am I a coward?
Who° calls me villain? Breaks my pate° across?
Plucks off my beard and blows it in my face?
Tweaks me by the nose? Gives me the lie i' the throat°   525
As deep as to the lungs? Who does me this?
Ha!
'Swounds,° I should take it. For it cannot be
But I am pigeon-livered° and lack gall°
To make oppression bitter, or ere this   530
I should have fatted° all the region kites
With this slave's offal.° Bloody, bawdy villain!
Remorseless, treacherous, lecherous, kindless° villain!
Oh, vengeance!
Why, what an ass am I! This is most brave,   535
That I, the son of a dear father murdered,
Prompted to my revenge by Heaven and Hell,
Must, like a whore, unpack my heart with words
And fall a-cursing like a very drab,°
A scullion!°   540
Fie upon 't! Foh! About, my brain! Hum, I have heard

---

504 **her working:** i.e., the effect of imagination; **wanned:** went pale   506 **function:** behavior
513 **general ear:** ears of the audience   514 **free:** innocent   518 **muddy-mettled:** made of mud,
not iron; **peak:** mope   519 **John-a-dreams:** "Sleepy Sam"; **unpregnant . . . cause:** barren of plans
for vengeance   521 **property:** personality   523–26 **Who . . . this:** Hamlet runs through all the
insults which provoked a resolute man to mortal combat   523 **pate:** head   525 **lie. . . throat:** the
bitterest of insults   528 **'Swounds:** by God's wounds   529 **pigeon-livered:** "as gentle as a dove";
gall: spirit   531 **fatted:** made fat   532 **I . . . offal:** before this I would have fed this slave's (i.e.,
the King's) gut to the kites   533 **kindless:** unnatural   539 **drab:** whore   540 **scullion:** the lowest
of the kitchen servants; perhaps the word should be "stallion" = male prostitute

That guilty creatures sitting at a play
Have by the very cunning of the scene
Been struck so to the soul that presently°
They have proclaimed their malefactions;   545
For murder, though it have no tongue, will speak
With most miraculous organ. I'll have these players
Play something like the murder of my father
Before mine uncle. I'll observe his looks,
I'll tent° him to the quick. If he but blench,°   550
I know my course. The spirit that I have seen
May be the Devil, and the Devil hath power
To assume a pleasing shape. Yea, and perhaps
Out of my weakness and my melancholy,
As he is very potent with such spirits,   555
Abuses me to damn me.° I'll have grounds
More relative° than this. The play's the thing
Wherein I'll catch the conscience of the King.   [*Exit.*]

ACT III

Scene I. A room in the castle.

[*Enter* KING, QUEEN, POLONIUS, OPHELIA, ROSENCRANTZ, *and*
GUILDENSTERN.]

KING   And can you, by no drift of circumstance,°
    Get from him why he puts on this confusion,
    Grating° so harshly all his days of quiet
    With turbulent and dangerous lunacy?
ROSENCRANTZ   He does confess he feels himself distracted,   5
    But from what cause he will by no means speak.
GUILDENSTERN   Nor do we find him forward to be sounded,°
    But, with a crafty madness, keeps aloof
    When we would bring him on to some confession
    Of his true state.
QUEEN   Did he receive you well?   10
ROSENCRANTZ   Most like a gentleman.
GUILDENSTERN   But with much forcing of his disposition.°

544 **presently:** immediately   550 **tent:** probe; **blench:** flinch   556 **Abuses . . . me:** i.e., deceives
me so that I may commit the sin of murder, which will bring me to damnation   557 **relative:**
convincing

III.i.1 **drift of circumstance:** circumstantial evidence, hint   3 **grating:** disturbing   7 **forward**
. . . sounded: eager to be questioned   12 **much . . . disposition:** making a great effort to be civil to
us

ROSENCRANTZ   Niggard of question,° but of our demands
    Most free in his reply.
QUEEN   Did you assay him
    To any pastime?°   15
ROSENCRANTZ   Madam, it so fell out that certain players
    We o'erraught° on the way. Of these we told him,
    And there did seem in him a kind of joy
    To hear of it. They are about the Court,
    And, as I think, they have already order   20
    This night to play before him.
POLONIUS   'Tis most true.
    And he beseeched me to entreat your Majesties
    To hear and see the matter.
KING   With all my heart, and it doth much content me
    To hear him so inclined.   25
    Good gentlemen, give him a further edge,
    And drive his purpose on to these delights.
ROSENCRANTZ   We shall, my lord.
               [*Exeunt* ROSENCRANTZ *and* GUILDENSTERN.]
KING   Sweet Gertrude, leave us too,
    For we have closely° sent for Hamlet hither,
    That he, as 'twere by accident, may here   30
    Affront° Ophelia.
    Her father and myself, lawful espials,°
    Will so bestow ourselves that, seeing unseen,
    We may of their encounter frankly judge
    And gather by him, as he is behaved,°   35
    If 't be the affliction of his love or no
    That thus he suffers for.
QUEEN   I shall obey you.
    And for your part, Ophelia, I do wish
    That your good beauties be the happy cause
    Of Hamlet's wildness. So shall I hope your virtues   40
    Will bring him to his wonted way again,
    To both your honors.
OPHELIA   Madam, I wish it may.   [*Exit* QUEEN.]
POLONIUS   Ophelia, walk you here. Gracious,° so please you,
    We will bestow ourselves. [*To* OPHELIA] Read on this book,°
    That show of such an exercise may color   45
    Your loneliness. We are oft to blame in this—
    'Tis too much proved—that with devotion's visage

---

13 Niggard of question: not asking many questions   **14–15 Did . . . pastime:** did you try to
interest him in any amusement   **17 o'erraught:** overtook   **29 closely:** secretly   **31 Affront:**
encounter   **32 lawful espials:** who are justified in spying on him   **35 by . . . behaved:** from him,
from his behavior   **43 Gracious:** your Majesty—addressed to the King   **44 book:** i.e., of
devotions

And pious action we do sugar o'er
The Devil himself.

KING [*Aside*]   Oh, 'tis too true!
How smart a lash that speech doth give my conscience!   50
The harlot's cheek, beautied with plastering art,
Is not more ugly to the thing that helps it°
Than is my deed to my most painted° word.
Oh, heavy burden!

POLONIUS   I hear him coming. Let's withdraw, my lord.   55

[*Exeunt* KING *and* POLONIUS.]

[*Enter* HAMLET.]

HAMLET   To be, or not to be—that is the question.
Whether 'tis nobler in the mind to suffer
The slings and arrows of outrageous fortune,
Or to take arms against a sea of troubles
And by opposing end them. To die, to sleep—   60
No more, and by a sleep to say we end
The heartache and the thousand natural shocks
That flesh is heir to. 'Tis a consummation
Devoutly to be wished. To die, to sleep,
To sleep—perchance to dream. Aye, there's the rub,°   65
For in that sleep of death what dreams may come
When we have shuffled off this mortal coil°
Must give us pause. There's the respect°
That makes calamity of so long life.
For who would bear the whips and scorns of time,   70
The oppressor's wrong, the proud man's contumely°
The pangs of déspised love, the law's delay,
The insolence of office° and the spurns
That patient merit of the unworthy takes,°
When he himself might his quietus° make   75
With a bare bodkin?° Who would fardels° bear,
To grunt and sweat under a weary life,
But that the dread of something after death,
The undiscovered country from whose bourn°
No traveler returns, puzzles the will,   80
And makes us rather bear those ills we have
Than fly to others that we know not of?

52 **ugly . . . it:** i.e., lust, which is the cause of its artificial beauty   53 **painted:** made-up   65 **rub:** impediment   67 **shuffled . . . coil:** cast off this fuss of life   68 **respect:** reason   71 **contumely:** insulting behavior   73 **insolence of office:** insolent behavior of government officials   73–74 **spurns . . . takes:** insults which men of merit have patiently to endure from the unworthy   75 **quietus:** discharge   76 **bodkin:** dagger; **fardels:** burdens   79 **bourn:** boundary

Thus° conscience does make cowards of us all,
And thus the native hue° of resolution
Is sicklied o'er with the pale cast° of thought,   85
And enterprises of great pitch° and moment
With this regard their currents turn awry
And lose the name of action.—Soft you now!
The fair Ophelia! Nymph, in thy orisons°
Be all my sins remembered.

OPHELIA   Good my lord,   90
How does your Honor for this many a day?

HAMLET   I humbly thank you—well, well, well.

OPHELIA   My lord, I have remembrances of yours
That I have longed long to redeliver.
I pray you now receive them.

HAMLET   No, not I.   95
I never gave you aught.

OPHELIA   My honored lord, you know right well you did,
And with them words of so sweet breath composed
As made the things more rich. Their perfume lost,
Take these again, for to the noble mind   100
Rich gifts wax poor when givers prove unkind.
There, my lord.

HAMLET   Ha, ha! Are you honest?°

OPHELIA   My lord?

HAMLET   Are you fair?   105

OPHELIA   What means your lordship?

HAMLET   That if you be honest and fair, your honesty should admit no
discourse to your beauty.°

OPHELIA   Could beauty, my lord, have better commerce than with
honesty?   110

HAMLET   Aye, truly, for the power of beauty will sooner transform
honesty from what it is to a bawd° than the force of honesty can
translate beauty into his likeness. This was sometime a paradox, but
now the time gives it proof. I did love you once.

OPHELIA   Indeed, my lord, you made me believe so.   115

HAMLET   You should not have believed me, for virtue cannot so inocu-
late our old stock but we shall relish° of it. I loved you not.

OPHELIA   I was the more deceived.

HAMLET   Get thee to a nunnery. Why wouldst thou be a breeder of
sinners? I am myself indifferent honest, but yet I could accuse me of   120

83–88 Thus . . . action: the religious fear that death may not be the end makes men shrink from
heroic actions   84 native hue: natural color   85 cast: color   86 pitch: height   89 orisons:
prayers   103 honest: chaste   107–08 That . . . beauty: if you are chaste and beautiful, your
chastity should allow no approach to your beauty   112 bawd: brothel-keeper   117 relish: have
some trace

such things that it were better my mother had not borne me. I am very proud, revengeful, ambitious, with more offenses at my beck° than I have thoughts to put them in, imagination to give them shape, or time to act them in. What should such fellows as I do crawling between heaven and earth? We are arrant knaves all. Believe none of   125
us. Go thy ways to a nunnery.° Where's your father?

OPHELIA   At home, my lord.

HAMLET   Let the doors be shut upon him, that he may play the fool nowhere but in 's own house. Farewell.

OPHELIA   Oh, help him, you sweet Heavens!   130

HAMLET   If thou dost marry, I'll give thee this plague for thy dowry: Be thou as chaste as ice, as pure as snow—thou shalt not escape calumny.° Get thee to a nunnery, go. Farewell. Or if thou wilt needs marry, marry a fool, for wise men know well enough what monsters° you make of them. To a nunnery, go, and quickly too. Farewell.   135

OPHELIA   O heavenly powers, restore him!

HAMLET   I have heard your paintings° too, well enough. God hath given you one face and you make yourselves another. You jig, you amble, and you lisp, and nickname God's creatures, and make your wantonness your ignorance.° Go to, I'll no more on 't—it hath made me mad.   140
I say we will have no more marriages. Those that are married already, all but one, shall live; the rest shall keep as they are. To a nunnery, go.   [*Exit.*]

OPHELIA   Oh, what a noble mind is here o'erthrown!
The courtier's, soldier's, scholar's, eye, tongue, sword—   145
The expectancy and rose° of the fair state,
The glass° of fashion and the mold of form,°
The observed of all observers—quite, quite down!
And I, of ladies most deject and wretched,
That sucked the honey of his music vows,   150
Now see that noble and most sovereign reason,
Like sweet bells jangled, out of tune and harsh,
That unmatched° form and feature of blown° youth
Blasted with ecstasy.° Oh, woe is me,
To have seen what I have seen, see what I see!   155

[*Reenter* KING *and* POLONIUS.]

KING   Love! His affections° do not that way tend,
Nor what he spake, though it lacked form a little,

---

122 **beck:** call   126 **nunnery:** i.e., a place where she will be removed from temptation   132–33 **calumny:** slander   134 **monsters:** horned beasts, cuckolds   137 **paintings:** using make-up   139–40 **nickname . . . ignorance:** give things indecent names and pretend to be too simple to understand their meanings   146 **expectancy . . . rose:** bright hope; the rose is used as a symbol for beauty and perfection   147 **glass:** mirror; **mold of form:** perfect pattern of manly beauty   153 **unmatched:** unmatchable; **blown:** perfect, like an open flower at its best   154 **Blasted . . . ecstasy:** ruined by madness   156 **affections:** state of mind

Was not like madness. There's something in his soul
O'er which his melancholy sits on brood,°
And I do doubt the hatch and the disclose°   160
Will be some danger. Which for to prevent,
I have in quick determination
Thus set it down: He shall with speed to England,
For the demand of our neglected tribute.
Haply the seas and countries different   165
With variable objects° shall expel
This something-settled° matter in his heart
Whereon his brains still beating puts him thus
From fashion of himself.° What think you on 't?

POLONIUS   It shall do well. But yet do I believe   170
The origin and commencement of his grief
Sprung from neglected love. How now, Ophelia!
You need not tell us what Lord Hamlet said,
We heard it all. My lord, do as you please,
But, if you hold it fit, after the play   175
Let his Queen mother all alone entreat him
To show his grief. Let her be round° with him,
And I'll be placed, so please you, in the ear
Of all their conference. If she find him not,
To England send him, or confine him where   180
Your wisdom best shall think.

KING   It shall be so.
Madness in great ones must not unwatched go.   [*Exeunt.*]

Scene II. A hall in the castle.

[*Enter* HAMLET *and* PLAYERS.]

HAMLET   Speak the speech,° I pray you, as I pronounced it to you,
trippingly on the tongue. But if you mouth° it, as many of your
players do, I had as lief the town crier spoke my lines. Nor do not saw
the air too much with your hand, thus, but use all gently. For in the
very torrent, tempest, and, as I may say, whirlwind of passion, you   5
must acquire and beget a temperance that may give it smoothness.
Oh, it offends me to the soul to hear a robustious° periwig-pated
fellow tear a passion to tatters, to very rags, to split the ears of the

---

159 **sits . . . brood**: sits hatching   160 **doubt . . . disclose**: suspect the brood which will result
166 **variable objects**: novel sights   167 **something-settled**: somewhat settled; i.e., not yet
incurable   168–69 **puts . . . himself**: i.e., separates him from his normal self   177 **round**: direct

III.ii.1 **the speech**: which he has written   2 **mouth**: "ham" it   7 **robustious**: ranting

groundlings,° who for the most part are capable of nothing but inexplicable dumb shows° and noise. I would have such a fellow   10 whipped for o'erdoing Termagant°—it out-Herods Herod. Pray you, avoid it.

FIRST PLAYER   I warrant your Honor.

HAMLET   Be not too tame neither, but let your own discretion be your tutor. Suit the action to the word, the word to the action, with this   15 special observance, that you o'erstep not the modesty of nature. For anything so overdone is from° the purpose of playing, whose end, both at the first and now, was and is to hold as 'twere the mirror up to Nature—to show Virtue her own feature, scorn her own image, and the very age and body of the time his form° and pressure.° Now this   20 overdone or come tardy off, though it make the unskillful laugh, cannot but make the judicious grieve, the censure of the which one° must in your allowance o'erweigh a whole theater of others. Oh, there be players that I have seen play, and heard others praise—and that highly, not to speak it profanely—that neither having the accent of   25 Christians nor the gait of Christian, pagan, nor man, have so strutted and bellowed that I have thought some of Nature's journeymen° had made men, and not made them well, they imitated humanity so abominably.

FIRST PLAYER   I hope we have reformed that indifferently° with us, sir.   30

HAMLET   Oh, reform it altogether. And let those that play your clowns speak no more than is set down for them. For there be of them that will themselves laugh, to set on some quantity of barren spectators to laugh too, though in the meantime some necessary question of the play be then to be considered. That's villainous, and shows a most   35 pitiful ambition in the fool that uses it. Go, make you ready.

[*Exeunt* PLAYERS.]

[*Enter* POLONIUS, ROSENCRANTZ, *and* GUILDENSTERN.]

How now, my lord! Will the King hear this piece of work?

POLONIUS   And the Queen too, and that presently.

HAMLET   Bid the players make haste.   [*Exit* POLONIUS.]

Will you two help to hasten them?   40

ROSENCRANTZ, GUILDENSTERN   We will, my lord.

[*Exeunt* ROSENCRANTZ *and* GUILDENSTERN.]

HAMLET   What ho! Horatio!

---

9 **groundlings:** the poorer spectators, who stood in the yard of the playhouse   10 **dumb shows:** an old-fashioned dramatic device; before a tragedy, and sometimes before each act, the characters mimed the action which was to follow   11 **Termagant:** God of the Saracens, who, like Herod, was presented in early stage plays as a roaring tyrant   17 **from:** contrary to   20 **very . . . pressure:** an exact reproduction of the age; **form:** shape; **pressure:** imprint   22 **the . . . one:** i.e., the judicious spectator   27 **journeymen:** hired workmen, not masters of the trade   30 **indifferently:** moderately

[*Enter* HORATIO.]

HORATIO   Here, sweet lord, at your service.
HAMLET   Horatio, thou art e'en as just a man
    As e'er my conversation coped° withal.   45
HORATIO   Oh, my dear lord—
HAMLET   Nay, do not think I flatter
    For what advancement may I hope from thee,
    That no revénue has but thy good spirits
    To feed and clothe thee? Why should the poor be flattered?
    No, let the candied tongue lick absurd pomp   50
    And crook the pregnant hinges of the knee
    Where thrift may follow fawning.° Dost thou hear?
    Since my dear soul was mistress of her choice
    And could of men distinguish, her election
    Hath sealed° thee for herself. For thou has been   55
    As one in suffering all that suffers nothing,
    A man that fortune's buffets and rewards
    Hast ta'en with equal thanks. And blest are those
    Whose blood and judgment are so well commingled
    That they are not a pipe for fortune's finger   60
    To sound what stop she please. Give me that man
    That is not passion's slave, and I will wear him
    In my heart's core—aye, in my heart of heart,
    As I do thee. Something too much of this.
    There is a play tonight before the King.   65
    One scene of it comes near the circumstance
    Which I have told thee of my father's death.
    I prithee when thou seest that act afoot,
    Even with the very comment° of thy soul
    Observe my uncle. If his occulted° guilt   70
    Do not itself unkennel° in one speech
    It is a damnèd ghost that we have seen
    And my imaginations are as foul
    As Vulcan's° stithy.° Give him heedful note,°
    For I mine eyes will rivet to his face,   75
    And after we will both our judgments join
    In censure of his seeming.°
HORATIO   Well, my lord.
    If he steal aught the whilst this play is playing,
    And 'scape detecting, I will pay the theft.

---

45 **coped:** met   51–52 **crook ... fawning:** bend the ready knees whenever gain will follow
flattery   55 **sealed:** set a mark on   69 **comment:** close observation   70 **occulted:** concealed
71 **unkennel:** come to light; lit., force a fox from his hole   74 **Vulcan:** the blacksmith god; **stithy:**
smithy; **heedful note:** careful observation   77 **seeming:** looks

HAMLET   They are coming to the play. I must be idle.°   80
Get you a place.

[*Danish march. A flourish. Enter* KING, QUEEN, POLONIUS, OPHE-
LIA, ROSENCRANTZ, GUILDENSTERN, *and other* LORDS *attendant,
with the* GUARD *carrying torches.*]

KING   How fares our cousin Hamlet?

HAMLET   Excellent, i' faith, of the chameleon's dish. I eat the air, promise-crammed. You cannot feed capons so.°

KING   I have nothing with this answer,° Hamlet. These words are not   85
mine.

HAMLET   No, nor mine now.° [*To* POLONIUS] My lord, you played once
i' the university, you say?

POLONIUS   That did I, my lord, and was accounted a good actor.

HAMLET   What did you enact?   90

POLONIUS   I did enact Julius Caesar. I was killed i' the Capitol. Brutus
killed me.

HAMLET   It was a brute part of him to kill so capital a calf there. Be the
players ready?

ROSENCRANTZ   Aye, my lord, they stay upon your patience.°   95

QUEEN   Come hither, my dear Hamlet, sit by me.

HAMLET   No, good Mother, here's metal more attractive.

POLONIUS   [*To the* KING]   Oh ho! Do you mark that?

HAMLET   Lady, shall I lie in your lap?

[*Lying down at* OPHELIA'S *feet*]

OPHELIA   No, my lord.   100

HAMLET   I mean, my head upon your lap?

OPHELIA   Aye, my lord.

HAMLET   Do you think I meant country matters?°

OPHELIA   I think nothing, my lord.

HAMLET   That's a fair thought to lie between maids' legs.   105

OPHELIA   What is, my lord?

HAMLET   Nothing.

OPHELIA   You are merry, my lord.

HAMLET   Who, I?

OPHELIA   Aye, my lord.   110

HAMLET   Oh God, your only jig-maker.° What should a man do but be

___

80 be idle: seem crazy   **83–84 Excellent . . . so:** Hamlet takes "fare" literally as "what food are
you eating"; the chameleon was supposed to feed on air; **promise-crammed:** stuffed, like a fattened
chicken (*capon*), but with empty promises   **85 I . . . answer:** I cannot make any sense of your
answer   **87 nor . . . now:** i.e., once words have left the lips they cease to belong to the speaker   **95
stay . . . patience:** wait for you to be ready   **104 country matters:** something sexual (with the
obvious pun)   **111 jig-maker:** composer of jigs

merry? For look you how cheerfully my mother looks, and my father died within 's two hours.

OPHELIA   Nay, 'tis twice two months, my lord.

HAMLET   So long? Nay, then, let the Devil wear black, for I'll have a suit   115
of sables.° Oh heavens! Die two months ago, and not forgotten yet? Then there's hope a great man's memory may outlive his life half a year. But, by 'r Lady, he must build churches then, or else shall he suffer not thinking on, with the hobbyhorse,° whose epitaph is "For, oh, for oh, the hobbyhorse is forgot."   120

[*Hautboys*° *play. The dumb show enters. Enter a* KING *and a* QUEEN *very lovingly, the* QUEEN *embracing him and he her. She kneels, and makes show of protestation unto him. He takes her up, and declines his head upon her neck, lays him down upon a bank of flowers. She, seeing him asleep, leaves him. Anon comes in a fellow, takes off his crown, kisses it, and pours poison in the* KING'S *ears, and exits. The* QUEEN *returns, finds the* KING *dead, and makes passionate action. The* POISONER, *with some two or three Mutes, comes in again, seeming to lament with her. The dead body is carried away. The* POISONER *woos the* QUEEN *with gifts. She seems loath and unwilling awhile, but in the end accepts his love.*   Exeunt.]

OPHELIA   What means this, my lord?

HAMLET   Marry, this is miching mallecho.° It means mischief.

OPHELIA   Belike this show imports the argument° of the play.

[*Enter* PROLOGUE.]

HAMLET   We shall know by this fellow. The players cannot keep counsel, they'll tell all.   125

OPHELIA   Will he tell us what this show meant?

HAMLET   Aye, or any show that you'll show him. Be not you ashamed to show, he'll not shame to tell you what it means.

OPHELIA   You are naught,° you are naught. I'll mark the play.

PROLOGUE   For us, and for our tragedy,   130
                           Here stooping to your clemency,
                           We beg your hearing patiently.

HAMLET   Is this a prologue, or the posy of a ring?°

OPHELIA   'Tis brief, my lord.

HAMLET   As woman's love.   135

[*Enter two* PLAYERS, KING *and* QUEEN.]

115–16 **suit of sables:** a quibble on "sable," black, and "sable," gown trimmed with sable fur, worn by wealthy old gentlemen   119 **hobbyhorse:** imitation horse worn by performers in a morris dance, an amusement much disapproved of by the godly   **s.d. Hautboys:** oboes   122 **miching mallecho:** slinking mischief   123 **argument:** plot; she is puzzled by the dumb show   129 **naught:** wicked   133 **posy . . . ring:** it was a pretty custom to inscribe rings with little mottoes or messages, which were necessarily brief

PLAYER KING Full° thirty times hath Phoebus' cart° gone round
　　Neptune's° salt wash and Tellus'° orbèd ground,
　　And thirty dozen moons with borrowed sheen°
　　About the world have times twelve thirties been,
　　Since love our hearts and Hymen° did our hands　　　　　140
　　Unite commutual° in most sacred bands.
PLAYER QUEEN So many journeys may the sun and moon
　　Make us again count o'er ere love be done!
　　But, woe is me, you are so sick of late,
　　So far from cheer and from your former state,　　　　　145
　　That I distrust° you. Yet, though I distrust,
　　Discomfort you, my lord, it nothing must.
　　For women's fear and love holds quantity°
　　In neither aught or in extremity.°
　　Now what my love is, proof hath made you know,　　　　150
　　And as my love is sized, my fear is so.
　　Where love is great, the littlest doubts are fear,
　　Where little fears grow great, great love grows there.
PLAYER KING Faith, I must leave thee,° love, and shortly too,
　　My operant powers° their functions leave to do.　　　　155
　　And thou shalt live in this fair world behind,
　　Honored, beloved, and haply one as kind
　　For husband shalt thou—
PLAYER QUEEN　　　　　　　　Oh, confound the rest!
　　Such love must needs be treason in my breast.
　　In second husband let me be accurst!　　　　　　　　　160
　　None wed the second but who killed the first.
HAMLET [*Aside*] Wormwood,° wormwood.
PLAYER QUEEN The instances° that second marriage move
　　Are base respects of thrift,° but none of love.
　　A second time I kill my husband dead　　　　　　　　　165
　　When second husband kisses me in bed.
PLAYER KING I do believe you think what now you speak,
　　But what we do determine oft we break.
　　Purpose is but the slave to memory,
　　Of violent birth but poor validity,　　　　　　　　　170
　　Which now, like fruit unripe, sticks on the tree
　　But fall unshaken when they mellow be.
　　Most necessary 'tis that we forget
　　To pay ourselves what to ourselves is debt.

136–209 **Full . . . twain:** the play is deliberately written in crude rhyming verse, full of ridiculous and bombastic phrases　136 **Phoebus' cart:** the chariot of the sun　137 **Neptune:** the sea god; **Tellus:** the earth goddess　138 **borrowed sheen:** light borrowed from the sun　140 **Hymen:** god of marriage　141 **commutual:** mutually　146 **distrust:** am anxious about　148 **quantity:** proportion　149 **In . . . extremity:** either nothing or too much　154 **leave thee:** i.e., die　155 **operant powers:** bodily strength　162 **Wormwood:** bitterness　163 **instances:** arguments　164 **respects of thrift:** considerations of gain

What to ourselves in passion we propose,   175
The passion ending, doth the purpose lose.
The violence of either grief or joy
Their own enactures° with themselves destroy.
Where joy most revels, grief doth most lament,
Grief joys, joy grieves, on slender accident.   180
This world is not for aye,° nor 'tis not strange
That even our loves should with our fortunes change,
For 'tis a question left us yet to prove
Whether love lead fortune or else fortune love.
The great man down, you mark his favorite flies,   185
The poor advanced makes friends of enemies.
And hitherto doth love on fortune tend,
For who not needs shall never lack a friend,
And who in want a hollow friend doth try
Directly seasons° him his enemy.   190
But, orderly to end where I begun,
Our wills and fates do so contráry run
That our devices still are overthrown,
Our thoughts are ours, their ends none of our own.
So think thou wilt no second husband wed,   195
But die thy thoughts when thy first lord is dead.

PLAYER QUEEN   Nor earth to me give food nor Heaven light!
    Sport and repose lock from me day and night!
    To desperation turn my trust and hope!
    An anchor's° cheer in prison be my scope!   200
    Each opposite that blanks the face of joy
    Meet what I would have well and it destroy!
    Both here and hence pursue me lasting strife
    If, once a widow, ever I be wife!

HAMLET   If she should break it now!   205

PLAYER KING   'Tis deeply sworn. Sweet, leave me here a while.
    My spirits grow dull, and fain I would beguile
    The tedious day with sleep.   [*Sleeps.*]

PLAYER QUEEN   Sleep rock thy brain,
    And never come mischance between us twain!   [*Exit.*]

HAMLET   Madam, how like you this play?   210

QUEEN   The lady doth protest too much, methinks.

HAMLET   Oh, but she'll keep her word.

KING   Have you heard the argument?° Is there no offense in 't?

HAMLET   No, no, they do but jest, poison in jest—no offense i' the
    world.   215

KING   What do you call the play?

---

178 **enactures:** performances   181 **aye:** ever   190 **seasons:** ripens into   200 **anchor:** anchorite,
hermit   213 **argument:** plot; when performances were given at Court, it was sometimes customary
to provide a written or printed synopsis of the story for the distinguished spectators

HAMLET   *The Mousetrap.*° Marry, how? Tropically.° This play is the
image of a murder done in Vienna. Gonzago is the Duke's name, his
wife, Baptista. You shall see anon. 'Tis a knavish piece of work, but
what o' that? Your Majesty, and we that have free° souls, it touches us   220
not. Let the galled jade wince, our withers are unwrung.°

[*Enter* LUCIANUS.]

This is one Lucianus, nephew to the King.
OPHELIA   You are as good as a chorus, my lord.
HAMLET   I could interpret between you and your love, if I could see the
puppets dallying.°   225
OPHELIA   You are keen, my lord, you are keen.°
HAMLET   It would cost you a groaning to take off my edge.
OPHELIA   Still better, and worse.
HAMLET   So you must take your husbands.° Begin, murderer. Pox, leave
thy damnable faces and begin. Come, the croaking raven doth bellow   230
for revenge.
LUCIANUS   Thoughts black, hands apt, drugs fit, and time agreeing,
Confederate season, else no creature° seeing,
Thou mixture rank of midnight weeds collected,
With Hecate's ban° thrice blasted, thrice infected,   235
Thy natural magic and dire property°
On wholesome life usurp immediately.

[*Pours the poison into the sleeper's ear.*]

HAMLET   He poisons him i' the garden for his estate.° His name's
Gonzago. The story is extant, and written in very choice Italian. You
shall see anon how the murderer gets the love of Gonzago's wife.   240
OPHELIA   The King rises.
HAMLET   What, frighted with false fire!°
QUEEN   How fares my lord?
POLONIUS   Give o'er the play.
KING   Give me some light. Away!   245
POLONIUS   Lights, lights, lights!
                              [*Exeunt all but* HAMLET *and* HORATIO.]
HAMLET   "Why, let the stricken deer go weep,

---

217 **Mousetrap:** the phrase was used of a device to entice a person to his own destruction;
Tropically: figuratively, with a pun on "trap"   220 **free:** innocent   221 **galled . . . unwrung:** let
a nag with a sore back flinch when the saddle is put on; our shoulders (being ungalled) feel no pain
225 **puppets dallying:** Elizabethan puppets were crude marionettes, popular at fairs. While the
figures were put through their motions, the puppet master explained what was happening   226
keen: (a) sharp, (b) "horny"   229 **So . . . husbands:** i.e., as the marriage service expresses it, "for
better, for worse"   233 **Confederate . . . creature:** the opportunity conspiring with me, no other
creature   235 **Hecate's ban:** the curse of Hecate, goddess of witchcraft   236 **property:** nature
238 **estate:** kingdom   442 **false fire:** a mere show

The hart ungallèd play,
For some must watch while some must sleep.
   Thus runs the world away."   250
Would not this, sir, and a forest of feathers°—if the rest of my
fortunes turn Turk° with me—with two Provincial roses° on my
razed° shoes, get me a fellowship° in a cry° of players, sir?

HORATIO   Half a share.

HAMLET   A whole one, I.   255
"For thou dost know, O Damon° dear,
   This realm dismantled° was
Of Jove himself, and now reigns here
   A very, very—pajock."°

HORATIO   You might have rhymed.   260

HAMLET   O good Horatio, I'll take the ghost's word for a thousand
pound. Didst perceive?

HORATIO   Very well, my lord.

HAMLET   Upon the talk of the poisoning?

HORATIO   I did very well note him.   265

HAMLET   Ah, ha! Come, some music! Come, the recorders!°
"For if the King like not the comedy,
Why then, belike, he likes it not, perdy."°
Come, some music!

[*Reenter* ROSENCRANTZ *and* GUILDENSTERN.]

GUILDENSTERN   Good my lord, vouchsafe me a word with you.   270

HAMLET   Sir, a whole history.

GUILDENSTERN   The King, sir—

HAMLET   Aye, sir, what of him?

GUILDENSTERN   Is in his retirement marvelous distempered.°

HAMLET   With drink, sir?   275

GUILDENSTERN   No, my lord, rather with choler.°

HAMLET   Your wisdom should show itself more richer to signify this to
the doctor, for for me to put him to his purgation° would perhaps
plunge him into far more choler.

GUILDENSTERN   Good my lord, put your discourse into some frame,°   280
and start not so wildly from my affair.

HAMLET   I am tame, sir. Pronounce.

GUILDENSTERN   The Queen your mother, in most great affliction of
spirit, hath sent me to you.

---

251 **forest of feathers**: set of plumes, much worn by players   252 **turn Turk**: turn heathen, and
treat me cruelly; **Provincial roses**: rosettes, worn on the shoes   253 **razed**: slashed, ornamented
with cuts; **fellowship**: partnership; **cry**: pack   256 **Damon**: Damon and Pythias were legendary
types of perfect friends   257 **dismantled**: robbed   259 **pajock**: peacock, a strutting, lecherous
bird   266 **recorders**: wooden flutes   268 **perdy**: by God   274 **distempered**: disturbed; but
Hamlet takes the word in its other sense of "drunk"   276 **choler**: anger, which Hamlet again
pretends to understand as meaning "biliousness"   278 **purgation**: laxative   280 **frame**: order

HAMLET   You are welcome.   285

GUILDENSTERN   Nay, good my lord, this courtesy is not of the right breed. If it shall please you to make me a wholesome answer, I will do your mother's commandment. If not, your pardon and my return shall be the end of my business.

HAMLET   Sir, I cannot.   290

GUILDENSTERN   What, my lord?

HAMLET   Make you a wholesome answer, my wit's diseased. But, sir, such answer as I can make you shall command, or rather, as you say, my mother. Therefore no more, but to the matter. My mother, you say—   295

ROSENCRANTZ   Then thus she says. Your behavior hath struck her into amazement and admiration.°

HAMLET   Oh, wonderful son that can so astonish a mother! But is there no sequel at the heels of this mother's admiration? Impart.

ROSENCRANTZ   She desires to speak with you in her closet ere you go to   300
bed.

HAMLET   We shall obey, were she ten times our mother. Have you any further trade with us?

ROSENCRANTZ   My lord, you once did love me.

HAMLET   So I do still, by these pickers and stealers.°   305

ROSENCRANTZ   Good my lord, what is your cause of distemper? You do surely bar the door upon your own liberty if you deny your griefs to your friend.

HAMLET   Sir, I lack advancement.°

ROSENCRANTZ   How can that be when you have the voice of the King   310
himself for your succession in Denmark?

HAMLET   Aye, sir, but "While the grass grows"°—the proverb is something musty.

[*Reenter* PLAYERS *with recorders.*]

Oh, the recorders! Let me see one. To withdraw° with you—why do you go about to recover the wind° of me, as if you would drive me 315
into a toil?°

GUILDENSTERN   O my lord, if my duty be too bold, my love is too unmannerly.°

HAMLET   I do not well understand that. Will you play upon this pipe?

GUILDENSTERN   My lord, I cannot.   320

---

297 admiration: wonder   305 pickers . . . stealers: i.e., hands, an echo from the Christian's duty in the catechism to keep his hands "from picking and stealing"   309 advancement: promotion; Hamlet harks back to his previous interview with Rosencrantz and Guildenstern   312 While . . . grows: the proverb ends "the steed starves"   314 withdraw: go aside; Hamlet leads Guildenstern to one side of the stage   315 recover . . . wind: a hunting metaphor; approach me with the wind against you   316 toil: net   317–18 if . . . unmannerly: if I exceed my duty by asking these questions, then my affection for you shows lack of manners; i.e., forgive me if I have been impertinent

HAMLET   I pray you.

GUILDENSTERN   Believe me, I cannot.

HAMLET   I do beseech you.

GUILDENSTERN   I know no touch of it, my lord.

HAMLET   It is as easy as lying. Govern these ventages° with your fingers   325
and thumb, give it breath with your mouth, and it will discourse most
eloquent music. Look you, these are the stops.

GUILDENSTERN   But these cannot I command to any utterance of harmony, I have not the skill.

HAMLET   Why, look you now, how unworthy a thing you make of me!   330
You would play upon me, you would seem to know my stops, you
would pluck out the heart of my mystery, you would sound me from
my lowest note to the top of my compass—and there is much music,
excellent voice, in this little organ—yet cannot you make it speak.
'Sblood, do you think I am easier to be played on than a pipe? Call me   335
what instrument you will, though you can fret° me, you cannot play
upon me.

[*Reenter* POLONIUS.]

God bless you, sir!

POLONIUS   My lord, the Queen would speak with you, and presently.

HAMLET   Do you see yonder cloud that's almost in shape of a camel?   340

POLONIUS   By the mass, and 'tis like a camel indeed.

HAMLET   Methinks it is like a weasel.

POLONIUS   It is backed like a weasel.

HAMLET   Or like a whale?

POLONIUS   Very like a whale.   345

HAMLET   Then I will come to my mother by and by. They fool me to the
top of my bent.° I will come by and by.

POLONIUS   I will say so.   [*Exit* POLONIUS.]

HAMLET   "By and by" is easily said. Leave me, friends.
                              [*Exeunt all but* HAMLET.]

'Tis now the very witching time° of night,   350
When churchyards yawn and Hell itself breathes out
Contagion to this world. Now could I drink hot blood,
And do such bitter business as the day
Would quake to look on. Soft! Now to my mother.
O heart, lose not thy nature, let not ever   355
The soul of Nero° enter this firm bosom.
Let me be cruel, not unnatural.
I will speak daggers to her, but use none.
My tongue and soul in this be hypocrites,

---

325 **ventages:** finger holes   336 **fret:** annoy, with a pun on the frets on stringed instruments   347
bent: capacity   350 **witching time:** when witches perform their foul rites   356 **Nero:** Nero
killed his own mother

How in my words soever she be shent,°   360
To give them seals° never, my soul, consent!   [*Exit.*]

Scene III. *A room in the castle.*

[*Enter* KING, ROSENCRANTZ, *and* GUILDENSTERN.]

KING   I like him not, nor stands it safe with us
    To let his madness range.° Therefore prepare you.
    I your commission will forthwith dispatch,
    And he to England shall along with you.
    The terms of our estate° may not endure   5
    Hazard so near us as doth hourly grow
    Out of his lunacies.
GUILDENSTERN   We will ourselves provide.
    Most holy and religious fear it is
    To keep those many many bodies safe
    That live and feed upon your Majesty.   10
ROSENCRANTZ   The single and peculiar° life is bound
    With all the strength and armor of the mind
    To keep itself from noyance,° but much more
    That spirit upon whose weal° depends and rests
    The lives of many. The cease of majesty°   15
    Dies not alone, but like a gulf° doth draw
    What's near it with it. It is a massy° wheel
    Fixed on the summit of the highest mount,
    To whose huge spokes ten thousand lesser things
    Are mortised° and adjoined; which, when it falls,   20
    Each small annexment, petty consequence,°
    Attends the boisterous ruin. Never alone
    Did the King sigh but with a general groan.
KING   Arm you, I pray you, to this speedy voyage,
    For we will fetters put upon this fear,   25
    Which now goes too free-footed.
ROSENCRANTZ, GUILDENSTERN   We will haste us.
               [*Exeunt* ROSENCRANTZ *and* GUILDENSTERN.]

[*Enter* POLONIUS.]

360 **shent:** rebuked   361 **give . . . seals:** ratify words by actions

III.iii.2 range: roam freely   **5 terms . . . estate:** i.e., one in my position   **11 peculiar:** individual   **13 noyance:** injury   **14 weal:** welfare   **15 cease of majesty:** death of a king   **16 gulf:** whirlpool   **17 massy:** massive   **20 mortised:** firmly fastened   **21 annexment . . . consequence:** attachment, smallest thing connected with it

POLONIUS   My lord, he's going to his mother's closet.
    Behind the arras I'll convey myself
    To hear the process. I'll warrant she'll tax° him home.
    And, as you said,° and wisely was it said,   30
    'Tis meet that some more audience than a mother,
    Since nature makes them partial, should o'erhear
    The speech, of vantage.° Fare you well, my liege.
    I'll call upon you ere you go to bed
    And tell you what I know.
KING   Thanks, dear my lord.   [*Exit* POLONIUS.]   35
    Oh, my offense is rank,° it smells to Heaven.
    It hath the primal eldest curse° upon 't,
    A brother's murder. Pray can I not,
    Though inclination be as sharp as will.°
    My stronger guilt defeats my strong intent,   40
    And like a man to double business bound,
    I stand in pause where I shall first begin,
    And both neglect. What if this cursèd hand
    Were thicker than itself with brother's blood,
    Is there not rain enough in the sweet heavens   45
    To wash it white as snow? Whereto serves mercy
    But to confront the visage of offense?
    And what's in prayer but this twofold force,
    To be forestalled° ere we come to fall
    Or pardoned being down? Then I'll look up,   50
    My fault is past. But oh, what form of prayer
    Can serve my turn? "Forgive me my foul murder"?
    That cannot be, since I am still possessed
    Of those effects° for which I did the murder—
    My crown, mine own ambition, and my Queen.   55
    May one be pardoned and retain the offense?°
    In the corrupted currents of this world
    Offense's gilded hand may shove by justice,
    And oft 'tis seen the wicked prize itself
    Buys out the law. But 'tis not so above.   60
    There is no shuffling, there the action lies
    In his true nature,° and we ourselves compelled
    Even to the teeth and forehead of our faults
    To give in evidence. What then? What rests?
    Try what repentance can. What can it not?   65
    Yet what can it when one cannot repent?

29 tax: censure   **30 as . . . said:** actually Polonius himself had said it   **33 of vantage:** from a place of vantage; i.e., concealment   **36 rank:** foul   **37 primal . . . curse:** the curse laid upon Cain, the first murderer, who also slew his brother   **39 will:** desire   **49 forestalled:** prevented   **54 effects:** advantages   **56 offense:** i.e., that for which he has offended   **61–62 there . . . nature:** in heaven the case is tried on its own merits

Oh, wretched state! Oh, bosom black as death!
Oh, limèd° soul, that struggling to be free
Art more engaged! Help, angels! Make assay!°
Bow, stubborn knees, and heart with strings of steel,   70
Be soft as sinews of the newborn babe!
All may be well.   [*Retires and kneels.*]

[*Enter* HAMLET.]

HAMLET   Now might I do it pat, now he is praying,
And now I'll do 't. And so he goes to Heaven,
And so am I revenged. That would be scanned: 75
A villain kills my father, and for that
I, his sole son, do this same villain send
To Heaven.
Oh, this is hire and salary, not revenge,
He took my father grossly,° full of bread,   80
With all his crimes broad blown, as flush° as May,
And how his audit stands who knows save Heaven?
But in our circumstance and course of thought,°
'Tis heavy with him. And am I then revenged,
To take him in the purging of his soul,   85
When he is fit and seasoned, for his passage?
No.
Up, sword, and know thou a more horrid hent.°
When he is drunk asleep, or in his rage,
Or in the incestuous pleasure of his bed—   90
At gaming, swearing, or about some act
That has no relish of salvation in 't—
Then trip him, that his heels may kick at Heaven
And that his soul may be as damned and black
As Hell, whereto it goes. My mother stays.   95
This physic° but prolongs thy sickly days.   [*Exit.*]
KING [*Rising*]   My words fly up, my thoughts remain below.
Words without thoughts never to Heaven go.   [*Exit.*]

Scene IV. The Queen's closet.

[*Enter* QUEEN *and* POLONIUS.]

68 limèd: caught as in birdlime   **69 assay:** attempt   **80 grossly:** i.e., when he was in a state of sin
81 broad . . . flush: in full blossom, as luxuriant   **83 circumstance . . . thought:** as it appears to
my mind   **88 hent:** opportunity   **96 physic:** medicine

POLONIUS   He will come straight. Look you lay home to° him.
　　Tell him his pranks have been too broad° to bear with,
　　And that your grace hath screened and stood between
　　Much heat and him. I'll sconce me° even here.
　　Pray you, be round with him.   5
HAMLET [*Within*]   Mother, Mother, Mother!
QUEEN   I'll warrant you,
　　Fear me not. Withdraw, I hear him coming.
　　　　　　　　　　　　[POLONIUS *hides behind the arras.*]

[*Enter* HAMLET.]

HAMLET   Now, Mother, what's the matter?
QUEEN   Hamlet, thou hast thy father much offended.
HAMLET   Mother, you have my father much offended.   10
QUEEN   Come, come, you answer with an idle° tongue.
HAMLET   Go, go, you question with a wicked tongue.
QUEEN   Why, how now, Hamlet!
HAMLET   What's the matter now?
QUEEN   Have you forgot me?
HAMLET   No, by the rood,° not so.
　　You are the Queen, your husband's brother's wife,   15
　　And—would it were not so!—you are my mother.
QUEEN   Nay, then, I'll set those to you that can speak.
HAMLET   Come, come, and sit you down. You shall not budge,
　　You go not till I set you up a glass°
　　Where you may see the inmost part of you.   20
QUEEN   What wilt thou do? Thou wilt not murder me?
　　Help, help, ho!
POLONIUS [*Behind*]   What ho! Help, help, help!
HAMLET [*Drawing*]   How now! A rat? Dead, for a ducat, dead!

[*Makes a pass through the arras.*]

POLONIUS [*Behind*]   Oh, I am slain!   [*Falls and dies.*]
QUEEN   Oh me, what hast thou done?   25
HAMLET   Nay, I know not. Is it the King?
QUEEN   Oh, what a rash and bloody deed is this!
HAMLET   A bloody deed! Almost as bad, good Mother,
　　As kill a king and marry with his brother.
QUEEN   As kill a king!
HAMLET   Aye, lady, 'twas my word.   30

III.iv.1 **lay . . . to:** be strict with   2 **broad:** unrestrained; Polonius is thinking of the obvious
insolence of the remarks about second marriage in the play scene   4 **sconce me:** hide myself   11
idle: foolish   14 **rood:** crucifix   19 **glass:** looking-glass

[*Lifts up the arras and discovers* POLONIUS.]

Thou wretched, rash, intruding fool, farewell!
I took thee for thy better. Take thy fortune.
Thou find'st to be too busy is some danger.
Leave wringing of your hands. Peace! Sit you down,
And let me wring your heart. For so I shall   35
If it be made of penetrable stuff,
If damnèd custom have not brassed° it so
That it be proof and bulwark against sense.
QUEEN   What have I done that thou darest wag thy tongue
In noise so rude against me?
HAMLET   Such an act   40
That blurs the grace and blush of modesty,
Calls virtue hypocrite, takes off the rose
From the fair forehead of an innocent love,
And sets a blister° there—makes marriage vows
As false as dicers' oaths. Oh, such a deed   45
As from the body of contraction° plucks
The very soul, and sweet religion makes
A rhapsody of words.° Heaven's face doth glow,
Yes, this solidity and compound mass,°
With tristful visage, as against the doom,°   50
Is thought-sick at the act.
QUEEN   Aye me, what act
That roars so loud and thunders in the index?°
HAMLET   Look here upon this picture,° and on this,
The counterfeit presentment° of two brothers.
See what a grace was seated on this brow—   55
Hyperion's curls, the front° of Jove himself,
An eye like Mars, to threaten and command,
A station° like the herald Mercury°
New-lighted on a heaven-kissing hill,
A combination° and a form indeed   60
Where every god did seem to set his seal
To give the world assurance of a man.
This was your husband. Look you now what follows.
Here is your husband, like a mildewed ear,
Blasting his wholesome brother. Have you eyes?   65
Could you on this fair mountain leave to feed

37 **brassed:** made brazen   44 **sets a blister:** brands as a harlot   46 **contraction:** the marriage
contract   48 **rhapsody of words:** string of meaningless words   49 **mass:** solid earth   50 **tristful
... doom:** sorrowful face, as in anticipation of Doomsday   52 **index:** prologue   53 **picture:**
modern producers usually interpret the pictures as miniatures, Hamlet wearing one of his father,
Gertrude one of Claudius   54 **counterfeit presentment:** portrait   56 **front:** forehead   58
station: figure; **Mercury:** messenger of the gods, and one of the most beautiful   60 **combination:**
i.e., of physical qualities

And batten° on this moor? Ha! Have you eyes?
You cannot call it love, for at your age
The heyday° in the blood is tame, it's humble,
And waits upon the judgment. And what judgment   70
Would step from this to this? Sense° sure you have,
Else could you not have motion.° But sure that sense
Is apoplexed;° for madness would not err,
Nor sense to ecstasy° was ne'er so thralled°
But it reserved some quantity of choice   75
To serve in such a difference.° What devil was 't
That thus hath cozened° you at hoodman-blind?°
Eyes without feeling, feeling without sight,
Ears without hands or eyes, smelling sans° all,
Or but a sickly part of one true sense   80
Could not so mope.°
Oh, shame! Where is thy blush? Rebellious° Hell,
If thou canst mutine° in a matron's bones,
To flaming youth let virtue be as wax
And melt in her own fire. Proclaim no shame   85
When the compulsive ardor° gives the charge,
Since frost itself as actively doth burn,
And reason panders° will.

QUEEN   O Hamlet, speak no more.
Thou turn'st mine eyes into my very soul,
And there I see such black and grainèd° spots   90
As will not leave their tinct.°

HAMLET   Nay, but to live
In the rank sweat of an enseamèd° bed,
Stewed in corruption, honeying and making love
Over the nasty sty—

QUEEN   Oh, speak to me no more,
These words like daggers enter in my ears.   95
No more, sweet Hamlet!

HAMLET   A murderer and a villain,
A slave that is not twentieth part the tithe°
Of your precedent° lord, a vice of kings,°
A cutpurse° of the empire and the rule,

---

67 **batten:** glut yourself   69 **heyday:** excitement   71 **Sense:** feeling   72 **motion:** desire   73
apoplexed: paralyzed   74 **ecstasy:** excitement, passion; **thralled:** enslaved   76 **serve . . . differ-**
ence: to enable you to see the difference between your former and your present husband   77
cozened: cheated; **hoodman-blind:** blindman's-buff   79 **sans:** without   81 **mope:** be dull   82–
88 **Rebellious . . . will:** i.e., if the passion (*Hell*) of a woman of your age is uncontrollable
(*rebellious*), youth can have no restraints; there is no shame in a young man's lust when the elderly are
just as eager and their reason (which should control desire) encourages them   83 **mutine:** mutiny
86 **compulsive ardor:** compelling lust   88 **panders:** acts as go-between   90 **grainèd:** dyed in the
grain   91 **tinct:** color   92 **enseamèd:** greasy   97 **tithe:** tenth part   98 **precedent:** former; **vice**
of kings: caricature of a king   99 **cutpurse:** thief

That from a shelf the precious diadem stole   100
    And put it in his pocket!

QUEEN   No more!

HAMLET   A king of shreds and patches—

[*Enter* GHOST.]

Save me, and hover o'er me with your wings,
    You heavenly guards! What would your gracious figure?

QUEEN   Alas, he's mad!   105

HAMLET   Do you not come your tardy son to chide
    That, lapsed in time and passion, lets go by
    The important acting of your dread command?°
    Oh, say!

GHOST   Do not forget. This visitation   110
    Is but to whet thy almost blunted purpose.
    But look, amazement on thy mother sits.
    Oh, step between her and her fighting soul.
    Conceit° in weakest bodies strongest works.
    Speak to her, Hamlet.

HAMLET   How is it with you, lady?   115

QUEEN   Alas, how is 't with you
    That you do bend your eye on vacancy°
    And with the incorporal° air do hold discourse?
    Forth at your eyes your spirits wildly peep,
    And as the sleeping soldiers in the alarm,   120
    Your bedded° hairs, like life in excrements,°
    Start up and stand an° end. O gentle son,
    Upon the heat and flame of thy distemper°
    Sprinkle cool patience. Whereon do you look?

HAMLET   On him, on him! Look you how pale he glares!   125
    His form and cause conjoined,° preaching to stones,
    Would them make capable.° Do not look upon me,
    Lest with this piteous action you convert
    My stern effects.° Then what I have to do
    Will want true color—tears perchance for blood.   130

QUEEN   To whom do you speak this?

HAMLET   Do you see nothing there?

QUEEN   Nothing at all, yet all that is I see.

HAMLET   Nor did you nothing hear?

107–08 **That . . . command:** who has allowed time to pass and passion to cool, and neglects the
urgent duty of obeying your dread command   114 **Conceit:** imagination   117 **vacancy:** empty
space   118 **incorporal:** bodiless   121 **bedded:** evenly laid; **excrements:** anything that grows out
of the body, such as hair or fingernails; here hair   122 **an:** on   123 **distemper:** mental disturbance
126 **form . . . conjoined:** his appearance and the reason for his appearance joined   127 **capable:**
i.e., of feeling   128–29 **convert . . . effects:** change the stern action which should follow

QUEEN   No, nothing but ourselves.
HAMLET   Why, look you there! Look how it steals away!
    My father, in his habit° as he lived!   135
    Look where he goes, even now, out at the portal!   [*Exit* GHOST.]
QUEEN   This is the very coinage of your brain.
    This bodiless creation ecstasy°
    Is very cunning in.
HAMLET   Ecstasy!
    My pulse, as yours, doth temperately keep time,   140
    And makes as healthful music. It is not madness
    That I have uttered. Bring me to the test
    And I the matter will reword, which madness
    Would gambol° from. Mother, for love of grace,
    Lay not that flattering unction° to your soul,   145
    That not your trespass but my madness speaks.
    It will but skin and film the ulcerous place,
    Whiles rank corruption, mining° all within,
    Infects unseen. Confess yourself to Heaven,
    Repent what's past, avoid what is to come,   150
    And do not spread the compost on the weeds
    To make them ranker. Forgive me this my virtue,
    For in the fatness° of these pursy° times
    Virtue itself of vice must pardon beg—
    Yea, curb° and woo for leave to do him good.   155
QUEEN   O Hamlet, thou hast cleft my heart in twain.
HAMLET   Oh, throw away the worser part of it,
    And live the purer with the other half.
    Good night. But go not to my uncle's bed.
    Assume a virtue if you have it not.   160
    That° monster, custom, who all sense doth eat,
    Of habits devil, is angel yet in this,
    That to the use° of actions fair and good
    He likewise gives a frock or livery
    That aptly° is put on. Refrain tonight,   165
    And that shall lend a kind of easiness
    To the next abstinence, the next more easy.
    For use almost can change the stamp° of nature,
    And either the Devil,° or throw him out
    With wondrous potency. Once more, good night.   170
    And when you are desirous to be blest,
    I'll blessing beg of you. For this same lord,

135 **habit:** garment   138 **ecstasy:** madness   144 **gambol:** start away   145 **unction:** healing
ointment   148 **mining:** undermining   153 **fatness:** grossness; **pursy:** bloated   155 **curb:** bow
low   161–65 **That . . . on:** i.e., custom (bad habits) like an evil monster destroys all sense of good
and evil, but yet can become an angel (good habits) when it makes us perform good actions as
mechanically as we put on our clothes   163 **use:** practice   165 **aptly:** readily   168 **stamp:**
impression   169 **either the Devil:** some verb such as "shame" or "curb" has been omitted

[*Pointing to* POLONIUS]

I do repent; but Heaven hath pleased it so,
To punish me with this, and this with me,
That I must be their scourge and minister.   175
I will bestow° him, and will answer well
The death I gave him. So again good night.
I must be cruel only to be kind.
Thus bad begins, and worse remains behind.
One word more, good lady.

QUEEN   What shall I do?   180
HAMLET   Not this, by no means, that I bid you do.
Let the bloat° king tempt you again to bed,
Pinch wanton° on your cheek, call you his mouse,
And let him, for a pair of reechy° kisses
Or paddling in your neck with his damned fingers,   185
Make you to ravel° all this matter out,
That I essentially am not in madness,
But mad in craft. 'Twere good you let him know.
For who that's but a Queen, fair, sober, wise,
Would from a paddock,° from a bat, a gib,°   190
Such dear concernings hide? Who would do so?
No, in despite of sense and secrecy,
Unpeg the basket on the house's top,
Let the birds fly, and like the famous ape,°
To try conclusions,° in the basket creep   195
And break your own neck down.

QUEEN   Be thou assured if words be made of breath
And breath of life, I have no life to breathe
What thou hast said to me.

HAMLET   I must to England. You know that?
QUEEN   Alack,   200
I had forgot. 'Tis so concluded on.

HAMLET   There's letters sealed, and my two schoolfellows,
Whom I will trust as I will adders fanged,
They bear the mandate.° They must sweep my way,
And marshal me to knavery. Let it work,   205
For 'tis the sport to have the enginer°
Hoist with his own petar.° And 't shall go hard
But I will delve one yard below their mines
And blow them at the moon: Oh, 'tis most sweet

176 bestow: get rid of   182 bloat: bloated   183 wanton: erotically   184 reechy: foul   186
ravel: unravel, reveal   190 paddock: toad; gib: tomcat   194 famous ape: the story is not known,
but evidently told of an ape that let the birds out of their cage and, seeing them fly, crept into the cage
himself and jumped out, breaking his own neck   195 try conclusions: repeat the experiment
204 mandate: command   206 enginer: engineer   207 petar: land mine

When in one line two crafts° directly meet.   210
This man shall set me packing.
I'll lug the guts into the neighbor room.
Mother, good night. Indeed this counselor
Is now most still, most secret, and most grave
Who was in life a foolish prating knave.   215
Come, sir, to draw toward an end with you.
Good night, Mother.

> [*Exeunt severally,* HAMLET *dragging in* POLONIUS.]

ACT IV

Scene I. A room in the castle.

[*Enter* KING, QUEEN, ROSENCRANTZ, *and* GUILDENSTERN.]

KING   There's matter° in these sighs, these profound heaves,
  You must translate. 'Tis fit we understand them.
  Where is your son?
QUEEN   Bestow this place° on us a little while.

> [*Exeunt* ROSENCRANTZ *and* GUILDENSTERN.]

  Ah, mine own lord, what have I seen tonight!   5
KING   What, Gertrude? How does Hamlet?
QUEEN   Mad as the sea and wind when both contend
  Which is the mightier. In his lawless fit,
  Behind the arras hearing something stir,
  Whips out his rapier, cries "A rat, a rat!"   10
  And in this brainish apprehension° kills
  The unseen good old man.
KING   Oh, heavy deed!
  It had been so with us had we been there.
  His liberty is full of threats to all,
  To you yourself, to us, to everyone.   15
  Alas, how shall this bloody deed be answered?
  It will be laid to us, whose providence°
  Should have kept short,° restrained and out of haunt,°
  This mad young man. But so much was our love
  We would not understand what was most fit,   20
  But, like the owner of a foul disease,

---

210 **crafts:** devices

IV.i.1 **matter:** something serious   4 **Bestow ... place:** give place, leave us   11 **brainish
apprehension:** mad imagination   17 **providence:** foresight   18 **short:** confined; **out of haunt:**
away from others

To keep it from divulging° let it feed
Even on the pith° of life. Where is he gone?
QUEEN   To draw apart the body he hath killed,
    O'er whom his very madness, like some ore   25
    Among a mineral of metals base,
    Shows itself pure. He weeps for what is done.
KING   O Gertrude, come away!
    The sun no sooner shall the mountains touch
    But we will ship him hence. And this vile deed   30
    We must, with all our majesty and skill,
    Both countenance° and excuse. Ho, Guildenstern!

[*Reenter* ROSENCRANTZ *and* GUILDENSTERN.]

    Friends both, go join you with some further aid.
    Hamlet in madness hath Polonius slain,
    And from his mother's closet hath he dragged him.   35
    Go seek him out, speak fair, and bring the body
    Into the chapel. I pray you, haste in this.
                [*Exeunt* ROSENCRANTZ *and* GUILDENSTERN.]
    Come, Gertrude, we'll call up our wisest friends,
    And let them know both what we mean to do
    And what's untimely done,°   40
    Whose whisper o'er the world's diameter
    As level as the cannon to his blank°
    Transports his poisoned shot, may miss our name
    And hit the woundless air. Oh, come away!
    My soul is full of discord and dismay.   [*Exeunt.*]   45

Scene II. Another room in the castle.

[*Enter* HAMLET.]

HAMLET   Safely stowed.
ROSENCRANTZ, GUILDENSTERN [*Within*]   Hamlet! Lord Hamlet!
HAMLET   But soft, what noise? Who calls on Hamlet?
    Oh, here they come.

[*Enter* ROSENCRANTZ *and* GUILDENSTERN.]

ROSENCRANTZ   What have you done, my lord, with the dead body?   5

22 **divulging**: becoming known   23 **pith**: marrow   32 **countenance**: take responsibility for   40
done: a half-line has been omitted; some editors fill the gap with "So, haply slander"   42 **blank**:
target

HAMLET   Compounded it with dust, whereto 'tis kin.

ROSENCRANTZ   Tell us where 'tis, that we may take it thence
    And bear it to the chapel.

HAMLET   Do not believe it.

ROSENCRANTZ   Believe what?   10

HAMLET   That I can keep your counsel and not mine own. Besides, to be
    demanded of a sponge! What replication° should be made by the son
    of a king?

ROSENCRANTZ   Take you me for a sponge, my lord?

HAMLET   Aye, sir, that soaks up the King's countenance,° his rewards, his   15
    authorities. But such officers do the King best service in the end. He
    keeps them, like an ape, in the corner of his jaw, first mouthed, to be
    last swallowed. When he needs what you have gleaned, it is but
    squeezing you and, sponge, you shall be dry again.

ROSENCRANTZ   I understand you not, my lord.   20

HAMLET   I am glad of it. A knavish speech sleeps in a foolish ear.°

ROSENCRANTZ   My lord, you must tell us where the body is, and go with
    us to the King.

HAMLET   The body is with the King, but the King is not with the body.°
    The King is a thing—   25

GUILDENSTERN   A thing, my lord?

HAMLET   Of nothing. Bring me to him. Hide fox, and all after.° [*Exeunt.*]

Scene III. Another room in the castle.

[*Enter* KING, *attended.*]

KING   I have sent to seek him, and to find the body.
    How dangerous is it that this man goes loose!
    Yet must not we put the strong law on him.
    He's loved of the distracted° multitude,
    Who like not in their judgment but their eyes;°   5
    And where 'tis so, the offender's scourge is weighed,
    But never the offense. To bear° all smooth and even,
    This sudden sending him away must seem
    Deliberate pause.° Diseases desperate grown
    By desperate appliance are relieved,   10
    Or not at all.

IV.ii.12 **replication:** answer   15 **countenance:** favor   21 **A ... ear:** a fool never understands
the point of a sinister speech   24 **The ... body:** this plays on the notion that a king had two
"bodies," one physical (the king as man), the other figurative (body of authority)   27 **Hide ...
after:** a form of the game of hide-and-seek; with these words Hamlet runs away from them

IV.iii.4 **distracted:** bewildered   5 **like ... eyes:** whose likings are swayed not by judgment but by
looks   7 **bear:** make   9 **Deliberate pause:** the result of careful planning

[*Enter* ROSENCRANTZ.]
>   How now! What hath befall'n?
ROSENCRANTZ   Where the dead body is bestowed, my lord,
We cannot get from him.
KING   But where is he?
ROSENCRANTZ   Without, my lord, guarded, to know your pleasure.
KING   Bring him before us.   15
ROSENCRANTZ   Ho, Guildenstern! Bring in my lord.

[*Enter* HAMLET *and* GUILDENSTERN.]

KING   Now, Hamlet, where's Polonius?
HAMLET   At supper.
KING   At supper! Where?
HAMLET   Not where he eats, but where he is eaten. A certain convoca-   20
tion of politic worms° are e'en at him. Your worm is your only
emperor for diet. We fat all creatures else to fat us, and we fat
ourselves for maggots. Your fat king and your lean beggar is but
variable service,° two dishes, but to one table. That's the end.
KING   Alas, alas!   25
HAMLET   A man may fish with the worm that hath eat of a king, and eat
of the fish that hath fed of that worm.
KING   What dost thou mean by this?
HAMLET   Nothing but to show you how a king may go a progress°
through the guts of a beggar.   30
KING   Where is Polonius?
HAMLET   In Heaven—send thither to see. If your messenger find him
not there, seek him i' the other place yourself. But indeed if you find
him not within this month, you shall nose him as you go up the stairs
into the lobby.   35
KING [*To some* ATTENDANTS]   Go seek him there.
HAMLET   He will stay till you come.   [*Exeunt* ATTENDANTS.]
KING   Hamlet, this deed, for thine especial safety,
Which we do tender,° as we dearly grieve
For that which thou hast done, must send thee hence   40
With fiery quickness. Therefore prepare thyself.
The bark is ready and the wind at help,°
The associates tend,° and every thing is bent°
For England.
HAMLET   For England?
KING   Aye, Hamlet.
HAMLET   Good.

20–21 **convocation . . . worms:** an assembly of political-minded worms   24 **variable service:**
choice of alternatives   29 **go a progress:** make a state journey   39 **tender:** regard highly   42 **at
help:** favorable   43 **associates tend:** your companions are waiting; **bent:** ready

KING   So is it if thou knew'st our purposes.   45

HAMLET   I see a cherub that sees them. But, come, for England! Farewell, dear Mother.

KING   Thy loving father, Hamlet.

HAMLET   My mother. Father and mother is man and wife, man and wife
is one flesh, and so, my mother. Come, for England!   [*Exit.*]   50

KING   Follow him at foot,° tempt him with speed aboard.
Delay it not, I'll have him hence tonight.
Away! For everything is sealed and done
That else leans on the affair. Pray you make haste.
                    [*Exeunt* ROSENCRANTZ *and* GUILDENSTERN.]
And, England, if my love thou hold'st at aught—   55
As my great power thereof may give thee sense,
Since yet thy cicatrice° looks raw and red
After the Danish sword, and thy free awe°
Pays homage to us—thou mayst not coldly set
Our sovereign process,° which imports at full,   60
By letters congruing° to that effect,
The present° death of Hamlet. Do it, England,
For like the hectic° in my blood he rages,
And thou must cure me. Till I know 'tis done,
Howe'er my haps,° my joys were ne'er begun.   [*Exit.*]   65

Scene IV. *A plain in Denmark.*

[*Enter* FORTINBRAS, *a* CAPTAIN, *and* SOLDIERS, *marching.*]

FORTINBRAS   Go, Captain, from me greet the Danish King.
Tell him that by his license Fortinbras
Craves the conveyance of a promised march°
Over his kingdom. You know the rendezvous.
If that His Majesty would aught with us,   5
We shall express our duty in his eye,°
And let him know so.

CAPTAIN   I will do 't, my lord.

FORTINBRAS   Go softly on.
                        [*Exeunt* FORTINBRAS *and* SOLDIERS.]

[*Enter* HAMLET, ROSENCRANTZ, GUILDENSTERN, *and others.*]

51 at foot: at his heels   57 cicatrice: scar   58 free awe: voluntary submission   59–60 coldly
. . . process: hesitate to carry out our royal command   61 congruing: agreeing   62 present:
immediate   63 hectic: fever   65 Howe'er my haps: whatever may happen to me

IV.iv.3 Craves . . . march: asks for permission to transport his army, as had already been
promised   6 in . . . eye: in person

HAMLET Good sir, whose powers° are these?
CAPTAIN They are of Norway, sir.   10
HAMLET How purposed, sir, I pray you?
CAPTAIN Against some part of Poland.
HAMLET Who commands them, sir?
CAPTAIN The nephew to old Norway, Fortinbras.
HAMLET Goes it against the main° of Poland, sir,   15
  Or for some frontier?
CAPTAIN Truly to speak, and with no addition,°
  We go to gain a little patch of ground
  That hath in it no profit but the name.
  To pay five ducats, five, I would not farm it,   20
  Nor will it yield to Norway or the Pole
  A ranker° rate should it be sold in fee.°
HAMLET Why, then the Polack never will defend it.
CAPTAIN Yes, it is already garrisoned.
HAMLET Two thousand souls and twenty thousand ducats   25
  Will not debate the question of this straw.
  This is the imposthume of° much wealth and peace,
  That inward breaks, and shows no cause without
  Why the man dies. I humbly thank you, sir.
CAPTAIN God be wi' you, sir.   [*Exit.*]
ROSENCRANTZ   Will 't please you go, my lord?   30
HAMLET I'll be with you straight. Go a little before.
                                    [*Exeunt all but* HAMLET.]
  How all occasions do inform against° me
  And spur my dull revenge! What is a man
  If his chief good and market° of his time
  Be but to sleep and feed? A beast, no more.   35
  Sure, He that made us with such large discourse,
  Looking before and after,° gave us not
  That capability and godlike reason
  To fust° in us unused. Now whether it be
  Bestial oblivion, or some craven scruple   40
  Of thinking too precisely on the event—
  A thought which, quartered, hath but one part wisdom
  And ever three parts coward—I do not know
  Why yet I live to say "This thing's to do,"
  Sith I have cause, and will, and strength, and means   45
  To do 't. Examples gross as earth exhort me.
  Witness this army, of such mass and charge,°
  Led by a delicate and tender Prince

9 **powers:** forces 15 **main:** mainland 17 **addition:** exaggeration 22 **ranker:** richer; **in fee:** with possession as freehold 27 **imposthume of:** inward swelling caused by 32 **inform against:** accuse 34 **market:** profit 36–37 **such . . . after:** intelligence that enables us to consider the future and the past 39 **fust:** grow musty 47 **charge:** expense

Whose spirit with divine ambition puffed
Makes mouths at the invisible event,°   50
Exposing what is mortal and unsure
To all that fortune, death, and danger dare,
Even for an eggshell. Rightly to be great
Is not to stir without great argument,
But greatly to find quarrel in a straw   55
When honor's at the stake.° How stand I then,
That have a father killed, a mother stained,
Excitements of my reason and my blood,
And let all sleep while to my shame I see
The imminent death of twenty thousand men   60
That for a fantasy and trick of fame
Go to their graves like beds, fight for a plot
Whereon the numbers cannot try the cause,°
Which is not tomb enough and continent°
To hide the slain? Oh, from this time forth,   65
My thoughts be bloody or be nothing worth!   [*Exit.*]

Scene V. Elsinore. A room in the castle.

[*Enter* QUEEN, HORATIO, *and a* GENTLEMAN.]

QUEEN   I will not speak with her.
GENTLEMAN   She is importunate, indeed distract.°
   Her mood will needs be pitied.
QUEEN   What would she have?
GENTLEMAN   She speaks much of her father, says she hears
   There's tricks° i' the world, and hems° and beats her heart,   5
   Spurns enviously° at straws, speaks things in doubt
   That carry but half-sense. Her speech is nothing,
   Yet the unshaped use° of it doth move
   The hearers to collection.° They aim° at it,
   And botch° the words up fit to their own thoughts,   10
   Which, as her winks and nods and gestures yield them,
   Indeed would make one think there might be thought,
   Though nothing sure, yet much unhappily.

50 Makes . . . event: mocks at the unseen risk   53–56 Rightly . . . stake: true greatness is a
matter of fighting not for a mighty cause but for the merest trifle when honor is concerned   63
Whereon . . . cause: a piece of ground so small that it would not hold the combatants   64
continent: large enough to contain

IV.v.2 distract: out of her mind   5 tricks: trickery; hems: makes significant noises   6 Spurns
enviously: kicks spitefully   8 unshaped use: disorder   9 collection: i.e., attempts to find a
sinister meaning; aim: guess   10 botch: patch

HORATIO   'Twere good she were spoken with, for she may strew
    Dangerous conjectures in ill-breeding minds.   15
QUEEN   Let her come in.   [*Exit* GENTLEMAN.]
    [*Aside*] To my sick soul, as sin's true nature is,
    Each toy° seems prologue to some great amiss.°
    So full of artless jealousy is guilt,
    It spills itself in fearing to be spilt.°   20

    [*Reenter* GENTLEMAN, *with* OPHELIA.]

OPHELIA   Where is the beauteous Majesty of Denmark?
QUEEN   How now, Ophelia!
OPHELIA   [*Sings.*]
      "How should I your truelove know
        From another one?
    By his cockle hat° and staff   25
        And his sandal shoon."°
QUEEN   Alas, sweet lady, what imports this song?
OPHELIA   Say you? nay, pray you, mark. [*Sings.*]
      "He is dead and gone, lady,
        He is dead and gone,   30
    At his head a grass-green turf,
        At his heels a stone."
    Oh, oh!
QUEEN   Nay, but, Ophelia—
OPHELIA   Pray you, mark. [*Sings.*]
    "White his shroud as the mountain snow—"   35

    [*Enter* KING.]

QUEEN   Alas, look here, my lord.
OPHELIA   [*Sings.*]
      "Larded° with sweet flowers,
    Which bewept to the grave did go
      With truelove showers."°
KING   How do you, pretty lady?   40
OPHELIA   Well, God 'ild° you! They say the owl was a baker's daughter.°
    Lord, we know what we are but know not what we may be. God be at
    your table!
KING   Conceit upon her father.

---

18 **toy:** trifle; **amiss:** calamity   20 **It . . . split:** guilt reveals itself by its efforts at concealment   25
cockle hat: a hat adorned with a cockleshell worn by pilgrims   26 **sandal shoon:** sandals, the
proper footwear of pilgrims   37 **Larded:** garnished   39 **truelove showers:** the tears of his faithful
love   41 **'ild** (yield): reward; **owl . . . daughter:** an allusion to a legend that Christ once went into a
baker's shop and asked for bread; the baker's wife gave him a piece but was rebuked by her daughter
for giving him too much; thereupon the daughter was turned into an owl

OPHELIA   Pray you let's have no words of this, but when they ask you   45
   what it means, say you this [*Sings*]:
         "Tomorrow is Saint Valentine's day,°
            All in the morning betime,
         And I a maid at your window,
            To be your Valentine.   50

         "Then up he rose, and donned his clothes,
            And dupped° the chamber door,
         Let in the maid, that out a maid
            Never departed more."
KING   Pretty Ophelia!   55
OPHELIA   Indeed, la, without an oath, I'll make an end on 't. [*Sings.*]
         "By Gis° and by Saint Charity,
            Alack, and fie for shame!
         Young men will do 't, if they come to 't,
            By cock, they are to blame.   60
         Quoth she, before you tumbled me,
            You promised me to wed."
      He answers:
         "So would I ha' done, by yonder sun,
            An thou hadst not come to my bed."   65
KING   How long hath she been thus?
OPHELIA   I hope all will be well. We must be patient. But I cannot
   choose but weep to think they should lay him i' the cold ground. My
   brother shall know of it. And so I thank you for your good counsel.
   Come, my coach! Good night, ladies, good night, sweet ladies, good   70
   night, good night.   [*Exit.*]
KING   Follow her close,° give her good watch, I pray you.
                                                      [*Exit* HORATIO.]
      Oh, this is the poison of deep grief. It springs
      All from her father's death. O Gertrude, Gertrude,
      When sorrows come, they come not single spies,°   75
      But in battalions! First, her father slain;
      Next, your son gone, and he most violent author°
      Of his own just remove. The people muddied,
      Thick and unwholesome in their thoughts and whispers,
      For good Polonius' death. And we have done but greenly°   80
      In huggermugger° to inter him. Poor Ophelia
      Divided from herself and her fair judgment,
      Without the which we are pictures, or mere beasts.

47 **Saint . . . day:** February 14, the day when birds are supposed to mate; according to the old belief
the first single man then seen by a maid is destined to be her husband   52 **dupped:** opened   57–
60 **Gis . . . cock:** for "Jesus" and "God," both words being used instead of the sacred names, like the
modern "Jeez" and "Gee"; **cock** is probably also the obscene pun   72 **close:** closely   75 **spies:**
scouts   77 **author:** cause   80 **done . . . greenly:** shown immature judgment   81 **huggermug-
ger:** secret haste

Last, and as much containing as all these,
Her brother is in secret come from France,   85
Feeds on his wonder, keeps himself in clouds,
And wants not buzzers° to infect his ear
With pestilent speeches of his father's death,
Wherein necessity, of matter beggared,
Will nothing stick our person to arraign°   90
In ear and ear. O my dear Gertrude, this,
Like to a murdering piece,° in many places
Gives me superfluous death.

[*A noise within*]

QUEEN   Alack, what noise is this?
KING   Where are my Switzers?° Let them guard the door.

[*Enter another* GENTLEMAN.]

What is the matter?
GENTLEMAN   Save yourself, my lord.   95
The ocean, overpeering of his list,°
Eats not the flats° with more impetuous haste
Than young Laertes, in a riotous head,°
O'erbears your officers. The rabble call him lord,
And as the world were now but to begin,   100
Antiquity forgot, custom not known,
The ratifiers and props of every word,°
They cry "Choose we—Laertes shall be King!"
Caps, hands, and tongues applaud it to the clouds—
"Laertes shall be King, Laertes King!"   105
QUEEN   How cheerfully on the false trail they cry!
Oh, this is counter,° you false Danish dogs!

[*A noise within*]

KING   The doors are broke.

[*Enter* LAERTES, *armed*, DANES *following*.]

LAERTES   Where is this King? Sirs, stand you all without.

---

87 buzzers: scandalmongers   **89–90 Wherein . . . arraign:** in which, knowing nothing of the true facts, he must necessarily accuse us   **92 murdering piece:** cannon loaded with grapeshot   **94 Switzers:** Swiss bodyguard   **96 overpeering . . . list:** looking over its boundary; i.e., flooding the mainland   **97 Eats . . . flats:** floods not the flat country   **98 in . . . head:** with a force of rioters **101–02 Antiquity . . . word:** forgetting ancient rule and ignoring old custom, by which all promises must be maintained   **107 counter:** in the wrong direction of the scent

DANES   No, let's come in.

LAERTES   I pray you, give me leave.   110

DANES   We will, we will.   [*They retire without the door.*]

LAERTES   I thank you. Keep the door. O thou vile King,
Give me my father!

QUEEN   Calmly, good Laertes.

LAERTES   That drop of blood that's calm proclaims me bastard,
Cries cuckold to my father, brands the harlot   115
Even here, between the chaste unsmirchèd brows
Of my true mother.

KING   What is the cause, Laertes,
That thy rebellion looks so giantlike?
Let him go, Gertrude. Do not fear° our person.
There's such divinity doth hedge a king°   120
That treason can but peep to what it would,
Acts little of his will. Tell me, Laertes,
Why thou art thus incensed. Let him go, Gertrude.
Speak, man.

LAERTES   Where is my father?

KING   Dead.

QUEEN   But not by him.   125

KING   Let him demand his fill.

LAERTES   How came he dead? I'll not be juggled with.
To Hell, allegiance! Vows, to the blackest devil!
Conscience and grace, to the profoundest pit!
I dare damnation. To this point I stand,   130
That both the worlds I give to negligence.
Let come what comes, only I'll be revenged
Most throughly for my father.

KING   Who shall stay you?

LAERTES   My will, not all the world.
And for my means, I'll husband them so well   135
They shall go far with little.

KING   Good Laertes,
If you desire to know the certainty
Of your dear father's death, is 't writ in your revenge
That, swoopstake,° you will draw both friend and foe,
Winner and loser?   140

LAERTES   None but his enemies.

KING   Will you know them, then?

LAERTES   To his good friends thus wide I'll ope my arms,
And like the kind life-rendering pelican,°
Repast° them with my blood.

---

119 fear: fear for   120 divinity . . . king: divine protection surrounds a king as with a hedge
139 swoopstake: "sweeping the board"   143 life-rendering pelican: the mother pelican was
supposed to feed her young with blood from her own breast   144 Repast: feed

KING   Why, now you speak
  Like a good child and a true gentleman.   145
  That I am guiltless of your father's death,
  And am most sensibly in grief for it,
  It shall as level° to your judgment pierce
  As day does to your eye.
DANES [*Within*]   Let her come in.
LAERTES   How now! What noise is that?   150

[*Reenter* OPHELIA.]

  O heat, dry up my brains! Tears seven times salt
  Burn out the sense and virtue of mine eye!
  By Heaven, thy madness shall be paid with weight
  Till our scale turn the beam.° O rose of May!°
  Dear maid, kind sister, sweet Ophelia!   155
  Oh heavens! Is 't possible a young maid's wits
  Should be as mortal as an old man's life?
  Nature is fine in love, and where 'tis fine
  It sends some precious instance of itself
  After the thing it loves.°   160
OPHELIA [*Sings.*]
      "They bore him barefaced on the bier,
      Hey non nonny, nonny, hey nonny,
      And in his grave rained many a tear—"
  Fare you well, my dove!
LAERTES   Hadst thou thy wits and didst persuade revenge,   165
  It could not move thus.
OPHELIA [*Sings.*]
      "You must sing down a-down
      An you call him a-down-a."
  Oh, how the wheel° becomes it! It is the false steward, that stole his
  master's daughter.   170
LAERTES   This nothing's more than matter.°
OPHELIA   There's° rosemary, that's for remembrance —pray you, love,
  remember. And there is pansies, that's for thoughts.
LAERTES   A document° in madness, thoughts and remembrance fitted.

---

148 **level:** clearly   154 **turn . . . beam:** weigh down the beam of the scale; **rose of May:** perfection
of young beauty   158–60 **Nature . . . loves:** i.e., her love for her father was so exquisite that she
has sent her sanity after him   169 **wheel:** explained variously as the spinning wheel, Fortune's
wheel, or the refrain; the likeliest explanation is that she breaks into a little dance at the words "You
must sing," and that the *wheel* is the turn as she circles round   171 **This . . . matter:** this nonsense
means more than sense   172–78 **There's . . . died:** in the language of flowers, each has its peculiar
meaning, and Ophelia distributes them appropriately: for her brother, rosemary (remembrance) and
pansies (thoughts); for the King, fennel (flattery) and columbine (thanklessness); for the Queen, rue,
called also herb o' grace (sorrow), and daisy (light of love); neither is worthy of violets (faithfulness)
174 **document:** instruction

OPHELIA   There's fennel for you, and columbines. There's rue for you,   175
and here's some for me—we may call it herb of grace o' Sundays. Oh,
you must wear your rue with a difference. There's a daisy. I would
give you some violets, but they withered all when my father died.
They say a' made a good end. [*Sings.*]
                "For bonny sweet Robin is all my joy."
LAERTES   Thought and affliction, passion, Hell itself,   180
She turns to favor° and to prettiness.
OPHELIA [*Sings.*]
        "And will a' not come again?
        And will a' not come again?
            No, no, he is dead,   185
            Go to thy deathbed,
        He never will come again.

        "His beard was as white as snow,
        All flaxen was his poll.°
            He is gone, he is gone,   190
            And we cast away moan.
        God ha' mercy on his soul!"
And of all Christian souls, I pray God. God be wi' you.   [*Exit.*]
LAERTES   Do you see this, O God?
KING   Laertes, I must commune with your grief,   195
Or you deny me right. Go but apart,
Make choice of whom your wisest friends you will,
And they shall hear and judge 'twixt you and me.
If by direct or by collateral° hand
They find us touched,° we will our kingdom give,   200
Our crown, our life, and all that we call ours,
To you in satisfaction. But if not,
Be you content to lend your patience to us
And we shall jointly labor with your soul
To give it due content.
LAERTES   Let this be so.   205
His means of death, his obscure funeral,
No trophy, sword, nor hatchment° o'er his bones,
No noble rite nor formal ostentation,
Cry to be heard, as 'twere from Heaven to earth,
That I must call 't in question.
KING   So you shall,   210
And where the offense is let the great ax fall.
I pray you, go with me.   [*Exeunt.*]

182 favor: charm   189 flaxen ... poll: white as flax was his head   199 collateral: i.e., as an
accessory   200 touched: implicated   207 hatchment: device of the coat of arms carried in a
funeral and hung up over the tomb

Scene VI. Another room in the castle.

[*Enter* HORATIO *and a* SERVANT.]

HORATIO   What are they that would speak with me?
SERVANT   Seafaring men, sir. They say they have letters for you.
HORATIO   Let them come in.   [*Exit* SERVANT.]
  I do not know from what part of the world
  I should be greeted, if not from Lord Hamlet.   5

[*Enter* SAILORS.]

FIRST SAILOR   God bless you, sir.
HORATIO   Let Him bless thee too.
FIRST SAILOR   He shall, sir, an 't please Him. There's a letter for you, sir.
  It comes from the ambassador that was bound for England—if your
  name be Horatio, as I am let to know it is.   10
HORATIO [*Reads.*]   "Horatio, when thou shalt have overlooked° this, give
  these fellows some means° to the King. They have letters for him. Ere
  we were two days old at sea, a pirate of very warlike appointment°
  gave us chase. Finding ourselves too slow of sail, we put on a
  compelled valor, and in the grapple I boarded them. On the instant   15
  they got clear of our ship, so I alone became their prisoner. They have
  dealt with me like thieves of mercy; but they knew what they did—I
  am to do a good turn for them. Let the King have the letters I have
  sent, and repair thou to me with much speed as thou wouldest fly
  death. I have words to speak in thine ear will make thee dumb, yet are 20
  they much too light for the bore of the matter.° These good fellows
  will bring thee where I am. Rosencrantz and Guildenstern hold their
  course for England. Of them I have much to tell thee. Farewell.
                                "He that thou knowest thine,
                                                    "HAMLET"   25

  Come, I will make you way for these your letters,
  And do 't the speedier that you may direct me
  To him from whom you brought them.   [*Exeunt.*]

Scene VII. Another room in the castle.

[*Enter* KING *and* LAERTES.]

KING   Now must your conscience my acquittance seal,
  And you must put me in your heart for friend,

IV.vi.11 **overlooked:** read   **12 means:** access   **13 appointment:** equipment   **21 too . . .**
matter: i.e., words fall short, like a small shot fired from a cannon with too wide a bore

Sith you have heard, and with a knowing ear,
That he which hath your noble father slain
Pursued my life.

LAERTES   It well appears. But tell me   5
Why you proceeded not against these feats,°
So crimeful and so capital° in nature,
As by your safety, wisdom, all things else,
You mainly were stirred up.

KING   Oh, for two special reasons,
Which may to you perhaps seem much unsinewed,°   10
But yet to me they're strong. The Queen his mother
Lives almost by his looks, and for myself—
My virtue or my plague, be it either which—
She's so conjunctive° to my life and soul
That as the star moves not but° in his sphere,   15
I could not but by her. The other motive
Why to a public count° I might not go
Is the great love the general gender° bear him,
Who, dipping all his faults in their affection,°
Would, like the spring that turneth wood to stone,°   20
Convert his gyves to graces.° So that my arrows,
Too slightly timbered° for so loud a wind,
Would have reverted to my bow again
And not where I had aimed them.

LAERTES   And so have I a noble father lost,   25
A sister driven into desperate terms,°
Whose worth, if praises may go back again,°
Stood challenger on mount of all the age
For her perfections.° But my revenge will come.

KING   Break not your sleeps for that. You must not think   30
That we are made of stuff so flat and dull
That we can let our beard be shook with danger
And think it pastime. You shortly shall hear more.°
I loved your father, and we love ourself,
And that, I hope, will teach you to imagine—   35

[*Enter a* MESSENGER, *with letters.*]

How now! What news?

IV.vii.6 **feats:** acts   7 **capital:** deserving death   10 **unsinewed:** weak, flabby   14 **conjunctive:** joined inseparably   15 **moves ... but:** moves only in   17 **count:** trial   18 **general gender:** common people   19 **dipping ... affection:** gilding his faults with their love   20 **like ... stone:** in several places in England there are springs of water so strongly impregnated with lime that they will quickly cover with stone anything placed in them   21 **Convert ... graces:** regard his fetters as honorable ornaments   22 **timbered:** shafted   26 **terms:** condition   27 **if ... again:** if one may praise her for what she used to be   28–29 **Stood ... perfections:** i.e., her worth challenged the whole world to find one as perfect   33 **hear more:** i.e., when news comes from England that Hamlet is dead

MESSENGER   Letters, my lord, from Hamlet.
    This to your Majesty, this to the Queen.
KING   From Hamlet! Who brought them?
MESSENGER   Sailors, my lord, they say—I saw them not.
    They were given me by Claudio, he received them   40
    Of him that brought them.
KING   Laertes, you shall hear them.
    Leave us.   [*Exit* MESSENGER.]

[*Reads*] "High and Mighty, you shall know I am set naked° on your
kingdom. Tomorrow shall I beg leave to see your kingly eyes, when I
shall, first asking your pardon thereunto, recount the occasion of my   45
sudden and more strange return.

                                                        "HAMLET"

    What should this mean? Are all the rest come back?
    Or is it some abuse,° and no such thing?
LAERTES   Know you the hand?   50
KING   'Tis Hamlet's character.° "Naked!"
    And in a postscript here, he says "alone."
    Can you advise me?
LAERTES   I'm lost in it, my lord. But let him come.
    It warms the very sickness in my heart   55
    That I shall live and tell him to his teeth
    "Thus didest thou."
KING   If it be so, Laertes—
    As how should it be so, how otherwise?—
    Will you be ruled by me?
LAERTES   Aye, my lord,
    So you will not o'errule° me to a peace.   60
KING   To thine own peace. If he be now returned,
    As checking at° his voyage, and that he means
    No more to undertake it, I will work him
    To an exploit now ripe in my device,
    Under the which he shall not choose but fall.   65
    And for his death no wind of blame shall breathe,
    But even his mother shall uncharge the practice°
    And call it accident.
LAERTES   My lord, I will be ruled,
    The rather if you could devise it so
    That I might be the organ.°
KING   It falls right.   70

43 **naked**: destitute   49 **abuse**: attempt to deceive   51 **character**: handwriting   60 **o'errule**:
command   62 **checking at**: swerving aside from   67 **uncharge . . . practice**: not suspect that his
death was the result of the plot   70 **organ**: instrument

You have been talked of since your travel much,
And that in Hamlet's hearing, for a quality
Wherein they say you shine. Your sum of parts°
Did not together pluck such envy from him
As did that one, and that in my regard   75
Of the unworthiest siege.°
LAERTES   What part is that, my lord?
KING   A very ribbon in the cap of youth,
    Yet needful too; for youth no less becomes
    The light and careless livery that it wears
    Than settled age his sables and his weeds,°   80
    Importing health and graveness. Two months since,
    Here was a gentleman of Normandy.
    I've seen myself, and served against, the French,
    And they can well° on horseback; but this gallant
    Had witchcraft in 't, he grew unto his seat,   85
    And to such wondrous doing brought his horse
    As had he been incorpsed and deminatured°
    With the brave beast. So far he topped my thought°
    That I, in forgery of shapes and tricks,
    Come short of what he did.
LAERTES   A Norman was 't?   90
KING   A Norman.
LAERTES   Upon my life, Lamond.
KING   The very same.
LAERTES   I know him well. He is the brooch° indeed
    And gem of all the nation.
KING   He made confession° of you,   95
    And gave you such a masterly report
    For art and exercise in your defense,
    And for your rapier most especial,
    That he cried out 'twould be a sight indeed
    If one could match you. The scrimers° of their nation,   100
    He swore, had neither motion, guard, nor eye
    If you opposed them. Sir, this report of his
    Did Hamlet so envenom with his envy
    That he could nothing do but wish and beg
    Your sudden coming o'er to play with him.   105
    Now, out of this—
LAERTES   What out of this, my lord?
KING   Laertes, was your father dear to you?

73 **sum of parts**: accomplishments as a whole   76 **siege**: seat, place   80 **sables ... weeds**:
dignified robes   84 **can well**: can do well   87 **incorposed ... deminatured**: of one body   88
topped my thought: surpassed what I could imagine   93 **brooch**: ornament   95 **confession**:
report   100 **scrimers**: fencers

Or are you like the painting of a sorrow,
A face without a heart?

LAERTES   Why ask you this?

KING   Not that I think you did not love your father,   110
But that I know love is begun by time,
And that I see, in passages of proof,°
Time qualifies the spark and fire of it.
There lives within the very flame of love
A kind of wick or snuff° that will abate it.   115
And nothing is at a like goodness still,°
For goodness, growing to a pleurisy,°
Dies in his own too much. That we would do
We should do when we would; for this "would" changes
And hath abatements and delays as many   120
As there are tongues, are hands, are accidents,
And then this "should" is like a spendthrift° sigh
That hurts by easing. But to the quick o' the ulcer.°
Hamlet comes back. What would you undertake
To show yourself your father's son in deed   125
More than in words?

LAERTES   To cut his throat i' the church.°

KING   No place indeed should murder sanctuarize,°
Revenge should have no bounds. But, good Laertes,
Will you do this, keep close within your chamber.
Hamlet returned shall know you are come home.   130
We'll put on those° shall praise your excellence
And set a double varnish on the fame
The Frenchman gave you, bring you in fine° together
And wager on your heads. He, being remiss,
Most generous and free from all contriving,   135
Will not peruse the foils, so that with ease,
Or with a little shuffling, you may choose
A sword unbated,° and in a pass of practice°
Requite him for your father.

LAERTES   I will do 't,
And for that purpose I'll anoint my sword.   140
I bought an unction° of a mountebank°
So mortal that but dip a knife in it,

---

112 **passages of proof:** experiences which prove   115 **snuff:** before the invention of self-
consuming wicks for candles, the wick smoldered and formed a ball of soot which dimmed the light
and gave out a foul smoke   116 **still:** always   17 **pleurisy:** fullness   122 **spendthrift:** wasteful,
because sighing was supposed to be bad for the blood   123 **quick ... ulcer:** i.e., to come to the
real issue; **quick:** flesh, sensitive part   126 **cut ... church:** i.e., to commit murder in a holy place,
which would bring Laertes in danger of everlasting damnation   127 **sanctuarize:** give sanctuary
to   131 **put ... those:** set on some   133 **fine:** short   138 **unbated:** not blunted; **pass of
practice:** treacherous thrust   141 **unction:** poison; **mountebank:** quack doctor

Where it draws blood no cataplasm° so rare,
Collected from all simples° that have virtue
Under the moon,° can save the thing from death   145
That is but scratched withal. I'll touch my point
With this contagion, that if I gall° him slightly,
It may be death.

KING   Let's further think of this,
Weigh what convenience both of time and means
May fit us to our shape.° If this should fail,   150
And that our drift look through our bad performance,°
'Twere better not assayed. Therefore this project
Should have a back or second, that might hold
If this did blast in proof.° Soft! Let me see—
We'll make a solemn wager on your cunnings.   155
I ha't.
When in your motion you are hot and dry—
As make your bouts° more violent to that end—
And that he calls for drink, I'll have prepared him
A chalice° for the nonce,° whereon but sipping,   160
If he by chance escape your venomed stuck,°
Our purpose may hold there. But stay, what noise?

[*Enter* QUEEN.]

How now, sweet Queen!

QUEEN   One woe doth tread upon another's heel,
So fast they follow. Your sister's drowned, Laertes.   165

LAERTES   Drowned! Oh, where?

QUEEN   There is a willow grows aslant a brook
That shows his hoar° leaves in the glassy stream.
There with fantastic garlands did she come
Of crowflowers, nettles, daisies, and long purples   170
That liberal° shepherds give a grosser name,
But our cold maids do dead-men's-fingers call them.
There on the pendent° boughs her coronet weeds°
Clambering to hang, an envious sliver° broke,
When down her weedy trophies and herself   175
Fell in the weeping brook. Her clothes spread wide,

143 **cataplasm:** poultice   144 **simples:** herbs   145 **Under ... moon:** herbs collected by moonlight were regarded as particularly potent   147 **gall:** break the skin   149–50 **Weigh ... shape:** consider the best time and method of carrying out our plan   151 **drift ... performance:** intention be revealed through bungling   154 **blast in proof:** break in trial, like a cannon which bursts when being tested   158 **bouts:** attacks, in the fencing match   160 **chalice:** cup; **nonce:** occasion   161 **stuck:** thrust   168 **hoar:** gray   171 **liberal:** coarse-mouthed   173 **pendent:** hanging over the water; **coronet weeds:** wild flowers woven into a crown   174 **envious sliver:** malicious branch

And mermaidlike awhile they bore her up—
Which time she chanted snatches of old tunes,
As one incapable° of her own distress,
Or like a creature native and indued°   180
Unto that element. But long it could not be
Till that her garments, heavy with their drink,
Pulled the poor wretch from her melodious lay°
To muddy death.
LAERTES   Alas, then she is drowned!
QUEEN   Drowned, drowned.   185
LAERTES   Too much of water hast thou, poor Ophelia,
And therefore I forbid my tears. But yet
It is our trick°—Nature her custom holds,
Let shame say what it will. When these° are gone,
The woman will be out.° Adieu, my lord.   190
I have a speech of fire that fain° would blaze
But that this folly douts° it.   [*Exit.*]
KING   Let's follow, Gertrude.
How much I had to do to calm his rage!
Now fear I this will give it start again,
Therefore let's follow.   [*Exeunt.*]   195

ACT V

Scene I. A churchyard.

[*Enter two* CLOWNS,° *with spades, etc.*]

FIRST CLOWN   Is she to be buried in Christian burial° that willfully seeks
   her own salvation?
SECOND CLOWN   I tell thee she is, and therefore make her grave
   straight.° The crowner° hath sat on her, and finds it Christian burial.
FIRST CLOWN   How can that be, unless she drowned herself in her own   5
   defense?
SECOND CLOWN   Why, 'tis found so.
FIRST CLOWN   It must be "se offendendo,"° it cannot be else. For here

---

179 incapable: not realizing   180 indued: endowed; i.e., a creature whose natural home is the water (*element*)   183 lay: song   187–88 But ... trick: it is our habit; i.e., to break into tears at great sorrow   189 these: i.e., my tears   190 woman ... out: I shall be a man again   191 fain: willingly   192 douts: puts out

V.i.s.d. Clowns: countrymen   1 Christian burial: suicides were not allowed burial in consecrated ground, but were buried at crossroads; the gravediggers and the priest are professionally scandalized that Ophelia should be allowed Christian burial solely because she is a lady of the Court   4 straight: straightway; crowner: coroner   8 se offendendo: for *defendendo,* in self-defense

lies the point. If I drown myself wittingly,° it argues an act, and an act
hath three branches—it is to act, to do, and to perform. Argal,° she   10
drowned herself wittingly.

SECOND CLOWN   Nay, but hear you, goodman delver.°

FIRST CLOWN   Give me leave. Here lies the water, good. Here stands the
man, good. If the man go to this water and drown himself, it is will he,
nill he° he goes, mark you that; but if the water come to him and   15
drown him, he drowns not himself. Argal, he that is not guilty of his
own death shortens not his own life.

SECOND CLOWN   But is this law?

FIRST CLOWN   Aye, marry, is 't, crowner's quest° law.

SECOND CLOWN   Will you ha' the truth on 't? If this had not been a   20
gentlewoman, she should have been buried out o' Christian burial.

FIRST CLOWN   Why, there thou say'st. And the more pity that great folks
should have countenance° in this world to drown or hang themselves
more than their even° Christian. Come, my spade. There is no ancient
gentlemen but gardeners, ditchers, and gravemakers. They hold up   25
Adam's profession.

SECOND CLOWN   Was he a gentleman?

FIRST CLOWN   A' was the first that ever bore arms.°

SECOND CLOWN   Why, he had none.

FIRST CLOWN   What, art a heathen? How dost thou understand the   30
Scripture? The Scripture says Adam digged. Could he dig without
arms? I'll put another question to thee. If thou answerest me not to
the purpose, confess thyself—

SECOND CLOWN   Go to.

FIRST CLOWN   What is he that builds stronger than either the mason, the   35
shipwright, or the carpenter?

SECOND CLOWN   The gallows-maker, for that frame outlives a thousand
tenants.

FIRST CLOWN   I like thy wit well, in good faith. The gallows does well,
but how does it well? It does well to those that do ill. Now thou dost   40
ill to say the gallows is built stronger than the church; argal, the
gallows may do well to thee. To 't again, come.

SECOND CLOWN   Who builds stronger than a mason, a shipwright, or a
carpenter?

FIRST CLOWN   Aye, tell me that, and unyoke.°   45

SECOND CLOWN   Marry, now I can tell.

FIRST CLOWN   To 't.

SECOND CLOWN   Mass,° I cannot tell.

---

9 **wittingly:** with full knowledge   10 **Argal:** for the Latin *ergo*, therefore   12 **delver:** digger
14–15 **will he, nill he:** willy-nilly, whether he wishes or not   19 **quest:** inquest   23 **countenance:** favor   24 **even:** fellow   28 **bore arms:** had a coat of arms—the outward sign of a
gentlemen   45 **unyoke:** finish the job, unyoking the plow oxen being the end of the day's work
48 **Mass:** by the mass

[*Enter* HAMLET *and* HORATIO, *afar off.*]

FIRST CLOWN   Cudgel thy brains no more about it, for your dull ass will
not mend his pace with beating, and when you are asked this question   50
next, say "A gravemaker." The houses that he makes last till
Doomsday. Go, get thee to Yaughan,° fetch me a stoup° of liquor.
                                        [*Exit* SECOND CLOWN.]

[FIRST CLOWN *digs, and sings.*]

       "In youth, when I did love, did love,
         Methought it was very sweet,
       To contract; oh, the time, for-a my behoove,°   55
         Oh, methought, there-a was nothing-a meet."
HAMLET   Has this fellow no feeling of his business, that he sings at grave-
making?
HORATIO   Custom hath made it in him a property of easiness.°
HAMLET   'Tis e'en so. The hand of little employment hath the daintier   60
sense.°
FIRST CLOWN [*Sings.*]
       "But age, with his stealing steps,
         Hath clawed me in his clutch,
       And hath shipped me intil the land°
         As if I had never been such."   65

[*Throws up a skull.*]

HAMLET   That skull had a tongue in it, and could sing once. How the
knave jowls° it to the ground, as if it were Cain's jawbone, that did the
first murder! It might be the pate of a politician which this ass now
o'erreaches°—one that would circumvent God, might it not?
HORATIO   It might, my lord.   70
HAMLET   Or of a courtier, which could say "Good morrow, sweet lord!
How dost thou, good lord?" This might be my lord Such-a-one that
praised my lord Such-a-one's horse when he meant to beg it, might it
not?
HORATIO   Aye, my lord.   75
HAMLET   Why, e'en so. And now my Lady Worm's chapless,° and
knocked about the mazzard° with a sexton's spade. Here's fine revolu-

52 **Yaughan:** apparently an innkeeper near the Globe Theatre; **stoup:** large pot   55 **behoove:**
benefit   59 **property of easiness:** careless habit   60–61 **hand . . . sense:** those who have little to
do are the most sensitive   74 **shipped . . . land:** shoved me into the ground   67 **jowls:**
dashes   69 **o'erreaches:** gets the better of   76 **chapless:** without jaws   77 **mazzard:** head, a slang
word; lit., drinking-bowl

tion, an we had the trick to see 't. Did these bones cost no more the
breeding but to play at loggats° with 'em? Mine ache to think on 't.

FIRST CLOWN [*Sings.*]

> "A pickax and a spade, a spade,   80
>   For and a shrouding sheet—
> Oh, a pit of clay for to be made
>   For such a guest is meet."

[*Throws up another skull.*]

HAMLET   There's another. Why may not that be the skull of a lawyer?°
Where be his quiddities now, his quillets, his cases, his tenures, and   85
his tricks? Why does he suffer this rude knave now to knock him
about the sconce° with a dirty shovel, and will not tell him of his
action of battery? Hum! This fellow might be in 's time a great buyer
of land, with his statutes, his recognizances, his fines, his double
vouchers, his recoveries. Is this the fine° of his fines and the recovery   90
of his recoveries, to have his fine pate full of fine dirt? Will his
vouchers vouch him no more of his purchases, and double ones too,
than the length and breadth of a pair of indentures? The very
conveyances of his lands will hardly lie in this box,° and must the
inheritor himself have no more, ha?   95

HORATIO   Not a jot more, my lord.

HAMLET   Is not parchment made of sheepskins?

HORATIO   Aye, my lord, and of calfskins too.

HAMLET   They are sheep and calves which seek out assurance in that. I
will speak to this fellow. Whose grave's this, sirrah?   100

FIRST CLOWN   Mine, sir. [*Sings.*]

> "Oh, a pit of clay for to be made
>   For such a guest is meet."

HAMLET   I think it be thine indeed, for thou liest in 't.

FIRST CLOWN   You lie out on 't, sir, and therefore 'tis not yours. For my   105
part, I do not lie in 't, and yet it is mine.

HAMLET   Thou dost lie in 't, to be in 't, and say it is thine. 'Tis for the
dead, not for the quick, therefore thou liest.

FIRST CLOWN   'Tis a quick lie, sir, 'twill away again, from me to you.

HAMLET   What man dost thou dig it for?   110

FIRST CLOWN   For no man, sir.

HAMLET   What woman, then?

---

79 loggats: a game in which billets of wood or bones were stuck in the ground and knocked over by
throwing at them   **84–93 lawyer . . . indentures:** Hamlet strings out a number of the legal phrases
loved by lawyers: *quiddities:* subtle arguments; *quillets:* quibbles; *tenures:* titles to property;
tricks: knavery; *statutes:* bonds; *recognizances:* obligations; *fines:* conveyances; *vouchers:* guaran-
tors; *recoveries:* transfers; *indentrues:* agreements   **87 sconce:** head; lit., blockhouse   **90 fine:**
ending   **94 box:** coffin

FIRST CLOWN   For none, neither.

HAMLET   Who is to be buried in 't?

FIRST CLOWN   One that was a woman, sir, but, rest her soul, she's dead.   115

HAMLET   How absolute° the knave is! We must speak by the card,° or equivocation° will undo us. By the Lord, Horatio, this three years I have taken note of it—the age is grown so picked° that the toe of the peasant comes so near the heel of the courtier, he galls his kibe.° How long hast thou been a gravemaker?   120

FIRST CLOWN   Of all the days i' the year, I came to 't that day that our last King Hamlet o'ercame Fortinbras.

HAMLET   How long is that since?

FIRST CLOWN   Cannot you tell that? Every fool can tell that. It was that very day that young Hamlet was born, he that is mad, and sent into England.   125

HAMLET   Aye, marry, why was he sent into England?

FIRST CLOWN   Why, because a' was mad. A' shall recover his wits there, or, if a' do not, 'tis no great matter there.

HAMLET   Why?   130

FIRST CLOWN   'Twill not be seen in him there—there the men are as mad as he.

HAMLET   How came he mad?

FIRST CLOWN   Very strangely, they say.

HAMLET   How "strangely"?   135

FIRST CLOWN   Faith, e'en with losing his wits.

HAMLET   Upon what ground?

FIRST CLOWN   Why, here in Denmark. I have been sexton here, man and boy, thirty years.

HAMLET   How long will a man lie i' the earth ere he rot?   140

FIRST CLOWN   I' faith, if a' be not rotten before a' die—as we have many pocky° corses nowadays that will scarce hold the laying in—a' will last you some eight year or nine year. A tanner will last you nine year.

HAMLET   Why he more than another?

FIRST CLOWN   Why, sir, his hide is so tanned with his trade that a' will keep out water a great while, and your water is a sore decayer of your whoreson° dead body. Here's a skull now. This skull has lain in the earth three and twenty years.   145

HAMLET   Whose was it?

FIRST CLOWN   A whoreson mad fellow's it was. Whose do you think it was?   150

HAMLET   Nay, I know not.

FIRST CLOWN   A pestilence on him for a mad rogue! A' poured a flagon

116 **absolute:** exact; **by . . . card:** exactly; the card is the mariner's compass   117 **equivocation:** ambiguity   118 **picked:** refined   118–19 **toe . . . kibe:** i.e., the peasant follows the courtier so closely that he rubs the courtier's heel into a blister   142 **pocky:** syphilitic   147 **whoreson:** "son of a bitch"

of Rhenish on my head once. This same skull, sir, was Yorick's skull, the King's jester.   155

HAMLET   This?

FIRST CLOWN   E'en that.

HAMLET   Let me see. [*Takes the skull.*] Alas, poor Yorick! I knew him, Horatio—a fellow of infinite jest, of most excellent fancy. He hath borne me on his back a thousand times, and now how abhorred in my   160 imagination it is! My gorge rises at it. Here hung those lips that I have kissed I know not how oft. Where be your gibes now? Your gambols? Your songs? Your flashes of merriment that were wont to set the table on a roar? Not one now, to mock your own grinning? Quite chop-fallen?° Now get you to my lady's chamber and tell her, let her   165 paint an inch thick, to this favor° she must come—make her laugh at that. Prithee, Horatio, tell me one thing.

HORATIO   What's that, my lord?

HAMLET   Dost thou think Alexander looked o' this fashion i' the earth?

HORATIO   E'en so.   170

HAMLET   And smelt so? Pah!

[*Puts down the skull.*]

HORATIO   E'en so, my lord.

HAMLET   To what base uses we may return, Horatio! Why may not imagination trace the noble dust of Alexander till he find it stopping a bunghole?°   175

HORATIO   'Twere to consider too curiously° to consider so.

HAMLET   No, faith, not a jot, but to follow him thither with modesty enough and likelihood to lead it. As thus: Alexander died, Alexander was buried, Alexander returneth into dust; the dust is earth; of earth we make loam;° and why of that loam, whereto he was converted,   180 might they not stop a beer barrel?

> "Imperious Caesar, dead and turned to clay,
>   Might stop a hole to keep the wind away.
>   Oh, that that earth which kept the world in awe
>   Should patch a wall to expel the winter's flaw!"°   185

But soft! But soft! Aside—here comes the King.

[*Enter* PRIESTS, *etc., in procession; the corpse of Ophelia,* LAERTES *and* MOURNERS *following;* KING, QUEEN, *their trains, etc.*]

The Queen, the courtiers—who is this they follow?
And with such maimèd° rites? This doth betoken

---

165 **chop-fallen:** downcast, with a pun on "chapless"   166 **favor:** appearance, especially in the face
175 **bunghole:** the hole in a beer barrel   176 **curiously:** precisely   180 **loam:** mixture of clay
and sand, used in plastering walls   185 **flaw:** blast   188 **maimèd:** curtailed

The corse they follow did with desperate hand
Fordo° its own life. 'Twas of some estate.°   190
Couch° we awhile, and mark.   [*Retiring with* HORATIO.]
LAERTES   What ceremony else?
HAMLET   That is Laertes, a very noble youth. Mark.
LAERTES   What ceremony else?
FIRST PRIEST   Her obsequies have been as far enlarged   195
   As we have warranty.° Her death was doubtful,
   And but that great command o'ersways the order,°
   She should in ground unsanctified have lodged
   Till the last trumpet; for° charitable prayers,
   Shards,° flints, and pebbles should be thrown on her.   200
   Yet here she is allowed her virgin crants,°
   Her maiden strewments° and the bringing home
   Of bell and burial.
LAERTES   Must there no more be done?
FIRST PRIEST   No more be done.
   We should profane the service of the dead   205
   To sing a requiem and such rest to her
   As to peace-parted souls.°
LAERTES   Lay her i' the earth.
   And from her fair and unpolluted flesh
   May violets spring! I tell thee, churlish priest,
   A ministering angel shall my sister be   210
   When thou liest howling.
HAMLET   What, the fair Ophelia!
QUEEN [*Scattering flowers*] Sweets to the sweet. Farewell!
   I hoped thou shouldst have been my Hamlet's wife,
   I thought thy bride bed to have decked, sweet maid,
   And not have strewed thy grave.
LAERTES   Oh, treble woe   215
   Fall ten times treble on that cursèd head
   Whose wicked deed thy most ingenious sense°
   Deprived thee of! Hold off the earth a while
   Till I have caught her once more in mine arms.

[*Leaps into the grave.*]

   Now pile your dust upon the quick° and dead   220
   Till of this flat a mountain you have made

---

190 **Fordo:** destroy; **estate:** high rank   191 **Couch:** lie down   195–96 **Her . . . warranty:** the funeral rites have been as complete as may be allowed   197 **but . . . order:** if the King's command had not overruled the proper procedure   199 **for:** instead of   200 **Shards:** pieces of broken crockery   201 **crants:** wreaths of flowers   202 **maiden strewments:** the flowers strewn on the corpse of a maiden   207 **peace-parted souls:** souls which departed in peace, fortified with the rites of the Church   217 **most . . . sense:** lively intelligence   220 **quick:** living

To o'ertop old Pelion° or the skyish head
Of blue Olympus.
HAMLET [*Advancing*] What is he whose grief
  Bears such an emphasis? Whose phrase of sorrow
  Conjures the wandering stars and makes them stand   225
  Like wonder-wounded hearers? This is I,
  Hamlet the Dane.

[*Leaps into the grave.*]

LAERTES   The Devil take thy soul!

[*Grappling with him*]

HAMLET   Thou pray'st not well.
  I prithee, take thy fingers from my throat,
  For though I am not splenitive° and rash,   230
  Yet have I in me something dangerous,
  Which let thy wisdom fear. Hold off thy hand.
KING   Pluck them asunder.
QUEEN   Hamlet, Hamlet!
ALL   Gentlemen—
HORATIO   Good my lord, be quiet.

[*The* ATTENDANTS *part them, and they come out of the grave.*]

HAMLET   Why, I will fight with him upon this theme   235
  Until my eyelids will no longer wag.
QUEEN   O my son, what theme?
HAMLET   I loved Ophelia. Forty thousand brothers
  Could not, with all their quantity of love,
  Make up my sum. What wilt thou do for her?   240
KING   Oh, he is mad, Laertes.
QUEEN   For love of God, forbear him.°
HAMLET   'Swounds, show me what thou'lt do.
  Woo 't weep? Woo 't fight? Woo 't fast? Woo 't tear thyself?
  Woo 't drink up eisel?° Eat a crocodile?   245
  I'll do 't. Dost thou come here to whine?
  To outface° me with leaping in her grave?
  Be buried quick with her, and so will I.
  And if thou prate of mountains, let them throw
  Millions of acres on us, till our ground,   250

---

222 Pelion: when the giants fought against the gods in order to reach Heaven, they tried to pile
Mount Pelion and Mount Ossa on Mount Olympus, the highest mountain in Greece   **230
splenitive:** hot-tempered   **242 forbear him:** leave him alone   **245 eisel:** vinegar   **247 outface:**
browbeat

Singeing his pate against the burning zone,
Make Ossa° like a wart! Nay, an thou 'lt mouth,
I'll rant as well as thou.

QUEEN   This is mere madness.
And thus awhile the fit will work on him.
Anon, as patient as the female dove   255
When that her golden couplets° are disclosed,°
His silence will sit drooping.

HAMLET   Hear you, sir.
What is the reason that you use me thus?
I loved you ever. But it is no matter,
Let Hercules himself do what he may,   260
The cat will mew and dog will have his day.°   [*Exit.*]

KING   I pray thee, good Horatio, wait upon him.   [*Exit* HORATIO.]
[*To* LAERTES] Strenghten your patience in our last night's speech.
We'll put the matter to the present push.°
Good Gertrude, set some watch over your son.   265
This grave shall have a living monument.°
An hour of quiet shortly shall we see,
Till then, in patience our proceeding be.   [*Exeunt.*]

Scene II. A hall in the castle.

[*Enter* HAMLET *and* HORATIO.]

HAMLET   So much for this, sir. Now shall you see the other.
You do remember all the circumstance?
HORATIO   Remember it, my lord!
HAMLET   Sir, in my heart there was a kind of fighting
That would not let me sleep. Methought I lay   5
Worse than the mutines in the bilboes.° Rashly,
And praised be rashness for it, let us know,
Our indiscretion sometime serves us well
When our deep plots do pall.° And that should learn° us
There's a divinity that shapes our ends,   10
Roughhew them how we will.
HORATIO   That is most certain.
HAMLET   Up from my cabin,

---

252 **Ossa:** See l. 222, n.   256 **couplets:** eggs, of which the dove lays two only; **disclosed:**
hatched   260–61 **Let . . . day:** i.e., let this ranting hero have his turn; mine will come sometime
264 **push:** test; lit., thrust of a pike   266 **living monument:** with the double meaning of "lifelike
memorial" and "the death of Hamlet"

V.ii.6 **mutines . . . bilboes:** mutineers in the shackles used on board ship   9 **pall:** fail; **learn:** teach

My sea gown° scarfed° about me, in the dark
Groped I to find out them,° had my desire,
Fingered their packet, and in fine withdrew   15
To mine own room again, making so bold,
My fears forgetting manners, to unseal
Their grand commission where I found, Horatio—
Oh royal knavery!—an exact command,
Larded° with many several sorts of reasons,   20
Importing Denmark's health and England's too,
With, ho! such bugs° and goblins in my life°
That, on the supervise,° no leisure bated,°
No, not to stay the grinding of the ax,
My head should be struck off.

HORATIO   Is 't possible?   25

HAMLET   Here's the commission. Read it at more leisure
But wilt thou hear me how I did proceed?

HORATIO   I beseech you.

HAMLET   Being thus benetted round with villainies—
Ere I could make prologue to my brains,   30
They had begun the play—I sat me down,
Devised a new commission, wrote it fair.
I once did hold it, as our statists° do,
A baseness to write fair,° and labored much
How to forget that learning, but, sir, now   35
It did me yeoman's service.° Wilt thou know
The effect of what I wrote?

HORATIO   Aye, good my lord.

HAMLET   An earnest conjuration from the King,
As England was his faithful tributary,
As love between them like the palm might flourish,   40
As peace should still her wheaten garland wear
And stand a comma 'tween their amities,°
And many suchlike "Ases"° of great charge,°
That, on the view and knowing of these contents,
Without debatement° further, more or less,   45
He should the bearers put to sudden death,
Not shriving time allowed.°

HORATIO   How was this sealed?

HAMLET   Why, even in that was Heaven ordinant.°

13 **sea gown:** a thick coat with a high collar worn by seamen; **scarfed:** wrapped   14 **them:** i.e.,
Rosencrantz and Guildenstern   20 **Larded:** garnished   22 **bugs:** bugbears; **in my life:** so long as I
was alive   23 **supervise:** reading; **bated:** allowed   33 **statists:** statesmen   34 **fair:** legibly   36
yeoman's service: faithful service   42 **stand . . . amities:** be a connecting link of their friendship
43 **"Ases":** official documents were written in flowery language full of metaphorical clauses
beginning with "As"; Hamlet; puns on "asses"; **great charge:** "great weight" and "heavy burden"
45 **debatement:** argument   47 **Not . . . allowed:** without giving them time even to confess their
sins   48 **ordinant:** directing, in control

I had my father's signet in my purse,
Which was the model° of that Danish seal—   50
Folded the writ° up in the form of the other,
Subscribed° it, gave 't the impression,° placed it safely,
The changeling° never known. Now the next day
Was our sea fight, and what to this was sequent°
Thou know'st already.   55

HORATIO   So Guildenstern and Rosencrantz go to 't.

HAMLET   Why, man, they did make love to this employment.
They are not near my conscience, their defeat°
Does by their own insinuation° grow.
'Tis dangerous when the baser nature comes   60
Between the pass° and fell° incensèd points
Of mighty opposites.

HORATIO   Why, what a King is this!

HAMLET   Does it not, think'st thee, stand me now upon—
He that hath killed my King and whored my mother,
Popped in between the election and my hopes,°   65
Thrown out his angle° for my proper° life,
And with such cozenage°—is 't not perfect conscience,
To quit° him with this arm? And is 't not to be damned,
To let this canker° of our nature come
In further evil?   70

HORATIO   It must be shortly known to him from England
What is the issue of the business there.

HAMLET   It will be short. The interim is mine,
And a man's life's no more than to say "One."
But I am very sorry, good Horatio,   75
That to Laertes I forgot myself,
For by the image of my cause I see
The portraiture of his. I'll court his favors.
But, sure, the bravery° of his grief did put me
Into a towering passion.

HORATIO   Peace! Who comes here?   80

[*Enter* OSRIC.°]

OSRIC   Your lordship is right welcome back to Denmark.

50 **model:** copy   51 **writ:** writing   52 **Subscribed:** signed; **impression:** of the seal   53
changeling: lit., an ugly child exchanged by the fairies for a fair one   54 **sequent:** following   58
defeat: destruction   59 **by . . . insinuation:** because they insinuated themselves into this business   61 **pass:** thrust; **fell:** fierce   65 **Popped . . . hopes:** as is from time to time shown in the play,
the Danes chose their King by election   66 **angle:** fishing rod and line; **proper:** own   67
cozenage: cheating   68 **quit:** pay back   69 **canker:** maggot   79 **bravery:** excessive show   **s.d.**
Osric: Osric is a specimen of the fashionable, effeminate courtier; he dresses prettily and talks the
jargon of his class, which at this time affected elaborate and allusive metaphors and at all costs
avoided saying plain things plainly

HAMLET   I humbly thank you, sir. Dost know this water fly?

HORATIO   No, my good lord.

HAMLET   Thy state is the more gracious,° for 'tis a vice to know him. He
hath much land, and fertile. Let a beast be lord of beasts and his crib   85
shall stand at the King's mess.° 'Tis a chough,° but, as I say, spacious°
in the possession of dirt.

OSRIC   Sweet lord, if your lordship were at leisure, I should impart a
thing to you from His Majesty.

HAMLET   I will receive it, sir, with all diligence of spirit. Put your bonnet   90
to his right use,° 'tis for the head.

OSRIC   I thank your lordship, it is very hot.

HAMLET   No, believe me, 'tis very cold. The wind is northerly.

OSRIC   It is indifferent° cold, my lord, indeed.

HAMLET   But yet methinks it is very sultry and hot, for my complexion—   95

OSRIC   Exceedingly, my lord. It is very sultry, as 'twere—I cannot tell
how. But, my lord, His Majesty bade me signify to you that he has
laid a great wager on your head. Sir, this is the matter—

HAMLET   I beseech you, remember—

[HAMLET *moves him to put on his hat.*]

OSRIC   Nay, good my lord, for mine ease, in good faith. Sir, here is newly   100
come to Court Laertes—believe me, an absolute° gentleman, full of
most excellent differences,° of very soft society° and great showing.°
Indeed, to speak feelingly° of him, he is the card or calendar of
gentry,° for you shall find in him the continent of what part a
gentleman would see.°   105

HAMLET   Sir,° his definement suffers no perdition in you, though I know
to divide him inventorially would dizzy the arithmetic of memory,
and yet but yaw° neither, in respect of his quick sail. But in the verity
of extolment, I take him to be a soul of great article, and his infusion
of such dearth and rareness as, to make true diction of him, his   110

---

84 Thy . . . gracious: you are in the better state   85–86 Let . . . mess: i.e., any man, however low,
who has wealth enough will find a good place at Court   85 crib: manger   86 mess: table; chough:
jackdaw (chatterbox); spacious: wealthy   90–91 Put . . . use: i.e., put your hat on your head; Osric
is so nice-mannered that he cannot bring himself to wear his hat in the presence of the Prince   94
indifferent: moderately   101 absolute: perfect   102 differences: qualities peculiar to himself;
soft society: gentle breeding; great showing: distinguished appearance   103 feelingly: with
proper appreciation   103–04 card . . . gentry: the very fashion plate of what a gentleman should
be   104–05 continent . . . see: all the parts that should be in a perfect gentleman   106–12 Sir . . .
more: Hamlet retorts in similar but even more extravagant language; this is too much for Osric (and
for most modern readers); Hamlet's words may be paraphrased: "Sir, the description of this perfect
gentleman loses nothing in your account of him; though I realize that if one were to try to enumerate
his excellences, it would exhaust our arithmetic, and yet"—here he changes the image to one of
sailing—"we should still lag behind him as he outsails us. But in the true vocabulary of praise, I take
him to be a soul of the greatest worth, and his perfume"—i.e., his personal essence—"so scarce and
rare that to speak truly of him, the only thing like him is his own reflection in his mirror, and
everyone else who tries to follow him merely his shadow"   108 yaw: fall off from the course laid

semblable is his mirror, and who else would trace him, his umbrage—
nothing more.

OSRIC   Your lordship speaks most infallibly of him.

HAMLET   The concernancy,° sir? Why do we wrap the gentleman in our
more rawer breath?°   115

OSRIC   Sir?°

HORATIO   Is 't not possible to understand in another tongue? You will do
't, sir, really.

HAMLET   What imports the nomination° of this gentleman?

OSRIC   Of Laertes?   120

HORATIO   His purse is empty already, all's golden words are spent.

HAMLET   Of him, sir.

OSRIC   I know you are not ignorant—

HAMLET   I would you did, sir. Yet, in faith, if you did, it would not much
approve° me. Well, sir?   125

OSRIC   You are not ignorant of what excellence Laertes is—

HAMLET   I dare not confess that, lest I should compare with him in
excellence, but to know a man well were to know himself.

OSRIC   I mean, sir, for his weapon,° but in the imputation° laid on him by
them, in his meed° he's unfellowed.°   130

HAMLET   What's his weapon?

OSRIC   Rapier and dagger.

HAMLET   That's two of his weapons, but, well.

OSRIC   The King, sir, hath wagered with him six Barbary horses, against
the which he has imponed,° as I take it, six French rapiers and   135
poniards, with their assigns,° as girdle, hanger,° and so—three of the
carriages, in faith, are very dear to fancy,° very responsive to° the hilts,
most delicate carriages, and of very liberal conceit.°

HAMLET   What call you the carriages?

HORATIO   I knew you must be edified by the margent° ere you had done.   140

OSRIC   The carriages, sir, are the hangers.

HAMLET   The phrase would be more germane° to the matter if we could
carry a cannon by our sides. I would it might be hangers till then. But,
on—six Barbary horses against six French swords, their assigns, and
three liberal-conceited carriages. That's the French bet against the   145
Danish. Why is this "imponed," as you call it?

OSRIC   The King, sir, hath laid, sir, that in a dozen passes between
yourself and him, he shall not exceed you three hits. He hath laid on

---

114 **concernancy:** i.e., what is all this talk about?   114–15 **Why . . . breath:** why do we discuss
the gentleman with our inadequate voices?   116 **Sir:** Osric is completey baffled   119 **nomina-
tion:** naming   125 **approve:** commend   119 **his weapon:** i.e., skill with his weapon; **imputa-
tion:** reputation   130 **meed:** merit; **unfellowed:** without an equal   135 **imponed:** laid down as a
stake   136 **assigns:** that which goes with them; **hanger:** straps by which the scabbard was hung
from the belt; for specimens   137 **dear to fancy:** of beautiful design; **responsive to:** matching
138 **liberal conceit:** elaborately artistic   140 **edified . . . margent:** informed by the notes; in
Shakespeare's time the notes were often printed in the margin   142 **germane:** related

twelve for nine, and it would come to immediate trial if your lordship
would vouchsafe the answer.   150

HAMLET   How if I answer no?

OSRIC   I mean, my lord, the opposition of your person in trial.

HAMLET   Sir, I will walk here in the hall. If it please His Majesty, it is the
breathing-time of day with me.° Let the foils be brought, the gentleman willing, and the King hold his purpose, I will win for him an I   155
can. If not, I will gain nothing but my shame and the odd hits.

OSRIC   Shall I redeliver you e'en so?

HAMLET   To this effect, sir, after what flourish° your nature will.

OSRIC   I commend my duty to your lordship.

HAMLET   Yours, yours. [*Exit* OSRIC.] He does well to commend it   160
himself, there are no tongues else for 's turn.

HORATIO   This lapwing° runs away with the shell on his head.

HAMLET   He did comply with his dug° before he sucked it. Thus has
he—and many more of the same breed that I know the drossy° age
dotes on—only got the tune of the time and outward habit of   165
encounter,° a kind of yesty collection° which carries them through
and through the most fond° and winnowed° opinions—and do but
blow them to their trial, the bubbles are out.°

[*Enter a* LORD.]

LORD   My lord, His Majesty commended him to you by young Osric,
who brings back to him that you attend him in the hall. He sends to   170
know if your pleasure hold to play with Laertes, or that you will take
longer time.

HAMLET   I am constant to my purposes, they follow the King's pleasure.
If his fitness speaks, mine is ready, now or whensoever, provided I be
so able as now.   175

LORD   The King and Queen and all are coming down.

HAMLET   In happy time.°

LORD   The Queen desires you to use some gentle entertainment° to
Laertes before you fall to play.

HAMLET   She well instructs me.   [*Exit* LORD.]   180

HORATIO   You will lose this wager, my lord.

---

154 **breathing-time . . . me:** time when I take exercise   158 **flourish:** elaborate phrasing   162
lapwing: a pretty, lively little bird; it is so lively that it can run about the moment it is hatched   163
did . . . dug: was ceremonious with the nipple; i.e., behaved in this fantastic way from his infancy
164 **drossy:** scummy, frivolous   165–66 **tune . . . encounter:** i.e., they sing the same tune as
everyone else and have the same society manners   166 **yesty collection:** frothy catchwords   167
fond: foolish; **winnowed:** light as chaff; winnowing is the process of fanning the chaff from the
grain   167–68 **do . . . out:** force them to make sense of their words and they are deflated, as
Hamlet has just deflated Osric   177 **In . . . time:** at a good moment   178 **gentle entertainment:**
kindly treatment; i.e., be reconciled after the brawl in the churchyard

HAMLET   I do not think so. Since he went into France I have been in continual practice, I shall win at the odds. But thou wouldst not think how ill all's here about my heart—but it is no matter.

HORATIO   Nay, good my lord—   185

HAMLET   It is but foolery, but it is such a kind of gaingiving° as would perhaps trouble a woman.

HORATIO   If your mind dislike anything, obey it. I will forestall their repair hither and say you are not fit.

HAMLET   Not a whit, we defy augury.° There's special providence in the   190
fall of a sparrow.° If it be now, 'tis not to come; if it be not to come, it will be now; if it be not now, yet it will come. The readiness is all. Since no man has aught of what he leaves, what is 't to leave betimes? Let be.

[*Enter* KING, QUEEN, LAERTES, *and* LORDS, OSRIC *and other*
ATTENDANTS *with foils; a table and flagons of wine on it.*]

KING   Come, Hamlet, come, and take this hand from me.   195

[*The* KING *puts* LAERTES' *hand into* HAMLET'S.]

HAMLET   Give me your pardon, sir. I've done you wrong,
But pardon 't, as you are a gentleman.
This presence° knows,
And you must needs have heard, how I am punished
With sore distraction. What I have done   200
That might your nature, honor, and exception°
Roughly awake, I here proclaim was madness.
Was 't Hamlet wronged Laertes? Never Hamlet.
If Hamlet from himself be ta'en away,°
And when he's not himself does wrong Laertes,   205
Then Hamlet does it not, Hamlet denies it.
Who does it, then? His madness. If 't be so,
Hamlet is of the faction that is wronged,
His madness is poor Hamlet's enemy.
Sir, in this audience   210
Let my disclaiming from a purposed evil°
Free me so far in your most generous thoughts
That I have shot mine arrow o'er the house,
And hurt my brother.

LAERTES   I am satisfied in nature,

---

186 **gaingiving:** misgiving   190 **augury:** omens   190–91 **special . . . sparrow:** the idea comes
from Matthew 10:29: "Are not two sparrows sold for a farthing? and one of them shall not fall to the
ground without your Father"   198 **presence:** the whole Court   201 **exception:** resentment   204
If . . . away: i.e., Hamlet mad is not Hamlet   211 **Let . . . evil:** let my declaration that I did not
intend any harm

Whose motive, in this case, should stir me most   215
To my revenge. But in my terms of honor
I stand aloof, and will no reconcilement
Till by some elder masters of known honor
I have a voice and precedent of peace
To keep my name ungored.° But till that time   220
I do receive your offered love like love
And will not wrong it.

HAMLET   I embrace it freely,
And will this brother's wager frankly play.
Give us the foils. Come on.

LAERTES   Come, one for me.

HAMLET   I'll be your foil,° Laertes. In mine ignorance   225
Your skill shall, like a star i' the darkest night,
Stick° fiery off indeed.

LAERTES   You mock me, sir.

HAMLET   No, by this hand.

KING   Give them the foils, young Osric. Cousin Hamlet,
You know the wager?

HAMLET   Very well, my lord.   230
Your Grace has laid the odds o' the weaker side.

KING   I do not fear it, I have seen you both.
But since he is bettered,° we have therefore odds.

LAERTES   This is too heavy, let me see another.

HAMLET   This likes° me well. These foils have all a length?°   235

[*They prepare to play.*]

OSRIC   Aye, my good lord.

KING   Set me the stoups° of wine upon that table.
If Hamlet give the first or second hit,
Or quit° in answer of the third exchange,
Let all the battlements their ordnance fire.   240
The King shall drink to Hamlet's better breath,
And in the cup a union° shall he throw
Richer than that which four successive kings
In Denmark's crown have worn. Give me the cups,
And let the kettle° to the trumpet speak,   245
The trumpet to the cannoneer without,
The cannon to the Heavens, the Heaven to earth,

219–20 I . . . ungored: I bear you no grudge so far as concerns my personal feelings, which would most readily move me to vengeance; but as this matter touches my honor, I cannot accept your apology until I have been assured by those expert in matters of honor that I may do so without loss of reputation   225 foil: Hamlet puns on the other meaning of foil—tin foil set behind a gem to give it luster   227 Stick . . . off: shine out   233 bettered: considered your superior   235 likes: pleases; have . . . length: are all of equal length   237 stoups: drinking-vessels   239 quit: strike back   242 union: a large pearl   245 kettle: kettledrum

"Now the King drinks to Hamlet." Come, begin,
And you, the judges, bear a wary eye.
HAMLET   Come on, sir.
LAERTES   Come, my lord.   [*They play.*]
HAMLET   One.
LAERTES   No.
HAMLET   Judgment.   250
OSRIC   A hit, a very palpable hit.
LAERTES   Well, again.
KING   Stay, give me drink. Hamlet, this pearl is thine°—
Here's to thy health.

[*Trumpets sound, and cannon shot off within.*]

                    Give him the cup.
HAMLET   I'll play this bout first. Set it by a while.
Come. [*They play.*] Another hit, what say you?   255
LAERTES   A touch, a touch, I do confess.
KING   Our son shall win.
QUEEN   He's fat and scant of breath.
Here, Hamlet, take my napkin, rub thy brows.
The Queen carouses to thy fortune, Hamlet.
HAMLET   Good madam!
KING   Gertrude, do not drink.   260
QUEEN   I will, my lord, I pray you pardon me.

[*She drinks.*]

KING [*Aside*]   It is the poisoned cup, it is too late.
HAMLET   I dare not drink yet, madam—by and by.
QUEEN   Come, let me wipe thy face.
LAERTES   My lord, I'll hit him now.
KING   I do not think 't.   265
LAERTES [*Aside*]   And yet 'tis almost against my conscience.
HAMLET   Come, for the third, Laertes. You but dally.
I pray you pass with your best violence,
I am afeard you make a wanton of me.°
LAERTES   Say you so? Come on.   270

[*They play.*]

OSRIC   Nothing, neither way.

---

252 **this . . . thine:** with these words the King drops the poisoned pearl into the cup intended for
Hamlet   269 **make . . . me:** treat me like a child by letting me win

LAERTES   Have at you now!

[LAERTES *wounds* HAMLET; *then, in scuffling, they change rapiers,*
and HAMLET *wounds* LAERTES.]

KING   Part them, they are incensed.
HAMLET   Nay, come, again.

[*The* QUEEN *falls.*]

OSRIC   Look to the Queen there, ho!
HORATIO   They bleed on both sides. How is it, my lord?
OSRIC   How is 't, Laertes?   275
LAERTES   Why, as a woodcock to mine own springe,° Osric,
   I am justly killed with mine own treachery.
HAMLET   How does the Queen?
KING   She swounds to see them bleed.
QUEEN   No, no, the drink, the drink!—O my dear Hamlet—
   The drink, the drink! I am poisoned.   [*Dies.*]   280
HAMLET   Oh, villainy! Ho! Let the door be locked.
   Treachery! Seek it out.

[LAERTES *falls.*]

LAERTES   It is here, Hamlet. Hamlet, thou art slain.
   No medicine in the world can do thee good,
   In thee there is not half an hour of life.   285
   The treacherous instrument is in thy hand,
   Unbated and envenomed. The foul practice
   Hath turned itself on me. Lo, here I lie
   Never to rise again. Thy mother's poisoned.
   I can no more. The King, the King's to blame.   290
HAMLET   The point envenomed too!
   Then, venom, to thy work.

[*Stabs the* KING.]

ALL   Treason! Treason!
KING   Oh, yet defend me, friends, I am but hurt.
HAMLET   Here, thou incestuous, murderous, damnèd Dane,   295
   Drink off this potion. Is thy union° here?
   Follow my mother.   [KING *dies.*]
LAERTES   He is justly served.

276 springe: snare   296 union: pearl

It is a poison tempered° by himself.
Exchange forgiveness with me, noble Hamlet.
Mine and my father's death come not upon thee,   300
Nor thine on me!   [*Dies.*]

HAMLET   Heaven make thee free of it! I follow thee.
I am dead, Horatio. Wretched Queen, adieu!
You that look pale and tremble at this chance,
That are but mutes or audience to this act,   305
Had I but time—as this fell° sergeant, Death,
Is strict in his arrest—oh, I could tell you—
But let it be. Horatio, I am dead,
Thou livest. Report me and my cause aright
To the unsatisfied.°

HORATIO   Never believe it.   310
I am more an antique Roman° than a Dane.
Here's yet some liquor left.

HAMLET   As thou 'rt a man,
Give me the cup. Let go—by Heaven, I'll have 't.
O good Horatio, what a wounded name,
Things standing thus unknown, shall live behind me!   315
If thou didst ever hold me in thy heart,
Absent thee from felicity a while,
And in this harsh world draw thy breath in pain
To tell my story.

[*March afar off, and shot within.*]

          What warlike noise is this?

OSRIC   Young Fortinbras, with conquest come from Poland,   320
To the ambassadors of England gives
This warlike volley.

HAMLET   Oh, I die, Horatio,
The potent poison quite o'ercrows° my spirit.
I cannot live to hear the news from England,
But I do prophesy the election° lights   325
On Fortinbras. He has my dying voice.°
So tell him, with the occurrents, more and less,
Which have solicited.° The rest is silence.   [*Dies.*]

HORATIO   Now cracks a noble heart. Good night, sweet Prince,
And flights of angels sing thee to thy rest!   330

[*March within.*]

298 tempered: mixed   306 fell: dread   310 unsatisfied: who do not know the truth   311
antique Roman: like Cato and Brutus, who killed themselves rather than survive in a world which
was unpleasing to them   323 o'ercrows: overpowers   325 election: as King of Denmark   326
voice: support   327–28 occurrents . . . solicited: events great and small which have caused me to
act

Why does the drum come hither?

[*Enter* FORTINBRAS, *and the* ENGLISH AMBASSADORS, *with drum, colors, and* ATTENDANTS.]

FORTINBRAS   Where is this sight?
HORATIO   What is it you would see?
  If aught of woe or wonder, cease your search.
FORTINBRAS   This quarry cries on havoc.° O proud Death,
  What feast is toward° in thine eternal cell   335
  That thou so many princes at a shot
  So bloodily hast struck?
FIRST AMBASSADOR   The sight is dismal,
  And our affairs from England come too late.
  The ears are senseless that should give us hearing,
  To tell him his commandment is fulfilled,   340
  That Rosencrantz and Guildenstern are dead.
  Where should we have our thanks?
HORATIO   Not from his mouth
  Had it the ability of life to thank you.
  He never gave commandment for their death.
  But since, so jump° upon this bloody question,   345
  You from the Polack wars, and you from England,
  Are here arrived, give order that these bodies
  High on a stage be placèd to the view,
  And let me speak to the yet unknowing world
  How these things came about. So shall you hear   350
  Of carnal, bloody, and unnatural acts,
  Of accidental judgments, casual slaughters,
  Of deaths put on by cunning and forced cause,
  And, in this upshot, purposes mistook
  Fall'n on the inventors' heads. All this can I   355
  Truly deliver.
FORTINBRAS   Let us haste to hear it,
  And call the noblest to the audience.
  For me, with sorrow I embrace my fortune.
  I have some rights of memory° in this kingdom,
  Which now to claim my vantage° doth invite me.   360
HORATIO   Of that I shall have also cause to speak,
  And from his mouth whose voice will draw on more.°
  But let this same be presently performed,

---

334 quarry... havoc: heap of slain denotes a pitiless slaughter   **335 toward:** being prepared
345 jump: exactly   **359 rights of memory:** rights which will be remembered; i.e., with the
disappearance of all the family of the original King Hamlet, the situation reverts to what it was before
the death of Fortinbras' father   **360 vantage:** advantage   **362 voice... more:** i.e., Hamlet's dying
voice will strengthen your claim

Even while men's minds are wild, lest more mischance
On plots and errors happen.
FORTINBRAS   Let four captains   365
Bear Hamlet, like a soldier, to the stage.
For he was likely, had he been put on,°
To have proved most royally. And for his passage
The soldiers' music and the rites of war
Speak loudly for him.   370
Take up the bodies. Such a sight as this
Becomes the field, but here shows much amiss.
Go, bid the soldiers shoot.
    [*A dead march. Exeunt, bearing off the bodies; after which a peal of
                                                        ordnance is shot off.*]

Questions for Writing and Discussion

1.   Why do you think Hamlet spurns Ophelia in Act III, scene i? Is this a
deliberate cruelty? Or has he been led to misunderstand her?

2.   What reason does Hamlet give for disposing of Rosencrantz and Guildenstern
as he does (Act V, scene ii, lines 57–62)? What does his notion of the clash of
"mighty opposites" suggest about the part a hero must play in any tragedy, and the
part he plays in his own?

3.   We are told in Act I, scene i, that Fortinbras' father was vanquished by
Hamlet's father. At the end of the play, however, Fortinbras presides over the
restoration of domestic tranquillity in Denmark, and has lived to see Hamlet
vanquished. If we take Fortinbras to be yet another avenger, but different in kind
from both Hamlet and Laertes, what sort of dramatic point is made by the swift
progress of his military career in the background of Hamlet's difficult quest for
revenge (consult Hamlet's soliloquy at Act IV, scene iv)? Is there a sense in which
Laertes posed a threat to the political stability of Denmark (see Act IV, scene v,
lines 95–105)? Is this true of Hamlet also? Why does Fortinbras order that Hamlet
be given a soldier's burial?

4.   Compare Ophelia's description of Hamlet (Act III, scene i, lines 144–55) with
Osric's description of Laertes (Act V, scene ii, lines 100–05). What is added to
your understanding of the two characters by these descriptions, and by the persons
who supply them?

5.   Hamlet twice compares his father to Hyperion, the last of the Titans (gods in
Greek myth who were deposed by the Olympians after a war in heaven). Clearly,
Hamlet intends to convey awe of his father; but what else could the comparison
suggest to an audience familiar with the conquest of the ancient Titans by the
upstart Olympians? How might the comparison be used in a psychoanalytic
interpretation of the play as described in the Introduction?

367 had . . . on: had he become King

HENRIK IBSEN

A Doll House

Introduction

First and foremost, *A Doll House* is a play. If saying that strikes you as excessively obvious, think for a moment of how easily, while reading Ibsen's work, we can forget that it is meant to be produced on the stage. One reason we can forget this is that the play reads so well. Yet everything about it—structure, characterization, language, ideas—is shaped for the most effective performance. So, as you become absorbed in reading this translation from the Norwegian original, there is a real point in constantly reminding yourself: *it's a play.*

That means you cannot expect from it the things you might from a novel—such as helpful asides and explanations from the author, descriptions of the historical background and physical setting, elaborate psychologizing about the characters. What you can expect are the elements that are distinctive to the play as a form—such as compact divisions into self-contained acts each of which builds up to its own climax, sharp confrontations between characters that help to compress the action into a relatively short time, and dialogue that reveals both the inner feelings of the characters and the special roles they have to undertake on stage.

Ideally, when reading a play, we ought to "see" it in our mind's eye as if it were being performed on stage. The reader becomes a sort of director making decisions on how the skeleton of the text will be given the flesh of drama.

But *A Doll House* is also a work crucially intertwined with the moral and spiritual history of modern humanity, especially with the troubled relationships between modern men and women. When the play was first put on the stage, its subject was considered daring, perhaps subversive; even today, a century later, it arouses strong feelings. At a recent New York revival, when Nora finally takes leave of her home in Act III, there were cheers from women, and some men, in the audience who saw her decision as an early instance of feminist rebellion.

The great Irish playwright, George Bernard Shaw, once said that "Nora's revolt is the end of a chapter in human history." We think he meant by this striking sentence that once Ibsen's play had become popular it was a good deal harder (though not impossible) for people to accept uncritically the kind of paternalistic domination to which Nora is subjected. So we have here one of those infrequent works of literature which immediately left their mark on the lives of many people; and one reason was that the play itself was deeply implicated with, and shaped by, a given moment of history.

Writing in the second half of the nineteenth century, Henrik Ibsen was one of the major figures in that "school" of European literature that we call realism. The realist writers sought to break with past forms and conventions of society—patriotism, religion, the family—which were commonly held to be sacred, or at least beyond criticism. They believed that everything in the life of their time had to be laid open to honest and scathing criticism. They wanted to probe beneath the appearances of things and to discover their inner reality. (All through the nineteenth century thoughtful minds kept asking: what is *really* the nature of our life, *really* the truth of our ideas, *really* the value of our society?) They often wrote out of an assumption that society had grown rigid, impersonal, cold; that it was denying the potential for human growth; that it had become necessary for men and women to question inherited beliefs in order to discover what really mattered in the years given to us. As a student of Ibsen's works, Ronald Peacock, has written: his plays "repeat the picture of the rebel against society, in the sense of integrity against hypocrisy, of independence against cowardice, of spiritual vitality against deadening convention. Ibsen creates a myth of the Truthful Man [and Woman]. . . ."

This effort to distinguish between external appearance and underlying reality became so strong a preoccupation of writers in the late nineteenth century that many people came to feel, perhaps a little narrowly, that the great function of literature was *moral criticism.* "Live better!" said the Russian writer Chekhov when asked what the central impulse of his work was, and Ibsen would surely have agreed with him.

A Doll House seems to begin mildly enough. Ibsen was using one of the standard conventions of European theatre: the domestic drama, in which conflicts and troubles between members of a family are brought to a sharp and rapid climax. The conflict between Nora and Torvald is not, however, a mere routine family argument such as can develop at any time between wife and husband. No; in the context of the play it rapidly becomes a conflict between two visions or styles of life. Faintly at the outset and much more so at the end, Nora represents an effort to grapple honestly with the realities of our life and thereby to reach that tentative understanding which we call maturity; while Torvald represents the petty evasions, the cheerful lies and hypocrisies of a complacent middle-class existence. Between these two ways of life there can, finally, be no compromise—and that is what Nora comes to see in the overwhelming final act.

Here, we think, lies a major source of Ibsen's power as a playwright: he endows the seemingly small and trivial circumstances of an obscure Norwegian couple with a great power of reverberation. He sweeps all of us into an awareness that—even if we are not quite the "squirrel" that Nora pretends to be or not quite so stuffy as Torvald is—still, something of their torment remains our torment, and thereby something of their growth may be our growth. For what is at stake in the play is not just the question of women's rights, though in part it certainly *is* that; what is at stake is the struggle of a human being to discover the truth about herself.

George Bernard Shaw, writing at the turn of the century, understood very keenly the relationship between the specific issues raised by the play and the richer implications that we see behind those issues:

> [There are] both Ibsenites and anti-Ibsenites who seem to think that the [case of Nora is] meant to establish a golden rule for women who wish to be "emancipated"; the said golden rule being simply, Run away from your husband. But in Ibsen's view of life, that would come under the same condemnation as the ecclesiastical rule, Cleave to your husband until death do you part. Most people know of a case or two in which it would be wise for a wife to follow the example of Nora. . . . But they must also know cases in which the results of such a course would be tragi-comic. . . .

Still, there's a certain danger in what we (and Shaw, too) have just been saying. It is the danger of blunting the sharp edges of Nora's rebellion by using highfalutin phrases about growth, discovery, fulfillment, and so forth. Not that those phrases don't matter; they do matter, a great deal. But the *specific* content, the cutting edge, of Nora's final decision is the refusal of a woman to accept the humiliating role to which her lordly husband assigns her. Whatever larger implications we can draw from the play depend on this fact. That Ibsen meant to make a sharp statement about the condition of women, we can see from the notes he wrote for the play:

> A woman cannot be herself in the society of the present day, which is an exclusively masculine society, with laws framed by men and with a judicial system that judges feminine conduct from a masculine point of view.

Has the play become dated, then? Since it is no longer shocking or unusual for wives to leave their husbands, should we feel the play has lost its power to move us? We think not. Even the particular issues of women's rights are still very much with us. (By the way, it's worth noting that in the play itself there is no mention whatever of women's rights; what Ibsen does is to dramatize a situation, as a result of which critics and readers are led to reflect upon women's rights.) There are still plenty of doll houses in the world, still plenty of women who go through the shaming masquerade of making themselves into "squirrels" and "larks" in order to please their husbands. So, if the play is not finally about feminism, it takes off from the problems of women. If it opens into the largest questions about human freedom and responsibility, it starts out from the particular problem of what the rights and obligations of a middle-class wife should be.

All literature is like that: the larger implications emerge only out of particular stories and situations; the particular stories and situations move us only if they bear within themselves larger implications.

To grasp both the specific issues and the larger implications of *A Doll House,* we must have a clear understanding of what Ibsen has done with Nora. Anyone directing the play must make a clear decision as to how Nora will be played, especially in the first two acts. (The bang-up ending is relatively easy.)

A mistake that many directors and actresses have made with regard to Nora is to show her at the outset as *merely* the simpering if charming little ninny that she makes herself out to be in her husband's presence. As a result, it becomes hard to persuade the audience that suddenly, by the third act, she is capable of so extraordinary a step as leaving her husband and children in order to go off by herself. But this difficulty can be avoided by paying close attention to Ibsen's text, which shows us that even in the first act Nora is *playing a role,* consciously or semiconsciously *acting* the brainless little darling wife.*

Very soon, however—in fact, during the conversations she has in Act I with Mrs. Linde, Rank, and Krogstad—it becomes clear that Nora has a mind of her own, undeveloped perhaps but quick and bright. ("I'm capable of something too," she tells her friend Mrs. Linde, and once we learn what she has done for her husband, we gain some respect for her.)

The development of Nora in the third act is not so much a radical change as it is a sharp emergence. The "new" Nora has been there all along, but three-quarters hidden, deliberately keeping herself in shadow in order to placate her husband. The perceptive human being that we now recognize Nora to be is finally able to come out into the open.

Shocked by Torvald's mean-spirited response when he learns the truth about their situation, Nora emerges as a figure of mounting intelligence. She can speak such powerful lines as these:

> I've lived by doing tricks for you. . . .

> I have to stand completely alone, if I'm ever going to discover myself and the world out there.

> You never loved me. You've thought it fun to be in love with me, that's all.

These simple sentences, in the context of the play, descend like hammer blows. Once it becomes clear that the early Nora was probably capable of thinking them but found it prudent not to speak them, they gain the force of inevitability. And when Nora is seen in this way, the opening and closing

---

*In support of this view, we would quote from one critic of Ibsen, Hermann Weigand, who neatly sums up Nora's confused yet complex state of mind during the early part of the play:

   1) A certain degree of heroism must be conceded to the little woman who sacrifices her vanity year after year to live up to that irksome obligation [the debt]. . . . 2) At the same time she is self-conscious enough to underscore that aspect of the case to Kristine Linde. 3) She is tremendously proud of having kept her secret; as a matter of fact, however, her knowledge of Torvald's strict notions left no other course open to her. 4) In providing for the quarterly payments, she is incapable of any systematic saving. She lives from hand to mouth. . . . 5) She has been getting a great deal of childish fun out of working a bit now and then in secret. . . . 6) The play-acting to which she resorted to get money out of Torvald gave her the most perfect opportunity for self-expression. In opening her bagful of tricks, she was altogether herself. . . .

sections of the play come to seem closely knit, a movement of drama that reveals a growth of character.

Let us end, now, by coming back to the point we made at the beginning: *A Doll House* is a play that is designed to be vivid and exciting on the stage. Ibsen, of course, was concerned with human experience, but that concern always took the form of shaping experience into dramatic structures. At every point he works to make certain that the play moves rapidly, the characters are thrust into significant crises, and what we witness is an entanglement of suffering human beings at the climax of their trouble.

These are generalizations, but if you read the play carefully, we think you'll agree with them. To illustrate, let us just look at the first act in a bit of detail:

Opening: Nora and Torvald shown in characteristic relations. Nora stealthily eating macaroons, like a child who has to hide things from her daddy. Afraid of rebuke by her husband. He quickly "labels" her—squirrel, lark, little spendthrift. Taking advantage of this, she tries to wheedle some money out of him, though we don't yet know what she needs it for. So, for the moment, we may accept Torvald's smug assumption that it's because she can't manage properly. Full of self-importance, he gives her some. It's "a doll house," and Nora the doll. All of this—just a few minutes.

Enter Mrs. Linde: a force of complication and disturbance. The first tightening of emotions. At a quick glance it may seem Nora is lucky, Mrs. Linde deprived; but as their conversation develops, it comes to seem more complicated. The plot is being unfolded through their talk—we get a richer view of Nora: she isn't a flighty creature; she has been doing something on the sly because she knows she has to pander to her husband's vanity. Rapid stroke by stroke, Ibsen prepares for the clash to come.

Now Krogstad: further disturbance, but notice that Ibsen brings him onto the stage for just a minute, so as to establish a point of contrast. He is a key figure in the plot, as we'll learn a bit later, importantly connected with both Nora and Mrs. Linde. But so far we're being teased with just a glimpse of him. He withdraws, and Rank appears, the character who serves as detached observer, a semiphilosophical voice.

A Moment of Gaiety: tension having been built up, Ibsen now teases us a little and lightens the tone of things. Torvald promises to help Mrs. Linde get a job; the children come in, noisy and happy; Nora is delighted with them (this establishes how attached she is to them and how much of a wrench it will be when she leaves).

Krogstad Again: now the major climax of the act, an open confrontation between Nora and Krogstad. The whole story becomes clear, and Nora is left in a state of acute anxiety. She tries to charm Torvald with chatter about her costume in order to protect him from the threat Krogstad represents; but he, stuffy and righteous as we have come to know him, pontificates about Krogstad's bad character, without realizing, of course, that each word fills Nora with a kind of terror.

Last Moment: just before the curtain goes down, Nora is overcome with the thought that a trap is closing in upon her and there seems nothing she can do to escape it. The fearful power of circumstances, the wretchedness of people unable to reach one another with an honest word. . . .

The first act, then, is brilliantly constructed, with a maximum of dramatic economy and thrust. Everything has been set up to prepare for the clash that is to come. The remaining acts we leave to you.

A Doll House *

CHARACTERS OF THE PLAY

TORVALD HELMER, *a lawyer*
NORA, *his wife*
DR. RANK
MRS. LINDE
NILS KROGSTAD, *a bank clerk*
THE HELMERS' THREE SMALL CHILDREN
ANNE-MARIE, *their nurse*
HELENE, *a maid*
A DELIVERY BOY

The action takes place in HELMER'S *residence.*

ACT I

A comfortable room, tastefully but not expensively furnished. A door to the right in the back wall leads to the entryway, another to the left leads to HELMER'S *study. Between these doors, a piano. Midway in the left-hand wall a door, and further back a window. Near the window a round table with an armchair and a small sofa. In the right-hand wall, toward the rear a door, and nearer the foreground a porcelain stove with two armchairs and a rocking chair beside it. Between the stove and the side door, a small table. Engravings on the walls. An etagére with china figures and other small art objects; a small bookcase with richly bound books; the floor carpeted; a fire burning in the stove. It is a winter day.*

A bell rings in the entryway; shortly after we hear the door being unlocked. NORA *comes into the room, humming happily to herself; she is wearing street clothes and carries an armload of packages, which she puts down on the table to the right. She has left the hall door open; and through it a* DELIVERY BOY *is seen, holding a Christmas tree and a basket which he gives to the* MAID *who let them in.*

NORA   Hide the tree well, Helene. The children mustn't get a glimpse of it till
this evening, after it's trimmed. *(To the* DELIVERY BOY, *taking out her purse)*
How much?

DELIVERY BOY   Fifty, ma'am.

NORA   There's a crown. No, keep the change. *(The* BOY *thanks her and leaves.*
NORA *shuts the door. She laughs softly to herself while taking off her street
things. Drawing a bag of macaroons from her pocket, she eats a couple, then steals
over and listens at her husband's study door.)* Yes, he's home. *(Hums again as
she moves to the table, right.)*

HELMER   *(from the study)*   Is that my little lark twittering out there?

NORA   *(busy opening some packages)*   Yes, it is.

HELMER   Is that my squirrel rummaging around?

NORA   Yes!

HELMER   When did my squirrel get in?

NORA   Just now. *(Putting the macaroon bag in her pocket and wiping her mouth)*
Do come in, Torvald, and see what I've bought.

HELMER   Can't be disturbed. *(After a moment he opens the door and peers in, pen
in hand.)* Bought, you say? All that there? Has the little spendthrift been
out throwing money around again?

NORA   Oh, but Torvald, this year we really should let ourselves go a bit. It's the
first Christmas we haven't had to economize.

HELMER   But you know we can't go squandering.

NORA   Oh yes, Torvald, we can squander a little now. Can't we? Just a tiny,
wee bit. Now that you've got a big salary and are going to make piles and
piles of money.

HELMER   Yes—starting New Year's. But then it's a full three months till the
raise comes through.

NORA   Pooh! We can borrow that long.

HELMER   Nora! *(Goes over and playfully takes her by the ear)* Are your scatter-
brains off again? What if today I borrowed a thousand crowns, and you
squandered them over Christmas week, and then on New Year's Eve a roof
tile fell on my head, and I lay there—

NORA   *(putting her hand on his mouth)* Oh! Don't say such things!

HELMER   Yes, but what if it happened—then what?

NORA   If anything so awful happened, then it just wouldn't matter if I had
debts or not.

HELMER   Well, but the people I'd borrowed from?

NORA   Them? Who cares about them! They're strangers.

HELMER   Nora, Nora, how like a woman! No, but seriously, Nora, you know
what I think about that. No debts! Never borrow! Something of freedom's
lost—and something of beauty, too—from a home that's founded on
borrowing and debt. We've made a brave stand up to now, the two of us;
and we'll go right on like that the little while we have to.

NORA   *(going toward the stove)* Yes, whatever you say, Torvald.

HELMER   *(following her)* Now, now, the little lark's wings mustn't droop.

Come on, don't be a sulky squirrel. *(Taking out his wallet)* Nora, guess what I have here.

NORA   *(turning quickly)* Money!

HELMER   There, see. *(Hands her some notes)* Good grief, I know how costs go up in a house at Christmastime.

NORA   Ten—twenty—thirty—forty. Oh, thank you. Torvald; I can manage no end on this.

HELMER   You really will have to.

NORA   Oh yes, I promise I will! But come here so I can show you everything I bought. And so cheap! Look, new clothes for Ivar here—and a sword. Here a horse and a trumpet for Bob. And a doll and a doll's bed here for Emmy; they're nothing much, but she'll tear them to bits in no time anyway. And here I have dress material and handkerchiefs for the maids. Old Anne-Marie really deserves something more.

HELMER   And what's in that package there?

NORA   *(with a cry)* Torvald, no! You can't see that till tonight!

HELMER   I see. But tell me now, you little prodigal, what have you thought of for yourself?

NORA   For myself? Oh, I don't want anything at all.

HELMER   Of course you do. Tell me just what—within reason—you'd most like to have.

NORA   I honestly don't know. Oh, listen, Torvald—

HELMER   Well?

NORA   *(fumbling at his coat buttons, without looking at him)* If you want to give me something, then maybe you could—you could—

HELMER   Come on, out with it.

NORA   *(hurriedly)* You could give me money, Torvald. No more than you think you can spare, then one of these days I'll buy something with it.

HELMER   But Nora—

NORA   Oh, please, Torvald darling, do that! I beg you, please. Then I could hang the bills in pretty gilt paper on the Christmas tree. Wouldn't that be fun?

HELMER   What are those little birds called that always fly through their fortunes?

NORA   Oh yes, spendthrifts; I know all that. But let's do as I say, Torvald; then I'll have time to decide what I really need most. That's very sensible, isn't it?

HELMER   *(smiling)* Yes, very—that is, if you actually hung onto the money I give you, and you actually used it to buy yourself something, But it goes for the house and for all sorts of foolish things, and then I only have to lay out some more.

NORA   Oh, but Torvald—

HELMER   Don't deny it, my dear little Nora. *(Putting his arm around her waist)* Spendthrifts are sweet, but they use up a frightful amount of money. It's incredible what it costs a man to feed such birds.

NORA   Oh, how can you say that! Really, I save everything I can.

HELMER   *(laughing)* Yes, that's the truth. Everything you can. But that's nothing at all.

NORA   *(humming, with a smile of quiet satisfaction)* Hm, if you only knew what expenses we larks and squirrels have, Torvald.

HELMER   You're an odd little one. Exactly the way your father was. You're never at a loss for scaring up money; but the moment you have it, it runs right out through your fingers; you never know what you've done with it. Well, one takes you as you are. It's deep in your blood. Yes, these things are hereditary, Nora.

NORA   Ah, I could wish I'd inherited many of Papa's qualities.

HELMER   And I couldn't wish you anything but just what you are, my sweet little lark. But wait; it seems to me you have a very—what should I call it?—a very suspicious look today—

NORA   I do?

HELMER   You certainly do. Look me straight in the eye.

NORA   *(looking at him)* Well?

HELMER   *(shaking an admonitory finger)* Surely my sweet tooth hasn't been running riot in town today, has she?

NORA   No. Why do you imagine that?

HELMER   My sweet tooth really didn't make a little detour through the confectioner's?

NORA   No, I assure you, Torvald—

HELMER   Hasn't nibbled some pastry?

NORA   No, not at all.

HELMER   Not even munched a macaroon or two?

NORA   No, Torvald, I assure you, really—

HELMER   There, there now. Of course I'm only joking.

NORA   *(going to the table, right)* You know I could never think of going against you.

HELMER   No, I understand that; and you *have* given me your word. *(Going over to her)* Well, you keep your little Christmas secrets to yourself, Nora darling. I expect they'll come to light this evening, when the tree is lit.

NORA   Did you remember to ask Dr. Rank?

HELMER   No. But there's no need for that; it's assumed he'll be dining with us. All the same, I'll ask him when he stops by here this morning. I've ordered some fine wine. Nora, you can't imagine how I'm looking forward to this evening.

NORA   So am I. And what fun for the children, Torvald!

HELMER   Ah, it's so gratifying to know that one's gotten a safe, secure job, and with a comfortable salary. It's a great satisfaction, isn't it?

NORA   Oh, its wonderful!

HELMER   Remember last Christmas? Three whole weeks before, you shut yourself in every evening till long after midnight, making flowers for the Christmas tree, and all the other decorations to surprise us. Ugh, that was the dullest time I've ever lived through.

NORA   It wasn't at all dull for me.

HELMER   *(smiling)* But the outcome *was* pretty sorry, Nora.

NORA   Oh, don't tease me with that again. How could I help it that the cat came in and tore everything to shreds.

HELMER   No, poor thing, you certainly couldn't. You wanted so much to please us all, and that's what counts. But it's just as well that the hard times are past.

NORA   Yes, it's really wonderful.

HELMER   Now I don't have to sit here alone, boring myself, and you don't have to tire your precious eyes and your fair little delicate hands—

NORA   *(clapping her hands)* No, is it really true, Torvald, I don't have to? Oh, how wonderfully lovely to hear! *(Taking his arm)* Now I'll tell you just how I've thought we should plan things. Right after Christmas—*(The doorbell rings.)* Oh, the bell. *(Straightening the room up a bit)* Somebody would have to come. What a bore!

HELMER   I'm not at home to visitors, don't forget.

MAID   *(from the hall doorway)* Ma'am, a lady to see you—

NORA   All right, let her come in.

MAID *(to* HELMER)   And the doctor's just come too.

HELMER   Did he go right to my study?

MAID   Yes, he did.

*(*HELMER *goes into his room. The* MAID *shows in* MRS. LINDE, *dressed in traveling clothes, and shuts the door after her.)*

MRS. LINDE   *(in a dispirited and somewhat hesitant voice)* Hello, Nora.

NORA *(uncertain)*   Hello—

MRS. LINDE   You don't recognize me.

NORA   No, I don't know—but wait, I think—*(Exclaiming)* What! Kristine! Is it really you?

MRS. LINDE   Yes, it's me.

NORA   Kristine! To think I didn't recognize you. But then, how could I? *(More quietly)* How you've changed, Kristine!

MRS. LINDE   Yes, now doubt I have. In nine—ten long years.

NORA   Is it so long since we met! Yes, it's all of that. Oh, these last eight years have been a happy time, believe me. And so now you've come in to town, too. Made the long trip in the winter. That took courage.

MRS. LINDE   I just got here by ship this morning.

NORA   To enjoy yourself over Christmas, of course. Oh, how lovely! Yes, enjoy ourselves, we'll do that. But take your coat off. You're not still cold? *(Helping her)* There now, let's get cozy here by the stove. No, the easy chair there! I'll take the rocker here. *(Seizing her hands)* Yes, now you have your old look again; it was only in that first moment. You're a bit pale, Kristine— and maybe a bit thinner.

MRS. LINDE   And much, much older, Nora.

NORA   Yes, perhaps, a bit older; a tiny, tiny bit; not much at all. *(Stopping short; suddenly serious)* Oh, but thoughtless me, to sit here, chattering away. Sweet, good Kristine, can you forgive me?

MRS. LINDE   What do you mean, Nora?

NORA *(softly)*   Poor Kristine, you've become a widow.

MRS. LINDE   Yes, three years ago.

NORA   Oh, I knew it, of course; I read it in the papers. Oh Kristine, you must believe me; I often thought of writing you then, but I kept postponing it, and something always interfered.

MRS. LINDE   Nora dear, I understand completely.

NORA   No, it was awful of me, Kristine. You poor thing, how much you must have gone through. And he left you nothing?

MRS. LINDE   No.

NORA   And no children?

MRS. LINDE   No.

NORA   Nothing at all, then?

MRS. LINDE   Not even a sense of loss to feed on.

NORA *(looking incredulously at her)*   But Kristine, how could that be?

MRS. LINDE *(smiling wearily and smoothing her hair)*   Oh, sometimes it happens, Nora.

NORA   So completely alone. How terribly hard that must be for you. I have three lovely children. You can't see them now; they're out with the maid. But now you must tell me everything—

MRS. LINDE   No, no, no, tell me about yourself.

NORA   No, you begin. Today I don't want to be selfish. I want to think only of you today. But there *is* something I must tell you. Did you hear of the wonderful luck we had recently?

MRS. LINDE   No, what's that?

NORA   My husband's been made manager in the bank, just think!

MRS. LINDE   Your husband? How marvelous!

NORA   Isn't it? Being a lawyer is such an uncertain living, you know, especially if one won't touch any cases that aren't clean and decent. And of course Torvald would never do that, and I'm with him completely there. Oh, we're simply delighted, believe me! He'll join the bank right after New Year's and start getting a huge salary and lots of commissions. From now on we can live quite differently—jus as we want. Oh, Kristine, I feel so light and happy! Won't it be lovely to have stacks of money and not a care in the world?

MRS. LINDE   Well, anyway, it would be lovely to have enough for necessities.

NORA   No, not just for necessities, but stacks and stacks of money!

MRS. LINDE *(smiling)*   Nora, Nora, aren't you sensible yet? Back in school you were such a free spender.

NORA *(with a quiet laugh)*   Yes, that's what Torvald still says. *(Shaking her finger)* But "Nora, Nora" isn't as silly as you all think. Really, we've been in no position for me to go squandering. We've had to work, both of us.

MRS. LINDE   You too?

NORA Yes, at odd jobs—needlework, crocheting, embroidery, and such—
(*Casually*) and other things too. You remember that Torvald left the
department when we were married? There was no chance of promotion in
his office, and of course he needed to earn more money. But that first year
he drove himself terribly. He took on all kinds of extra work that kept him
going morning and night. It wore him down, and then he fell deathly ill.
The doctors said it was essential for him to travel south.

MRS. LINDE Yes, didn't you spend a whole year in Italy?

NORA That's right. It wasn't easy to get away, you know. Ivar had just been
born. But of course we had to go. Oh, that was a beautiful trip, and it saved
Torvald's life. But it cost a frightful sum, Kristine.

MRS. LINDE I can well imagine.

NORA Four thousand, eight hundred crowns it cost. That's really a lot of
money.

MRS. LINDE But it's lucky you had it when you needed it.

NORA Well, as it was, we got it from Papa.

MRS. LINDE I see. It was just about the time your father died.

NORA Yes, just about then. And, you know, I couldn't make the trip out to
nurse him. I had to stay here, expecting Ivar any moment, and with my
poor sick Torvald to care for. Dearest Papa, I never saw him again, Kristine.
Oh, that was the worst time I've known in all my marriage.

MRS. LINDE I know how you loved him. And then you went off to Italy?

NORA Yes. We had the means now, and the doctors urged us. So we left a
month after.

MRS. LINDE And your husband came back completely cured?

NORA Sound as a drum!

MRS. LINDE But—the doctor?

NORA Who?

MRS. LINDE I thought the maid said he was a doctor, the man who came in
with me.

NORA Yes, that was Dr. Rank—but he's not making a sick call. He's our
closest friend, and he stops by at least once a day. No, Torvald hasn't had a
sick moment since, and the children are fit and strong, and I am, too.
(*Jumping up and clapping her hands*) Oh, dear God, Kristine, what a lovely
thing to live and be happy! But how disgusting of me—I'm talking of
nothing but my own affairs. (*Sits on a stool close by* KRISTINE, *arms resting
across her knees*) Oh, don't be angry with me! Tell me, is it really true that
you weren't in love with your husband? Why did you marry him, then?

MRS. LINDE My mother was still alive, but bedridden and helpless—and I had
two younger brothers to look after. In all conscience, I didn't think I could
turn him down.

NORA No, you were right there. But was he rich at the time?

MRS. LINDE He was very well off, I'd say. But the business was shaky, Nora.
When he died, it all fell apart, and nothing was left.

NORA And then—?

MRS. LINDE Yes, so I had to scrape up a living with a little shop and a little teaching and whatever else I could find. The last three years have been like one endless workday without a rest for me. Now it's over, Nora. My poor mother doesn't need me, for she's passed on. Nor the boys, either; they're working now and can take care of themselves.

NORA   How free you must feel—

MRS. LINDE   No—only unspeakably empty. Nothing to live for now. *(Standing up anxiously)* That's why I couldn't take it any longer out in that desolate hole. Maybe here it'll be easier to find something to do and keep my mind occupied. If I could only be lucky enough to get a steady job, some office work—

NORA   Oh, but Kristine, that's so dreadfully tiring, and you already look so tired. It would be much better for you if you could go off to a bathing resort.

MRS. LINDE   *(going toward the window)*   I have no father to give me travel money, Nora.

NORA   *(rising)*   Oh, don't be angry with me.

MRS. LINDE   *(going to her)*   Nora dear, don't you be angry with me. The worst of my kind of situation is all the bitterness that's stored away. No one to work for, and yet you're always having to snap up your opportunities. You have to live; and so you grow selfish. When you told me the happy change in your lot, do you know I was delighted less for your sakes than for mine?

NORA   How so? Oh, I see. You think maybe Torvald could do something for you.

MRS. LINDE   Yes, that's what I thought.

NORA   And he will, Kristine! Just leave it to me; I'll bring it up so delicately— find something attractive to humor him with. Oh, I'm so eager to help you.

MRS. LINDE   How very kind of you, Nora, to be so concerned over me— doubly kind, considering you really know so little of life's burdens yourself.

NORA   I—? I know so little—?

MRS. LINDE   *(smiling)*   Well, my heavens—a little needlework and such— Nora, you're just a child.

NORA   *(tossing her head and pacing the floor)*   You don't have to act so superior.

MRS. LINDE   Oh?

NORA   You're just like the others. You all think I'm incapable of anything serious—

MRS. LINDE   Come now—

NORA   That I've never had to face the raw world.

MRS. LINDE   Nora dear, you've just been telling me all your troubles.

NORA   Hm! Trivia! *(Quietly)* I haven't told you the big thing.

MRS. LINDE   Big thing? What do you mean?

NORA   You look down on me so, Kristine, but you shouldn't. You're proud that you worked so long and hard for your mother.

MRS. LINDE   I don't look down on a soul. But it is true; I'm proud—and happy, too—to think it was given to me to make my mother's last days almost free of care.

NORA   And you're also proud thinking of what you've done for your brothers.

MRS. LINDE   I feel I've a right to be.

NORA   I agree. But listen to this, Kristine—I've also got something to be proud and happy for.

MRS. LINDE   I don't doubt it. But whatever do you mean?

NORA   Not so loud. What if Torvald heard! He mustn't, not for anything in the world. Nobody must know, Kristine. No one but you.

MRS. LINDE   But what is it, then?

NORA   Come here. *(Drawing her down beside her on the sofa)* It's true—I've also got something to be proud and happy for. I'm the one who saved Torvald's life.

MRS. LINDE   Saved—? Saved how?

NORA   I told you about the trip to Italy. Torvald never would have lived if he hadn't gone south—

MRS. LINDE   Of course, your father gave you the means—

NORA *(smiling)*   That's what Torvald and all the rest think, but—

MRS. LINDE   But—?

NORA   Papa didn't give us a pin. I was the one who raised the money.

MRS. LINDE   You? The whole amount?

NORA   Four thousand, eight hundred crowns. What do you say to that?

MRS. LINDE   But Nora, how was it possible? Did you win the lottery?

NORA *(disdainfully)*   The lottery? Pooh! No art to that.

MRS. LINDE   But where did you get it from then?

NORA *(humming, with a mysterious smile)*   Hmm, tra-la-la-la.

MRS. LINDE   Because you couldn't have borrowed it.

NORA   No? Why not?

MRS. LINDE   A wife can't borrow without her husband's consent.

NORA *(tossing her head)*   Oh, but a wife with a little business sense, a wife who knows how to manage—

MRS. LINDE   Nora, I simply don't understand—

NORA   You don't have to. Whoever said I *borrowed* the money? I could have gotten it other ways. *(Throwing herself back on the sofa)* I could have gotten it from some admirer or other. After all, a girl with my ravishing appeal—

MRS. LINDE   You lunatic.

NORA   I'll bet you're eaten up with curiosity, Kristine.

MRS. LINDE   Now listen here, Nora—you haven't done something indiscreet?

NORA *(sitting up again)*   Is it indiscreet to save your husband's life?

MRS. LINDE   I think it's indiscreet that without his knowledge you—

NORA   But that's the point: he mustn't know! My Lord, can't you understand? He mustn't ever know the close call he had. It was to *me* the doctors came to say his life was in danger—that nothing could save him but a stay in the south. Didn't I try strategy then! I began talking about how lovely it would be for me to travel abroad like other young wives; I begged and I cried; I told him please to remember my condition, to be kind and indulge me; and then I dropped a hint that he could easily take out a loan. But at that, Kristine, he nearly exploded. He said I was frivolous, and it was his duty as man of the house not to indulge me in whims and fancies—as I think he called them. Aha, I thought, now you'll just have to be saved—and that's when I saw my chance.

MRS. LINDE   And your father never told Torvald the money wasn't from him?

NORA   No, never. Papa died right about then. I'd considered bringing him into my secret and begging him never to tell. But he was too sick at the time—and then, sadly, it didn't matter.

MRS. LINDE   And you've never confided in your husband since?

NORA   For heaven's sake, no! Are you serious? He's so strict on that subject. Besides—Torvald, with all his masculine pride—how painfully humiliating for him if he ever found out he was in debt to me. That would just ruin our relationship. Our beautiful happy home would never be the same.

MRS. LINDE   Won't you ever tell him?

NORA   *(thoughtfully, half smiling)*   Yes—maybe sometime, years from now, when I'm no longer so attractive. Don't laugh! I only mean when Torvald loves me less than now, when he stops enjoying my dancing and dressing up and reciting for him. Then it might be wise to have something in reserve — *(Breaking off)*   How ridiculous! That'll never happen — Well, Kristine, what do you think of my big secret? I'm capable of something too, hm? You can imagine, of course, how this thing hangs over me. It really hasn't been easy meeting the payments on time. In the business world there's what they call quarterly interest and what they call amortization, and these are always so terribly hard to manage. I've had to skimp a little here and there, wherever I could, you know. I could hardly spare anything from my house allowance, because Torvald has to live well. I couldn't let the children go poorly dressed; whatever I got for them, I felt I had to use up completely—the darlings!

MRS. LINDE   Poor Nora, so it had to come out of your own budget, then?

NORA   Yes, of course. But I was the one most responsible, too. Every time Torvald gave me money for new clothes and such, I never used more than half; always bought the simplest, cheapest outfits. It was a godsend that everything looks so well on me that Torvald never noticed. But it did weigh me down at times, Kristine. It *is* such a joy to wear fine things. You understand.

MRS. LINDE   Oh, of course.

NORA   And then I found other ways of making money. Last winter I was lucky enough to get a lot of copying to do. I locked myself in and sat writing every evening till late in the night. Ah, I was tired so often, dead tired. But still it was wonderful fun, sitting and working like that, earning money. It was almost like being a man.

MRS. LINDE   But how much have you paid off this way so far?

NORA   That's hard to say, exactly. These accounts, you know, aren't easy to figure. I only know that I've paid out all I could scrape together. Time and again I haven't known where to turn. *(Smiling)* Then I'd sit here dreaming of a rich old gentleman who had fallen in love with me—

MRS. LINDE   What! Who is he?

NORA   Oh, really! And that he'd died, and when his will was opened, there in big letters it said, "All my fortune shall be paid over in cash, immediately, to that enchanting Mrs. Nora Helmer."

MRS. LINDE   But Nora dear—who *was* this gentleman?

NORA   Good grief, can't you understand? The old man never existed; that was only something I'd dream up time and again whenever I was at my wits' end for money. But it makes no difference now; the old fossil can go where he pleases for all I care; I don't need him or his will—because now I'm free. (*Jumping up*) Oh, how lovely to think of that, Kristine! Carefree! To know you're carefree, utterly carefree, to be able to romp and play with the children, and to keep up a beautiful, charming home—everything just the way Torvald likes it! And think, spring is coming, with big blue skies. Maybe we can travel a little then. Maybe I'll see the ocean again. Oh yes, it *is* so marvelous to live and be happy!

(*The front doorbell rings.*)

MRS. LINDE (*rising*)   There's the bell. It's probably best that I go.

NORA   No, stay. No one's expected. It must be for Torvald.

MAID (*from the hall doorway*)   Excuse me, ma'am—there's a gentleman here to see Mr. Helmer, but I didn't know—since the doctor's with him—

NORA   Who is the gentleman?

KROGSTAD (*from the doorway*)   It's me, Mrs. Helmer.

(MRS. LINDE *starts and turns away toward the window.*)

NORA (*stepping toward him, tense, her voice a whisper*)   You? What is it? Why do you want to speak to my husband?

KROGSTAD   Bank business—after a fashion. I have a small job in the investment bank, and I hear now your husband is going to be our chief—

NORA   In other words, it's—

KROGSTAD   Just dry business, Mrs. Helmer. Nothing but that.

NORA   Yes, then please be good enough to step into the study. (*She nods indifferently, as she sees him out by the hall door, then returns and begins stirring up the stove.*)

MRS. LINDE   Nora—who was that man?

NORA   That was a Mr. Krogstad—a lawyer.

MRS. LINDE   Then it really was him.

NORA   Do you know that person?

MRS. LINDE   I did once—many years ago. For a time he was a law clerk in our town.

NORA   Yes, he's been that.

MRS. LINDE   How he's changed.

NORA   I understand he had a very unhappy marriage.

MRS. LINDE   He's a widower now.

NORA   With a number of children. There now, it's burning. *(She closes the stove door and moves the rocker a bit to one side.)*

MRS. LINDE   They say he has a hand in all kinds of business.

NORA   Oh? That may be true; I wouldn't know. But let's not think about business. It's so dull.

(DR. RANK enters from HELMER'S study.)

RANK *(still in the doorway)*   No, no, really—I don't want to intrude, I'd just as soon talk a little while with your wife. *(Shuts the door, then notices* MRS. LINDE*)* Oh, beg pardon, I'm intruding here too.

NORA   No, not at all. *(Introducing him)* Dr. Rank, Mrs. Linde.

RANK   Well now, that's a name much heard in this house. I believe I passed the lady on the stairs as I came.

MRS. LINDE   Yes, I take the stairs very slowly. They're rather hard on me.

RANK   Uh-hm, some touch of internal weakness?

MRS. LINDE   More overexertion, I'd say.

RANK   Nothing else? Then you're probably here in town to rest up in a round of parties?

MRS. LINDE   I'm here to look for work.

RANK   Is that the best cure for overexertion?

MRS. LINDE   One has to live, Doctor.

RANK   Yes, there's a common prejudice to that effect.

NORA   Oh, come on, Dr. Rank—you really do want to live yourself.

RANK   Yes, I really do. Wretched as I am, I'll gladly prolong my torment indefinitely. All my patients feel like that. And it's quite the same, too, with the morally sick. Right at this moment there's one of those moral invalids in there with Helmer—

MRS. LINDE *(softly)*   Ah!

NORA   Who do you mean?

RANK   Oh, it's a lawyer, Krogstad, a type you wouldn't know. His character is rotten to the root—but even he began chattering all-importantly about how he had to *live*.

NORA   Oh? What did he want to talk to Torvald about?

RANK   I really don't know. I only heard something about the bank.

NORA   I didn't know that Krog—that this man Krogstad had anything to do with the bank.

RANK   Yes, he's gotten some kind of berth down there. *(To* MRS. LINDE*)* I don't know if you also have, in your neck of the woods, a type of person who scuttles about breathlessly, sniffing out hints of moral corruption, and then maneuvers his victim into some sort of key position where he can keep an eye on him. It's the healthy these days that are out in the cold.

MRS. LINDE   All the same, it's the sick who most need to be taken in.

RANK *(with a shrug)*   Yes, there we have it. That's the concept that's turning society into a sanatorium.

(NORA, *lost in her thoughts, breaks out into quiet laughter and claps her hands.*)

RANK Why do you laugh at that? Do you have any real idea of what society is?

NORA What do I care about dreary old society? I was laughing at something quite different—something terribly funny. Tell me, Doctor—is everyone who works in the bank dependent now on Torvald?

RANK Is that what you find so terribly funny?

NORA (*smiling and humming*) Never mind, never mind! (*Pacing the floor*) Yes, that's really immensely amusing: that we—that Torvald has so much power now over all those people. (*Taking the bag out of her pocket*) Dr. Rank, a little macaroon on that?

RANK See here, macaroons! I thought they were contraband here.

NORA Yes, but these are some that Kristine gave me.

MRS. LINDE What? I—?

NORA Now, now, don't be afraid. You couldn't possibly know that Torvald had forbidden them. You see, he's worried they'll ruin my teeth. But hmp! Just this once! Isn't that so, Dr. Rank? Help yourself! (*Puts a macaroon in his mouth*) And you too, Kristine. And I'll also have one, only a little one— or two, at the most. (*Walking about again*) Now I'm really tremendously happy. Now there's just one last thing in the world that I have an enormous desire to do.

RANK Well! And what's that?

NORA It's something I have such a consuming desire to say so Torvald could hear.

RANK And why can't you say it?

NORA I don't dare. It's quite shocking.

MRS. LINDE Shocking?

RANK Well, then it isn't advisable. But in front of us you certainly can. What do you have such a desire to say so Torvald could hear?

NORA I have such a huge desire to say—to hell and be damned!

RANK Are you crazy?

MRS. LINDE My goodness, Nora!

RANK Go on, say it. Here he is.

NORA (*hiding the macaroon bag*) Shh, shh, shh!

(HELMER *comes in from his study, hat in hand, overcoat over his arm.*)

NORA (*going toward him*) Well, Torvald dear, are you through with him?

HELMER Yes, he just left.

NORA Let me introduce you—this is Kristine, who's arrived here in town.

HELMER Kristine—? I'm sorry, but I don't know—

NORA Mrs. Linde, Torvald dear. Mrs. Kristine Linde.

HELMER Of course. A childhood friend of my wife's, no doubt?

MRS. LINDE Yes, we knew each other in those days.

NORA   And just think, she made the long trip down here in order to talk with you.

HELMER   What's this?

MRS. LINDE   Well, not exactly—

NORA   You see, Kristine is remarkably clever in office work, and so she's terribly eager to come under a capable man's supervision and add more to what she already knows—

HELMER   Very wise, Mrs. Linde.

NORA   And then when she heard that you'd become a bank manager—the story was wired out to the papers—then she came in as fast as she could and—Really, Torvald, for my sake you can do a little something for Kristine, can't you?

HELMER   Yes, it's not at all impossible. Mrs. Linde, I suppose you're a widow?

MRS. LINDE   Yes.

HELMER   Any experience in office work?

MRS. LINDE   Yes, a good deal.

HELMER   Well, it's quite likely that I can make an opening for you—

NORA *(clapping her hands)*   You see, you see!

HELMER   You've come at a lucky moment, Mrs. Linde.

MRS. LINDE   Oh, how can I thank you?

HELMER   Not necessary. *(Putting his overcoat on)* But today you'll have to excuse me—

RANK   Wait, I'll go with you. *(He fetches his coat from the hall and warms it at the stove.)*

NORA   Don't stay out long, dear.

HELMER   An hour; no more.

NORA   Are you going too, Kristine?

MRS. LINDE *(putting on her winter garments)*   Yes, I have to see about a room now.

HELMER   Then perhaps we can all walk together.

NORA *(helping her)*   What a shame we're so cramped here, but it's quite impossible for us to—

MRS. LINDE   Oh, don't even think of it! Good-bye, Nora dear, and thanks for everything.

NORA   Good-bye for now. Of course you'll be back again this evening. And you too, Dr. Rank. What? If you're well enough? Oh, you've got to be! Wrap up tight now.

(In a ripple of small talk the company moves out into the hall; children's voices are heard outside on the steps.)

NORA   There they are! There they are! *(She runs to open the door. The children come in with their nurse,* ANNE-MARIE.*)* Come in, come in! *(Bends down and kisses them)* Oh, you darlings—! Look at them, Kristine. Aren't they lovely!

RANK   No loitering in the draft here.

HELMER   Come, Mrs. Linde—this place is unbearable now for anyone but mothers.

(DR. RANK, HELMER, *and* MRS. LINDE *go down the stairs.* ANNE-MARIE *goes into the living room with the children.* NORA *follows, after closing the hall door.*)

NORA   How fresh and strong you look. Oh, such red cheeks you have! Like apples and roses. (*The children interrupt her throughout the following.*) And it was so much fun? That's wonderful. Really? You pulled both Emmy and Bob on the sled? Imagine, all together! Yes, you're a clever boy, Ivar. Oh, let me hold her a bit, Anne-Marie. My sweet little doll baby! (*Takes the smallest from the nurse and dances with her*) Yes, yes, Mama will dance with Bob as well. What? Did you throw snowballs? Oh, if I'd only been there! No, don't bother, Anne-Marie—I'll undress them myself. Oh yes, let me. It's such fun. Go in and rest; you look half frozen. There's hot coffee waiting for you on the stove. (*The nurse goes into the room to the left. Nora takes the children's winter things off, throwing them about, while the children talk to her all at once.*) Is that so? A big dog chased you? But it didn't bite? No, dogs never bite little, lovely doll babies. Don't peek in the packages, Ivar! What is it? Yes, wouldn't you like to know. No, no, it's an ugly something. Well? Shall we play? What shall we play? Hide-and-seek? Yes, let's play hide-and-seek. Bob must hide first. I must? Yes, let me hide first. (*Laughing and shouting, she and the children play in and out of the living room and the adjoining room to the right. At last* NORA *hides under the table. The children come storming in, search, but cannot find her, then hear her muffled laughter, dash over to the table, lift the cloth and find her. Wild shouting. She creeps forward as if to scare them. More shouts. Meanwhile, a knock at the hall door; no one has noticed it. Now the door half opens, and* KROGSTAD *appears. He waits a moment; the game goes on.*)

KROGSTAD   Beg pardon, Mrs. Helmer—

NORA (*with a strangled cry, turning and scrambling to her knees*)   Oh! what do you want?

KROGSTAD   Excuse me. The outer door was ajar; it must be someone forgot to shut it—

NORA (*rising*)   My husband isn't home, Mr. Krogstad.

KROGSTAD   I know that.

NORA   Yes—then what do you want here?

KROGSTAD   A word with you.

NORA   With—? (*To the children, quietly*) Go in to Anne-Marie. What? No, the strange man won't hurt Mama. When he's gone, we'll play some more. (*She leads the children into the room to the left and shuts the door after them. Then, tense and nervous*) You want to speak to me?

KROGSTAD   Yes, I want to.

NORA   Today? But it's not yet the first of the month—

KROGSTAD   No, it's Christmas Eve. It's going to be up to you how merry a Christmas you have.

NORA   What is it you want? Today I absolutely can't—

KROGSTAD   We won't talk about that till later. This is something else. You do have a moment to spare, I suppose?

NORA   Oh yes, of course—I do, except—

KROGSTAD   Good. I was sitting over at Olsen's Restaurant when I saw your husband go down the street—

NORA   Yes?

KROGSTAD   With a lady.

NORA   Yes. So?

KROGSTAD   If you'll pardon my asking: wasn't that lady a Mrs. Linde?

NORA   Yes.

KROGSTAD   Just now come into town?

NORA   Yes, today.

KROGSTAD   She's a good friend of yours?

NORA   Yes, she is. But I don't see—

KROGSTAD   I also knew her once.

NORA   I'm aware of that.

KROGSTAD   Oh? You know all about it. I thought so, Well, then let me ask you short and sweet: is Mrs. Linde getting a job in the bank?

NORA   What makes you think you can cross-examine me, Mr. Krogstad—you, one of my husband's employees? But since you ask, you might as well know—-yes, Mrs. Linde's going to be taken on at the bank. And I'm the one who spoke for her, Mr. Krogstad. Now you know.

KROGSTAD   So I guessed right.

NORA   *(pacing up and down)*   Oh, one does have a tiny bit of influence, I should hope. Just because I am a woman, don't think it means that—When one has a subordinate position, Mr. Krogstad, one really ought to be careful about pushing somebody who—hm—

KROGSTAD   Who has influence?

NORA   That's right.

KROGSTAD   *(in a different tone)*   Mrs. Helmer, would you be good enough to use your influence on my behalf?

NORA   What? What do you mean?

KROGSTAD   Would you please make sure that I keep my subordinate position in the bank?

NORA   What does that mean? Who's thinking of taking away your position?

KROGSTAD   Oh, don't play the innocent with me. I'm quite aware that your friend would hardly relish the chance of running into me again; and I'm also aware now whom I can thank for being turned out.

NORA   But I promise you—

KROGSTAD   Yes, yes, yes, to the point: there's still time, and I'm advising you to use your influence to prevent it.

NORA   But Mr. Krogstad, I have absolutely no influence.

KROGSTAD   You haven't? I thought you were just saying—

NORA   You shouldn't take me so literally. I! How can you believe that I have any such influence over my husband?

KROGSTAD   Oh, I've known your husband from our student days. I don't think the great bank manager's more steadfast than any other married man.

NORA   You speak insolently about my husband, and I'll show you the door.

KROGSTAD   The lady has spirit.

NORA   I'm not afraid of you any longer. After New Year's, I'll soon be done with the whole business.

KROGSTAD *(restraining himself)*   Now listen to me, Mrs. Helmer. If necessary, I'll fight for my little job in the bank as if it were life itself.

NORA   Yes, so it seems.

KROGSTAD   It's not just a matter of income; that's the least of it. It's something else—All right, out with it! Look, this is the thing. You know, just like all the others, of course, that once, a good many years ago, I did something rather rash.

NORA   I've heard rumors to that effect.

KROGSTAD   The case never got into court; but all the same, every door was closed in my face from then on. So I took up those various activities you know about. I had to grab hold somewhere; and I dare say I haven't been among the worst. But now I want to drop all that. My boys are growing up. For their sakes, I'll have to win back as much respect as possible here in town. That job in the bank was like the first rung in my ladder. And now your husband wants to kick me right back down in the mud again.

NORA   But for heaven's sake, Mr. Krogstad, it's simply not in my power to help you.

KROGSTAD   That's because you haven't the will to—but I have the means to make you.

NORA   You certainly won't tell my husband that I owe you money?

KROGSTAD   Hm—what if I told him that?

NORA   That would be shameful of you. *(Nearly in tears)* This secret—my joy and my pride—that he should learn it in such a crude and disgusting way— learn it from you. You'd expose me to the most horrible unpleasantness—

KROGSTAD   Only unpleasantness?

NORA *(vehemently)*   But go on and try. It'll turn out the worse for you, because then my husband will really see what a crook you are, and then you'll *never* be able to hold your job.

KROGSTAD   I asked if it was just domestic unpleasantness you were afraid of?

NORA   If my husband finds out, then of course he'll pay what I owe at once, and then we'd be through with you for good.

KROGSTAD *(a step closer)*   Listen, Mrs. Helmer—you've either got a very bad memory, or else no head at all for business. I'd better put you a little more in touch with the facts.

NORA   What do you mean?

KROGSTAD   When your husband was sick, you came to me for a loan of four thousand, eight hundred crowns.

NORA   Where else could I go?

KROGSTAD   I promised to get you that sum—

NORA   And you got it.

KROGSTAD   I promised to get you that sum, on certain conditions. You were so involved in your husband's illness, and so eager to finance your trip, that I guess you didn't think out all the details. It might just be a good idea to remind you. I promised you the money on the strength of a note I drew up.

NORA   Yes, and that I signed.

KROGSTAD   Right. But at the bottom I added some lines for your father to guarantee the loan. He was supposed to sign down there.

NORA   Supposed to? He did sign.

KROGSTAD   I left the date blank. In other words, your father would have dated his signature himself. Do you remember that?

NORA   Yes, I think—

KROGSTAD   Then I gave you the note for you to mail to your father. Isn't that so?

NORA   Yes.

KROGSTAD   And naturally you sent it at once—because only some five, six days later you brought me the note, properly signed. And with that, the money was yours.

NORA   Well, then; I've made my payments regularly, haven't I?

KROGSTAD   More or less. But—getting back to the point—those were hard times for you then, Mrs. Helmer.

NORA   Yes, they were.

KROGSTAD   Your father was very ill, I believe.

NORA   He was near the end.

KROGSTAD   He died soon after?

NORA   Yes.

KROGSTAD   Tell me, Mrs. Helmer, do you happen to recall the date of your father's death? The day of the month, I mean.

NORA   Papa died the twenty-ninth of September.

KROGSTAD   That's quite correct; I've already looked into that. And now we come to a curious thing—*(Taking out a paper)* which I simply cannot comprehend.

NORA   Curious thing? I don't know—

KROGSTAD   This is the curious thing: that your father co-signed the note for your loan three days after his death.

NORA   How—? I don't understand.

KROGSTAD   Your father died the twenty-ninth of September. But look. Here your father dated his signature October second. Isn't that curious, Mrs. Helmer? *(NORA is silent.)* Can you explain it to me? *(NORA remains silent.)* It's also remarkable that the words "October second" and the year aren't written in your father's hand, but rather in one that I think I know. Well, it's easy to understand. Your father forgot perhaps to date his signature, and then someone or other added it, a bit sloppily, before anyone knew of his death. There's nothing wrong in that. It all comes down to the signature. And there's no question about *that*, Mrs. Helmer. It really *was* your father who signed his own name here, wasn't it?

NORA *(after a short silence, throwing her head back and looking squarely at him)* No, it wasn't. I signed Papa's name.

KROGSTAD Wait, now—are you fully aware that this is a dangerous confession?

NORA Why? You'll soon get your money.

KROGSTAD Let me ask you a question—why didn't you send the paper to your father?

NORA That was impossible. Papa was so sick. If I'd asked him for his signature, I also would have had to tell him what the money was for. But I couldn't tell him, sick as he was, that my husband's life was in danger. That was just impossible.

KROGSTAD Then it would have been better if you'd given up the trip abroad.

NORA I couldn't possibly. The trip was to save my husband's life. I couldn't give that up.

KROGSTAD But didn't you ever consider that this was a fraud against me?

NORA I couldn't let myself be bothered by that. You weren't any concern of mine. I couldn't stand you, with all those cold complications you made, even though you knew how badly off my husband was.

KROGSTAD Mrs. Helmer, obviously you haven't the vaguest idea of what you've involved yourself in. But I can tell you this: it was nothing more and nothing worse than I once did—and it wrecked my whole reputation.

NORA You? Do you expect me to believe that you ever acted bravely to save your wife's life?

KROGSTAD Laws don't inquire into motives.

NORA Then they must be very poor laws.

KROGSTAD Poor or not—if I introduce this paper in court, you'll be judged according to law.

NORA This I refuse to believe. A daughter hasn't a right to protect her dying father from anxiety and care? A wife hasn't a right to save her husband's life? I don't know much about laws, but I'm sure that somewhere in the books these things are allowed. And you don't know anything about it— you who practice the law? You must be an awful lawyer, Mr. Krogstad.

KROGSTAD Could be. But business—the kind of business we two are mixed up in—don't you think I know about that? All right. Do what you want now. But I'm telling you *this:* if I get shoved down a second time, you're going to keep me company.   *(He bows and goes out through the hall.)*

NORA *(pensive for a moment, then tossing her head)* Oh, really! Trying to frighten me! I'm not so silly as all that. *(Begins gathering up the children's clothes, but soon stops)* But—? No, but that's impossible! I did it out of love.

THE CHILDREN *(in the doorway, left)* Mama, that strange man's gone out the door.

NORA Yes, yes, I know it. But don't tell anyone about the strange man. Do you hear. Not even Papa!

THE CHILDREN No, Mama. But now will you play again?

NORA No, not now.

THE CHILDREN   Oh, but Mama, you promised.

NORA   Yes, but I can't now. Go inside; I have too much to do. Go in, go in, my sweet darlings. (*She herds them gently back in the room and shuts the door after them. Settling on the sofa, she takes up a piece of embroidery and makes some stitches, but soon stops abruptly.*) No! (*Throws the work aside, rises, goes to the hall door and calls out*) Helene! Let me have the tree in here. (*Goes to the table, left, opens the table drawer, and stops again*) No, but that's utterly impossible!

MAID   (*with the Christmas tree*)   Where should I put it, Ma'am?

NORA   There. The middle of the floor.

MAID   Should I bring anything else?

NORA   No, thanks. I have what I need.

(*The* MAID, *who has set the tree down, goes out.*)

NORA   (*absorbed in trimming the tree*)   Candles here—and flowers here. That terrible creature! Talk, talk, talk! There's nothing to it at all. The tree's going to be lovely. I'll do anything to please you, Torvald. I'll sing for you, dance for you—

(HELMER *comes in from the hall, with a sheaf of papers under his arm.*)

NORA   Oh! You're back so soon?

HELMER   Yes. Has anyone been here?

NORA   Here? No.

HELMER   That's odd. I saw Krogstad leaving the front door.

NORA   So? Oh yes, that's true. Krogstad was here a moment.

HELMER   Nora, I can see by your face that he's been here, begging you to put in a good word for him.

NORA   Yes.

HELMER   And it was supposed to seem like your own idea? You were to hide it from me that he'd been here. He asked you that, too, didn't he?

NORA   Yes, Torvald, but—

HELMER   Nora, Nora, and you could fall for that? Talk with that sort of person and promise him anything? And then in the bargain, tell me an untruth.

NORA   An untruth—?

HELMER   Didn't you say that no one had been here? (*Wagging his finger*) My little songbird must never do that again. A songbird needs a clean beak to warble with. No false notes. (*Putting his arm about her waist*) That's the way it should be, isn't it? Yes, I'm sure of it. (*Releasing her*) And so, enough of that. (*Sitting by the stove*) Ah, how snug and cozy it is here. (*Leafing among his papers*)

NORA   (*busy with the tree, after a short pause*)   Torvald!

HELMER   Yes.

NORA   I'm so much looking forward to the Stenborgs' costume party, day after tomorrow.

HELMER   And I can't wait to see what you'll surprise me with.

NORA   Oh, that stupid business.

HELMER   What?

NORA   I can't find anything that's right. Everything seems so ridiculous, so inane.

HELMER   So my little Nora's come to *that* recognition?

NORA   (*going behind his chair, her arms resting on its back*)   Are you very busy, Torvald?

HELMER   Oh—

NORA   What papers are those?

HELMER   Bank matters.

NORA   Already?

HELMER   I've gotten full authority from the retiring management to make all necessary changes in personnel and procedure. I'll need Christmas week for that. I want to have everything in order by New Year's.

NORA   So that was the reason this poor Krogstad—

HELMER   Hm.

NORA   (*still leaning on the chair and slowly stroking the nape of his neck*)   If you weren't so very busy, I would have asked you an enormous favor, Torvald.

HELMER   Let's hear. What is it?

NORA   You know, there isn't anyone who has your good taste—and I want so much to look well at the costume party. Torvald, couldn't you take over and decide what I should be and plan my costume?

HELMER   Ah, is my stubborn little creature calling for a lifeguard?

NORA   Yes, Torvald, I can't get anywhere without your help.

HELMER   All right—I'll think it over. We'll hit on something.

NORA   Oh, how sweet of you. (*Goes to the tree again. Pause.*) Aren't the red flowers pretty—? But tell me, was it really such a crime that this Krogstad committed?

HELMER   Forgery. Do you have any idea what that means?

NORA   Couldn't he have done it out of need?

HELMER   Yes, or thoughtlessness, like so many others. I'm not so heartless that I'd condemn a man categorically for just one mistake.

NORA   No, of course not, Torvald!

HELMER   Plenty of men have redeemed themselves by openly confessing their crimes and taking their punishments.

NORA   Punishment—?

HELMER   But now Krogstad didn't go that way. He got himself out by sharp practices, and that's the real cause of his moral breakdown.

NORA   Do you really think that would—?

HELMER   Just imagine how a man with that sort of guilt in him has to lie and cheat and deceive on all sides, has to wear a mask even with the nearest and dearest he has, even with his own wife and children. And with the children, Nora—that's where it's most horrible.

NORA   Why?

HELMER   Because that kind of atmosphere of lies infects the whole life of a home. Every breath the children take in is filled with the germs of something degenerate.

NORA (*coming closer behind him*)   Are you sure of that?

HELMER   Oh, I've seen it often enough as a lawyer. Almost everyone who goes bad early in life has a mother who's a chronic liar.

NORA   Why just—the mother?

HELMER   It's usually the mother's influence that's dominant, but the father's works in the same way, of course. Every lawyer is quite familiar with it. And still this Krogstad's been going home year in, year out, poisoning his own children with lies and pretense; that's why I call him morally lost. (*Reaching his hands out toward her*) So my sweet little Nora must promise me never to plead his cause. Your hand on it. Come, come, what's this? Give me your hand. There, now. All settled. I can tell you it'd be impossible for me to work alongside of him. I literally feel physically revolted when I'm anywhere near such a person.

NORA (*withdraws her hand and goes to the other side of the Christmas tree*)   How hot it is here! And I've got so much to do.

HELMER (*getting up and gathering his papers*)   Yes, and I have to think about getting some of these read through before dinner. I'll think about your costume, too. And something to hang on the tree in gilt paper, I may even see about that. (*Putting his hand on her head*) Oh you, my darling little songbird.   (*He goes into his study and closes the door after him.*)

NORA (*softly, after a silence*)   Oh, really! it isn't so. It's impossible. It must be impossible.

ANNE-MARIE (*in the doorway, left*)   The children are begging so hard to come in to Mama.

NORA   No, no, no, don't let them in to me! You stay with them, Anne-Marie.

ANNE-MARIE   Of course, Ma'am. (*Closes the door*)

NORA (*pale with terror*)   Hurt my children—! Poison my home? (*A moment's pause; then she tosses her head.*) That's not true. Never. Never in all the world.

ACT II

Same room. Beside the piano the Christmas tree now stands stripped of ornament, burned-down candle stubs on its ragged branches. NORA'S *street clothes lie on the sofa.* NORA, *alone in the room, moves restlessly about; at last she stops at the sofa and picks up her coat.*

NORA (*dropping the coat again*)   Someone's coming! (*Goes toward the door, listens*) No—there's no one. Of course—nobody's coming today, Christmas Day—or tomorrow, either. But maybe—(*Opens the door and looks out*) No, nothing in the mailbox. Quite empty. (*Coming forward*) What nonsense! He won't do anything serious. Nothing terrible could happen. It's impossible. Why, I have three small children.

(ANNE-MARIE, *with a large carton, comes in from the room to the left.*)

ANNE-MARIE   Well, at last I found the box with the masquerade clothes.
NORA   Thanks. Put it on the table.
ANNE-MARIE *(does so)*   But they're all pretty much of a mess.
NORA   Ahh! I'd love to rip them in a million pieces!
ANNE-MARIE   Oh, mercy, they can be fixed right up. Just a little patience.
NORA   Yes, I'll go get Mrs. Linde to help me.
ANNE-MARIE   Out again now? In this nasty weather? Miss Nora will catch
   cold—get sick.
NORA   Oh, worse things could happen—How are the children?
ANNE-MARIE   The poor mites are playing with their Christmas presents, but—
NORA   Do they ask for me much?
ANNE-MARIE   They're so used to having Mama around, you know.
NORA   Yes, but Anne-Marie, I *can't* be together with them as much as I was.
ANNE-MARIE   Well, small children get used to anything.
NORA   You think so? Do you think they'd forget their mother if she was gone
   for good?
ANNE-MARIE   Oh, mercy—gone for good!
NORA   Wait, tell me, Anne-Marie—I've wondered so often—how could you
   ever have the heart to give your child over to strangers?
ANNE-MARIE   But I had to, you know, to become little Nora's nurse.
NORA   Yes, but how could you *do* it?
ANNE-MARIE   When I could get such a good place? A girl who's poor and
   who's gotten in trouble is glad enough for that. Because that slippery fish,
   he didn't do a thing for me, you know.
NORA   But your daughter's surely forgotten you.
ANNE-MARIE   Oh, she certainly has not. She's written to me, both when she
   was confirmed and when she was married.
NORA *(clasping her about the neck)*   You old Anne-Marie, you were a good
   mother for me when I was little.
ANNE-MARIE   Poor little Nora, with no other mother but me.
NORA   And if the babies didn't have one, then I know that you'd—What silly
   talk! *(Opening the carton)* Go in to them. Now I'll have to—Tomorrow you
   can see how lovely I'll look.
ANNE-MARIE   Oh, there won't be anyone at the party as lovely as Miss
   Nora.   *(She goes off into the room, left.)*
NORA *(begins unpacking the box, but soon throws it aside)*   Oh, if I dared to go
   out. If only nobody would come. If only nothing would happen here while
   I'm out. What craziness—nobody's coming. Just don't think. This muff—
   needs a brushing. Beautiful gloves, beautiful gloves. Let it go. Let it go!
   One, two, three, four, five, six— *(With a cry)* Oh, there they are! *(Poises to
   move toward the door, but remains irresolutely standing.* MRS. LINDE *enters from
   the hall, where she has removed her street clothes.)*
NORA   Oh, it's you, Kristine. There's no one else out there? How good that
   you've come.

MRS. LINDE I hear you were up asking for me.

NORA Yes, I just stopped by. There's something you really can help me with. Let's get settled on the sofa. Look, there's going to be a costume party tomorrow evening at the Stenborgs' right above us, and now Torvald wants me to go as a Neapolitan peasant girl and dance the tarantella that I learned in Capri.

MRS. LINDE Really, you are giving a whole performance?

NORA Torvald says yes, I should. See, here's the dress. Torvald had it made for me down there; but now it's all so tattered that I just don't know—

MRS. LINDE Oh, we'll fix that up in no time. It's nothing more than the trimmings—they're a bit loose here and there. Needle and thread? Good, now we have what we need.

NORA Oh, how sweet of you!

MRS. LINDE (*sewing*) So you'll be in disguise tomorrow, Nora. You know what? I'll stop by then for a moment and have a look at you all dressed up. But listen, I've absolutely forgotten to thank you for that pleasant evening yesterday.

NORA (*getting up and walking about*) I don't think it was as pleasant as usual yesterday. You should have come to town a bit sooner, Kristine— Yes, Torvald really knows how to give a home elegance and charm.

MRS. LINDE And you do, too, if you ask me. You're not your father's daughter for nothing. But tell me, is Dr. Rank always so down in the mouth as yesterday?

NORA No, that was quite an exception. But he goes around critically ill all the time—tuberculosis of the spine, poor man. You know, his father was a disgusting thing who kept mistresses and so on—and that's why the son's been sickly from birth.

MRS. LINDE (*lets her sewing fall to her lap*) But my dearest Nora, how do you know about such things?

NORA (*walking more jauntily*) Hmp! When you've had three children, then you've had a few visits from—women who know something of medicine, and they tell you this and that.

MRS. LINDE (*resumes sewing; a short pause*) Does Dr. Rank come here every day?

NORA Every blessed day. He's Torvald's best friend from childhood, and *my* good friend, too. Dr. Rank almost belongs to this house.

MRS. LINDE But tell me—is he quite sincere? I mean, doesn't he rather enjoy flattering people?

NORA Just the opposite. Why do you think that?

MRS. LINDE When you introduced us yesterday, he was proclaiming that he'd often heard my name in this house; but later I noticed that your husband hadn't the slightest idea who I really was. So how could Dr. Rank—?

NORA But it's all true, Kristine. You see, Torvald loves me beyond words, and, as he puts it, he'd like to keep me all to himself. For a long time he'd almost be jealous if I even mentioned any of my old friends back home. So of course I dropped that. But with Dr. Rank I talk a lot about such things, because he likes hearing about them.

MRS. LINDE   Now listen, Nora; in many ways you're still like a child. I'm a good deal older than you, with a little more experience. I'll tell you something; you ought to put an end to all this with Dr. Rank.

NORA   What should I put an end to?

MRS. LINDE   Both parts of it, I think. Yesterday you said something about a rich admirer who'd provide you with money—

NORA   Yes, one who doesn't exist—worse luck. So?

MRS. LINDE   Is Dr. Rank well off?

NORA   Yes, he is.

MRS. LINDE   With no dependents?

NORA   No, no one. But—

MRS. LINDE   And he's over here every day?

NORA   Yes, I told you that.

MRS. LINDE   How can a man of such refinement be so grasping?

NORA   I don't follow you at all.

MRS. LINDE   Now don't try to hide it, Nora. You think I can't guess who loaned you the forty-eight hundred crowns?

NORA   Are you out of your mind? How could you think of such a thing! A friend of ours, who comes here every single day. What an intolerable situation that would have been!

MRS. LINDE   Then it really wasn't him.

NORA   No, absolutely not. It never even crossed my mind for a moment—And he had nothing to lend in those days; his inheritance came later.

MRS. LINDE   Well, I think that was a stroke of luck for you, Nora dear.

NORA   No, it never would have occurred to me to ask Dr. Rank— Still, I'm quite sure that if I had asked him—

MRS. LINDE   Which you won't, of course.

NORA   No, of course not. I can't see that I'd ever need to. But I'm quite positive that if I talked to Dr. Rank—

MRS. LINDE   Behind your husband's back?

NORA   I've got to clear up this other thing; *that's* also behind his back. I've *got* to clear it all up.

MRS. LINDE   Yes, I was saying that yesterday, but—

NORA   *(pacing up and down)*   A man handles these problems so much better than a woman—

MRS. LINDE   One's husband does, yes.

NORA   Nonsense. *(Stopping)* When you pay everything you owe, then you get your note back, right?

MRS. LINDE   Yes, naturally.

NORA   And can rip it into a million pieces and burn it up—that filthy scrap of paper!

MRS. LINDE   *(looking hard at her, laying her sewing aside, and rising slowly)*   Nora, you're hiding something from me.

NORA   You can see it in my face?

MRS. LINDE   Something's happened to you since yesterday morning. Nora, what is it?

NORA (*hurrying toward her*)   Kristine! (*Listening*) Shh! Torvald's home. Look, go in with the children a while. Torvald can't bear all this snipping and stitching. Let Anne-Marie help you.

MRS. LINDE (*gathering up some of the things*)   All right, but I'm not leaving here until we've talked this out. (*She disappears into the room, left, as* TORVALD *enters from the hall.*)

NORA   Oh, how I've been waiting for you, Torvald dear.

HELMER   Was that the dressmaker?

NORA   No, that was Kristine. She's helping me fix up my costume. You know, it's going to be quite attractive.

HELMER   Yes, wasn't that a bright idea I had?

NORA   Brilliant! But then wasn't I good as well to give in to you?

HELMER   Good—because you give in to your husband's judgment? All right, you little goose, I know you didn't mean it like that. But I won't disturb you. You'll want to have a fitting, I suppose.

NORA   And you'll be working?

HELMER   Yes. (*Indicating a bundle of papers*) See. I've been down to the bank. (*Starts toward his study*)

NORA   Torvald.

HELMER (*stops*)   Yes.

NORA   If your little squirrel begged you, with all her heart and soul, for something—?

HELMER   What's that?

NORA   Then would you do it?

HELMER   First, naturally, I'd have to know what it was.

NORA   Your squirrel would scamper about and do tricks, if you'd only be sweet and give in.

HELMER   Out with it.

NORA   Your lark would be singing high and low in every room—

HELMER   Come on, she does that anyway.

NORA   I'd be a wood nymph and dance for you in the moonlight.

HELMER   Nora—don't tell me it's that same business from this morning?

NORA (*coming closer*)   Yes, Torvald, I beg you, please!

HELMER   And you actually have the nerve to drag that up again?

NORA   Yes, yes, you've got to give in to me; you have to let Krogstad keep his job in the bank.

HELMER   My dear Nora, I've slated his job for Mrs. Linde.

NORA   That's awfully kind of you. But you could just fire another clerk instead of Krogstad.

HELMER   This is the most incredible stubbornness! Because you go and give an impulsive promise to speak up for him, I'm expected to—

NORA   That's not the reason, Torvald. It's for your own sake. That man does writing for the worst papers; you said it yourself. He could do you any amount of harm. I'm scared to death of him—

HELMER   Ah, I understand. It's the old memories haunting you.

NORA   What do you mean by that?

HELMER   Of course, you're thinking about your father.

NORA   Yes, all right. Just remember how those nasty gossips wrote in the papers about Papa and slandered him so cruelly. I think they'd have had him dismissed if the department hadn't sent you up to investigate, and if you hadn't been so kind and open-minded toward him.

HELMER   My dear Nora, there's a notable difference between your father and me. Your father's official career was hardly above reproach. But mine is; and I hope it'll stay that way as long as I hold my position.

NORA   Oh, who can ever tell what vicious minds can invent? We could be so snug and happy now in our quiet, carefree home—you and I and the children, Torvald! That's why I'm pleading with you so—

HELMER   And just by pleading for him you make it impossible for me to keep him on. It's already known at the bank that I'm firing Krogstad. What if it's rumored around now that the new bank manager was vetoed by his wife—

NORA   Yes, what then—?

HELMER   Oh yes—as long as your little bundle of stubbornness gets her way—! I should go and make myself ridiculous in front of the whole office—give people the idea I can be swayed by all kinds of outside pressure. Oh, you can bet I'd feel the effects of that soon enough! Besides—there's something that rules Krogstad right out at the bank as long as I'm the manager.

NORA   What's that?

HELMER   His moral failings I could maybe overlook if I had to—

NORA   Yes, Torvald, why not?

HELMER   And I hear he's quite efficient on the job. But he was a crony of mine back in my teens—one of those rash friendships that crop up again and again to embarrass you later in life. Well, I might as well say it straight out: we're on a first-name basis. And that tactless fool makes no effort at all to hide it in front of others. Quite the contrary—he thinks that entitles him to take a familiar air around me, and so every other second he comes booming out with his "Yes, Torvald!" and "Sure thing, Torvald!" I tell you, it's been excruciating for me. He's out to make my place in the bank unbearable.

NORA   Torvald, you can't be serious about all this.

HELMER   Oh no? Why not?

NORA   Because these are such petty considerations.

HELMER   What are you saying? Petty? You think I'm petty!

NORA   No, just the opposite, Torvald dear. That's exactly why—

HELMER   Never mind. You call my motives petty; then I might as well be just that. Petty! All right! We'll put a stop to this for good. (*Goes to the hall door and calls*) Helene!

NORA   What do you want?

HELMER   *(searching among his papers)*   A decision. *(The* MAID *comes in.)* Look here; take this letter; go out with it at once. Get hold of a messenger and have him deliver it. Quick now. It's already addressed. Wait, here's some money.

MAID   Yes, sir.   *(She leaves with the letter.)*

HELMER   *(straightening his papers)*   There, now, little Miss Willful.

NORA   *(breathlessly)*   Torvald, what was that letter?

HELMER   Krogstad's notice.

NORA   Call it back, Torvald! There's still time. Oh, Torvald, call it back! Do it for my sake—for your sake, for the children's sake! Do you hear, Torvald; do it! You don't know how this can harm us.

HELMER   Too late.

NORA   Yes, too late.

HELMER   Nora dear, I can forgive you this panic, even though basically you're insulting me. Yes, you are! Or isn't it an insult to think that I should be afraid of a courtroom hack's revenge? But I forgive you anyway, because this shows so beautifully how much you love me. *(Takes her in his arms)* This is the way it should be, my darling Nora. Whatever comes, you'll see: when it really counts, I have strength and courage enough as a man to take on the whole weight myself.

NORA   *(terrified)*   What do you mean by that?

HELMER   The whole weight, I said.

NORA   *(resolutely)*   No, never in all the world.

HELMER   Good. So we'll share it, Nora, as man and wife. That's as it should be. *(Fondling her)* Are you happy now? There, there, there—not these frightened dove's eyes. It's nothing at all but empty fantasies—Now you should run through your tarantella and practice your tambourine. I'll go to the inner office and shut both doors, so I won't hear a thing; you can make all the noise you like. *(Turning in the doorway)* And when Rank comes, just tell him where he can find me.

(He nods to her and goes with his papers into the study, closing the door.)

NORA   *(standing as though rooted, dazed with fright, in a whisper)*   He really could do it. He will do it. He'll do it in spite of everything. No, not that, never, never! Anything but that! Escape! A way out—*(The doorbell rings.)* Dr. Rank! Anything but that! Anything, whatever it is! *(Her hands pass over her face, smoothing it; she pulls herself together, goes over and opens the hall door.* DR. RANK *stands outside, hanging his fur coat up. During the following scene, it begins getting dark.)*

NORA   Hello, Dr. Rank. I recognized your ring. But you mustn't go in to Torvald yet; I believe he's working.

RANK   And you?

NORA   For you, I always have an hour to spare—you know that. *(He has entered, and she shuts the door after him.)*

RANK   Many thanks. I'll make use of these hours while I can.

NORA   What do you mean by that? While you can?

RANK   Does that disturb you?

NORA   Well, it's such an odd phrase. Is anything going to happen?

RANK   What's going to happen is what I've been expecting so long—but I honestly didn't think it would come so soon.

NORA *(gripping his arm)*   What is it you've found out? Dr. Rank, you have to tell me!

RANK *(sitting by the stove)*   It's all over with me. There's nothing to be done about it.

NORA *(breathing easier)*   Is it you—then—?

RANK   Who else? There's no point in lying to one's self. I'm the most miserable of all my patients, Mrs. Helmer. These past few days I've been auditing my internal accounts. Bankrupt! Within a month I'll probably be laid out and rotting in the churchyard.

NORA   Oh, what a horrible thing to say.

RANK   The thing itself is horrible. But the worst of it is all the other horror before it's over. There's only one final examination left; when I'm finished with that, I'll know about when my disintegration will begin. There's something I want to say. Helmer with his sensitivity has such a sharp distaste for anything ugly. I don't want him near my sickroom.

NORA   Oh, but Dr. Rank—

RANK   I won't have him in there. Under no condition. I'll lock my door to him—As soon as I'm completely sure of the worst, I'll send you my calling card marked with a black cross, and you'll know then the wreck has started to come apart.

NORA   No, today you're completely unreasonable. And I wanted you so much to be in a really good humor.

RANK   With death up my sleeve? And then to suffer this way for somebody else's sins. Is there any justice in that? And in every single family, in some way or another, this inevitable retribution of nature goes on—

NORA *(her hands pressed over her ears)*   Oh, stuff! Cheer up! Please—be gay!

RANK   Yes, I'd just as soon laugh at it all. My poor, innocent spine, serving time for my father's gay army days.

NORA *(by the table, left)*   He was so infatuated with asparagus tips and *pâté de foie gras,* wasn't that it?

RANK   Yes—and with truffles.

NORA   Truffles, yes. And then with oysters, I suppose?

RANK   Yes, tons of oysters, naturally.

NORA   And then the port and champagne to go with it. It's so sad that all these delectable things have to strike at our bones.

RANK   Especially when they strike at the unhappy bones that never shared in the fun.

NORA   Ah, that's the saddest of all.

RANK *(looks searchingly at her)*   Hm.

NORA *(after a moment)*   Why did you smile?

RANK   No, it was you who laughed.

NORA   No, it was you who smiled, Dr. Rank!

RANK *(getting up)* You're even a bigger tease than I'd thought.

NORA I'm full of wild ideas today.

RANK That's obvious.

NORA *(putting both hands on his shoulders)* Dear, dear Dr. Rank, you'll never die for Torvald and me.

RANK Oh, that loss you'll easily get over. Those who go away are soon forgotten.

NORA *(looks fearfully at him)* You believe that?

RANK One makes new connections, and then—

NORA Who makes new connections?

RANK Both you and Torvald will when I'm gone. I'd say you're well under way already. What was that Mrs. Linde doing here last evening?

NORA Oh, come—you can't be jealous of poor Kristine?

RANK Oh yes, I am. She'll be my successor here in the house. When I'm down under, that woman will probably—

NORA Shh! Not so loud. She's right in there.

RANK Today as well. So you see.

NORA Only to sew on my dress. Good gracious, how unreasonable you are. *(Sitting on the sofa)* Be nice now, Dr. Rank. Tomorrow you'll see how beautifully I'll dance, and you can imagine then that I'm dancing only for you—yes, and of course for Torvald, too—that's understood. *(Takes various items out of the carton)* Dr. Rank, sit over here and I'll show you something.

RANK *(sitting)* What's that?

NORA Look here. Look.

RANK Silk stockings.

NORA Flesh-colored. Aren't they lovely? Now it's so dark here, but tomorrow—No, no, no, just look at the feet. Oh well, you might as well look at the rest.

RANK Hm—

NORA Why do you look so critical? Don't you believe they'll fit?

RANK I've never had any chance to form an opinion on that.

NORA *(glancing at him a moment)* Shame on you. *(Hits him lightly on the ear with the stockings)* That's for you. *(Puts them away again)*

RANK And what other splendors am I going to see now?

NORA Not the least bit more, because you've been naughty. *(She hums a little and rummages among her things.)*

RANK *(after a short silence)* When I sit here together with you like this, completely easy and open, then I don't know—I simply can't imagine— whatever would have become of me if I'd never come into this house.

NORA *(smiling)* Yes, I really think you feel completely at ease with us.

RANK *(more quietly, staring straight ahead)* And then to have to go away from it all—

NORA Nonsense, you're not going away.

RANK *(his voice unchanged)* —and not even be able to leave some poor show of gratitude behind, scarcely a fleeting regret—no more than a vacant place that anyone can fill.

NORA   And if I asked you now for—? No—

RANK   For what?

NORA   For a great proof of your friendship—

RANK   Yes, yes?

NORA   No, I mean—for an exceptionally big favor—

RANK   Would you really, for once, make me so happy?

NORA   Oh, you haven't the vaguest idea what it is.

RANK   All right, then tell me.

NORA   No, but I can't, Dr. Rank—it's all out of reason. It's advice and help, too—and a favor—

RANK   So much the better. I can't fathom what you're hinting at. Just speak out. Don't you trust me?

NORA   Of course. More than anyone else. You're my best and truest friend, I'm sure. That's why I want to talk to you. All right, then, Dr. Rank: there's something you can help me prevent. You know how deeply, how inexpressibly dearly Torvald loves me; he'd never hesitate a second to give up his life for me.

RANK   (*leaning close to her*)   Nora—do you think he's the only one—

NORA   (*with a slight start*)   Who—?

RANK   Who'd gladly give up his life for you.

NORA   (*heavily*)   I see.

RANK   I swore to myself you should know this before I'm gone. I'll never find a better chance. Yes, Nora, now you know. And also you know now that you can trust me beyond anyone else.

NORA   (*rising, natural and calm*)   Let me by.

RANK   (*making room for her, but still sitting*)   Nora—

NORA   (*in the hall doorway*)   Helene, bring the lamp in. (*Goes over to the stove*) Ah, dear Dr. Rank, that was really mean of you.

RANK   (*getting up*)   That I've loved you just as deeply as somebody else? Was *that* mean?

NORA   No, but that you came out and told me. That was quite unnecessary—

RANK   What do you mean? Have you known—?

(*The* MAID *comes in with the lamp, sets it on the table, and goes out again.*)

RANK   Nora—Mrs. Helmer—I'm asking you: have you known about it?

NORA   Oh, how can I tell what I know or don't know? Really, I don't know what to say—Why did you have to be so clumsy, Dr. Rank! Everything was so good.

RANK   Well, in any case, you now have the knowledge that my body and soul are at your command. So won't you speak out?

NORA   (*Looking at him*)   After that?

RANK   Please, just let me know what it is.

NORA   You can't know anything now.

RANK   I have to. You mustn't punish me like this. Give me the chance to do whatever is humanly possible for you.

NORA   Now there's nothing you can do for me. Besides, actually, I don't need any help. You'll see—it's only my fantasies. That's what it is. Of course! *(Sits in the rocker, looks at him, and smiles)* What a nice one you are, Dr. Rank. Aren't you a little bit ashamed, now that the lamp is here?

RANK   No, not exactly. But perhaps I'd better go—for good?

NORA   No, you certainly can't do that. You must come here just as you always have. You know Torvald can't do without you.

RANK   Yes, but *you?*

NORA   You know how much I enjoy it when you're here.

RANK   That's precisely what threw me off. You're a mystery to me. So many times I've felt you'd almost rather be with me than with Helmer.

NORA   Yes—you see, there are some people that one loves most and other people that one would almost prefer being with.

RANK   Yes, there's something to that.

NORA   When I was back home, of course I loved Papa most. But I always thought it was so much fun when I could sneak down to the maids' quarters, because they never tried to improve me, and it was always so amusing, the way they talked to each other.

RANK   Aha, so it's *their* place that I've filled.

NORA   *(jumping up and going to him)*   Oh, dear sweet Dr. Rank, that's not what I meant at all. But you can understand that with Torvald it's just the same as with Papa—

(The MAID *enters from the hall.)*

MAID   Ma'am—please! *(She whispers to* NORA *and hands her a calling card.)*

NORA   *(glancing at the card)*   Ah! *(Slips in into her pocket)*

RANK   Anything wrong?

NORA   No, no, not at all. It's only some—it's my new dress—

RANK   Really? But—there's your dress.

NORA   Oh, that. But this is another one—I ordered it—Torvald mustn't know—

RANK   Ah, now we have the big secret.

NORA   That's right. Just go in with him—he's back in the inner study. Keep him there as long as—

RANK   Don't worry. He won't get away.   *(Goes into the study.)*

NORA   *(to the* MAID*)*   And he's standing waiting in the kitchen.

MAID   Yes, he came up by the back stairs.

NORA   But didn't you tell him somebody was here?

MAID   Yes, but that didn't do any good.

NORA   He won't leave?

MAID   No, he won't go till he's talked with you, ma'am.

NORA   Let him come in, then—but quietly. Helene, don't breathe a word about this. It's a surprise for my husband.

MAID   Yes, yes, I understand—   *(Goes out.)*

NORA   This horror—it's going to happen. No, no, no, it can't happen, it mustn't. *(She goes and bolts* HELMER'S *door. The* MAID *opens the hall door for* KROGSTAD *and shuts it behind him. He is dressed for travel in a fur coat, boots and a fur cap.)*

NORA   *(going toward him)*   Talk softly. My husband's home.

KROGSTAD   Well, good for him.

NORA   What do you want?

KROGSTAD   Some information.

NORA   Hurry up, then. What is it?

KROGSTAD   You know, of course, that I got my notice.

NORA   I couldn't prevent it, Mr. Krogstad. I fought for you to the bitter end, but nothing worked.

KROGSTAD   Does your husband's love for you run so thin? He knows everything I can expose you too, and all the same he dares to—

NORA   How can you imagine he knows anything about this?

KROGSTAD   Ah, no—I can't imagine it either, now. It's not at all like my fine Torvald Helmer to have so much guts—

NORA   Mr. Krogstad, I demand respect for my husband!

KROGSTAD   Why, of course—all due respect. But since the lady's keeping it so carefully hidden, may I presume to ask if you're also a bit better informed than yesterday about what you've actually done?

NORA   More than you ever could teach me.

KROGSTAD   Yes, I *am* such an awful lawyer.

NORA   What is it you want from me?

KROGSTAD   Just a glimpse of how you are, Mrs. Helmer. I've been thinking about you all day long. A cashier, a night-court scribbler, a—well, a type like me also has a little of what they call a heart, you know.

NORA   Then show it. Think of my children.

KROGSTAD   Did you or your husband ever think of mine? But never mind. I simply wanted to tell you that you don't need to take this thing too seriously. For the present, I'm not proceeding with any action.

NORA   Oh no, really! Well—I knew that.

KROGSTAD   Everything can be settled in a friendly spirit. It doesn't have to get around town at all; it can stay just among us three.

NORA   My husband may never know anything of this.

KROGSTAD   How can you manage that? Perhaps you can pay me the balance?

NORA   No, not right now.

KROGSTAD   Or you know some way of raising the money in a day or two?

NORA   No way that I'm willing to use.

KROGSTAD   Well, it wouldn't have done you any good, anyway. If you stood in front of me with a fistful of bills, you still couldn't buy your signature back.

NORA   Then tell me what you're going to do with it.

KROGSTAD   I'll just hold onto it—keep it on file. There's no outsider who'll even get wind of it. So if you've been thinking of taking some desperate step—

NORA   I have.

KROGSTAD   Been thinking of running away from home—

NORA   I have!

KROGSTAD   Or even of something worse—

NORA   How could you guess that?

KROGSTAD   You can drop those thoughts.

NORA   How could you guess I was thinking of *that*?

KROGSTAD   Most of us think about *that* at first. I thought about it too, but I discovered I hadn't the courage—

NORA   (*lifelessly*)   I don't either.

KROGSTAD   (*relieved*)   That's true, you haven't the courage? You too?

NORA   I don't have it—I don't have it.

KROGSTAD   It would be terribly stupid, anyway. After that first storm at home blows out, why, then—I have here in my pocket a letter for your husband—

NORA   Telling everything?

KROGSTAD   As charitably as possible.

NORA   (*quickly*)   He mustn't ever get that letter. Tear it up. I'll find some way to get money.

KROGSTAD   Beg pardon, Mrs. Helmer, but I think I just told you—

NORA   Oh, I don't mean the money I owe you. Let me know how much you want from my husband, and I'll manage it.

KROGSTAD   I don't want any money from your husband.

NORA   What do you want, then?

KROGSTAD   I'll tell you what. I want to recoup, Mrs. Helmer; I want to get on in the world—and there's where your husband can help me. For a year and a half I've kept myself clean of anything disreputable—all that time struggling with the worst conditions; but I was satisfied, working my way up step by step. Now I've been written right off, and I'm just not in the mood to come crawling back. I tell you, I want to move on. I want to get back in the bank—in a better position. Your husband can set up a job for me—

NORA   He'll never do that!

KROGSTAD   He'll do it. I know him. He won't dare breathe a word of protest. And once I'm in there together with him, you just wait and see! Inside of a year, I'll be the manager's right-hand man. It'll be Nils Krogstad, not Torvald Helmer, who runs the bank.

NORA   You'll never see the day!

KROGSTAD   Maybe you think you can—

NORA   I have the courage now—for *that*.

KROGSTAD   Oh, you don't scare me. A smart, spoiled lady like you—

NORA   You'll see; you'll see!

KROGSTAD   Under the ice, maybe? Down in the freezing, coal-black water?

There, till you float up in the spring, ugly, unrecognizable, with your hair falling out—

NORA   You don't frighten me.

KROGSTAD   Nor do you frighten me. One doesn't do these things, Mrs. Helmer. Besides, what good would it be? I'd still have him safe in my pocket.

NORA   Afterwards? When I'm no longer—?

KROGSTAD   Are you forgetting that *I'll* be in control then over your final reputation? (NORA *stands speechless, staring at him.*) Good; now I've warned you. Don't do anything stupid. When Helmer's read my letter, I'll be waiting for his reply. And bear in mind that it's your husband himself who's forced me back to my old ways. I'll never forgive him for that. Good-bye, Mrs. Helmer.   *(He goes out through the hall.)*

NORA *(goes to the hall door, opens it a crack, and listens)*   He's gone. Didn't leave the letter. Oh no, no, that's impossible too! *(Opening the door more and more)* What's that? He's standing outside—not going downstairs. He's thinking it over? Maybe he'll—? *(A letter falls in the mailbox; then* KROGSTAD'S *footsteps are heard, dying away down a flight of stairs.* NORA *gives a muffled cry and runs over toward the sofa table. A short pause.)* In the mailbox. *(Slips warily over to the hall door)* It's lying there. Torvald, Torvald—now we're lost!

MRS. LINDE *(entering with the costume from the room, left)*   There now, I can't see anything else to mend. Perhaps you'd like to try—

NORA *(in a hoarse whisper)*   Kristine, come here.

MRS. LINDE *(tossing the dress on the sofa)*   What's wrong? You look upset.

NORA   Come here. See that letter? *There!* Look—through the glass in the mailbox.

MRS. LINDE   Yes, yes, I see it.

NORA   That letter's from Krogstad—

MRS. LINDE   Nora—it's Krogstad who loaned you the money!

NORA   Yes, and now Torvald will find out everything.

MRS. LINDE   Believe me, Nora, it's best for both of you.

NORA   There's more you don't know. I forged a name.

MRS. LINDE   But for heaven's sake—?

NORA   I only want to tell you that, Kristine, so that you can be my witness.

MRS. LINDE   Witness? Why should I—?

NORA   If I should go out of my mind—it could easily happen—

MRS. LINDE   Nora!

NORA   Or anything else occurred—so I couldn't be present here—

MRS. LINDE   Nora, Nora, you aren't yourself at all!

NORA   And someone should try to take on the whole weight, all of the guilt, you follow me—

MRS. LINDE   Yes, of course, but why do you think—?

NORA   Then you're the witness that it isn't true, Kristine. I'm very much myself; my mind right now is perfectly clear; and I'm telling you: nobody else has known about this; I alone did everything. Remember that.

MRS. LINDE   I will. But I don't understand all this.

NORA   Oh, how could you ever understand it? It's the miracle now that's going to take place.

MRS. LINDE   The miracle?

NORA   Yes, the miracle. But it's so awful, Kristine. It mustn't take place, not for anything in the world.

MRS. LINDE   I'm going right over and talk with Krogstad.

NORA   Don't go near him; he'll do you some terrible harm!

MRS. LINDE   There was a time once when he'd gladly have done anything for me.

NORA   He?

MRS. LINDE   Where does he live?

NORA   Oh, how do I know? Yes. *(Searches in her pocket)* Here's his card. But the letter, the letter—!

HELMER *(from the study, knocking on the door)*   Nora!

NORA *(with a cry of fear)*   Oh! What is it? What do you want?

HELMER   Now, now, don't be so frightened. We're not coming in. You locked the door—are you trying on the dress?

NORA   Yes, I'm trying it. I'll look just beautiful, Torvald.

MRS. LINDE *(who has read the card)*   He's living right around the corner.

NORA   Yes, but what's the use? We're lost. The letter's in the box.

MRS. LINDE   And your husband has the key?

NORA   Yes, always.

MRS. LINDE   Krogstad can ask for his letter back unread; he can find some excuse—

NORA   But it's just this time that Torvald usually—

MRS. LINDE   Stall him. Keep him in there. I'll be back as quick as I can. *(She hurries out through the hall entrance.)*

NORA *(goes to* HELMER's *door, opens it, and peers in)*   Torvald!

HELMER *(from the inner study)*   Well—does one dare set foot in one's own living room at last? Come on, Rank, now we'll get a look—*(In the doorway)* But what's this?

NORA   What, Torvald dear?

HELMER   Rank had me expecting some grand masquerade.

RANK *(in the doorway)*   That was my impression, but I must have been wrong.

NORA   No one can admire me in my splendor—not until tomorrow.

HELMER   But Nora dear, you look so exhausted. Have you practiced too hard?

NORA   No, I haven't practiced at all yet.

HELMER   You know, it's necessary—

NORA   Oh, it's absolutely necessary, Torvald. But I can't get anywhere without your help. I've forgotten the whole thing completely.

HELMER   Ah, we'll soon take care of that.

NORA   Yes, take care of me, Torvald, please! Promise me that? Oh, I'm so nervous. That big party— You must give up everything this evening for me. No business—don't even touch your pen. Yes? Dear Torvald, promise?

HELMER   It's a promise. Tonight I'm totally at your service—you little helpless thing. Hm—but first there's one thing I want to—(*Goes toward the hall door*)
NORA   What are you looking for?
HELMER   Just to see if there's any mail.
NORA   No, no, don't do that, Torvald!
HELMER   Now what?
NORA   Torvald, please. There isn't any.
HELMER   Let me look, though. (*Starts out.* NORA, *at the piano, strikes the first notes of the tarantella.* HELMER, *at the door, stops.*) Aha!
NORA   I can't dance tomorrow if I don't practice with you.
HELMER   (*going over to her*)   Nora dear, are you really so frightened?
NORA   Yes, so terribly frightened. Let me practice right now; there's still time before dinner. Oh, sit down and play for me, Torvald. Direct me. Teach me, the way you always have.
HELMER   Gladly, if it's what you want. (*Sits at the piano*)
NORA   (*snatches the tambourine up from the box, then a long, varicolored shawl, which she throws around herself, whereupon she springs forward and cries out*)   Play for me now! Now I'll dance!

(HELMER *plays and* NORA *dances.* RANK *stands behind* HELMER *at the piano and looks on.*)

HELMER   (*as he plays*)   Slower. Slow down.
NORA   Can't change it.
HELMER   Not so violent, Nora!
NORA   Has to be just like this.
HELMER   (*stopping*)   No, no, that won't do at all.
NORA   (*laughing and swinging her tambourine*)   Isn't that what I told you?
RANK   Let me play for her.
HELMER   (*getting up*)   Yes, go on. I can teach her more easily then.

(RANK *sits at the piano and plays;* NORA *dances more and more wildly.* HELMER *has stationed himself by the stove and repeatedly gives her directions; she seems not to hear them; her hair loosens and falls over her shoulders; she does not notice, but goes on dancing.* MRS. LINDE *enters.*)

MRS. LINDE   (*standing dumbfounded at the door*)   Ah—!
NORA   (*still dancing*)   See what fun, Kristine!
HELMER   But Nora darling, you dance as if your life were at stake.
NORA   And it is.
HELMER   Rank, stop! This is pure madness. Stop it, I say!

(RANK *breaks off playing, and* NORA *halts abruptly.*)

HELMER   (*going over to hear*)   I never would have believed it. You've forgotten everything I taught you.

NORA *(throwing away the tambourine)*   You see for yourself.

HELMER   Well, there's certainly room for instruction here.

NORA   Yes, you see how important it is. You've got to teach me to the very last minute. Promise me that, Torvald?

HELMER   You can bet on it.

NORA   You mustn't, either today or tomorrow, think about anything else but me; you mustn't open any letters—or the mailbox—

HELMER   Ah, it's still the fear of that man—

NORA   Oh yes, yes, that too.

HELMER   Nora, it's written all over you—there's already a letter from him out there.

NORA   I don't know. I guess so. But you mustn't read such things now; there mustn't be anything ugly between us before it's all over.

RANK *(quietly to* HELMER*)*   You shouldn't deny her.

HELMER *(putting his arm around her)*   The child can have her way. But tomorrow night, after you've danced—

NORA   Then you'll be free.

MAID *(in the doorway, right)*   Ma'am, dinner is served.

NORA   We'll be wanting champagne, Helene.

MAID   Very good, ma'am.   *(Goes out)*

HELMER   So—a regular banquet, hm?

NORA   Yes, a banquet—champagne till daybreak! *(Calling out)* And some macaroons, Helene. Heaps of them—just this once.

HELMER *(taking her hands)*   Now, now, now—no hysterics. Be my own little lark again.

NORA   Oh, I will soon enough. But go on in—and you, Dr. Rank. Kristine, help me put up my hair.

RANK *(whispering, as they go)*   There's nothing wrong—really wrong, is there?

HELMER   Oh, of course not. It's nothing more than this childish anxiety I was telling you about.   *(They go out, right.)*

NORA   Well?

MRS. LINDE   Left town.

NORA   I could see by your face.

MRS. LINDE   He'll be home tomorrow evening. I wrote him a note.

NORA   You shouldn't have. Don't try to stop anything now. After all, it's a wonderful joy, this waiting here for the miracle.

MRS. LINDE   What is it you're waiting for?

NORA   Oh, you can't understand that. Go in to them, I'll be along in a moment.

(MRS. LINDE goes into the dining room. NORA stands a short while as if composing herself; then she looks at her watch.)

NORA   Five. Seven hours to midnight. Twenty-four hours to the midnight after, and then the tarantella's done. Seven and twenty-four? Thirty-one hours to live.

HELMER (*in the doorway, right*)   What's become of the little lark?
NORA (*going toward him with open arms*)   Here's your lark!

ACT III

*Same scene. The table, with chairs around it, has been moved to the center of the
room. A lamp on the table is lit. The hall door stands open. Dance music drifts
down from the floor above.* MRS. LINDE *sits at the table, absently paging through
a book, trying to read, but apparently unable to focus her thoughts. Once or twice
she pauses, tensely listening for a sound at the outer entrance.*

MRS. LINDE (*glancing at her watch*)   Not yet—and there's hardly any time left.
   If only he's not—(*Listening again*) Ah, there he is. (*She goes out in the hall
   and cautiously opens the outer door. Quiet footsteps are heard on the stairs. She
   whispers.*) Come in. Nobody's here.
KROGSTAD (*in the doorway*)   I found a note from you at home. What's back of
   all this?
MRS. LINDE   I just *had* to talk to you.
KROGSTAD   Oh? And it just *had* to be here in this house?
MRS. LINDE   At my place it was impossible; my room hasn't a private entrance.
   Come in; we're all alone. The maid's asleep, and the Helmers are at the
   dance upstairs.
KROGSTAD (*entering the room*)   Well, well, the Helmers are dancing tonight?
   Really?
MRS. LINDE   Yes, why not?
KROGSTAD   How true—why not?
MRS. LINDE   All right, Krogstad, let's talk.
KROGSTAD   Do we two have anything more to talk about?
MRS. LINDE   We have a great deal to talk about.
KROGSTAD   I wouldn't have thought so.
MRS. LINDE   No, because you've never understood me, really.
KROGSTAD   Was there anything more to understand—except what's all too
   common in life? A calculating woman throws over a man the moment a
   better catch comes by.
MRS. LINDE   You think I'm so thoroughly calculating? You think I broke it off
   lightly?
KROGSTAD   Didn't you?
MRS. LINDE   Nils—is that what you really thought?
KROGSTAD   If you cared, then why did you write me the way you did?
MRS. LINDE   What else could I do? If I had to break off with you, then it was
   my job as well to root out everything you felt for me.
KROGSTAD (*wringing his hands*)   So that was it. And this—all this, simply for
   money!

MRS. LINDE   Don't forget I had a helpless mother and two small brothers. We couldn't wait for you, Nils; you had such a long road ahead of you then.

KROGSTAD   That may be; but you still hadn't the right to abandon me for somebody else's sake.

MRS. LINDE   Yes—I don't know. So many, many times I've asked myself if I did have that right.

KROGSTAD *(more softly)*   When I lost you, it was as if all the solid ground dissolved from under my feet. Look at me; I'm a half-drowned man now, hanging onto a wreck.

MRS. LINDE   Help may be near.

KROGSTAD   It was near—but then you came and blocked it off.

MRS. LINDE   Without my knowing it, Nils. Today for the first time I learned that it's you I'm replacing at the bank.

KROGSTAD   All right—I believe you. But now that you know, will you step aside?

MRS. LINDE   No, because that wouldn't benefit you in the slightest.

KROGSTAD   Not "benefit" me, hm! I'd step aside anyway.

MRS. LINDE   I've learned to be realistic. Life and hard, bitter necessity have taught me that.

KROGSTAD   And life's taught me never to trust fine phrases.

MRS. LINDE   Then life's taught you a very sound thing. But you do have to trust in actions, don't you?

KROGSTAD   What does that mean?

MRS. LINDE   You said you were hanging on like a half-drowned man to a wreck.

KROGSTAD   I've good reason to say that.

MRS. LINDE   I'm also like a half-drowned woman on a wreck. No one to suffer with; no one to care for.

KROGSTAD   You made your choice.

MRS. LINDE   There wasn't any choice then.

KROGSTAD   So—what of it?

MRS. LINDE   Nils, if only we two shipwrecked people could reach across to each other.

KROGSTAD   What are you saying?

MRS. LINDE   Two on one wreck are at least better off than each on his own.

KROGSTAD   Kristine!

MRS. LINDE   Why do you think I came into town?

KROGSTAD   Did you really have some thought of me?

MRS. LINDE   I have to work to go on living. All my born days, as long as I can remember, I've worked, and it's been my best and my only joy. But now I'm completely alone in the world; it frightens me to be so empty and lost. To work for yourself—there's no joy in that. Nils, give me something— someone to work for.

KROGSTAD   I don't believe all this. It's just some hysterical feminine urge to go out and make a noble sacrifice.

MRS. LINDE   Have you ever found me to be hysterical?

KROGSTAD   Can you honestly mean this? Tell me—do you know everything
  about my past?

MRS. LINDE   Yes.

KROGSTAD   And you know what they think I'm worth around here.

MRS. LINDE   From what you were saying before, it would seem that with me
  you could have been another person.

KROGSTAD   I'm positive of that.

MRS. LINDE   Couldn't it happen still?

KROGSTAD   Kristine—you're saying this in all seriousness? Yes, you are! I can
  see it in you. And do you really have the courage, then—?

MRS. LINDE   I need to have someone to care for; and your children need a
  mother. We both need each other. Nils, I have faith that you're good at
  heart—I'll risk everything together with you.

KROGSTAD *(gripping her hands)*   Kristine, thank you, thank you—Now I know
  I can win back a place in their eyes. Yes—but I forgot—

MRS. LINDE *(listening)*   Shh! The tarantella. Go now! Go on!

KROGSTAD   Why? What is it?

MRS. LINDE   Hear the dance up there? When that's over, they'll be coming
  down.   •

KROGSTAD   Oh, then I'll go. But—it's all pointless. Of course, you don't know
  the move I made against the Helmers.

MRS. LINDE   Yes, Nils, I know.

KROGSTAD   And all the same, you have the courage to—?

MRS. LINDE   I know how far despair can drive a man like you.

KROGSTAD   Oh, if I only could take it all back.

MRS. LINDE   You easily could—your letter's still lying in the mailbox.

KROGSTAD   Are you sure of that?

MRS. LINDE   Positive. But—

KROGSTAD *(looks at her searchingly)*   Is that the meaning of it, then? You'll have
  your friend at any price. Tell me straight out. Is that it?

MRS. LINDE   Nils—anyone who's sold herself for somebody else once isn't
  going to do it again.

KROGSTAD   I'll demand my letter back.

MRS. LINDE   No, no.

KROGSTAD   Yes, of course. I'll stay here till Helmer comes down; I'll tell him
  to give me my letter again—that it only involves my dismissal—that he
  shouldn't read it—

MRS. LINDE   No, Nils, don't call the letter back.

KROGSTAD   But wasn't that exactly why you wrote me to come here?

MRS. LINDE   Yes, in that first panic. But it's been a whole day and night since
  then, and in that time I've seen such incredible things in this house.
  Helmer's got to learn everything; this dreadful secret has to be aired; those
  two have to come to a full understanding; all these lies and evasions can't go
  on.

KROGSTAD   Well, then, if you want to chance it. But at least there's one thing I
  can do, and do right away—

MRS. LINDE *(listening)*   Go now, go quick! The dance is over. We're not safe another second.

KROGSTAD   I'll wait for you downstairs.

MRS. LINDE   Yes, please do; take me home.

KROGSTAD   I can't believe it; I've never been so happy. *(He leaves by way of the outer door; the door between the room and the hall stays open.)*

MRS. LINDE *(straightening up a bit and getting together her street clothes)*   How different now! How different! Someone to work for, to live for—a home to build. Well, it is worth the try! Oh, if they'd only come! *(Listening)* Ah, there they are. Bundle up. *(She picks up her hat and coat.* NORA'S *and* HELMER'S *voices can be heard outside; a key turns in the lock, and* HELMER *brings* NORA *into the hall almost by force. She is wearing the Italian costume with a large black shawl about her; he has on evening dress, with a black domino open over it.)*

NORA *(struggling in the doorway)*   No, no, no, not inside! I'm going up again. I don't want to leave so soon.

HELMER   But Nora dear—

NORA   Oh, I beg you, please, Torvald. From the bottom of my heart, *please*— only an hour more!

HELMER   Not a single minute, Nora darling. You know our agreement. Come on, in we go; you'll catch cold out here. *(In spite of her resistance, he gently draws here into the room.)*

MRS. LINDE   Good evening.

NORA   Kristine!

HELMER   Why, Mrs. Linde—are you here so late?

MRS. LINDE   Yes, I'm sorry, but I did want to see Nora in costume.

NORA   Have you been sitting here, waiting for me?

MRS. LINDE   Yes. I didn't come early enough; you were all upstairs; and then I thought I really couldn't leave without seeing you.

HELMER *(removing* NORA'S *shawl)*   Yes, take a good look. She's worth looking at, I can tell you that, Mrs. Linde. Isn't she lovely?

MRS. LINDE   Yes, I should say—

HELMER   A dream of loveliness, isn't she? That's what everyone thought at the party, too. But she's horribly stubborn—this sweet little thing. What's to be done with her? Can you imagine, I almost had to use force to pry her away.

NORA   Oh, Torvald, you're going to regret you didn't indulge me, even for just a half hour more.

HELMER   There, you see. She danced her tarantella and got a tumultuous hand—which was well earned, although the performance may have been a bit too naturalistic—I mean it rather overstepped the proprieties of art. But never mind—what's important is, she made a success, an overwhelming success. You think I could let her stay on after that and spoil the effect? Oh no; I took my lovely little Capri girl—my capricious little Capri girl, I should say—took her under my arm; one quick tour of the ballroom, a curtsy to every side, and then—as they say in novels—the beautiful vision disappeared. An exit should always be effective, Mrs. Linde, but that's what

I can't get Nora to grasp. Phew, it's hot in here. *(Flings the domino on a chair and opens the door to his room)* Why's it dark in here? Oh yes, of course. Excuse me. *(He goes in and lights a couple of candles.)*

NORA *(in a sharp, breathless whisper)*   So?

MRS. LINDE *(quietly)*   I talked with him.

NORA   And—?

MRS. LINDE   Nora—you must tell your husband everything.

NORA *(dully)*   I knew it.

MRS. LINDE   You've got nothing to fear from Krogstad, but you have to speak out.

NORA   I won't tell.

MRS. LINDE   Then the letter will.

NORA   Thanks, Kristine. I know now what's to be done. Shh!

HELMER *(reentering)*   Well, then, Mrs. Linde—have you admired her?

MRS. LINDE   Yes, and now I'll say good night.

HELMER   Oh, come, so soon? Is this yours, this knitting?

MRS. LINDE   Yes, thanks. I nearly forgot it.

HELMER   Do you knit, then?

MRS. LINDE   Oh yes.

HELMER   You know what? You should embroider instead.

MRS. LINDE   Really? Why?

HELMER   Yes, because it's a lot prettier. See here, one holds the embroidery so, in the left hand, and then one guides the needle with the right—so—in an easy, sweeping curve—right?

MRS. LINDE   Yes, I guess that's—

HELMER   But, on the other hand, knitting—it can never be anything but ugly. Look, see here, the arms tucked in, the knitting needles going up and down—there's something Chinese about it. Ah, that was really a glorious champagne they served.

MRS. LINDE   Yes, good night, Nora, and don't be stubborn anymore.

HELMER   Well put, Mrs. Linde!

MRS. LINDE   Good night, Mr. Helmer.

HELMER *(accompanying her to the door)*   Good night, good night. I hope you get home all right. I'd be very happy to—but you don't have far to go. Good night, good night. *(She leaves. He shuts the door after her and returns.)* There, now, at last we got her out the door. She's a deadly bore, that creature.

NORA   Aren't you pretty tired, Torvald?

HELMER   No, not a bit.

NORA   You're not sleepy?

HELMER   Not at all. On the contrary, I'm feeling quite exhilarated. But you? Yes, you really look tired and sleepy.

NORA   Yes, I'm very tired. Soon now I'll sleep.

HELMER   See! You see! I was right all along that we shouldn't stay longer.

NORA   Whatever you do is always right.

HELMER *(kissing her brow)*   Now my little lark talks sense. Say, did you notice what a time Rank was having tonight?

NORA   Oh, was he? I didn't get to speak with him.

HELMER   I scarcely did either, but it's a long time since I've seen him in such high spirits. *(Gazes at her a moment, then comes nearer her)* Hm—it's marvelous, though, to be back home again—to be completely alone with you. Oh, you bewitchingly lovely young woman!

NORA   Torvald, don't look at me like that!

HELMER   Can't I look at my richest treasure? At all that beauty that's mine, mine alone—completely and utterly.

NORA *(moving around to the other side of the table)*   You mustn't talk to me that way tonight.

HELMER *(following her)*   The tarantella is still in your blood, I can see—and it makes you even more enticing. Listen. The guests are beginning to go. *(Dropping his voice)* Nora—it'll soon be quiet through this whole house.

NORA   Yes, I hope so.

HELMER   You do, don't you, my love? Do you realize—when I'm out at a party like this with you—do you know why I talk to you so little, and keep such a distance away; just send you a stolen look now and then—you know why I do it? It's because I'm imagining then that you're my secret darling, my secret young bride-to-be, and that no one suspects there's anything between us.

NORA   Yes, yes; oh, yes, I know you're always thinking of me.

HELMER   And then when we leave and I place the shawl over those fine young rounded shoulders—over that wonderful curving neck—then I pretend that you're my young bride, that we're just coming from the wedding, that for the first time I'm bringing you into my house—that for the first time I'm alone with you—completely alone with you, your trembling young beauty! All this evening I've longed for nothing but you. When I saw you turn and sway in the tarantella—my blood was pounding till I couldn't stand it— that's why I brought you down here so early—

NORA   Go away, Torvald! Leave me alone. I don't want all this.

HELMER   What do you mean? Nora, you're teasing me. You will, won't you? Aren't I your husband—?

(A knock at the outside door)

NORA *(startled)*   What's that?

HELMER *(going toward the hall)*   Who is it?

RANK *(outside)*   It's me. May I come in a moment?

HELMER *(with quiet irritation)*   Oh, what does he want now? *(Aloud)* Hold on. *(Goes and opens the door)* Oh, how nice that you didn't just pass us by!

RANK   I thought I heard your voice, and then I wanted so badly to have a look in. *(Lightly glancing about)* Ah, me, these old familiar haunts. You have it snug and cozy in here, you two.

HELMER   You seemed to be having it pretty cozy upstairs, too.

RANK   Absolutely. Why shouldn't I? Why not take in everything in life? As much as you can, anyway, and as long as you can. The wine was superb—

HELMER   The champagne especially.

RANK   You noticed that too? It's amazing how much I could guzzle down.

NORA   Torvald also drank a lot of champagne this evening.

RANK   Oh?

NORA   Yes, and that always makes him so entertaining.

RANK   Well, why shouldn't one have a pleasant evening after a well-spent day?

HELMER   Well spent? I'm afraid I can't claim that.

RANK   *(slapping him on the back)*   But I can, you see!

NORA   Dr. Rank, you must have done some scientific research today.

RANK   Quite so.

HELMER   Come now—little Nora talking about scientific research!

NORA   And can I congratulate you on the results?

RANK   Indeed you may.

NORA   Then they were good?

RANK   The best possible for both doctor and patient—certainty.

NORA   *(quickly and searchingly)*   Certainty?

RANK   Complete certainty. So don't I owe myself a gay evening afterwards?

NORA   Yes, you're right, Dr. Rank.

HELMER   I'm with you—just so long as you don't have to suffer for it in the morning.

RANK   Well, one never gets something for nothing in life.

NORA   Dr. Rank—are you very fond of masquerade parties?

RANK   Yes, if there's a good array of odd disguises—

NORA   Tell me, what should we two go as at the next masquerade?

HELMER   You little featherhead—already thinking of the next!

RANK   We two? I'll tell you what: you must go as Charmed Life—

HELMER   Yes, but find a costume for *that!*

RANK   Your wife can appear just as she looks every day.

HELMER   That was nicely put. But don't you know what you're going to be?

RANK   Yes, Helmer, I've made up my mind.

HELMER   Well?

RANK   At the next masquerade I'm going to be invisible.

HELMER   That's a funny idea.

RANK   They say there's a hat—black, huge—have you never heard of the hat that makes you invisible? You put it on, and then no one on earth can see you.

HELMER   *(suppressing a smile)*   Ah, of course.

RANK   But I'm quite forgetting what I came for. Helmer, give me a cigar, one of the dark Havanas.

HELMER   With the greatest pleasure. *(Holds out his case)*

RANK   Thanks. *(Takes one and cuts off the tip)*

NORA   *(striking a match)*   Let me give you a light.

RANK   Thank you. *(She holds the match for him; he lights the cigar.)*   And now good-bye.

HELMER   Good-bye, good-bye, old friend.

NORA   Sleep well, Doctor.

RANK   Thanks for that wish.

NORA   Wish me the same.

RANK   You? All right, if you like—Sleep well. And thanks for the light.

(He nods to them both and leaves.)

HELMER *(his voice subdued)*   He's been drinking heavily.

NORA *(absently)*   Could be. (HELMER *takes his keys from his pocket and goes out in the hall.*) Torvald—what are you after?

HELMER   Got to empty the mailbox; it's nearly full. There won't be room for the morning papers.

NORA   Are you working tonight?

HELMER   You know I'm not. Why—what's this? Someone's been at the lock.

NORA   At the lock—?

HELMER   Yes, I'm positive. What do you suppose—? I can't imagine one of the maids—? Here's a broken hairpin. Nora, it's yours—

NORA *(quickly)*   Then it must be the children—

HELMER   You'd better break them of that. Hm, hm—well, opened it after all. *(Takes the contents out and calls into the kitchen)* Helene! Helene, would you put out the lamp in the hall. *(He returns to the room, shutting the hall door, then displays the handful of mail.)* Look how it's piled up. *(Sorting through them)* Now what's this?

NORA *(at the window)*   The letter! Oh, Torvald, no!

HELMER   Two calling cards—from Rank.

NORA   From Dr. Rank?

HELMER *(examining them)*   "Dr. Rank, Consulting Physician." They were on top. He must have dropped them in as he left.

NORA   Is there anything on them?

HELMER   There's a black cross over the name. See? That's a gruesome notion. He could almost be announcing his own death.

NORA   That's just what he's doing.

HELMER   What! You've heard something? Something he's told you?

NORA   Yes. That when those cards came, he'd be taking his leave of us. He'll shut himself in now and die.

HELMER   Ah, my poor friend! Of course I knew he wouldn't be here much longer. But so soon— And then to hide himself away like a wounded animal.

NORA   If it has to happen, then it's best it happens in silence—don't you think so, Torvald?

HELMER *(pacing up and down)*   He'd grown right into our lives. I simply can't imagine him gone. He with his suffering and loneliness—like a dark cloud setting off our sunlit happiness. Well, maybe it's best this way. For him, at least. *(Standing still)* Any maybe for us too, Nora. Now we're thrown back on each other, completely. *(Embracing her)* Oh you, my darling wife, how can I hold you close enough? You know what, Nora—time and again I've wished you were in some terrible danger, just so I could stake my life and soul and everything, for your sake.

NORA (*tearing herself away, her voice firm and decisive*)   Now you must read your
    mail, Torvald.
HELMER   No, no, not tonight. I want to stay with you, dearest.
NORA   With a dying friend on your mind?
HELMER   You're right. We've both had a shock. There's ugliness between us—
    these thoughts of death and corruption. We'll have to get free of them first.
    Until then—we'll stay apart.
NORA (*clinging about his neck*)   Torvald—good night! Good night!
HELMER (*kissing her on the cheek*)   Good night, little songbird. Sleep well, Nora.
    I'll be reading my mail now.
            (*He takes the letters into his room and shuts the door after him.*)
NORA (*with bewildered glances, groping about, seizing* HELMER'S *domino, throwing
    it around her, and speaking in short, hoarse, broken whispers*)   Never see him
    again. Never, never. (*Putting her shawl over her head*) Never see the
    children either—them, too. Never, never. Oh, the freezing black water!
    The depths—down—Oh, I wish it were over—He has it now; he's reading
    it—now. Oh no, no, not yet. Torvald, good-bye, you and the children—
    (*She starts for the hall; as she does,* HELMER *throws open his door and stands
    with an open letter in his hand.*)
HELMER   Nora!
NORA (*screams*)   Oh—!
HELMER   What is this? You know what's in this letter?
NORA   Yes, I know. Let me go! Let me out!
HELMER (*holding her back*)   Where are you going?
NORA (*struggling to break loose*)   You can't save me, Torvald!
HELMER (*slumping back*)   True! Then it's true what he writes? How horrible!
    No, no, it's impossible—it can't be true.
NORA   It *is* true. I've loved you more than all this world.
HELMER   Ah, none of your slippery tricks.
NORA (*taking one step toward him*)   Torvald—!
HELMER   What *is* this you've blundered into!
NORA   Just let me loose. You're not going to suffer for my sake. You're not
    going to take on my guilt.
HELMER   No more playacting. (*Locks the hall door*) You stay right here and give
    me a reckoning. You understand what you've done? Answer! You
    understand?
NORA (*looking squarely at him, her face hardening*)   Yes. I'm beginning to
    understand everything now.
HELMER (*striding about*)   Oh, what an awful awakening! In all these eight
    years—she who was my pride and joy—a hypocrite, a liar—worse,
    worse—a criminal! How infinitely disgusting it all is! The shame! (NORA
    says nothing and goes on looking straight at him. He stops in front of her.) I
    should have suspected something of the kind. I should have known. All
    your father's flimsy values— Be still! All your father's flimsy values have
    come out in you. No religion, no morals, no sense of duty— Oh, how I'm

punished for letting him off! I did it for your sake, and you repay me like this.

NORA   Yes, like this.

HELMER   Now you've wrecked all my happiness—ruined my whole future. Oh, it's awful to think of. I'm in a cheap little grafter's hands; he can do anything he wants with me, ask for anything, play with me like a puppet— and I can't breathe a word. I'll be swept down miserably into the depths on account of a featherbrained woman.

NORA   When I'm gone from this world, you'll be free.

HELMER   Oh, quit posing. Your father had a mess of those speeches too. What good would that ever do me if you were gone from this world, as you say? Not the slightest. He can still make the whole thing known; and if he does, I could be falsely suspected as your accomplice. They might even think that I was behind it—that I put you up to it. And all that I can thank you for— you that I've coddled the whole of our marriage. Can you see now what you've done to me?

NORA   *(icily calm)*   Yes.

HELMER   It's so incredible, I just can't grasp it. But we'll have to patch up whatever we can. Take off the shawl. I said, take it off! I've got to appease him somehow or other. The thing has to be hushed up at any cost. And as for you and me, it's got to seem like everything between us is just as it was—to the outside world, that is. You'll go right on living in this house, of course. But you can't be allowed to bring up the children; I don't dare trust you with them— Oh, to have to say this to someone I've loved so much! Well, that's done with. From now on happiness doesn't matter; all that matters is saving the bits and pieces, the appearance—*(The doorbell rings. HELMER starts.)* What's that? And so late. Maybe the worst—? You think he'd—? Hide, Nora! Say you're sick. *(NORA remains standing motionless. HELMER goes and opens the door.)*

MAID   *(half dressed, in the hall)*   A letter for Mrs. Helmer.

HELMER   I'll take it. *(Snatches the letter and shuts the door)* Yes, it's from him. You don't get it; I'm reading it myself.

NORA   Then read it.

HELMER *(by the lamp)*   I hardly dare. We may be ruined, you and I. But—I've got to know. *(Rips open the letter, skims through a few lines, glances at an enclosure, then cries out joyfully)* Nora! *(NORA looks inquiringly at him.)* Nora! Wait—better check it again— Yes, yes, it's true. I'm saved. Nora, I'm saved!

NORA   And I?

HELMER   You too, of course. We're both saved, both of us. Look. He's sent back your note. He says he's sorry and ashamed—that a happy develop- ment in his life—oh, who cares what he says! Nora, we're saved! No one can hurt you. Oh, Nora, Nora—but first, this ugliness all has to go. Let me see—*(Takes a look at the note)* No, I don't want to see it; I want the whole thing to fade like a dream. *(Tears the note and both letters to pieces, throws them into the stove and watches them burn)* There—now there's nothing left— He wrote that since Christmas Eve you— Oh, they must have been three terrible days for you, Nora.

NORA   I fought a hard fight.

HELMER   And suffered pain and saw no escape but— No, we're not going to dwell on anything unpleasant. We'll just be grateful and keep on repeating: it's over now, it's over! You hear me, Nora? You don't seem to realize—it's over. What's it mean—that frozen look? Oh, poor little Nora, I understand. You can't believe I've forgiven you. But I have, Nora; I swear I have. I know that what you did, you did out of love for me.

NORA   That's true.

HELMER   You loved me the way a wife ought to love her husband. It's simply the means that you couldn't judge. But you think I love you any the less for not knowing how to handle your affairs? No, no—just lean on me: I'll guide you and teach you. I wouldn't be a man if this feminine helplessness didn't make you twice as attractive to me. You mustn't mind those sharp words I said—that was all in the first confusion of thinking my world had collapsed. I've forgiven you, Nora; I swear I've forgiven you.

NORA   My thanks for your forgiveness.   *(She goes out through the door, right.)*

HELMER   No, wait— *(Peers in)* What are you doing in there?

NORA *(inside)*   Getting out of my costume.

HELMER *(by the open door)*   Yes, do that. Try to calm yourself and collect your thoughts again, my frightened little songbird. You can rest easy now; I've got wide wings to shelter you with. *(Walking about close by the door)* How snug and nice our home is, Nora. You're safe here; I'll keep you like a hunted dove I've rescued out of a hawk's claws. I'll bring peace to your poor, shuddering heart. Gradually it'll happen, Nora; you'll see. Tomorrow all this will look different to you; then everything will be as it was. I won't have to go on repeating I forgive you; you'll feel it for yourself. How can you imagine I'd ever conceivably want to disown you—or even blame you in any way? Ah, you don't know a man's heart, Nora. For a man there's something indescribably sweet and satisfying in knowing he's forgiven his wife—and forgiven her out of a full and open heart. It's as if she belongs to him in two ways now: in a sense he's given her fresh into the world again, and she's become his wife and his child as well. From now on that's what you'll be to me—you little, bewildered, helpless thing. Don't be afraid of anything, Nora; just open your heart to me, and I'll be conscience and will to you both—*(NORA enters in her regular clothes.)* What's this? Not in bed? You've changed your dress?

NORA   Yes, Torvald, I've changed my dress.

HELMER   But why now, so late?

NORA   Tonight I'm not sleeping.

HELMER   But Nora dear—

NORA *(looking at her watch)*   It's still not so very late. Sit down, Torvald; we have a lot to talk over. *(She sits at one side of the table.)*

HELMER   Nora—what is this? That hard expression—

NORA   Sit down. This'll take some time. I have a lot to say.

HELMER (*sitting at the table directly opposite her*)   You worry me, Nora. And I don't understand you.

NORA   No, that's exactly it. You don't understand me. And I've never understood you either—until tonight. No, don't interrupt. You can just listen to what I say. We're closing out accounts, Torvald.

HELMER   How do you mean that?

NORA (*after a short pause*)   Doesn't anything strike you about our sitting here like this?

HELMER   What's that?

NORA   We've been married now eight years. Doesn't it occur to you that this is the first time we two, you and I, man and wife, have ever talked seriously together?

HELMER   What do you mean—seriously?

NORA   In eight whole years—longer even—right from our first acquaintance, we've never exchanged a serious word on any serious thing.

HELMER   You mean I should constantly go and involve you in problems you couldn't possibly help me with?

NORA   I'm not talking of problems, I'm saying that we've never sat down seriously together and tried to get to the bottom of anything.

HELMER   But dearest, what good would that ever do you?

NORA   That's the point right there: you've never understood me. I've been wronged greatly, Torvald—first by Papa, and then by you.

HELMER   What! By us—the two people who've loved you more than anyone else?

NORA (*shaking her head*)   You never loved me. You've thought it fun to be in love with me, that's all.

HELMER   Nora, what a thing to say!

NORA   Yes, it's true now, Torvald. When I lived at home with Papa, he told me all his opinions, so I had the same ones too; or if they were different I hid them, since he wouldn't have cared for that. He used to call me his doll-child, and he played with me the way I played with my dolls. Then I came into your house—

HELMER   How can you speak of our marriage like that?

NORA (*unperturbed*)   I mean, then I went from Papa's hands into yours. You arranged everything to your own taste, and so I got the same taste as you—or I pretended to; I can't remember. I guess a little of both, first one, then the other. Now when I look back, it seems as if I'd lived here like a beggar—just from hand to mouth. I've lived by doing tricks for you, Torvald. But that's the way you wanted it. It's a great sin what you and Papa did to me. You're to blame that nothing's become of me.

HELMER   Nora, how unfair and ungrateful you are! Haven't you been happy here?

NORA   No, never. I thought so—but I never have.

HELMER   Not—not happy!

NORA   No, only lighthearted. And you've always been so kind to me. But our home's been nothing but a playpen. I've been your doll-wife here, just as at home I was Papa's doll-child. And in turn the children have been my dolls. I thought it was fun when you played with me, just as they thought it fun when I played with them. That's been our marriage, Torvald.

HELMER   There's some truth in what you're saying—under all the raving exaggeration. But it'll all be different after this. Playtime's over; now for the schooling.

NORA   Whose schooling—mine or the children's?

HELMER   Both yours and the children's, dearest.

NORA   Oh, Torvald, you're not the man to teach me to be a good wife to you.

HELMER   And you can say that?

NORA   And I—how am I equipped to bring up children?

HELMER   Nora!

NORA   Didn't you say a moment ago that that was no job to trust me with?

HELMER   In a flare of temper! Why fasten on that?

NORA   Yes, but you were so very right. I'm not up to the job. There's another job I have to do first. I have to try to educate myself. You can't help me with that. I've got to do it alone. And that's why I'm leaving you now.

HELMER   *(jumping up)*   What's that?

NORA   I have to stand completely alone, if I'm ever going to discover myself and the world out there. So I can't go on living with you.

HELMER   Nora, Nora!

NORA   I want to leave right away. Kristine should put me up for the night—

HELMER   You're insane! You've no right! I forbid you!

NORA   From here on, there's no use forbidding me anything. I'll take with me whatever is mine. I don't want a thing from you, either now or later.

HELMER   What kind of madness is this!

NORA   Tomorrow I'm going home—I mean, home where I came from. It'll be easier up there to find something to do.

HELMER   Oh, you blind, incompetent child!

NORA   I must learn to be competent, Torvald.

HELMER   Abandon your home, your husband, your children! And you're not even thinking what people will say.

NORA   I can't be concerned about that. I only know how essential this is.

HELMER   Oh, it's outrageous. So you'll run out like this on your most sacred vows.

NORA   What do you think are my most sacred vows?

HELMER   And I have to tell you that! Aren't they your duties to your husband and children?

NORA   I have other duties equally sacred.

HELMER   That isn't true. What duties are they?

NORA   Duties to myself.

HELMER   Before all else, you're a wife and a mother.

NORA   I don't believe in that anymore. I believe that, before all else, I'm a human being, no less than you—or anyway, I ought to try to become one. I know the majority thinks you're right, Torvald, and plenty of books agree with you, too. But I can't go on believing what the majority says, or what's written in books. I have to think over these things myself and try to understand them.

HELMER   Why can't you understand your place in your own home? On a point like that, isn't there one everlasting guide you can turn to? Where's your religion?

NORA   Oh, Torvald, I'm really not sure what religion is.

HELMER   What—?

NORA   I only know what the minister said when I was confirmed. He told me religion was this thing and that. When I get clear and away by myself, I'll go into that problem too. I'll see if what the minister said was right, or, in any case, if it's right for me.

HELMER   A young woman your age shouldn't talk like that. If religion can't move you, I can try to rouse your conscience. You do have some moral feeling? Or, tell me—has that gone too?

NORA   It's not easy to answer that, Torvald. I simply don't know. I'm all confused about these things. I just know I see them so differently from you. I find out, for one thing, that the law's not at all what I'd thought—but I can't get it through my head that the law is fair. A woman hasn't a right to protect her dying father or save her husband's life! I can't believe that.

HELMER   You talk like a child. You don't know anything of the world you live in.

NORA   No, I don't. But now I'll begin to learn for myself. I'll try to discover who's right, the world or I.

HELMER   Nora, you're sick; you've got a fever. I almost think you're out of your head.

NORA   I've never felt more clearheaded and sure in my life.

HELMER   And—clearheaded and sure—you're leaving your husband and children?

NORA   Yes.

HELMER   Then there's only one possible reason.

NORA   What?

HELMER   You no longer love me.

NORA   No. That's exactly it.

HELMER   Nora! You can't be serious!

NORA   Oh, this is so hard, Torvald—you've been so kind to me always. But I can't help it. I don't love you anymore.

HELMER   (*struggling for composure*)   Are you also clearheaded and sure about that?

NORA   Yes, completely. That's why I can't go on staying here.

HELMER   Can you tell me what I did to lose your love?

NORA   Yes, I can tell you. It was this evening when the miraculous thing didn't come—then I knew you weren't the man I'd imagined.

HELMER   Be more explicit; I don't follow you.

NORA   I've waited now so patiently eight long years—for, my Lord, I know miracles don't come every day. Then this crisis broke over me, and such a certainty filled me: *now* the miraculous event would occur. While Krogstad's letter was lying out there, I never for an instant dreamed that you could give in to his terms. I was so utterly sure you'd say to him: go on, tell your tale to the whole wide world. And when he'd done that—

HELMER   Yes, what then? When I'd delivered my own wife into shame and disgrace—!

NORA   When he'd done that, I was so utterly sure that you'd step forward, take the blame on yourself and say: I am the guilty one.

HELMER   Nora—!

NORA   You're thinking I'd never accept such a sacrifice from you? No, of course not. But what good would my protests be against you? That was the miracle I was waiting for, in terror and hope. And to stave that off, I would have taken my life.

HELMER   I'd gladly work for you day and night, Nora—and take on pain and deprivation. But there's no one who gives up honor for love.

NORA   Millions of women have done just that.

HELMER   Oh, you think and talk like a silly child.

NORA   Perhaps. But you neither think nor talk like the man I could join myself to. When your big fright was over—and it wasn't from any threat against me, only for what might damage you—when all the danger was past, for you it was just as if nothing had happened. I was exactly the same, your little lark, your doll, that you'd have to handle with double care now that I'd turned out so brittle and frail. *(Gets up)* Torvald—in that instant it dawned on me that for eight years I've been living here with a stranger, and that I'd even conceived three children—oh, I can't stand the thought of it! I could tear myself to bits.

HELMER *(heavily)*   I see. There's a gulf that's opened between us—that's clear. Oh, but Nora, can't we bridge it somehow?

NORA   The way I am now, I'm no wife for you.

HELMER   I have the strength to make myself over.

NORA   Maybe—if your doll gets taken away.

HELMER   But to part! To part from you! No, Nora, no—I can't imagine it.

NORA *(going out, right)*   All the more reason why it has to be. *(She reenters with her coat and a small overnight bag, which she puts on a chair by the table.)*

HELMER   Nora, Nora, not now! Wait till tomorrow.

NORA   I can't spend the night in a strange man's room.

HELMER   But couldn't we live here like brother and sister—

NORA   You know very well how long that would last. *(Throws her shawl about her)* Good-bye, Torvald. I won't look in on the children. I know they're in better hands than mine. The way I am now, I'm no use to them.

HELMER   But someday, Nora—someday—?

NORA   How can I tell? I haven't the least idea what'll become of me.

HELMER   But you're my wife, now and wherever you go.

NORA   Listen, Torvald—I've heard that when a wife deserts her husband's house just as I'm doing, then the law frees him from all responsibility. In any case, I'm freeing you from being responsible. Don't feel yourself bound, any more than I will. There has to be absolute freedom for us both. Here, take your ring back. Give me mine.

HELMER   That too?

NORA   That too.

HELMER   There it is.

NORA   Good. Well, now it's all over. I'm putting the keys here. The maids know all about keeping up the house—better than I do. Tomorrow, after I've left town, Kristine will stop by to pack up everything that's mine from home. I'd like those things shipped to me.

HELMER   Over! All over! Nora, won't you ever think about me?

NORA   I'm sure I'll think of you often, and about the children and the house here.

HELMER   May I write you?

NORA   No—never. You're not to do that.

HELMER   Oh, but let me send you—

NORA   Nothing. Nothing.

HELMER   Or help you if you need it.

NORA   No. I accept nothing from strangers.

HELMER   Nora—can I never be more than a stranger to you?

NORA   *(picking up the overnight bag)*   Ah, Torvald—it would take the greatest miracle of all—

HELMER   Tell me the greatest miracle!

NORA   You and I both would have to transform ourselves to the point that— Oh, Torvald, I've stopped believing in miracles.

HELMER   But I'll believe. Tell me! Transform ourselves to the point that—?

NORA   That our living together could be a true marriage.

(She goes out down the hall.)

HELMER   *(sinks down on a chair by the door, face buried in his hands)*   Nora! Nora! *(Looking about and rising)* Empty. She's gone. *(A sudden hope leaps in him)* The greatest miracle—?

(From below, the sound of a door slamming shut)

Translated by Rolf Fjelde

Questions for Writing and Discussion.

1.   A high point in the play comes when Nora dances the tarantella. Apart from the fact that it gives the leading actress a chance for a "bang-up scene" (provided she can dance!), what significance does this have in the play? Could it be said, and with how much plausibility, that Nora's dance symbolizes the whole relationship she has to her husband? But in what way does the dance also symbolize, perhaps, her growing readiness to break out of the role she has previously accepted?

2. At the end of the second act, Nora says she is waiting for a "miracle?" What does she mean? And what is the reality she encounters? How does the ending of the second act prepare for the third?

3. One problem in producing the play would be Torvald. Can he be made to seem anything but hopelessly stuffy, pompous, dull? Wouldn't there be a danger that the actor assigned to this part might slide into mere caricature because he wanted, at all costs, to make Torvald vivid? Is there any redeeming humanity in Torvald—see, especially, the conclusion of the play?

4. To have a very tightly constructed play, the author has to make certain that the minor characters have definite and limited functions. (By the way, *why* minor characters at all?) Consider the minor characters one by one, and see whether, or how, they contribute to the development of the play.

5. Do you think it appropriate to see the play as a tract in behalf of feminism? If you were watching the play in a theatre, and a good actress was performing Nora, do you think you'd be inclined to applaud her speeches when she tells her husband she is leaving? Why? Why not?

AUGUST STRINDBERG

The Stronger

Introduction

In one of his encounters with Rosencrantz and Guildenstern, whose role at Elsinore he is trying to puzzle out, Hamlet says: "Man delights not me; nor woman neither, though by your smiling you seem to say so." The latter part of the sentence gives us a signal of nervous anticipation on Hamlet's side, and implies an unwritten stage direction: *after the phrase, "Man delights not me," Rosencrantz and Guildenstern begin to smile.* And it is with that smile of male fellowship that the scene is usually played. But suppose we in the audience saw that throughout the scene Rosencrantz and Guildenstern did not smile once. We would then have learned something unexpected about Hamlet in what looks like an otherwise unpromising bit of dialogue: that he is suspicious to the point of paranoia; quick to attribute motives or judgments to others, which their actions do not confirm; fearful of being seen through and overruled; chronically anxious. Now, imagine an entire play in which one character tries to outwit and overwhelm another by anticipating responses that we in the audience do not see, and by responding to unwritten stage directions that stay unwritten in the performance. This character is the Mrs. X whose monologue Strindberg entitles *The Stronger*.

As *Hamlet* is usually performed, the encounter we have mentioned is one of many occasions for a display of Hamlet's mastery: *he* knows what *they* are thinking. Here is an apparently similar moment in *The Stronger:*

> Well, perhaps it's not right to make fun of one's husband like this. He's sweet anyhow, and a good, dear husband. You ought to have had a husband like him, Amelia. What are you laughing at? What is it? Eh? And, you see, I know he is faithful to me. Yes, I know it. He told me himself—what *are* you giggling at?

By no stretch of the imagination can we call this a display of Mrs. X's mastery. It is too apprehensive, too unsure of itself. And while we can imagine many looks

943

corresponding to these words, the most effective performance would doubtless show Miss Y with a quiet and barely visible suppressed smile, never once breaking into a giggle. Mrs. X is losing control; she is, as we like to say, "giving herself away"; yet the progress of her monologue shows something far more terrible than our phrase implies. For she is creating out of herself the figure that haunts her—indeed, the figure that she thinks has already invaded her being and drained away her individual life. And she accomplishes her act of self-destruction without beginning to understand her own complicity in it. She places her faith in, and feels she is relying on, nothing more than the everyday world of fact and gossip.

It would be pleasantly uplifting to say that the play carries a moral: "All of our demons are pure fabrications. We can live happily if only we let up on ourselves." But the play really encourages no such reading. Miss Y may be harmless outside of what Mrs. X makes of her. Or she may not be. What we can say with certainty is that, in the play, Miss Y is as much Mrs. X's creation as, in the haunted mind of the speaker herself, Mrs. X is Miss Y's. About Miss Y we hardly get "objective" information, but we do know that she remains silent: this would seem to indicate that she understands Mrs. X's psychological war better than Mrs. X herself. Whatever Miss Y is, she stays the same throughout the monologue, and Mrs. X does not. Since it *is* simply a monologue, it may be asked why Strindberg should have written it as a play and not as a story. We can offer one possible answer. The work that we have to do in completing our idea of Miss Y is like the work an actor does in completing his or her idea of any character at all, about whom a play tells hardly anything compared to what is needed in performance. By calling attention to the uneasily close relation between our idea of character and the details of performance, *The Stronger* makes us ponder all we may have assumed too quickly in our idea of character itself.

The Stronger

CHARACTERS OF THE PLAY

MISS Y., *actress, unmarried*
MRS. X., *actress, married*
A WAITRESS

Scene: A corner of a ladies' café (in Stockholm in the eighteen eighties). Two small wrought-iron tables, a red plush settee and a few chairs.

   MISS Y. *is sitting with a half-empty bottle of beer on the table before her, reading an illustrated weekly which from time to time she exchanges for another.*

   MRS. X. *enters, wearing a winter hat and coat and carrying a decorative Japanese basket.*

MRS. X.   Why, Millie, my dear, how are you? Sitting here all alone on Christmas Eve like some poor bachelor.

(MISS Y. *looks up from her magazine, nods, and continues to read.*)

MRS. X.   You know it makes me feel really sad to see you. Alone. Alone in a café and on Christmas Eve of all times. It makes me feel as sad as when once in Paris I saw a wedding party at a restaurant. The bride was reading a comic paper and the bridegroom playing billiards with the witnesses. Ah me, I said to myself, with such a beginning how will it go, and how will it end? He was playing billiards on his wedding day! And she, you were going to say, was reading a comic paper on hers. But that's not quite the same.

(A WAITRESS *brings a cup of chocolate to* MRS. X. *and goes out.*)

MRS. X.   Do you know, Amelia, I really believe now you would have done better to stick to him. Don't forget I was the first who told you to forgive him. Do you remember? Then you would be married now and have a home. Think how happy you were that Christmas when you stayed with your fiancé's people in the country. How warmly you spoke of domestic happiness! You really quite longed to be out of the theatre. Yes, Amelia dear, home is best—next best to the stage, and as for children—but you couldn't know anything about that.

(MISS Y.'S *expression is disdainful.* MRS. X. *sips a few spoonfuls of chocolate, then opens her basket and displays some Christmas presents.*)

THE STRONGER From *Six Plays of Strindberg,* translated by Elizabeth Sprigge. Copyright 1955 by Elizabeth Sprigge. Reprinted by permission of Curtis Brown, Ltd.

MRS. X.   Now you must see what I have bought for my little chicks. *(Takes out a doll.)* Look at this. That's for Lisa. Do you see how she can roll her eyes and turn her head. Isn't she lovely? And here's a toy pistol for Maja.*

(She loads the pistol and shoots it at MISS Y. *who appears frightened.)*

MRS. X.   Were you scared? Did you think I was going to shoot you? Really, I didn't think you'd believe that of me. Now if *you* were to shoot *me* it wouldn't be so surprising, for after all I did get in your way, and I know you never forget it—although I was entirely innocent. You still think I intrigued to get you out of the Grand Theatre, but I didn't. I didn't, however much you think I did. Well, it's no good talking, you will believe it was me . . . *(Takes out a pair of embroidered slippers.)* And these are for my old man, with tulips on them that I embroidered myself. As a matter of fact I hate tulips, but he has to have tulips on everything.

*(*MISS Y. *looks up, irony and curiosity in her face.)*

MRS. X.   *(putting one hand in each slipper)* Look what small feet Bob has, hasn't he? And you ought to see the charming way he walks—you've never seen him in slippers, have you?

*(*MISS Y. *laughs.)*

MRS. X.   Look, I'll show you.

(She makes the slippers walk across the table, and MISS Y. *laughs again.)*

MRS. X.   But when he gets angry, look, he stamps his foot like this. "Those damn girls who can never learn how to make coffee! Blast! That silly idiot hasn't trimmed the lamp properly!" Then there's a draught under the door and his feet get cold. "Hell, it's freezing, and the damn fools can't even keep the stove going!"

(She rubs the sole of one slipper against the instep of the other. MISS Y. *roars with laughter.)*

MRS. X.   And then he comes home and has to hunt for his slippers, which Mary has pushed under the bureau . . . Well, perhaps it's not right to make fun of one's husband like this. He's sweet anyhow, and a good, dear husband. You ought to have had a husband like him, Amelia. What are you laughing at? What is it? Eh? And, you see, I know he is faithful to me. Yes, I know it. He told me himself—what *are* you giggling at?—that while I was on tour in Norway that horrible Frederica came and tried to seduce him. Can you

*Pronounced *Maja.*

imagine anything more abominable? *(Pause)* I'd have scratched her eyes out if she had come around while I was at home. *(Pause)* I'm glad Bob told me about it himself, so I didn't just hear it from gossip. *(Pause)* And, as a matter of fact, Frederica wasn't the only one. I can't think why, but all the women in the Company seem to be crazy about my husband. They must think his position gives him some say in who is engaged at the Theatre. Perhaps you have run after him yourself? I don't trust you very far, but I know he has never been attracted by you, and you always seemed to have some sort of grudge against him, or so I felt.

(Pause. They look at one another guardedly.)

MRS. X.   Do come and spend Christmas Eve with us tonight, Amelia—just to show that you're not offended with us, or anyhow not with me. I don't know why, but it seems specially unpleasant not to be friends with you. Perhaps it's because I did get in your way that time . . . *(Slowly)* or—I don't know—really, I don't know at all why it is.

(Pause. MISS Y. *gazes curiously at* MRS. X.*)*

MRS. X.   *(thoughtfully)*   It was so strange when we were getting to know one another. Do you know, when we first met, I was frightened of you, so frightened I didn't dare let you out of my sight. I arranged all my goings and comings to be near you. I dared not be your enemy, so I became your friend. But when you came to our home, I always had an uneasy feeling, because I saw my husband didn't like you, and that irritated me—like when a dress doesn't fit. I did all I could to make him be nice to you, but it was no good—until you went and got engaged. Then you became such tremendous friends that at first it looked as if you only dared show your real feelings then—when you were safe. And then, let me see, how was it after that? I wasn't jealous—that's queer. And I remember at the christening, when you were the godmother, I told him to kiss you. He did, and you were so upset . . . As a matter of fact, I didn't notice that then . . . I didn't think about it afterwards either . . . I've never thought about it—until *now!* *(Rises abruptly.)* Why don't you say something? You haven't said a word all this time. You've just let me go on talking. You have sat there with your eyes drawing all these thoughts out of me—they were there in me like silk in a cocoon—thoughts . . . Mistaken thoughts? Let me think. Why did you break off your engagement? Why did you never come to our house after that? Why don't you want to come to us tonight?

(MISS Y. makes a motion, as if about to speak.)

MRS. X.   No. You don't need to say anything, for now I see it all. That was why—and why—and why. Yes. Yes, that's why it was. Yes, yes, all the pieces fit together now. That's it. I won't sit at the same table as you. *(Moves* *her things to the other table.)* That's why I have to embroider tulips, which I loathe, on his slippers—because you liked tulips. *(Throws the slippers on the floor.)* That's why we have to spend the summer on the lake—because you couldn't bear the seaside. That's why my son had to be called Eskil—because it was your father's name. That's why I had to wear your colours, read your books, eat the dishes you liked, drink your drinks—your chocolate, for instance. That's why—oh my God, it's terrible to think of, terrible! Everything, everything came to me from you—even your passions. Your soul bored into mine like a worm into an apple, and ate and ate and burrowed and burrowed, till nothing was left but the skin and a little black mould. I wanted to fly from you, but I couldn't. You were there like a snake, your black eyes fascinating me. When I spread my wings, they only dragged me down. I lay in the water with my feet tied together, and the harder I worked my arms, the deeper I sank—down, down, till I reached the bottom, where you lay in waiting like a giant crab to catch me in your claws—and now here I am. Oh how I hate you! I hate you, I hate you! And you just go on sitting there, silent, calm, indifferent, not caring whether the moon is new or full, if it's Christmas or New Year, if other people are happy or unhappy. You don't know how to hate or to love. You just sit there without moving—like a cat* at a mouse-hole. You can't drag your prey out, you can't chase it, but you can out-stay it. Here you sit in your corner—you know they call it the rat-trap after you—reading the papers to see if anyone's ruined or wretched or been thrown out of the Company. Here you sit sizing up your victims and weighing your chances—like a pilot his shipwrecks for the salvage. *(Pause.)* Poor Amelia! Do you know, I couldn't be more sorry for you. I know you are miserable, miserable like some wounded creature, and vicious because you are wounded. I can't be angry with you. I should like to be, but after all you are the small one—and as for your affair with Bob, that doesn't worry me in the least. Why should it matter to me? And if you, or somebody else taught me to drink chocolate, what's the difference? *(Drinks a spoonful. Smugly.)* Chocolate is very wholesome anyhow. And if I learnt from you how to dress, *tant mieux!*—that only gave me a stronger hold over my husband, and you have lost what I gained. Yes, to judge from various signs, I think you have now lost him. Of course, you meant me to walk out, as you once did, and which you're now regretting. But I won't do that, you may be sure. One shouldn't be narrow-minded, you know. And why should nobody else want what I have? *(Pause.)* Perhaps, my dear, taking everything into consideration, at this moment it is I who am the stronger. You never got anything from me, you just gave away—from yourself. And now, like the thief in the night, when you woke up I had what you had lost. Why was it then that everything you touched became worthless and sterile? You couldn't keep a man's love—for all your tulips and your passions—but I could. You couldn't learn the art of living from your books—but I learnt it. You bore no little

*In Swedish, "stork."

Eskil, although that was your father's name. *(Pause.)* And why is it you are silent—everywhere, always silent? Yes, I used to think this was strength, but perhaps it was because you hadn't anything to say, because you couldn't think of anything. *(Rises and picks up the slippers.)* Now I am going home, taking the tulips with me—*your* tulips. You couldn't learn from others, you couldn't bend, and so you broke like a dry stick. I did not. Thank you, Amelia, for all your good lessons. Thank you for teaching my husband how to love. Now I am going home—to love him.   *(Exit.)*

Translated by Elizabeth Sprigge

Questions for Writing and Discussion

1. What is your initial response to Mrs. X's firing the toy pistol at Miss Y, followed by her amusement at the fright she causes? After reading the entire play, how would you interpret the gesture? Is this interpretation different from your initial one?

2. Why might the stage direction, "Miss Y makes a motion, as if about to speak," be used by Strindberg to mark a turning point in the play? In fact, what happens to Mrs. X after that point?

3. From Miss Y's silence, and the few stage directions for her responses, how would you describe her? Is she just anyone?

4. Mrs. X defines herself throughout the play—first happily, then bitterly, at last with a fierce display of satisfaction—by her vivid and specific sense of "the woman's role." Would you say she has found peace of mind by the end of the play? Why, or why not?

5. Which of the two women do you think is "the stronger" named in the title? Why?

LILLIAN HELLMAN

The Little Foxes

Introduction

The Little Foxes has been one of the most successful American plays of the twentieth century. This is due partly to its author's gift for stagecraft, that is, skilled management in the portrayal of human conflicts so as to create vivid situations in the theatre. The conflict in *The Little Foxes* concerns a particular family, the Hubbards, through which gradations of evil are explored; but it also draws upon certain crucial aspects of American life some eighty years ago that extend far beyond the particular experience of the Hubbards. It draws upon the Southern myth, the central story about life in the South that has, with variations, often been repeated this past century.

The Southern myth is a story of what happened to the defeated homeland after the Civil War, how it suffered through years of humiliation and then gradually pulled itself together by abandoning its own traditions and adopting the values of its enemy, the commercial North. Thereby honor was abandoned and prosperity began.

Many Southern writers of the twentieth century—such as the great novelist William Faulkner and the talented playwrights Lillian Hellman and Tennessee Williams—have found themselves driven by the pressures of shared communal memory—by the pressures of interwoven love and revulsion—to keep returning to the archetypal story of their culture. In *The Little Foxes* Lillian Hellman shares with William Faulkner a fascination with that part of the Southern myth which shows how a tough, aggressive, greedy, amoral new class of merchants and capitalists arose in the late nineteenth-century South, replacing the defeated and often demoralized planter aristocracy. Thus in Act I, only a few minutes after the play opens, there is a crucial exchange between Mr. Marshall, the suave businessman from Chicago, and the Hubbards on the subject of the Southern aristocracy. Out of either politeness or ignorance, or perhaps both, Mr. Marshall mistakes what the Hubbards represent socially in the South of 1900, and the hardheaded Ben Hubbard quickly sets the record straight.

"Southern aristocrats," says Ben, "have *not* kept together and have *not* kept what belonged to them." It is they, the Hubbards, who have taken over the wealth of the local Southern aristocrats—but, as Ben realistically adds, "we are not aristocrats."

Now this sets the record straight not only for Mr. Marshall, but more important, for the theatre audience, which Hellman shrewdly suspects is not very knowledgeable about class distinctions in the South. Ben Hubbard makes it clear that his family is part of what we would now call the new bourgeoisie, the entrepreneurial class that evolved after the defeat of the planter aristocracy in the Civil War.

This new class, as shown by Hellman, is energetic, ambitious, rapacious, without moral scruples; yet by itself it cannot get very far. It simply lacks the capital for large-scale commercial or industrial development. It must therefore ally itself with "foreign," that is Northern, money, here represented by the cultivated but tough Mr. Marshall from Chicago. Thereby the Hubbards complete, once and for all, the break from the traditions of the Old South—indeed, in order to succeed the Hubbards must be more rapacious, more exploitative than even Northern big money. Lillian Hellman takes pains to show that even before the appearance of Mr. Marshall and his Chicago money, the Hubbards have been greedy and disloyal. They cheat their customers and treat the local blacks with a meanness that Birdie, the beaten and frightened remnant of the Old South, finds abhorrent. (She is distressed, for instance, by Oscar's wanton shooting of the game that the blacks badly need for food.) It would be sentimental to suppose—and Lillian Hellman makes sure we do not suppose—that the Hubbards, or the class they personify, have been "corrupted" by Northern money. No; it is their inner corruption that prepares them for the alliance with Northern big money.

Until now, in developing her plot and her characters, Hellman has followed closely the traditional contours of Southern myth. But at one major point in the play she goes further, showing evidence of the liberal and radical ideas of the 1930s which influenced her thinking. In Act II Ben Hubbard, who serves as the central intelligence (but not the moral center) of the play, reports on a conversation he had with Mr. Marshall:

> There'll be no trouble from anybody, white or black. Marshall said that to me. "What about strikes? That's all we've had in Massachusetts for the last three years." I say to him, "What's a strike? I never heard of one. Come South, Marshall. We got good folks and we don't stand for any fancy fooling."

Here a new element has been added to the Southern myth by Hellman—that at least for some decades to come the South will serve as a source of cheap labor for Northern capital, with people like the Hubbards doing the dirty work for the Northern owners and, of course, themselves profiting hugely.

So it is important to note that while Hellman uses the Southern myth, she is not its captive. She writes about the South, in part because that is where she herself comes from; but she writes about it from a considerable moral and psychic distance. Thus, she uses the device, also important in the novels of Faulkner, of the aging black servant, in this play Addie, who serves as the moral conscience of the play. Addie is the one character who, in her mixture of clear-sightedness and helplessness, understands and judges, apparently as the author herself would like the audience to understand and judge. Brief but strong, Addie's judgment comes in Act III, when she talks about the Hubbards and people like them:

> Yeah, they got mighty well off cheating niggers. Well, there are people who eat the earth and eat all the people on it like in the Bible with the locusts. Then there are people who stand around and watch them eat it. *(Softly)* Sometimes I think it ain't right to stand and watch them do it.

The force of Addie's remarks is magnified by the fact that they are immediately followed with a little speech by Birdie in which she expresses a feeble nostalgia for "the old days" ("if we could only go back to Lionnet," her family's plantation now taken over by the Hubbards). We are not expected to take Birdie seriously as a moral agent opposing the evil of the Hubbards; her very name suggests feebleness, just as, by the way, the name of the ruthless Hubbard sister, Regina (Latin for *queen*), suggests strength. Addie's central speech is repeated at the close of the play by Regina's daughter, Zan, who vows to move beyond the weakness of her father Horace and her aunt Birdie and to fight "hard" against the values of the Hubbards. She'll "be fighting . . . someplace where people don't just stand around and watch." Thereby Hellman grafts a mildly liberal or even Marxist conclusion onto the Southern myth.

So far we have discussed *The Little Foxes* in terms of its underlying social scheme or pattern of meaning; but when you read the play or see it on the stage, what you immediately encounter is a drama of individual figures. We have been trying to trace the story behind the story, to examine the bones of history on which Hellman has put the flesh of drama. When we now turn to the drama itself, what is likely to strike us first of all is how sharply and simply all the characters are drawn. Except perhaps for Ben, who does reveal a certain charming complexity in the candor of his evil, all the characters in the play can seem one-dimensional, as if meant to embody just a single dominant or even obsessive trait. *The Little Foxes* has in fact a component of melodrama, in that characters are shown through unshaded and simplified portrayal in order to make an unambiguous moral point. It would not be hard to describe the major figures in *The Little Foxes* in the following way:

> *Ben Hubbard,* the cynical, undeluded entrepreneur aware of his place in history and of the moral price he has to pay for it

> *Regina,* a figure reminding us a little of Lady Macbeth—ambitious, ruthless, prepared to drive her husband to death in order to achieve her ends

> *Birdie,* the decayed aristocrat remembering days of lost glory, now victimized by the New South

Addie, the grumpy, loyal black servant, critical of the whites behind their backs and sometimes to their faces, who carries within herself the best of the old world

Yet here we come to a crucial difference in *genres,* or kinds of literary works. If *The Little Foxes* were a novel, the blocklike simplicity of the characterization and plot could be a drawback, for it would be hard to read a full-length book in which the characters did not show at least a little more complexity, variety, even unexpectedness. But in a play, where everything has to be concentrated into a few hours on a stage and there is not much need or possibility for extensive psychological probing into the depths of character, the method Hellman uses in *The Little Foxes* can be effective and powerful.

When you read a play, it often helps to imagine it being performed on the stage—performed by resourceful actors who can take its plot and its fierce cues of characterization and make them into something tensely dramatic and significant. For remember what Lillian Hellman once said in an interview: "A play is not only on paper. It is there to share with actors, directors, scene designers, electricians."

Now, we aren't saying here that the drama as a form can never yield richer and subtler kinds of characterization than this play provides. Still, it's plain that, by working up a tight (if not always entirely plausible) plot and a series of fiercely-sketched outlines of character, Hellman gives a good director and skillful actors what they need for making a vital work of theatre.

Certain technical details reinforce this judgment. Act I ends, a little shockingly, when Oscar Hubbard slaps his wife Birdie: it comes as both a sign of the Hubbard morality at its most despicable and as a suggestive symbol of the relationship between "new" and "old" South. Act II has an even more shocking climax, when Regina tells her husband, the dying Horace, a weak but decent man: "I hope you die. I hope you die soon. *(Smiles)* I'll be waiting for you to die." The brutality of the Hubbard code, which until now we have seen mainly in its public aspect, is here revealed in a personal dimension.

Then in Act III Hellman introduces very skillfully a quiet interlude, a change of pace. The play is going to end with Regina's triumph over her brothers and Zan's rebellion against Regina; but now, at the start of the act, as a contrast in tone and mood, there is a restrained interval—very effectively written— bringing together Horace, Birdie, Zan, and Addie, the characters who themselves are not actively evil but who are either helpless before it, like Birdie and Addie, or who don't know how to fight it, like Horace and Zan. This is the quiet before the storm, a device that playwrights often use in starting a final act. But the quiet, of course, does not and cannot last very long; soon the little foxes will enter, in a concluding paroxysm of strife and moral ugliness, to "spoil the vines."

The Little Foxes

CHARACTERS OF THE PLAY

ADDIE
CAL
BIRDIE HUBBARD
OSCAR HUBBARD
LEO HUBBARD
REGINA GIDDENS
WILLIAM MARSHALL
BENJAMIN HUBBARD
ALEXANDRA GIDDENS
HORACE GIDDENS

ACT I

Scene: *The living room of the Giddens house, in a small town in the deep South, the Spring of 1900. Upstage is a staircase leading to the second story. Upstage, right, are double doors to the dining room. When these doors are open we see a section of the dining room and the furniture. Upstage, left, is an entrance hall with a coat rack and umbrella stand. There are large lace-curtained windows on the left wall. The room is lit by a center gas chandelier and painted china oil lamps on the tables. Against the wall is a large piano. Downstage, right, are a high couch, a large table, several chairs. Against the left back wall are a table and several chairs. Near the window there are a smaller couch and tables. The room is good-looking, the furniture expensive; but it reflects no particular taste. Everything is of the best and that is all.*

At Rise: ADDIE, *a tall, nice-looking Negro woman of about fifty-five, is closing the windows. From behind the closed dining-room doors there is the sound of voices. After a second,* CAL, *a middle-aged Negro, comes in from the entrance hall carrying a tray with glasses and a bottle of port.* ADDIE *crosses, takes the tray from him, puts it on table, begins to arrange it.*

ADDIE *(pointing to the bottle)* You gone stark out of your head?
CAL No, smart lady, I ain't. Miss Regina told me to get out that bottle. *(Points to bottle)* That very bottle for the mighty honored guest. When Miss Regina changes orders like that you can bet your dime she got her reason.
ADDIE *(points to dining room)* Go on. You'll be needed.

CAL Miss Zan she had two helpings frozen fruit cream and she tell that honored guest, she tell him that you make the best frozen fruit cream in all the South.

ADDIE *(smiles, pleased)* Did she? Well, see that Belle saves a little for her. She like it right before she go to bed. Save a few little cakes, too, she like—

The dining-room doors are opened and quickly closed again by BIRDIE HUBBARD. BIRDIE *is a woman of about forty, with a pretty, well-bred, faded face. Her movements are usually nervous and timid, but now, as she comes running into the room, she is gay and excited.* CAL *turns to* BIRDIE.

BIRDIE Oh, Cal. *(Closes door)* I want you to get one of the kitchen boys to run home for me. He's to look in my desk drawer and— *(To* ADDIE*)* My, Addie. What a good supper! Just as good as good can be.

ADDIE You look pretty this evening, Miss Birdie, and young.

BIRDIE *(laughing)* Me, young? *(Turns back to* CAL*)* Maybe you better find Simon and tell him to do it himself. He's to look in my desk, the left drawer, and bring my music album right away. Mr. Marshall is very anxious to see it because of his father and the opera in Chicago. *(To* ADDIE*)* Mr. Marshall is such a polite man with his manners and very educated and cultured and I've told him all about how my mama and papa used to go to Europe for the music—*(Laughs; to* ADDIE*)* Imagine going all the way to Europe just to listen to music. Wouldn't that be nice, Addie? Just to sit there and listen and— *(Turns and steps to* CAL*)* Left drawer, Cal. Tell him that twice because he forgets. And tell him not to let any of the things drop out of the album and to bring it right in here when he comes back.

The dining-room doors are opened and quickly closed by OSCAR HUBBARD. *He is a man in his late forties.*

CAL Yes'm. But Simon he won't get it right. But I'll tell him.

BIRDIE Left drawer, Cal, and tell him to bring the blue book and—

OSCAR *(sharply)* Birdie.

BIRDIE *(turning nervously)* Oh, Oscar. I was just sending Simon for my music album.

OSCAR *(to* CAL*)* Never mind about the album. Miss Birdie has changed her mind.

BIRDIE But, really, Oscar. Really I promised Mr. Marshall. I—

[CAL *looks at them, exits.*]

OSCAR Why do you leave the dinner table and go running about like a child?

BIRDIE *(trying to be gay)* But, Oscar, Mr. Marshall said most specially he *wanted* to see my album. I told him about the time Mama met Wagner, and Mrs. Wagner gave her the signed program and the big picture. Mr. Marshall wants to see that. Very, very much. We had such a nice talk and—

OSCAR *(taking a step to her)* You have been chattering to him like a magpie.

You haven't let him be for a second. I can't think he came South to be bored with you.

BIRDIE (*quickly, hurt*)   He wasn't bored. I don't believe he was bored. He's a very educated, cultured gentleman. (*Her voice rises.*) I just don't believe it. You always talk like that when I'm having a nice time.

OSCAR (*turning to her, sharply*)   You have had too much wine. Get yourself in hand now.

BIRDIE (*drawing back, about to cry, shrilly*)   What am I doing? I am not doing anything. What am I doing?

OSCAR (*taking a step to her, tensely*)   I said get yourself in hand. Stop acting like a fool.

BIRDIE (*turns to him, quietly*)   I don't believe he was bored. I just don't believe it. Some people like music and like to talk about it. That's all I was doing.

LEO HUBBARD *comes hurrying through the dining-room door. He is a young man of twenty, with a weak kind of good looks.*

LEO   Mama! Papa! They are coming in now.

OSCAR (*softly*)   Sit down, Birdie. Sit down now. (BIRDIE *sits down, bows her head as if to hide her face.*)

The dining-room doors are opened by CAL. *We see people beginning to rise from the table.* REGINA GIDDENS *comes in with* WILLIAM MARSHALL. REGINA *is a handsome woman of forty.* MARSHALL *is forty-five, pleasant-looking, self-possessed. Behind them comes* ALEXANDRA GIDDENS, *a very pretty, rather delicate-looking girl of seventeen. She is followed by* BENJAMIN HUBBARD, *fifty-five, with a large jovial face and the light graceful movements that one often finds in large men.*

REGINA   Mr. Marshall, I think you're trying to console me. Chicago may be the noisiest, dirtiest city in the world but I should still prefer it to the sound of our horses and the smell of our azaleas. I should like crowds of people, and theatres, and lovely women— *Very* lovely women, Mr. Marshall?

MARSHALL (*crossing to sofa*)   In Chicago? Oh, I suppose so. But I can tell you this: I've never dined there with three *such* lovely ladies.

ADDIE *begins to pass the port.*

BEN   Our Southern women are well favored.

LEO (*laughs*)   But one must go to Mobile for the ladies, sir. Very elegant worldly ladies, too.

BEN (*looks at him very deliberately*)   Worldly, eh? *Worldly,* did you say?

OSCAR (*hastily, to* LEO)   Your uncle Ben means that worldliness is not a mark of beauty in any woman.

LEO (*quickly*)   Of course, Uncle Ben. I didn't mean—

MARSHALL   Your port is excellent, Mrs. Giddens.

REGINA   Thank you, Mr. Marshall. We had been saving that bottle, hoping we could open it just for you.

ALEXANDRA (*as* ADDIE *comes to her with the tray*)   Oh. May I *really*, Addie?

ADDIE   Better ask Mama.

ALEXANDRA   May I, Mama?

REGINA (*nods, smiles*)   In Mr. Marshall's honor.

ALEXANDRA (*smiles*)   Mr. Marshall, this will be the first taste of port I've ever had.

ADDIE *serves* LEO.

MARSHALL   No one ever had their first taste of a better port. (*He lifts his glass in a toast; she lifts hers; they both drink.*) Well, I suppose it is all true, Mrs. Giddens.

REGINA   What is true?

MARSHALL   That you Southerners occupy a unique position in America. You live better than the rest of us, you eat better, you drink better. I wonder you find time, or want to find time, to do business.

BEN   A great many Southerners don't.

MARSHALL   Do all of you live here together?

REGINA   Here with me? (*Laughs*) Oh, no. My brother Ben lives next door. My brother Oscar and his family live in the next square.

BEN   But we are a very close family. We've always *wanted* it that way.

MARSHALL   That is very pleasant. Keeping your family together to share each other's lives. My family moves around too much. My children seem never to come home. Away at school in the winter; in the summer, Europe with their mother—

REGINA (*eagerly*)   Oh, yes. Even down here we read about Mrs. Marshall in the society pages.

MARSHALL   I dare say. She moves about a great deal. And all of you are part of the same business? Hubbard Sons?

BEN (*motions to* OSCAR)   Oscar and me. (*Motions to* REGINA) My sister's good husband is a banker.

MARSHALL (*looks at* REGINA, *surprised*)   Oh.

REGINA   I am so sorry that my husband isn't here to meet you. He's been very ill. He is at Johns Hopkins. But he will be home soon. We think he is getting better now.

LEO   I work for Uncle Horace. (REGINA *looks at him.*) I mean I work for Uncle Horace at his bank. I keep an eye on things while he's away.

REGINA (*smiles*)   Really, Leo?

BEN (*looks at* LEO, *then to* MARSHALL)   Modesty in the young is as excellent as it is rare. (*Looks at* LEO *again*)

OSCAR (*to* LEO)   Your uncle means that a young man should speak more modestly.

LEO (*hastily, taking a step to* BEN)   Oh, I didn't mean, sir—

MARSHALL   Oh, Mrs. Hubbard. Where's that Wagner autograph you promised to let me see? My train will be leaving soon and—

BIRDIE   The autograph? Oh. Well. Really, Mr. Marshall, I didn't mean to chatter so about it. Really I— *(Nervously, looking at* OSCAR*)* You must excuse me. I didn't get it because, well, because I had—I—I had a little headache and—

OSCAR   My wife is a miserable victim of headaches.

REGINA *(quickly)*   Mr. Marshall said at supper that he would like you to play for him, Alexandra.

ALEXANDRA *(who has been looking at* BIRDIE*)*   It's not I who play well, sir. It's my aunt. She plays just wonderfully. She's my teacher. *(Rises; eagerly)* May we play a duet? May we, Mama?

BIRDIE *(taking* ALEXANDRA'S *hand)*   Thank you, dear. But I have my headache now. I—

OSCAR *(sharply)*   Don't be stubborn, Birdie. Mr. Marshall wants you to play.

MARSHALL   Indeed I do. If your headache isn't—

BIRDIE *(hesitates, then gets up, pleased)*   But I'd like to, sir. Very much. *(She and* ALEXANDRA *go to the piano.)*

MARSHALL   It's very remarkable how you Southern aristocrats have kept together. Kept together and kept what belonged to you.

BEN   You misunderstand, sir. Southern aristocrats have *not* kept together and have *not* kept what belonged to them.

MARSHALL *(laughs, indicates room)*   You don't call this keeping what belongs to you?

BEN   But we are not aristocrats. *(Points to* BIRDIE *at the piano)* Our brother's wife is the only one of us who belongs to the Southern aristocracy.

BIRDIE *looks towards* BEN.

MARSHALL *(smiles)*   My information is that you people have been here, and solidly here, for a long time.

OSCAR   And so we have. Since our great-grandfather.

BEN *(smiles)*   Who was *not* an aristocrat, like Birdie's.

MARSHALL *(a little sharply)*   You make great distinctions.

BEN   Oh, they have been made for us. And maybe they are important distinctions. *(Leans forward, intimately)* Now you take Birdie's family. When my great-grandfather came here they were the highest-tone plantation owners in this state.

LEO *(steps to* MARSHALL, *proudly)*   My mother's grandfather was *governor* of the state before the war.

OSCAR   They owned the plantation, Lionnet. You may have heard of it, sir?

MARSHALL *(laughs)*   No, I've never heard of anything but brick houses on a lake, and cotton mills.

BEN   Lionnet in its day was the best cotton land in the South. It still brings us in a fair crop. *(Sits back)* Ah, they were great days for those people—even when I can remember. They had the best of everything. *(*BIRDIE *turns to* *them.)* Cloth from Paris, trips to Europe, horses you can't raise any more, niggers to lift their fingers—

BIRDIE *(suddenly)* We were good to our people. Everybody knew that. We were better to them than—

MARSHALL *looks up at* BIRDIE.

REGINA Why, Birdie. You aren't playing.

BEN But when the war comes these fine gentlemen ride off and leave the cotton, *and* the women, to rot.

BIRDIE My father was killed in the war. He was a fine soldier, Mr. Marshall. A fine man.

REGINA Oh, certainly, Birdie. A famous soldier.

BEN *(to* BIRDIE*)* But that isn't the tale I am telling Mr. Marshall. *(To* MAR-SHALL*)* Well, sir, the war ends. *(*BIRDIE *goes back to piano.)* Lionnet is almost ruined, and the sons finish ruining it. And there were thousands like them. Why? *(Leans forward)* Because the Southern aristocrat can adapt himself to nothing. Too high-tone to try.

MARSHALL Sometimes it is difficult to learn new ways. *(*BIRDIE *and* ALEXAN-DRA *begin to play.* MARSHALL *leans forward, listening.)*

BEN Perhaps, perhaps. *(He sees that* MARSHALL *is listening to the music. Irritated, he turns to* BIRDIE *and* ALEXANDRA *at the piano, then back to* MARSHALL.*)* You're right, Mr. Marshall. It is difficult to learn new ways. But maybe that's why it's profitable. *Our* grandfather and *our* father learned the new ways and learned how to make them pay. They work. *(Smiles nastily) They* are in trade. Hubbard Sons, Merchandise. Others, Birdie's family, for example, look down on them. *(Settles back in chair)* To make a long story short, Lionnet now belongs to *us.* *(*BIRDIE *stops playing.)* Twenty years ago we took over their land, their cotton, and their daughter. *(*BIRDIE *rises and stands stiffly by the piano.* MARSHALL, *who has been watching her, rises.)*

MARSHALL May I bring you a glass of port, Mrs. Hubbard?

BIRDIE *(softly)* No, thank you, sir. You are most polite.

REGINA *(sharply, to* BEN*)* You are boring Mr. Marshall with these ancient family tales.

BEN I hope not. I hope not. I am trying to make an important point—*(Bows to* MARSHALL*)* for our future business partner.

OSCAR *(to* MARSHALL*)* My brother always says that it's folks like us who have struggled and fought to bring to our land some of the prosperity of your land.

BEN Some people call that patriotis

REGINA *(laughs gaily)* I hope you don't find my brothers too obvious, Mr. Marshall. I'm afraid they mean that this is the time for the ladies to leave the gentlemen to talk business.

MARSHALL *(hastily)* Not at all. We settled everything this afternoon. *(*MAR-

SHALL *looks at his watch.)* I have only a few minutes before I must leave for
the train. *(Smiles at her)* And I insist they be spent with you.

REGINA   *And* with another glass of port.

MARSHALL   Thank you.

BEN *(to* REGINA*)*   My sister is right. *(To* MARSHALL*)* I am a plain man and I am
trying to say a plain thing. A man ain't only in business for what he can get
out of it. It's got to give him something here. *(Puts hand to his breast)* That's
every bit as true for the nigger picking cotton for a silver quarter, as it is for
you and me. *(*REGINA *gives* MARSHALL *a glass of port.)* If it don't give him
something here, then he don't pick the cotton right. Money isn't all. Not by
three shots.

MARSHALL   Really? Well, I always thought it was a great deal.

REGINA   And so did I, Mr. Marshall.

MARSHALL *(leans forward; pleasantly, but with meaning)*   Now you don't have to
convince me that you are the right people for the deal. I wouldn't be here if
you hadn't convinced me six months ago. You want the mill here, and I
want it here. It isn't my business to find out *why* you want it.

BEN   To bring the machine to the cotton, and not the cotton to the machine.

MARSHALL *(amused)*   You have a turn for neat phrases, Hubbard. Well, however grand your reasons are, mine are simple: I want to make money and I
believe I'll make it on you. *(As* BEN *starts to speak, he smiles.)* Mind you, I
have no objections to more high-minded reasons. They are mighty valuable
in business. It's fine to have partners who so closely follow the teachings of
Christ. *(Gets up)* And now I must leave for my train.

REGINA   I'm sorry you won't stay over with us, Mr. Marshall, but you'll come
again. Any time you like.

BEN *(motions to* LEO, *indicating the bottle)*   Fill them up, boy, fill them up. *(*LEO
moves around filling the glasses as BEN *speaks.)* Down here, sir, we have a
strange custom. We drink the *last* drink for a toast. That's to prove that the
Southerner is always still on his feet for the last drink. *(Picks up his glass)* It
was Henry Frick, your Mr. Henry Frick, who said, "Railroads are the
Rembrandts of investments." Well, *I* say, "Southern cotton mills *will be* the
Rembrandts of investment." So I give you the firm of Hubbard Sons and
Marshall, Cotton Mills, and to it a long and prosperous life.

They all pick up their glasses. MARSHALL *looks at them, amused. Then he, too,
lifts his glass, smiles.*

OSCAR   The children will drive you to the depot. Leo! Alexandra! You will
drive Mr. Marshall down.

LEO *(eagerly, looks at* BEN *who nods)*   Yes, sir. *(To* MARSHALL*)* Not often Uncle
Ben lets *me* drive the horses. And a beautiful pair they are. *(Starts for hall)*
Come on, Zan.

ALEXANDRA   May I drive tonight, Uncle Ben, please? I'd like to and—

BEN *(shakes his head, laughs)*   In your evening clothes? Oh, no, my dear.

ALEXANDRA   But Leo always—*(Stops, exits quickly)*
REGINA   I don't like to say good-bye to you, Mr. Marshall.
MARSHALL   Then we won't say good-bye. You have promised that you would
come and let me show you Chicago. Do I have to make you promise again?
REGINA *(looks at him as he presses her hand)*   I promise again.
MARSHALL *(touches her hand again, then moves to* BIRDIE*)*   Good-bye, Mrs.
Hubbard.
BIRDIE *(shyly, with sweetness and dignity)*   Good-bye, sir.
MARSHALL *(as he passes* REGINA*)*   Remember.
REGINA   I will.
OSCAR   We'll see you to the carriage.

[MARSHALL *exits, followed by* BEN *and* OSCAR.]

For a second REGINA *and* BIRDIE *stand looking after them. Then* REGINA
throws up her arms, laughs happily.

REGINA   And there, Birdie, goes the man who has opened the door to our
future.
BIRDIE *(surprised at the unaccustomed friendliness)*   What?
REGINA *(turning to her)*   *Our future.* Yours and mine, Ben's and Oscar's, the
children— *(Looks at* BIRDIE'S *puzzled face, laughs)* Our future! *(Gaily)* You
were charming at supper, Birdie. Mr. Marshall certainly thought so.
BIRDIE *(pleased)*   Why, Regina! Do you think he did?
REGINA   Can't you tell when you're being admired?
BIRDIE   Oscar said I bored Mr. Marshall. *(Then quietly)* But he admired *you.*
He told me so.
REGINA   What did he say?
BIRDIE   He said to me, "I hope your sister-in-law will come to Chicago.
Chicago will be at her feet." He said the ladies would bow to your manners
and the gentlemen to your looks.
REGINA   Did he? He seems a lonely man. Imagine being lonely with all that
money. I don't think he likes his wife.
BIRDIE   Not like his wife? What a thing to say.
REGINA   She's away a great deal. He said that several times. And once he made
fun of her being so social and high-tone. But that fits in all right. *(Sits back,
arms on back of sofa, stretches)* Her being social, I mean. She can introduce
me. It won't take long with an introduction from her.
BIRDIE *(bewildered)*   Introduce you? In Chicago? You mean you really might
go? Oh, Regina, you can't leave here. What about Horace?
REGINA   Don't look so scared about everything, Birdie. I'm going to live in
Chicago. I've always wanted to. And now there'll be plenty of money to go
with.
BIRDIE   But Horace won't be able to move around. You know what the doctor
wrote.
REGINA   There'll be millions, Birdie, millions. You know what I've always said
when people told me we were rich? I said I think you should either be a

nigger or a millionaire. In between, like us, what for? (*Laughs; looks at* BIRDIE) But I'm not going away tomorrow, Birdie. There's plenty of time to worry about Horace when he comes home. If he ever decides to come home.

BIRDIE   Will we be going to Chicago? I mean, Oscar and Leo and me?

REGINA   You? I shouldn't think so. (*Laughs*) Well, we must remember tonight. It's a very important night and we mustn't forget it. We shall plan all the things we'd like to have and then we'll really have them. Make a wish, Birdie, any wish. It's bound to come true now.

BEN *and* OSCAR *enter*.

BIRDIE (*laughs*)   Well. Well, I don't know. Maybe. (REGINA *turns to look at* BEN.) Well, I guess I'd know right off what I wanted.

OSCAR *stands by the upper window, waves to the departing carriage.*

REGINA (*looks up at* BEN, *smiles. He smiles back at her.*)   Well, you did it.

BEN   Looks like it might be we did.

REGINA (*springs up, laughs*)   Looks like it! Don't pretend. You're like a cat who's been licking the cream. (*Crosses to wine bottle*) Now we must all have a drink to celebrate.

OSCAR   The children, Alexandra and Leo, make a very handsome couple, Regina. Marshall remarked himself what fine young folks they were. How well they looked together!

REGINA (*sharply*)   Yes. You said that before, Oscar.

BEN   Yes, sir. It's beginning to look as if the deal's all set. I may not be a subtle man—but— (*Turns to them; after a second*) Now somebody ask me how I know the deal is set.

OSCAR   What do you mean, Ben?

BEN   You remember I told him that down here we drink the *last* drink for a toast?

OSCAR (*thoughtfully*)   Yes. I never heard that before.

BEN   Nobody's ever heard it before. God forgives those who invent what they need. I already had his signature. But we've all done business with men whose word over a glass is better than a bond. Anyway it don't hurt to have both.

OSCAR (*turns to* REGINA)   You understand what Ben means?

REGINA (*smiles*)   Yes, Oscar. I understand. I understood immediately.

BEN (*looks at her admiringly*)   Did you, Regina? Well, when he lifted his glass to drink, I closed my eyes and saw the bricks going into place.

REGINA   And *I* saw a lot more than that.

BEN   Slowly, slowly. As yet we have only our hopes.

REGINA   Birdie and I have just been planning what we want. I know what I want. What will you want, Ben?

BEN   Caution. Don't count the chickens. (*Leans back, laughs*) Well, God would allow us a little daydreaming. Good for the soul when you've worked hard enough to deserve it. *(Pauses)* I think I'll have a stable. For a long time I've had my good eyes on Carter's in Savannah. A rich man's pleasure, the sport of kings, why not the sport of Hubbards? Why not?

REGINA *(smiles)*   Why not? What will you have, Oscar?

OSCAR   I don't know. *(Thoughtfully)* The pleasure of seeing the bricks grow will be enough for me.

BEN   Oh, of course. Our *greatest* pleasure will be to see the bricks grow. But we are all entitled to a little side indulgence.

OSCAR   Yes, I suppose so. Well, then, I think we might take a few trips here and there, eh, Birdie?

BIRDIE *(surprised at being consulted)*   Yes, Oscar. I'd like that.

OSCAR   We might even make a regular trip to Jekyll Island. I've heard the Cornelly place is for sale. We might think about buying it. Make a nice change. Do you good, Birdie, a change of climate. Fine shooting on Jekyll, the best.

BIRDIE   I'd like—

OSCAR *(indulgently)*   What would you like?

BIRDIE   *Two* things. Two things I'd like most.

REGINA   Two! I should like a thousand. You are modest, Birdie.

BIRDIE *(warmly delighted with the unexpected interest)*   I should like to have Lionnet back. I know you own it now, but I'd like to see it fixed up again, the way Mama and Papa had it. Every year it used to get a nice coat of paint—Papa was very particular about the paint—and the lawn was so smooth all the way down to the river, with the trims of zinnias and red-feather plush. And the figs and blue little plums and the scuppernongs— *(Smiles; turns to* REGINA*)* The organ is still there and it wouldn't cost much to fix. We could have parties for Zan, the way Mama used to have for me.

BEN   That's a pretty picture, Birdie. Might be a most pleasant way to live. *(Dismissing* BIRDIE*)* What do you want, Regina?

BIRDIE *(very happily, not noticing that they are no longer listening to her)*   I could have a cutting garden. Just where Mama's used to be. Oh, I do think we could be happier there. Papa used to say that *nobody* had ever lost their temper at Lionnet, and *nobody* ever would. Papa would never let anybody be nasty-spoken or mean. No, sir. He just didn't like it.

BEN   What do you want, Regina?

REGINA   I'm going to Chicago. And when I'm settled there and know the right people and the right things to buy—because I certainly don't now—I shall go to Paris and buy them. *(Laughs)* I'm going to leave you and Oscar to count the bricks.

BIRDIE   Oscar. Please let me have Lionnet back.

OSCAR *(to* REGINA*)*   You are serious about moving to Chicago?

BEN   She is going to see the great world and leave us in the little one. Well, we'll come and visit you and meet all the great and be proud to think you are our sister.

REGINA *(gaily)*   Certainly. And you won't even have to learn to be subtle, Ben. Stay as you are. You will be rich and the rich don't have to be subtle.

OSCAR   But what about Alexandra? She's seventeen. Old enough to be thinking about marrying.

BIRDIE   And, Oscar, I have one more wish. Just one more wish.

OSCAR *(turns)*   What is it, Birdie? What are you saying?

BIRDIE   I want you to stop shooting. I mean, so much. I don't like to see animals and birds killed just for the killing. You only throw them away—

BEN *(to* REGINA*)*   It'll take a great deal of money to live as you're planning, Regina.

REGINA   Certainly. But there'll be plenty of money. You have estimated the profits very high.

BEN   I have—

BIRDIE *(*OSCAR *is looking at her furiously)*   And you never let anybody else shoot, and the niggers need it so much to keep from starving. It's wicked to shoot food just because you like to shoot, when poor people need it so—

BEN *(laughs)*   I have estimated the profits very high—for myself.

REGINA   What did you say?

BIRDIE   I've always wanted to speak about it, Oscar.

OSCAR *(slowly, carefully)*   What are you chattering about?

BIRDIE *(nervously)*   I was talking about Lionnet and—and about your shooting—

OSCAR   You are exciting yourself.

REGINA *(to* BEN*)*   I didn't hear you. There was so much talking.

OSCAR *(to* BIRDIE*)*   You have been acting very childish, very excited, all evening.

BIRDIE   Regina asked me what I'd like.

REGINA   What did you say, Ben?

BIRDIE   Now that we'll be so rich everybody was saying what they would like, so *I* said what *I* would like, too.

BEN   I said— *(He is interrupted by* OSCAR.*)*

OSCAR *(to* BIRDIE*)*   Very well. We've all heard you. That's enough now.

BEN   I am waiting. *(They stop.)* I am waiting for you to finish. You and Birdie. Four conversations are three too many. *(*BIRDIE *slowly sits down.* BEN *smiles, to* REGINA.*)* I said that I had, and I do, estimate the profits very high—for myself, and Oscar, of course.

REGINA *(slowly)*   And what does that mean?

BEN *shrugs, looks towards* OSCAR.

OSCAR *(looks at* BEN, *clears throat)*   Well, Regina, it's like this. For forty-nine per cent Marshall will put up four hundred thousand dollars. For fifty-one per cent—*(Smiles archly)* a controlling interest, mind you, we will put up two hundred and twenty-five thousand dollars besides offering him certain benefits that our (*Looks at* BEN) local position allows us to manage. Ben means that two hundred and twenty-five thousand dollars is a lot of money.

REGINA   I know the terms and I know it's a lot of money.

BEN (*nodding*)   It is.

OSCAR   Ben means that we are ready with our two-thirds of the money. Your third, Horace's I mean, doesn't seem to be ready. (*Raises his hand as* REGINA *starts to speak*) Ben has written to Horace, I have written, and you have written. He answers. But he never mentions this business. Yet we have explained it to him in great detail and told him the urgency. Still he never mentions it. Ben has been very patient, Regina. Naturally, you are our sister and we want you to benefit from anything we do.

REGINA   And in addition to your concern for me, you do not want control to go out of the family. (*To* BEN) That right, Ben?

BEN   That's cynical. (*Smiles*) Cynicism is an unpleasant way of saying the truth.

OSCAR   No need to be cynical. We'd have no trouble raising the third share, the share that you want to take.

REGINA   I am sure you could get the third share, the share you were saving for me. But that would give you a strange partner. And strange partners sometimes want a great deal. (*Smiles unpleasantly*) But perhaps it would be wise for you to find him.

OSCAR   Now, now. Nobody says we *want* to do that. We would like to have you in and you would like to come in.

REGINA   Yes. I certainly would.

BEN (*laughs, puts up his hand*)   But we haven't heard from Horace.

REGINA   I've given my word that Horace will put up the money. That should be enough.

BEN   Oh, it was enough. I took your word. But I've got to have more than your word now. The contracts will be signed this week, and Marshall will want to see our money soon after. Regina, Horace has been in Baltimore for five months. I know that you've written him to come home, and that he hasn't come.

OSCAR   It's beginning to look as if he doesn't want to come home.

REGINA   Of course he wants to come home. You can't move around with heart trouble at any moment you choose. You know what doctors are like once they get their hands on a case like this—

OSCAR   They can't very well keep him from answering letters, can they? (REGINA *turns to* BEN.) They couldn't keep him from arranging for the money if he wanted to—

REGINA   Has it occurred to you that Horace is also a good business man?

BEN   Certainly. He is a shrewd trader. Always has been. The bank is proof of that.

REGINA   Then, possibly, he may be keeping silent because he doesn't think he is getting enough for his money. (*Looks at* OSCAR) Seventy-five thousand he has to put up. That's a lot of money, too.

OSCAR   Nonsense. He knows a good thing when he hears it. He knows that we can make *twice* the profit on cotton goods manufactured *here* than can be made in the North.

BEN   That isn't what Regina means. *(Smiles)* May I interpret you, Regina? *(To* OSCAR*)* Regina is saying that Horace wants *more* than a third of our share.

OSCAR   But he's only putting up a third of the money. You put up a third and you get a third. What else *could* he expect?

REGINA   Well, *I* don't know. I don't know about these things. It would seem that if you put up a third you should only get a third. But then again, there's no law about it, is there? I should think that if you knew your money was very badly needed, well, you just might say, I want more, I want a bigger share. You boys have done that. I've heard you say so.

BEN   *(after a pause, laughs)* So you believe he has deliberately held out? For a larger share? *(Leaning forward)* Well, I *don't* believe it. But I *do* believe that's what *you* want. Am I right, Regina?

REGINA   Oh, I shouldn't like to be too definite. But I *could* say that I wouldn't like to persuade Horace unless he did get a larger share. I must look after his interests. It seems only natural—

OSCAR   And where would the larger share come from?

REGINA   I don't know. That's not my business. *(Giggles)* But perhaps it could come off your share, Oscar.

REGINA *and* BEN *laugh.*

OSCAR *(rises and wheels furiously on both of them as they laugh)*   What kind of talk is this?

BEN   I haven't said a thing.

OSCAR *(to* REGINA*)*   You are talking very big tonight.

REGINA *(stops laughing)*   Am I? Well, you should know me well enough to know that I wouldn't be asking for things I didn't think I could get.

OSCAR   Listen. I don't believe you can even get Horace to come home, much less get money from him or talk quite so big about what you want.

REGINA   Oh, I can get him home.

OSCAR   Then why haven't you?

REGINA   I thought I should fight his battles for him, before he came home. Horace is a very sick man. And even if *you* don't care how sick he is, I do.

BEN   Stop this foolish squabbling. How can you get him home?

REGINA   I will send Alexandra to Baltimore. She will ask him to come home. She will say that she *wants* him to come home, and that *I* want him to come home.

BIRDIE *(suddenly)*   Well, of course she wants him here, but he's sick and maybe he's happy where he is.

REGINA *(ignores* BIRDIE, *to* BEN*)*   You agree that he will come home if she asks him to, if she says that I miss him and want him—

BEN *(looks at her, smiles)*   I admire you, Regina. And I agree. That's settled now and— *(Starts to rise)*

REGINA *(quickly)* But before she brings him home, I want to know what he's going to get.

BEN What do you want?

REGINA Twice what you offered.

BEN Well, you won't get it.

OSCAR *(to REGINA)* I think you've gone crazy.

REGINA I don't want to fight, Ben—

BEN I don't either. You won't get it. There isn't any chance of that *(Roguishly)* You're holding us up, and that's not pretty, Regina, not pretty. *(Holds up his hand as he sees she is about to speak)* But we need you, and I don't want to fight. Here's what I'll do: I'll give Horace forty per cent instead of the thirty-three and a third he really should get. I'll do that, provided he is home and his money is up within two weeks. How's that?

REGINA All right.

OSCAR I've asked before: where is this extra share coming from?

BEN *(pleasantly)* From you. From your share.

OSCAR *(furiously)* From me, is it? That's just fine and dandy. That's my reward. For thirty-five years I've worked my hands to the bone for you. For thirty-five years I've done all the things you didn't want to do. And this is what I—

BEN *(turns slowly to look at OSCAR. OSCAR breaks off.)* My, my. I am being attacked tonight on all sides. First by my sister, then by my brother. And I ain't a man who likes being attacked. I can't believe that God wants the strong to parade their strength, but I don't mind doing it if it's got to be done. *(Leans back in his chair)* You ought to take these things better, Oscar. I've made you money in the past. I'm going to make you more money now. You'll be a very rich man. What's the difference to any of us if a little more goes here, a little less goes there—it's all in the family. And it will stay in the family. I'll never marry. *(ADDIE enters, begins to gather the glasses from the table. OSCAR turns to BEN.)* So my money will go to Alexandra and Leo. They may even marry some day and— *(ADDIE looks at BEN.)*

BIRDIE *(rising)* Marry—Zan and Leo—

OSCAR *(carefully)* That would make a great difference in my feelings. If they married.

BEN Yes, that's what I mean. Of course it would make a difference.

OSCAR *(carefully)* Is that what *you* mean, Regina?

REGINA Oh, it's too far away. We'll talk about it in a few years.

OSCAR I want to talk about it now.

BEN *(nods)* Naturally.

REGINA There's a lot of things to consider. They are first cousins, and—

OSCAR That isn't unusual. Our grandmother and grandfather were first cousins.

REGINA *(giggles)* And look at us.

BEN *giggles.*

OSCAR *(angrily)* You're both being very gay with my money.

BEN *(sighs)*   These quarrels. I dislike them so. *(Leans forward to* REGINA*)* A marriage might be a very wise arrangement, for several reasons. And then, Oscar has given up something for you. You should try to manage something for him.

REGINA   I haven't said I was opposed to it. But Leo is a wild boy. There were those times when he took a little money from the bank and—

OSCAR   That's all past history—

REGINA   Oh, I know. And I know all young men are wild. I'm only mentioning it to show you that there are considerations—

BEN *(irritated because she does not understand that he is trying to keep* OSCAR *quiet)*   All right, so there are. But please assure Oscar that you will think about it very seriously.

REGINA *(smiles, nods)*   Very well. I assure Oscar I will think about it seriously.

OSCAR *(sharply)*   That is not an answer.

REGINA *(rises)*   My, you're in a bad humor and you shall put me in one. I have said all that I am willing to say now. After all, Horace has to give his consent, too.

OSCAR   Horace will do what you tell him to.

REGINA   Yes, I think he will.

OSCAR   And I have your word that you will try to—

REGINA *(patiently)*   Yes, Oscar. You have my word that I will think about it. Now do leave me alone.

There is the sound of the front door being closed.

BIRDIE   I—Alexandra is only seventeen. She—

REGINA *(calling)*   Alexandra? Are you back?

ALEXANDRA   Yes, Mama.

LEO *(comes into the room)*   Mr. Marshall got off safe and sound. Weren't those fine clothes he had? You can always spot clothes made in a good place. Looks like maybe they were done in England. Lots of men in the North send all the way to England for their stuff.

BEN *(to* LEO*)*   Were you careful driving the horses?

LEO   Oh, yes, sir. I was.

ALEXANDRA *has come in on* BEN'S *question, hears the answer, looks angrily at* LEO.

ALEXANDRA   It's a lovely night. You should have come, Aunt Birdie.

REGINA   Were you gracious to Mr. Marshall?

ALEXANDRA   I think so, Mama. I liked him.

REGINA   Good. And now I have great news for you. You are going to Baltimore in the morning to bring your father home.

ALEXANDRA *(gasps, then delighted)*   Me? Papa said I should come? That must mean— *(Turns to* ADDIE*)* Addie, he must be well. Think of it, he'll be back home again. We'll bring him home.

REGINA   You are going alone, Alexandra.

ADDIE (ALEXANDRA *has turned in surprise*)   Going alone? Going by herself? A child that age! Mr. Horace ain't going to like Zan traipsing up there by herself.

REGINA (*sharply*)   Go upstairs and lay out Alexandra's things.

ADDIE   He'd expect me to be along—

REGINA   I'll be up in a few minutes to tell you what to pack. (ADDIE *slowly begins to climb the steps. To* ALEXANDRA) I should think you'd like going alone. At your age it certainly would have delighted me. You're a strange girl, Alexandra. Addie has babied you so much.

ALEXANDRA   I only thought it would be more fun if Addie and I went together.

BIRDIE (*timidly*)   Maybe I could go with her, Regina. I'd really like to.

REGINA   She is going alone. She is getting old enough to take some responsibilities.

OSCAR   She'd better learn now. She's almost old enough to get married. (*Jovially, to* LEO, *slapping him on shoulder*) Eh, son?

LEO   Huh?

OSCAR (*annoyed with* LEO *for not understanding*)   Old enough to get married, you're thinking, eh?

LEO   Oh, yes, sir. (*Feebly*) Lots of girls get married at Zan's age. Look at Mary Prester and Johanna and—

REGINA   Well, she's not getting married tomorrow. But she is going to Baltimore tomorrow, so let's talk about that. (*To* ALEXANDRA) You'll be glad to have Papa home again.

ALEXANDRA   I wanted to go before, Mama. You remember that. But you said *you* couldn't go, and that *I* couldn't go alone.

REGINA   I've changed my mind. (*Too casually*) You're to tell Papa how much you missed him, and that he must come home now—for your sake. Tell him that you *need* him home.

ALEXANDRA   Need him home? I don't understand.

REGINA   There is nothing for you to understand. You are simply to say what I have told you.

BIRDIE (*rises*)   He may be too sick. She couldn't do that—

ALEXANDRA   Yes. He may be too sick to travel. I couldn't make him think he had to come home for me, if he is too sick to—

REGINA (*looks at her, sharply, challengingly*)   You *couldn't* do what I tell you to do, Alexandra?

ALEXANDRA (*quietly*)   No. I couldn't. If I thought it would hurt him.

REGINA (*after a second's silence, smiles pleasantly*)   But you are doing this for Papa's own good. (*Takes* ALEXANDRA'S *hand*) You must let me be the judge of his condition. It's the best possible cure for him to come home and be taken care of here. He mustn't stay there any longer and listen to those alarmist doctors. You are doing this entirely for his sake. Tell your papa that I want him to come home, that I miss him very much.

ALEXANDRA (*slowly*) Yes, Mama.

REGINA (*to the others; rises*)   I must go and start getting Alexandra ready now. Why don't you all go home?

BEN (*rises*) I'll attend to the railroad ticket. One of the boys will bring it over. Good night, everybody. Have a nice trip, Alexandra. The food on the train is very good. The celery is so crisp. Have a good time and act like a little lady.   [*Exits.*]

REGINA   Good night, Ben. Good night Oscar— (*Playfully*) Don't be so glum, Oscar. It makes you look as if you had chronic indigestion.

BIRDIE Good night, Regina.

REGINA   Good night, Birdie.   [*Exits upstairs.*]

OSCAR (*starts for hall*) Come along.

LEO (*to* ALEXANDRA)   Imagine your not wanting to go! What a little fool you are. Wish it were me. What I could do in a place like Baltimore!

ALEXANDRA (*angrily, looking away from him*)   Mind your business. I can guess the kind of things *you* could do.

LEO (*laughs*) Oh, no, you couldn't.   [*He exits.*]

REGINA (*calling from the top of the stairs*)   Come on, Alexandra.

BIRDIE (*quickly, softly*) Zan.

ALEXANDRA   I don't understand about my going, Aunt Birdie. (*Shrugs*) But anyway, Papa will be home again. (*Pats* BIRDIE's *arm*) Don't worry about me. I can take care of myself. Really I can.

BIRDIE (*shakes her head, softly*)   That's not what I'm worried about. Zan—

ALEXANDRA (*comes close to her*)   What's the matter?

BIRDIE   It's about Leo—

ALEXANDRA (*whispering*)   He beat the horses. That's why we were late getting back. We had to wait until they cooled off. He always beats the horses as if—

BIRDIE (*whispering frantically, holding* ALEXANDRA's *hands*)   He's my son. My own son. But you are more to me—more to me than my own child. I love you more than anybody else—

ALEXANDRA   Don't worry about the horses. I'm sorry I told you.

BIRDIE (*her voice rising*)   *I am not worrying about the horses.* I am worrying about *you.* You are *not* going to marry Leo. I am not going to let them do that to you—

ALEXANDRA   Marry? To Leo? (*Laughs*) I wouldn't marry, Aunt Birdie. I've never even thought about it—

BIRDIE   But they have thought about it. (*Wildly*) Zan, I couldn't stand to think about such a thing. You and—

OSCAR *has come into the doorway on* ALEXANDRA's *speech. He is standing quietly, listening.*

ALEXANDRA (*laughs*)   But I'm not going to marry. And I'm certainly not going to marry Leo.

BIRDIE   Don't you understand? They'll make you. They'll make you—
ALEXANDRA (*takes* BIRDIE'S *hands, quietly, firmly*)   That's foolish, Aunt Birdie. I'm grown now. Nobody can make me do anything.
BIRDIE   I just couldn't stand—
OSCAR (*sharply*)   Birdie. (BIRDIE *looks up, draws quickly away from* ALEXAN-DRA. *She stands rigid, frightened. Quietly*) Birdie, get your hat and coat.
ADDIE (*calls from upstairs*)   Come on, baby. Your mama's waiting for you, and she ain't nobody to keep waiting.
ALEXANDRA   All right. (*Then softly, embracing* BIRDIE) Good night, Aunt Birdie. (*As she passes* OSCAR) Good night, Uncle Oscar. (BIRDIE *begins to move slowly towards the door as* ALEXANDRA *climbs the stairs.* ALEXANDRA *is almost out of view when* BIRDIE *reaches* OSCAR *in the doorway. As* BIRDIE *quickly attempts to pass him, he slaps her hard, across the face.* BIRDIE *cries out, puts her hand to her face. On the cry,* ALEXANDRA *turns, begins to run down the stairs.*) Aunt Birdie! What happened? What happened? I—
BIRDIE (*softly, without turning*)   Nothing, darling. Nothing happened. (*Quickly, as if anxious to keep* ALEXANDRA *from coming close*) Now go to bed. (OSCAR *exits.*) Nothing happened. (*Turns to* ALEXANDRA, *who is holding her hand.*) I only—I only twisted my ankle. (*She goes out.* ALEXANDRA *stands on the stairs looking after her as if she were puzzled and frightened.*)

ACT II

Scene: *Same as Act One. A week later, morning.*

At Rise: *The light comes from the open shutter of the right window; the other shutters are tightly closed.* ADDIE *is standing at the window, looking out. Near the dining-room doors are brooms, mops, rags, etc. After a second,* OSCAR *comes into the entrance hall, looks in the room, shivers, decides not to take his hat and coat off, comes into the room. At the sound of the door,* ADDIE *turns to see who has come in.*

ADDIE (*without interest*)   Oh, it's you, Mr. Oscar.
OSCAR   What is this? It's not night. What's the matter here? (*Shivers*) Fine thing at this time of the morning. Blinds all closed. (ADDIE *begins to open shutters.*) Where's Miss Regina? It's cold in here.
ADDIE   Miss Regina ain't down yet.
OSCAR   She had any word?
ADDIE (*wearily*)   No, sir.
OSCAR   Wouldn't you think a girl that age could get on a train at one place and have sense enough to get off at another?
ADDIE   Something must have happened. If Zan say she was coming last night,

she's coming last night. Unless something happened. Sure fire disgrace to
let a baby like that go all that way alone to bring home a sick man without—

OSCAR   You do a lot of judging around here, Addie, eh? Judging of your white
folks, I mean.

ADDIE *(looks at him, sighs)*   I'm tired. I been up all night watching for them.

REGINA *(speaking from the upstairs hall)*   Who's downstairs, Addie? *(She appears
in a dressing gown, peers down from the landing.* ADDIE *picks up broom,
dustpan and brush and exits.)* Oh, it's you Oscar. What are you doing here so
early? I haven't been down yet. I'm not finished dressing.

OSCAR *(speaking up to her)*   You had any word from them?

REGINA   No.

OSCAR   Then something certainly has happened. People don't just say they are
arriving on Thursday night, and they haven't come by Friday morning.

REGINA   Oh, nothing has happened. Alexandra just hasn't got sense enough to
send a message.

OSCAR   If nothing's happened, then why aren't they here?

REGINA   You asked me that ten times last night. My, you do fret so, Oscar.
Anything might have happened. They may have missed connections in
Atlanta, the train may have been delayed—oh, a hundred things could have
kept them.

OSCAR   Where's Ben?

REGINA *(as she disappears upstairs)*   Where should he be? At home, probably.
Really, Oscar, I don't tuck him in his bed and I don't take him out of it.
Have some coffee and don't worry so much.

OSCAR   Have some coffee? There isn't any coffee. *(Looks at his watch, shakes his
head. After a second* CAL *enters with a large silver tray, coffee urn, small cups,
newspaper.)* Oh, there you are. Is everything in this fancy house always late?

CAL *(looks at him, surprised)*   You ain't out shooting this morning, Mr. Oscar?

OSCAR   First day I missed since I had my head cold. First day I missed in eight
years.

CAL   Yes, sir. I bet you. Simon he say you had a mighty good day yesterday
morning. That's what Simon say. *(Brings* OSCAR *coffee and newspaper)*

OSCAR   Pretty good, pretty good.

CAL *(laughs, slyly)*   Bet you got enough bobwhite and squirrel to give every
nigger in town a Jesus-party. Most of 'em ain't had no meat since the cotton
picking was over. Bet they'd give anything for a little piece of that meat—

OSCAR *(turns his head to look at* CAL)   Cal, if I catch a nigger in this town going
shooting, you know what's going to happen.

LEO *enters.*

CAL *(hastily)*   Yes, sir, Mr. Oscar. I didn't say nothing about nothing. It was
Simon who told me and— Morning, Mr. Leo. You gentlemen having your
breakfast with us here?

LEO   The boys in the bank don't know a thing. They haven't had any message.
         [CAL *waits for an answer, gets none, shrugs, moves to door, exits.*]
OSCAR *(peers at* LEO*)*   What you doing here, son?
LEO   You told me to find out if the boys at the bank had any message from
         Uncle Horace or Zan—
OSCAR   I told you if they had a message to bring it here. I told you that if they
         didn't have a message to stay at the bank and do your work.
LEO   Oh, I guess I misunderstood.
OSCAR   You didn't misunderstand. You just were looking for any excuse to
         take an hour off. *(*LEO *pours a cup of coffee.)* You got to stop that kind of
         thing. You got to start settling down. You going to be a married man one of
         these days.
LEO   Yes, sir.
OSCAR   You also got to stop with that woman in Mobile. *(As* LEO *is about to
         speak)* You're young and I haven't got no objections to outside women.
         That is, I haven't got no objections as long as they don't interfere with
         serious things. Outside women are all right in their place, but *now* isn't their
         place. You got to realize that.
LEO *(nods)*   Yes, sir. I'll tell her. She'll act all right about it.
OSCAR   Also, you got to start working harder at the bank. You got to convince
         your Uncle Horace you going to make a fit husband for Alexandra.
LEO   What do you think has happened to them? Supposed to be here last
         night— *(Laughs)* Bet you Uncle Ben's mighty worried. Seventy-five thou-
         sand dollars worried.
OSCAR *(smiles happily)*   Ought to be worried. Damn well ought to be. First he
         don't answer the letters, then he don't come home— *(Giggles)*
LEO   What will happen if Uncle Horace don't come home or don't—
OSCAR   Or don't put up the money? Oh, we'll get it from outside. Easy
         enough.
LEO *(surprised)*   But *you* don't want outsiders.
OSCAR   What do I care who gets my share? I been shaved already. Serve Ben
         right if he had to give away some of his.
LEO   Damn shame what they did to you.
OSCAR *(looking up the stairs)*   Don't talk so loud. Don't you worry. When I die,
         you'll have as much as the rest. You might have yours *and* Alexandra's. I'm
         not so easily licked.
LEO   I wasn't thinking of myself, Papa—
OSCAR   Well, you should be, you should be. It's every man's duty to think of
         himself.
LEO   You think Uncle Horace don't want to go in on this?
OSCAR *(giggles)*   That's my hunch. He hasn't showed any signs of loving it yet.
LEO *(laughs)*   But he hasn't listened to Aunt Regina yet, either. Oh, he'll go
         along. It's too good a thing. Why wouldn't he want to? He's got plenty and
         plenty to invest with. He don't even have to sell anything. Eighty-eight
         thousand worth of Union Pacific bonds sitting right in his safe-deposit box.
         All he's got to do is open the box.

OSCAR   *(after a pause, looks at his watch)* Mighty late breakfast in this fancy
     house. Yes, he's had those bonds for fifteen years. Bought them when they
     were low and just locked them up.

LEO   Yea. Just has to open the box and take them out. That's all. Easy as easy
     can be. *(Laughs)* The things in that box! There's all those bonds, looking
     mighty fine. *(OSCAR slowly puts down his newspaper and turns to* LEO.*)* Then
     right next to them is a baby shoe of Zan's and a cheap old cameo on a string,
     and, *and*—nobody'd believe this—a piece of an old violin. Not even a
     whole violin. Just a piece of an old thing, a piece of a violin.

OSCAR   *(very softly, as if he were trying to control his voice)*   A piece of a violin!
     What do you think of that!

LEO   Yes sirree. A lot of other crazy things, too. A poem, I guess it is, signed
     with his mother's name, and two old schoolbooks with notes and— *(LEO
     catches* OSCAR'S *look. His voice trails off. He turns his head away.)*

OSCAR   *(very softly)*   How do you know what's in the box, son?

LEO   *(stops, draws back, frightened, realizing what he has said)*   Oh, well. Well, er.
     Well, one of the boys, sir. It was one of the boys at the bank. He took old
     Manders' keys. It was Joe Horns. He just up and took Manders' keys and,
     and—well, took the box out. *(Quickly)* Then they all asked me if I wanted
     to see, too. So I looked a little, I guess, but then I made them close up the
     box quick and I told them never—

OSCAR   *(looks at him)*   Joe Horns, you say? He opened it?

LEO   Yes, sir, yes, he did. My word of honor. *(Very nervously looking away)* I
     suppose that don't excuse *me* for looking— *(Looking at* OSCAR*)* but I did
     make him close it up and put the keys back in Manders' drawer—

OSCAR   *(leans forward, very softly)*   Tell me the truth, Leo. I am not going to be
     angry with you. Did you open the box yourself?

LEO   *No, sir, I didn't.* I told you I didn't. No, I—

OSCAR   *(irritated, patient)*   I am *not* going to be angry with you. *(Watching* LEO
     carefully) Sometimes a young fellow deserves credit for looking round him
     to see what's going on. Sometimes that's a good sign in a fellow your age.
     (OSCAR rises.) Many great men have made their fortune with their eyes.
     Did you open the box?

LEO   *(very puzzled)*   No. I—

OSCAR   *(moves to* LEO*)*   Did you open the box? It may have been—well, it may
     have been a good thing if you had.

LEO   *(after a long pause)*   I opened it.

OSCAR   *(quickly)*   Is that the truth? *(LEO nods.)* Does anybody else know that
     you opened it? Come, Leo, don't be afraid of speaking the truth to me.

LEO   No. Nobody knew. Nobody was in the bank when I did it. But—

OSCAR   Did your Uncle Horace ever know you opened it?

LEO   *(shakes his head)*   He only looks in it once every six months when he cuts
     the coupons, and sometimes Manders even does that for him. Uncle
     Horace don't even have the keys. Manders keeps them for him. Imagine
     not looking at all that. You can bet if I had the bonds, I'd watch 'em like—

OSCAR   If you had them. *(LEO watches him.)* If you had them. Then you could have a share in the mill, you and me. A fine, big share, too. *(Pauses, shrugs)* Well, a man can't be shot for wanting to see his son get on in the world, can he, boy?

LEO *(looks up, begins to understand)*   No, he can't. Natural enough. *(Laughs)* But I haven't got the bonds and Uncle Horace has. And now he can just sit back and wait to be a millionaire.

OSCAR *(innocently)*   You think your Uncle Horace likes you well enough to lend you the bonds if he decides not to use them himself?

LEO   Papa, it must be that you haven't had your breakfast! *(Laughs loudly)* Lend me the bonds! My God—

OSCAR *(disappointed)*   No, I suppose not. Just a fancy of mine. A loan for three months, maybe four, easy enough for us to pay it back then. Anyway, this is only April— *(Slowly counting the months on his fingers)* and if he doesn't look at them until Fall, he wouldn't even miss them out of the box.

LEO   That's it. He wouldn't even miss them. Ah, well—

OSCAR   No, sir. Wouldn't even miss them. How could he miss them if he never looks at them? *(Sighs as* LEO *stares at him)* Well, here we are sitting around waiting for him to come home and invest his money in something he hasn't lifted his hand to get. But I can't help thinking he's acting strange. You laugh when I say he could lend you the bonds if he's not going to use them himself. But would it hurt him?

LEO *(slowly looking at* OSCAR)   No. No, it wouldn't.

OSCAR   People ought to help other people. But that's not always the way it happens. (BEN *enters, hangs his coat and hat in hall. Very carefully)* And so sometimes you got to think of yourself. *(As* LEO *stares at him,* BEN *appears in the doorway.)* Morning, Ben.

BEN *(coming in, carrying his newspaper)*   Fine sunny morning. Any news from the runaways?

REGINA *(on the staircase)*   There's no news or you would have heard it. Quite a convention so early in the morning, aren't you all? *(Goes to coffee urn)*

OSCAR   You rising mighty late these days. Is that the way they do things in Chicago society?

BEN *(looking at his paper)*   Old Carter died up in Senateville. Eighty-one is a good time for us all, eh? What do you think has really happened to Horace, Regina?

REGINA   Nothing.

BEN *(too casually)*   You don't think maybe he never started from Baltimore and never intends to start?

REGINA *(irritated)*   Of course they've started. Didn't I have a letter from Alexandra? What is so strange about people arriving late? He has that cousin in Savannah he's so fond of. He may have stopped to see him. They'll be along today some time, very flattered that you and Oscar are so worried about them.

BEN   I'm a natural worrier. Especially when I am getting ready to close a business deal and one of my partners remains silent *and* invisible.

REGINA *(laughs)* Oh, is that it? I thought you were worried about Horace's health.

OSCAR Oh, that too. Who could help but worry? I'm worried. This is the first day I haven't shot since my head cold.

REGINA *(starts towards dining room)* Then you haven't had your breakfast. Come along. *(OSCAR and LEO follow her.)*

BEN Regina. *(She turns at dining-room door.)* That cousin of Horace's has been dead for years and, in any case, the train does not go through Savannah.

REGINA *(laughs, continues into dining room, seats herself)* Did he die? You're always remembering about people dying. *(BEN rises.)* Now I intend to eat my breakfast in peace, and read my newspaper.

BEN *(goes toward dining room as he talks)* This is second breakfast for me. My first was bad. Celia ain't the cook she used to be. Too old to have taste any more. If she hadn't belonged to Mama, I'd send her off to the country.

OSCAR *and* LEO *start to eat.* BEN *seats himself.*

LEO Uncle Horace will have some tales to tell, I bet. Baltimore is a lively town.

REGINA *(to CAL)* The grits isn't hot enough. Take it back.

CAL Oh, yes'm. *(Calling into kitchen as he exits)* Grits didn't hold the heat. Grits didn't hold the heat.

LEO When I was at school three of the boys and myself took a train once and went over to Baltimore. It was so big we thought we were in Europe. I was just a kid then—

REGINA I find it very pleasant *(ADDIE enters)* to have breakfast alone. I hate chattering before I've had something hot. *(CAL closes the dining-room doors.)* Do be still, Leo.

ADDIE *come into the room, begins gathering up the cups, carries them to the large tray. Outside there are the sounds of voices. Quickly* ADDIE *runs into the hall. A few seconds later she appears again in the doorway, her arm around the shoulders of* HORACE GIDDENS, *supporting him.* HORACE *is a tall man of about forty-five. He has been good looking, but now his face is tired and ill. He walks stiffly, as if it were an enormous effort, and carefully, as if he were unsure of his balance.* ADDIE *takes off his overcoat and hangs it on the hall tree. She then helps him to a chair.*

HORACE How are you, Addie? How have you been?

ADDIE I'm all right, Mr. Horace. I've just been worried about you.

ALEXANDRA *enters. She is flushed and excited, her hat awry, her face dirty. Her arms are full of packages, but she comes quickly to* ADDIE.

ALEXANDRA Now don't tell me how worried you were. We couldn't help it and there was no way to send a message.

ADDIE   *(begins to take packages from* ALEXANDRA*)*   Yes, sir, I was mighty
   worried.
ALEXANDRA   We had to stop in Mobile over night. Papa—*(Looks at him)* Papa
   didn't feel well. The trip was too much for him, and I made him stop and
   rest— *(As* ADDIE *takes the last package)* No, don't take that. That's father's
   medicine. I'll hold it. It mustn't break. Now, about the stuff outside. Papa
   must have his wheel chair. I'll get that and the valises—
ADDIE   *(very happy, holding* ALEXANDRA'S *arms)*   Since when you got to carry
   your own valises? Since when I ain't old enough to hold a bottle of
   medicine? *(*HORACE *coughs.)* You feel all right, Mr. Horace?
HORACE   *(nods)*   Glad to be sitting down.
ALEXANDRA   *(opening package of medicine)*   He doesn't feel all right. *(*ADDIE
   looks at her, then at HORACE.*)* He just says that. The trip was very hard on
   him, and now he must go right to bed.
ADDIE   *(looking at him carefully)*   Them fancy doctors, they give you help?
HORACE   They did their best.
ALEXANDRA   *(has become conscious of the voices in the dining room)*   I bet Mama
   was worried. I better tell her we're here now. *(She starts for door.)*
HORACE   Zan. *(She stops.)* Not for a minute, dear.
ALEXANDRA   Oh, Papa, you feel bad again. I knew you did. Do you want your
   medicine?
HORACE   No, I don't feel that way. I'm just tired, darling. Let me rest a little.
ALEXANDRA   Yes, but Mama will be mad if I don't tell her we're here.
ADDIE   They're all in there eating breakfast.
ALEXANDRA   Oh, are they all here? Why do they *always* have to be here? I was
   hoping Papa wouldn't have to see anybody, that it would be nice for him
   and quiet.
ADDIE   Then let your papa rest for a minute.
HORACE   Addie, I bet your coffee's as good as ever. They don't have such good
   coffee up North. *(Looks at the urn)* Is it as good, Addie? *(*ADDIE *starts for
   coffee urn.)*
ALEXANDRA   No. Dr. Reeves said not much coffee. Just now and then. I'm the
   nurse now, Addie.
ADDIE   You'd be a better one if you didn't look so dirty. Now go and take a
   bath, Miss Grown-up. Change your linens, get out a fresh dress and give
   your hair a good brushing—go on—
ALEXANDRA   Will you be all right, Papa?
ADDIE   Go on.
ALEXANDRA   *(on stairs, talks as she goes up)*   The pills Papa must take once every
   four hours. And the bottle only when—only if he feels very bad. Now
   don't move until I come back and don't talk much and remember about his
   medicine, Addie—
ADDIE   Ring for Belle and have her help you and then I'll make you a fresh
   breakfast.
ALEXANDRA   *(as she disappears)*   How's Aunt Birdie? Is she here?
ADDIE   It ain't right for you to have coffee? It will hurt you?

HORACE *(slowly)*   Nothing can make much difference now. Get me a cup, Addie. *(She looks at him, crosses to urn, pours a cup.)* Funny. They can't make coffee up North. (ADDIE *brings him a cup.)* They don't like red pepper, either. *(He takes the cup and gulps it greedily.)* God, that's good. You remember how I used to drink it? Ten, twelve cups a day. So strong it had to stain the cup. *(Then slowly)* Addie, before I see anybody else, I want to know why Zan came to fetch me home. She's tried to tell me, but she doesn't seem to know herself.

ADDIE *(turns away)*   I don't know. All I know is big things are going on. Everybody going to be high-tone rich. Big rich. You too. All because smoke's going to start out of a building that ain't even up yet.

HORACE   I've heard about it.

ADDIE   And, er—*(Hesitates—steps to him)* And—well, Zan, she going to marry Mr. Leo in a little while.

HORACE *(looks at her, then very slowly)*   What are you talking about?

ADDIE   That's right. That's the talk, God help us.

HORACE *(angrily)*   What's the talk?

ADDIE   I'm telling you. There's going to be a wedding— *(Angrily turns away)* Over my dead body there is.

HORACE *(after a second, quietly)*   Go and tell them I'm home.

ADDIE *(hesitates)*   Now you ain't to get excited. You're to be in your bed—

HORACE   Go on, Addie. Go and say I'm back. (ADDIE *opens dining-room doors. He rises with difficulty, stands stiff, as if he were in pain, facing the dining room.)*

ADDIE   Miss Regina. They're home. They got here—

REGINA   Horace! (REGINA *quickly rises, runs into the room. Warmly)* Horace! you've finally arrived. *(As she kisses him, the others come forward, all talking together.)*

BEN *(in doorway, carrying a napkin)*   Well, sir, you had us all mighty worried. *(He steps forward. They shake hands.* ADDIE *exits.)*

OSCAR   You're a sight for sore eyes.

HORACE   Hello, Ben.

LEO *enters, eating a biscuit.*

OSCAR   And how you feel? Tip-top, I bet, because that's the way you're looking.

HORACE *(coldly, irritated with* OSCAR'S *lie)*   Hello, Oscar. Hello, Leo, how are you?

LEO *(shaking hands)*   I'm fine, sir. But a lot better now that you're back.

REGINA   Now sit down. What did happen to you and where's Alexandra? I am so excited about seeing you that I almost forgot about her.

HORACE   I didn't feel good, a little weak, I guess, and we stopped over night to rest. Zan's upstairs washing off the train dirt.

REGINA   Oh, I am so sorry the trip was hard on you. I didn't think that—

HORACE   Well, it's just as if I had never been away. All of you here—

BEN   Waiting to welcome you home.

BIRDIE *bursts in. She is wearing a flannel kimono and her face is flushed and excited.*

BIRDIE *(runs to him, kisses him)*   Horace!

HORACE *(warmly pressing her arm)*   I was just wondering where you were, Birdie.

BIRDIE *(excited)*   Oh, I would have been here. I didn't know you were back until Simon said he saw the buggy. *(She draws back to look at him. Her face sobers.)* Oh, you don't look well, Horace. No, you don't.

REGINA *(laughs)*   Birdie, what a thing to say—

HORACE *(looking at* OSCAR*)*   Oscar thinks I look very well.

OSCAR *(annoyed; turns on* LEO*)*   Don't stand there holding that biscuit in your hand.

LEO   Oh, well. I'll just finish my breakfast, Uncle Horace, and then I'll give you all the news about the bank—   [*He exits into the dining room.*]

OSCAR   And what is that costume you have on?

BIRDIE *(looking at* HORACE*)*   Now that you're home, you'll feel better. Plenty of good rest and we'll take such fine care of you. *(Stops)* But where is Zan? I missed her so much.

OSCAR   I asked you what is that strange costume you're parading around in?

BIRDIE *(nervously, backing towards stairs)*   Me? Oh! It's my wrapper. I was so excited about Horace I just rushed out of the house—

OSCAR   Did you come across the square dressed that way? My dear Birdie, I—

HORACE *(to* REGINA, *wearily)*   Yes, it's just like old times.

REGINA *(quickly to* OSCAR*)*   Now, no fights. This is a holiday.

BIRDIE *(runs quickly up the stairs)*   Zan! Zannie!

OSCAR   Birdie! *(She stops.)*

BIRDIE   Oh. Tell Zan I'll be back in a little while. *(Whispers)* Sorry, Oscar.
                                                                            [*Exits.*]

REGINA *(to* OSCAR *and* BEN*)*   Why don't you go finish your breakfast and let Horace rest for a minute?

BEN *(crossing to dining room with* OSCAR*)*   Never leave a meal unfinished. There are too many poor people who need the food. Mighty glad to see you home, Horace. Fine to have you back. Fine to have you back.

OSCAR *(to* LEO *as* BEN *closes dining-room doors)*   Your mother has gone crazy. Running around the streets like a woman—

The moment REGINA *and* HORACE *are alone, they become awkward and self-conscious.*

REGINA *(laughs awkwardly)*   Well. Here we are. It's been a long time. *(*HORACE *smiles.)* Five months. You know, Horace, I wanted to come and be with you in the hospital, but I didn't know where my duty was. Here, or with you. But you know how much I *wanted* to come.

HORACE   That's kind of you, Regina. There was no need to come.

REGINA   Oh, but there was. Five months lying there all by yourself, no kinfolks, no friends. Don't try to tell me you didn't have a bad time of it.

HORACE   I didn't have a bad time. *(As she shakes her head, he becomes insistent.)* No, I didn't, Regina. Oh, at first when I—when I heard the news about myself—but after I got used to that, I liked it there.

REGINA   You *liked* it? *(Coldly)* Isn't that strange. You liked it so well you didn't want to come home?

HORACE   That's not the way to put it. *(Then, kindly, as he sees her turn her head away)* But there I was and I got kind of used to it, kind of to like lying there and thinking. *(Smiles)* I never had much time to think before. And time's become valuable to me.

REGINA   It sounds almost like a holiday.

HORACE *(laughs)*   It was, sort of. The first holiday I've had since I was a little kid.

REGINA   And here I was thinking you were in pain and—

HORACE *(quietly)*   I was in pain.

REGINA   And instead you were having a holiday! A holiday of thinking. Couldn't you have done that here?

HORACE   I wanted to do it before I came here. I was thinking about us.

REGINA   About us? About you and me? Thinking about you and me after all these years. *(Unpleasantly)* You shall tell me everything you thought—some day.

HORACE *(there is silence for a minute)*   Regina. *(She turns to him.)* Why did you send Zan to Baltimore?

REGINA   Why? Because I wanted you home. You can't make anything suspicious out of that, can you?

HORACE   I didn't mean to make anything suspicious about it. *(Hesitantly, taking her hand)* Zan said you wanted me to come home. I was so pleased at that and touched, it made me feel good.

REGINA *(taking away her hand, turns)*   Touched that I should want you home?

HORACE *(sighs)*   I'm saying all the wrong things as usual. Let's try to get along better. There isn't so much more time. Regina, what's all this crazy talk I've been hearing about Zan and Leo? Zan and Leo marrying?

REGINA *(turning to him, sharply)*   Who gossips so much around here?

HORACE *(shocked)*   Regina!

REGINA *(annoyed, anxious to quiet him)*   It's some foolishness that Oscar thought up. I'll explain later. I have no intention of allowing any such arrangement. It was simply a way of keeping Oscar quiet in all this business I've been writing you about—

HORACE *(carefully)*   What has Zan to do with any business of Oscar's? Whatever it is you had better put it out of Oscar's head immediately. You know what I think of Leo.

REGINA   But there's no need to talk about it now.

HORACE   There is no need to talk about it ever. Not as long as I live. (HORACE *stops, slowly turns to look at her.)* As long as I live. I've been in a hospital for

five months. Yet since I've been here you have not once asked me about—
about my health. *(Then gently)* Well, I suppose they've written you. I can't
live very long.

REGINA *(coldly)*   I've never understood why people have to talk about this kind
of thing.

HORACE *(there is a silence. Then he looks up at her, his face cold)*   You misunderstand. I don't intend to gossip about my sickness. I thought it was only fair
to tell you. I was not asking for your sympathy.

REGINA *(sharply, turns to him)*   What do the doctors think caused your bad
heart?

HORACE   What do you mean?

REGINA   They didn't think it possible, did they, that your fancy women may
have—

HORACE *(smiles unpleasantly)*   Caused my heart to be bad? I don't think that's
the best scientific theory. You don't catch heart trouble in bed.

REGINA *(angrily)*   I didn't think you did. I only thought you might catch a bad
conscience—in bed, as you say.

HORACE   I didn't tell them about my bad conscience. Or about my fancy
women. Nor did I tell them that my wife has not wanted me in bed with her
for— *(Sharply)* how long is it, Regina? (REGINA *turns to him.*) Ten years?
Did you bring me home for this, to make me feel guilty again? That means
you want something. But you'll not make me feel guilty any more. My
"thinking" has made a difference.

REGINA   I see that it has. *(She looks towards dining-room door; then comes to him,
her manner warm and friendly)* It's foolish for us to fight this way. I didn't
mean to be unpleasant. I was stupid.

HORACE *(wearily)*   God knows I didn't either. I came home wanting so much
not to fight, and then all of a sudden there we were. I got hurt and—

REGINA *(hastily)*   It's all my fault. I didn't ask about—about your illness
because I didn't want to remind you of it. Anyway I never believe doctors
when they talk about— *(Brightly)* when they talk like that.

HORACE *(not looking at her)*   Well, we'll try our best with each other. *(He rises.)*

REGINA *(quickly)*   I'll try. Honestly, I will. Horace, Horace, I know you're
tired but, but—couldn't you stay down here a few minutes longer? I want
Ben to tell you something.

HORACE   Tomorrow.

REGINA   I'd like to now. It's very important to me. It's very important to all of
us. *(Gaily, as she moves toward dining room)* Important to your beloved
daughter. She'll be a very great heiress—

HORACE   Will she? That's nice.

REGINA *(opens doors)*   Ben, are you finished breakfast?

HORACE   Is this the mill business I've had so many letters about?

REGINA *(to BEN)*   Horace would like to talk to you now.

HORACE   Horace would not like to talk to you now. I am very tired, Regina—

REGINA *(comes to him)*   Please. You've said we'll try our best with each other.
I'll try. Really, I will. Please do this for me now. You will see what I've done

while you've been away. How I watched your interests. *(Laughs gaily)* And I've done very well too. But things can't be delayed any longer. Everything must be settled this week— (HORACE *sits down.* BEN *enters.* OSCAR *has stayed in the dining room, his head turned to watch them.* LEO *is pretending to read the newspaper.)* Now you must tell Horace all about it. Only be quick because he is very tired and must go to bed. (HORACE *is looking up at her. His face hardens as she speaks.)* But I think your news will be better for him than all the medicine in the world.

BEN *(looking at* HORACE)   It could wait. Horace may not feel like talking today.

REGINA   What an old faker you are! You know it can't wait. You know it must be finished this week. You've been just as anxious for Horace to get here as I've been.

BEN *(very jovial)*   I suppose I have been. And why not? Horace has done Hubbard Sons many a good turn. Why shouldn't I be anxious to help him now?

REGINA *(laughs)*   Help him! Help him when you need him, that's what you mean.

BEN   What a woman you married, Horace. *(Laughs awkwardly when* HORACE *does not answer)* Well, then I'll make it quick. You know what I've been telling you for years. How I've always said that every one of us little Southern business men had great things— *(Extends his arm)* —right beyond our finger tips. It's been my dream: my dream to make those fingers grow longer. I'm a lucky man, Horace, a lucky man. To dream and to live to get what you've dreamed of. That's *my* idea of a lucky man. *(Looks at his fingers as his arm drops slowly)* For thirty years I've cried bring the cotton mills to the cotton. (HORACE *opens medicine bottle.)* Well, finally I got up nerve to go to Marshall Company in Chicago.

HORACE   I know all this. *(He takes the medicine.* REGINA *rises, steps to him.)*

BEN   Can I get you something?

HORACE   Some water, please.

REGINA *(turns quickly)*   Oh, I'm sorry. Let me. *(Brings him a glass of water. He drinks as they wait in silence.)* You feel all right now?

HORACE   Yes. You wrote me. I know all that.

OSCAR *enters from dining room.*

REGINA *(triumphantly)*   But you don't know that in the last few days Ben has agreed to give us—you, I mean—a much larger share.

HORACE   Really? That's very generous of him.

BEN *(laughs)*   It wasn't so generous of me. It was smart of Regina.

REGINA *(as if she were signaling* HORACE)   I explained to Ben that perhaps you hadn't answered his letters because you didn't think he was offering you enough, and that the time was getting short and you could guess how much he needed you—

HORACE *(smiles at her, nods)*   And I could guess that he wants to keep control in the family?

REGINA (*to* BEN, *triumphantly*)   Exactly. (*To* HORACE) So I did a little bargaining for you and convinced my brothers they weren't the only Hubbards
who had a business sense.

HORACE   Did you have to convince them of that? How little people know
about each other! (*Laughs*) But you'll know better about Regina next time,
eh, Ben? (BEN, REGINA, HORACE *laugh together.* OSCAR'S *face is angry.*)
Now let's see. We're getting a bigger share. (*Looking at* OSCAR) Who's
getting less?

BEN   Oscar.

HORACE   Well, Oscar, you've grown very unselfish. What's happened to you?

LEO *enters from dining room.*

BEN (*quickly, before* OSCAR *can answer*)   Oscar doesn't mind. Not worth fighting
about now, eh, Oscar?

OSCAR (*angrily*)   I'll get mine in the end. You can be sure of that. I've got my
son's future to think about.

HORACE (*sharply*)   Leo? Oh, I see. (*Puts his head back, laughs.* REGINA *looks at
him nervously.*) I am beginning to see. Everybody will get theirs.

BEN   I knew you'd see it. Seventy-five thousand, and that seventy-five thousand will make you a million.

REGINA (*steps to table, leaning forward*)   It will, Horace, it will.

HORACE   I believe you. (*After a second*) Now I can understand Oscar's self-
sacrifice, but what did you have to promise Marshall Company besides the
money you're putting up?

BEN   They wouldn't take promises. They wanted guarantees.

HORACE   Of what?

BEN (*nods*)   Water power. Free and plenty of it.

HORACE   You got them that, of course.

BEN   Cheap. You'd think the Governor of a great state would make his price a
little higher. From pride, you know. (HORACE *smiles.* BEN *smiles.*) Cheap
wages. "What do you mean by cheap wages?" I say to Marshall. "Less than
Massachusetts," he says to me, "and that averages eight a week." "Eight a
week! By God," I tell him, "*I'd* work for eight a week myself." Why, there
ain't a mountain white or a town nigger but wouldn't give his right arm for
three silver dollars every week, eh, Horace?

HORACE   Sure. And they'll take less than that when you get around to playing
them off against each other. You can save a little money that way, Ben.
(*Angrily*) And make them hate each other just a little more than they do
now.

REGINA   What's all this about?

BEN (*laughs*)   There'll be no trouble from anybody, white or black. Marshall
said that to me. "What about strikes? That's all we've had in Massachusetts
for the last three years." I say to him, "What's a strike? I never heard of one.
Come South, Marshall. We got good folks and we don't stand for any fancy
fooling."

HORACE   You're right. *(Slowly)* Well, it looks like you made a good deal for
yourselves, and for Marshall, too. *(To* BEN) Your father used to say he
made the thousands and you boys would make the millions. I think he was
right. *(Rises)*

REGINA *(they are all looking at* HORACE. *She laughs nervously)*   Millions for *us,*
too.

HORACE   Us? You and me? I don't think so. We've got enough money, Regina.
We'll just sit by and watch the boys grow rich. *(They watch* HORACE *tensely
as he begins to move towards the staircase. He passes* LEO, *looks at him for a
second.)* How's everything at the bank, Leo?

LEO   Fine, sir. Everything is fine.

HORACE   How are all the ladies in Mobile? *(*HORACE *turns to* REGINA,
sharply) Whatever made you think I'd let Zan marry—

REGINA   Do you mean that you are turning this down? Is it possible that's what
you mean?

BEN   No, that's not what he means. Turning down a fortune. Horace is tired.
He'd rather talk about it tomorrow—

REGINA   We can't keep putting it off this way. Oscar must be in Chicago by the
end of the week with the money and contracts.

OSCAR *(giggles, pleased)*   Yes, sir. Got to be there end of the week. No sense
going without the money.

REGINA *(tensely)*   I've waited long enough for your answer, I'm not going to
wait any longer.

HORACE *(very deliberately)*   I'm very tired now, Regina.

BEN *(hastily)*   Now, Horace probably has his reasons. Things he'd like
explained. Tomorrow will do. I can—

REGINA *(turns to* BEN, *sharply)*   I want to know his reasons now! *(Turns back to*
HORACE.)

HORACE *(as he climbs the steps)*   I don't know them all myself. Let's leave it at
that.

REGINA   We shall not leave it at that! We have waited for you here like
children. Waited for you to come home.

HORACE   So that you could invest my money. So this is why you wanted me
home? Well, I had hoped— *(Quietly)* If you are disappointed, Regina, I'm
sorry. But I must do what I think best. We'll talk about it another day.

REGINA   We'll talk about it now. Just you and me.

HORACE *(looks down at her; his voice is tense)*   Please, Regina. It's been a hard
trip. I don't feel well. Please leave me alone now.

REGINA *(quietly)*   I want to talk to you, Horace. I'm coming up. *(He looks at her
for a minute, then moves on again out of sight. She begins to climb the stairs.)*

BEN *(softly;* REGINA *turns to him as he speaks)*   Sometimes it is better to wait for
the sun to rise again. *(She does not answer.)* And sometimes, as our mother
used to tell you, *(*REGINA *starts up stairs.)* it's unwise for a good-looking
woman to frown. *(*BEN *rises, moves towards stairs.)* Softness and a smile do
more to the heart of men— *(She disappears.* BEN *stands looking up the stairs.
There is a long silence. Then, suddenly,* OSCAR *giggles.)*

OSCAR   Let us hope she'll change his mind. Let us hope. *(After a second* BEN *crosses to table, picks up his newspaper.* OSCAR *looks at* BEN. *The silence makes* LEO *uncomfortable.)*

LEO   The paper says twenty-seven cases of yellow fever in New Orleans. Guess the flood-waters caused it. *(Nobody pays attention.)* Thought they were building the levees high enough. Like the niggers always say: a man born of woman can't build nothing high enough for the Mississippi. *(Gets no answer, gives an embarrassed laugh)*

Upstairs there is the sound of voices. The voices are not loud, but BEN, OSCAR, LEO *become conscious of them.* LEO *crosses to landing, looks up, listens.*

OSCAR *(pointing up)*   Now just suppose she don't change his mind? Just suppose he keeps on refusing?

BEN *(without conviction)*   He's tired. It was a mistake to talk to him today. He's a sick man, but he isn't a crazy one.

OSCAR *(giggles)*   But just suppose he is crazy. What then?

BEN *(puts down his paper, peers at* OSCAR*)*   Then we'll go outside for the money. There's plenty who would give it.

OSCAR   And plenty who will want a lot for what they give. The ones who are rich enough to give will be smart enough to want. That means we'd be working for them, don't it, Ben?

BEN   You don't have to tell me the things I told you six months ago.

OSCAR   Oh, you're right not to worry. She'll change his mind. She always has. *(There is a silence. Suddenly* REGINA'S *voice becomes louder and sharper. All of them begin to listen now. Slowly* BEN *rises, goes to listen by the staircase.* OSCAR, *watching him, smiles. As they listen* REGINA'S *voice becomes very loud.* HORACE'S *voice is no longer heard.)* Maybe. But I don't believe it. I never did believe he was going in with us.

BEN *(turning on him)*   What the hell do you expect me to do?

OSCAR *(mildly)*   Nothing. You done your almighty best. Nobody could blame you if the whole thing just dripped away right through our fingers. You can't do a thing. But there may be something I could do for us. *(OSCAR rises.)* Or, I might better say, Leo could do for us. *(BEN stops, turns, looks at* OSCAR. LEO *is staring at* OSCAR.*)* Ain't that true, son? Ain't it true, you might be able to help your own kinfolks?

LEO *(nervously taking a step to him)*   Papa, I—

BEN *(slowly)*   How would he help us, Oscar?

OSCAR   Leo's got a friend. Leo's friend owns eighty-eight thousand dollars in Union Pacific bonds. *(BEN turns to look at* LEO.*)* Leo's friend don't look at the bonds much—not for five or six months at a time.

BEN *(after a pause)*   Union Pacific. Uh, huh. Let me understand. Leo's friend would—would lend him these bonds and he—

OSCAR *(nods)*   Would be kind enough to lend them to us.

BEN   Leo.

LEO *(excited, comes to him)*   Yes, sir?

BEN   When would your friend be wanting the bonds back?

LEO *(very nervous)*   I don't know. I— well, I—

OSCAR *(sharply; steps to him)*   You told me he won't look at them until Fall—

LEO   Oh, that's right. But I—not till Fall. Uncle Horace never—

BEN *(sharply)*   Be still.

OSCAR *(smiles at LEO)*   Your uncle doesn't wish to know your friend's name.

LEO *(starts to laugh)*   That's a good one. Not know his name—

OSCAR   Shut up, Leo! (LEO *turns away slowly, moves to table.* BEN *turns to* OSCAR.) He won't look at them until September. That gives us five months. Leo will return the bonds in three months. And we'll have no trouble raising the money once the mills are going up. Will Marshall accept bonds?

BEN *stops to listen to sudden sharp voices from above. The voices are now very angry and very loud.*

BEN *(smiling)*   Why not? Why not? *(Laughs.)* Good. We are lucky. We'll take the loan from Leo's friend—I think he will make a safer partner than our sister. *(Nods towards stairs, turns to* LEO) How soon can you get them?

LEO   Today. Right now. They're in the safe-deposit box and—

BEN *(sharply)*   I don't want to know where they are.

OSCAR *(laughs)*   We will keep it secret from you. *(Pats* BEN'S *arm)*

BEN *(smiles)*   Good. Draw a check for our part. You can take the night train for Chicago. Well, Oscar *(holds out his hand),* good luck to us.

OSCAR   Leo will be taken care of?

LEO   I'm entitled to Uncle Horace's share. I'd enjoy being a partner—

BEN *(turns to stare at him)*   You would? You can go to hell, you little— *(Starts towards* LEO*)*

OSCAR *(nervously)*   Now, now. He didn't mean that. I only want to be sure he'll get something out of all this.

BEN   Of course. We'll take care of him. We won't have any trouble about that. I'll see you at the store.

OSCAR *(nods)*   That's settled then. Come on, son. *(Starts for door)*

LEO *(puts out his hand)*   I didn't mean just that. I was only going to say what a great day this was for me and— *(*BEN *ignores his hand.)*

BEN   Go on.

LEO *looks at him, turns, follows* OSCAR *out.* BEN *stands where he is, thinking. Again the voices upstairs can be heard.* REGINA'S *voice is high and furious.* BEN *looks up, smiles, winces at the noise.*

ALEXANDRA *(upstairs)*   Mama—Mama—don't . . . *(The noise of running footsteps is heard and* ALEXANDRA *comes running down the steps, speaking as she comes.)* Uncle Ben! Uncle Ben! Please go up. Please make Mama stop. Uncle Ben, he's sick, he's so sick. How can Mama talk to him like that— please, make her stop. She'll—

BEN   Alexandra, you have a tender heart.

ALEXANDRA (*crying*)   Go on up, Uncle Ben, please—

Suddenly the voices stop. A second later there is the sound of a door being slammed.

BEN   Now you see. Everything is over. Don't worry. (*He starts for the door.*) Alexandra, I want you to tell your mother how sorry I am that I had to leave. And don't worry so, my dear. Married folk frequently raise their voices, unfortunately. (*He starts to put on his hat and coat as* REGINA *appears on the stairs.*)

ALEXANDRA (*furiously*)   How can you treat Papa like this? He's sick. He's very sick. Don't you know that? I won't let you.

REGINA   Mind your business, Alexandra. (*To* BEN—*her voice is cold and calm*) How much longer can you wait for the money?

BEN (*putting on his coat*)   He has refused? My, that's too bad.

REGINA   He will change his mind. I'll find a way to make him. What's the longest you can wait now?

BEN   I could wait until next week. But I can't wait until next week. (*He giggles, pleased at the joke.*) I could but I can't. Could and can't. Well, I must go now. I'm very late—

REGINA (*coming downstairs towards him*)   You're not going. I want to talk to you.

BEN   I was about to give Alexandra a message for you. I wanted to tell you that Oscar is going to Chicago tonight, so we can't be here for our usual Friday supper.

REGINA (*tensely*)   Oscar is going to Chi— (*Softly*) What do you mean?

BEN   Just that. Everything is settled. He's going on to deliver to Marshall—

REGINA (*taking a step to him*)   I demand to know what— You are lying. You are trying to scare me. *You haven't got the money.* How could you have it? You can't have— (BEN *laughs.*) You will wait until I—

HORACE *comes into view on the landing.*

BEN   You are getting out of hand. Since when do I take orders from you?

REGINA   Wait, you— (BEN *stops.*) How *can* he go to Chicago? Did a ghost arrive with the money? (BEN *starts for the hall.*) I don't believe you. Come back here. (REGINA *starts after him.*) Come back here, you— (*The door slams. She stops in the doorway, staring, her fists clenched. After a pause she turns slowly.*)

HORACE (*very quietly*)   It's a great day when you and Ben cross swords. I've been waiting for it for years.

ALEXANDRA   Papa, Papa, please go back! You will—

HORACE   And so they don't need you, and so you will not have your millions, after all.

REGINA (*turns slowly*)   You hate to see anybody live now, don't you? You hate to think that I'm going to be alive and have what I want.

HORACE   I should have known you'd think that was the reason.

REGINA   Because you're going to die and you know you're going to die.

ALEXANDRA *(shrilly)*   Mama! Don't—Don't listen, Papa. Just don't listen. Go away—

HORACE   Not to keep you from getting what you want. Not even partly that. *(Holding to the rail)* I'm sick of you, sick of this house, sick of my life here. I'm sick of your brothers and their dirty tricks to make a dime. There must be better ways of getting rich than cheating niggers on a pound of bacon. Why should I give you the money? *(Very angrily)* To pound the bones of this town to make dividends for you to spend? You wreck the town, you and your brothers, *you* wreck the town and live on it. Not me. Maybe it's easy for the dying to be honest. But it's not my fault I'm dying. *(ADDIE enters, stands at door quietly.)* I'll do no more harm now. I've done enough. I'll die my own way. And I'll do it without making the world any worse. I leave that to you.

REGINA *(looks up at him slowly, calmly)*   I hope you die. I hope you die soon. *(Smiles)* I'll be waiting for you to die.

ALEXANDRA *(shrieking)*   Papa! Don't— Don't listen— Don't—

ADDIE   Come here, Zan. Come out of this room.

ALEXANDRA *runs quickly to* ADDIE, *who holds her.* HORACE *turns slowly and starts upstairs.*

ACT III

Scene: *Same as Act One. Two weeks later. It is late afternoon and it is raining.*

At Rise: HORACE *is sitting near the window in a wheel chair. On the table next to him is a safe-deposit box, and a small bottle of medicine.* BIRDIE *and* ALEXANDRA *are playing the piano. On a chair is a large sewing basket.*

BIRDIE *(counting for* ALEXANDRA*)*   One and two and three and four. One and two and three and four. *(Nods—turns to* HORACE.*)* We once played together, Horace. Remember?

HORACE *(has been looking out of the window)*   What, Birdie?

BIRDIE   We played together. You and me.

ALEXANDRA   *Papa* used to play?

BIRDIE   Indeed he did. *(ADDIE appears at the door in a large kitchen apron. She is wiping her hands on a towel.)* He played the fiddle and very well, too.

ALEXANDRA *(turns to smile at* HORACE*)*   I never knew—

ADDIE   Where's your mama?

ALEXANDRA   Gone to Miss Safronia's to fit her dresses.

ADDIE *nods, starts to exit.*

HORACE   Addie.

ADDIE   Yes, Mr. Horace.

HORACE   (*speaks as if he had made a sudden decision*)   Tell Cal to get on his things. I want him to go an errand.

ADDIE *nods, exits.* HORACE *moves nervously in his chair, looks out of the window.*

ALEXANDRA   (*who has been watching him*)   It's too bad it's been raining all day, Papa. But you can go out in the yard tomorrow. Don't be restless.

HORACE   I'm not restless, darling.

BIRDIE   I remember so well the time we played together, your papa and me. It was the first time Oscar brought me here to supper. I had never seen all the Hubbards together before, and you know what a ninny I am and how shy. (*Turns to look at* HORACE) You said you could play the fiddle and you'd be much obliged if I'd play with you. I was obliged to *you,* all right, all right. (*Laughs when he does not answer her*) Horace, you haven't heard a word I've said.

HORACE   Birdie, when did Oscar get back from Chicago?

BIRDIE   Yesterday. Hasn't he been here yet?

ALEXANDRA   (*stops playing*)   No. Neither has Uncle Ben since—since that day.

BIRDIE   Oh, I didn't know it was *that* bad. Oscar never tells me anything—

HORACE   (*smiles, nods*)   The Hubbards have had their great quarrel. I knew it would come some day. (*Laughs*) It came.

ALEXANDRA   It came. It certainly came all right.

BIRDIE   (*amazed*)   But Oscar was in such a good humor when he got home, I didn't—

HORACE   Yes, I can understand that.

ADDIE *enters carrying a large tray with glasses, a carafe of elderberry wine and a plate of cookies, which she puts on the table.*

ALEXANDRA   Addie! A party! What for?

ADDIE   Nothing for. I had the fresh butter, so I made the cakes, and a little elderberry does the stomach good in the rain.

BIRDIE   Isn't this nice! A party just for us. Let's play party music, Zan.

ALEXANDRA *begins to play a gay piece.*

ADDIE   (*to* HORACE, *wheeling his chair to center*)   Come over here, Mr. Horace, and don't be thinking so much. A glass of elderberry will do more good.

ALEXANDRA *reaches for a cake.* BIRDIE *pours herself a glass of wine.*

ALEXANDRA   Good cakes, Addie. It's nice here. Just us. Be nice if it could always be this way.

BIRDIE *(nods happily)*   Quiet and restful.

ADDIE   Well, it won't be that way long. Little while now, even sitting here, you'll hear the red bricks going into place. The next day the smoke'll be pushing out the chimneys and by church time that Sunday every human born of woman will be living on chicken. That's how Mr. Ben's been telling the story.

HORACE *(looks at her)*   They believe it that way?

ADDIE   Believe it? They use to believing what Mr. Ben orders. There ain't been so much talk around here since Sherman's army didn't come near.

HORACE *(softly)*   They are fools.

ADDIE *(nods, sits down with the sewing basket)*   You ain't born in the South unless you're a fool.

BIRDIE *(has drunk another glass of wine)*   But we didn't play together after that night. Oscar said he didn't like me to play on the piano. *(Turns to* ALEXANDRA*)* You know what he said that night?

ALEXANDRA   Who?

BIRDIE   Oscar. He said that music made him nervous. He said he just sat and waited for the next note. (ALEXANDRA *laughs.)* He wasn't poking fun. He meant it. Ah, well— *(She finishes her glass, shakes her head.* HORACE *looks at her, smiles.)* Your papa don't like to admit it, but he's been mighty kind to me all these years. *(Running the back of her hand along his sleeve)* Often he'd step in when somebody said something and once— *(She stops, turns away, her face still.)* Once he stopped Oscar from— *(She stops, turns. Quickly)* I'm sorry I said that. Why, here I am so happy and yet I think about bad things. *(Laughs nervously)* That's not right, now, is it? *(She pours a drink.* CAL *appears in the door. He has on an old coat and is carrying a torn umbrella.)*

ALEXANDRA   Have a cake, Cal.

CAL *(comes in, takes a cake)*   Yes'm. You want me, Mr. Horace?

HORACE   What time is it, Cal?

CAL   'Bout ten minutes before it's five.

HORACE   All right. Now you walk yourself down to the bank.

CAL   It'll be closed. Nobody'll be there but Mr. Manders, Mr. Joe Horns, Mr. Leo—

HORACE   Go in the back way. They'll be at the table, going over the day's business. *(Points to the deposit box)* See that box?

CAL *(nods)*   Yes, sir.

HORACE   You tell Mr. Manders that Mr. Horace says he's much obliged to him for bringing the box, it arrived all right.

CAL *(bewildered)*   He know you got the box. He bring it himself Wednesday. I opened the door to him and he say, "Hello, Cal, coming on to summer weather."

HORACE   You say just what I tell you. Understand?

BIRDIE *pours another drink, stands at table.*

CAL   No, sir. I ain't going to say I understand. I'm going down and tell a man he give you something he already know he give you, and you say "understand."

HORACE   Now, Cal.

CAL   Yes, sir. I just going to say you obliged for the box coming all right. I ain't going to understand it, but I'm going to say it.

HORACE   And tell him I want him to come over here after supper, and to bring Mr. Sol Fowler with him.

CAL *(nods)*   He's to come after supper and bring Mr. Sol Fowler, your attorney-*at*-law, with him.

HORACE *(smiles)*   That's right. Just walk right in the back room and say your piece. *(Slowly)* In front of everybody.

CAL   Yes, sir.   [*Mumbles to himself as he exits*]

ALEXANDRA *(who has been watching* HORACE*)*   Is anything the matter, Papa?

HORACE   Oh, no. Nothing.

ADDIE   Miss Birdie, that elderberry going to give you a headache spell.

BIRDIE *(beginning to be drunk; gaily)*   Oh, I don't think so. I don't think it will.

ALEXANDRA *(as* HORACE *puts his hand to his throat)*   Do you want your medicine, Papa?

HORACE   No, no. I'm all right, darling.

BIRDIE   Mama used to give me elderberry wine when I was a little girl. For hiccoughs. *(Laughs)* You know, I don't think people get hiccoughs any more. Isn't that funny? (BIRDIE *laughs.* HORACE *and* ALEXANDRA *laugh.)* I used to get hiccoughs just when I shouldn't have.

ADDIE *(nods)*   And nobody gets growing pains no more. That is funny. Just as if there was some style in what you get. One year an ailment's stylish and the next year it ain't.

BIRDIE *(turns)*   I remember. It was my first big party, at Lionnet I mean, and I was so excited, and there I was with hiccoughs and Mama laughing. *(Softly—looking at carafe)* Mama always laughed. *(Picks up carafe)* A big party, a lovely dress from Mr. Worth in Paris, France, and hiccoughs. *(Pours drink)* My brother pounding me on the back and Mama with the elderberry bottle, laughing at me. Everybody was on their way to come, and I was such a ninny, hiccoughing away. *(Drinks)* You know, that was the first day I ever saw Oscar Hubbard. The Ballongs were selling their horses and he was going there to buy. He passed and lifted his hat—we could see him from the window—and my brother, to tease Mama, said maybe we should have invited the Hubbards to the party. He said Mama didn't like them because they kept a store, and he said that was old-fashioned of her. *(Her face lights up.)* And then, and *then,* I saw Mama angry for the first time in my life. She said that wasn't the reason. She said she was old-fashioned, but not that way. She said she was old-fashioned enough not to like people who killed animals they couldn't use, and who made their money charging awful interest to poor, ignorant niggers and cheating them on what they bought. She was very angry, Mama was. I had never seen her face like that. And then suddenly she laughed and said, "Look, I've frightened Birdie out of the hiccoughs." *(Her head drops; then softly)* And so she had. They were all gone. *(Moves to sofa, sits)*

ADDIE   Yeah, they got mighty well off cheating niggers. Well, there are people who eat the earth and eat all the people on it like in the Bible with the locusts. Then there are people who stand around and watch them eat it. *(Softly)* Sometimes I think it ain't right to stand and watch them do it.

BIRDIE *(thoughtfully)*   Like I say, if we could only go back to Lionnet. Everybody'd be better there. They'd be good and kind. I like people to be kind. *(Pours drink)* Don't you, Horace; don't you like people to be kind?

HORACE   Yes, Birdie.

BIRDIE *(very drunk now)*   Yes, that was the first day I ever saw Oscar. Who would have thought— *(Quickly)* You all want to know something? Well, I don't like Leo. My very own son, and I don't like him. *(Laughs, gaily)* My, I guess I even like Oscar more.

ALEXANDRA   Why did you marry Uncle Oscar?

ADDIE *(sharply)*   That's no question for you to be asking.

HORACE *(sharply)*   Why not? She's heard enough around here to ask anything.

ALEXANDRA   Aunt Birdie, why did you marry Uncle Oscar?

BIRDIE   I don't know. I thought I liked him. He was kind to me and I thought it was because he liked me too. But that wasn't the reason— *(Wheels on* ALEXANDRA*)* Ask why *he* married *me*. I can tell you that: He's told it to me often enough.

ADDIE *(leaning foward)*   Miss Birdie, don't—

BIRDIE *(speaking very rapidly, tensely)*   My family was good and the cotton on Lionnet's fields was better. Ben Hubbard wanted the cotton and *(rises)* Oscar Hubbard married it for him. He was kind to me, then. He used to smile at me. He hasn't smiled at me since. Everybody knew that's what he married me for. *(*ADDIE *rises.)* Everybody but me. Stupid, stupid me.

ALEXANDRA *(to* HORACE, *holding his hand, softly)*   I see. *(Hesitates)* Papa, I mean— when you feel better couldn't we go away? I mean, by ourselves. Couldn't we find a way to go—

HORACE   Yes, I know what you mean. We'll try to find a way. I promise you, darling.

ADDIE *(moves to* BIRDIE*)*   Rest a bit, Miss Birdie. You get talking like this you'll get a headache and—

BIRDIE *(sharply, turning to her)*   I've never had a headache in my life. *(Begins to cry hysterically)* You know it as well as I do. *(Turns to* ALEXANDRA*)* I never had a headache, Zan. That's a lie they tell for me. I drink. All by myself, in my own room, by myself, I drink. Then, when they want to hide it, they say, "Birdie's got a headache again"—

ALEXANDRA *(comes to her quickly)*   Aunt Birdie.

BIRDIE *(turning away)*   Even you won't like me now. You won't like me any more.

ALEXANDRA   I love you. I'll always love you.

BIRDIE *(furiously)*   Well, don't. Don't love me. Because in twenty years you'll just be like me. They'll do all the same things to you. *(Begins to laugh hysterically)* You know what? In twenty-two years I haven't had a whole day of happiness. Oh, a little, like today with you all. But never a single, whole day. I say to myself, if only I had one more *whole* day, then— *(The laugh stops.)* And that's the way you'll be. And you'll trail after them, just like me, hoping they won't be so mean that day or say something to make you feel so bad—only you'll be worse off because you haven't got my Mama to remember— *(Turns away, her head drops. She stands quietly, swaying a little, holding onto the sofa.* ALEXANDRA *leans down, puts her cheek on* BIRDIE'S *arm.)*

ALEXANDRA *(to* BIRDIE*)*   I guess we were all trying to make a happy day. You know, we sit around and try to pretend nothing's happened. We try to pretend we are not here. We make believe we are just by ourselves, some place else, and it doesn't seem to work. *(Kisses* BIRDIE'S *hand)* Come now, Aunt Birdie, I'll walk you home. You and me. (She takes BIRDIE'S *arm. They move slowly out.)*

BIRDIE *(softly as they exit)*   You and me.

ADDIE *(after a minute)*   Well. First time I ever heard Miss Birdie say a word. *(*HORACE *looks at her.)* Maybe it's good for her. I'm just sorry Zan had to hear it. *(*HORACE *moves his head as if he were uncomfortable.)* You feel bad, don't you? *(He shrugs.)*

HORACE   So you didn't want Zan to hear? It would be nice to let her stay innocent, like Birdie at her age. Let her listen now. Let her see everything. How else is she going to know that she's got to get away? I'm trying to show her that. I'm trying, but I've only got a little time left. She can even hate me when I'm dead, if she'll only learn to hate and fear this.

ADDIE   Mr. Horace—

HORACE   Pretty soon there'll be nobody to help her but you.

ADDIE *(crossing to him)*   What can I do?

HORACE   Take her away.

ADDIE   How can I do that? Do you think they'd let me just go away with her?

HORACE   I'll fix it so they can't stop you when you're ready to go. You'll go, Addie?

ADDIE *(after a second, softly)*   Yes, sir. I promise. *(He touches her arm, nods.)*

HORACE *(quietly)*   I'm going to have Sol Fowler make me a new will. They'll make trouble, but you make Zan stand firm and Fowler'll do the rest. Addie, I'd like to leave you something for yourself. I always wanted to.

ADDIE *(laughs)*   Don't you do that, Mr. Horace. A nigger woman in a white man's will! I'd never get it nohow.

HORACE   I know. But upstairs in the armoire drawer there's seventeen hundred dollar bills. It's money left from my trip. It's in an envelope with your name. It's for you.

ADDIE   Seventeen hundred dollar bills! My God, Mr. Horace, I won't know how to count up that high. *(Shyly)* It's mighty kind and good of you. I don't know what to say for thanks—

CAL *(appears in doorway)*   I'm back. *(No answer)* I'm back.

ADDIE   So we see.

HORACE   Well?

CAL   Nothing. I just went down and spoke my piece. Just like you told me. I say, "Mr. Horace he thank you mightily for the safe box arriving in good shape and he say you come right after supper to his house and bring Mr. Attorney-at-law Sol Fowler with you." Then I wipe my hands on my coat. Every time I ever told a lie in my whole life, I wipe my hands right after. Can't help doing it. Well, while I'm wiping my hands, Mr. Leo jump up and say to me, "What box? What you talking about?"

HORACE   (*smiles*)   Did he?

CAL   And Mr. Leo say he got to leave a little early cause he got something to do. And then Mr. Manders say Mr. Leo should sit right down and finish up his work and stop acting like somebody made him Mr. President. So he sit down. Now, just like I told you, Mr. Manders was mighty surprised with the message because he knows right well he brought the box— (*Points to box, sighs*) But he took it all right. Some men take everything easy and some do not.

HORACE   (*puts his head back, laughs*)   Mr. Leo was telling the truth; he *has* got something to do. I hope Manders don't keep him too long. (*Outside there is the sound of voices.* CAL *exits.* ADDIE *crosses quickly to* HORACE, *puts basket on table, begins to wheel his chair towards the stairs. Sharply*) No. Leave me where I am.

ADDIE   But that's Miss Regina coming back.

HORACE   (*nods, looking at door*)   Go away, Addie.

ADDIE   (*hesitates*)   Mr. Horace. Don't talk no more today. You don't feel well and it won't do no good—

HORACE   (*as he hears footsteps in the hall*)   Go on.

She looks at him for a second, then picks up her sewing from table and exits as REGINA *comes in from hall.* HORACE'S *chair is now so placed that he is in front of the table with the medicine.* REGINA *stands in the hall, shakes umbrella, stands it in the corner, takes off her cloak and throws it over the banister. She stares at* HORACE.

REGINA   (*as she takes off her gloves*)   We had agreed that you were to stay in your part of this house and I in mine. This room is *my* part of the house. Please don't come down here again.

HORACE   I won't.

REGINA   (*crosses towards bell cord*)   I'll get Cal to take you upstairs.

HORACE   (*smiles*)   Before you do I want to tell you that after all, we have invested our money in Hubbard Sons and Marshall, Cotton Manufacturers.

REGINA   (*stops, turns, stares at him*)   What are you talking about? You haven't seen Ben— When did you change your mind?

HORACE   I didn't change my mind. *I* didn't invest the money. (*Smiles*) It was invested for me.

REGINA   (*angrily*)   What—?

HORACE   I had eighty-eight thousand dollars' worth of Union Pacific bonds in that safe-deposit box. They are not there now. Go and look. (*As she stares at him, he points to the box.*) Go and look, Regina. (*She crosses quickly to the box, opens it.*) Those bonds are as negotiable as money.

REGINA (*turns back to him*)   What kind of joke are you playing now? Is this for my benefit?

HORACE   I don't look in that box very often, but three days ago, on Wednesday it was, because I had made a decision—

REGINA   I want to know what you are talking about.

HORACE (*sharply*)   Don't interrupt me again. Because I had made a decision, I sent for the box. The bonds were gone. Eighty-eight thousand dollars gone. (*He smiles at her.*)

REGINA (*after a moment's silence, quietly*)   Do you think I'm crazy enough to believe what you're saying?

HORACE (*shrugs*)   Believe anything you like.

REGINA (*stares at him, slowly*)   Where did they go to?

HORACE   They are in Chicago. With Mr. Marshall, I should guess.

REGINA   What did they do? Walk to Chicago? Have you really gone crazy?

HORACE   Leo took the bonds.

REGINA (*turns sharply then speaks softly, without conviction*)   I don't believe it.

HORACE (*leans forward*)   I wasn't there but I can guess what happened. This fine gentleman, to whom you were willing to marry your daughter, took the keys and opened the box. You remember that the day of the fight Oscar went to Chicago? Well, he went with my bonds that his son Leo had stolen for him. (*Pleasantly*) And for Ben, of course, too.

REGINA (*slowly, nods*)   When did you find out the bonds were gone?

HORACE   Wednesday night.

REGINA   I thought that's what you said. Why have you waited three days to do anything? (*Suddenly laughs*) This *will* make a fine story.

HORACE (*nods*)   Couldn't it?

REGINA (*still laughing*)   A fine story to hold over their heads. How could they be such fools? (*Turns to him*)

HORACE   But I'm not going to hold it over their heads.

REGINA (*the laugh stops*)   What?

HORACE (*turns his chair to face her*)   I'm going to let them keep the bonds—as a loan from you. An eighty-eight-thousand-dollar loan; they should be grateful to you. They will be, I think.

REGINA (*slowly, smiles*)   I see. You are punishing me. But I won't let you punish me. If you won't do anything, I will. Now. (*She starts for door.*)

HORACE   You won't do anything. Because you can't. (REGINA *stops.*) It won't do you any good to make trouble because I shall simply say that I lent them the bonds.

REGINA (*slowly*)   You would do that?

HORACE   Yes. For once in your life I am tying your hands. There is nothing for you to do. (*There is silence. Then she sits down.*)

REGINA   I see. You are going to lend them the bonds and let them keep all the profit they make on them, and there is nothing I can do about it. Is that right?

HORACE   Yes.

REGINA *(softly)*   Why did you say that I was making this gift?

HORACE   I was coming to that. I am going to make a new will, Regina, leaving you eighty-eight thousand dollars in Union Pacific bonds. The rest will go to Zan. It's true that your brothers have borrowed your share for a little while. After my death I advise you to talk to Ben and Oscar. They won't admit anything and Ben, I think, will be smart enough to see that he's safe. Because I knew about the theft and said nothing. Nor will I say anything as long as I live. Is that clear to you?

REGINA *(nods, softly, without looking at him)*   You will not say anything as long as you live.

HORACE   That's right. And by that time they will probably have replaced your bonds, and then they'll belong to you and nobody but us will ever know what happened. *(Stops, smiles)* They'll be around any minute to see what I am going to do. I took good care to see that word reached Leo. They'll be mighty relieved to know I'm going to do nothing and Ben will think it all a capital joke on you. And that will be the end of that. There's nothing you can do to them, nothing you can do to me.

REGINA   You hate me very much.

HORACE   No.

REGINA   Oh, I think you do. *(Puts her head back, sighs)* Well, we haven't been very good together. Anyway, I don't hate you either. I have only contempt for you. I've always had.

HORACE   From the very first?

REGINA   I think so.

HORACE   I was in love with *you*. But why did *you* marry *me?*

REGINA   I was lonely when I was young.

HORACE   *You* were lonely?

REGINA   Not the way people usually mean. Lonely for all the things I wasn't going to get. Everybody in this house was so busy and there was so little place for what I wanted. I wanted the world. Then, and then— *(Smiles)* Papa died and left the money to Ben and Oscar.

HORACE   And you married me?

REGINA   Yes, I thought— But I was wrong. You were a small-town clerk then. You haven't changed.

HORACE *(nods, smiles)*   And that wasn't what you wanted.

REGINA   No. No, it wasn't what I wanted. *(Pauses, leans back; pleasantly)* It took me a little while to find out I had made a mistake. As for you—I don't know. It was almost as if I couldn't stand the kind of man you were— *(Smiles; softly)* I used to lie there at night, praying you wouldn't come near—

HORACE   Really? It was as bad as that?

REGINA (*nods*)   Remember when I went to Doctor Sloan and I told you he said there was something the matter with me and that you shouldn't touch me any more?

HORACE   I remember.

REGINA   But you believed it. I couldn't understand that. I couldn't understand that anybody could be such a soft fool. That was when I began to despise you.

HORACE (*puts his hand to his throat, looks at the bottle of medicine on table*)   Why didn't you leave me?

REGINA   I told you I married you for something. It turned out it was only for this. (*Carefully*) This wasn't what I wanted, but it was something. I never thought about it much but if I had (HORACE *puts his hand to his throat.*) I'd have known that you would die before I would. But I couldn't have known that you would get heart trouble so early and so bad. I'm lucky, Horace. I've always been lucky. (HORACE *turns slowly to the medicine.*) I'll be lucky again.

HORACE *looks at her. Then he puts his hand to his throat. Because he cannot reach the bottle he moves the chair closer. He reaches for the medicine, takes out the cork, picks up the spoon. The bottle slips and smashes on the table. He draws in his breath, gasps.*

HORACE   Please. Tell Addie— The other bottle is upstairs. (REGINA *has not moved. She does not move now. He stares at her. Then, suddenly as if he understood, he raises his voice. It is a panic-stricken whisper, too small to be heard outside the room.*) Addie! Addie! Come— (*Stops as he hears the softness of his voice. He makes a sudden, furious spring from the chair to the stairs, taking the first few steps as if he were a desperate runner. On the fourth step he slips, gasps, grasps the rail, makes a great effort to reach the landing. When he reaches the landing, he is on his knees. His knees give way, he falls on the landing, out of view.* REGINA *has not turned during his climb up the stairs. Now she waits a second. Then she goes below the landing, speaks up.*)

REGINA   Horace. Horace. (*When there is no answer, she turns, calls*) Addie! Cal! Come in here. (*She starts up the steps.* ADDIE *and* CAL *appear. Both run towards the stairs.*) He's had an attack. Come up here. (*They run up the steps quickly.*)

CAL   My God. Mr. Horace—

They cannot be seen now.

REGINA (*her voice comes from the head of the stairs*)   Be still, Cal. Bring him in here.

Before the footsteps and the voices have completely died away, ALEXANDRA *appears in the hall door, in her raincloak and hood. She comes into the room, begins to unfasten the cloak, suddenly looks around, sees the empty wheel chair, stares, begins to move swiftly as if to look in the dining room. At the same moment* ADDIE *runs down the stairs.* ALEXANDRA *turns and stares up at* ADDIE.

ALEXANDRA   Addie! What?

ADDIE   (*takes* ALEXANDRA *by the shoulders*)   I'm going for the doctor. Go upstairs.

ALEXANDRA *looks at her, then quickly breaks away and runs up the steps.* ADDIE *exits. The stage is empty for a minute. Then the front door bell begins to ring. When there is no answer, it rings again. A second later* LEO *appears in the hall, talking as he comes in.*

LEO   (*very nervous*)   Hello. (*Irritably*) Never say any use ringing a bell when a door was open. If you are going to ring a bell, then somebody should answer it. (*Gets in the room, looks around, puzzled, listens, hears no sound*) Aunt Regina. (*He moves around restlessly.*) Addie. (*Waits*) Where the hell— (*Crosses to the bell cord, rings it impatiently, waits, gets no answer, calls*) Cal! Cal! (CAL *appears on the stair landing.*)

CAL   (*his voice is soft, shaken*)   Mr. Leo. Miss Regina says you stop that screaming noise.

LEO   (*angrily*)   Where is everybody?

CAL   Mr. Horace he got an attack. He's bad. Miss Regina says you stop that noise.

LEO   Uncle Horace— What— What happened? (CAL *starts down the stairs, shakes his head, begins to move swiftly off.* LEO *looks around wildly.*) But when— You seen Mr. Oscar or Mr. Ben? (CAL *shakes his head. Moves on.* LEO *grabs him by the arm.*) Answer me, will you?

CAL   No, I ain't seen 'em. I ain't got time to answer you. I got to get things.

[CAL *runs off.*]

LEO   But what's the matter with him? When did this happen— (*Calling after* CAL) You'd think Papa'd be some place where you could find him. I been chasing him all afternoon.

OSCAR *and* BEN *come into the room, talking excitedly.*

OSCAR   I hope it's not a bad attack.

BEN   It's the first one he's had since he came home.

LEO   Papa, I've been looking all over town for you and Uncle Ben—

BEN   Where is he?

OSCAR   Addie said it was sudden.

BEN   (*to* LEO)   Where is he? When did it happen?

LEO   Upstairs. Will you listen to me, please? I been looking for you—

OSCAR   (*to* BEN)   You think we should go up? (BEN, *looking up the steps, shakes his head.*)

BEN   I don't know. I don't know.

OSCAR *(shakes his head)*   But he was all right—

LEO *(yelling)*   *Will you listen to me?*

OSCAR *(sharply)*   What is the matter with you?

LEO   I been trying to tell you. I been trying to find you for an hour—

OSCAR   Tell me what?

LEO   Uncle Horace knows about the bonds. He knows about them. He's had the box since Wednesday—

BEN *(sharply)*   Stop shouting! What the hell are you talking about?

LEO *(furiously)*   I'm telling you he knows about the bonds. Ain't that clear enough—

OSCAR *(grabbing* LEO'S *arm)*   You God-damn fool! Stop screaming!

BEN   Now what happened? Talk quietly.

LEO   You heard me. Uncle Horace knows about the bonds. He's known since Wednesday.

BEN *(after a second)*   How do you know that?

LEO   Because Cal comes down to Manders and says the box came O.K. and—

OSCAR *(trembling)*   That might not mean a thing—

LEO *(angrily)*   No? It might not, huh? Then he says Manders should come here tonight and bring Sol Fowler with him. I guess that don't mean a thing either.

OSCAR *(to* BEN)   Ben— What— Do you think he's seen the—

BEN *(motions to the box)*   There's the box. *(Both* OSCAR *and* LEO *turn sharply.* LEO *makes a leap to the box.)* You ass. Put it down. What are you going to do with it, eat it?

LEO   I'm going to— *(Starts)*

BEN *(furiously)*   Put it down. Don't touch it again. Now sit down and shut up for a minute.

OSCAR   Since Wednesday. *(To* LEO*)* You said he had it since Wednesday. Why didn't he say something— *(To* BEN*)* I don't understand—

LEO *(taking a step)*   I can put it back. I can put it back before anybody knows.

BEN *(who is standing at the table, softly)*   He's had it since Wednesday. Yet he hasn't said a word to us.

OSCAR   Why? Why?

LEO   What's the difference why? He was getting ready to say plenty. He was going to say it to Fowler tonight—

OSCAR *(angrily)*   Be still. *(Turns to* BEN, *looks at him, waits)*

BEN *(after a minute)*   I don't believe that.

LEO *(wildly)*   *You* don't believe it? What do I care what *you* believe? I do the dirty work and then—

BEN *(turning his head sharply to* LEO*)*   I'm remembering that. I'm remembering that, Leo.

OSCAR   What do you mean?

LEO   You—

BEN *(to* OSCAR*)*   If you don't shut that little fool up, I'll show you what I mean. For some reason he knows, but he don't say a word.

OSCAR   Maybe he didn't know that *we*—

BEN (*quickly*) That *Leo*— He's no fool. Does Manders know the bonds are missing?

LEO How could I tell? I was half crazy. I don't think so. Because Manders seemed kind of puzzled and—

OSCAR But we got to find out— (*He breaks off as* CAL *comes into the room carrying a kettle of hot water.*)

BEN How is he, Cal?

CAL I don't know, Mr. Ben. He was bad. (*Going towards stairs*)

OSCAR But when did it happen?

CAL (*shrugs*) He wasn't feeling bad early. (ADDIE *comes in quickly from the hall.*) Then there he is next thing on the landing, fallen over, his eyes tight—

ADDIE (*to* CAL) Dr. Sloan's over at the Ballongs. Hitch the buggy and go get him. (*She takes the kettle and cloths from him, pushes him, runs up the stairs.*) Go on.   [*She disappears.* CAL *exits.*]

BEN Never seen Sloan anywhere when you need him.

OSCAR (*softly*) Sounds bad.

LEO He would have told *her* about it. Aunt Regina. He would have told his own wife—

BEN (*turning to* LEO) Yes, he might have told her. But they weren't on such pretty terms and maybe he didn't. Maybe he didn't. (*Goes quickly to* LEO) Now, listen to me. If she doesn't know, it may work out all right. If she does know, you're to say he lent you the bonds.

LEO Lent them to me! Who's going to believe that?

BEN Nobody.

OSCAR (*to* LEO) Don't you understand? It can't do no harm to say it—

LEO Why should I say he lent them to me? Why not to you? (*Carefully*) Why not to Uncle Ben?

BEN (*smiles*) Just because he didn't lend them to me. Remember that.

LEO But all he has to do is say he didn't lend them to me—

BEN (*furiously*) But for some reason, he doesn't seem to be talking, does he? (*There are footsteps above. They all stand looking at the stairs.* REGINA *begins to come slowly down.*) What happened?

REGINA He's had a bad attack.

OSCAR Too bad. I'm so sorry we weren't here when—when Horace needed us.

BEN When *you* needed us.

REGINA (*looks at him*) Yes.

BEN How is he? Can we—can we go up?

REGINA (*shakes her head*) He's not conscious.

OSCAR (*pacing around*) It's that—it's that bad? Wouldn't you think Sloan could be found quickly, just once, just once?

REGINA I don't think there is much for him to do.

BEN Oh, don't talk like that. He's come through attacks before. He will now.

REGINA *sits down. After a second she speaks softly.*

REGINA   Well. We haven't seen each other since the day of our fight.

BEN *(tenderly)*   That was nothing. Why, you and Oscar and I used to fight when we were kids.

OSCAR *(hurriedly)*   Don't you think we should go up? Is there anything we can do for Horace—

BEN   You don't feel well. Ah—

REGINA *(without looking at them)*   No, I don't. *(Slight pause)* Horace told me about the bonds this afternoon. *(There is an immediate shocked silence.)*

LEO   The bonds. What do you mean? What bonds? What—

BEN *(looks at him furiously; then to REGINA)*   The Union Pacific bonds? *Horace's* Union Pacific bonds?

REGINA   Yes.

OSCAR *(steps to her, very nervously)*   Well. Well what—what about them? What—what could he say?

REGINA   He said that Leo had stolen the bonds and given them to you.

OSCAR *(aghast, very loudly)*   That's ridiculous. Regina, absolutely—

LEO   I don't know what you're talking about. What would I—Why—

REGINA *(wearily to BEN)*   Isn't it enough that he stole them from me? Do I have to listen to this in the bargain?

OSCAR   You are talking—

LEO   I didn't steal anything. I don't know why—

REGINA *(to BEN)*   Would you ask them to stop that, please?

There is silence for a minute. BEN *glowers at* OSCAR *and* LEO.

BEN   Aren't we starting at the wrong end, Regina? What did Horace tell you?

REGINA *(smiles at him)*   He told me that Leo had stolen the bonds.

LEO   I didn't steal—

REGINA   Please. Let me finish. Then he told me that he was going to pretend that he had lent them to you (LEO *turns sharply to* REGINA, *then looks at* OSCAR, *then looks back at* REGINA) as a present from me—to my brothers. He said there was nothing I could do about it. He said the rest of his money would go to Alexandra. That is all.

There is a silence. OSCAR *coughs,* LEO *smiles slyly.*

LEO *(taking a step to her)*   I told you he had lent them— I could have told you—

REGINA *(ignores him, smiles sadly at BEN)*   So I'm very badly off, you see. *(Carefully)* But Horace said there was nothing I could do about it as long as he was alive to say he had lent you the bonds.

BEN   You shouldn't feel that way. It can all be explained, all be adjusted. It isn't as bad—

REGINA   So you, at least, are willing to admit that the bonds were stolen?

(OSCAR *laughs nervously*)

BEN　I admit no such thing. It's possible that Horace made up that part of the story to tease you— *(Looks at her)* Or perhaps to punish you.

REGINA *(sadly)*　It's not a pleasant story. I feel bad, Ben, naturally. I hadn't thought—

BEN　Now you shall have the bonds safely back. That was the understanding wasn't it Oscar?

OSCAR　Yes.

REGINA　I'm glad to know that. *(Smiles)* Ah, I had greater hopes—

BEN　Don't talk that way. That's foolish. *(Looks at his watch)* I think we ought to drive out for Sloan ourselves. If we can't find him we'll go over to Senateville for Doctor Morris. And don't think I'm dismissing this other business. I'm not. We'll have it all out on a more appropriate day.

REGINA *(looks up, quietly)*　I don't think you had better go yet. I think you had better stay and sit down.

BEN　We'll be back with Sloan.

REGINA　Cal has gone for him. I don't want you to go.

BEN　Now don't worry and—

REGINA　You will come back in this room and sit down. I have something more to say.

BEN *(turns, comes towards her)*　Since when do I take orders from you?

REGINA *(smiles)*　You don't—yet. *(Sharply)* Come back, Oscar. You too, Leo.

OSCAR *(sure of himself, laughs)*　My dear Regina.

BEN *(softly, pats her hand)*　Horace has already clipped your wings and very wittily. Do I have to clip them, too? *(Smiles at her)* You'd get farther with a smile, Regina. I'm a soft man for a woman's smile.

REGINA　I'm smiling, Ben. I'm smiling because you are quite safe while Horace lives. But I don't think Horace will live. And if he doesn't live I shall want seventy-five per cent in exchange for the bonds.

BEN *(steps back, whistles, laughs)*　Greedy! What a greedy girl you are! You want so much of everything.

REGINA　Yes. And if I don't get what I want I am going to put all three of you in jail.

OSCAR *(furiously)*　You're mighty crazy. Having just admitted—

BEN　And on what evidence would you put Oscar and Leo in jail?

REGINA *(laughs, gaily)*　Oscar, listen to him. He's getting ready to swear that it was you and Leo! What do you say to that? *(OSCAR turns furiously towards BEN.)* Oh, don't be angry, Oscar. I'm going to see that he goes in with you.

BEN　Try anything you like, Regina, *(Sharply)* And now we can stop all this and say good-bye to you. *(ALEXANDRA comes slowly down the steps.)* It's his money and he's obviously willing to let us borrow it. *(More pleasantly)* Learn to make threats when you can carry them through. For how many years have I told you a good-looking woman gets more by being soft and appealing? Mama used to tell you that. *(Looks at his watch)* Where the hell is Sloan? *(To OSCAR)* Take the buggy and— *(As BEN turns to OSCAR, he sees ALEXANDRA. She walks stiffly. She goes slowly to the lower window, her head bent. They all turn to look at her.)*

OSCAR (*after a second, moving toward her*) What? Alexandra—(*She does not answer. After a second,* ADDIE *comes slowly down the stairs, moving as if she were very tired. At foot of steps, she looks at* ALEXANDRA, *then turns and slowly crosses to door and exits.* REGINA *rises.* BEN *looks nervously at* ALEXANDRA, *at* REGINA. *As* ADDIE *passes him, irritably to* ALEXANDRA) Well, what is— (*turns into room—sees* ADDIE *at foot of steps*)—what's? (BEN *puts up a hand, shakes his head.*) My God, I didn't know—who *could* have known—I didn't know he was that sick. Well, well—I—(REGINA *stands quietly, her back to them.*)

BEN (*softly, sincerely*) Seems like yesterday when he first came here.

OSCAR (*sincerely, nervously*) Yes, that's true. (*Turns to* BEN) The whole town loved him and respected him.

ALEXANDRA (*turns*) Did you love him, Uncle Oscar?

OSCAR Certainly, I— What a strange thing to ask! I—

ALEXANDRA Did you love him, Uncle Ben?

BEN (*simply*) He had—

ALEXANDRA (*suddenly starts to laugh very loudly*) And you, Mama, did you love him, too?

REGINA I know what you feel, Alexandra, but please try to control yourself.

ALEXANDRA (*still laughing*) I'm trying, Mama. I'm trying very hard.

BEN Grief makes some people laugh and some people cry. It's better to cry, Alexandra.

ALEXANDRA (*the laugh has stopped; tensely moves toward* REGINA) What was Papa doing on the staircase?

BEN *turns to look at* ALEXANDRA.

REGINA Please go and lie down, my dear. We all need to get over shocks like this. (ALEXANDRA *does not move,* REGINA'S *voice becomes softer, more insistent.*) Please go, Alexandra.

ALEXANDRA No, Mama. I'll wait. I've got to talk to you.

REGINA Later. Go and rest now.

ALEXANDRA (*quietly*) I'll wait, Mama. I've plenty of time.

REGINA (*hesitates, stares, makes a half shrug, turns back to* BEN) As I was saying. Tomorrow morning I am going up to Judge Simmes. I shall tell him about Leo.

BEN (*motioning toward* ALEXANDRA) Not in front of the child, Regina. I—

REGINA (*turns to him; sharply*) I didn't ask her to stay. Tomorrow morning I go to Judge Simmes—

OSCAR And what proof? What proof of all this—

REGINA (*turns sharply*) None. I won't need any. The bonds are missing and they are with Marshall. That will be enough. If it isn't, I'll add what's necessary.

BEN I'm sure of that.

REGINA (*turns to* BEN) You can be quite sure.

OSCAR We'll deny—

REGINA   Deny your heads off. You couldn't find a jury that wouldn't weep for a woman whose brothers steal from her. And you couldn't find twelve men in this state you haven't cheated and hate you for it.

OSCAR   What kind of talk is this? You couldn't do anything like that! We're your own brothers. *(Points upstairs)* How can you talk that way when upstairs not five minutes ago—

REGINA *(slowly)*   There are people who can never go back, who must finish what they start. I am one of those people, Oscar. *(After a slight pause)* Where was I? *(Smiles at* BEN*)* Well, they'll convict you. But I won't care much if they don't. *(Leans forward; pleasantly)* Because by that time you'll be ruined. I shall also tell my story to Mr. Marshall, who likes me, I think, and who will not want to be involved in your scandal. A respectable firm like Marshall and Company. The deal would be off in an hour. *(Turns to them angrily)* And you know it. Now I don't want to hear any more from any of you. *You'll do no more bargaining in this house.* I'll take my seventy-five per cent and we'll forget the story forever. That's one way of doing it, and the way I prefer. You know me well enough to know that I don't mind taking the other way.

BEN *(after a second, slowly)*   None of us have ever known you well enough, Regina.

REGINA   You're getting old, Ben. Your tricks aren't as smart as they used to be. *(There is no answer. She waits, then smiles.)* All right. I take it that's settled and I get what I asked for.

OSCAR *(furiously to* BEN*)*   Are you going to let her do this—

BEN *(turns to look at him, slowly)*   You have a suggestion?

REGINA *(puts her arms above her head, stretches, laughs)*   No, he hasn't. All right. Now, Leo, I have forgotten that you ever saw the bonds. *(Archly, to* BEN *and* OSCAR*)* And as long as you boys both behave yourselves, I've forgotten that we ever talked about them. You can draw up the necessary papers tomorrow.

BEN *laughs.* LEO *stares at him, starts for door. Exits.* OSCAR *moves towards door angrily.* REGINA *looks at* BEN*, nods, laughs with him. For a second,* OSCAR *stands in the door, looking back at them. Then he exits.*

REGINA   You're a good loser, Ben. I like that.

BEN *(he picks up his coat, then turns to her)*   Well, I say to myself, what's the good? You and I aren't like Oscar. We're not sour people. I think that comes from a good digestion. Then, too, one loses today and wins tomorrow. I say to myself, years of planning and I get what I want. Then I don't get it. But I'm not discouraged. The century's turning, the world is open. Open for people like you and me. Ready for us, waiting for us. After all this is just the beginning. There are hundreds of Hubbards sitting in rooms like this throughout the country. All their names aren't Hubbard, but they are all Hubbards and they will own this country some day. We'll get along.

REGINA *(smiles)*   I think so.

BEN   Then, too, I say to myself, things may change. (*Looks at* ALEXANDRA) I
       agree with Alexandra. What is a man in a wheel chair doing on a staircase? I
       ask myself that.

REGINA (*looks up at him*)   And what do you answer?

BEN   I have no answer. But maybe some day I will. Maybe never, but maybe
       some day. (*Smiles; pats her arm*) When I do, I'll let you know. (*Goes towards
       hall*)

REGINA   When you do, write me. I will be in Chicago. (*Gaily*) Ah, Ben, if Papa
       had only left me his money.

BEN   I'll see you tomorrow.

REGINA   Oh, yes. Certainly. You'll be sort of working for me now.

BEN   (*as he passes* ALEXANDRA, *smiles*)   Alexandra, you're turning out to be a
       right interesting girl. (*Looks at* REGINA) Well, good night all.   [*He exits.*]

REGINA   (*Sits quietly for a second, stretches, turns to look at* ALEXANDRA)   What
       do you want to talk to me about, Alexandra?

ALEXANDRA (*slowly*)   I've changed my mind. I don't want to talk. There's
       nothing to talk about now.

REGINA   You're acting very strange. Not like yourself. You've had a bad shock
       today. I know that. And you loved Papa, but you must have expected this to
       come some day. You knew how sick he was.

ALEXANDRA   I knew. We all knew.

REGINA   It will be good for you to get away from here. Good for me, too.
       Time heals most wounds, Alexandra. You're young, you shall have all the
       things I wanted. I'll make the world for you the way I wanted it to be for
       me. (*Uncomfortably*) Don't sit there staring. You've been around Birdie so
       much you're getting just like her.

ALEXANDRA (*nods*)   Funny. That's what Aunt Birdie said today.

REGINA (*nods*)   Be good for you to get away from all this.

       ADDIE *enters.*

ADDIE   Cal is back, Miss Regina. He says Dr. Sloan will be coming in a few
       minutes.

REGINA   We'll go in a few weeks. A few weeks! That means two or three
       Saturdays, two or three Sundays. (*Sighs*) Well, I'm very tired. I shall go to
       bed. I don't want any supper. Put the lights out and lock up. (ADDIE *moves
       to the piano lamp, turns it out.*) You go to your room, Alexandra. Addie will
       bring you something hot. You look very tired. (*Rises; to* ADDIE) Call me
       when Dr. Sloan gets here. I don't want to see anybody else. I don't want any
       condolence calls tonight. The whole town will be over.

ALEXANDRA   Mama, I'm not coming with you. I'm not going to Chicago.

REGINA (*turns to her*)   You're very upset, Alexandra.

ALEXANDRA (*quietly*)   I mean what I say. With all my heart.

REGINA   We'll talk about it tomorrow. The morning will make a difference.

ALEXANDRA   It won't make any difference. And there isn't anything to talk

about. I am going away from you. Because I want to. Because I know Papa
would want me to.

REGINA (*puzzled, careful, polite*) You *know* your papa wanted you to go away
from me?

ALEXANDRA Yes.

REGINA (*softly*) And if I say no?

ALEXANDRA (*looks at her*) Say it, Mama, say it. And see what happens.

REGINA (*softly, after a pause*) And if I make you stay?

ALEXANDRA That would be foolish. It wouldn't work in the end.

REGINA You're very serious about it, aren't you? (*Crosses to stairs*) Well, you'll
change your mind in a few days.

ALEXANDRA You only change your mind when you want to. And I won't want
to.

REGINA (*going up the steps*) Alexandra, I've come to the end of my rope.
Somewhere there has to be what I want, too. Life goes too fast. Do what
you want; think what you want; go where you want. I'd like to keep you
with me, but I won't make you stay. Too many people used to make me do
too many things. No, I won't make you stay.

ALEXANDRA You couldn't, Mama, because I want to leave here. As I've never
wanted anything in my life before. Because now I understand what Papa
was trying to tell me. (*Pause*) All in one day: Addie said there were people
who ate the earth and other people who stood around and watched them do
it. And just now Uncle Ben said the same thing. Really, he said the same
thing. (*Tensely*) Well, tell him for me, Mama, I'm not going to stand around
and watch you do it. Tell him I'll be fighting as hard as he'll be fighting
(*rises*) some place where people don't just stand around and watch.

REGINA Well, you have spirit, after all. I used to think you were all sugar
water. We don't have to be bad friends. I don't want us to be bad friends,
Alexandra. (*Starts, stops, turns to* ALEXANDRA.) Would you like to come
and talk to me, Alexandra? Would you—would you like to sleep in my
room tonight?

ALEXANDRA (*takes a step towards her*) Are you afraid, Mama?

REGINA *does not answer. She moves slowly out of sight.* ADDIE *comes to*
ALEXANDRA, *presses her arm.*

Questions for Writing and Discussion

1.   In this play Ben Hubbard is the center of intelligence and Addie the center of
moral awareness. How well do these terms fit Ben and Addie? What are the risks,
or the possible rewards, when a writer separates the center of intelligence from the
moral center (since in many works of literature the two functions are assumed by
one character)?

2.   Every once in a while Ben Hubbard delivers himself of a piece of canned wisdom, a sententious remark. What is the purpose of these? How do they reveal aspects of Ben's character? Do they also serve the purpose of delivering some (questionable?) generalizations about what is happening?

3.   A subplot concerns the relationship between Oscar Hubbard and his wife Birdie. This serves the obvious purpose of contributing a little to the picture of Hubbard wickedness. But does it tell us more about the background, the underlying themes of the play?

4.   Distinguish among the kinds of wickedness represented in the Hubbard family. How do these relate to one another? Do you find it hard to believe in such unrelieved evil, or do you think there is plenty of evidence for accepting it as realistic?

5.   There are characters in plays who are necessary to the plot yet not vividly drawn in their own right. One such is Zan, the seventeen-year-old daughter of Regina, who at the start is seen rather conventionally but at the end has to carry the moral idea, or message, of the play. Suppose you were assigned this part—how would you perform it so as to make Zan credible in both the first and the third acts? Imagine yourself as either an actress or a director.

6.   Horace, Birdie, and Alexandra all are, or were, musical. Oscar has said that music makes him nervous. Does music stand for anything in human character beyond mere social refinement? Why does Horace keep a part of a broken violin in the safe-deposit box?

7.   Ben observes that "A good-looking woman gets more by being soft and appealing." How does this apply to both Hubbard marriages? What is the relation of sexuality to power in both cases?

TENNESSEE WILLIAMS

Cat on a Hot Tin Roof

Introduction:
An Imaginary Notebook of an Imaginary Director

Some directors, before undertaking a play, write notes to themselves, clues and hints as to what they should do when they try to move from script to stage. Here are some imaginary notes by an imaginary director trying to figure out the play and how to cope with it.

1. "Human kind"—who said it?—"cannot bear much reality." This single sentence compresses, I would guess, the intended meaning of Williams' play—but with the addition that the need a playwright has for *dramatizing* his ideas necessarily leads him to show a group of characters with *varying* and *changing* capacities for facing reality. It's the *varying* and *changing* that count most.

So I see a spectrum of characters in "Cat." There are the simple, auxiliary figures like Gooper and Mae who understand nothing about life or love or death, but act simply out of blunt greed and conscious falsity. They're two dimensional, and can't be played any other way. Don't try to make them more complicated. There's Big Mama, who combines self-deception with sudden moments of courage in about equal amounts. And there are Margaret and Big Daddy, who at least know that there *is* a reality out there, usually painful and requiring exertions of honesty to reach. Not that they (or anyone) quite manage to keep looking at that reality throughout, or with steady courage, since one of the things Williams has in mind here is the difficulty, perhaps the impossibility, of reaching the truth even when you steadily want to reach it. (Note: one of the more touching moments in the play is in Act II. Big Daddy and Brick do finally try to speak honestly but fail, partly because they fall back into their customary styles of response, Big Daddy into loud rant and Brick into wry evasion. But more, and here I think Williams is on to something, Americans seem always to believe that anything can be solved by sincerity, a good heart-to-heart talk, a rap session. But Williams seems to be saying, no, that's not so, sometimes heart-to-heart brings nothing but torment.)

Perhaps the play should be taken to suggest that reality or truth is not some final fixed object or state of being; it may be no more than our yearning, a chimera of our troubled consciousness. At best, it may be some limit toward which to strain—and strain because we know we can't reach it.

If the play is performed with this problematic emphasis in mind, it will hold up better than if we look for some definite idea, which it probably can't yield. On the other hand, if I complicate it too much for the actors, they might become nervous and imprecise.

2. One big problem we'll have to face is how to cope with the *hysteria* that seems to beset the main characters most of the time. If you're reading, you can cool it off, so to speak, by putting the book down and taking a rest; but the spectator in the theatre can't do that. Williams says, in his Notes for the Designer, that the play "deals with human extremities of emotion." Does he perhaps indulge those "extremities" too much at certain points, in a sort of wanton surrender to the nerves of his characters?

But remember:

a) The action does take place at a moment of crisis when all the major characters—Big Daddy, Margaret, Brick—have lost their grip on themselves;

b) The play can't be done in a "realistic" style; it has to be seen as another example of American grotesque, in which all expressions and situations are distorted or exaggerated in order to get (it is hoped) at the essence of things. And what is the essence in this play? Uncertainty, fear, panic, loneliness.

3. Brick will be the hardest role to bring out, because he is the least clearly conceived of the major characters. He is recessive rather than assertive; he does not want to act; he changes a lot. Margaret and Big Daddy—juicy roles, with the danger of being "hammed up," especially if I don't keep the actors in check. But Brick, because he has to be done in a style subordinate to the high jinks of Margaret and Big Daddy, needs special help in defining, shading, protecting.

I see the central weakness of the play as the Brick–Skipper relation. Sure, my literary friends will tell me that it draws from a traditional motif of American literature—the friendship, pure and therapeutic, between two male friends (Huck–Jim; Ishmael–Queequeg; Natty Bumpo–his Indian friend.) But in Williams' (oversophisticated? perhaps even decadent?) treatment, this theme loses some of its nineteenth-century moral strength and takes on a clinical aspect. It's hard to accept at face value Brick's view of his friendship with Skipper (and I wish Williams hadn't made Skipper into a sort of dummy, suggesting unhappy associations with Lenny in Steinbeck's *Of Mice and Men*.)

But it is part of the play and has to be kept in. Otherwise, the Brick–Margaret relationship would become incomprehensible. All one can do is to hope that the passages in which the Skipper story is told are handled with speed and restraint. We just have to get past them as best we can.

4. Where is the real emotional energy of this play? In the two strong characters, Margaret and Big Daddy. They have *will;* they are ready to impose that will on others. They are ruthless, but *they know it.* If anything can redeem them, that's it. They do want a piece of reality, as much as they can absorb.

A big problem: without being too explicit or wrenching the text, how can I suggest that there is a certain connection between Margaret and Big Daddy, some unspoken sense each has that in the crises and decisions of this moment each knows that it is the other—and finally no one else—who counts. Each of them loves Brick, each talks to Brick; but each is also talking *through* or *past* Brick, in order to reach one another. The currents of psychic energy that matter most run between Margaret and Big Daddy, but they run apart from or underneath the words.

So the actors who play these two parts have to be trained to suggest an intense awareness of one another, a tension of constantly watching one another; but at all costs, avoid explicit signs of flirtation between them. You can't keep an audience from being suspicious, but you can keep the actors from confirming the suspicions with a sledge hammer.

5. Big Mama. Two dangers: (a) to do her entirely in caricature, the self-deluded, silly, noisy, vulgar Southern old doll or (b) to take too seriously the changes in her that do occur in Acts II and III, thereby missing the element of parody in her last speech or two. Something genuine is revealed in her under all that stress; but the foolishness of a lifetime can't be shaken off in half an hour. Still, which actress will be able to resist a heartbreaking switch from Big Mama as drip to Big Mama as sudden wise lady?

6. Williams makes a big deal out of Southern gentility—the falsities and evasions it encourages, all those "Yaiss's" and all that sweet talk. This is handy enough, since there's a tradition in the American theatre of using the manners and mannerisms of that gentility. It helps save us time by quickly establishing the social milieu, the code of manners in which we develop the action. But there's a trap here—that the audience may take the whole thing as still another slap at "the degenerate South," as if only in the South do people evade and lie! My problem will be to indicate, somehow, that what Williams is showing here has its "universal" implications, yet I can't let it go stuffy or pompous.

How do we do that?

7. Act I—no major difficulties. Williams starts with the traditional device of having two major characters—Margaret and Brick—fill in the background of the story. Margaret's humor about the "no-neck monsters" is a strong opening, and here the actress can work it to the hilt. The play, in general, seems a little overheated, and any humorous relief should be welcomed. Then the tension between Margaret and Brick is developed further—it's a good first act.

Acts II and III will give us trouble. There are too many climaxes, too many outbursts of rhetoric, probably too many words. You must face the danger of wearing out the audience with Big Mama's shrieking (which actress in that part wouldn't shriek?), Big Daddy's ranting, Gooper and Mae's venality, etc. If I were free to, I'd cut a little, tone down some of the confrontations. The ending—Margaret blackmailing Brick into bed—is strong, but make sure the tenderness also comes through. By then, the audience may be wrung out.

8. A small problem, but interesting: although I feel that Williams sometimes lets his language get away from him, there are, on the other hand, a number of passages in which he puts a general remark—an aphorism or epigram—into the mouth of a character, and most of these seem pretty good. (For example, when Margaret says in Act I, Brick has "the charm of the defeated," or Brick in Act II, "Mendacity is a system that we live in. Liquor is one way out an' death's the other," or when Margaret says to Brick in Act I, "I'm not living with you. We occupy the same cage.")

How to play such lines? The first answer would be "naturally," but that's not a very good answer, since nothing in this play is "natural"; everything is inflamed, strange, oversize. Still, don't let the actors read such sentences as if they had suddenly come up with a nugget of wisdom and were overawed. In a play where so much is overstated, maybe the best kind of emphasis is understatement.

9. Finally, the biggest problem of all: there are two versions of Act III. Williams explains this circumstance by telling what happened when the director of the first Broadway production, Elia Kazan, read the original version of the play:

> ... he was excited by it, but he had definite reservations about it which were concentrated in the third act. The gist of his reservations can be listed as three points: one, he felt that Big Daddy was too vivid and important a character to disappear from the play except as an offstage cry after the second act curtain; two, he felt that the character of Brick should undergo some apparent mutation as a result of the virtual vivisection that he undergoes in his interview with his father in Act Two. Three, he felt that the character of Margaret, while he understood that I ... liked her myself, should be, if possible, more clearly sympathetic to an audience.
>
> It was only the third of these suggestions that I embraced wholeheartedly from the outset. ... I didn't want Big Daddy to reappear in Act Three and I felt that the moral paralysis of Brick was a root thing in his tragedy, and to show a dramatic progression would obscure the meaning of that tragedy in him. ...

Yet, in the reworked version that Williams finally did under Kazan's pressure, at least some of the changes that Kazan had asked for were made. So, which do we use—the play as first written or the play as first produced?

I opt for the play as first written. The changes induced by Kazan made the play more "dramatic" but less coherent. You don't need Big Daddy on stage in Act III because he has already done all he can, already shot his bolt, in the previous act. There's enough conflict, enough confusion, without him. Williams was quite right in what he said about Brick—to show him changing very much in Act III would be to make his character highly unpersuasive, since someone with his kind of problems doesn't change very quickly (and remember, the action of the play is continuous, all in *one* evening). As for Margaret, she has surely won the sympathy of the audience by the end of Act II! Only an utterly incompetent actress could fail to do that.

So I think the play as Williams first wrote it is clearer, sharper, less cluttered, even if it allows for fewer melodramatic high jinks of the kind that Kazan wanted in Act III. The dramatic, in any case, isn't a quality that emerges from violent face-to-face shouting; it emerges from a persuasive evocation of deep inner conflicts within and among human beings: it comes from truth, not noise.

Cat on a Hot Tin Roof

CHARACTERS OF THE PLAY

MARGARET
BRICK
MAE, *sometimes called Sister Woman*
BIG MAMA
DIXIE, *a little girl*
BIG DADDY
REVEREND TOOKER
GOOPER, *sometimes called Brother Man*
DOCTOR BAUGH, *pronounced "Baw"*
LACEY, *a Negro servant*
SMOKEY, *another*
Another little girl and two small boys

NOTES FOR THE DESIGNER

The set is the bed-sitting-room of a plantation home in the Mississippi Delta. It is along an upstairs gallery which probably runs around the entire house; it has two pairs of very wide doors opening onto the gallery, showing white balustrades against a fair summer sky that fades into dusk and night during the course of the play, which occupies precisely the time of its performance, excepting, of course, the fifteen minutes of intermission.

Perhaps the style of the room is not what you would expect in the home of the Delta's biggest cotton-planter. It is Victorian with a touch of the Far East. It hasn't changed much since it was occupied by the original owners of the place, Jack Straw and Peter Ochello, a pair of old bachelors who shared this room all their lives together. In other words, the room must evoke some ghosts; it is gently and poetically haunted by a relationship that must have involved a tenderness which was uncommon. This may be irrelevant or unnecessary, but I once saw a reproduction of a faded photograph of the verandah of Robert Louis Stevenson's home on that Samoan Island where he spent his last years, and there was a quality of tender light on weathered wood, such as porch furniture made of bamboo and wicker, exposed to tropical suns and tropical rains, which came to mind when I thought about the set for this play, bringing also to mind the grace and comfort of light, the reassurance it gives, on a late and fair afternoon in summer, the way that no matter what, even dread of death, is gently touched and soothed by it. For the set is the background for a play that deals with human extremities of emotion, and it needs that softness behind it.

The bathroom door, showing only pale-blue tile and silver towel racks, is in one side wall; the hall door in the opposite wall. Two articles of furniture need mention: a big double bed which staging should make a functional part of the set as often as suitable, the surface of which should be slightly raked to make figures on it seen more easily; and against the wall space between the two huge double doors upstage: a monumental monstrosity peculiar to our times, a *huge* console combination of radio-phonograph (Hi-Fi with three speakers) TV set *and* liquor cabinet, bearing and containing many glasses and bottles, all in one piece, which is a composition of muted silver tones, and the opalescent tones of reflecting glass, a chromatic link, this thing, between the sepia (tawny gold) tones of the interior and the cool (white and blue) tones of the gallery and sky. This piece of furniture (?!), this monument, is a very complete and compact little shrine to virtually all the comforts and illusions behind which we hide from such things as the characters in the play are faced with. . . .

The set should be far less realistic than I have so far implied in this description of it. I think the walls below the ceiling should dissolve mysteriously into air; the set should be roofed by the sky; stars and moon suggested by traces of milky pallor, as if they were observed through a telescope lens out of focus.

Anything else I can think of? Oh, yes, fanlights (transoms shaped like an open glass fan) above all the doors in the set, with panes of blue and amber, and above all, the designer should take as many pains to give the actors room to move about freely (to show their restlessness, their passion for breaking out) as if it were a set for a ballet.

An evening in summer. The action is continuous, with two intermissions.

ACT I

At the rise of the curtain someone is taking a shower in the bathroom, the door of which is half open. A pretty young woman, with anxious lines in her face, enters the bedroom and crosses to the bathroom door.

MARGARET (*shouting above roar of water*)   One of those no-neck monsters hit me with a hot buttered biscuit so I have t' change!

(MARGARET'S *voice is both rapid and drawling. In her long speeches she has the vocal tricks of a priest delivering a liturgical chant, the lines are almost sung, always continuing a little beyond her breath so she has to gasp for another. Sometimes she intersperses the lines with a little wordless singing, such as "Da-da-daaaa!"*

Water turns off and BRICK *calls out to her, but is still unseen. A tone of politely feigned interest, masking indifference, or worse, is characteristic of his speech with* MARGARET.)

BRICK   Wha'd you say, Maggie? Water was on s' loud I couldn't hearya. . . .
MARGARET   Well, I!—just remarked that!—one of th' no-neck monsters messed up m' lovely lace dress so I got t'—cha-a-ange. . . .

(*She opens and kicks shut drawers of the dresser.*)

BRICK   Why d'ya call Gooper's kiddies no-neck monsters?
MARGARET   Because they've got no necks! Isn't that a good enough reason?
BRICK   Don't they have any necks?
MARGARET   None visible. Their fat little heads are set on their fat little bodies without a bit of connection.
BRICK   That's too bad.
MARGARET   Yes, it's too bad because you can't wring their necks if they've got no necks to wring! Isn't that right, honey?

(*She steps out of her dress, stands in a slip of ivory satin and lace.*)

Yep, they're no-neck monsters, all no-neck people are monsters . . .

(*Children shriek downstairs.*)

Hear them? Hear them screaming? I don't know where their voice-boxes are located since they don't have necks. I tell you I got so nervous at that table tonight I thought I would throw back my head and utter a scream you could hear across the Arkansas border an' parts of Louisiana an' Tennessee. I said to your charming sister-in-law, Mae, honey, couldn't you feed those precious little things at a separate table with an oilcloth cover? They make such a mess an' the lace cloth looks *so* pretty! She made enormous eyes at me and said, "Ohhh, noooooo! On Big Daddy's birthday? Why, he would never forgive me!" Well, I want you to know, Big Daddy hadn't been at the table two minutes with those five no-neck monsters slobbering and drooling over their food before he threw down his fork an' shouted, "Fo' God's sake, Gooper, why don't you put them pigs at a trough in th' kitchen?"— Well, I swear, I simply could have di-ieed!

Think of it, Brick, they've got five of them and number six is coming. They've brought the whole bunch down here like animals to display at a county fair. Why, they have those children doin' tricks all the time! "Junior, show Big Daddy how you do this, show Big Daddy how you do that, say your little piece fo' Big Daddy, Sister. Show your dimples, Sugar. Brother, show Big Daddy how you stand on your head!"—It goes on all the time, along with constant little remarks and innuendos about the fact that you and I have not produced any children, are totally childless and therefore totally useless!—Of course it's comical but it's also disgusting since it's so obvious what they're up to!

BRICK (*without interest*)   What are they up to, Maggie?

MARGARET   Why, you know what they're up to!

BRICK (*appearing*)   No, I don't know what they're up to.

(*He stands there in the bathroom doorway drying his hair with a towel and hanging onto the towel rack because one ankle is broken, plastered and bound. He is still slim and firm as a boy. His liquor hasn't started tearing him down outside. He has the additional charm of that cool air of detachment that people have who have given up the struggle. But now and then, when disturbed, something flashes behind it, like lightning in a fair sky, which shows that at some deeper level he is far from peaceful. Perhaps in a stronger light he would show some signs of deliquescence, but the fading, still warm, light from the gallery treats him gently.*)

MARGARET   I'll tell you what they're up to, boy of mine!—They're up to cutting you out of your father's estate, and—

(*She freezes momentarily before her next remark. Her voice drops as if it were somehow a personally embarrassing admission.*)

—Now we know that Big Daddy's dyin' of—*cancer*. . . .

(*There are voices on the lawn below: long-drawn calls across distance.* MARGARET *raises her lovely bare arms and powders her armpits with a light sigh.*

She adjusts the angle of a magnifying mirror to straighten an eyelash, then rises fretfully saying:)

There's so much light in the room it—

BRICK (*softly but sharply*)   Do we?

MARGARET   Do we what?

BRICK   Know Big Daddy's dyin' of cancer?

MARGARET   Got the report today.

BRICK   Oh . . .

MARGARET (*letting down bamboo blinds which cast long, gold-fretted shadows over the room*)   Yep, got th' report just now . . . it didn't surprise me, Baby. . . .

(Her voice has range, and music; sometimes it drops low as a boy's and you have a sudden image of her playing boy's games as a child.)

I recognized the symptoms soon's we got here last spring and I'm willin' to bet you that Brother Man and his wife were pretty sure of it, too. That more than likely explains why their usual summer migration to the coolness of the Great Smokies was passed up this summer in favor of—hustlin' down here ev'ry whipstitch with their whole screamin' tribe! And why so many allusions have been made to Rainbow Hill lately. You know what Rainbow Hill is? Place that's famous for treatin' alcoholics an' dope fiends in the movies!

BRICK   I'm not in the movies.

MARGARET   No, and you don't take dope. Otherwise you're a perfect candidate for Rainbow Hill, Baby, and that's where they aim to ship you—over my dead body! Yep, over my dead body they'll ship you there, but nothing would please them better. Then Brother Man could get a-hold of the purse strings and dole out remittances to us, maybe get power-of-attorney and sign checks for us and cut off our credit wherever, whenever he wanted! Son-of-a-bitch!—How'd you like that, Baby?—Well, you've been doin' just about ev'rything in your power to bring it about, you've just been doin' ev'rything you can think of to aid and abet them in this scheme of theirs! Quittin' work, devoting yourself to the occupation of drinkin'!—Breakin' your ankle last night on the high school athletic field: doin' what? Jumpin' hurdles? At two or three in the morning? Just fantastic! Got in the paper. *Clarksdale Register* carried a nice little item about it, human interest story about a well-known former athlete stagin' a one-man track meet on the Glorious Hill High School athletic field last night, but was slightly out of condition and didn't clear the first hurdle! Brother Man Gooper claims he exercised his influence t' keep it from goin' out over AP or UP or every goddam "P."

But, Brick? You still have one big advantage!

(During the above swift flood of words, BRICK *has reclined with contrapuntal leisure on the snowy surface of the bed and has rolled over carefully on his side or belly.)*

BRICK *(wryly)*   Did you *say* something, Maggie?

MARGARET   Big Daddy dotes on you, honey. And he can't stand Brother Man and Brother Man's wife, that monster of fertility, Mae; she's downright odious to him! Know how I know? By little expressions that flicker over his face when that woman is holding fo'th on one of her choice topics such as— how she refused twilight sleep!—when the twins were delivered! Because she feels motherhood's an experience that a woman ought to experience fully!—in order to fully appreciate the wonder and beauty of it! HAH!

(This loud "HAH!" is accompanied by a violent action such as slamming a drawer shut.)

—and how she made Brother Man come in an' stand beside her in the delivery room so he would not miss out on the "wonder and beauty" of it either!—producin' those no-neck monsters. . . .

(A speech of this kind would be antipathetic from almost anybody but MARGARET; *she makes it oddly funny, because her eyes constantly twinkle and her voice shakes with laughter which is basically indulgent.)*

—Big Daddy shares my attitude toward those two! As for me, well—I give him a laugh now and then and he tolerates me. In fact!—I sometimes suspect that Big Daddy harbors a little unconscious "lech" fo' me. . . .

BRICK   What makes you think that Big Daddy has a lech for you, Maggie?

MARGARET   Way he always drops his eyes down my body when I'm talkin' to him, drops his eyes to my boobs an' licks his old chops! Ha ha!

BRICK   That kind of talk is disgusting.

MARGARET   Did anyone ever tell you that you're an ass-aching Puritan, Brick?

I think it's mighty fine that that ole fellow, on the doorstep of death, still takes in my shape with what I think is deserved appreciation!

And you wanta know something else? Big Daddy didn't know how many little Maes and Goopers had been produced! "How many kids have you got?" he asked at the table, just like Brother Man and his wife were new acquaintances to him! Big Mama said he was jokin', but that ole boy wasn't jokin', Lord, no!

And when they infawmed him that they have five already and were turning out number six!—the news seemed to come as a sort of unpleasant surprise . . .

(Children yell below.)

Scream, monsters!

(Turns to BRICK *with a sudden, gay, charming smile which fades as she notices that he is not looking at her but into fading gold space with a troubled expression. It is constant rejection that makes her humor "bitchy.")*

Yes, you should of been at that supper-table, Baby.

(Whenever she calls him "baby" the word is a soft caress.)

Y'know, Big Daddy, bless his ole sweet soul, he's the dearest ole thing in the world, but he does hunch over his food as if he preferred not to notice anything else. Well, Mae an' Gooper were side by side at the table, direckly across from Big Daddy, watchin' his face like hawks while they jawed an' jabbered about the cuteness an' brilliance of th' no-neck monsters!

(*She giggles with a hand fluttering at her throat and her breast and her long throat arched.*
    She comes downstage and recreates the scene with voice and gesture.)

And the no-neck monsters were ranged around the table, some in high chairs and some on th' *Books of Knowledge,* all in fancy little paper cups in honor of Big Daddy's birthday, and all through dinner, well, I want you to know that Brother Man an' his partner never once, for one moment, stopped exchanging pokes an' pinches an' kicks an' signs an' signals!—Why, they were like a couple of cardsharps fleecing a sucker.—Even Big Mama, bless her ole sweet soul, she isn't th' quickest an' brightest thing in the world, she finally noticed, at last, an' said to Gooper, "Gooper, what are you an' Mae makin' all these signs at each other about?"—I swear t' goodness, I nearly choked on my chicken!

(MARGARET, *back at the dressing-table, still doesn't see* BRICK. *He is watching her with a look that is not quite definable.—Amused? shocked? contemptuous?—part of those and part of something else.*)

Y'know—your brother Gooper still cherishes the illusion he took a giant step up on the social ladder when he married Miss Mae Flynn of the Memphis Flynns.

(MARGARET *moves about the room as she talks, stops before the mirror, moves on.*)

But I have a piece of Spanish news for Gooper. The Flynns never had a thing in this world but money and they lost that, they were nothing at all but fairly successful climbers. Of course, Mae Flynn came out in Memphis eight years before I made my debut in Nashville, but I had friends at Ward-Belmont who came from Memphis and they used to come to see me and I used to go to see them for Christmas and spring vacations, and so I know who rates an' who doesn't rate in Memphis society. Why, y'know ole Papa Flynn, he barely escaped doing time in the Federal pen for shady manipulations on th' stock market when his chain stores crashed, and as for Mae having been a cotton carnival queen, as they remind us so often, lest we forget, well, that's one honor that I don't envy her for!—Sit on a brass throne on a tacky float an' ride down Main Street, smilin', bowin', and blowin' kisses to all the trash on the street—

(*She picks out a pair of jeweled sandals and rushes to the dressing-table.*)

Why, year before last, when Susan McPheeters was singled out fo' that honor, y' know what happened to her? Y'know what happened to poor little Susie McPheeters?

BRICK (*absently*)   No. What happened to little Susie McPheeters?

MARGARET   Somebody spit tobacco juice in her face.

BRICK (*dreamily*)   Somebody spit tobacco juice in her face?

MARGARET   That's right, some old drunk leaned out of a window in the Hotel Gayoso and yelled, "Hey, Queen, hey, hey, there, Queenie!" Poor Susie looked up and flashed him a radiant smile and he shot out a squirt of tobacco juice right in poor Susie's face.

BRICK   Well, what d'you know about that.

MARGARET (*gaily*)   What do I know about it? I was there, I saw it!

BRICK (*absently*)   Must have been kind of funny.

MARGARET   Susie didn't think so. Had hysterics. Screamed like a banshee. They had to stop th' parade an' remove her from her throne an' go on with—

(*She catches sight of him in the mirror, gasps slightly, wheels about to face him. Count ten.*)

—Why are you looking at me like that?

BRICK (*whistling softly, now*)   Like what, Maggie?

MARGARET (*intensely, fearfully*)   The way y' were lookin' at me just now, befo' I caught your eye in the mirror and you started t' whistle! I don't know how t' describe it but it froze my blood!—I've caught you lookin' at me like that so often lately. What are you thinkin' of when you look at me like that?

BRICK   I wasn't conscious of lookin' at you, Maggie.

MARGARET   Well, I was conscious of it! What were you thinkin'?

BRICK   I don't remember thinking of anything, Maggie.

MARGARET   Don't you think I know that—? Don't you—?—Think I know that—?

BRICK (*cooly*)   Know *what*, Maggie?

MARGARET (*struggling for expression*)   That I've gone through this—*hideous!*—transformation, become—*hard!* Frantic!

(*Then she adds, almost tenderly:*)

—*cruel!!*

That's what you've been observing in me lately. How could y' help but observe it? That's all right. I'm not—thin-skinned any more, can't afford t' be thin-skinned any more.

(*She is now recovering her power.*)

—But Brick? Brick?

BRICK   Did you say something?

MARGARET   I was *goin' t'* say something: that I get—lonely. Very!

BRICK   Ev'rybody gets that . . .

MARGARET   Living with someone you love can be lonelier—than living entirely *alone!*—if the one that y' love doesn't love you. . . .

(*There is a pause.* BRICK *hobbles downstage and asks, without looking at her:*)

BRICK   Would you like to live alone, Maggie?

(*Another pause: then—after she has caught a quick, hurt breath:*)

MARGARET   *No!—God!—I wouldn't!*

(*Another gasping breath. She forcibly controls what must have been an impulse to cry out. We see her deliberately, very forcibly, going all the way back to the world in which you can talk about ordinary matters.*)

Did you have a nice shower?

BRICK   Uh-huh.

MARGARET   Was the water cool?

BRICK   No.

MARGARET   But it made y' feel fresh, huh?

BRICK   Fresher. . . .

MARGARET   I know something would make y' feel *much* fresher!

BRICK   What?

MARGARET   An alcohol rub. Or cologne, a rub with cologne!

BRICK   That's good after a workout but I haven't been workin' out, Maggie.

MARGARET   You've kept in good shape, though.

BRICK (*indifferently*)   You think so, Maggie?

MARGARET   I always thought drinkin' men lost their looks, but I was plainly mistaken.

BRICK (*wryly*)   Why, thanks, Maggie.

MARGARET   You're the only drinkin' man I know that it never seems t' put fat on.

BRICK   I'm gettin' softer, Maggie.

MARGARET   Well, sooner or later it's bound to soften you up. It was just beginning to soften up Skipper when—

(*She stops short.*)

I'm sorry. I never could keep my fingers off a sore—I wish you *would* lose your looks. If you did it would make the martyrdom of Saint Maggie a little more bearable. But no such goddam luck. I actually believe you've gotten better looking since you've gone on the bottle. Yeah, a person who didn't

know you would think you'd never had a tense nerve in your body or a
strained muscle.

*(There are sounds of croquet on the lawn below: the click of mallets, light voices,
near and distant.)*

Of course, you always had that detached quality as if you were playing a
game without much concern over whether you won or lost, and now that
you've lost the game, not lost but just quit playing, you have that rare sort
of charm that usually only happens in very old or hopelessly sick people,
the charm of the defeated.—You look so cool, so cool, so enviably cool.

(Music is heard.)

They're playing croquet. The moon has appeared and it's white, just
beginning to turn a little bit yellow. . . .

You were a wonderful lover. . . .

Such a wonderful person to go to bed with, and I think mostly because you
were really indifferent to it. Isn't that right? Never had any anxiety about it,
did it naturally, easily, slowly, with absolute confidence and perfect calm,
more like opening a door for a lady or seating her at a table than giving
expression to any longing for her. Your indifference made you wonderful
at lovemaking—*strange?*—but true. . . .

You know, if I thought you would never, never, *never* make love to me
again— I would go downstairs to the kitchen and pick out the longest and
sharpest knife I could find and stick it straight into my heart, I swear that I
would!

But one thing I don't have is the charm of the defeated, my hat is still in the
ring, and I am determined to win!

(There is the sound of croquet mallets hitting croquet balls.)

—What is the victory of a cat on a hot tin roof?—I wish I knew. . . .

Just staying on it, I guess, as long as she can. . . .

(More croquet sounds.)

Later tonight I'm going to tell you I love you an' maybe by that time you'll
be drunk enough to believe me. Yes, they're playing croquet. . . .

Big Daddy is dying of cancer. . . .

What were you thinking of when I caught you looking at me like that?
Were you thinking of Skipper?

(BRICK *takes up his crutch, rises.*)

Oh, excuse me, forgive me, but laws of silence don't work! No, laws of silence don't work. . . .

(BRICK *crosses to the bar, takes a quick drink, and rubs his head with a towel.*)

Laws of silence don't work. . . .

When something is festering in your memory or your imagination, laws of silence don't work, it's just like shutting a door and locking it on a house on fire in hope of forgetting that the house is burning. But not facing a fire doesn't put it out. Silence about a thing just magnifies it. It grows and festers in silence, becomes malignant. . . .

Get dressed, Brick.

(*He drops his crutch.*)

BRICK   I've dropped my crutch.

(*He has stopped rubbing his hair dry but still stands hanging onto the towel rack in a white towel-cloth robe.*)

MARGARET   Lean on me.
BRICK   No, just give me my crutch.
MARGARET   Lean on my shoulder.
BRICK   *I don't want to lean on your shoulder, I want my crutch!*

(*This is spoken like sudden lightning.*)

Are you going to give me my crutch or do I have to get down on my knees on the floor and—
MARGARET   *Here, here, take it, take it!*

(*She has thrust the crutch at him.*)

BRICK (*hobbling out*)   Thanks . . .
MARGARET   We mustn't scream at each other, the walls in this house have ears. . . .

(*He hobbles directly to liquor cabinet to get a new drink.*)

—but that's the first time I've heard you raise your voice in a long time, Brick. A crack in the wall?—Of composure?

—I think that's a good sign. . . .

A sign of nerves in a player on the defensive!

(BRICK *turns and smiles at her cooly over his fresh drink.*)

BRICK   It just hasn't happened yet, Maggie.
MARGARET   What?
BRICK   The click I get in my head when I've had enough of this stuff to make me peaceful. . . .

Will you do me a favor?
MARGARET   Maybe I will. What favor?
BRICK   Just, just keep your voice down!
MARGARET (*in a hoarse whisper*)   I'll do you that favor, I'll speak in a whisper, if not shut up completely, if *you* will do *me* a favor and make that drink your last one till after the party.
BRICK   What party?
MARGARET   Big Daddy's birthday party.
BRICK   Is this Big Daddy's birthday?
MARGARET   You know this is Big Daddy's birthday!
BRICK   No, I don't, I forgot it.
MARGARET   Well, I remembered it for you. . . .

(*They are both speaking as breathlessly as a pair of kids after a fight, drawing deep exhausted breaths and looking at each other with faraway eyes, shaking and panting together as if they had broken apart from a violent struggle.*)

BRICK   Good for you, Maggie.
MARGARET   You just have to scribble a few lines on this card.
BRICK   You scribble something, Maggie.
MARGARET   It's got to be your handwriting; it's your present, I've given him my present; it's got to be your handwriting!

(*The tension between them is building again, the voices becoming shrill once more.*)

BRICK   I didn't get him a present.
MARGARET   I got one for you.
BRICK   All right, You write the card, then.
MARGARET   And have him know you didn't remember his birthday?
BRICK   I didn't remember his birthday.
MARGARET   You don't have to prove you didn't!
BRICK   I don't want to fool him about it.
MARGARET   Just write "Love, Brick!" for God's—
BRICK   No.

MARGARET   You've *got* to!

BRICK   I don't have to do anything I don't want to do. You keep forgetting the conditions on which I agreed to stay on living with you.

MARGARET *(out before she knows it)*   I'm not living with you. We occupy the same cage.

BRICK   You've got to remember the conditions agreed on.

MARGARET   They're impossible conditions!

BRICK   Then why don't you—?

MARGARET   HUSH! Who is out there? Is somebody at the door?

(There are footsteps in hall.)

MAE *(outside)*   May I enter a moment?

MARGARET   Oh, *you!* Sure. Come in, Mae.

(MAE enters bearing aloft the bow of a young lady's archery set.)

MAE   Brick, is this thing yours?

MARGARET   Why, Sister Woman—that's my Diana Trophy. Won it at the intercollegiate archery contest on the Ole Miss campus.

MAE   It's a mighty dangerous thing to leave exposed round a house full of nawmal rid-blooded children attracted t'weapons.

MARGARET   "Nawmal rid-blooded children attracted t'weapons" ought t'be taught to keep their hands off things that don't belong to them.

MAE   Maggie, honey, if you had children of your own you'd know how funny that is. Will you please lock this up and put the key out of reach?

MARGARET   Sister Woman, nobody is plotting the destruction of your kiddies. —Brick and I still have our special archers' license. We're goin' deer-huntin' on Moon Lake as soon as the season starts. I love to run with dogs through chilly woods, run, run leap over obstructions—

(She goes into the closet carrying the bow.)

MAE   How's the injured ankle, Brick?

BRICK   Doesn't hurt. Just itches.

MAE   Oh, my! Brick—Brick, you should've been downstairs after supper! Kiddies put on a show. Polly played the piano, Buster an' Sonny drums, an' then they turned out the lights an' Dixie an' Trixie puhfawmed a toe dance in fairy costume with *spahkluhs!* Big Daddy just beamed! He just beamed!

MARGARET *(from the closet with a sharp laugh)*   Oh, I bet. It breaks my heart that we missed it!

(She reenters.)

But Mae? Why did y'give dawgs' names to all your kiddies?

MAE   *Dogs'* names?

(MARGARET *has made this observation as she goes to raise the bamboo blinds,* *since the sunset glare has diminished. In crossing she winks at* BRICK.)

MARGARET (*sweetly*)   Dixie, Trixie, Buster, Sonny, Polly!—Sounds like four dogs and a parrot . . . animal act in a circus!

MAE   Maggie?

(MARGARET *turns with a smile.*)

Why are you so catty?

MARGARET   Cause I'm a cat! But why can't *you* take a joke, Sister Woman?

MAE   Nothin' pleases me more than a joke that's funny. You know the real names of our kiddies. Buster's real name is Robert. Sonny's real name is Saunders. Trixie's real name is Marlene and Dixie's—

(*Someone downstairs calls for her.* "Hey, Mae!"—*She rushes to door, saying:*)

Intermission is over!

MARGARET (*as* MAE *closes door*)   I wonder what Dixie's real name is?

BRICK   Maggie, being catty doesn't help things any . . .

MARGARET   I know! *WHY!*—Am I so catty?—Cause I'm consumed with envy an' eaten up with longing?—Brick, I've laid out your beautiful Shantung silk suit from Rome and one of your monogrammed silk shirts. I'll put your cuff-links in it, those lovely star sapphires I get you to wear so rarely. . . .

BRICK   I can't get trousers on over this plaster cast.

MARGARET   Yes, you can, I'll help you.

BRICK   I'm not going to get dressed, Maggie.

MARGARET   Will you just put on a pair of white silk pajamas?

BRICK   Yes, I'll do that, Maggie.

MARGARET   *Thank* you, thank you so *much!*

BRICK   Don't mention it.

MARGARET   *Oh, Brick!* How long does it have t' go on? This punishment? Haven't I done time enough, haven't I served my term, can't I apply for a— pardon?

BRICK   Maggie, you're spoiling my liquor. Lately your voice always sounds like you'd been running upstairs to warn somebody that the house was on fire!

MARGARET   Well, no wonder, no wonder. Y'know what I feel like, Brick?

(*Children's and grownups' voices are blended, below, in a loud but uncertain rendition of* "My Wild Irish Rose.")

I feel all the time like a cat on a hot tin roof!

BRICK   Then jump off the roof, jump off it, cats can jump off roofs and land on their four feet uninjured!

MARGARET   Oh, yes!

BRICK   Do it!—fo' God's sake, do it . . .

MARGARET   Do what?

BRICK   Take a lover!

MARGARET   I can't see a man but you! Even with my eyes closed, I just see you! Why don't you get ugly, Brick, why don't you please get fat or ugly or something so I could stand it?

(*She rushes to hall door, opens it, listens.*)

The concert is still going on! Bravo, no-necks, bravo!

(*She slams and locks door fiercely.*)

BRICK   What did you lock the door for?

MARGARET   To give us a little privacy for a while.

BRICK   You know better, Maggie.

MARGARET   No, I don't know better. . . .

(*She rushes to gallery doors, draws the rose-silk drapes across them.*)

BRICK   Don't make a fool of yourself.

MARGARET   I don't mind makin' a fool of myself over you!

BRICK   I mind, Maggie. I feel embarrassed for you.

MARGARET   Feel embarrassed! But don't continue my torture. I can't live on and on under these circumstances.

BRICK   You agreed to—

MARGARET   I know but—

BRICK   —Accept that condition!

MARGARET   *I CAN'T! CAN'T CAN'T!*

(*She seizes his shoulder.*)

BRICK   Let go!

(*He breaks away from her and seizes the small boudoir chair and raises it like a lion-tamer facing a big circus cat.*
    Count five. She stares at him with her fist pressed to her mouth, then bursts into shrill, almost hysterical laughter. He remains grave for a moment, then grins and puts the chair down.
    BIG MAMA *calls through closed door.*)

BIG MAMA   Son? Son? Son?

BRICK   What is it, Big Mama?

BIG MAMA (*outside*)   Oh son! We got the most wonderful news about Big Daddy. I just had t' run up an' tell you right this—

(*She rattles the knob.*)

—What's this door doin', locked, faw? You all think there's robbers in the house?

MARGARET   Big Mama, Brick is dressin', he's not dressed yet.

BIG MAMA   That's all right, it won't be the first time I've seen Brick not dressed. Come on, open this door!

(MARGARET, *with a grimace, goes to unlock and open the hall door, as* BRICK *hobbles rapidly to the bathroom and kicks the door shut.* BIG MAMA *has disappeared from the hall.*)

MARGARET   Big Mama?

(BIG MAMA *appears through the opposite gallery doors behind* MARGARET, *huffing and puffing like an old bulldog. She is a short, stout woman; her sixty years and 170 pounds have left her somewhat breathless most of the time; she's always tensed like a boxer, or rather, a Japanese wrestler. Her "family" was maybe a little superior to* BIG DADDY's, *but not much. She wears a black or silver lace dress and at least half a million in flashy gems. She is very sincere.*)

BIG MAMA (*loudly, startling* MARGARET)   Here—I come through Gooper's and Mae's gall'ry door. Where's Brick? *Brick*—Hurry on out of there, son, I just have a second and want to give you the news about Big Daddy.—I hate locked doors in a house. . . .

MARGARET (*with affected lightness*)   I've noticed you do, Big Mama, but people have got to have *some* moments of privacy, don't they?

BIG MAMA   No, ma'am, not in *my* house. (*Without pause*) Whacha took off you' dress faw? I thought that little lace dress was so sweet on yuh, honey.

MARGARET   I thought it looked sweet on me, too, but one of m' cute little table-partners used it for a napkin so—!

BIG MAMA (*picking up stockings on floor*)   What?

MARGARET   You know, Big Mama, Mae and Gooper's so touchy about those children—thanks, Big Mama . . .

(BIG MAMA *has thrust the picked-up stockings in* MARGARET's *hand with a grunt.*)

—that you just don't dare to suggest there's any room for improvement in their—

BIG MAMA   Brick, hurry out!—Shoot, Maggie, you just don't like children.

MARGARET   I do SO like children! Adore them!—well brought up!

BIG MAMA (*gentle—loving*)   Well, why don't you have some and bring them up well, then, instead of all the time pickin' on Gooper's an' Mae's?

GOOPER (*shouting up the stairs*)   Hey, hey, Big Mama, Betsy an' Hugh got to go, waitin' t' tell yuh g'by!

BIG MAMA   Tell 'em to hold their hawses, I'll be right down in a jiffy!

(She turns to the bathroom door and calls out.)

Son? Can you hear me in there?

(There is a muffled answer.)

We just got the full report from the laboratory at the Ochsner Clinic, completely negative, son, ev'rything negative, right on down the line! Nothin' a-tall's wrong with him but some little functional thing called a spastic colon. Can you hear me, son?

MARGARET   He can hear you, Big Mama.

BIG MAMA   Then why don't he say something? God Almighty, a piece of news like that should make him shout. It made *me* shout, I can tell you. I shouted and sobbed and fell right down on my knees!—Look!

(She pulls up her skirt.)

See the bruises where I hit my kneecaps? Took both doctors to haul me back on my feet!

(She laughs—she always laughs like hell at herself.)

Big Daddy was furious with me! But ain't that wonderful news?

(Facing bathroom again, she continues:)

After all the anxiety we been through to git a report like that on Big Daddy's birthday? Big Daddy tried to hide how much of a load that news took off his mind, but didn't fool *me*. He was mighty close to crying about it *himself!*

(Goodbyes are shouted downstairs, and she rushes to door.)

Hold those people down there, don't let them go! —Now, git dressed, we're all comin' up to this room fo' Big Daddy's birthday party because of your ankle.—How's his ankle, Maggie?

MARGARET   Well, he broke it, Big Mama.

BIG MAMA   I know he broke it.

(A phone is ringing in hall. A Negro voice answers: "Mistuh Polly's res'dence.")

I mean does it hurt him much still.

MARGARET   I'm afraid I can't give you that information, Big Mama. You'll have to ask Brick if it hurts much still or not.

SOOKEY *(in the hall)*   It's Memphis, Mizz Polly, it's Miss Sally in Memphis.

BIG MAMA   Awright, Sookey.

(BIG MAMA *rushes into the hall and is heard shouting on the phone.*)

Hello, Miss Sally. How are you, Miss Sally?—Yes, well, I was just gonna call you about it. *Shoot!*—

(*She raises her voice to a bellow.*)

Miss Sally? Don't ever call me from the Gayoso Lobby, too much talk goes on in that hotel lobby, no wonder you can't hear me! Now listen, Miss Sally. They's nothin' serious wrong with Big Daddy. We got the report just now, they's nothin' wrong but a thing called a—spastic! *SPASTIC!*—colon . . .

(*She appears at the hall door and calls to* MARGARET.)

—Maggie, come out here and talk to that fool on the phone. I'm shouted breathless!

MARGARET (*goes out and is heard sweetly at phone*)　Miss Sally? This is Brick's wife, Maggie. So nice to hear your voice. Can you hear *mine?* Well, *good!*— Big Mama just wanted you to know that they've got the report from the Ochsner Clinic and what Big Daddy has is a spastic colon. Yes. Spastic colon, Miss Sally. That's right, spastic colon. *G'bye, Miss Sally, hope I'll see you real soon!*

(*Hangs up a little before Miss Sally was probably ready to terminate the talk. She returns through the hall door.*)

She heard me perfectly. I've discovered with deaf people the thing to do is not shout at them but just enunciate clearly. My rich old Aunt Cornelia was deaf as the dead but I could make her hear me just by sayin' each word slowly, distinctly, close to her ear. I read her the *Commercial Appeal* ev'ry night, read her the classified ads in it, even, she never missed a word of it. But was she a mean ole thing! Know what I got when she died? Her unexpired subscriptions to five magazines and the Book-of-the-Month Club and a LIBRARY full of ev'ry dull book ever written! All else went to her hellcat of a sister . . . meaner than she was, even!

(BIG MAMA *has been straightening things up in the room during this speech.*)

BIG MAMA (*closing closet door on discarded clothes*)　*Miss Sally sure is a case!* Big Daddy says she's always got her hand out fo' something. He's not mistaken. That poor ole thing always has her hand out fo' somethin'. I don't think Big Daddy gives her as much as he should.

(*Somebody shouts for her downstairs and she shouts:*)

I'm comin'!

(She starts out. At the hall door, turns and jerks a forefinger, first toward the bathroom door, then toward the liquor cabinet, meaning: "Has Brick been drinking?" MARGARET *pretends not to understand, cocks her head and raises her brows as if the pantomimic performance was completely mystifying to her.*

BIG MAMA *rushes back to* MARGARET:)

Shoot! Stop playin' so dumb!—I mean has he been drinkin' that stuff much yet?

MARGARET *(with a little laugh)*   Oh! I think he had a highball after supper.

BIG MAMA   Don't laugh about it!—Some single men stop drinkin' when they git married and others start! Brick never touched liquor before he—!

MARGARET *(crying out)*   *THAT'S NOT FAIR!*

BIG MAMA   Fair or not fair I want to ask you a question, one question: D'you make Brick happy in bed?

MARGARET   Why don't you ask if he makes *me* happy in bed?

BIG MAMA   Because I know that—

MARGARET   *It works both ways!*

BIG MAMA   Something's not right! You're childless and my son drinks!

(Someone has called her downstairs and she has rushed to the door on the line above. She turns at the door and points at the bed.)

—When a marriage goes on the rocks, the rocks are *there,* right *there!*

MARGARET   *That's*—

*(BIG MAMA *has swept out of the room and slammed the door.)*

—not—*fair . . .*

*(MARGARET *is alone, completely alone, and she feels it. She draws in, hunches her shoulders, raises her arms with fists clenched, shuts her eyes tight as a child about to be stabbed with a vaccination needle. When she opens her eyes again, what she sees is the long oval mirror and she rushes straight to it, stares into it with a grimace and says: "Who are you?"—Then she crouches a little and answers herself in a different voice which is high, thin, mocking: "I am Maggie the Cat!"—Straightens quickly as bathroom door opens a little and* BRICK *calls out to her.)*

BRICK   Has Big Mama gone?

MARGARET   She's gone.

(He opens the bathroom door and hobbles out, with his liquor glass now empty, straight to the liquor cabinet. He is whistling softly. MARGARET'S *head pivots on her long, slender throat to watch him.*

She raises a hand uncertainly to the base of her throat, as if it was difficult for her to swallow, before she speaks.)

You know, our sex life didn't just peter out in the usual way, it was cut off short, long before the natural time for it to, and it's going to revive again, just as sudden as that. I'm confident of it. That's what I'm keeping myself attractive for. For the time when you'll see me again like other men see me. Yes, like other men see me. They still see me, Brick, and they like what they see. Uh-huh. Some of them would give their—

Look, Brick!

(She stands before the long oval mirror, touches her breast and then her hips with her two hands.)

How high my body stays on me!—Nothing has fallen on me—not a fraction. . . .

(Her voice is soft and trembling: a pleading child's. At this moment as he turns to glance at her—a look which is like a player passing a ball to another player, third down and goal to go—she has to capture the audience in a grip so tight that she can hold it till the first intermission without any lapse of attention.)

Other men still want me. My face looks strained, sometimes, but I've kept my figure as well as you've kept yours, and men admire it. I still turn heads on the street. Why, last week in Memphis everywhere that I went men's eyes burned holes in my clothes, at the country club and in restaurants and department stores, there wasn't a man I met or walked by that didn't just eat me up with his eyes and turn around when I passed him and look back at me. Why, at Alice's party for her New York cousins, the best lookin' man in the crowd—followed me upstairs and tried to force his way in the powder room with me, followed me to the door and tried to force his way in!

BRICK   Why didn't you let him, Maggie?

MARGARET   Because I'm not that common, for one thing. Not that I wasn't almost tempted to. You like to know who it was? It was Sonny Boy Maxwell, that's who!

BRICK   Oh, yeah, Sonny Boy Maxwell, he was a good end-runner but had a little injury to his back and had to quit.

MARGARET   He has no injury now and has no wife and still has a lech for me!

BRICK   I see no reason to lock him out of a powder room in that case.

MARGARET   And have someone catch me at it? I'm not that stupid. Oh, I might sometime cheat on you with someone, since you're so insultingly eager to have me do it!—But if I do, you can be damned sure it will be in a place and a time where no one but me and the man could possibly know. Because I'm not going to give you any excuse to divorce me for being unfaithful or anything else. . . .

BRICK   Maggie, I wouldn't divorce you for being unfaithful or anything else. Don't you know that? Hell. I'd be relieved to know that you'd found yourself a lover.

MARGARET   Well, I'm taking no chances. No, I'd rather stay on this hot tin roof.

BRICK   A hot tin roof's 'n uncomfo'table place t' stay on. . . .

(He starts to whistle softly.)

MARGARET *(through his whistle)*   Yeah, but I can stay on it just as long as I have to.

BRICK   You could leave me, Maggie.

(He resumes whistle. She wheels about to glare at him.)

MARGARET   *Don't want to and will not!* Besides if I did, you don't have a cent to pay for it but what you get from Big Daddy and he's dying of cancer!

(For the first time a realization of BIG DADDY'S *doom seems to penetrate to* BRICK'S *consciousness, visibly, and he looks at* MARGARET.)

BRICK   Big Mama just said he *wasn't,* that the report was okay.

MARGARET   That's what she thinks because she got the same story that they gave Big Daddy. And was just as taken in by it as he was, poor ole things. . . .

But tonight they're going to tell her the truth about it. When Big Daddy goes to bed, they're going to tell her that he is dying of cancer.

(She slams the dresser drawer.)

—It's malignant and it's terminal.

BRICK   Does Big Daddy know it?

MARGARET   Hell, do they *ever* know it? Nobody says, "You're dying." You have to fool them. They have to fool *themselves.*

BRICK   Why?

MARGARET   *Why?* Because human beings dream of life everlasting, that's the reason! But most of them want it on earth and not in heaven.

(He gives a short, hard laugh at her touch of humor.)

Well. . . . *(She touches up her mascara.)* That's how it is, anyhow. . . . *(She looks about.)* Where did I put down my cigarette? Don't want to burn up the home-place, at least not with Mae and Gooper and their five monsters in it!

(She has found it and sucks at it greedily. Blows out smoke and continues:)

So this is Big Daddy's last birthday. And Mae and Gooper, they know it, oh, *they* know it, all right. They got the first information from the Ochsner

Clinic. That's why they rushed down here with their no-neck monsters. Because. Do you know something? Big Daddy's made no will? Big Daddy's never made out any will in his life, and so this campaign's afoot to impress him, forcibly as possible, with the fact that you drink and I've borne no children!

(He continues to stare at her a moment, then mutters something sharp but not audible and hobbles rather rapidly out onto the long gallery in the fading, much faded, gold light.)

MARGARET *(continuing her liturgical chant)*   Y'know, I'm *fond* of Big Daddy, I am genuinely fond of that old man, I really *am,* you know. . . .

BRICK *(faintly, vaguely)*   Yes, I know you are. . . .

MARGARET   I've always sort of admired him in spite of his coarseness, his four-letter words and so forth. Because Big Daddy *is* what he *is,* and he makes no bones about it. He hasn't turned gentleman farmer, he's still a Mississippi red neck, as much of a red neck as he must have been when he was just overseer here on the old Jack Straw and Peter Ochello place. But he got hold of it an' built it into th' biggest an' finest plantation in the Delta.— I've always *liked* Big Daddy. . . .

(She crosses to the proscenium.)

Well, this is Big Daddy's last birthday. I'm sorry about it. But I'm facing the facts. It takes money to take care of a drinker and that's the office that I've been elected to lately.

BRICK   You don't have to take care of me.

MARGARET   Yes, I do. Two people in the same boat have got to take care of each other. At least you want money to buy more Echo Spring when this supply is exhausted, or will you be satisfied with a ten-cent beer?

Mae an' Gooper are plannin' to freeze us out of Big Daddy's estate because you drink and I'm childless. But we can defeat that plan. We're *going* to defeat that plan!

Brick, y'know, I've been so God damn disgustingly poor all my life! —That's the *truth,* Brick!

BRICK   I'm not sayin' it isn't.

MARGARET   Always had to suck up to people I couldn't stand because they had money and I was poor as Job's turkey. You don't know what that's like. Well, I'll tell you, it's like you would feel a thousand miles away from Echo Spring!—And had to get back to it on that broken ankle . . . without a crutch!

That's how it feels to be as poor as Job's turkey and have to suck up to relatives that you hated because they had money and all you had was a bunch of hand-me-down clothes and a few old moldy three per cent government bonds. My daddy loved his liquor, he fell in love with his liquor the way you've fallen in love with Echo Spring!—And my poor Mama, having to maintain some semblance of social position, to keep appearances up, on an income of one hundred and fifty dollars a month on those old government bonds!

When I came out, the year that I made my debut, I had just two evening dresses! One Mother made me from a pattern in *Vogue,* the other a hand-me-down from a snotty rich cousin I hated!

—The dress that I married you in was my grandmother's weddin' gown. . . .

So that's why I'm like a cat on a hot tin roof!

(BRICK *is still on the gallery. Someone below calls up to him in a warm Negro voice, "Hiya, Mistuh Brick, how yuh feelin'?"* BRICK *raises his liquor glass as if that answered the question.)*

MARGARET   You can be young without money but you can't be old without it. You've got to be old *with* money because to be old without it is just too awful, you've got to be one or the other, either *young* or *with money,* you can't be old and *without* it.—That's the *truth,* Brick. . . .

(BRICK *whistles softly, vaguely.)*

Well, now I'm dressed, I'm all dressed, there's nothing else for me to do.

(Forlornly, almost fearfully)

I'm dressed, all dressed, nothing else for me to do. . . .

(She *moves about restlessly, aimlessly, and speaks, as if to herself.)*

I know when I made my mistake.—What am I—? Oh!—my bracelets. . . .

(She *starts working a collection of bracelets over her hands onto her wrists, about six on each, as she talks.)*

I've thought a whole lot about it and now I know when I made my mistake. Yes, I made my mistake when I told you the truth about that thing with Skipper. Never should have confessed it, a fatal error, tellin' you about that thing with Skipper.

BRICK   Maggie, shut up about Skipper. I mean it, Maggie; you got to shut up about Skipper.

MARGARET   You ought to understand that Skipper and I—

BRICK   You don't think I'm serious, Maggie? You're fooled by the fact that I am saying this quiet? Look, Maggie. What you're doing is a dangerous thing to do. You're—you're—you're—foolin' with something that—nobody ought to fool with.

MARGARET   This time I'm going to finish what I have to say to you. Skipper and I made love, if love you could call it, because it made both of us feel a little bit closer to you. You see, you son of a bitch, you asked too much of people, of me, of him, of all the unlucky poor damned sons of bitches that happen to love you, and there was a whole pack of them, yes, there was a pack of them besides me and Skipper, you asked too goddam much of people that loved you, you—superior creature!—you godlike being!— And so we made love to each other to dream it was you, both of us! Yes, yes, yes! Truth, truth! What's so awful about it? I like it, I think the truth is—yeah! I shouldn't have told you. . . .

BRICK   (*holding his head unnaturally still and uptilted a bit*)   It was Skipper that told me about it. Not you, Maggie.

MARGARET   I told you!

BRICK   After he told me!

MARGARET   What does it matter who—?

(BRICK *turns suddenly out upon the gallery and calls:*)

BRICK   Little girl! Hey, little girl!

LITTLE GIRL   (*at a distance*)   What, Uncle Brick?

BRICK   Tell the folks to come up!—Bring everybody upstairs!

MARGARET   I can't stop myself! I'd go on telling you this in front of them all, if I had to!

BRICK   Little girl! Go on, go on, will you? Do what I told you, call them!

MARGARET   Because it's got to be told and you, you!—you never let me!

(*She sobs, then controls herself, and continues almost calmly.*)

It was one of those beautiful, ideal things they tell about in the Greek legends, it couldn't be anything else, you being you, and that's what made it so sad, that's what made it so awful, because it was love that never could be carried through to anything satisfying or even talked about plainly. Brick, I tell you, you got to believe me, Brick, I *do* understand all about it! I—I think it was—*noble!* Can't you tell I'm sincere when I say I respect it? My only point, the only point that I'm making, is life has got to be allowed to continue even after the *dream* of life is—all—over. . . .

(BRICK *is without his crutch. Leaning on furniture, he crosses to pick it up as she continues as if possessed by a will outside herself.*)

Why I remember when we double-dated at college, Gladys Fitzgerald and I and you and Skipper, it was more like a date between you and Skipper. Gladys and I were just sort of tagging along as if it was necessary to chaperone you!—to make a good public impression—

BRICK *(turns to face her, half lifting his crutch)*   Maggie, you want me to hit you with this crutch? Don't you know I could kill you with this crutch?

MARGARET   Good Lord, man, d' you think I'd care if you did?

BRICK   One man has one great good true thing in his life. One great good thing which is true!—I had friendship with Skipper.—You are naming it dirty!

MARGARET   I'm not naming it dirty! I am naming it clean.

BRICK   Not love with you, Maggie, but friendship with Skipper was that one great true thing, and you are naming it dirty!

MARGARET   Then you haven't been listenin', not understood what I'm saying! I'm naming it so damn clean that it killed poor Skipper!—You two had something that had to be kept on ice, yes, incorruptible, yes!—and death was the only icebox where you could keep it. . . .

BRICK   I married you, Maggie. Why would I marry you, Maggie, if I was—?

MARGARET   Brick, don't brain me yet, let me finish!—I know, believe me I know, that it was only Skipper that harbored even any *unconscious* desire for anything not perfectly pure between you two!—Now let me skip a little. You married me early that summer we graduated out of Ole Miss, and we were happy, weren't we, we were blissful, yes, hit heaven together ev'ry time that we loved! But that fall you an' Skipper turned down wonderful offers of jobs in order to keep on bein' football heroes—pro-football heroes. You organized the Dixie Stars that fall, so you could keep on bein' team-mates forever! But somethin' was not right with it!—*Me included!*—between you. Skipper began hittin' the bottle . . . you got a spinal injury—couldn't play the Thanksgivin' game in Chicago, watched it on TV from a traction bed in Toledo. I joined Skipper. The Dixie Stars lost because poor Skipper was drunk. We drank together that night all night in the bar of the Blackstone and when cold day was comin' up over the Lake an' we were comin' out drunk to take a dizzy look at it, I said, "SKIPPER! STOP LOVIN' MY HUSBAND OR TELL HIM HE'S GOT TO LET YOU ADMIT IT TO HIM!"—one way or another!

HE SLAPPED ME HARD ON THE MOUTH!—then turned and ran without stopping once, I am sure, all the way back into his room at the Blackstone. . . .

—When I came to his room that night, with a little scratch like a shy little mouse at his door, he made that pitiful, ineffectual little attempt to prove that what I had said wasn't true. . . .

*(*BRICK *strikes at her with crutch, a blow that shatters the gemlike lamp on the table.)*

—In this way, I destroyed him, by telling him truth that he and his world which he was born and raised in, yours and his world, had told him could not be told?

—From then on Skipper was nothing at all but a receptable for liquor and drugs. . . .

—Who shot cock-robin? I with my—

(She throws back her head with tight shut eyes.)

—merciful arrow!

(BRICK *strikes at her; misses.*)

Missed me!—Sorry,—I'm not tryin' to whitewash my behavior, Christ, no! Brick, I'm not good. I don't know why people have to pretend to be good, nobody's good. The rich or the well-to-do can afford to respect moral patterns, conventional moral patterns, but I could never afford to, yeah, but—I'm honest! Give me credit for just that, will you *please?*—Born poor, raised poor, expect to die poor unless I manage to get us something out of what Big Daddy leaves when he dies of cancer! But Brick?!—*Skipper is dead! I'm alive!* Maggie the cat is—

(BRICK *hops awkwardly forward and strikes at her again with his crutch.*)

—alive! I am alive, alive! I am . . .

(He hurls the crutch at her, across the bed she took refuge behind, and pitches forward on the floor as she completes her speech.)

—alive!

(*A little girl,* DIXIE, *bursts into the room, wearing an Indian war bonnet and firing a cap pistol at* MARGARET *and shouting: "Bang, bang, bang!"*
    Laughter downstairs floats through the open hall door. MARGARET *had crouched gasping to bed at child's entrance. She now rises and says with cool fury:*)

Little girl, your mother or someone should teach you—*(Gasping)*—to knock at a door before you come into a room. Otherwise people might think that you—lack—good breeding. . . .

DIXIE   Yanh, yanh, yanh, what is Uncle Brick doin' on th' floor?

BRICK   I tried to kill your Aunt Maggie, but I failed—and I fell. Little girl, give me my crutch so I can get up off th' floor.

MARGARET   Yes, give your uncle his crutch, he's a cripple, honey, he broke his ankle last night jumping hurdles on the high school athletic field!

DIXIE   What were you jumping hurdles for, Uncle Brick?

BRICK   Because I used to jump them, and people like to do what they used to do, even after they've stopped being able to do it. . . .

MARGARET   That's right, that's your answer, now go away, little girl.

(DIXIE *fires cap pistol at* MARGARET *three times.*)

Stop, you stop that, monster! You little no-neck monster!

(She seizes the cap pistol and hurls it through gallery doors.)

DIXIE *(with a precocious instinct for the cruelest thing)*   You're *jealous!* —You're just jealous because you can't have babies!

(She sticks out her tongue at MARGARET *as she sashays past her with her stomach stuck out, to the gallery.* MARGARET *slams the gallery doors and leans panting against them. There is a pause.* BRICK *has replaced his spilt drink and sits, faraway, on the great four-poster bed.)*

MARGARET   You see?—they gloat over us being childless, even in front of their five little no-neck monsters!

(Pause, Voices approach on the stairs.)

Brick?—I've been to a doctor in Memphis, a—a gynecologist. . . .

I've been completely examined, and there is no reason why we can't have a child whenever we want one. And this is my time by the calendar to conceive. Are you listening to me? Are you? Are you LISTENING TO ME!

BRICK   Yes, I hear you, Maggie.

(His attention returns to her inflamed face.)

—But how in hell on earth do you imagine—that you're going to have a child by a man that can't stand you?

MARGARET   That's a problem that I will have to work out.

(She wheels about to face the hall door.)

Here they come!

(The lights dim.)

CURTAIN

ACT II

(There is no lapse of time. MARGARET *and* BRICK *are in the same positions they held at the end of Act I.)*

MARGARET *(at door)*   Here they come!

(BIG DADDY *appears first, a tall man with a fierce, anxious look, moving careful-ly not to betray his weakness even, or especially, to himself.*)

BIG DADDY   Well, Brick.
BRICK   Hello, Big Daddy.—Congratulations!
BIG DADDY   —Crap. . . .

(*Some of the people are approaching through the hall, others along the gallery: voices from both directions.* GOOPER *and* REVEREND TOOKER *become visible outside gallery doors, and their voices come in clearly.*
   They pause outside as GOOPER *lights a cigar.*)

REVEREND TOOKER (*vivaciously*)   Oh, but St. Paul's in Grenada has three memorial windows, and the latest one is a Tiffany stained-glass window that cost twenty-five hundred dollars, a picture of Christ the Good Shepherd with a Lamb in His arms.
GOOPER   Who give that window, Preach?
REVEREND TOOKER   Clyde Fletcher's widow. Also presented St. Paul's with a baptismal font.
GOOPER   Y'know what somebody ought t' give your church is a *coolin'* system, Preach.
REVEREND TOOKER   Yes, siree, Bob! And y'know what Gus Hamma's family gave in his memory to the church at Two Rivers? A complete new stone parish-house with a basketball court in the basement and a—
BIG DADDY (*uttering a loud barking laugh which is far from truly mirthful*)   Hey, Preach! What's all this talk about memorials, Preach? Y' think somebody's about t' kick off around here? 'S that it?

(*Startled by this interjection,* REVEREND TOOKER *decides to laugh at the question almost as loud as he can.*
   How he would answer the question we'll never know, as he's spared that embarrassment by the voice of GOOPER'S *wife,* MAE, *rising high and clear as she appears with* "DOC" BAUGH, *the family doctor, through the hall door.*)

MAE (*almost religiously*)   —Let's see now, they've had their *tyyy*-phoid shots, and their tetanus shots, their diphtheria shots and their hepatitis shots and their polio shots, they got *those* shots every month from May through September, and—Gooper? Hey! Gooper!—What all have the kiddies been shot faw?
MARGARET (*overlapping a bit*)   Turn on the Hi-Fi, Brick! Let's have some music t' start off th' party with!

(*The talk becomes so general that the room sounds like a great aviary of chattering birds. Only* BRICK *remains unengaged, leaning upon the liquor cabinet with his faraway smile, an ice cube in a paper napkin with which he now and then rubs his forehead. He doesn't respond to* MARGARET'S *command. She bounds forward and stoops over the instrument panel of the console.*)

GOOPER   We gave 'em that thing for a third anniversary present, got three speakers in it.

(*The room is suddenly blasted by the climax of a Wagnerian opera or a Beethoven symphony.*)

BIG DADDY   *Turn that dam thing off!*

(*Almost instant silence, almost instantly broken by the shouting charge of* BIG MAMA, *entering through hall door like a charging rhino.*)

BIG MAMA   *Wha's my Brick, wha's mah precious baby!!*
BIG DADDY   *Sorry! Turn it back on!*

(*Everyone laughs very loud.* BIG DADDY *is famous for his jokes at* BIG MAMA'*s expense, and nobody laughs louder at these jokes than* BIG MAMA *herself, though sometimes they're pretty cruel and* BIG MAMA *has to pick up or fuss with something to cover the hurt that the loud laugh doesn't quite cover.*
    On this occasion, a happy occasion because the dread in her heart has also been lifted by the false report on BIG DADDY'*s condition, she giggles, grotesquely, coyly, in* BIG DADDY'*s direction and bears down upon* BRICK, *all very quick and alive.*)

BIG MAMA   Here he is, here's my precious baby! What's that you've got in your hand? You put that liquor down, son, your hand was made fo' holdin' somethin' better than that!
GOOPER   Look at Brick put it down!

(BRICK *has obeyed* BIG MAMA *by draining the glass and handing it to her. Again everyone laughs, some high, some low.*)

BIG MAMA   Oh, you bad boy, you, you're my bad little boy. Give Big Mama a kiss, you bad boy, you!—Look at him shy away, will you? Brick never liked bein' kissed or made a fuss over, I guess because he's always had too much of it!
Son, you turn that thing off!

(BRICK *has switched on the TV set.*)

I can't stand TV, radio was bad enough but TV has gone it one better, I mean—(*Plops wheezing in chair*)—one worse, ha ha! Now what'm I sittin' down here faw? I want t' sit next to my sweetheart on the sofa, hold hands with him and love him up a little!

(BIG MAMA *has on a black and white figured chiffon. The large irregular patterns, like the markings of some massive animal, the luster of her great diamonds and many pearls, the brilliants set in the silver frames of her glasses, her riotous voice, booming laugh, have dominated the room since she entered.* BIG DADDY *has been regarding her with a steady grimace of chronic annoyance.*)

BIG MAMA *(still louder)*   Preacher, Preacher, hey, Preach! Give me you' hand an' help me up from this chair!

REVEREND TOOKER   None of your tricks, Big Mama!

BIG MAMA   What tricks? You give me you' hand so I can get up an'—

(REVEREND TOOKER *extends her his hand. She grabs it and pulls him into her lap with a shrill laugh that spans an octave in two notes.*)

Ever seen a preacher in a fat lady's lap? Hey, hey, folks! Ever seen a preacher in a fat lady's lap?

(BIG MAMA *is notorious throughout the Delta for this sort of inelegant horse-play.* MARGARET *looks on with indulgent humor, sipping Dubonnet "on the rocks" and watching* BRICK, *but* MAE *and* GOOPER *exchange signs of humorless anxiety over these antics, the sort of behavior which* MAE *thinks may account for their failure to quite get in with the smartest young married set in Memphis, despite all. One of the Negroes,* LACEY *or* SOOKEY, *peeks in, cackling. They are waiting for a sign to bring in the cake and champagne. But* BIG DADDY'S *not amused. He doesn't understand why, in spite of the infinite mental relief he's received from the doctor's report, he still has these same old fox teeth in his guts. "This spastic thing sure is something," he says to himself, but aloud he roars at* BIG MAMA:)

BIG DADDY   BIG MAMA, WILL YOU QUIT HORSIN'?—You're too old an' too fat fo' that sort of crazy kid stuff an' besides a woman with your blood-pressure—she had two hundred last spring!—is riskin' a stroke when you mess around like that . . .

BIG MAMA   *Here comes Big Daddy's birthday!*

(Negroes *in white jackets enter with an enormous birthday cake ablaze with candles and carrying buckets of champagne with satin ribbons about the bottle necks.*

MAE *and* GOOPER *strike up song, and everybody, including the Negroes and Children, joins in. Only* BRICK *remains aloof.*)

EVERYONE
    Happy birthday to you.
    Happy birthday to you.
    Happy birthday, Big Daddy—

(Some sing: "Dear, Big Daddy!")

Happy birthday to you.

(Some sing: "How old are you?")

(MAE has come down center and is organzing her children like a chorus. She gives them a barely audible: "One, two, three!" and they are off in the new tune.)

CHILDREN
Skinamarinka—dinka—dink
Skinamarinka—do
We love you.
Skinamarinka—dinka—dink
Skinamarinka—do.

(All together, they turn to BIG DADDY.*)*

Big Daddy, you!

(They turn back front, like a musical comedy chorus.)

We love you in the morning;
We love you in the night.
We love you when we're with you,
And we love you out of sight.
Skinamarinka—dinka—dink
Skinamarinka—do.

(MAE turns to BIG MAMA.*)*

Big Mama, too!

(BIG MAMA bursts into tears. The Negroes leave.)

BIG DADDY   Now Ida, what the hell is the matter with you?
MAE   She's just so happy.
BIG MAMA   I'm just so happy, Big Daddy, I have to cry or something.

(Sudden and loud in the hush:)

Brick, do you know the wonderful news that Doc Baugh got from the clinic about Big Daddy? Big Daddy's one hundred per cent!
MARGARET   Isn't that wonderful?
BIG MAMA   He's just one hundred per cent. Passed the examination with flying colors. Now that we know there's nothing wrong with Big Daddy but a

spastic colon, I can tell you something. I was worried sick, half out of my mind, for fear that Big Daddy might have a thing like—

(MARGARET *cuts through this speech, jumping up and exclaiming shrilly:*)

MARGARET   Brick, honey, aren't you going to give Big Daddy his birthday present?

(*Passing by him, she snatches his liquor glass from him.*
She picks up a fancily wrapped package.)

Here it is, Big Daddy, this is from Brick!

BIG MAMA   This is the biggest birthday Big Daddy's ever had, a hundred presents and bushels of telegrams from—
MAE (*at same time*)   What is it, Brick?
GOOPER   I bet 500 to 50 that Brick don't *know* what it is.
BIG MAMA   The fun of presents is not knowing what they are till you open the package. Open your present, Big Daddy.
BIG DADDY   Open it you'self. I want to ask Brick somethin'! Come here, Brick.
MARGARET   Big Daddy's callin' you, Brick.

(*She is opening the package.*)

BRICK   Tell Big Daddy I'm crippled.
BIG DADDY   I see you're crippled. I want to know how you got crippled.
MARGARET (*making diversionary tactics*)   Oh, look, oh, look, why, it's a cashmere robe!

(*She holds the robe up for all to see.*)

MAE   You sound surprised, Maggie.
MARGARET   I never saw one before.
MAE   That's funny.—*Hah!*
MARGARET (*turning on her fiercely, with a brilliant smile*)   Why is it funny? All my family ever had was family—and luxuries such as cashmere robes still surprise me!
BIG DADDY (*ominously*)   Quiet!
MAE (*heedless in her fury*)   I don't see how you could be so surprised when you bought it yourself at Loewenstein's in Memphis last Saturday. You know how I know?
BIG DADDY   I said, Quiet!
MAE   —I know because the salesgirl that sold it to you waited on me and said, Oh, Mrs. Pollitt, your sister-in-law just bought a cashmere robe for your husband's father!

MARGARET   Sister Woman! Your talents are wasted as a housewife and mother, you really ought to be with the FBI or—
BIG DADDY   QUIET!

(REVEREND TOOKER'S *reflexes are slower than the others'. He finishes a sentence after the bellow.*)

REVEREND TOOKER (*to* DOC BAUGH)   —the Stork and the Reaper are running neck and neck!

(*He starts to laugh gaily when he notices the silence and* BIG DADDY'S *glare. His laugh dies falsely.*)

BIG DADDY   Preacher, I hope I'm not butting in on more talk about memorial stained-glass windows, am I, Preacher?

(REVEREND TOOKER *laughs feebly, then coughs dryly in the embarrassed silence.*)

Preacher?
BIG MAMA   Now, Big Daddy, don't you pick on Preacher!
BIG DADDY (*raising his voice*)   You ever hear that expression all hawk and no spit? You bring that expression to mind with that little dry cough of yours, all hawk an' no spit. . . .

(*The pause is broken only by a short startled laugh from* MARGARET, *the only one there who is conscious of and amused by the grotesque.*)

MAE (*raising her arms and jangling her bracelets*)   I wonder if the mosquitoes are active tonight?
BIG DADDY   What's that, Little Mama? Did you make some remark?
MAE   Yes, I said I wondered if the mosquitoes would eat us alive if we went out on the gallery for a while.
BIG DADDY   Well, if they do, I'll have your bones pulverized for fertilizer!
BIG MAMA (*quickly*)   Last week we had an airplane spraying the place and I think it done some good, at least I haven't had a—
BIG DADDY (*cutting her speech*)   Brick, they tell me, if what they tell me is true, that you done some jumping last night on the high school athletic field?
BIG MAMA   Brick, Big Daddy is talking to you, son.
BRICK (*smiling vaguely over his drink*)   What was that, Big Daddy?
BIG DADDY   They said you done some jumping on the high school track field last night.
BRICK   That's what they told me, too.
BIG DADDY   Was it jumping or humping that you were doing out there? What were you doing out there at three A.M., layin' a woman on that cinder track?

BIG MAMA   Big Daddy, you are off the sick-list, now, and I'm not going to excuse you for talkin' so—

BIG DADDY   Quiet!

BIG MAMA   —*nasty* in front of Preacher and—

BIG DADDY   *QUIET!*—I ast you, Brick, if you was cuttin' you'self a piece o' poon-tang last night on that cinder track? I thought maybe you were chasin' poon-tang on that track an' tripped over something in the heat of the chase—'sthat it?

(GOOPER *laughs, loud and false, others nervously following suit.* BIG MAMA *stamps her foot, and purses her lips, crossing to* MAE *and whispering something to her as* BRICK *meets his father's hard, intent, grinning stare with a slow, vague smile that he offers all situations from behind the screen of his liquor.*)

BRICK   No, sir, I don't think so. . . .

MAE (*at the same time, sweetly*)   Reverend Tooker, let's you and I take a stroll on the widow's walk.

(*She and the preacher go out on the gallery as* BIG DADDY *says:*)

BIG DADDY   Then what the hell were you doing out there at three o'clock in the morning?

BRICK   Jumping the hurdles, Big Daddy, runnin' and jumpin' the hurdles, but those high hurdles have gotten too high for me, now.

BIG DADDY   Cause you was drunk?

BRICK (*his vague smile fading a little*)   Sober I wouldn't have tried to jump the *low* ones. . . .

BIG MAMA (*quickly*)   Big Daddy, blow out the candles on your birthday cake!

MARGARET (*at the same time*)   I want to propose a toast to Big Daddy Pollitt on his sixty-fifth birthday, the biggest cotton-planter in—

BIG DADDY (*bellowing with fury and disgust*)   I told you to stop it, now stop it, quit this—!

BIG MAMA (*coming in front of* BIG DADDY *with the cake*)   Big Daddy, I will not allow you to talk that way, not even on your birthday, I—

BIG DADDY   I'll talk like I want to on my birthday, Ida, or any other goddam day of the year and anybody here that don't like it knows what they can do!

BIG MAMA   You don't mean that!

BIG DADDY   What makes you think I don't mean it?

(*Meanwhile various discreet signals have been exchanged and* GOOPER *has also gone out on the gallery.*)

BIG MAMA   I just know you don't mean it.

BIG DADDY   You don't know a goddam thing and you never did!

BIG MAMA   Big Daddy, you don't mean that.

BIG DADDY   Oh, yes, I do, oh, yes, I do, I mean it! I put up with a whole lot of crap around here because I thought I was dying. And you thought I was dying and you started taking over, well, you can stop taking over now, Ida, because I'm not gonna die, you can just stop now this business of taking over because you're not taking over because I'm not dying, I went through the laboratory and the goddam exploratory operation and there's nothing wrong with me but a spastic colon. And I'm not dying of cancer which you thought I was dying of. Ain't that so? Didn't you think that I was dying of cancer, Ida?

(*Almost everybody is out on the gallery but the two old people glaring at each other across the blazing cake.*
   BIG MAMA'S *chest heaves and she presses a fat fist to her mouth.*
   BIG DADDY *continues, hoarsely:*)

Ain't that so, Ida? Didn't you have an idea I was dying of cancer and now you could take control of this place and everything on it? I got that impression, I seemed to get that impression. Your loud voice everywhere, your fat old body butting in here and there!

BIG MAMA   Hush! The Preacher!

BIG DADDY   Rut the goddam preacher!

(BIG MAMA *gasps loudly and sits down on the sofa which is almost too small for her.*)

Did you hear what I said? I said rut the goddam preacher!

(*Somebody closes the gallery doors from outside just as there is a burst of fireworks and excited cries from the children.*)

BIG MAMA   I never seen you act like this before and I can't think what's got in you!

BIG DADDY   I went through all that laboratory and operation and all just so I would know if you or me was boss here! Well, now it turns out that I am and you ain't—and that's my birthday present—and my cake and champagne!—because for three years now you been gradually taking over. Bossing. Talking. Sashaying your fat old body around the place I made! I made this place! I was overseer on it! I was the overseer on the old Straw and Ochello plantation. I quit school at ten! I quit school at ten years old and went to work like a nigger in the fields. And I rose to be overseer of the Straw and Ochello plantation. And old Straw died and I was Ochello's partner and the place got bigger and bigger and bigger and bigger and bigger! I did all that myself with no goddam help from you, and now you think you're just about to take over. Well, I am just about to tell you that you are not just about to take over, you are not just about to take over a God damn thing. Is that clear to you, Ida? Is that very plain to you, now? Is

that understood completely? I been through the laboratory from A to Z.
I've had the goddam exploratory operation, and nothing is wrong with me
but a spastic colon—made spastic, I guess, by *disgust!* By all the goddam
lies and liars that I have had to put up with, and all the goddam hypocrisy
that I lived with all these forty years that we been livin' together!

Hey! Ida!! Blow out the candles on the birthday cake! Purse up your lips
and draw a deep breath and blow out the goddam candles on the cake!

BIG MAMA   Oh, Big Daddy, oh, oh, oh, Big Daddy!

BIG DADDY   What's the matter with you?

BIG MAMA   *In all these years you never believed that I loved you??*

BIG DADDY   Huh?

BIG MAMA   *And I did, I did so much, I did love you!* —I even loved your hate and
your hardness, Big Daddy!

(She sobs and rushes awkwardly out onto the gallery.)

BIG DADDY *(to himself)   Wouldn't it be funny if that was true. . . .*

(A pause is followed by a burst of light in the sky from the fireworks.)

BRICK! HEY, BRICK!

*(He stands over his blazing birthday cake.
     After some moments,* BRICK *hobbles in on his crutch, holding his glass.*
     MARGARET *follows him with a bright, anxious smile.)*

I didn't call you, Maggie. I called Brick.

MARGARET   I'm just delivering him to you.

(She kisses BRICK *on the mouth which he immediately wipes with the back of his
hand. She flies girlishly back out.* BRICK *and his father are alone.)*

BIG DADDY   Why did you do that?

BRICK   Do what, Big Daddy?

BIG DADDY   Wipe her kiss off your mouth like she'd spit on you.

BRICK   I don't know. I wasn't conscious of it.

BIG DADDY   That woman of yours has a better shape on her than Gooper's but
somehow or other they got the same look about them.

BRICK   What sort of look is that, Big Daddy?

BIG DADDY   I don't know how to describe it but it's the same look.

BRICK   They don't look peaceful, do they?

BIG DADDY   No, they sure in hell don't.

BRICK   They look nervous as cats?

BIG DADDY   That's right, they look nervous as cats.

BRICK   Nervous as a couple of cats on a hot tin roof?

BIG DADDY   That's right, boy, they look like a couple of cats on a hot tin roof. It's funny that you and Gooper being so different would pick out the same type of woman.

BRICK   Both of us married into society, Big Daddy.

BIG DADDY   Crap . . . I wonder what gives them both that look?

BRICK   Well. They're sittin' in the middle of a big piece of land, Big Daddy, twenty-eight thousand acres is a pretty big piece of land and so they're squaring off on it, each determined to knock off a bigger piece of it than the other whenever you let it go.

BIG DADDY   I got a surprise for those women. I'm not gonna let it go for a long time yet if that's what they're waiting for.

BRICK   That's right, Big Daddy. You just sit tight and let them scratch each other's eyes out. . . .

BIG DADDY   You bet your life I'm going to sit tight on it and let those sons of bitches scratch their eyes out, ha ha ha. . . .

But Gooper's wife's a good breeder, you got to admit she's fertile. Hell, at supper tonight she had them all at the table and they had to put a couple of extra leafs in the table to make room for them, she's got five head of them, now, and another one's comin'.

BRICK   Yep, number six is comin'. . . .

BIG DADDY   Brick, you know, I swear to God, I don't know the way it happens?

BRICK   The way what happens, Big Daddy?

BIG DADDY   You git you a piece of land, by hook or crook, an' things start growin' on it, things accumulate on it, and the first thing you know it's completely out of hand, completely out of hand!

BRICK   Well, they say nature hates a vacuum, Big Daddy.

BIG DADDY   That's what they say, but sometimes I think that a vacuum is a hell of a lot better than some of the stuff that nature replaces it with.

Is someone out there by that door?

BRICK   Yep.

BIG DADDY   Who?

(*He has lowered his voice.*)

BRICK   Someone int'rested in what we say to each other.

BIG DADDY   Gooper?—*GOOPER!*

(*After a discreet pause,* MAE *appears in the gallery door.*)

MAE   Did you call Gooper, Big Daddy?

BIG DADDY   Aw, it was you.

MAE   Do you want Gooper, Big Daddy?

BIG DADDY   No, and I don't want you. I want some privacy here, while I'm having a confidential talk with my son Brick. Now it's too hot in here to close them doors, but if I have to close those rutten doors in order to have a private talk with my son Brick, just let me know and I'll close 'em. Because I hate eavesdroppers, I don't like any kind of sneakin' an' spyin'.

MAE   Why, Big Daddy—

BIG DADDY   You stood on the wrong side of the moon, it threw your shadow!

MAE   I was just—

BIG DADDY   You was just nothing but *spyin'* an' you *know* it!

MAE *(begins to sniff and sob)*   Oh, Big Daddy, you're so unkind for some reason to those that really love you!

BIG DADDY   Shut up, shut up, shut up! I'm going to move you and Gooper out of that room next to this! It's none of your goddam business what goes on in here at night between Brick an' Maggie. You listen at night like a couple of rutten peek-hole spies and go and give a report on what you hear to Big Mama an' she comes to me and says they say such and such and so and so about what they heard goin' on between Brick an' Maggie, and Jesus, it makes me sick. I'm goin' to move you an' Gooper out of that room, I can't stand sneakin' an' spyin', it makes me sick. . . .

(MAE throws back her head and rolls her eyes heavenward and extends her arms as if invoking God's pity for this unjust martyrdom; then she presses a handkerchief to her nose and flies from the room with a loud swish of skirts.)

BRICK *(now at the liquor cabinet)*   They listen, do they?

BIG DADDY   Yeah. They listen and give reports to Big Mama on what goes on in here between you and Maggie. They say that—

(He stops as if embarrassed.)

—You won't sleep with her, that you sleep on the sofa. Is that true or not true? If you don't like Maggie, get rid of Maggie!—What are you doin' there now?

BRICK   Fresh'nin' up my drink.

BIG DADDY   Son, you know you got a real liquor problem?

BRICK   Yes, sir, yes, I know.

BIG DADDY   Is that why you quit sports-announcing, because of this liquor problem?

BRICK   Yes, sir, yes, sir, I guess so.

(He smiles vaguely and amiably at his father across his replenished drink.)

BIG DADDY   Son, don't guess about it, it's too important.

BRICK *(vaguely)*   Yes, sir.

BIG DADDY   And listen to me, don't look at the damn chandelier. . . .

(Pause. BIG DADDY'S *voice is husky.)*

—Somethin' else we picked up at th' big fire-sale in Europe.

(Another pause.)

Life is important. There's nothing else to hold onto. A man that drinks is throwing his life away. Don't do it, hold onto your life. There's nothing else to hold onto. . . .

Sit down over here so we don't have to raise our voices, the walls have ears in this place.

BRICK *(hobbling over to sit on the sofa beside him)*   All right, Big Daddy.

BIG DADDY   Quit!—how'd that come about? Some disappointment?

BRICK   I don't know. Do you?

BIG DADDY   I'm askin' you, God damn it! How in hell would I know if you don't?

BRICK   I just got out there and found that I had a mouth full of cotton. I was always two or three beats behind what was goin' on on the field and so I—

BIG DADDY   Quit!

BRICK *(amiably)*   Yes, quit.

BIG DADDY   Son?

BRICK   Huh?

BIG DADDY *(inhales loudly and deeply from his cigar; then bends suddenly a little forward, exhaling loudly and raising a hand to his forehead)*   —Whew!—ha ha!—I took in too much smoke, it made me a little light-headed. . . .

(The mantel clock chimes.)

Why is it so damn hard for people to talk?

BRICK   Yeah. . . .

(The clock goes on sweetly chiming till it has completed the stroke of ten.)

—Nice peaceful-soundin' clock, I like to hear it all night. . . .

(He slides low and comfortable on the sofa; BIG DADDY *sits up straight and rigid with some unspoken anxiety. All his gestures are tense and jerky as he talks. He wheezes and pants and sniffs through his nervous speech, glancing quickly, shyly, from time to time, at his son.)*

BIG DADDY   We got that clock the summer we wint to Europe, me an' Big Mama on that damn Cook's Tour, never had such an awful time in my life, I'm tellin' you, son, those gooks over there, they gouge your eyeballs out in their grand hotels. And Big Mama bought more stuff than you could haul in a couple of boxcars, that's no crap. Everywhere she wint on this whirlwind tour, she bought, bought, bought. Why, half that stuff she bought is still crated up in the cellar, under water last spring?

(He laughs.)

That Europe is nothin' on earth but a great big auction, that's all it is, that bunch of old worn-out places, it's just a big fire-sale, the whole rutten thing, an' Big Mama wint wild in it, why, you couldn't hold that woman with a mule's harness! Bought, bought, bought!—lucky I'm a rich man, yes siree, Bob, an' half that stuff is mildewin' in th' basement. It's lucky I'm a rich man, it sure is lucky, well, I'm a rich man, Brick, yep, I'm a mighty rich man.

(His eyes light up for a moment.)

Y'know how much I'm worth? Guess, Brick! Guess how much I'm worth!

(Brick smiles vaguely over his drink.)

Close on ten million in cash an' blue chip stocks, outside, mind you, of twenty-eight thousand acres of the richest land this side of the valley Nile!

(A puff and crackle and the night sky blooms with an eerie greenish glow. Children shriek on the gallery.)

But a man can't buy his life with it, he can't buy back his life with it when his life has been spent, that's one thing not offered in the Europe fire-sale or in the American markets or any markets on earth, a man can't buy his life with it, he can't buy back his life when his life is finished. . . .

That's a sobering thought, a very sobering thought, and that's a thought that I was turning over in my head, over and over and over—until today. . . .

I'm wiser and sadder, Brick, for this experience which I just gone through. They's one thing else that I remember in Europe.

BRICK   What is that, Big Daddy?

BIG DADDY   The hills around Barcelona in the country of Spain and the children running over those bare hills in their bare skins beggin' like starvin' dogs with howls and screeches, and how fat the priests are on the streets of Barcelona, so many of them and so fat and so pleasant, ha ha!—Y'know I could feed that country? I got money enough to feed that goddam country, but the human animal is a selfish beast and I don't reckon the money I passed out there to those howling children in the hills around Barcelona would more than upholster one of the chairs in this room, I mean pay to put a new cover on this chair!

Hell, I threw them money like you'd scatter feed corn for chickens, I threw money at them just to get rid of them long enough to climb back into th' car and—drive away. . . .

And then in Morocco, them Arabs, why, prostitution begins at four or five, that's no exaggeration, why, I remember one day in Marrakech, that old walled Arab city, I set on a broken-down wall to have a cigar, it was fearful hot there and this Arab woman stood in the road and looked at me till I was embarrassed, she stood stock still in the dusty hot road and looked at me till I was embarrassed. But listen to this. She had a naked child with her, a little naked girl with her, barely able to toddle, and after a while she set this child on the ground and give her a push and whispered something to her.

This child come toward me, barely able t' walk, come toddling up to me and—

Jesus, it makes you sick t' remember a thing like this! It stuck out its hand and tried to unbutton my trousers!

That child was not yet five! Can you believe me? Or do you think that I am making this up? I wint back to the hotel and said to Big Mama, Git packed! We're clearing out of this country. . . .

BRICK   Big Daddy, you're on a talkin' jag tonight.

BIG DADDY (*ignoring this remark*)   Yes, sir, that's how it is, the human animal is a beast that dies but the fact that he's dying don't give him pity for others, no, sir, it—

—Did you say something?

BRICK   Yes.

BIG DADDY   What?

BRICK   Hand me over that crutch so I can get up.

BIG DADDY   Where you goin'?

BRICK   I'm takin' a little short trip to Echo Spring.

BIG DADDY   To where?

BRICK   Liquor cabinet. . . .

BIG DADDY   Yes, sir, boy—

(*He hands* BRICK *the crutch.*)

—the human animal is a beast that dies and if he's got money he buys and buys and buys and I think the reason he buys everything he can buy is that in the back of his mind he has the crazy hope that one of his purchases will be life everlasting!—Which it never can be. . . . The human animal is a beast that—

BRICK (*at the liquor cabinet*)   Big Daddy, you sure are shootin' th' breeze here tonight.

(*There is a pause and voices are heard outside.*)

BIG DADDY   I been quiet here lately, spoke not a word, just sat and stared into space. I had something heavy weighing on my mind but tonight that load was took off me. That's why I'm talking.—The sky looks diff'rent to me. . . .

BRICK   You know what I like to hear most?
BIG DADDY   What?
BRICK   Solid quiet. Perfect unbroken quiet.
BIG DADDY   Why?
BRICK   Because it's more peaceful.
BIG DADDY   Man, you'll hear a lot of that in the grave.

(*He chuckles agreeably.*)

BRICK   Are you through talkin' to me?
BIG DADDY   Why are you so anxious to shut me up?
BRICK   Well, sir, ever so often you say to me, Brick, I want to have a talk with
    you, but when we talk, it never materializes. Nothing is said. You sit in a
    chair and gas about this and that and I look like I listen. I try to look like I
    listen, but I don't listen, not much. Communication is—awful hard between
    people an'—somehow between you and me, it just don't—
BIG DADDY   Have you ever been scared? I mean have you ever felt downright
    terror of something?

(*He gets up.*)

Just one moment. I'm going to close these doors. . . .

(*He closes doors on gallery as if he were going to tell an important secret.*)

BRICK   What?
BIG DADDY   Brick?
BRICK   Huh?
BIG DADDY   Son, I thought I had it!
BRICK   Had what? Had what, Big Daddy?
BIG DADDY   Cancer!
BRICK   Oh . . .
BIG DADDY   I thought the old man made out of bones had laid his cold and
    heavy hand on my shoulder!
BRICK   Well, Big Daddy, you kept a tight mouth about it.
BIG DADDY   A pig squeals. A man keeps a tight mouth about it, in spite of a
    man not having a pig's advantage.
BRICK   What advantage is that?
BIG DADDY   Ignorance—of mortality—is a comfort. A man don't have that
    comfort, he's the only living thing that conceives of death, that knows what
    it is. The others go without knowing, which is the way that anything living
    should go, go without knowing, without any knowledge of it, and yet a pig
    squeals, but a man sometimes, he can keep a tight mouth about it. Some-
    times he—

(There is a deep, smoldering ferocity in the old man.)

—can keep a tight mouth about it. I wonder if—

BRICK   What, Big Daddy?

BIG DADDY   A whiskey highball would injure this spastic condition?

BRICK   No, sir, it might do it good.

BIG DADDY *(grins suddenly, wolfishly)*   Jesus, I can't tell you! The sky is open! Christ, it's open again! It's open, boy, it's open!

(BRICK looks down at his drink.)

BRICK   You feel better, Big Daddy?

BIG DADDY   Better? Hell! I can breathe!—All of my life I been like a doubled up fist. . . .

(He pours a drink.)

—Poundin', smashin', drivin'!—now I'm going to loosen these doubled up hands and touch things *easy* with them. . . .

(He spreads his hands as if caressing the air.)

You know what I'm contemplating?

BRICK *(vaguely)*   No, sir. What are you contemplating?

BIG DADDY   Ha ha!—*Pleasure!*—pleasure with *women!*

(BRICK'S smile fades a little but lingers.)

Brick, this stuff burns me!—

—Yes, boy. I'll tell you something that you might not guess. I still have desire for women and this is my sixty-fifth birthday.

BRICK   I think that's mighty remarkable, Big Daddy.

BIG DADDY   Remarkable?

BRICK   *Admirable,* Big Daddy.

BIG DADDY   You're damn right it is, remarkable and admirable both. I realize now that I never had me enough. I let many chances slip by because of scruples about it, scruples, convention—crap. . . . All that stuff is bull, bull, bull!—It took the shadow of death to make me see it. Now that shadow's lifted, I'm going to cut loose and have, what is it they call it, have me a—ball!

BRICK   A ball, huh?

BIG DADDY   That's right, a ball, a ball! Hell!—I slept with Big Mama till, let's see, five years ago, till I was sixty and she was fifty-eight, and never even liked her, never did!

(The phone has been ringing down the hall. BIG MAMA *enters, exclaiming:)*

BIG MAMA   Don't you men hear that phone ring? I heard it way out on the gall'ry.

BIG DADDY   There's five rooms off this front gall'ry that you could go through. Why do you go through this one?

*(*BIG MAMA *makes a playful face as she bustles out the hall door.)*

Hunh!—Why, when Big Mama goes out of a room, I can't remember what that woman looks like, but when Big Mama comes back into the room, boy, then I see what she looks like, and I wish I didn't!

(Bends over laughing at this joke till it hurts his guts and he straightens with a grimace. The laugh subsides to a chuckle as he puts the liquor glass a little distrustfully down on the table.

   BRICK *has risen and hobbled to the gallery doors.)*

Hey! Where you goin'?

BRICK   Out for a breather.

BIG DADDY   Not yet you ain't. Stay here till this talk is finished, young fellow.

BRICK   I thought it was finished, Big Daddy.

BIG DADDY   It ain't even begun.

BRICK   My mistake. Excuse me. I just wanted to feel that river breeze.

BIG DADDY   Turn on the ceiling fan and set back down in that chair.

*(*BIG MAMA'S *voice rises, carrying down the hall.)*

BIG MAMA   Miss Sally, you're a case! You're a caution, Miss Sally. Why didn't you give me a chance to explain it to you?

BIG DADDY   Jesus, she's talking to my old maid sister again.

BIG MAMA   Well, goodbye, now, Miss Sally. You come down real soon, Big Daddy's dying to see you! Yaisss, goodbye, Miss Sally. . . .

(She hangs up and bellows with mirth. BIG DADDY *groans and covers his ears as she approaches.*

   Bursting in:)

Big Daddy, that was Miss Sally callin' from Memphis again! You know what she done, Big Daddy? She called her doctor in Memphis to git him to tell her what that spastic thing is! Ha-*HAAAA!*—And called back to tell me how relieved she was that—Hey! Let me in!

*(*BIG DADDY *has been holding the door half closed against her.)*

BIG DADDY   Naw I ain't. I told you not to come and go through this room. You just back out and go through those five other rooms.

BIG MAMA   Big Daddy? Big Daddy? Oh, Big Daddy!—You didn't mean those things you said to me, did you?

(He shuts door firmly against her but she still calls.)

Sweetheart? Sweetheart? Big Daddy? You didn't mean those awful things you said to me?—I know you didn't. I know you didn't mean those things in your heart. . . .

(The childlike voice fades with a sob and her heavy footsteps retreat down the hall. BRICK has risen once more on his crutches and starts for the gallery again.)

BIG DADDY   All I ask of that woman is that she leave me alone. But she can't admit to herself that she makes me sick. That comes of having slept with her too many years. Should of quit much sooner but that old woman she never got enough of it—and I was good in bed . . . I never should of wasted so much of it on her. . . . They say you got just so many and each one is numbered. Well, I got a few left in me, a few, and I'm going to pick me a good one to spend 'em on! I'm going to pick me a choice one, I don't care how much she costs, I'll smother her in—minks! Ha ha! I'll strip her naked and smother her in minks and choke her with diamonds! Ha ha! I'll strip her naked and choke her with diamonds and smother her with minks and hump her from hell to breakfast. *Ha aha ha ha ha!*

MAE *(gaily at door)*   Who's that laughin' in there?

GOOPER   Is Big Daddy laughin' in there?

BIG DADDY   Crap!—them two—*drips.* . . .

(He goes over and touches BRICK'S shoulder.)

Yes, son. Brick, boy.—I'm—*happy*! I'm happy, son, I'm happy!

(He chokes a little and bites his under lip, pressing his head quickly, shyly against his son's head and then, coughing with embarrassment, goes uncertainly back to the table where he set down the glass. He drinks and makes a grimace as it burns his guts. BRICK sighs and rises with effort.)

What makes you so restless? Have you got ants in your britches?

BRICK   Yes, sir . . .

BIG DADDY   Why?

BRICK   —Something—hasn't—happened. . . .

BIG DADDY   Yeah? What is that!

BRICK *(sadly)*   —the click. . . .

BIG DADDY   Did you say click?

BRICK   Yes, click.

BIG DADDY   What click?

BRICK   A click that I get in my head that makes me peaceful.

BIG DADDY   I sure in hell don't know what you're talking about, but it disturbs me.

BRICK   It's just a mechanical thing.

BIG DADDY   What is a mechanical thing?

BRICK   This click that I get in my head that makes me peaceful. I got to drink till I get it. It's just a mechanical thing, something like a—like a—like a—

BIG DADDY   Like a—

BRICK   Switch clicking off in my head, turning the hot light off and the cool night on and—

(He looks up, smiling sadly.)

—all of a sudden there's—peace!

BIG DADDY *(whistles long and soft with astonishment; he goes back to* BRICK *and clasps his son's two shoulders)*   Jesus! I didn't know it had gotten that bad with you. Why, boy, you're—*alcoholic!*

BRICK   That's the truth, Big Daddy. I'm alcoholic.

BIG DADDY   This shows how I—let things go!

BRICK   I have to hear that little click in my head that makes me peaceful. Usually I hear it sooner than this, sometimes as early as—noon, but—

—Today it's—dilatory. . . .

—I just haven't got the right level of alcohol in my bloodstream yet!

(This last statement is made with energy as he freshens his drink.)

BIG DADDY   Uh-huh. Expecting death made me blind. I didn't have no idea that a son of mine was turning into a drunkard under my nose.

BRICK *(gently)*   Well, now you do, Big Daddy, the news has penetrated.

BIG DADDY   UH-huh, yes, now I do, the news has—penetrated. . . .

BRICK   And so if you'll excuse me—

BIG DADDY   No, I won't excuse you.

BRICK   —I'd better sit by myself till I hear that click in my head, it's just a mechanical thing but it don't happen except when I'm alone or talking to no one. . . .

BIG DADDY   You got a long, long time to sit still, boy, and talk to no one, but now you're talkin' to me. At least I'm talking to you. And you set there and listen until I tell you the conversation is over!

BRICK   But this talk is like all the others we've ever had together in our lives! It's nowhere, nowhere!—it's—it's *painful,* Big Daddy. . . .

BIG DADDY   All right, then let it be painful, but don't you move from that chair!—I'm going to remove that crutch. . . .

(He seizes the crutch and tosses it across room.)

BRICK   I can hop on one foot, and if I fall, I can crawl!

BIG DADDY   If you ain't careful you're gonna crawl off this plantation and then, by Jesus, you'll have to hustle your drinks along Skid Row!

BRICK   That'll come, Big Daddy.

BIG DADDY   Naw, it won't. You're my son and I'm going to straighten you out; now that *I'm* straightened out, I'm going to straighten out you!

BRICK   Yeah?

BIG DADDY   Today the report come in from Ochsner Clinic. Y'know what they told me?

(His face glows with triumph.)

The only thing that they could detect with all the instruments of science in that great hospital is a little spastic condition of the colon! And nerves torn to pieces by all that worry about it.

(A little girl bursts into room with a sparkler clutched in each fist, hops and shrieks like a monkey gone mad and rushes back out again as BIG DADDY *strikes at her.*

Silence. The two men stare at each other. A woman laughs gaily outside.)

I want you to know I breathed a sigh of relief almost as powerful as the Vicksburg tornado!

BRICK   You weren't ready to go?

BIG DADDY   GO WHERE?—crap. . . .

—When you are gone from here, boy, you are long gone and no where! The human machine is not no different from the animal machine or the fish machine or the bird machine or the reptile machine or the insect machine! It's just a whole God damn lot more complicated and consequently more trouble to keep together. Yep. I thought I had it. The earth shook under my foot, the sky come down like the black lid of a kettle and I couldn't breathe!—Today!!—that lid was lifted, I drew my first free breath in—how many years?—*God! —three.* . . .

(There is laughter outside, running footsteps, the soft, plusby sound and light of exploding rockets.

BRICK *stares at him soberly for a long moment; then makes a sort of startled sound in his nostrils and springs up on one foot and hops across the room to grab his crutch, swinging on the furniture for support. He gets the crutch and flees as if in horror for the gallery. His father seizes him by the sleeve of his white silk pajamas.)*

Stay here, you son of a bitch!—till I say go!

BRICK   I can't.

BIG DADDY   You sure in hell will, God damn it.

BRICK   No, I can't. We talk, you talk, in—circles! We get no where, no where! It's always the same, you say you want to talk to me and don't have a ruttin' thing to say to me!

BIG DADDY   Nothin' to say when I'm tellin' you I'm going to live when I thought I was dying?!

BRICK   Oh—*that!*—Is that what you have to say to me?

BIG DADDY   Why, you son of a bitch! Ain't that, ain't that—*important?!*

BRICK   Well, you said that, that's said, and now I—

BIG DADDY   Now you set back down.

BRICK   You're all balled up, you—

BIG DADDY   I ain't balled up!

BRICK   You are, you're all balled up!

BIG DADDY   Don't tell me what I am, you drunken whelp! I'm going to tear this coat sleeve off if you don't set down!

BRICK   Big Daddy—

BIG DADDY   Do what I tell you! I'm the boss here, now! I want you to know I'm back in the driver's seat now!

(BIG MAMA *rushes in, clutching her great heaving bosom.*)

What in hell do you want in here, Big Mama?

BIG MAMA   Oh, Big Daddy! Why are you shouting like that? I just cain't *stainnnnnnnd*—it. . . .

BIG DADDY (*raising the back of his hand above his head*)   GIT!—outa here.

(*She rushes back out, sobbing.*)

BRICK (*softly, sadly*)   Christ. . . .

BIG DADDY (*fiercely*)   Yeah! Christ!—is right . . .

(BRICK *breaks loose and hobbles toward the gallery.*
    BIG DADDY *jerks his crutch from under* BRICK *so he steps with the injured ankle. He utters a hissing cry of anguish, clutches a chair and pulls it over on top of him on the floor.*)

Son of a—tub of—hog fat. . . .

BRICK   Big Daddy! Give me my crutch.

(BIG DADDY *throws the crutch out of reach.*)

Give me that crutch, Big Daddy.

BIG DADDY   Why do you drink?

BRICK   Don't know, give me my crutch!

BIG DADDY   You better think why you drink or give up drinking!

BRICK   Will you please give me my crutch so I can get up off this floor?

BIG DADDY   First you answer my question. Why do you drink? Why are you throwing your life away, boy, like somethin' disgusting you picked up on the street?

BRICK *(getting onto his knees)*   Big Daddy, I'm in pain, I stepped on that foot.

BIG DADDY   Good! I'm glad you're not too numb with the liquor in you to feel some pain!

BRICK   You—spilled my—drink . . .

BIG DADDY   I'll make a bargain with you. You tell me why you drink and I'll hand you one. I'll pour you the liquor myself and hand it to you.

BRICK   Why do I drink?

BIG DADDY   Yea! Why?

BRICK   Give me a drink and I'll tell you.

BIG DADDY   Tell me first!

BRICK   I'll tell you in one word.

BIG DADDY   What word?

BRICK   DISGUST!

(The clock chimes softly, sweetly. BIG DADDY *gives it a short, outraged glance.)*

Now how about that drink?

BIG DADDY   What are you disgusted with? You got to tell me that, first. Otherwise being disgusted don't make no sense!

BRICK   Give me my crutch.

BIG DADDY   You heard me, you got to tell me what I asked you first.

BRICK   I told you, I said to kill my disgust!

BIG DADDY   DISGUST WITH WHAT!

BRICK   You strike a hard bargain.

BIG DADDY   What are you disgusted with?—an' I'll pass you the liquor.

BRICK   I can hop on one foot, and if I fall, I can crawl.

BIG DADDY   You want liquor that bad?

BRICK *(dragging himself up, clinging to bedstead)*   Yeah, I want it that bad.

BIG DADDY   If I give you a drink, will you tell me what it is you're disgusted with, Brick?

BRICK   Yes, sir, I will try to.

(The old man pours him a drink and solemnly passes it to him. There is silence as Brick drinks.)

Have you ever heard the word "mendacity"?

BIG DADDY   Sure. Mendacity is one of them five dollar words that cheap politicians throw back and forth at each other.

BRICK   You know what it means?

BIG DADDY   Don't it mean lying and liars?

BRICK   Yes, sir, lying and liars.

BIG DADDY   Has someone been lying to you?

CHILDREN (*chanting in chorus offstage*)
>   We want Big Dad-dee!
>   We want Big Dad-dee!

(GOOPER *appears in the gallery door.*)

GOOPER   Big Daddy, the kiddies are shouting for you out there.
BIG DADDY (*fiercely*)   Keep out, Gooper!
GOOPER   'Scuse *me!*

(BIG DADDY *slams the doors after* GOOPER.)

BIG DADDY   Who's been lying to you, has Margaret been lying to you, has your
>   wife been lying to you about something, Brick?
BRICK   Not her. That wouldn't matter.
BIG DADDY   Then who's been lying to you, and what about?
BRICK   No one single person and no one lie. . . .
BIG DADDY   Then what, what then, for Christ's sake?
BRICK   —The whole, the whole—thing. . . .
BIG DADDY   Why are you rubbing your head? You got a headache?
BRICK   No, I'm tryin' to—
BIG DADDY   —Concentrate, but you can't because your brain's all soaked with
>   liquor, is that the trouble? Wet brain!

(*He snatches the glass from* BRICK'S *hand.*)

What do you know about this mendacity thing? Hell! I could write a book
on it! Don't you know that? I could write a book on it and still not cover the
subject? Well, I could, I could write a goddam book on it and still not cover
the subject anywhere near enough!!—Think of all the lies I got to put up
with!—Pretenses! Ain't that mendacity? Having to pretend stuff you don't
think or feel or have any idea of? Having for instance to act like I care for
Big Mama!—I haven't been able to stand the sight, sound, or smell of that
woman for forty years now!—even when I *laid* her!—regular as a piston. . . .

Pretend to love that son of a bitch of a Gooper and his wife Mae and those
five same screechers out there like parrots in a jungle? Jesus! Can't stand to
look at 'em!

Church!—it bores the Bejesus out of me but I go!—I go an' sit there and
listen to the fool preacher!

Clubs!—Elks! Masons! Rotary!—*crap!*

(*A spasm of pain makes him clutch his belly. He sinks into a chair and his voice is
softer and hoarser.*)

You I *do* like for some reason, did always have some kind of real feeling for—affection—respect—yes, always. . . .

You and being a success as a planter is all I ever had any devotion to in my whole life!—and that's the truth. . . .

I don't know why, but it is!

I've lived with mendacity!—Why can't *you* live with it? Hell, you *got* to live with it, there's nothing *else* to *live* with except mendacity, is there?

BRICK   Yes, sir. Yes, sir there is something else that you can live with!

BIG DADDY   What?

BRICK *(lifting his glass)*   This!—Liquor. . . .

BIG DADDY   That's not living, that's dodging away from life.

BRICK   I want to dodge away from it.

BIG DADDY   Then why don't you kill yourself, man?

BRICK   I like to drink. . . .

BIG DADDY   Oh, God, I can't talk to you. . . .

BRICK   I'm sorry, Big Daddy.

BIG DADDY   Not as sorry as I am. I'll tell you something. A little while back when I thought my number was up—

(This speech should have torrential pace and fury.)

—before I found out it was just this—spastic—colon. I thought about you. Should I or should I not, if the jig was up, give you this place when I go—since I hate Gooper an' Mae an' know that they hate me, and since all five same monkeys are little Maes an' Goopers.—And I thought, No!—Then I thought, Yes!—I couldn't make up my mind. I hate Gooper and his five same monkeys and that bitch Mae! Why should I turn over twenty-eight thousand acres of the richest land this side of the valley Nile to not my kind?—But why in hell, on the other hand, Brick—should I subsidize a goddam fool on the bottle?—Liked or not liked, well, maybe even—*loved!*—Why should I do that?—Subsidize worthless behavior? Rot? Corruption?

BRICK *(smiling)*   I understand.

BIG DADDY   Well, if you do, you're smarter than I am, God damn it, because I don't understand. And this I will tell you frankly. I didn't make up my mind at all on that question and still to this day I ain't made out no will!—Well, now I don't *have* to. The pressure is gone. I can just wait and see if you pull yourself together or if you don't.

BRICK   That's right, Big Daddy.

BIG DADDY   You sound like you thought I was kidding.

BRICK *(rising)*   No, sir, I know you're not kidding.

BIG DADDY   But you don't care—?

BRICK *(hobbling toward the gallery door)*   No, sir, I don't care. . . .

Now how about taking a look at your birthday fireworks and getting some of that cool breeze off the river?

(He stands in the gallery doorway as the night sky turns pink and green and gold with successive flashes of light.)

BIG DADDY   *WAIT!*—Brick. . . .

(His voice drops. Suddenly there is something shy, almost tender, in his restraining gesture.)

Don't let's—leave it like this, like them other talks we've had, we've always—talked around things, we've—just talked around things for some rutten reason, I don't know what, it's always like something was left not spoken, something avoided because neither of us was honest enough with the—other. . . .

BRICK   I never lied to you, Big Daddy.

BIG DADDY   Did I ever to *you?*

BRICK   No, sir. . . .

BIG DADDY   Then there is at least two people that never lied to each other.

BRICK   But we've never *talked* to each other.

BIG DADDY   We can *now*.

BRICK   Big Daddy, there don't seem to be anything much to say.

BIG DADDY   You say that you drink to kill your disgust with lying.

BRICK   You said to give you a reason.

BIG DADDY   Is liquor the only thing that'll kill this disgust?

BRICK   Now. Yes.

BIG DADDY   But not once, huh?

BRICK   Not when I was still young an' believing. A drinking man's someone who wants to forget he isn't still young an' believing.

BIG DADDY   Believing what?

BRICK   Believing. . . .

BIG DADDY   Believing *what?*

BRICK *(stubbornly evasive)*   Believing. . . .

BIG DADDY   I don't know what the hell you mean by believing and I don't think you know what you mean by believing, but if you still got sports in your blood, go back to sports announcing and—

BRICK   Sit in a glass box watching games I can't play? Describing what I can't do while players do it? Sweating out their disgust and confusion in contests I'm not fit for? Drinkin' a coke, half bourbon, so I can stand it? That's no goddam good any more, no help—time just outran me, Big Daddy—got there first . . .

BIG DADDY   I think you're passing the buck.

BRICK   You know many drinkin' men?

BIG DADDY *(with a slight, charming smile)*   I have known a fair number of that species.

BRICK   Could any of them tell you why he drank?

BIG DADDY   Yep, you're passin' the buck to things like time and disgust with "mendacity" and—crap!—if you got to use that kind of language about a thing, it's ninety-proof bull, and I'm not buying any.

BRICK   I had to give you a reason to get a drink!

BIG DADDY   You started drinkin' when your friend Skipper died.

(Silence for five beats. Then BRICK *makes a startled movement, reaching for his crutch.)*

BRICK   What are you suggesting?

BIG DADDY   I'm suggesting nothing.

(The shuffle and clop of BRICK'S *rapid hobble away from his father's steady, grave attention.)*

—But Gooper an' Mae suggested that there was something not right exactly in your—

BRICK   *(stopping short downstage as if backed to a wall)* "Not right"?

BIG DADDY   Not, well, exactly *normal* in your friendship with—

BRICK   They suggested that, too? I thought that was Maggie's suggestion.

*(*BRICK'S *detachment is at last broken through. His heart is accelerated; his forehead sweat-beaded; his breath becomes more rapid and his voice hoarse. The thing they're discussing, timidly and painfully on the side of* BIG DADDY, *fiercely, violently on* BRICK'S *side, is the inadmissible thing that Skipper died to disavow between them. The fact that if it existed it had to be disavowed to "keep face" in the world they lived in, may be at the heart of the "mendacity" that* BRICK *drinks to kill his disgust with. It may be the root of his collapse. Or maybe it is only a single manifestation of it, not even the most important. The bird that I hope to catch in the net of this play is not the solution of one man's psychological problem. I'm trying to catch the true quality of experience in a group of people, that cloudy, flickering, evanescent—fiercely charged!—interplay of live human beings in the thundercloud of a common crisis. Some mystery should be left in the revelation of character in a play, just as a great deal of mystery is always left in the revelation of character in life, even in one's own character to himself. This does not absolve the playwright of his duty to observe and probe as clearly and deeply as he* legitimately *can: but it should steer him away from "pat" conclusions, facile definitions which make a play just a play, not a snare for the truth of human experience.*

The following scene should be played with great concentration, with most of the power leashed but palpable in what is left unspoken.)

Who else's suggestion is it, is it *yours?* How many others thought that
Skipper and I were—

BIG DADDY *(gently)*   Now, hold on, hold on a minute, son.—I knocked around
in my time.

BRICK   What's that got to do with—

BIG DADDY   I said 'Hold on!'—I bummed, I bummed this country till I was—

BRICK   Whose suggestion, who else's suggestion is it?

BIG DADDY   Slept in hobo jungles and railroad Y's and flophouses in all cities
before I—

BRICK   Oh, *you* think so, too, you call me your son and a queer. Oh! Maybe
that's why you put Maggie and me in this room that was Jack Straw's and
Peter Ochello's, in which that pair of old sisters slept in a double bed where
both of 'em died?

BIG DADDY   *Now just don't go throwing rocks at—*

(Suddenly REVEREND TOOKER *appears in the gallery doors, his head slightly,
playfully, fatuously cocked, with a practised clergyman's smile, sincere as a bird-
call blown on a hunter's whistle, the living embodiment of the pious, conventional
lie.*

　　BIG DADDY *gasps a little at this perfectly timed, but incongruous,
apparition.)*

—What're you lookin' for, Preacher?

REVEREND TOOKER   The gentleman's lavatory, ha ha!—heh, heh . . .

BIG DADDY *(with strained courtesy)*   —Go back out and walk down to the other
end of the gallery, Reverend Tooker, and use the bathroom connected with
my bedroom, and if you can't find it, ask them where it is!

REVEREND TOOKER   Ah, thanks.

(He goes out with a deprecatory chuckle.)

BIG DADDY   It's hard to talk in this place . . .

BRICK   Son of a—!

BIG DADDY *(leaving a lot unspoken)*   —I seen all things and understood a lot of
them, till 1910. Christ, the year that—I had worn my shoes through,
hocked my—I hopped off a yellow dog freight car half a mile down the
road, slept in a wagon of cotton outside the gin—Jack Straw an' Peter
Ochello took me in. Hired me to manage this place which grew into this
one.—When Jack Straw died—why, old Peter Ochello quit eatin' like a
dog does when its master's dead, and died, too!

BRICK   Christ!

BIG DADDY   I'm just saying I understand such—

BRICK *(violently)*   Skipper is dead. I have not quit eating!

BIG DADDY   No, but you started drinking.

(BRICK *wheels on his crutch and hurls his glass across the room shouting:*)

BRICK   YOU THINK SO, TOO?
BIG DADDY   *Shhh!*

(*Footsteps run on the gallery. There are women's calls.*
   BIG DADDY *goes toward the door.*)

Go way!—Just broke a glass. . . .

(BRICK *is transformed, as if a quiet mountain blew suddenly up in volcanic flame.*)

BRICK   You think so, too? You think so, too? You think me an' Skipper did, did, did!—*sodomy!*—together?
BIG DADDY   Hold—!
BRICK   That what you—
BIG DADDY   —*ON*—a minute!
BRICK   You think we did dirty things between us, Skipper an'—
BIG DADDY   Why are you shouting like that? Why are you—
BRICK   —Me, is that what you think of Skipper, is that—
BIG DADDY   —so excited? I don't think nothing. I don't know nothing. I'm simply telling you what—
BRICK   You think that Skipper and me were a pair of dirty old men?
BIG DADDY   Now that's—
BRICK   Straw? Ochello? A couple of—
BIG DADDY   Now just—
BRICK   —ducking sissies? Queers? Is that what you—
BIG DADDY   Shhh.
BRICK   —think?

(*He loses his balance and pitches to his knees without noticing the pain. He grabs the bed and drags himself up.*)

BIG DADDY   Jesus!—Whew. . . . Grab my hand!
BRICK   Naw, I don't want your hand. . . .
BIG DADDY   Well, I want yours. Git up!

(*He draws him up, keeps an arm about him with concern and affection.*)

You broken out in a sweat! You're panting like you'd run a race with—
BRICK (*freeing himself from his father's hold*)   Big Daddy, you shock me, Big Daddy, you, you—*shock* me! Talkin' so—

(*He turns away from his father.*)

—casually!—about a—thing like that . . .

—Don't you know how people *feel* about things like that? How, how *disgusted* they are by things like that? Why, at Ole Miss when it was discovered a pledge to our fraternity, Skipper's and mine, did a, *attempted* to do a, unnatural thing with—

We not only dropped him like a hot rock!—We told him to git off the campus, and he did, he got!—All the way to—

(He halts, breathless.)

BIG DADDY   —Where?
BRICK   —North Africa, last I heard!
BIG DADDY   Well, I have come back from further away than that, I have just now returned from the other side of the moon, death's country, son, and I'm not easy to shock by anything here.

(He comes downstage and faces out.)

Always, anyhow, lived with too much space around me to be infected by ideas of other people. One thing you can grow on a big place more important than cotton!—is *tolerance!*—I grown it.

(He returns toward BRICK.*)*

BRICK   Why can't exceptional friendship, *real, real, deep, deep friendship!* between two men be respected as something clean and decent without being thought of as—
BIG DADDY   It can, it is, for God's sake.
BRICK   —*Fairies.* . . .

(In his utterance of this word, we gauge the wide and profound reach of the conventional mores he got from the world that crowned him with early laurel.)

BIG DADDY   I told Mae an' Gooper—
BRICK   Frig Mae and Gooper, frig all dirty lies and liars!—Skipper and me had a clean, true thing between us?—had a clean friendship, practically all our lives, till Maggie got the idea you're talking about. Normal? No!—It was too rare to be normal, any true thing between two people is too rare to be normal. Oh, once in a while he put his hand on my shoulder or I'd put mine on his, oh, maybe even, when we were touring the country in pro-football an' shared hotel-rooms we'd reach across the space between the two beds and shake hands to say goodnight, yeah, one or two times we—
BIG DADDY   Brick, nobody thinks that that's not normal!
BRICK   Well, they're mistaken, it was! It was a pure an' true thing an' that's not normal.

(They both stare straight at each other for a long moment. The tension breaks and both turn away as if tired.)

BIG DADDY   Yeah, it's—hard t'—talk. . . .
BRICK   All right, then, let's—let it go. . . .
BIG DADDY   Why did Skipper crack up? Why have you?

(BRICK looks back at his father again. He has already decided, without knowing that he has made this decision, that he is going to tell his father that he is dying of cancer. Only this could even the score between them: one inadmissible thing in return for another.)

BRICK *(ominously)*   All right. You're asking for it, Big Daddy. We're finally going to have that real true talk you wanted. It's too late to stop it, now, we got to carry it through and cover every subject.

(He hobbles back to the liquor cabinet.)

Uh-huh.

(He opens the ice bucket and picks up the silver tongs with slow admiration of their frosty brightness.)

Maggie declares that Skipper and I went into pro-football after we left "Ole Miss" because we were scared to grow up . . .

(He moves downstage with the shuffle and clop of a cripple on a crutch. As MARGARET did when her speech became "recitative," he looks out into the house, commanding its attention by his direct, concentrated gaze—a broken, "tragically elegant" figure telling simply as much as he knows of "the Truth":)

—Wanted to—keep on tossing—those long, long!—high, high!—passes that—couldn't be intercepted except by time, the aerial attack that made us famous! And so we did, we did, we kept it up for one season, that aerial attack, we held it high!—Yeah, but—

—that summer, Maggie, she laid the law down to me, said, Now or never, and so I married Maggie. . . .
BIG DADDY   How was Maggie in bed?
BRICK *(wryly)*   Great! the greatest!

(BIG DADDY nods as if he thought so.)

She went on the road that fall with the Dixie Stars. Oh, she made a great show of being the world's best sport. She wore a—wore a—tall bearskin cap! A shako, they call it, a dyed moleskin coat, a moleskin coat dyed red!—Cut up crazy! Rented hotel ballrooms for victory celebrations, wouldn't cancel them when it—turned out—defeat. . . .

MAGGIE THE CAT! Ha ha!

(BIG DADDY *nods*.)

—But Skipper, he had some fever which came back on him which doctors couldn't explain and I got that injury—turned out to be just a shadow on the X-ray plate—and a touch of bursitis. . . .

I lay in a hospital bed, watched our games on TV, saw Maggie on the bench next to Skipper when he was hauled out of a game for stumbles, fumbles!—Burned me up the way she hung on his arm!—Y'know, I think that Maggie had always felt sort of left out because she and me never got any closer together than two people just get in bed, which is not much closer than two cats on a—fence humping. . . .

So! She took this time to work on poor dumb Skipper. He was a less than average student at Ole Miss, you know that, don't you?!—Poured in his mind the dirty, false idea that what we were, him and me, was a frustrated case of that ole pair of sisters that lived in this room, Jack Straw and Peter Ochello!—He, poor Skipper, went to bed with Maggie to prove it wasn't true, and when it didn't work out, he thought it *was* true!—Skipper broke in two like a rotten stick—nobody ever turned so fast to a lush—or died of it so quick. . . .

—Now are you satisfied?

(BIG DADDY *has listened to this story, dividing the grain from the chaff. Now he looks at his son.*)

BIG DADDY   Are *you* satisfied?
BRICK   With what?
BIG DADDY   That half-ass story!
BRICK   What's half-ass about it?
BIG DADDY   Something's left out of that story. What did you leave out?

(*The phone has started ringing in the hall. As if it reminded him of something,* BRICK *glances suddenly toward the sound and says:*)

BRICK   Yes!—I left out a long-distance call which I had from Skipper, in which he made a drunken confession to me and on which I hung up!—last time we spoke to each other in our lives. . . .

(*Muted ring stops as someone answers phone in a soft, indistinct voice in hall.*)

BIG DADDY   You hung up?

BRICK   Hung up. Jesus! Well—

BIG DADDY   Anyhow now!—we have tracked down the lie with which you're disgusted and which you are drinking to kill your disgust with, Brick. You been passing the buck. This disgust with mendacity is disgust with yourself.

You!—dug the grave of your friend and kicked him in it!—before you'd face truth with him!

BRICK   *His* truth, not *mine!*

BIG DADDY   His truth, okay! But you wouldn't face it with him!

BRICK   Who *can* face truth? Can *you?*

BIG DADDY   Now don't start passin' the rutten buck again, boy!

BRICK   *How about these birthday congratulations, these many, many happy returns of the day, when ev'rybody but you knows there won't be any!*

(Whoever has answered the hall phone lets out a high, shrill laugh; the voice becomes audible saying: "no, no, you got it all wrong! Upside down! Are you crazy?"

　　BRICK *suddenly catches his breath as he realized that he has made a shocking disclosure. He hobbles a few paces, then freezes, and without looking at his father's shocked face, says:)*

Let's, let's—go out, now, and—

*(*BIG DADDY *moves suddenly forward and grabs hold of the boy's crutch like it was a weapon for which they were fighting for possession.)*

BIG DADDY   Oh, no, no! No one's going out! What did you start to say?

BRICK   I don't remember.

BIG DADDY   "Many happy returns when they know there won't be any"?

BRICK   Aw, hell, Big Daddy, forget it. Come on out on the gallery and look at the fireworks they're shooting off for your birthday. . . .

BIG DADDY   First you finish that remark you were makin' before you cut off. "Many happy returns when they know there won't be any"?—Ain't that what you just said?

BRICK   Look, now. I can get around without that crutch if I have to but it would be a lot easier on the furniture an' glassware if I didn' have to go swinging along like Tarzan of th'—

BIG DADDY   FINISH! WHAT YOU WAS SAYIN'!

(An eerie green glow shows in sky behind him.)

BRICK *(sucking the ice in his glass, speech becoming thick)* Leave th' place to Gooper and Mae an' their five little same little monkeys. All I want is—

BIG DADDY   "LEAVE TH' PLACE," did you say?

BRICK *(vaguely)*   All twenty-eight thousand acres of the richest land this side of the valley Nile.

BIG DADDY   Who said I was "leaving the place" to Gooper or anybody? This is
my sixty-fifth birthday! I got fifteen years or twenty years left in me! I'll
outlive *you!* I'll bury you an' have to pay for your coffin!

BRICK   Sure. Many happy returns. Now let's go watch the fireworks, come on,
let's—

BIG DADDY   Lying, have they been lying? About the report from th'—clinic?
Did they, did they—find something?—*Cancer.* Maybe?

BRICK   Mendacity is a system that we live in. Liquor is one way out an' death's
the other. . . .

(*He takes the crutch from* BIG DADDY'S *loose grip and swings out on the gallery
leaving the doors open.*
A song, "Pick a Bale of Cotton," is heard.)

MAE (*appearing in door*)   Oh, Big Daddy, the field-hands are singin' fo' you!

BIG DADDY (*shouting hoarsely*)   BRICK! BRICK!

MAE   He's outside drinkin', Big Daddy.

BIG DADDY   BRICK!

(MAE *retreats, awed by the passion of his voice. Children call* BRICK *in tones
mocking* BIG DADDY. *His face crumbles like broken yellow plaster about to fall
into dust.*
There is a glow in the sky. BRICK *swings back through the doors, slowly,
gravely, quite soberly.*)

BRICK   I'm sorry, Big Daddy. My head don't work any more and it's hard for
me to understand how anybody could care if he lived or died or was dying
or cared about anything but whether or not there was liquor left in the
bottle and so I said what I said without thinking. In some ways I'm no better
than the others, in some ways worse because I'm less alive. Maybe it's being
alive that makes them lie, and being almost *not* alive makes me sort of
accidentally truthful—I don't know but—anyway—we've been friends . . .

—And being friends is telling each other the truth. . . .

(*There is a pause.*)

You told *me!* I told *you!*

(*A child rushes into the room and grabs a fistful of firecrackers and runs out
again.*)

CHILD (*screaming*)   Bang, bang, bang, bang, bang, bang, bang, bang, bang!

BIG DADDY (*slowly and passionately*)   CHRIST—DAMN—ALL—LYING
SONS OF—LYING BITCHES!

(He straightens at last and crosses to the inside door. At the door he turns and looks back as if he had some desperate question he couldn't put into words. Then he nods reflectively and says in a hoarse voice:)

Yes, all liars, all liars, all lying dying liars!

(This is said slowly, slowly, with a fierce revulsion. He goes on out.)

—Lying! Dying! Liars!

(His voice dies out. There is the sound of a child being slapped. It rushes, hideously bawling, through room and out the hall door.
    BRICK *remains motionless as the lights dim out and the curtain falls.)*

CURTAIN

ACT III

There is no lapse of time.
MAE *enters with* REVEREND TOOKER.

MAE   Where is Big Daddy! Big Daddy?
BIG MAMA *(entering)*   Too much smell of burnt fireworks makes me feel a little
    bit sick at my stomach.—Where is Big Daddy?
MAE   That's what I want to know, where has Big Daddy gone?
BIG MAMA   He must have turned in, I reckon he went to baid. . . .

    (GOOPER enters.)

GOOPER   Where is Big Daddy?
MAE   We don't know where he is!
BIG MAMA   I reckon he's gone to baid.
GOOPER   Well, then, now we can talk.
BIG MAMA   What *is* this talk, *what* talk?

    (MARGARET appears on gallery, talking to DR. BAUGH.)

MARGARET *(musically)*   My family freed their slaves ten years before abolition,
    my great-great grandfather gave his slaves their freedom five years before
    the war between the States started!
MAE   Oh, for God's sake! Maggie's climbed back up in her family tree!
MARGARET *(sweetly)*   What Mae?—Oh, where's Big Daddy?!

(The pace must be very quick. Great Southern animation.)

BIG MAMA *(addressing them all)*　I think Big Daddy was just worn out. He loves his family, he loves to have them around him, but it's a strain on his nerves. He wasn't himself tonight, Big Daddy wasn't himself, I could tell he was all worked up.

REVEREND TOOKER　I think he's remarkable.

BIG MAMA　Yaisss! Just remarkable. Did you all notice the food he ate at that table? Did you all notice the supper he put away? Why, he ate like a hawss!

GOOPER　I hope he doesn't regret it.

BIG MAMA　Why, that man—ate a huge piece of cawn-bread with molasses on it! Helped himself twice to hoppin' john.

MARGARET　Big Daddy loves hoppin' john.—We had a real country dinner.

BIG MAMA *(overlapping* MARGARET*)*　Yais, he simply adores it! An' candied yams? That man put away enough food at that table to stuff a nigger *field-hand!*

GOOPER *(with grim relish)*　I hope he don't have to pay for it later on. . . .

BIG MAMA *(fiercely)*　What's *that,* Gooper?

MAE　Gooper says he hopes Big Daddy doesn't suffer tonight.

BIG MAMA　Oh, shoot, Gooper says, Gooper says! Why should Big Daddy suffer for satisfying a normal appetite? There's nothin' wrong with that man but nerves, he's sound as a dollar! And now he knows he is an' that's why he ate such a supper. He had a big load off his mind, knowin' he wasn't doomed t'—what he thought he was doomed to. . . .

MARGARET *(sadly and sweetly)*　Bless his old sweet soul. . . .

BIG MAMA *(vaguely)*　Yais, bless his heart, wher's Brick?

MAE　Outside.

GOOPER　—Drinkin' . . .

BIG MAMA　I know he's drinkin'. You all don't have to keep tellin' *me* Brick is drinkin'. Cain't I see he's drinkin' without you continually tellin' me that boy's drinkin'?

MARGARET　Good for you, Big Mama!

(She applauds.)

BIG MAMA　Other people *drink* and *have* drunk an' will *drink,* as long as they make that stuff an' put it in bottles.

MARGARET　That's the truth. I never trusted a man that didn't drink.

MAE　Gooper never drinks. Don't you trust Gooper?

MARGARET　Why, Gooper don't you drink? If I'd known you didn't drink, I wouldn't of made that remark—

BIG MAMA　*Brick?*

MARGARET　—at least not in your presence.

(She laughs sweetly.)

BIG MAMA   *Brick!*

MARGARET   He's still on the gall'ry. I'll go bring him in so we can talk.

BIG MAMA (*worriedly*)   I don't know what this mysterious family conference is
about.

(*Awkward silence.* BIG MAMA *looks from face to face, then belches slightly and
mutters, "Excuse me. . . ." She opens an ornamental fan suspended about her
throat, a black lace fan to go with her black lace gown and fans her wilting
corsage, sniffing nervously and looking from face to face in the uncomfortable
silence as* MARGARET *calls "Brick?" and* BRICK *sings to the moon on the
gallery.*)

I don't know what's wrong here, you all have such long faces! Open that
door on the hall and let some air circulate through here, will you please,
Gooper?

MAE   I think we'd better leave that door closed, Big Mama, till after the talk.

BIG MAMA   Reveren' Tooker, will *you* please open that door?!

REVEREND TOOKER   I sure will, Big Mama.

MAE   I just didn't think we ought t' take any chance of Big Daddy hearin' a
word of this discussion.

BIG MAMA   *I swan!* Nothing's going to be said in Big Daddy's house that he
cain't hear if he wants to!

GOOPER   Well, Big Mama, it's—

(MAE *gives him a quick, hard poke to shut him up. He glares at her fiercely as she
circles before him like a burlesque ballerina, raising her skinny bare arms over her
head, jangling her bracelets, exclaiming:*)

MAE   *A breeze! A breeze!*

REVEREND TOOKER   I think this house is the coolest house in the Delta.—Did
you all know that Halsey Banks' widow put air-conditioning units in the
church and rectory at Friar's Point in memory of Halsey?

(*General conversation has resumed; everybody is chatting so that the stage sounds
like a big bird-cage.*)

GOOPER   Too bad nobody cools your church off for you. I bet you sweat in
that pulpit these hot Sundays, Reverend Tooker.

REVEREND TOOKER   Yes, my vestments are drenched.

MAE (*at the same time to* DR. BAUGH)   You think those vitamin B_{12} injections
are what they're cracked up t' be, Doc Baugh?

DOCTOR BAUGH   Well, if you want to be stuck with something I guess they're
as good to be stuck with as anything else.

BIG MAMA (*at gallery door*)   *Maggie, Maggie, aren't you comin' with Brick?*

MAE (*suddenly and loudly, creating a silence*)   *I have a strange feeling, I have a
peculiar feeling!*

BIG MAMA (*turning from gallery*)   What feeling?

MAE   That Brick said somethin' he shouldn't of said t' Big Daddy.

BIG MAMA   Now what on earth could Brick of said t' Big Daddy that he shouldn't say?

GOOPER   Big Mama, there's somethin'—

MAE   NOW, WAIT!

(*She rushes up to* BIG MAMA *and gives her a quick hug and kiss.* BIG MAMA *pushes her impatiently off as the* REVEREND TOOKER'S *voice rises serenely in a little pocket of silence:*)

REVEREND TOOKER   Yes, last Sunday the gold in my chasuble faded into th' purple. . . .

GOOPER   Reveren' you must of been preachin' hell's fire last Sunday!

(*He guffaws at this witticism but the* REVEREND *is not sincerely amused. At the same time* BIG MAMA *has crossed over to* DR. BAUGH *and is saying to him:*)

BIG MAMA (*her breathless voice rising high-pitched above the others*)   In my day they had what they call the Keeley cure for heavy drinkers. But now I understand they just take some kind of tablets, they call them "Annie Bust" tablets. But *Brick* don't need to take *nothin'*.

(BRICK *appears in gallery doors with* MARGARET *behind him.*)

BIG MAMA (*unaware of his presence behind her*)   That boy is just broken up over Skipper's death. You know how poor Skipper died. They gave him a big, big dose of that sodium amytal stuff at his home and then they called the ambulance and give him another big, big dose of it at the hospital and that and all of the alcohol in his system fo' months an' months just proved too much for his heart. . . . I'm scared of needles! I'm more scared of a needle than the knife. . . . I think more people have been needled out of this world than—

(*She stops short and wheels about.*)

OH!—here's Brick! My precious baby—

(*She turns upon* BRICK *with short, fat arms extended, at the same time uttering a loud, short sob, which is both comic and touching.*

BRICK *smiles and bows slightly, making a burlesque gesture of gallantry for* MAGGIE *to pass before him into the room. Then he hobbles on his crutch directly to the liquor cabinet and there is absolute silence, with everybody looking at* BRICK *as everybody has always looked at* BRICK *when he spoke or moved or appeared. One by one he drops ice cubes in his glass, then suddenly, but not quickly, looks back over his shoulder with a wry, charming smile, and says:*)

BRICK   I'm sorry! Anyone else?

BIG MAMA *(sadly)*   No, son. I *wish* you wouldn't!

BRICK   I wish I didn't have to, Big Mama, but I'm still waiting for that click in my head which makes it all smooth out!

BIG MAMA   Aw, Brick, you—BREAK MY HEART!

MARGARET *(at the same time)*   *Brick, go sit with Big Mama!*

BIG MAMA   I just cain't *staiiiiiiiii-nnnnnd*—it. . . .

(She sobs.)

MAE   Now that we're all assembled—

GOOPER   We kin talk. . . .

BIG MAMA   Breaks my heart. . . .

MARGARET   Sit with Big Mama, Brick, and hold her hand.

(BIG MAMA sniffs very loudly three times, almost like three drum beats in the pocket of silence.)

BRICK   You do that, Maggie. I'm a restless cripple. I got to stay on my crutch.

(BRICK hobbles to the gallery door; leans there as if waiting.

MAE sits beside BIG MAMA, while GOOPER moves in front and sits on the end of the couch, facing her. REVEREND TOOKER moves nervously into the space between them; on the other side, DR. BAUGH stands looking at nothing in particular and lights a cigar. MARGARET turns away.)

BIG MAMA   Why're you all *surroundin'* me—like this? Why're you all starin' at me like this an' makin' signs at each other?

(REVEREND TOOKER steps back startled.)

MAE   Calm yourself, Big Mama.

BIG MAMA   Calm you'self, *you'self*, Sister Woman. How could I calm myself with everyone starin' at me as if big drops of blood had broken out on m'face? What's this all about, Annh! What?

(GOOPER coughs and takes a center position.)

GOOPER   Now, Doc Baugh.

MAE   Doc Baugh?

BRICK *(suddenly)*   SHHH!—

(Then he grins and chuckles and shakes his head regretfully.)

—Naw!—that wasn't th' click.

GOOPER   Brick, shut up or stay out there on the gallery with your liquor! We

got to talk about a serious matter. Big Mama wants to know the complete
truth about the report we got today from the Ochsner Clinic.

MAE *(eagerly)*   —on Big Daddy's condition!

GOOPER   Yais, on Big Daddy's condition, we got to face it.

DOCTOR BAUGH   Well. . . .

BIG MAMA *(terrified, rising)*   Is there? Something? Something that I? Don't—
Know?

(In these few words, this startled, very soft, question, BIG MAMA *reviews the
history of her forty-five years with* BIG DADDY, *her great, almost embarrassingly
true-hearted and simple-minded devotion to* BIG DADDY, *who must have had
something* BRICK *has, who made himself loved so much by the "simple expedient"
of not loving enough to disturb his charming detachment, also once coupled, like*
BRICK'S, *with virile beauty.*

BIG MAMA *has a dignity at this moment: she almost stops being fat.)*

DOCTOR BAUGH *(after a pause, uncomfortably)*   Yes?—Well—

BIG MAMA   I!!!—want to—*knowwwwwww. . . .*

*(Immediately she thrusts her fist to her mouth as if to deny that statement.
    Then, for some curious reason, she snatches the withered corsage from her breast
and hurls it on the floor and steps on it with her short, fat feet.)*

—*Somebody must be lyin'!*—*I want to know!*

MAE   Sit down, Big Mama, sit down on this sofa.

MARGARET *(quickly)*   Brick, go sit with Big Mama.

BIG MAMA   *What is it, what is it?*

DOCTOR BAUGH   I never have seen a more thorough examination than Big
Daddy Pollitt was given in all my experience with the Ochsner Clinic.

GOOPER   It's one of the best in the country.

MAE   It's *THE* best in the country—bar *none!*

(For some reason she gives GOOPER *a violent poke as she goes past him. He slaps
at her hand without removing his eyes from his mother's face.)*

DOCTOR BAUGH   Of course they were ninety-nine and nine-tenths percent
sure before they even started.

BIG MAMA   Sure of what, sure of what, sure of—*what?*—*what!*

(She catches her breath in a startled sob. MAE *kisses her quickly. She thrusts* MAE
fiercely away from her, staring at the doctor.)

MAE   Mommy, be a brave girl!

BRICK *(in the doorway, softly)*
    "By the light, by the light,
    Of the sil-ver-ry mo-ooo-n . . ."

GOOPER Shut up!—Brick.
BRICK Sorry. . . .

(*He wanders out on the gallery.*)
DOCTOR BAUGH But now, you see, Big Mama, they cut a piece off this growth, a specimen of the tissue and—
BIG MAMA Growth? You told Big Daddy—
DOCTOR BAUGH Now wait.
BIG MAMA (*fiercely*) You told me and Big Daddy there wasn't a thing wrong with him but—
MAE Big Mama, they always—
GOOPER Let Doc Baugh talk, will yuh?
BIG MAMA —little spastic condition of—

(*Her breath gives out in a sob.*)

DOCTOR BAUGH Yes, that's what we told Big Daddy. But we had this bit of tissue run through the laboratory and I'm sorry to say the test was positive on it. It's—well—malignant. . . .

(*Pause.*)

BIG MAMA —Cancer?! Cancer?!

(DR. BAUGH *nods gravely.*
BIG MAMA *gives a long gasping cry.*)

MAE and GOOPER Now, now, now, Big Mama, you had to know. . . .
BIG MAMA *WHY DIDN'T THEY CUT IT OUT OF HIM? HANH? HANH?*
DOCTOR BAUGH Involved too much, Big Mama, too many organs affected.
MAE Big Mama, the liver's affected and so's the kidneys, both! It's gone way past what they call a—
GOOPER A surgical risk.
MAE —Uh-huh. . . .

(BIG MAMA *draws a breath like a dying gasp.*)

REVEREND TOOKER Tch, tch, tch, tch, tch!
DOCTOR BAUGH Yes, it's gone past the knife.
MAE *That's why he's turned yellow, Mommy!*
BIG MAMA *Git away from me, git away from me, Mae!*

(*She rises abruptly.*)

I want Brick! Where's Brick? Where is my only son?

MAE Mama! Did she say "*only* son"?

GOOPER What does that make *me*?

MAE A sober responsible man with five precious children!—*Six!*

BIG MAMA I want Brick to tell me! Brick! Brick!

MARGARET (*rising from her reflections in a corner*) Brick was so upset he went back out.

BIG MAMA *Brick!*

MARGARET Mama, let *me* tell you!

BIG MAMA No, no, leave me alone, you're not my blood!

GOOPER *Mama, I'm your son!* Listen to *me!*

MAE Gooper's your son, Mama, he's your first-born!

BIG MAMA Gooper never liked Daddy.

MAE (*as if terribly shocked*) That's not TRUE!

(*There is a pause. The minister coughs and rises.*)

REVEREND TOOKER (*to* MAE) I think I'd better slip away at this point.

MAE (*sweetly and sadly*) Yes, Doctor Tooker, you go.

REVEREND TOOKER (*discreetly*) Goodnight, goodnight, everybody, and God bless you all . . . on this place. . . .

(*He slips out.*)

DOCTOR BAUGH That man is a good man but lacking in tact. Talking about people giving memorial windows—if he mentioned one memorial window, he must have spoke of a dozen, and saying how awful it was when somebody died intestate, the legal wrangles, and so forth.

(MAE *coughs, and points at* BIG MAMA.)

DOCTOR BAUGH Well, Big Mama. . . .

(*He sighs.*)

BIG MAMA It's all a mistake, I know it's just a bad dream.

DOCTOR BAUGH We're gonna keep Big Daddy as comfortable as we can.

BIG MAMA Yes, it's just a bad dream, that's all it is, it's just an awful dream.

GOOPER In my opinion Big Daddy is having some pain but won't admit that he has it.

BIG MAMA Just a dream, a bad dream.

DOCTOR BAUGH That's what lots of them do, they think if they don't admit they're having the pain they can sort of escape the fact of it.

GOOPER (*with relish*) Yes, they get sly about it, they get real sly about it.

MAE Gooper and I think—

GOOPER Shut up, Mae!—Big Daddy ought to be started on morphine.

BIG MAMA Nobody's going to give Big Daddy morphine.

DOCTOR BAUGH   Now, Big Mama, when that pain strikes it's going to strike mighty hard and Big Daddy's going to need the needle to bear it.

BIG MAMA   I tell you, nobody's going to give him morphine.

MAE   Big Mama, you don't want to see Big Daddy suffer, you know you—

(GOOPER *standing beside her gives her a savage poke.*)

DOCTOR BAUGH (*placing a package on the table*)   I'm leaving this stuff here, so if there's a sudden attack you all won't have to send out for it.

MAE   I know how to give a hypo.

GOOPER   Mae took a course in nursing during the war.

MARGARET   Somehow I don't think Big Daddy would want Mae to give him a hypo.

MAE   You think he'd want *you* to do it?

(DR. BAUGH *rises.*)

GOOPER   Doctor Baugh is goin'.

DOCTOR BAUGH   Yes, I got to be goin'. Well, keep your chin up, Big Mama.

GOOPER (*with jocularity*)   She's gonna keep *both* chins up, aren't you Big Mama?

(BIG MAMA *sobs.*)

Now stop that, Big Mama.

MAE   Sit down with me, Big Mama.

GOOPER (*at door with* DR. BAUGH)   Well, Doc, we sure do appreciate all you done. I'm telling you, we're surely obligated to you for—

(DR. BAUGH *has gone without a glance at him.*)

GOOPER   —I guess that doctor has got a lot on his mind but it wouldn't hurt him to act a little more human. . . .

(BIG MAMA *sobs.*)

Now be a brave girl, Mommy.

BIG MAMA   It's not true, I know that it's just not true!

GOOPER   Mama, those tests are infallible!

BIG MAMA   Why are you so determined to see your father daid?

MAE   Big Mama!

MARGARET (*gently*)   I know what Big Mama means.

MAE (*fiercely*)   Oh, do you?

MARGARET   (*quietly and very sadly*)   Yes, I think I do.

MAE   For a newcomer in the family you sure do show a lot of understanding.

MARGARET   Understanding is needed on this place.

MAE   I guess you must have needed a lot of it in your family, Maggie, with your father's liquor problem and now you've got Brick with his!

MARGARET   Brick does not have a liquor problem at all. Brick is devoted to Big Daddy. This thing is a terrible strain on him.

BIG MAMA   Brick is Big Daddy's boy, but he drinks too much and it worries me and Big Daddy, and, Margaret, you've got to cooperate with us, you've got to cooperate with Big Daddy and me in getting Brick straightened out. Because it will break Big Daddy's heart if Brick don't pull himself together and take hold of things.

MAE   Take hold of *what* things, Big Mama?

BIG MAMA   The place.

(There is a quick violent look between MAE *and* GOOPER.)

GOOPER   Big Mama, you've had a shock.

MAE   Yais, we've all had a shock, but . . .

GOOPER   Let's be realistic—

MAE   —Big Daddy would never, would *never,* be foolish enough to—

GOOPER   —put this place in irresponsible hands!

BIG MAMA   Big Daddy ain't going to leave the place in anybody's hands; Big Daddy is *not* going to die. I want you to get that in your heads, all of you!

MAE   Mommy, Mommy, Big Mama, we're just as hopeful an' optimistic as you are about Big Daddy's prospects, we have faith in *prayer*—but nevertheless there are certain matters that have to be discussed an' dealt with, because otherwise—

GOOPER   Eventualities have to be considered and now's the time. . . . Mae, will you please get my briefcase out of our room?

MAE   Yes, honey.

(She rises and goes out through the hall door.)

GOOPER *(standing over* BIG MAMA)   Now Big Mom. What you said just now was not at all true and you know it. I've always loved Big Daddy in my own quiet way. I never made a show of it, and I know that Big Daddy has always been fond of me in a quiet way, too, and he never made a show of it neither.

*(*MAE *returns with* GOOPER'S *briefcase.)*

MAE   Here's your briefcase, Gooper, honey.

GOOPER *(handing the briefcase back to her)*   Thank you. . . . Of ca'use, my relationship with Big Daddy is different from Brick's.

MAE   You're eight years older'n Brick an' always had t'carry a bigger load of th' responsibilities than Brick ever had t'carry. He never carried a thing in his life but a football or a highball.

GOOPER   Mae, will y'let me talk, please?

MAE   Yes, honey.

GOOPER   Now, a twenty-eight thousand acre plantation's a mighty big thing t'run.

MAE   Almost singlehanded.

(MARGARET *has gone out onto the gallery, and can be heard calling softly to* BRICK.)

BIG MAMA   You never had to run this place! What are you talking about? As if Big Daddy was dead and in his grave, you had to run it? Why, you just helped him out with a few business details and had your law practice at the same time in Memphis!

MAE   Oh, Mommy, Mommy, Big Mommy! Let's be fair! Why, Gooper has given himself body and soul to keeping this place up for the past five years since Big Daddy's health started failing. Gooper won't say it, Gooper never thought of it as a duty, he just did it. And what did Brick do? Brick kept living in his past glory at college! Still a football player at twenty-seven!

MARGARET (*returning alone*)   Who are you talking about, now? Brick? A football player? He isn't a football player and you know it. Brick is a sport's announcer on TV and one of the best-known ones in the country!

MAE   I'm talking about what he was.

MARGARET   Well, I wish you would just stop talking about my husband.

GOOPER   I've got a right to discuss my brother with other members of MY OWN family which don't include *you*. Why don't you go out there and drink with Brick?

MARGARET   I've never seen such malice toward a brother.

GOOPER   How about his for me? Why, he can't stand to be in the same room with me!

MARGARET   This is a deliberate campaign of vilification for the most disgusting and sordid reason on earth, and I know what it is! It's *avarice, avarice, greed, greed!*

BIG MAMA   *Oh, I'll scream! I will scream in a moment unless this stops!*

(GOOPER *has stalked up to* MARGARET *with clenched fists at his sides as if he would strike her.* MAE *distorts her face again into a hideous grimace behind* MARGARET'S *back.*)

MARGARET   We only remain on the place because of Big Mom and Big Daddy. If it is true what they say about Big Daddy we are going to leave here just as soon as it's over. Not a moment later.

BIG MAMA (*sobs*)   Margaret. Child. Come here. Sit next to Big Mama.

MARGARET   Precious Mommy. I'm sorry, I'm so sorry, I—!

(*She bends her long graceful neck to press her forehead to* BIG MAMA'S *bulging shoulder under its black chiffon.*)

GOOPER   How beautiful, how touching, this display of devotion!

MAE   Do you know why she's childless? She's childless because that big beautiful athlete husband of hers won't go to bed with her!

GOOPER   You jest won't let me do this in a nice way, will yah? Aw right—Mae and I have five kids with another one coming! I don't give a goddam if Big Daddy likes me or don't like me or did or never did or will or will never! I'm just appealing to a sense of common decency and fair play. I'll tell you the truth. I've resented Big Daddy's partiality to Brick ever since Brick was born, and the way I've been treated like I was just barely good enough to spit on and sometimes not even good enough for that. Big Daddy is dying of cancer, and it's spread all through him and it's attacked all his vital organs including the kidneys and right now he is sinking into uremia, and you all know what uremia is, it's poisoning of the whole system due to the failure of the body to eliminate its poisons.

MARGARET *(to herself, downstage, hissingly)*   *Poisons, poisons! Venomous thoughts and words! In hearts and minds!—That's poisons!*

GOOPER *(overlapping her)*   I am asking for a square deal, and I expect to get one. But if I don't get one, if there's any peculiar shenanigans going on around here behind my back, or before me, well, I'm not a corporation lawyer for nothing, I know how to protect my own interests.—*OH! A late arrival!*

(BRICK *enters from the gallery with a tranquil, blurred smile, carrying an empty glass with him.*)

MAE   Behold the conquering hero comes!

GOOPER   The fabulous Brick Pollitt! Remember him?—Who could forget him!

MAE   He looks like he's been injured in a game!

GOOPER   Yep, I'm afraid you'll have to warm the bench at the Sugar Bowl this year, Brick!

(MAE *laughs shrilly.*)

Or was it the Rose Bowl that he made that famous run in?

MAE   The punch bowl, honey. It was in the punch bowl, the cut-glass punch bowl!

GOOPER   Oh, that's right, I'm getting the bowls mixed up!

MARGARET   Why don't you stop venting your malice and envy on a sick boy?

BIG MAMA   *Now you two hush, I mean it, hush, all of you, hush!*

GOOPER   All right, Big Mama. A family crisis brings out the best and the worst in every member of it.

MAE   *That's* the truth.

MARGARET   *Amen!*

BIG MAMA   *I said, hush!* I won't tolerate any more catty talk in my house.

(MAE *gives* GOOPER *a sign indicating briefcase.*
   BRICK'S *smile has grown both brighter and vaguer. As he prepares a drink, he sings softly:*)

BRICK
   Show me the way to go home,
   I'm tired and I wanta go to bed,
   I had a little drink about an hour ago—
GOOPER (*at the same time*)   Big Mama, you know it's necessary for me t'go back to Memphis in th' mornin' t'represent the Parker estate in a lawsuit.

(MAE *sits on the bed and arranges papers she has taken from the briefcase.*)

BRICK (*continuing the song*)
   Wherever I may roam,
   On land or sea or foam.
BIG MAMA   Is it, Gooper?
MAE   Yaiss.
GOOPER   That's why I'm forced to—to bring up a problem that—
MAE   Somethin' that's too important t'be put off!
GOOPER   If Brick was sober, he ought to be in on this.
MARGARET   Brick is present; we're here.
GOOPER   Well, good. I will now give you this outline my partner, Tom Bullitt, an' me have drawn up—a sort of dummy—trusteeship.
MARGARET   Oh, that's it! You'll be in charge an' dole out remittances, will you?
GOOPER   This we did as soon as we got the report on Big Daddy from th' Ochsner Laboratories. We did this thing, I mean we drew up this dummy outline with the advice and assistance of the Chairman of the Boa'd of Directors of th' Southern Plantahs Bank and Trust Company in Memphis, C. C. Bellowes, a man who handles estates for all th' prominent fam'lies in West Tennessee and th' Delta.
BIG MAMA   Gooper?
GOOPER (*crouching in front of* BIG MAMA)   Now this is not—not final, or anything like it. This is just a preliminary outline. But it does provide a basis—a design—a—possible, feasible—*plan!*
MARGARET   Yes, I'll bet.
MAE   It's a plan to protect the biggest estate in the Delta from irresponsibility an'—
BIG MAMA   Now you listen to me, all of you, you listen here! They's not goin' to be any more catty talk in my house! And Gooper, you put that away before I grab it out of your hand and tear it right up! I don't know what the hell's in it, and I don't want to know what the hell's in it. I'm talkin' in Big Daddy's language now; I'm his *wife,* not his *widow,* I'm still his *wife!* And I'm talkin' to you in his language an'—

GOOPER   Big Mama, what I have here is—

MAE   Gooper explained that it's just a plan. . . .

BIG MAMA   I don't care what you got there. Just put it back where it came from, an' don't let me see it again, not even the outside of the envelope of it! Is that understood? Basis! Plan! Preliminary! Design! I say—what is it Big Daddy always says when he's disgusted?

BRICK *(from the bar)*   Big Daddy says "crap" when he's disgusted.

BIG MAMA *(rising)*   That's right—*CRAP!* I say *CRAP* too, like Big Daddy!

MAE   Coarse language doesn't seem called for in this—

GOOPER   Somethin' in me is *deeply outraged* by hearin' you talk like this.

BIG MAMA   *Nobody's goin' to take nothin'*—till Big Daddy lets go of it, and maybe, just possibly, not—not even then! No, not even then!

BRICK

You can always hear me singin' this song,
Show me the way to go home.

BIG MAMA   Tonight Brick looks like he used to look when he was a little boy, just like he did when he played wild games and used to come home all sweaty and pink-cheeked and sleepy, with his—red curls shining. . . .

(She comes over to him and runs her fat shaky hand through his hair. He draws aside as he does from all physical contact and continues the song in a whisper, opening the ice bucket and dropping in the ice cubes one by one as if he were mixing some important chemical formula.)

BIG MAMA *(continuing)*   Time goes by so fast. Nothin' can outrun it. Death commences too early—almost before you're half-acquainted with life—you meet with the other. . . .

Oh, you know we just got to love each other an' stay together, all of us, just as close as we can, especially now that such a *black* thing has come and moved into this place without invitation.

(Awkwardly embracing BRICK, *she presses her head to his shoulder.*
   GOOPER *has been returning papers to* MAE *who has restored them to briefcase with an air of severely tried patience.)*

GOOPER   Big Mama? Big Mama?

(He stands behind her, tense with sibling envy.)

BIG MAMA *(oblivious of* GOOPER*)*   Brick, you hear me, don't you?

MARGARET   Brick hears you, Big Mama, he understands what you're saying.

BIG MAMA   Oh, Brick, son of Big Daddy! Big Daddy does so love you! Y'know what would be his fondest dream come true? If before he passed on, if Big Daddy has to pass on, you gave him a child of yours, a grandson as much like his son as his son is like Big Daddy!

MAE (*zipping briefcase shut: an incongruous sound*)   Such a pity that Maggie an'
Brick can't oblige!

MARGARET (*suddenly and quietly but forcefully*)   Everybody listen.

(*She crosses to the center of the room, holding her hands rigidly together.*)

MAE   Listen to what, Maggie?

MARGARET   I have an announcement to make.

GOOPER   A sports announcement, Maggie?

MARGARET   Brick and I are going to—*have a child!*

(BIG MAMA *catches her breath in a loud gasp.*)

(*Pause.* BIG MAMA *rises.*)

BIG MAMA   Maggie! Brick! This is too good to believe!

MAE   That's right, too good to believe.

BIG MAMA   Oh, my, my! This is Big Daddy's dream, his dream come true! I'm
going to tell him right now before he—

MARGARET   We'll tell him in the morning. Don't disturb him now.

BIG MAMA   I want to tell him before he goes to sleep, I'm going to tell him his
dream's come true this minute! And Brick! A child will make you pull
yourself together and quit this drinking!

(*She seizes the glass from his hand.*)

The responsibilities of a father will—

(*Her face contorts and she makes an excited gesture; bursting into sobs, she rushes
out, crying.*)

I'm going to tell Big Daddy right this minute!

(*Her voice fades out down the hall.*
    BRICK *shrugs slightly and drops an ice cube into another glass.* MARGARET
*crosses quickly to his side, saying something under her breath, and she pours the
liquor for him, staring up almost fiercely into his face.*)

BRICK (*coolly*)   Thank you, Maggie, that's a nice big shot.

(MAE *has joined* GOOPER *and she gives him a fierce poke, making a low hissing
sound and a grimace of fury.*)

GOOPER (*pushing her aside*)   Brick, could you possibly spare me one small shot
of that liquor?

BRICK   Why, help yourself, Gooper boy.

GOOPER   I will.

MAE *(shrilly)*   Of course we know that this is—

GOOPER   *Be still, Mae!*

MAE   I won't be still! I know she's made this up!

GOOPER   God damn it, I said to shut up!

MARGARET   Gracious! I didn't know that my little announcement was going to provoke such a storm!

MAE   *That* woman isn't *pregnant!*

GOOPER   Who said she was?

MAE   *She* did.

GOOPER   The doctor didn't. Doc Baugh didn't.

MARGARET   I haven't gone to Doc Baugh.

GOOPER   Then who'd you go to, Maggie?

MARGARET   One of the best gynecologists in the South.

GOOPER   Uh huh, uh huh!—I see. . . .

(He takes out pencil and notebook.)

—May we have his name, please?

MARGARET   No, you may not, Mister Prosecuting Attorney!

MAE   He doesn't have any name, he doesn't exist!

MARGARET   Oh, he exists all right, and so does my child, Brick's baby!

MAE   You can't conceive a child by a man that won't sleep with you unless you think you're—

(BRICK has turned on the phonograph. A scat song cuts MAE'S speech.)

GOOPER   *Turn that off!*

MAE   We know it's a lie because we hear you in here; he won't sleep with you, we hear you! So don't imagine you're going to put a trick over on us, to fool a dying man with a—

(A long drawn cry of agony and rage fills the house. MARGARET turns phonograph down to a whisper.
The cry is repeated.)

MAE *(awed)*   Did you hear that, Gooper, did you hear that?

GOOPER   Sounds like the pain has struck.

MAE   Go see, Gooper!

GOOPER   Come along and leave these love birds together in their nest!

(He goes out first, MAE follows but turns at the door, contorting her face and hissing at MARGARET:)

MAE   *Liar!*

(She slams the door.

   MARGARET *exhales with relief and moves a little unsteadily to catch hold of*
BRICK'S *arm.)*

MARGARET   Thank you for—keeping still . . .
BRICK   OK, Maggie.
MARGARET   It was gallant of you to save my face!
BRICK   —It hasn't happened yet.
MARGARET   What?
BRICK   The click. . . .
MARGARET   —the click in your head that makes you peaceful, honey?
BRICK   Uh-huh. It hasn't happened. . . . I've got to make it happen before I can
   sleep. . . .
MARGARET   —I—know what you—mean. . . .
BRICK   Give me that pillow in the big chair, Maggie.
MARGARET   I'll put it on the bed for you.
BRICK   No, put it on the sofa, where I sleep.
MARGARET   Not tonight, Brick.
BRICK   I want it on the sofa. That's where I sleep.

*(He has hobbled to the liquor cabinet. He now pours down three shots in quick
succession and stands waiting, silent. All at once he turns with a smile and says:)*

   There!
MARGARET   What?
BRICK   The *click*. . . .

*(His gratitude seems almost infinite as he hobbles out on the gallery with a drink.
We hear his crutch as he swings out of sight. Then, at some distance, he begins
singing to himself a peaceful song.*

   MARGARET *holds the big pillow forlornly as if it were her only companion, for
a few moments, then throws it on the bed. She rushes to the liquor cabinet, gathers
all the bottles in her arms, turns about undecidedly, then runs out of the room
with them, leaving the door ajar on the dim yellow hall.* BRICK *is heard hobbling
back along the gallery, singing his peaceful song. He comes back in, sees the pillow
on the bed, laughs lightly, sadly, picks it up. He has it under his arm as*
MARGARET *returns to the room.* MARGARET *softly shuts the door and leans
against it, smiling softly at* BRICK.*)*

MARGARET   Brick, I used to think that you were stronger than me and I didn't
   want to be overpowered by you. But now, since you've taken to liquor—
   you know what?—I guess it's bad, but now I'm stronger than you and I can
   love you more truly!

   Don't move that pillow. I'll move it right back if you do!

—Brick?

(She turns out all the lamps but a single rose-silk-shaded one by the bed.)

I really have been to a doctor and I know what to do and—Brick?—this is my time by the calendar to conceive!

BRICK   Yes, I understand, Maggie. But how are you going to conceive a child by a man in love with his liquor?

MARGARET   By locking his liquor up and making him satisfy my desire before I unlock it!

BRICK   Is that what you've done, Maggie?

MARGARET   Look and see. That cabinet's mighty empty compared to before!

BRICK   Well, I'll be a son of a—

(He reaches for his crutch but she beats him to is and rushes out on the gallery, hurls the crutch over the rail and comes back in, panting.
There are running footsteps. BIG MAMA *bursts into the room, her face all awry, gasping, stammering.)*

BIG MAMA   Oh, my God, oh, my God, oh, my God, where is it?

MARGARET   Is this what you want, Big Mama?

*(*MARGARET *hands her the package left by the doctor.)*

BIG MAMA   I can't bear it, oh, God! Oh, Brick! Brick, baby!

(She rushes at him. He averts his face from her sobbing kisses. MARGARET *watches with a tight smile.)*

My son, Big Daddy's boy! Little Father!

(The groaning cry is heard again. She runs out, sobbing.)

MARGARET   And so tonight we're going to make the lie true, and when that's done, I'll bring the liquor back here and we'll get drunk together, here, tonight, in this place that death has come into. . . .

—What do you say?

BRICK   I don't say anything. I guess there's nothing to say.

MARGARET   Oh, you weak people, you weak, beautiful people!—who give up.—What you want is someone to—

(She turns out the rose-silk lamp.)

—take hold of you.—Gently, gently, with love! And—

(The curtain begins to fall slowly.)

I *do* love you, Brick, I *do!*
BRICK *(smiling with charming sadness)*   Wouldn't it be funny if that was true?

THE CURTAIN COMES DOWN

THE END

Questions for Writing and Discussion

1.   We all know that human beings are changeable, inconsistent, and not entirely comprehensible, yet in a play it is also necessary that they be shown with *some* consistency and comprehensibility. One of the most interesting characters in this play, Big Mama, clearly gave the author some troubles, in that he wanted to show her inner conflicts while yet making her a coherent and credible figure. Discuss the character of Big Mama as it is presented from act to act, with the changes Tennessee Williams suggests in her behavior and attitudes.

2.   In the editors' comments about this play, the problem of its "emotional temperature" is briefly discussed—that is, the problem of hysteria, the pitch of feeling, the excess of emotion. How do you respond to this, not as something you might encounter in real life, but as you read it on the page or, more important, imagine it on the stage?

3.   The "Southern aspect" of this play—decayed gentility, a tendency toward grand rhetoric, certain attitudes toward the relations between the sexes—is obviously important. Do you think that the play becomes too "special," too much of a case study of a particular culture (the culture of the South), or does it have, for you, larger implications and values? Do you think it would be possible to shift the play from the Mississippi Delta in which Williams puts it to, say, upstate New York or North Dakota and still retain the drama he has presented? Would there be gains? Would there be losses?

COPYRIGHTS AND ACKNOWLEDGMENTS

The authors wish to thank the following for permission to reprint the poetry used in this book:

INDEX OF AUTHORS AND TITLES

FICTION

POETRY